The INTERNATIONAL CRITICAL COMMENTARY
on the Holy Scriptures of the Old and New Testaments

GENERAL EDITORS

G. I. DAVIES, F.B.A.
Emeritus Professor of Old Testament Studies in the University of Cambridge
Fellow of Fitzwilliam College

AND

C. M. TUCKETT
Emeritus Professor of New Testament in the University of Oxford
Fellow of Pembroke College

FORMERLY UNDER THE EDITORSHIP OF

J. A. EMERTON, F.B.A., C. E. B. CRANFIELD, F.B.A. and G. N. STANTON
General Editors of the New Series

S. R. DRIVER
A. PLUMMER
C. A. BRIGGS
Founding Editors

A CRITICAL AND EXEGETICAL COMMENTARY

ON

ECCLESIASTES

BY

STUART WEEKS

Professor of Old Testament and Hebrew, Durham University

IN TWO VOLUMES

VOLUME 1

Introduction and Commentary on Ecclesiastes 1.1–5.6

t&tclark

LONDON • NEW YORK • OXFORD • NEW DELHI • SYDNEY

T&T CLARK
Bloomsbury Publishing Plc
50 Bedford Square, London, WC1B 3DP, UK
1385 Broadway, New York, NY 10018, USA

BLOOMSBURY, T&T CLARK and the T&T Clark logo are trademarks of
Bloomsbury Publishing Plc

First published in Great Britain 2020
Paperback edition published 2025

Copyright © Stuart Weeks, 2020

Stuart Weeks has asserted his right under the Copyright, Designs and Patents Act, 1988, to be identified as the Author of this work.

All rights reserved. No part of this publication may be reproduced or transmitted in any form or by any means, electronic or mechanical, including photocopying, recording, or any information storage or retrieval system, without prior permission in writing from the publishers.

Bloomsbury Publishing Plc does not have any control over, or responsibility for, any third-party websites referred to or in this book. All internet addresses given in this book were correct at the time of going to press. The author and publisher regret any inconvenience caused if addresses have changed or sites have ceased to exist, but can accept no responsibility for any such changes.

The NewJerusalemU, GraecaU and TranslitLSU fonts used to print this work are available from Linguist's Software, Inc., PO Box 580, Edmonds, WA 98020-0580 USA.
Tel (425) 775-1130. www.linguistsoftware.com

A catalogue record for this book is available from the British Library.

A catalog record for this book is available from the Library of Congress.

ISBN: HB: 978-0-5670-3113-6
PB: 978-0-5677-1715-3
ePDF: 978-0-5676-9352-5

Series: International Critical Commentary

Typeset by Forthcoming Publications (www.forthpub.com)

To find out more about our authors and books visit www.bloomsbury.com and sign up for our newsletters.

For my mother, Moyra Weeks

CONTENTS OF VOLUME I

General Editors' Preface — ix
Preface — xi
Bibliography of Works Cited — xv
List of Abbreviations and Sigla — lxvii

INTRODUCTION — 1

COMMENTARY

1.1
SUPERSCRIPTION — 229

1.2-3
THE CHALLENGE — 248

INTRODUCTION TO 1.4-11 — 261
EVIDENCE FROM THE WORLD — 261
1.4 — 270
1.5-6 — 274
1.7 — 295
1.8 — 303
1.9-11 — 311

INTRODUCTION TO 1.12–2.11 — 327
EVIDENCE FROM EXPERIENCE — 327
1.12-13 — 331
1.14-15 — 342
1.16-18 — 350
2.1-2 — 364
2.3 — 376
2.4-11 — 387

INTRODUCTION TO 2.12-26	420
REFLECTIONS ON EXPERIENCE	420
2.12	424
2.13-17	434
2.18-23	447
2.24-26	466
INTRODUCTION TO 3.1-15	482
THE WORK OF GOD AND HUMANS	482
3.1-8	485
3.9-15	501
INTRODUCTION TO 3.16-22	531
HIDDEN DISTINCTIONS	531
3.16-17	535
3.18-21	543
3.22	562
INTRODUCTION TO 4.1-16	565
WORK AND OTHER PEOPLE	565
4.1-3	569
4.4-6	580
4.7-12	589
4.13-16	604
INTRODUCTION TO 4.17–5.6 (ET 5.1-7)	624
SPEAKING TO GOD	624
4.17–5.2	627
5.3-6	642

GENERAL EDITORS' PREFACE

Much scholarly work has been done on the Bible since the publication of the first volumes of the International Critical Commentary in the 1890s. New linguistic, textual, historical and archaeological evidence has become available, and there have been changes and developments in methods of study. In the twenty-first century there will be as great a need as ever, and perhaps a greater need, for the kind of commentary that the International Critical Commentary seeks to supply. The series has long had a special place among works in English on the Bible, because it has sought to bring together all the relevant aids to exegesis, linguistic and textual no less than archaeological, historical, literary and theological, to help the reader to understand the meaning of the books of the Old and New Testaments. In the confidence that such a series meets a need, the publishers and the editors are commissioning new commentaries on all the books of the Bible. The work of preparing a commentary on such a scale cannot but be slow, and developments in the past half-century have made the commentator's task yet more difficult than before, but it is hoped that the remaining volumes will appear without too great intervals between them. No attempt has been made to secure a uniform theological or critical approach to the problems of the various books, and scholars have been selected for their scholarship and not for their adherence to any school of thought. It is hoped that the new volumes will attain the high standards set in the past, and that they will make a significant contribution to the understanding of the books of the Bible.

G. I. D.
C. M. T.

PREFACE

Ecclesiastes has been treated already in the ICC series, and George Barton's 1908 commentary remains a valuable resource, often cited. Barton necessarily engaged, though, with the scholarship on Ecclesiastes of his own time, much of which was pre-occupied with issues that proved to be of limited interest to subsequent generations. In his own preface, indeed, he felt obliged to write: 'Those who expect to find here the advocacy of new and startling theories of this fascinatingly perplexing book will be disappointed. In the judgment of the writer there has been something too much of these things in the recent literature on Qoheleth.' Arguably, in fact, he wrote at just the wrong time: no modern period has been entirely free of attempts to slice the book into layers, or to butcher it altogether, but in the work of scholars like Siegfried, Haupt, and, rather differently, Zapletal, the end of the nineteenth and beginning of the twentieth century saw redactional bloodthirstiness of an unprecedented sort. More recent scholars have largely, and rightly, backed away from that whole approach, and although scholarship on Ecclesiastes has yet to achieve even the limited consensus that Barton hoped his own commentary would promote, it has tended to concern itself with very different issues, sometimes returning to questions that had preoccupied scholars long before his time. Things have changed in other areas as well. Although new discoveries have by no means rendered obsolete the extraordinary text-critical work by scholars like Euringer and McNeile, which did much to inform Barton's commentary, they have entirely changed the scholarly perspective on some issues, while modern approaches in linguistics and lexicography are markedly different to those of his era.

So long as texts remain important to us, there will always be a need for new commentaries on them: the texts may not change, but the way we read and receive them most assuredly will. I offer the excuse of Barton's partial redundancy, therefore, not because a new commentary on Ecclesiastes needs an excuse, but because this commentary is not entirely 'new' in that sense: to a great extent, it is merely informed by more recent data and engages with more recent scholarship. Although, to be sure, it has also been influenced by more recent developments in areas like literary theory, and by modern sensitivities in some areas that were less troubling to earlier generations, there is little in much of my text that would have seemed alien to Barton or his contemporaries. If in very many respects, however, this is a rather old-fashioned piece of work, I feel no need to apologize. Our engagement with a text in every age also requires us to have a form of that text that we can trust (or at least agree), and an understanding of the ways in which its words can be read. Establishing those things for Ecclesiastes, so far as is possible on the evidence available, has been my primary purpose, as will be clear from the proportion of space devoted to text-critical and philological issues. Although I have suggested many new readings or interpretations myself, moreover, I have also made an effort throughout to show that, despite the difficulties and the plurality of opinions, reading Ecclesiastes should not be a free-for-all, and that many of the ways in which particular passages have been understood (often by very fine scholars) are either wholly speculative or demonstrably wrong. There are many problems, and many places where more than one reading is possible, but the accretion of suggestions over the centuries has made it much harder than it should be for readers to determine what the text certainly does or does not say, and much easier for the less conscientious simply to cherry-pick suggestions that suit their own interpretations.

To that extent, at least, this is intended to be a commentary for commentators, who will find, I hope, not just my opinion, but also all the information that they need to reach their own conclusions about the more controversial passages. For that reason, the philological and text-critical notes are undoubtedly daunting for the non-specialist, although by translating readings where appropriate, I hope I have at least made it possible for those without any expertise in the languages to get a good sense of the issues, and for those with a limited knowledge to work their way through them. I have, in any case, summarized key issues from the notes in the main commentary, which is pitched at a more general audience. Inevitably, this main commentary is more particularly an expression of my own views, although I have tried to summarize and engage with those of others, and again to clear away some of the assumptions and speculations that have established themselves over the years.

The main commentary is also, perhaps, significantly less old-fashioned, and I am not sure how Barton or his contemporaries would have reacted to my understanding of the book as a thought-provoking entertainment, loosely in the form of a memoir, or to my suspicion that it devotes great effort to undermining some of the ideas that are often considered to be its key assumptions. Given the history of the book's interpretation, however, and despite my predecessor's optimism that he might recall critics to some consensus of judgment, I am very sure indeed that my ideas will no more unify scholarship around them than have those of any other commentator on Ecclesiastes. If this book is not to prove wholly ephemeral, I hope that it will make some lasting contribution to scholarly housekeeping—throwing out the rubbish, polishing the silverware, and upgrading the appliances—at least until such time as a new ICC is due.

A number of previous scholars have commented on how time-consuming and frustrating it is to work closely with Ecclesiastes, and had I paid more attention to those comments when I took this task on more than a decade ago, I might not have agreed so readily: on a personal note, I owe thanks and apologies to friends, family and colleagues who have put up with the extent to which it has gradually taken over my life and consumed my waking hours. Equally, I am grateful to the many colleagues and students, especially at Durham, who have discussed the text with me over the past decade, and made it possible to share the otherwise very lonely task of writing a commentary. My particular gratitude, however, is reserved for Graham Davies, who as series editor has contributed so much to the closing stages of this volume, and whose encouragement has been important throughout the many years it has taken. I am also indebted to Duncan Burns, who has worked so hard on the material at the production stage, and saved me from many infelicities.

The commentary has spread into a second volume, but the nature of Ecclesiastes is such that it is difficult to talk sensibly about any of it without having examined it all. Accordingly, the critical notes and much of the commentary are all but complete for that volume, and I hope that it will appear reasonably soon after this first.

Durham, January 2019

BIBLIOGRAPHY OF WORKS CITED

Works marked with an asterisk are cited by author's name alone, or by author and date where that is necessary to avoid confusion. Other works are cited by short title. Citations are *ad loc.* unless otherwise specified in the text.

*Aalders, G. C., *Het boek de Prediker* (COut; Kampen, 1948).
Ackroyd, P. R., 'The Meaning of Hebrew דור Considered', *JSS* 13 (1968): 3-10.
Adriaen, M., 'S. Hieronymi Presbyteri Commentarius in Ecclesiasten', in *S. Hieronymi Presbyteri Opera I,1* (CCSL 72; Turnhout, 1959), 247-361.
Aejmelaeus, A., 'Function and Interpretation of כי in Biblical Hebrew', *JBL* 105 (1986): 193-209.
—'Textual History of the Septuagint and the Principles of Critical Editing', in A. P. Otero and P. T. Morales (eds.), *The Text of the Hebrew Bible and its Editions: Studies in Celebration of the Fifth Centennial of the Complutensian Polyglot* (STHB 1; Leiden/Boston, 2017), 160-79.
Aitken, J. K., 'Rhetoric and Poetry in Greek Ecclesiastes', *BIOSCS* 38 (2005): 55-77.
—'Ecclesiastes', in *The T&T Clark Companion to the Septuagint* (Bloomsbury Companions; London, 2015), 365-69.
Albright, W. F., 'Some Canaanite-Phoenician Sources of Hebrew Wisdom', in M. Noth and D. W. Winton Thomas (eds.), *Wisdom in Israel and in the Ancient Near East* (VTSup 3; Leiden, 1955), 1-15.
Alexander, P. S., 'Why No Textual Criticism in Rabbinic Midrash? Reflections on the Textual Culture of the Rabbis', in G. J. Brooke (ed.), *Jewish Ways of reading the Bible* (JSSSup 11; Oxford, 2000), 175-90.
—'"Translation and Midrash Completely Fused Together"? The Form of the Targums to Canticles, Lamentations and Qohelet', *AS* 9 (2011): 83-99.
—'Profile Targum Qohelet', *AS* 9 (2011): 101-14.
*Allgeier, A., *Das Buch des Predigers oder Koheleth Übersetzt und Erklärt* (HSAT 6.2; Bonn, 1925).
Alster, B., *Wisdom of Ancient Sumer* (Bethesda, 2005).
Alter, R., *The Wisdom Books: Job, Proverbs, and Ecclesiastes. A Translation with Commentary* (New York/London, 2010).
Amir, Y., 'Doch ein griechischer Einfluss auf das Buch Kohelet?', in *Studien zum antiken Judentum* (BEATAJ 2; Frankfurt a.M., 1985), 35-50. An earlier version of this study appeared in Hebrew as 'לבעיית היחס בין קוהלת לחכמת יוון' = 'On the Problem of the Relationship between Ecclesiastes and the Wisdom of Greece', *Beth Mikra* 10/23-4 (1965): 36-42.

Andersen, F. I., and A. D. Forbes, *Spelling in the Hebrew Bible: Dahood Memorial Lecture* (BibOr 41; Rome, 1986).

Anderson, W. H. U., 'The Curse of Work in Qoheleth: An Exposé of Genesis 3:17-19 in Ecclesiastes', *EQ* 70 (1998): 99-113.

—'The Poetic Inclusio of Qoheleth in Relation to 1,2 and 12,8', *SJOT* 12 (1998): 203-13.

Annus, A., and A. Lenzi, *Ludlul bēl nēmeqi: The Standard Babylonian Poem of the Righteous Sufferer: Introduction, Cuneiform Text, and Transliteration with a Translation and Glossary* (Publications of the Foundation for Finnish Assyriological Research 2; State Archives of Assyria Cuneiform Texts 7; Helsinki, 2010).

Antic, R., 'Cain, Abel, Seth, and the Meaning of Human Life as Portrayed in the Books of Genesis and Ecclesiastes', *AUSS* 44 (2006): 203-11.

Aptowitzer, V., *Das Schriftwort in der Rabbinischer Literatur* (The Library of Biblical Studies; New York, 1970).

Archer, G. L., 'The Linguistic Evidence for the Date of Ecclesiastes', *JETS* 12 (1969): 167-81.

Aslanov, C., 'La Place du *Venetus Graecus* dans l'histoire des traductions grecques de la Bible', *Revue de Philologie, de Littérature et d'Histoire Anciennes* 73 (1999): 155-74.

Assmann, J., 'Schrift, Tod und Identität: Das Grab als Vorschule der Literatur im alten Ägypten', in A. Assmann, J. Assmann, and C. Hardmeier (eds.), *Schrift und Gedächtnis, Beitrage zur Archäologie der literarischen Kommunikation* (Munich, 1983), 64-93.

Asurmendi, J., *Du non-sens: L'Ecclésiaste* (Lectio Divina; Paris, 2012).

Atkinson, T., *Singing at the Winepress: Ecclesiastes and the Ethics of Work* (London/New York, 2015).

Auffret, P., '"Rien du tout de nouveau sous le soleil". Étude stucturelle de Qoh 1,4-11', *FO* 26 (1989): 145-66.

Aune, D. E., 'On the Origins of the "Council of Javneh" Myth', *JBL* 110 (1991): 491-93.

Azevedo, J., 'Ethiopian Manuscripts of the Book of Ecclesiastes—Part I', *Hermenêutica* 2 (2002): 61-80.

Azize, J., 'The Genre of Qohelet', *Davar Logos* 2 (2003): 123-38.

Backhaus, F. J., *»Den Zeit und Zufall trifft sie alle«: Studien zur Komposition und zum Gottesbild im Buch Qohelet* (BBB 83; Frankfurt a.M., 1993).

—'Qohelet und Sirach', *BN* 69 (1993): 32-55.

—'Die Pendenskonstruktion im Buch Qohelet', *ZAH* 8 (1995): 1-30.

—*«Es gibt nichts Besseres für den Menschen» [Koh. 3, 22]. Studien zur Komposition und zur Weisheitskritik im Buch Kohelet* (BBB 121; Bodenheim a.R., 1998).

—'Ekklesiastes', in M. Karrer, W. Kraus, E. Bons, and K. Brodersen (eds.), *Septuaginta Deutsch: Erläuterungen und Kommentare zum griechischen Alten Testament*. Vol. 2, *Psalmen bis Daniel* (Stuttgart, 2011), 2001-28.

*Baer, S. ספר אסתר קהלת קינות רות השירים שיר מגלות: חמש *Quinque volumina: Canticum Canticorum Ruth Threni Ecclesiastes Esther* (Leipzig, 1886).
Baldwin, J., 'Is There Pseudonymity in the Old Testament?', *Themelios* 4 (1978): 6-12.
Bar-Ilan, M., 'Writing in Ancient Israel and Early Judaism. Part Two: Scribes and Books in the Late Second Commonwealth and Rabbinic Period', in M. J. Mulder (ed.), *Mikra: Text, Translation, Reading and Interpretation of the Hebrew Bible in Ancient Judaism and Early Christianity* (Peabody, 2004), 21-38. Originally published as the second volume of *Compendia rerum Iudaicarum ad Novum Testamentum* in Assen and Philadelphia, 1988.
Barag, G., '"קהלת" היא מה?'= 'What is "Qohelet"?', *Tarbiz* 21 (1950): 101-105.
Baranowski, K. J., 'The Article in the Book of Qoheleth', in G. Geiger (ed.), Ἐν πάσῃ γραμματικῇ καὶ σοφίᾳ. En pāsē grammatikē kai sophiā: *Saggi di linguistica ebraica in onore di Alviero Niccacci, ofm* (Studium Biblicum Franciscanum 78; Milan, 2011), 31-51.
Barbour, J., '"Like an Error Which Proceeds from the Ruler": The Shadow of Saul in Qoheleth 4:17–5:6', in M. Augustin and H. M. Niemann (eds.), *Thinking Towards New Horizons: Collected Communications to the XIXth Congress of the International Organization for the Study of the Old Testament, Ljubljana 2007* (BEATAJ 55; Frankfurt a.M./New York, 2008), 121-28.
—*The Story of Israel in the Book of Qohelet: Ecclesiastes as Cultural Memory* (Oxford Theological Monographs; Oxford, 2012).
Bardski, K., 'The Snowball and the Cord of Three Stands: Qoh 4:12b in the Rabbinic Tradition', in N. Calduch-Benages (ed.), *Wisdom for Life: Essays Offered to Honor Prof. Maurice Gilbert, SJ on the Occasion of his Eightieth Birthday* (BZAW 445; Berlin/Boston, 2014), 156-67.
Barnes, J., 'L'Ecclésiaste et le scepticisme Grec', *RTP* 131 (1999): 103-14. The original English text has been published subsequently as 'Scepticism and the Book of Ecclesiastes', in his *Proof, Knowledge, and Scepticism* (Essays in Ancient Philosophy; Oxford, 2014), 611-24.
Barr, J., *Biblical Words for Time* (SBT 33; London, 1962).
—'Vocalization and the Analysis of Hebrew among the Ancient Translators', in B. Hartmann et al. (ed.), *Hebräische Wortforschung: Festschrift zum 80. Geburtstag von Walter Baumgartner* (VTSup 16; Leiden, 1967), 1-11.
—*Comparative Philology and the Text of the Old Testament* (Oxford, 1968).
—'Reading a Script without Vowels', in W. Haas (ed.), *Writing Without Letters* (Mont Follick Series 4; Manchester/Totowa, 1976), 71-100.
—'A New Look at Kethibh-Qere', in *Remembering All the Way: A Collection of Old Testament Studies Published on the Occasion of the Fortieth Anniversary of the Oudtestamentisch Werkgezelschap in Nederland* (OTS 21; Leiden, 1981), 19-37.
—*The Variable Spellings of the Hebrew Bible: The Schweich Lectures of the British Academy 1986* (Oxford, 1989).

—'"Determination" and the Definite Article in Biblical Hebrew', *JSS* 34 (1989): 307-35.
Barthélemy, D., *Les Devanciers d'Aquila: première publication intégrale du texte des fragments du Dodécaprophéton trouvés dans le désert de Juda, précédée d'une étude sur les traductions et recensions grecques de la Bible réalisées au premier siècle de notre ère sous l'influence du rabbinat palestinien* (VTSup 10; Leiden, 1963).
—'Qui est Symmaque?', *CBQ* 36 (1974): 451-65.
—*Studies in the Text of the Old Testament: An Introduction to the Hebrew Old Testament Text Project* (Textual Criticism and the Translator 3; Winona Lake, 2012).
*Bartholomew, C. G., *Ecclesiastes* (Baker Commentary on the Old Testament Wisdom and Psalms; Grand Rapids, 2009).
*Barton, G. A., *A Critical and Exegetical Commentary on the Book of Ecclesiastes* (ICC; Edinburgh/New York, 1908).
Barton, J., *The Spirit and the Letter: Studies in the Biblical Canon* (Hulsean Lectures 1990; London, 1997).
*Barucq, A., *Ecclésiaste Qohéleth: Traduction et commentaire* (Verbum Salutis; Paris, 1968).
*Bauer, H., and P. Leander, *Historische Grammatik der hebräischen Sprache des Alten Testaments* (Halle a.S., 1922).
Beckwith, R., *The Old Testament Canon of the New Testament Church and Its Background in Early Judaism* (Grand Rapids, 1985).
Bellia, G., and A. Passaro (eds.), *Il Libro del Qohelet. Tradizione, redazione, teologia* (Cammini nello Spirito. Biblica 44; Milan, 2001).
Ben Zvi, E., 'The Prophetic Book: A Key Form of Prophetic Literature', in M. A. Sweeney and E. Ben Zvi (eds.), *The Changing Face of Form Criticism for the Twenty-First Century* (Grand Rapids/Cambridge, 2003), 276-97.
*Bennett, S. J., *Ecclesiastes / Lamentations: A Commentary in the Wesleyan Tradition* (New Beacon Bible Commentary; Kansas City, 2010).
Benoit, P., J. T. Milik, and R. de Vaux (eds.), *Les Grottes de Murabbaʿât* (DJD 2; Oxford, 1961).
Berger, S., 'Notice sur quelques textes latins inédits de l'Ancien Testament', *Notices et extraits des manuscrits de la Bibliothèque nationale et autres bibliothèques* 34 (1895): 119-52.
Berlejung, A., and P. van Hecke (eds.), *The Language of Qohelet in its Context: Essays in Honour of Prof. A. Schoors on the Occasion of his Seventieth Birthday* (OLA 164; Louvain, 2007).
Berner, C., 'Der ferne Gott als Richter? Zur theologischen Deutung weltlicher Ungerechtigkeit im Koheletbuch', *ZTK* 108 (2011): 253-69.
Bertram, G., 'Hebräischer und griechischer Qohelet. Ein Beitrag zur Theologie der hellenistischen Bibel', *ZAW* 64 (1952): 26-49.
Bianchi, F., '«Essi non hanno chi li consoli» (Qo 4,1)', *RivB* 40 (1992): 299-307.

—'The Language of Qohelet: A Bibliographical Survey', *ZAW* 105 (1993): 210-23.
—'"Ma Dio ricerca ciò che è scomparso"? (Qo 3,15b). La Storia, la memoria e il tempo nel libro di Qohelet', *RivB* 42 (1994): 59-73.
—'C'è una "Teologia della prova" in Qohelet? Osservazioni filologiche e bibliche su Qo 3,18', in R. Fabris (ed.), *Initium Sapientiae. Scritti in onore di Franco Festorazzi nel suo 70° compleanno* (RivBSup 36; Bologna, 2000), 163-78.
—'Il metodo del Qohelet: il poema iniziale (1,1-18)', *Parole di Vita* 48 (2003): 18-24.
*Bickell, G., *Der Prediger über den Wert des Daseins: Wiederherstellung des bisher zerstücketten Textes, Uebersetzung und Erklärung* (Innsbruck: Wagner, 1884).
Bickerman, E. J., *Four Strange Books of the Bible: Jonah, Daniel, Koheleth, Esther* (New York, 1967).
Bidder, R., *Ueber Koheleths Stellung zum Unsterblichkeitsglauben: ein Beitrag zu gerechter Beurtheilung des Buches Koheleth* (Erlangen, 1875).
Binder, G., and L. Liesenborghs (eds.), *Kommentar zum Ecclesiastes (Tura-Papyrus), Teil I.1: Kommentar zu Eccl. Kap. 1, 1-2, 14 (Einleitung, Text, Ubersetzung, Indices)* (PTA 25; Bonn, 1979).
Birnbaum, E., *Der Koheletkommentar des Hieronymus: Einleitung, revidierter Text, Übersetzung und Kommentierung* (CSEL Extra seriem; Berlin/Boston, 2014).
Birnbaum, E., and L. Schwienhorst-Schönberger (eds.), *Hieronymus als Exeget und Theologe: interdisziplinäre Zugänge zum Koheletkommentar des Hieronymus*, 2014).
Bishop, E. F. F., 'A Pessimist in Palestine', *PEQ* 100 (1968): 33-41.
Blenkinsopp, J., 'Ecclesiastes 3.1-15: Another Interpretation', *JSOT* 20 (1995): 55-64.
Boda, M. J., T. Longman, and C. G. Rata (eds.), *The Words of the Wise Are Like Goads: Engaging Qoheleth in the 21st Century* (Winona Lake, 2013).
Bolin, T. M., *Ecclesiastes and the Riddle of Authorship* (BibleWorld; New York/ London, 2017).
Bons, E., 'Zur Gliederung und Kohärenz von Koh 1,12–2,11', *BN* 24 (1984): 73-93.
—'šiddā w=šiddōt: Überlegungen zum Verständnis eines Hapaxlegomenons', *BN* 36 (1987): 12-16.
Bonwetsch, N., and H. Achelis (eds.), *Hippolytus Werke. 1. Bd Exegetische und homiletische Schriften*, Vol. 1.1 (GCS; Leipzig, 1897).
[Boutauld, M.], *Les Conseils de la sagesse, ou le recueïl des maximes de Salomon les plus necessaires à l'homme pour se conduire sagement, avec des reflexions sur ces maximes*. (Paris, 1677). See Weeks, *Making of Many Books*, §257.
Brady, C. M. M., 'Exegetical Similarities and the Liturgical Use of the Targumim of the Megilloth', *AS* 12 (2014): 108-20.

Brandscheidt, R., *Weltbegeisterung und Offenbarungsglaube: literar-, form- und traditionsgeschichtliche Untersuchung zum Buch Kohelet* (TThSt 64; Trier, 1999).
Braun, R., *Kohelet und die frühhellenistische Popularphilosophie* (BZAW 130; Berlin, 1973).
Brenner, A., 'M Text Authority in Biblical Love Lyrics: The Case of Qoheleth 3.1-9 and Its Textual Relatives', in A. Brenner and F. van Dijk-Hemmes (eds.), *On Gendering Texts: Female and Male Voices in the Hebrew Bible* (Biblical Interpretation Series 1; Leiden, 1993), 133-63.
*Brenz (Brentius), J., *Ecclesiastes Solomonis: Cum commentariis, iuxta piis atque eruditis Iohannis Brentii, per Hiobem Gast e Germano in Latinum tralatus: Epistola nuncupatoria ad Illustriss. Principem Hessorum Philippum* (Haguenau, 1528).
Brock, S. P., *The Bible in the Syriac Tradition* (Gorgias Handbooks; Piscataway, 2nd edn, 2006).
Brooke, G. J., 'Reading the Plain Meaning of Scripture in the Dead Sea Scrolls', in G. J. Brooke (ed.), *Jewish Ways of Reading the Bible* (JSSSup 11; Oxford, 2000), 67-90.
Brooke, G. J., and P. van Hecke (eds.), *Goochem in Mokum, Wisdom in Amsterdam: Papers on Biblical and Related Wisdom Read at the Fifteenth Joint Meeting of the Society for Old Testament Study and the Oudtestamentisch Werkgezelschap, Amsterdam, July 2012* (OTS 68; Leiden/Boston, 2016).
Brown, W. P., *Character in Crisis: A Fresh Approach to the Wisdom Literature of the Old Testament* (Grand Rapids/Cambridge, 1996).
*—*Ecclesiastes* (Interpretation; Louisville, 2000).
Broyde, M. J., 'Defilement of the Hands, Canonization of the Bible, and the Special Status of Esther, Ecclesiastes, and Song of Songs', *Judaism* 44 (1995): 65-79.
Bühlmann, A., 'The Difficulty of Thinking in Greek and Speaking in Hebrew (Qoheleth 3.18; 4.13-16; 5.8)', *JSOT* 90 (2000): 101-108.
Bundvad, M., *Time in the Book of Ecclesiastes* (Oxford Theology and Religion Monographs; Oxford, 2015).
Burkes, S. L., *Death in Qoheleth and Egyptian Biographies of the Late Period* (SBLDS 170; Atlanta, 1999).
Burkitt, F. C., *Fragments of the Books of Kings, according to the translation of Aquila from a MS. formerly in the Geniza at Cairo, now in the possession of C. Taylor D.D. Master of S. Johns College and S. Schechter, M.A. University Reader in Talmudic literature* (Cambridge, 1897).
—'Is Ecclesiastes a Translation?', *JTS* (Old Series) 23 (1921): 22-26.
Byargeon, R. W., 'The Significance of Ambiguity in Ecclesiastes 2,24-26', in Schoors (ed.), *Qohelet in the Context*, 367-72.
Caminos, R. A., *A Tale of Woe: From a Hieratic Papyrus in the A.S. Pushkin Museum of Fine Arts in Moscow* (Oxford, 1977).

Caneday, A. B., 'Qoheleth: Enigmatic Pessimist or Godly Sage?', *Grace Theological Journal* 7 (1986): 21-56.
Canellis, A., 'Le *Commentaire sur l'Ecclésiaste* de saint Jérôme', in L. Mellerin (ed.), *La réception du Livre de Qohélet: Ier–XIIIe siècle* (Cerf Patrimoines; Paris, 2016), 205-27.
Cannon, W. W., 'Jerome and Symmachus: Some Points in the Vulgate Translation of Koheleth', *ZAW* 45 (1927): 191-99.
Caquot, A., and H. Zafrani, *La Version arabe de la Bible de Sa'adya Gaon: l'Ecclésiaste et son commentaire "Le Livre de l'ascèse"* (Collection judaïsme en terre d'Islam 4; Paris, 1989).
Carasik, M., 'Exegetical Implications of the Masoretic Cantillation Marks in Ecclesiastes', *HS* 42 (2001): 145-65.
—'Qohelet's Twists and Turns', *JSOT* 28 (2003): 192-209.
Carbajosa, I., 'Prolegomena to a (Critical) Edition of Syrohexapla', in A. P. Otero and P. T. Morales (eds.), *The Text of the Hebrew Bible and its Editions: Studies in Celebration of the Fifth Centennial of the Complutensian Polyglot* (STHB 1; Leiden/Boston, 2017), 255-85.
Carlebach, J., *Das Buch Koheleth. Ein Deutungsversuch* (Frankfurt a.M., 1936).
Carrière, J.-M., '«Tout est vanité»: l'un des concepts de Qohélet', *EstBib* 55 (1997): 297-311, reprinted 463-77 after errors.
Casanowicz, I. M., 'The Book of Ecclesiastes in the Septuagint Version', *Johns Hopkins University Circulars* 10 (1891): 117-18.
Caspari, C. P., *Das Buch Hiob (1,1–38,16) in Hieronymus's Uebersetzung aus der alexandrinischen Version nach einer St Gallener Handschrift saec. VIII* (Oslo, 1893).
Castellino, G. R., 'Qohelet and his Wisdom', *CBQ* 30 (1968): 15-28.
Cazelles, H., 'Conjonctions de subordination dans la langue de Qohelet', *GLECS* 8 (1957): 21-22.
Ceriani, A. M. (ed.), *Codex Syro-Hexaplaris Ambrosianus Photolithographice Editus* (Monumenta Sacra et Profana ex codicibus praesertim Bibliothecae Ambrosianae 7; Milan, London, 1874).
Cheyne, T. K., *Job and Solomon or the Wisdom of the Old Testament* (London, 1887).
—*Jewish Religious Life after the Exile* (American Lectures on the History of Religions: Third Series 3; New York/London, 1898).
Chiesa, B., *L'Antico Testamento ebraico secondo la tradizione* palestinese (Turin, 1978).
—*The Emergence of Hebrew Biblical Pointing: The Indirect Sources* (Judentum und Umwelt 1; Frankfurt a.M., 1979).
Christianson, E. S., 'Qoheleth and the Existential Legacy of the Holocaust', *HeyJ* 38 (1997): 35-50.
—*A Time to Tell: Narrative Strategies in Ecclesiastes* (JSOTSup 280; Sheffield, 1998).

—'Qoheleth and the/His Self among the Deconstructed', in Schoors (ed.), *Qohelet in the Context*, 425-33.
—*Ecclesiastes through the Centuries* (BBC; Malden, 2007).
*Clarke, A., *The Holy Bible, Containing the Old and New Testaments: The text carefully printed from the most correct copies of the present authorised translation, including the marginal readings and parallel texts: with a commentary and critical notes; designed as a help to a better understanding of the sacred writings Volume III Job to Solomon's Songs* (London, 2nd edn, 1854).
Clarke, E. G., 'Reflections on the Preparation of a Critical Edition of the Targum of Koheleth', *Textus* 16 (1991): 79-94.
Clemens, D. M., 'The Law of Sin and Death: Ecclesiastes and Genesis 1–3', *Themelios* 19 (1994): 5-8.
Clines, D. J. A., 'Predestination in the Old Testament', in D. J. A. Clines (ed.), *On the Way to the Postmodern: Old Testament Essays 1967–1998. Volume 2* (JSOTSup 293; Sheffield, 1998), 524-41.
Cohen, M., ''aššūrênû 'attâ sᵉbābûnî (Q. sᵉbābûnû) (Psaume XVII 11A)', *VT* 41 (1991): 137-44.
Cohen, Y., *Wisdom from the Late Bronze Age* (SBLWAW 29; Atlanta, 2013).
Collins, N. L., 'Who Wanted a Translation of the Pentateuch into Greek?', in G. J. Brooke (ed.), *Jewish Ways of Reading the Bible* (JSSSup 11; Oxford, 2000), 20-57.
Condamin, A., 'Études sur l'Ecclésiaste', *RB* 8–9 (1899–1900): 8, 493-509; 9, 30-44, 354-77.
Cook, Johann, 'Aspects of the Relationship between the Septuagint Versions of Kohelet and Proverbs', in Schoors (ed.), *Qohelet in the Context*, 481-92.
Cook, John A., 'The Verb in Qohelet', in Boda, Longman, and Rata (eds.), *The Words of the Wise*, 309-42.
Coppens, J., 'La structure de l'Ecclésiaste', in M. Gilbert (ed.), *La sagesse de l'Ancien Testament* (BETL 51; Leuven, 1979), 288-92.
Corley, J., 'Qoheleth and Sirach: A Comparison', in N. Calduch-Benages (ed.), *Wisdom for Life: Essays Offered to Honor Prof. Maurice Gilbert, SJ on the Occasion of his Eightieth Birthday* (BZAW 445; Berlin/Boston, 2014), 145-55.
Corré, A. D., 'A Reference to Epispasm in Koheleth', *VT* 4 (1954): 416-18.
Crenshaw, J. L., 'The Eternal Gospel (Ecclesiastes 3:11)', in J. L. Crenshaw and J. T. Willis (eds.), *Essays in Old Testament Ethics (J. Philip Hyatt memoriam)* (New York, 1974), 23-55.
—'The Shadow of Death in Qoheleth', in J. G. Gammie et al. (eds.), *Israelite Wisdom: Theological and Literary Essays in Honor of Samuel Terrien* (New York, 1978), 205-16.
—'The Expression *mî yôdēaʿ* in the Hebrew Bible', *VT* 36 (1986): 274-88.
*—*Ecclesiastes: A Commentary* (OTL; London, 1988).
—'Prohibitions in Proverbs and Qoheleth', in E. Ulrich, J. W. Wright, R. P. Carroll, and P. R. Davies (eds.), *Priests, Prophets and Scribes* (JSOTSup 149; Sheffield, 1992), 115-24.

—'Qoheleth's Understanding of Intellectual Inquiry', in Schoors (ed.), *Qohelet in the Context*, 205-24.
—'Qoheleth's Quantitative Language', in Berlejung and van Hecke (eds.), *The Language of Qohelet*, 1-22.
—'Qoheleth in Historical Context', *Bib* 88 (2007): 285-99.
—*Qoheleth: The Ironic Wink* (Studies on Personalities of the Old Testament; Columbia, 2013).
de Crom, D., 'The Book of Canticles in Codex Graecus Venetus 7', in N. R. M. de Lange, J. G. Krivoruchko, and C. Boyd-Taylor (eds.), *Jewish Reception of Greek Bible Versions: Studies in their Use in Late Antiquity and the Middle Ages* (TSMEMJ 23; Tübingen, 2009), 287-301.
Cross, F. M., 'The Oldest Manuscripts from Qumran', *JBL* 74 (1955): 147-72.
Crüsemann, F., 'Die unveränderbare Welt. Überlegungen zur "Krisis der Weisheit" beim Prediger (Kohelet)', in W. Schotroff and W. Stegemann (eds.), *Der Gott der kleinen Leute: sozialgeschichtliche Bibelauslegungen. Bd.1 Altes Testament* (Munich, 1979), 80-104. ET 'The Unchangeable World: The "Crisis of Wisdom" in Koheleth', in *God of the Lowly: Socio-Historical Interpretations of the Bible* (Maryknoll, 1984), 57-77.
Dahan, G., 'L'Ecclésiaste contre Aristote? Les commentaires de Eccl 1,13 et 17-18 aux XIIe et XIIIe siècles', in J. F. Meirinhos (ed.), *Itinéraires de la raison: études de philosophie médiévale offertes à Maria Cândida Pacheco* (Louvain-la-Neuve, 2005), 205-33.
Dahl, G., 'The "Three Heights" of Joshua 17.11', *JBL* 53 (1934): 381-83.
Dahood, M. J., 'Canaanite-Phoenician Influence in Qoheleth' (PhD diss.; The Johns Hopkins University, 1951).
—'Canaanite-Phoenician Influence in Qoheleth', *Bib* 33 (1952): 30-52, 191-221.
—'The Language of Qoheleth', *CBQ* 14 (1952): 227-32.
—'Qoheleth and Recent Discoveries', *Bib* 39 (1958): 302-18.
—'Qoheleth and Northwest Semitic Philology', *Bib* 43 (1962): 349-65.
—'The Phoenician Background of Qoheleth', *Bib* 47 (1966): 264-82.
—'Scriptio Defectiva in Qoheleth 4,10a', *Bib* 49 (1968): 243.
—'Hebrew–Ugaritic Lexicography VI', *Bib* 49 (1968): 355-69.
D'Alario, V., *Il Libro del Qohelet. Struttura letteraria e retorica* (RivBSup 27; Bologna, 1992).
—'"Chi sa se lo spirito dell'uomo sale in alto...?" (Qo 3,21). Un testo problematico sul tema dell'immortalità', in G. Lorizio (ed.), *Morte e sopravvivenza* (Saggi 32; Rome, 1995), 211-22.
—'Liberté de Dieu ou Destin? Un Autre Dilemme dans l'Interprétation du Qohélet', in Schoors (ed.), *Qohelet in the Context*, 457-63.
—'L'assurdità del male nella teodicea del Qohelet', in R. Fabris (ed.), *Initium Sapientiae. Scritti in onore di Franco Festorazzi nel suo 70° compleanno* (RivBSup 36; Bologna, 2000), 179-97.

—'Qohelet e l'Apocalittica. Il significato del termine 'ôlām in Qo 3,11', in A. Casalegno (ed.), *Tempo ed Eternità: In dialogo con Ugo Vanni S.I.* (San Paolo, 2002), 73-88.

Davila, J., 'Qoheleth and Northern Hebrew', *Maarav* 5–6 (1990): 69-87.

*Davis, E. F., *Proverbs, Ecclesiastes, and the Song of Songs* (Westminster Bible Companion; Louisville, 2000).

Day, J., 'Foreign Semitic Influence on the Wisdom of Israel and its Appropriation in the Book of Proverbs', in J. Day et al. (eds.), *Wisdom in Ancient Israel*, 55-70.

Day, J., R. P. Gordon, and H. G. M. Williamson (eds.), *Wisdom in Ancient Israel: Essays in Honour of J. A. Emerton* (Cambridge, 1995).

*Delitzsch, Franz, *Biblischer Commentar über die poetischen Bücher des Alten Testaments Vol 4: Hoheslied und Koheleth Mit Excursen von Consul D Wetzstein* (Leipzig, 1875); ET *Commentary on the Song of Songs and Ecclesiastes* (Clark's Foreign Theological Library Fourth Series 54; Edinburgh, 1877).

Delitzsch, Friedrich, *Wo lag das Paradies? Eine biblisch-assyriologische Studie mit zahlreichen assyriologischen Beiträgen zur biblischen Länder- und Völkerkunde und einer Karte Babyloniens* (Leipzig, 1881).

Dell, K. J., 'Ecclesiastes as Wisdom: Consulting Early Interpreters', *VT* 44 (1994): 301-29. A revised version appears in her *Interpreting Ecclesiastes*, 9-36.

—'The Cycle of Life in Ecclesiastes', *VT* 59 (2009): 181-89. A revised version appears in her *Interpreting Ecclesiastes*, 59-67.

—*Interpreting Ecclesiastes: Readers Old and New* (CrStHB 3; Winona Lake, 2013).

—'Exploring Intertextual Links between Ecclesiastes and Genesis 1–11', in Dell and Kynes (eds.), *Reading Ecclesiastes Intertextually*, 3-14.

—'Ecclesiastes as Mainstream Wisdom (without Job)', in Brooke and van Hecke (eds.), *Goochem*, 43-52.

Dell, K. J., and W. Kynes (eds.), *Reading Ecclesiastes Intertextually* (LHBOTS 587; London/New York, 2014).

Delsman, W. C., 'Zur Sprache des Buches Koheleth', in *Von Kanaan bis Kerala: Festschrift für Prof. Mag. Dr. J. P. M. van der Ploeg O.P. zur Vollendung des siebzigsten Lebensjahres am 4. Juli 1979. Überreicht von Kollegen, Freunden und Schülern* (AOAT 211; Neukirchen-Vluyn/Kevelaer, 1982), 341-65.

—'Die Inkongruenz im Buch Qoheleth', in K. Jongeling, H. Murre-van den Berg, and L. van Rompay (eds.), *Studies in Hebrew and Aramaic Syntax Presented to Professor J. Hoftijzer on the Occasion of his Sixty-fifth Birthday* (SSLL 17; Leiden/New York/København/Köln, 1991), 27-37.

—*Die Datierung des Buches Qoheleth: Eine sprachwissenschaftliche Analyse* (Nijmegen, 2000).

Dempster, S. G., 'Ecclesiastes and the Canon', in Boda, Longman, and Rata (eds.), *The Words of the Wise*, 387-400.

Derenbourg, J., 'Notes detachées sur l'Ecclésiaste', *REJ* 1 (1880): 165-85.

Des Rochettes, J., 'Qohélet ou l'humour noir à la recherche de Dieu dans un contexte hébraïco-hellénique', in A. Marchadour (ed.), *L'évangile exploré: Mélanges offerts à Simon Légasse à l'occasion de ses soixante-dix ans* (Paris, 1996), 49-71.

*Desvoeux, A. V., *A Philosophical and Critical Essay on Ecclesiastes Wherein the Author's Design is stated; his Doctrine vindicated; his Method explained in an Analytical Paraphrase annexed to a New Version of the Text from the Hebrew; and the Differences between that new Translation and the received Version accounted for in Philological Observations* (London, 1760).

Dewald, C., 'Narrative Surface and Authorial Voice in Herodotus' Histories', *Arethusa* 20 (1987): 147-70.

Diebner, B. J., 'Die biblischen Texte des Hamburger Papyrus Bilinguis 1 (Cant, Lam Co., Eccl Gr. et Co.) in ihrem Verhältnis zum Text der Septuaginta besonders des Kodex B (Vat. Gr. 1209): Beobachtungen und methodische Bemerkungen', in T. Orlandi and F. Wisse (eds.), *Acts of the Second International Congress of Coptic Study, Roma, 22–26 September 1980* (Rome, 1985), 59-74.

Diebner, B. J., R. Kasser, and A. Kropp (eds.), *Hamburger Papyrus Bil. 1: Die alttestamentlichen Texte des Papyrus Bilinguis 1 der Staats- und Universitätsbibliothek Hamburg* (CO 18; Geneva, 1989).

Diesel, A. A., R. G. Lehmann, E. Otto, and A. Wagner (eds.), *"Jedes Ding hat seine Zeit..."*. *Studien zur israelitischen und altorientalischen Weisheit. Diethelm Michel zum 65. Geburtstag* (BZAW 241; Berlin, 1996).

Díez Macho, A., 'Tres nuevos manuscritos "palestinenses"', *EstBib* 13 (1954): 247-65.

—'La cantilación protomasorética del Pentateuco (MS. 191 del Seminario Teologico Judio de Nueva York)', *EstBib* 18 (1959): 223-51.

Díez Merino, L., *Targum de Qohelet. Edición Príncipe del Ms. Villa-Amil n.o 5 de Alfonso de Zamora* (BHBib 13; Madrid, 1987).

Dillmann, A., 'Über Baal mit dem weiblichen Artikel (ἡ Βάαλ)', in *Monatsberichte der Königlich Preußischen Akademie der Wissenschaften zu Berlin. Aus dem Jahre 1881* (Berlin, 1882), 601-20.

—'Über die griechische Übersetzung des Qoheleth', *SPAW* (Berlin, 1892), 3-16.

Döller, J., 'Altorientalisches Weltbild im Kohelet (1,5-7)', *Der Katholik: Zeitschrift für katholische Wissenschaft und kirchliches Leben* 35 (3rd series) (1907): 361-64.

Dölsch (Dolscius), P., Ἐκκλεσιαστης Σολομωντος Ἐμμέτ- ρως Μεταφρασθεὶς ὑπὸ Παύλου τοῦ Δολσκίου Πλαέως (Leipzig, 1559).

Dorp, J. van, 'Enkele aantekeningen bij de vertaling van Prediker 3:5a', *ACEBT* 21 (2004): 117-23.

Dörsing, F., *Lehre mich doch, daß es ein Ende mit mir haben muß: Die Sicht des Menschen im Buch des Predigers Salomo* (Frankfurt a.M., 1997).

Dotan, A., 'Deviation in Gemination in the Tiberian Vocalization.', in E. Fernández Tejero (ed.), *Estudios masoréticos: V Congreso de la IOMS: dedicados a Harry M. Orlinsky* (Madrid, 1983), 63-77.
Drewes, B. F., 'Prediker in Indonesië en elders: Contextueel uitgelegd', *ACEBT* 21 (2004): 81-93. ET 'Reading the Bible in Context: An Indonesian and a Mexican Commentary on Ecclesiastes: Contextual Interpretations', *Exchange* 34 (2005): 120-33.
Driver, G. R., 'Supposed Arabisms in the Old Testament', *JBL* 55 (1936): 101-20.
—'Problems and Solutions', *VT* 4 (1954): 225-45.
—'Reflections on Recent Articles', *JBL* 73 (1954): 125-36.
—'Abbreviations in the Massoretic Text', *Textus* 1 (1960): 112-31.
—'Once Again Abbreviations', *Textus* 4 (1964): 76-94.
Dubarle, A. M., 'Δραξασθε παιδειας (Ps., II, 12)', *RB* 62 (1955): 511-12.
Dundua, N., 'The Textual Value of the Old Georgian Version of Ecclesiastes', in W. Kraus, M. van der Meer, and M. Meiser (eds.), *XV Congress of the International Organization for Septuagint and Cognate Studies: Munich, 2013* (SBLSCS 64; Atlanta, 2016), 231-39.
Duport, J., Σολομῶν ἔμμετρος, *sive Tres libri Solomonis scilicet, Proverbia, Ecclesiastes, Cantica, Graeco carmine donati* (Cambridge, 1646).
Dyk, J. W., and E. Talstra, 'Paradigmatic and Syntagmatic Features in Identifying Subject and Predicate in Nominal Clauses.', in C. L. Miller (ed.), *The Verbless Clause in Biblical Hebrew. Linguistic Approaches, Volume 1* (LSAWS; Winona Lake, 1999), 133-85.
Eaton, M., *Ecclesiastes: An introduction and commentary* (TOTC 16; Leicester, 1983).
Ehlich, K., 'Hebel–Metaphern der Nichtigkeit', in Diesel et al. (eds.), *"Jedes Ding hat seine Zeit..."*, 49-64.
*Ehrlich, A. B., 'Koheleth', in *Randglossen zur hebräischen Bibel. Textkritisches, sprachliches und sachliches Vol. 7* (Leipzig, 1914), 55-108.
*Eichhorn, D. M., *Musings of the Old Professor: The Meaning of Koheles: A New Translation of and Commentary on the Book of Ecclesiastes* (New York, 1963).
Elgvin, T., 'The Use of Scripture in 1Q/4QMysteries', in E. G. Chazon and B. Halpern-Amaru (eds.), *New Perspectives on Old Texts: Proceedings of the Tenth International Symposium of the Orion Center for the study of the Dead Sea Scrolls and associated literature, 9–11 January, 2005* (STDJ 88; Leiden/ Boston, 2010), 117-31.
Ellermeier, F., 'Das Verbum חוש in Koh 2,25. Eine exegetische, auslegungsgeschichtliche und semasiologische Untersuchung', *ZAW* 75 (1963): 197-217.
—*Qohelet. Teil 1 Abschnitt 1. Untersuchungen zum Buche Qohelet* (Herzberg a.H., 1967).
—*Qohelet. Teil 1 Abschnitt 2. Einzelfrage Nr. 7. Das Verbum חוש in Qoh 2,25. Akkadisch ḫâšu(m) "sich sorgen" im Lichte neu veröffentlicher Texte* (Herzberg a.H., 2nd edn, 1970).

—'Der Harem Qohelet/Salomos—vorläufiges Warnsignal zu Qoh. 2,8', in *Sibyllen-Musikanten-Haremsfrauen* (ThOrAr 2; Herzberg a.H., 1970), 22-27.

Elliott, M. W., 'Temporality in Our Hearts? Qoheleth 3:11 One More Time', in S. Fischer and M. Grohmann (eds.), *Weisheit und Schöpfung: Festschrift für James Alfred Loader zum 65. Geburtstag* (WAS 7, 2010), 79-90.

Ellis, E., 'Reconsidering the Fear of God in Job 37:14-24 and Qohelet 3:1-17 in the Light of Rudolf Otto's *Das Heilige*', *OTE* 28 (2015): 53-69.

*Elster, E., *Commentar über den Prediger Salomo* (Göttingen, 1855).

*Enns, P., *Ecclesiastes* (THOTC; Grand Rapids, 2011).

Eph'al, I., and J. Naveh, *Aramaic Ostraca of the Fourth Century BC from Idumaea* (Jerusalem, 1996).

Ernst, D., and A. Lange, '4681. 4QFragment Mentioning Qoh 1:8-9', in *Qumran Cave 4 XXVI Cryptic Texts and Miscellanea, Part1* (DJD 36; Oxford, 2000), p. 422, pl. XXIX.

Esh, S., 'Variant Readings in Mediaeval Hebrew Commentaries', *Textus* 5 (1966): 84-92.

*Euringer, S., *Der Masorahtext des Koheleth kritisch untersucht* (Leipzig, 1890).

*Ewald, H., *Die poetischen Bücher des Alten Bundes erklärt Vierter Theil Sprüche Salomo's Kohélet Zusätze zu den frühern Theilen und Schluss* (Göttingen, 1837). Cited as 'Ewald 1837'.

*—*Die Dichter des Alten Bundes: Die salomonischen Schriften*, vol. 2 (Göttingen, 2nd edn, 1867).

Ewald, J. L., *Salomo: Versuch einer psychologisch - biographischen Darstellung* (Leipzig/Gera, 1800).

*Farmer, K. A., *Who Knows What Is Good? A Commentary on the Books of Proverbs and Ecclesiastes* (ITC; Grand Rapids, 1991).

Faur, J., *The Horizontal Society: Understanding the Covenant and Alphabetic Judaism* (2 vols.; Boston, 2008).

Fernández, A., 'Es Ecclesiastes una Versión?', *Bib* 3 (1922): 45-50.

Fidler, R., 'Qoheleth in "The House of God": Text and Intertext in Qoh 4:17–5:6 (Eng. 5:1-7)', *HS* 47 (2006): 7-21.

*Field, F., *Origenis Hexaplorum quae supersunt; sive veterum interpretum graecorum in totum Vetus Testamentum fragmenta Post Flaminium Nobilium, Drusium, et Montefalconium, adhibita etiam versione Syro-Hexaplari, concinnavit, emendavit, et multis partibus auxit Fridericus Field* (Oxford, 1875). Field, *Auctarium*, is published as an appendix, with additional readings.

Fisch, H., 'Qohelet: A Hebrew Ironist', in *Poetry with a Purpose: Biblical Poetics and Interpretation* (Indiana Studies in Biblical Literature; Indianapolis, 1988), 158-78.

Fisch, M., 'Ecclesiastes (Qohelet) in Context—A Study of Wisdom as Constructive Skepticism', in I. C. Jarvie and N. Laor (eds.), *Critical Rationalism: Essays for Joseph Agassi Vol. 2, The Social Sciences and the humanities* (BSPS 162; Dordrecht, London, 1995), 167-85.

Fischer, A. A., 'Beobachtungen zur Komposition von Kohelet 1,3–3,15', *ZAW* 103 (1991): 72-86.
—*Skepsis oder Furcht Gottes? Studien zur Komposition und Theologie des Buches Kohelet* (BZAW 247; Berlin/New York, 1997).
—'Kohelet und die frühe Apokalyptik. Eine Auslegung von Koh 3,16-21', in Schoors (ed.), *Qohelet in the Context*, 339-56.
Fischer, S., 'Zur Übersetzung von Kohelet 2,25. Wer isst und sorgt sich ohne mich?', *Fund* 3 (1995): 219-23.
—*Die Aufforderung zur Lebensfreude im Buch Kohelet und seine Rezeption der ägyptischen Harfnerlieder* (WAS 2; Frankfurt a.M., 1999).
—'Qohelet and "Heretic" Harpers' Songs', *JSOT* 26 (2002): 105-21.
Fitzmyer, J. A., *The Aramaic Inscriptions of Sefire* (BibOr 19; Rome, 1967).
Flesher, P. V. M., 'The Wisdom of the Sages: Rabbinic rewriting of Qohelet', in E. M. Meyers and P. V. M. Flesher (eds.), *Aramaic in Postbiblical Judaism and Early Christianity: Papers from the 2004 National Endowment for the Humanities Summer Seminar at Duke University* (DJSS 3; Winona Lake, 2010), 269-79.
Flesher, P. V. M., and B. Chilton, *The Targums: A Critical Introduction* (Leiden, 2011).
Fontaine, C. R., 'Ecclesiastes', in C. A. Newsom and S. H. Ringe (eds.), *The Women's Bible Commentary* (Louisville/London, 1992), 153-55.
Foresti, F., '*'āmāl* in Koheleth: "Toil" or "Profit"', *Ephemerides Carmeliticae* 31 (1980): 415-30.
Forman, C. C., 'Koheleth's Use of Genesis', *JSS* 5 (1960): 256-63.
Fox, M. V., 'Frame-Narrative and Composition in the Book of Qohelet', *HUCA* 48 (1977): 83-106.
—'A Study of Antef', *Orientalia* 46 (1977): 393-423.
—'The Identification of Quotations in Biblical Literature', *ZAW* 92 (1980): 416-31.
—*The Song of Songs and the Ancient Egyptian Love Songs* (Madison/London, 1985).
—'The Meaning of *Hebel* for Qohelet', *JBL* 105 (1986): 409-27.
—'Qohelet's Epistemology', *HUCA* 58 (1987): 137-55.
—'Qohelet 1.4', *JSOT* 40 (1988): 109.
*—*Qohelet and his Contradictions* (JSOTSup 71; Sheffield, 1989). Cited as 'Fox 1989'.
—'What Happens in Qohelet 4:13-16?', *JHebS* 1 (1997).
—'Who Can Learn? A Dispute in Ancient Pedagogy', in M. L. Barré (ed.), *Wisdom, You Are My Sister: Studies in Honor of Roland E. Murphy, O. Carm., on the Occasion of his Eightieth Birthday* (CBQMS 29; Washington, 1997), 62-77.
—'Words for Folly', *ZAH* 10 (1997): 4-15.
—'The Inner-Structure of Qohelet's Thought', in Schoors (ed.), *Qohelet in the Context*, 225-38.

—'Time in Qohelet's "Catalogue of Times"', *JNSL* 24 (1998): 25-39.
*—*A Time to Tear Down and a Time to Build Up: A Rereading of Ecclesiastes* (Grand Rapids/Cambridge, 1999).
—*Ecclesiastes. The Traditional Hebrew Text with the New JPS Translation* (JPSBC; Philadelphia, 2004).
Fredericks, D. C., *Qoheleth's Language: Re-evaluating Its Nature and Date* (ANETS 3; Lewiston/Queenston/Lampeter, 1988).
—*Coping with Transience: Ecclesiastes on Brevity in Life* (BibSem 18; Sheffield, 1993).
Freedman, D. N., and J. Lundbom, 'דּוֹר, *dôr*', in *TDOT* 3:169-81.
Frydrych, T., *Living under the Sun: Examination of Proverbs & Qoheleth* (VTSup 90; Leiden/Boston/Köln, 2002).
Fuller, R., 'The Form and Formation of the Book of the Twelve: The Evidence from the Judean Desert', in J. W. Watts and P. R. House (eds.), *Forming Prophetic Literature: Essays on Isaiah and the Twelve in Honor of John D. W. Watts* (JSOTSup 235; Sheffield, 1996), 86-102.
Gadd, C. J., 'Tablets from Chagar Bazar and Tall Brak, 1937–38', *Iraq* 7 (1940): 22-66.
Galling, K., 'Kohelet-Studien', *ZAW* 50 (1932): 276-99.
*—'Der Prediger', in *Die fünf Megilloth* (HAT 1/18; Tübingen, 1940), 47-90.
—'Das Rätsel der Zeit im Urteil Kohelets (Koh 3, 1-15)', *ZTK* 58 (1961): 1-15.
*—'Der Prediger', in *Die fünf Megilloth* (HAT 1/18; Tübingen, 2nd edn, 1969), 73-125. Cited as 'Galling 1969'.
Gammie, J. G., 'Spatial and Ethical Dualism in Jewish Wisdom and Apocalyptic Literature', *JBL* 93 (1974): 356-85.
—'Stoicism and Anti-Stoicism in Qoheleth', *HAR* 9 (1985): 169-87.
Garfinkel, S., 'Qoheleth: The Philosopher Means Business', in K. F. Kravitz and D. M. Sharon (eds.), *Bringing the Hidden to Light: The Process of Interpretation. Studies in honor of Stephen A. Geller* (Winona Lake, 2007), 51-62.
Garr, W. R., and S. E. Fassberg (eds.), *A Handbook of Biblical Hebrew. Volume 1: Periods, Corpora, and Reading Traditions* (Winona Lake, 2016).
Garrett, D. A., 'Qoheleth on the Use and Abuse of Political Power', *TJ* NS 8 (1987): 159-77.
Garuti, P., 'Une Route qui mène à Rome...ou dans l'environs (Qo 4,13-16)', in J. E. Aguilar Chiu, K. J. O'Mahony, and M. Roger (eds.), *Bible et Terre Sainte: Mélanges Marcel Beaudry* (Bern, 2008), 105-18.
Gasquet, F. A. (ed.), *Biblia sacra iuxta latinam vulgatam versionem* (18 vols.; Rome, 1926–1995).
Gault, B. P., 'A Reexamination of "Eternity" in Ecclesiastes 3:11', *BSac* 165 (2008): 39-57.
von Gebhardt, O., *Graecus Venetus: Pentateuchi, Proverbiorum, Ruth, Cantici, Ecclesiastae, Threnorum, Danielis Version Graeca; ex unico Bibliothecae S. Marci Venetae codice* (Leipzig, 1875).

*Geier, M., *In Salomonis Ecclesiasten commentarius succinctus, dilucidus, fontiumque praecipue Ebraeorum mentem genuinam una cum usu evolvens* (Leipzig, 1668).

Gentry, P. J., 'Hexaplaric Materials in Ecclesiastes and the Rôle of the Syro-Hexapla', *AS* 1 (2003): 5-28.

—'The Relationship of Aquila and Theodotion to the Old Greek of Ecclesiastes in the Marginal Notes of the Syro-Hexapla', *AS* 2 (2004): 63-84.

—'Propaedeutic to a Lexicon of the Three: The Priority of a New Critical Edition of Hexaplaric Fragments', *AS* 2 (2004): 145-74.

—'The Role of the "Three" in the Text History of the Septuagint: II. Aspects of interdependence of the Old Greek and the Three in Ecclesiastes', *AS* 4 (2006): 153-92.

—'The Text of the Old Testament', *JETS* 52 (2009): 19-45.

*—(ed.), *Septuaginta: Vetus Testamentum Graecum. Auctoritate Academiae Scientiarum Gottingensis editum. Vol. XI, 2 Ecclesiastes* (Göttingen, forthcoming).

Gericke, J. W., 'Injustice under the Sun? A New Perspective on Possible Allusions to Ancient Near Eastern Solar Mythology in Qohelet', *OTE* 16 (2003): 244-58.

—'Axiological assumptions in Qohelet: A Historical-Philosophical Clarification', *Verbum et Ecclesia* 33 (2012): art. 515, 6 pages.

—'Qohelet's Concept of Deity: A Comparative-Philosophical Perspective', *Verbum et Ecclesia* 34 (2013): art. 743, 8 pages.

—'A Comprehensive Typology of Philosophical Perspectives on Qohelet', *Verbum et Ecclesia* 36 (2015): art. 1358, 7 pages.

—'A Comprehensive Philosophical Approach to Qohelet's Epistemology: Original Research', *HTS Theological Studies* 71 (2015): 1-9.

Gerleman, G., 'Die sperrende Grenze. Die Wurzel *ʿlm* im Hebräischen', *ZAW* 91 (1979): 338-49.

Gese, H., 'Die Krisis der Weisheit bei Koheleth', in *Les Sagesses du Proche-Orient Ancien. Colloque de Strasbourg 17–19 mai 1962* (Travaux du Centre d'Études Supérieures Spécialisé d'Histoire des Religions de Strasbourg; Paris, 1963), 139-51. ET 'The Crisis of Wisdom in Koheleth', in J. L. Crenshaw (ed.), *Theodicy in the Old Testament* (Issues in Religion and Theology 4; Philadelphia/London, 1983), 141-53.

—'Zur Komposition des Koheletbuches', in H. Cancik, H. Lichtenberger, and P. Schäfer (eds.), *Geschichte—Tradition—Reflexion: Festschrift für Martin Hengel zum 70. Geburtstag: Bd.1, Judentum* (Tübingen, 1996), 69-98.

Giambrone, A., 'Aquila's Greek Targum: Reconsidering the Rabbinical Setting of an Ancient Translation', *HTR* 110 (2017): 24-45.

Gianto, A., 'The Theme of Enjoyment in Qohelet', *Bib* 73 (1992): 528-33.

—'Human Destiny in Emar and Qohelet', in Schoors (ed.), *Qohelet in the Context*, 473-79.

Gil, M., *A History of Palestine, 634–1099* (trans. E. Broido; Cambridge/New York, 1992).

Gilbert, M., 'Qohelet et Ben Sira', in Schoors (ed.), *Qohelet in the Context*, 161-79.

Ginsberg, H. L., 'Review of *A Grammar of the Phoenician Language* by Zellig S. Harris', *JBL* 56 (1937): 138-43.
—'"King of Kings" and "Lord of Kingdoms"', *AJSL* 57 (1940): 71-74.
—*Studies in Koheleth* (TSJTSA 17; New York, 1950).
—'Supplementary Studies in Kohelet', *Proceedings of the American Academy of Jewish Research* 21 (1952): 35-62.
—'The Structure and Contents of the Book of Koheleth', in M. Noth and D. W. Thomas (eds.), *Wisdom in Israel and in the Ancient Near East* (VTSup 3; Leiden, 1955), 138-49.
*— קֹהֶלֶת =*Qohelet* (A New Commentary on the Torah, the Prophets and the Holy Writings; Tel-Aviv/Jerusalem, 1961).
—'The Quintessence of Koheleth', in A. Altmann (ed.), *Biblical and Other Studies* (STLI 1; Cambridge, MA, 1963), 47-59.
*Ginsburg, C. D., *Coheleth, Commonly Called the Book of Ecclesiastes: Translated from the original Hebrew, with a commentary, historical and critical* (London, 1861).
—*The Massorah: Compiled from Manuscripts Alphabetically and Lexically Arranged* (4 vols.; London, 1880).
—*Introduction to the Massoretico-critical Edition of the Hebrew Bible* (London, 1897).
—*The Writings Diligently Revised According to the Massorah and the Early Editions: With the Various Readings from the Manuscripts and the Ancient Versions* (London, 1926).
Ginzberg, L., 'Die Haggada bei den Kirchenvätern. V. Der Kommentar des Hieronymus zu Koheleth', in V. Aptowitzer and A. Z. Schwarz (eds.), *Abhandlungen zur Erinnerung an Hirsch Perez Chajes* (Veröffentlichungen der Alexander Kohut Memorial Foundation 7; Vienna, 1933), 22-50.
Giostra, A., '"Accomodar i pronunciati delle Sacre Lettere" L'interpretazione di Ecclesiaste 1,4-6 tra i primi sostenitori della Teoria Copernicana', *StPat* 53 (2006): 391-424.
Glasser, É., *Le Procès du bonheur par Qohelet* (Lectio Divina 61; Paris, 1970).
Gnanaraj, D., *The Language of Qoheleth: An Evaluation of the Recent Scholarly Studies* (Delhi, 2012).
Goldingay, J., and D. Payne, *A Critical and Exegetical Commentary on Isaiah 40–55: Volume I, Introduction and commentary on Isaiah 40–44.23* (ICC; London/New York, 2006).
*Goldman, Y. A. P. (commentary on the critical apparatus of Qoheleth in *BHQ*, fascicle 18, 64*-112*).
—'Le texte massorétique de Qohélet, témoin d'un compromis théologique entre les "disciples des sages" (Qoh 7,23-24; 8,1; 7,19)', in Y. A. P. Goldman, A. van der Kooij, and R. D. Weis (eds.), *Sôfer Mahîr: Essays in Honour of Adrian Schenker Offered by Editors of Biblia Hebraica Quinta* (VTSup 110; Leiden/Boston, 2006), 69-93.

Gómez Aranda, M., *El Comentario de Abraham Ibn Ezra al Libro Del Eclesiastés: Introducción,Traducción y Edición Critica* (Textos y estudios "Cardenal Cisneros" de la Biblia Políglota Matritense 56; Madrid, 1994).

—'Grammatical Remarks in *The Commentary of Abraham Ibn Ezra on Qohelet*', *Sefarad* 56 (1996): 61-82.

—'The Influence of Isaac Ibn Ghayyat on Abraham Ibn Ezra's Commentary on Ecclesiastes', *JJS* 63 (2012): 84-104.

Good, E. M., 'The Unfilled Sea: Style and meaning in Ecclesiastes 1:2-11', in J. G. Gammie and et al. (eds.), *Israelite Wisdom: Theological and Literary Essays in Honor of Samuel Terrien* (New York, 1978), 59-73.

—*Irony in the Old Testament* (BLS 3; Sheffield, 2nd edn, 1981).

Goodman, M., 'Sacred Scripture and "Defiling the Hands"', *JTS* 41 (1990): 99-107.

Goodrich, R. J., and D. J. D. Miller (eds.), *St Jerome: Commentary on Ecclesiastes* (Ancient Christian Writers: The Works of the Fathers in Translation 66; New York/Mahwah, 2012).

Gordis, R., 'Ecclesiastes 1:17: Its Text and Interpretation', *JBL* 56 (1937): 323-30.

—'Quotations in Wisdom Literature', *JQR* 30 (1939): 123-47.

—'The Original Language of Qohelet', *JQR* 37 (1946): 67-84.

—'Quotations as a Literary Usage in Biblical, Oriental, and Rabbinic Literature', *HUCA* 22 (1949): 157-219.

—'The Translation Theory of Qohelet Re-Examined', *JQR* 40 (1949): 103-16.

—'Koheleth: Hebrew or Aramaic?', *JBL* 71 (1952): 93-109.

—'Was Koheleth a Phoenician? Some Observations on Methods in Research', *JBL* 74 (1955): 103-14.

—'Qoheleth and Qumran: A Study of Style', *Bib* 41 (1960): 395-410.

—Koheleth—The Man and his World: A study of Ecclesiastes (New York, 3rd edn, 1968).

Gordon, C. H., 'השפעה צפון-ישראלית על העברית שלאחר-גלות בבל', *EI* 3 (1954): 104-105; ET 'North Israelite Influence on Postexilic Hebrew', *IEJ* 5 (1955): 85-88.

Görg, M., 'Zu einer bekannten Paronomasie in Koh 2,8', *BN* 90 (1997): 5-7.

Gorssen, L., 'La cohérence de la conception de Dieu dans l'Ecclésiaste', *ETL* 46 (1970): 282-324.

Goshen-Gottstein, M. H., 'Hebrew Biblical Manuscripts: Their History and their Place in the HUBP Edition', *Bib* 48 (1967): 243-90.

Grabbe, L. L., *Comparative Philology and the Text of Job: a Study in Methodology* (SBLDS 34; Missoula, 1977).

—'Aquila's Translation and Rabbinic Exegesis', *JJS* 33 (1982): 527-36.

*Graetz, H., *Kohélet* קהלת *oder der Salomonische Prediger Übersetzt und kritisch erläutert Nebst Anhang über Kohélet's Stellung im Kanon, über die griechische Uebersetzung desselben und über Graecismen darin und einem Glossar* (Leipzig, 1871).

Graves, M., *Jerome's Hebrew Philology: A Study Based on his Commentary on Jeremiah* (VCSup 90; Leiden/Boston, 2007).
—'Glimpses into the History of the Hebrew Bible Through the Vulgate Tradition, with Special Reference to Vulgate MS θ^G', in A. P. Otero and P. T. Morales (eds.), *The Text of the Hebrew Bible and its Editions: Studies in Celebration of the Fifth Centennial of the Complutensian Polyglot* (STHB 1; Leiden/Boston, 2017), 217-54.
Greenberg, M., 'נסה in Exodus 20:20 and the Purpose of the Sinaitic Theophany', *JBL* 79 (1960): 273-76.
Greenstein, E. L., 'Sages with a Sense of Humor: The Babylonian Dialogue between a Master and His Servant and the Book of Qohelet', in R. J. Clifford (ed.), *Wisdom Literature in Mesopotamia and Israel* (SBLSS 36; Atlanta, 2007), 55-65.
Greenwood, K. R., 'Debating Wisdom: The Role of Voice in Ecclesiastes', *CBQ* 74 (2012): 476-91.
Gregory, B. C., 'A Reassessment of Sirach's Relationship to Qoheleth: A Case Study of Qoheleth 3:15 and Sirach 5:3', in Dell and Kynes (eds.), *Reading Ecclesiastes Intertextually*, 189-200.
Griffith, S. H., *The Bible in Arabic: The Scriptures of the "People of the Book" in the Language of Islam* (Princeton, 2013).
Grimm, W., 'Ueber die Stelle Koheleth 3,11^b', *ZWT* 23 (1880): 274-79.
Grimme, H., 'Babel und Koheleth-Jojakhin', *OLZ* 8 (1905): 432-38.
*de Groot (Grotius), H., *Annotata ad Vetus Testamentum*, vol. 1 (Paris, 1664).
Gropp, D. M., 'The Origin and Development of the Aramaic *šallîṭ* Clause', *JNES* 52 (1993): 31-36.
Grossberg, D., 'Form and Content and their Correspondence', *HS* 41 (2000): 47-52.
Günther, J., 'Der Zusammenhang in Koh 3 11-15', *ZAW* 51 (1933): 79-80.
Gutridge, C. A., 'The Sacrifice of Fools and the Wisdom of Silence: Qoheleth, Job and the Presence of God', in A. Rapoport-Albert and G. Greenberg (eds.), *Biblical Hebrews, Biblical Texts. Essays in Memory of Michael P. Weitzman* (JSOTSup 333; Sheffield, 2001), 83-99.
Gwynn, R. M., 'Notes on the Vocabulary of Ecclesiastes in Greek', *Hermathena* 19 (1920): 115-22.
ter Haar Romeny, R. B., *A Syrian in Greek Dress: The Use of Greek, Hebrew, and Syriac Biblical Texts in Eusebius of Emesa's Commentary on Genesis* (Louvain, 1997).
Haden, N. K., 'Qohelet and the Problem of Alienation', *CSR* 17 (1987): 52-66.
Hallock, R. T., *Persepolis Fortification Tablets* (OIP 92; Chicago, 1969).
Halperin, D. J., 'The "Book of Remedies," the Canonization of the Solomonic Writings, and the Riddle of Pseudo-Eusebius', *JQR* 72 (1982): 269-92.
Hankins, C. D., 'The Internal Infinite: Deleuze, Subjectivity, and Moral Agency in Ecclesiastes', *JSOT* 40 (2015): 43-59.

BIBLIOGRAPHY OF WORKS CITED

Hardt, H. von der, *Jesu Jojadae, summorum inter Judaeos pontificum filii et fratris, Coheleth prosopopeia Salomonis, omnium opinione obscurissimum librum, dilucide et curate ex linguae indole, historia et antiquitate* (Helmstedt, 1714).

Harrison, C. R., 'Qoheleth among the Sociologists', *BibInt* 5 (1997): 160-80.

Hasel, G. F., 'יָעַץ, *yāg*ʿ', in *TDOT* 5:385-93.

Haupt, P., 'The Book of Ecclesiastes', in *Oriental Studies: A Selection of the Papers read before the Oriental Club of Philadelphia 1888–1894* (Boston, 1894), 242-78.

*—*Koheleth oder Weltschmerz in der Bible: Ein Lieblingsbuch Friedrichs des Grossen* (Leipzig, 1905).

Hayman, A. P., 'Qohelet and the Book of Creation', *JSOT* 16 (1991): 93-111.

—'Qohelet, the Rabbis and the Wisdom Text from the Cairo Geniza', in A. G. Auld (ed.), *Understanding Poets and Prophets. Essays in Honour of George Wishart Anderson* (JSOTSup 152; Sheffield, 1993), 149-65.

Hays, J. D., 'Verb Forms in the Expository Discourse Sections of Ecclesiastes', *JOTT* 7 (1995): 9-18.

Heard, R. C., 'The Dao of Qoheleth. An Intertextual Reading of the Daode Jing and the Book of Ecclesiastes', *Jian Dao* 5 (1996): 65-93.

Hecke, P. van, 'The Verbs ראה and שמע in the Book of Qohelet: A Cognitive-Semantic Perspective', in Berlejung and van Hecke (eds.), *The Language of Qohelet*, 203-20.

*Heiligstedt, A., *Franc Jos Valent Dominic Maureri Commentarius grammaticus historicus criticus in Vetus Testamentum: in usum maxime gymnasiorum et academiarum adornatus: Vol IV Sect II Commentarium in Ecclesiasten et Canticum Canticorum continens* (Leipzig, 1848).

Heim, K., 'Hyper-Ambiguity in Ecclesiastes' (Paper presented at the annual meeting of the SBL; Denver, November 18, 2018).

*Heinemann, M., קֹהֶלֶת: *Uebersetzung des Koheleth, nebst grammatisch exegetischem Commentar* (Berlin, 1831).

Hendel, R., *Steps to a New Edition of the Hebrew Bible* (Atlanta, 2016).

Hengel, M., *Judentum und Hellenismus: Studien zu ihrer Begegnung unter besonderer Berücksichtigung Palästinas bis zur Mitte des 2. Jh. v. Chr* (WUNT 10; Tübingen, 2nd edn, 1973). ET *Judaism and Hellenism: Studies in their encounter in Palestine during the early Hellenistic period* (2 vols.; Philadelphia, 1974).

Herrmann, W., 'Zu Koheleth 3, 14', in W. Herrmann (ed.), *Von Gott und den Göttern. Gesammelte Aufsätze zum Alten Testament* (BZAW 259; Berlin, 1999), 1-6.

*Hertzberg, H. W., *Der Prediger (Qohelet)* (KAT 16/4; Leipzig, 1932). Cited as 'Hertzberg 1932'.

—'Palästinische Bezüge im Buche Kohelet', *ZDPV* 73 (1957): 113-24.

*—*Der Prediger* (KAT 17/4; Gütersloh, 2nd edn, 1963).

*Herzfeld, L., קֹהֶלֶת *übersetzt und erläutert* (Braunschweig, 1838).

Hieke, T., 'Wie hast du's mit der Religion? Sprechhandlungen und Wirkintentionen in Kohelet 4,17–5,6', in Schoors (ed.), *Qohelet in the Context*, 319-38.
Hinz, W., 'Die elamischen Buchungstäfeichen der Darius-Zeit', *Orientalia* 39 (1970): 421-40.
—*Altiranisches Sprachgut der Nebenüberlieferungen* (GO III, 3; Wiesbaden, 1975).
Hirshman, M. G., 'Qohelet's Reception and Interpretation in Early Rabbinic Literature', in J. L. Kugel (ed.), *Studies in Ancient Midrash* (Cambridge, MA, 2001), 87-99.
Hitzig, F., 'Ueber die Stelle Prediger 3,11', *TSK* 12 (1839): 513-18.
*—'Der Prediger Salomo's', in *Kurzgefasstes exegetisches Handbuch zum Alten Testament: Siebente Lieferung* (Leipzig, 1847), 113-221.
—'Zur Exegese und Kritik des Buches Kohelet', *ZWT* 14 (1871): 566-75.
Hobbins, J. F., 'The Poetry of Qohelet', in Boda, Longman, and Rata (eds.), *The Words of the Wise*, 163-92.
*Hodgson, B., *Ecclesiastes: A New Translation from the Original Hebrew* (Oxford/London, 1790).
Hoffmann, F., and J. F. Quack, *Anthologie der demotischen Literatur* (EQÄ 4; Berlin, 2007).
Holland, F. T., 'Heart of Darkness: A Study of Qohelet 3:1-15', *PIBA* 17 (1994): 81-101.
Holm-Nielsen, S., 'On the Interpretation of Qoheleth in Early Christianity', *VT* 24 (1974): 168-77.
Holmstedt, R., 'אֲנִי וְלִבִּי The Syntactic Encoding of the Collaborative Nature of Qohelet's Experiment', *JHebS* 9 (2009).
—'The Grammar of שׁ and אשׁר in Qohelet', in Boda, Longman, and Rata (eds.), *The Words of the Wise*, 283-307.
—*The Relative Clause in Biblical Hebrew* (LSAWS 10; Winona Lake, 2016).
Hügel, K., 'Eine queere Lesart von Kohelet 4,9-12', *SJOT* 28 (2014): 104-15.
Humbert, P., 'Qoheléth', *RTP* 3 (1915): 253-77.
—*Recherches sur les sources égyptiennes de la littérature sapientiale d'Israël* (Mémoires de l'Université de Neuchâtel 7; Neuchâtel, 1929).
Hunter, A. J., 'An Awfully Beastly Business: Some Thoughts on *behēmāh* in Jonah and Qoheleth', in Brooke and van Hecke (eds.), *Goochem*, 82-94.
Hurvitz, A., 'The Chronological Significance of "Aramaisms" in Biblical Hebrew', *IEJ* 18 (1968): 234-40.
—'The Language of Qoheleth and Its Historical Setting within Biblical Hebrew', in Berlejung and van Hecke (eds.), *The Language of Qohelet*, 23-34.
—*A Concise Lexicon of Late Biblical Hebrew: Linguistic innovations in the Writings of the Second Temple period* (VTSup 160; Leiden/Boston, 2014).
Hyvärinen, K., *Die Übersetzung von Aquila* (CB 10; Uppsala, 1977).
Ingram, D., *Ambiguity in Ecclesiastes* (LHBOTS 431; New York/London, 2006).
—'The Riddle of Qohelet and Qohelet the Riddler', *JSOT* 37 (2013): 485-509.
Irwin, W. A., 'Ecclesiastes 3,18', *AJSL* 56 (1939): 298-99.

—'A Rejoinder', *AJSL* 58 (1941): 100-101.
—'Ecclesiastes 4:13-16', *JNES* 3 (1944): 255-57.
Isaksson, B., *Studies in the Language of Qoheleth: With Special Emphasis on the Verbal System* (SSU 10; Uppsala, 1987).
—'The Syntax of the Narrative Discourse in Qohelet', in Berlejung and van Hecke (eds.), *The Language of Qohelet*, 35-46.
James, K. W., 'Ecclesiastes: Precursor of Existentialists', *The Bible Today* 22 (1984): 85-90.
Janichs, G., *Animadversiones criticae in versionem Syriacam Peschitthonianam librorum Koheleth et Ruth. Dissertatio Inauguralis* (Leipzig, 1869).
Janzen, J. G., 'Qohelet on Life "Under the Sun"', *CBQ* 70 (2008): 465-83.
Japhet, S., '"Goes to the South and Turns to the North" (Ecclesiastes 1:6): The Sources and History of the Exegetical Traditions', *JSQ* 1 (1993): 289-322.
Japhet, S., and R. B. Salters, *The Commentary of R. Samuel Ben Meir Rashbam on Qoheleth* (Jerusalem/Leiden, 1985).
Jarick, J., 'Aquila's *Koheleth*', *Textus* 15 (1990): 131-39.
—'Theodore of Mopsuestia and the Text of Ecclesiastes', in L. Greenspoon and O. Munnich (eds.), *VIII Congress of the International Organization for Septuagint and Cognate Studies. Paris 1992* (SBLSCS 41; Atlanta, 1995), 367-85.
—'The Bible's "Festival Scrolls" among the Dead Sea Scrolls', in S. E. Porter and C. A. Evans (eds.), *The Scrolls and the Scriptures: Qumran Fifty Years After* (JSPSup 26; Sheffield, 1997), 170-82.
—'The Hebrew Book of Changes: Reflections on *hakkōl hebel* and *lakkōl z^{e}mān* in Ecclesiastes', *JSOT* 90 (2000): 79-99.
—'Ecclesiastes among the Comedians', in Dell and Kynes (eds.), *Reading Ecclesiastes Intertextually*, 176-88.
—'Ecclesiastes among the Tragedians', in Brooke and van Hecke (eds.), *Goochem*, 95-107.
Jasper, F. N., 'Ecclesiastes: A Note for Our Time', *Int* 31 (1967): 259-73.
Jastram, N. R., 'The Severus Scroll and Rabbi Meir's Torah', in E. Martín Contreras and L. Miralles-Maciá (eds.), *The Text of the Hebrew Bible: From the Rabbis to the Masoretes* (JAJSup 13; Göttingen, 2014), 137-45.
Jastrow, Marcus, *A Dictionary of the Targumim, the Talmud Babli and Yerushalmi, and the Midrashic Literature* (London/New York, 1903).
*Jastrow, Morris, *A Gentle Cynic, Being a Translation of the Book of Koheleth Commonly Known as Ecclesiastes, Stripped of Later Additions: Also its Origin, Growth and Interpretation* (Philadelphia/London, 1919).
Jayādvaita Swami (Jay Israel), *Vanity Karma: Ecclesiastes, the Bhagavad-Gītā, and the Meaning of Life* (Los Angeles, 2015).
Jenner, K. D., '10c4 – I/II Kings (II,4), Proverbs, Ecclesiastes, and Song of Songs (II,5)', in P. B. Dirksen and M. J. Mulder (eds.), *The Peshiṭta: Its Early Text and History: Papers Read at the Peshiṭta Symposium Held at Leiden 30–31 August 1985* (MPIL 4; Leiden, 1988), 279-89.

Jenni, E., 'Das Wort *ʿōlām* im Alten Testament', *ZAW* 64–65 (1952): 64, 197-248; 65, 1-35.

—*Die hebräischen Präpositionen 1. Die Präposition Beth* (Stuttgart, 1992).

Johnston, C., 'The Alleged Grecisms of Ecclesiastes', *Johns Hopkins University Circulars* 10 (1891): 118-19.

Johnstone, W., '"The Preacher" as Scientist', *SJT* 20 (1967): 210-21.

Jones, B. W., 'From Gilgamesh to Qoheleth', in W. W. Hallo, B. W. Jones, and G. L. Mattingly (eds.), *The Bible in the Light Of Cuneiform Literature: Scripture in Context 3* (ANETS 8; Lewiston/Queenston/Lampeter, 1990), 349-79.

Jones, S. C., 'Solomon's Table Talk: Martin Luther on the Authorship of Ecclesiastes', *SJOT* 28 (2014): 81-90.

Jong, S. de, '"Quitate de mi Sol!" Eclesiastés y la tecnocracia helenística', *RIBLA* 11 (1992): 75-85.

—'A Book on Labour: The Structuring Principles and the Main Theme of the Book of Qohelet', *JSOT* 17 (1992): 107-16.

—'Qohelet and the Ambitious Spirit of the Ptolemaic Period', *JSOT* 19 (1994): 85-96.

Joosten, J., 'The Syntax of Volitive Verbal Forms in Qoheleth in Historical Perspective', in Berlejung and van Hecke (eds.), *The Language of Qohelet*, 47-61.

—'The Tiberian Vocalization and the Hebrew of the Second Temple Period', in E. Tigchelaar and P. Van Hecke (eds.), *Hebrew of the Late Second Temple Period: Proceedings of a Sixth International Symposium on the Hebrew of the Dead Sea Scrolls and Ben Sira* (STDJ 114; Leiden/Boston, 2015), 25-36.

Joüon, P., 'Sur le nom de "Qoheleth"', *Bib* 2 (1921): 53-54.

—'Notes de syntaxe hébraïque', *Bib* 2 (1921): 223-29.

—'Notes philologiques sur le texte Hébreu d'Ecclésiaste', *Bib* 11 (1930): 419-25.

Kahle, P., *The Cairo Geniza* (Oxford, 2nd edn, 1959).

Kaiser, G. P. C., *Koheleth, das Collectivum der Davidischen Könige in Jerusalem: ein historisches Lehrgedicht über den Umsturz des jüdischen Staates. Uebersetzt und mit historischen und philologisch-kritischen bemerkungen erläutert* (Erlangen, 1823).

Kaiser, O., *Der Mensch unter dem Schicksal. Studien zur Geschichte, Theologie und Gegenwartsbedeutung der Weisheit* (BZAW 161; Berlin/New York, 1985).

—'Die Sinnkrise bei Kohelet', in *Der Mensch unter dem Schicksal*, 91-109.

—'Judentum und Hellenismus. Ein Beitrag zur Frage nach dem hellenistischen Einfluß auf Kohelet und Jesus Sirach', in *Der Mensch unter dem Schicksal*, 135-53. Previously published in *Verkündigung und Forschung* 27 (1982): 68-86.

—'Qoheleth', in J. Day et al. (eds.), *Wisdom in Ancient Israel*, 83-93.

Kamano, N., 'Character and Cosmology: Rhetoric of Qoh 1,3–3,9', in Schoors (ed.), *Qohelet in the Context*, 419-24.

—*Cosmology and Character: Qoheleth's Pedagogy from a Rhetorical-Critical Perspective* (BZAW 312; Berlin/New York, 2002).

*Kamenetzky, A. S., 'Die Pšiṭa zu Ḳoheleth textkritisch und in ihrem Verhältnis zu dem massoretischen Text, der Septuaginta und den andern alten griechischen Versionen', ZAW 24 (1904): 181-239.
—'Das Koheleth-Rätsel', ZAW 29 (1909): 63-69.
—'Die Rätselname Koheleth', ZAW 34 (1914): 225-28.
—'Die ursprünglich beabsichtigte Aussprache des Pseudonyms קהלת', OLZ 24 (1921): cols. 11-15.
Kedar-Kopfstein, B., 'Jewish Traditions in the Writings of Jerome', in D. R. G. Beattie and M. J. MacNamara (eds.), *The Aramaic Bible Targums in their Historical Context* (JSOTSup 166; Sheffield, 1994), 420-30.
Kelly, J. R., 'Sources of Contention and the Emerging Reality Concerning Qohelet's Carpe Diem Advice', *Antiguo Oriente* 8 (2010): 117-34.
*Kennicott, B., *Vetus Testamentum Hebraicum cum Variis Lectionibus* (2 vols.; Oxford, 1776-80).
Khan, G., 'The Medieval Karaite Tradition of Hebrew Grammar', *Asociacion Española de Orientalistas* 38 (2002): 51-76.
—'The Languages of the Old Testament', in J. Carleton Paget and J. Schaper (eds.), *The New Cambridge History of the Bible: From the Beginnings to 600* (Cambridge, 2013), 1-21.
Klein, C., *Kohelet und die Weisheit Israels: Eine formgeschichtliche Studie* (BWANT 132; Stuttgart, 1994).
Klein, J., '"The Ballad about Early Rulers" in Eastern and Western Traditions', in K. van Lerberghe and G. Voet (eds.), *Languages and Cultures in Contact: At the Crossroads of Civilizations in the Syro-Mesopotamian Realm: Proceedings of the 42th RAI* (OLA 96; Leuven, 1999), 203-16.
Klostermann, E., *De libri Coheleth versione Alexandrina: Dissertatio Inauguralis* (Kiel, 1892).
*Knobel, A., *Commentar über das Buch Koheleth* (Leipzig, 1836).
Knobel, P. S., 'Targum Qoheleth: A Linguistic and Exegetical Inquiry' (PhD diss.; Yale University, 1976).
—*The Targum of Qohelet* (The Aramaic Bible 15; Edinburgh/Collegeville, 1991).
Knopf, C. S., 'The Optimism of Koheleth', *JBL* 49 (1930): 195-99.
Koenen, K., 'Zu den Epilogen des Buches Qohelet', *BN* 72 (1994): 24-27.
Koh, Y. V., *Royal Autobiography in the Book of Qoheleth* (BZAW 369; Berlin/New York, 2006).
*Köhlmoos, M., *Kohelet. Der Prediger Salomo* (Das Alte Testament Deutsch Neues Göttinger Bibelwerk 16/5; Göttingen/Bristol, 2015).
van der Kooij, A., 'Standardization or Preservation? Some Comments on the Textual History of the Hebrew Bible in the Light of Josephus and Rabbinic Literature', in E. Martín Contreras and L. Miralles-Maciá (eds.), *The Text of the Hebrew Bible: From the Rabbis to the Masoretes* (JAJSup 13; Göttingen, 2014), 63-78.
Koosed, J. L., *(Per)mutations of Qohelet: Reading the body in the book* (LHBOTS 429; New York/London, 2006).

Korpel, M. C. A., and J. M. Oesch (eds.), *Delimitation Criticism: A New Tool in Biblical Scholarship* (Pericope 1; Assen, 2000).
Kotjatko-Reeb, J., 'Koh 3,1-8: Infinitive und Verbalnomina nach dem Zeitnomen עת im Hebräischen', in J. Kotjatko-Reeb et al. (eds.), *Nichts Neues unter der Sonne?*, 55-74.
Kotjatko-Reeb, J. et al. (eds.), *Nichts Neues unter der Sonne? Zeitvorstellungen im Alten Testament: Festschrift für Ernst-Joachim Waschke zum 65. Geburtstag* (BZAW 450; Berlin, 2014).
Kreuzer, S., *Bible in Greek: Translation, Transmission, and Theology of the Septuagint* (Atlanta, 2015).
Krochmal, N., מורה נבוכי הזמן : ספר מורה אמונה צרופה ומלמד חכמת ישראל = *A Guide for the Perplexed of this Time* (Lviv, 1851). Prepared for posthumous publication by L. Zunz.
Kroker, E., *D. Martin Luthers Werke Kritische Gesamtausgabe. Werke. Tischreden, 1. Band* (Weimar, 1912).
Krüger, T., 'Dekonstruktion und Rekonstruktion prophetischer Eschatologie im Qohelet-Buch', in Diesel et al. (eds.), *"Jedes Ding hat seine Zeit..."*, 107-29.
—'Das Gute und die Güter: Erwägungen zur Bedeutung von טוב und טובה im Qoheletbuch', *TZ* 53 (1997): 53-63.
—'Die Rezeption der Tora im Buch Kohelet', in L. Schwienhorst-Schönberger (ed.), *Das Buch Kohelet. Studien zur Struktur, Geschichte, Rezeption und Theologie* (BZAW 254; Berlin/New York, 1997), 303-25.
—'Qoh 2,24-26 und die Frage nach dem "Guten" im Qohelet-Buch', in *Kritische Weisheit. Studien zur weisheitlichen Traditionskritik im Alten Testament* (Zürich, 1997), 131-49.
—'Le Livre de Qohéleth dans le contexte de la littérature juive des IIIe et IIe siècles avant Jésus-Christ', *RTP* 131 (1999): 135-62.
*—*Kohelet: (Prediger)* (BKAT 19; Neukirchen-Vluyn, 2000). ET *Qoheleth A Commentary* (Hermeneia; Minneapolis, 2004).
—'"And They Have No Comforter": Job and Ecclesiastes in Dialogue', in Dell and Kynes (eds.), *Reading Ecclesiastes Intertextually*, 94-105.
Kugel, J. L., 'Qohelet and Money', *CBQ* 51 (1989): 32-49.
—'Wisdom and the Anthological Temper', *Prooftexts* 17 (1997): 9-32.
Kustár, Z., 'Neue Sichten—neue Schichten: Skizze einer Redaktionsgeschichte des Buches Kohelet', in J. Kotjatko-Reeb et al. (eds.), *Nichts Neues unter der Sonne?*, 279-92.
Kynes, W., *An Obituary for Wisdom Literature: The Birth, Death, and Intertextual Reintegration of a Biblical Corpus* (New York, 2018).
Labate, A., 'L'apporto della Catena Hauniense sull' Ecclesiaste per il testo delle versioni greche di Simmaco e della LXX', *RivB* 35 (1987): 57-61.
Labendz, J. R., 'Aquila's Bible Translation in Late Antiquity: Jewish and Christian Perspectives', *HTR* 102 (2009): 353-88.
Lambert, W. G., 'Some New Babylonian Wisdom Literature', in J. Day et al. (eds.), *Wisdom in Ancient Israel*, 30-42.

Lamparter, H., *Das Buch der Weisheit Prediger und Sprüche* (BAT 16; Stuttgart, 2nd edn, 1959).
*Lampe, G. W. H. (ed.), *A Patristic Greek Lexicon* (Oxford, 1961).
Lane, D. J., 'Qoheleth', in *The Old Testament in Syriac according to the Peshiṭta Version: Edited on Behalf of the International Organization for the Study of the Old Testament by the Peshiṭta Institute, Leiden. Part II, fasc. 5 Proverbs, Wisdom of Solomon, Ecclesiastes, Song of Songs* (Leiden, 1979).
—'"Lilies That Fester...": The Peshiṭta Text of Qoheleth (Peshiṭta Institute Communication)', *VT* 29 (1979): 481-90.
Lange, A., 'In Diskussion mit dem Tempel. Zur Auseinandersetzung zwischen Kohelet und weisheitlichen Kreisen am Jerusalemer Tempel', in Schoors (ed.), *Qohelet in the Context*, 113-59.
—'Pre-Maccabean Literature from the Qumran Library and the Hebrew Bible', *DSD* 13 (2006): 277-305.
—'"They confirmed the reading" (*y. Ta'an.* 4.68a): The Textual Standardization of Jewish Scriptures in the Second Temple Period', in A. Lange et al. (eds.), *From Qumran to Aleppo*, 29-80.
Lange, A., M. Weigold, and J. Zsengellér (eds.), *From Qumran to Aleppo: A Discussion with Emanuel Tov about the Textual History of Jewish Scriptures in Honor of his 65th birthday* (FRLANT 230; Göttingen, 2009).
de Lange, N., 'The Letter to Africanus: Origen's Recantation?', in E. A. Livingstone (ed.), *Studia Patristica: Papers Presented to the Seventh International Conference on Patristic Studies Held in Oxford 1975. Part II Monastica et Ascetica, Orientalia, E Saeculo Secundo, Origen, Athanasius, Cappadocian Fathers, Chrysostom, Augustine* (Berlin, 1985), 242-44.
—'The Revival of the Hebrew Language in the Third Century CE', *JSQ* 3 (1996): 342-58.
—'9. A Greek Translation of Kohelet (Ecclesiastes)', in *Greek Jewish Texts from the Cairo Genizah* (TSAJ 51, 1996), 71-78.
—*Japheth in the Tents of Shem: Greek Bible Translations in Byzantine Judaism* (Tübingen, 2015).
Lauha, A., 'Die Krise des religiösen Glaubens bei Kohelet', in M. Noth and D. W. Thomas (eds.), *Wisdom in Israel and in the Ancient Near East* (VTSup 3; Leiden, 1955), 183-91.
*—*Kohelet* (BKAT 19; Neukirchen-Vluyn, 1978).
—'Kohelets Verhältnis zur Geschichte', in J. Jeremias and L. Perlitt (eds.), *Die Botschaft und die Boten. Festschrift für Hans Walter Wolff zum 70. Geburstag* (Neukirchen-Vluyn, 1981), 393-401.
Laurent, F., '"L'homme est-il supérieur à la bête?" Le doute de Qohéleth (Qo 3,16-21)', *RSR* 91 (2003): 11-43.
—'Les paroles du Qohéleth et le jugement: *mišpāṭ – šāpaṭ*', in E. Bons, C. Coulot, D. Fricker, R. Kuntzmann, and J. Schlosser (eds.), *Le jugement dans l'un et l'autre testament* (Lectio divina 197; Paris, 2004), 1:243-70.

—'Le livre de Qohéleth ou la retenue de l'écriture', *RevScRel* 79 (2005): 5-22.
Lavoie, J.-J., 'À quoi sert-il de perdre sa vie à la gagner? Le repos dans le Qohelet', *ScEs* 44 (1992): 331-47.
—'De l'inconvénient d'être né. Étude de Qohélet 4,1-3', *SR* 24 (1995): 297-308.
—'Critique cultuelle et doute existentiel: étude de Qo 4,17–5,6', *SR* 26 (1997): 147-67.
—'Il y a un temps pour tout, mais tout est pour rien. Quelques observations à partir de Qohéleth 3,1-9', *RECAPO* 6 (1997): 20-44.
—'Puissance divine et finitude humaine selon Qohélet 3,10-15', *SR* 31 (2002): 283-96.
—'Habēl habālīm hakol hābel. Histoire de l'interprétation d'une formule célèbre et enjeux culturels', *ScEs* 58 (2006): 219-49.
—'Activité, sagesse et finitude humaine. Étude de Qohélet 1,12-18', *LTP* 63 (2007): 87-111.
—'Ironie et ambiguïtés en Qohélet 4,13-16', *SR* 37 (2008): 15-39.
—'De l'exégèse historico-critique à l'herméneutique *queer*: analyse de Qohélet 4,9-12', *Theoforum* 40 (2009): 185-209.
—'Où en sont les études sur le livre de Qohélet?', *LTP* 69 (2013): 95-133.
—'L'expérimentation de la jouissance: Étude de Qohélet 2,1-3', *LTP* 72 (2016): 145-72.
Lavoie, J.-J., and M. Mehramooz, 'Quelques remarques sur les manuscrits judéo-persans du Qohélet de la Bibliothèque nationale de France', *Religiologiques* 17 (1998): 192-215.
—'Le texte hébreu et la traduction judéo-persanne du Qohélet: à partir des manuscripts 116 et 117 de la Bibliothèque nationale de France', *LTP* 56 (2000): 489-508.
—'Étude de quelques mots obscurs du Qohélet à la lumière de l'histoire de l'exégèse et des manuscrits judéo-persans de la Bibliothèque nationale de France', *SR* 29 (2000): 183-97.
Leanza, S., 'Sulle fonti del commentario all'Ecclesiaste di Girolamo', *ASE* 3 (1986): 173-99.
—'Le tre versioni geronimiane dell'Ecclesiaste', *ASE* 4 (1987): 87-108.
— 'Sul Commentario all' Ecclesiaste di Girolamo. Il Problema Esegetico', in Y.-M. Duval (ed.), *Jérôme entre l'occident et l'orient. XVIe centenaire du départ de saint Jérôme de Rome et de son installation à Bethléem. Actes du Colloque de Chantilly (Septembre 1986)* (Paris, 1988), 267-82.
Lee, B., 'A Specific Application of the Proverb in Ecclesiastes 1:15', *JHebS* 1 (1997).
Lee, E. P., *The Vitality of Enjoyment in Qohelet's Theological Rhetoric* (BZAW 353; Berlin/New York, 2005).
Lee, J. A. L., *A Lexical Study of the Septuagint Version of the Pentateuch* (SBLSCS 14; Chico, 1983).

Lees, F. R., and D. Burns, 'The Book of Ecclesiastes', in *The Temperance Bible-Commentary: giving at one view version, criticism and exposition in regard to all passages of Holy Writ bearing on "wine" and "strong drink", or illustrating the principles of the temperance reformation* (London, 1868), 147-49.
Leiman, S. Z., 'Masorah and Halakhah: a Study in Conflict', in M. Cogan, B. L. Eichler, and J. H. Tigay (eds.), *Tehillah le-Moshe: Biblical and Judaic Studies in Honor of Moshe Greenberg* (Winona Lake, 1997), 291-306.
Leithart, P. J., 'Solomon's Sexual Wisdom: Qohelet and the Song of Songs in the Postmodern Condition', in Boda, Longman, and Rata (eds.), *The Words of the Wise*, 443-60.
Lemaire, A., *Nouvelles inscriptions araméennes d'Idumée. Tome II Collections Moussaïeff, Jeselsohn, Welch et divers* (TransSup 9; Paris, 2002).
*Leupold, H. C., *Exposition of Ecclesiastes* (Grand Rapids, 1952).
Levine, B. A., 'The Semantics of Loss: Two Exercises in Biblical Hebrew Lexicography', in Z. Zevit, S. Gitin, and M. Sokoloff (eds.), *Solving Riddles and Untying Knots: Biblical, Epigraphic, and Semitic Studies in Honor of Jonas C. Greenfield* (Winona Lake, 1995), 137-58.
Levine, É., *The Aramaic Version of Qohelet* (New York, 1978).
—'Qohelet's Fool: A Composite Portrait', in Y. T. Radday and A. Brenner (eds.), *On Humour and the Comic in the Hebrew Bible* (JSOTSup 92; Sheffield, 1990), 277-94.
—'The Humor in Qohelet', *ZAW* 109 (1997): 71-83.
Levinson, B. M., *A More Perfect Torah: At the Intersection of Philology and Hermeneutics in Deuteronomy and the Temple Scroll* (CrStHB 1; Winona Lake, 2013).
—'"Better that you should not vow than that you vow and not fulfill": Qoheleth's Use of Textual Allusion and the Transformation of Deuteronomy's Law of Vows', in Dell and Kynes (eds.), *Reading Ecclesiastes Intertextually*, 28-41.
Levy, A., *Das Targum zu Koheleth nach südarabischen Handschriften* (Breslau, 1905).
Levy, B. B., *Fixing God's Torah: The Accuracy of the Hebrew Bible Text in Jewish Law* (New York/Oxford, 2001).
Levy, J., *Neuhebräisches und chaldäisches Wörterbuch über die Talmudim und Midraschim* (4 vols.; Leipzig, 1876).
Levy, L., 'Das Steinewerfen in Koheleth 3,5, in der Deukalionsage und im Hermeskult', *MGWJ* 55 (1911): 531-42.
*—*Das Buch Qoheleth Ein Beitrag zur Geschichte des Sadduzäismus Kritisch untersucht, übersetzt und erklärt* (Leipzig, 1912).
Lichtheim, M., 'The Songs of the Harpers', *JNES* 4 (1945): 178-212.
—*Ancient Egyptian Literature: Volume I. The Old and Middle Kingdoms* (Berkeley/Los Angeles/London, 1973).

—*Ancient Egyptian Literature: Volume II. The New Kingdom* (Berkeley/Los Angeles/London, 1976).
—*Ancient Egyptian Literature: Volume III. The Late Period* (Berkeley/Los Angeles/London, 1980).
—*Late Egyptian Wisdom Literature in the International Context* (OBO 52; Fribourg/Göttingen, 1983).
—*Ancient Egyptian Autobiographies Chiefly of the Middle Kingdom: A Study and an Anthology* (OBO 84; Fribourg/Göttingen, 1988).
Lieberman, S., *Hellenism in Jewish Palestine: Studies in the Literary Transmission, Beliefs and Manners of Palestine in the I Century B.C.E.–IV Century C.E.* (New York, 2nd edn, 1962).
—*Greek in Jewish Palestine: Studies in the Life and Manners of Jewish Palestine in the II–IV Centuries C.E.* (New York, 2nd edn, 1965).
Lim, T. H., 'The Defilement of the Hands as a Principle Determining the Holiness of Scriptures', *JTS* 61 (2010): 501-15.
Linafelt, T., and F. W. Dobbs-Allsopp, 'Poetic Line Structure in Qoheleth 3:1', *VT* 60 (2010): 249-59.
Linde, C., *How to Correct the* Sacra Scriptura? *Textual Criticism of the Latin Bible between the Twelfth and Fifteenth Century* (Medium Aevum Monograph 29; Oxford, 2012).
Liphschitz, N., *Timber in Ancient Israel: Dendroarchaeology and Dendrochronology* (Tel Aviv, 2007).
Lipschitz, N., and G. Biger, 'The Timber Trade in Ancient Palestine', *Tel Aviv* 22 (1995): 121-27.
*Lipschütz, L., *Kitāb al-Khilaf: Mishael ben Uzziel's Treatise on the Differences between Ben Asher and Ben Naphtali* (Publications of the Hebrew University Bible Project Monograph Series 2; Jerusalem, 1965).
Litteral, J. (ed.), *Commentary on Ecclesiastes by St. Jerome* (trans. R. MacGregor; Ancient Bible Commentaries in English; Ashland, 2014).
Loader, J. A., 'Qohelet 3:2-8—A "Sonnet" in the Old Testament', *ZAW* 81 (1969): 239-42.
—*Polar Structures in the Book of Qohelet* (BZAW 152; Berlin, 1979).
*—*Ecclesiastes: A Practical Commentary* (Text and Interpretation; Grand Rapids, 1986).
Loevy, J., *Libri Kohelet; versio arabica quam composuit Ibn-Ghijâth. Dissertatio inauguralis quam ad summos in philosophia honores ab amplissimo philosophorum ordine Lipsiensi rite capessendos scripsit Jacobus Loevy* (Leiden, 1884).
Loewenclau, I. von, 'Kohelet und Sokrates – Versuch eines Vergleiches', *ZAW* 98 (1986): 327-38.
Lohfink, N., 'Technik und Tod nach Koheleth', in H. Schlier, E. von Severus, J. Sudbrack, and A. Pereira (eds.), *Strukturen christlicher Existenz. Beiträge zur Erneuerung des geistlichen Lebens* (Würzburg, 1968), 27-35.

—'Warum ist der Tor unfähig, böse zu handeln? (Koh 4,17)', in F. Steppat (ed.), *XXI. Deutscher Orientalistentag, vom 24. bis 29. März 1980 in Berlin: Vorträge* (ZDMGSup 5; Wiesbaden, 1983), 113-20.
—'Die Wiederkehr des immer Gleichen. Eine frühe Synthese zwischen griechischem und jüdischem Weltgefühl in Kohelet 1,4-11', *AF* 53 (1985): 125-49.
—'Gegenwart und Ewigkeit. Die Zeit im Buch Kohelet', *Geist und Leben* 60 (1987): 2-12.
—'Koh 1,2 „Alles ist Windhauch"–universale oder anthropologische Aussage?', in R. Mosis and L. Ruppert (eds.), *Der Weg zum Menschen. Zur philosophischen und theologischen Anthropologie. Für Alfons Deissler* (Freiburg i.B./ Basel/Vienna, 1989), 201-16.
—'Das Koheletbuch: Strukturen und Struktur', in L. Schwienhorst-Schönberger (ed.), *Das Buch Kohelet. Studien zur Struktur, Geschichte, Rezeption und Theologie* (BZAW 254; Berlin/New York, 1997), 39-121.
—'Ist Kohelets הבל-Aussage erkenntnistheoretisch gemeint?', in Schoors (ed.), *Qohelet in the Context*, 41-59.
*—*Kohelet* (NEchtB 1; Würzburg, 6th edn, 2009); ET *Qoheleth: A Continental Commentary* (CC; Minneapolis, 2003).
Longacre, D., 'Reconsidering the Date of the En-Gedi Leviticus Scroll (EGLev): Exploring the Limitations of the Comparative-Typological Paleographic Method', *Textus* 27 (2018): 44-84.
Longman III, T., *Fictional Akkadian Autobiography: A Generic and Comparative Study* (Winona Lake, 1991).
*—*The Book of Ecclesiastes* (NICOT; Grand Rapids, 1998).
—'Determining the Historical Context of Ecclesiastes', in Boda, Longman, and Rata (eds.), *The Words of the Wise*, 89-102.
—'Qoheleth as Solomon: "For what can anyone who comes after the king do?" (Ecclesiastes 2:12)', in Dell and Kynes (eds.), *Reading Ecclesiastes Intertextually*, 42-56.
—'The "Fear of God" in the Book of Ecclesiastes', *BBR* 25 (2015): 13-21.
Loretz, O., 'Zur Darbietungsform der "Ich-Erzählung" im Buche Qohelet', *CBQ* 25 (1963): 46-59.
—*Qohelet und der alte Orient. Untersuchungen zu Stil und theologischer Thematik des Buches Qohelet* (Freiburg i.B./Basel/Vienna, 1964).
—'Anfänge jüdischer Philosophie nach Qohelet 1,1-11 und 3,1-15', *UF* 23 (1991): 223-44.
—'Poetry and Prose in the Book of Qohelet (1:1–3:22; 7:23–8:1; 9:6-10; 12:8-14)', in J. C. de Moor and W. G. E. Watson (eds.), *Verse in Ancient Near Eastern Prose* (AOAT 42; Kevelaer/Neukirchen-Vluyn, 1993), 155-89.
—'Eiliges Gebet, Eid und Gelübde in Ugarit und Israel nach RS 15.10 und Qohelet 4,17–5,6; 8,2-3', in R. Albertz (ed.), *Kult, Konflikt und Versöhnung. Beiträge zur kultischen Sühne in religiösen, sozialen und politischen Auseinandersetzungen des antiken Mittelmeerraumes* (AOAT 285; Münster, 2001), 99-121.

Lowth, R., *De Sacra Poesi Hebraeorum: Praelectiones academicae Oxonii habitae: subjicitur metricae Harianae brevis confutatio: & oratio Crewiana* (Oxford, 1753). ET *Lectures on the Sacred Poetry of the Hebrews: To which are added, the principal notes of Professor Michaelis and notes by the translator and others* (London/Dublin/Glasgow/Sydney, 4th edn, 1839).

*Luther, M., *Ecclesiastes Solomonis, cum annotationibus Doc. Mart Luth.* (Wittemberg, 1532); ET *An exposition of Salomons booke called Ecclesiastes or the preacher: Seene and allowed* (London, 1573).

Lux, R., '"Ich, Kohelet, bin Konig...": Die Fiktion als Schlüssel zur Wirklichkeit in Kohelet 1,12–2,26', *EvT* 50 (1990): 331-42.

—'Tod und Gerechtigkeit im Buch Kohelet', in A. Berlejung and B. Janowski (eds.), *Tod und Jenseits im alten Israel und in seiner Umwelt* (FAT 64; Tübingen, 2009), 43-65.

*Luzzatto, S. D. (SHaDaL), 'פירוש קהלת'= 'Commentary on Qohelet', *Ozar Nechmad* 4 (1863): 47-92.

Lyons, W. J., '"Outing" Qoheleth: On the Search for Homosexuality in the Wisdom Tradition', *Theology & Sexuality* 12 (2006): 181-202.

*Lys, D., *L'Ecclésiaste ou que vaut la vie? Traduction, introduction générale, commentaire de 1/1 à 4/3* (Paris, 1977).

—'L'Être et le temps: Communication de Qohèlèth', in M. Gilbert (ed.), *La Sagesse de l'Ancien Testament* (BETL 51; Leuven, 1979), 249-58.

MacDonald, D. B., 'Old Testament Notes', *JBL* 18 (1899): 212-15.

Machinist, P., 'Fate, *miqreh*, and Reason: Some Reflections on Qohelet and Biblical Thought', in Z. Zevit, S. Gitin, and M. Sokoloff (eds.), *Solving Riddles and Untying Knots. Biblical, epigraphic, and Semitic Studies in Honor of Jonas C. Greenfield* (Winona Lake, 1995), 159-75.

*McNeile, A. H., *An Introduction to Ecclesiastes with Notes and Appendices* (Cambridge, 1904).

Malessa, M., 'Biblisch-hebräisch דִּבֶּר אֶל/לְ- und אֵת עִם/דִּבֶּר im Vergleich', in M. F. J. Baasten and W. T. van Peursen (eds.), *Hamlet on a Hill: Semitic and Greek Studies Presented to Professor T. Muraoka on the Occasion of his Sixty-Fifth Birthday* (OLA 118; Leuven/Paris/Dudley, 2003), 333-40.

Manfredi, S., 'Qohelet in dialogo: una sfida intertestuale', in Bellia and Passaro (eds.), *Il Libro del Qohelet*, 293-313.

Mangan, C., 'Some Similarities between Targum Job and Targum Qohelet', in D. R. G. Beattie and M. J. MacNamara (eds.), *The Aramaic Bible Targums in their Historical Context* (JSOTSup 166; Sheffield, 1994), 349-53.

Mann, J., *The Jews in Egypt and in Palestine under the Fāṭimid Caliphs: A Contribution to their Political and Communal History based Chiefly on Genizah Material Hitherto Unpublished* (2 vols.; London, 1920).

Manns, F., 'Le Targum de Qohelet: Manuscrit Urbinati 1. Traduction et commentaire', *LASBF* 42 (1992): 145-98.

—'Les Traditions targumiques dans le commentaire de Qohelet de St Jérôme', *Did* 35 (2005): 65-83.

Marböck, J., 'Kohelet und Sirach. Eine vielschichtige Beziehung', in L. Schwienhorst-Schönberger (ed.), *Das Buch Kohelet. Studien zur Struktur, Geschichte, Rezeption und Theologie* (BZAW 254; Berlin/New York, 1997), 275-301.

Margoliouth, D. S., 'Ecclesiastes and Ecclesiasticus', *The Expositor (Seventh Series)* 5 (1908): 118-26.

—'The Prologue of Ecclesiastes', *The Expositor (Eighth Series)* 2 (1911): 463-70.

*Marshall, P. S., 'A Critical Edition of the Hexaplaric Fragments of Ecclesiastes' (PhD diss.; The Southern Baptist Theological Seminary, 2007).

Martin, G. D., *Multiple Originals: New Approaches to Hebrew Bible Textual Criticism* (Atlanta, 2010).

Maussion, M., *Le Mal, le bien et le jugement de Dieu dans le livre de Qohélet* (OBO 190; Fribourg/Göttingen, 2003).

Mazzinghi, L., 'Il mistero del tempo: sul termine 'ōlām in Qo 3,11', in R. Fabris (ed.), *Initium Sapientiae. Scritti in onore di Franco Festorazzi nel suo 70° compleanno* (RivBSup 36; Bologna, 2000), 147-61.

—'Qohelet and Enochism: A Critical Relationship', *Hen* 24 (2002): 157-67.

—'The Verbs מצא "to Find" and בקש "to Search" in the Language of Qoheleth. An Exegetical Study', in Berlejung and van Hecke (eds.), *The Language of Qohelet*, 91-120.

Meade, J., and P. J. Gentry, 'Evaluating Evaluations: The Commentary of *BHQ* and the Problem of הוֹלֵלוֹת in Ecclesiastes 1:17', in G. Bonney and R. Vincent (eds.), *Sophia-Paideia: Sapienza e Educazione (Sir 1,27). Miscellanea di studi offerti in onore del prof. Don Mario Cimosa* (BibScRel 34; Rome, 2012), 197-212.

Meek, R. L., 'The Meaning of הבל in Qohelet: An Intertextual Suggestion', in Boda, Longman, and Rata (eds.), *The Words of the Wise*, 241-56.

—'"I Was King Over Israel in Jerusalem": Inerrancy and Authorial Ambiguity in Ecclesiastes', *JESOT* 4 (2015): 63-85.

—'Twentieth- and Twenty-First-Century Readings of *Hebel* (הֶבֶל) in Ecclesiastes', *CBR* 14 (2016): 279-97.

Mehlman, B. H., and S. M. Limmer, *Medieval Midrash: The House for Inspired Innovation* (BRLJ 52; Leiden/Boston, 2017).

*Melanchthon, P., *Enarratio brevis Concionum Libri Salomonis, cuius Titulus est Ecclesiastes* (Wittenberg, 1550).

Mercati, G., *Se la versione dall'ebraico del Codice Veneto Greco VII sia di Simone Atumano, arcivescovo di Tebe: Ricerca storia, con notizie e documenti sulla vita dell'Atumano* (StT 30; Rome, 1916).

Mercer, S. A. B., *The Ethiopic Text of the Book of Ecclesiastes* (ORS 6; London, 1931).

Méthot, J.-F., 'Remarques sur la formalisation de Qo 1,18: "Qui augmente la conneaissance augmente la souffrance"', *ScEs* 59 (2007): 27-33.

Michaud, R., *Qohélet et l'hellénisme. La literature de Sagesse. Histoire et théologie* (Paris, 1987).

Michel, D., 'Qohelet-Probleme. Überlegungen zu Qoh 8,2-9 und 7,11-14', *ThViat* 15 (1979): 81-103.
*—*Qohelet* (EdF 258; Darmstadt, 1988).
—*Untersuchungen zur Eigenart des Buches Qohelet* (BZAW 183; Berlin/New York, 1989).
—'Kohelet und die Krise der Weisheit. Anmerkungen zur Person, Zeit und Umwelt Kohelets', *BK* 45 (1990): 2-6.
—'Weisheit und Apokalyptik', in A. S. van der Woude (ed.), *The Book of Daniel in the Light of New Findings* (BETL 106; Leuven, 1993): 413-34.
Middeldorpf, H., *Codex Syriaco-Hexaplaris: liber quartus Regum e codice parisiensi, Jesaias, duodecim Prophetae minores, Proverbia, Jobus, Canticum threni, Ecclesiastes e codice mediolanensi* (Berlin, 1835).
*Miletto, G., *L'Antico Testamento ebraico nella tradizione babilonese I frammenti dell Genizah* (Quaderni di Henoch 3; Turin, 1987).
Miller, D. B., 'Qohelet's Symbolic Use of הבל', *JBL* 117 (1998): 437-54.
—'Power in Wisdom: The Suffering Servant of Ecclesiastes 4', in T. Grimsrud and L. L. Johns (eds.), *Peace and Justice Shall Embrace: Power and Theopolitics in the Bible. Fs. Millard Lind* (Telford/Scottdale, 1999), 145-73.
—'What the Preacher Forgot: The Rhetoric of Ecclesiastes', *CBQ* 62 (2000): 215-35.
—*Symbol and Rhetoric in Ecclesiastes: The Place of Hebel in Qoheleth's Work* (SBLABib 2; Atlanta, 2002).
*—*Ecclesiastes* (Scottdale, 2010).
Miller, R. D., 'Orality and Performance in Ancient Israel', *RevScRel* 86 (2012): 183-94.
Mills, M. E., *Reading Ecclesiastes: A Literary and Cultural Exegesis* (Heythrop Studies in Contemporary Philosophy, Religion & Theology; Aldershot, 2003).
Min, Y.-J., 'How Do the Rivers Flow? (Ecclesiastes 1.7)', *BT* 42 (1991): 226-30.
Mizrahi, N., 'Qohelet 6:5b in Light of 4QQoh^a ii 2 and Rabbinic Literature', *Textus* 21 (2002): 159-74.
Montfaucon, B. de, *Origenis Hexaplorum quae supersunt, multi partibus auctiora quam a Flaminio Nobilio et Joanne Drusio edita fuerint* (Paris, 1713).
Montgomery, J. A., 'Notes on Ecclesiastes', *JBL* 43 (1924): 241-44.
Moore, G. F., 'The Vulgate Chapters and Numbered Verses in the Hebrew Bible', *JBL* 12 (1893): 73-78.
Mopsik, C., *L'Ecclésiaste et son double Araméen: Qohélet et son Targoum* (Les Dix Paroles; Rieux-en-Val, 1990).
Morag, S., 'On the Historical Validity of the Vocalization of the Hebrew Bible', *JAOS* 94 (1974): 307-15.
Moran, W. L., 'Amarna Glosses', *RA* 69 (1975): 147-58.
Moreno García, A., and J. Boira Sales, 'Concepción Jeronimiana de los sentidos bíblicos en el comentario a Qohélet', *EstBib* 55 (1997): 239-62.
Moreschini, C., *S. Hieronymi Presbyteri Opera III Opera Polemica 2 Dialogus Adversus Pelagianos* (CCSL 80; Turnholt, 1990).

Morse, B., 'Introduction to a Dandy: Part I, The Assembler Reassembled', *Biblical Interpretation* 22 (2014): 132-45.

—'Introduction to a Dandy: Part II: Qoheleth's Turn, with Duchamp at Monte Carlo', *Biblical Interpretation* 22 (2014): 233-52.

Moss, S. A., 'Ecclesiastes 1:4: A Proof Text for Reincarnation', *JBQ* 21 (1993): 28-30.

Mroczek, E., '"Aramaisms" in Qohelet: Methodological Problems in Identification and Interpretation', in Boda, Longman, and Rata (eds.), *The Words of the Wise*, 343-63.

Muilenburg, J., 'A Qoheleth Scroll from Qumran', *BASOR* 135 (1954): 20-28.

Mulder, J. S. M., 'Qoheleth's Division and Also its Main Point', in *Von Kanaan bis Kerala: Festschrift für Prof. Mag. Dr. J. P. M. van der Ploeg O.P. zur Vollendung des siebzigsten Lebensjahres am 4. Juli 1979. Überreicht von Kollegen, Freunden und Schülern* (AOAT 211; Neukirchen-Vluyn/Kevelaer, 1982), 149-59.

Müller, H.-P., 'Wie sprach Qohälät von Gott?', *VT* 18 (1968): 507-21.

—'Theonome Skepsis und Lebensfreude. Zu Koh 1,12-3,15', *BZ* 30 (1986): 1-19.

—'Der unheimliche Gast. Zum Denken Kohelets', *ZTK* 84 (1987): 440-67.

—'Kolloquialsprache und Volksreligion in den Inschriften von Kuntillet ʿAǧrūd und Ḫirbet el-Qōm', *ZAH* 5 (1992): 15-51.

—'Kohelet und Amminadab', in Diesel et al. (eds.), *"Jedes Ding hat seine Zeit..."*, 149-65.

—'Travestien und geistige Landschaften. Zum Hintergrund einiger Motive bei Kohelet und im Hohenlied', *ZAW* 109 (1997): 557-74.

Muraoka, T., 'On the So-Called *dativus ethicus* in Hebrew', *JTS* n.s. 29 (1978): 495-98.

Murphy, R. E., *Wisdom Literature: Job, Proverbs, Ruth, Canticles, Ecclesiastes, and Esther* (FOTL 13; Grand Rapids, 1981).

*—*Ecclesiastes* (WBC 23A; Dallas, 1992).

Mutius, H.-G. von, 'Eine talmudische Textvariante zu Kohelet 5,9 und ihr Verhältnis zur LXX', *BN* 144 (2010): 87-93.

*Nachtigal, J. C. C., *Koheleth, oder die Versammlung der Weisen, gewöhnlich genannt der Prediger Salomo's* (Halle a.S., 1798).

Naveh, J., and S. Shaked, *Aramaic Documents from Ancient Bactria from the Khalili Collections* (London, 2012).

*Negenman, J., *Prediker* (Belichting van het bijbelboek; Boxtel/Leuven, 1988).

Neher, A., *Notes sur Qohélét (L'Ecclésiaste)* (Paris, 1951).

Niccacci, A., 'Qohelet. Analisi sintattica, traduzione, composizione', *LASBF* 54 (2004): 53-94.

Niehr, H., 'Zur Semantik von nordwestsemitisch ʿlm als "Unterwelt" und "Grab"', in B. Pongratz-Leisten, H. Kühne, and P. Xella (eds.), *Ana šadî Labnāni lū allik : Beiträge zu altorientalischen und mittelmeerischen Kulturen: Festschrift für Wolfgang Röllig* (Kevelaer, 1997): 295-305.

Noegel, S. B., '"Word Play" in Qoheleth', *JHebS* 7 (2007): article 4.

North, R., 'Brain and Nerve in the Biblical Outlook', *Bib* 74 (1993): 577-97.
Norton, G. J., 'Cautionary Reflections on a Re-edition of Fragments of Hexaplaric Material', in G. J. Norton and S. Pisano (eds.), *Tradition of the Text: Studies offered to Dominique Barthélemy in Celebration of his 70th Birthday* (OBO 109; Fribourg/Göttingen, 1991), 129-55.
—*Frederick Field's Prolegomena to Origenis hexaplorum quae supersunt, sive veterum interpretum Graecorum in totum Vetus Testamentum fragmenta* (Paris, 2005).
O'Dowd, R., *The Wisdom of Torah: Epistemology in Deuteronomy and the Wisdom Literature* (FRLANT; Göttingen, 2009).
Ofer, Y., 'The *Jerusalem Crown* and its Editorial Principles', in M. Glatzer (ed.), כתר ירושלים *Jerusalem Crown: The Bible of the Hebrew University of Jerusalem. Companion Volume* (Jerusalem/Basel, 2002), 33-38.
Ogden, G. S., 'The "Better"-Proverb (Tôb-Spruch), Rhetorical Criticism, and Qoheleth', *JBL* 96 (1977): 489-505.
—'Qoheleth's Use of the "Nothing Is Better"-Form', *JBL* 98 (1979): 339-50.
—'Historical Allusion in Qoheleth IV 13-16?', *VT* 30 (1980): 309-15.
—'The Mathematics of Wisdom: Qoheleth IV 1-12', *VT* 34 (1984): 446-53.
—'The Interpretation of דור in Ecclesiastes 1.4', *JSOT* 11 (1986): 91-92.
*—*Qoheleth* (RNBC; Sheffield, 2nd edn, 2007).
Oh, M., *Sprachliche Gestaltung und Semantik: Untersuchungen zu den biblischen Büchern Proverbien und Kohelet* (KTR 13; Berlin, 2014).
van Oorschot, J., 'König und Mensch: Biografie und Autobiografie bei Kohelet und in der alttestamentlichen Literaturgeschichte', in A. Berlejung and R. Heckl (eds.), *Mensch und König: Studien zur Anthropologie des Alten Testaments: Rüdiger Lux zum 60. Geburtstag* (Herders biblische Studien 53; Freiburg i.B., 2008), 109-22.
Orni, E., and E. Efrat, 'Atmospheric Pressure and Winds', in *Geography of Israel* (Jerusalem, 3rd edn, 1971), 139-42.
Osborne, C., 'Was Verse the Default Form for Presocratic Philosophy?', in C. Atherton (ed.), *Form and Content in Didactic Poetry* (NCLS 5; Bari, 1998), 23-35.
Osinkina, L., 'The Textual History of Ecclesiastes in Church Slavonic' (PhD diss.; University of Oxford, 2008).
Ostriker, A., 'Ecclesiastes as Witness: A Personal Essay', *APR* 34 (2005): 7-13.
*van der Palm, J. H., *Ecclesiastes Philologice et Critice Illustratus* (Leiden, 1784).
Parkinson, R., *The Tale of Sinuhe and Other Ancient Egyptian Poems 1940–1640 BC* (Oxford, 1997).
Paulson, G. N., 'The Use of Qoheleth in Bonhoeffer's "Ethics"', *Word and World* 18 (1990): 307-13.
Penkower, J. S., 'An Eleventh- or Twelfth-Century Masoretic Bible Codex (Jeremiah, Zechariah, Proverbs, and Chronicles): Its Place among Eastern Codices', *Textus* 27 (2018): 85-110.

BIBLIOGRAPHY OF WORKS CITED

Pennacchini, B., 'Qohelet ovvero il libro degli assurdi', *Euntes Docete* 30 (1977): 491-510.
Perdue, L. G., *Wisdom and Creation: The Theology of Wisdom Literature* (Nashville, 1994).
—'Wisdom and Apocalyptic: The Case of Qoheleth', in F. García Martínez (ed.), *Wisdom and Apocalypticism in the Dead Sea Scrolls and in the Biblical Tradition* (BETL 168; Leuven, 2003), 231-58.
Perles, F., 'A Miscellany of Lexical and Textual Notes on the Bible: Chiefly in Connection with the Fifteenth Edition of the Lexicon by Gesenius-Buhl', *JQR* 2 (1911): 97-132.
Perles, J., 'Thron und Circus des Königs Salomo', *MGWJ* 21 (1872): 122-39.
Perowne, J. J. S., 'Ecclesiastes', *The Expositor* 10 (1879): 61-74, 165-72, 313-20.
Perrin, N., 'Messianism in the Narrative Frame of Ecclesiastes?', *RB* 108 (2001): 37-60.
*Perry, T. A., *Dialogues with Kohelet: The Book of Ecclesiastes. Translation and commentary* (University Park, 1993).
—'A Poetics of Absence: The Structure and Meaning of Genesis 1.2', *JSOT* 18 (1993): 3-11.
—*The Book of Ecclesiastes (Qohelet) and the Path to Joyous Living* (New York, 2015).
Petau (Petauius), D., ΔΙΟΝΥΣΙΟΥ ΤΟΥ ΠΕΤΑΒΙΟΥ ΑΥΡΗΛΙΑΝΕΩΣ τοῦ ἐκ τῆς ἑταιρείας Ιησου Ελληνικα ἔπη παντοδαπὰ, μ[ε]τ[α] καὶ τῆς Λατινικῆς ἑρμενείας. Ὠν τὰ πρῶτα ἔχει ὁ τοῦ Σολομῶντος Εκκλησιατὴς ἐμμέτρως μεταφρασθεὶς (Paris, 1641).
Petschenig, M. (ed.), *Iohannis Cassiani Conlationes XXIIII* (CSEL 13; Vienna, 1886).
Philippus Presbyter, *Philippi Presbyteri... In historiam Iob commentariorvm libri tres* (Basel, 1527).
Phillips, K., 'A New Codex from the Scribe Behind the Leningrad Codex: L17', *TynBul* 68 (2017): 1-29.
Pinçon, B., 'Le Dieu de Qohélet', *RevScRel* 85 (2011): 411-25.
Pinder, M., and G. Parthey (eds.), *Ravennatis Anonymi Cosmographia et Guidonis Geographica. Ex libris manu scriptis* (Berlin, 1860).
Pinker, A., 'Qohelet 4,13-16', *SJOT* 22 (2008): 176-94.
—'The Principle of Irreversibility in Kohelet 1,15 and 7,13', *ZAW* 120 (2008): 387-403.
—'Intrusion of Ptolemaic Reality on Cultic Practices in Qoh 4:17', *JHebS* 9 (2009).
—'Qohelet 2,12b', *BZ* 53 (2009): 94-105.
—'Qohelet 3,18: A Test?', *SJOT* 23 (2009): 282-96.
—'Anthropomorphic Conception of the Sun in Qohelet 1:5', *SEE-J Hiphil* 7 (2010).
—'Experimenting with Entertainment in Qoheleth 2:1-3', *ABR* 58 (2010): 17-35.
—'How Should We Understand Ecclesiastes 2:26?', *JBQ* 38 (2010): 219-29.

—'Qohelet 3:14-15', *BZ* 54 (2010): 253-71.
—'A Reevaluation of the Kesil's Image in the Book of Qohelet', *SJOT* 25 (2011): 49-74.
—'An Interpretation of Qohelet 5:17-19 based on Intertextuality Considerations', *BeO* 53 (2011): 65-86.
—'The Oppressed in Qohelet 4:1', *VT* 61 (2011): 393-405.
Piotti, F., 'La lingua dell' Ecclesiaste e lo sviluppo storico dell' Ebraico', *BeO* 15 (1973): 185-96.
—'Osservazioni su alcuni usi linguistici dell' Ecclesiaste', *BeO* 19 (1977): 49-56.
—'Osservazioni su alcuni problemi esegetici nel libro dell' Ecclesiaste: Studio I', *BeO* 20 (1978): 169-81.
—'La descrizione degli elementi naturali in Qo 1,4-7. Problemi esegetici e linguistici', *BeO* 46 (2004): 207-48.
—'Osservazioni sul metodo di ricerca di Qohelet', *BeO* 48 (2006): 129-68.
—'Percezione del "Disordine" e "Timore di Dio" in Qohelet (I): *Distorsione* (עוח) e *abominio* (תועבה) nei testi normativi, profetici e sapienziali', *BeO* 51 (2009): 3-32.
—'Percezione del "Disordine" e "Timore di Dio" in Qohelet (II): Aspetti della *distorsione* (עוח) in Qohelet', *BeO* 51 (2009): 101-31.
—'Percezione del "Disordine" e "Timore di Dio" in Qohelet (III): Il credo di Qohelet tra disordine percepito e timore di Dio', *BeO* 52 (2010): 3-33.
—*Qohelet: La ricerca del senso della vita* (Antico e Nuovo Testamento 18; Brescia, 2012).
—'Lavoro e pigrizia in Qo 4,4-6 alla luce del libro dei Proverbi', *BeO* 55 (2013): 185-216.
du Plessis, S. J., 'Aspects of Morphological Peculiarities of the Language of Qoheleth', in I. H. Eybers et al. (eds.), *De Fructu Oris Sui: Essays in Honour of Adrianus Van Selms* (POS 9; Leiden, 1971), 164-80.
Plumptre, E. H., 'The Author of Ecclesiastes', *Expositor* 11 (1880): 401-30.
*—*Ecclesiastes: Or, the Preacher: With Notes and Introduction* (CBSC; Cambridge, 1881).
*Podechard, E., *L'Ecclésiaste* (EBib; Paris, 1912).
—'La composition du livre de l'Ecclésiaste', *RB* 9 (1912): 161-91.
Polk, T., 'The Wisdom of Irony: A Study of *hebel* and Its Relation to Joy and the Fear of God in Ecclesiastes', *StudBT* 6 (1976): 3-17.
Porten, B., and A. Yardeni, *Textbook of Aramaic Documents from Ancient Egypt*. Vol. 1, *Letters* (Jerusalem, 1986).
—*Textbook of Aramaic Documents from Ancient Egypt*. Vol. 3, *Literature, Accounts, Lists* (Jerusalem, 1993).
*Power, A. D., *Ecclesiastes: Or, The Preacher: A New Translation, with Introd., Notes, Glossary and Index* (London, 1952).
Power, E., 'Corrections from the Hebrew in the Theodulfian Mss. of the Vulgate', *Bib* 5 (1924): 233-58.
Powicke, M., *Stephen Langton* (Oxford, 1928).

*Provan, I., *Ecclesiastes, Song of Songs* (The NIV Application Commentary; Grand Rapids, 2001).

—'Fresh Perspectives on Ecclesiastes: "Qohelet for Today"', in Boda, Longman, and Rata (eds.), *The Words of the Wise*, 401-16.

Puech, É., 'Un nouveau fragment du manuscrit[b] de l'Ecclésiaste (4QQohélet[b] ou 4Q110)', *RevQ* 19 (2000): 617-21.

—'Qohelet a Qumran', in Bellia and Passaro (eds.), *Il Libro del Qohelet*, 144-70.

de Pury, A., 'Qohéleth et le canon des Ketubim', *RTP* 131 (1999): 163-98.

Qimron, E., *The Hebrew of the Dead Sea Scrolls* (HSS 29; Atlanta, 1986).

Quack, J. F., 'Über die mit ʿnḫ gebildeten Namensformen und die Vokalisation einiger Verbalformen', *GM* 123 (1991): 91-100.

—*Die Lehren des Ani: ein neuägyptischer Weisheitstext in seinem kulturellen Umfeld* (OBO 141; Fribourg/Göttingen, 1994).

—'The Interaction of Egyptian and Aramaic Literature', in O. Lipschits, G. N. Knoppers, and M. Oeming (eds.), *Judah and the Judeans in the Achaemenid Age: Negotiating Identity in an International Context* (Winona Lake, 2011), 375-401.

*Rahlfs, A., *Septuaginta. Id est Vetus Testamentum graece iuxta LXX interpretes* (Stuttgart, 2nd edn, 1979). Ecclesiastes is on pp. 238-60 of the second volume.

Rainey, A. F., 'A Second Look at Amal in Qoheleth', *CTM* 36 (1965): 805.

Rajak, T., '"Torah shall go forth from Zion": Common Judaism and the Greek Bible', in W. O. McCready and A. Reinhartz (eds.), *Common Judaism: Explorations in Second-Temple Judaism* (Minneapolis, 2008), 145-58.

Ramond, S., 'Y a-t-il de l'ironie dans le livre de Qohelet?', *VT* 60 (2010): 621-40.

Ranston, H., 'Ecclesiastes and Theognis', *AJSL* 34 (1918): 99-122.

—'Koheleth and the Early Greeks', *JTS* 24 (1923): 160-69.

—*Ecclesiastes and the Early Greek Wisdom Literature* (London, 1925).

Ratzabi, Y., 'Massoretic Variants to the Five Scrolls from a Babylonian-Yemenite MS', *Textus* 5 (1966): 93-113.

*Ravasi, G., *Qohelet* (La Parola di Dio; Milan, 2nd edn, 1991).

de Regt, L. J., 'Signs of Redactional Development in Some Old Testament Texts and the Translator', *JNSL* 30 (2004): 81-97.

Reider, J., 'Etymological Studies in Biblical Hebrew', *VT* 2 (1952): 113-30.

*Renan, E., *L'Ecclésiaste traduit de l'hébreu avec une étude sur l'age et le caractère du livre* (Oeuvres Complètes de Ernest Renan 7; Paris, 1955). Originally published Paris, 1882. ET *Cohelet, or, The Preacher Translated from the Hebrew: With a study on the age and character of the book* (London, 1884).

Rendsburg, G. A., 'Dual Personal Pronouns and Dual Verbs in Hebrew', *JQR* 73 (1982): 38-58.

—'The Galilean Background of Mishnaic Hebrew', in L. I. Levine (ed.), *The Galilee in Late Antiquity* (New York, 1992), 225-40.

Renehan, R., 'The Greek Anthropocentric View of Man', *HSCP* 85 (1981): 239-59.

Revell, E. J., 'The Oldest Evidence for the Hebrew Accent System', *BJRL* 54 (1972): 214-22.
—'The Voweling of "*i* Type" Segolates in Tiberian Hebrew', *JNES* 44 (1985): 319-28.
Reymond, E. D., *Qumran Hebrew: An Overview of Orthography, Phonology, and Morphology* (Atlanta, 2014).
Rizzi, G., 'Tradizione e intertestualità nell'ermeneutica Giudaica di lingua Greca e Aramaica di Qo 1,1-3. Una prospettiva di ricerca', in Bellia and Passaro (eds.), *Il Libro del Qohelet*, 227-55.
Robinson, J. T., *Asceticism, Eschatology, Opposition to Philosophy: The Arabic Translation and Commentary of Salmon ben Yeroḥam on Qohelet (Ecclesiastes)* (Leiden, 2012).
Rofé, A., 'המלאך׳ בקהלת ה, ה לאור נוסחת ויכוח חכמתית'= "The Angel" in Qohelet 5:5 in the Light of a Wisdom Dialogue Formula', *EI* 14 (1978): 105-109.
—'Biblical Antecedents of the Targumic Solution of Metaphors (Ps 89:41-42; Ezek 22:25-28; Gen 49:8-9,14-15)', in J. Krašovec (ed.), *The Interpretation of the Bible: The International Symposium in Slovenia* (JSOTSup 289; Sheffield, 1998), 333-38.
—'La formula sapienzale "Non dire..." e l'angelo di Qo 5,5', in Bellia and Passaro (eds.), *Il Libro del Qohelet*, 217-26.
—'The Wisdom Formula "Do Not Say..." and the Angel in Qohelet 5.5', in J. C. Exum and H. G. M. Williamson (eds.), *Reading from Right to Left: Essays on the Hebrew Bible in Honour of David J. A. Clines* (JSOTSup 373; London/New York, 2003), 364-76.
Rose, M., 'Querdenken mit und über Qohelet', *TZ* 53 (1997): 83-96.
—'De la "Crise de la sagesse" à la "Sagesse de la Crise"', *RTP* 131 (1999): 115-34.
—*Rien de nouveau: Nouvelles approches du livre de Qoheleth: avec une bibliographie, 1988–1998, élaborée par Béatrice Perregaux Allisson* (OBO 168; Fribourg/Göttingen, 1999).
Rosenmüller, E. F. K., *Salomonis regis et sapientis quae perhibentur scripta* (2 vols.; Ern. Frid. Car. Rosenmülleri Scholia In Vetus Testamentum 9; Leipzig, 1830).
Rosenthal, G. S., '*Tikkun ha-Olam*: The Metamorphosis of a Concept', *The Journal of Religion* 85 (2005): 214-40.
*de Rossi, G. B., *Variae Lectiones Veteris Testamenti Librorum: Ex immensa manuscriptorum editorumque codicum congerie haustae et ad Samaritanum textum, ad vetustissimas versiones, ad accuratiores sacrae criticae fontes ac leges examinatae* (Parma, 1784–88).
Rosso Ubigli, L., 'Qohelet di fronte all'apocalittica', *Hen* 5 (1986): 209-33.
Roth, W. M. W., 'A Study of the Classical Hebrew Verb *ṣkl*', *VT* 18 (1968): 69-78.
Rousseau, F., 'Structure de Qohelet I 4-11 et plan du livre', *VT* 31 (1981): 200-17.

Rudman, D., 'A Contextual Reading of Ecclesiastes 4:13-16', *JBL* 116 (1997): 57-73.
—'Qohelet's Use of לפני', *JNSL* 23 (1997): 143-50.
—'A Note on the Dating of Ecclesiastes', *CBQ* 61 (1999): 47-52.
—'4QInstruction & Ecclesiastes: A Comparative Study', *Qumran Chronicle* 9 (2000): 153-63.
—*Determinism in the Book of Ecclesiastes* (JSOTSup 316; Sheffield, 2001).
—'The Use of הבל as an Indicator of Chaos in Ecclesiastes', in Berlejung and van Hecke (eds.), *The Language of Qohelet*, 121-41.
Rütersworden, U., 'Erwagungen zur alttestamentlichen Paradiesvorstellung', *TLZ* 123 (1998): 1153-62.
Şahin, B., 'Die Sprache Der Meder' (Lizentiatsarbeit diss.; University of Zurich, 2004).
Salters, R. B., 'The Word for "God" in the Peshiṭta of Koheleth', *VT* 21 (1971): 251-54.
—'Qoheleth and the Canon', *ExpTim* 86 (1975): 339-42.
—'A Note on the Exegesis of Ecclesiastes 3.15b', *ZAW* 88 (1976): 419-22.
—'Notes on the History of the Interpretation of Koh. 5:5', *ZAW* 90 (1978): 95-101.
—'Notes on the Interpretation of Qoh 6_2', *ZAW* 91 (1979): 282-89.
—'Observations on the Septuagint of Ecclesiastes', *OTE* 5 (1992): 163-74.
—'Observations on the Peshitta of Ecclesiastes', *OTE* 8 (1995): 388-97.
—'Textual Criticism and Qoheleth', *JNSL* 23 (1997): 53-71.
—'Observations on the Targum to Qoheleth', *JNSL* 24 (1998): 13-24.
Salyer, G., *Vain Rhetoric: Private Insight and Public Debate in Ecclesiastes* (JSOTSup 327; Sheffield, 2001).
Salzberger, M., 'Septuagintalübersetzung zum Buche Kohelet', *MGWJ* 22 (1873): 168-74.
Samet, N., 'Qohelet 1,4 and the Structure of the Book's Prologue', *ZAW* 126 (2014): 92-100.
—'Religious Redaction in Qohelet in Light of Mesopotamian Vanity Literature', *VT* 65 (2015): 1-16.
—'The Gilgamesh Epic and the Book of Qohelet: A New Look', *Bib* 96 (2015): 375-90.
—'The Validity of the Masoretic Text as a Basis for Diachronic Linguistic Analysis of Biblical Texts: Evidence from Masoretic vocalisation', *JSem* 25 (2016): 1064-79.
Sandberg, R., 'Qohelet and the Rabbis', in Boda, Longman, and Rata (eds.), *The Words of the Wise*, 37-54.
Sanders, P., 'The Ashkar-Gilson Manuscript: Remnant of a Proto-Masoretic model scroll of the Torah', *JHebS* 14 (2014): article 7.
de Savignac, J., 'La sagesse du Qôhéléth et l'épopée de Gilgamesh', *VT* 28 (1978): 318-23.

Schellenberg, A., *Erkenntnis als Problem. Qohelet und die alttestamentliche Diskussion um das menschliche Erkennen* (OBO 188; Fribourg/Göttingen, 2002).
—'Qohelet's Use of the Word עִנְיָן: Some observations on Qoh 1,13; 2,23.26; 3,10, and 8,16', in Berlejung and van Hecke (eds.), *The Language of Qohelet*, 143-55.
*—*Kohelet* (ZBKAT 17; Zürich, 2013).
Schenke, H.-M., and R. Kasser (eds.), *Papyrus Michigan 3520 und 6868(a): Ecclesiastes, Erster Johannesbrief und Zweiter Petrusbrief im fayumischen Dialekt* (TUGAL 151; Berlin/New York, 2003).
Schneck, R., 'Qohélet y la Guerra Amazónica, 1995: una nota teológica', *Theologica Xaveriana* 115 (1995): 321-25.
Schlögl, N., 'Qohelet 4, 13-16', *WZKM* 33 (1926): 163-65.
Schmidt, J., 'Koheleth 4:17', *ZAW* 17 (1940): 279-80.
Schoors, A., 'The Particle כִּי', *OTS* 21 (1981): 240-76.
—'Kethibh-Qere in Ecclesiastes', in J. Quaegebeur (ed.), *Studia Paulo Naster Oblata II: Orientalia Antiqua* (OLA 13; Leuven, 1982), 215-22.
—'La Structure littéraire de Qohéleth', *OLP* 13 (1982): 91-116.
—'The Peshitta of Kohelet and Its Relation to the Septuagint', in C. Laga, J. A. Munitz, and L. V. Rompay (eds.), *After Chalcedon: Studies in Theology and Church History Offered to Professor Albert Van Roey for His Seventieth Birthday* (OLA 18; Leuven, 1985), 347-57.
—'The Use of Vowel Letters in Qoheleth', *UF* 20 (1988): 277-86.
—*The Preacher Sought to Find Pleasing Words: A Study of the Language of Qoheleth: Part I Grammar* (OLA 41; Leuven, 1992).
—'The Verb ראה in the Book of Qoheleth', in Diesel et al. (eds.), *"Jedes Ding hat seine Zeit..."*, 227-41.
—(ed.), *Qohelet in the Context of Wisdom* (BETL 136; Leuven, 1998).
— 'The Word ṭwb in the Book of Qoheleth', in M. Dietrich and I. Kottsieper (eds.), *"Und Mose schrieb dieses Lied auf". Studien zum Alten Testament und zum Alten Orient. Festschrift für Oswald Loretz zur Vollendung seines 70. Lebensjahres mit Beiträgen von Freunden, Schülern und Kollegen* (AOAT 250; Münster, 1998), 685-700.
—'(Mis)use of Intertextuality in Qoheleth Exegesis', in A. Lemaire and M. Sæbø (eds.), *Congress Volume: Oslo 1998* (VTSup 80; Leiden, 2000), 45-59.
—*The Preacher Sought to Find Pleasing Words. A Study of the Language of Qoheleth: Part II Vocabulary* (OLA 143; Leuven, Paris, Dudley, 2004).
*—*Ecclesiastes* (HCOT; Leuven, Paris, Walpole, 2013).
Schorch, S., 'The Septuagint and the Vocalization of the Hebrew Text of the Torah', in M. K. H. Peters (ed.), *XII Congress of the International Organisation for Septuagint and Cognate Studies, Leiden 2004* (SBLSCS 54; Leiden/Boston, 2006), 41-54.

Schultz, R. L., 'Qoheleth and Isaiah in Dialogue', in Dell and Kynes (eds.), *Reading Ecclesiastes Intertextually*, 57-70.
—'Was Qohelet an Eschatological or an Anti-Apocalyptic Sage? *Hebel*, the Evil Day, and Divine Judgment in the Book of Ecclesiastes', in M. J. Boda, Russell L. Meeks, and William R. Osborne, (eds.), *Riddles and Revelations: Explorations into the Relationship between Wisdom and Prophecy in the Hebrew Bible* (LHBOTS 634; London/New York, 2018), 199-214.
Schunck, K.-D., 'Drei Seleukiden im Buche Kohelet?', *VT* 9 (1959): 192-201.
Schwartz, M. J., 'Koheleth and Camus: Two Views of Achievement', *Judaism* 35 (1986): 29-34.
Schwarzschild, R., 'The Syntax of אשר in Biblical Hebrew with Special Reference to Qoheleth', *HS* 31 (1990): 7-39.
Schwienhorst-Schönberger, L., „*Nicht im Menschen gründet das Glück" (Koh 2,24): Kohelet im Spannungsfeld jüdischer Weisheit und hellenistischer Philosophie* (Herders biblische Studien 2; Freiburg i.B., 1994).
—'Neues unter der Sonne: Zehn Jahre Kohelet-Forschung (1987–1997)', *Theologische Revue* 94 (1998): 363-76.
—'Neuere Veroffentlichungen zum Buch Kohelet (1998–2003)', *TLZ* 128 (2003): 1123-38.
—Kohelet (HTKAT; Freiburg i.B./Basel/Vienna, 2004).
Scippa, V., '"Il tutto fece bello nel suo tempo…". La bellezza in Qohelet', *Asp* 53 (2006): 263-84.
Sciumbata, M. P., 'Peculiarità e motivazioni della struttura lessicale dei verbi della "conoscenza" in Qohelet. Abbozzo di una storia dell'epistemologia ebraico-biblica', *Hen* 18 (1996): 235-49.
*Segal, B. J., *Kohelet's Pursuit of Truth: A New Reading of Ecclesiastes* (Jerusalem, 2016).
Segal, E., '*Aristeas* or Haggadah: Talmudic Legend and the Greek Bible in Palestinian Judaism', in W. O. McCready and A. Reinhartz (eds.), *Common Judaism: Explorations in Second-Temple Judaism* (Minneapolis, 2008), 159-72.
Segal, J. B., *Aramaic Texts from North Saqqâra, with some Fragments in Phoenician* (London, 1983).
Segal, M. H., 'The Promulgation of the Authoritative Text of the Hebrew Bible', *Journal of Biblical Literature* 72 (1953): 35-47.
Segal, M., E. Tov, W. B. Seales, C. S. Parker, P. Shor, Y. Porath, and A. Yardeni, 'An Early Leviticus Scroll from En-Gedi: Preliminary publication', *Textus* 26 (2016): 29-58.
Segert, S., *A Grammar of Phoenician and Punic* (Munich, 1976).
Seow, C. L., 'Qohelet's Autobiography', in A. B. Beck, A. H. Bartelt, P. R. Raabe, and C. A. Franke (eds.), *Fortunate the Eyes that See: Essays in Honor of David Noel Freedman in Celebration of his Seventieth Birthday* (Grand Rapids/ Cambridge, 1995), 275-87.
—'Linguistic Evidence and the Dating of Qohelet', *JBL* 115 (1996): 643-66.

—'The Socioeconomic Context of "The Preacher's" Hermeneutic', *PSB* 17 (1996): 168-95.
*—*Ecclesiastes: A New Translation with Introduction and Commentary* (AB 18C; New York/London/Toronto/Sydney/Auckland, 1997).
—'Beyond Mortal Grasp: The Usage of *hebel* in Ecclesiastes', *ABR* 48 (2000): 1-16.
Seufert, M., 'The Presence of Genesis in Ecclesiastes', *WTJ* 78 (2016): 75-92.
Seybold, K., 'Reverenz und Gebet: Erwägungen zu der Wendung Hillā Panîm', *ZAW* 88 (1976): 2-16.
Shaffer, A., 'ט–יב ,ד קוהלת של המיסופוטאמי הרקע' = 'The Mesopotamian Background of Qohelet 4:9-12', *EI* 8 (1967): 246-50.
—'המשלש 'החוט מקור על חדשות ידיעות' = 'New Light on the "Three-ply Cord"', *EI* 9 (1969): 159-60.
Sharp, C. J., 'Ironic Representation, Authorial Voice, and Meaning in Qohelet', *BibInt* 12 (2004): 37-68.
Sheppard, G. T., 'The Epilogue to Qoheleth as Theological Commentary', *CBQ* 39 (1977): 182-89.
Shields, M. A., 'Ecclesiastes and the End of Wisdom', *TynBul* 50 (1999): 117-39.
—*The End of Wisdom: A Reappraisal of the Historical and Canonical Function of Ecclesiastes* (Winona Lake, 2006).
Shuster, M., 'Being as Breath, Vapor as Joy: Using Martin Heidegger to Re-read the Book of Ecclesiastes', *JSOT* 33 (2008): 219-44.
*Sicker, M., *Kohelet: The Reflections of a Judean Prince, a New Translation and Commentary* (New York/Lincoln/Shanghai, 2006).
*Siegfried, D. C., *Prediger und Hoheslied Übersetzt und erklärt* (HAT II, 3/2; Göttingen, 1898).
Simon-Shoshan, M., '"The Heavens Proclaim the Glory of God...": A Study in Rabbinic Cosmology', *BDD* 20 (2008): 67-96.
Sirat, C., *Les Papyrus en caractères hébraïques trouvés en Egypte* (Paris, 1985).
—'Genesis Discovery', *Genizah Fragments* 23 (1992): 2.
—'Earliest known Sefer Torah', *Genizah Fragments* 24 (1992): 3.
Smelik, K. A. D., 'A Re-interpretation of Ecclesiastes 2,12b', in Schoors (ed.), *Qohelet in the Context*, 385-89.
Smelik, W., 'Code-Switching: The Public Reading of the Bible in Hebrew, Aramaic and Greek', in L. Morenz and S. Schorch (eds.), *Was ist ein Text? Alttestamentliche, ägyptologische und altorientalistische Perspektiven* (Berlin, 2007), 123-51.
Smit, E. J., 'The Tell Siran Inscription: Linguistic and Historical Implications', *Tydskrif vir Semitistiek/ Journal for Semitics* 1 (1989): 108-17.
Sneed, M. R., '(Dis)closure in Qohelet: Qohelet Deconstructed', *JSOT* 27 (2002): 115-26.
—'Is the "Wisdom Tradition" a Tradition?', *CBQ* 73 (2011): 50-71.
—*The Politics of Pessimism in Ecclesiastes: A Social-Science Perspective* (SBLAIL 12; Atlanta, 2012).

Spangenberg, I. J. J., 'Die Struktuur en stekkening van Prediker 4:17–5:6', *NGTT* 30 (1989): 260-69.
—'Quotations in Ecclesiastes: An Appraisal', *OTE* 4 (1991): 19-35.
—'A Century of Wrestling with Qohelet', in Schoors (ed.), *Qohelet in the Context*, 61-91.
Sperber, A., 'Hebrew Based upon Greek and Latin Transliterations', *HUCA* 12–13 (1937): 103-274.
—*A Historical Grammar of Biblical Hebrew* (Leiden, 1966).
—*The Bible in Aramaic, Vol. 4A* (Leiden, 1968).
*Spohn, G. L., *Der Prediger Salomo: aus dem hebräischen aufs neue übersetzt und mit kritischen Anmerkungen begleitet: Nebst einer Beilage, welche Varianten zu dem Prediger in den LXX. aus zweyen Manuskripten und dem Olympiodor enthält* (Leipzig, 1785).
Staples, W. E., 'The Meaning of ḥēpeṣ in Ecclesiastes', *JNES* 24 (1965): 110-12.
Starowieyski, M., 'Le Livre de l'Ecclésiaste dans l'antiquité chrétienne', in S. G. Hall (ed.), *Gregory of Nyssa: Homilies on Ecclesiastes. An English Version with Supporting Studies. Proceedings of the Seventh International Colloquium on Gregory of Nyssa (St. Andrews, 5–10 September 1990)* (Berlin/New York, 1993), 405-40.
Stephanus, I., 'Qohelet', *RIBLA* 15 (1993): 75-85.
Stern, D., 'The Hebrew Bible in Europe in the Middle Ages: A Preliminary Typology', *JSIJ* 11 (2012): 235-322.
Strack, H. L., *Prolegomena critica in Vetus Testamentum Hebraicum, quibus agitur i, De codicibus et deperditis et adhuc exstantibus, ii, De textu Bibliorum Hebraicorum qualis Talmudistarum temporibus fuerit* (Leipzig, 1873).
*Strobel, A., *Das Buch Prediger (Kohelet)* (Die Welt der Bibel; Dusseldorf, 1967).
Stronach, D., 'The Garden as a Political Statement: Some Case Studies from the Near East in the First Millennium B.C.', *BAI* 4 (1990): 171-80.
*Stuart, M., *A Commentary on Ecclesiastes* (New York, 1851).
Sun, C., 'Ecclesiastes among the Megilloth: Death as the Interthematic Link', *BBR* 27 (2017): 185-206.
Sutcliffe, E. F., 'St. Jerome's Pronunciation of Hebrew', *Biblica* 29 (1948): 112-25.
Sutcliffe, J., *A Commentary on the Old and New Testament: In which the sacred text is illustrated with copious notes, theological, historical, and critical; with improvements and reflections at the end of each chapter* (London, 1834).
*Swete, H. B., *The Old Testament in Greek according to the Septuagint. Vol. 2 Chronicles–Tobit* (Cambridge, 3rd edn, 1922).
Talmon, S., 'Double Readings in the Massoretic Text', *Textus* 1 (1960): 144-84.
—'The Three Scrolls of the Law that Were Found in the Temple Court', *Textus* 2 (1962): 14-27.
—'Aspects of the Textual Transmission of the Bible in the Light of Qumran Manuscripts', *Textus* 4 (1964): 95-132.
—'Fragments of Two Leviticus Scrolls from Masada', *Textus* 19 (1998): 27-44.

Tamez, E., 'Ecclesiastes 3:1-8: A Latin American Perspective', in P. Pope-Levison and J. R. Levison (eds.), *Return to Babel* (Louisville, 1999), 75-80.
*—*When the Horizons Close: Rereading Ecclesiastes* (Maryknoll, 2000). ET of *Cuando los horizontes se cierran: Relectura del libro de Eclesiastés o Qohelet* (San José, Costa Rica, 1998).
—'Ecclesiastes: A Reading from the Periphery', *Int* 55 (2001): 250-59.
Taradach, M., 'La figure insolite de Salomon dans TgQo 1,12 dans les Talmuds et quelques Midrašim', in F. Raurell, D. Roure, and P.-R. Tragan (eds.), *Tradició i traducció de la paraula: miscellània Guiu Camps* (SDM 47; Montserrat, 1993), 325-35.
Taradach, M., and J. Ferrer, *Un Targum de Qohélet. Ms. M-2 de Salamanca, Editio Princeps. Texte araméen, traduction et commentaire critique* (MdB 37; Geneva, 1998).
Taylor, C., 'On Some Verses of Qoheleth', *JPh* 2 (1869): 296-310.
Tchernetska, N., J. Olszowy-Schlanger, and N. de Lange, 'An Early Hebrew-Greek Biblical Glossary from the Cairo Genizah', *REJ* 166 (2007): 91-128.
Teicher, J. L., 'The Ben Asher Bible Manuscripts', *JJS* 2 (1950): 17-25.
Thackeray, H. S., *A Grammar of the Old Testament in Greek according to the Septuagint. Vol. I: Introduction, Orthography and Accidence* (Cambridge, 1909).
*Thilo, M., *Der Prediger Salomo Neu Übersetzt und auf seinen Gedankengang untersucht* (Bonn, 1923).
Thompson, H., *The Coptic (Sahidic) Version of Certain Books of the Old Testament: From a Papyrus in the British Museum* (London/Edinburgh/New York/Toronto/Melbourne, 1908).
Thurn, H., 'Zum Text des Hieronymus-Kommentars zum Kohelet', *BZ* 33 (1989): 234-44.
Tin-Sheung, W., 'Qoheleth 1:3-11: Prose or Poetry?', *Jian Dao* 14 (2000): 25-47.
Tita, H., 'Ist die thematische Einheit Koh 4,17–5,6 eine Anspielung auf die Salomoerzählung? Aporien der religionskritischen Interpretation', *BN* 84 (1996): 87-102.
van der Toorn, K., 'Echoes of Gilgamesh in the Book of Qohelet? A Reassessment of the Intellectual Sources of Qohelet', in W. H. van Soldt (ed.), *Veenhof Anniversary Volume: Studies presented to Klaas R. Veenhof on the Occasion of his Sixty-Fifth Birthday* (Uitgaven van het Nederlands Historisch-Archaeologisch Instituut te Istanbul 89; Leiden, 2001), 503-14.
Torrey, C. C., 'The Question of the Original Language of Qoheleth', *JQR* 39 (1948): 151-60.
—'The Problem of Ecclesiastes IV 13-16', *VT* 2 (1952): 175-77.
Tov, E., 'The Nature of the Large-Scale Differences between the LXX and MT S T V, compared with Similar Evidence in Other Sources', in A. Schenker (ed.), *The Earliest Text of the Hebrew Bible: The Relationship between the Masoretic Text and the Hebrew Base of the Septuagint Reconsidered* (SBLSCS 52; Atlanta, 2003), 121-44.

—'The Reading Tradition of the MT Group Compared with That of the Septuagint', *JNSL* 40 (2014): 1-16.
*Treier, D. J., *Proverbs & Ecclesiastes* (Brazos theological commentary on the Bible; Grand Rapids, 2011).
Tremblay, H., 'Qohélet 1,18. Histoire du texte et de son interprétation', *ScEs* 59 (2007): 5-25.
Trompelt, K., 'Die masoretische Akzentuation als Spiegel abweichender Texttraditionen', in A. Lange et al. (eds.), *From Qumran to Aleppo*, 176-88.
Tuan, Y.-F., *The Hydrologic Cycle and the Wisdom of God: A Theme in Geoteleology* (University of Toronto Department of Geography Research Publications 1; Toronto, 1968).
Tuplin, C., *Achaemenid Studies* (Historia Einzelschriften 99; Stuttgart, 1996).
Tur-Sinai, N. H. (=Harry Torczyner), 'Dunkle Bibelstellen', in K. Budde (ed.), *Vom alten Testament Karl Marti zum Siebzigsten Geburtstage gewidmet von Freunden, Fachgenossen und Schülern* (BZAW 41; Giessen, 1925), 274-80.
—'דברי קהלת'='The Words of Qohelet', in הלשון והספר: עיונות יסוד במדע הלשון ובמקורותיה בספרות = *The Language and the Book* (Jerusalem, 1950), 2:389-408.
*Tyler, T., *Ecclesiastes: A contribution to its interpretation; containing an introduction to the book; an exegetical analysis; and a translation, with notes* (London/Edinburgh, 1874).
Uehlinger, C., 'Qohelet im Horizont mesopotamischer, levantinischer und ägyptischer Weisheitsliteratur der persischen und hellenistischen Zeit', in L. Schwienhorst-Schönberger (ed.), *Das Buch Kohelet. Studien zur Struktur, Geschichte, Rezeption und Theologie* (BZAW 254; Berlin/New York, 1997), 155-247.
Ugwueye, L. E., 'God-Justice versus Evil in *Qoheleth*: A Materialist Interpretation', *MJSS* 5 (2014): 528-32.
Ullendorff, E., 'The Meaning of קהלת', *VT* 12 (1962): 215.
Ulrich, E., 'Ezra and Qoheleth Manuscripts from Qumran (4QEzra, 4QQohA,B)', in E. Ulrich, J. W. Wright, R. P. Carroll, and P. R. Davies (eds.), *Priests, Prophets and Scribes* (JSOTSup 149; Sheffield, 1992), 139-57.
—'109. 4QQoh^a', in *Qumran Cave 4 XI: Psalms to Chronicles* (DJD 16; Oxford, 2000), 221-26, pl. XXV.
—'110. 4QQoh^b', in *Qumran Cave 4 XI: Psalms to Chronicles* (DJD 16; Oxford, 2000), 227, pl. XXVI.
*Umbreit, F. W. C., *Koheleth's des weisen königs Seelenkampf: oder philosophische Betrachtungen über das höchste Gut aus dem hebräischen übersetzt und als ein ganzes dargestellt, ein versuch* (Gotha, 1818).
Vaccari, A., '"Stultorum infinitus est numerus" (Eccl, 1,15 Vulg.)', *VD* 8 (1928): 81-84.
—'Recupero d'un lavoro critico di S. Girolamo', in A. Vaccari (ed.), *Scritti di Erudizione e di filologia* (SeL 67; Rome, 1958), 83-146.
Vajda, G., *Deux commentaires Karaïtes sur l'Ecclésiaste* (Leiden, 1971).

Van Seters, J., 'Did the *Sopherim* Create a Standard Edition of the Hebrew Scriptures?', in E. Martín Contreras and L. Miralles-Maciá (eds.), *The Text of the Hebrew Bible: From the Rabbis to the Masoretes* (JAJSup 13; Göttingen, 2014), 47-61.

Vattioni, F., 'Due note sull'Ecclesiaste', *AION* 17 (1967): 157-63.

Verheij, A. J. C., 'Paradise Retried: On Qohelet 2.4-6', *JSOT* 16 (1991): 113-15.

—'Words Speaking for Themselves: On the Poetics of Qohelet 1:4-7', in J. Dyk (ed.), *Give Ear to my Words: Psalms and Other Poetry in and Around the Hebrew Bible: Essays in Honour of Professor N. A. van Uchelen* (Amsterdam, 1996), 183-88.

Viano, M., *The Reception of Sumerian Literature in the Western Periphery* (Antichistica 9: Studi orientali 4; Venice, 2016).

Vignolo, R., 'Maschera e sindrome regale: Interpretazione ironico-psicanalitica di Qoh 1,12–2,26', *Teología* 26 (2001): 12-64.

*Vílchez Líndez, J., *Eclesiastés o Qohélet* (NBE: Sapiencales 3; Estella, Navarra, 1994).

Vinel, F., 'Accumulation de ὅτι dans l'Ecclésiaste: brouillage du sens ou force rhétorique?', in B. A. Taylor (ed.), *IX Congress of the International Organization for Septuagint and Cognate Studies: Cambridge, 1995* (SBLSCS 45; Atlanta, 1997), 391-401.

—'Le Texte Grec de l'Ecclésiaste et ses caractéristiques: une relecture critique de l'histoire de la royauté', in Schoors (ed.), *Qohelet in the Context*, 283-302.

—L'Ecclésiaste: Traduction du texte grec de la Septante: Introduction et notes (La Bible d'Alexandrie 18; Paris, 2002).

Vonach, A., 'Die sogenannte "Kanon- oder Ptahotepformel". Anmerkungen zu Tradition und Kontext einer markanten Verwendung', *PzB* 6 (1997): 73-80.

Waard, J. de, 'The Translator and Textual Criticism (with Particular Reference to Eccl 2,25)', *Bib* 60 (1979): 509-29.

Wagner, M., *Die lexicalischen und grammatikalischen Aramaismen im alttestamentlichen Hebräisch* (BZAW 96; Berlin, 1966).

Wazana, N., 'A Case of the Evil Eye: Qohelet 4:4-8', *JBL* 126 (2007): 685-702.

Weber, R., B. Fischer, J. Gribomont, H. F. D. Sparks, W. Thiele, and R. Gryson (eds.), *Biblia Sacra iuxta Vulgatam Versionem* (Stuttgart, 5th edn, 2007).

Weeks, S., 'Whose Words? Qoheleth, Hosea and Attribution in Biblical Literature', in P. J. Harland and C. T. R. Hayward (eds.), *New Heaven and New Earth: Prophecy and the Millennium. Essays in Honour of Anthony Gelston* (VTSup 77; Leiden/Boston/Köln, 1999), 151-70.

—*Instruction and Imagery in Proverbs 1–9* (Oxford, 2007).

—'Predictive and Prophetic Literature: Can Neferti Help Us Read the Bible?', in J. Day (ed.), *Prophecy and the Prophets in Ancient Israel: Proceedings of the Oxford Old Testament Seminar* (LHBOTS 531; London/New York, 2010), 25-46.

—*An Introduction to the Study of Wisdom Literature* (T&T Clark Approaches to Biblical Studies; London, 2010).

—*Ecclesiastes and Scepticism* (LHBOTS 541; New York/London, 2012).
—'"Fear God and Keep His Commandments": Could Qohelet Have Said This?', in B. U. Schipper and D. A. Teeter (eds.), *Wisdom and Torah: The Reception of 'Torah' in the Wisdom Literature of the Second Temple Period* (JSJSup 163; Leiden/Boston, 2013), 101-18.
—'Restoring the Greek Tobit', *JSJ* 44 (2013): 1-15.
—'Notes on Some Hebrew Words in Ecclesiastes', in J. K. Aitken, J. M. S. Clines, and C. M. Maier (eds.), *Interested Readers: Essays on the Hebrew Bible in Honor of David J. A. Clines* (Atlanta, 2013), 373-84.
—*The Making of Many Books: Printed Works on Ecclesiastes 1523–1875* (Winona Lake, 2014).
—'The Inner-Textuality of Qoheleth's Monologue', in Dell and Kynes (eds.), *Reading Ecclesiastes Intertextually*, 142-53.
—'Wisdom, Form and Genre', in M. Sneed (ed.), *Was There a Wisdom Tradition? New Prospects in Israelite Wisdom Studies* (Atlanta, 2015), 161-77.
—'Divine Judgment and Reward in Ecclesiastes', in Brooke and van Hecke (eds.), *Goochem*, 155-66.
—'Is "Wisdom Literature" a Useful Category?', in H. Najman, J.-S. Rey, and E. Tigchelaar (eds.), *Tracing Sapiential Traditions in Ancient Judaism* (Leiden/Boston, 2016), 3-23.
Weeks, S., S. J. Gathercole, and L. T. Stuckenbruck (eds.), *The Book of Tobit: Texts from the Principal Ancient and Medieval Traditions: With Synopsis, Concordances, and Annotated Texts in Aramaic, Hebrew, Greek, Latin, and Syriac* (Fontes et subsidia ad Bibliam pertinentes 3; Berlin, 2004).
Weinberg, J. P., 'Authorship and Author in the Ancient Near East and in the Hebrew Bible', *HS* 44 (2003): 157-69.
Weisman, Z., 'Elements of Political Satire in Koheleth 4, 13-16; 9, 13-16', *ZAW* 111 (1999): 547-60.
Weiss, J., 'The Masorah of The Jewish Theological Seminary of America Library Manuscript 232 (E. N. Adler Ms. 346)' (PhD diss.; The Graduate School of The Jewish Theological Seminary, 2009).
Weitzman, M. P., *The Syriac Version of the Old Testament: An Introduction* (Cambridge, 1999).
Wente, E. F., 'Egyptian "Make Merry" Songs Reconsidered', *JNES* 21 (1962): 118-28.
Wernberg-Møller, P. C. H., 'The Old Accusative Case Ending in Biblical Hebrew: Observations on הַמְּנוּחָה in Psalm 116: 15', *JSS* 33 (1988): 155-64.
Wernik, U., 'Will the Real Homosexual in the Bible Please Stand Up?', *Theology & Sexuality* 11 (2005): 47-64.
West, M. L., *Iambi et Elegi Graeci* (Oxford, 2nd edn, 1989).
Westenholz, J. G., *Legends of the Kings of Akkade: The Texts* (Winona Lake, 1997).

Whitley, C. F., 'Has the Particle שם an Asseverative Force?', *Bib* 55 (1974): 394-98.
*—*Koheleth: His Language and Thought* (BZAW 148; Berlin/New York, 1979).
Whybray, R. N., 'The Identification and Use of Quotations in Ecclesiastes', in J. A. Emerton (ed.), *Congress Volume, Vienna, 1980* (VTSup 32; Leiden, 1981), 435-51.
—'Qoheleth, Preacher of Joy', *JSOT* 7 (1982): 87-98.
—'Ecclesiastes 1.5-7 and the Wonders of Nature', *JSOT* 13 (1988): 105-12.
*—*Ecclesiastes* (NCB; Grand Rapids/London, 1989).
—'"A Time to Be Born and a Time to Die": Some Observations on Ecclesiastes 3:2-8', in M. Mori, H. Ogawa, and M. Yoshikawa (eds.), *Near Eastern Studies Dedicated to H.I.H. Prince Takahito Mikasa* (Bulletin of the Middle Eastern Culture Centre in Japan 5; Wiesbaden, 1991), 469-83.
Wickes, W., *A Treatise on the Accentuation of the Twenty-One So-Called Prose Books of the Old Testament: With a Facsimile of a Page of the Codex Assigned to Ben-Asher in Aleppo* (Oxford, 1887).
*Wildeboer, G., 'Der Prediger', in *Die fünf Megillot (Das Hohelied, Das Buch Ruth, Die Klagelieder, Der Prediger, Das Buch Esther)* (KHC 17; Freiburg i.B./Leipzig/Tübingen, 1898), 109-68.
Wilkins, A. S., *M. Tulli Ciceronis Rhetorica. Tomus II Brutus; Orator; De Optimo Genere Oratorum; Partitiones Oratoriae; Topica* (OCT; Oxford, 1903).
Williams, M. H., *The Monk and the Book: Jerome and the Making of Christian Scholarship* (Chicago, 2006).
Willmes, B., *Menschliches Schicksal und ironische Weisheitskritik im Koheletbuch: Kohelets Ironie und die Grenzen der Exegese* (Biblisch-theologische Studien 39; Neukirchen-Vluyn, 2000).
Wilson, A. M., 'The Particle את in Hebrew', *Hebraica* 6 (1890): 139-50, 212-24.
Wilson, G. H., '"The Words of the Wise": The Intent and Significance of Qohelet 12:9-14', *JBL* 103 (1984): 175-92.
Wilson, L., 'Artful Ambiguity in Ecclesiastes 1,1-11. A Wisdom Technique?', in Schoors (ed.), *Qohelet in the Context*, 357-65.
Wise, M. O., 'A Calque from Aramaic in Qoheleth 6:12; 7:12; and 8:13', *JBL* 109 (1990): 249-57.
Wright, A. G., 'The Riddle of the Sphinx: The Structure of the Book of Qoheleth', *CBQ* 30 (1968): 313-34.
—'The Riddle of the Sphinx Revisited: Numerical Patterns in the Book of Qoheleth', *CBQ* 42 (1980): 35-51.
—'"For Everything There Is a Season": The Structure and Meaning of the Fourteen Opposites (Ecclesiastes 3,2-8)', in M. Carrez, J. Doré, and P. Grelot (eds.), *De la Tôrah au Messie: Études d'exégèse et d'herméneutique bibliques offertes à Henri Cazelles pour ses 25 années d'enseignement à l'Institut Catholique de Paris (Octobre 1979)* (Paris, 1981), 321-28.
—'Additional Numerical Patterns in Qoheleth', *CBQ* 45 (1983): 32-43.

—'The Poor but Wise Youth and the Old but Foolish King (Qoh 4:13-16)', in M. L. Barré (ed.), *Wisdom, You Are my Sister: Studies in Honor of Roland E. Murphy, O.Carm., on the Occasion of his Eightieth Birthday* (CBQMS 29; Washington, 1997), 142-54.

*Wright, C. H. H., *The Book of Koheleth, Commonly Called Ecclesiastes: Considered in relation to modern criticism, and to the doctrines of modern pessimism, with a critical and grammatical commentary and a revised translation (Donnellan Lectures 1880–81)* (London, 1883).

Wright, J. R., 'Commentary on Ecclesiastes', in *Proverbs, Ecclesiastes, Song of Solomon* (ACCS: Old Testament IX; Downers Grove, 2005), 190-285.

Wyatt, N., *Religious Texts from Ugarit: The Words of Ilimilku and his Colleagues* (BibSem 53; Sheffield, 1998).

Yardeni, A., *The Book of Hebrew Script: History, Palaeography, Script Styles, Calligraphy and Design* (Jerusalem, 1997).

Yeard, F. (John), *A New Paraphrase upon Ecclesiastes: With an analysis and notes. Proving, that the preacher introduces a refin'd sensualist, to oppugn and invalidate his penitential animadversions and exhortations* (London, 1701).

Yeivin, I., 'The Division into Sections in the Book of Psalms', *Textus* 7 (1969): 76-102.

—*Bible-Hagiographa: Codex Berlin Or. Qu. 680 - Codex New York, JTS 510* (Jerusalem, 1972).

—*Introduction to the Tiberian Masorah* (trans. E. J. Revell; SBLMasS 5; Missoula, 1980).

Yesudian-Storfjell, S. C., 'The Reception of Qoheleth in a Selection of Rabbinic, Patristic and Nonconformist Texts' (PhD diss.; University of Sheffield, 2003).

*Yi, Y. Y., 'Translation Technique of the Greek Ecclesiastes' (PhD diss.; The Southern Baptist Theological Seminary, 2005). Published as *The Greek Ecclesiastes: Translation Technique and Identity* (Saarbrücken, 2009).

Young, I., *Diversity in Pre-exilic Hebrew* (FAT 5; Tübingen, 1993).

Young, I., and R. Rezetko, with the assistance of M. Ehrensvärd, *Linguistic Dating of Biblical Texts* (2 vols.; London, 2008).

Youngblood, R. F., 'Qoheleth's "Dark House" (Eccl. 12:5)', *JETS* 29 (1986): 397-410.

*Zapletal, V., *Das Buch Kohelet: Kritisch und metrisch untersucht übersetzt und erklärt* (Freiburg i.B., 2nd edn, 1911).

*Zer-Kavod, M., 'קהלת'='Qohelet', in חמש מגילות: רות, שיר השירים, קהלת, איכה, אסתר = *The Five Megillot* (Jerusalem, 1990). Originally published 1973.

Zevit, Z., 'The Linguistic and Contextual Arguments in Support of a 3m.s. Suffix -*y*', *UF* 9 (1977): 315-28.

Ziegler, J., 'Die Wiedergabe der nota accusativi *'et*, *'aet*- mit σύν', *ZAW* 100 (1988): 222-33.

—'Der Gebrauch des Artikels in der Septuaginta des Ecclesiastes', in D. Fraenkel, U. Quast, and J. W. Wevers (eds.), *Studien zur Septuaginta: Robert Hanhart zu Ehren* (AAWG.PH 190; MSU 20; Göttingen, 1990), 83-120.

Zimmerli, W., *Die Weisheit des Predigers Salomo* (Aus der Welt der Religion. Biblische Reihe 11; Berlin, 1936).

—'Das Buch Kohelet: Traktat oder Sentenzensammlung?', *VT* 24 (1974): 221-30.

*—'Das Buch des Predigers Salomo', in H. Ringgren and W. R. Zimmerli, *Sprüche, Prediger* (ATD 16; Göttingen, 3rd edn, 1980), 123-253.

Zimmermann, F., 'The Root *KAHAL* in Some Scriptural Passages', *JBL* 50 (1931): 311-12.

—'Notes on Some Difficult Old Testament Passage (*sic*)', *JBL* 55 (1936): 303-308.

—'On Eccles. 3:18', *AJSL* 58 (1941): 100.

—'The Aramaic Provenance of Qohelet', *JQR* 36 (1945): 17-45.

—'The Question of Hebrew in Qohelet', *JQR* 40 (1949): 79-102.

*—*The Inner World of Qohelet: With Translation and Commentary* (New York, 1973).

Zirkel, G., *Untersuchungen über den Prediger: nebst kritischen und philologischen Bemerkungen* (Würzburg, 1792).

*Zöckler, O., *Das Hohelied und der Prediger Theologisch-homiletisch bearbeitet* (THBW AT 13; Bielefeld/Leipzig, 1868); ET *Ecclesiastes: or, Koheleth* (New York, 1898).

*Zorell, F., *Lexicon Hebraicum et Aramaicum Veteris Testamenti* (2 vols.; Rome, 1946–1954).

ABBREVIATIONS AND SIGLA

AAWG.PH	Abhandlungen der Akademie der Wissenschaften in Göttingen, Philologisch-Historische Klasse
AB	Anchor Bible
ABR	*Australian Biblical Review*
ACCS	Ancient Christian Commentary on Scripture
ACEBT	*Amsterdamse Cahiers voor Exegese van de Bijbel en zijn Tradities*
AF	*Archivo di Filosofia*
AION	*Annali Istituto Orientale di Napoli*
AJSL	*American Journal of Semitic Languages and Literature*
ANETS	Ancient Near Eastern Texts and Studies
AOAT	Alter Orient und Altes Testament
APR	*American Poetry Review*
AS	*Aramaic Studies*
ASE	*Annali di storia dell'esegesi*
Asp	*Asprenas. Rivista di scienze teologiche*
ATD	Das Alte Testament Deutsch
AUSS	*Andrews University Seminary Studies*
BAI	*Bulletin of the Asia Institute*
BASOR	*Bulletin of the American Schools of Oriental Research*
BAT	Die Botschaft des alten Testaments,
BBB	Bonner biblische Beiträge
BBC	Blackwell Bible Commentaries
BBR	*Bulletin for Biblical Research*
BDAG	W. Bauer, F. W. Danker, W. F. Arndt, and F. W. Gingrich, *Greek-English Lexicon of the New Testament and Other Early Christian Literature* (3rd ed.; Chicago & London, 2000)
BDB	F. Brown, S. R. Driver, and C. A. Briggs, *A Hebrew and English Lexicon of the Old Testament* (Oxford, 1906)
BDD	*Bekhol Derakhekha Daehu Journal of Torah and Scholarship*
BEATAJ	Beiträge zur Erforschung des Alten Testaments und des antiken Judentum
BeO	*Bibbia e oriente*
BETL	Bibliotheca ephemeridum theologicarum lovaniensium
BH^1	*Biblia Hebraica* (Stuttgart, 1905–1906). The text of Ecclesiastes was prepared by S. R. Driver

BH^3	Biblia Hebraica (Stuttgart, 3rd edn, 1929–37). The text of Ecclesiastes was prepared by F. Horst.
BHBib	Bibliotheca Hispana Bíblica
BHQ	Biblia Hebraica Quinta Editione (Stuttgart, 2004-). The text of Ecclesiastes was prepared by Y. A. P. Goldman.
BHS	Biblia Hebraica Stuttgartensia (5th ed.; Stuttgart, 1990). The text of Ecclesiastes was prepared by F. Horst.
Bib	Biblica
BibInt	Biblical Interpretation
BibOr	Biblica et Orientalia
BibScRel	Biblioteca di Scienze Religiose
BibSem	The Biblical Seminar
BIOSCS	Bulletin of the International Organization for Septuagint and Cognate Studies
BJRL	Bulletin of the John Rylands University Library of Manchester
BK	Bibel und Kirche
BKAT	Biblischer Kommentar Altes Testament
BLS	Bible and Literature Series
BN	Biblische Notizen
BRLJ	The Brill Reference Library of Judaism
BSac	Bibliotheca sacra
BSPS	Boston Studies in the Philosophy of Science
BWANT	Beiträge zur Wissenschaft vom Alten und Neuen Testament
BZ	Biblische Zeitschrift
BZAW	Beihefte zur Zeitschrift für die alttestamentliche Wissenschaft
CAD	The Assyrian Dictionary of the Oriental Institute of the University of Chicago (Chicago & Glückstadt, 1956–2010)
CB	Coniectanea biblica
CBQ	Catholic Biblical Quarterly
CBQMS	Catholic Biblical Quarterly Monograph Series
CBR	Currents in Biblical Research
CBSC	The Cambridge Bible for Schools and Colleges
CC	Continental Commentaries
CCSL	Corpus Christianorum: Series Latina
CIS	Corpus Inscriptionum Semiticarum
CO	Cahiers d'Orientalisme
COut	Commentar op het Oude Testament
CrStHB	Critical Studies in the Hebrew Bible
CSEL	Corpus Scriptorum Ecclesiasticorum Latinorum
CSR	Christian Scholars Review
CTM	Concordia Theological Monthly
DCH	D. J. A. Clines (ed.), Dictionary of Classical Hebrew (Sheffield, 1993–2016)

Did	*Didaskalia. Revista da Faculdade de teologia de Lisboa*
DJD	Discoveries in the Judaean Desert
DJSS	Duke Judaic Studies Series
DSD	*Dead Sea Discoveries*
EBib	Études Bibliques
EdF	Erträge der Forschung
EI	*Eretz-Israel*
EQ	*Evangelical Quarterly*
EQÄ	Einführungen und Quellentexte zur Ägyptologie
EstBib	*Estudios bíblicos*
ET	English translation
ETL	*Ephemerides theologicae lovanienses*
EvT	*Evangelische Theologie*
ExpTim	*Expository Times*
FAT	Forschungen zum Alten Testament
FO	*Folia orientalia*
FOTL	Forms of the Old Testament Literature
FRLANT	Forschungen zur Religion und Literatur des Alten und Neuen Testaments
FSBP	Fontes et subsidia ad Bibliam pertinentes
Fund	*Fundamentum: Zeitschrift der Freien Evangelisch-Theologischen Akademie Basel*
GCS	Die griechischen christlichen Schriftsteller der ersten drei Jahrhunderte herausgegeben von der Kirchenväter
GKC	W. Gesenius, *Gesenius' Hebrew Grammar. As edited and enlarged by the late E. Kautzsch... Second English edition. Revised in accordance with the twenty-eighth German edition, 1909, by A. E. Cowley* (Oxford, 2nd edn, 1910)
GLECS	*Comptes rendus du Groupe Linguistique d'Etudes Chamito-Semitiques*
GM	*Göttinger Miszellen*
GO	Göttinger Orientforschungen
HALOT	L. Koehler, W. Baumgartner, and J. J. Stamm, *The Hebrew and Aramaic Lexicon of the Old Testament. Translated and edited under the supervision of M. E. J. Richardson* (4 vols; Leiden, Boston & Köln, 1994–99)
HAR	Hebrew Annual Review
HAT	Handbuch zum Alten Testament
HCM	Holmstedt, R. D., J. A. Cook, and P. S. Marshall, *Qoheleth: A handbook on the Hebrew text* (Baylor handbook on the Hebrew Bible; Waco, 2017).
HCOT	Historical Commentary on the Old Testament
Hen	*Henoch*

HeyJ	*Heythrop Journal*
HS	*Hebrew Studies*
HSAT	*Die Heilige Schrift des Alten Testaments*
HSCP	*Harvard Studies in Classical Philology*
HSS	Harvard Semitic Studies
HTKAT	Herders theologischer Kommentar zum Alten Testament
HTR	*Harvard Theological Review*
HUCA	*Hebrew Union College Annual*
ICC	International Critical Commentary
IEJ	*Israel Exploration Journal*
Int	*Interpretation*
ITC	International Theological Commentary
JAJSup	Journal of Ancient Judaism Supplements
JAOS	*Journal of the American Oriental Society*
JBL	*Journal of Biblical Literature*
JBQ	*Jewish Bible Quarterly*
JESOT	*Journal for the Evangelical Study of the Old Testament*
JETS	*Journal of the Evangelical Theological Society*
JHebS	*Journal of Hebrew Scriptures*
JJS	*Journal of Jewish Studies*
J-M	P. Joüon, *A Grammar of Biblical Hebrew*. Translated and revised by T. Muraoka (2 vols.; Subsidia biblica, 14/1-2; Rome, 1991)
JNES	*Journal of Near Eastern Studies*
JNSL	*Journal of Northwest Semitic Languages*
JOTT	*Journal of Translation and Textlinguistics*
JPh	*Journal of Philology*
JPSBC	The JPS Bible Commentary
JQR	*Jewish Quarterly Review*
JSem	*Journal of Semitics*
JSIJ	*Jewish Studies, an Internet Journal*
JSJ	*Journal for the Study of Judaism in the Persian, Hellenistic, and Roman Periods*
JSJSup	Supplements to the Journal for the Study of Judaism
JSOT	*Journal for the Study of the Old Testament*
JSOTSup	Journal for the Study of the Old Testament Supplement Series
JSPSup	Journal for the Study of the Pseudepigrapha: Supplement Series
JSQ	*Jewish Studies Quarterly*
JSS	*Journal of Semitic Studies*
JSSSup	Journal of Semitic Studies Supplement Series
JTS	*Journal of Theological Studies*
KAI	H. Donner and W. Röllig, *Kanaanäische und aramäische Inschriften* (Wiesbaden, 2nd edn, 1966–69)

ABBREVIATIONS AND SIGLA

KAT	Kommentar zum Alten Testament
KHC	Kurzer Hand-Commentar zum Alten Testament
kjv	King James Version
KTR	Kieler Theologische Reihe
KTU	M. Dietrich, O. Loretz, and J. Sanmartín, *Die keilalphabetischen Texte aus Ugarit* (Alter Orient und Altes Testament, 24; Kevelaer & Neukirchen-Vluyn, 1976; 3rd edn. Munster, 2013)
LASBF	*Liber annuus Studii biblici franciscani*
LHBOTS	Library of Hebrew Bible / Old Testament Studies
lit.	literally
LSAWS	Linguistic Studies in Ancient West Semitic
LSJ	H. G. Liddell, R. Scott, H. S. Jones, *A Greek-English Lexicon* (9th ed.; Oxford, 1996)
LTP	*Laval Theologique et Philosophique*
MdB	Le Monde de la Bible
MGWJ	*Monatsschrift für Geschichte und Wissenschaft des Judentums*
MJSS	*Mediterranean Journal of Social Sciences*
MM	J. H. Moulton and G. Milligan, *The Vocabulary of the Greek Testament* (London, 1930)
MPIL	Monographs of the Peshiṭta Institute Leiden
MSU	Mitteilungen des Septuaginta-Unternehmens
NBE	Nueva Biblia Española
NCB	New Century Bible Commentary
NCLS	Nottingham Classical Literature Studies
NEchtB	Die Neue Echter Bibel
NGTT	*Nederduitse gereformeerde teologiese tydskrif*
NICOT	New International Commentary on the Old Testament
NJPS	New Jewish Publication Society translation
NT	New Testament
OBO	Orbis biblicus et orientalis
OCT	Oxford Classical Texts
OIP	The University of Chicago Oriental Institute Publications
OLA	Orientalia lovaniensia analecta
OLP	*Orientalia lovaniensia periodica*
OLZ	*Orientalistische Literaturzeitung*
ORS	Oriental Research Series
OTE	*Old Testament Essays*
OTL	Old Testament Library
OTS	*Oudtestamentische Studiën / Old Testament Studies* (journal)
OTS	Oudtestamentische Studiën / Old Testament Studies (series)
PAAJR	Proceedings of the American Academy of Jewish Research
PAT	D. R. Hillers and E. Cussini, *Palmyrene Aramaic Texts* (Baltimore and London, 1996)

PEQ	*Palestine Exploration Quarterly*
PG	Patrologia graeca (Patrologiae cursus completus: Series Graeca). Edited and published by J.-P. Migne. 162 vols. Paris: 1857–86
PIBA	*Proceedings of the Irish Biblical Association*
PL	Patrologia latina (Patrologiae cursus completus: Series Latina). Edited and published by J.-P. Migne. 217 vols. Paris: 1844–64
POS	Pretoria Oriental Series
PSB	*Princeton Seminary Bulletin*
PTA	Papyrologische Texte und Abhandlungen
PzB	*Protokolle zur Bibel*
RA	*Revue d'Assyriologie*
RB	*Revue biblique*
RECAPO	*Revue d'Études des Civilisations Anciennes du Proche-Orient*
REJ	*Revue des études juives*
RevQ	*Revue de Qumran*
RevScRel	*Revue des sciences religieuses*
RIBLA	*Revista de interpretación bíblica latino-americana*
RivB	*Rivista biblica italiana*
RivBSup	Supplementi alla Rivista Biblica
RNBC	Readings: A New Biblical Commentary
RSR	*Recherches de science religieuse*
RSV	Revised Standard Version
RTP	*Revue de théologie et de philosophie*
SBL	Society of Biblical Literature
SBLABib	Society of Biblical Literature Academia Biblica
SBLAIL	SBL Ancient Israel and Its Literature
SBLDS	Society of Biblical Literature Dissertation Series
SBLMasS	Society of Biblical Literature Masoretic Studies
SBLSCS	Society of Biblical Literature Septuagint and Cognate Studies
SBLSS	Society of Biblical Literature Symposium Series
SBLWAW	Society of Biblical Literature Writings from the Ancient World
SBT	Studies in Biblical Theology
ScEs	*Science et esprit*
SDM	Scripta et documenta
SEE-J Hiphil	Scandinavian Evangelical E-Journal: Hiphil
SeL	Storia e Letteratura
SJOT	*Scandinavian Journal of the Old Testament*
SJT	*Scottish Journal of Theology*
SPAW	*Sitzungsberichte der Königlich preussischen Akademie der Wissenschaften*
SR	*Studies in Religion*
SSLL	Studies in Semitic Languages and Linguistics

SSU	Acta Universitatis Upsaliensis: Studia Semitica Upsaliensia
StudBT	*Studia Biblica et Theologica*
STDJ	Studies on the Texts of the Desert of Judah
STHB	Supplements to the Textual History of the Bible
STLI	Studies and Texts (Philip W. Lown Institute of Advanced Judaic Studies)
StPat	*Studia Patavina*
StT	Studi e Testi, Biblioteca apostolica vaticana
TAD	B. Porten and A. Yardeni (eds.), *Textbook of Aramaic Documents from Ancient Egypt* (3 vols.; Jerusalem, 1986–93)
TDOT	G. J. Botterweck and H. Ringgren (eds.), *Theological Dictionary of the Old Testament* (Grand Rapids, 1974–2006)
THBW	Theologisch-homiletisches Bibelwerk
ThOrAr	Theologische und orientalische Arbeiten
THOTC	The Two Horizons Old Testament Commentary
ThViat	*Theologia viatorum*
TJ	*Trinity Journal*
TLZ	*Theologische Literaturzeitung*
TOTC	Tyndale Old Testament commentaries
TransSup	Supplément à Transeuphratène
TSAJ	Texte und Studien zum Antiken Judentum
TSJTSA	Texts and Studies of the Jewish Theological Seminary of America
TSK	*Theologische Studien und Kritiken*
TSMEMJ	Texts and Studies in Medieval and Early Modern Judaism
TThSt	Trierer theologische Studien
TUGAL	Texte und Untersuchungen zur Geschichte der altchristlichen Literatur
TynBul	*Tyndale Bulletin*
TZ	*Theologische Zeitschrift*
UF	*Ugarit-Forschungen*
VCSup	Supplements to Vigiliae Christianae
VD	*Verbum domini*
VT	*Vetus Testamentum*
VTSup	Vetus Testamentum Supplements
WAS	Wiener alttestamentliche Studien
WBC	Word Biblical Commentary
WTJ	*The Westminster Theological Journal*
WUNT	Wissenschaftliche Untersuchungen zum Neuen Testament
WZKM	*Wiener Zeitschrift für die Kunde des Morgenlandes*
ZAH	*Zeitschrift für Althebräistik*
ZAW	*Zeitschrift für die alttestamentliche Wissenschaft*

ZBKAT	Zurcher Bibelkommentare. Altes Testament
ZDMGSup	Zeitschrift der deutschen morgenländischen Gesellschaft: Supplementbände
ZDPV	*Zeitschrift des deutschen Palästina-Vereins*
ZTK	*Zeitschrift für Theologie und Kirche*
ZWT	*Zeitschrift für wissenschaftliche Theologie*

Textual sigla (see pp. 199-228), below, for details and editions cited)

G	Greek Septuagint
GB	Codex Vaticanus
GS	Codex Sinaiticus
Hie	Lemma of Jerome's commentary
La	Old Latin
M	The common or usual reading of Masoretic texts
MA	Aleppo Codex
ML	Leningrad Codex, ms EBP. I B 19a
S	Syriac (Peshitta)
Syh	Syro-Hexapla
V	Vulgate
T	Targum
α'	Aquila's text
θ'	Theodotion's text
σ'	Symmachus' text
*	Used with another siglum to indicate what is taken to be the original reading in that textual tradition; in particular, G* is the 'Old Greek'.

INTRODUCTION

A very great deal has been written about Ecclesiastes over the last two millennia.[1] The inclination of earlier generations was to read it, and to qualify its claims, in the light of other biblical literature, with the result that it has not always had the reputation for subversiveness that it has tended to enjoy in modern scholarship. Its provocative tone, however, and its concern with the human condition have always attracted interest.[2] It is also a very difficult

---

[1] For commentaries from the third to sixteenth centuries, see Starowieyski, 'Le Livre de l'Ecclésiaste dans l'antiquité chrétienne', 424-40; for commentaries and other studies 1523–1875, Weeks, *The Making of Many Books*; for 1875–1988, Reinhard Lehmann's bibliography in Michel, *Untersuchungen*, 291-322; for 1988–1998, Béatrice Perrigaux Allison's bibliography in Rose, *Rien de nouveau*, 557-629. I am aware of more than 800 studies that have appeared since then. About a hundred of those published between 2000 and 2013 are surveyed in Lavoie, 'Les Études'; cf. also Schwienhorst-Schönberger, 'Neues unter der Sonne', for 1987–1997, and 'Neuere Veroffentlichungen', for 1998–2003.

[2] If Ecclesiastes was ever at risk of being excluded from the biblical canon, it is not clear that its more difficult assertions were the reason. The Talmud includes a lengthy discussion of Ecclesiastes and Proverbs (see *b. Šabbat* 30b), in the course of which it is suggested that earlier sages had wished to suppress both books because they were self-contradictory (Dell, 'Ecclesiastes as Wisdom', 313-17, helpfully presents translations of this and other relevant passages). The Mishnah (*Yadayim* 3.5) also seems to suggest that the status of Ecclesiastes was disputed by the early rabbis, although it gives no explicit reason, and the book is linked here instead with Song of Songs (cf. *b. Megillah* 7a, which also talks about Esther). There is a reference in this discussion to a declaration in favour of both books, and Graetz, in an appendix to his commentary (147-73) hypothesized that there had been a 'Council of Jamnia' (or 'Yavneh') at which the contents of the Jewish canon had been finalized, and the canonical status of Ecclesiastes established. Aune, 'Origins', suggests that Graetz was influenced by a similar suggestion in Spinoza's *Tractatus Theologico-Politicus* (which can be found at the end of ch. 10). That view is no longer generally held (cf. Dempster, 'Canon', 391-92): it is unlikely that any formal decision about the book's status was ever made within Judaism, and the nature of any controversy surrounding it is unclear. The mishnaic discussion speaks mysteriously in terms of books that are accepted to be sacred 'defiling the hands', and some apparently supposed that Ecclesiastes did not do so—but this very concept may have been poorly understood by the rabbis themselves, and it is interpreted in various ways by modern scholars; see, e.g., Barton, *The Spirit and the Letter*, 108-21; Broyde, 'Defilement'; Goodman, 'Sacred Scripture'; Lim, 'Defilement'; Beckwith, *Canon*, 278-81. Strikingly, when

book, not only in the sense that its claims have so often seemed to need such qualification, but also in the more basic sense that it is hard to read: generations of commentators have struggled to understand what the text actually says or means at many points. Luther was probably right to suspect that some engage with it principally for the pleasure of wrestling with its puzzles,[3] but this has also, of course, been the source of much confusion and frustration, and it has compounded the broader problems of interpretation. Although a great deal has been written, therefore, it would be hard to claim that a great deal has been agreed amongst scholars, or that any consensus is ever likely to emerge around some issues.

In his important recent commentary, and in a series of other works spanning several decades, Anton Schoors has put every subsequent commentator in his debt by gathering many of the different opinions on particular points, and at that level it does remain possible to discuss and adjudicate between them—as I have tried to do in my own commentary, below.[4] It is a lot more difficult, however, to

---

R. Simeon claims in the Tosefta (*Yadayim* 2.14) that Ecclesiastes does not defile the hands, it is simply because he believes it to have been written by Solomon himself, rather than through divine inspiration. We do, to be sure, find early Jewish suspicions about the book's ideas described in Jerome's commentary to 12.13-14 and in Leviticus Rabbah (28.1): Halperin, 'Book of Remedies', explores the various stories and traditions that arose around the 'Solomonic' books more generally. However, although rabbis and interpreters of various generations seem to have understood the book to have been the subject of controversy at some point in the past, they do not seem to have shared any single or consistent view of the reasons for that controversy, and they certainly did not avoid using Ecclesiastes themselves: Bickerman, *Four Strange Books*, 153, claims that, 'Of its 222 verses, 122 are quoted in rabbinic sources'.

[3] In the preface of his commentary; the 1573 English translation speaks of 'eche man labouryng to frame diverse of the sayinges therein to his owne profession, or rather opinion whether for that their curiositie was delighted in strange, obscure and unwonted matters: or else for that in such obscure and darke writyngs, it is easie for a man to fayne what hee phansieth and supposeth'. Salyer, *Vain Rhetoric*, 146-47, compares the book to a Rubik's Cube, presenting stimulating problems that are 'there to be solved by engaging the reader's mind' (146). Given the notorious problems presented by its language alone, I am not sure on what basis Davis (166) claims that 'Koheleth's language is invariably simple'.

[4] There is a significant overlap, of course, between Schoors' 2013 commentary and his earlier works—in particular *The Preacher* I and II. The commentary became available only after I had finished a significant proportion of my own work, and I have retained existing references to these other studies, but noted places where the views expressed in his commentary differ.

give any similar overview of ideas about the book's themes and message, or about aspects of its structure and presentation. In part, this is simply because there are so many: even in 1861, Christian Ginsburg's 'Historical Sketch of the Exegesis of the Book' ran from page 27 to page 243 of his commentary while barely scratching the surface of many issues, and much has been written since then. The greater problem, though, is that scholars find many different sorts of interconnection, so that it is not simply a matter of some scholars believing the book to say one thing while another group believes it to say something different. Writing of scholarship on Ecclesiastes in the late sixteenth century, which was a lot less diverse in its views than is current scholarship, Ginsburg remarked that 'Every fresh commentator either actually or virtually regards all his predecessors as having misunderstood Coheleth' (73)—and Eric Christianson, in *Ecclesiastes through the Centuries*, sets that alongside many similar observations by others, among the *testimonia* that preface his own excellent history of the book's reception.

Rather than try to aggregate all these views, I have opted in the introduction to set out my own, and to use these, so far as practical, as a framework for the discussion of other opinions in key areas. It may be taken as a given that, since scholars disagree with each other on so many points, little that I say would win the assent of every other commentator, although I have tried to indicate where my opinions represent the view of a minority, or are cries in the wilderness. I should stress also, however, that even where there is some consensus with respect to the interpretation of specific passages, the fact of consensus does not always put that interpretation beyond question: some understandings survive, I think, more through their appeal to past authority than through any inherent credibility (4.5 offers a parade example). Certain of the broader claims often made about the book seem similarly rooted in habit or inertia, and I have attempted to question these thoroughly, even where I agree with them myself.

After some experimentation, it has proved easiest to deal with the important issues in two main discussions, respectively covering the internal matters of presentation and content, and the external matters of date and context—although there is necessarily some overlap between them. The third main part of the introduction is quite different in character, and addresses the textual history of the book. I have prefaced it with an overview for those readers who would prefer not to grapple with the drier technical issues, but I have also gone considerably further than other commentators in setting out the background to the key versions of Ecclesiastes. There are several reasons for this, the most important being that our understanding of certain issues has been transformed in the last few decades. The character and context of the Septuagint translation of the book, in particular, is much better understood, and this has consequences for the weight that we should give to its testimony. Although, furthermore, it is now more than a quarter of a century since the initial publication of the fragments from Ecclesiastes found among the Dead Sea Scrolls at Qumran, these have been undeservedly neglected by most recent commentators. At a more fundamental level, though, disagreements continue to simmer in text-critical circles around important aspects of the Hebrew text, such as the real antiquity of the vocalization applied to it in medieval times, the date at which, and extent to which the consonantal text became fixed, and the proper approach to variants recorded only in late manuscripts. In most respects, I think, my opinions here are not out of step with the majority of other scholars who have worked with the texts and versions, but they may well be unfamiliar to those who do not work in this area, and it seems important, in any case, to state them: there are several places in the commentary where I have adopted readings that have been ignored or rejected by previous commentators, and this section of the introduction offers a background, a context, and, I hope, part of the justification for those decisions.

A. *The Presentation and Content of the Book*

It is as difficult to pull apart the various elements of the discourse in Ecclesiastes as it is to separate the significance of its words from the way they are presented. Rather than try to do either, I have opted, therefore, to present here a single brief account of the book, covering both aspects together—although we shall have to return to some questions again later, when we look at the style and affinities. As I have suggested already, a proper discussion of the many and varied past interpretations would fill several volumes in itself, so this account is necessarily of my own views, though I have tried to indicate the main areas of disagreement between scholars.

Since a detailed study of all the key passages will be offered in the commentary, furthermore, I have not attempted to offer at this point similarly detailed arguments in support of particular interpretations.

1. *Attribution and Authorship*

The bulk of the material that makes up Ecclesiastes is introduced to us as 'the words of Qohelet' in 1.1: 'Qohelet' is a mysterious epithet, not clearly either a name or a title, and its meaning is uncertain.[5] That verse also informs us, however, that Qohelet was 'son of David, king in Jerusalem', and 1.12 then goes on to say that he was 'king over Israel in Jerusalem'. Since there were, strictly speaking, no other descendants of David who ruled 'Israel' (as opposed to Judah) from Jerusalem, readers have long taken this to mean that Qohelet must have been King Solomon. That, of course, suits well the association of Solomon with the collection or composition of aphorisms attested in 1 Kgs 4.32 and in the titles of the book of Proverbs, but if we are supposed to be hearing the voice of Solomon, then it is not clear why we are being told about 'the words of Qohelet'. If Solomon or Qohelet is also the author of the book, furthermore, then whose is the voice that talks about them in 1.1 and the epilogue of 12.9-14?

We shall look at the attributions to Solomon and Qohelet in more detail later, but the assumption I shall make in this commentary, mostly in line with other recent commentators, is that the book is a 'work of imagination' (Segal, 1), and that the identity of its actual author is unknown to us. This author, however, was responsible for creating both the speech that is attributed to Qohelet—a fictional or fictionalized character—and an epilogue which comments on that speech.[6] Modern scholars have tended to regard the link with

---

[5] Because the book itself is named after this protagonist, there is some scope for confusion. Throughout the commentary, I have followed the convention of referring to the book as 'Ecclesiastes' and the character as 'Qohelet'. The latter, incidentally, reflects the usual Jewish pronunciation: 'Qoheleth'—with an aspirated 't'—is, in principle, a more accurate transliteration of the word from biblical Hebrew, and is used by many other writers. On the meaning of 'Qohelet', see the notes on 1.1, below.

[6] See especially Fox, 'Frame-Narrative'. I have discussed the issue at much greater length in Weeks, *Ecclesiastes and Scepticism*, 13-19.

Solomon as a facet of this presentation: the character Qohelet is portrayed as taking on, at least for a short part of the book, the identity of Solomon. I doubt myself that that is the case, for reasons which will become clear, but suspect instead that, if the information in 1.1 and 1.12 is not just a curiously half-hearted, secondary attempt to identify Qohelet as Solomon, then it is intended to place the words of Qohelet on a par with the 'Solomonic' sayings in Proverbs.

Of course, many scholars until quite recently have worked on the rather different assumptions either that some historical 'Qohelet' himself wrote the book,[7] and that the superscription and epilogue are simply additions to his original words,[8] or that an editor has

---

[7] This permitted much speculation about his background, based either on assumptions about the social context of such authors or on the details offered by Qohelet within the book. Among the latter, Plumptre's essay 'The Author of Ecclesiastes' (cf. pp. 36-55 of his commentary) is particularly memorable, tracing as it does at length Qohelet's childhood and youth, his period of reckless sensuality, his friendship with a fellow Jew, and his passion for a woman who turned out to be false, before he was able to settle down with a family and confront old age. A number of recent studies have reacted strongly (and quite rightly, I think) against such readings, sometimes drawing out more general problems that surround the whole notion of autobiography or the literary first person. See, e.g., Salyer, *Vain Rhetoric*; Mills, *Reading Ecclesiastes*; more briefly, Koosed, *(Per)mutations*, 27-33.

[8] A minority position, most famously voiced by Graetz (47-49) but expounded more recently (and a little differently) by Wilson, 'Words of the Wise', holds that the epilogue was not just added to an original version of Ecclesiastes, but to the emergent canon of the Writings, or some part of it (Proverbs and Ecclesiastes in Wilson's view). De Pury, 'Qohéleth', 191-95, takes it, indeed, to identify Qohelet as the editor responsible for that collection. As noted by Graetz, the earliest exponent of this theory appears to have been Krochmal, in the eleventh chapter of his *Guide* (see especially p. 119, misprinted as '191' in the first edition). Cheyne, in *Job and Solomon*, 232-34, gives a useful account of its nineteenth-century reception (although he misunderstands Graetz's reference, and cites Krochmal's book as a journal), but goes on to show just how speculative it is. Sun, 'Ecclesiastes', treats the question in a different context, suggesting that the theme of death in the book as a whole has led to its inclusion among the Megilloth, more particularly, as a counterweight to themes in the other books, 'but the epilogist may disagree with some of Qoheleth's views and side with the rest of the Megilloth' (190). I doubt myself that such deliberations were involved in the creation of that corpus, and although the specific claim about the epilogue may have weight in a final-form reading of the books together, it hardly speaks to the original intention behind its composition.

presented to us in this book words that were originally spoken by that historical Qohelet, and memorized or recorded in another form previously. It is difficult to disprove such assumptions, but they should not be our default position. Before Roman times, authorial attribution in the modern sense was not a general feature of ancient Near Eastern literature: most texts are anonymous, and those that give names at all (which tend to be confined to particular genres) do so not through a desire to identify the author, so much as to provide a 'voice', context or authority for their content. The simplest way to put it is that they bear the name of their principal character (who might or might not actually have existed as a person), and not that of their author—rather as Daniel Defoe originally presented *Robinson Crusoe* as a memoir by Crusoe himself.[9]

Many texts, Jewish and otherwise, certainly adopt this convention, and in those where it is possible that the named individuals may actually have been involved in the composition, that is probably not the reason why they have been named. None of this, it should be emphasized, is because the real authors were attempting to mislead their readers. Ancient attitudes to 'pseudonymity' are complicated, and the term itself is somewhat misleading, but although the boundaries between author and character were sometimes blurred,[10]

---

[9] Provan puts a common assumption into words by insisting (29-30) that 'There is no good reason to doubt that [Qohelet] existed and worked just as the author who quotes his words asserts to us (12:9–10); it would be curious to receive the speaker's words from this author and yet reject his rather clear testimony about their originator'. Such third-person presentations of fictional or fictionalized protagonists are not themselves uncommon in ancient literature, however, with *Ahiqar* (see below) offering a lengthy example, and one might as well say that the long third-person subtitle of Defoe's novel, which summarizes the story, is itself evidence for the historicity of Crusoe. When such views are expressed by explicitly religious commentators, it is tempting to suggest that they arise from a certain discomfort with the idea that a text could be both fictional and canonical. It would be fair to note also, however, that scholars have often been slow to recognize fiction elsewhere among ancient texts: the basic historicity of Ahiqar as a person has often been defended, for instance, however historically improbable the portrayals of his life might seem, and the fictional Egyptian *Tale of Sinuhe* (which we shall also encounter later) was commonly read as a true story by earlier commentators. It might be better to say that orientalizing scholarship has tended to struggle with the idea that such relatively sophisticated, 'realistic' fiction, arguably pioneered in the modern West by Defoe, was pre-empted by other cultures.

[10] See Weeks, 'Predictive and Prophetic', 35. The terminology itself creates problems. Baldwin, 'Is There Pseudonymity?', 8, denies its applicability here,

it is likely that ancient audiences were in general as aware of the conventions that governed attribution as modern readers are of those that govern, say, a first-person novel, with its own adoption of another voice by the author—and they are unlikely to have shared Koosed's reaction, in her *(Per)mutations*, that 'Qohelet, whoever he is, is lying to me' (24). In the case of Ecclesiastes, matters are further complicated, however, because the attribution to 'Qohelet' is not straightforwardly an attribution to a named individual, and Koosed rightly goes on to say that 'the author is using a persona who is writing under a pseudonym whose meaning we do not understand', which 'obfuscates rather than illuminates identity'. That obfuscation may have been present from the outset, but if the author was playing with the conventions in some way that his audience *did* understand, it may no longer be possible for us to share that understanding.

Michael Fox, who has done more than anyone else to shift perceptions away from a simple identification of Qohelet as the author, speaks also of the material not attributed to Qohelet in the book (principally the epilogue) as a 'frame' for the speech, and correspondingly of a 'frame narrator', who is in some sense no less a 'character' than is Qohelet.[11] What we hear in the book, therefore, is

saying that 'Qoheleth is no more pretending to be Solomon than Shakespeare is pretending to be Hamlet, but he is inviting his readers to see life through the eyes of that superbly endowed king'—which I would take to be the very essence of pseudonymity in ancient literature. Given the scope for confusion, however, it is perhaps best avoided, and Meek, 'I was King', 75-77, points out that we are not, of course, actually offered the name Solomon, strictly making the term inaccurate as well (except, perhaps, when applied to 'Qohelet').

[11] Fox, 'Frame-Narrative', 91-92. So dominant in the twentieth century was the assumption that the epilogue is secondary, that it is easy to forget that by taking it as integral, Fox is reinstating a view that had been maintained previously by commentators as notable as Herzfeld, Hitzig (who speaks of the real author talking about his fictitious creation in 12.9-11) and Delitzsch (who is scathing about those scholars who confuse the book's protagonist with its author). Where Fox is more innovative, is in his insistence that not even the epilogue simply presents the voice of the author. In general, his view is supported by a certain consistency between monologue and epilogue. Fox does not argue the point himself, and it is difficult to make strong claims on the basis of just a few verses, but the language of the monologue is distinctive and probably idiomatic (as we shall see later), and there is no reason to suppose that the epilogue is different in this respect—note, for instance, the use of š- in 12.9 (see Delitzsch, 215, who examines the matter in

never strictly the voice of the author, as such, but separate voices or identities adopted by the author. This is important for understanding the role and nature of the epilogue, which reacts to Qohelet and his words, but it also underscores the point that Qohelet himself need not be treated merely as a cypher for the author. In a work like Job, with multiple characters offering different opinions, it is easy to be aware that the author may share the views of no single character, but we should also be conscious that the use of Qohelet's voice permits the author of Ecclesiastes to express provocative opinions that may likewise not have been his own. Correspondingly, he might not have expected his audience to accept all of those opinions, or to acquiesce in Qohelet's idiosyncratic take on the world, while some of the ways in which his protagonist is presented may have been designed to shape perceptions of Qohelet alongside his actual words. As with much ancient literature, it can be helpful to treat what we are reading not as an essay in which an author speaks to us directly, but as something closer to a dramatic performance, in which we are supposed to react to the claims and viewpoints of a character who speaks before us.

2. *The Character of the Monologue*

The author probably does intend us, though, to understand the totality of Qohelet's words as a single speech: they are structured with matching declarations in 1.2 and 12.8 which seem designed to bring them back to where they started, and the constant, thematic statements about the 'vanity' of particular phenomena themselves tie the intervening materials to those declarations. It is not unreasonable, therefore, to speak of 1.2–12.8 as a 'monologue', and there are no explicit counter-indications that different parts were supposed to have been uttered at different times—although, as will

detail). This suggests, of course, that the author has made no attempt to distinguish between the two voices, at least in terms of the sort of Hebrew that they use, but it is also, of course, an argument against the epilogue as a whole being the work of some later redactor, who would have had no obvious reason to avoid using more conventional literary Hebrew. Similarly, we may note the uses of *ʾlhym* in 12.13-14, which accord with Qohelet's usage in the monologue; Sheppard, 'The Epilogue', 184, notes that Proverbs, in contrast, always uses the divine name when it talks about fearing God.

become clear, this monologue recounts Qohelet's observations and experience over a period of time, and might loosely be described as a sort of fictive intellectual memoir. At many points, however, the book feels much more like an anthology or collection, held together by aspects of its language and expression, but thematically and stylistically diverse.

This diversity is apparent even in the first three chapters, which are generally regarded as the most coherent, because although it is possible to see a progression of ideas through Qohelet's prologue about natural phenomena (1.4-11), his first-person account of his efforts to find something meaningful for humans in life (1.12–2.11), his reflections on those efforts (2.12-26), and his subsequent statements about God and the world (3.1-15), the way he talks about them fits no simple pattern. After that point, the work will be punctuated by other set-piece compositions—notably the further memoir in 7.23–8.1 and the description of a death in 12.3-5, which follows almost seamlessly from the commendations of living life properly in 11.7–12.2. There will also be some lengthy, if looser, discussions which draw together various materials and ideas around a theme—wealth and the enjoyment of property in 5.7–6.9, for instance, or the issues around human ignorance and misperception that dominate 8.5b through to 9.3 (or even, arguably, 9.12). Large parts of the book are filled, however, either by much shorter, even looser series of sayings and admonitions, or by the very brief, seemingly miscellaneous materials that make up much of chs. 7 and 10. There is, as we shall see, a certain rhyme and reason behind it, but this irregularity has frustrated attempts to find a 'structure' for the monologue that is anything more than a rather vague description of it,[12] and

---

[12] As may be clear from my own presentation here, I think we can go no further than loosely to group consecutive passages as 'sections' when they share common themes or formal features—which is the approach of, e.g., Schoors, 'La Structure littéraire de Qohéleth' (an article that includes a helpful survey of previous attempts). Other commentators have sometimes tried to find much broader sections (there is another helpful review of some key proposals in Lohfink, 'Strukturen', 39-52, and an excellent overview of the scholarship in d'Alario, *Qohelet*, 17-58). Seow (46-47), for instance, breaks the book into two major sections, with the division after 6.9, and each of these into two further sections, with sub-divisions after 4.16 and 8.17. In doing so, he is adapting the proposals of Backhaus, *Den Zeit*, who places the first sub-division instead after 3.22. When, however, these sub-divisions bear labels like 'everything is elusive' (6.10–8.17), or the first and

has fuelled other attempts to revise and re-order the book, on an assumption that such apparent chaos could result only from disintegration or thoughtless redaction of the text.[13] More generally, it

third are supposed to be 'reflection' while the second and fourth are 'ethics', it becomes reasonable to ask whether there is any genuine relationship between the descriptions and much of the content. If, say, 7.8-10 seem neither reflective nor concerned with elusiveness, placing them in such a section seems at best misleading; at worst, it can force a reading of them that is entirely inappropriate. Equally, if the structural markers are supposed to be clear, then it is a problem that searches for the same sort of markers turn up different results: Niccacci, 'Qohelet', also identifies two major sections, which he sees as parallel to each other, but for him, the break is after 7.14, a long way from Seow's 6.9, and for Castellino, 'Qohelet', the break falls at 4.17. Although scholars often look for them, there is no particular reason, in fact, to suppose that ancient writers (any more than modern ones) habitually built their compositions around balanced structures. The very different attempt of Wright, 'Riddle of the Sphinx', to identify structure through the book's repetition of phrases and motifs may point to a way in which the writer has attempted to impose some order in the later, more miscellaneous parts of the book, although his own results are optimistic in their precision (as are those of Mulder, 'Division', which offers a revision of Wright's hypothesis). That article should be distinguished, however, from his later 'Riddle of the Sphinx Revisited', and 'Additional Numerical Patterns', which offer a far less plausible account based on word and verse counts (later imitated in Stephanus, 'Qohelet', which consequently identifies 4.1-16 and 8.17–9.15, a little unexpectedly, as the book's central texts). This technique—which seems to reflect what Asurmendi, *Du non-sens*, 16, calls 'le penchant ludique de l'exégèse pour le Meccano', loosely, the way exegetes love to play with texts as though with Meccano—is applied on a smaller scale in Wright's 'For Everything There Is a Season'. For a different but not wholly dissimilar attempt to demonstrate structural coherence, at least in the first two chapters, see especially Bons, 'Zur Gliederung'.

[13] Paul Haupt, not an admirer of the many interpolators he believed to have ruined the book, suggested that, 'If the book in its present shape should have been written by one author, he must have been a duplex personality of the HYDE-JEKYLL type. But the book we have is not intact. It reminds me of the remains of a daring explorer who has met with some terrible accident, leaving his shattered form exposed to the encroachments of all sorts of foul vermin.' See 'The Book of Ecclesiastes', 254. Bickell's slightly earlier commentary is arranged on the premise (3-4) that, although there had been some hostile interpolation, the main problem with the order was that the original pages of Ecclesiastes had become disordered—which is improbable, since the book is unlikely to have been transmitted in a codex (with pages, as opposed to a scroll) earlier than the time at which it was translated into Greek, and the Septuagint Greek version has the same order as the standard Hebrew text. Cheyne, *Job and Solomon*, 204, advances the not dissimilar idea that 'from chap. iii onwards we have before us the imperfectly

has encouraged rather atomistic readings of Ecclesiastes, as a loose assemblage of different sayings or poems (so, e.g., Galling), perhaps even (as we shall see) reflecting different viewpoints.

The dissatisfaction that many readers have found in this aspect of the book, however, may be as much as anything a product of modern tastes and assumptions—as Good (*Irony*, 171) puts it, 'Perhaps we are too certain we know what a "book" is'.[14] While it is true that Ecclesiastes closely resembles no other ancient composition in every respect, it is not difficult to find parallels to these particular characteristics—whether in the sudden shifts of style and topic that mark much of the Hebrew prophetic literature, or in the often baffling arrangement of aphorisms and admonitions in ancient instructions and sayings-collections.[15] Among the latter, the famous *Sayings of Ahiqar* frames a very mixed group of sayings within a story of betrayal and high politics (presented, like Qohelet's speech, as a first-person memoir in the oldest version that we have), and, rather differently, the Jewish book of Tobit moves disconcertingly from first-person memoir to third-person narrative,[16] incorporating a number of set-piece prayers and sequences of admonitions, which to our eye appear simply intrusive. Rather than try to explain all such examples in terms of diverse sources or problems in transmission, it seems easier to accept that ancient audiences tolerated, and probably even enjoyed, such variations and shifts of tone. Without excluding the possibility that some may indeed have arisen in the course of transmission, we should certainly not assume that their

---

worked-up meditations of an otherwise unknown writer, found after his death in proximity to a highly finished fragment which apparently professed to be the work of king Solomon'.

[14] Similarly Canaday, 'Qoheleth', 33, 'In many respects the book defies the Western mind that looks for clear breaks in thought around which it may be outlined'. See also, e.g., Salyer, *Vain Rhetoric*, 147-48.

[15] Lange, 'Pre-Maccabean Literature', 300-304, goes so far as to suggest that the 'seemingly random combination of different sapiential subgenres' (303) is actually a mark of the instruction genre, to which Ecclesiastes must accordingly belong, even if it lacks other key features.

[16] Events are seen wholly from Tobit's viewpoint up to the point when he prays in ch. 3, and the narrative switches to third-person as soon as it extends its scope to events in distant Media of which he was unaware. This illustrates very well the extent to which person and perspective can be connected in ancient literature—but it is as jarring to us as the sudden break from Janet Leigh's point of view in Hitchcock's *Psycho*, when the character she plays is killed.

presence in Ecclesiastes marks the book as composite or its text as corrupt.

Again, indeed, it may be more helpful to think of the material as dramatic or performative. Qohelet is not a comedian,[17] but his monologue resembles many modern stand-up routines, moving as they do through different topics with a mixture of anecdotes, one-liners, and maybe even poems.[18] This is a performance rather like those, designed so that each part of it can be relished in its own right, and is not a logical disquisition—a fact that is never clearer than at those points where, as we shall see later, economy or clarity of sense seem to have been sacrificed in favour of sound and style. As Alter (*Wisdom Books*, 342) puts it, moreover, 'the relative looseness of form admirably suits the mobility of Qohelet's thought'. We know very little about the way in which ancient compositions were 'used' by their readership, but there are grounds to suppose that many would actually have been performed before an audience (see, e.g., Miller, 'Orality and Performance'), and it is certainly not difficult to imagine that this was the case with Ecclesiastes—Christianson (*Time to Tell*, 257) visualizes the monologue as a 'one-man play' (cf. Salyer, *Vain Rhetoric*, 186-87).

---

[17] The 'humorous' reading of the book in Des Rochettes, 'L'Humour noir', consists principally of imagining different expressions on Qohelet's face, rather than identifying places where the text actually appears to be funny, but many readers have found a certain wryness, and Fisch, 'Qohelet', 173, speaks of 'the playfulness, the sense of being amused at one's own expense that are the mark of the ironic consciousness'. Jarick, in 'Ecclesiastes among the Comedians', seeks more precisely to find points of contact between the book and Athenian comedy, and finds many. Whatever we make of those individually, they show, at least, that the Athenian writers were capable of presenting extremely cynical and pessimistic claims in a context where the audience was expecting to laugh, and that we cannot easily judge the tone of a piece simply by the sentiments that we find in it. I am inclined myself (like Greenstein, 'Sages', and Levine, 'Qohelet's Fool', 'Humor') to think that there probably is humour in the book, and at least a humorous use at times of the grotesque and unexpected, but suspect that Qohelet's own part is often as the straight man, who might make us laugh, but does not laugh with us.

[18] Shortly after I had first written this, I received a proposal for a paper by Knut Heim ('Hyper-Ambiguity in Ecclesiastes'), subsequently delivered at the 2018 SBL conference, in which he claims a little differently, although along the same lines, that, 'It is as if Qoheleth speaks in the mode of modern stand-up comedians, where social critique is expressed regularly through indirection, innuendo, and humor, where the real meaning of what is being said only emerges from the speaker's intonation (pitch, pause, speed, tone, stress, emphasis, etc.)'.

3. *Qohelet's Ideas*

It is hard simply to summarize Qohelet's ideas without doing some injustice to them: they are strongly interconnected, and the monologue develops various of them in different directions. It is best to sketch this development as a whole before trying to address some key points individually.

(a) *Outline*

Qohelet begins with a declaration of his themes: 'Vapour of vapours! ... Vapour of vapours! It is all vapour! What profit is there for a human in any of his business, at which he works beneath the sun?' (1.1-3). We shall look shortly at the meaning of *hebel*, the term that I have translated 'vapour' here: suffice it to say that the vapour which concerns him is immediately linked to human activity in these verses. Qohelet, however, pursues neither his statement nor his question straight away. Instead, he presents two very different blocks of evidence that will form the basis for his claims. The first, in 1.4-11, begins by contrasting the transience of humans with the permanence of the world, and goes on to describe a series of phenomena that each in their own way reaches a conclusion, but does so repeatedly: a sun that rises and sets, but then rises again to do the same, a wind that blows, then blows again, and rivers that run into the sea without ever filling it, so continue to run. Even human actions can be similar: I take the proper sense of 1.8 to be that we do not use words up when we speak, or fill our eyes and ears by seeing and hearing (although other commentators commonly see an exclamation of wonder here). Qohelet claims, accordingly, that all this movement and activity belie a fundamentally static situation, in which there is no change and nothing is new: anything that seems novel does so only because everything is ultimately forgotten.

In 1.12, there is a significant change of style and tone. Qohelet's second tranche of evidence will be derived from his own experience. He begins by summarizing his brief, initial enquiries into the role of humans within the world, into the nature of the wisdom that he uses to address that issue, and into pleasure. These lead him to find human achievements merely vapour, wisdom a source of pain, and pleasure pointless. In what I take to be a second phase, therefore, he sets out to undertake a much longer experiment in 2.3-10, which involves constructing a whole business and livelihood for himself, and enables him also to enjoy a luxurious, wealthy lifestyle. When he comes to assess the results of this in 2.11, however, he finds that it too is vapour, which has failed to grant him the sort of profit that he really wants.

It is from the results of this experiment that Qohelet's insights and ideas begin to flow. In the first place, he understands that his wisdom has not really done him any good. It has made him no profit, and since he will die just like a fool, his earlier accumulation of wisdom was just another vapour: in a reference back to 1.11, he suggests that people forget about such equality at death because they forget about everything. With regard to this, it is important for us to be aware that Qohelet (like at least most of his contemporaries) has no belief in an afterlife where the dead might be rewarded or punished, or might even be fully conscious (cf. 9.10), so if there is any profit to be gained at all by humans, it must be while they are alive.

The reason why Qohelet feels that he has made no profit, despite becoming wealthy, is not stated explicitly: 2.11 says merely that when he turns to examine his achievements, he finds them to be vapour, and declares that there is 'no profit under the sun'. His understanding becomes clearer in 2.12b, however, and then in 2.18-23, when, after talking about the implications for the usefulness of wisdom, he goes on to spell out the problem that his business will outlast him and pass to somebody else (so is not really *his*). The more immediate concern that pre-occupies him in these verses, though, is that the business may pass to somebody who may have no wisdom, and who may have done nothing to earn it. Correspondingly, he comes to understand in 2.24 that the qualities and situations of individual humans are not connected directly to their own character, but are a matter of divine dispensation—and in 2.26 he probably goes on to reject the idea that they are straightforwardly a result of reward and punishment.

There is another significant change of style at the beginning of ch. 3, but the ideas here mark a continuation. The famous sequence of paired actions in 3.2-8 has attracted various interpretations. I share the view that it makes the point (drawn out in 3.10-11) that anything humans do must be good in its time, because everything that humans do is ordained by God. By implication, humans make no real decisions, and no action can be inherently bad. All that humans can do for themselves is to take pleasure and seek to do good (3.12). In 3.9-15, Qohelet again refers back to 1.4-11, but he now links the permanence of the world and the ignorance of humans to divine action: God maintains that permanence and conceals his achievements from humans, so that he provokes their fear, and God is responsible for every genuine initiative.

By 3.15, therefore, Qohelet has established a particular understanding of human life within the world, and presented his reasons for that understanding: his investigations have led him to understand that humans misapprehend the nature of a world about which they can know little, and so believe that they can achieve more for themselves than is actually possible. Everything they do is in fact done on behalf of God, and nothing that they achieve is really achieved by or for themselves. There are some chinks left open in this. Most notably, at 2.10 Qohelet observes that he found pleasure in the creation of his business, and that this was in some sense his 'share'—an idea that is picked up again in 3.12-13, where such pleasure is described as a gift or payment from God, and that is going to become a very prominent concern as the monologue goes on. Such pleasure is not, in Qohelet's terms, a 'profit' that can balance out the expenditure of effort involved in living, but it is at least some compensation for all the work and hardship. In 3.12-13 this is also set alongside an idea of 'doing good in one's life', which is not explained, but which perhaps indicates an idea that, even if humans cannot control their actions and outcomes, they have some responsibility for their motives.

After 3.15, Qohelet continues to draw further conclusions and to make new observations, but in a less clearly structured way. The first of these are very important. In 3.16-17, he affirms, despite the deterministic worldview that he has just espoused, and apparently despite the evidence of his own eyes, that God will judge humans. In the obscure 3.18-22, he also insists, probably in connection with this judgment, that humans are different from animals, even though the visible evidence makes the death, and so the nature, of both seem identical. These are significant counterweights to what he has said previously, insofar as they represent dogmatic beliefs that Qohelet holds despite the evidence, not apparent deductions from his investigations. They also, though, develop further his theme that the appearance of the world is misleading, and that what humans actually see can lead them to misunderstand their situation. In 3.22, commending pleasure in one's achievements again, he adds the observation, which will be repeated often, that nobody can see what will happen after them, and this is another aspect of the problem: we do not understand the world, and so our place in it, but we also have no way to adapt our behaviour to a hidden future, perhaps by trying to leave some mark behind us.

Much of what follows defies summary, and Qohelet explores a number of different areas. Sometimes he explicitly elaborates upon or qualifies the core ideas that he has set out in the first three chapters, and he retains a particular interest in the issues of what is good for humans, of wisdom, and of pleasure, which were set out programmatically in 1.12–2.2. Often, though, he merely brings his own, very distinct perspective to bear on topics that are tangential to these issues—among the declarations that follow swiftly after ch. 3, we find, for instance, the value of other people assessed by 4.9-12 purely in terms of material advantage (warmth, rather than any other reason, is notably offered as the motivation to share a bed with someone), while 4.17–5.6 depict communications with God as an avoidable risk, and sacrifice as something that only fools have to do.

Very broadly speaking, chs. 4 and 5 cover various aspects of human life—our relationships with other humans, with God, and with wealth. From 5.12, a series of examples, or parables, take up this last theme, and provide an opportunity for Qohelet to emphasize from various angles his understanding that wealth means nothing without the ability, granted by God, to take satisfaction from what one has; ch. 6 concludes with affirmations that humans have no power to challenge their situation or to understand their own lives. In the more miscellaneous 7.1–8.9, the principal theme is wisdom, which we shall look at in more detail below, and the monologue includes a further passage of memoir, but 7.13-18 do pick up earlier interests again, and include the provocative suggestion that we should not be more righteous or wise than needs be, and that it is simply fear of God that will get us through, while 8.2-5a depict the dangers of royal anger—perhaps to make a similar point about fear. The fear of God recurs again in 8.10-17, where Qohelet reiterates and builds upon his points that what we see of the world may mislead us, that there is nothing good for us except to find pleasure in what we do, and that God deliberately hides his achievements—which even the wise will be unable to discover.

The beginning of ch. 9 seems to mark a sort of break, in which Qohelet mulls over his observations in order to draw conclusions about the divine control of both righteous and wicked, and the human inability to understand God's attitude to them when everyone seems to meet the same fate—a problem that leads them to behave badly and to cling to life. In 9.7-10, this culminates in Qohelet's strongest and most famous statement of his belief that we should find pleasure in what we do, backed by a claim that our work has already been accepted by God. In 9.11 Qohelet then introduces a new idea of unpredictability, linked to his beliefs about human ignorance, but also probably drawing on the problem of undifferentiated outcomes: time and chance can affect everybody, while nobody knows when their time will come—in a chilling image, humans are like trapped birds or netted fish, awaiting the return of the hunter.

This idea may be picked up in the difficult 10.5-10, but those verses are followed by what seems to be a series of miscellaneous sayings up to the beginning of ch. 11, where Qohelet apparently warns against over-cautiousness in the face of ignorance: if we try to predict what is happening, we will never accomplish anything. From 11.7, this becomes a further commendation to enjoy life and find pleasure, motivated by an awareness of coming death, and in 12.3-5 Qohelet describes a death in a household (often interpreted as an allegory of old age). Even as the corpse goes to its grave, however, this is against the background of a fertile natural world that will go on, taking us back to 1.4, and after a short sequence of images that highlight the violence and wastefulness of death, Qohelet finally repeats his declaration that 'everything is vapour'.

It should be very apparent from all of this that we are not dealing with a carefully structured argument in the monologue, and even in the first three chapters there is sometimes more rhetoric than logic behind Qohelet's claims. It should also be evident, however, that Qohelet's ideas are cumulative: most of the assertions that he makes in later chapters depend on points that he has already made, and there is a deliberate effort early in the book to lay a groundwork, to which Qohelet himself not infrequently appeals. If we elaborate a little less than he does, the basic assumptions can be stated straightforwardly: activity within the world all contributes toward endless processes that are under the control of God, and human actions are no exception. Although they expend effort in living, therefore, nothing that humans achieve is achieved simply for themselves. This means both that they receive no permanent, material compensation for their efforts—making it impossible to 'profit' from their work—and that their situation in life is a result of divine intentions rather than of their own worthiness. Humans have no insight into the larger processes within which their lives are lived, and this leads to a series of problems: they do not know what will happen or understand what is happening, which can lead them to draw false conclusions and to pursue pointless ambitions. In the face of all this, the best they can do to offset the cost of their efforts is to try to find pleasure in them, while the only way that they can deal with the uncertainties is to treat God with the respect that he wants, and in the expectation that he will ultimately act with justice.

In fact, Qohelet devotes relatively little space to his practical suggestions for coping with the situation in which humans find themselves, and much of his emphasis is instead on his own observations and, as we shall see, on the problems that surround human perception. If he actually does believe all this, however, then some of his early statements and actions seem puzzling. Why would he seek to find a good in human efforts, for example (2.3), when his understandings of the world and of profit would seem to preclude such a possibility almost by definition? And why would he have accumulated wisdom (1.16) when the unknowability of the world so limits its usefulness? Qohelet, indeed, asks himself that question in 2.15, shortly after declaring the impossibility of profit in 2.11, and it seems clear that we must reckon with a development in his ways of looking at the world. Another, more positive aspect of this is reflected in the emphasis that he comes to place on pleasure, which he had dismissed as useless in 2.1. As I have suggested above, therefore, we have to see a narrative dimension to Qohelet's account from 1.12 onwards, and I doubt that his intellectual development is restricted to the first two chapters: a further short memoir in ch. 7 seems to suggest, as we shall see, that he has continued to move on.[19] Since his account of the world in 1.4-11

---

[19] As Mills says in *Reading Ecclesiastes*, 20, 'Qohelet, the older sage, waits at the end of the story for his younger self to develop and achieve that breadth of experience which will produce the final moral vision of the narration'. Segal

seems to embody many of his fully fledged beliefs, however, it is also likely that we are supposed to regard those verses as a sort of prelude. To make his case, Qohelet presents a particular perspective on the world, then an account of his experiences, but for this second approach to addressing the points in 1.2-3, he steps backward to a time when he first became king, according to 1.12, and when he did not yet have that perspective, then shows us how he came to gain it.

(b) *The* hebel *Statements*
I have already mentioned the way that a certain unity is imposed on the monologue by, to use the traditional translation for a moment, statements about the 'vanity' of various phenomena, which tie into the programmatic declarations at 1.2 and 12.8, that 'everything is vanity'. In the form 'This (also) is vanity', such statements occur nineteen times, in 1.14; 2.1, 11 (twice), 15, 17, 19, 21, 23, 26; 4.4, 8, 16; 5.9; 6.2, 9; 7.6; 8.10, 14. Among these, 4.7-8 and 8.14 introduce a situation as 'a vanity', and then subsequently describe it again, using the more formulaic comment. Rarely, Qohelet also makes pronouncements using the 'this (also) is...wording, but without using 'vanity' at all (cf. 1.17; 5.15). Clearly, these statements are supposed to draw out and embody some or all of Qohelet's key ideas, and the Hebrew word *hebel*, which lies behind the traditional translation, also appears outside them. So 3.19 uses 'for everything is *hebel*' as support for an assertion, rather than as a description, while in 11.8 Qohelet claims that 'everything which comes is *hebel*', and in 11.10 calls youth *hebel*. In the difficult 5.7, the plural of this noun is used in conjunction with dreams and words, and 6.11 also identifies *hebel* as a product of speech. In 6.12, 7.15 and 9.9, we find *hebel* used attributively to characterize lives, or the days of one's life, and in 6.4 it is associated with the circumstances into which a premature child is born. Not surprisingly, translators have struggled to find any English word that fits all of these contexts, but, more importantly, commentators have also failed to reach any consensus over the principal connotation of

devotes a whole discussion (107-12) to change within the book, observing (107) that, 'Set against Kohelet's observations of an un-understandable, unchangeable world is the man himself, who ever so subtly grows and develops. It is he who changes; he is not at the end of the book who he was at the beginning.'

hebel in the book (Meek, 'Readings', offers a helpful overview of the various opinions).

The basic sense of the word is unproblematic, and the difficulty lies in the fact that Qohelet uses it metaphorically: *hebel* is connected in some way with air, or the movement of air (which is why I translated it earlier as 'vapour'), and this literal sense probably underpins both Isa 57.13, where wind and *hebel* will together snatch something away, and the second part of Ps 62.10 (ET 62.9), where humans are even lighter on the scales than *hebel*. It is difficult to be more precise than that, although we may reasonably presume that *hebel* must have been differentiated from simple nothingness, or from air itself (if that was a concept familiar to the original audience) by some quality of movement, temperature or effect. Post-biblical usage, in fact, does suggest that *hebel* is typically exhaled or exuded in some way: the word, or its Aramaic cognate, is used of breath, vapour, the hot air from cooking, and the lethal miasma of a pit or a marsh. The notions of hot air, breath or exhalation are not excluded by the passages from Isaiah and Psalm 62, while there may even be a play between literal and figurative meanings in Job 35.16, where it is *hebel*, 'hot air', that is said by Elihu to open Job's mouth, when 'without knowledge he multiplies words'. There is no good reason to suppose, therefore, that the underlying idea in biblical usage was very different from that in post-biblical Hebrew, and strictly speaking, then, Qohelet is declaring everything to be 'hot air', 'vapour', or something similar.

Of course, it may be as misleading to leave metaphors untranslated as to substitute an interpretation, and if there were any evidence *hebel* had acquired a fixed sense or connotation other than 'vapour' in biblical Hebrew, then by leaving it untranslated we would risk opening the term up to a wider range of interpretations than the author might originally have intended.[20] It does not seem

---

[20] Although he speaks of it as being used metaphorically, Fredericks, in *Coping*, 15, sees attempts to understand *hebel* in terms of vapour as 'etymological', and Good, *Irony*, 177, speaks of vapour as the 'etymological basis' of the noun. Such descriptions are misleading: even were we to suppose that the metaphor had come to convey a fixed sense, we would not normally understand *hebel* in that sense to be a new word, etymologically derived from *hebel* as vapour. This understanding apparently frees Good to pursue his rendering of *hebel* in terms of 'irony', an understanding derived entirely from contextual considerations, which Polk, 'The

likely, however, that *hebel* ever settled down to convey any single meaning, and so, for example, Ps 144.4 is able to use *hebel* as a figure for transience and insignificance, while Isa 30.7 uses it of 'useless' or 'insubstantial' Egyptian aid, and Prov 31.30 contrasts beauty in a woman with piety, calling it *hebel* in order to evoke both insignificance and transience together. Although *hebel* may have come to have certain particular connotations or extended meanings, the biblical evidence suggests that, on the whole, it remained very much a live metaphor, through which writers could use the figure of breath or vapour to convey, separately or simultaneously, a variety of ideas.[21]

Naturally, these associations largely flow from the nature and characteristics of 'vapour' itself, which is ephemeral, and which can have a presence or existence while possessing no actual substance or ability to affect anything—it has been suggested that a comparable figure in English might be 'a bubble' (Burkitt, 'Is Ecclesiastes a Translation?', 28; cf. Zimmerli, *Die Weisheit*, 16). In a few places, however, the imagery seems to depend not on the nature of vapour itself, but on the nature of interactions with vapour, which can be felt but not grasped, or can be blown at people, so that it is a source of confusion or frustration (see, e.g., Ps 39.7 [ET 39.6], where the word cannot imply the same as in the preceding verse, or Job 27.12). A verb derived from the noun has corresponding implications of confusion or deception: it is used of being misguided (Ps 62.11 [ET 62.10]) or of misleading others (Jer 23.16), and the noun perhaps takes on this connotation where it is used with the verb (2 Kgs 17.15; cf. Jer 2.5; Job 27.12).

Given the wide range of possible meanings that can be attached to such a metaphor, it seems likely that the original audience would have to have been guided to Qohelet's intended sense by their understanding of the contexts in which he uses it. An important clue is also offered, however, by the way he links *hebel* to other expressions from an early point, and most notably to the alliterative descriptions *rĕʿût rûaḥ* and *raʿyôn rûaḥ*, which are found a number

---

Wisdom of Irony', 8, rightly criticizes as based on an idea that 'words are simply empty ciphers, completely dependent upon context to fill them with sense' (although he himself sees irony as central to Qohelet's message).

[21] See especially Miller, 'Qohelet's Symbolic Use of הבל', and his *Symbol and Rhetoric*.

of times (see 1.14; 2.11, 17, 26; 4.4, 6; 6.9; and 1.17; 4.16).²² The sense of these is not itself entirely undisputed, but the second word in each, the common term *rûaḥ*, is itself used of breath or wind, and the link with *hebel* suggests that a similar metaphor of air is being used. Neither *rĕʿût* nor *raʿyôn* appears as a Hebrew word elsewhere in biblical literature, but both do appear there as Aramaic words: *rĕʿût* with reference to royal and divine wishes or decisions in Ezra (5.17; 7.18), and *raʿyôn* referring to thoughts or worries in Daniel (2.29, 30; 4.16 [ET 4.19]; 5.6, 10; 7.28). Since there are many other connections with Aramaic in Ecclesiastes, it is hard to ignore these established uses, and they point to *rĕʿût rûaḥ* meaning something like 'wishing for wind', and *raʿyôn rûaḥ* either the same, or possibly 'worrying about wind'—although, since *rûaḥ* can also mean 'spirit', they could alternatively connote 'wishing' and 'worrying' by one's spirit, and there may even be a play on both senses.²³

The more precise implications of these expressions may be apparent from other usage: 5.15 uses a similar figure of 'toiling for *rûaḥ*' either to describe the zero net gain of a human at death, or with ironic reference to their (ultimately pointless) reasons for working. This understanding is compatible with the one occasion when *raʿyôn* appears in Ecclesiastes without *rûaḥ*: in 2.22 the *raʿyôn* of a human heart is set beside physical toil, in a context which suggests that it means mental labour, ambition, or anxiety. This verse might be compared with 4.6, which does not use *rĕʿût rûaḥ* as a simple comment on a situation, in the normal way, but again links it with physical toil, counting both as less desirable than a little tranquillity. Such references suggest that we are dealing with a way of talking about human motivation and pre-occupation, and both expressions apparently connote some sort of pointless anxiety,

---

²² It is possible that whereas the traditional Hebrew text has two expressions, the other ancient versions were based on texts which had only *rĕʿût rûaḥ*: see the note at 1.14.

²³ Hosea 12.2 uses the expression רעה רוח in parallel with רדף קדים, 'chases the East wind', and the Hebrew verb רעה there probably means 'herds, shepherds': the meaning of the imagery is not entirely clear, but it is associated with the Northern Kingdom's betrayal of God and cultivation of relationships with Assyria and Egypt, so perhaps conveys an idea of effort that will ultimately prove futile. Several of the ancient translations connect Qohelet's usage with רעה, probably because of this passage, but if they are right to do so, the sense is probably similar to that derived from the Aramaic.

desire ('wishful thinking'), or even labour. This suits the context of Qohelet's initial statements about *hebel*, which throughout 1.2–2.11 is associated with human efforts, and it seems highly likely that the use in conjunction with these other expressions would have led the audience to think of the broader *hebel* metaphor, at least initially, in terms of futility and pointless aspiration, rather than of, say, transience or any of its other established implications.

Without going through all the instances in detail here, it becomes clear as the book progresses that when Qohelet singles out particular situations as *hebel*, he is not referring to precisely the same sort of issue in every case. What the various situations do seem to have in common, however, is that they each involve a problem of human perception or expectation: an activity or a phenomenon is *hebel* when humans are driven to think or act in some way by a false or faulty apprehension of what they are doing. Typically, it is the misguided action or effort itself which attracts the description, but Qohelet also uses *hebel* to describe situations which can or do cause such misguidedness, because humans misinterpret what they see in them—the prosperity of a man who will not enjoy it, for instance (6.2), or the continuing good health of the wicked, which conceals the fact of divine judgment (8.10-14). To put that in the terms of the metaphor itself, what Qohelet sees in each case is something like an attempt to return the touch of a breath of wind on our skin, and the broader expectation of humans that they can grasp what they can sense.[24] When he talks in 2.15, for instance, about his own past

---

[24] It is tempting to compare a well-known Greek analogy. Monimus of Syracuse, who was active in the fourth century BCE, is reputed to have claimed that τῦφος τὰ πάντα, perhaps literally 'Everything is smoke'—a claim that is naturally reminiscent of Qohelet's belief that 'Everything is *hebel*'. Where this claim is preserved much later in Sextus Empiricus, Πρὸς λογικούς (*Against the Logicians*), it is glossed as οἴησις τῶν οὐκ ὄντων ὡς ὄντων, loosely 'trying to treat things that don't exist as though they did exist'. The term τῦφος, to be sure, may already have lost much of its metaphorical quality, if it ever possessed such: the cognate verb is used of smoking, but the noun seems to have drawn its sense of 'delusion' or 'self-satisfaction' from its use to describe fevers and delirium. I doubt, furthermore, that Monimus was directly an influence on Ecclesiastes, as is sometimes suggested (e.g. by Amir, 'Doch ein griechischer Einfluss?'), let alone that Qohelet's claims are intended specifically to echo Monimus (as Köhlmoos claims at 1.2): the Greek debate about reality and knowability is conducted at a much greater level of abstraction and generalization than is Qohelet's discourse. All the same, Monimus makes a point that is very similar to Qohelet's, about the

efforts to be wise, which are now revealed to have gained him no real advantage over the fool, the illusion lies in the false or thoughtless expectations that had motivated him, while in 5.9 it lies in the pursuit by others of a fulfilment that they will never find.

This mismatch between expectation and reality may induce a sense of frustration or futility, but *hebel* does not in itself describe that sense, and those whose motivations are *hebel* (in Qohelet's view, at least) may never realize that fact for themselves. If the elusiveness of air is a key element of the metaphor, moreover, that quality does not adequately describe Qohelet's use of it: the problems that he sees lie not simply in the qualities of *hebel*, but in the false expectations that it can engender. An appreciation of this underpins what has certainly been the most influential modern interpretation of *hebel* and Qohelet's description of situations as *hebel*, which draws on existentialist ideas of 'absurdity', and which is especially associated with the work of Michael Fox. According to this understanding:

> Underlying Qohelet's *hebel*-judgments is an assumption that the system should be rational, which, for Qohelet, means that actions should invariably produce appropriate consequences. In fact, Qohelet stubbornly expects them to do so. Qohelet believes in the rule of divine justice. That is why he does not merely resign himself to the violations of equity he observes. He is shocked by them: they clash with his belief that the world must work equitably. These violations are offensive to reason. They are absurd. (Fox, 'The Meaning of *Hebel* for Qohelet', 426)

This captures very well the mismatch between expectations and reality that seems to be embodied in Qohelet's use of *hebel* as a metaphor, but it also imports ideas that are expressed directly nowhere else in the book, and ignores some that are. As we have seen, Qohelet believes strongly in divine judgment, but also in divine control of events: when he sees circumstances that seem to stand in contradiction to the former, it drives him to emphasize the latter. Correspondingly, the problem in a passage like 8.10-14 is not that the world is irrational, but that what humans can perceive of

inability of humans to distinguish what is real, and it might not be inappropriate to suggest that, if such ideas had any more general currency when the book was written, they would have informed the audience's understanding of Qohelet's claims.

God's work does not enable them to understand it, so that their own reasoning and subsequent behaviour is based on a false perception. In, say, 5.18–6.2, on the other hand, the illusion lies in the identical appearance of those who can enjoy what they have and those who cannot. To be sure, this means that from a human perspective the world or things within it may seem bent or crooked (cf. 1.15; 7.13)—and the fact of possession without enjoyment is a hard thing for humans to put up with (cf. 6.1). The essence of Qohelet's message, however, is not that the world is working wrongly, but that humans cannot see it properly—because it is clearly no part of God's intention that they should do so. To that extent, nobody and nothing—least of all 'the system'—is irrational or at fault. The individual mismatches of expectation that Qohelet isolates are merely symptomatic of the fact that 'all is *hebel*', and that human understandings must necessarily be based on information that is limited, and potentially misleading.

There is a relationship between this and existentialist conceptions of the absurd, and it is not at all inappropriate to read Ecclesiastes in dialogue with such approaches to the problem of human existence in the world—indeed, it would not be wholly anachronistic to say that, in some important respects, Qohelet addresses key issues of existentialism in ways that would not be entirely alien to that tradition.[25] The translation of *hebel* as 'absurdity' helps to bring out such connections, but at the same time it potentially imputes to Qohelet, certainly in Fox's understanding, a view of the cosmos

---

[25] The link is made explicitly in a popular article that appeared shortly before Fox's: James, 'Ecclesiastes: Precursor of Existentialists', which examines it, however, only in a very general way, and around the same time Schwartz, 'Koheleth and Camus', compared Ecclesiastes with Camus' portrayal of Sisyphus (although he noted differences between them). The issue had been in the air a long time, though: well before all these, and in 1968, the same year that Barucq pre-empted Fox by characterizing *hebel* as 'absurdité' (as Pennacchini, 'Qohelet', was later also to do in 1977), Gordis devoted a chapter of his third edition (111-21) to denying the validity of such comparisons. Ingram, *Ambiguity*, 96 n. 25, mentions some other works, and there is a useful list of studies in Gericke, 'Comprehensive Typology', 3-4, to which we might add Christianson, 'Existential Legacy', a powerful reading that looks at existential attitudes to the holocaust. Among those who oppose the comparison, Shuster, 'Being as Breath', explicitly rejects existentialism in favour of a comparison with Heidegger, and Sneed, *Politics of Pessimism*, 168-70, declares that Qohelet is 'no modern existentialist', while Ehlich, 'Metaphern', 59-61, offers some thoughtful qualifications.

as meaningless or irrational that he would only hold if he believed God himself to be irrational.[26] What he actually seems to believe, rather, is simply that humans try to live meaningfully in a world that is itself meaningful, but are prevented from aligning themselves properly to that world by the limits of their own perception[27]—a belief, that, as we shall see, leads him to emphasize the limits of human wisdom.

It is difficult always to exclude other nuances in some places, and in 9.9, for instance, *hebel* surely carries some additional or even alternative implication that human life is ephemeral and transitory.[28] What *hebel* seems principally to represent for Qohelet, however, is

---

[26] On the pursuit of meaning that Fox sees as a counterpart to the declarations of absurdity, see his 'Inner-Structure'. The same issue can be raised, I think, in respect of Rudman's idea (in 'The Use of הבל') that the various implications of *hebel* are linked by the idea of chaos, and that Qoheleth 'believed the world was under the dominion of chaos' (141).

[27] Haden, 'Qoheleth', discusses the issues usefully in terms of 'alienation' and 'epistemic distance', making the important point also that, as Qohelet's own declarations about God show, God in the book is not supposed to be wholly unknowable—although he then goes on to attribute to Qohelet a theology that is more conventional, I think, than the text itself suggests. It is also interesting to compare Atkinson's summary of an emphasis found in the interpretations both of Bonaventure and of Luther: 'the problem Solomon is confronting is not creation in itself, but the way in which humanity *sees* it and responds to it in word and deed' (*Singing*, 191; his italics).

[28] Fredericks, *Coping*, sees this as the primary sense, while allowing for other nuances elsewhere. Against readings that permit various implications, Fox argues (35-36) that *hebel* cannot have different meanings in different places 'because then the summary "All is *hebel*" would be meaningless. Indeed, it would be specious reasoning or a rhetorical device—arguing from disparate categories that share only a multivalent label.' That is fair so long as it is not taken too far: we could equally argue that Qohelet is indeed more rhetor than logician, and that the use of a multivalent metaphor permits him to conjure a unity that would be impossible were his language more precise. Were we to insist, on the other hand, that he is genuinely trying to make an argument here, then we should also need to bear in mind that *hebel* lends itself to the sort of equivocation, intentional or otherwise, that is found repeatedly even in the works of Plato. Reviewing various translations of *hebel*, Alter, *Wisdom Books*, 340, offers the important reminder that 'all of these English equivalents are more or less right, and abstractions being what they are, each one has the effect of excluding the others and thus limiting the scope of the Hebrew metaphor'. Alter accordingly opts to retain that metaphor in his own translation, rendering the noun as 'mere breath', but I am not sure that that has the same range of resonances for a modern audience that *hebel* would have had for an ancient one.

bound up with this misapprehension by humans of the world, and of their place within it: they invest effort for things they cannot gain, or for reasons which are false, while they fail to pursue or to accomplish the only truly beneficial option which is open to them—pleasure in their activities—either because their concerns lie elsewhere, or because they have been misled into behaviour which may shorten their lives or prevent their enjoyment. What confronts humans is *hebel* because it is misleading or illusory, but what they typically do in response to it is also *hebel* because it is misguided or deluded. Without an equivalent, established metaphor in English, it is difficult to translate *hebel* in a way that reflects all the different nuances, even if we are willing to sacrifice the continuity of Qohelet's usage by adopting different terms in different contexts. The idea of an illusion, however, and of corresponding human delusion or confusion, comes close to catching the sense of *hebel* both in Ecclesiastes and in many of the other texts where it is used, so I have generally adopted those in my translation.[29]

Beyond the issue of meaning and translation, though, it is important also to appreciate the function of *hebel* as a unifying structural device, which holds much of the monologue together while simultaneously serving to separate particular observations and discussions from each other. It is striking, therefore, although rarely remarked upon until quite recently,[30] that Qohelet continues to use the word

---

[29] I would distinguish this from the interpretation in terms of epistemological scepticism which Michel, *Untersuchungen*, 40-51, adopts (on that, see Lohfink, 'הבל-Aussage') and Seow's comparable idea that Qohelet is depicting the world as incomprehensible (see 'Beyond', 15-16). Fisch, 'Constructive Skepticism', understands the issue in similar terms, but prefers to think in terms of the 'tentativity' with which humans are forced to act, unable to achieve certainty in the world. He speaks of Qohelet's problem (177) as 'divining...the possibility, meaning and prospects of rational and progressive action in conditions of thorough (epistemic) uncertainty'. Qohelet's use of the term, I think, expresses not his belief that humans cannot know reality, so much as his belief that they misapprehend it, and that it lends itself to such misapprehension. A significant part of the problem is that they do not always, or even usually, recognize the limitations, and so do not act, perhaps, as tentatively as they should.

[30] Carrière, 'Tout est vanité', extrapolates a pattern in Qohelet's use of the word from Wright's observation (in "The Riddle of the Sphinx Revisited', 44), that the numerical value of *hebel* (5+2+30-37) is equal to the number of times it occurs in the book. His numerological suggestions are unconvincing (and we may note that Wright's original count required him to delete one use as secondary,

after 8.14, but stops using his 'This (also) is *hebel*' formula at that point, with some four chapters of the book still to go. The simplest explanation for this, of course, would be that after this point, the monologue no longer introduces new situations or phenomena that Qohelet wants to characterize this way, and it is certainly true that what immediately follows (at least up to 9.12) could be understood as a sort of summary or extrapolation. We might perhaps have expected some such statement in connection with 9.13-15, but Qohelet instead derives from that a series of sayings about wisdom, and after this, down to ch. 12, his speech consists mostly of sayings and admonitions, with only occasional observations of situations that might earlier have attracted the formula. Without putting too much weight on the absence, it might be reasonable to suggest that the cessation of this formula is a structural device in itself, as much as was its presence in the earlier chapters: towards the end of the book we move into a phase where Qohelet is no longer concerned to draw out the misperceptions that lie behind human situations and behaviour, but to draw some wider conclusions and to offer some broader, more miscellaneous advice that loosely relates to those conclusions. Segal (108) notes the disappearance of the first-person perspective toward the end of the monologue (after 9.13, the only first-person suffix is in 12.1, where it does not refer to Qohelet, and the independent pronoun last appears in 9.16; the last first-person verb is in 10.7): this perhaps also reflects the extent to which the discourse shifts away from the personal engagement and examination that turned earlier chapters more visibly into a quest.

which Carrière does not); the divisions that he imposes also seem arbitrary. Carrière does, however, draw attention to the shift in Qohelet's discourse, and the more varied uses of *hebel* in the last chapters. Ingram, *Ambiguity*, 127-28, sets out in detail the uneven distribution of the term, and Segal picks this up as an instance of change within the monologue (108), going on to suggest (136-37) that there is a shift away from using it to characterize situations, and toward using it as a way to describe the fleetingness of life (cf. 6.12; 7.15; 9.9). I am myself inclined to think that this is indicative more of changes in the content than of some attempt to depict Qohelet becoming 'less enamored of the word' (136), although those changes may themselves, of course, be an aspect of Qohelet's characterization. Gianto, 'Theme of Enjoyment', argues that the change after 8.14 marks the gradual emergence of pleasure as an alternative to the reality of *hebel*, which seems to place too much weight on that particular theme in the closing chapters, but may be closer to the mark.

(c) *Wisdom*

Word distributions and frequencies are not always a very useful way to approach a text, but given Qohelet's undoubted concern with wisdom, it is interesting to observe just where he uses terms from the relevant Hebrew root ḤKM. These appear no fewer than 53 times, across 44 of the book's 222 verses (although two are in the epilogue at 12.9 and 11, so are not actually uses by Qohelet himself), and this frequency is similar to that found in the book of Proverbs, which is around two-and-a-half times longer and has 104 occurrences—it is slightly higher, if anything. Of course, wisdom is not always his focus when Qohelet uses the vocabulary of wisdom, but it would be fair to say that Qohelet refers to no other of his preoccupations so often—*hebel* appears an impressive 38 times, but eight of these are in 1.2 and 12.8—and from those raw data alone, we might well conclude that Ecclesiastes is very much a book about wisdom. The terminology is distributed irregularly, however, with the relevant words falling largely in 1.13–2.26 (17 uses), 7.4–8.5 (16), and 9.10–10.12 (13). Around 90% of Qohelet's own uses, therefore, are to be found in less than 40% of the verses in the monologue, and all the way between the end of ch. 2 and the beginning of ch. 7, such vocabulary only appears twice: at 4.13, where wisdom is an attribute of the youth but not the issue at stake, and at 6.8, where Qohelet apparently reaches back to 2.13-16 in order to draw an analogy.[31]

This concentration correlates with Qohelet's concerns in the first two chapters, where wisdom is a key tool in his investigations, and then a target of his concerns in the angry reflections that follow. In ch. 7 through to the beginning of ch. 8, moreover, wisdom is itself the principal topic of Qohelet's discourse. It is difficult to generalize about the second half of ch. 9 and the first of ch. 10, but wisdom and the wise appear in lists at 9.10-11, and most of the other uses are in sayings about wisdom. We find a lot of references to wisdom, in other words, when Qohelet is talking either about the

---

[31] It is harder to judge the 36 uses of the verb *ydʿ*, 'know', because Qohelet does not use it typically of human knowledge in some more general way, but of things that he or others know. The cognate noun *dʿt*, however, is commonly used in association with 'wisdom', and has a similar distribution (it appears in 1.16, 18; 2.21, 26; 7.12; 9.10; 12.9).

experiences that shaped his views or when wisdom itself is at the centre of his attention, but the concept is notably rare in the middle of the monologue, where he talks about divine action and human behaviour.

After such a virtual absence of references in chs. 3–6, the way Qohelet then deals with wisdom in ch. 7 is all the more intriguing. Much of this chapter is very difficult to interpret, for various reasons, but in 7.1-6 Qohelet presents wisdom in ways that might seem less than appealing: where the mind of fools is like a house of celebration, that of the wise is like a house of mourning, and the wise offer rebukes where fools offer songs and laughter. In 7.7, 11-12, and probably 19, the power of wisdom is heavily qualified, and, perhaps in another reference back to 2.15, 7.16 warns against being unnecessarily wise. Qohelet has included wisdom in none of his previous recommendations or admonitions, and when he does finally turn to it, his commendation is, therefore, lukewarm at best—he makes folly sound a lot more appealing. Similar qualifications are attached in chs. 9 and 10: the wise are as liable as anyone to suffer the vagaries of chance (9.11), wisdom is likely to go unheeded however useful it may be (9.13-18), and the benefits of wisdom are contingent on the profit or advantage it offers (10.10). In 10.2 and 12-13, to be sure, the wise man acts as a foil to the fool, but these are really the only points at which Qohelet adopts a conventional attitude towards wisdom.

In the course of 7.23–8.1, Qohelet undertakes a quest to find wisdom (probably, as we shall see, wisdom personified as a woman), and this episode is especially interesting because, up to this point, the Qohelet who had so magnified his own wisdom in 1.16 has made no subsequent mention of it since 2.15. When he does finally talk about that wisdom now, it is no longer in terms of how wise he has been: instead, Qohelet declares that he wants to be wise, but finds it beyond him. After recounting his failure to discover wisdom, he goes on both to speak bitterly of wisdom as a woman who traps men when God wills it, and to finish in 8.1, furthermore, with a declaration that probably pairs wisdom's capacity to enlighten with its tendency to dishearten. It is not entirely clear how we are supposed to understand all this—and the text is probably damaged at points, making the task harder. It seems unlikely, however, either that Qohelet is seeking simply to supplement his existing wisdom with some more insightful form of wisdom, or that he has suffered an intellectual decline. When the tool with which he made his enquiries in 1.13 seems now to be utterly beyond his grasp in 7.23-24, the point seems rather to be that his reflections have changed his relationship with wisdom. We might say that his heart is no longer in it, even if he wishes otherwise, although Qohelet himself suggests that he no longer feels trapped by wisdom's own heart: his new incapacity is also a form of liberation, and when he sets out to find wisdom, it is less to embrace than to accuse her (a point that has been lost in the Hebrew text, but not in the Greek). In any case, we shall hear nothing more of Qohelet's own wisdom until the epilogue.

In its treatment both of wisdom generally and of Qohelet's wisdom in particular, the book depicts a significant shift away from Qohelet's enthusiastic embrace of it in 1.12–2.10 toward something that we might almost call a loss of faith. At the outset of his enquiries, wisdom was not just a tool (1.13; 2.3, 9), but one of the primary objects of his investigations (1.17-18; 2.12; 8.16); his confidence in wisdom, however, seems to have survived neither his immediate conclusions, nor his broader reflections on the world—which is hardly surprising once he has come to realize its limitations. From an acknowledgment as early as 1.18 that wisdom can be a source of pain, Qohelet has realized in 2.13-16 that this pain comes with no corresponding gain: wisdom merely allows him to perceive his fate more clearly, not to change it. By 8.5-9, his list of 'what the wise man knows' consists entirely of known unknowns and of situations that cannot be changed, while 8.17–9.1 stress both that the wise can know no more than anybody else about what God has done, and that the wise are as much under God's control as everybody else. Although he never condemns wisdom, therefore, and continues occasionally to contrast it favourably with folly, the view of the world that Qohelet has developed excludes the possibility that wisdom might ever achieve anything that he regards as important.[32]

---

[32] Sharp, 'Representation', 65, suggests: 'The book is working as hard as it possibly can, with rhetorical tools as sophisticated as those one might encounter in any work of literature ancient or contemporary, to make the point that "Qohelet's" reliance on wisdom alone is precisely not a viable way to live'.

(d) *The Basis of Qohelet's Ideas*

What we have seen already about the *hebel* declarations and about Qohelet's attitudes to wisdom merely emphasizes what is surely a major theme of the monologue more generally: human ignorance is determined by the nature of the world, and by the deliberate design of God, with the consequence that human perception is unreliable. We may reasonably ask, therefore, on what basis Qohelet presumes to offer us his own insights as reliable, and how he can claim to know anything about what is supposed to be unknown. Is this merely a literary device, which introduces, in effect, an omniscient narrator, or is Qohelet's knowledge plausible despite his denials of human knowledge?

The book offers no direct answer to that question, and although Qohelet himself has much to say about knowledge and ignorance, epistemology itself is nowhere addressed directly as a concern. That has not, however, prevented scholars from enquiring into Qohelet's epistemology, and there has been some very important work in this area, even if, as is so often the case when we are dealing with Ecclesiastes, no consensus has been achieved.[33] In this respect, some issues are complicated by problems surrounding the interpretation of particular passages: 7.27 has often been read, for example, in terms of inductive reasoning (quite wrongly, I think).[34] The principal difficulty, however, has proved to be the significance that different scholars attach to Qohelet's many statements about having 'seen' or 'observed' particular phenomena, and to his use of ideas associated with those observations. In particular, some have been drawn

---

[33] There is a helpful recent overview of scholarship in Gericke, 'Comprehensive Philosophical Approach', who notes the more detailed surveys in O'Dowd, *The Wisdom of Torah*, 138-42, and Schellenberg, *Erkenntnis*, 35-60.

[34] In fact, a great deal of the discussion in this area has based itself on some of the most difficult passages in the book. For details see the commentary and notes, but, in short, I doubt that there is any 'testing' in 2.1 and 7.23, or that Qohelet's references to 'finding' ever imply anything more than 'encountering' or 'discovering' (as in 7.29): they do not embody some idea of arriving at a conclusion or understanding as the result of calculation. In 7.27, Qohelet is encountering one woman after another in the hope or expectation of thereby encountering something that he seeks, and although it has become very common to read this as 'adding one thing to another to find the sum' (as the RSV puts it), such an understanding requires us, for no good reason, to insert an extra verb, to read one preposition as though it were another, and to imbue the (admittedly difficult) final noun with a sense that it possesses clearly nowhere else.

to see in them an approach that is specifically empirical: Qohelet seems to be extrapolating conclusions directly from his experience in such cases, not importing them dogmatically or reasoning his way to them on the basis of other conclusions.[35]

If Qohelet were indeed an empiricist at heart, then his conclusions would certainly stand in strong contrast to his methods. In most cases where he describes a situation, however, Qohelet seems concerned to illustrate his existing beliefs, rather than actually to derive any new understanding. The most important potential exceptions are in the first two chapters, where he carries out his investigations and draws conclusions from them, but these need to be read with some caution. In particular, the rejection in 2.11 of his own works, and consequently of any possible profit for humans, seems not to be derived from his actual experience of building businesses—all apparently successful ones—but from his insistence that to qualify as a 'profit' what one owns must be something that can only be earned, and that can never belong to anybody else subsequently.[36] His conclusion, in other words, is derived not from his experience, but from the application to it of a presupposition. Interestingly, what does come out of his experience, according to the previous verse, is an appreciation of pleasure, which Qohelet had earlier tested experimentally in 2.1 as well: what Qohelet gains in these chapters is not a new knowledge validated by experience, but an understanding that there can be value in the very act of experiencing something.

It is also important to be clear, whatever weight one puts on Qohelet's claims to experience, that much of his worldview is

---

[35] See, e.g., Fox, 'Qohelet's Epistemology'; Piotti, 'Osservazioni sul Metodo'; and, more strongly, Hayman, 'Qohelet and the Book of Creation', 98-99; Sciumbata, 'Peculiarità e motivazioni'. Schellenberg's study of Qohelet's empiricism in *Erkenntnis*, 161-91, leads her to understand his appeals to individual experience in terms of his belief that human knowledge is limited to what happens within the world, where only experiential and empirical enquiries are possible (196). I am more sympathetic to the view of Johnstone, in 'Preacher as Scientist', 219, that Qohelet 'sets out deliberately to observe in an empirical way... But...nothing observable is in the end valid, as giving the final truth about life, or as providing satisfaction, meaning, or profit.'

[36] Qohelet's take on all human property is very like that expressed in a familiar advertising slogan: 'You never really own a Patek Philippe, you merely look after it for the next generation' (Leagas Delaney agency, 1976–present).

derived from dogmatic statements, which, far from being affirmed by his observations, often stand in contradiction to them (cf. Gericke, 'Concept of Deity', 3). Indeed, since the whole problem of perception is rooted, for him, in an understanding that the world we can see does not adequately represent the world as it really is, perception is problematized by his *belief* in a different, unobservable reality.[37] In Qohelet's 'real' world, God differentiates and judges humans, or treats them according to their fear of him, and he arranges human lives according to his own preferences, but little or none of this is visible to humans (cf. Piotti, 'Percezione II'). In the 'real' world, likewise, there is a meaning and a reason for events that seem random and unpredictable to humans with their restricted insight. To his audience, who would surely have shared his belief in the validity of these religious beliefs, Qohelet is effectively saying that, if the world as we see it seems not to reflect them, it is not because they are unreal, but because we cannot properly see the world.

This is a dogmatic, theological conservatism, but its implications are radical in other areas. Most importantly, if such realities are invisible to us, or even hidden from us, then this fact inevitably casts doubt on claims made about revelation and about the capacities of human wisdom. Qohelet has nothing to say directly about the former, although the context of his comments about dreams in 5.2 and 5.6 suggests that they may be a dismissal of individual aspirations to gain insight directly from God (see the commentary).[38]

---

[37] O'Dowd, *The Wisdom of Torah*, 144, suggests that Qohelet 'creates irony by juxtaposing his *a priori* worldview alongside his experiential knowledge without offering an explanation', and later (149) that 'It is these unexpected turns from empirical to rational/traditional judgments which force readers to question Qohelet's epistemological foundations and his relation to his tradition'. That may be so for readers whose focus is on Qohelet himself, but where such juxtapositions are clearly deliberate, it seems more probable that they are intended to address human perceptions in general, rather than Qohelet's in particular.

[38] I doubt that those comments are directed consciously at the claims of apocalyptic literature (cf. Rosso Ubigli, 'Qohelet di fronte', 227-28; Mazzinghi, 'Enochism', 161-64), not least because I understand them to be set within the context of his advice about the temple in particular. More generally, though, if Qohelet is making a deliberate reference to Deut 23.22 (ET 23.21) in 5.3—on which, see below—then he does cite the Torah, and although 4.17 seems to cast doubt on the need for anyone but fools to sacrifice, it is doubtful that we can read that as an outright rejection of legal prescriptions. Equally, the limits placed on

He has a great deal to say about wisdom, however, much of which denies its ability to rise above the mundane, and qualifies its usefulness even there. Qohelet's understanding is also radical, of course, in other respects: a dogmatic belief in divine determinism has consequences for the reality of human choice, and, as ch. 3 shows, for the whole concept of any action being inherently good or bad (an idea that will be picked up in ch. 9). On the other hand, his ideas about pleasure arise, by elimination, from the beliefs that drive Qohelet to exclude any other form of compensation. Again, though, such ideas are drawn out as the logical consequence of Qohelet's beliefs, not as the result of observation—which could not itself reveal them. We might, therefore, properly add to a description of Qohelet as dogmatist the qualification that he implicitly reasons on the basis of his dogmas—but it would be misleading to think of him as an empiricist.

Having said that his audience would most likely have shared some of Qohelet's beliefs, finally, it is important to stress that they might have had somewhat greater difficulty accepting either some of his extrapolations from those beliefs, or some of his other dogmatic ideas. Qohelet's restrictive definition of profit, most notably, is crucial in the account of his own development, but it is difficult to believe that many would have shared such a definition, or would have reacted as Qohelet does when he turns to inspect his achievements in 2.11. This is something that we shall consider shortly, when we look at the characterization of Qohelet, but more immediately it should alert us to an element of artificiality in the account of his thinking. It is interesting to examine the epistemological assumptions of the monologue, in a way that the book

human knowledge by Qohelet do not exclude the possibility of accepting prophecy or the Torah as sources of revelation, and it seems likely that Qohelet's ideas about judgment and divine control, as well as his more general reference to, e.g., righteousness, are implicitly rooted in a piety that would necessarily draw on some sort of revelation. While he shows no specific interest in the topic, therefore (as Schultz, 'Was Qohelet', 212, points out), we should probably not take his silence to suggest that the worldview attributed to Qohelet would have been understood by his audience to exclude altogether the possibility of divine communication with humans. On the other hand, Qohelet clearly does not presume the sort of links between Torah and wisdom that we find in Prov 1–9 and Ben Sira, or the corresponding portrayals of law as a source of insight into the will of God more generally.

itself does not, but there are peculiarities and idiosyncrasies here that would surely have struck the original audience—perhaps more forcefully than they strike modern readers, who are accustomed to find the unfamiliar in an ancient text—and we should be wary of assuming that Qohelet is always adopting, or even attempting to model common beliefs and approaches in this area.

4. *The Epilogue and the Portrayal of Qohelet*

Qohelet presents himself to us in the monologue as a man who has devoted much of his life to answering certain questions, but who has found no adequate answers. He tells us of his own resentments, and sometimes of his incapacities, as well as of his many observations, and there is an invitation throughout for us to engage with him as a fellow human. His monologue ends, moreover, with dramatic, jarring images of death, culminating in a bleak restatement of the claim with which he began. It is more than a little disconcerting, therefore, when the last few verses of the book take pains to inform us that Qohelet was actually a writer and crafter of words, that all books like this are intended to be painful—so it's probably not a good idea to read any more—and that we should just fear God and do what he says. The problem is not simply that these statements seem out of step with all that has been said so far, but that they positively dismantle it: every effort that has been made to engage our sympathies, to provoke our laughter, anger or sadness, is revealed as deliberate manipulation by a clever writer, working in a tradition that specializes in such manipulation. With a metatheatrical flourish, this whole book, so concerned with illusion and misplaced belief, is shown to have been a sort of illusion itself, and, by implication, our suspension of disbelief as we listened to Qohelet merely another symptom of a broader problem: the imagery used is of sheep-herding, and it is we, the audience, who have been the sheep.[39]

---

[39] So, a little differently, Koosed, *(Per)mutations*, 110: 'Qoh 12:11–12 does not fit comfortably with the book as a whole. In fact, it seems to undermine the very activity of study and book writing without which this book would never have come into existence.' She goes on to point out (111) that 'a book that begins with the emptiness of life…could not believe its own self to be full of weighty meaning'.

Going beyond this, whoever is speaking to us at the end of the book not only reminds us that it was all just a story, but then warns us against any other such painful books, and finally sends us away with some more conventional advice to be pious. For the only time in Ecclesiastes, moreover, we are addressed as 'my child' in 12.12, which seems to establish the speaker's tone here as that of a concerned parent, and we hardly need the other literary resonances of that expression, so popular in Proverbs, to discern a critical comment on advice literature more generally: 'The words of wise men are like goads, and like embedded spikes... There is much working on books without end, and much study is a wearying of the flesh' (12.11-12). For all that the admonition here might seem to say 'this is the only advice you should ever read'—which would be respectful, if a little odd—there is also an implication that we might have done better not even to have read this one, and that the subsequent advice to 'Fear God and keep his commandments' is all we really need. Despite some praise for Qohelet's talents as a writer and a teller of truth, therefore, the epilogue—'the first commentary on the book', as Dell describes it ('Ecclesiastes as Wisdom', 309)—is hardly a ringing endorsement of his monologue, and seems more concerned that we should not worry about it too much.[40]

It is hard to believe that this is just clumsiness—the result, perhaps, of some later writer who wished to praise Qohelet inadvertently undercutting what had been said: there is no obvious place in such an attempt for 12.11-12 (which is why, perhaps, scholars who take such an approach to the problem usually end up finding multiple later editors—Koenen, 'Zu den Epilogen', is a notable exception). While it is commonly suggested, moreover, that the last two verses, 12.13-14, were added to make the book more palatable to orthodox readers (whatever that might have meant at the time), it is likewise difficult to imagine who might have felt this way about the book but nevertheless wanted to commend it—or who might have thought, for that matter, that two such conventional verses would actually make up for the more than two hundred verses that had gone before. It is altogether simpler to suppose that the author of the monologue has merely adopted another voice here, to say something about that

---

[40] Scholars have paid curiously little attention to the tensions between the monologue and the epilogue, but see the thoughtful remarks in Laurent, 'Le Livre', 8-14.

monologue, even if it seems to follow that, in some sense, he must wish to distance the book as a whole from the words of its key protagonist (see my 'Fear God').

In his new persona as epilogist, the author now takes the stage that Qohelet has vacated, and turns his views back on him.[41] Qohelet was indeed wise, while his teaching and his carefully crafted words have persisted beyond him and continue to convey a knowledge of the truth—but that is something about which we should be concerned. Such truth is painful, and to hear the words of Qohelet or of other wise men is potentially to experience all the downsides of wisdom that Qohelet has been so concerned to emphasize. The epilogue draws out, then, the irony that is inherent in a book of 'wisdom' that regards wisdom without enthusiasm, and disengages us from the rhetoric that might sweep us up into sharing Qohelet's bleak outlook. Insofar as we can judge the tone of such things, I think that it does so rather playfully: the imagery of spikes and goads is a bit too vivid, perhaps, and the dismissal of endless books a bit too world-weary for us to take the statements as entirely earnest. Besides, if the author was really so concerned about the effects, he could simply not have written the book in the first place (and if these are not words from the author, we could say much the same of any later editor who wrote them, presumably under no compulsion to transmit the book). If this strange epilogue is indeed a little tongue-in-cheek, however, it makes some important points, both about the character of what has preceded, and about the ways in which we should react to it. If the author does distance himself from Qohelet at this crucial point, furthermore, then it raises legitimate questions about how we are supposed to view that character elsewhere in the book.

Those questions are difficult to answer in full. In matters like the idiosyncrasy of Qohelet's language (which we shall look at later), his curious name, and his apparent fondness for commercial terminology like 'profit' and 'loss' (cf. 1.15),[42] we can see that there was

---

[41] Willmes, *Menschliches Schicksal*, 240, speaks aptly of the epilogue presenting 'eine ironische Parabase': in early Greek comedy, the parabasis is a sort of intermission, during which, with the actors absent, the chorus sets aside its role within the play to step forward and address the audience directly on some topic, often to do with the play or the playwright.

[42] See Weeks, *Ecclesiastes and Scepticism*, 34-36, and the works cited there in n. 50.

probably scope for the author to have shaped perceptions of his character by the audience. We ourselves lack sufficient knowledge of the context to be sure just how they would have reacted—although it is probably possible to say that there is little in any of these to suggest that he was being portrayed as either the regal or the scholarly figure that many commentators have wanted to find (or, for that matter, as the dandy that Morse memorably constructs in his two-part 'Introduction'). What does come across more clearly is Qohelet's extraordinary materialism. The monologue begins with the question that will dominate his concerns—'What profit is there for a human in any of his business, at which he works beneath the sun?'—and if we construe that merely as a question about the meaning or purpose of human life, then it seems unexceptionable. As Qohelet goes on, however, it becomes clear that he really does mean, very literally, a 'profit': he wants to know what a human can achieve so that in death they have more than they had at birth, and accordingly have something concrete to show for all the hard work of living.

That is something, perhaps, about which fewer people would be concerned, and even if the original audience might have shared his disbelief in any meaningful afterlife, it seems difficult to accept that they would, as readily as Qohelet, have rejected the significance of any mark that they might leave on posterity. Not many other people, I suspect, would ever likewise have rejected all they had made for themselves simply because they would no longer be the owner when they died (2.18-19), and although many have doubtless sympathized with the calls to enjoyment of life for which Qohelet is famous, such enjoyment remains second-best for Qohelet himself: it is what we all have to settle for, not what he really wants. Qohelet understands the world in a way that makes the profit he desires inherently unobtainable, and it is doubtful that his audience would fully have shared either his understanding of the world or his desire for such a particular sort of profit.

If we think also of his initial inability to see the purpose of pleasure (2.2) or recall, say, his deadpan delivery of the sayings in 7.1-6, which commend melancholy and the rebukes of the wise above the celebration and laughter of the foolish, then we might also suspect that Qohelet is being portrayed as somewhat less than fun-loving, for all his calls to enjoy life. Although there is doubtless some movement in his ideas about such matters, as I have noted above, the only point at which he actually depicts *himself* as finding pleasure is in 2.10, where he declares that he enjoyed the creation and running of his business, while 2.1 probably depicts pleasure as something that he could only experience by force-feeding it to himself. We could easily go into some other curious aspects of the monologue, and most especially 4.9-12, where Qohelet commends company with no apparent concept of companionship,[43] but it should be clear already that Qohelet does not naturally place value in things which represent neither a material gain nor a definable benefit—even pleasure only has meaning to him when he becomes able to accept it as such.

The fact that this strange and disconsolate figure calls on us to find pleasure in what we do has provoked a certain amount of debate about whether his message is ultimately optimistic or pessimistic. Of course, if we are supposed to share Qohelet's values, then we are presumably supposed also to share his sense that the joy to be found in work is a poor substitute for the profit that he actually seeks, even if he is keen to promote it as better than nothing. If it is reasonable to suggest as I have, though, that his views about profit were unlikely to have been commonplace, then it is doubtful that we are supposed to share his disappointment in finding no such profit. Qohelet has lost a shilling and found sixpence, but what he commends is likely to be seen as a pure gain by anyone else. To that extent, at least, the book perhaps invites us to see Qohelet as Whybray does in 'Qoheleth, Preacher of Joy', even though this far from joyous preacher clearly does not view his own words in that way. If it is also reasonable to suggest from the perspective of any normal audience, ancient or modern, that Qohelet in 7.1-6 unconsciously promotes the fools, with their joy, singing and laughter, over the wise with their morbidity, vexation, melancholy and rebukes, then there is at least one other issue over which the author probably intends his readers to part company with Qohelet (at least

---

[43] Lavoie, 'Analyse de Qohélet 4,9-12', 208, observes how those verses outline the benefits of company 'de manière froide et sans émotions', 'coldly and emotionlessly'. Fontaine, never keen to find the best in Qohelet, says in 'Ecclesiastes', 154, that he 'views companionship solely from the perspective of what it can do for the ego in control', but even the more sympathetic Jasper, 'Note for our Time', 266, remarks that 'the motive of self-interest is not absent even here. It is still more a matter of what is advantageous than of what is right.'

initially), and there may be other, less obvious ones. It seems less likely that the author wishes us to embrace Qohelet's most idiosyncratic positions than that they are intended to engage our interest without compelling our agreement.

Taken with what is said in the epilogue about the words of the wise, it is tempting to see a satirical edge to all this, and Qohelet has indeed been viewed as a parody of some archetypal wise man (see especially Shields, 'Ecclesiastes and the End of Wisdom', and *The End of Wisdom*, which correspondingly adopt an understanding of the epilogue that makes it central to the purposes of the book).[44] The principal difficulty with that reading in particular is that we have no evidence for such an archetype ever having existed: even without getting into vexed questions about whether 'wise men' ever constituted an identifiable class, none of the many things said about them elsewhere suggests that Qohelet might be an exaggerated embodiment of some ideal. At least for the first few chapters, furthermore, he does not use the sort of admonitory or aphoristic styles associated with 'the wise' elsewhere, so if there is any sort of satire on ideas, it is not obviously matched by any consistent literary parody. If Qohelet's concerns point to him being any sort of 'type', it is more probably a businessman than a sage: it is in that sphere that we might expect such an assessment of life in terms of profit and loss, and I have some suspicion that the audience was intended to see him in such terms—but in chs. 5 and 6 he is fiercely critical himself of attitudes shaped by wealth. More generally, though, it is far from clear that we are supposed to find Qohelet actually unsympathetic as a person: even when we may not be expected to share his outlook or opinions, he has not obviously been set up for us to ridicule or reject. The condescension of the epilogue, on the other hand, and its implicit insults to our intelligence, make it hard to believe that we

---

[44] Longman, 38, suggests not dissimilarly that the epilogue reveals Qohelet's monologue to have been a teaching device, used by the speaker 'in order to instruct his son (12:12) concerning the dangers of speculative, doubting wisdom in Israel'. Bolin, *Ecclesiastes*, 69, sees this as 'overtly theological' and 'one-sided', allowing Longman to identify the supposedly more orthodox epilogist as 'the inspired biblical author'—although Longman himself goes no further than to suggest that this is how the book came to be included in the canon. At the very least, this sort of reading does play into the conventional dichotomy in interpretations of the book between poorly defined 'orthodox' and 'subversive' views, of which Bolin (64-67) is more generally—and rightly—critical.

are supposed to accept it uncritically as a revelation of Qohelet's inadequacies—even before we try to explain its complimentary evaluations of Qohelet himself.

Having said that the style of the book does not suggest a direct parody of existing advice literature, though, I should add that Qohelet probably does engage with such literature all the same. The key passage is the difficult 7.23-29, which we have touched on already, and in which Krüger is right, I think, to see Qohelet as talking about a personification of wisdom as a woman. More broadly, this description of 'woman Wisdom' probably forms part of an account in which Qohelet, having struggled to be wise, sets out unsuccessfully to find her. Such personifications of wisdom probably originated in the complex imagery of Proverbs 1–9, although they are found in Ben Sira and other subsequent literature (see my *Instruction and Imagery*, 158-69), so when Qohelet sets out to find a literal woman, and fails to do so despite encountering numerous people, he engages an established imagery on its own terms, probably in order to contradict the assertion of Proverbs 1–9 that wisdom is easily accessible—in that work, she stands in the street, not 'far, and deep, deep down' (7.23). This corresponds to his own more cautious attitudes toward wisdom, which we have looked at already, but it also contributes toward the picture of Qohelet that the author paints for us. As in the earlier memoir of ch. 2, Qohelet acts here, and does not just talk, but even more than in that previous account, he behaves with a sort of literal-minded naivety, treating a familiar image as though it were a reality, and conducting a painstaking enquiry for a woman who does not exist.

Of course, there is a literary conceit involved, but that naivety only adds to a sense that Qohelet behaves sometimes almost as an *idiot savant*, and that what distinguishes him from other people is not merely intelligence, but a resistance to compromise and illusion that comes close to being an incapacity. He is by no means immune to emotion, but when Qohelet looks at a world which appears not to affirm his beliefs, he does not follow others in altering those beliefs, or flinch from accepting truths that are painful to him. The author has created him not as an 'everyman', but as somebody whose unusual perspective sets him apart from most other humans in a way that those other humans might find disconcerting, and forces him to acknowledge truths that bring him no benefit or happiness. He has prepared a speech for woman Wisdom, but he engages explicitly with other people nowhere else: the only conversations that he reports are with or in his own heart (e.g. 1.16-17; 2.1, 15; 3.17-18; 7.25), and this imagery of the self as companion is again distinctive enough to suggest that the author uses it deliberately, to portray Qohelet as unusually self-contained—if not actually lonely.[45]

We are probably supposed to imagine that it is his wisdom, mentioned so early in his account as exceeding that of others, which has shaped Qohelet and his perceptions. This adds piquancy to his sense, in ch. 7, that he is no longer wise or capable of wisdom, and explains his subsequent treatment of wisdom—if 7.26 is indeed talking about personified wisdom, furthermore, then Qohelet views himself as having been caught previously in a trap (a part of which is constituted by wisdom's own 'heart'). The caution expressed in the epilogue corresponds to this portrayal: wisdom is a source of pain, not happiness, and Qohelet's whole unhappy discourse exemplifies that fact. Qohelet has been too wise (2.15), and himself commends others not to make the same mistake (7.16), so that in this respect the monologue and epilogue are actually in accord.[46] Qohelet, furthermore, does not benefit personally from revealing the true state of the world, and since the principal belief that he derives from his experience is that humans should accept and enjoy what they have, it is doubtful that he understands this truth itself to be of benefit to his audience. Although it first ensures that we

---

[45] Fontaine, 'Ecclesiastes', 154, reads this rather differently: 'Significantly, the author never speaks of entering a meaningful relationship and so lives in a world where he is the only true subject. Nature, women, and other social inferiors remain objects for his use, so naturally he suffers the boredom of the elite who exist in a world populated only by themselves.' With respect to the 'heart', Koosed, *(Per)mutations*, 46-47, draws attention to the fact that, despite 42 uses in the book, 'heart' has received much less attention than other supposed key terms, and goes on to suggest (51) that 'There is a split at the root of Qohelet's identity between his I and his heart'. She does not follow this up systematically, but the usage is certainly distinctive, and represents, I think, a significant aspect of Qohelet's portrayal, which enables him to act and speak cooperatively, as it were, while remaining isolated. In more than half the uses that Koosed lists, though, the heart is not Qohelet's own, and in, e.g., 11.9-10, the same virtual dichotomy is attributed by Qohelet to others. This is an aspect not just of Qohelet, therefore, but of the anthropology attributed to him.

[46] Perry, *Book of Ecclesiastes*, 6, suggests that Qohelet offers 'his own curriculum vitae as an example not to follow', and whether or not that is entirely true of Qohelet himself, I think it is probably true of the book as a whole.

are disengaged from Qohelet's rhetoric, and itself emphasizes piety over pleasure, the epilogue not only picks up much of Qohelet's vocabulary (as we shall see when we turn to it in the commentary), but also offers strong continuity, therefore, both with the portrayal of Qohelet in the monologue and with an important aspect of his message. Qohelet cultivated wisdom to the point that he was forced to an unhappy realization of the limits set on life: we should not do the same.

5. *Unity and Coherence*

From all that has been said so far, it will be clear that I consider Ecclesiastes to be essentially the work of a single writer, not only when it comes to the relationship between the superscription, monologue and epilogue, but also with respect to the monologue itself. To be sure, Qohelet's words do not always flow smoothly, as a single, coherent discussion, but they are framed as a broadly sequential series of experiences, and of reflections arising from those experiences, which, at least until the end of ch. 8, are commonly conscripted to illustrate the specific points about vapour and profit which transcend his individual observations. It is also true, as we shall see later, that Qohelet probably draws sometimes on existing materials, and it is very likely, furthermore, that the text has become damaged at points in the course of transmission—there are even a few places in which it would not be unreasonable to suppose that it has been subject to more deliberate alteration. I see no strong grounds, however, on which to suppose either that the 'monologue' was in fact written in the first place to embody a variety of voices or opinions, or that such variety has been introduced by any extensive reworking of the monologue after it had first been composed. In this respect, my approach corresponds to that of many other recent commentators, but the book has often been read very differently in the past, and some of those older approaches continue to exercise an influence.

Here it is necessary to distinguish between several different sorts of claim. Perhaps the most basic and important is an idea found even amongst very early readers of the book, that Qohelet actively contradicts himself at various points and in respect of various issues (I have explored this at more length in 'Inner-Textuality'). This has often been used to justify other assumptions, and at one level it is probably true: there are significant tensions between some of Qohelet's ideas—most notably his determinism and his insistence on divine judgment—which might be considered theological contradictions (although they are rarely described as such on the many occasions when they appear in other writings). The more direct contradictions that are usually singled out, however, can generally be explained either in terms of Qohelet's changing ideas, or as a consequence of failures to recognize the way in which Qohelet often qualifies his statements and ideas. An example of the first is provided easily enough by his attitude to pleasure, which is dismissed as useless in 2.2, even though Qohelet will later commend it at many different points as the only real benefit available to humans, and explicitly praise it in 8.15. It is doubtful, in fact, that he regards it as any more 'useful', in his terms, even in those later passages, but the important point, anyway, is that Qohelet's experiences after 2.2 force him to a re-evaluation of his initial opinions. Qohelet's struggles to be wise at the end of ch. 7 present a similar contrast with his claims to have been exceptionally wise in 1.16, and are surely to be explained in much the same way—but are no less problematic, of course, for scholars who read the monologue more as a static statement of opinions, than as an account of experience and development. In his recent commentary, Segal presents (110-11) a relatively long list of 'contradictions' that he thinks can be explained in these terms.

Other apparent contradictions seem specifically formulated to make a point. In 2.13-15, for instance, wisdom has an 'advantage', but Qohelet sees no genuine benefit: all wisdom does is show us an uncomfortable truth, without enabling us to change the future. In 8.10-14, rather differently, Qohelet protests the reality of divine judgment, in the face of common human experience and of apparent exceptions, explicitly to make the point that what we see is illusory. If we fail to take the point in either case, then of course there is an inconsistency—but we will not read such passages better by taking everything that Qohelet says as a statement of dogma, subject to no qualification. He is not saying 'wisdom is advantageous' or that 'God rewards and punishes' then immediately contradicting himself, but setting those statements beside observations in order to say something about either the statement or the observation. To the extent that he presents a superficial contradiction that invites resolution, we might well say that contradictions are a significant component of Qohelet's discourse—but such cases do not imply incoherence.

Many interpreters, however, have seen contradictions in the book as symptomatic of a broader issue, and understood there to be several different viewpoints on display in the monologue, even where these do not actively contradict each other. Broadly speaking, the various expressions of this understanding involve any of three assumptions: (1) the book actually contained from the outset a dialogue, or an interplay between several different characters; (2) the book includes quotations of other viewpoints, to which Qohelet reacts; or (3) the book began with the expression of a single viewpoint, but has been supplemented with material that expresses other views.[47] Such assumptions allow a passage like 8.10-14 simply to be broken into different parts, so that, say, the more conventional sentiments of 8.12b-13 can be understood either to provoke a contrary reaction in 8.14, or to have been added as a way of softening the claim in that verse.

In the text as we have it, at least, there is no punctuation or any other way to differentiate the supposedly different views without reference solely to their content, and some early attempts to restore the book, based on more 'objective' assumptions that it was originally written in metrical verse, resulted in such savage, procrustean amputations that they have long been discredited.[48] Despite the linguistic peculiarities that we shall explore later, furthermore, no part of the book has self-evidently been composed in a different style or dialect of Hebrew which might enable us to distinguish it. Without such external criteria available, therefore, all three of these approaches present the same methodological difficulty: commentators who wish to separate the various viewpoints that they find are obliged first to define them, and then to apply their pre-determined

---

[47] I do not include here the various attempts (e.g. Galling; Fischer, *Skepsis*) to see the book as an anthology from the outset, because those attempts are generally driven by formal or form-critical considerations, rather than by a concern to explain different opinions. Indeed, they usually attribute most of the material to a single author.

[48] See especially Zapletal, *Das Buch Kohelet*; Haupt. Loretz, 'Poetry and Prose', has more recently taken an opposite approach, seeking to identify additions to the book in verse.

templates to the text—which is is no more scientific a procedure than Michelangelo removing the stone that was not David. Even if one of the many attempts to isolate separate voices did actually stumble upon original distinctions, we should have no way to know it or to prove it, and if the book really is composite, then we have no agreed basis for distinguishing separate voices or recovering an original version.

Martin Rose, unusual amongst recent scholars in his determination to find redactional layers throughout the book, apparently sees the current tendency to treat it as a unified work in terms of a passing modern fad, tied up with 'final-form' readings of texts (see his *Rien de nouveau*, 21-28), and, to be sure, the development of biblical criticism over the last few centuries has owed much to the recognition that some texts certainly are composite. It should not be our default position, however, that any text must either have been created from the wholesale redaction of sources, or have itself been subjected to extensive later editing, especially if the content as it stands can be explained without resort to such complications. In the particular case of Ecclesiastes, the approach that we take must be determined, to a great extent, by the limits of our tolerance for its formal and ideological inconsistencies. It is also important, however, to balance those considerations against the undoubted complexity of solutions which attempt to segregate the material.[49] Rose's own work, for example, involves an assumption that the original text was very brief and preserved only in scattered parts of chs. 1–3, 8, and 12, sometimes only as short phrases within verses:

---

[49] Redactional theories about Ecclesiastes generally envisage something much less simple than the sort of variation between different versions of Mesopotamian 'vanity' texts (see below) to which Samet draws attention in her 'Religious Redaction'. To be fair, she presents these only as potential analogies to the more straightforward addition of an epilogue to the book (although she includes no examples of an epilogue, as such), and they undoubtedly demonstrate ways in which ancient texts could undergo change and development, albeit in a very different context and over a very long period. Even in such cases, however, where we know that there has been change, it is difficult to associate such change specifically with attempts to qualify or alter the message: from many variants, Samet selects only a few instances where that may have been the case, and even those involve unprovable assumptions about the coherence and compatibility of particular themes.

this text has then been revised and supplemented, with the revised version itself then subsequently revised and supplemented again by a third hand. Brandscheidt (*Weltbegeisterung*) similarly identifies a composition that has twice been revised by others, and subjected to some additional supplementation—although she does not otherwise duplicate Rose's results—and Kustár ('Neue Sichten') finds an original work that has undergone no fewer than four stages of redaction. Köhlmoos' identification of additions, principally in the first and last chapters, by a writer 'Z' (for 'Zweite Generation', 'second-generation'), who is variously described as an author or editor, is simpler—although she too claims that there are further additions to be found.[50] In no such studies, however, are the processes that are assumed to have given rise to the finished text depicted as entirely straightforward, and we may reasonably ask whether they provide an economic explanation for that text.[51] As Jarick, 'Festival Scrolls', 177-79, points out, furthermore, those processes would have to have been accomplished swiftly, given the relatively short space of time between the likely date of composition and the earliest attestations of the text (on both of which, see below). If they remove inconsistencies within Qohelet's speech, finally, they do so only by

---

[50] Köhlmoos' presentation is unusual inasmuch as her 'Z' is not used primarily to resolve tensions or contradictions, but is depicted as sharpening the pessimism of the book, aligning it with outside traditions, and setting it more firmly against other incipient movements within Judaism. Although she claims, without specifics, that the 'Z' material exhibits stylistic differences, no very clear reason is offered for distinguishing this material.

[51] Or a necessary one. Of Siegfried's earlier but not dissimilar idea, that the original book was extensively supplemented by four further writers or glossators, with two epilogists and two editors subsequently inserting additional material, Barton (28) comments, 'It is built upon the supposition that absolutely but one type of thought can be harbored by a human mind while it is composing a book' (although he himself then goes on to identify additions by an editor and a Pharisaic glossator, 44-46). Condamin observes no less bluntly in 'Études', 8:503, that 'cependant cette méthode d'exégèse, en ce qui concerne l'Ecclésiaste, est entachée d'un vice radical: l'arbitraire', 'so far as Ecclesiastes is concerned, this method of exegesis is besmirched by a radical vice: arbitrariness', and goes on to note, in the course of a very thorough discussion, that Wildeboer's commentary, also then recently published, had found no need to divide Ecclesiastes that way. More recent commentators have sometimes gone further than denying a need: Gese, 'Komposition', for instance, argues that sections often characterized as secondary are in fact crucial to the structure of the book.

suggesting that subsequent editors have deliberately created such inconsistencies, and raising a whole new set of questions.[52]

Attempts to isolate different voices within the original composition, rather than in redactional layers, go back much further: Podechard ('Composition', 161-62) notes uses of this explanation even in patristic exegesis, and Bolin (*Ecclesiastes*, 69-71) discusses its role in Gregory of Nyssa's interpretation. At the beginning of the eighteenth century, John Yeard understood the monologue in terms of a Solomonic discourse which was interrupted at points by a 'Worldling'—so 2.24, for instance, could be understood as a declaration by this sensualist, followed by Solomon's response, with the worldling taking over completely for a while in 8.14–9.18.[53] More than a century later, and a little differently, Joseph Sutcliffe was to declare in the introduction to his commentary on Ecclesiastes that:

> This book is called in Hebrew קהלת CHOHELETH, convocator, or one who has collected the systems of moralists... It comprises a review of life, in which five speakers at least are introduced: the disgusted courtier—the philosopher—the stoick—the epicure—the preacher. Hence it abounds with variation of opinion, with discordant sentiments, and systems at issue with one another. For want of distinguishing those speakers, whose notions the preacher attacks,

---

[52] I shall not go into the broader issues here, but the Targum (see below) provides an interesting illustration of ways in which the meaning of a canonical text could be transformed by retaining but re-contextualizing its words. Hayman, 'Qohelet', 156-59, shows a slightly different way in which another early Jewish text counters Ecclesiastes through selective quotation and re-interpretation, and goes on to explore the similar treatments in rabbinic literature. If an editor did feel, for some unknown reason, a need to retain and transmit the words of a non-canonical work with which they disagreed, it is not clear why they would instead simply have included explicit qualifications and contradictions; cf. the forceful polemic against this approach in Provan, 32-33, and on Rose's assumptions in particular, see Weeks, *Ecclesiastes and Scepticism*, 10. In that respect, Coppens, in 'La structure', makes a more plausible claim when he supposes that the book emerged in stages, but that the same author was responsible for every stage—although his identification of the different elements is, naturally, highly speculative.

[53] Yeard, *New Paraphrase*. The author's name has been misprinted 'Ycard' on the title-page, and is often cited accordingly (the error is even replicated in a later re-print of the work); the 'F.' has also caused confusion, but probably stands for 'Father'. Similar views were expressed in the eighteenth century by, e.g., Moses Mendelssohn, Johann Herder and Johann Eichhorn—see Weeks, *The Making of Many Books*, 81-82, 114, 116-17, 119.

as in chap. 12, men have wrested the sentiments in this book to their own destruction. They are ignorant that the preacher, towards the close especially, speaks like himself, and as a sincere believer in Moses and the prophets. "Fear God, and keep his commandments, for this is the whole duty of man."

Heinemann's commentary of 1831 (p. 3) had a little earlier expressed a similar idea, and the looser notion that Qohelet cites a variety of opinions goes back among modern scholars at least to de Groot's commentary of 1644. It is not a view restricted to earlier such scholars, moreover, and among the important twentieth-century commentators, Levy, for instance, takes Qohelet at various points to be quoting and responding to the opinions of others (he reads 7.6b, for example, as the beginning of a response to views quoted in 7.1-6a), while Michel's commentary sees lengthy citations with responses as a key component of the monologue.[54] Modern writers who take this approach have more generally, though, moved away from any notion that the book is a formal dialogue or deliberate collection of different opinions, toward the rather different idea that Qohelet cites and responds, in a more restricted way, to existing sayings and aphorisms, which would have been recognized as such by the original audience.[55] This understanding, most closely associated with Gordis and Whybray, can offer such recognition as a partial explanation, at least, for the otherwise puzzling lack of any formal differentiation between the different voices—although Gordis also sometimes translates Qohelet's own words as introductions to the

---

[54] Helpfully, there is a list in his slightly later study: Michel, *Untersuchungen*, 245-46. Michel offers a justification for his approach in 'Qohelet-Probleme'.

[55] Michel aside, Perry, *Dialogues*, is the principal exception: Perry reads the book as a dialogic essay in which we hear two voices, belonging respectively to the pessimistic Qohelet ('K'), and a presenter ('P'), who responds to him. See also Loewenclau, 'Kohelet und Sokrates', which compares Qohelet's discourse to a Socratic dialogue, and more recently Greenwood, 'Debating Wisdom'. The approach should be distinguished from that of Zimmerli, who sees the book not as a formal dialogue, but as one side of a debate, in which Qohelet engages with a more conventional wisdom represented especially in Proverbs: the conventional wise man is a *Gesprächspartner*, or 'interlocutor' in a less formal sense, but Qohelet's own claims are only to be understood in the light of the claims he is attacking. See especially his Introduction (pp. 128-30), and 'Traktat oder Sentenzensammlung?'

thoughts of others—and even some scope for identification of likely quotations using form-critical techniques.[56]

I have distinguished the 'dialogue' and 'quotation' approaches above—although, truth be told, advocates of each sometimes make no clear distinction between them—principally because it is much easier to defend the possibility of isolated quotations in the text than to explain why any formal dialogue or interplay of voices seems to have been constructed so chaotically, and without any indication of the separate speakers. Being more defensible, however, does not imply that the approach is any more likely to be correct. To be sure, it is highly likely that Qohelet's words do include existing sayings, even if the epilogue at 12.9 probably does not, as often claimed, explicitly depict him as a collector of such sayings. As Fox has pointed out, though, in his 'Identification of Quotations' (a thoroughly sensible article on the subject), this does not make any significant difference to what we understand Qohelet to be saying, just so long as he is citing opinions with which he agrees. The difficulties begin if, like Gordis and others, we take any of his citations to be expressions of sentiments with which he disagrees. The supposition that when Qohelet says X then Y this should sometimes be interpreted '(people say) X (but I say) Y', is open to the very basic methodological questions that I have touched on with respect to all ideas about multiple voices in the monologue. As Fox puts it, moreover, 'Recognition of quotations…may become an all-purpose tool for artificial elimination of difficulties', and we cannot just label anything awkward as a quotation while retaining any semblance of exegetical integrity.

That is not to say, of course, that there are no expressions in the book of viewpoints with which Qohelet disagrees, and I take 1.10 and 2.26, in different ways, to include just such expressions. In those verses, though, the external claims are clearly marked and dismissed. Elsewhere, in 11.3-6 for example (and probably in the sayings that immediately precede those verses), Qohelet offers and then explicitly undermines advice that is deliberately absurd, and in

---

[56] Apart from their commentaries, see especially Gordis, 'Quotations in Wisdom Literature', and 'Quotations as a Literary Usage'; Whybray, 'Identification and Use'. A similar line has been pursued more recently in Spangenberg, 'Quotations in Ecclesiastes'.

7.1-6, I think, he makes claims designed to alienate the audience, which perhaps help drive him to a re-evaluation of his own assumptions. It would be wrong, therefore, to insist that every statement in the monologue offers an opinion with which Qohelet consistently agrees, but I doubt that the presence of such passages can be used to justify the identification of multiple, unmarked quotations: where they are not clearly marked, indeed, the extraordinary character of their content makes it likely that Qohelet is at best satirizing, rather than citing, the opinions of others.

More generally, matters are complicated, of course, by the relationship between Qohelet and the author of the book: it would not be difficult to make the case that any apparent tensions or inconsistencies in the monologue result from a conscious decision to draw these out, and that the writer does not intend us to find Qohelet entirely coherent. Such might be described, perhaps, as the presence in the text not of different voices, but of different intentions. I doubt, in fact, that we are supposed to be driven into disagreement specifically with Qohelet's views on, say, determinism or the afterlife, by our reaction to the problems that he uncovers—with the exception of wisdom, about which Qohelet is ultimately critical himself, no single issue, after all, receives sufficient focus. It seems no less unlikely, on the other hand, that Qohelet is simply a mouthpiece for the author's own opinions on every matter, and a degree of inconsistency could well be an element of his characterization.

If we insist on finding incoherence then that, or some other deliberate purpose, provides a simpler explanation either than a complicated literary history or the inclusion from the outset of unmarked, contrary opinions that do not belong to Qohelet himself. In some cases, furthermore, and perhaps especially with regard to aspects of Qohelet's determinism, it may be that we find difficulties which would not have been apparent to the author or the original audience, and that we are, in effect, holding the book to too high a standard. In any case, though, it will be clear already that I consider the actual degree of contradiction and incoherence often to have been overstated. On those few occasions when we do encounter potential instances, the proper approach is to seek an explanation in each case which does not simply remove material from the reckoning.

6. *Summary: the nature and purpose of the book*

Ecclesiastes presents itself as the words of a very clever but rather unusual individual, Qohelet, who has devoted his life to the pursuit of a particular problem. In a world where humans each make only a brief appearance, to live lives and to act out roles assigned to them within processes beyond their comprehension, what can they actually achieve on their own behalf and for their own benefit? From the outset, Qohelet examines alongside this the quality of wisdom and the experience of pleasure. Anticipating at first that wisdom will supply his answers, he very rapidly becomes disillusioned with it, to the point that he eventually finds himself incapable of being wise any more. Having initially dismissed pleasure as pointless, however, he comes to appreciate that it is, in fact, the only genuine compensation that humans will receive from God for their efforts, which offer them benefits only if they can find satisfaction in what they are doing. The scope of Qohelet's enquiries is very wide, and he examines various spheres of human life. Human relationships with the world are characterized almost throughout, however, by the failure of humans to appreciate the limitations that are placed upon them: they try to grasp what cannot be held, and to have some impact upon what cannot be influenced.

Despite the serious tone of Qohelet's remarks the book is also an entertainment, however, with its contents carefully crafted, as we shall see later, and its themes expressed in a wide variety of different ways. Whatever we are supposed to make of Qohelet from listening to his words, moreover, an epilogue suggests that we should not, perhaps, take them entirely to heart. It would probably not be correct, therefore, to see the book specifically as some sort of polemic, even if it does offer a significant critique of any human pretensions to wisdom and self-determination, and perhaps accordingly of other literature that promoted such ideas. It may have been a desire to advertise Ecclesiastes as on a par with such literature that motivated the inclusion of hints that Qohelet was Solomon, or like Solomon, but even that is not carried through with any great conviction. Especially given the mysterious epithet 'Qohelet' itself, therefore, and the character's eventual denial of his own wisdom, it seems unlikely that his words are really being attributed to Solomon, or that Qohelet is being set up as some alternative source of authority. We may like to place works within some broader intellectual movement or debate, and, as we shall see later, it is possible to align Qohelet's ideas with those of certain other works. The book itself offers little reason, though, to read it specifically as an attempt to overturn established ideas or to pick a fight with other authors, and its provocations are of a different order: Ecclesiastes invites us not to adopt some particular view of the world, but to react to the strong, often startling views of its protagonist. Ostriker ('Ecclesiastes', 8) talks of Qohelet inventing 'the thrill of disillusion', and claims 'a bracing exhilaration rises from his caustic treatment of everyone else's values'—which, I think, is very much the sort of response the book is after.

B. *The Date and Context of Ecclesiastes*

1. *Date*

For those interested in the history of ideas or in the development of early Judaism, the date of Ecclesiastes is potentially important, and a clear understanding of the context within which it was composed would certainly help us to assess more clearly the potential influences upon it from other sources: it is hard for us to talk about the book in relation to other texts or ideas without knowing, at least in very broad terms, when it was written. It is doubtful, on the other hand, that our understanding and interpretation of the book's message depends to any significant degree on its date: this is not a work explicitly intended to address a particular contemporary or historical situation, and it sets out, indeed, to tackle questions that are essentially universal—even if ultimately the constraints that Qohelet places upon the world involve presuppositions that not everyone would always have shared. If there are any allusions to particular people or events—which I am inclined to doubt—it is not clear that we would miss much by overlooking them. From an exegetical point of view, therefore, we can get along without requiring any absolute consensus in this area, so it may be a little surprising to find just how much has been written on this question in modern scholarship.

Two manuscripts of Ecclesiastes were found among the Dead Sea Scrolls, and we shall look at these in more detail below. The earlier (4QQoh[a]) has been dated palaeographically to the first half of the second century BCE—more precisely to around 175–150 BCE—and although this has not been confirmed by carbon-dating, so far as I am aware, such datings have proved broadly reliable.[57] We can consider a date around 150 BCE, therefore, as absolutely the last point at which the book might have been composed. This excludes some of the very latest dates that had been suggested previously,[58] but it is doubtful that we can establish any date still earlier than that, which would narrow the field further. The only significant argument made on linguistic grounds for the latest possible date has been that of Seow, who claims (in 'Linguistic Evidence', 653-54) that the use of a term *šlṭ*, particularly in 2.19, reflects a legal terminology that was confined to the Persian period. I shall discuss that in the notes to 2.19: suffice it to say here that the argument cannot be sustained. The many verbal resemblances between Ecclesiastes and Ben Sira that were identified by an earlier generation of scholars might also have trimmed off a few decades: there is some consensus that Ben Sira belongs to the first quarter of the second century, and if it actually cites Ecclesiastes, then Ecclesiastes itself is unlikely to have been written after the third. Those resemblances have been scrutinized in a series of studies over the last twenty-five years, however, and there is now much less confidence that Ben Sira knew Ecclesiastes.[59] More recently, there have been suggestions that allusions to Ecclesiastes are to be found in 1Q/4QMysteries, a work that is commonly dated around 200 BCE (see especially Lange, 'In Diskussion'). As Elgvin's review of these (in 'Use of Scripture', 128-29) shows, however, the only striking link is that work's single use of a Hebrew expression found otherwise only in 6.8 (*mh ywtr l-*, 'what is the advantage for?'; cf. 7.11 *ytr l-*, 'an advantage

---

[57] On the hand, see especially Cross, 'Oldest Manuscripts', 162; Muilenburg, 'A Qoheleth Scroll', 23-24. The word 'broadly' should be emphasized: the accuracy of such datings depends to a great extent on the availability of comparative materials, and can be affected by such factors as the length of a scribe's career.

[58] Graetz, arguing (12-13) that 8.3 must be referring to a tyrannical foreign king who was actually present in Palestine, and that 10.16 points to him being a *parvenu*, famously placed the book in the reign of Herod, a view that was also espoused by Cheyne in his *Jewish Religious Life*, 200-203. Cheyne notes the story in *b. Baba Batra* 4a, where Baba b. Buta, blinded and imprisoned by Herod, cites 10.20 as his reason for not cursing him.

[59] See especially Backhaus, 'Qohelet und Sirach'; Marböck, 'Kohelet und Sirach'; Gilbert, 'Qohelet et Ben Sira'; Gregory, 'Reassessment'. Marböck surveys earlier scholarship on the issue, and Gregory provides an overview of the more recent developments.

for'). This may belong with the linguistic evidence to which we shall turn shortly, but it does not show a knowledge of Ecclesiastes in particular. Goff ('Wisdom', 216) also dismisses those links, although he does suggest (223-24) that a passage in 4QInstruction, commonly dated to the third century, might respond to Ecclesiastes in a more general way. That is not impossible, but the text does not show a clear knowledge of the book. Rudman ('4QInstruction') in fact, reverses the order, and suggests that Ecclesiastes is responding to the sort of ideas found in 4QInstruction.

If we have to settle for the mid-second century as the latest date that can be established, matters are a little less clear cut when it comes to the earliest.[60]

(a) *Linguistic Evidence*

Much of the discussion about date has been driven in the past by the questions around the book's apparent attribution to Solomon (on which, see the commentary at 1.1). As is often noted, Huig de Groot (who wrote under the Latinized name 'Grotius') was the first modern scholar to raise these questions in his 1644 commentary,[61] but it is important to appreciate that he did so not because he was

---

[60] Delsman, *Datierung*, provides a helpful overview of the questions, and covers in more detail many of the issues that I shall discuss below. See also, more concisely, Longman, 'Determining'. To the normal evidence, Longman (96) adds the references to 'silver' or 'money' in 5.9; 7.12; and 10.19, which he takes to 'reflect a time after coinage has been introduced into Palestine' under the Persians. That may be true, but earlier uses, like Judg 9.4, undermine the probative value of those references.

[61] On the basis of a passage in the *Table Talk*, Ginsburg suggested long ago (on pp. 145-46 of his commentary) that Martin Luther, in fact, had much earlier attributed the book to Ben Sira, and that view, picked up by some others in the following decades, has more recently been affirmed by Bartholomew (p. 44 of his). Luther says of the book he is describing, however, that 'es viel seiner Lehre hat, wie man sich im Hausregiment halten soll. Dazu so ists wie ein Talmud aus vielen Büchern zusammen gezogen', 'it contains much useful information about how a household should be run. Furthermore, it is like a Talmud, drawn together out of many books': by no stretch of the imagination is this a recognisable description of Ecclesiastes, a book on which Luther had himself lectured. It seems certain that the record of this conversation has confused Ecclesiastes with Ecclesiasticus (Ben Sira). See Kroker, *D. Martin Luthers Werke Kritische Gesamtausgabe. Werke. Tischreden, 1. Band*, 207, for the text, and Jones, 'Solomon's Table Talk', for a more comprehensive refutation. Bolin, *Ecclesiastes*, 40-41, has some caustic

unable to reconcile the content with Solomon, but because he perceived the language of the book to demand a date of composition much later than the time of Solomon:

> *Ego...Solomonis esse non puto, sed scriptum serius sub illius regis, tanquam poenitentia ducti, nomine. Argumentum eius rei habeo multa uocabula, quae non alibi quam in Daniele, Esdra & Chaldeis interpretibus reperias* (521).

> ...I do not consider it Solomon's, but to have been written later in the name of that king, as though he were being driven by repentance. As an argument for that case, I have many items of vocabulary which you will not find anywhere else other than in Daniel, Ezra, and among the Aramaic translators.

De Groot then expanded on this in his note on 12.11 (pp. 539-40), which he believes to be talking about the actual authors of the book,

> *id est, qui haec colligerent, ac sub persona Solomonis in unum corpus congererent, mandatum habuere ab uno pastore, id est, ut puto, Zorobabele, qui, ob res tenues Iudaeorum, & Persici imperii reverentiam, regem se dicere non ausus, quanquam inter suos pro rege habebatur, nomen usurpauit modestius pastoris*

> That is, those who were to collect these things, and under the *persona* of Solomon bring them together into a single body of work, had a mandate to do so from a 'single shepherd'—that is, I think, Zerubbabel, who, because of the tenuous position of the Jews and out of a healthy respect for the Persian empire, dared not speak of himself as 'king' (though he was treated as a king among his own people) and took on the title of a more humble shepherd.

In other words, he understood Ecclesiastes to have been produced under the orders of a much later 'son of David', Zerubbabel, who was not willing to describe himself as a king, rather than as a shepherd (12.11; cf. Zech 11), but who laid claim to the identity of his royal predecessor.[62] His key evidence for this was that the vocabulary

---

remarks about the role of this idea in conservative debates about authorship, and takes pleasure 'in the irony that, to support the claim that Solomon didn't write something he was thought to have written, appeal was made to something Luther was thought to have said that he didn't say'.

[62] The same attribution is made in Weinberg, 'Authorship and Author', 166-69, which cites de Groot on the dating, but seems to be unaware that he linked the book to Zerubbabel. Weinberg, who in the same article attributes Job to Elihu,

of the book seems much closer to that of books written nearer the time of Zerubbabel, and this evidence naturally, therefore, became the initial point of departure both for those scholars who chose to follow de Groot, at least in denying Solomonic authorship, and for those who sought to prove him wrong. Since de Groot wrote, it would probably be fair to say that the language of Ecclesiastes has been subjected to closer examination, and been the object of more discussion than that of any other book in the Bible.[63]

To put the issues in a nutshell, there is a general agreement that Ecclesiastes uses many terms that are otherwise attested most commonly, sometimes only, in relatively late biblical literature or in much later rabbinic texts, and that elements of its syntax resemble later, not earlier Hebrew. For the great majority of scholars, this is an overwhelming argument for placing the book in the Persian or Hellenistic periods. Those who argue for an earlier date on various grounds generally point out, on the other hand, that terms which are only attested late need not have originated late, that other factors may have influenced the form or selection of words, and that there is little in the language of the book that is wholly without precedent in earlier compositions, even if some features are more common in later ones. At the risk of caricature, this has usually been in essence a debate between those who believe that a late date offers a single, simple explanation for at least most of the linguistic data, and those who seek a range of other explanations for those data because they find a late date incompatible with the contents or the attribution of the book.

---

believes (161) that where the author of a text 'was forgotten or it was considered undesirable to mention him' in a genre where it was conventional to provide an author's name, the name 'could be invented as in the cases of Job and Qohelet'. This is a misunderstanding, I think, of pseudonymity in ancient literature, but there have been a number of similar attempts to identify Qohelet as the *nom de plume* or *nom de guerre* of some known historical figure. Weinberg himself notes (166) a suggestion by J. Klausner in 1954, that the book was written by Hyrcanus, son of Joseph, which has recently been picked up by Sicker (4-11), while not long after de Groot, Hermann von der Hardt made a convoluted attempt to link it with the obscure Joshua son of Joiada, who is mentioned by Josephus in *Antiquities* 11.7.1: see his *Jesu Jojadae*. Grimme, 'Babel', associates it with Jehoiachin.

[63] There is a useful (if partisan) overview of modern scholarship in Gnanaraj, *Language of Qoheleth*. See also Bianchi, 'The Language of Qohelet'. Discussions of particular words and constructions are surveyed magisterially in Schoors, *The Preacher* I and *The Preacher* II.

Admittedly, matters have become yet more complicated over the last few decades. On the one hand, the discovery of the Qumran texts has made it clear that we cannot envisage the development of Hebrew in terms of a straight line, and certain of the features that link Ecclesiastes with later, mishnaic Hebrew, are absent or rare within those texts. Recent scholarship has also shown a much greater reluctance both to accept at face value the dates that are claimed by some biblical texts and to retain dates that have traditionally been assigned to others, so that it is more difficult to say with precision what is 'early' and what is 'late'—a problem compounded by the recognition of different registers of Hebrew, which led some late compositions to employ an earlier, conservative form of the language. Franz Delitzsch is often quoted as saying (in his commentary, p. 197) that, 'Wenn das B. Koheleth altsalomonisch wäre, so gäbe es keine Geschichte der hebräischen Sprache', 'if the Book of Qohelet were early and Solomonic, there would be no history of the Hebrew language', but although they might approve the general sentiment, few scholars today would subscribe to the rather simplistic model of development that lies behind that remark.

The question has been further complicated by several attempts to suggest that the book's Hebrew reflects the strong influence of some other language, either because it is a translation,[64] or because it was composed in a locality where such an influence was to be found

---

[64] For several decades in the twentieth century, a number of scholars held that Ecclesiastes was written originally in Aramaic. Although the idea had earlier been canvassed by Margoliouth, 'Ecclesiastes and Ecclesiasticus', 120, this was first formally proposed in a short note by Burkitt, 'Is Ecclesiastes a Translation?', and adopted swiftly by Fernández, 'Es Ecclesiastes una Versión?', who thought that further evidence was to be found in the difficulties surrounding השני in 4.15. Frank Zimmermann later made a more wide ranging case in two articles, 'Aramaic Provenance', and 'The Question of Hebrew in Qohelet', and was supported by Torrey, 'Question'. The best known statement of the position, though, has probably been that of H. L. Ginsberg, proposed in *Studies*, and defended in 'Supplementary Studies'. See also his 'The Quintessence of Koheleth'. Robert Gordis long supplied the principal arguments against the position, in 'The Original Language of Qohelet'; 'Translation Theory'; and 'Koheleth: Hebrew or Aramaic?' So far as I am aware, the theory has not found support more recently, and Charles Whitley's substantial examination demonstrates the considerable obstacles that lie in the way of any attempt to resurrect it; see especially his summary (106-10).

more generally.⁶⁵ Those attempts are not implausible in principle, and it is very likely that the book of Tobit, for instance, was translated from Aramaic into Hebrew because Hebrew literature carried greater prestige.⁶⁶ The particular arguments adduced for such a background to Ecclesiastes, however, have won few supporters, and if the purpose of a translation was indeed to situate the book within the Hebrew literary canon, it would seem strange for the translator to have adopted what most commentators regard as a curious, non-standard sort of Hebrew.⁶⁷

Although de Groot and many subsequent commentators focused on the use of 'Aramaisms' and on the attestations of particular vocabulary in late literature, the Hebrew of Ecclesiastes also shows affinities with later texts in certain aspects of its syntax—perhaps most notably the total displacement of the third-person plural feminine suffix pronoun *-hn* by its masculine equivalent *-hm* (see, e.g., Schoors, *The Preacher* I, 162-63). In other respects, however, its language is simply unexpected. To take a famous example,

---

⁶⁵ Following his thesis—'Canaanite-Phoenician Influence in Qoheleth'—a series of articles by Mitchell Dahood drew attention to supposed influences on Qohelet from Phoenician language and orthography: see especially 'The Language of Qoheleth'; most of the others are listed in the bibliography, but see also Weeks, *Ecclesiastes and Scepticism*, 41 n. 58. William Albright broadly accepted these suggestions by his student, and himself claimed that the author of Ecclesiastes 'was an influential Jew who lived...probably in southern Phoenicia'; his writings were intended to be Hebrew, but 'their written form betrays Phoenician influence in spelling, morphology, syntax, vocabulary, and content'; see Albright, 'Some Canaanite-Phoenician Sources', 15. Archer, 'Linguistic Evidence', has also defended Dahood, but most other scholars have been less sympathetic; see, e.g., Gordis, 'Was Koheleth a Phoenician?' and 'Qoheleth and Qumran'. Whitley reviews most of his suggestions, concluding that they often help to throw light on particular usages, but do not add up to evidence for his theory (111-18). Seow, 'Linguistic Evidence', 654-57, concludes that 'The possibility that some idioms in Qohelet are a result of Phoenician influences cannot be ruled out even though that possibility cannot be demonstrated beyond question'. Similar caution is expressed in Schoors' two volumes on the language of the book (see n. 63), which examine most of the proposals in detail.

⁶⁶ This is likely to be true not only of the single Hebrew text found at Qumran (where at least four Aramaic texts were discovered), but also, much later, of one of the medieval Hebrew versions: H6 in Weeks, Gathercole, and Stuckenbruck, *The Book of Tobit*.

⁶⁷ Delsman, 'Zur Sprache', offers a handy summary of the *hapax legomena* and other distinctive features in the language of the book.

Ecclesiastes very often uses *š-*, prefixed to the following word, where biblical Hebrew would typically use the relative particle *'šr*. This is an old usage, but one that is unusual and largely confined to poetic contexts in the Bible: it only becomes so commonplace in the Hebrew of much later rabbinic literature, and before that in Ecclesiastes, Song of Songs, and the Copper Scroll (3Q15) from Qumran. Of course, Song of Songs is another 'Solomonic' work, the date of which is itself disputed, but this is a somewhat eclectic group of texts, and it is hard to say why they alone should have pre-empted rabbinic usage in this respect. The most likely explanation is that *š-* was more common in speech, either as a colloquial[68] or as a dialectical form,[69] than it is in pre-rabbinic literature, and that these works represent a less standard, literary register of Hebrew than do others. We shall touch on this again below, but it is very difficult to be more precise than that—or to exclude the possibility that some of the book's other characteristics, usually attributed to a late date, are actually to be explained in the same way.

We should not try to suggest, then, that every peculiarity of the Hebrew in Ecclesiastes can be explained by dating the book late:

[68] Wise, 'A Calque', 250, sees 'Hebrew of a type much closer to the spoken language than that of any other postexilic book of the Bible—and, in fact, than that of most Hebrew works of the entire Second Temple period', and Isaksson, *Studies*, 138, remarks similarly that 'the idiom of Qoheleth in many respects comes closer to the spoken language than the "standard" narrative Hebrew'. See also Müller, 'Kolloquialsprache', 17, which sees colloquial features in both Ecclesiastes and Song of Songs. Since we obviously have no direct access to ancient spoken Hebrew, documentary texts are particularly important as a source of insight, and links with the Copper Scroll especially so: the errors and orthographic curiosities of that text might be taken to suggest that its writer had little concern with (or perhaps knowledge of) scribal niceties and conventions; cf. Piotti, 'La lingua', 193-94.

[69] The idea that the language of Ecclesiastes represents a northern dialect of Hebrew cannot be divorced altogether from Dahood's suggestions of Phoenician influence (see n. 65), but the case has been put on broader grounds in Davila, 'Qoheleth and Northern Hebrew', and Ecclesiastes is sometimes cited in studies that attempt to find the roots of mishnaic Hebrew in the North; see, e.g., Gordon, 'North Israelite Influence'; Rendsburg, 'Galilean Background'. Seow, 'Linguistic Evidence', 665, voices a not uncommon suspicion when he says more generally 'the possibility that the Hebrew of Qohelet reflects a non-Judean dialect cannot be ruled out, although it is difficult to identify the dialect specifically'. Our actual knowledge of specific Hebrew dialects is so limited, however, that almost any statement in this area is highly speculative.

it is not simply the language typical of literature from any period, so far as we know, but has its own, distinctive character—and that distinctiveness is no doubt compounded by the differences between the content of the book and that of most other early Hebrew literature. Correspondingly, it would be difficult to prove beyond doubt on the basis of its Hebrew alone that the book dates to any period in particular. On the other hand, its distinctiveness tells against Ecclesiastes being a translation, and is explained no more easily by those who favour an early date than by those who would put it late. It seems unlikely, furthermore, that everything which distinguishes this book from others linguistically can be attributed to factors other than date: de Groot's observations about vocabulary remain valid, and it is manifestly simpler to explain 'late' expressions in the book as the result of a late date of composition than in any other way.[70]

To take just a few clear examples of these: *ḥwṣ mn*, 'except for', is found nowhere in biblical Hebrew other than 2.25, but is common in later Hebrew; *kbr*, 'already', is used in later Hebrew and nine times in Ecclesiastes, but nowhere else in the Bible; the noun *zmn*, 'occasion', is used in 3.1 and elsewhere only in the indisputably late books of Ezra, Nehemiah, Esther, and Daniel;[71] *kʾḥd* is similarly found with the sense 'together' or 'alike' only in 11.6 and other late texts. Many other terms can and have been adduced, but these four examples are particularly striking because we have no reason to believe that any of them is colloquial or dialectal, and none of them has a meaning that is in any way technical or obscure. We may freely allow, of course, that any one of these expressions might actually be early, and have avoided inclusion in earlier Hebrew

---

[70] Studies of the syntax and other characteristics of the language are necessarily more complicated, not least because comparisons have to be made with materials that are generally very different in terms of style or content, while Ecclesiastes itself arguably contains different types of discourse, in which verbal or other elements may behave differently (cf. Hays, 'Verb Forms'). Isaksson, *Studies*, is reluctant to draw conclusions about date from his examination of verbs, but see, e.g., Joosten, 'Volitive Verbal Forms', and Cook, 'The Verb in Qohelet', for more positive affirmations that the language is late in this respect also.

[71] Hurvitz, 'Language of Qoheleth', 26-29, offers a detailed study of this word, concluding that it 'came into Late Biblical Hebrew from Aramaic no earlier than the second half of the fifth century BCE'. Mroczek, 'Aramaisms', 350-51, protests unpersuasively that a cognate was used earlier in Akkadian, and that *zmn* may simply have been unusual in pre-exilic Hebrew.

literature simply by chance. The odds shift significantly, however, with each additional case, and if we factor in expressions that are not unknown in earlier texts but much more common in later ones, then it is much harder to explain Ecclesiastes as a product of the monarchic than of some later period.[72]

Particular issues surround the use in the book of expressions that probably did not originate in Hebrew. Aramaic terms predominate in this category, but are generally unhelpful as a criterion for dating: although the influence of Aramaic is undoubtedly more marked in many texts that can be dated late, various forms of Aramaic are likely to have influenced Hebrew throughout its history. It can sometimes be difficult, furthermore, to say for certain whether a word originated in Aramaic rather than in Hebrew, or whether it might, indeed, have been inherited from elsewhere by both languages. Particular words or phrases may be noted, of course, and we might observe, for example, that the noun *šlṭwn* used in 8.4 and 8.8, is found in no early Hebrew sources, while the cognate verb *šlṭ*, used in 2.19; 5.18; 6.2 and 8.9, is found elsewhere only in Est 9.1 and Neh 5.15 (see, e.g., Hurvitz, 'Chronological Significance', 239). These Aramaic terms do not seem to have entered the vocabulary of Hebrew writers before the Persian period, and they represent common but quite nuanced ideas around the exercise of power: if they were known earlier, it is hard to explain why they were not used.[73] Indeed, if these are actually uses by the cosmopolitan Solomon—which is the sort of explanation favoured by early opponents of de Groot—then

---

[72] In his review of the vocabulary, Fredericks, *Qoheleth's Language*, 206-207, allows that *ḥwṣ mn* and *kʾḥd* are late, also adding *tqp*, 'prevail'—although he sees the last as a possible Aramaism and the others as calques on Aramaic expressions. The extremely strict criteria that he applies, including the exclusion from consideration of talmudic (as opposed to mishnaic) Hebrew, set the hurdle extremely high for the inclusion of anything as either late Hebrew or Aramaic, and are open to criticism. All the same, after such methodological purism, it is curious to find in his conclusion that since these accepted words 'have parallels only in Imperial Aramaic or LBH [Late Biblical Hebrew]' they 'may give slight evidence of a later writing than the grammar alone would suggest, thus a date in the pre-exilic era, in the eighth or seventh century B.C. might be recommended' (263). This is a methodologically indefensible compromise.

[73] From the same root, we do have השליט in Gen 42.6, as Mroczek, 'Aramaisms', 348, notes. That may, of course, say more about the date of the Joseph story in its present form than about the antiquity of the usage.

we have to explain either how he expected his fellow Jews to understand them, or why nobody else chose to use them for the next few hundred years. While we must not take the presence of Aramaic as definitive proof for a late date in itself, individual cases can potentially provide solid evidence.[74]

The number of expressions from other languages is much smaller, and where Hebrew terms have been described as calques on foreign phrases, rather than actual borrowings, it is more difficult to make secure connections. Without the complication of a long relationship, which affects the evaluation of Aramaic usages, such loanwords do offer, however, evidence that is potentially more specific. The most important instance is the word *prds*, which occurs in 2.5, and elsewhere in Neh 2.8 and Ct 4.13.[75] This is related not only to our own word 'paradise', but to the Greek παράδεισος, the earliest appearances of which are in Xenophon's fourth-century descriptions of wooded estates used by the Persian kings:[76] the context and presentation of the term suggest that he is using it as a loanword. In Old Persian, *paridaida* would refer to 'walling around', but that term does not actually appear in any of our limited Old Persian

---

[74] The same is potentially true for the many links with Phoenician that have been claimed by Dahood, and Seow, 'Linguistic Evidence', 656, is attracted to his idea that 'beneath the sun', a common expression in Ecclesiastes, should be linked to some Persian-period uses of this expression: see the notes at 1.3. In general, though, whether Dahood has made his case or not, the potential influence of Phoenician is not so linked to any particular period that it can be used as a criterion for dating.

[75] The most comprehensive discussion that I know of this word's use in Greek and Near Eastern sources is to be found in Tuplin, *Achaemenid Studies*, 80-131; see also Stronach, 'The Garden'.

[76] Xenophon *Anabasis* 1.2.7 describes an area bisected by a river and filled with wild animals, which Cyrus used to hunt (also mentioned in his *Cyropaedia* 1.3.14), while 2.4.14 describes a large, beautiful and heavily forested area (cf. Plutarch, *Artaxerxes* 25, where trees are similarly the dominant feature). The *Hellenica* (4.1.15) again speaks of wild animals in such areas. Stronach, 'The Garden', 179 n. 36, summarizes: 'From most extant classical accounts it does in fact appear that the term "paradise" was used to refer to a park-like estate in which the regular features included trees, other produce, running water, and animals for hunting'. Tuplin, *Achaemenid Studies*, argues persuasively that, although the same term is used for both in descriptions of the Persian context, we should distinguish between 'paradises' used for hunting and 'botanical' ones (see especially pp. 100, 108-109).

sources, and the *pairi-daêzãn* found in much later Avestan Persian refers to something different.⁷⁷ The anomalous *-s-* (rather than *-d-*) suggests, in fact, that the Persians may themselves have adopted it originally as a loanword, or used a dialectal form: the Achaemenid kings took over from Median ones, who would have used the term *paridaiza* (see Şahin, 'Die Sprache Der Meder', 106), and they perhaps inherited this term along with an existing institution. For a few scholars over the years, though, the discrepancy has suggested a possibility that the word might have entered Hebrew independently, and might possibly have done so before the rise of the Achaemenid empire led to a more widespread adoption of Persian terminology— were there any weight in that possibility, of course, the term would be of limited value as a criterion for dating. Indeed, if it was not borrowed as a Persian term at all, but directly from, say, Sanskrit (where the cognate term is *paridhis*) or some other language, then it would be useless to protest even that other Persian loanwords commonly identified in Hebrew seem to appear only in literature generally dated to the Persian period and later.⁷⁸

Against such speculative possibilities, however, we should take note of two facts. The first is that the word came to be adopted in a number of other languages during the Achaemenid period, but in none, so far as we can tell, before that period. The second, not unrelated fact is that it seems to have been borrowed initially to describe a phenomenon or phenomena associated with Persia and its monarchy in particular. This is obvious in Xenophon, of course, but we may note that the Hebrew *prds* in Neh 2.8 also refers to an Achaemenid royal forest, from which timber can be extracted, and the limited uses of the word in Akkadian (which begin shortly after the conquest of Babylon, and probably all date from the Achaemenid period, see *CAD*) seem to associate it with the grounds of a palace. In Ptolemaic Greek documents from Egypt, we find a more extended use of παράδεισος to describe not parks, as such, but a variety of orchards or similar plots of land, sometimes very

---

⁷⁷ In *Videvdat* 3.18; 5.49 = 7.64 it appears in the expression *pairi-daêzãn pairi-daêzayãn*, referring to the erection of a cell or enclosure in which an unclean man or woman is to be imprisoned, and literally means 'building a barrier around'.

⁷⁸ For an older opinion that the word may be much earlier than Persian, see, e.g., Delitzsch, *Wo lag das Paradies?*, 95-97. On the dating of other Persian loanwords found in the Hebrew Bible, see Seow, 'Linguistic Evidence', 647-48.

small,[79] and if the Elamite word *partetaš* is a borrowing of *paridaida / paridaiza*, which is far from certain, then it is possible that the word had a wider application inside Persia itself as early as the fifth century.[80] The later Greek usage is essentially the same as that found in subsequent Hebrew and Jewish Aramaic sources, and fits well with the uses in Eccles 2.5 and Ct 4.13; if Lemaire is right to read *prds* in a fourth-century Aramaic document from Idumea, which is talking about olives, then that too is presumably referring to a grove or orchard.[81]

All of this is compatible with a simple supposition that, whether it originated in Persian or not, *paridaida / paridaiza* was picked up in other languages during the period of the Achaemenid empire, initially to describe particular types of land associated with the

---

[79] We shall touch on this development below and in the notes to 2.5.

[80] *Partetaš* is attested in a large number of the Persepolis fortification texts. The claim that it is a borrowing from Old Persian is found in, e.g., Hinz, 'Die elamischen Buchungstäfeichen', 425; cf. his *Altiranisches Sprachgut*, 179. Hallock, the editor of the texts in question, had already addressed a similar suggestion by Benveniste, pointing out that the Elamite usually refers to a place where fruit or grain is to be stored, generally after being deposited to someone's account, which hardly suits the presumed sense of the Persian; see Hallock, *Persepolis Fortification Tablets*, 15. In a few places (e.g. tablets 150, 1815), the *partetaš* seems to be a place where workers are located, so we are dealing with something more than a cupboard, and Hinz thinks of a 'domain', but the reference is apparently to a structure or institution that is at least partially covered. Although the Persepolis tablets naturally include many loanwords from Persian, the link is very uncertain and remains controversial; if there was a borrowing, though, perhaps it was of the Persian word in its literal sense, not of the possibly Median technical term. For a helpful discussion, with a fuller account of the debate, see Tuplin, *Achaemenid Studies*, 93-96.

[81] Lemaire, *Nouvelles inscriptions araméennes*, 208. Lemaire is discussing the ostracon published as no. 186 in Eph'al and Naveh, *Aramaic Ostraca*, 84; the editors read the awkward *prws*, which they translate 'divided (?)'. Judging from the photograph (p. 85), both readings are possible. The next word is more difficult to read: the editors understand *'l*, so that the product is 'divided to 10', which also seems awkward. Were we to read *prds*, we should perhaps expect a proper name, as in the *gnt qws*, 'the grove of Qaus', which is found on the preceding ostracon 185. The texts in this corpus probably date from around 362–312 BCE (cf. Lemaire's discussion on pp. 199-201), so this use of *prds* may be from around the same time as an occurrence found in 4Q206 frag. 3, 21 (1 En 32.3), which refers to a *prds qšṭ'*, 'the grove of truth' or 'righteousness', characterized by tall trees, and another on 6Q8 frag. 2, 3, which lacks a clear context. I am aware of no earlier uses in Aramaic.

Persian crown, but thereafter more generally in some of those languages to describe plantations or agricultural plots that had no royal connection, and that could vary greatly in size. The particular associations of 'building round' with land or trees is not inherent in the etymology of the word, and the Sanskrit equivalent is not typically used in the same way: if *prds* entered Hebrew quite independently from some other Indo-European source, it is unlikely that it would have done so bearing these same connotations. If it did come from Persian, on the other hand, but entered Hebrew earlier than it entered other languages, then it is hard to see what, before Achaemenid times, would have necessitated the borrowing of a term that was strongly associated at first with land belonging to the Persian crown. Any moderately sensible explanation that did not involve the dating of Ecclesiastes at some point in the fifth century or later would have to envisage a much more complicated double borrowing, in which the term first entered Hebrew from some unknown source, with a more general meaning that happened to coincide with later Greek and Aramaic uses, and was then re-interpreted or re-borrowed in Nehemiah to correspond with Persian usage—and that is essentially the implication of, for example, Young and Rezetko's claim that the word might have come from Sanskrit, or via some unattested Indo-European language (*Linguistic Dating*, 1:301-302; cf. Young, *Diversity*, 161-62).

If that more complicated explanation did not already strain credulity, then it is surely rendered wholly untenable by the fact that Ecclesiastes contains a second term that is most readily understood as a loanword from Persian: *ptgm* in 8.11 (although Young and Rezetko in the same place try to link this also with Sanskrit or some other language; cf. Young, *Diversity*, 70-71). We know less about the history of this word, and it is correspondingly harder to place the borrowing in a broader context, but it appears in no Hebrew sources that might be considered earlier than the Achaemenid period (the only other biblical use is in Est 1.20), and, although our earlier sources are admittedly less numerous, attestations in Aramaic are all from the fifth century or later (see Seow, 'Linguistic Evidence', 650). Among these we might note a use that illustrates how such terms came to be transferred from one language to another through administrative use: an Aramaic letter written in 353 BCE by a Persian official in the satrapy of Bactria uses *ptgm* to describe an 'official notification' or 'protest' against the taxation of royal camel-keepers (which cannot be delivered because the other official concerned has gone away before it can be issued to him), and the Aramaic letters in this corpus more generally contain a large number of Persian words (see Naveh and Shaked, *Aramaic Documents*, 68-69). With local administrators applying them to official procedures and institutions in their communications, it is not hard to see how or why such 'Persianisms' appeared in Hebrew and Aramaic during more than two centuries of Persian dominance in the Near East (just as, conversely, many Aramaic words travelled in the other direction, eventually appearing in Middle Persian). In the case of neither *prds* nor *ptgm*, moreover, do we have either attested alternatives from any other period that offer an equally plausible origin, or any reason to view the normal derivations as problematic. A date for Ecclesiastes in the Persian period or later, therefore, makes it easy to explain the presence of these two words, and conforms with ample other evidence; a date any earlier than that would require resort to complicated and unnecessarily speculative explanations for each.

Looking later still, it is unlikely that any of the words used in Ecclesiastes are Greek in origin, but it has often been suggested that particular expressions reflect Greek rather than Hebrew usage.[82] Of course, it is not easy to verify such claims: similar idioms can develop independently, and, when foreign influence does seem probable, it can be hard to exclude other potential sources: Qohelet's references to activity 'under the sun', for instance, undoubtedly match a familiar Greek usage, but the same expression is found in Phoenician inscriptions (see Seow on 1.3), while it would not be astonishing if the author came up with the phrase without knowing either the Greek or the Phoenician uses. Other proposals are discussed in the notes to the commentary, but the most compelling

---

[82] Although parallels had long been noted, it seems to have been Zirkel, in his 1792 *Untersuchungen*, who first suggested that the author was more familiar with Greek than Hebrew (see especially 118-19)—his idea, and even the way he expressed it, is echoed (apparently unconsciously) in the title of Buhlmann's more recent 'Thinking in Greek'. Subsequent reactions have ranged from eager acceptance (Graetz devotes a whole appendix to his consideration of instances) to outright rejection (as, e.g., Johnston, 'Alleged Grecisms'; cf. Kaiser, 'Judentum und Hellenismus', 137-38).

case for specifically Greek influence can be made for the use of ʿśh in 6.12 to mean 'spend (a period of time)': that verb (which usually means 'make') does not take a period of time as a direct object anywhere else in Hebrew to give such a sense, but Greek readily refers to 'making a day', or some other period, when it means 'spending' it. Of course, we cannot exclude the possibility of a parallel semantic development in Hebrew, but the idiom is absent from later Hebrew texts, so any such development would have to have been localized or short-lived.[83] Greek influence on the author's Hebrew offers a simpler explanation in this case.

Having said above that *prds* was not necessarily derived directly from Persian, moreover, it is important to note the possibility that its use in 2.5 reflects Greek rather than Persian usage.[84] Neither there nor in Ct 4.13, where the reference is to a pomegranate orchard, do we find any link with Persia, and Ct 4.13, at least, definitely has no royal connection. This aligns the usage with the very common uses of παράδεισος, in Greek papyri and other sources, to indicate orchards and groves that varied greatly in size and content.[85] That

---

[83] I am not sure what Seow, 'Linguistic Evidence', 658-59, is trying to demonstrate by noting a parallel in Middle Egyptian, and one possible use in Akkadian of a similar idiom: Greek is a more probable source of influence than either, even if 'there is nothing distinctly Hellenistic about the idiom'.

[84] Greek influence on agricultural terminology in the Hellenistic period is by no means improbable. There is another possible instance in the fourth-century Aramaic ostraca from Idumea which we encountered above (n. 81) in connection with *prds*: a word *kph* occurs several times (185:3; 189:4; 193:2; cf. *kpy* 188:4), and the editors suggest very plausibly that it is a borrowing from the Greek κῆπος, 'orchard, grove'; see Ephʿal and Naveh, *Aramaic Ostraca*, 84.

[85] Lee, *Lexical Study*, 53-56, shows that by the third century BCE the word had been popularized in Greek, and it appears in papyri as a common agricultural term: 'It is clear first of all that a παράδεισος was composed chiefly of fruit-trees of various kinds... παράδεισοι are mentioned frequently in the papyri and were clearly a common feature of agriculture in Ptolemaic Egypt... A παράδεισος, then, may be defined as "an area of cultivated ground containing chiefly fruit-trees, at times also other types of tree, vines, and possibly other plants, and perhaps protected by a wall." There is no exact equivalent to this term in English. "Orchard" is probably the nearest to it. "Garden" is unsatisfactory...' (pp. 54-55). Gwynn, 'Notes', 121, observes also a link with vegetables. This sense appears in the Septuagint (e.g. Jer 36.5 [= M 29.5], where παράδεισοι produce fruit), and the Greek Sir 24.30-31 speaks of irrigating a παράδεισος alongside a κῆπος; the issue of Septuagint usage is complicated, however, both by issues of translational equivalence and, perhaps, by a growing association of 'paradise'

seems to be a secondary development within the Greek spoken in areas formerly ruled by Persia, not indicating a shift in reference from high-status to low-status property, so much as a willingness to apply the foreign word to more familiar local environments. It is important exegetically—as we shall see in the commentary, a sense similar to that in Ct 4.13 is more appropriate for *prds* in Eccles 2.5 than is some idea of 'royal parks'—but it also has implications for the date. Whether the shift has actually been influenced by the shift in Greek (and possibly Aramaic), or whether it has happened independently in Hebrew, the fact that Eccles 2.5 and Ct 4.13 both show such assimilation of this foreign word does suggest that those passages post-date its initial introduction. It perhaps implies more specifically, indeed, that both are later than Neh 2.8, and were composed at a point when *prds* had already become a normal agricultural term in Hebrew, as it is in later rabbinic texts.[86]

In any case, from all that has been said, it will be clear that the linguistic data do not offer absolute certainty in the area of dating. Even making allowance for the fact that the Hebrew of Ecclesiastes is simply peculiar in some ways, they do, however, make it highly unlikely that the book was written before the Achaemenid period, and offer some grounds to suppose that it may be later. Any scholar wishing to date the work earlier has to explain not only the presence in the text of Hebrew words and usages that are rare or unknown in earlier Hebrew, but also the appearance of expressions seemingly borrowed from other languages that, so far as we know, exercised little or no influence on Hebrew before this time. There remains a

with the 'garden of God'. The size, distribution, and many other details about παράδεισοι are discussed in Tuplin, *Achaemenid Studies*, 80-131. He calculates from a large sample (p. 98) that the median size of Egyptian παράδεισοι is only about 0.25 hectares, and the commonest size in one region is only half that. For comparison, a soccer pitch conforming to FIFA standards can be 0.62 ha to 0.82 ha in area, and Major League Baseball fields vary between 0.83 ha and 1.12 ha, so the latter could accommodate three or four middling παράδεισοι.

[86] So Bickerman, *Four Strange Books*, 141, '...*pardes* means orchard; that is how *paradeisos* was used by the Greek administration... Therefore, Ecclesiastes must have been written in the third century, when Jerusalem and Palestine were under the domination of the Ptolemies.' Given the broad usage of *ptgm* as well, I doubt that the appearance of these words in the book can be taken to suggest the sort of knowledge of, or preoccupation with Persian royal ideology, in particular, which Bolin, *Ecclesiastes*, 48-49, sees behind Qohelet's depictions of kingship and God.

healthy debate around these issues, and discussions have certainly moved on from the simplistic paradigms with which some earlier scholars worked. The existence of the debate, however, should not be taken to suggest that there are broad divisions within scholarship over this matter: the overwhelming majority of scholars who have worked with the book believe that the language of Ecclesiastes dates it no earlier than about the fifth century, and they have good reasons for doing so.

(b) *Historical References*
I have already expressed some scepticism toward the idea that the book contains allusions to specific people or events, but ancient readers and modern commentators alike have long tried to identify such references. Some early Jewish interpreters viewed Ecclesiastes as a work of prophecy, and in his commentary Jerome reports a reading of 12.2-7 as a prediction of events that will befall Israel with the coming of Babylonian and Roman invaders, and the subsequent destructions of the Jerusalem temple. Such predictive readings aside, interpreters have generally found two different sorts of reference: to earlier historical events or biblical stories, and to more contemporary figures and situations.

The two scholars most closely associated with the former see different forces at work: for Gottlieb Kaiser, writing his *Koheleth, das Collectivum* in 1823, Ecclesiastes was a symbolic, almost allegorical account of the Judahite monarchy, while Jennie Barbour, writing her *The Story of Israel* much more recently, sees the book less as a sort of riddle, and more as a work that bears an unconscious cultural, intertextual imprint, with its discourse shaped by the 'historical habit of imagination' (3) which she attributes to the Jewish intellectual culture of the time. In practice, though, this does not always lead them to very different results. Both notably, although in different ways, see Qohelet as a 'collective' (Kaiser) or 'composite' (Barbour) representative of monarchy, while on a more specific level, the brief story in 9.13-15, for instance, is read by Kaiser (114-15) as an account of the Babylonian siege of Jerusalem, with Jeremiah as the poor, wise man, while for Barbour it is a reflection on the Assyrian attack in 701, with Isaiah in that role. Where they differ most obviously is in their assessment of the links that they find: Kaiser is largely content just to identify the kings and stories, while Barbour explores more wide-ranging implications—so, for instance, she takes Qohelet to have transformed the account of 701 from a celebration into a critique.

It is difficult to evaluate such readings. They necessarily rely, of course, on specific understandings of a text that is often difficult—and in the case of 9.13-15, for instance, my own understanding that Qohelet is saying that the city would not be saved were it attacked, and not talking about its actual salvation, makes it much more difficult to see a link with 701. In general, Barbour's broader conceptualization allows her to escape the constraints imposed on Kaiser's allegorical approach, which often seems forced. Its very breadth, on the other hand, presents methodological problems of its own: should we follow Barbour (119-22), for instance, in linking the anonymity of the king in this story with a similar tendency to anonymize in Ben Sira, and thence to an implicit critique of royalty? Or should we simply observe that none of the many characters mentioned by Qohelet bears a name, which might be taken as an attempt to ensure that they are read as types, not as historical individuals? It is a reasonable supposition that Qohelet's discourse has been shaped by the literary and intellectual presuppositions of the book's author, and it is interesting to identify possible influences, but when we make this a matter of allusion, or assign to it even an unconscious purpose, then there is a real risk of emphasizing some links over others without good reason.

For practical purposes, then perhaps the most important point to be made here is that significant uncertainties surround all the identifications proposed by both Kaiser and Barbour, making it difficult to adduce them as evidence for the date of Ecclesiastes. If both of them are right to see references to the fall of Jerusalem at different points, then these analyses, to be sure, lend some additional weight to the linguistic evidence placing the book after the period of the monarchy—although the texts that they adduce are so susceptible to other interpretations that this weight is very limited. Considering the broader issues, however, we may reasonably ask how plausible such approaches to the book are in the first place. Whether Qohelet shows an explicit interest or not in history is largely a matter of how one understands certain of his statements. If (with Barbour, 40-41) we read 1.13-14 or 8.16 as declarations that Qohelet investigated everything 'that has been done', then there might indeed be an implication that he has studied human history. In the context of the question that ends 1.13, however, and of the actual investigations that follow, commentators have generally been more inclined to take his topic as 'all that humans do'. Shortly before, in 1.11, Qohelet has declared that 'there is no memory of the earlier times', and although this has been variously understood, it is hardly an acclamation of the past as important. Whatever significance we attach to intertextuality as a way of reading Ecclesiastes, therefore, to see it actually as a deliberate work of history, in any sense, seems to stand in virtual contradiction to the ideas of its protagonist.

The other approach to events in Ecclesiastes, which seeks contemporary references, is obviously different in this respect, and does not impute to Qohelet a particular historical consciousness. Indeed, since many of his statements about wealth and society are clearly 'political' in a general way, it would be by no means astonishing if he were to address the contemporary context more specifically. The problem is that, if he does at all, he does not do so in a way that is explicit to us. Again, moreover, much tends to depend on the understanding of texts that are difficult—most notably 4.13-16, where many scholars have been inclined to find a tale of contemporary politics,[87] while others (myself included) find no tale at all. A distinction has to be made, of course, between readings that presume a certain date, and those that adduce evidence for dating. For example, if we suppose that Ecclesiastes dates to Ptolemaic times, then the situation described in 5.7-8 may well be an accurate reflection of the contemporary situation—but the description is far too generic for us to declare that Qohelet can only be talking about those times. Unfortunately, almost all the potentially relevant material falls into that category, and we can hardly specify that the concerns of, say, 10.20, would only have been felt in some particular period.[88] Studies that attempt to understand the book against the social and political background of the Persian

---

[87] E.g., Schunck, 'Drei Seleukiden'; Ogden, 'Historical Allusion'; Fox, 'What Happens?'

[88] Addressing himself to Seow, 'Socioeconomic Context', James Crenshaw rightly asks, 'Apart from the problem presented by any literary work...how many eras of the past are distinctive enough to be recognizable millennia later?'; see his 'Qoheleth's Understanding', 210. Proven adds the further objection that the writer may have imagined Qohelet into contexts or situations that were not his own: 'The imagination of the commentator has not come near to reckoning with the imagination of the speaker' (28).

(e.g. Seow, 21-35) or Hellenistic[89] periods are quite legitimate and may throw light on the content, but the fact that they find a fit does not in itself offer evidence for that date.

Such evidence, in the form of more specific allusions, is harder to find. Krüger makes a suggestion in passing that Qohelet's characteristic expression 'under the sun' is a veiled reference to an association between Ptolemy V and the sun-god, which would be a little more plausible if the use of that expression were not so often varied by 'under the heavens', which can carry no such nuance—an argument also against Gericke ('Injustice') which sees a more general polemic against solar mythology. If 4.13-16 does include a reference to royal succession, then it is apparently not specific enough, because a number of different players have been suggested—while no very good fit, on the other hand, has been found for 10.16-17, if that is likewise not just a pair of general aphorisms (the key passages and suggestions are summarized in Lauha, 'Verhältnis'). In short, therefore, modern scholars have found no difficulty in reading Ecclesiastes against the background of various periods (just as their predecessors read the book against a Solomonic background), but little or nothing has been identified that points unequivocally to one specific period.

(c) *Literary References*

There is one very close parallel between Ecclesiastes and another composition: the first part of 5.3 resembles the first part of Deut 23.22 (ET 23.21):

> Eccles 5.3: *kʾšr tdr ndr lʾlhym ʾl tʾḥr lšlmw*, 'when you have vowed a vow to God, do not delay to fulfil it.

> Deut 23.22: *ky tdr ndr lyhwh ʾlhyk lʾ tʾḥr lšlmw*, 'if you have vowed a vow to YHWH your God, do not delay to fulfil it.

---

[89] E.g. Jong, 'Ambitious Spirit'; cf. his 'Quitate de mi Sol'; Tamez, 'Reading from the Periphery'. More self-consciously 'sociological' approaches to Ecclesiastes have started to play a significant role in recent scholarship; see, e.g., Harrison, 'Qoheleth', and especially Sneed, *Politics of Pessimism*. Although these potentially illuminate important aspects of the book, they are vulnerable, of course, to problems of interpretation in key passages, and often open to the charge of neglecting both the significance of literary convention in the book and the distinctions that have to be made between the author and his protagonist.

It seems highly probable that there is literary dependence here, or at least that the text in Ecclesiastes involves a recollection of that in Deuteronomy—especially since the subsequent 5.4 can then be read as paraphrasing the next two verses of Deuteronomy.[90] More loosely, the repeated statement in 4.1 'and there is no-one to comfort them' is strongly reminiscent of expressions that occur in Lam 1.2, 9, 16, 17, 21, and the language of seeking and finding in 7.28 is close to that of Ct 3.1-4. It is a reasonable supposition that these resemblances in Lamentations and Song of Songs represent deliberate allusion (as Seow points out in the latter case), although the allusion might conceivably be to the traditions of composition in which those texts are usually understood to stand, rather than directly to the texts themselves. Since no precise dates are agreed for these texts, the references do not help us to pin down the date of Ecclesiastes, although they probably exclude the monarchic period. If there is a reference to personified wisdom in ch. 7, as I have suggested above, then this would point to a date in or after the Persian period: that concept was probably not familiar before Proverbs 1–9, which is itself usually dated to that time.[91] Although links with the early chapters of Genesis are also commonly asserted, I doubt that there is any specific reference.[92] If there were, it would again add little to our knowledge of the date.

---

[90] See especially Levinson, *A More Perfect Torah*, and his 'Better that You Should Not Vow'. Levinson sees a deliberate re-working of the Deuteronomic law to present the breaking of vows as a risky sort of foolishness, rather than as a punishable breach of the Torah.

[91] On the probability that the personification originated in Prov 1–9, see Weeks, *Instruction and Imagery*, 124-25, and on the date, 156-58.

[92] The name 'Abel' is written the same way as *hebel*, and this has sometimes provided ammunition for ingenuity in the exegesis of both Gen 4 and Ecclesiastes. Neher, *Notes*, 73-91, pursues the connection at length, seeing also an evocation of Cain's name (*qyn*) in 2.7's *qnyty* ('I acquired'; cf. likewise Treier at 1.2) and *mqnh* ('cattle'), along with a reference to Seth in 4.15, and his analysis has been elaborated more recently in Antic, 'Cain, Abel, Seth'. Whatever the heuristic value of making that link, however, I doubt that it was intended by the author of the book, or that it is indicative, as is also often suggested, of a broader reference to the early chapters of Genesis (so, e.g., Clemens, 'The Law of Sin and Death'; Forman, 'Koheleth's Use of Genesis'; Meek, 'Meaning'; Seufert, 'Presence of Genesis'; and cf. Krüger, 'Rezeption'). Dell's critical examination of the suggested links ('Exploring') concludes (12-13) that the strongest evidence is found in the link between Eccles 3.20; 12.7 and Gen 2.7; 3.19, but, she

INTRODUCTION

Links to other compositions are more difficult to assess, and, as we shall see below, there are many connections with other literature which do not amount to direct citations or allusions in Ecclesiastes. It has long been noted, however, that 9.7-9 bear a resemblance to advice offered in the Old Babylonian version of the epic of Gilgamesh, and follow the sequence of that advice very closely while omitting certain elements of it (so, e.g., Loretz, *Qohelet und der alte Orient*, 116-22; Day, 'Foreign Semitic', 59-61). The threefold cord of 4.12, furthermore, also appears among the Gilgamesh materials as a symbol of strength in numbers (see, e.g., Shaffer, 'הרקע המיסופוטאמי' and 'ידיעות חדשות'; de Savignac, 'La Sagesse', 322; Jones, 'Gilgamesh, 367-68). Samet ('Gilgamesh Epic') suggests also that the associations of sunlight with life and darkness with death in 11.7-8 have their origin in yet another passage from Gilgamesh. For the purpose of dating Ecclesiastes, of course, none of this is especially helpful: the Gilgamesh traditions are very much earlier even than Solomon. It is interesting to observe, however, that the various passages involved occur together in no single version of the epic that has survived. It is by no means certain that the author of Ecclesiastes drew them directly from a Gilgamesh text,[93] and it is possible that they have been mediated through another composition or compositions, but should either a new version of the epic, or a copy of an intermediary ever be found, it could provide potentially important evidence.

Finally, the famous saying in 11.1, about scattering bread on water, is often perceived to have a close counterpart in an Egyptian text, conventionally known as the *Instruction of 'Onchsheshonqy* (although the protagonist's name should probably, in fact, be pronounced 'Chasheshonqy').[94] In 19, 10 this advises 'Do a good deed and throw (it) in the flood: when (the flood) dries up you will

---

says, 'scholars have tended to build a higher edifice upon this evidence than I believe the comparison really deserves'; so, similarly, Michel, 67-73. Much rests on common vocabulary, which is explicable in other ways, and not especially striking in its quantity.

[93] See especially the reservations expressed in Uehlinger, 'Qohelet im Horizont', 180-92; van der Toorn, 'Echoes'. The latter does, however, suggest (506) that the later standard version of the epic is presented as *narû* literature, and can claim some generic affinity with Ecclesiastes.

[94] See Quack, 'Namensformen', 91 n. 3. Quack himself uses 'Chascheschonqi'.

find it'.⁹⁵ The Egyptian text is known from slightly later manuscripts, but was probably first composed in the fifth or sixth century BCE, so if there were a clear relationship with Ecclesiastes, this would be useful evidence for dating. Although the resemblance here is intriguing, however, it is doubtful that the sayings are close enough to posit any direct connection between them.

(d) *Summary*

Connections with other texts tend to affirm that Ecclesiastes was written after the period of the Judahite monarchy, and probably no earlier than the Persian period. The linguistic evidence points in very much the same direction, although the presence of at least one probable borrowing from Greek usage suggests a date of composition in Hellenistic times. A date in the late sixth or fifth century cannot be excluded, therefore, but it is more likely that the book was composed no earlier than the late fourth century. If we add in the evidence for the latest date and round the numbers a little, then realistically the possible range is approximately 500–150 BCE, the probable approximately 300–150 BCE. Most scholars correspondingly take the third century to be the likeliest century of composition.

2. *Location, Contexts and the Book's Universalism*

Qohelet locates himself in Jerusalem (1.12, 16; 2.7, 9), as does the superscription to the book in 1.1, but there are otherwise no more explicit geographical references than there are historical ones. It is far from certain, moreover, that the author wrote the book in the same place that he set it—especially since, if that desire is original, the choice of Jerusalem may have been determined by the desire to associate Qohelet with Solomon. Amongst the various mentions of the climate, plants, and animals, or the details offered of everyday life, none seems incompatible with a Palestinian setting, but unless we suppose that 4.17 implies ready access to the Jerusalem Temple in particular, none actually demands such a setting.⁹⁶ The suspicion

---

[95] See Lichtheim, *Ancient Egyptian Literature III*, 174; more recently Hoffmann and Quack, *Anthologie*, 292.

[96] Humbert, *Recherches*, 113, suggests that the description of the wind blowing North/South in 1.6 would fit an Egyptian context better than a Palestinian

of some scholars, that the language shows northern dialectal features, might well place Ecclesiastes outside Jerusalem, but it is difficult to confirm that suspicion (see n. 69, above). In short, therefore, we do not know where the book was composed.

It is equally difficult to say anything about the social setting. The advice about a king in 8.2-4 is probably conventional in nature, and warns about the dangers of interactions with the powerful: it should certainly not be read as a clue that the author was personally familiar with the royal court—whichever court that might have been at the time the book was written—or that he expected his audience to be. Ecclesiastes is not a volume on court etiquette. More generally, the tone of the book is often didactic, but that does not mean that its purpose was pedagogical, or that we should see it as a school-book. It is tempting to be literal-minded about such things, and an over-emphasis on them has often influenced understandings both of Ecclesiastes and of Proverbs, which has its own didactic tone and a lot more sayings about kings. It is important to appreciate, however, both that these works draw in some ways on longstanding literary traditions and, rather differently, that the interests of their authors and audiences could extend beyond their own immediate experience—those same readers will be getting advice about sowing seed in 11.6.

If we should not make too much of some topics, however, there are certain concerns or emphases in the text that do stick out a little. The references to sacrifice and to vows in 4.17–5.5 are picked up, for example, in 9.2, where those who do and don't sacrifice, and those who do and don't make vows are portrayed as separate groups, analogous to the righteous and wicked, or the clean and unclean. No other such specific behaviours are singled out in that list, and we might reasonably speculate that sacrifice and vows were topics of particular interest to the author. It is striking, though, that the issues around them would have been potentially of concern even to non-Jews, and they draw attention to an important aspect

---

one, and Hertzberg, 'Palästinische Bezüge', 113-14, tries to counter that by talking about shifts through those points. I doubt that the wind is even the subject (see the commentary), but this would be slim evidence in any case. The rest of Hertzberg's article affirms more the possibility than the probability of a Palestinian context, while Bishop, 'A Pessimist in Palestine', places the book in a Palestinian context without really considering any alternatives.

of Qohelet's discourse: in addressing the plight *of* humanity, he commonly addresses himself *to* that humanity as a whole. It hardly needs saying that none of the everyday, worldly situations described in the book are characterized in a way that makes them specifically Jewish. It should be observed also, however, that Qohelet's 'monotheistic' discourse about God would have been perfectly at home within polytheistic religious traditions (see Weeks, *Introduction*, 118).[97] When he also avoids use of the divine name throughout, therefore, Qohelet is able to address even religious concerns that would have been, in effect, universal.

There is no good reason to doubt that Ecclesiastes was composed by a Jew, or that its composition in Hebrew would have restricted its reception to a Jewish or Samaritan audience. Even though the epilogue adopts a much more Deuteronomic tone in its closing lines, however, the book presents itself throughout as a reflection on issues that would have concerned Jews and gentiles alike, and avoids limiting its scope or assumptions. Correspondingly, when it talks about a temple in 4.17, we are probably not supposed to understand that the advice offered was directed only towards Jews in Jerusalem, or only, indeed, towards Jews. That is not to say, of course, that everyone in the ancient world would have shared, say, Qohelet's theological presuppositions, any more than every Jew would have done, but it seems likely that the book embodies a deliberate and self-conscious attempt to address universal questions in a universal way.[98]

---

[97] Frydrych, *Living*, 107-108, makes much of Qohelet's monotheism to suggest that he has in mind a similarly monotheistic, Jewish audience, but misses the point that many ancient writers, whether of Egyptian instructions or of Greek philosophy, spoke of 'God' or 'the god' in contexts where divinity or divine power in general were at issue.

[98] The point is put emphatically by Humbert, in 'Qoheléth', 257-58, which speaks of the vastness of Qohelet's horizon. It is what I take to be the clarity of the book's intentions in this respect, among other things, that makes me reluctant to follow some other scholars in finding constant allusions and references in Ecclesiastes to literature and ideas that were more particularly Jewish. Arguably, an important side-effect in modern times has been to facilitate comparisons not just with philosophical traditions, but with quite different religious traditions: see, e.g., the comparisons with Chinese thought by Heard and Jarick mentioned elsewhere, and Jayādvaita, *Vanity Karma*, which interweaves a critical reading of the text with references to Sanskrit literature. Such comparisons have a long history: cf. Weeks, *The Making of Many Books*, §284. Jayādvaita himself pushes

There is no reason to suppose that this intention was motivated by ideological opposition to more specifically Jewish religious concerns, and although the author might not himself have advocated all the positions held by Qohelet, there is no indication that he understood his protagonist actually to contradict whatever he took to be core Jewish positions. Equally, the book shows none of the interest in reconciling Jewish particularism with theological universalism that we find in, say, Philo or Ben Sira. The author more likely understands his text to transcend such issues, focusing as it does on questions around divine governance and the relationship of individuals to God, which might broadly be considered common religious ground. This has a counterpart in the advice that Qohelet offers, so when in particular he commends fear of God, which was a very widespread concept in the ancient world, this could be interpreted in terms of Torah piety by a Jew, just as it could be interpreted in other terms by someone else. Likewise, his warnings about vows carry the same weight whichever god is involved, and religious affiliation is relevant to few, if any, of his many admonitions and observations.

It is hard to know whether ancient readers would have regarded this attempt as successful, and whether Qohelet really finds common ground. Perhaps the most we can say is that, whatever other problems they had with the book, early Jewish and Christian interpreters found no apparent difficulty in accepting its theology. For our present purposes, though, this universalism creates certain difficulties. If Qohelet shows a particular concern with vows and sacrifices, as we noted above, it is reasonable to suppose that these were of interest to the author—but they may have been of interest precisely because they offered an opportunity to explore an issue of interest to everybody, not because they were especially controversial in the time or place where the author worked. It is difficult to establish the precise historical context of much ancient literature, but if we have reason to suppose that Ecclesiastes has been designed deliberately

---

the question further (48-51), citing with some amusement the doubts of Stuart, 140-43, that Qohelet would have reached the same conclusions had he lived in the more stimulating intellectual climate of post-Enlightenment Europe, and suggesting that the modern world, on the contrary, might only affirm Qohelet in his despair. I am inclined to agree that the author probably considered the issues timeless as well as universal—which may be one reason for the lack of historical as well as religious specificity.

to transcend its own context, then the task may be all but impossible, leaving us with the hope only that the author has overlooked clues to that context, and with the possibility that the very fact of the attempt is a clue.

There might be some mileage in that last possibility if we are willing to suppose that some environments are more conducive to such efforts than others. Older ideas of an 'international' wisdom movement, for instance, could furnish an explanation for universalism in wisdom literature by supposing that its authors adopted a supranational ideology. Still earlier generations of scholars might have pointed to the cosmopolitanism of Solomon's court. If it is not difficult to identify or invent environments that would nurture a universalistic outlook, however, it is very hard either to choose between them, or to deny that such an outlook might arise even in an unpromising context. Although we can discern the author's purpose, furthermore, we cannot so easily establish his motivation.

In the book of Job, to which we shall return again below, we have another Jewish composition that aspires to address universal issues, and that book goes so far as to make its various characters explicitly non-Jewish. Ecclesiastes is not unique in this respect, therefore, and it is likely that we are dealing not with a specific reaction to historical circumstance—Jewish engagement with Hellenism, say, or with the realities of rule by a foreign empire—but with a generic mode of discourse. Just as Greek and Roman philosophical discussions of religion are far removed from the depictions of the gods in Homer or Vergil, and even from the everyday realities of religious performance, so works like Job and Ecclesiastes seek to explore the universal by placing themselves outside the particular. If we have to be rather vague about the historical and geographical context within which Ecclesiastes was composed, therefore, comparisons with other literature do offer possibilities for contextualizing the book in a different way.

3. *Style*

Before turning to such comparisons, it is important to say a little about the style of the book—not least because our previous discussion of its language may have left an impression that Ecclesiastes is not somehow as 'literary' as many of the texts with which, as we shall see, it stands closest comparison. In particular, if that language does indeed stand closer to the vernacular, or to some dialect of Hebrew, then it is easy to assume that it does so because the author was not attempting to adopt a formal, literary style. Robert Lowth, indeed, said of Ecclesiastes in 1753 that:

> The style of this work is...singular; the language is generally low, I might almost call it mean or vulgar; it is frequently loose, unconnected, approaching to the incorrectness of conversation; and possesses very little of the poetical character, even in the composition and structure of the periods: which peculiarity may possibly be accounted for from the nature of the subject. Contrary to the opinion of the Rabbies, Ecclesiastes has been classed among the poetical books; though if their authority and opinions were of any weight or importance, they might, perhaps, on this occasion, deserve some attention.[99]

Lowth himself accepted the view of Desvoeux, that the book was 'written in prose, but that it contains many scraps of poetry, introduced as occasion served',[100] but a continuing uncertainty over this point is illustrated by the ways in which different modern translations present Ecclesiastes, laying out very variable amounts of its content as poetry or prose.[101] The difficulty arises, of course, because although there are passages in biblical Hebrew that scholars would generally assign without much debate to one category or the other, there is also a middle ground (as in English composition), and a lot of the material in this book occupies that ground. Matters are further complicated by disagreements of a more technical sort around, for instance, the role and nature of metre in Hebrew verse, and, as I mentioned earlier, attempts to recover or restore a metrical framework in Ecclesiastes were very influential on its interpretation for a brief period around the end of the nineteenth century and beginning of the twentieth.

---

[99] See Lowth, *De sacra poesi Hebraeorum*, 239; this translation is from Lowth, *Lectures*, 271.

[100] Lowth expresses the opinion in a footnote on the page cited. Desvoeux did not publish his commentary until 1760, but in his preface (p. vii) describes a Latin treatise circulated to 'some learned friends' in 1736, and it is apparently this that Lowth himself cites. In his commentary, Desvoeux discusses the issue on pp. 339-47.

[101] Hobbins, 'Poetry', offers a helpful overview of the scholarship and issues, along with its own proposals.

We do not need to discuss those technical issues in detail here, beyond acknowledging that it is difficult to find any sustained metre or rhythm in the book. The use of parallelism has generally been considered a more obvious marker of Hebrew verse, and in the book of Proverbs this commonly characterizes aphoristic literature as well. There are clear instances of it in 1.15, 'bent, it was beyond fixing, and as a loss, it was beyond counting', in 7.8, 'better is the end of speech than its beginning, better long of spirit than lofty of spirit', and in 10.12, 'the words of a wise man's mouth attract favour, but the lips of a fool consume him'. Other examples, not always so clear, may be identified elsewhere, but the device is not common in the book—at least in the way we normally expect to find it, with balanced clauses set in parallel. If we look at, say, 1.4, then what we find is actually rather different: two very short clauses set in parallel, but constituting a single idea, which is then contrasted with the next, longer clause: 'one generation goes, another generation comes, while the world stays forever constant'. Something similar happens shortly afterwards, in 1.7, while in 1.9 a third clause explains and builds on the previous, parallel ones. In 3.1-8, the first verse has parallel clauses, but it introduces something that at once goes far beyond normal parallelism, and at the same time falls short of it: the fourteen pairs that follow are not paired clauses, but short, mostly two-word phrases.

The book, in fact, shows a considerable fondness for constructing different types of statement out of short units that repeat or contrast with each other. Note, for instance, the first parts of 3.19, 'for what befalls humans, and what befalls animals, just one thing befalls them: as the death of this one, so the death of that, and there is one breath for all'. That verse exemplifies a particular tendency to repeat the same term three times in a sentence (so Segal, 13; who lists also 1.2, 6; 3.20; 7.28; 8.8, 14, 17; 9.6; 12.8—others could be added), but we find similar accumulations in, for example, the beginning of 6.3: 'if a man has children a hundred times, and lives many years, and the days of his years are going to be a lot, but his self is not satisfied by his good fortune'. This fondness, indeed, is one of the things that make the book difficult to read at many points, as it is not always clear how the parts fit together. It also results in a complexity that often seems unnecessary: do we really need in 9.12, for example, analogies with both netted fish and trapped birds? Having already noted the neat parallelism of 10.12, which employs a playful imagery of mouths and lips, we might also observe, moreover, that 10.13 goes on to explain the point—surely quite needlessly—and 10.14 to add a further, related point. Qohelet does not self-evidently share the view that brevity is the soul of wit: when he is not cramming extra words or clauses into his constructions, he builds or elaborates on them to add extra cases or new issues.[102] In this respect, it would be hard to say that he is trying to be poetic, but what he does create is something much denser and more intricate than most biblical prose.

Some of this may be down to a deliberate characterization of Qohelet himself as talkative or pompous, and some probably has an emphatic function. It seems more doubtful, though, that any of it would come across as plain or vulgar, and although the monologue does have the sort of conversational looseness that Lowth discerns when we consider broader matters of structure and arrangement, the sentences individually give a very different impression. This impression is heightened when we consider the points at which a very deliberate effort seems to have been made to polish the language, sometimes at the expense of the sense. The most famous example is probably *ṭwb šm mšmn ṭwb* at the beginning of 7.1, which has been commended by many commentators for its stylishness—although many have then struggled to find a meaningful connection with what follows. In 3.18, as I shall argue in the commentary, rhythm and assonance have been given such priority over clarity that the verse has become almost baffling. More broadly, the repetitions of 'generation' in 1.4 and of 'the sun' in 1.5 are probably more a matter of rhythm than of parallelism, and 1.4-7 as a whole is marked by strong assonance—a consideration for which may also have guided, for example, the choice of vocabulary in 3.3, or the omission of prepositions in 3.4.

Where the sense is not obviously affected, it can be hard to judge whether similar concerns have influenced the composition of say, 6.11, or the use of alliterative expressions like *ḥkmh wḥšbwn* and

---

[102] Kugel, 'Wisdom', 25-26, makes a similar point in a different way: looking at 4.9-12, he claims that Qohelet 'takes a perfectly good mashal and, instead of just citing it, interrupts it with a long, prosy parade of illustrations... It is almost as if Qohelet cannot stand the symmetry, the poetry, of wisdom.'

mr mmwt in 7.25-26. In general, though, the text gives a strong impression of having been composed with a concern for its sound as well as its meaning, and it would not be too much to say that some of it seems very carefully crafted. This is something that we tend to associate with Hebrew poetry more than with prose: consisting as it does mostly of narrative, however, our biblical Hebrew prose corpus contains little that is comparable in theme or tone to much of what we find in Ecclesiastes.[103] If we are to avoid sharp dichotomies, then the best way to view this is probably not in terms of 'poetic prose', or of some mixture between poetry and prose. A description as 'rhetorical' might be closer to the mark, but what the evidence of stylistic care really points to is a much more general concern with words, of the sort which distinguishes 'good' from 'bad' speech and writing. Combined with the other indications of compositional complexity, it tends to tell against any idea that the style is purely conversational: too much work has gone into shaping this material for it to be likely that any original listener would have taken it that way.

Judging by the character of the Hebrew, however, it does seem likely that the author has deliberately avoided using a formal, literary register,[104] and if we are to explain the anomaly, it may be helpful to recall the resemblance already noted between the Hebrew of Ecclesiastes and that of Song of Songs. Whether or not the materials in the latter actually were drawn from a long tradition of singing (and I am inclined to think that they were), they were probably at least intended to resemble songs in that tradition, which would have lain some way outside any formal, scribal traditions of literary composition. If the Hebrew in Song of Songs is an elevated but non-literary register of Hebrew, then we should perhaps suppose that the same is

---

[103] This potentially complicates comparisons such as that made in Joosten, 'Volitive Verbal Forms', 53-56, which observes that Ecclesiastes does not follow the 'classical rules of word-order in volitive clauses' (54). Classically, those rules do not apply to poetry, and so the book may be breaking them for reasons of style rather than (or as well as) date—although date is more clearly the explanation for the book's non-volitive uses of weyiqtol forms, which Joosten goes on to explore.

[104] It is difficult to say whether the register ever shifts within the book. Whybray, 'Time to Be Born', 471, notes that 3.2-8 uses vocabulary that is largely classical, and avoids expressions elsewhere characteristic of the book, but that may be simply a product of the subject-matter and of the constraints on the syntax in those verses.

true of that in Ecclesiastes: the author uses it, in other words, either because he is unaware of 'literary' Hebrew, or because he wishes to avoid that label. The latter seems more likely, but it is hard to say precisely what his intention might have been. One possibility is that he is imitating some other tradition of oral performance, and it is not impossible that there were performers who delivered at least loosely comparable material. Another is that he either wants to impart a particular tone and perspective, or to avoid any connotations attached in his own context to works written in a more standard literary Hebrew. Whatever the case, though, none of this means that Ecclesiastes is not 'literary' in some sense: it is written in an elevated style, but without the more-or-less conservative forms of Hebrew that were generally employed for literary compositions.[105]

4. *Literary and Intellectual Contexts*

We have touched already on the appearance in Ecclesiastes of some material that has probably been adapted from other texts, and of possible allusions to other literature. It is difficult to know how much else we would discover if more ancient texts were available to us, but what we do have is enough to show that the author did not compose his book in some sort of literary isolation: it draws on and reacts to a potentially broad range of existing works, which would themselves in turn have been influenced by others. To the extent that we can establish its place in the broader field of

---

[105] I am correspondingly reluctant to accept the conclusion of Carlebach, *Das Buch Koheleth*, 64, that the colloquialisms of the book represent a special *Sprache der Weisen*, 'language of the wise', which is intended to be plain and clear: we would not naturally apply such a description to Song of Songs, with its comparable language, while the (itself rarely plain) language of Proverbs generally shows few of the features usually associated with Ecclesiastes. Young, *Diversity*, 155, comes to a similar conclusion by identifying the language as dialectal then adding ideas about the place of composition and details from the epilogue to deduce that the language is 'specifically that of a Jerusalem "Wisdom school"', which heaps speculation upon speculation. Without prejudice to the question of the book's possible dialectal background (see n. 69), it might be more accurate to draw an analogy with modern literature written in dialect, like Irvine Welsh's *Trainspotting*, or the Uncle Remus tales of Joel Chandler Harris (upon which Fox draws for an analogy to the book's narration): the language in such works is not standard literary English, but that does not make them by any means devoid of literary technique.

ancient literature, we can better understand the intentions behind Ecclesiastes, the ways in which it might have been received, and perhaps even the original resonance of themes and expressions in the book.

(a) *The Question of Genre*

The task would be easier, perhaps, if Ecclesiastes itself were not so unusual. As I noted earlier, many elements of its composition are familiar—the format of the content as a speech, for example, or the book's sudden shifts of tone—and we shall see shortly that some of its key ideas had a long pre-history. No other known work, however, puts these things together in quite the same way, and we have no reason to suppose that Ecclesiastes is the sole survivor from some otherwise lost corpus: in certain respects it was probably very original in its day, and there are still few works like it. It is not unique in its uniqueness, however, and we possess other ancient compositions that are similarly hard to identify as members of a class, except in some very general way. Although it is helpful to discuss Ecclesiastes in terms of genre, therefore, it must be with an awareness both that its generic affinities with other texts do not imply some broader identity, and that genre has limitations as a concept when we are discussing most texts, ancient or modern.

To take the second point first, it is not difficult to identify indications of generic awareness in the ancient world, even beyond the reach of Aristotle. The Bible itself offers obvious examples in the anthologization of texts: Proverbs, Psalms, and the book of the Twelve Minor Prophets all offer instances where texts regarded as similar in some sense have been brought together, and it is possible that, for example, the Song of Songs should be regarded in the same way. Elsewhere, and rather differently, the most famous example of an established genre is probably that of the *sbᵓyt*, or 'instruction', in ancient Egypt: a large number of texts over a long period adopted this description of themselves, and with it a self-presentation as advice offered by an individual to his son or successor (see Weeks, *Instruction and Imagery*, 4-32). The conventions of the 'instruction' genre, if not its label, were familiar outside Egypt, and we have instances in Proverbs. The collectors of Proverbs, however, have set these alongside other types of material in their own anthology: what identified a text as suitable for the collection, therefore, could embrace the features that made it an instruction, but were clearly not the same. Whether it is being imposed by an author or a collector, as this example illustrates, a generic label is not exclusive, and need apply only to one aspect of a work.

A different implication of this can be identified amongst the Egyptian instructions themselves: their conventional self-presentation constrains their content, but only to a limited extent, and instructions can contain a wide variety both of advice and of material that is not strictly advice—the New Kingdom *Instruction of Any*, for instance, turns into a dialogue about the value of education.[106] Just as different generic descriptions can be attached to the same text to describe different relationships with other texts, so when genre is used to describe a text, it does so only in respect of particular aspects: if something was called an instruction, readers could expect it to frame its content in a particular way, but could not anticipate other aspects of theme or style. In practice, this means that when a label is used to describe a wide range of texts, it may convey very little about them. If we consider how little Jonah, say, has in common with Micah, or either of those books with Haggai, we might suspect that a book qualified for the Twelve by dint of little more than being short enough, and featuring a prophet in some way: it is not easy to identify or create a genre 'prophetic book' that entails anything more but can still contain all of the Twelve, let alone other works traditionally described that way (although Ben Zvi makes a valiant effort in 'The Prophetic Book').

If we are to use genres descriptively to align different compositions with each other, then the consequence of all this is that we may do better to use multiple labels to represent different affinities than to squeeze texts into single categories. In the book of Lamentations, for example, it is clearly helpful to think of the materials both as laments and as acrostic poems—our own categories aside, it is likely that both types of composition would have been familiar to ancient writers, and that there is a deliberate attempt to bring them together in the poetry. Collapsing the two into a notion of, say, 'acrostic laments', would merely render both useless, inasmuch

---

[106] See Fox, 'Who Can Learn?', and on the text more generally Quack, *Die Lehren des Ani*.

as it would make Lamentations *sui generis* instead of drawing out its separate associations with other acrostic poems and with other laments. It is correspondingly important to recognize that while a generic label may describe both thematic and compositional aspects of a work—and does so helpfully in the case of instructions—formal, structural elements may also be independent of theme, and represent a separate set of affinities.

This approach is potentially very constructive when it comes to Ecclesiastes, because although 'genre' might be too loaded a description for some of its associations with other literature, it is fair to say that while we find some of the book's most important ideas expressed elsewhere in texts like Job that are formally quite different, key aspects of its formal presentation also correspond to those of texts with very different interests. If we compare Ecclesiastes with the book of Hosea, for instance, it is obvious from the outset that the two share little in common when it comes to their subject-matter or concerns. Formally, however, we do find in Hosea not only a similar presentation of the content as speech, but, more specifically, a superscription and an epilogue that comments on that content, as well as an initial narrative and elements of memoir that form a basis for some of what follows. These two books are about very different things, but they are constructed in ways that at least stand comparison. If making such comparisons feels transgressive, in a discipline so long conditioned by form-critical sensibilities, then we might perhaps recall again that formal resemblances to the prophetic books were an important influence on early Jewish interpretations of Ecclesiastes.[107] At the very least, though, it is important to recognize that situating Ecclesiastes in its broader literary context must involve the recognition of affinities that may be compositional, as well as thematic.

(b) *Compositional Affinities with Other Literature*
Having touched on some of the problems that can arise from trying to assign a single generic label to a single text, and before turning to particular formal aspects of Ecclesiastes, it is important also to say something about the assignment of texts as groups to genres. This

---

[107] I have written on issues of genre more generally, especially in respect of Proverbs and Ecclesiastes, in Weeks, 'Wisdom, Form and Genre'.

has played a significant role in modern discussions of 2.4-9 and the material around it in particular, as we shall see, but it is relevant also to the consideration of other materials where commentators have understood generic affiliations to imply that texts would have been read in a particular way.

There is nothing illegitimate about this in itself: it is fundamental to the very notion of genre, after all, that response to a text may be influenced by a perception of its relationship with other texts. The difficulty is that, as we have seen already, different perceptions may be at work, and not all of them will align with those of the original author or audience. To take an obvious example, Lucian's *Uerae Historiae*, written in the second century CE, has often been associated with modern science fiction, and certainly fits many definitions of such fiction, but we may be equally certain, of course, that science fiction was not among the many types of composition that Lucian would have set out to parody, or that his audience would have known. If scholars naturally avoid reading such self-evidently anachronistic genres back into the consciousness of ancient writers, however, they are not always so cautious when it comes to genres that are modern creations based on the reading of ancient texts. In the case of Ecclesiastes, its common designation as 'wisdom literature' furnishes an important but rather complicated example of this: the designation is old (although not nearly so old as the texts), but only in relatively modern times came to be treated as something like a description of genre, with an implication that the book should be understood especially in relation to other books labelled that way (see, e.g., Weeks, 'Useful Category'; Sneed, 'Wisdom Tradition'; Kynes, *Obituary*, 25-104).

It is easier to see the general issue more clearly, however, if we look at something more precise—say, Seow's claim, in his commentary on the first few words of 1.12, that 'The style here imitates the self-presentation formula of kings in the royal inscriptions of the ancient Near East'. Seow goes on to state more specifically that, 'in the West Semitic examples', the king is typically introduced using precisely the wording that we find in 1.12, with a first-person pronoun followed by a proper name: 'I, Qohelet'. Seow makes the point at greater length in a separate article ('Qohelet's Autobiography', 279-84), and he is by no means the only one to do so, although there are variations on the theme within scholarship: Longman, in his *Fictional Akkadian Autobiography*, for instance, looks particularly to fictional royal autobiographies in Akkadian rather than to West Semitic inscriptions. In any case, though, the implication of the similarities is commonly taken to be that ancient readers would have understood 1.12 and the memoir that follows as an example of, or at least a literary pastiche of a royal inscription or memoir—despite the fact that becoming king in 1.12 is the only specifically royal action ascribed to Qohelet.

This is attractive, but it rests on the idea that certain royal inscriptions or memoirs constitute a specific genre, recognizable by its phraseology, and it is very difficult to substantiate that idea. In part, the problem is not that we cannot find enough royal texts with particular features, but that such features appear in many texts that are not royal—we find 'I, wisdom', for instance, in Prov 8.12, and 'I, Tobit' in Tobit 1.3, both employing what is supposed by this theory to be an exclusively royal form of self-presentation. It is also true, however, that the various texts in Akkadian which present themselves as royal inscriptions or accounts do not otherwise share any particular set of characteristics that would identify them as members of a specific, recognizable genre—Longman has been heavily criticized for his arbitrary isolation of certain texts to create the more formally consistent group with which he compares Ecclesiastes (see especially Westenholz, *Legends*, 16-24). Generic definitions deployed in this discussion seem to be the product of an entirely modern selectivity, and although it is reasonable to suppose that ancient readers would have seen a formal self-presentation of a familiar sort in 1.12, we really have no grounds to suppose more precisely that this would in itself have led them to take what follows as specifically 'royal'—even before we ask questions about the likelihood of those readers having any familiarity with, say, foreign tomb-inscriptions or centuries-old texts in Akkadian.

It can be more difficult to identify the problems when vaguer claims are made on the basis of fewer, or more loosely related materials. The story of the great king and the small city in 9.14-15, for example, has been labelled in a number of different ways by scholars, and there is nothing inherently wrong in describing it as, say, a 'parable'—that term, which I shall use myself at various points, summarizes a particular understanding of its style, function and historicity (so, e.g., Loader, *Polar Structures*, 24). It is potentially problematic, however, if we take this to be a description of genre (so, e.g., Barucq, 164) and link it to passages like Prov 24.30-34:

Murphy does that, in the same place (*Wisdom Literature*, 130) that he talks about a genre 'reflection', which 'designates a text that is characterized by observation and thought, and hence has a fairly loose structure'. Grouping texts this way can be convenient, and can have some heuristic value, but we have no basis for supposing that those groupings correspond to any specific ancient understanding, and there is a significant risk that talking about them as 'genres' will turn extrinsic classifications into conscious, intrinsic allusions: the idea that Ecclesiastes deploys 'parables' or 'example stories' conventionally has greatly complicated the study of 4.13-16, for instance, while Murphy's category of 'reflection' (picked up by Dell, in 'Mainstream', 45-46) imposes an artificial consistency on materials that are stylistically and thematically diverse. We do not need to avoid describing texts, but using the discourse of genre to do so can impute a false objectivity to our observations, and, without careful qualification, an unevidenced historical reality to our classifications.

(c) *The First-Person Perspective*

As we turn to look at some of the book's compositional characteristics, therefore, it is important to say not only that the first-person perspective adopted in Qohelet's monologue, which is one of the most obvious of these, is a feature of many other ancient texts, but also that those texts vary greatly in character.[108] If this is a mark of genre at all, it is certainly not the mark of any single genre that would universally have been recognized as distinct on this ground alone.

At least in Egypt, the use of the first person in much earlier literature is perhaps to be associated both directly and indirectly with the tradition of 'tomb autobiographies'—first-person memorializations

---

[108] This formal aspect of the work has received less attention than it deserves, but see especially Loretz, 'Ich-Erzählung', who recognizes the conventional nature of the presentation. The neglect may be due to the continuing tendency of many commentators, as Loretz notes (56-57), to confuse the "I" of the book with the "I" of its author. This distinction is important, and when Koh, *Royal Autobiography*, 199, talks about 'Qoheleth's personal struggle' and the tension between the wisdom tradition and 'his own experience in life', van Oorschot, 'König', 120, rightly responds that such expressions belong in the context of a novel about Qohelet, not an academic study.

of the dead that were composed for presentation in their tomb.[109] 'Autobiography' may be a misnomer, not only because it is unlikely that they were actually composed by the individuals they memorialize, but also because they can contain reflections and admonitions that go beyond a simple account of lives lived (cf. Burkes, *Death in Qoheleth*, 171-76). In any case, though, the influence of that tradition can be seen not only in the appearance of a fictionalized memoir, the Middle Kingdom *Tale of Sinuhe*,[110] but also in the rise of the instruction genre, with its conventional, testamentary context. More broadly, it probably contributed to the shaping of much literature as speech, and when stories or other material are being presented as the words of a particular individual, this individual naturally speaks in the first person—the story of the *Shipwrecked Sailor* offers an interesting example.[111] We should not, however, exaggerate the extent to which the first-person perspective is used otherwise. An account set at the end of the Twentieth Dynasty, or the beginning of the Twenty-first—so in the eleventh century BCE—is a fictionalized report of an expedition by a royal official, Wenamun, and adopts the first person to accord with this presentation.[112] It may in fact have been composed slightly later, but does not mark a broader tradition, and is the last known, free-standing narrative to do so. As Quack has observed ('Interaction', 384), 'All tales from Egypt attested during the first millennium BCE are third-person narratives'.

Although some of these texts do include reflections on human life or didactic elements, Qohelet's monologue differs from them, as from the Mesopotamian *narû*-literature—which has already been mentioned in the guise of Longman's 'fictional autobiographies', and which presents narratives and prophecies from a first-person,

---

[109] For this view, see Assmann, 'Schrift, Tod und Identität'. On the early manifestations, see especially Lichtheim, *Ancient Egyptian Autobiographies*, and more generally Burkes, *Death in Qoheleth*, 171-208.

[110] Translated in Lichtheim, *Ancient Egyptian Literature I*, 222-35; Parkinson, *Tale of Sinuhe*, 21-53.

[111] Lichtheim, *Ancient Egyptian Literature I*, 211-15, and Parkinson, *Tale of Sinuhe*, 89-101. The first-person narrative is framed by a short third-person narrative, and includes within itself a first-person memoir by another character.

[112] Lichtheim, *Ancient Egyptian Literature II*, 224-30. The text was found with another work, *The Tale of Woe* (Papyrus Pushkin 127), which is also written in the first person but presented as a letter of complaint, and the epistolary form is known elsewhere in ancient literature: see Caminos, *A Tale of Woe*, 79.

royal perspective—in that it focuses very little on narrative or on events: the occurrences and accomplishments recounted in chs. 1–2, and then in ch. 7, presumably would have required considerable time (had they been real), but are passed over swiftly. Whatever we may glean about him from the way he is portrayed, Qohelet shows hardly any interest in telling us about himself, or about any aspect of his life that lies outside his reflections, his enquiries, and his development as a consequence of those enquiries.[113] Such a limited amount of autobiography might incline us to look more toward instructions as a parallel, but if there are any hints at all of the conventional context for instructions, they are in the address to the young in 11.9 and in the epilogue's use of 'my son' at 12.12, both of which occur far too late to drive a reading in those terms. The content of instructions is not fixed, but it is worth noting also that Qohelet offers no advice, as such, before the end of ch. 4, and does not do so consistently even after that point. Some scholars have wanted to see a testamentary quality in Qohelet's words, and the emphasis on death at the close of the monologue might support such a reading: it can hardly be presumed, though, on the basis of any close resemblance either to tomb autobiographies or to instructions.[114]

---

[113] So similarly, Fisch, 'Qohelet', 158-59, who goes on to compare the book with other famous literary 'voyages of self-discovery'. Christianson's thoughtful 'Qoheleth and the/his Self' explores ways in which this last aspect functions to draw out more general issues about the self and personal development—an idea which is also central, a little differently, to studies such as Gese, 'Krisis', and Brown, *Character in Crisis*, 120-50. When talking about the first-person presentation in formal terms, it is important to bear this dimension in mind: among the many and various compositions in the Hebrew Bible, only the book of Jeremiah, perhaps, comes close to the same consciousness of self, and Qohelet's sense of alienation, both from the world and from his younger, more confident self, which is expressed especially in chs. 2 and 7, is important for understanding both what he says, and the appeal of his monologue to many readers over the centuries.

[114] As suggested by Perdue, *Wisdom & Creation*, 202. Perdue finds a lot of connections for Ecclesiastes. In 'Wisdom and Apocalyptic', 234-35, he claims that Ecclesiastes appropriates 'the royal testament, a form found especially in ancient Egypt'. Of the six works that he cites, however, one does not exist (and probably never did), two have nothing directly to do with royalty, and a fourth is royal only inasmuch as it is attributed to a vizier. The instructions of Merikare and Amenemhet are indeed attributed to kings, but the former is a sort of *Fürstenspiegel*, and the latter engages mainly with events around the assassination of Amenemhet, who 'writes' it posthumously (Bolin, *Ecclesiastes*, 47, is right to doubt the significance of *Amenemhet* for understanding Ecclesiastes, but wrong to

In fact, Qohelet's use of the first person is far more reminiscent of two uses found in Greek literature, where first-person memoirs and narratives are not a common form: the authorial 'I' adopted most notably by Herodotus, who comments some forty times this way on his own narrative in the *Histories*, highlighting his own role as collector and commentator (see especially Dewald, 'Narrative Surface'), and the 'lyric I' of Greek lyric poetry—the persona adopted by the poets through which they express experience and emotion. The latter is especially important because, as we shall see, there are also important thematic links between Ecclesiastes and the lyric poetry of Theognis, who frequently uses the first person. This is arguably a usage that is also comparable to the first-person perspective adopted by speakers in the Song of Songs, which has its own first-person counterparts in Egyptian and Mesopotamian literature, and it is more loosely related to the first person of many psalms, hymns and prayers—including works like the Mesopotamian *Ludlul bēl nēmeqi* ('I Will Praise the Lord of Wisdom'), which recounts (in the first person) the sufferings endured by an individual, or the shorter but similar composition found at Ugarit on tablet RS 25.460.[115] The sort of usage found in Herodotus is less commonly attested elsewhere, although we do sometimes find something similar in references to teaching, as in Prov 22.20-21, or in the epilogue to the Egyptian *Instruction of Ptahhotep* (Pap. Prisse 15.8).[116]

Having seen some examples already, it may be important to point out that the first-person perspective plays at least as great a role in Hebrew literature as in any other ancient corpus. The instances are very diverse, and range from, say, the framing of Deuteronomy

suggest that the king's death is merely assumed by scholars—it is a crucial issue). This is not a specific form or genre in any meaningful sense. Later, Perdue was to claim in 'Mortality', 108-109, that 'Qohelet's literary form approximates the form of testamentary literature in Israel and Judaism' (he cites Gen 49 and the Testaments of the Twelve Patriarchs), but he also claimed resemblances to Egyptian tomb autobiographies, which are very different. Except that some of them belong to the broader genre of 'instruction', these texts have little in common with each other, and almost nothing in common with Ecclesiastes beyond a first-person perspective.

[115] See Annus and Lenzi, *Ludlul bēl nēmeqi*; Cohen, *Wisdom*, 165-75.

[116] Translated in Lichtheim, *Ancient Egyptian Literature I*, 61-80; Parkinson, *Tale of Sinuhe*, 246-72.

and of materials in Proverbs as speech, through to the accounts of experience and expressions of hope in many psalms. Some result from an explicit interplay of voices, as in Job and Song of Songs, others from the introduction of characters who speak, as in Proverbs 1–9 or Lamentations, and still others from the apparent presentation of accounts as though they were reports—Nehemiah offering the simplest example of that last. The prophetic books, of course, offer numerous cases, not only because they present speeches in which God talks in the first person, but also because the prophets themselves sometimes offer first-person reports of visions, of symbolic actions, and even of their own, sometimes complicated interactions with God: Jeremiah and Ezekiel both open with extensive first-person discourses.

These uses sometimes raise interesting questions or issues (see my 'Whose Words?'), as when Hosea 2, for example, has God speak initially in the first person as the prophet addressing his children, or when we stop to wonder who is supposed to be receiving Nehemiah's report or various of the prophetic accounts. Issues of historicity aside, the first-person perspective can function as an interesting and sophisticated literary device, and Jewish writers were clearly aware of its possibilities. Its use persists into other and subsequent Jewish literature, whether in the vision reports of Enoch or the memoir that begins the book of Tobit (which, as I mentioned earlier, shifts into the third person as soon as the scope of the narrative moves beyond Tobit's own perspective). In Ben Sira, the conventional, first-person voice of a 'parent' appears occasionally (e.g. 16.24), rather as in Proverbs 1–9, but we also hear an authorial voice (e.g. 33.17; 34.11-12; 39.32) and are offered a highly stylized memoir in ch. 51 (if that is not secondary). Without multiplying examples, it should be obvious that first-person discourse plays a significant and diverse role over a long period and across a wide range of Jewish compositions.

Such range and diversity is important in itself, because it suggests that the presentation of material in Ecclesiastes as a first-person monologue would probably not, in itself, have sent any strong signals about the generic affiliations of the book: Qohelet is one speaker among many in Jewish literature, and those many are restricted to no narrow range of themes or topics. Even, or perhaps especially when combined with elements of memoir, this presentation is unlikely to have shaped expectations about what was to follow, except insofar as it would have led the audience to anticipate the expression of a personal viewpoint, not the claims of an omniscient narrator[117]—and from that point of view, of course, it is interesting that we are only introduced properly to Qohelet after the sweeping assertions of 1.2-11. We are dealing, therefore, with something that may have been important as a literary device, but probably was not in itself a freestanding mark of genre.

Going beyond the perspective involved, it is important to say a little about the function of memoir itself in the book, which has often been tied up with discussions of its epistemology. As I have emphasized above, Qohelet does not use the brief account of his accomplishments in ch. 2 as a way to glorify himself—it provides instead the basis for his claims about the futility of accomplishment—and this distinguishes that account very strongly from the sort of royal inscriptions often associated with it. We might well be tempted, therefore, to see this and Qohelet's other claims to experience as comparable rather to the sort of accounts that we find in Proverbs 7 and 24.30-34, where the speaker claims to have seen a particular event or situation. In the first of these, the observation is followed (from 7.22) by an interpretation of what is really going on, and admonitions against being caught the same way; in the second, the observation provokes reflection and a suitable aphorism. Leaving aside questions about empiricism in either case, it is interesting to ask whether Qohelet's observations and reflections might be understood as an extended form of such accounts, and so, perhaps, as a particular development within established conventions of didactic literature.

---

[117] The implications of the first-person presentation are explored very fruitfully and at length by Salyer in *Vain Rhetoric*, and he notes in his preface (13-14) that, 'By choosing to base the rhetoric of the book essentially on the strengths and weaknesses of Qoheleth's "I", the implied author spurned the aura of "omnisciency" which surrounds so many of the Canon's third-person narrators'. One consequence is that 'At issue in the book of Ecclesiastes is the rhetorical question of how does one validate the "truth", or perhaps, wisdom of the individual'. As will become clear, I am inclined to think that this is an important element of the author's strategy, and that his presentation of Qohelet is sometimes intended to provoke doubt or create distance in a way that would be much harder if the monologue were simply an unvoiced essay. Segal, 106, puts it well when he says that 'the reader is invited into a complex relationship with the character and his words'.

That these accounts do resemble some of what we find in Qohelet's monologue seems undeniable: in 8.10, for instance, Qohelet observes a situation which he believes to be misleading, and in 9.16 he extrapolates conclusions from another situation. Far more typically, however, his 'observations' are not of things seen through a window or in passing, but of situations carefully crafted to illustrate a point, and presented as indicative of a broader problem—ch. 6 offers a few examples. The events of the first two chapters seem even more distant: they represent not the observation but the creation of a situation, deliberately to answer a question. Whatever the resemblances, furthermore, the implications are limited. Accounts such as those in Proverbs 7 and 24 are rare, and those two instances are also very different from each other in both form and intention: the first is not a 'real' observation, but a device enabling the speaker to witness an interaction—to be, as it were, a fly on the wall—and the second constructs a background for what was apparently an established aphorism (cf. Prov 6.10-11). We may reasonably doubt, therefore, both that they are 'conventional' in any meaningful sense, and that they intentionally reflect some specific methodology.

Qohelet's own observations, moreover, are varied, and it is sometimes difficult to say whether they are actually accounts of 'experiences' at all. In 3.16-22, for example, he seems to begin with an observation about the omnipresence of evil that is based not on seeing some single instance, but on a concatenation of experiences, then to end by 'seeing' only in the sense of discovering a lesson to be taken away from his reflections on experience. In places like 4.15, it is hard to know even whether Qohelet 'saw' something, or is claiming to 'have seen', possibly over a long period. This is rather more like the first-person testimonies that we find in, for example, Job 4.8; 15.17, where the speakers declare what their past experience has taught them, or those in Ps 37.25-26, 35-36, where such experience is instantiated through depictions of the righteous and wicked seen as individuals: it is not self-evidently the purpose of such declarations to suggest that broader principles have been extrapolated from specific observations, and their reference, we might say, is to 'experience', not 'experiences'.

The monologue, then, mixes specific actions and observations with more general reflections and perceptions in a way that makes it difficult to generalize about the basis of Qohelet's own opinions, let alone to link his expressions of experience to particular epistemological ideas or to some nascent empiricism. All that we can say, perhaps, is that his frequent personalization of his claims makes many of them different in character from the sort of unqualified assertions that are more typical in, say, Proverbs. Qohelet roots most of his statements in his own reflections, and does not attempt to present them simply as universal truths that might be acknowledged by anybody: in doing so, he is able to adduce evidence, and to lend them the authority of his vaunted wisdom—but he also makes it potentially easier, of course, for the audience to distance themselves from his opinions, and even for himself to move on from them. In any case, it is doubtful that the author has adopted this type of presentation simply in conformity to some established tradition of extrapolating truths from physical observations: there is no evidence for such a tradition, and, much of the time, that is not what Qohelet actually does.

(i) *The* hebel *statements*

We discussed earlier the use of claims that various phenomena are 'vapour' as a device that unifies the monologue, both through the matching claims of 1.2 and 12.8, and through the accumulation of more specific assertions across the first eight chapters. Whether we see this principally as an aspect of structure or of argumentation, it is extremely unusual, and it is difficult to find any close analogy in ancient literature: there are certainly no grounds to suppose this is a technique that readers would have found familiar.

It does not offer a precise parallel, but a Demotic instruction found on Papyrus Insinger and several other manuscripts is interesting in this respect.[118] This Ptolemaic work is more regularly structured than Ecclesiastes, organizing its predominantly one-line sayings by subject-matter into separate, numbered teachings. Except for the last, each of the teachings which has been preserved closes with a comment that (in Lichtheim's translation) 'The fate

---

[118] See especially Lichtheim, *Late Egyptian Wisdom Literature*, 107-234. There is also an English translation in Lichtheim, *Ancient Egyptian Literature III*, 184-217, but the German translation in Hoffmann and Quack, *Anthologie*, 239-73 (under the heading 'Das große demotische Weisheitsbuch'), incorporates more of the text known from manuscripts other than Insinger, and is consequently more complete.

and the fortune that come, it is the god who determines them', or some minor variant on that. The point is often preceded with other comments about divine action, or by the inclusion of sayings which contradict sayings already presented in that teaching. What appear to be a lot of miscellaneous aphorisms, when they are considered separately, are deployed in this way to demonstrate a single overall point, that human fortunes and affairs are under divine control.

Setting aside the interest that Ecclesiastes and this Egyptian work both show in relativizing the value of wisdom and advice, their shared desire to find a common thread running through a variety of issues does make them stand out. There is no reason, however, to suspect any direct link between them, and there is no close resemblance between them in other respects: they are unlikely to be isolated representatives of some more widespread type of composition.

(ii) *Ecclesiastes and advice literature*

To the extent that one may be expected to learn from it, much literature is didactic, while not every text that is commonly labelled 'didactic' in a more specific way actually provides useful advice—Papyrus Insinger's core message, indeed, seems to be that no advice is really useful, despite its didactic presentation. That is true of Ecclesiastes also, at least to some extent, and both works illustrate the fact that aphoristic observations need not always be intended to modify behaviour. Categories like 'advice literature', therefore, need to be treated with some caution: there is much even in Proverbs that can be described only very loosely as 'advice'. If we set aside the indicative and aphoristic for the moment, however, it is undoubtedly true that Ecclesiastes contains admonitions that seem to link it, broadly at least, to some of the materials in Proverbs and in other ancient compositions—most notably instructions.

It is also true, however, that no direct admonitions are to be found in the monologue before several occur together in 4.17–5.6.[119] The following verse contains what is formally an admonition ('don't be

---

[119] Miller, 'Rhetoric', 228, makes the interesting suggestion that this is a rhetorical strategy: Qohelet works on challenging and 'destabilizing' the assumptions of his audience before he starts telling them what to do. Christianson, in *A Time to Tell*, 244-45, notes more generally a sharp shift to second-person address in the second half of the book, culminating in ch. 11, which displaces the

surprised if'), even though it does not really commend any behaviour, but there are no more until 7.10. A number of commands follow swiftly in 7.13-17, 21, 27-29, although only four of these advise more than looking at something, and then a series of imperatives occur together in 8.2-3, all relating to the same situation. Further linked admonitions are found together in 9.7-10, one isolated prohibition in 10.4, and finally a few on different topics in 10.20; 11.1-2, 6, 9-10; 12.1. It is difficult to count them without imposing complicated definitions,[120] but it would be hard on any reckoning to claim that admonitions occupy a lot of space in the monologue; they do not occur, furthermore, until four chapters have already passed, and after that they are mostly grouped together around particular themes or situations, sometimes with long gaps between the groups.[121] Qohelet's monologue contains admonitions, but in no formal sense can it be described overall as admonitory.[122]

As already noted, it is hard to distinguish aphoristic advice from what is merely observational, and it is often difficult, moreover, to recognize what is actually aphoristic. Taking account of the fact, though, that it is the juxtaposition of sayings which characterizes their use in Proverbs and comparable literature, we might recognize strings of indicative sayings or aphorisms in 4.5-6, 9-14; 5.9-11; 7.1-9, 11-12; 9.16–10.3; 10.8-19. Other scattered statements might

first-person forms that had dominated the first half, and which draws readers into what had previously been Qohelet's more private ruminations. That is an attractive idea, if it is not pushed too far.

[120] Crenshaw, 'Prohibitions', 120-21, indicates the variety of vetitive expressions that Qohelet uses, and his positive admonitions similarly take no single form, so identification depends either on an understanding of the sense in each case, which may sometimes be open to challenge, or an artificial restriction of the description to particular forms.

[121] De Jong, 'Book on Labour', attempts to identify the structure of the book as one of alternating sections of observation and instruction. What he observes, I think, is rather the inclusion of admonitory material, at irregular intervals and in passages of irregular length, within a discourse that is primarily, in his terms, 'observation'.

[122] The long delay, in particular, seems to me to be an obstacle to the formal aspect of Dell's attempt ('Mainstream', 44-45) to tie Ecclesiastes and Proverbs together as 'wisdom literature' through their use of similar forms: there is material in Ecclesiastes that clearly resembles material in Proverbs, but this material does not characterize the book as a whole. I have already expressed my doubts about the comparability of Qohelet's memoir with passages like Prov 24.30-34, which Dell also adduces.

well be understood as aphorisms, but, as with admonitions, the overall numbers are not high, and this sort of material is again often concentrated into particular passages.[123] Someone who read only the sayings and admonitions in 7.1-22 or 9.16–11.6 might be forgiven for thinking that they were reading a text very similar to Proverbs. Equally, though, it is doubtful that anyone who read just chs. 1–3, 6, most of 8–9, or 12, would see any resemblance at all. To be sure, Ecclesiastes contains types of aphorism that are well known to us from elsewhere, such as the 'better than' sayings found in, for example, 4.6 and 7.1. More than half the book, however, contains little or nothing that is formally close to the sorts of material found commonly in Proverbs, or in other works commonly linked to Proverbs.

This is important because we do sometimes find aphoristic and admonitory literature employed in other types of text. Tobit 4.3-19, for example, although badly damaged in the principal Greek text, contains a long section of admonitory parental instruction,[124] and Psalm 34 also adopts the conventions of instruction in its second half, offering a series of admonitions and then of aphorisms. Such cases tend to suggest that advice literature could not only be used as a secondary genre in works that would not primarily be described that way—rather as a novel might *include* a letter or a poem without *becoming* a letter or a poem—but could be used that way almost conventionally. The proportion and distribution do not suggest that quite the same is happening in Ecclesiastes, but neither do they suggest that the book has been designed primarily to be read in the light of existing advice literature: like some other texts, it exploits and reacts to such literature without belonging to it.

(iii) *Summary*

There are, of course, many other aspects of the book that might be investigated, but even this cursory survey of some obvious formal features tends to affirm both the distinctiveness of Ecclesiastes and

---

[123] After acknowledging the difficulties, Klein, *Kohelet*, 68, furnishes a list of 'Sprüche' which are discussed individually in his Chapter 4.2. These include both admonitions and aphorisms, and his definitions are generous, but the list shows a significant concentration in chs. 4–5 and 7–11, with only one or two in each of the other chapters.

[124] For an attempt to recreate the original, see Weeks, 'Restoring the Greek Tobit'.

its rootedness in existing conventions. The original audience would surely have found nothing strange about its first-person presentation and its use of memoir, but it seems equally clear that they would not have associated either characteristic with any single type of composition, let alone read in details about Qohelet's status. Likewise, no ancient audience is likely to have ignored the links with admonitory and aphoristic literature in the second half of the book, but, especially in the light of the cumulative argument which lends coherence to its content, they would probably not have been led by these to read it as an instruction or collection. Overall, the book has many familiar features, but it does not fall into any simple category.

Without going into a detailed analysis of all its components it is important to point out, furthermore, that we have no close parallels to some of the book's most famous passages: the overview of the world and its nature in 1.4-11, the list of times in 3.1-8, or the account of a death that dominates the first part of ch. 12. The nature of the last is disputed, of course, but it is possible to treat these three passages broadly as a group: each involves a sequence or sequences of phenomena set in parallel to make a point or, in that last case, to depict a situation. It is possible to adduce analogies, but at this level of abstraction, of course, we are dealing not so much with a particular type of composition as with a compositional device: none of the three passages has any obviously closer parallel in ancient literature, and it is unlikely that any of them represent some common type that the audience would instantly have recognized. If we acknowledge links elsewhere in Ecclesiastes with reports, instructions and aphoristic collections, we must also acknowledge that much in the book has no such obvious links.

That said, our tendency to categorize and classify material means that any difficulty in classification can give a potentially false impression. So far as we can tell, Ecclesiastes was indeed very original in many respects—but the same could be said of more than a few ancient compositions, and our labelling of others can conceal great variety even within the broader categories. Ancient literature, like modern, may operate with certain conventions, but it is far from tediously formulaic. It is impossible to judge how the original audience would have reacted to the formal aspects of Ecclesiastes, but there is no reason to suspect that they would have found it strangely or disturbingly different from anything they had encountered before. The same may be true of its message.

(d) *Thematic Affinities with Other Literature*
The sheer quantity of comparable material makes it difficult to outline in any detail here the various ways in which some of the principal themes and ideas found in Ecclesiastes resonate with those of other ancient texts. It is easiest, perhaps, simply to offer some of the most compelling examples,[125] and to begin with a work that has its origins in the early second millennium BCE, but is known in versions from various places in Syria and Mesopotamia through to the seventh century. It is generally called the *Ballad of Early Rulers*, and this translation of the Sumerian version is adapted from Alster's presentation of the text:[126]

> With Eni the plans are drawn.
> According to the decisions of the gods, lots are allotted.
> Since time immemorial there has been [w]ind![127]
> Has there ever been a time when you did not hear this from the mouth of a predecessor?
> Above them were those (kings), (and above) those kings were others.
> Above (are) the houses where they lived, [below (are)] their everlasting houses.
> Like the remote heavens, no hand, indeed, has ever reached them.
> Like the depth of the underworld (lit. earth), one knows nothing (about it/them).
> All life is an illusion (lit. 'the turning of the eye').
> The life of mankind was not [intended to last for ever].
> Where is Alulu, the king [who reigned 36,000 years?]
> ...
> Where are those great kings, from former days till now?
> They are no longer engendered, they are no longer born.
> Life onto which no light is shed, how can it be more valuable than death?
> Young man, let me truly instruct you about your god!
> Chase away grief from depression! Spurn silence!

---

[125] Both the texts treated here are also compared with Ecclesiastes in Gianto, 'Human Destiny'.

[126] Alster, *Wisdom of Ancient Sumer*, 312-17; Alster offers editions of all three known versions on pp. 288-322, and sayings in the other versions are often strikingly reminiscent of Qohelet, e.g. from the Neo-Assyrian text, lines 5-6: "Whatever the heart('s desires[?]) are on earth, they are no good, [they evaporate (?)] in "wind(?)" / The task of a scholar's pupil does not yield a joyous heart' (Alster, 321). Slightly more recent presentations are available in Cohen, *Wisdom*, 129-50. For a useful overview of the texts and of the debate surrounding the relationships between them, see Viano, *Reception*, 298-310.

[127] The reading of this line is uncertain; see Cohen, *Wisdom*, 140-42.

> Instead of a single day's joy, let there come a long day of 36,000
> years <of silence!>
> As for her little child, may Siraš rejoice over you!
> These are the regulations of righteous mankind!

Obviously, the text is not easy in places, and it is important not to force the resemblances—but it is also hard not to be struck by them: human lives are divinely determined, brief and illusory; even the famous will be forgotten and their lives left no more meaningful than death; a long, silent death is coming, so the young should learn to be loud and joyful (the goddess Siraš is associated with beer). It is little wonder, perhaps, that some scholars have seen this poem as evidence for the rootedness of Ecclesiastes in Mesopotamian traditions, if not as a direct influence upon its composition.[128]

Probably of similar antiquity, although it is known directly only from Late Bronze Age copies found outside Mesopotamia, is a work that takes the form of an instruction offered to his son by one Šūpê-amēli, followed by the son's response: this is probably the text known under the title *Šimâ Milka* ('Heed the advice!') in an Old Babylonian catalogue of literary works.[129] It is the son's response that is interesting here. After challenging the advice to establish a household by referring to animals that have none, and then noting how a date grove subsists without having to do any work itself, he turns to the associated topics of property and mortality:

> My father, you built a house,
> You elevated high the door; sixty cubits is the width of your (house).
> —but what have you achieved?
> Just as much as [your] house's loft is full, so too its storage room is full of grain.
> —but upon the day of your death (only) nine bread portions of offerings will be counted and placed at your head.
> From your household (var. 'capital') of a thousand sheep
> —(only) a goat, a fine garment—that will be your own [sha]re.

---

[128] So, e.g., Lambert, 'Some New Babylonian Wisdom Literature', 37-42; Klein, 'The Ballad about Early Rulers'; Alster, *Wisdom of Ancient Sumer*, 297.

[129] See, most recently, Cohen, *Wisdom*, 81-128. There is a list of previous editions there, and in my *Ecclesiastes and Scepticism*, 17 n. 10.

Your money? It will be lost! (var. 'From the money which you acquired either bribes or taxes [will be left]')

Few are the days in which we eat bread,
—but many will be the days in which our teeth will be idle.
Few are the days in which we look at the Sun,
—but many will be the days in which we will sit in the shadows.
The Netherworld is teeming, but its inhabitants lie sleeping.
Ereškigal (goddess of the underworld) is our mother and we her children.
At the gate of the netherworld, blinds have been placed,
So that the living will not be able to see the dead.[130]

The first point here, of course, is that the father, who has built a large house and filled its stores with grain, will receive only a few offerings of bread at death; from his wealth and huge flocks he will get only a goat and a garment. He will not really be able to use even these, however, because the many days of death that follow a brief life under the sun will be spent asleep, in a place that is concealed from mortals. Between them, the *Ballad* and *Šimâ Milka* show that the consequences of death for the living—including the loss of their property—were already a concern in Mesopotamian literature centuries before the composition of Ecclesiastes, and this concern was addressed in ways that are sometimes strikingly similar. The distribution of both texts, furthermore, makes it clear that they were known outside Mesopotamia itself before the end of the second millennium.

Other scholars, though, have looked elsewhere, and particular attention has been paid to an Egyptian text which describes itself, perhaps fictionally, as a harper's song from the tomb of King Intef (there were several kings with this name at the end of the third millennium)—its actual date and origin are disputed:[131]

---

[130] The translation here is Cohen's, slightly modified for clarity: see his *Wisdom*, 99-101.

[131] This translation is the one I offered in *Ecclesiastes and Scepticism*, 137-38; the readings and understandings of the Egyptian that I have adopted are discussed in detail there. I have based it on the transcriptions of Papyrus Harris 500 (BM Papyrus 10060), col. VI, 2–VII, 3, and on the fragmentary copy from the tomb of Paatenemheb (the Leyden fragment), in Fox, 'A Study of Antef', 405-406. As before, I have taken liberties with the presentation of the text for the sake of

> *The song which is in the tomb of Intef, the justified, which is in front of the harpist:*
> This noble is flourishing: fate is good, perishing good.
> A generation has been going, another staying on,
> Since the time of the ancients.
> The divine dead who existed long ago, are at peace in their pyramids;
> Nobles become spirits, likewise buried in their pyramids.
>
> Those who built tombs—their places are no more:
> see what has been done with them!
> I have heard the words of Imhotep and of Djedef-Hor,
> widely quoted as their sayings.
> See the places belonging to them, their walls crumbled away—
> their places are no more, as though they had never existed.
> None comes from there
> to say how they are doing, to say what they are doing
> until he has made our hearts whole,
> until we pass swiftly to the place they went.
>
> But be happy in your heart:
> Forgetfulness performs the spirit-making rite for you.
> Follow your heart while you exist,
> put myrrh upon your head, dress yourself in fine linen,
> anoint yourself with true wonders of divine stuff.
> Keep adding to your happiness, let your heart never slacken.
> Follow your heart and your happiness, do your things on earth.
> Let your heart never perish, until there comes to you that day of lament:
> the Weary-Hearted One doesn't hear their lament,
> weeping doesn't save a man from the netherworld.
>
> *Refrain*: Have a holiday—never tire of it!
> No one can have his things go with him.
> There is none who goes comes back again.

Again, this poem proposes that life should be enjoyed because death is unknown, and its expression of that enjoyment is strongly reminiscent of Qohelet's words at 9.8—which, as we saw above, find a parallel also in the Mesopotamian Gilgamesh traditions. We also find references to forgetfulness and the loss of property here, and the poem's attitude towards death stands in strong contrast, of

clarity. For collected translations of harpers' songs, see especially Lichtheim, 'The Songs of the Harpers', and Wente, 'Egyptian "Make Merry" Songs Reconsidered'. Fox also gives a translation and a transcription of Papyrus Harris in his *Song of Songs*, 345-47, 378-80.

course, both to the assumptions of the Egyptian funerary cult, and to the detailed claims made about the afterlife in some other Egyptian texts. This attracts criticism in another song (see Lichtheim, 'The Songs of the Harpers', 197-98), but much of the content is highly conventional, in fact, and found in other harpers' songs and funerary inscriptions. This is true even of the initial reference to the coming and going of generations, which is sometimes linked elsewhere to natural phenomena. Just before it too commends rejoicing in life, for instance, the *Song of Khai-Inheret* remarks that:

> (As) the waters go downstream
> And the north wind goes upstream,
> (So) every man (goes) to his (appointed) hour.[132]

Of course, the reference here is to the Nile, and the theme seems to be very different from that expressed by Qohelet in 1.6-7, but there are enough points of contact with Egyptian harpers' songs more generally that Stefan Fischer (in his his *Die Aufforderung zur Lebensfreude*, and 'Qohelet and "Heretic" Harpers' Songs') has seen them as a major influence on Ecclesiastes. Certain of the themes in the Intef song, moreover, recur many centuries later in tomb autobiographies from the Late Period. For example,

> O my brother, my husband,
> Friend, high priest!
> Weary not of drink and food,
> Of drinking deep and loving!
> Celebrate the holiday,
> Follow your heart day and night,
> Let not care into your heart,
> Value the years spent on earth!
> The west [i.e. the place of the afterlife], it is a land of sleep,
> Darkness weighs on the dwelling-place
> Those who are there sleep in their mummy-forms.
> They wake not to see their brothers,
> They see not their fathers, their mothers,
> Their hearts forgot their wives, their children.[133]

---

[132] From Lichtheim, 'The Songs of the Harpers', 201.
[133] From the Stela of Taimhotep. Translation from Lichtheim, *Ancient Egyptian Literature III*, 62-63. See also Burkes, *Death in Qoheleth*, 190-97; Burkes' excellent study considers more generally the developments in attitudes to death which are reflected both in such texts and in Ecclesiastes.

At the very least, then, Mesopotamia can claim no monopoly on the idea that humans should be motivated by the prospect of death to enjoy their lives while they can. As has long been recognized, however, some of the most striking resemblances to Ecclesiastes are to be found in a body of literature that comes neither from Egypt nor from Mesopotamia: the works of Theognis, who was a Greek lyric poet of the sixth or late seventh century BCE. 'Theognidea' were widely cited in classical literature, and many of the quotations ascribed to him were probably not, in fact, his work. Authentic or not, however, a few examples indicate the numerous correspondences of thought and expression which led Ranston, a century ago, to suggest a relationship with Ecclesiastes:[134]

> Nobody, Cyrnus, is himself responsible for loss and profit,
> but gods are the givers of both these things.
> Nor does does any human labour knowing, at heart,
> whether he is moving to a good conclusion or a bad.
> For often, expecting to do badly he does well,
> and expecting to do well he does badly.
> Nor do as many things come to a man as he wants:
> for he holds the means of terrible hardship.
> We humans value vanities, knowing nothing,
> but gods bring everything to a conclusion
> according with their own purpose.   (Theognis 133-142)[135]

> The best of all things for humans is not to be born,
> nor see the rays of the dazzling sun
> —but once born, to pass as swiftly as possible through the gates of Hades
> and lie with much earth heaped over.   (Theognis 425-428)

> I'll make one suggestion to all humans: while you still are young,
> having a bright bloom, and soundness of mind at heart,
> enjoy what you have. For there is no growing young
> twice comes from the gods, nor release from death
> for mortal humans...   (Theognis 1007-1011)

> Respect and fear the gods, Cyrnus, for it is this that restrains a man
> From doing or speaking impiety.   (Theognis 1179-1180)

---

[134] Ranston, 'Ecclesiastes and Theognis'; see also his 'Koheleth and the Early Greeks' and *Ecclesiastes and the Early Greek Wisdom Literature*.
[135] My translations appeared originally (alongside the Greek text) in *Ecclesiastes and Scepticism*, 135-36, and are based on the text in West, *Iambi et Elegi Graeci*, 180, 194, 21, and 231.

Here we have again the issues of providence and of living life in the face of death, but also notions of profit, of unpredictability, of illusion as a consequence of ignorance, and even of fearing the divine. Living is described as 'seeing the sun' (cf. also Theognis 567-570; 1143; or elsewhere as 'being seen by the sun', cf. Theognis 167-168; 615-616; 847-850; 1183-1184), and deemed worse than never being born (cf. Eccles 4.2-3). Elsewhere, Theognis, like Qohelet, talks to his heart (Theognis 213; 877-878), and in a discussion about spending wealth at 903-930, he draws a comparison between two men he has seen, who each behaved differently, which is very reminiscent of Qohelet's anonymous illustrations. Unless we date Ecclesiastes very early, Ranston's suspicion that Theognis was a major, although probably indirect influence on the book, hardly seems unreasonable—even if that seems to leave us with three wholly different traditions as potential suppliers.[136]

It is unlikely that the author of Ecclesiastes would have known Middle or Late Egyptian—and Middle Kingdom compositions were probably little known even in Egypt by the Achaemenid period.[137] It is also highly improbable that he would have known Sumerian, or have had any practical reason by Achaemenid times to have learned even Akkadian, so while we cannot absolutely exclude the possibility, the chances seem slim that he would actually have read any of the Near Eastern texts directly (so, similarly, van der Toorn, 'Echoes', 512; cf. Bolin, *Ecclesiastes*, 47). If Ecclesiastes is

---

[136] I am speaking broadly here. Hengel, *Judentum und Hellenismus*, 226-27 ET 1:123, notes a number of Greek epitaphs that express similar sentiments, and that the *carpe diem* theme, in particular, was widespread in the Hellenistic world, while Jarick, in 'Ecclesiastes among the Comedians', finds many parallels in Athenian comedy, and Bolin, *Ecclesiastes*, 49-50, finds parallels in Greek legends about wise kings. It is not unreasonable, at any rate, to speak of Theognis as representative of a tradition somewhat wider than Greek lyric poetry, and the ideas expressed in Egypt and Mesopotamia seem not to have been confined to single types of composition. It might not be inappropriate even to speak of three different cultures (while allowing, of course, that those cultures never existed wholly in isolation from each other).

[137] Cf. Quack, 'Interaction', 375: 'there is no evidence that literary texts in classical Middle Egyptian language were created anew during the Late period. As a matter of fact, they even seem to have died out during that period; there is no single manuscript of a Middle Egyptian literary composition later than the Saïtic period'. The 26th, Saite Dynasty was the last to rule Egypt before the Persian conquest in 525 BCE.

as late as most scholars assume, then a knowledge of Greek and of the famous Theognis seems more plausible. It is hardly less likely, however, that these themes and motifs circulated much more generally, in both literary and oral traditions, across much of the eastern Mediterranean and Near East, and it is difficult to say how far any given manifestation of them was shaped by any other.[138] It should not astonish us that different writers, in different regions and over a long period of time, might have engaged with the issues of life and living that are faced by all humans, or that they might sometimes have reached similar conclusions. That is not to say that the resemblances between Ecclesiastes and other texts reflect no more than coincidence, and it seems no more likely that the author knew none of these other texts and traditions, mediated in some form or another, than that he knew all of them. What they show, rather, is that many of the key images, reflections and conclusions attributed to Qohelet might well have been familiar already to the original audience, whatever their context: despite the investigative fiction that it adopts, the book is not proclaiming new discoveries, but at least partly re-framing ideas that were ancient and widespread.

In passing, it should be observed that all of this is relevant to the way we contextualize Ecclesiastes within the Judaism of its time. Unless we are willing to assign a similar cause to every manifestation (as, apparently, does Crüsemann, 'Die unveränderbare Welt', 88 ET 63), the many appearances of such ideas in ancient literature make it unlikely that their appearance in our book can only be explained as the consequence of particular historical events, or as a reaction in the author's own society either to some loss of

---

[138] Van der Toorn, 'Echoes', 511, cautions against 'the blurring vision by which distinct traditions are seen as one abstract whole', but Kelly, 'Sources', addresses this complaint directly in a wide-ranging survey of the materials that resemble 9.7-9. He concludes, rightly I think, that the themes and idioms are too prevalent for us to identify any particular literary source for them, at least amongst those that are extant, and defends Murphy's contention (xlv) that the similarities to other literature found in Ecclesiastes 'witness to certain relatively common ideas of the ancient world'. Van der Toorn himself is arguably guilty of a different sort of 'blurring' when he acknowledges a lack of any precise correspondence to Greek philosophical literature, but insists that Qohelet owes an 'unmistakable debt to the spirit of Greek popular philosophy' (513), as though that were some single, distinct and readily defined entity (see below on Braun).

confidence, or against more 'optimistic' or 'orthodox' literature. I doubt we can even say very generally, as Crenshaw ('Qoheleth in Historical Context', 288) claims, that they point to a community 'struggling to grasp the implications of a loss of certainty', or that they point, indeed, to the 'struggles' of 'a community' in any way at all. These are conventional themes, not certainly expressive even of real anxieties, and cannot constantly be characterized as the recurrent symptoms of societal or intellectual 'crises' (however fond German-speaking scholars, especially, may be of that terminology—see, e.g., Lauha, 'Die Krise des religiösen Glaubens'; Gese 'Krisis'; Michel, 'Kohelet und die Krise'; Kaiser 'Die Sinnkrise').

Rose ('Crise') rejects the notion of a crisis for other reasons: defining 'wisdom' methodologically, he sees a continuity between Ecclesiastes and earlier works. Without subscribing to that view in particular, it does seem important nonetheless to stress the continuity of these ideas, which seem to have been deep-seated as well as widely distributed, and in each culture to have co-existed with very different beliefs—probably without significant friction. It is far from clear, furthermore, that such different beliefs or emphases were associated with different groups or sections of society, although it is very possible that, at any given point, they represent different registers of each culture. Even were we to suppose, for some reason, that Ecclesiastes must represent some independent formulation of similar ideas, then the very fact that such co-existence marks diversity elsewhere would make it unreasonable to insist that Ecclesiastes must reflect a special break within Judaism, or that it would even necessarily have been regarded by contemporaries as subversive or polemical in any meaningful way. As it is, the fairest assumption we can make is that the book draws not on some recently dug, communal well of resentment or despair, but on motifs and traditions of expression that were known in the region long before there even was a Jewish nation or community, and very likely co-existed with other ideas and traditions throughout the history of that community.[139]

---

[139] Such objections can also be levelled, of course, against explanations of the book in terms of a personal crisis. Broadly psychological treatments go back further than one might expect (see especially Johann Ewald's 1800 *Salomo*, which discusses Ecclesiastes in the ninth chapter), and aspects of Ecclesiastes are

The long history and wide distribution of ideas is also important when we turn more particularly to consider the not uncommon claim that Ecclesiastes has been influenced or provoked by Greek philosophy. Of course, any examination of that claim runs at once into problems of definition: Theognis could be (and sometimes is) called a philosopher, just as much pre-Socratic philosophy could as well be called poetry.[140] Both would most likely have been familiar to Greeks through symposia, and it is doubtful that any significant distinction would originally have been seen between them. Plato (*Laws* 1.630; *Meno* 95-96) is clear and explicit that Theognis is a poet, but cites him as a source of moral claims or insights, so to the extent that Ecclesiastes resembles Theognis, it seems unlikely that anyone familiar with Greek traditions would have refused to link the book with what we might now recognize as philosophy. This is in essence, though, a problem of generic labelling similar to those that we have encountered already, and the fact that an ancient audience might not have made the same clear distinctions as a modern one does not legitimize a blurring of our own categories—a difficulty that is evident, for instance, in the notion found in Braun's *Popularphilosophie* of a Greek 'popular philosophy'. That concept incorporates all sorts of gnomic, dramatic, and other materials, providing a wealth of analogies to particular topics or expressions in Ecclesiastes, but Braun then uses those as the basis of claims for a direct relationship with thinkers like the Cynics or Sceptics, whom

---

often attributed to facets of the author's personality (see, e.g., Galling, 'Kohelet-Studien', 281), but it is Zimmermann who most famously claims (IX), that the book 'is a mirror of the chain of neuroses that afflicted' Qohelet. The fact that many of its ideas are very old would make it difficult, furthermore, to use those ideas themselves as a criterion for dating Ecclesiastes, either relatively (perhaps by treating them as a reaction against material in Proverbs), or absolutely (perhaps by associating Qohelet's materialism with Ptolemaic commerce, as various scholars have done more casually).

[140] See Osborne, 'Was Verse the Default Form for Presocratic Philosophy?', who notes (28-29) that for this period 'the quantity of known prose philosophy is tiny...up to Heraclitus we have only one sentence of prose, and that is not prosaic in its style of diction', and who argues (30-31) that 'the normal way to publish one's thoughts to a large audience, probably predominantly listeners rather than readers, was in poetic recitation', with prose becoming a mass medium for philosophy perhaps only after its encounter in fifth-century Athens with the rhetorical tradition of public speaking—up to that point, it is rarer, and addressed only to a smaller literate audience.

we would more naturally describe as 'philosophers', but with whom Qohelet has little specifically in common (see also the critique of Braun in Kaiser, 'Judentum und Hellenismus', 138-40).

The problem is made no easier by the fact that we do not operate with clear-cut definitions of our own. To put it plainly, though, if we try to read Theognis in terms of the ontological, cosmological, and epistemological discourse usually associated with subsequent understandings of the Greek philosophical tradition, then it proves difficult to do so without reading in more than is explicitly stated. However ancient readers might have classified Theognis, we would not commonly place his work in our category of philosophy, or assume that a resemblance to his work implied a close connection also with, say, Plato, or the Stoic tradition. Correspondingly, when we read Ecclesiastes, it is easy to find superficial resemblances to philosophical themes and concerns, but difficult to find anything that is inherently 'philosophical' except on a very broad definition. When Qohelet talks about the world in the first chapter, for example, it would be a considerable stretch to say that his analogies are scientific or cosmological: he is not attempting to explain natural phenomena, but using the common experience of them to make a point. Likewise, although his reservations about the scope of human wisdom might be called epistemological in some very broad sense, it would be misleading to understand them as an exercise in epistemology: Qohelet never concerns himself with *how* we know anything. The monologue, to be sure, includes arguments of a sort, but there is no interest in argumentation or critical thinking, and although (as we saw earlier) much weight has been placed on an apparent reference to Qohelet's thought-processes in 7.27, the verse could hardly sustain such weight even if it certainly contained such a reference.

Whether or not Qohelet actually 'does' philosophy on any measure, moreover, the very clear resemblances between Ecclesiastes and other ancient texts make it difficult to sustain any specific claim that the author must have been writing with an awareness of Greek philosophical texts or systems in particular—even Theognis is probably at best a contemporary of the early pre-Socratics, while the Mesopotamian and Egyptian materials are largely much older. To the extent that such works address issues of life and living that were also of interest to subsequent, self-consciously philosophical writers, it is inevitable that there should be points of contact, and unsurprising that there might be points of agreement as well. For very much the same reason, it is not unhelpful to bring any such works into dialogue with philosophy, and a number of writers have done this very productively with Ecclesiastes. From a historical point of view, however, the book can itself be called philosophical only in a very general way, and there are no good reasons to suppose that it was composed in reaction to, or even with any specific awareness of, the Greek or any other recognized philosophical tradition. Barnes, an expert in the Greek tradition, concludes memorably and unequivocally (in 'L'Ecclésiaste', 114 [624 in the English version]), that 'the Preacher has no interest in Greek philosophy, a subject about which he knows nothing whatsoever; and—for all the text reveals—he has no interest in or knowledge of Greek culture'.

Finally, having observed some sometimes striking resemblances between Ecclesiastes and literature from other cultures, it is important to ask, of course, whether counterparts to its major themes and ideas were also to be found in earlier Hebrew literature. To the extent that the biblical texts may be only a subset of that literature, it is, of course, difficult to answer the question with any certainty, and the presence of analogous concerns in literature from so many other traditions raises the strong possibility that they were present also in earlier Hebrew oral traditions, or in texts that are now lost to us—just as it is likely that Song of Songs presents only a fragment of the tradition that it represents. At the very least, we should not use the absence of closely analogous works to suggest in itself that Ecclesiastes must be radically discontinuous with anything that went before. Even without speculating beyond the evidence that we do possess, however, it is possible to see some connections in earlier literature.

Most obviously, of course, the determinism that is so central to Qohelet's thinking is not confined to Ecclesiastes, and explicit statements about the divine control of individual lives appear in Proverbs (e.g. 19.21; 21.30-31), although the consequences are not drawn out there. There is a less general resemblance, perhaps, in Ps 39.5-7 (ET 39.4-6), which Crenshaw ('Qoheleth in Historical Context', 295-97) sees as especially close to Ecclesiastes. This is set within a first-person account and associates the transience of human life with ignorance about the future ('one heaps [things] up and knows not who will gather them'). More broadly, the psalm is punctuated by references to *hebel*, two of them in a repeated statement that identifies every human as *hebel*, and its plea to God seems to be for respite from his attentions, so that the psalmist can find a little happiness in his brief life before death. That plea finds a close parallel in Job 10.20, and it is the book of Job, of course, that has most often been set beside Ecclesiastes, and classed with it as 'sceptical' or 'pessimistic' literature.

Such descriptions tend to raise more questions than they answer, and can be misleading if taken to suggest that Job and Ecclesiastes always sing in harmony (whether or not the author of Ecclesiastes knew Job, as, e.g., Krüger, 'Dialogue', 104, suspects). Both, to be sure, formally develop their discourse as a response to some particular event—the destruction of Job's prosperous life and the failure of Qohelet's experiment to supply what he wanted—and both have a clear interest in issues around divine justice. Arguably, indeed, that interest is more precisely in the hiddenness of divine justice, and the consequent misperceptions that this can create: Job's principal concern is not that God might be unjust (a possibility that never occurs to Qohelet), but that his own problems are being perceived by others as divine punishment. For all its discursiveness at various points, however, it is not clear that the book of Job ever really ventures far beyond these concerns with justice, and with the inability of humans to constrain or comprehend the divine. In Ecclesiastes, on the other hand, those issues are less at the forefront of Qohelet's concerns, and act more as a starting-point or background for his concern with how humans should live. Likewise, Job 28 famously discusses the inaccessibility of wisdom, and perhaps suggests that God has established a monopoly in it, but although Qohelet is no less concerned with wisdom, his emphasis is more upon its inherent pains and limitations. There are differences between them, then, which should not be understated, but both books do depict humans struggling with problems that flow from a belief in absolute divine sovereignty over the world, and with the constraints that it places upon them. Without the presence of the other, each would seem more isolated in the biblical canon, and Job provides the clearest evidence that the author of Ecclesiastes was not the only Jewish writer interested in such problems.

(e) *Summary*

Because it has been preserved for us in the context of a scriptural canon, within which it has memorably been described (in

Kaiser, 'Qoheleth', 84) as a 'ghost at the banquet', and perhaps also because we have become disinclined to make comparisons across the boundaries of categories like 'prophecy' and 'wisdom', Ecclesiastes may seem to us more distinct from other literature than it actually was. Nevertheless, in some important respects, Ecclesiastes is indeed an unusual and original book. Perhaps most strikingly, its organization around a recurring theme enables it to present a sort of cumulative argument in favour of the claim that brackets Qohelet's monologue, and in doing so it also manages to impose coherence on a diverse range of materials. The book as a whole belongs to no known 'type' of composition, and some of its most memorable passages have no obvious precedent. In other ways, however, it seems deeply rooted in existing literature, both formally and thematically: the book incorporates certain styles and ideas that are well attested, and its novelty lies above all in the way it combines and deploys these.

If we accept a date in the Ptolemaic period, then it is difficult to resist a comparison with Theognis, whose poems are written from the perspective of a gently cynical, world-weary aristocrat. Qohelet seems to see the world in much the same way, even though his temperament is, perhaps, portrayed rather differently. Apart from the obvious difference that Theognis writes in verse, what distinguishes the two, above all, is that Qohelet's pronouncements and shifts of tone do not constitute formally separate compositions, but are set together as phases of a single monologue, orientated superficially around a single issue, with short narrative, memoir elements offering an explanation for his attitudes and understandings. For an audience that might have been familiar with Theognis, or at least aware of the similar ideas that were manifested in a wide range of ancient literature, it seems likely that this broad coherence and aggregation of separate themes would have been the book's most original contribution. If that audience was also familiar with the combination of pronouncement and first-person narrative that marks some of the prophetic literature, then the similar approach in Ecclesiastes might itself have seemed less striking than the application of this style to a very different topic. Of course, we can only speculate, but it seems likely that any audience would have seen the book, one way or another, as bringing together in a new way elements that were often already familiar.

C. *The Text of Ecclesiastes*

Although in a fragment from Qumran (4QQoh^a, see below) we do possess one unusually early witness to a small portion of the Hebrew text of Ecclesiastes, most of our witnesses reflect the text as it stood in about the first to second centuries CE or later. As will become clear, there are numerous minor differences between them, and these sometimes include different wordings or suggest very different understandings. They all seem, however, to embody what is basically the same version, and there is no reason to suppose that, at least by this time, the book existed in radically different versions or recensions. Theories that it evolved through a process of substantial revision or supplementation, therefore, cannot appeal directly to text-critical evidence. The various witnesses do often suggest, on the other hand, that the book already provided something of a challenge to its readers: there are many points at which they show varying interpretations, or seem to struggle to understand the text. These difficulties themselves doubtless contributed to the rise of some variants, as attempts were made to ease them, or to adjust the text in the direction of particular understandings, and so although many variants are the result of simple errors in reading or copying, text-critical issues cannot entirely be disconnected from problems of meaning and comprehension. Indeed, it is important to appreciate that the different ancient versions, and even individual copies of the text, are witnesses not only to its form, but to the history of its interpretation.[141]

Accordingly, in the notes to the text I have made an effort to explain how the different versions arrived at their individual readings, rather than simply to select what I take to be the earliest reading. It will become apparent very quickly from these notes, I think, not only that no single version has a monopoly on 'good'

---

[141] Brooke, 'Reading the Plain Meaning', 83, 89, is surely right to wonder 'whether any scribe in the late second temple period would have considered himself to be a mere copyist; they were expositors of the plain meaning of the text, copying it out verbatim for the most part, but enhancing it in many small but intriguing ways', and to suggest that 'modern scholars should be wary of distinguishing between matters they may deem to be in the realm of textual criticism and the scribal transmission of texts and those which can more obviously be described as exegetical or eisegetical'.

readings, but also that in many places there are no strong grounds on which to choose between different readings. Sometimes this is because different variants of the text can each make an equally strong claim to represent an earlier text; sometimes, less helpfully, it is because any single earlier reading has been lost, and can no longer be established from the witnesses that we possess. Both situations lend support in different ways to the common modern opinion that we cannot and should not use textual witnesses simply to reconstruct some single ancestral text—which may never have been familiar to more than a few readers, even if it ever actually existed. Of course, none of that prevents us from attempting to identify the earliest readings available where we can do so, and when engaging with a book that has provoked so much debate about its author's intentions, we can legitimately seek to come as close as possible to that author's words.

As well as appreciating the limitations, it is important that we understand the different character of each witness to the text, and the problems involved in using it for text-critical purposes. These are discussed individually in the sections that follow, but it may be helpful also to begin with a less technical overview of the situation.

The two earliest Hebrew manuscripts of Ecclesiastes that we possess were both discovered amongst the Dead Sea Scrolls at Qumran. One of these, usually dated to the first half of the second century BCE (4QQoh^a), contains small portions of the text between 5.13 and 7.20; the other, 4QQoh^b, which may be as late as the first century CE, contains even smaller fragments from between 1.8 and 1.15. The Hebrew text as a whole is not attested directly in manuscripts earlier than the tenth century. These much later copies, on which most modern translations are based, reflect the culmination of some centuries of work by Jewish scholars known as 'Masoretes', and the Masoretic version (with the siglum **M**) contains a consonantal text supplemented by vowel-points, accents and certain other annotations that were intended, amongst other things, to promote accurate transmission.[142] The source of the vocalization

---

[142] This should properly be distinguished from the pre-Masoretic text, of course, and when scholars speak in shorthand of 'emending' the text of M, they are proposing not to change M, as such, but of borrowing and altering its text as a starting-point for restoring an earlier form.

employed has been much debated, and is discussed at length below. Where the Qumran discoveries tend to reflect a situation in which many texts with different readings co-existed, the earliest Masoretic manuscripts present a much less variable text, and reflect a movement toward significantly greater conformity that seems to have preceded the Masoretes themselves. In reducing the number of variants, however, the scribal tradition sometimes excluded readings that were earlier than those actually adopted, and we have access to these now only via versions in other languages, translated from copies of the Hebrew that had not yet been lost, discarded, or brought into alignment.

Of particular importance in this respect is a Greek translation (**G**), probably made some time in or shortly before the first century CE, but perhaps as late as the second century, which was to become the standard version of Ecclesiastes in the Septuagint Greek Bible of the Eastern churches (although it was itself almost certainly the work of a Jewish scholar and intended originally for Jewish use). In line with conventions that we find in some other Greek translations of the period, the creator of this Greek Ecclesiastes opted to keep as close as he could to the Hebrew source-text or texts with which he was working, and produced a translation that is not easy to read in Greek, but from which it is usually possible not only to reconstruct the underlying Hebrew with a high degree of probability, but also to determine the way in which the translator was parsing and interpreting his unpointed Hebrew text.

We may reasonably assume that he considered his source text or texts the best available to him, and that he drew on whatever traditions or information were known to him when it came to interpretation of those texts, since it was almost certainly the intention of this translator to produce a version that would itself facilitate discussion and interpretation in Jewish circles—and that would, accordingly, need to have been acceptable to informed readers. On a fairly conservative estimate, however, the consonantal Hebrew reflected in his translation differed from the Masoretic text of M^L (on which, see below) in more than a hundred places, and while most of the differences are small, many make a difference to the meaning. There are numerous other places in which the translator probably read the same consonants, but seems to have vocalized them differently, and some in which he even divided the words or clauses of his source differently—all, perhaps, in line with traditions of reading or interpretation that differed from those known to the Masoretes (although they may have been no less ancient). While it is not always possible to choose, it is clear nevertheless that in some of these cases the Greek has preserved an earlier reading of the consonants than the one adopted by the Masoretes, and between them the two versions sometimes supply enough evidence to reconstruct a text that has been preserved fully in neither.

Our greatest problem in this respect lies in reconstructing the original text of the Greek. Probably in the second century CE, three further Greek versions appeared, revising G or providing wholly new translations of the Hebrew. These are attributed to Aquila (α'), Theodotion (θ') and Symmachus (σ'), and readings from them are commonly preserved in manuscript annotations or through direct citations in other works. Generally, although not in every case, they draw on versions of the Hebrew that were closer to the Masoretic tradition than was the source-text of G, and so while they furnish some interesting readings of their own, they differ much less from M. The difficulty lies in the fact that readings from these versions, probably along with other revisions of the text toward the Hebrew, have found their way into the manuscript tradition of G—perhaps in some cases simply because they offer clearer or better Greek—with the result that the text of G has itself at various points been brought closer to M in some or all of the surviving manuscripts. From a practical point of view, this problem has been compounded by the fact that Rahlfs' edition of the Greek Ecclesiastes—the edition most commonly used by modern scholars—not only tends to favour readings close to the Hebrew even when they are sometimes poorly attested in Greek, but also has in places itself 'restored' the text of G on the basis of the text in Saint Jerome's Latin commentary (**Hie**). This was written in the late fourth century, before his more famous translation in the Vulgate (**V**), and Jerome himself used not just G, but Hebrew sources which were again much closer to M; he also drew on the Three, especially Symmachus. Accordingly, that edition brings the text of G into even closer alignment with M, with the result that many important differences between them have commonly been obscured or overlooked.

Similar but more intractable problems surround the use of the Syriac version (**S**), which is a witness simultaneously to the Hebrew and the Greek texts. Where G reflects an underlying consonantal text different from that of M, S supports G slightly more than half the time—but this is not a simple matter of shared Hebrew sources: S exhibits some readings that had developed within the G tradition after it had been translated (such as a gloss found at the end of 2.15), and which must have been derived from Greek manuscripts. Sometimes different Syriac manuscripts individually support M or G where they differ, suggesting that this 'mixture' is in part a result of revisions over time, but it is also likely that the translation was informed by both versions from the outset, and scholars have sometimes suggested that the translator of S used the Greek as a sort of 'crib' when he struggled with the Hebrew. Correspondingly, S can be helpful as a witness to the text of G or M, and provides a few interesting readings of its own, but where G and M offer different readings, it cannot easily be used as an independent witness in support of either.

The Targum of Ecclesiastes (**T**) is a relatively late Jewish translation into Aramaic, and, as we would expect, it commonly supports the readings of M. On a number of occasions, though, it supports G against M, sometimes in a striking way. Since it is most unlikely to have been influenced by G itself, or by any of the other ancient translations that were themselves based on G, this probably indicates that its sources shared some readings or understandings with the source-text of G, despite the relatively late date of T itself. In general, though, a degree of caution is required in the text-critical use of T: it interprets and embellishes the text extensively, even if it is not usually difficult to tell what text lies behind its changes. Of course, while making life difficult for the text critic, these characteristics also offer valuable insights into the way that the text was read and understood. A different problem, for which there is no such silver lining, is the fact that the textual history of T itself is complicated in places, and there is no very helpful critical edition.

Voicing what seems to be quite a common assumption, Longman (25) claims that the ancient versions 'add little to our understanding of the text, since, except for orthography, they essentially agree with the Masoretic Text'. This is not really true, and judging by the evidence of these various witnesses, it would be difficult to claim that the Hebrew text of Ecclesiastes has been transmitted to us in a pristine state. There are many differences between them, many of those differences seem to reflect differences between Hebrew manuscripts that go back to the period before the Hebrew became more fixed, and, where it is possible to judge, M by no means always seems to reflect the more original reading.[143] In a few places, furthermore, it is likely that the text is corrupt, but none of the witnesses enable us to repair it with any degree of confidence. Most of the variations, it should be emphasized, however, are in formal terms very minor: they involve such things as the addition or omission of conjunctions, or the reading of graphically similar characters as, say, ד rather than ר, ו rather than י, or ב rather than כ. In a work where the expression of ideas is often very compact,

---

[143] As will become clear in the notes to individual verses, it is often difficult to choose between variant readings, and in many cases unnecessary to do so. Although, correspondingly, there are not a few other places where its originality is doubtful in 1.1–5.6—the text covered by this first volume—I have rejected the majority consonantal text of M outright only in some eight instances. In two of these there is no significant change to the sense, but M is relatively late or in a clear minority (with no reason otherwise to prefer it): I read with 4QQoh[b] אשר נעשו, 'which are achieved', for M שנעשה (with the same sense) at 1.14, and בירושלם, 'in Jerusalem', for M על ירושלם, 'over Jerusalem', at 1.16, with all the other versions and many Hebrew manuscripts. In a few other places I read the text attested by other versions where it gives a better sense or syntax: so, singular עשהו, 'he has done', for plural M עשוהו in 2.12; העמל, 'the business', with an article for M עמל in 4.4. The versional evidence is less clear cut in 1.10, where I read plural היו, 'were' for M היה, 'was', but the syntactical considerations compelling. In 2.12, the ancient translations do not directly attest a more original reading, but help to show what has gone wrong where the text is apparently corrupt: G and σ' reflect an unexpected המילך, 'the advice', which is probably the source of M המלך, 'the king', but resulted, I think, from metathesis of two characters in an original מה ילך, 'what will he bring?'. Finally, there are two places where I would emend without any versional support, but where there are widely acknowledged to be difficulties in the text or tradition: I take the M שואף, 'drawing' of 1.5 to be an error for שב ואף, 'returns and then', and M המלאך, the messenger', in 5.5 to have added an article to an original מלאך, 'your fulfilling', after it had been misunderstood. In both these cases, I am following or adapting suggestions made by other scholars. Some earlier exegetes made very many more emendations (and a number of these have left a mark on the apparatus of *BHS*), but, for comparison, *BHQ* proposes some nineteen changes here, and although there is little consistency around the actual changes that commentators more generally would make, this sort of number currently seems typical. All that said, there are some substantially greater problems in the second half of the book, as we shall see in the second volume.

though, and in which readers have long struggled to establish just what is being said, even such apparently minor changes can make a significant difference, and have sometimes provoked further changes by scribes seeking to make sense of what they have found. As I said at the outset, indeed, it seems likely that some changes have been motivated in the first place by a desire to 'clarify' the text in favour of certain interpretations, and so, as often elsewhere, the text-critical issues can be bound up tightly with other problems.

1. *Hebrew Texts*

(a) *The Qumran fragments*

(i) *4QQoh^a*

The fragments from this leather scroll, recovered from cave 4 at Qumran in 1952, were first described in detail by James Muilenburg ('A Qoheleth Scroll') in 1954, and subsequently published alongside the fragments of 4QQoh^b by Eugene Ulrich—initially in a 1992 article ('Ezra and Qoheleth Manuscripts', 142-47), and then more formally in the Discoveries in the Judaean Desert series (Ulrich, '4QQoh^{a}'). Alternative presentations of the text from both manuscripts are also offered by Puech ('Qohelet a Qumran'). Seven fragments have been identified altogether: the largest, fragment 1, contains four complete lines from the top of one column (fragment 1, col ii) of the original scroll, and increasingly less of the following three lines. To the right of this column, eight lines are preserved from the preceding column (frag 1, col i), but we only have a few words from the end of each line; to the left, there is a correction inserted into the top margin, followed by four lines from the next column (frag 1, col iii), but, again, we only have a small amount of text, this time from the beginning of each line. The other fragments (probably including the tiny fragment 2, which is hard to place with certainty) belong to the lower half of the same section of scroll, but we have no material extant for the middle of this section. Each column probably had twenty lines originally, but for column ii, the best preserved, we now have text or traces only for six or seven lines at the top, and nine at the bottom (with some extra material written additionally in the top and bottom margins—see figure).

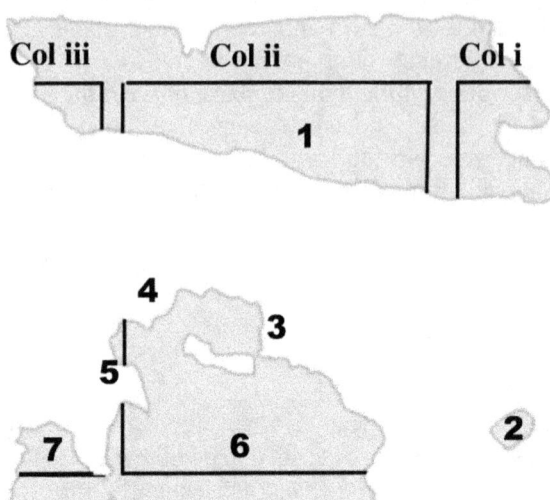

The text originally represented in the three columns corresponds to 5.13 to 7.20. Not all of this has survived, of course, but we can read some or all of:

5.13-17:	frag. 1, col i, lines 1-8
6.3-8:	frag. 1, col ii, lines 1-7
6.12–7.6:	frags. 3-6, col ii, lines 12-20
7.7-10:	frag. 1, col iii, lines 1-5
7.19-20:	frag. 7, col iii, lines 18-20

The manuscript is well-written, and Muilenberg ('A Qoheleth Scroll', 23) says of it that 'The writing is a beautiful specimen of Essene scribal art. The letters are large and spacious, superbly wrought both in their prevailing uniformity and in the artistic flourishes of which the scribe appears to be especially fond. The writing is never crowded or crabbed; each letter stands out sharply and clearly.' Since the script is generally dated to the second quarter of the second century (175–150 BCE), it is questionable, of course, whether it can strictly be considered an Essene product at all (whatever position we adopt on the background of the scrolls more generally), and the manuscript is probably among the earliest of those found at Qumran, pre-dating the establishment of any community there. Its clarity, however, is indisputable, and it is worth observing that the ease with which undamaged portions can be read is enhanced by the use both of generous spaces between words and of distinct final forms for כ, מ, נ, and פ (no final צ is extant in the text, but it is likely that the scribe used final forms for all five of the letters which were later to take these forms more consistently).[144]

(α) *Problems in the text*. For all its virtues, the manuscript does contain some corrections, and there are some especially significant problems at the bottom of column ii and the top of column iii, which affect the reading of 7.6-7. These seem to have arisen principally from the scribe's initial omission of the words הלך ובחושך at the beginning of column ii, line 2, where at first he jumped straight to שמו. Realising this whilst the ink was still wet, but after he had already continued, he erased שמו by smearing it, and then inserted הלך ובחושך שמו in the top margin. Perhaps to avoid entanglement with the first line of column ii, which was, of course, already written, he placed the insertion so that it began above the last word of that line, but extended across the space that was to lie above the (as yet unwritten) column iii. He also placed the insertion in parentheses (the fact that traces of the opening parenthesis collide with the ה suggest that this may have been an afterthought). Beneath the insertion, it is still possible to see the top of the vertical ruling that marks the righthand boundary of column iii; there is also a horizontal line visible, marking the upper limit of the first line. These rules are visible as faint lines elsewhere on the manuscript, but here they appear to have been inked, perhaps to reinforce the

---

[144] The use of final forms even at this early stage of transmission would, on the face of it, have deterred certain common scribal errors, such as metathesis or the wrong division of words. That we do find apparent instances of such errors in the text of Ecclesiastes, even when those letters are involved, is probably to be put down to persistent inconsistency in their use. The Masoretic text of M^L itself preserves the writing לםרבה with a medial 'final' ם at Isa 9.6, and in, e.g., Neh 2.13, the writing המפרוצים (*K^ethîbh*) has probably been brought about by the use of a medial מ in final position: the *Q^erê* directs that this should be two words, הם פרוצים. Some instances are attested for the lost Severus Scroll (see below), and there are many examples in earlier manuscripts, mostly of a medial form used at the end of a word, but sometimes of a final form used in the middle; see conveniently Talmon, 'Fragments', 35-36. It would not be surprising either if such usages actually lay behind some errors in our text, or if scribes consolidated errors by 'correcting' the forms after transposition or misdivision.

separation between the first line of column iii and the text that has been inserted above it.

As we should expect, the scribe seems to have begun writing the first line of column iii straight below the horizontal rule, and although the column breaks off quite quickly, there is space here for seven or eight characters. Only one is visible, however—an initial/medial מ, three or four characters from the start of the line—although traces are visible on either side of it. Given the good preservation of the surrounding text, Ulrich is probably correct to suggest that the first words of line 1 have been deliberately erased. The result looks something like this:

(הלך ובחושך שמו)
מ   line 1
חכם ויעוה   line 2

The matter is complicated by several other factors. The first is physical: there is a tear extending horizontally between lines 1 and 2 from the left side of the fragment to the beginning of the column. This would not matter, except that the characters which follow חכם in line 2 are written above the line—their baseline is the same as the topline of חכם *ḥkm*. The tear, therefore, runs through the upper parts of these letters, making them difficult to read, especially since they appear to have been written not only above the line, but also somewhat smaller than is usual elsewhere on the manuscript. There are no obvious marks or traces on the surface to suggest that this is because the scribe is avoiding an erasure or a fault in the leather. Ulrich reads them as a simple continuation of the text after חכם, and restores ויעוה (cf. Prov 12.8), which would be a variant on M ויאבד; that reading had been adopted previously by Muilenburg also ('A Qoheleth Scroll', 27). This works well in terms of line-length, permitting him to restore lines 2-4, for which we only have one or two words at the start of each line, and line 5, where we only have the top of a ל, with a good fit both to the expected width of the column and to the text of M. This restoration may be correct, but given their curious size and position (about which Ulrich has nothing to say), we should not exclude the possibility that the letters following חכם in line 2 are a correction to the deleted material in line 1, written beneath that line because the top margin was already occupied: the length of lines in the manuscript is not so regular that the scribe could not have fitted the requisite material while writing line 2 around that correction.

Whatever has happened in line 2, the first line raises questions of its own. The only words in M between the end of 7.6 and the חכם of 7.7, which starts line 2 here, are the opening words of 7.7, כי העשק יהולל. That is sufficient text, however, to fill less than half a line on this manuscript, so either there was material in line 1 that is not present in M, or the apparent deletions at the beginning of the line extended for much of its length and reflect the correction of a very significant error. Some weight might be lent to the latter possibility by the scribe's treatment of the previous verse, at the bottom of the preceding column ii: here the הבל which concludes 7.6 is written in the bottom margin, and the זה that precedes it extends a little awkwardly into the left-hand margin. To be sure, the scribe might have wished to avoid starting a new column with the single last word of a preceding sentence, but he could have written at least the זה there as well, and there is nothing in the writing of the last line to suggest that he was trying to squeeze in a few extra letters. More importantly, the הבל lies at the very edge of the fragment that we possess, but this would have put it neither at the start of the line, nor beneath the זה which precedes it—and which must surely have preceded it immediately in the copyist's text: it is highly improbable that there is anything missing between these words in M. If the first line of the next column did begin with a calamitous error, then הבל, or perhaps זה הבל, may have been restored here as part of the effort to correct that error, and the scroll perhaps only partially unrolled to write הבל in its current awkward position, about a third of the way along the original line.

It is true, on the other hand, that some commentators had already wondered, long before the discovery of this manuscript, whether something might be missing before 7.7 in M and the other ancient versions: the כי, usually 'for', which begins the verse does not self-evidently pick up anything in 7.6. If the traces in the first line of column iii (and possibly the superlinear characters after חכם in the next line) are the damaged remnants of such material, then there is enough space for a short saying, about twenty characters long; if the line begins, however, with essentially blank space, where a deleted text once stood, there is correspondingly less room for any additional material, and if the manuscript actually did have a plus, then it may have involved just a few words—perhaps a command or prohibition.

(β) *Relationship with Masoretic texts.* The problems in 7.6-7, outlined in the last section, make it difficult to evaluate the readings of 4QQoh[a] at the point where it potentially diverges most from the consonantal text adopted by the Masoretes. Other differences are discussed in more detail in the notes, but may be summarized here:

	M[L]	4QQoh[a]	notes
5.14	כאשר	כיא	see the notes on this verse
5.15	וגם	גם	
5.16	וכעס	כעס	
5.16	יאכל	יאכל ≠	reading uncertain, but no ל
5.17	בכל	בכול	orthographic
6.3	ממנו הנפל	הנפל ממנו	
6.4	ובחשך (twice)	ובחושך	orthographic
	בא	בה	orthographic?
	ילך	הלך	
6.5	לא...לא	לוא...לוא	orthographic
	נחת	נוחת	
6.6	ואלו	ואם לוא	
	לא	לוא	orthographic
	הלא	הלוא	orthographic
	הכל	הכול	orthographic
6.7	כל	כול	orthographic
	לא	לוא	orthographic
6.8	כי מה	כמה	
	להלך נגד	להלך נגד ≠	traces do not match M
6.12	אשר מי יניד	יֹנִ[י]ד שׁמׁ[	So Puech. Ulrich reads [שׁמׁ]יֹ and also questions whether there is sufficient space for the full text of M בחיים...לאדם
		ש- for אשר	
7.2	משתה	מ[ש]חה	
	הוא	ה[ו]אה	longer form of pronoun
	סוף כל	כול סוף	

INTRODUCTION

7.3	משחק	משחוק	orthographic
	ייטב לב	יי[טבלב	written as a single word
7.4	בבית	בית	possibly twice
7.5	לשמוע	לשמוע	orthographic
	נערת	נערות	plural for singular
	מאיש שמע	מלמוע corrected to מלשמוע	
7.6	שחק	שחוק	orthographic
	וגם	גם	
7.7	ויאבד	וי֯ע֯וֹ֯ד֯]	see discussion above
7.8	מראשיתו	מרשיתו	orthographic
7.19	תעזר	תעז	
	אשר	ש-	אשר היו in
7.20	אשר	ש-	אשר יעשה in

It will be clear from this list that 4QQoh^a makes greater use of *plene* spellings with ו as a vowel-letter than does the consonantal text of M^L or other Masoretic manuscripts, and this sometimes reveals a different interpretation of the text—in 7.5, for example, the reading נערות takes the noun to be plural, where M and the other ancient versions see a feminine singular construct in נערת. Other variations that might be orthographic are found less consistently, or are perhaps to be understood in another way. Despite Muilenburg's suggestion ('A Qoheleth Scroll', 24), it is unlikely that כמה in 6.8 is a 'Phoenician spelling' of the כי מה found in M (see the note 'then how' at 6.8), and the reasons for the spelling כיא in 5.14 need to be evaluated in the light of the fact that the manuscript uses כי elsewhere, in 6.4 and 7.6. The בה (for בא) in 6.4 is also curious, given that the word is spelled בא in 5.14, and may reflect simple carelessness or lack of concern; although that is probably not true, as Goldman claims, of the spelling of הוא as הואה in 7.2 (if the reconstruction is correct)—see the note 'this is the whole end of a human' there. The absence of א from מראשיתו in 7.8, on the other hand, reflects quite a common tendency to omit א even when it is serving as a radical and not as a vowel-letter (the scribes may not always have made a clear distinction). It is difficult, of course, to judge how far the spellings in this manuscript represent those used originally by the author of the book, and how far those in M correspondingly reflect assimilation to later practices. The same can be said for the probable use of -ש in several places where M has the alternative אשר.

(ii) *4QQoh^b*

A second witness recovered from cave 4 at Qumran, and also edited (in part, at least) by Ulrich ('Ezra and Qoheleth Manuscripts', 148; '4QQoh[b]'), is less substantial. As presented in DJD, it consists of two very small leather fragments which both belonged originally to the same column of a scroll. Each contains a few words from three or four generously spaced lines of that column, and although the fragments cannot be joined directly, the last line of fragment 1 contains the top of a ל which would originally have been on the same line as, and followed, the words in the first line of fragment 2. The text starts at 1.10 כבר and the penultimate line of fragment 2 has אשר נעשו תחת, which corresponds to שנעשו תחת in 1.14 of the M text. The few words on each line are clearly separated, and the hand is neat: the small amount of material that remains does not, however, provide a very sturdy basis for palaeographic dating. Ulrich puts the manuscript in the middle of the first century BCE, but allows that it could be as late as the early first century CE; it is, at least, considerably later than 4QQoh[a].

In the same year that Ulrich's official edition appeared, a fragment of manuscript was published by D. Ernst and A. Lange in a different volume of DJD under the title '4QFragment Mentioning Qoh 1:8-9 (4Q468l)'. This very small fragment, about a centimetre high and 2.5 centimetres wide, contains text from two lines, on the second of which we find משמוע מה ש[. This is a sequence found elsewhere only in Eccles 1.8-9 (although the vowel-letter ו is absent from the text of M), and the trace of a character before the sequence would also fit the ן of אזן, which precedes it in M. It is a reasonable supposition, therefore, that the second line contains text from Ecclesiastes. Of the first line, however, Ernst and Lange say:

> The few characters of line 1 do not correspond to the preceding text in the book of Qohelet. Thus 4Q468l either attests to a free and independent text of Qohelet (cf. 4QQoh[b]) or preserves a text alluding to Qoh 1:8-9. The latter seems more probable as the few characters of line 2 provide insufficient evidence to speculate on a third copy of Qohelet at Qumran.

It is difficult to ignore the fact, however, that at the beginning of the first line we do find the characters יג (although Ernst and Lange strangely read וגע[: the initial י could conceivably be a ו—the bottom is missing—but the ע is beyond doubt). These are followed by a *vacat*, and the photographs suggest surface damage, which has also erased the tail of the ע. It is not a great stretch to see a link between these initial characters and the יגעים of 1.8 in M: indeed, it would be a curious coincidence if they were not connected, so it seems that at least part of the first line also contains text from 1.8. The difficulties only arise after the *vacat*, where Ernst and Lange restore the remaining slight traces as]ש̇[ ]נ̇[ ]ל̇[ ]ק̇. Setting those aside for a moment, it is also important to observe that the spacing between the lines on this fragment is similar to that on the two fragments published by Ulrich, and that where the letter-forms can be compared, the handwriting seems strikingly similar on all three fragments. Accordingly, Emile Puech (in 'Un nouveau fragment') was swift to jump in and suggest that Ernst and Lange had failed to realize that this is, in fact, another fragment of 4QQoh^b, and he was surely right to do so.

Given the problems in the last line of the text published by Ulrich, which does not seem to correspond to the M text of Ecclesiastes (see below), it is not impossible both that this new fragment 4Q468l belongs to 4QQoh^b, and that, at the same time, Ernst and Lange were right to see in the first line something different from the M text. Much hinges here, however, on the apparent ק immediately after the lacuna: the subsequent traces are very slight, although it may be said that, from the more recent high-resolution photographs, it is difficult to see any basis at all for the נ that they find among them. The ק, however, is an illusion: the topline of the characters lies along the edge of the fragment, and, as Puech (618) observes, the supposed ק should actually be construed as ל, with the top of the ל lost above the break. There is a similar instance in the second line of 4QQoh^b, where a break in the top makes לוא look like קא. Although the remains of an א that Puech claims to find immediately afterwards are probably a tear in the edge of the leather rather than actually a trace of ink, we can legitimately read [א]לו [ם]יגע here, which fits M. The remainder of the line is sketchier. A partial character that Puech identifies as the ו of יוכל could as well be the י, and although he claims to find evidence of the א and ש from איש, the traces are too slight to be determinative one way or the other. It is highly probable, however, that the first line of the fragment contains throughout a text similar to that found in M, and that 4Q468l is simply, therefore, a fragment of 4QQoh^b containing an earlier portion of the text. It probably comes from very slightly higher in the same column as the other fragments—there may be as little as a single line missing between them.

Taking all the material together, we have text from:

1.8-9:	4Q468l lines 1-2
1.10-12:	Ulrich frag. 1, lines 1-3
1.13:	Ulrich frag 2, lines 4-5; frag 1, line 4 (only the ל of על)
1.14:	Ulrich frag 2, lines 5-6
1.15:	On line 7, see below

The unhappy timing of the various publications means that 4Q468l is lacking from the *editio princeps* of 4QQoh^b, and because it precedes the other fragments, a proper account of the text would re-number the lines for the purpose of reference to readings. Puech, indeed, offers such a re-numbering, but he also restores and lays out very differently the text of the fragments published by Ulrich,[145] and there is considerable scope for confusion here, so I have retained separate numbering.

(α) *Problems in the text*. The last line (7) of the portion published by Ulrich has two clear characters and the trace of a third: Ulrich presents these as]גבו˚[, but the final trace could belong to any of a number of different characters, whilst there is considerable unmarked space before the ג, probably a break between words. Recent photographs show more clearly traces of the upright from another character before this space, so it might be better to represent the text as]˚גב˚[. This corresponds to nothing in the M text of 1.14-15: indeed the combination גב does not occur in the book until 5.7, and even were we to discount the ב for some reason, the reading could not correspond to the next ג, in 1.16 הגדלתי. Correspondingly, this manuscript either contained only an extract from Ecclesiastes, followed by some other material, or had a text in 1.14-15 that differed from the text of M: there is nothing in M

---

[145] 'Un nouveau fragment', 619. Puech's reconstruction problematically has to include a supposed 2 cm lacuna at the beginning of one line for him to achieve the fit that he wants.

that could have left these traces. Especially taking account of the material from 4Q468l, the extract here would have to have been so long that we can probably discount the possibility that Ecclesiastes was simply being cited. If we are dealing with a textual variant, however, it is obviously difficult to say whether what we have here is a plus, or an alternative to something in the text of M. Puech's reconstruction leads him to read גבו]ר after the place where M has לתקן in 1.15, and to read להיות גבור in place of לתקן. However, if we are indeed to read גבור, as seems very likely, then it would more logically have served as a subject for the first יוכל in that verse, giving 'crooked, a strong man could not straighten (it)...'. The strongest objection to this is that the trace preceding גב, although it is tall, is not so tall as the ל found elsewhere in the manuscript, making it difficult to restore יוכל there; the ink of the trace fades fast towards the top, though, and the upper part of an ל may simply have been lost—its height makes it difficult to associate the trace with any other character.

(β) *Relationship with Masoretic texts*. With only a small amount of text preserved, the number of variants is necessarily small as well, and may be summarized as:

	M^L	4QQoh^b	notes
1.8	לא	לוא	orthographic
	משמע	משמוע	orthographic
1.10	לעלמים	לעולמים	orthographic
1.11	לא	לוא	orthographic
1.14	שנעשו	אשר נעשו	
1.14/1.15	לא יוכל לתקן	לוא יוכ[ל גבו]ר לתקן ?	see above

As in 4QQoh^a, there is a tendency toward a greater use of *plene* spellings with ו as a vowel-letter than in M. Although 4QQoh^a has two or three cases of -ש where M has אשר, on the other hand, we find an instance here of the opposite.

(b) *Masoretic texts (**M**)*
The standard critical edition of the Masoretic version is now *Biblia Hebraica Quinta Editione* (*BHQ*), published by the Deutsche Bibelgesellschaft in Stuttgart. Fascicle 18 (*General Introduction*

and Megilloth), which includes the edition of Ecclesiastes by Y. A. P. Goldman, was published in 2004. The text is based on manuscript EBP. I B 19a of the St Petersburg State Library, better known as Codex Leningrad (M^L), which was produced in Cairo, probably in 1008 or 1009 CE (the information given by the codex itself offers dates between 1008 and 1013). This is later, therefore, than the famous Aleppo Codex (M^A), which was written around 930, but is the earliest complete manuscript of the Hebrew Bible because the latter has been damaged, and significant portions are missing—including the entire text of Ecclesiastes. The *BHQ* text is intended to reproduce M^L in all but some specific aspects of layout, and is effectively a diplomatic edition. In the commentary, I have cited the text and apparatus as '*BHQ*', the editor's critical notes as 'Goldman'.

(i) *The Consonantal Text*
Writing at the end of the first century CE, or the beginning of the second, but alluding to the earlier admonition in Deut 4.2, Josephus famously claimed about his fellow Jews that

δῆλον δ' ἐστὶν ἔργῳ, πῶς ἡμεῖς πρόσιμεν τοῖς ἰδίοις γράμμασι· τοσούτου γὰρ αἰῶνος ἤδη παρῳχηκότος οὔτε προσθεῖναί τις οὐδὲν οὔτε ἀφελεῖν αὐτῶν οὔτε μεταθεῖναι τετόλμηκεν, πᾶσι δὲ σύμφυτόν ἐστιν εὐθὺς ἐκ πρώτης γενέσεως Ἰουδαίοις τὸ νομίζειν αὐτὰ θεοῦ δόγματα καὶ τούτοις ἐμμένειν καὶ ὑπὲρ αὐτῶν, εἰ δέοι, θνήσκειν ἡδέως.

There is a visible indication of the way we approach our own scriptures: though such a long time has already passed, nobody has dared to add to or subtract from them, or make any change, but it is innate in all Jews, from the moment of their birth, to reckon them the teachings of God, to abide by them, and further, if needs be, happily to die for them. (*Contra Apion* 1.42; my translation)

We find echoes of a similar idea in *b. ʿErubin* 13a, where R. Meir is cited indirectly as talking of his studies with R. Akiba and R. Ishmael. When asked by the latter about his profession, he says that he is a scribe, and is told:

בני הוי זהיר במלאכתך שמלאכתך מלאכת שמים היא שמא אתה מחסר אות אחת
או מייתר אות אחת נמצאת מחריב את כל העולם כולו

My son, be careful in your profession—for your profession is a heavenly profession—lest you leave out a single character or add a single character, so that you end up destroying all the world completely.

That passage forms part of a much longer conversation about the use of קנקנתום (copper or iron sulphate) in R. Meir's ink, in which the issue is that this substance preserves the ink but makes it impossible to blot out curses in water, as demanded by Num 5.23. It is just one aspect, therefore, of a broader rabbinic concern with the production and treatment of scrolls, more particularly Torah scrolls, but its specific reference to accurate preservation of the text only reinforces an impression that Judaism went to extraordinary lengths to safeguard the integrity of its biblical text. Indeed, the idea expressed by Josephus, of an unaltered, unalterable text, has long had a grip on the imagination of Jewish readers, even if the reality is more probably that there were differences between biblical texts throughout their history, and that even when modern printing enabled the production of an unalterable text, that text was still far from unaltered.[146] The idea has not been without influence in more modern scholarship as well, and as Martin Goodman (in 'Sacred Scripture', 106) has remarked sceptically, 'It is tempting, particularly perhaps for biblical scholars, to assume that people who believe that a text is sacred will go to great trouble to ensure its precise transmission'—he goes on to note of Josephus himself that he 'could vary the biblical text considerably, while claiming, however speciously, to reproduce it with complete accuracy'.

Late in the second half of the first millennium CE, this desire to preserve and to consolidate the text (along with other concerns, as we shall see) found expression in the development of biblical texts equipped with vowel and cantillation marks that fixed the pronunciation, and in which the text itself was supplemented by an apparatus of lists and annotations designed, at least in part, to secure its safe transmission. Little is known about the early 'Masoretes' whose work is represented in these manuscripts,[147] and who seem

---

[146] On the continuing problems caused by the clash between ideal and reality, see especially Levy, *Fixing*, which also touches on issues around the association of the biblical writings with the Temple (7-13).

[147] The term 'masorah' itself is older, and has been picked up from such uses as the famous *m. 'Abot* 3:13, מסרת סיג לתורה, 'tradition is a fence for the Torah', or

to have been active from at least the middle of the eighth century in Babylon, Jerusalem and Tiberias. Equally, we do not have sufficient evidence to reconstruct with confidence the historical development of the various elements that characterize their texts—although we do know that the conventions developed in Tiberias, which eventually dominated the tradition from about the end of the ninth century, were not originally without rivals: texts using the Palestinian and Babylonian systems of vocalization have been known to Western scholars since the nineteenth century. Beyond frequent references to different 'western' (Tiberian) and 'eastern' (Babylonian) habits, however, Masoretic sources typically refer only to a small number of named individuals. We can say with some confidence that the ben Asher family in Tiberias was involved over several generations, and perhaps for as long as two centuries, but that in itself indicates the extent to which this may have been a family-scale undertaking. Although their work was to prove extremely influential, therefore, it is better to think of these Masoretes as an assortment of connected and highly specialized scholars than as any sort of large, institutionalized body. The influence that they came to exercise was ultimately derived from their reputation rather than from any official standing, and did not involve any ability to command the destruction or replacement of manuscripts created by others.[148]

---

b. *Megillah* 3a, where the divisions of the text into units of sense are identified as traditions (מסורת) which have been forgotten and then revived. In b. *Sukkah* 6b and in b. *Qiddušin* 18b it apparently refers specifically to the spelling of the biblical text (in the latter, as opposed to the conventional pronunciation); see below.

[148] A list of Tiberian scholars that has been preserved in manuscripts of Aaron ben Asher's treatise on accents, *Diqduqe ha-Ṭeʿamim*, names only some fifteen or sixteen individuals from about the end of the eighth century to the beginning of the tenth (some confusion in the text makes it difficult to count). These include the father and son Riqat and Abraham ben Riqat, along with several generations of the ben Asher family. See Mann, *Jews in Egypt*, 2:43-49; Chiesa, *Emergence*, 38-41, 81-82; Gil, *A History of Palestine*, 179. One of the others, Pinḥas, is named as 'head of the yeshiva', but this speaks more to the social status of the individuals concerned than to the 'official' status of their project. The list talks of 'many others whose names are not recalled here', and is doubtless not comprehensive: rather later, Ibn Ezra speaks of fifteen scholars who attest to their scrutiny of scrolls (see n. 190, below), although it is not clear whether he is talking about a group of contemporaries or (as seems more likely) about a series of correctors whose work has been recorded over time.

The work of the Masoretes marks a significant stage in what had undoubtedly been a much longer process. Despite the claim made by Josephus, the Qumran scrolls attest to considerable textual diversity even in his lifetime. This diversity is further affirmed by the first Greek translations of the biblical texts, which frequently differ from their later Masoretic counterparts in ways that are most readily explained as a reflection of variants within the early Hebrew tradition itself—and in the Pentateuch there are many striking agreements between the Greek and Samaritan traditions that confirm just such an origin.[149] However, we find a marked tendency to agree more closely with the Masoretic readings even in the later translations by the Three (Aquila, Symmachus and Theodotion, of whom more below), which were all probably produced within the century following Josephus' remarks: although we must be wary of falling into the trap of assuming that the readings they followed were the only readings available to them, it does seem likely that this reflects increasing conformity in the text more generally, or at least the emergence of a majority text.

It is hard to say whether this is the consequence of any deliberate policy. To be sure, earlier references indicate an interest in the text that foreshadows the work of the Masoretes, and *b. Qiddušin* 30a famously speaks of scribes counting all the words of the Torah and of the Psalms in order to establish their midpoints: the passage is concerned to explain the name 'scribe', which is etymologically connected with numbers and counting in Hebrew, but the practice to which it refers—a technique for checking the accuracy of a copy—was to become well-known as a component of the Masoretic tradition. Another discussion, attested in several places, is rather obscure, but probably reflects a rabbinic understanding, at least, that the text of the Torah had been consolidated in the Temple period

---

[149] It is worth mentioning also the Severus Scroll, said to have been looted after the destruction of the Jerusalem Temple, but later donated to a synagogue by the Emperor Severus. Readings from this Torah scroll that differ from Masoretic readings are attested in several late sources and sometimes associated with R. Meir, who apparently knew it, or who made copies (in his capacity as a scribe) that agreed with it. See especially Ginsburg, *Introduction*, 410-20; Lieberman, *Hellenism in Jewish Palestine*, 23-25; Jastram, 'Severus Scroll'; Segal, 'Promulgation', 46-47. Readings attributed to other lost manuscripts are detailed in Strack, *Prolegomena*, 14-29.

by taking the majority reading at points where several manuscripts differed from each other.[150] The difficulty lies not in establishing that there might have been a keen interest in consolidating and preserving the text, but in identifying who, if anybody, would have been in a position to impose such conformity, and on what basis they did so.

For the pre-rabbinic era, the evidence that we possess makes it difficult to draw any general conclusions about the production and control of texts. To be sure, it is not unreasonable to suppose that diverse textual traditions complicated the development of exegetical approaches based on close reading, or that some readers might have found the level of diversity attested at Qumran so problematic that they would have attempted to do something about it. If that ever was the case, however, we have no direct evidence for such efforts beyond the late and difficult account just mentioned. More general claims for the preservation and dissemination of 'special' texts by the religious authorities are speculative and founded on very slender evidence; we may legitimately doubt, anyway, that such protection would have been extended over any length of time to all the works that now comprise the Hebrew canon.[151] For the

---

[150] The accounts are presented and discussed in, e.g., Talmon, 'The Three Scrolls'; see also Levy, *Fixing*, 7-12. Interpretations of the significance vary considerably. The story has developed in various different directions, and it would be rash to treat it as a reliable historical source for Second Temple practices. For a more sceptical approach, see, e.g., Van Seters, '*Sopherim*', 54-57.

[151] It is probable that some writings were kept in the Temple, and there are later references to a ספר עזרה, 'the scroll of the Temple Court', but ideas that an effort was made to maintain a perfect text rest principally on the very problematic account mentioned already. 2 Macc 2.13-15 talks about the collecting together of books, *m. Mo'ed Qaṭan* 3.4 about the general prohibition on writing or correcting books during the intermediate days of Pesach and Sukkot, and *b. Kettubot* 106a about the payment of correctors from Temple funds, but though these and various other references have sometimes been taken to point in that direction, nothing else directly indicates any involvement of the Temple in maintaining the biblical text, as opposed to retaining copies of the Torah and maybe some other works. Presumably these would have enjoyed some status, and they certainly did retrospectively (*y. Sanhedrin* 13a, for instance, speaks of the king being required to copy for himself a text of the Torah, which is corrected against the ספר עזרה), but whether they were actually superior copies is hard to say; *pace* van der Kooij, 'Standardization or Preservation?', 70-71, the account in the *Letter of Aristeas* (29-31, 46), which speaks of the High Priest sending a copy of the Torah, suggests no more than that he had access to one. (Whether the *Letter* shows any concern,

centuries after the destruction of the Temple, our evidence suggests that texts were commonly produced by professional scribes, who worked on a commercial basis rather than under the auspices of any institution—and to a greater or lesser extent, this may have been true in earlier times as well.

As we have already noted, R. Meir was one such scribe, and so scribes clearly could be scholars. It is unlikely, however, that most of them were, or even that their profession offered any equivalent prestige: an interesting passage in *b. Pesaḥim* 50b sheds some light on the book trade when it talks directly about the scribes who produce scrolls, phylacteries and *mezuzot*, stressing that neither they nor the merchants who sell their products are fated ever to become wealthy from them, because were they to do so, they would stop.[152] For a later period in Palestine and Egypt, Gil (*A History of Palestine*, 232) notes that by the eleventh century 'Book production evidently provided many of the Palestinians [whose documents have survived] with a livelihood'. Whether they typically made much money even then, however, is questionable. A contract from that period (Cambridge University Library T-S 10J5.15) does show that Samuel ben Jacob, the scribe of M[L], was able late in his career to command a fee of 25 dinars for copying and pointing the eight books of the Prophets and the Writings,[153] and at the time, this would have

---

indeed, with the replacement of existing, inferior copies depends on the meaning of ἀμελέστερον...σεσήμανται [30], which has been much debated: I doubt that verb can be used of copying, and Demetrius is probably claiming no more than that the Jewish writings had been misrepresented.) Equally, it is a stretch to see in the ספר מוגה of *b. Pesaḥim* 112a any sort of reference to a special, 'corrected' edition of the biblical text, as does, e.g., Tov, 'Large-scale Differences', 139 n. 56. The point of the advice there is simply that you should not teach a child from a book that has not been checked, since it is hard to un-teach an error. With regard to Ecclesiastes in particular, it is questionable in any case whether the book would have had sufficient authority in Second Temple times to have warranted special treatment, and unlikely that copies would have been required for synagogue use.

[152] Bar-Ilan, 'Writing', 22, speaks in terms of scribal status having become diminished in this period. Whether all copyists earlier had a higher social status, however, is questionable: it seems more likely that the term ספר simply characterized a wider range of occupations or affiliations in earlier texts, including high-status official roles.

[153] See Ben Outhwaite, 'Samuel ben Jacob: The Leningrad Codex B19a and T-S 10J5.15', *Fragment of the Month*: Jan. 2016, https://www.repository.cam.ac.uk//handle///-FOTM_January-VoR.pdf (cf. https://doi.org/10.17863/CAM.7894).

been equivalent to about ten times the monthly salary of a skilled labourer, or around five times that of a master craftsman. Such fees, however, were probably not typical. Gil (233-34) also notes the sale of a complete (but presumably unpointed) bible around this time for 13 dinars, and an offer to a widow of 12 dinars for four bibles with minor damage. These are still substantial sums of money, but if we take into account the cost of materials and the amount of time required to copy an entire bible, then it seems unlikely that most scribes were making much more of a living than did other skilled labourers, and their livelihood may have been somewhat precarious. We have a number of letters from the scribe Israel ben Nathan, who was responsible for that 13-dinar bible, in which he is very actively touting for work and begging favours from wealthy supporters— not least, as he observes in one such letter, because there were not always enough local scholars in need of his services. There is likely to have been some variability over the centuries, but although their longer texts were clearly too expensive for most people to have bought, the picture painted by the available evidence is of modestly paid professionals either working to commission or, perhaps more commonly, copying whatever texts they thought they would be able to sell. So far as we can tell, this was never either a guild that might have held meetings to thrash out the fine details of the biblical text, or a group of scholars with wealth and time on its hands, capable of deliberately and collectively reducing textual variation.

There are potentially significant gaps in our knowledge, of course, but the limited evidence that we possess does not point to any obvious mechanism or central source of authority that might have brought about the reduction in textual diversity that seems to be suggested by the relative congruity between the later translations, and between those translations and the Masoretic readings. On the face of it, furthermore, this narrowing of the textual tradition seems to be affirmed by the limited number of surviving Hebrew manuscripts that have been placed, not all uncontroversially, in the period between about the late first and the eighth centuries.[154] Some

---

[154] On such texts in general, see Gentry, 'The Text of the Old Testament', 21-22; Hendel, *Steps*, 203-204; Longacre, 'Reconsidering'. On Wadi Murabbaʿat: Benoit, Milik, and Vaux, *Les Grottes de Murabbaʿât*, 75-79, 181-205; Fuller, 'Form and Formation', 88 n. 5. On the En-Gedi Leviticus Scroll: Segal et al., 'An Early Leviticus Scroll'; Longacre, 'Reconsidering' (which argues plausibly for

caution is needed, given that very little text altogether is preserved. These manuscripts, however, generally point to the dominance of readings that were very close to those adopted in the early Masoretic manuscripts, although with a few substantial variants and a significant amount of orthographic variation, especially in the use of vowel-letters.[155] Indirect evidence for the period paints a slightly more complicated picture. If we focus on Ecclesiastes for a moment, we may observe that although, as we have already noted, the Three agree with the later Masoretic texts in many places where those texts differ from the earlier Greek translation, they by no means do so in every case.[156] If this might be put down to their still relatively early date, it is more difficult to discount the much later evidence of the Targum. While this Aramaic translation is prone to extensive elaboration and is sometimes dependant on traditions known from other Hebrew literature, there is no reason to suppose that it drew directly on other, non-Hebrew textual traditions with their roots in a much earlier period. It is surprising, therefore, not only to find a number of places where the Targum diverges sharply from the

---

a third-fourth century date, rather than first-second). On T-S NS 4.3 and T-S NS 3.21: Sirat, 'Genesis Discovery'; 'Earliest known Sefer Torah'; Yardeni, *Hebrew Script*, 80, 93. On Berlin Staatlichen Museen p 10598, Ashmolean Antinoopolis Pap.47 and 48, and 49 and 50, Bodleian Ms. Heb d.89: Sirat, *Les Papyrus*, 32-38; Yardeni, *Hebrew Script*, 73, 85. On London Manuscript and Ashkar-Gilson Hebrew Manuscript 2: Sanders, 'Ashkar-Gilson'.

[155] The orthographic variations in the first-century CE Mur 88 from Wadi Murabba'at have been summarized helpfully by Fuller, who notes among other things that: four times it has ע for M^L א; 13 times it has a *plene* spelling with ו when M^L does not, and conversely it is written six times defectively when M^L is *plene* with ו; similarly, ten times Mur 88 is written *plene* with י when M^L is not, and once it is written defectively when M^L is *plene*; see Fuller, 'Form and Formation', 88 n. 5. Elsewhere, uses and non-uses of ו and י vowel-letters constitute the most common basis for variation from M^L, but as Sanders, 'Ashkar-Gilson', points out with respect to the seventh-/eighth-century London Manuscript and Ashkar-Gilson Hebrew Manuscript, these and similar variations may correspond to readings in other Masoretic manuscripts.

[156] So, e.g., at Eccles 7.14, α', and θ' appear to have read חיה, which is rendered as ζῆθι, 'live', rather than M היה, 'be'; in 9.2 σ' ἄδηλα, 'obscure', reflects הבל, 'vanity', for the second הכל, 'all', in M, and the *propterea quod*, 'because', attributed to σ' by Jerome, reflects באשר for M כאשר; in 9.14 σ' ἀποτείχισμα, 'stockades', reflects מצורים for M מצודים. Should all of these be attributed to the influence of G, we can look at, say, 7.25 where σ' has read a plural ἐπίστανται, '(they do not) know' (= ידעו), for M ידע, '(he does not) know'.

Masoretic text as we know it, but some where in doing so it agrees with the Greek: there are notable instances in 7.21, where both supply 'the wicked' as a subject for the verb, in 10.1 where each in a different way preserves the same element from a long-corrupted text, in 10.3 where both have 'everyone' rather than 'to everyone', and in 5.8, where both probably preserve the original preposition. Other examples are less striking, but the number overall and the nature of some of the correspondences make it difficult simply to blame them all on coincidence, while the very different character of the Greek translation makes it no easier to believe that both translators were just adopting similar interpretations of their material, and altering their texts accordingly. It is particularly noteworthy, moreover, that in several of these cases the Targum and the Greek both preserve a reading that is almost certainly closer to the original than is the reading to be found in the major Masoretic manuscripts. In passing, we might note also in 6.5 some close correspondences to the readings of Symmachus and the Vulgate, which may have roots in Jewish interpretative tradition. Unless we are to find a way of placing the Targum much earlier than the late first millennium date which is usually assigned to it—and that would be difficult—we can only reasonably assume that, at least in some places, it had access to readings or interpretations that had found their way through whatever bottleneck reduced the diversity among texts between Qumran and Aquila, but not into the Masoretic manuscripts.

We shall touch below on the issue of apparent discrepancies between Talmudic and Masoretic readings, which again indicate a degree of continuing textual variety, but, looking once more beyond Ecclesiastes, it is interesting to note a certain amount of evidence from sources that are less commonly cited. For instance, one analysis of Eusebius of Emesa's 'Hebrew' readings from the fourth century (ter Haar Romeny, *A Syrian in Greek Dress*, 57-64) has found a number of cases in which the reading cannot be reconciled with the consonantal text of M, and several more which have apparently vocalized the text differently. Eusebius was probably relying on information from others for his readings, and we should not put too much weight on most of them. We may also note, however, some of the corrections explicitly based on a Hebrew text which were much later offered to Latin readings in one of the Theodulphian Bibles, and which are examined by Graves ('Glimpses'; see also Power, 'Corrections'). These commonly agree with M^L, but Graves' study of 1 Samuel identifies five places where the corrections reflect significant differences in the consonants or vocalization, and he notes that in two of those the corrector found a text that probably agreed against M^L with the Hebrew used by Jerome. Even in the ninth century, therefore, a text that was essentially 'Masoretic' in its readings could apparently still preserve what are likely to have been earlier variants, absent from the key early Masoretic manuscripts with which we are familiar. A Hebrew–Greek glossary of Exodus, Isaiah, and Jeremiah, probably written around the same time and designed to help learners of Hebrew, seems likewise to have been based on a Hebrew text that differed from M^L.[157] This list could certainly be extended: we shall note a number of places, for example, where Jerome's own work on Ecclesiastes appears to reflects a different Hebrew basis, and many of his other works suggest a continuing degree of diversity in the Hebrew textual tradition of his time.[158]

Overall, though, we find evidence that seems to point in two different directions: toward the existence and dominance of texts close to the basic consonantal texts adopted by the Masoretes, and

---

[157] See Tchernetska, Olszowy-Schlanger, and de Lange, 'Early Hebrew-Greek Biblical Glossary'; de Lange, *Japheth*, 88-89. Many of the variants involve simply the *plene* or defective writing of medial/final vowel-letters, but three are more substantial. A few signs may be vowel-points, and, if so, the editors note also that תמצו from Isa 66.11 seems to have been vocalized with *pataḥ* under the ה rather than the *qameṣ* of M^L. Some caution is necessary, as the glossary is the lower text of a palimpsest and many readings are uncertain, but if the editors are correct in their suspicion that it is actually based on a Masoretic text, since nearly half the words glossed have also been annotated by the Masoretes, then that text was unusually deviant.

[158] In addition to variants reflected in his own translations, we may note especially Jerome's comment on Hab 2.19, that the reading רוח rather than כל רוח is to be found in certain Hebrew manuscripts (which he associates with Aquila's reading there, although Field does not appear to pick up this element of the citation). Similarly, in his *Epistle* 106, he comments that the Greek version of Ps 35.10 has 'Lord!' twice (as, indeed, some manuscripts do), but that many Hebrew exemplars do not have it even once. Such comments indicate not only, of course, his awareness of specific variants, but his understanding that there was sufficient diversity in the tradition to require the use of multiple witnesses. On Jerome's use of different manuscripts, see, e.g., Graves, *Jerome's Hebrew Philology*, 54; Linde, *Sacra Scriptura?*, 106. A long list of places where Jerome or Origen appears to have read a text different from M, or to have pronounced the consonants differently, is offered in Sperber, *Historical Grammar*, 119-20.

at the same time toward a continuing, if limited, variety within the Hebrew textual tradition as a whole. The simplest explanation for this is that, at some point probably during the first two centuries CE or a little earlier, the number and hence the diversity of Hebrew biblical texts declined steeply in what were to become the principal centres of Hebrew scholarship, so that when the tradition re-established itself, it was on the basis of a very few exemplars. A significant loss of manuscripts during the brutal Jewish revolts of this period, in Palestine and elsewhere, along with the rise of new exegetical approaches, may well have contributed to such a decline, as is very often suggested. It may also be symptomatic, however, simply of a much broader decline in the use of Hebrew and of Hebrew texts (and we shall touch a little later on the significant role of Greek in the synagogue and elsewhere). If the scribal production of texts was indeed dependant to any great extent upon a commercial demand for those texts, then any such collapse in the market is likely to have reduced the number of active scribes and limited the diversity of exemplars, perhaps for several generations, and it may also have concentrated production of new texts within particular circles, perhaps some time before the revolts.[159] In any case, though, it seems likely that, initially at least, the narrowing of the textual tradition was accomplished as much by circumstance as by design—and in that case, although the readings that were preserved may have been no less early than many others, and although they may have been preserved in texts associated with specific groups, it is unlikely that they were preserved because any authority had formally evaluated them as more original than those others.

As the Hebrew text re-asserted itself, probably in the course of the third century, it was under the influence of various factors—not the least of them the very sort of expectation that Josephus voices, but also now the requirements of midrashic or halakhic exegesis, the influence of communal reading in the synagogue, and perhaps the need to establish consensus around passages which were the subject of disputes within Judaism or between rabbinic Jews and other groups with a stake in the biblical text. It is not unlikely, moreover, that scribes generally created new copies based

---

[159] Lange, 'Textual Standardization', makes a good case for textual consolidation in the course of the first century BCE, perhaps earlier in Egypt than in Palestine, although his account of the mechanisms depends heavily on much later sources.

on exemplars associated with the revival, and that as the textual tradition grew back after its decimation, it was with a narrower genetic basis, as well as under new constraints. Of course, such a situation may have facilitated the elimination (or incorporation, cf. Talmon, 'Double Readings') of whatever variants remained, but they were not driven out of the tradition altogether, and managed to survive in manuscripts like the one used in France by Theodulph or his informant, and perhaps closer to home in sources used by the Targum. When the Masoretes began their work, therefore, the text had essentially been reduced to one main type, although a certain degree of variation persisted.

This never quite went away, and even within the texts of the Masoretic tradition, it is important to recognize that at no point was there ever absolute agreement over every detail even of the consonantal text, let alone of the pointing that was subsequently applied to it. This fact was acknowledged, and Masoretic lists or annotations regularly refer to different 'western' and 'eastern' readings of words. Although these references are very variable and sometimes contradictory, they probably do reflect an accurate understanding that there were divergences between the Masoretic traditions of Palestinian and Babylonian scholarship, which is borne out to some extent by the Babylonian manuscripts that we possess. It is difficult, however, to identify any manuscripts that possess only 'eastern' or 'western' readings. The problem may be not that all our manuscripts are 'mixed' in that respect, but that 'eastern' and 'western' are being used as labels to legitimize known variants, and perhaps especially those that fall into particular categories. We also have long, and again rather variable lists of differences between ben Asher and a rival, ben Naphtali, and of points on which they agreed with each other against other Masoretes.[160] Although a high proportion of these involve different uses of the sign *metheg*, with only a few touching on anything more substantial, we may once more suspect that the Masoretic notes are drawing other variants into the established category of 'ben Asher' and 'ben Naphtali' differences: even our earliest manuscripts never conform wholly to the readings of one or the other (although the Aleppo Codex comes very close in the text that is extant).

---

[160] Although it has not gone without criticism, Lipschütz, *Kitāb al-Khilaf*, is the most convenient edition of an early version.

There were certainly variants within the tradition, then, even if they were generally minor in nature, and the tradents do not pretend otherwise. Perhaps the most significant issue that confronted efforts to consolidate the text, is one that lies behind many of the 'western'/'eastern' variants: inconsistent orthography, and especially the sort of variations in the use of vowel-letters that we find also in comparisons of earlier consonantal texts with M^L. In the passage that has already been mentioned from *b. Qiddušin* 30a, clauses and letters are actually cited for the midpoints under discussion, but anyone who cares to count the text in a Masoretic codex or in any modern edition will find it very difficult to replicate the findings, or even come close to the same conclusions (which differ, indeed, from those of the Masoretes themselves). One problem is drawn out when the passage goes on to discuss an issue that arises from the count, and the sages involved suggest that a scroll be brought so that they can count the letters for themselves. Either the objection raised to this, or the explanation offered when they fail—the text is very concise as always, and could be understood either way—is that the rabbis, unlike the scribes, have no expertise in בחסירות ויתרות, that is to say, in defective and *plene* spellings, which respectively omit or include optional vowel-letters. A possible implication of this response is that the sages realized their Torah scroll might not contain the same spellings as that used by the scribes, but the reference to the expertise of those scribes, not shared by the rabbis, suggests a more fundamental difficulty—that some or all vowel-letters were not to be included, and that only the scribes knew which letters should actually be counted (which imputes to them, of course, a certain knowledge of grammar as well as of spelling).

Another passage from the Talmud is interesting, and perhaps rather contradictory in this respect. In *b. Sanhedrin* 4b (cf. *Menaḥot* 34b), which is more broadly preoccupied with the authority of the spoken Torah and the traditional vocalization of the text, the structure of phylacteries is addressed with reference to Exod 13.16; Deut 6.8 and Deut 11.18. Rabbi Ishmael is credited with the ruling that they should have four compartments because in the first two passages the word טוטפה is spelled defectively and could be read as singular, while in the third it is spelled *plene* as טוטפות, which (according to Ishmael) has to be read as plural, and so stands for two—the three passages therefore combine to make four. The ruling is cited here because Ishmael's argument involves ignoring what was taken to be the established pronunciation of the word (which was the same in every case) in order to exploit the other possibilities permitted by the consonants, and he wants to read the *waw* as a vowel-letter signifying not 'u' but 'o'. Correspondingly, the issue at stake is the propriety of reading against the grain, as it were, which was to prove a popular feature of Jewish exegesis for centuries to come (and which we shall encounter again shortly). The tractate goes on to explore other instances and to acknowledge basic disagreements over the matter, but it incidentally highlights the difficulties and potential ambiguities that could be created by the presence or absence of vowel-letters, particularly in an environment where the natural sense of the text could be less important than its potential meanings.[161]

In the case of the fragments of Ecclesiastes from Qumran, we have already seen the considerable extent to which the orthography of earlier manuscripts can differ from that found more typically in Masoretic texts. For long-established texts like the Pentateuch, such differences might conceivably be explained by consolidation of the texts around still earlier readings or manuscripts that pre-dated expansions in the use of vowel-letters (although certain spellings known from early inscriptions are notably rare or absent), but at least in a late book like Ecclesiastes it seems more likely that there has been some revision of the spelling toward the conservative scribal norms of a subsequent period, and it is difficult to distinguish tendencies between the various books that would suggest they have gone through different processes.[162] There is still a degree of

---

[161] Compare the similar reckoning in *b. Sukkah* 6b, which is connected with an assertion about the authoritative status of the conventional pronunciation, and the other examples noted in Andersen and Forbes, *Spelling*, 74-75. It is worth mentioning here also the very clever interpretation in Buber's text of *Midrash Tanḥuma*, Behar 1 (cf. Re'eh 4), which comes close to being a scribal joke: Ephron in Gen 23.16 makes a loss (חסר) on his deal with Abraham because for the first time in this verse his name appears without a vowel-letter, that is to say, with a defective spelling (חסר).

[162] Cf. Barr, *Variable Spellings*, 20: 'it is likely that few parts, or no parts, of the Hebrew Bible, as they lie before us in the Masoretic text, stand in the spelling in which they were first written, or in which their final redaction took place'. Barr goes on to demonstrate in great detail the absence of evidence for distinct orthographic histories within the biblical corpus, even where distinct practices

freedom and variation across the corpus, however, which suggests the development at some point, at least, of a reluctance to override whatever spellings had been received—even sometimes when the Masoretic notes demanded it. Even if the scribes and Masoretes did make some changes to that spelling, they have ultimately not attempted to impose collectively any tightly drawn set of conventions—which is most likely one reason that the use of *plene* and defective spellings is so erratic even within single Masoretic codices. It is also plainly true, however, that such usage was similarly erratic across the tradition.

Comparing the Leningrad and Aleppo codices, *BHQ* notes (p. xx) that the differences between their consonantal texts involve principally the presence or absence of medial vowel-letters, and variability of this sort is attested by other early Masoretic manuscripts. Without travelling to distant libraries, it is currently difficult to ascertain the readings of all the other important manuscripts in this respect. However, even a quick glance through (incomplete) photographs of Codex Sassoon 1053, which is probably slightly earlier but generally very close to M^L (cf. Yeivin, *Introduction*, 21-22), picks up such variations as הוללת in Eccles 1.17 where M^L has הוללות, העננות in 2.8 where M^L has תענוגת, יתר in 2.15 where M^L has יותר, האחרנים in 4.16 where M^L has האחרונים, משתדר in 5.4 where M^L has משתדור, המשל in 10.4 where M^L has המושל, and שמר in 8.2 and 12.13 where M^L has שמור—all cases where M^L writes the word *plene*, with *waw* serving as a vowel-letter, but Sassoon 1053 does not (or, in 2.8, has the *waw* in a different place). On the other hand, in 1.10 we find מלפנינו, with *yod* as a vowel-letter, where M^L has just מלפנו. The text of 1.10, 17;

can be identified—a conclusion that stands at some distance from the slightly earlier, more optimistic conclusions in Andersen and Forbes, *Spelling*. Of course, this means that we should treat with very great caution any attempts to date the composition of texts on the basis of the spelling preserved in Masoretic texts—as Seow has tried to do for Ecclesiastes in Seow, 'Linguistic Evidence', 644-46; cf. Schoors, *The Preacher* I, 221. On the variability of spelling specifically in Ecclesiastes, see Schoors, 'Vowel Letters', 284-85. Some caution has to be attached to general claims such as that of Khan, 'Languages', 5, that 'the text had been fixed not only in content but also in orthography by the third century BC. This orthography is broadly uniform across all biblical books'—at least if such claims are understood to suggest that all manuscripts preserved a common spelling after that point, which is patently not true.

2.8 and 12.13 is no longer extant in another manuscript of similar antiquity, British Museum MS Or. 9879 (see Yeivin, *Introduction*, 29), but it agrees with Sassoon 1053 at 2.15, 4.16, 5.4, 8.2 and 10.4,[163] suggesting—on the assumption that the M^L readings were not confined to M^L—that we are looking not at random variations or errors, but at two distinct forms of the consonantal text of Ecclesiastes. Different spellings were not, perhaps, still being generated in these traditions, at least on any large scale, but earlier variations had become fixed in different ways—and it is quite possible, of course, that other forms persisted as well, and are simply not reflected in the surviving manuscripts. The variable writing of שמר is characterized as a matter of eastern/western variation by the Masoretic notes, but although M^L famously includes Babylonian elements in its Masorah (cf. Phillips, 'A New Codex', 29), none of these manuscripts is 'eastern', and it is unlikely that the differences are to be explained simply using that paradigm. In any case, even at the relatively advanced stage when these manuscripts were produced, the Masoretic pointing was still being applied to texts with variable orthography; at least when any significant numbers of manuscripts had survived from an earlier period, that pointing had probably evolved, furthermore, against a background of even greater variety.

If it was apparently not a priority for those creating Masoretic texts either to regularize or to eliminate any variation in orthography when there was no effect on the sense, this was perhaps because, as the passage from *b. Qidduŝin* implies, vowel-letters were not at some early stage regarded as core elements of the text in the same way, and so could be handled more loosely, or perhaps because, as the case in *b. Sanhedrin* illustrates, they were at once unimportant to those who emphasized traditional pronunciation but potentially very important to those who did not. In any case, when the various Masoretic manuscripts consolidated them individually, they effectively consolidated variety within the Masoretic tradition as a whole: there is not, strictly, a single 'Masoretic' reading of any of the words we have just noted, and the manuscript tradition continued both to preserve such variety, and to generate new variations. Alongside the other differences that we find, or that

---

[163] Note also in Or. 9879 the defective לחבק at 3.5.

the Masoretic notes acknowledge, they are an important reminder that 'the Masoretic text' was never entirely monolithic, even in the earliest manifestations of it that we possess.[164] In practical terms, they also indicate that *plene* or defective spellings are unlikely to have been fixed from a very early stage, and this often helps us to understand differences between ancient witnesses to the text.[165]

More generally, the Masoretic tradition probably represents a bottleneck within a bottleneck: from the narrower textual tradition of the first few centuries CE, it has distilled a tradition that is yet narrower while never quite achieving a single text that is agreed in every detail. At least in the case of Ecclesiastes, however, there are reasons to suppose that it neither embraced nor wholly extinguished all those variants that had survived the initial narrowing, some of which appear to have influenced the Targum—despite the pictures painted in some earlier scholarship of rabbis and Masoretes ordering the systematic suppression of rival texts (see Goshen-Gottstein, 'Hebrew Biblical Manuscripts', 265 n. 1). To a greater or lesser extent this was probably true of other books, and it can lead to some interesting discrepancies. For a reader of M^L, for example, the account of R. Ishmael's argument in *b. Sanhedrin*, which I mentioned above, might seem deeply confusing: it is posited on a *plene* spelling in Deut 11.18 which has been rejected by the scribe or his forebears, and so makes no sense in terms of that text. There are some other striking examples of such variation, and when, for

---

[164] In 'The Masoretic Text: A Critical Evaluation', which was published as a prologue to the 1966 Ktav (New York) reprint of Ginsburg's *Introduction*, Harry Orlinsky accordingly proclaims: 'There never was, and there never can be, a single fixed masoretic text of the Bible!' (p. xviii). With, say, the Greek Septuagint translation, it is a reasonable supposition that the translator produced a single form of his text, and it is essentially this that we are attempting to describe when we talk about the 'Old Greek', or 'G*'. There is no equivalent 'M*', however, and although it is convenient to talk generally about 'the Masoretic text' when we are describing the high proportion of material that the various manuscripts have in common, the expression can be misleading if we take it to imply that there was ever some single form in that tradition too.

[165] Weiss, 'The Masorah', 58-59, helpfully tabulates orthographic variants between early Masoretic texts of Nahum, for which we have rather more witnesses, and this gives a better sense of the variety. See also the statistics for variants across Jeremiah and Chronicles in Penkower, 'Codex', 92-95. For an account of variants from M^L in two much later texts of Ecclesiastes, see Lavoie and Mehramooz, 'Le texte hébreu et la traduction judéo-persanne', 505-506.

instance, M at Isa 58.7 reads פרס, while *b. Baba Batra* 9a rests an interpretation upon the use of ש in a word it spells פרוש, then we have to presume that the Masoretes and their successors, who surely knew of that exegesis, did not care that their reading actively contradicted it.[166] Later readers found such contradictions profoundly problematic (see Leiman, 'Masorah and Halakhah'), but unless we try to impute some anti-rabbinic motive, perhaps by reverting to older ideas that the Masoretes were Karaites, it seems simpler to suggest that the Masoretic texts were not primarily intended to establish some single consonantal text that could be used for every purpose, whatever ambitions have been projected on to the Masoretes by others.

There was variety in the Hebrew textual tradition, then, before and during the period when the ben Ashers and others were at work. That variety persists among the texts regarded as authoritative by early medieval Jewish commentators,[167] and it only becomes more marked in the larger corpus of manuscripts from subsequent centuries, as we shall see later. The Masoretic texts do not themselves embody the whole range of that variety, but, equally, they do not reduce the tradition to a single form. Indeed, although in most of the cases we have noted the issue is no more than a matter of variant spellings, it is likely that the Masoretic tradition as a whole continued to transmit certain well-established consonantal variants that went far beyond the orthographic. Over a long period, for instance, many readers of Babylonian texts would apparently have read ילך rather than יאכל in Eccles 5.16, and understood the man described there to be 'walking', not 'eating' in darkness (see the notes to that verse). Such variants, which demand a quite different pronunciation, lead us into broader questions about how the text was read and pronounced.

---

[166] The scale of the differences between M and the biblical citations in the Talmud became very clear in the (incomplete) work of Victor Aptowitzer, published initially in five parts between 1906 and 1915, but gathered conveniently in *Schriftwort*.

[167] See, e.g., Barr, *Variable Spellings*, 9-10, which includes an example from Rashi, and on some 39 variants attested by Rashbam, see Esh, 'Variant Readings in Mediaeval Hebrew Commentaries'.

(ii) *Vocalization*

Going beyond whatever further limitations may have been imposed on variation between the consonantal texts to which the Masoretic pointing was originally applied, it is the fixing of the pronunciation that constitutes the most important part of the Masoretic project. From a text-critical perspective, however, Masoretic work in this area presents a problem, because it is difficult to evaluate the origin or date of the vowels and accents that were applied to individual words or phrases. Addressing that problem, furthermore, can potentially entail engagement with a variety of different claims and debates that have emerged over the centuries, with a risk of blurring the specific issues at stake. In particular, therefore, it is important to make a clear distinction from the outset between claims about the antiquity of the pronunciation in a general sense, and about the antiquity of the pronunciation applied to specific words. We need not suppose that the Masoretes were applying pronunciations current in the language of their own time, or even applying some late and artificial understanding of Hebrew, in order to claim that the way in which they vocalized the consonantal text at any given place might not be the way in which the author or the earliest readers would have expected it to be vocalized.

We have already seen examples in 4QQoh[a] at 7.5, where the inclusion of a vowel-letter shows that a noun was being read as plural, although the Masoretes and others later read it as singular, and at 6.5, where the spelling נוחת (cf. Sir 30.17) is similarly incompatible with the pointing of נחת in M as *naḥat*. Below we shall note a significant number of words that were clearly construed and pronounced by the translator of G in a way that was different from the Masoretic understanding, even when it is unlikely that he was confronted by any different spelling. In a purely consonantal script, such ambiguities are inevitable if no single vocalization is demanded by the context, and if the author of Ecclesiastes originally had the option to indicate some particular pronunciations by his use of vowel-letters, then the erratic treatment and transmission of those letters, which we have already observed above, has at least seriously eroded the clarity of his intentions. On the face of it, therefore, it would seem that we have to accept the possibility of reading certain words in more than one way, and to pin down the intended meaning, when we can, through a consideration of meaning and context. This remains largely true even if we suppose the Masoretic vocalizations to pre-date the Masoretes themselves: those vocalizations would only have any claim to particular authority if they were based on an accurate oral transmission of the text that went back to the author himself, or at least to a much earlier period, when the orthography of the text might have offered clearer guidance, and the readers have been more familiar with the book's idiom.

The existence of just such a tradition is accepted by some scholars, who correspondingly accord a greater weight to the Masoretic vocalization of specific words than to the rival vocalizations reflected in other versions. Again, this needs to be distinguished from more general phenomena. To take a well-known instance of the latter, Jerome talks in his commentary on Dan 11.45 about the unaspirated pronunciation of the פ in אפדנו, noting that פ elsewhere in Hebrew (at least as he knew it) was always aspirated, and the exceptional pointing with *dageš* in M seems to affirm a similar pronunciation (see, e.g., Kahle, *The Cairo Geniza*, 181-82; Khan, 'Languages', 10). Such a pronunciation may indeed go back to the origins of the term as a loanword from Persian, but there is no evidence that the pronunciation was in conflict with some more modern version, and the preservation of archaic or foreign pronunciations for particular words is not in itself an unusual phenomenon. Whatever else it tells us about the Masoretic knowledge of biblical Hebrew, that case does not imply that the whole text of Daniel was being transmitted orally, and with its vowels unaltered.

In fact, such a transmission would be remarkable, and perhaps more remarkable than might seem obvious at first. Confronting a tendency by some scholars to disregard the Masoretic vocalization altogether, James Barr in a famous work (*Comparative Philology*, 194) described the implausible picture painted by such scholars of '(a) a long period during which the consonantal text was cherished and transmitted, and (b) a late and arbitrary process by which a vocalization was more or less imposed on this text by men who indeed tried their best to understand it but were handicapped by the limitations of their knowledge of Hebrew...and by the narrowness of their understanding of these particular texts'. He went on to note (196) both the indications of vocalization even in the consonantal text and 'the tradition of vocalization which was passed on... Week by week and year by year, Moses and the prophets were read... [T]he biblical text was transmitted also in a spoken form; the text was publicly read and the mode of reading was passed on.'

All that is fair, and Barr's point is well taken, but it needs some qualification. Barr himself has elsewhere discussed at length, as we have seen, the highly inconsistent character of 'indications of vocalization...in the consonantal text', while the lectionary cycle meant that passages were repeated only at long intervals (probably every third year), and some books, including Ecclesiastes, may not have been read aloud in such settings until a relatively late date. To be sure, such general usage tells against the late imposition of some brand new set of readings, but, even setting aside broader questions about the currency of Hebrew in the synagogue, this usage does not constitute a mechanism for the accurate and detailed preservation of specific pronunciations in ambiguous contexts: many analogies could be adduced to show that simple use or repetition does not guarantee the precise preservation of pronunciations in the face of other influences.

In practical terms, therefore, Barr's observation, and the arguments that he goes on to make against the artificiality of the Masoretic pronunciation, should certainly caution us against arbitrary vocalizations which contradict the understanding of all our witnesses—which was his intention. They do not in themselves, however, offer a compelling reason for us automatically to prefer the vocalization of M to that of other witnesses, and we do not have to make a choice simply between accepting the vocalization as ancient in its entirety, and discounting it completely: there is a great deal of space between those two positions.[168] To re-state the distinction made already, moreover, the principal issue at stake here is not really the linguistic status of the Hebrew represented by the pointing, so much as the existence and nature of a reading tradition behind the Masoretic pronunciation. Without getting drawn into the debate over language, I think we can reasonably acknowledge the likelihood both that the Masoretes vocalize the text in a way that would have been distinct from other contemporary pronunciations

---

[168] It is correspondingly unfortunate that much of the discussion in this area has seemed unusually polarized. Writing in the 1970s, Grabbe felt able to remark that, since the great debates over the antiquity of the vowel-points in the seventeenth century, 'the treatment of the value of the MT vowel pointing has wavered between practically blind conservatism and almost complete disregard'; Grabbe, *Comparative Philology*, 179.

of Hebrew, and that this vocalization reflects, at least in certain demonstrable respects, a much earlier pronunciation.[169] Elements of this pronunciation can be shown, on the basis of earlier orthography, to have existed many centuries before the Masoretes worked, but are not usually reflected explicitly in the orthography of biblical manuscripts from the first half of the first millennium, or in the transliterations of Jerome and others—the most widely quoted example is the pronunciation of suffix pronouns with a vowel following the consonant.

If we are to go further, and to claim that the Masoretic vocalization preserves much earlier (or even original) ways of reading each word of each text, and so transmits an early interpretation in places where the consonants could be understood in more than one way, then we are claiming, in effect, that the pronunciation of many thousands of words would have to have been retained somehow without alteration for a period of at least half a millennium, and possibly much longer. Since nobody could have known in advance which pronunciations might become lost, this would seem to imply either that some method of marking the vowels was in existence long before the systems that we know, which is extremely unlikely for many reasons, or that all the biblical texts were being memorized in their entirety and passed down with a high level of accuracy over many generations, which would be a feat surely worthy of more remark than we actually find in ancient sources.[170] Such a

---

[169] For an overview of the debates surrounding this issue, see Grabbe, *Comparative Philology*, 179-97.

[170] In his commentary on Isaiah (at 58.2), Jerome famously refers to the ability of Jews in general at the synagogue to chant from memory the books of Moses and of the prophets. However—setting aside vexed questions about Jerome's actual experience of the synagogue—even if there was an emphasis on memorization in the education of all, it is likely that the precise recitation of material in large quantities would have been a skill possessed only by a few. If Jerome's remark is not simply an exaggeration, therefore, it may attest no more than the sort of corporate endeavour that can guide even the unchurched through a liturgy. When memorization of the biblical text is discussed at *b. Megillah* 18b, it is noted that R. Meir was able to reproduce the scroll of Esther from memory, and that R. Hananel was once found writing Torah scrolls the same way (despite an opinion that a biblical text should never be copied except directly from another text), while the equivalent passage at *y. Megillah* 4.1 includes the boasts of others that they can write the entirety of scripture from memory. Such abilities, however, are

scenario is not impossible, but it would raise a lot of questions—not least as to why, if they valued the precise pronunciation highly enough to make such efforts, these unusually literate people would have entrusted it for centuries to the vagaries of human memory, even after becoming familiar with scripts that recorded vowels. If they were memorizing it, on the other hand, for some different reason—perhaps for self-improvement or because some prestige was attached to the accomplishment—it is doubtful that they would have preserved the *minutiae* that distinguished, say, a particular ancient pronunciation from a more recent one.[171]

Such a big claim requires correspondingly strong evidence, and this has been sought in attempts to demonstrate 'historical' vocalizations that preserve accurate pronunciations unassisted by the consonantal text. Jan Joosten, for instance, points out (in 'The Tiberian Vocalization', 26) that 'The distinction between long and short forms in the prefix conjugation of middle weak verbs or in

---

clearly depicted as exceptional even among the rabbis: the Babylonian version describes the words of the Torah in terms of Prov 23.5, 'When your eyes light upon it, it is gone', to describe how difficult such memorization is, and to single out R. Meir (who was, we may recall, a professional scribe) as untypical. In the same discussion at *b. Megillah* 18b, there are references to a reader restoring from memory words that have been omitted in a scroll, but also to readers accidentally omitting text themselves or reading while half-asleep, and there is certainly no expectation of memorization. Arguably, the strongest evidence (although it is not early) is for the learning of the Pentateuch off by heart: *Midrash Tanḥuma*, Ki Tissa 16, speaks of students learning the Torah through a process of repeating what their teacher has said until they are able to recite it along with the teacher—but it is unclear what the scope of this learning is, and the same homily goes on to speak of the inability of Moses to memorize the entire Torah on Sinai, because 'its length is more than that of the earth' (Job 11.9)—God finally just gives him a summary of the basics. (The account is very different in the version published by Buber, which lacks the references both to study and to the forgetfulness of Moses.)

[171] The memorization of lengthy texts is not in itself unusual, but what is proposed constitutes something more complicated than, say, the *tajwid* which governs the pronunciation of the Qurʾan by the *huffaz* who have memorized it. It is noteworthy even in that case, though, that the absence of vowels in the text early in its existence led to multiple variations in the pronunciation of the Qurʾan, and, indeed, to the subsequent acceptance of parallel traditions even after vocalization marks had been introduced. It is difficult to locate any close parallel to the supposed preservation of specific pronunciations, not least because the motive behind such memorizations is indeed generally prestigious or educational, and they are not specifically intended to conserve the material.

the Hiphil of strong verbs...does not blindly follow the spelling. Long forms written defectively are almost always correctly pointed by the Masoretes.' Such observations have to confront the difficulty that, as we have seen, the consonantal texts to which the Masoretic vocalization was applied seem still to have been very fluid and inconsistent with respect to spelling, and especially in their use of vowel-letters. Even where the proper pointing was not indicated clearly by the context, therefore, it is not unreasonable to suggest that, in such instances, the vowels were first applied to manuscripts with *plene* spelling, or were informed by an awareness of such spelling in other manuscripts. Masoretic manuscripts were commonly produced by a *naqdan* who added the pointing and annotations to a consonantal text that had been copied by a scribe, but even in the case of M[L], where Samuel ben Jacob both copied the text and added the pointing, there are numerous places where the Masoretic annotations contradict the text, and presume different spellings.[172] When the spellings that we have are defective, therefore, we certainly cannot presuppose that the vocalizations must have been based on some other source of information: they may simply go back to manuscripts with *plene* spellings.[173]

Similar difficulties confront Nili Samet in 'Validity', the only detailed attempt to demonstrate the presence of early vocalizations

---

[172] Ofer, 'The *Jerusalem Crown*', 35, observes: 'In the Prophets section of the Leningrad Codex, there are more than two hundred and fifty words whose spelling does not accord with the Masorah. In the Cairo manuscript [of the prophets], there are three hundred such words, and in the Prophets section of Sassoon 1053, there are about five hundred such instances'. Ofer focuses on the Prophets because he is concerned to draw a contrast with the more consistent Aleppo Codex: the discrepancies, of course, extend far beyond that section in M[L]. See also Andersen and Forbes, *Spelling*, 78-79, which notes instances where M[L] conversely introduces what may be new masoretic notes to match readings that are not found in other early manuscripts.

[173] Segal, 'Promulgation', 42, seeks to justify the idea of memorized readings not from internal but from talmudic evidence, claiming that, 'Where...the defective spelling may involve a possible misunderstanding of the correct meaning of the word, the scribes handed down orally the correct pronunciation'. For evidence, he points to a discussion in *b. Nedarim* 37b, other aspects of which we shall consider below, and in particular a phrase מקרא סופרים found there. The sense of that is disputed, and the description unclear, but the instances given do not suggest that it has anything to do with defective writings (even if we are happy to rely on the Talmud as evidence for scribal practices many centuries earlier).

in Ecclesiastes, where she tries to show that the Masoretic vocalization in respect of three separate phenomena in the book represents a departure from Masoretic norms, and reflects the preservation of Second Temple pronunciations compatible with the late date of the book. Another example, mentioned by Samet, was also adduced some years ago by Shelomo Morag (in 'Historical Validity', 308-309), and involves the pointing of the relative pronoun -שׁ with *šewa* before a pronoun in (M^L and other early manuscripts of) 2.22 and in 3.18. This is a pronunciation found in Hebrew texts with Babylonian vocalization, and it is known more broadly in post-biblical Hebrew, but it contradicts the usual early Masoretic pointing of -שׁ with the vowel *segol* (there is no other instance of שְׁהוּא, but cf. שֶׁהֵם at Ct 6.5; Lam 4.9). This is, however, the least convincing case, because Morag offers no evidence for such a pronunciation in Second Temple times, and merely speculates that it might also have been a feature of some earlier Hebrew dialect: whatever has provoked the exceptional pointing, its origins are more likely to be later, and although Morag draws attention here to an inconsistency in the Masoretic pointing (which is hardly an unusual phenomenon in itself), this may simply be a reflection of contemporary speaking habits, rather than of some historical preservation.[174]

Samet's own examples are more complicated. Two involve what are essentially orthographic questions: the consistent pointing of the feminine demonstrative זו with *ḥolem*, as *zōh*, which is rare outside the book, and the pointing of certain forms from weak *lamed-ʾaleph* verbs as if they were *lamed-he*, or *vice versa*. The latter is particularly striking because it is *not* consistent: the same participle חוטא is vocalized properly (that is, according to Masoretic norms) at 7.26

---

[174] See Bar-Asher's comments in Garr and Fassberg, *Handbook*, 208-209: he suspects that the two isolated uses here 'may have been grafted onto the consonantal text from a late tradition'. Of course, because the limitations of the evidence make it difficult to identify earlier pronunciations, let alone pronunciations that existed in Second Temple times but that were definitely no longer current, there are always going to be problems with this sort of approach. Making a somewhat different point, in his subsequent discussion of the way וּלְדוֹ is pointed in 1 Chr 3.5 and 20.8, Morag suggests that such late vocalizations are somehow connected to the late date of the books concerned, but whatever the case with Chronicles, it should be borne in mind that the Masoretes would have attributed Ecclesiastes to Solomon, and that nobody considered it 'late', so far as we know, before the seventeenth century.

as *ḥōṭē*ʾ, but then at 8.12; 9.2, 18 it appears in the form *ḥōṭe*ʾ, as though the verb were not חטא but חטה.¹⁷⁵ This is not really covered by Samet's belief that 'the Masoretes had a tradition which instructed them to treat third *ʾālep* and third *hê* participles in Qoheleth differently than those of other books' (1070): preservation of such distinctions between separate instances would require instructions for each occurrence, not just such a general admonition.¹⁷⁶ It would seem more economical, though, to suppose that what we have in both cases is further evidence for the initial instability of orthography within the textual tradition adopted by the Masoretes: at some earlier stage of the text's development, the vowels have been specified for (or with some consciousness of) a consonantal text that had writings like זו and (inconsistently) חוטא / חוטה but have then been applied to a text with the more conventional זה and (consistently) חטא.¹⁷⁷ This extends somewhat beyond the issue of *plene* and

---

¹⁷⁵ It is not clear to me why Samet does not include in her list ולחוטא in 2.26, but it is noteworthy that the participle there is pointed *ḥōṭeʾ* in Mᴸ (and Sassoon 1053), but *ḥōṭēʾ* in MS Or. 9879. Ginsburg, *Writings* (cf. his *Massorah*, 4:379-80), indicates similar variation among later manuscripts for this and all the other occurrences.

¹⁷⁶ Samet does not investigate the Masorah, but we may note that Mᴸ has appropriate annotations (or at least a circellus) at every place except 9.18 (where the pointing has presumably been extrapolated from the preceding two instances). MS Or. 9879, on the other hand, has Masoretic annotations at 7.26 and 9.2 to remind the scribe of the proper pointing, but not at 2.26 (where, as we saw in the last note, it differs from Mᴸ, perhaps because the *naqdan* had not yet encountered the peculiarity), 8.12, or 9.18. The Masoretes were evidently aware of the odd vocalization, although there is some irregularity both in the vocalization itself and in the notes designed to protect it. More importantly, though, the very existence of the notes shows that the word was being treated exceptionally, and it is questionable whether we can extrapolate anything about the vocalization more generally from such explicitly 'protected' oddities.

¹⁷⁷ The existence of such spellings is well established: for the writings זו and חוטה in particular at Qumran, see Reymond, *Qumran Hebrew*, 154, 189. We shall look below at the difficulties involved in using later medieval manuscripts, but it is worth noting that זו is attested among these as a variant at every point where the feminine זה occurs in the book, and in addition to the manuscripts cited in Kennicott and Ginsburg, *Writings*, we may also note זו at Eccles 9.13 in the Babylonian text of Ms BM 2333, Ratzabi, 'Masoretic Variants', 106. Because זו is rather rare in the Masoretic text, this is not a particularly easy error for the later scribes to have made, and, as Ginsburg's apparatus suggests, pointing זה as masculine would have presented a greater temptation to the careless; cf. also Lavoie and Mehramooz, 'Le texte hébreu et la traduction judéo-persane', 500-501. It is

defective writings that we addressed above, but it would suit either the Masoretic convention of a *naqdan* applying his vowels to a text furnished separately by a scribe or the possibility that the vowels were inherited from a reading tradition that was based on a text with such spellings, but was itself of no particular antiquity.[178] It provides, furthermore, an explanation that is both simpler and more complete. In a sense, of course, this might mean that the Masoretic pointing does indeed preserve a historical pronunciation (depending on how much we wish to read into such orthographic variation), but it does not imply the existence of a comprehensive, early tradition.

Samet's third example is different, and concerns the pointing of seven different nouns according to a pattern of vocalization that is associated with Late Biblical Hebrew—the *qitlôn* pattern rather than the classical *qittālôn*; both patterns are used in post-biblical Hebrew. It should be noted at once that six of the nouns on her list occur nowhere in the Bible outside Ecclesiastes, and they may all be late arrivals in Hebrew. This is significant when we are assessing the language of the book, but Samet is using them to set up what is essentially a straw man: there is no reason to suppose that, without pressure from a reading tradition, the Masoretes would have

---

not impossible, therefore, that the writings with וו preserve, albeit erratically, a reading older than that in M^L. In his *Massorah*, III, 71, however, Ginsburg cites וו as an attested *Q^erê* reading in each verse, and it is impossible to exclude that usage as a source for the variant. As regards the verb, it is interesting to compare the variable writings בה and בא that we noted in 4QQoh^a, above: early scribes may not have made the distinctions between types of verb that are generally reflected in Masoretic vocalization. That we do not find such writings generally in M would seem to suggest not that the Masoretes had access consistently to manuscripts in which such spellings were never used, but rather that there has been some scribal move toward greater conformity in this area, perhaps informed by a clearer consciousness that these are lexical, rather than simply orthographic distinctions.

[178] We have already noted the many discrepancies between text and Masorah in M^L, and Trompelt, 'Die masoretische Akzentuation', discusses two instances in Isaiah where the Masoretic accents are apparently based on variant texts, and stand in tension with other elements of the pointing. Vocalizations reflecting variant orthography, therefore, would hardly stand in isolation, and it is important to recognize the extent to which Masoretic texts typically conflate traditions that may have had disparate origins. Elsewhere in Ecclesiastes, it is interesting to note, for example, the unexpected vocalization of יניד in 10.20, pointed apparently as a jussive despite the parallel יוליך, which is not, and there this pointing has probably been provoked by a defective writing יגד, which is attested as a *Q^erê* and was probably an early variant.

exercised some archaizing principle that forced them to overrule the contemporary pronunciations that they knew for particular words in favour of theoretical ancient pronunciations attested nowhere else. The six tell us little other than that, as we have already acknowledged, the vocalization is not simply an artificial construction. Much rests, therefore, on זכרון, which is vocalized as *zikrôn* in 1.11a and 2.16, over against the classical *zikkārôn*. That classical form, however, appears in 1.11b immediately after the first use of *zikrôn*, and Samet, surprisingly, does not discuss the problem this raises for her view, that the Masoretes deliberately chose to point the absolute form of the noun using a Late Biblical Hebrew pattern particularly in Ecclesiastes because they were instructed by their tradition to do so. At best, they are being inconsistent in a way that would again have required very specific information, but it is altogether more likely that they are vocalizing *zikrôn* in both 1.11a and in 2.16 as a construct form of the classical *zikkārôn* (cf. Lev 23.24, linked to these uses by the Masoretic notes that again protect the readings), rather than as an absolute form on the *qitlôn* pattern. This is the understanding of most commentators. Samet does not show, therefore, that the Masoretes are behaving in any way unusually when they vocalize these words, or provide any reason to suppose that they were drawing on a reading tradition that provided historical pronunciations specifically for this book.

Such approaches are perhaps fated always to fall foul of the textual complexities and the difficulty of establishing Masoretic intentions in many places: it seems unlikely that the internal evidence of the vocalization could ever furnish an argument strong enough to support any supposition that biblical texts were transmitted orally from an early point in their history, in a way that preserved original readings. That is not to say, however, that the Masoretic vocalization must have been entirely the invention of the Masoretes themselves, and we do have a certain amount of external evidence that sheds some light on its history—and, indeed, on the motivations that lay behind the Masoretic project.

This evidence is to be found principally in the Babylonian Talmud, and in the relationships between that corpus and the Masoretic text, so it is important to be clear from the outset that we face text-critical complications in this direction as well. In particular, the complicated textual tradition of the Talmud has been subject to the influence of the biblical text, so that where distinctions between the two might originally have been clear, it is likely that they have been assimilated over the course of time. This has happened in the case of *b. Makkot* 10a, noted by Mutius ('Eine talmudische Textvariante') which clearly depends on a reading לו in Eccles 5.9, even though the Masoretic לא has come to dominate the textual tradition. The Talmudic version in that case may not represent a huge difference in pronunciation, but it does reflect a significantly different understanding. We also have to deal with aspects of rabbinic exegesis that can tend to mislead. In *b. Ta'anit* 7b, for instance, we are urged to adopt a pronunciation in 8.1 that had been followed by the translator of the Greek but was not picked up by the Masoretes—their reading is specifically rejected. Such admonitions to 'read not X but Y' (אל תקרי...אלא...), however, are a commonplace of Talmudic discourse, and are often used seemingly just to draw out an additional interpretation: they cannot be employed straightforwardly to determine any normative pronunciation, although they possibly do sometimes indicate an awareness of textual variants (see especially Talmon, 'Aspects', 126-29), and more certainly illustrate the ambivalence toward fixed pronunciations that we encountered earlier in the case of R. Ishmael.[179]

For all that such problems can complicate the issues, however, they cannot conceal a strong Talmudic interest in the idea of a received, traditional pronunciation, which may on occasion differ from the text or from the most natural reading of the text. Such differences create a problem of authority in halakhic discussions, and engender what is portrayed as a long-running disagreement between those who favour adherence to the pronunciation suggested by the spelling (the מסורת) in their text, and those who would follow a traditional pronunciation (the מקרא). A list of important rabbis who prefer that traditional pronunciation is given in *b. Sanhedrin* 4a, where the initial point at stake is a rather complicated one about the reading of ירשיען as singular or plural in Exod 22.8, but the principle is illustrated with reference to the possibility of reading שבעם in

---

[179] As Alexander, 'Why No Textual Criticism?', 182 puts it, 'Behind the written text of Scripture stands, so to speak, a grander and more complex Torah which is accessed through the narrow door of the finite words written in the Sefer Torah'. The *'al tiqrei* principle 'On the face of it...seems to show the rabbis starting from a text, which in principle they regarded as inviolable and absolutely fixed, and, as it were, artificially creating textual variants!'

Lev 12.5 as 'seventy (days)' (with a plural ending, as in Dan 9.24) rather than the conventional 'two weeks' (with a dual ending). In *b. Qiddušin* 18b, a distinction is similarly made between the views of rabbis Eliezer, Akiba and Simon: the first attributes authority to the מסורת, the second to the מקרא, and the third to both. The argument in that passage is over בבגדו בה in Exod 21.8, which Eliezer reads as 'dealt faithlessly with her' and Akiba as '(spread) his garment over her'. Likewise, in *b. Kerithot* 17b, rabbis Assi and Huna differ over the relative authority of מסורת and מקרא for the interpretation of מצות in Lev 5.17—either a singular or a defectively written plural construct form—and in *b. Pesaḥim* 86b rabbis Judah and Simon disagree about whether to understand יאכל in Exod 12.46 as an (active) qal form (the מסורת), or as a (passive) niph'al (the מקרא).

There are many similar discussions of words presented without formal debate, and it is in this area that text-critical issues create the most difficulties: the rabbis do not generally treat *plene* and defective spellings as precise orthographic equivalents, but apparently tend to suppose instead that when something *could* be written with a vowel-letter, it *should* be written that way.[180] Correspondingly, if a word does not have a vowel-letter, then any possible reading that does not treat it as a defective spelling can be regarded as the more natural,[181] and this leads to contradictions between the 'natural' and the 'traditional' that would have been complicated from the outset by orthographic variations, and that have sometimes now been rendered quite obscure or meaningless in many manuscripts. Where the issue is clear, however, there is also a clear correspondence between the Masoretic pointing of words and the readings regarded in the Talmud as 'traditional', suggesting very strongly that the

---

[180] The concise discussion of errors in Torah scrolls, at *b. Menaḥot* 29b, is difficult to follow at points, but it appears to claim that accidental writings *plene* were not to be taken as errors that would disqualify a scroll from subsequent correction, while defective writings were (since to correct them would leave the manuscript speckled or patchy). Andersen and Forbes, *Spelling*, 73, suggest that this would have led to a gradual increase in the number of vowel-letters, and would seem to imply a lack of rabbinic concern with such issues. It seems more likely, though, that the *plene* spellings (or possibly extraneous letters more generally) were acceptable simply because they could be corrected without interpolation: there is no implied expectation that they should be allowed to stand.

[181] See similarly, e.g., the treatment of Num 7.19 הקרב in Buber's version of *Midrash Tanḥuma*, Naso 22.

Masoretes were concerned not to vocalize their text 'naturally', or even to explore the potential ambiguities which are often the focus of the Talmud itself, but simply to reproduce the 'traditional' pronunciation.[182] That concern is also manifest in other places, when the Masoretes use their notes, for instance, to support euphemistic substitutions or traditional readings of words and passages that are advocated by the Talmud but differ from the text: there is not complete concord between the two at every such point, probably in part because of differences between the texts that each used, but the overlap is significant enough to exclude coincidence.[183]

There can be no real doubt, in other words, that the Masoretic text largely supports, through its pointing and annotations, a tradition of pronunciation that is also attested in the Babylonian Talmud, even if it is not always explicitly commended there. The Talmud itself associates support for that tradition with rabbis as early as Akiba, in the first or second century, and although it indicates an

---

[182] So, in the instances described above, the Masoretes point ירשיעֶנּ as plural at Exod 22.8, שבעים as dual at Lev 12.5, בגד as 'garment' at Exod 21.8, מצות as plural at Lev 5.17, and יאכל as a niph'al in Exod 12.46, in every case following the מקרא, the reading tradition as it is reported by the Babylonian Talmud, against what the rabbis (including those who supported that tradition) took to be the implication of the consonantal spelling. Elsewhere note, e.g., *b. Baba Meṣi'a* 22b, which worries about the conventional pronunciation of יתן in Lev 11.38 as passive, which is again the reading of M, when there is no indication of this in the consonantal text.

[183] All but one of the instances given in *b. Nedarim* 37b, of words that are not found in the text but are to be read, have a corresponding *Q^erê* in M; that one (at Ruth 2.11) is characterized instead by the Masoretes as an 'eastern' / 'western' variant. The list is not presented as complete, so is not strictly contradicted by the fact that Masoretic texts identify other examples (e.g. at 2 Sam 18.20); cf. Ginsburg, *Introduction*, 312-15. The subsequent list of words that are written but are not to be read is also largely supported, although textual variation has affected cases like that of Deut 6.1; see Samuel Loewinger's prologue to Aptowitzer, *Schriftwort*, xv–xxv. The other classes of reading mentioned in *b. Nedarim* 37a-38a are either presented without examples or obscure. On euphemisms and emendations, see Ginsburg, *Introduction*, 345-63. More broadly, the Talmud is not unaware of *Q^erê* / *K^ethîbh* as a phenomenon, and here there is again much agreement: see, e.g., the unedifying *b. Soṭah* 42b on 1 Sam 17.7 and 23, *b. 'Erubin* 26a on 2 Kgs 20.4, or *b. Yoma* 21b on Hag 1.8, all instances which are picked up in M. Note also, though, *b. Sanhedrin* 20a on 2 Sam 3.35: כתיב להכרות וקרינן להברות, 'it is written *lhkrwt* but we read *lhbrwt*': this is not supported by a *Q^erê* in M^L, probably because the consonantal tradition of M differed here from that of the Talmud, and already had להברות (although, perhaps under the influence of the Talmud, להכרות is found as the *K^ethîbh* in some later manuscripts).

awareness of divergences over details, it clearly understands this tradition to be ancient: *b. Nedarim* 37a-38a notes that Exod 19.9 is sub-divided differently in Palestine and Babylon, so this is not an entirely unified tradition, but the same passage also has R. Isaac declare that certain prescribed readings that run against the text are '*halakha* to Moses from Sinai'—a technical description that characterizes them as incontestable, without any need for scriptural support (see conveniently Faur, *The Horizontal Society*, 2:68-70). Such an understanding associates the traditional pronunciation with the idea of an Oral Torah, and Philip Alexander ('Why No Textual Criticism?', 186) describes the broader context: 'As it developed the rabbinic doctrine of Scripture located inspiration ever more precisely in the graphic form of the consonantal text as it is found in the Synagogue Sifrei Torah. These constituted the Written Torah. The vowels and accents belonged to the Oral Torah.'

If this tradition was indeed ancient and authoritative, however, then even a limited degree of diversity within it could not begin to explain the fact that earlier versions frequently diverge from M. When the G translation of Ecclesiastes was prepared, to take an example at hand, it is apparent not only that the translator had a Hebrew consonantal text which differed from M in numerous places, and so could not conceivably have been read aloud in the same way, but also that when he was confronted with the same consonants, he often construed them quite differently.[184] If M reflects a reading tradition, then that tradition was clearly either ignored by or unknown to the translator.[185] If we can put that down to the

---

[184] See the list below. Tov, 'Reading Tradition', 13-14, counts 29 places in Genesis, 13 in Exodus and 40 in Leviticus, where the Greek translation reflects a different vocalization—so Ecclesiastes is not untypical in this respect despite the relatively late date of the translation (although the translation technique may also make any differences more obvious). It is a matter of one's expectation, whether these numbers seem small or large, but it is important to bear in mind that considerations of sense and context will guide readers to the same understanding and reading in the great majority of places, so the numbers should not be evaluated as a proportion of all words, but of all genuinely ambiguous words.

[185] Attempts to explain the origin of the vocalizations adopted by the Septuagint translators in terms of transcriptions, independent reading traditions and memorization have been reviewed in Schorch, 'The Septuagint and the Vocalization of the Hebrew Text of the Torah', which adds the further suggestion that they may have depended on parabiblical texts. There are indeed occasional indications that some translators were aware of Jewish reading traditions concerning particular

possibility that G originated in different circles, perhaps with their own traditions, the same cannot be said in the case of Aquila, whose strong links with rabbinic Judaism are hardly in doubt, but whose text likewise exhibits more differences from M than we should expect if he were following the same or a similar reading tradition (and not only in Ecclesiastes). More broadly, of course, some of the orthographic choices made in the scribal tradition might well be taken to suggest that the scribes who created the texts adopted by the Masoretes did not themselves necessarily pronounce them in the same way.[186] If the tradition only emerged after the major translations had been completed, on the other hand, and at a time when the consonantal text had become more firmly established in something like its present form, then it is much easier for us to understand not only why other versions might reflect different readings or pronunciations, but also why the vocalization seems in some places to embody adaptation to a corrupt consonantal reading—an early and authoritative tradition, indeed, might be expected to have prevented, or at least to have curbed the very emergence of any serious errors in the text, which led it to differ from the memorized version. In this context, it is interesting to recall the discussion of המסורת שכחום וחזרו ויסדום in *b. Megillah* 3a, which we noted earlier in connection with

words, perhaps most notably when in translations of the historical books we find traces of an early attempt to reproduce a euphemistic $Q^e rê$ / $K^e thîbh$ tradition in treatments of the name 'Baal': in early versions of the Greek, it was given a feminine article (as at Rom 11.4), probably to guide readers to the pronunciation αἰσχύνη, 'shame', which is a parallel to the substitution of 'Ishbosheth' and 'Mephibosheth' for Ishbaal and Meribaal / Me(m)phibaal in the Hebrew text. See Dillmann, 'Über Baal'. If any were following a particular reading tradition more generally, however, rather than simply translating to the best of their knowledge and understanding, the many differences make it unlikely that this was the same tradition later reflected in M.

[186] Within Ecclesiastes, it is interesting to note a possible example in 4.10, where the Masoretes point ואילו as though it were an unusual compounding of the two words ואי לו, 'and woe to him'. The writing as a single word, however, is found consistently in early manuscripts, and it seems likely that the scribes understood themselves to be dealing with the late conditional conjunction אילו, which T also understands here. The strangeness of the writing (which stands in contrast to the אי לך of 10.16) led many later scribes, familiar with the Masoretic vocalization, to split the words. In view of the understanding in the Targum and Midrash, the spelling עלם in 3.11 may also reflect a scribal understanding different from that of the Masoretes, and this is probably true likewise of שכלות in 1.17 (although the Masoretic interpretation is less clear cut there).

the name of the Masoretes: that text seems to suggest that an authoritative tradition of pronunciation survived at least until the time of Ezra and Nehemiah, but was then forgotten and re-instated only when the major targumim were produced (and perhaps re-instated through them). That offers a reason for earlier scribes and scholars to have been ignorant of the tradition, but it also, of course, suggests that even advocates of that tradition did not understand it to have existed uninterrupted for centuries.

None of this has to mean that no established reading tradition yet existed at all in the earlier period when these texts and translations were produced, but it does suggest, at the very least, that no single tradition yet enjoyed the sort of status attributed to their tradition by the Masoretes.[187] What we see in the rabbinic debates about authority is, perhaps, the initial, still controversial emergence of traditional readings as a source of authority, at least with respect to the Torah. This may have begun as early as the first and second centuries, if it was indeed associated with Akiba and others of his time (although that is a sizable 'if': issues of historicity aside, it is difficult to say whether or not interpretations attributed to the early rabbis are simply being presented in the light of a later paradigm). The Talmud suggests, however, that even much later the process had yet to win over everybody, and it offers little reason to suppose that significant efforts had, or would have been made at an earlier stage to fix or transmit such readings across the Bible as a whole.

We should not neglect the strong possibility, furthermore, that it is the Babylonian Talmud itself which brings the reading tradition into prominence, some centuries after the period in which most of the ancient versions had been produced, and that the Masoretic agreement with many of the vocalizations and substitutions proposed in the Talmud results not from any independent knowledge, but from conformity to an idea expounded in this relatively new corpus (and perhaps involves some direct borrowing from it). From that point of view, it is interesting to note not only that the vocalization of texts probably began amongst the Babylonian Jews, but also how much harder it is to find in the earlier Jerusalem Talmud any clear

---

[187] We might add to the evidence an interesting anomaly noted in Weitzman, *The Syriac Version*, 99-100, who observes the clear dependence of a passage in the Haggadah upon a pronunciation of Isa 63.8-9 that is reflected in the Septuagint but not M.

counterpart to the Babylonian Talmud's developed ideas about distinct text and reading traditions, or even a recognition of the issues, while Jerome's many comments about Hebrew include no apparent reference to such ideas.[188] It would not be unreasonable to suspect, therefore, that the 'authoritative' reading tradition, at least in its full-fledged form, is a relatively late product of Babylonian Judaism, and that the Masoretic project itself is a response to the rise of that tradition, which draws the Talmudic ideas together with a more standardized consonantal text and a particular pronunciation of Hebrew, to create a version of it that offers a precision far beyond the aspirations of the rabbis themselves. Indeed, it would not be difficult to argue that the principal aim of the Masoretes, at least in the first instance, was to preserve and systematize this newly authoritative tradition of pronunciation, and that their concerns with the Talmud and with the consonantal text extended no further than was necessary to achieve that aim. As we have seen already, the Masoretes were apparently quite prepared to ignore consonantal

[188] Jerome's remarks about Jewish pronunciation in his commentary on Titus 3.9 (PL 26, col. 594; CCSL 77c, p. 64) refer only to the willingness of Jews to make fun of aspirant learners of Hebrew when they mispronounce biblical names because they have misunderstood the derivations, or commit other, similar blunders. In his Epistle 36 to Damasus (PL 26, col. 458; CSEL 54.1; p. 280; CCSL 54, p. 279), dealing with the different vocalizations by the Septuagint and Aquila of וחמשים in Exod 13.18, he speaks of the way in which *Aquilam uero et in ceteris et in hoc maxime loco proprie transtulisse omnis Iudaea conclamat et synagogarum consonant uniuersa subsellia*, 'all Judea cries together that Aquila has translated properly in general and especially in this place, while the benches of the synagogue are in complete agreement', before explaining the ambiguity of the consonantal text—but this very language of consensus is notable for its lack of any reference to an authoritative tradition, and elsewhere Jerome speaks of the need to exercise judgment or to take account of context in the vocalization of ambiguous words or in the pronunciation of ש as ś or š (see his commentaries on, e.g., Isa 2.22; 9.7; Jer 9.21; also Kedar-Kopfstein, 'Traditions', 425-26). There is nothing to suggest that his informants have drawn his attention to such a tradition, and where he follows what are $Q^e r\hat{e}$ or $K^e th\hat{i}bh$ readings in M, he shows no awareness of any distinction. It is hard to gauge precisely the extent to which Jerome's many transliterations of Hebrew words reflect pronunciations different from those attested in M, or to evaluate the extent to which he is relying on Jewish informants in every case, but we may note, for instance, *sadda et saddoth* in 2.8, where M has *šiddāh* and *šiddôt*: it is unlikely that he failed to seek advice about the pronunciation of this notorious crux. The vocalization in M, on the other hand, looks very much as though it reflects the etymological speculations reported in *b. Giṭṭin* 68a; see the note.

readings demanded by the Talmud, and so it is unlikely that they were trying to produce some sort of 'Talmudic Bible', while their relatively relaxed attitude towards orthographic variation stands in contrast to the detailed debates over minor matters of accentuation that are attributed to them in early sources.

In any case, though, while it is not hard to connect the ideas behind M with a reading tradition, it is very difficult to find external evidence that would enable us securely to locate that tradition much earlier than the Babylonian Talmud. Even if we accept the claims made there that link it to Akiba and other early rabbis, this is still a long way from the time that the texts themselves were composed, and they offer no reason to push it back still further into Second Temple times. To be sure, the traditions depicted in the Talmud and reflected in the work of the Masoretes could well have transmitted particular interpretations and pronunciations from a much earlier time, but if the evaluation of specific pronunciations as authoritative itself emerged only relatively late, then it is hard to justify, on external grounds, any more general supposition that earlier tradents would have invested the effort into memorization of all such pronunciations.

This is not the place to examine in detail the relationship between the Masoretic presentation of the text and the traditions of reading preserved in the Talmud. Despite the obvious affinities between the two, however, and the strong possibility that it is a Talmudic idea that has inspired the work of the Masoretes, the Babylonian Talmud could clearly not have been the sole source of Masoretic understandings. To whatever extent they relied on 'traditional' pronunciations, it is likely, in fact, both that the Masoretes attempted to systematize their material in the light of grammatical or other understandings, and that their work initially incorporated or tried to deal with a degree of variety amongst the known understandings and pronunciations of the text.[189]

---

[189] It would be difficult to make a thorough investigation of variant vocalizations during the period at which the Masoretes were working, but we might note, e.g., a case at 1.10 רבד, where the interpretation of the Midrash, probably to be dated somewhere between the late seventh and early tenth centuries, seems to rest on a pronunciation adopted by G, but not by M. Such a case implies that more than one pronunciation might have been current even in learned circles, and even going beyond deliberate ambiguities elicited for exegetical purposes.

With respect to the former, accounts from the period of the Tiberian Masoretes and a little later stress the persistence in Tiberias of a Hebrew marked by perfect enunciation and a mastery of the language's principles, not of a tradition that preserved historical pronunciations for individual words—beyond particular instances of $Q^e r\hat{e}$ / $K^e th\hat{i}bh$ and suchlike, they had a tradition, we might say, more of 'how to read', than of 'what to read' (see especially the tenth- to twelfth-century accounts cited in Chiesa, *Emergence*, 9-13). Even if those are somewhat romanticized projections, based on the nuanced character of the Tiberian pointing, the early descriptions that we have are of the Masoretes constantly scrutinizing and re-scrutinizing their work, and accord more with an idea that they were establishing the proper text in accordance with conventions and existing texts, than with any sense that they were simply aligning every word to an agreed oral version.[190] It has been suggested very plausibly, moreover, that in M^L itself there are clear signs of adaptation in the pointing toward the ben Asher norms (see, e.g., Dotan, 'Deviation'), and to whatever extent any *naqdan* set out initially just to record a known pronunciation of the text, it is clear that the tradition over time also attempted in certain respects to standardize its readings. As for variety within the Masoretic tradition, we might recall that, in looking earlier at Samet's study, we encountered a case of variant vocalization in 2.26, and although there is no thorough

---

[190] Talking about a particular spelling, Ibn Ezra claims in his commentary on Exod 25.31 that, 'I have examined books which had been scrutinized by the sages of Tiberias, and (in relation to which) fifteen of their elders have sworn that they gave consideration (הסתכלו) three times to every word, to every point, to every *plene* and to every defective spelling'. In his famous commendation of the ben Asher scroll (*Mishneh Torah*: Tefillin, Mezuzah and the Torah Scroll, 8.4), which probably did much to spread the reputation of the Tiberian Masoretes amongst Jews internationally, Maimonides says that ben Asher 'corrected it (שהגיהו) and scrutinized it in fine detail (ודקדק בו) for many years and corrected it (והגיהו, as before) many times'—information that he may have derived from a colophon, if Teicher, 'The Ben Asher Bible Manuscripts', 22, is correct. The meaning of הגיה here is obviously close to 'correcting' or 'proofreading', as in modern Hebrew, but דקדק, implies a different sort of examination; see Khan, 'Medieval Karaite Tradition', 57-58. He notes, among other things, that the cognate noun is used in the title of the Masorete Aaron ben Asher's treatise on the accents, which, as Khan himself puts it, 'formulated rules for the occurrence of…fine distinctions in form with regard to vowels and accents', and later became associated specifically with the study of grammar.

collection of data on the topic, variations in the vocalization of Masoretic manuscripts are by no means unknown elsewhere.[191] It is hard in any given case, of course, to say whether these are the result of error, outside influences or variant traditions, and the controversies around the nature of *Qᵉrê* / *Kᵉthîbh* readings make it difficult to claim without qualification that some of those might also reflect an attempt to preserve other variants. Neither the internal nor the external evidence, however, suggests that Masoretic texts emerged simply as a record of some universally agreed pronunciation: they are the product of a scholarly enterprise that undoubtedly involved some degree of interpretation, systematization, and reconciliation. Even on the most optimistic view of the reading tradition's precision and antiquity, therefore, it must patently have been subject to an undefinable degree of adaptation and change within the Masoretic tradition.

Finally, and on a related point, Goldman in *BHQ* sometimes speaks of M readings in Ecclesiastes as 'theologically' motivated (see, e.g., his remarks on 1.12, 13; 2.12; 3.11, 19), and it is easy to gain the impression from his edition that M reflects a very particular point of view. In part, this is down to his use of the common and convenient convention (which I follow myself) that permits commentators to say things like, 'M understands such-and-such', as though M were an individual rather than a tradition. It would be unwise, obviously, to take this convention too literally, or to seek in M the sort of consistent viewpoint that might more legitimately be sought in, say, one of the Greek translations. It probably is true, though, that M can be called interpretative in several respects. We cannot deny the possibility, for instance, or even the probability, that the Masoretes picked up specific theological interpretations of the text: they were likely working against a background of rabbinic interpretation which freely decontextualized and re-interpreted texts, so that readings which had become familiar, or even traditional, might

---

[191] Another example in Ecclesiastes—the pointing by M^L and Or 9879 of מקרה in its several occurrences at 3.19—will be discussed in the notes to that verse. Instances from later manuscripts are to be found in the apparatus of Ginsburg's edition (see n. 199), and those from the early JTS ms 232 (probably written around 1000 CE) are listed in Weiss, 'The Masorah', 65. More broadly, see the descriptions of manuscripts in Yeivin, *Introduction*, 23-28, which typically note common divergences from standard vocalization.

nevertheless have originated in understandings that were motivated by no concern with original sense or authorial intention—and this may also be true, of course, in the case of the other versions.[192] To that extent, the Masoretic presentation might be regarded as potentially interpretative even if the Masoretes themselves were seeking merely to fix and preserve a pronunciation.

In a much broader sense, moreover, the very act of vocalizing a consonantal text involved a degree of interpretation on the part of the Masoretes or their forebears. Authors and readers working with unvocalized texts have to deal with a much greater potential for ambiguity and confusion, and the mechanics of composition and interpretation are correspondingly different.[193] Where such a text has been left open to different readings, either accidentally or deliberately, vocalization fixes a particular understanding to the exclusion of others—and in doing so may actively suppress an author's intention to permit multiple interpretations,[194] or their willingness to tolerate different pronunciations that would not affect the sense (which I suspect to be true of, e.g., נעשה at 1.9). In that broader sense, what the Masoretes were doing might be considered inherently interpretative, and if they also actively chose between rival pronunciations, or themselves provided readings—say, where the text had become difficult or corrupt—then we might go so far as to say that the Masoretes were interpreters in a more specific way as well, and not merely inheritors of interpretations. It is naturally difficult to say, however, what they determined and what they inherited, so although Goldman may well have identified some places where the text of M preserves readings that originated in theological considerations (I doubt that is true of all his examples), we should not take his observations cumulatively to imply that the Masoretes must consciously have promulgated some particular theological orthodoxy, and there is certainly little or no sign that they have used their notations deliberately to alter or to minimize the many statements by Qohelet that could have been considered problematic.

---

[192] Goldman, 'Disciples des Sages', makes a case that the M presentation of certain passages in chs. 7 and 8 preserves interpretations that arose in the light of rabbinic concerns about Ecclesiastes and its status.

[193] On the ancient reading of unvocalized texts, see especially Barr, 'Vocalization', and more generally his essay 'Reading a Script without Vowels'.

[194] This is a theme pursued at some length in Martin, *Multiple Originals*.

(iii) *Summary*

As may be very clear by now, there are many different factors to be considered when we evaluate Masoretic manuscripts as witnesses to the text of Ecclesiastes. To be sure, there is no reason to doubt that they preserve, in slightly differing forms, a consonantal text that goes back to a time much earlier than the earliest Masoretes. That particular version of the text, though, is likely to have survived more by chance than because any earlier authority considered it inherently superior—and we should bear in mind, of course, that any ancient evaluation of 'superiority' would, in any case, likely have differed significantly from a modern, text-critical evaluation. It is also probable, moreover, both that the text had undergone orthographic revisions in the course of its transmission, and that, at least in this respect, it remained somewhat unstable even at the point when scholars began to annotate it with indications of the pronunciation.

Their motivation for doing so is likely to have been mixed. I have emphasized here the links with a tendency to place 'traditional' or 'received' pronunciation on a par with ideas about an 'oral Torah', which became prominent in the Babylonian Talmud early in the sixth century CE—although the Talmud itself suggests an earlier rabbinic interest in the idea. It is not improbable, of course, that more practical concerns also played a part, and the Talmud itself also betrays a consciousness of differences between biblical and contemporary Hebrew which could have caused a problem for readers.[195] In any case, however, it is unlikely that the new systems of vocalization and pronunciation were able to draw systematically upon oral traditions of recitation that preserved the pronunciation of particular words from some very much earlier time: arguments

---

[195] So *b. Ḥullin* 137b declares that לשון תורה לעצמה לשון חכמים לעצמן, 'the tongue of the Torah is for itself, the tongue of the sages for itself', when demanding use of the mishnaic rather than a biblical form of a plural, and the same tag is repeated in *b. ʿAbodah Zarah* 58b with respect to using a mishnaic verb rather than its biblical equivalent. In *b. Nedarim* 49a, a question about vows revolves around the differing semantic range of a term in biblical usage and in different dialects, and *b. Šabbat* 36a lists three objects that can cause confusion because the word once used to describe each of them now commonly refers to something different. The perception is not confined to the Babylonian sages: *y. Sukkah* 17b refers to teaching 'the tongue of the Torah', and *y. Nedarim* 24b is also concerned with language and vows.

in favour of such traditions are stymied by issues of orthographic inconsistency, on the one hand, and, on the other, by the absence of any evidence for their influence on earlier sources. While we need hardly deny, therefore, that Masoretic texts may very often preserve early understandings, the Masoretes may well have relied in many cases on later but well-established interpretations, or on their own reckonings of proper grammar and pronunciation: Masoretic texts are not artificial constructions, spun wholly from new cloth, but neither are they endowed with some special ability to transcend the already complicated exegetical history of biblical texts.

In practical terms and for our purposes, then, it would be difficult to justify setting the early Masoretic readings on a pedestal. So far as we can tell from the evidence of those other books for which there are more pre-Masoretic Hebrew witnesses, it seems likely that, except in orthographic details, the consonantal texts in Masoretic manuscripts generally preserve readings at least as old as those that were found by the translators of G and the other early versions. Without discounting the possibility that the pointing may also reflect an early understanding in any given place, however, we have no good reason to treat that pointing as authoritative by default. To be sure, the Masoretes should not be overruled arbitrarily, and speculative pronunciations that have no basis in any version should be treated with hardly less caution than speculative emendations of the consonants. We cannot presuppose, however, that any particular vocalization in M must be considered inherently more authentic somehow than a rival vocalization reflected in an earlier source, or that it is even necessarily much older than the earliest manuscripts in which it appears. Accordingly, we should not place the onus on other versions somehow to 'prove' that they are more accurate. On the contrary, it is important for us to recognize both that readers in the first half of the first millennium CE seem sometimes to have read the same passage in different ways, perhaps supported by varying traditions of reading and interpretation, and that none of these readers had privileged access to the original intentions of the author.

(iv) *Later Masoretic variants*

Scholars tend to reserve the term 'Masorete' for the ben Ashers and their near-contemporaries, but the 'Masoretic' texts subsequently based on their work, like M^L, continued to appear long afterwards, and we have vastly more Hebrew biblical manuscripts from the later centuries between the end of the first millennium, when Codex Leningrad and the Aleppo Codex were produced, and the appearance of the first printed Hebrew biblical texts, in the late fifteenth century. Not all of these can be described as 'Masoretic', not least because they include unpointed synagogue scrolls and texts created for a variety of other purposes, but it would be a little arbitrary to deny that description to the large number that were constructed on the same principles as the earlier codices—typically, as in earlier times, with a *naqdan* employed to point, correct and annotate a consonantal text that had been copied by a scribe. Despite a marked tendency in general to deprecate their value relative to the Tiberian manuscripts, some of these later texts are very fine, and Cambridge MS Add. 1753, indeed, is widely regarded as one of the best witnesses that we possess to the ben Asher text of the Hagiographa, even though it was only produced in about the fifteenth century.[196]

It is difficult, however, to establish the relationships between different Hebrew manuscripts, or to identify the sort of groups and families that are found among manuscripts in, say, the Septuagint tradition. That problem, indeed, may stem in part from the very methods that were employed to create them, since they were not simply copied one from another, but subject both to emendation in accordance with whatever knowledge and traditions the *naqdan* possessed, and to variation between the consonantal texts with which the *naqdanim* were supplied.[197] External evidence also testifies to the potential complexity of the inter-relationships. Gil, for instance, notes a letter written in November 1061 by the scribe

---

[196] See, e.g., Yeivin, 'Division into Sections', 80. The manuscript is collated in *BHQ*, cf. *BHQ* XXIII–XXIV.

[197] The separation of responsibilities has another consequence which may have been important for the development of Masoretic texts even at an early stage: the *naqdan* could correct the consonants in a particular copy, but it is not clear that scribes would necessarily have emended their own model texts in the light of such corrections, even if they saw them, so that to some extent the consonants and the Masoretic apparatus may constitute not a single tradition, but two traditions that co-exist and intersect. The same scribes who created a text to which Masoretic annotations and pointing were applied could also, of course, create texts for synagogue use, to which no such additions were to be made, and, correspondingly, pointing could in principle be added to existing texts that were originally intended to serve another purpose. There were exceptions, like Samuel ben Jacob, who acted as both scribe and *naqdan* for M^L (and very plausibly for several other manuscripts in our possession)—although even in his case, as already noted, we

Israel ben Nathan (whom we encountered earlier), which states his intention to focus on the copying of the Torah, since there was a greater demand for biblical texts than for the Mishnaic and Talmudic orders which other letters show to have made up the bulk of his work in the preceding two years. Having heard that there are reliable manuscripts to be found in al-Mahdiyya, he asks that some wealthy residents of that city (in modern Tunisia) be urged to acquire a bible for him to use as a basis for his copying. A slightly later letter from another scribe requests the transport of some uncorrected biblical texts from Fustat in Egypt to Ashkelon.[198] It is very clear both that the scribal business even in the eleventh century involved a wide-ranging, international transfer of texts, and that scribes frequently chose the models that they would use simply on the basis of reports and reputation: ben Nathan had no obvious reason himself to suppose that the al-Mahdiyya texts preserved readings any more authentic than others, but could sell copies on the assumption that clients would have heard the same recommendations of their reliability. It was to be a century or two before the fame of the Tiberian texts spread widely, and so led to a wider distribution of their readings for much the same reason—although even then scribes seem often to have preferred different exemplars (many of which may have been quite untouched by the Masoretes). If he is not just planning to sell them, the scribe in the second case, Nathan ha-Kohen ben Mevorakh, is probably seeking to correct manuscripts produced in Egypt against exemplars available in Palestine, and so to raise their value—presumably without any consciousness of how much this might make life difficult for future students of the textual history. Perhaps a little removed from the commercial hustle and bustle, there was undoubtedly some genuine scholarship on the text going on alongside all this, but it was not wholly disconnected—and scholars are mentioned as important clients for such scribes: we cannot isolate any simpler and purer tradition of transmission, and

---

find many startling discrepancies between the consonantal text and the Masorah which indicate a disjuncture between the two; see especially Phillips, 'A New Codex'.

[198] Gil, *A History of Palestine*, 233-34. On the other hand, the contract of Samuel ben Jacob to copy the prophets and writings, mentioned earlier, apparently mentions his intention to use as an exemplar a text that he had prepared previously for another client.

in the face of such complexity, it seems unlikely that we shall ever be in a strong position to trace in detail the relationships between the many manuscripts that have survived.

Broad groupings of the European texts into types (such as Stern, 'The Hebrew Bible in Europe') are helpful in some ways, but can do little justice to their many distinctions and interconnections. The most famous attempt at a collation, by Kennicott in 1776–1780, was a little later supplemented and corrected selectively by de Rossi in 1784–1788, but even though neither work usually examines variants other than in the consonantal text, it is difficult to make any proper assessment of the information that they offer without any true insight into the quality and inter-relationships of the many manuscripts that they list: the various editions of *BH* and *BHS* famously chose not even to specify what manuscripts were involved when citing variants from these sources in the apparatus. Some other works are more helpful in this respect, but the usefulness, for example, of Ginsburg's two attempts to create a text with a proper apparatus of variants (including vowels) is constrained by the limitations of the manuscripts that were available to him.[199]

The text-critical value of the later manuscripts is also problematic. Among the early, probably pre-Masoretic Hebrew manuscripts mentioned above is Berlin Staatliche Museen p 10598, which preserves a reading אל בני for M[L] לבני in Exod 3.14. That reading appears also at Qumran and in the Samaritan text, so it appears to be an early variant that managed to pass through the bottleneck of the first centuries CE, but was not picked up in the major Tiberian Masoretic manuscripts: that the reading is found in more than a dozen of Kennicott's manuscripts suggests, however, that it continued to circulate. The very early reading איביך from Mur 88 at Zeph 3.15 is also widely attested (see de Rossi), as is one of the readings from the Hebrew–Greek glossary, Exod 16.13 השליו for השלו, and three of the variants attested in the Theodulphian notes: לדרכו for M[L] לביתו in 1 Sam 23.18, the absence of אלהים supporting a reading אדני יהוה in

---

[199] C. D. Ginsburg, עשרים וארבעה ספרי הקדש: מדויקים היטב על פי המסורה ועל פי דפוסים ראשונים, עם חלופים והגהות מן כתבי יד עתיקים ותרגומים ישנים (2 vols.; London, 1894–1897); *The Old Testament diligently revised according to the Massorah and the early editions: with the various readings from the manuscripts and the ancient versions* (4 vols.; London, 1926); the volumes of the latter have individual titles—that containing Ecclesiastes is called *Writings* in this commentary.

2 Sam 7.25, and the loss of כל in 1 Sam 25.17. The first two of those Theodulphian readings are so strikingly different from the standard text of M that they are unlikely to have arisen separately and coincidentally. In short, therefore, for some of the later variants we have Hebrew witnesses that are themselves significantly earlier, and date to a period before or around the time that the major Tiberian Masoretic manuscripts were being produced.[200] It would not be easy to maintain a position, therefore, that all such variants are merely corruptions introduced into the Masoretic tradition after it had become more broadly disseminated, and many may have found their way into the tradition through the influence of, or perhaps even the application of Masorah to consonantal texts that had been transmitted in different circles. Whatever their ultimate influence, the ben Ashers did not kill off all rival readings or provide a single basis for all subsequent texts.

That said, however, it is no less clear that many of Kennicott's variants really are the consequence of late errors or confusions, and with both types co-existing in an undifferentiated mass, we have no easy way to distinguish old variants from new—except, unhelpfully, when we already have evidence of their antiquity. Even when we have earlier attestations, moreover, it is difficult to exclude the possibility of simple coincidence and polygenesis: whatever factors led to a variation in one place can lead to the appearance of a similar variation elsewhere. It may help to illustrate the problem if we take an example from Eccles 1.16, where M^L has Qohelet talk of everyone who was 'over' Jerusalem before him. That reading is supported by no other ancient version, and ranged against it we have not only the Greek, but both of Jerome's translations, the Syriac and the Targum, as well as a large number of the witnesses collated by Kennicott, de Rossi and Ginsburg. All of those texts prefer 'in' Jerusalem, which I happen to think is probably the original reading, but whether one is looking at the ancient versions or at the Kennicott manuscripts, it is

---

[200] From an earlier point in the tradition, although still within the bottleneck, we may also note various places where the readings of Jerome appear to reflect variants that are found among the later manuscripts; cf. Sperber, *Historical Grammar*, 114. It is harder to assess the significance of variants found in the Targum which appear also in the later manuscripts, such as the added ושחכמתי at 2.20: it is very possible that they have appeared in the tradition simply under the influence of the Targum.

hard to deny that this reading 'in' could have been influenced by the 'in Jerusalem' that appears in 1.12, and in the similar expressions at 2.7 and 2.9, or by a concern that Solomon did not really have many predecessors 'over' Jerusalem. If we did not have the earlier witnesses, indeed, we would almost certainly conclude that the medieval scribes made a change precisely on such grounds—and we cannot deny the possibility that they did so completely in ignorance of the earlier variant. It is hardly surprising, therefore, that attempts to discover 'new' early variants among the late manuscripts have yielded very slim pickings.[201]

Of course, this possibility of polygenesis makes it difficult to assign a relative value to the readings of any one manuscript, and the problem is compounded when little information is available on particular manuscripts, as is frequently the case. It may seem striking at first glance, for instance, to observe that there are some five occasions on which Kennicott's ms 17 (which he describes as thirteenth-century and Ashkenazi) appears to agree with the readings of the Greek text against M^L in Ecclesiastes (1.8, 16; 7.25; 9.2; 10.10), raising the possibility that it might prove a rich source of other early variants. A quick check reveals, however, that it frequently differs from M^L elsewhere as well, and Kennicott himself notes that the manuscript contains multiple variants: it seems all too possible, alas, that this manuscript simply contains so many errors that some are bound to correspond with readings in the Greek—although there is really no way to be sure without a thorough examination. Such problems make the information worse than useless, of course, when *BHS* or any other source notes the support for a reading of, say, two unnamed manuscripts, but it is not much more helpful just to supply a list of names and numbers. Where I refer to the later manuscripts in the commentary, therefore, I have generally provided a source—which I would urge anyone to consult before they are tempted to rely on those manuscripts as evidence for anything crucial. Because of the difficulties, these texts can at best add a little support to proposals based on the ancient versions for the existence of certain variants at an earlier date (which is why any wholesale exclusion from editions of M is difficult to justify). Their

---

[201] See especially Goshen-Gottstein, 'Hebrew Biblical Manuscripts', but also the very detailed account in Barthélemy, *Studies*, 256-382.

primary importance, however, is for establishing the later history of the manuscript tradition and its reception, not for reconstruction of the earlier textual tradition, and that is likely to remain the case unless we acquire much more information.[202]

In general, though, even if we cannot spot them, the evidence from earlier material does not really justify any deep pessimism about the ability of some variants to survive outside the Masoretic tradition, and to reach the later texts in an 'extramassoretic trickle', as Goshen-Gottstein puts it ('Hebrew Biblical Manuscripts', 280, 285). It is also by no means improbable that minor variants in Ecclesiastes might have survived elimination within early outposts of that tradition, and some work has been done in this area. Miletto's collection of variants from Babylonian manuscripts (*L'Antico Testamento*) is especially interesting in this respect, because we know that the Masoretic text and traditions developed at least slightly differently in Babylonian Judaism, even if the Masoretic account of the differences seems problematic in many ways. A good proportion of the 43 divergences from the text of *BHS* that he identifies in Ecclesiastes seem to be simple errors, sometimes confined to a single manuscript, but others (including 'in Jerusalem' at 1.16) match variants found elsewhere,[203] and it does seem likely that the list includes at least a few readings that have been preserved from an earlier stage in the history of the text—although it is, as

---

[202] In just under 35% of the places listed below where G appears to follow a consonantal text different from M^L, some counterpart to all or part of its apparent reading is found also amongst the later manuscripts. It is possible in every case, and perhaps probable in most, that the readings have arisen independently, and the more substantial differences in G generally have no such counterpart. I would be inclined to venture that, as well as the spelling זו for זה that has already been mentioned above, candidates for some continuity of transmission or of interpretative tradition are most likely to be found among: the 'in Jerusalem' of 1.16; the curious בינה of one manuscript at 1.18; בכל for the second מכל in 2.10; ממנו for ממני in 2.25; בעמלו for בכל עמלו in 3.13; באשר for כאשר in 4.17; גם for וגם in 7.6; ולבי for בלבי and והוללות for הוללות in 7.25; וישתבחו for וישתכחו in 8.10; the omission of כל ימי הבלך in 9.9; מצודים for מצודים in 9.14; and perhaps ובוקע for בוקע in 10.9. In no case, however, can coincidence or other factors be excluded with any confidence.

[203] The only precise match with G other than in 1.16 is at 2.10, where several manuscripts have the reading בכל, but Miletto notes a few other matches with variants in the G tradition, and claims other points of contact with S, V and T in particular.

with the Kennicott manuscripts, difficult to identify any such possibilities without the support of other witnesses or with any degree of certainty.

The Babylonian Masorah continued to be used by Yemenite Jews for a considerable time after it had largely been displaced elsewhere by the Tiberian, and Ratzabi ('Massoretic Variants') has collected a significant number of variants, in the consonantal text and in the pointing, that are to be found in the fifteenth- or sixteenth-century MS Bodleian 2333, where the text of Ecclesiastes (with Babylonian vocalization but no accents or Masorah) is accompanied by the philosophical commentary of Isaac Ibn Ghayyat. Ratzabi helpfully supplies variants, separately, from both the text and the commentary, as well as from the other works on the manuscript (Song of Songs and Lamentations, each with midrashim, and Esther with the Megillat Antiochus in Aramaic and Arabic). Many of those that he lists from the text of Ecclesiastes are striking, and they include not only, as we may have come to expect, the variant 'in Jerusalem' at 1.16, but a pointing of ודעת as a noun in the next verse, and a conjunction at the beginning of 3.21, which all agree with G, as well as agreements with Hie, V and T at 9.15 and 11.9. This very interesting manuscript cannot escape the issues that surround all the late texts, but its date alone does indicate the possible persistence of side-channels from the Babylonian tradition over a long period. Ecclesiastes here is not strictly a Masoretic text, and it is difficult to say whether we are talking about something that is basically a Masoretic or an extra-Masoretic transmission, but the character of the manuscript also shows how readings could be passed on in the broader Hebrew tradition as a whole without always being subject to the sort of checks and controls that were variably imposed by the Masoretes.

Working in a similar vein, but with a smaller corpus, Chiesa (in *L'Antico Testamento*) has examined variants amongst the texts with Palestinian pointing, the origin of which is rather mysterious, but the distinct nature of which might suggest a development that was similarly independent to at least some small degree. He took the curious decision, however, to use as his base text the Van der Hooght text of 1705: this had also been used as a base by Kennicott, which facilitates comparison with the Kennicott variants, but it is an eclectic text ultimately based on late codices *via* printed editions, so is often out of step with the earliest Masoretic manuscripts. Consequently, the two 'variants' that Chiesa identifies from a manuscript containing Eccles 11.1-9 and 12.3-9 (JTS MS 594, Box B, Envelope 12)—בילדותיך in 11.9 and הספדים in 12.5—actually accord with the readings of M^L. The only point at which its consonantal text differs from M^L, if we follow the transcriptions of Kahle and Diez Macho, is in fact at 12.5, where M^L has עולמו and the manuscript has the defective עלמו (which is not noted by Chiesa, because Van der Hooght also has the defective spelling!).[204] Since, according to Diez Macho, this manuscript has been copied from a text that dates to the seventh or eighth century, its readings are potentially early and important, but they actually affirm a certain continuity with the Tiberian tradition.

Overall, therefore, the manuscripts that are currently known do not by any means exclude the possibility that the Babylonian tradition preserved some early variants in Ecclesiastes, even if the limited evidence for the Palestinian tradition shows no more than the sort of orthographic variation that we have already found between Tiberian manuscripts. None of this seriously undermines the basic coherence of the Masoretic tradition as a whole, or enables us to identify early variants in late texts. However, alongside the mixed evidence that we saw earlier for the state of the text before and around the time that the Masoretic project began, it should also caution us against dogmatism in these matters. Early in the second millennium CE the reputation of the Tiberian Masorah did indeed permit the Tiberian texts to achieve a dominant position within a Judaism that had more broadly rekindled its interest in the Hebrew Bible over the preceding centuries, but this is unlikely to have resulted in the extinction of all other readings inside and outside the broader Masoretic tradition, a few of which probably preserved early variants. Such readings may have continued to exercise an influence, and sometimes, indeed, may even have found their way back into the later Masoretic texts. Because they mingle there with many more variants that did indeed arise much later, we cannot readily identify them or use them textcritically in anything more than a minor supporting role. We should not, however, buy into any simplistic and idealistic vision of the

---

[204] For the readings, see Chiesa, *L'Antico Testamento*, 235, and on the manuscript more generally, *idem*, 114-16; Díez Macho, 'Tres nuevos manuscritos', 249-53; 'La cantilación protomasorética', 240-48; Kahle, *The Cairo Geniza*, 336-44, pls. 5-6. The last two have transcriptions of the whole text.

Hebrew textual tradition narrowing to achieve some sort of purity and unity at Tiberias, after which it could only degenerate: the reality is much more interesting and complicated.

(v) *The division of the text in Ecclesiastes*
Although it was not without precedent,[205] the introduction of standardized chapter numbers in the biblical text is usually associated with the work of Stephen Langton in Paris at the beginning of the thirteenth century (see Powicke, *Stephen Langton*, 34-39). Divisions of the text by spacing, though, are found as early as the Qumran manuscripts, and Masoretic manuscripts include *parashot*, which use space to mark out sections, usually but not always to indicate the beginning of something new. They also divide the text into *sedarim*—liturgically orientated sections determined by length and marked by a *samekh* in the margin. *BHQ* notes (14*) that Ecclesiastes is always divided into four *sedarim* (marked at 1.1; 3.13; 7.1; 9.7), but its list of *parashot* in the three main manuscripts that were employed for the edition shows much less regularity, and such variation is typical (see, e.g., Penkower, 'Codex', 96-102). More consistently,[206] the Masoretic system divided the text at a lower level by using the sign : to close each verse (indeed, the sign is called *soph pasuq*, 'end of verse'), and these divisions are the basis for the numbered verses within each chapter that are found in modern bibles. Moore ('Chapters and Numbered Verses') placed the earliest such use around 1440, when R. Isaac Nathan used for his concordance of the Hebrew Bible a count of the Masoretic verses within each of Langton's chapters. The idea caught on in the course of the sixteenth century, though, and the Latin version published at Lyons by Antoine du Ry in 1528 already includes chapter numbers at the head of each chapter, and Arabic numerals in the margin, marking each verse, while the third edition of Bomberg's Hebrew Bible, published in 1546–1548, numbers every fifth verse.

Although they have all developed quite recently from the same Christian system of numbering chapters and Jewish system of verse-division, the numbers found in modern Hebrew bibles often

---

[205] Kreuzer, *Bible in Greek*, 259-61, notes the numbering of chapters in the book of Daniel on the Greek Papyrus 967, which has been dated to around 200 CE.
[206] But not with complete consistency: see, e.g., the apparatus of *BHS* at Exod 20.3-4, 8-9.

differ from those in other bibles as a consequence of interpretative or other decisions made at an early stage of this development. In Ecclesiastes, such an inconsistency affects the numbering of the verse that begins 'Watch your foot' either (in the Hebrew) at the end of ch. 4, or (in modern English and many other versions) at the beginning of ch. 5, and this leaves the verse-numbering out of step throughout the rest of ch. 5. In fact, though, English bibles, like the Hebrew, took the verse to be the last verse of ch. 4 throughout the sixteenth century: this was its position in Coverdale's translation, in the Geneva Bible and in the Douay-Rheims version. It was only in the Authorized Version of 1611 that it moved to ch. 5, perhaps under the influence of the German reformers. Luther's commentary, published in 1532 but based on lectures given in 1526, makes an explicit observation about the verse, that *hinc incipio caput quintum, est enim nouus locus*, 'I begin chapter 5 here, because it is a new topic'; it is also placed in ch. 5 by Johannes Brenz, a close ally of Luther, in his 1528 commentary (p. 94b), in the first edition of Luther's Bible, published in 1534, and in Philipp Melanchthon's commentary of 1550. In view of this disagreement, it is interesting to observe that one of the manuscripts collated by *BHQ* (M^{L34} = EBP. II B 34 in the Russian National Library, probably from the late tenth century) does show a 'closed' *parashah* at 4.16-17, indicating consciousness of a thematic break between those verses.

More generally, the delimitation of texts has become an object of considerable scholarly interest over the last two decades, and there is some consensus that scribes were quite commonly marking divisions of sense long before the formal punctuation of the Masoretic texts and of later Greek manuscripts.[207] In *b. Nedarim* 37a-38a, already mentioned above, a reference to פיסוק טעמים probably describes the separation of the text into units in the reading tradition. It is also clear, however, that division of the text could be variable, that divisions were not systematically marked at the level of individual sentences or 'verses' in prose, and that the reliance principally upon spacing to mark such divisions made them very vulnerable in the course of transmission to ignorance, carelessness,

---

[207] See especially Revell, 'Oldest Evidence', and more recently the programmatic Korpel and Oesch, *Delimitation Criticism*. Hobbins, 'Poetry', 169, emphasizes that these divisions are unlikely to go back to the authors of any material, and are not 'components of the text per se'.

or simple lack of room. From time to time, moreover, the M text is divided to suit a reading that is almost certainly secondary, and perhaps relatively late, indicating that there was scope for adaptation in the system (9.1-2 furnishes an example in Ecclesiastes). Without going into the broader issues here, we may note that there are a few places where the text of Ecclesiastes has clearly come to be construed differently in other traditions:

1.5-6:	G reads what is the last clause of v. 5 in M with v. 6.
3.17-18:	important manuscripts of G read the last word of 3.17 as the first of 3.18.
7.23-24:	G reads the first clause of 7.24 as continuing the last of 7.23.
8.2-3:	G, S read what is the first clause of v. 3 in M with v. 2.
12.9-10:	G, Hie read what is the last word of 12.9 in M with 12.10. S reads it in both places.
12.11-12:	G reads the first phrase of 12.12 in M with 12.11.

At least in some of these cases, it is difficult to be certain how far the differences go back to the original translators, who did not need to punctuate their own texts, and were not thereby forced to assign clauses to one verse or another where there was any ambiguity. There is also inconsistency between the manuscripts, especially in 1.5 where Rahlfs places an ἄνω τελεία (the raised point roughly equivalent to a semi-colon) after ἕλκει (cf., e.g., the Greek text on Hamburger Pap. Bil. 1, although that marks the break in a different way). Codex Sinaiticus, however, places one instead after the subsequent ἀνατέλλων (cf. M), and Vaticanus, which punctuates more sparingly anyway, has no punctuation in either place. Conversely, there are other places where the translators may have intended a division that is not found in M, but which has not been picked up consistently in subsequent punctuation. For example, it is possible in G to read the last clause of 8.5 with 8.6, which gives a much easier reading,[208] and to do much the same also at 10.10-11 and 12.4-5, which are all places where the Masoretic division groups the content in a way that is open to challenge. Of course, our own freedom to make such challenges is tied up with the more general questions about the antiquity of the readings

---

[208] This is probably, in fact, how Sinaiticus construes the text, with no break marked after πονηρόν.

implied by the Masoretic pointing. Even were we to regard that pointing as truly ancient, however, it would still be important to recognize its interpretative character, despite the influence that the punctuation has exercised on subsequent readings of the text—and I suspect that this influence has not been for the better in cases like 6.6; 7.28-29; 9.1-2; 11.4-5.

(vi) Q^{e}rê *and* K^{e}thîbh *in Ecclesiastes*
We have already talked about *Q^{e}rê* and *K^{e}thîbh* in general, but the confusing and occasionally misleading way in which such readings have sometimes been presented, especially in *BHS*, makes it useful to summarize the particular occurrences here. Such a summary may also help allay any tendency to assume that this is an area in which the Masoretic manuscripts are all clear cut and consistent.

The straightforward cases in M^L are:

	Q^{e}rê	*K^{e}thîbh*
4.8	עינו	עיניו
4.17	רגלך	רגליך
5.8	הוא	היא
5.10	ראות	ראית
5.17	חייו	חיו
6.10	שתקיף	שהתקיף
7.22	אתה	את
9.4	יחבר	יבחר
10.20	כנפים	הכנפים
12.6	ירתק	ירחק

At least, these should be straightforward: the manuscript marks them all clearly in the margin with ק and the word that is to be read out, but *BHS* does not reproduce the instance at 5.17 (it instead presents חייו in the apparatus as the reading of a Cairo Genizah manuscript).[209] That instance at 5.17 is lacking from Sassoon 1053,

---

[209] Horst, the editor, did include the M^L *Q^{e}rê* in his previous presentation of M^L for *BH³*, but here, in a comment well hidden among the cross-references to the Masorah Magna, he explains that he has suppressed it because it contradicts the Masoretic note—and this is clearly part of the broader, very problematic attempt

which has the *Qᵉrê* as its *Kᵉthîbh*, but much the same happens variably with all these readings in other, later manuscripts. In 6.10, on the other hand, MS Or 9879 similarly has the *Qᵉrê* שתקיף as its *Kᵉthîbh*, but no manuscripts seem to have התקיף, which *BHS* lists as a variant of the *Kᵉthîbh*. That reading, in fact, exists only as a hypothesis (see the notes to the verse), and is misleadingly described. Of course, this does not mean that there is never any variation between the *Qᵉrê* readings in the early tradition, and we may note that MS Or 9879, for example, spells the *Qᵉrê plene* as יחובר in 9.4. In the case of 6.10, again, Baer (81) has the *Qᵉrê* / *Kᵉthîbh* as a western tradition only; the 'eastern' reading is שתקיף for *Qᵉrê* and *Kᵉthîbh*.

In addition to those instances, there are three places where M^L does not present an explicit *Qᵉrê*, as such, but instead has a Masoretic comment that one of the letters in the word is superfluous (as shown in *BHQ*), and points the word accordingly:

	Kᵉthîbh	superfluous	implied *Qᵉrê*
10.3	כשהסכל	ה	כסכל
10.10	הכשיר	י	הכשר
12.5	וינאץ	א	וינץ

These are dealt with rather variably both in the manuscripts and in modern editions. *BHS* at 10.3 and 10.10 presents the Masoretic comment alongside a formal *Qᵉrê* annotation (which M^L has in neither place), but offers only the comment at 12.5. It is not clear whether it is merely being inconsistent in this respect, or trying to incorporate Masoretic annotations from other manuscripts: MS Or 9879 is lacking for the second two, but at 10.3 gives just a *Qᵉrê*, כסכל.

---

to reconcile text with Masorah in *BHS*. Horst cites a similar case at 2 Sam 18.18, where de Boer in *BHS* has done the same, for the same reason. The masoretic note, reproduced in *BHQ*, simply refers to the defective writing of the word in these passages and at 2 Kgs 25.30; Jer 52.33, and it is difficult on any reckoning to justify the omission. It is presumably because he is following *BHS* that Schoors, in 'Kethibh-Qere', his helpful review of each case, omits 5.17 but does include 10.3, 10 (see below).

We also have a number of *Qᵉrê* and *Kᵉthîbh* readings that are not found as marginal annotations in M^L, but are attested in Masoretic lists as purportedly *Qᵉrê* in the Babylonian, 'eastern' tradition. The following are taken variously from Baer (81, which notes sources), and Ginsburg (*Massorah* III, 71, which does not); Baer's readings in 8.2 and 12.13 have been corrected in the light of Ginsburg, *Introduction*, 235-36. From Ginsburg's rather fuller account of the formal lists that distinguish eastern and western readings in his *Introduction* (236-37), it is apparent that the situation was much more confused than a simple table can suggest, so although these are attested, the labels need to be treated with caution, and it is not clear how far the description is shoe-horning actual textual variants into the *Qᵉrê* / *Kᵉthîbh* paradigm. We might observe that in 5.5, the 'eastern' reading מעשי is supported by G, Hie, V, and T, and in 10.10 לו is probably reflected in manuscripts of G, if not the original translation: these readings, at least, were probably not confined to eastern manuscripts.

	Western	Eastern	M^L
1.13	על	אל	על
3.9	העושה	העושה	העושה
3.11	העלם	העולם	העלם
4.1	העשוקים^{1,2}	העשקים	העשקים
5.5	מעשה	מעשי	מעשה
7.2	משתה	המשתה	משתה
8.2	שמור	שמר	שמור
9.9	הוא	היא	הוא
10.10	לא	לו	לא
12.5	אל	על	אל
12.5	עלמו	עולמו	עולמו
12.12	מהם	מהמה	מהמה
12.13	שמר	שמור	שמור

Of these, Ginsburg (*Introduction*, 236-37) notes that the witnesses differ as to which reading in 3.9 is eastern and which western, while there is considerable confusion around the reading in 4.1: the lists agree that the second occurrence of העשקים/העשוקים is *plene* in the western reading, but disagree about the first occurrence, and about whether both occurrences are *plene* or defective in the eastern text.

To these, we may conveniently add a more straightforward reading from the early Babylonian Masoretic text preserved in Berlin Or. Qu. 680 and JTS 510, which has $K^e th\hat{\imath}bh$ היה and $Q^e r\hat{e}$ הוה at 2.22, where M^L simply has הוה.[210]

Finally, Ginsburg (*Massorah* III, 71) also includes the following:

	$Q^e r\hat{e}$	$K^e th\hat{\imath}bh$
2.2, 24; 5.15; 5.18; 7.23; 9.13	זו	זה
10.20	יגד	יגיד
11.9	ובמראה	ובמראי

It is not always easy to establish the relationship between these readings and the translations offered in the other ancient versions, not least because the differences between $Q^e r\hat{e}$ and $K^e th\hat{\imath}bh$ do not affect the sense in every case. There are a few places, however, where the $K^e th\hat{\imath}bh$ seems to be supported: by V at 4.8, by S at 10.10, by σ' and S at 12.5, and perhaps by G at 10.20. There is generally more support for the $Q^e r\hat{e}$: by all the versions except V at 4.8, by all at 4.17 and 9.4, by σ' and G at 10.10, and by G, Hie, and V at 12.5. The support for the consonantal text of the $Q^e r\hat{e}$, however, does not always extend to support for the vocalization of those consonants proposed by the Masoretes (9.4 provides a clear example), and this suggests that the translators have found the $Q^e r\hat{e}$ readings in their texts, rather than that they are aware of them from a reading tradition. We have no reason to suppose that they would already have been marked as $Q^e r\hat{e}$ / $K^e th\hat{\imath}bh$ in those texts (although it is possible that some manuscripts recorded more than one reading; cf. Talmon, 'Aspects', 107-25), and it is more likely that we are dealing with simple textual variation.

2. *Greek Texts*

The emphasis that Josephus and later generations placed upon the Hebrew text can obscure the fact that, as we have already noted, by about the second century CE, and perhaps for some time before, this text would have been readily comprehensible to relatively few Jews, in Palestine or elsewhere. Without going into all the issues and

---

[210] The reading is visible on p. 117 of the facsimile edition, Yeivin, *Bible-Hagiographa*.

debates that surround the question of Hebrew's decline as a spoken language, we can see a recognition of it even in the Mishnah, which explicitly permits a range of prayers, oaths, and blessings to be spoken in any language (*m. Soṭah* 7.2), and which speaks of scriptures being written in Greek (*m. Megillah* 1.8; cf. *y. Megillah* 1.9).[211] Noting such passages, de Lange has pointed out also the extent to which Hebrew inscriptions are outnumbered by Greek even in the catacombs at Beit She'arim, which are closely associated with the early rabbinic movement, and has suggested very plausibly that it was only in the course of the third century that the language saw a significant revival. Outside very particular scholarly and religious circles, at least, many Jews in the first and second centuries are correspondingly likely to have been more familiar with their scriptures in Greek than in Hebrew, and for certain communities outside Palestine, indeed, this would have been the case for some centuries before that, just as it would continue to be true in Byzantine Judaism for many centuries to come.[212] Although the Hebrew text surely retained its high status, therefore, the probable reality is that not many would have known it well.

With the Greek translations serving, in effect, as a proxy for the Hebrew, efforts were made from quite an early point to align them more closely to it, or perhaps, as the Hebrew tradition itself

---

[211] It is likely, in fact, that we possess some Greek biblical texts intended for use in the synagogue; cf. Revell, 'Oldest Evidence', 216-22.

[212] Even rather later and in Palestine, such was the familiarity still with Greek scripture and language, that in *y. Mo'ed Qaṭan* 3.7 and *y. Yoma* 3.8 we find references to Aquila's Greek translation of words, used to explicate the Hebrew, while *y. Sukkah* 3.5 and *y. Šabbat* 6.4 even include transliterations of his Greek: cf. Field at Ps 47.15; Dan 5.5; Lev 23.40; Isa 3.20—although it is questionable whether the rabbis would have had first-hand knowledge of the Septuagint Pentateuch, as is often assumed; cf. Segal, '*Aristeas* or Haggadah'. This is part of a broader cultural influence, and the Babylonian Talmud notes of R. Meir's controversial teacher that 'Greek tunes never ceased from his mouth' (*b. Ḥagigah* 15b). On the pervasiveness of Greek in Palestinian rabbinic literature more generally, see Lieberman, *Greek in Jewish Palestine*, and on the broader influence of Greek scriptures on Jewish communities and culture, see Rajak, '"Torah shall go forth"'. Rajak also notes in passing (152) evidence for the use of the Greek Pentateuch as a basis for legal decisions in some communities. Of course, none of this need imply that the earliest Greek translations were specifically motivated by the decline of Hebrew: see Collins, 'Who Wanted?'.

consolidated around a standard, to re-align them.[213] As we shall see, the translation of Ecclesiastes that was to become part of the Greek Bible was strongly influenced by such efforts: in its original form, characterized as the Old Greek (**G***), it was from the outset a close approximation to the Hebrew text as the translator knew it, and so an important witness to the development of the Hebrew, even before revisions in many manuscripts sought to align it with later Hebrew standards. Within a century or two of its appearance, however, it had been joined by other Greek translations, and still later Greek versions are known as well—two of which will be covered briefly here. From a much later time, we have translations that are entirely literary or academic exercises,[214] and this is perhaps true, to an extent, of the Codex Graecus Venetus. The earlier texts, however, are a testament to the continuing importance of Greek in Jewish communities, as well, of course, as in the early Church: this is almost certainly the language in which Ecclesiastes would have been known to most of its readers for several centuries, and to many for much longer.

(a) *The Septuagint (***G***)*
As I write, the critical edition in the Göttingen Septuagint edition is under preparation by Peter Gentry (who has kindly made available to me his draft). Until it appears, probably before this volume, the standard edition is that of Rahlfs, although the diplomatic edition of Swete is also of value, and is unaffected by the terrible decision that Rahlfs made to use Jerome's commentary as a source of 'Old Latin', which has been mentioned above. Because Jerome drew directly on a Hebrew text of his time, and on the versions of the Three, the use of his translation to correct the Greek has brought it much closer to M in many places, and left some important, distinctive readings buried in the apparatus. This goes beyond the more general tendency of many earlier scholars to suppose that, when different readings are available for G, the one closest to M is likely

---

[213] De Lange, 'Revival'. On the possibility that Greek translations may have been used liturgically to provide running translations from the Hebrew, like the Aramaic Targums, see Smelik, 'Code-switching', 136-37.
[214] Notably Dölsch (Dolscius), *Ecclesiastes Salomonis*; Petau (Petauius), *Ecclesiaste Salomonis paraphrasis*; Duport, *Tres libri Solomonis*, 157-219.

to be the most original—an idea that seems, on the face of it, to be simple common sense. The problem is that, for various reasons, the Greek tradition has been contaminated by later readings derived from Hebrew texts, so while a resemblance to M may indeed be a reflection simply of the original source with which the translator worked, it may also be the result of such contamination. Accordingly, each case has to be examined on its own merits, and this is one reason why the lack of a proper edition has been a serious obstacle to the text-critical study of Ecclesiastes: scholars have not had the information necessary to reach informed decisions about such cases, or, indeed, about many other issues in G.[215]

(i) *Background and Character*
The reasons for G's contamination are connected with what is probably, in any case, the best starting place for a description of this Greek version: its use in Origen's Hexapla. That extraordinary work, produced in the first half of the third century CE, famously aligned versions of the biblical text in parallel columns, and although many questions still surround the precise contents and arrangement, the intention behind it was probably to clarify the relationship between the various Greek texts used by Jews and Christians (so, e.g., Norton, 'Cautionary Reflections', 154)—although it is also arguable that it reflects an implicit belief in the superiority of the Hebrew text, and in the need to check the Greek versions against it (cf. de Lange, 'Letter to Africanus'). While various of the columns were taken up by the text of the Hebrew and texts or variants from the versions of the Three, the most important, therefore, included a Greek translation that was annotated to indicate its relationship with the Hebrew, with words or passages obelized if they had no Hebrew equivalent, and supplements added, marked by asterisks, if the Greek had no existing equivalent to the Hebrew—these supplements were taken from the Three, most commonly from the text attributed to Theodotion. Some of the base texts selected for this column were already well established, and whatever the facts behind the story told in the *Letter of Aristeas*, a 'Septuagint' version of the Pentateuch, for instance, had certainly been in existence long

---

[215] Useful general introductions include Aitken, 'Ecclesiastes'; Backhaus, 'Ekklesiastes'. The latter includes notes on the text, but currently the only full commentary on G is that of Vinel.

before Origen made use of it. The other Greek texts that were used, and that ultimately became part of the Greek Bible, have not always left any earlier mark, and we know nothing about the version of Ecclesiastes that Origen used beyond what we can glean from the text itself.

The most obvious characteristic of this is its very peculiar Greek. Any translator has to strike a balance between representing the characteristics of their source and conveying its sense. Defending his own translation of a letter by Epiphanius, Jerome famously wrote:

> Ego enim non solum fateor, sed libera uoce profiteor, me in interpretatione Graecorum...non uerbum e uerbo, sed sensum exprimere de sensu. (*Epistula* LVII, *Ad Pammachium*, 5. PL 22: 308; CSEL 54: 508)

> For I not only confess but freely proclaim that in interpreting from Greek...I express myself not word-for-word but sense-for-sense.

He went on to cite Cicero's prologue to his translations of Aeschines and Demosthenes:

> nec conuerti ut interpres sed ut orator, sententiis isdem et earum formis, tamquam figuris uerbis ad nostram consuetudinem aptis. In quibus non uerbum pro uerbo necesse habui reddere sed genus omne uerborum uimque seruaui. Non enim me adnumerare lectori putaui oportere, sed tamquam appendere. (*De Optimo Genere Oratorum* 5.14)[216]

> I have translated not as an interpreter but as an orator, with the same meanings, but with the forms—in terms of figures and words—adapted to our usage. In this I have not considered it necessary to render word-by-word, but have followed the style and emphasis of the words as a whole. For I have not thought of my obligation to the reader in terms of counting out, so much as weighing out.

This is not an uncommon approach, but Jerome makes an interesting exception: he has translated in that way *absque scripturis sanctis, ubi et uerborum ordo mysterium est*, 'except when it comes to the holy scriptures, where even the order of the words holds secrets'.

---

[216] Text from Wilkins, *Rhetorica*. The text cited for Jerome in PL and CSEL has minor differences.

It would be difficult to maintain that Jerome himself always kept this in mind, and the paraphrases that we find often in his Vulgate translation are much more reminiscent of Cicero's approach. In making this exception, however, he does express an understanding of the biblical text that characterizes a number of Greek translations and revisions, including the G version of Ecclesiastes.

Since the seminal work *Les devanciers d'Aquila* by Dominique Barthélemy in 1963, it has generally been understood that, from some point around the turn of the eras, attempts were made to bring certain of the existing Greek biblical translations into a much closer alignment with the Hebrew text with which the revisers were familiar, so that, in Cicero's terms, they would 'count out' the words of that Hebrew, rather than 'weigh' it. Because they characteristically use the Greek καί γε, 'and indeed', to render the Hebrew גם and וגם, 'also, 'and also', these are generally labelled *kaige*, and their distinctive style is found already in the Greek Minor Prophets scroll from Nahal Ḥever (8HevXII gr), usually dated to the first century BCE or CE. In the second century CE, the same general approach is adopted in the versions of Theodotion and Aquila, and it represents a sharp departure from the more 'sense-for-sense' technique found in some of the earlier translations. The G version of Qohelet clearly belongs broadly in this tradition, and the similarity of its translation technique to that of Aquila (who, according to Jerome, *studiosius verbum interpretatur ad verbum*, 'more studiously translates word-for-word'),[217] has long led many scholars to suppose that it was, in fact, composed by Aquila. That idea has always been problematic, not least because we have fragments of Aquila's version that do not correspond to G: if G is indeed the work of Aquila, therefore, then we have to identify those fragments as another edition of his translation,[218] as the mislabelled translation of Symmachus

---

[217] *Epistula* XXXVI, *Ad Damasum*, 12. PL 22: 457; CSEL 54: 278.

[218] So, e.g., Salzberger, 'Septuagintalübersetzung', and Barton (8-10), who cites the detailed analysis in McNeile, 115-34. The notion of a 'second edition' is not driven solely by the need to explain separate readings attributed to Aquila: Jerome speaks in a number of places about a second edition by Aquila, often citing separate readings for the first and second, as in, e.g., his commentary on Jer 13.12 (*Aquilae prima editio 'lagunculam', secunda ipsum 'nebel'*). The implication of these is generally that the second edition inclined toward transliteration and an even closer adherence to the Hebrew, which would actually accord with the sorts of distinction that we find between G and α' in Ecclesiastes. It is by no means clear,

INTRODUCTION

or Theodotion, or as a separate, very 'Aquilan' rendering by an unknown translator.[219] The complexities raised by that problem mean that, although authorship by Aquila cannot completely be excluded any more than it can be proved, it is a great deal simpler to assume that the resemblance of G to his work is not a matter of authorship, but of a shared attachment to similar principles of translation.[220] Its character does suggest, however, that G is unlikely

however, that any second edition extended beyond the books of Jeremiah, Ezekiel and Daniel—for which such references are found in Jerome. In his commentaries on Jeremiah (at 32.30) and on Nahum (at 3.1), Jerome also seems to refer in similar terms to a second edition by Symmachus, although the Nahum comment might be referring back to Aquila (...*quod interpretatus est Aquila... Symmachus autem... in altera eius editione...*). At Jer 29.17, however, his reference to *secunda* is almost certainly a reference to Aquila's second edition, not to a further edition by Theodotion, whose reading has just been mentioned. Jerome is well informed and quite specific, but it is hard to say where he has found his 'second edition' readings, and whether they represent a fresh translation of certain books or simply annotations to a text of α'. He makes no suggestion himself that G in Ecclesiastes is the work of Aquila. For the data in particular, see the discussion by Field (xxiv-xxvii), who lists the examples, and also a significant number of other places where two different readings have been attributed to Aquila; he offers a similar list for Symmachus on pp. xxxvi-xxxvii. In the helpful English translation by Gerard Norton, *Frederick Field's Prolegomena*, these are pp. 52-56 and 71-73. Despite the acknowledged slimness of the evidence, Giambrone, 'Aquila's Greek Targum', has recently suggested that the double edition is indicative of a move from something like an interlinear Targum through to a more ideological and exegetical project.

[219] Barthélemy, *Les devanciers d'Aquila*, 27-30, notes in particular renderings attributed to Aquila that seem more characteristic of Symmachus, but does not suggest outright that the 'Aquilan' readings should actually be attributed to Symmachus, as Beckwith, *Canon*, 472, avers. Beckwith himself argues (472-76) that these readings are actually from the original 'Septuagint' version, displaced by Aquila's.

[220] Dillmann, 'Über die griechische Übersetzung', argued against Aquila having been the translator, but took G as we have it to be an older translation that had undergone a revision based on Aquila's work. More recently, Barthélemy, *Les devanciers d'Aquila*, 21-33, has once again restated the argument for Aquila as translator, and is supported by, e.g., Salters 'Observations on the Septuagint', 166-69, but opposed by Hyvärinen, *Die Übersetzung von Aquila*, 88-99: Jarick, 'Aquila's *Koheleth*', finds much in the translation that is Aquilan, but doubts that the question can be resolved with any certainty. A significant part of the problem, of course, is that our witnesses to the readings of the Three are not always clear or reliable. Barthélemy makes much, for instance of the fact that in 5.18, the rendering of גם attributed to α' is the very un-Aquilan ἀλλὰ καί, but it is not difficult to

to have been produced much earlier than about the first century CE, and may be as late as the second, so not far off Aquila's time.[221]

To give a flavour of the translation,[222] it would seem helpful to take an example, so here are the M and G versions of 3.10 (set out left-to-right):

ראיתי	את	הענין	אשר	נתן	אלהים	לבני	האדם	לענות	בו
εἶδον	σὺν	τὸν περι-σπασμόν	ὃν	ἔδωκεν	ὁ θεὸς	τοῖς υἱοῖς	τοῦ ἀνθρώ-που	τοῦ περι-σπᾶσθαι	ἐν αὐτῷ
I saw		the work	which	has given	(the) God	to the sons	of man	to be busy	in it

What looks like one word in the Hebrew is often rendered with two in the Greek, because the word actually has a prefixed article or preposition—the only genuine plus in G is the article on 'God', for which there is no equivalent in M. Otherwise, there is a close correspondence that extends even to the representation of the object-marker: את has no equivalent in either English or Greek, but the translator (under particular circumstances) renders it using σὺν (see Yi, 68-73; Ziegler, 'Die Wiedergabe'). This is equivalent to another Hebrew word את, a preposition meaning 'with', but it cannot properly be read as 'with' in Greek, because the word that follows is in the wrong case. All the σὺν really does, then, is mark the presence of an object-marker in the underlying Hebrew, and it would be confusing to any reader of Greek unfamiliar with that purpose. Otherwise, we may note the precise correspondence of the Greek word-order to that of the Hebrew, and a general adoption of the Hebrew idiom even where it gives an awkward sense in Greek

---

accept Marshall's conclusion that two attributions, close to each other in ms. 248, have accidentally been swapped, and that this error has then been picked up in the only other witness, ms 161, which is dependant on 248 throughout.

[221] Some support for such a dating is offered also by the observations on late vocabulary in Gwynn, 'Notes', 121-22.

[222] On the translation technique, see especially the detailed study by Yi, although at a few points this is inclined to assume that the source-text of G was identical to M when it probably was not. As a much briefer overview, Casanowicz's 'Book of Ecclesiastes' is still useful, and although dated, Klostermann's *De libri Coheleth* has much helpful information, albeit in Latin.

(e.g. ἐν, 'in', for -בּ on the last word). The translation is not simply verbatim at every point, however: with לבני, the translator does not attempt to render the preposition, but instead uses the dative case to convey the sense (which is more natural Greek), and לענות is similarly translated not with a preposition, but with a Greek equivalent to the expression, τοῦ + infinitive. That is the way in which such expressions are handled elsewhere, and so this is not 'looseness' as such, but the use of equivalences for expressions rather than just words.

The general effect is to produce a text that would probably have seemed very strange (and occasionally, perhaps, incomprehensible) to a Greek-speaker with no Hebrew, but which would have enabled exegesis of the text with reasonable confidence that it was a close, isomorphic representation of the original. Since this was presumably the translator's purpose, he resists a purely mechanical rendering when it might be misleading: the Hebrew word רוח, for instance, can mean either 'wind' or 'spirit/breath', and different words are used accordingly at, for example, 3.19 and 11.4 (which sheds some interesting light on the translator's understanding in other places, such as 1.6 and 11.5).[223] In a few cases, he is forced further away from the Hebrew by similar considerations: at the beginning of 1.10, for instance, a purely verbatim rendering would have lost the conditional aspect inherent in the Hebrew and changed the sense, so he adopts a different construction. Within the constraints of his translation technique, furthermore, the translator sometimes tries to make the Greek itself as stylish and attractive as possible, so that this is ultimately rather a sophisticated rendering, however awkward it may seem superficially.[224] Its assumptions, however, and those that underpin the *kaige* way of doing things more generally, are clearly tied to haggadic interpretative techniques, which

---

[223] Bolin, *Ecclesiastes*, 106, repeats a common supposition when he claims that G 'is a rigid translation that consistently renders the same Hebrew word with the same Greek word every time, regardless of context', but this is simply untrue.

[224] See especially Aitken, 'Rhetoric and Poetry'. Earlier commentators tend to be less generous: see, e.g., Casanowicz, 'Book of Ecclesiastes', 117: 'the rendering of the book of Ecclesiastes does not betray a spark of appreciation for the genius of the Greek language. The translator follows so closely and so mechanically the Hebrew scroll before him that his translation is in reality Hebrew in Greek disguise.'

could involve the consideration of words and wording with little regard to their context, and for which an entirely 'sense-to-sense' translation would be useless.[225]

Such techniques are themselves employed in the later Targum, but it is doubtful that they underpin G's rendering itself, as Ginsburg suggests in his commentary (496): it is rarely likely, if ever, that the translator has deliberately taken the Hebrew in an unnatural sense to make some exegetical point, and beyond the broad requirement to interpret in order to translate, the translator's purpose is to facilitate, not himself to conduct exegesis. Since he applies his translation technique with great consistency, furthermore, his intention to produce an accurate representation of the Hebrew text makes G an extremely useful resource: so long as we can restore the original text of the Greek with confidence, we can usually discern with no less confidence the Hebrew source-text on which it was based. As already observed, however, it is that first step which can often cause difficulties.

It is a general problem for the study of the Greek Bible that the Greek text which Origen annotated and supplemented in order to align it with his Hebrew often came to be copied and transmitted without the annotations, and that the Hexapla accordingly gave rise to readings in many 'Origenic' manuscripts that have in effect been aligned with a Hebrew text—indeed, it has been suggested that Origen himself may have included readings from manuscripts that had already been revised toward the Hebrew.[226] More broadly, there are signs of other hebraizations, and hexaplaric readings seem all too

---

[225] The Hebrew-Greek glossary mentioned above (see n. 157) was presumably designed for readers with a little more Hebrew who wished to engage directly with the Hebrew text. The principle behind the verbatim Greek translations is essentially very similar, however, and it is interesting to note the observation by the editors (120-24) that many of the Greek terms used in the glossary may actually have been derived from Aquila's version.

[226] In his *Letter to Africanus*, 5 (PG 11:60-61), Origen speaks of his special effort '...to work with the translation of the Seventy, so that I might not impute any re-writing to the Churches under heaven... But I laboured not to be ignorant of their (variants) so that, debating with Jews, I should not present them with things that are not in their copies and so that I might make use of what they do have, even if it is not to be found in our books.' Whilst it shows his awareness of differences between copies of Septuagint texts and his willingness to employ readings found by the Jews but not by Christians, this probably falls short of an

frequently to have found their way out of the other Greek columns, containing the versions of the Three, and into many manuscripts of G. Sometimes the original reading is beyond recovery where it seems likely that this has happened; more often, the contamination creates variants, alongside the many others that arose in the Greek tradition, which have to be weighed and assessed—not an easy task for scholars working on Ecclesiastes, when little detailed information about the texts has been available. If this detracts a little from the value of G as a witness, then it should be borne in mind that, although the effect is generally to bring G closer to M, there are still many points at which they differ.[227]

(ii) *Differences between G and M*
The following tables 1-3 set out a fairly conservative list of the places at which G was probably translated from a consonantal text that differed from that of M, or, in at least one case, where variants in G reflect assimilation of the G text to a Hebrew text that differed from M (other, less clear-cut possibilities are discussed in the notes to the text). There are a few expressions where issues of translation technique may have been involved, and so I have not included, for example, the case that we just saw in 3.10, where G has '*the* God' and M has just 'God' (although Goldman in *BHQ* would attribute that to a different—and in his view more original—source-text). I have set alongside each reading the agreements of other ancient witnesses where these are extant and unambiguous. An asterisk indicates issues (normally of attribution) that complicate the agreement—these are detailed in the notes to the commentary; S, the Syriac text, is marked as 'M/G' where the text or textual tradition appears to agree with both (see below). We shall deal

explicit statement that he changed his text in the Hexapla, as Norton, 'Cautionary Reflections', 152, claims: his use of other readings is set in the context of his debating, not his editing.

[227] As Aejmelaeus, 'Textual History', 161, puts it: 'What characterizes the textual history of all the translated books of the Septuagint is the tendency to compare the Greek text with the Hebrew and to make adjustments accordingly. This has happened repeatedly in different phases of the textual history and under different circumstances. It is a challenge to the textual critic and renders textual criticism of the Septuagint different from that of all other antique texts. This cannot be overemphasized.'

with the other versions in more detail shortly, but for the moment this gives a rough idea of the support for each reading, and some overview of affinities between G, M, and the other versions.

It may be noted that a significant number of these cases involve the different reading of individual, potentially ambiguous characters, as when, in several places, the versions variously reflect כאשר and באשר. Most others involve changes that are minor, in graphical terms, but that can have a significant impact upon the meaning. Despite their quantity, therefore, these differences do not suggest that G used a source-text that we could usefully call a different recension or version of Ecclesiastes, and most of them probably reflect no more than the sort of divergences that typically arise from copying errors or from efforts to make sense of an awkward or damaged text.

In view of the questions raised above about a tradition of pronunciation that was supposedly preserved by the Masoretes, it seems worth listing also the places at which G seems to reflect a pronunciation different from that indicated by the vowels in M, and I have done so in table 4. Here I have not attempted to guess precisely how the translator did vocalize his text, nor have I included the various places at which the reading of G contradicts the construal of the text or grouping of words that is implied by the Masoretic accents. Even from the minimal data presented, though, it seems clear that, as we have already observed, if the translator of G relied on a tradition of pronunciation at all, then that tradition differed significantly from what we find in M. Of course, the very fact of so many consonantal differences would seem to affirm that fact as well. Where the two do correspond in such matters as the pointing of prepositions with articles, the correspondence is sometimes striking, but, in the light of the many differences, it should probably be attributed to a shared understanding or *sens linguistique*, rather than to a common tradition.

Table 1. *Pluses in G*

	M^L	G	α'	θ'	σ'	S	La	Hie	V	T
1.1	מלך	+ Ισραηλ				M	G	M	M	M
1.2	קהלת	+ article								
1.8	לא תשבע	+ cj.				G		M	M	G

INTRODUCTION

	M^L	G	α'	θ'	σ'	S	La	Hie	V	T
2.3	תרתי	+ cj.	G	G	M			M	M	M
2.26	גם	שגם כי גם or				M		M	M	M
3.1	זמן	+ article								
3.21	מי	+ cj.				G		G	M	M
4.4	עמל	+ article								
4.17	זבח	+ suffix, זבחך	M	M		M		M	M	M
5.19	מענה	+ suffix, מענהו		G	G			M	M	M
7.2	מלכת	+ relative pronoun, משלכת				G	M	M	M	M
	יתן	+ ἀγαθὸν		M	G	M		M	M	M
7.12	בצל¹	+ suffix בצלה		M	M			M	M	
7.21	ידברו	+ ἀσεβεῖς		M	G			M	M	G
7.25	הוללות	+ cj.				G		M	M	
7.26	אני	+ αὐτὴν καὶ ἐρῶ				M		M	M	M
7.28	אדם	+ cj.				M		M	M	M
8.16	חכמה	+ article								
9.2	לטוב	+ καὶ τῷ κακῷ				G	G	G	G	M
	שבועה	+ article								
9.9	ראה	+ cj.				G		M	M	M
	בחיים	+ σου				M/G		M	M	
10.1	רוקח	+ ἡδύσματος		G	G			M	M	G
11.8	אם	+ cj.				M		M	M	M
12.5	גם	+ cj.				G	G		G	M	M

Table 2. *Minuses in G*

	M^L	G	α'	θ'	σ'	S	Hie	V	T
2.12	כבר	ø		G		G		G	M
2.15	אז	ø				G	G	G	M
3.13	האדם	- article							
3.19	ומקרה²	- cj.				G	G	G	G
5.2	החלום	- article		G					
5.9	לא	ø	M*	M*		M	M	M	M
5.10	הטובה	- article							

5.12	רעה	ø			M	M	M	M	M
5.16	וחליו	- suffix				G	G	G	G
7.1	הולדו	- suffix	M			G	M	G	
7.6	כי	ø			M	M/G	M	M	M
7.21	הדברים	- article			M				
7.25	הסכלות	- article							
8.2	אני	ø			M	G	M	M	G
8.5	ומשפט	- cj.				M	M	M	
8.8	המות	- article							
8.17	האדם¹	- article			M				
	בשל	ø			M				
9.1	האדם	- article	M						
9.9	כל ימי הבלך	ø	M			G	M	M	G
10.1	יביע	ø			G	G	G	G	M?
10.10	לא	ø					M	M	M

Table 3. *Other consonantal differences in G*

	M^L	G reflects:	α′	θ′	σ′	S	Hie	V	T
1.13	הוא	כיא				M	M	M	M
1.16	עם לבי	בלבי	M			M	M	G	G
	על ירושלם	בירושלם				G	G	G	G
1.18	כעס	דעת	M	M	M	M	M	M	M
2.3	ביין	כיין		G		M	M		M
	השמים	השמש				G	G	G	M
2.10	מכל²	בכל			M	G	G		G
2.21	ולאדם שלא	ואדם שלו לא		G		M	M		M
2.24	ושתה והראה	וישתה ושיראה	G (part)			G	M	M	M
2.25	יחוש	ישתה	G^{mss}	G^{mss}	G^{mss}	G	G^{mss}	M	M
	ממני	ממנו				G	G	M	M
3.14	יעשה	עשה				G	G	G	M
3.16	הצדק	הצדיק	M			G	M	M	G
3.18	המה	וגם				M			M
3.19	כי מקרה	כמקרה* mss					M		M

INTRODUCTION

	M^L	G reflects:	α′	θ′	σ′	S	Hie	V	T
4.11	ולאחד	והאחד	M			G	G		M
4.17	כאשר	באשר		G		M	M		
5.5	המלאך	האלהים	M	M	M	G	M	M	M
5.8	בכל	על כל			G	M	M	G?	G
5.10	K ראית אם Q אם ראות	כי ראש ראות or כי ראשית ראות		M	M	M/G	M	M	M
5.16	יאכל	ובאבל or ואבל				M/G	M	M	M
6.4	ילך	הולך				M	G	G	M
6.12	ויעשם	ועשם			M	G	M	M	M
	כצל	בצל				M		M	M
7.2	מלכה	משלחה				G			M
	באשר	כאשר				G	M	M	
7.10	מחכמה	בחכמה				G			M
7.12	בצל²	כצל				G			M
7.14	היה	חיה	G	G	M	M	M	M	M
7.18	את כלם	הכל		G	M	M	G	G	M
7.19	תעז	תעזר	M*		M*	M	M	M	G
7.22	ידע	ירע	G			M	M	M	M
7.24	מה שהיה	משהיה				G	G	G	M
7.26	אסורים	אסור ב-	M			M	M	M	M
8.4	באשר	כאשר			M	G	G		M
8.6	רעת	דעת		G	M		M	M	M
8.8	במלחמה	ביום מלחמה			M	G	M	M	M
8.9	עת אשר	את אשר	M		M	M		M	M
8.10	ובאו	ובאים		M		G	M		M
	יהלכו	והלכו	G	G	M	M	M		M
	וישתכחו	וישתבחו			G	M	G	G	M
8.11	מעשה	מעשי				G	G	G	G*
8.12	מאת	מאז				M	M	M	M
8.13	כצל	בצל				M	M	M	M
8.16	כאשר	באשר					M		

	M^L	G reflects:	α'	θ'	σ'	S	Hie	V	T
9.1	ולבור את	ולבי ראה את				M	G	M	M	M
9.2	הכל	הבל				G	M/G			
	כאשר	באשר				G				
	הנשבע	כנשבע					G	G	G	G
9.5	יודעים¹	ידעו				M	M	M	M	
	עוד להם	להם עוד				G	G			
9.10	בכחך	ככחך				M	M		M	
9.11	לחכמים	לחכם	M	M	G	M	M	M	M
9.14	מצודים	מצורים			G	G	G	G	G	M
10.3	לכל	הכל				G	G	G	G	
10.10	הכשיר	הכשר				G	M	G	G	
10.14	שיהיה	שהיה				G	G	G	G	M
10.16	ארץ	עיר				M	G	M	M	M
11.5	כאשר	באשר	G			M	M	M	M	M
	אינך	אין	M			M	M	M	M	M
12.6	ונרץ from רצץ	וירץ from רוץ				G	M	M	G	
	אל	על					G	G	G	
12.9	וחקר	יחקר	M			M	M	M	M	

Table 4. *Different understandings in G that probably reflect a different pronunciation*

	M^L	G	α'	θ'	σ'	S	Hie	V	T
1.5	וזרח qatal	participle	M		G	M?	G	G	
1.10	דבר noun	verb				G	M		M
1.15	לתקן qal	pual				M	G	G	
1.17	ודעת infinitive	noun				G	G	G	G
2.3	נהג participle	qatal				M	G		G
2.4	מעשי plural	singular				M	M	M	M	M
2.12	המלך 'king'	'counsel'*	M	M	G	M	M	M	M
2.23	שכב qatal	participle					G	G	
3.5	מחבק: מן + infinitive	מן + noun				G	G		M

INTRODUCTION

	M^L	G	α'	θ'	σ'	S	Hie	V	T
3.16	רשע 'wickedness'	'wicked man'*				M?	M	M	G
3.18	ולראות qal	hiphil				G	G	G	G	M
3.19	מקרה^{1,2} absolute	construct					G	G		G
3.21	הירדת, העלה with articles	with interrogative -ה					G	G	G	G
4.11	וחם verb	noun					G		G
4.12	יתקפו singular with suffix	plural				M	M		
4.14	יצא qatal	yiqtol				M	M	G	G	M
4.17	מן + מתת: infinitive	noun	G	G	M*	G	G		
5.3	את object-marker	pronoun or pronoun + object-marker	G			M/G	M	M	G
5.7	במדינה with article	without article			G*				
	שמר participle	infinitive					M	M	M
5.10	ברבות infinitive	noun/ adjective				G	G	G	G
5.11	העבד participle	noun		M	M		M	M	M
	והשבע noun	verb			M	M	M	M	
	לעשיר noun	verb			M	M	M	M	
5.12	חולה participle	noun				G	G	G	G	M
5.14	ילך hiphil	qal				G	G	G	M	
5.16	וכעס verb	noun				G	G	G	G
6.3	רב adjective	noun				M	M	M	
6.6	פעמים dual	plural	G			M	M	M	M
6.10	ונודע participle	qatal				S	G	M	G
7.7	מתנה noun	noun + suffix pronoun	G	G	M	M/G	G	G	M

	M^L	G	α′	θ′	σ′	S	Hie	V	T
7.19	לחכם without article	with article			G*				
7.23	רחוקה adjective	verb				M	G	G	G
7.24	עמק עמק adjectives	adjective then noun					G	G	
7.25	רשע 'wickedness'	'wicked man'				M	M	M	M
8.1	מי כהחכם	מי כה חכם	G		G	M/G	G*		
	ישנא 'change'	'hate'				G	M	M	M
8.3	אל תבהל niphal	piel			G	G	G	G	G
8.9	לרע noun	verb				M	G	G	M	G
8.10	קברים participle	noun				M	M	M	M
8.11	נעשה qatal	participle			G	G	G	M	G
	מעשה noun	מן + participle (עשׂי?)				G	G	G	
8.12	ומאריך participle	מן + noun ארך			M	M	M	M	M
9.4	לכלב without article	with article							
10.5	יצא participle	qatal				M	G	M	M	M
10.6	במרומים with article	without article	G		G				
	בשפל with article	without article							
10.10	קהה piel	qal				G	G	G	G
10.17	בשתי :ב- + noun שתי	a verbal form from בוש				M			
11.8	שבא qatal	participle	G			M	G		
12.3	ביום with article	without article							

	M^L	G	α'	θ'	σ'	S	Hie	V	T
12.4	וסגרו pual	qal				M	G	G	
	בשפל infinitive	noun			M	G	G	G	
	הטחנה noun	participle				G	G	G	
12.5	יראו 'fear'	'see'			G		M	M	
	מגבה adjective 'high'	noun 'height'.			G	G	G	M	M
	והפר hiphil	hophal		M*	G		G	G	
	הלך participle	qatal				M			
	בשוק with article	without article							
12.6	ותרץ as from רוץ	from רצץ	M	M	G	G	M	M	G
12.9	ואזן verb	noun	M			M	M	M	M
	תקן verb	noun	M			M	M	M	M

(b) *The Three (α', σ', θ')*

Although many are also preserved in a small number of Greek manuscripts, the principal source for fragments of these three versions of Ecclesiastes is the Syro-Hexapla (see below), which presents them (usually in Syriac) as marginal readings. They are also sometimes found in ancient citations, and Jerome often talks about them in his commentary, occasionally giving Latin translations or citing Greek words. Building on several earlier efforts, the classic edition is Field, although this has been displaced for Ecclesiastes by Marshall, which benefits from discoveries made since Field's time.

The information that we have about the three individuals associated with these other hexaplaric versions is limited and sometimes unreliable. Writing in the late fourth century, Epiphanius offers descriptions of all three (in his *Weights and Measures*, 13-16). According to him, Aquila was from Sinope and was related by marriage to the emperor Hadrian (ruled 117–138 CE), who took him to Jerusalem as an interpreter. There he converted to Christianity, but was expelled from the Church and converted instead to Judaism, making a translation of the scriptures that was motivated by a desire to distort the Septuagint. Of Symmachus, Epiphanius has less to say: he was a Samaritan who lived in the time of Verus (according to the Syriac; that is, Marcus Aurelius, ruled 161 to 180) and who converted to Judaism because of a lack of recognition by his own people; his translation was motivated by a desire to undermine an existing translation current among the Samaritans. Otherwise, Epiphanius merely talks at length about what might have been involved in the process of being re-circumcised for such a conversion, and about surgical procedures for 'uncircumcision'— a topic that seems to intrigue and outrage him. Finally, Theodotion of Pontus is placed in the time of Commodus (ruled 177 to 192). Another proselyte, he converted to Judaism as a reaction against Marcionism, and produced a translation that frequently agreed with the Septuagint (to the extent that it is commonly seen now as a revision of the Septuagint, rather than an entirely new translation). Epiphanius is concerned to defend the Septuagint against its rivals, and has little kind to say about any of the Three, but he does also supply interesting information about the Hexapla and about two other translations used for some sections by Origen—claiming that they had been found in wine jars with other texts in Jericho and in Nicopolis. Enough verifiable information is included that his accounts cannot be rejected wholesale.

(i) *Aquila (α′)*

Indeed, numerous Talmudic references to עקילס הגר, 'Aquila the proselyte', do affirm Epiphanius' contention that he was a convert to Judaism, as does, for example, Jerome in *Epistulae* 57.11, and there are a number of Jewish accounts that link him to Hadrian.[228] The Jewish sources, however, frequently entangle Aquila with with the translator of the Targum Onqelos whose name אונקלוס is somewhat similar in Hebrew, and who is likewise commonly identified as a proselyte, but whose work, more importantly, represents for Babylonian Judaism something that is equivalent to

---

[228] These need to be regarded with some caution: conversations with emperors or other powerful Romans are a familiar *topos* in rabbinic literature. Although it is the hardest element to assess, however, the issue of Aquila's relationship to Hadrian and his social status is not irrelevant: Giambrone, 'Aquila's Greek Targum', 29-30, attempts to make a case that his translation would have required 'financial backing' and sponsorship, and argues that this must have been supplied by the rabbinic movement—a case that carries little weight if it is true that Aquila enjoyed independent wealth and belonged to the highest social class.

Aquila's. A comparison of parallel passages in the Jerusalem and Babylonian Talmuds indicates the scale of the problem: *y. Megillah* 1.9 talks about Aquila's translation into Greek, the corresponding *b. Megillah* 3a about the Onqelos translation into Aramaic—it goes on to compare this with Targum Jonathan. Those passages link Aquila with Rabbis Eliezer and Joshua, but elsewhere (*y. Qiddušin* 1.1, 5a) Aquila is mentioned in connection with R. Akiba, and in his commentary on Isa 8.11 Jerome speaks of *Akibas quem magistrum Aquilae proselyti autumat*, 'Akiba, who is supposed to be the teacher of the proselyte Aquila'. Aquila's translation famously promotes rendering את even when it is simply the object-marker—a habit that is adopted also in G, as we have seen above—and this would accord with such an association: *b. Baba Qamma* 41b discusses rabbinic arguments about assigning a sense to the particle for halakhic purposes, and depicts Akiba as finding a meaning for it even in Deut 6.13, which had defeated his predecessors.[229]

Recent scholarship has been inclined not to make too much of this, or to try to read into the rather slight associations with Akiba an exegetical purpose that corresponds to some particular Jewish approach. Grabbe remarks of Aquila, indeed, that 'he seems to have laboured in a way which has more in common with modern translators than with rabbinic exegetes. There is little to suggest that he tried to exemplify any of the exegeses current in his own day'[230]—which is much the same as I have suggested above about G. If the two are similar in important ways, however, there are still differences between them, and these are manifest in their treatment of two famous problems in Ecclesiastes. When dealing with both the protagonist Qohelet and his declarations about *hebel*, G opts for what are ultimately sense-to-sense translations, rendering

---

[229] Aquila's use of σύν to render the object-marker is similar to that of G. It is spelled out generally but succinctly in Burkitt, *Fragments*, 12: 'σύν is regularly used whenever את is followed by the Hebrew article or by כל. When את is used without the article, i.e. before proper names or nouns with suffixes, or in the construct state, the Greek article is used instead of σύν.' The effect is that the את is aways reflected in the Greek, either by σύν or by an article. See also the more detailed account in Barthélemy, *Les devanciers d'Aquila*, 22-25.

[230] Grabbe, 'Aquila's Translation', 536. Similarly, Labendz, 'Aquila's Bible Translation', who stresses the liminal character of Aquila in rabbinic sources, where he is esteemed simply as a translator. For a contrary view, see Giambrone, 'Aquila's Greek Targum'.

the former as a title 'assemblyman' or somesuch, and the latter as 'vanity'. In each case α', on the other hand, stands closer to the Hebrew, simply transliterating the word Qohelet, and retaining the metaphorical character of *hebel* by translating it as 'vapour'.

There are few variations from M not already listed in connection with G, but note:

	M^L	α' reflects:	
8.12	מאת	מ(ו)ת	so too σ' and θ'
12.5	וחתחתים	חת התתים or חת חתים	
	ותפר	ותפרה	

(ii) *Symmachus (σ')*

Writing in the early fourth century, somewhat before Epiphanius, Eusebius offers some of the same information about the Hexapla in his *Church History* 16-17. He has nothing to say about Aquila or Theodotion, but says of Symmachus that he was an Ebionite—an opinion that has influenced many scholars, but that is almost certainly wrong: there are many indications that Symmachus was Jewish, and Eusebius has probably misconstrued the information at his disposal. There is no particular reason, on the other hand, to reject Epiphanius' statement that he was a Samaritan convert, and it is possible, although by no means certain, that he should be identified with the Symmachus ben Joseph mentioned as a disciple of R. Meir in *b. ʿErubin* 13b (see especially Barthélemy, 'Qui est Symmaque?').

In any case, the translation by Symmachus is in some respects the very opposite of that by Aquila: its principal concern is to convey the sense of each passage, and it often paraphrases as necessary in order to do so. The result is a text that reads much more smoothly as Greek and that generally conveys a meaning much more clearly—but that inevitably incorporates a much greater degree of interpretation (although, like α', σ' does render *hebel* as 'vapour', and not everything in the translation is 'sense-for-sense'). The style and clarity seem to have been much admired, and this is probably one reason for Jerome's frequent engagement with σ' in his commentary, while his later Vulgate translation of Ecclesiastes has been influenced by it almost throughout (see Cannon, 'Jerome and Symmachus'). These characteristics mean that σ' has to be used with some caution as a witness to the Hebrew text, but all the same, in addition to those variances from M^L already listed in connection with other witnesses, we may note the following readings:

	M^L	σ'	
2.15	חכמתי verb	ἡ σοφία μου: noun + suffix	
5.11	שָׂבָע	πλησμονή = שֹׂבַע	
5.12	רעה noun	adjective	So also Hie, V, S^{mss}
6.5	נחת	ø	See the note to the text. The absence has given rise to an interpretation reflected also in V, T
7.9	לכעוס qal	לכעס piel	
7.25	ולבי	בלבי	So also V, T
8.10	וממקום	מקום	
10.15	ידע sing.	plural	So also La, Hie, V, S
12.6	ירחק Q / ירתק K	ינתק	So also Hie, V, S
12.10	וכתוב participle	וכתב qatal	So also V, S

(iii) *Theodotion (θ')*
The very limited information offered about Theodotion by Epiphanius notes the extent to which the version that is attributed to him agrees with G, and of all the Three versions, θ' does indeed commonly seem the closest to a straightforward revision of G towards the Hebrew. There are significant questions, moreover, around both the extent to which everything labelled θ' actually comes from the same source (especially since readings attributed to Theodotion are found in the New Testament and other Christian literature that was earlier than Theodotion), and the ways in which that material was presented and used by Origen—all of which might discourage us from rushing to draw general conclusions about it (cf. Norton, 'Cautionary Reflections', 145). In Ecclesiastes, the readings of θ' commonly coincide with those of α'. We may note one additional reading where it differs from M:

	M^L	θ'
8.10	וממקום	ממקום

(c) Two Other Greek Translations

It has become increasingly clear in recent years that Judaism did not simply abandon Greek as a language for biblical texts after the second century, and there are many signs of continuing engagement with existing texts and translations. There are also some new efforts, both to revise Greek texts in the light of the Hebrew text, and to create new translations. A proper treatment of these is outside the scope of this commentary, but I shall give brief introductions here to two manuscripts that are of direct relevance to Ecclesiastes, readings from which are mentioned from time to time in my notes.

(i) A Greek translation in Hebrew script from the Cairo Genizah (T-S Misc. 28.74)

This manuscript from the eleventh century or earlier is written in a vocalized Hebrew script, but the language is Greek.[231] The principal edition is de Lange's 'A Greek Translation', which lists some earlier publications (but see also his *Japheth*, 95-98, 167). Except that I have divided all the words, the transliteration here largely follows that of de Lange, and reproduces the spellings—in some cases the errors also—implied by the manuscript.

(2.13) ...παρα την χωρικιαν ωσεν περισσοτερον το φως παρα το σκοτος (2.14) ο σοφος οφθαλμοι αυτου εν κεφαλην αυτου και ο χωρικος εις το σκοτος πορευγομενος και εγνωσα γαρ εγω ως συναντιασμα εναν συναντιαζει των παντων αυτων (2.15) και ειπον εγω εν καρδιαν μου ως συναντιασμα του χωρικου [γα]ρ εγω συναντιαζει μου και δια τι εφρονεσα [ε]γω τοτεν περισσοτερον και ελαλησα εν καρδιαν μου ως γαρ τουτο ματαιον (2.16) οτι ουκ εστιν μνημοσυνον του σοφου μετα τον χωρικον εις τον αιωναν εν πληνθον των ημερω(ν) των ελχαμενων τα παντα ελησμοναιται και πως αποθνησκει ο σοφος μετα τον χωρικον (2.17) και εμισησα την ζωην οτι κακον επι εμεν το ποιμα ος εποιωθη απουκατω του ηλιου οτι το παν ματαιον και κακοτηταν πνεοματου (2.18) και εμισησα εγω συν παν χειμασιαν μου ος εγω χειμαζομενος απουκατω του ηλιου ως να αφησω αυτο του α(ν)θρωπου ος εσται οπιλθεν μου (2.19) και τις γινωσκει μη τι φρενιμος εστιν η χωρικος και

---

[231] The use of the square Hebrew/Aramaic script is perhaps connected with the idea expressed in *m. Yadayim* 4.5, that biblical manuscripts only render the hands unclean if written using that script. On the possibility that this combination was originally advocated or permitted in the Tosefta to *m. Megillah* 2.1, see Smelik, 'Code-switching', 144-46.

εξισιασει εν παν κοπον μου ος εκοπωθην απουκατω του ηλιου
γαρ τουτο ματαιον (2.20) και εγυρισα εγω το απευμεριμνει συν
την καρδιαν μου επι παν τον κοπον τον εκοπωθην απουκατω
του ηλιου (2.21) οτι εστιν ανθρωπος ος κοπος αυτου υπο
σοφιας και εν γνωσιν και εν ευθυοτηταν και του ανθρωπου ος
ουκ εκοπωθη εις αυτο διδει αυτου μερτικον αυτου γαρ τουτο
ματαιον και κακια πολλη (2.22) οτι τι ωφελει τον ανθρω[πον]
εν παν χειμασιαν αυτου και εν κακοτηταν καρδιας αυτου ος
αυτος χειμαζομ[ενος] απουκατου του ηλιου (2.23) οτι...

Each verse in the original begins with the initial word or phrase in Hebrew: these correspond to the readings of M^L, except at 2.20, where M^L וסבותי is written defectively as וסבתי—the sort of orthographic variation that we have encountered many times already. In general, such correspondence also characterizes the translation, which essentially renders the Hebrew as we know it from M, word-for-word in order. The most obvious exception is in 2.19, where there is no equivalent for ושחכמתי, 'and (for) which I have been wise'—this has apparently been lost in error from the text or its source-text. In 2.21, the rendering is odd enough to raise a slight suspicion that the translator read something different: we find εν γνωσιν and εν ευθυοτηταν, but υπο σοφιας, where the Hebrew has -ב in each case. That may just be interpretative (see the note), but in 2.16 the translation of the difficult בשכבר by εν πληνθον (= εν πληθον) to give 'in the fullness of days' seems likely to have been inspired by a reading of the כבר element either as כבד (cf. Exod 8.20; Isa 21.15) or, more likely, as the כביר of Isa 28.2 and elsewhere.

There is no clear dependence on G, but the verbatim translation and retention of the word-order are naturally reminiscent of it, and we may note not only the use of σὺν for the object-marker את, but also the stereotypical rendering of גם, 'also'. In this translation, however, both are handled differently. G uses σὺν for את in 2.17 (את החיים → σὺν τὴν ζωήν) and 2.18 (את כל עמלי → σὺν πάντα μόχθον μου); T-S Misc.28.74, on the other hand, has it at 2.18 (את כל עמלי → συν παν χειμασιαν μου) and 2.20 (את לבי → συν την καρδιαν μου), but not at 2.17. It is difficult to generalize from such a small sample, but this translator seems to share the view of G that את should be rendered when it occurs before כל, 'all', but not the view that it should be rendered before an article (cf. Yi, 70-71). G, on the other hand, never uses σὺν when translating את לבי (cf.

1.13; 2.10; 8.9, 16), and the rendering here in 2.20 does not accord with the habits of either G or α'. As for גם, 'also', G uses the conventional καί γε when it occurs in 2.14, 15 (twice), 19, and 21. T-S Misc.28.74 is no less consistent, but in each place uses the conjunction γάρ instead. This is closer phonetically to the Hebrew, and succeeds in rendering one Hebrew word with one Greek word, but since it means 'for', and usually explains what has gone before, it imparts a very strange sense to the Greek. The translator has clearly been at least as concerned as G and α' to represent the underlying Hebrew, but he appears to be doing so by using devices and conventions that differ from theirs.

(ii) *Codex Graecus Venetus (Marcianus gr. VII)*
This fourteenth-century manuscript contains renderings of the Pentateuch, Ruth, Proverbs, Ecclesiastes, Lamentations and Daniel into a self-consciously literary Greek, which uses Atticizing forms to represent Hebrew, and Doric for Aramaic. These are parts of a single undertaking, not miscellaneous translations that have been collected together, and the manuscript may be, at least in part, the autograph copy. The principal edition is von Gebhardt's *Graecus Venetus*, which claims that the translation is based on the Hebrew, and that it shows the influence of David Qimḥi's exegesis. There are some points of contact with G in Ecclesiastes, although it is hard to say whether these just represent a shared approach to translation:[232] while on the whole it reads much more smoothly, this translation has a similar concern to represent the Hebrew with some precision. The expertise in both Greek and Hebrew, along with the presence of elements that can be attributed both to Christian and to Jewish influences, has long sustained a suspicion that it is the work of the scholarly Simon Atumanus, bishop of Gerace in Calabria and archbishop of Thebes, who may have been a Jewish convert.[233]

---

[232] See Klostermann, *De libri Coheleth*, 52-54, who thinks that the translator had G at his side, and who notes in particular the use of ξύμπαντα (= σύμπαντα) where G has σὺν πάντα reflecting את כל at, e.g., 1.14. As we have seen something similar in T-S Misc. 28.74, however, this may be just a continuing attempt to deal with the object-marker, rather than a sign of direct dependence.
[233] See Mercati, *Codice Veneto Greco VII*; Aslanov, 'La Place', 156-58; de Crom, 'Book of Canticles', 299-301.

Its translations are often interesting, and I shall mention them from time to time in the course of the commentary—although we might note straightaway its rendering of 'Qohelet' with a feminine noun ἐκκλησιάστρια that is not, to my knowledge, found elsewhere, but which probably means 'a woman who assembles', and which takes very seriously, therefore, the gender of קהלת when it is construed as a participle (see the notes on 1.1). In text-critical terms, the late date might reasonably raise doubts about the value of this version, but, for the most part, the rendering of Ecclesiastes appears to reflect a Hebrew text that is close to M^L. On the rare occasions, therefore, when it obviously does differ (most notably in 1.16, where it is yet another witness to '*in* Jerusalem'), we cannot easily write off its readings simply as the consequence of late errors in its source-text. It is harder with this text than with G, however, to retrovert its Hebrew directly from the Greek, and some minor discrepancies are likely to be translational in nature: this translator is much readier, for instance, to render a Hebrew infinitive with a purpose clause when appropriate,rather than with a matching Greek infinitive.

3. *Latin Texts*

(a) *The 'Old Latin'* (**La**)
Some of the Greek Septuagint translations were themselves translated many times into Latin, but if this was the case with Ecclesiastes, then most of those 'Old Latin' translations have been lost—Jerome refers in his commentary to 'Latin manuscripts' at 1.1 and 2.5, and to a 'Latin translator' at 1.13, furnishing us with just a handful of explicit readings. What we do have, in addition to various brief citations in other works, are three versions associated with Jerome himself. Two of these are complete: the translation provided in his commentary (**Hie**), which was written in about 388–389 CE,[234] and his Vulgate translation (**V**), usually dated to

---

[234] See Williams, *The Monk and the Book*, 282. The primary evidence for the date is a reference in the preface to Jerome's reading of Ecclesiastes to Blesilla *ante hoc ferme quinquennium*, 'about five years ago': Blesilla died in 384, and this reference not only affirms that Ecclesiastes is amongst the earliest of Jerome's commentaries, but also suggests his prior familiarity with the book as a reason for his having embarked on this commentary before examining

397 or 398. At around the same time as the commentary, however, he also produced a translation of the Solomonic books explicitly based on the Septuagint versions, which seems to have been a revision of Old Latin translations and was part of a broader project (see Leanza, 'Le tre versione', 88). Fragments of this have been preserved in the late eighth-century Codex Sangallensis 11,[235] and they include from Ecclesiastes the text of 1.4-6, 9; 3.1-8; 4.10-11; 7.3-6, 10, 14, 29; 8.2; 9.4; 10.16, 20; 11.4. Vaccari ('Recupero') has attempted to identify citations from it in other sources, although, of course, it can be difficult to say whether particular citations are from Jerome's revised text or from existing Latin sources. Because of the revision, this may stand closer in many respects to Origen's adapted Greek text than to the Old Greek, so although it draws on probably pre-hexaplaric Latin translations and can conveniently be labelled as 'Old Latin' (**La**), it must be used with caution as a source for the readings of G. Of course, this version is a secondary translation from the Greek, so its principal significance, like that of some other versions not covered here, is as a witness to G. It also offers, however, a sort of baseline against which we can evaluate Jerome's other translations.

(b) *Jerome's Commentary (***Hie***)*
For his commentary, according to the account in its preface, Jerome translated from the Hebrew, but tended to follow the G rendering where this did not diverge too much, and sometimes took account of readings from the Three. This is, indeed, the impression given by the translation itself. It should be borne in mind, of course, both that he was writing for an audience that would have placed a high value on the Septuagint text, and that his own Hebrew scholarship was still at an early stage, so it is unsurprising that he goes on to acknowledge a certain conservatism in his rendering. While plainly preserving translations that go back to the Old Latin versions that he had revised, however, Jerome does make good use of his

---

other, more mainstream works. Blesilla, incidentally, did not follow Jerome from Rome to Bethlehem, as Holm-Nielsen, 'Interpretation', 174, suggests; on this and some other claims that he makes about Jerome's commentary, see Leanza, 'Sul Commentario', 279-80.

[235] Published in Berger, 'Notice', 137-42. See also Caspari, *Hiob*, 6-7.

other sources, and the body of the commentary itself is a valuable source of alternative readings and interpretations, some of which have explicitly been drawn from Jewish sources (on his sources more generally, see Leanza, 'Sulle fonti'; Manns, 'Traditions', discusses some 23 passages where he sees points of contact with the Targum's interpretation—some more convincing than others). The mixture of influences upon the work, however, also make it difficult to use as a witness to any single text (which is why Rahlfs' use of it to 'correct' G is so problematic). The standard edition is Adriaen's 'S. Hieronymi Presbyteri Commentarius in Ecclesiasten' (see also the notes on the text in Thurn, 'Zum Text'). The recently published Birnbaum, *Koheletkommentar*, offers a new edition with the Latin text (revised by M. Margoni-Kögler) and a German translation. Two translations into English have also appeared recently: Goodrich and Miller, *Jerome: Commentary*, and Litteral, *Commentary*; the latter, in particular, needs to be used with some caution. The character of the commentary, and of Jerome's readings, are discussed by Moreno García and Boira Sales ('Concepción'), and Canellis ('Le Commentaire', who provides, 213-14, a useful table of the Hebrew words that Jerome transliterates and discusses), while papers covering various aspects of it are edited by Birnbaum and Schwienhorst-Schönberger in *Hieronymus als Exeget*.

In addition to those already listed in connection with other witnesses, we may note the following variants.

	M^L	Hie	
2.12	עשוהו qatal, plural	עשהו participle, sing.	So too S, V.
6.10	שהיה	שיהיה	So too V.
7.25	כסל abstract noun	'fool' (כסיל?)	So too S, V, T.
9.15	מסכן חכם	מסכן וחכם	So too V, T.
11.9	ויטיבך	ויטיב	So too V, T. Cf. S.
12.5	ינאץ	ינץ	See the notes to this verse.

As we observed earlier (see n. 158), Jerome refers on various occasions in other works to consulting multiple Hebrew texts. If he did so for Ecclesiastes, his readings may not have been from a single manuscript, and may in principle represent a selected variant, rather than the only reading available to him.

(c) *The Vulgate (V)*

In his preface to the Vulgate (V) translation of the Solomonic books, probably completed in about 398 CE, Jerome speaks of a long illness that had prevented him from working, despite the many demands made upon him, but boasts of translating all three books in three days. This is doubtless an exaggeration, but his work on Ecclesiastes may indeed have been quite quick: while he did not simply repackage either of his previous translations for this new project, the many points of contact between Hie and V suggest that he did not start entirely afresh. On relatively rare occasions (e.g. in their handling of שילך in 5.14), each version shows a different understanding of the Hebrew, but they often correspond closely to each other, and the variations between them are commonly differences of expression rather than sense, so that to some extent Jerome may simply have been re-writing. As we have noted already, Jerome made heavy use of Symmachus and his paraphrases for V, and his concern in this version (which lacks, of course, the benefit of an accompanying commentary) is much more to convey a clear meaning, even where this requires significant departures from the Hebrew. So in 1.15, for example, Hie has the already somewhat interpretative *peruersus non poterit adornari et imminutio non poterit numerari*, 'a perverse man cannot be made beautiful, and a deficit cannot be counted', which draws on G, but in V this becomes (for reasons explored in the notes to that verse) *peruersi difficile corriguntur et stultorum infinitus est numerus*, 'the perverse are only corrected with difficulty, and the number of fools is infinite'.

The standard manual edition of the Vulgate is Weber et al., *Biblia Sacra*, although there can be good reasons to use the larger Gasquet, *Biblia sacra iuxta latinam vulgatam versionem* (Ecclesiastes is in vol. 11). The textual history is, as one might expect, very complicated. The Vulgate did not wholly displace the Old Latin versions for some centuries, and they exercised a significant influence upon its development, while some of the various attempts to deal with corruption of the text, which was widely acknowledged to be a problem in the Middle Ages, probably did more harm than good: for a very interesting survey, see Linde's *Sacra Scriptura?* The modern editions are based on early manuscripts, but cannot wholly sidestep the difficulties.

V has generally picked up the variants reflected in Hie, but note also:

	M^L	V	
2.1	נסה from אנסכה	*affluam* from נסך	Perhaps a Jewish interpretation
3.13	בכל עמלו	*de labore suo* = בעמלו	Also found in later Hebrew mss and one ms of Hie

4. Syriac Texts

(a) *The Peshitta (S)*

The origins of the standard Syriac translation remain obscure and controversial. By about the ninth century CE, it had acquired the overall label 'Peshitta', perhaps meaning 'straightforward', but, like the Septuagint, it consisted originally of a series of separate translations. The identity of the translators is unknown, but although the Peshitta was to become strongly associated with Syriac Christianity, it is usually now thought likely that they were Jewish, and, indeed, it has been argued in Weitzman's *The Syriac Version*, that they belonged to a non-rabbinic Jewish community which was absorbed into Christianity. Our earliest manuscripts date from the fifth and sixth centuries CE, but the translations themselves are likely to have been made several centuries earlier; there is a helpful overview in Brock's *The Bible in the Syriac Tradition*. Some, at least, probably made use of the Septuagint as well as Hebrew texts, and these include Ecclesiastes[236]—although, as noted earlier, the occasional appearance of Syriac variants reflecting the readings of both G and M suggest that revisions from the Greek or Hebrew have also been introduced into the textual tradition after the initial composition.[237] The standard edition of Ecclesiastes in

---

[236] Beyond particular agreements, it seems likely that the uses of σὺν for את in G more generally may have influenced the Syriac translator's use of the archaic Syriac ܝܬ *yt*, itself equivalent to את, rather than a specific determination to pursue the same translation technique.

[237] Such revision toward the Greek is common in the tradition as a whole. Meade and Gentry, 'Evaluating Evaluations', 14, try to use the date of S to exclude a late date in the second century for G, arguing (from Weitzman's

this version is Lane's 'Qoheleth', and Lane has also published a useful study ('Lilies') of the manuscript tradition and of some key textual issues. Collations from an additional manuscript are to be found in a study by Jenner ('10c4', 286-87). Much earlier, although without access to the best manuscripts, the text was also studied in detail by Kamanetzky, whose comments remain valuable, and I shall cite them often in the commentary. Several other scholars have also subjected S to close scrutiny.[238]

Its relationship with both M and G means that S cannot be used straightforwardly to support one against the other, but it is potentially an early source of variant readings from either. In addition to those listed already, we may note the following differences from M^L:

	M^L	S	
2.2	מהולל	מה הללו	
2.16	בשכבר	כשכבר	Note variant reading in S tradition
2.26	לתת	ולתת	
9.9	אשר נתן לך	∅	Absent also from some later Hebrew mss: see de Rossi
10.10	וחילים	וחללים	
12.5	יראו	ירא	The singular (as S) is presumed in *b. Šabbat* 152a
12.7	על	אל	

datings) that the Syriac translation of Ecclesiastes must have been made at some time between the translations of the Pentateuch in about 150 and the later books in about 200. Even if we accept that dating, however, the fact that errors in the textual transmission of G have been picked up by S do not demand that we date G 'between the first century BCE and the first century CE'. Leaving aside the fact that an early error could easily have found its way into S within a few decades, we can never be sure that when S reflects G it did so from the outset, since there is a high likelihood of subsequent revisions toward G. For a clear example of secondary revision towards the Hebrew, see the note on 'letting go of my concern with all the business' at 2.20.

[238] See especially Janichs, *Animadversiones*; Salters, 'Observations on the Peshitta'; Schoors, 'Peshitta'. The agreements of S with G and M are tabulated by Ginsburg in section E of the first appendix in his commentary, and by Gordis (140-43).

(b) *The Syro-Hexapla* (**Syh**)

The Syro-Hexapla is a translation into Syriac (mostly) of the annotated 'Septuagint' Greek column from Origen's Hexapla, made by Paul of Tella in about 615–617 CE. For Ecclesiastes and some other books (Psalms, Job, Proverbs, Song of Songs, Wisdom, Ben Sira, prophets) this is preserved principally in a late eighth- or early ninth-century manuscript that probably originated in Egypt, but is now in the Biblioteca Ambrosiana at Milan; a first volume, with the Pentateuch and historical books, was lost sometime after the mid-sixteenth century. An excellent facsimile edition of this manuscript serves as the standard edition: Ceriani's *Codex Syro-Hexaplaris Ambrosianus*. An earlier printed edition, Middeldorpf's *Codex Syriaco-Hexaplaris*, is useful at points but has many flaws. There is a helpful recent overview in Carbajosa's 'Prolegomena'.

Allowing for the difficulty that its readings must be translated back into Greek and for some probable errors in the transmission of both the Syriac and its Greek sources, the Syro-Hexapla is a very important resource for Origen's Greek text, and the codex also has many marginal annotations, commonly preserving readings from the Three. It would be a mistake, however, simply to assume that all the contents have been extracted and translated directly from the Hexapla itself, and Gentry (especially in 'Hexaplaric Materials') has made a strong case that the annotations, at least for Ecclesiastes, were originally created for use with a different Greek base-text, probably drawn from the catena tradition.

5. *The Targum* (**T**)

A comprehensive collation of the key manuscripts is still awaited for this Aramaic translation, and detailed study of the text involves using a number of books. Sperber's presentation in *The Bible in Aramaic* is generally acknowledged not to be one of his best, and there are alternatives with collations in Levy's *Das Targum zu Koheleth*, which uses mostly Yemenite texts, and Knobel's 'Targum Qoheleth', which employs a greater range. None of these is ideal, though, and no current edition can be considered the standard.[239]

---

[239] See especially Clarke, 'Reflections', which offers a critique of each, and a detailed description of the manuscripts. He proposes that the Paris manuscript

There are several editions of individual manuscripts: Levine, *Aramaic Version*; Díez Merino, *Targum de Qohelet*; Taradach and Ferrer, *Un Targum de Qohélet*. These all include translations (into English, sixteenth-century Latin, and French respectively), and translations with commentaries are also to be found in Knobel, *The Targum of Qohelet*; Manns, 'Le Targum de Qohelet'; Mopsik, *Double Araméen*. Ginsburg offers an English translation in the first appendix to his commentary.[240]

To understand the basic character of T as a translation, it is helpful to compare it with M, which is probably close at most points to the source-text used by the translator. Here is a translation of the Hebrew of 1.4 with a slightly adapted version of Knobel's translation in *The Targum of Qohelet*:

> M A **generation goes**, and a **generation comes**, **but the earth stands forever**.

> T King Solomon said through the spirit of prophecy, 'The good **generation** of righteous ones **goes** from the world because of the sins of the evil **generation** of wicked ones who will **come** after them. **But the earth stands forever** to bear the punishment which comes upon the world because of the sins of men.'

The most obvious feature, here and in most of T, is the way that the translator effectively writes around the text, taking the words of the original, but re-contextualizing them to produce a new meaning that may have little to do with the 'literal' sense of the text.[241] This

---

Bibliothèque nationale Héb. 110 should be used as the base-text for any future edition, and his own corrected transcription of the consonantal text from that manuscript is now available on the Comprehensive Aramaic Lexicon website.

[240] Other useful studies include: Alexander, 'Translation and Midrash', and 'Profile Targum Qohelet', on pp. 101-14; Brady, 'Exegetical Similarities'; Flesher, 'Wisdom of the Sages'; Flesher and Chilton, *The Targums*, 241-44; Mangan, 'Some Similarities'; Salters, 'Observations on the Targum'; Yesudian-Storfjell, 'Reception of Qoheleth', 53-99.

[241] On subsequent Jewish interpretations of 1.4, see Moss, 'Ecclesiastes 1:4'. Rashi also introduces the idea of an evil generation, but to make the point that what they steal will eventually be exacted from their descendants. The Midrash includes an interpretation in terms of resurrection, and there is a later Kabbalistic interpretation of the verse as referring to the transmigration of souls. If the Targum's reading seems unnatural, it is not, perhaps, untypical of the broader tradition of exegesis within which it stands.

is not the type of 'sense-for-sense' translation that we saw in Symmachus, and the term 'paraphrase', although often used of it, is not really appropriate for T: employing, rather, a sort of midrashic exegesis, it does not replace words so much as try, through its new contextualization, to bring out from them a sense that accords with the translator's beliefs (which are clearly not often the same as Qohelet's).[242] At times, the original can be all but buried beneath this exegesis, as in 12.3, where an allegorical reading in terms of old age leads the translator to replace words with interpretations of those words as symbols,[243] or 4.13-14, which he understands in terms of Abraham and Nimrod. The text can be significantly extended as well, by the inclusion of examples or anecdotes, as in 3.11, where T splits the beginning of the verse from the end, first noting the providential deferment of the division between the kingdoms until after the Temple had been built, and then the hiding of God's name on its foundation stone—this particular case exemplifies the Targum's strong interest in linking the text to the story of Solomon. More often, though, it is surprisingly easy to identify the words with which the translator has been working, and T can be a valuable witness to the text—very rarely, it even offers what is almost a straight, word-for-word translation (e.g. 6.1). A few additional variants may be added to those listed already:

---

[242] Des Rochettes, 'L'Humour noir', 58-62, runs through a series of passages in which the Targum seems to change the sense of statements that might be considered shocking. Of the re-interpretation, Flesher, 'Wisdom of the Sages', 279, concludes that 'The document that should be the prime container of wisdom thought has been hollowed out and refilled by a talmudic rabbinism... The Qohelet Targum, which as a translation replaced the Hebrew Qohelet for the vast majority of Jews who did not know Hebrew, is no longer the cogent and relentless perpetuator of ideas dangerous to the rabbinic perspective but the purveyor of a compelling statement of the rabbinic world view. The targumic response to wisdom is that it is dangerous; it can no longer be merely ignored but must be replaced.' See also Sandberg, 'Qohelet', 44, and Levine, *Aramaic Version*, 64-72, which sets the treatment in a broader context of suppression. It is difficult, however, to judge just how far this displacement of one world view by another was a conscious act, or how much attention the targumist would actually have paid to the literal or 'original' meaning.

[243] It is a commonplace of targumic technique to replace the figurative with the literal; see, e.g., Rofé, 'Biblical Antecedents', 333-34.

	M^L	T reflects:	
2.1	אנסכה	אנסנה	Cf. Midrash Rabbah
2.20	שעמלתי	ושחכמתי +	Cf. 2.19
3.19	אחד להם	אחד לכל	
6.3	רב adjective, 'much'	noun 'chief'	G also reads as a noun, but with a different sense
7.6	וגם	גם	So too 4QQoh^a. G καί γε could reflect either reading
10.10	יבר piel	qal	Probably also Hie, V

The homiletic character of the work may suggest that it arose in an educational context: it is probably too long to have accompanied the festival reading of Qohelet in the synagogue (so Brady, 'Exegetical Similarities', 120). Most scholars would also date it to somewhere in the second half of the first millennium. That is little enough to go on, and beyond that we know virtually nothing about the origin of T. We did observe above, however, the curious fact that T agrees with G against M at a number of points. Unless T is much earlier than commonly supposed, this cannot readily be compared to the links often noted between targums and the Peshitta in the Pentateuch. If we are not to put the parallels down to an improbable degree of coincidence, it more likely results from exposure to texts or interpretations that preserved older readings or understandings outside the scope of the Tiberian Masoretic tradition, and this perhaps gives the faintest glimpse into its environment. It is difficult to specify just what those might have been, however, and although it is clear that the targumist is not simply plucking all his interpretations from thin air—in a number of places T draws on traditions known from the Talmud or elsewhere—we know too little to speak with any precision about his sources, whether they were literary or traditional.

6. *Other Versions*

Translations of Ecclesiastes which are much later, or which are translations of translations, have a role to play in reconstructions of the textual history, and are naturally important for consideration of the book's reception in the communities that used them. Some are mentioned on occasion in the commentary, but the limits both of space and of my own competence mean that they have not received any systematic treatment. In some cases, furthermore, there is still very little information available. The list here covers both the more important versions, and those which have received some attention in recent scholarship.

Coptic: Coptic translations based on the Septuagint were produced very early, and offer an important witness, therefore, to the text of G; readings are accordingly collated in the apparatus of the Göttingen edition. The text of Ecclesiastes (up to 12.3) is preserved in Fayyumic Coptic, along with the Greek text (which provides an early witness to G), on the important papyrus Hamburgensis Bilingualis 1, which was written *circa* 300 CE: an edition of this was published in Diebner and Kasser (eds.), *Hamburger Papyrus Bil. 1*, 258-317 (with the Greek on 242-56); see also Diebner, 'Die biblischen Texte', 59-74. The Fayyumic is also found on the early fourth-century Papyrus Michigan 3520, and there are fragments on the slightly later Papyrus Michigan 6868(a): see Schenke and Kasser, *Papyrus Michigan 3520 und 6868(a)*. The incomplete and fragmentary Sahidic text that was published in Thompson, *Coptic (Sahidic) Version*, 37-43, is probably somewhat later: it includes partial text from 6.6–9.6. A number of other Sahidic manuscripts have been published, and will be listed in the Göttingen edition.

Ethiopic: Although the translation was probably accomplished at some point between about the fourth and seventh centuries CE, the manuscript evidence is much later. A critical edition collating 24 manuscripts, dated to the fifteenth to nineteenth centuries, was published in Mercer, *Ethiopic Text*, and a more recent assessment of the manuscripts appeared in Azevedo, 'Ethiopian Manuscripts Part I' (so far as I know, the promised part II has not appeared). The relationship between the Ethiopic and other versions of the biblical texts is notoriously complicated, and Mercer claims (23-26) that although the translator based his work on G (possibly using several different manuscripts), there is evidence for the influence upon the translation or transmission of Masoretic or pre-Masoretic Hebrew texts, of S, of V, and, to a limited extent, of the Coptic; the later transmission has been variously affected by Arabic translations and perhaps the Targum. It is hard to say how far some of the various agreements with other versions are the result of coincidence rather than influence, but, in any case, such potential complexity makes it difficult to use the Ethiopic tradition for text-critical purposes, at least in the present state of our knowledge.

Arabic and Judeo-Persian: On the complicated and sometimes controversial history of Arabic biblical translations more generally, see now Griffith's *The Bible in Arabic*. Judeo-Arabic translations are provided in two tenth-century Karaite commentaries: see Vajda, *Deux commentaires*; Robinson, *Asceticism*. A translation and commentary that was often formerly attributed to Saadia Gaon is now understood to be the work of the eleventh-century exegete Isaac Ibn Ghayyat; see Loevy, *Libri Kohelet*; Gómez Aranda, 'The Influence of Isaac Ibn Ghayyat'; this appears to be the translation that appeared in Walton's *Polyglot*, and a version in French can be found in Caquot and Zafrani, *La version arabe*. Two manuscripts from the thirteenth or fourteenth centuries, with a Hebrew text and Judeo-Persian translation, have been studied in detail by Jean-Jacques Lavoie and Minoo Mehramooz in 'Quelques remarques'; 'Étude de quelques mots obscurs'; and 'Le texte hébreu et la traduction judéo-persanne'. For text-critical purposes, the principal significance of all these versions lies in their witness to the Hebrew texts on which they were based.

Others: The Old Georgian version, translated some time before the seventh century and a useful, non-hexaplaric witness to the text of G, is described in Dundua, 'Textual Value'. The later, very complicated Church Slavonic tradition is studied in Osinkina, 'Textual History', which places the translation in the late medieval period, and identifies the source as Latin.

1.1

SUPERSCRIPTION

(1.1)   The words of Qohelet, son of David, king in Jerusalem.

Commentary

In the Introduction, I noted that many ancient compositions are formulated as direct speech, or presented as monologues delivered by a particular character. The superscriptions to such works should not be read as authorial attributions, in the modern sense, so much as identifications of the voice that we are hearing, but they are compatible with seeing the 'words' here as a single speech, sandwiched between the matching declarations of 1.2 and 12.8, rather than as a collection of things that Qohelet said at different times. Even if an ancient audience understood the book to be a monologue by somebody called Qohelet, however, the subsequent specification that this 'Qohelet' was a son of David and king in Jerusalem would immediately have revealed that the name was a pseudonym—at least to anyone who was aware that David's family and dynasty included no 'King Qohelet'. Later, in v. 12, the additional information is offered that he was 'king of Israel' in Jerusalem, which considerably narrows the range of possible individuals, and it is possible that 'son of David' here is already supposed to point to Solomon. However much it may imply it, however, at no stage does the book state explicitly that it is reporting Solomon's words, and the attribution is more immediately to 'Qohelet'—a mysterious term that raises problems of its own.

All of this has to be taken with a *caveat*, that we cannot be certain about the original wording of the superscription. To be sure, it is unlikely that Ecclesiastes was ever circulated in a form that lacked any superscription, and although 1.1 is not itself put on the lips of Qohelet, who will only introduce himself in 1.12, it is most probably the work of the book's creator. The Greek version, however, does include here the information that Qohelet was king 'of Israel', and we have no reason to suppose that this was absent from the Hebrew on which it was based, even if we do not find it before 1.12 in Masoretic texts. It is possible that this is the original reading, not least because the Greek 'king of Israel in Jerusalem' seems less odd than 'king in Jerusalem' (see the note, below), but it is commonly taken to be evidence of a tendency to make the superscription less vague, and more clearly an indication of Solomon. The Targum, furthermore, goes so far as to name Solomon explicitly here. If there is indeed some such progression towards greater specification of Qohelet's identity, then it is possible that all of our versions are witnesses merely to quite advanced stages of that progression, and a few scholars have suggested, in fact, that Qohelet was not originally identified here even as a king.[1] That idea would make it easier to reconcile this superscription with a general lack of interest in, or even knowledge of, Qohelet's kingship elsewhere in the book. Although attractive, however, it is purely conjectural and rests on no textual evidence. The issue of Qohelet's identification with Solomon is complicated, and it is not impossible that such a complication has

---

[1] I would not myself exclude the possibility that the references pointing to Solomon are a very early secondary addition or alteration to the original superscription and to 1.12. This specific view is not something that has long been recognized, as Fischer, *Skepsis*, 3, claims, and it is not, in fact, very widely held—but that may be because many past commentators have viewed the entire superscription as secondary and redactional, which is an assumption rooted in approaches to the compositional history of the book rather than to its attribution. Bickell was unusual in rejecting 1.12 as the work of a 'pseudo-Solomonic' interpolator, although he was supported by Haupt, 'The Book of Ecclesiastes', 252-53. Haupt also observed: 'The references and allusions to Solomon...are so scanty that it is hard to believe the original author meant to assume the mask of the famous king of Israel. Nor does the author of the epilogue appear to know anything of this assumption. After the second chapter there is no allusion to Solomon whatever' (253). Among more recent commentators, Galling 1969 and Lauha both mark 'son...Jerusalem' as secondary; cf. also Fox, 'Frame-Narrative', 85 n. 7, although Fox modifies his opinion in his later writings—as apparently does Schwienhorst-Schönberger, who in *Nicht im Menschen*, 9, followed Lauha. Questions about the originality of the second part usually arise from redactional theories, but note, e.g., Eichhorn: 'Since King Solomon ruled from 973–933 BCE and the Book of Qoheles was written about 200 BCE, this editorial presumption is without foundation in historical fact. Therefore these two verses [1.1 and 1.12] could not possibly have been part of the original text.'

been imposed upon the work in some later attempt to align it with the emerging Solomonic corpus of writings. No version of the book currently exists without it, however.

Pseudonymity is a commonplace of ancient literature; the vagueness of attribution found here is not, and it is difficult to find any direct parallel.[2] In form, the introduction is most similar to those found in Jer 1.1 ('The words of Jeremiah, the son of Hilkiah'), Prov 30.1 ('The words of Agur, son of Yakeh'), and Neh 1.1 ('The words of Nehemiah, the son of Hakaliah'), all of which include a patronymic comparable to the 'son of David' here, and the first two of which include further specifications of identity. There are also some looser similarities with other superscriptions, such as Amos 1.1 ('the words of'), and we should probably not read too much into the specifics of the presentation. As the text stands, however, it does seem especially reminiscent not just of Prov 31.1 ('The words of…, king of…'), but more especially of Prov 1.1 ('son of David, king of Israel'), which *does* refer explicitly to Solomon. Perhaps surprisingly, this resemblance is not picked up in early Jewish exegesis, which focuses more on other issues, but if it is deliberate then it may indicate a conscious link with that other book, in whatever form it existed at the time.[3]

Whatever its oddities, the connection forged here with Solomon was to exert a great influence on reception of the book, although in different ways at different times. The attributions of Proverbs and Song of Songs to Solomon did not present ancient readers with a problem: his famous wisdom suited the confident tone of Proverbs, and his no less famous love of women the erotic tone of the Song. There is no self-evident place in the biblical accounts of Solomon's reign, however, for the sort of disillusionment that seems to be

---

[2] Although see n. 10, below. Perry (178) makes the interesting suggestion that, rather than suppose the book to be seeking to gain acceptance by claiming Solomonic authorship, we should perhaps consider that 'Solomon is *not* named precisely in order *not* to abuse authority'. On that reckoning, to be sure, it is doing pretty much everything to misrepresent itself *except* name its royal author explicitly, but the fact that Solomon is not named does suggest something more subtle here than some clumsy attempt to attach his authority to an existing work.

[3] Midrash Qohelet, interestingly, links the superscription with Jer 1.1 and Amos 1.1 on the basis that in all three the words are attributed to the men themselves, rather than to God. Perrin, 'Messianism', 41-42, suggests the possibility that Prov 1.1 has, in fact, been the model for the superscription in Ecclesiastes.

expressed in Ecclesiastes. Although its epilogue commends piety and fear of God, moreover, the monologue seems to portray itself as the work of a man late in life—and it is Solomon's later years during which, according to the biblical histories, he was most worldly and least God-fearing. Since the book's attitudes to government and kings sometimes seem likewise discordant with the views one might expect from Solomon, or any other king, its attribution to Solomon forced readers in earlier generations to suppose that the biblical accounts of Solomon's reign were telling only part of his story, and for some it clearly became necessary to create a new context in which a penitent Solomon could look back on the vanity of those worldly things to which he had once been drawn.

In Jewish sources, this doubtless contributed to the rise of stories which introduced a new chapter into Solomon's life. In the Jerusalem Talmud (*y. Sanhedrin* 13a), God expels Solomon from his throne, replacing him with an angel who assumes his identity: when he goes around claiming to be the king, people show him the angel and beat him for lying. The Babylonian Talmud records (*b. Giṭṭin* 68b) that Solomon, having brought the demon Asmodeus to Jerusalem, is hurled an enormous distance by him, and has to find his way back as a beggar, while the demon, this time, assumes his identity. There is a debate between authorities, the Talmud notes, as to whether he succeeded in regaining the throne, or remained a commoner. The Targum (at 1.12) tells a briefer version of the same story, with Asmodeus sent directly by God to punish Solomon, and this is probably echoed in the Midrash Rabbah on the same verse, which alludes to Solomon having become a commoner after he was king, while elements of it are elaborated in subsequent Jewish legends about Solomon. Such stories, and others emphasizing Solomon's penitence, were clearly known to exist by Christian writers in various periods. In his own commentary on 1.12, for instance, Jerome claims that *aiunt Hebraei hunc librum Salomonis esse, paenitentiam agentis, quod in sapientia diuitiisque confisus, per mulieres offenderit deum*, 'The Jews say that this is a book of Solomon's doing penance, because having placed his trust in wisdom and wealth, he gave offence to God on account of women'. Some, indeed, have survived only in Christian sources, and several later medieval Christian writers quote a work, now lost, that cited unnamed 'Hebrew books' for a story that:

Solomon was dragged five times through the streets of the city by way of penitence. They say likewise that he went into the temple, which he had built, with five rods, and gave them to the experts in the law, so that he might be beaten with them. They, by mutual agreement, all said together that they would lay no hand on the Lord's anointed; then, frustrated by them, he brought about his own removal from the throne.[4]

These legends create a place for Ecclesiastes in the story of Solomon, but they also represent, at least in part, an attempt to affirm the fundamental piety of Solomon, whose later associations with magic, science, and demonology combined with the biblical accounts of his reign to make him an extremely ambivalent figure. Jerome's commentary on the closing verses of Ecclesiastes once again cites Jewish sources as raising the possibility that the book might seem *oblitterandus*, worthy of obliteration, alongside *cetera scripta Salomonis quae antiquata sunt, nec in memoria durauerunt*, 'other writings of Solomon that were left in the past and of which no memory persists'.

This encapsulates very well a Talmudic perception both that Solomon's works had once been controversial, and that not all had survived; 1 Kgs 5.12 [ET 4.32] is cited in support of the fact that there had once been, after all, three thousand sayings, along with a thousand and five songs—vastly more than are to be found in the books now extant. Early Christian writers, indeed, used a Septuagint text that spoke of five thousand songs, and a fragment of Hippolytus' commentary on Song of Songs interprets Prov 25.1 to suggest, similarly, that Hezekiah and his men had selected what was to survive from this original, much larger corpus (see Bonwetsch and Achelis, *Hippolytus Werke*, 343). Whilst both Jewish and Christian writers were willing to accept the value of the Solomonic books that had come down to them, it seems that they were also very happy to allow that not everything written by Solomon was equally valuable,

---

[4] From cols. 658-59 of Philip de Herving, 'Responsio de Damnatione Salomonis', PL 203, cols. 644-59: *Aiunt libri Hebraei Salomonem quinquies tractum fuisse per plateas civitatis, poenitentia causa. Item aiunt eum venisse in templum quod aedificaverat cum quinque virgis, et dedit eas legisperitis ut verberaretur ab illis. Qui communi accepto consilio dixerunt, quod in unctum Domini non mitterent manum. Inde frustratus ab illis, a se ipso est depositus de regno.* My translation. See Halperin, 'Book of Remedies', 287-88, who notes other citations of the text.

so that by the first few centuries of the Common Era, this attribution was not taken automatically as a guarantee of authority or of value. Indeed, Solomon's reputation may have required validation from these writings, at least as much as they required the prestige of his name, and it has even been suggested that Ecclesiastes and the Song of Songs became canonical 'probably despite their attribution, and not because of it' (Hirshman, 'Qohelet's Reception', 88, and cf. Dell, 'Ecclesiastes as Wisdom', 320; Sandberg, 'Qohelet', 42-43; for a contrary view see, e.g., Salters, 'Qoheleth and the Canon', 340-41). It is certainly true that claims about Solomon's penitence and reconciliation with God remained highly controversial within both Judaism and Christianity.

Despite the stories, attempts to read Ecclesiastes itself biographically, that is, as an account of Solomon's own experiences, were problematic in this period. I noted in the Introduction that R. Simeon is cited in the Tosefta (*Yadayim* 2.14) as claiming that Ecclesiastes could not 'defile the hands' (like truly sacred books) because it was written by Solomon himself, not through divine inspiration. The Christian commentator Didymus the Blind posed the related question '(Are the) "sayings of Ecclesiastes" on the writer's own behalf?', and answered his own question by observing that:

> Properly speaking, the author of the divinely inspired scriptures is the Spirit which prompts something to be said, but it is assisted by a wise man. For the Spirit has not invisibly written the letters and put down the words, but breathes them into a soul. And it may be that Solomon is the one writing these things, or that some of the wise wrote them. And perhaps we should do better to align ourselves with this (latter), lest anyone think that the speaker is speaking these things about himself.[5]

In other words, the fact that this inspired scripture has been mediated through a human writer should not lead us to understand it

---

[5] [ῥῆμα]τα ἐκκλησιαστοῦ ἐκ προσώπου τοῦ συγγραφέως; κυρίως μὲν ἐπὶ τῶν θεοπνεύστων γρ[αφ]ῶν συγγραφεύς ἐστιν τὸ πν(εῦμ)α τὸ ὑποβαλὸν αὐτῷ λαληθῆναι, ὑπηρετεῖται δὲ ὑπό τινος [σο]φοῦ. οὐδὲ γὰρ τὸ πν(εῦμ)α ἀοράτως ἐχάραξεν τὰ γράμματα καὶ τὰς λέξεις ἔθηκεν, ἀλλ' ἐνπ[νεῖ] ψυχῇ τινι ταῦτα. καὶ ἤτοι αὐτός ἐστιν ὁ γράφων αὐτὰ ὁ Σολομὼν ἢ τῶν σοφῶν τινες ἔγραψαν αὐτά. καὶ τάχα μᾶλλον τούτῳ ἀρέσκομεν, ἵνα μὴ δόξῃ τις περὶ αὐτοῦ λέγειν τὸν λέ[γο]ντα ταῦτα. From the Tura Papyrus, p. 7, lines 9-12. See Binder and Liesenborghs, *Kommentar*, 17-19. My translation.

simply as that human talking about himself, and we might do better to think of it as an anonymous work. Too close an identification of ideas as the product of individual human experience has to be reconciled with any belief that those ideas arose through divine inspiration, and Didymus is not alone in his recognition of this issue: the tension is evident elsewhere in, for example, Theodoret's commentary on the Song of Songs, which has its own attribution to Solomon.[6]

Although the Solomonic attribution of Ecclesiastes was still one of the many issues debated during the nineteenth century, even some leading conservative scholars of that era accepted the view first propounded by de Groot in 1644, that the book was in fact the product of a much later era (see the Introduction, pp. 55-79, above). That opinion is held by the great majority of modern commentators, who do not generally regard the attribution as a secondary addition to the book, but, to use the expression employed by de Groot himself (at 12.11) and a little later by Robert Lowth (*De sacra poesi Hebraeorum*, 239), take the author to be writing *sub persona Salomonis*, 'under the persona of Solomon'.[7] This has had significant consequences for interpretation, because it has often been presumed that, by adopting this disguise, the author intended the memoir of ch. 2, in particular, to be read as an account of Solomon's activities. Because modern scholars do not explain the content by inventing

---

[6] Christianson, *Ecclesiastes through the Centuries*, 95, and Bolin, *Ecclesiastes*, 37-38, both focus on the idea that Didymus is proposing here some alternative author (enhanced by Bolin's translation of τῶν σοφῶν τινες as 'some other wise person'). This is not really Didymus' concern, and the issue is not that 'it would be inappropriate for Solomon'—in particular—'to be speaking about himself', or that 'the potentially questionable content of Ecclesiastes may taint the figure of Solomon' (Bolin), but that any attribution to specific personal experience might detract from understanding the origin of the content to be divine. All the same, Didymus probably is evoking an idea that Solomon elsewhere collected or edited 'words of the wise' (cf. Prov 1.6; 22.17; 24.23), and suggesting that we should think in these, and not in biographical terms.

[7] Bolin, *Ecclesiastes*, 42, has rightly noted that George Gregory's ET of Lowth's book (270) renders the expression in terms of Solomon, as author, playing the role of someone investigating the issues with which the book is concerned. That sense is not naturally or even easily derived from the original Latin, which speaks of an argument about the vanity of human affairs, '(presented) through the character of Solomon struggling with a difficult question', but Lowth does not explicitly deny Solomonic authorship.

stories about Solomon, or shy away from identifying material as a (fictional) account of Solomon's own experiences, it might even be said that their readings are often far more 'Solomonic' than were those of early commentators.

As will become clear below, I doubt that the memoir is supposed to be read in such terms, and it is difficult, indeed, to identify anything outside 1.1 and 1.12 which seems to demand a particular association with Solomon: if we did not have the indirect identification supplied by these verses, it is very doubtful that anyone would ever have deduced such an association from the book's content.[8] The introduction of Solomon, moreover, brings an unprecedented degree of complexity into the presentation of the book: we are obliged either to assume that 'Qohelet' *is* Solomon, using another name for some reason, or that this Qohelet is pretending to be Solomon for at least part of his account.[9] Since commentators these days tend to treat Qohelet himself as a creation of the author, this amounts to having a writer take on a persona, and that persona then take on another persona. If it is neither the statement of a historical fact, however, nor an attempt to shape the way we read the memoir, what is the function of the attribution implied here?

The resemblance to Prov 1.1 and the absence of an explicit reference to Solomon both offer important clues, I think, to the author's (or possibly a redactor's) intention. Had Solomon been named,

---

[8] There have been some systematic attempts to find 'Solomonic' details outside the memoir: see especially Christianson, *A Time to Tell*; Koh, *Royal Autobiography*. What they uncover, however, are details that *can* be related to Solomon, rather than details that demand such a relationship. Tita's rather different attempt, in 'Thematische Einheit', to read 4.17–5.6 as 'Solomonic' is able to point to its setting in a temple, but beyond that rests on resemblances that are vague, slight, or (when he links vows with Solomon's prayer) positively forced. I am not persuaded either by Fidler's alternative attempt ('Text and Intertext') to link those verses with accounts in Genesis of Jacob at Bethel, or by the belief of Barbour (*The Story of Israel*, 98-105, cf. 'Like an Error') and Gutridge ('The Sacrifice of Fools') that they allude to the story of Saul, but both illustrate how such details can point in quite different directions (Gutridge even goes on to see a further link with Job 42.8).

[9] Cheyne, *Job and Solomon*, 238-39, tries to resolve the difficulty by taking up the view of Luzzatto, that Qohelet was the real name of the author, and was inserted by editors to replace explicit references to Solomon that they recognized to be pseudonymous. It is not clear why they should then, however, have left the indirect 'son of David' information.

convention would indeed have led readers to understand that they should be reading the book as though through his eyes—and not just the memoir portions—which is probably not what the writer wanted: Longman ('Determining', 91) puts it well when he says that the book, 'while encouraging an association between Qohelet and Solomon, discourages a reader from *identifying* Qohelet and Solomon'. By signalling a link to Solomon more indirectly, and perhaps even by evoking the first verse of Proverbs, the author is able to identify the literary context within which he wants his work to be understood. It will only be several chapters into the book that its audience will encounter admonitions and sayings of the sort that characterize Proverbs itself, but in this way they are alerted from the outset that Qohelet is going to be addressing comparable themes and ideas.[10] On that understanding, we are being told not that the book is 'Solomon-ic', but that it is 'Solomon-ish'.

Whatever we are supposed to understand by the implied link with Solomon, the content of the book is formally introduced as words attributed to a figure called 'Qohelet', or 'the Qohelet'—the term was variously understood by ancient translators and commentators as a proper name or title. The Septuagint translator, reading it as a title and connecting it with a Hebrew verb that means 'to assemble (people)', rendered it using a Greek word for somebody who belongs to or addresses an assembly, ἐκκλησιαστής, which was taken up by the Latin tradition as 'Ecclesiastes' (this is not itself a Latin word, as Davis, 166, suggests). Many modern translations have preferred to

---

[10] There is an analogy of sorts to this among the Middle Kingdom Egyptian instructions, which conventionally bore the name of a speaker whose background provides a context within which his words are to be understood. When one of these was instead entitled *The Instruction by a Man for his Son*, the intention seems to have been to retain the generic marker but avoid the specificity, allowing the advice to be taken as universal. See Weeks, *Instruction and Imagery*, 10, 13-14. Azize, 'Qohelet Afresh', 205-206, makes the interesting and provocative suggestion that 'Qohelet uses pseudonymity as an educational ploy to undercut pseudonymity as a means of giving a work spurious authority in the minds of its readers', which might equally have been the intention of the Middle Kingdom text. This would imply that the device is almost a parody of the attributions in Proverbs and elsewhere, which does not seem impossible, but which does not really address the problem of the double attribution. Glasser, *Le Procès*, 35, also sees a reaction to those attributions, and suggests that Qohelet is posing as an 'anti-Solomon', with Solomon himself, perhaps, included amongst the less wise who preceded him in Jerusalem (1.16).

substitute 'the preacher', which introduces a religious nuance that is absent from any understanding of the Hebrew, but it is far from certain that we are actually dealing with a title at all. The epithet will be discussed in more detail in the notes: here it may be enough to say only that it is difficult to treat 'Qohelet' either simply as a name or simply as a description, raising the possibility that it was supposed to have been treated as both from the outset, and that the speaker is presented as having adopted a description of himself as his name. However we take it, though, if the term was supposed to convey a meaning, then that meaning is unclear. Indeed, a number of commentators have suggested that this very lack of clarity is the point, and Ingram ('The Riddle of Qohelet') thinks that the name 'is presented to readers as a riddle to be solved' (508)—although it is not clear, if so, that the book ever gives us the answer.

If the reader is perhaps left a little confused with respect to identity, there is at least some familiar information about place. Qohelet is located firmly in Jerusalem, with this location reinforced explicitly several times in the first two chapters (cf. 1.12, 16; 2.7, 9). As Christianson notes (*A Time to Tell*, 74 n. 6), this provides a narrative background against which the reader may understand, for instance, the mention of an otherwise anonymous and generic temple in 4.17, and perhaps some of the more general political references. Although we do not know for sure to what extent other literature was already attributed to David and Solomon when the superscription was composed, it seems likely that the attribution would have emphasized not only the Jewish credentials of the book, but its affinities with existing works. The superscription, in other words, may have supplied the original audience with a great deal of information, even if it does not really perform its prime function of identifying the work's protagonist.

Notes

1.1 words] Although it has been suggested that דברי קהלת... should be considered a nominal sentence with ellipsis, equivalent to ...אלה דברי קהלת (cf. Prov 25.1; Lamparter actually translates 'Dies sind die Reden', and HCM with the equivalent 'these are the words'), titles and captions arguably form a special case syntactically; correspondingly, we should be wary also of placing too much weight on any distinction between 'words of Qohelet' and '*the* words of Qohelet' (see Ellermeier, *Qohelet I.1*, 161-66). G has ῥήματα here, but elsewhere, except in 8.1-5 (where it is a matter of stylistic variation), renders דברים with λόγοι; ῥῆμα has presumably been used either for stylistic effect, as Aitken, 'Rhetoric and Poetry', 70, suggests, or to impart a sense that these are Qohelet's 'sayings' or 'pronouncements'.[11] The Targum has פתגמי נבואה דאיתנבי קהלת, 'the words of prophecy that Qohelet prophesied', reflecting an understanding of the book which is echoed in some other early Jewish exegesis (and has perhaps influenced G). In 4.15, it introduces its historicized understanding of the verse with 'Solomon the prophet said through the spirit of prophecy from ייי', as a way of explaining his foreknowledge (cf. 1.2; 3.11; 10.7), but the idea of prophetic inspiration is also used to explain how Qohelet possesses knowledge beyond normal human access (cf. 3.14; 9.7). Knobel (*The Targum of Qohelet*, 5) notes the similar identification of Solomon as a prophet in the Targum of Song of Songs, and the statement in the Targum to 1 Kgs 5.13, that Solomon prophesied about the subsequent Davidic kings.

According to a Masoretic, perhaps originally scribal convention, דברי should be written דבריֿ, with an enlarged ר (cf. סוףֿ in 12.13); see, e.g., Ginsberg, *Writings*; Yeivin, *Introduction*, 47-48. Such writings generally indicate the start of a section, a character that is significant in some way (as, e.g., the midpoint of the Pentateuch in Lev 11.42), or a character that might be mis-read. They are adopted very irregularly, especially among early manuscripts, and the convention is not followed here, or usually elsewhere, by M^L.

1.1 Qohelet] Or perhaps 'a speaker'. On the epithet, see Weeks, *Ecclesiastes and Scepticism*, 180-96, where I have discussed the issues in more detail. We do not know what קהלת means,[12] or even whether it is supposed to mean anything at all: the erratic appearance of definite articles with it in the textual tradition makes it hard to know whether it was a name or a title,[13] and

---

[11] The unexpectedness of the translation is highlighted by Rizzi, 'Tradizione', 246 n. 118, who notes that ῥήματα is found nowhere else as the *incipit* of a book in the Septuagint, but observes that the singular is used by Aquila in rendering Mic 1.1.

[12] The *plene* spelling קוהלת is used in M^L only once, at 12.8, and although there is much manuscript support for the defective קהלת in that verse, there is very little for the *plene* anywhere else. So far as we can judge these things, therefore, it is likely that the defective spelling without ו is original.

[13] M has an article in 12.8, and the text should be divided to read an article in 7.27. G was probably translated from a Hebrew text that had definite articles in 1.2; 7.27 and 12.8: for a detailed presentation, see the posthumous article by Joseph Ziegler (edited by Fraenkel), 'Gebrauch', 94. This cannot be dismissed as just a careless inconsistency: names in Hebrew do not take an article, but, equally, if a title does not have an article, then it is most naturally read as indefinite, making this verse a reference to 'words of *a* qohelet'. Zimmermann summarized the problem long ago: 'Commentators pay scant attention to the fact that קוהלת as a name anomalously receives the definite article. If it is argued that קוהלת is an attribute of office or function and, therefore, might tolerate the definite article,

this confusion is manifested also among the versions. Aquila transliterates as κωλεθ (κωελεθ at 12.8, according to one manuscript), and S as ܩܘܗܠܬ *qwhlt*, suggesting that both read the word as a personal name, which seems to be the understanding of T as well. On the other hand, G renders with ἐκκλησιαστοῦ, from ἐκκλησιαστής, and Vinel notes the use of ἐξεκκλησιάζειν to render קהל in the Septuagint of 1 Kgs 8.1 (2 Chr 5.2); 12.21: the translator has taken it as a title, indicating a role in connection with 'assemblies', or 'assembling'.[14] In Plato and Aristotle, the Greek noun indicates someone active in the Athenian Ekklesia, the public assembly; it is not really equivalent simply to 'citizen', as Seow suggests, but is closer to the idea of a politician (Plumptre favours 'debater')—Aristotle (*Rhetoric* 1358b) speaks of the 'assemblyman' as the arbiter of things to come, as distinct from the judge, who is the arbiter of things past, and Aristophanes' comedy Ἐκκλησιάζουσαι is about women taking control of the Athenian assembly. It is not clear, however, that the translator would have understood the term in this classical sense; in his commentary, Jerome takes the Greek to describe one who gathers a crowd, and his proposed Latin equivalent, *concionator* (= *contionator*), can be used of a demagogue or rabble-rouser.[15] In any case, G reflects an old understanding, reflected also, perhaps, in Aquila's vocalization,[16] that קֹהֶלֶת is a participle from the qal stem of the verb קהל, and this is explained in the Midrash as a reference to Solomon

---

then it is strange that in the other verses of the book the name appears without the definite article'; see Zimmermann, 'Aramaic Provenance', 44. Baranowski, 'The Article', has presented detailed arguments against a tendency by commentators to suggest that the use of definite articles in the book more generally is erratic, so the issue cannot be seen just as one symptom of a larger problem. Cheyne, *Job and Solomon*, 234, takes the differences between 12.8 and 12.9-10 in this respect to indicate different epilogists, but does not address 7.27, or ask why one epilogist should contradict the other.

[14] The renderings of the other early Greek translators are uncertain. *HALOT* attributes the translation παροιμιάστης to Symmachus, probably on the basis of two Greek manuscripts which give that reading at 12.10. That word, not attested elsewhere, would mean something like 'aphorist', but it is almost certainly an error for the παροιμίας which has been preserved in a third manuscript, although assigned there to Aquila. The error has come about through assimilation to ἐκκλησιαστής, but the term originally translated 'words' in 12.9, not 'Qohelet'. See Marshall and my own note at 12.9. Since we have no evidence to the contrary, it is probable that Symmachus and Theodotion rendered the word in the same way as the Septuagint.

[15] Rizzi, 'Tradizione', 247 n. 119, does note some more positive uses of *contionator* in post-classical sources, so we should not assume that Jerome saw the term as derogatory. See also Loretz, *Qohelet und der alte Orient*, 146.

[16] Jerome represents the Hebrew as *coeleth* in his commentary, and although Eusebius (*Hist. Eccl.* 6.25.2) tells us that Origen also knew a Jewish pronunciation κωελθ, this may have been a corruption of κωελεθ.

who 'assembled' all the leaders of Israel in 1 Kgs 8.1.[17] Other commentators, as early as Rashi and Rashbam, offer the alternative explanation that Qohelet 'gathers' wisdom or wise things, but although some modern commentators have made similar suggestions,[18] the root QHL and its derivatives are used in Hebrew of assembling people, not things.

There are some significant obstacles in the way of reading קהלת as a participle. The verb קהל is not used anywhere else in the qal stem—the hiph'il is used for 'calling an assembly', the niph'al for 'coming together as an assembly'—but even if we allow that this might be an exceptional usage, the form of the participle is feminine, and Qohelet is not female.[19] The explanation usually offered, that the feminine form could be used conventionally for

---

[17] The idea is resurrected, apparently independently, in Longman, 'Qoheleth as Solomon', 48. Two alternative vocalizations have been proposed by Abraham Kamenetzky. In 'Das Koheleth-Rätsel', 66 n. 4, he suggested קְהֵלֶת q^ehelet, in the context of a hypothesis that דברי קהלת originally signified 'folk-sayings', or 'Worte, die für den allgemeinen Gebrauch bestimmt sind' ('sayings which are intended for general use'), and was misunderstood by a subsequent redactor. That vocalization is based on no specific evidence, and Kamenetzky abandoned the theory in his subsequent articles 'Die Rätselname Koheleth', and 'Die ursprünglich beabsichtigte Aussprache des Pseudonyms קהלת', *OLZ* 24 (1921): 11-15. However, he developed in these articles a new proposal that the author of the book was particularly influenced by the accounts of David and Solomon addressing assemblies of the people in Chronicles, and so named Solomon using the term קְהֵלֹת $q^ehilōt$, a (defective) plural form from the unusual word for assembly, קהלה used in Deut 33.4 and Neh 5.7 and in some rabbinic literature (cf. Jastrow, *Dictionary*); in support of such a form, he cites, amongst other things, the place name מקהלת *mqhlt* (Num 33.25-26). See especially 'Die ursprünglich beabsichtigte Aussprache', 12-13. Not dissimilarly, Margoliouth, 'Prologue', 464-65, suggests that the use of קהלה in Neh 5.7 shows that the noun had taken on the sense 'lecture', and that a book entitled 'Lectures' had become attributed to Qohelet when the title was confused with the author.

[18] So, e.g., Seow (97) notes the use of the cognate verb in Syriac to refer to compilation of a book, and suggests that 'Qohelet probably does mean "Gatherer" or "Collector"—whether of wisdom, wealth, or people'. Perry, *Book of Ecclesiastes*, 1, simply calls Qohelet 'the Collector', and claims that his 'words' are what he has collected—although he goes on to see a further reference to the 'convoking' of scholars and students.

[19] The first-person presentation in the monologue actually makes it difficult to identify Qohelet's sex, since Hebrew does not distinguish gender in that person. Masculine forms of the participle, however, are twice applied to Qohelet where the feminine could have been specified: ומוצא אני in 7.26 and ידע אני in 8.12, and although it is true that feminine forms can sometimes be neglected in favour of the masculine, we can contrast the use of the feminine with an explicitly feminine subject in 3.21. The epilogue, moreover, uses masculine forms of the verb in 12.9-10, while in 1.1 and 12, of course, Qohelet is a king and not a queen. Provan

titles, rests on evidence that is slim to non-existent,[20] and if there ever was such a convention, it is highly unlikely that it would have been familiar to the author or his readers.[21] More generally, 'assembler' is an odd description for Solomon: it is hardly his most obvious or relevant characteristic, and a lot more 'assembling' was done by figures like David or Moses. If we try to take the term as a name, on the other hand, then we run into the problem that there was no 'King Qohelet'.

There is a strong possibility that the word is neither a proper name nor a formal title, as such, but a description of what the speaker actually does, or of

(29) takes M's division of words as original in 7.27, making Qohelet the subject of a feminine verb and 'introducing an element of doubt into our minds about the gender of the speaker', but that reading is probably an error, albeit an error that is difficult to explain.

[20] Many commentators have noted the terms 'sons of הספרת (Ezra 2.55) / סופרת (Neh 7.57)' and 'sons of פכרת הצביים' which occur in parallel lists in Ezra 2.55-57 and Neh 7.57-59. These lists are of 'the sons of Solomon's servants', divided into separate categories and grouped with the נתינים, who are temple functionaries. The various groups are each 'sons of so-and-so', and the terms are probably to be considered personal, family names as they stand (although Margoliouth, 'Prologue', 464, suggests that סופרת could equally be a place-name). If they were originally titles, they might reflect the use of a final ת- to form such terms in the distant past, but that is highly speculative, and note, e.g., the similar personal name מספרת in Neh 7.7. A purported use of feminine forms for titles in Phoenician is also mentioned sometimes, and Segert, *Grammar*, 173 §62.13, claims that: 'Some titles of men are expressed by feminine nouns (cf. H. *qōhælæt*)'; cf. Schoors, *The Preacher* II, 438. Segert cites, however, only the titles רבת ממלכאת and רבת מאת, found only in Punic texts, which both employ the single term רבת. Donner and Röllig, in *KAI*, 2:111, deny that רבת is to be taken as feminine in the two passages cited by Segert, and argue from context (and in one case from the Numidian translation in a bilingual text) that the form is plural. Titles with a formation in –*t* are more securely attested in Arabic, as many scholars have noted, but it is hard to see what relevance those could have to a consideration of Hebrew usage before the Islamic period, unless Qohelet is supposed to be an Arab. Nouns with a feminine form are indeed used to represent occupations or professions in much later Hebrew, as Whitley (5) and Schoors, *The Preacher* II, 438, note. Each offers examples only in the plural from Hebrew and Aramaic, and the usage is generally as a collective designation, although we may note also the singular משואחא attested in *b. Baba Meṣiʿa* 107b for the plural משוכות, 'surveyors', which both scholars cite from *m. ʿErubin* 4:11. The origin of these rare forms is unclear, but they do not occur early, and they are specifications of occupation or skill, not titles. There is no attestation of such a form, moreover, with just –*t*.

[21] Mention should, perhaps, be made of the term *qāḫilatu* or *qāʾilatu*, which is listed in *CAD* as 'Either a (WSem.) personal name or a profession'. It occurs twice in Old Babylonian texts from Chagar Bazar, and is very unlikely to be connected to 'Qohelet', but in any case the reference in one of the texts is clearly to a female palace worker; cf. Gadd, 'Tablets', 55.

the capacity in which he is addressing the audience.²² If that is the case, then, grammatically, it would seem unlikely that the word should be read actually as a participle, and we would perhaps be dealing rather with a formation like that of מדעת in Ruth 3.2, where a 'feminine' form of מודע, being used as a substantive meaning 'relation', is applied to Boaz, a man.²³ There are no other obvious analogies in biblical usage, but given the general character of the Hebrew in Ecclesiastes, it might possibly be an idiomatic or dialectal word. In that case, furthermore, the irregular use of definite articles might not be a product simply of confusion in the course of transmission, and at least in this verse, where no version has an article, we could read קהלת as indefinite— making this 'words of a קהלת, the son of David...'

It would be very much harder to do so in 12.9-10, however, where there is also no article attested, but where it is hard to read anything but a name without speculative emendation. We would also certainly expect a proper name in the introductory formula with אני that begins 1.12, and a name would be the most obvious reading here in 1.1, both because the verse is offering an attribution and because קהלת precedes the patronymic בן דוד. If we take all these problems seriously (which most commentators have been strangely reluctant to do), then the other strong possibility is that we are indeed dealing

---

²² If we think in terms of him assembling a crowd, however, which is the most popular interpretation of the term, we should be aware that a קהל is not just any group. Fox has claimed (161) that 'The *qahal* is not necessarily a formal assembly. It can be an informal, non-institutional gathering, such as a *qahal* of peoples (Gen 28:3) or of ghosts (Prov 21:16). We might imagine him [Qohelet] speaking to any gathering of people.' Large assemblies, however, are precisely what the passages that he cites are talking about (the assembly of the shades, in the latter case), and all the biblical usage for קהל, 'assembly', is with reference to large public communities and assemblies or to mythological or metaphorical assemblies that can be understood in similar terms. This is essentially the use in later Hebrew as well: cf. Joüon, 'Sur le nom', who responds to, and correctly rejects Podechard's claim (134) that the term might refer to an assembly of sages. If there is a reference to assembling a crowd, then we should not think in terms of a group at the kerbside or a philosophical circle, despite the claims made by, e.g., Lohfink (11-12) or Michaud, *Qohélet et l'hellénisme*, 119, who envisages Qohelet strolling round the market-place, surrounded by his pupils and in earnest discussion with the traders. A קהל is something more like a public convocation. Negenman (12) suggests that 'Qohelet' refers to an informal office originally associated with such convocations before they were displaced by synagogues, and would translate it as 'Voorganger', a Dutch term that means 'preceder' or 'predecessor', but that is also applied to church ministers (cf. οἱ προηγούμενοι of the early churches). That fits the uses of קהל better, but is entirely speculative.

²³ Schoors, *The Preacher* II, 438-39, similarly rejects a construal of the form as a participle, but sees it as denominative, and a member of 'a well known class of nouns of the *qōtēl*-type, which are designations of occupations or social roles'. This may not be inaccurate, but it does not explain the ה-.

with a personal name, perhaps of a type like עלמת in 1 Chr 7.8; 8.32; 9.42. This is the name of a location in 1 Chr 6.45 (ET 6.60), and possibly offers an early example of a person being named after the place in which they were born or lived (so Schoors, *The Preacher* II, 437). If קהלת was a personal name of this sort, or was, say, a name that people would have associated on other grounds with a particular class, location or ethnicity, then it might have conveyed meaning in a way that had nothing to do with its etymology. Of course, if that were the case, however, then the subsequent assertion that Qohelet is a son of David forces us either to take it as an alternative name for some known king, or to assume that the author is inventing an otherwise unattested king of Israel.

There are difficulties involved, then, in reading 'Qohelet' either as a name or as a description, and it seems likely that there was uncertainty in this matter long before the versions that we possess expressed their divided opinions. It is very possible, furthermore, that this uncertainty provoked early changes to the use of definite articles within the text, thereby muddying the waters even further. We should also consider the possibility, however, that the ambiguity is original, and that the erratic articles arise from the author's own usage. If קהלת never originally took an article after all, then we can explain how some readers came to take it as a title if we suppose that they struggled to reconcile a name 'Qohelet' with the Solomonic attribution, but it is harder to say why they then only added articles in a few places to express their understanding. If קהלת always originally had an article, on the other hand, then why did anyone read it as a name? The difficulties are easier to understand as a product of inconsistency within the text than as a cause of that inconsistency (although copyists may, of course, have exacerbated matters).

It might be possible to construct an explanation based on taking the epilogue as secondary, and supposing that it introduced a misunderstanding of Qohelet as a name. That misunderstanding, however, would itself require some explanation, and it would seem more straightforward to suggest that the author himself treated Qohelet variably as both a name and a title—he is, as it were, 'Qohelet' by name, and 'a qohelet' by nature, rather like Bunyan's 'Christian'. In the story that it tells at 1.12, T presents 'Qohelet' as a name that Solomon has adopted after being expelled from his throne, and although that precise story has more probably been provoked by Ecclesiastes than informed it, there is something to be said for the idea that Qohelet is supposed to have adopted his role as his name: after the life of wisdom and material success that he rejected, he now also rejects or sets aside his previous identity, and describes himself only as 'Gatherer' or 'Speaker', or whatever it is that 'Qohelet' actually means.[24]

---

[24] The sense is not necessarily so portentous: Graetz (17) suggests that 'war es vielleicht nur ein Spitzname, der vielleicht den Eingeweihten in jener Zeit bekannt war', 'it was probably just a nickname, which was probably understood by those in the know at that time', and the sense of which is now unrecoverable.

I find that explanation appealing, but it could also be characterized as making a virtue of necessity. In the end, we have reasons to read both a name and a description, and we can treat this discrepancy as the consequence either of secondary confusion or of the author's original intent. What we cannot readily do is prove that 'Qohelet' was a name, a description, or both. I have opted in the end, therefore, simply to retain 'Qohelet' in my translation, here and below, but to use 'the Qohelet' where the textual evidence favours the reading of an article. This may be perpetuating a confusion in the text and tradition, or it may be broadly in line with the author's intention—although in that case the word should properly be translated. At the very least, though, it avoids forcing an issue where we have too little evidence to make a clear decision.

Finally, it should be said that if 'Qohelet' is a title or description, whether or not it is also a name, the precise sense is uncertain. The potential links with קהל naturally evoke the idea of an assembly, but it is harder to say whether a noun or qal participle would refer to someone who convenes, addresses or merely belongs to that assembly, and scholarly opinions vary. Other senses or derivations, moreover, have been suggested. Whitley, 6, for example, understands derivatives from the root to connote 'indictment' in Neh 5.7 and Job 11.10 and that the Syriac cognate may have the sense 'consider': he suggests that Qohelet is 'the Sceptic', and is followed by Michel. Ullendorff, 'The Meaning of קהלת', similarly notes the Nehemiah passage, and a Syriac sense 'litigious', calling Qohelet 'the arguer', while Zimmermann at one point argued, in 'The Root *KAHAL*', that the epithet referred to 'reproving'; he does not cite the passage from Job, but to Neh 5.7 adds Deut 33.4 and Sir 7.7. It is not necessary, however, to read that special sense in the passages cited, and there is no other evidence for such a connotation in Hebrew. Scholarly appeals to languages other than Hebrew and Syriac are less common, although Barag has gone so far as to find a special sense of 'old age' or 'maturity' through analogy with a supposed Arabic cognate; this is entirely speculative.[25] If the word is actually an acronym or cryptogram,[26] which seems unlikely but not impossible, then there is virtually no chance that we shall ever recover its meaning.

1.1 son of David] Seow notes that, in practice, the Hebrew Bible always uses בן דוד of an actual son of David, usually Solomon; it can in principle, however, refer to any of his descendants: Jesus is frequently addressed as 'son

---

[25] Barag, 'מה היא "קהלת"?'. He derives this sense from the development of nominal forms from the root كهل *khl*, and consequently translates 1.1 as '"דברי" זקנת (או בינת הזקנה) אשר לבן דוד"', 'words "from the son of David's old age (or discernment in old age)"' (103). Subsequent uses of 'Qohelet' are then secondary, and reflect a misunderstanding. See the comments of Schoors, *The Preacher* II, 433.

[26] So Renan (534-36): he believes that it conceals the name 'Solomon'.

of David' in the NT, and if that is explicable in terms of Christian messianic motives, the same is less probable when Mt 1.20 uses it also of Joseph, his father. Jastrow claims that the Hebrew construction shows the words בן דוד to be a secondary addition, but offers no specific basis for that claim.

1.1 king] This is most naturally read as a second attribute of Qohelet, and the accentuation points that way, but, in both M and the versions, it could in principle be taken as an attribute of David (a possibility which Longman is keen to emphasize). There is no good reason to suppose that it means some lesser official or counsellor here, as Albright and Ginsberg have suggested.[27] Bianchi, 'Il metodo', 19, makes the curious and fanciful claim that, as 'son' in Hebrew can have an additional sense of belonging to a group (cf. Amos 7.14), and 'king' could supposedly be used to refer to the head of a school or academy (a claim for which no evidence is adduced), the description here would elicit not only a reminiscence of Solomon, but an identification of Qohelet's place within the wisdom tradition.

1.1 in Jerusalem] S ܕܐܘܪܫܠܡ d'wršlm, Hie regis ierusalem, V regis Hierusalem all mean 'of Jerusalem'; this is usually considered a facilitatory change,[28] but it is not really an easier reading—kings of the Davidic line were never normally known as 'kings of Jerusalem'—and it might have some claim to reflect an early variant. G ἐν Ιερουσαλημ, like T דהוה בירושלם, supports the 'in Jerusalem' of M, but G also reads Ισραηλ before Jerusalem, to give 'king of Israel in Jerusalem'; this plus was present also in La texts, according to Jerome in his commentary, and is probably G*; it is deprecated by Jerome himself, however, and obelized in Syh (indicating that no corresponding words were found in the Hebrew). Commentators usually regard it as an expansion based on 1.12, which the Greek translator either added (uncharacteristically), or else found in his source.[29] The expansion does offset the general oddity of the note, and may have been intended to do so.

This oddity resides in the fact that, although it has some narrative utility, there is no obvious reason to describe the kingship in terms of the city rather than the state—so the statement here is a bit like speaking of the US President as 'the President in Washington', or the British Queen as 'the Queen in

---

[27] Albright, 'Some Canaanite-Phoenician Sources', 15 n. 2. Albright would revocalize 'môlēk...or mallāk'. Similarly, Ginsberg, Studies, 14, takes it to mean 'property-holder'; cf. his 'Structure', 148-49. Perrin, 'Messianism', 42 n. 21, raises but rejects the possibility of vocalizing מלך as a verb.

[28] So, e.g. Rizzi, 'Tradizione', 243 n. 91: 'PeshQo 1,1 ד interpreta il TM ב come relazione genitivale, per facilitare l'attribuzione salomonica', 'the ד [d-] interprets the ב of M as reflecting a genitive relationship in order to facilitate the Solomonic attribution' (although it is not clear exactly how it would facilitate it).

[29] Cf. Salters, 'Textual Criticism', 60, who notes that G's rendering resembles the מלך ישראל בשמרון of 2 Kgs 14.23, although it should be observed that בשמרון there may qualify the preceding verb, rather than being part of the title.

London'—not actually wrong, but off-key. Showing an awareness of this, Midrash Qohelet explains that Jerusalem is 'a place of kingship', and Ibn Ezra takes it to be the proper place for acquiring wisdom.[30] Reading rather a lot into it, Perrin ('Messianism', 47) thinks that the expression is used alongside 'Son of David' because both derive from post-exilic messianic speculation, and that the superscription as a whole, indeed, is not pseudepigraphical in a normal way, but is claiming that 'the words of Qohelet are spoken in the spirit of Solomon, as an extension of the Solomonic wisdom tradition'. Kennicott notes the interesting reading of one late Hebrew manuscript (his ms. 76, thirteenth century), which has expanded the description to 'king of Judah in Jerusalem'—a change comparable to the reading in G, although, if anything, it tends to open up the possibility that Qohelet is *not* Solomon.

The three other times when the noun מלך precedes בירושלם (1 Kgs 10.26 = 2 Chr 1.14; 2 Chr 9.25), the reference is to cavalry being 'with the king in Jerusalem'. On the 41 other occasions when we find מלך בירושלם, in Kings, Chronicles and Jer 52.1, מלך is a verb, and the expression is part of the formulaic 'reigned n years (months, days) in Jerusalem'. If בירושלם is indeed original here, therefore, it might conceivably be a deliberate echo of that formula, and it is tempting even to wonder whether the verb might have been intended ('the son of David reigning in Jerusalem'; cf. Jer 33.21), although we should probably then expect המלך.

---

[30] For Ibn Ezra's commentary, I have used Gómez Aranda, *El Comentario*. Linguistic observations from the commentary are helpfully collected also in his 'Grammatical Remarks'.

1.2-3

THE CHALLENGE

(1.2) A complete illusion! said Qohelet, A complete illusion! It is all an illusion! (1.3) What profit is there for a human in any of his business, at which he works beneath the sun?

Commentary

Verse 1.2 is more famously translated in the KJV as 'Vanity of vanities, saith the Preacher, vanity of vanities; all is vanity'; it is picked up in 12.8, at the end of the monologue, with the slightly shorter 'Vanity of vanities, saith the preacher; all is vanity'. More literally, however, we might say 'Vapour of vapours...all is vapour', which conjures up both the sense and the lack of precision in the original: Qohelet is using a familiar metaphor here, but, as we saw in the Introduction, 'vapour' (Hebrew *hebel*) can have a range of different implications when it is used metaphorically elsewhere in biblical literature. Equally, it is unclear just what he means by 'all', so that one reader familiar with, say, Ps 39.6 (ET 39.5) or Ps 144.4 might easily take this to be a statement that 'everyone lives just a short while',[1] but to another, perhaps thinking of Job 21.34 or 35.16, this could mean 'everything is futile or senseless'.

What Qohelet actually intends will become clearer as the book progresses, although it still evokes much argument. For the moment, readers are offered only a question which brings challenges of its own: what can humans gain from their activities in the world? Qohelet uses a term (*ytrwn*) that would have been most familiar in

---

[1] Midrash Rabbah, in fact, cites a rabbinic interpretation of 1.2 as an explanation of the figure in Ps 144.4a, with Ps 144.4b serving conversely as an explanation of 6.12: both are seen as pointing to a fundamental lack of substance.

mercantile and financial language,[2] and 'all the work' could as well mean 'any of the work', so that on the face of it the answer is trivial: anyone can make a profit by, say, selling a loaf of bread. It is the very fact that he poses the question which leads us to suspect that he is talking about something deeper or more lasting, but he does not yet specify quite what that something might be.[3] The question will itself be picked up subsequently in various forms, most explicitly in 3.9 and 5.15, but also notably in 2.11, where Qohelet declares that he has found no profit in his own activities. His negativity on the point makes it clear that Qohelet believes the proper answer here to be 'none', and although the question in 1.3 is not, perhaps, purely rhetorical—there will be a genuine attempt to address it in what follows—it functions in the first place to qualify the declaration of 1.2: in some sense, the fact that 'all is vapour' is to be deduced from, or at least associated with, the difficulty in establishing just what it is that humans gain from the efforts they invest while alive.

The issue is clarified no further at this point, although what follows will furnish a context in which both the statement of 1.2 and the question of 1.3 are to be understood. That the scope of what Qohelet is claiming remains so open, though, seems likely to be deliberate. When Qohelet does go on to make his meaning clearer, there will be a certain compelling logic to it: nobody could deny that there is no material gain to be achieved from a life in this world ('beneath the sun') if they shared Qohelet's assumption that this life is to be followed by an afterlife to which nothing can be taken, and in which no reward or punishment is to be found. His use of the term 'profit' already hints at the very materialistic accounting

---

[2] See the note, below. Plumptre helpfully says of *ytrwn* that, 'Its strict meaning is "that which remains,"—the surplus, if any, of the balance-sheet of life. It was, probably, one of the words which the commerce of the Jews, after the Captivity, had brought into common use.' He goes on, though, to say that 'The question is in substance, almost in form, identical with that of our times "Is life worth living?"'; this is true to an extent, although the English expression lacks not only the commercial edge, but the sense that Qohelet is seeking to find a profit, not merely to break even.

[3] Although Perdue is right to emphasize that *ytrwn* does not simply connote advantage or instant gain, there is little basis for his assertion that the root carries a sense of endurance: we might gloss it with the ambiguous 'what is left over', but cognate terms suggest that *ytrwn* is not so much what endures, as what remains over; cf. Perdue, *Wisdom & Creation*, 208. The broader sense of the question is not implied, therefore, by the choice of language.

that he intends, and perhaps alerts readers to the possibility that Qohelet views the world through a very particular lens; at this stage, however, his sweeping claims seem designed more to compel attention than active assent or dissent.

Although he has already been named by the superscription in the first verse, Qohelet will not introduce himself until v. 12, so that the intervening vv. 2-11 seem to sit outside the main part of the monologue. Furthermore, as we have already noted, 1.2 is picked up at the end of Qohelet's speech, in 12.8, so that its claim effectively frames that speech.[4] A few scholars, in fact, have seen this whole section as an intrusive editorial addition,[5] and many more have been inclined to question the originality of at least vv. 2 and 3.[6] There is no compelling reason, however, to assume that the foreshadowing of Qohelet's later themes in these verses must result from some secondary summarizing of his words. Such claims are generally associated with broader theories about an editorial framework, and often work with a conception of the book as rather miscellaneous: if we omit either 1.2-3 or, more drastically, 1.2-11, then it becomes

---

[4] It has often been suggested that 1.2 and 12.8 effectively offer a proposition and a declaration that the proposition is now proven; see, e.g., Barton at 12.8; Anderson, 'Poetic Inclusio'. Without discounting the importance of the link between the verses, however, I am not sure either that Qohelet's thought is so static, or that his argument is so single-minded as some presentations of the book as a simple thesis/validation-of-thesis model might suggest.

[5] The view of Loretz, *Qohelet und der alte Orient*, 144, and of Longman, that we do not hear Qohelet's own words until 1.12, draws on their ideas about the generic affiliations of the work with royal inscriptions. Whilst it is certainly true that 1.12 marks the start of something new and more personal, there are too many links with what follows for us to associate this simply with the framework of the book, and there are antecedents for such introductory material in other ancient literature. Fox, 'Frame-Narrative', 87 n. 11, notes that '...we cannot derive *rules* from one genre and make a work from another conform to them. *Qohelet* uses some formulas from royal pronouncements but is not one itself.'

[6] There are no grounds to suppose that the presence of either verse, or the juxtaposition of the two, results from secondary redaction of the book, as asserted by, e.g. Whybray: 'v.3 is editorial and is closely connected with v.2, the two verses together forming an attempt by an editor to summarize Qoheleth's teaching as a whole'; cf. Whybray, 'Wonders of Nature', 106. There is no consistency on the point, however, even amongst those who propose such a framework: Galling 1969 (80), for instance, happily assigns both verses to his redactor 'QR1', while Lauha views v. 3 as the original introduction, and Kaiser likewise sees v. 2 as certainly redactional, but observes of v. 3 merely that Qohelet 'did not necessarily write it himself'; cf. Kaiser, 'Qoheleth', 86.

much harder to establish a clear basis or focus for much of what follows.

If it was indeed the author's intention that his readers should qualify and contextualize Qohelet's claims in the light of what follows, then he did not reckon with the very different assumptions that would be brought to his work by a much later readership. Especially in Christian traditions, 1.2-3 came to be seen not as claims to be qualified, but as a key to the book, which states in stark terms the lack of meaning and value in a material, temporal world.

Another understanding, which has gained some very limited currency more recently, rests on a translation 'wealth' for the word that I have rendered 'business'. Accordingly, the NJPS version asks, 'What real value is there for a man in all the gains he makes beneath the sun?', and such renderings foster an interpretation of Qohelet's quest in financial or economic terms that go beyond his desire for 'profit': as one exponent puts it, 'Qoheleth wishes to answer the question of what one should do with the wealth one has accumulated', and is offering practical advice to the wealthy.[7] All else aside, it is unlikely that the key word can be translated that way (see the notes at 2.11), and that, correspondingly, the original audience could have understood this to be the point of Qohelet's question, but the interpretation illustrates again how open the text has been to a variety of subsequent readings, by audiences with a variety of different concerns.

Notes

1.2 complete illusion] Or possibly 'illusion after illusion'. On the term הבל, see the Introduction, pp. 20-29, above. Rabbinic interpretations preserved in Midrash Rabbah speak of 'seven הבלים' here (equated with 'ages of man' or the days of creation), with each plural counted as two.[8] The construction,

---

[7] Garfinkel, 'Qoheleth', 54. He goes on to note that Ginsberg, himself a strong exponent of the translation as 'wealth', was on the NJPS committee, and that Fox, in his JPSBC commentary on that version, instantly rejects it. Gericke, 'Axiological Assumptions', suggests rather differently that Qohelet 'constructs reality through an economic metaphor' (6), and that *hebel* connotes 'worthlessness' in the sense of 'lacking any absolute value'—an understanding that struggles to explain many uses of the word in the book.

[8] This and other early interpretations are very helpfully presented and discussed in Lavoie, 'Habēl habālīm', 228-32.

הבל הבלים (traditionally 'vanity of vanities'), however, is usually taken to be similar to that found in 'song of songs', 'holy of holies', or the less well-known 'slave of slaves' (Gen 9.25) and 'heaven(s) of heavens' (1 Kgs 8.27).[9] Although this idiom is commonly described as 'expressive of the superlative idea' (Barton; cf. GKC §133 i, which regards it as a periphrasis for the superlative), that description is misleading. 'Superlative' is a term that can be used of adjectives, or of substantivized adjectives, and sometimes of adverbs, but not of nouns: while the 'holy of holies' may be 'the holiest (place)', the 'song of songs' is not 'the most song-like song'. It is also doubtful that a superlative, as such, would make much sense here, given either the referent or the metaphorical quality of הבל: if '*all*' is the *most* הבל, what is left to be *less* הבל? Or is one sort of vapour more vaporous than another? Ellermeier argues with some justice that a thing must be either הבל or not הבל—it cannot be more or less הבל.[10] It is better to say, then, that such expressions assert not a simple superlative, but rather that something is the very model or epitome of its type; in English we might call the 'song of songs' the 'ultimate' song.

Ellermeier himself, in fact, pursues a different path, translating '"הבל", immer wieder "הבל"', which we might paraphrase as 'הבל after הבל', or 'one הבל after another'. His main justification for this is that Qohelet's use of הכל הבל elsewhere is always to characterize something specific and concrete (1.14; 2.11, 17; 3.19), so that this verse is better understood as a summary reference to all such individual verdicts. Fox rightly objects that Ellermeier can adduce no other instances of the 'superlative' construction being used iteratively like this,[11] but it is possible that we should not think in terms of that construction at all. Although he speaks of 'Verallgemeinerung' ('generalization') rather than

---

[9] A number of other examples could be cited, but it is important to note that not all such expressions have quite the same meaning. In Num 3.32, for instance, Eleazar is 'keeper of the keepers' of the sanctuary, and in Ezek 26.7 Nebuchadrezzar is 'king of kings'; such cases do not so much single out the individual from the group, as express their relationship to the rest of the group. The same is possibly true, of course, in Gen 9.25.

[10] See Ellermeier, *Qohelet I.1*, 99. Fox, 'Frame-Narrative', 84 n. 5, objects that הבל can, in fact, have different degrees if understood in terms of 'absurdity', but that objection only has real force if the literal sense of the word has been all but subsumed by the metaphorical, which is doubtful. Midrash Qohelet does cite one rabbinic understanding of this verse in which it is likened to a man setting seven pots, one on top of another, until the steam (הבל) that emerges from the last has become so attenuated that it altogether lacks substance; this shows, to be sure, that הבל can be more or less substantial, but not really that הבל can be more or less הבל.

[11] Fox, 'Frame-Narrative', 84 n. 5. D'Alario, *Qohelet*, 64 n. 4, responds that הבל may be given an iterative aspect here by the repetition of the term, if not by the 'superlative' itself. The question may, of course, be considered in isolation from Ellermeier's broader theories about the composition of the book, although he draws on this verse to justify them.

iteration, Allgeier's comparisons with the (probably) iterative expressions in Ps 72.5's דור דורים (which also occurs in Isa 51.8, Ps 102.25) and Judg 5.30's רחם רחמתים, suggest that he likewise considers an iterative interpretation possible here. Those comparisons do indeed raise the possibility that we are dealing with a different sort of expression, in which a singular (presumably absolute) form is juxtaposed asyndetically with a dual or plural form of the same noun to denote a series. How far the existence of such an expression can be considered established outside the cliché with דור, however, is another matter.[12] It is attractive to suppose that Qohelet is here prefiguring his more specific observations, and declaring, in effect, that all one can encounter is הבל after הבל, but since it is not certain that the Hebrew can bear that sense, I have opted to retain the more classic translation, with the 'superlative' construction.

As the Masoretes probably read it this way, and as that construction involves placing a noun in the construct state before the plural of the same noun in the absolute, הֲבֵל must be a construct form of הֶבֶל, both on the two occasions when it appears here, and in the corresponding 12.8, but the vocalization is unexpected. To be sure, the expectations of commentators appear to differ in the matter: Delitzsch and Lauha, for instance, think it should be הֲבֵל, while, e.g., Barton and Whitley expect the construct to be the same as the absolute. A noun like חֶדֶר (cs. חֲדַר or חֶדֶר) illustrates the sort of problems involved in dealing with segholates,[13] and we should certainly avoid jumping (with, e.g., HCM) to the conclusion that this is an Aramaism (cf., e.g., עֲבֵד in Dan 6.21, equiv. to Heb. עֶבֶד);[14] J-M §96 A e suggests that הֲבֵל arises from a parallel absolute form הֲבֵל. In any case, Jerome's commentary attests a pronunciation *abal abalim*, which may reflect a more conventional הֲבַל הֲבָלִים in his time.[15]

---

[12] דור and other terms can be used in another, much more common construction, where two instances of the singular form can be linked by a conjunction to mean 'each and every' instance. See, e.g., the repeated uses in Esth 9.28 and 1 Chr 28.14-16. This construction, however, is distinct in both form and meaning.

[13] On the place of הבל within the segholates, see Revell, 'Voweling', 322.

[14] Du Plessis, 'Aspects', 169, notes שְׁנֵי in Deut 28.4; 18.51 and חֲדַר in 2 Kgs 20.30, and declares that 'these forms and הֲבֵל are without doubt following the morphology of the Aramaic nouns like צְלֵם, עֲבֵד and others'. It is difficult to know, of course, whether we are looking in each case at ancient pronunciations which have been preserved, but the more examples adduced, the more likely it seems that we are dealing with something which should be regarded as Hebrew, whatever its origin.

[15] On Jerome's Hebrew, see, e.g., Sutcliffe, 'St. Jerome's Pronunciation of Hebrew'; Sutcliffe points out, *inter alia*, that Jerome's pronunciation was constrained by practices current among the Jews by whom he was taught, and does not always recognize distinctions which would have been made both in the classical tongue and in the Tiberian pointing. Sperber, 'Hebrew Based upon Greek

The versions present no surprises here. S ܗܒܠ ܗܒܠܝܢ *hbl hblyn* is a virtual transliteration of the Hebrew, which, as Kamenetzky, 206, notes, hardly corresponds to Syriac usage (contrast Syh ܣܪܝܩܘܬܐ *sryqwt'*). Aitken ('Rhetoric and Poetry', 71) suggests that G's rendering, by chance or design, gives a stylish iambic rhythm μᾰτᾱιὄτῆς ׀ μᾰτᾱιὄτῆιτῶν; the choice of noun reflects standard Septuagint practice in the rendering of הבל, and effectively fixes a certain interpretation of the Hebrew metaphor in terms of 'unfruitfulness' or 'uselessness'.[16] Holm-Nielsen's claim, that this 'twists the meaning of the word in an ethical direction', arguably imputes a stronger ethical sense to the Greek term than general usage of the more common μάταιος would suggest,[17] but the Three avoid the problem by offering variations on ἀτμὸς (or ἀτμὶς) ἀτμῶν (or ἀτμίδων), which all refer to steam or vapour and so preserve the metaphorical quality.[18] Like all these, T clearly reflects the same text as M, but it places the saying in a vision of the future, where Solomon sees his work rendered futile by the division of the kingdom under his son.

1.2 said Qohelet] Or 'says Qohelet'. אמר is rendered as a past tense by G εἶπεν (cf. Hie, V, *dixit*), but more commonly with a present tense in modern translations. This is not problematic in grammatical terms, but it does tend to obscure the original presentation of what follows as a monologue, placed in the mouth of Qohelet—a very common form of presentation in biblical and other literature, which sometimes places such speeches in particular narrative contexts. We are being told, literally, that he said these words, rather than being offered an insight into his current opinions.

and Latin Transliterations', 218, compares the Babylonian pointing of הֶבֶל with Jerome's account, and notes the attestation αβλη for Origen's transliteration of הַבְלִי in Ps 31.7 (ET 31.6).

[16] הבל is sometimes rendered using other words, or with forms from the adjective μάταιος (e.g. 1 Kgs 16. 13, 26), but ματαιότης is used in Pss 31.7, 62.10 (ET 62.9), and several other times in the Psalms. The noun also appears three times in the NT, so unless we date the translation of G unusually early, it is unlikely that the translator actually coined the term, as Jarick suggests ('Tragedians', 104).

[17] Holm-Nielsen 'Interpretation', 170. Holm-Nielsen draws on Bertram, 'Hebräischer und griechischer', who also examines this rendering (30-33), but more explicitly associates it with notions of sinfulness. Even if the translation was originally motivated by theological concerns, which seems questionable, its use in Ecclesiastes surely reflects no more than the adoption of an established equivalent for הבל.

[18] It is difficult to disentangle the precise readings of each, or to distinguish uses of ἀτμὶς and ἀτμὸς: where the evidence is in Greek, the translators are referred to collectively; where the translators are specified, the evidence is in Syriac. Marshall tentatively assigns: α' and θ': (1) ἀτμὸς ἀτμῶν (or ἀτμίδων)... (2) ἀτμὸς ἀτμῶν (or ἀτμίδων) τὰ πάντα ἀτμὸς (or ἀτμὶς); σ': (1) ἀτμὸς ἀτμοῦ... (2) ...ἀτμὸς (or ἀτμὶς).

Where M here has קהלת, G has ὁ ἐκκλησιαστής with an article, making this the only place (apart from the problematic 7.27) where M and G disagree about the determination of 'Qohelet': otherwise, they both have an article at 12.8, while neither has an article at 1.1, 12; 12.9, 10. It may be significant in some unknown way that, as Goldman points out, in each of the other places where both have, or may originally have had, an article, קהלת follows אמר, as here, but it is difficult to avoid the fact that both witnesses display an awkward inconsistency: if 'Qohelet' is a title, it ought to have an article on every occcurrence, but if it is a name, it ought never to take an article. This is connected, of course, to more fundamental questions about the nature of the epithet (addressed above), but neither M nor G reflects a systematic understanding one way or the other. It is difficult to see why, therefore, the fact that the translator of G may have found הקהלת in his source-text makes that reading superior to קהלת in M (any more than it could be declared inferior), or why we should therefore emend the text to הַקְּהֵלָה, as *BHQ* proposes.[19]

1.2 it is all an illusion] Lit. 'the all (is) הבל'; G τὰ πάντα ματαιότης; Hie, V *omnia uanitas* retain the non-verbal character of the clause, against normal Greek and Latin syntax. This alliterative expression recurs not only in 12.8, but also in 1.14 and 2.11, as a conclusion drawn from Qohelet's further observations, and in 2.17; 3.19 as a basis for other conclusions.

The expression הכל is often treated as loaded, bearing some particular implication that would have specified immediately the scope of Qohelet's claim here. Pursuing such a line, Amir, 'Doch ein griechischer Einfluss?', 36, counts 58 uses of הכל in the Hebrew Bible, 17 of them in Qohelet, with the numbers increasing to 76 and 23 if forms with prefixed prepositions are included. His precise numbers are open to challenge (especially when he talks in the German version about Ecclesiastes having ten chapters), but he does have a fair point that Qohelet uses the expression unusually often. It is harder to say whether, as he claims, the disproportion is even more evident when we restrict our attention to passages where it means 'everything' in a general way, rather than 'all of' some specified thing: there is no clear antecedent for Qohelet's statement here, but we cannot always say with certainty when he is being 'general' (see, e.g., Christianson, *A Time to Tell*, 88-89). In any case, though, it is not inconceivable that the frequency of הכל would, as Amir implies, have suggested to anyone familiar with Greek philosophy and its discourse about 'the all', that the scope of Qohelet's enquiries was similar. His usage of the expression is not unique, however, and certainly does not demand such a reading; the frequency, moreover, would not be evident to an audience at this stage. Lohfink's contrary argument in 'Koh 1,2', that Qohelet must here be talking in a more limited way about human possessions, rests on the

---

[19] J. Ziegler's posthumous 'Gebrauch', 94, lists the evidence, with the G variants, and notes the discrepancy in M between 1.2 and 12.8, but does not propose emendation.

assumption (which I share in the commentary) that the 'all' will be specified by what follows. There is no more merit, however, in his argument from usage elsewhere that הכל *must* be limited in scope than there is in Amir's argument that it *must* be unlimited. הכל does not in itself either enforce or preclude any particular understanding of what 'everything' might be. Whatever we gather about his intentions here from our understanding of Qohelet's subsequent words, there is no reason to suppose that the expression takes on some single sense in his usage, and Crenshaw, 'Quantitative', 10, rightly emphasizes its 'ambiguity and openness'.

If there is a lack of precision in the expression, that may be a consequence more of stylistic concerns than of any deliberate desire to confuse, and the assonance of הכל הבל is self-evident. Jarick, 'Book of Changes', 79-82, notes also the strong visual resemblance of the words in Hebrew—although he acknowledges that this might be lost on an audience that only heard the text read—and the way that their juxtaposition compactly transforms 'everything' into 'nothing'. It is less obvious, I think, that we can reasonably speak of this as poetic parallelism, as he further suggests, unless we are willing to dispense with the assumption that this is a non-verbal clause, and even then a poetic presentation would more naturally set the words הכל הבל in parallel with הבל הבלים than with each other.

1.3 profit] Other words from the root are quite widely attested in biblical Hebrew, but יתרון itself is confined to Ecclesiastes (1.3; 2.11, 13 twice; 3.9; 5.8, 15; 7.12; 10.10, 11); this need not imply that the word is a new coinage, and it is widely supposed that the term is an established commercial one. The similar יתרן is attested in two Aramaic texts from Saqqara: one of these offers little context, but in the other there is a reference to יתרן כספא זי קים בשנת ||| ||||, 'the balance of money remaining in year 6', apparently referring to a profit or surplus; a related term יתרא appears in another text, which reads ויתרא מן אב '...and the surplus from Ab...'[20] The Hebrew יתרון, then, is probably what remains over after accounts have been settled, the net profit (cf. Akkadian *[w]atartu[m]*). G's περισσεία is not used in the Septuagint outside Ecclesiastes, but appears in the NT and occasionally elsewhere with the sense 'abundance' or 'superfluity'; MM notes that it is used for monetary surplus in two Greek inscriptions. The associated adjective is used in the Septuagint to render other forms from the Hebrew root. Although it seems flatter, the τί πλέον of α' and σ' can have the sense 'what use is it...?', so may be quite a clever rendering of the Hebrew as a Greek idiom.

---

[20] See Segal, *Aramaic Texts*, 34, 38, 124; the texts cited are his nos. 19 (l. 2) and 23 (rev. l. 3); no. 149 l. 2 reads just ויתר[ח]:, so the sense of the word is uncertain here. Seow notes the first, and refers to the edition of Porten and Yardeni, *Textbook*, 3:2.11.6.

1.3 a human] Lit. 'the human' (אדם). Kennicott notes לאיש in a single thirteenth-century manuscript. This seems not so much an error as a deliberate substitution, but the reason for it is unclear. Dahood, 'Canaanite-Phoenician', 202-203, sees Phoenician influence in the book's preference for אדם over איש, but this is more probably an aspect of its subject-matter: cf. Piotti, 'Usi Linguistici', 49-51.

1.3 in any of] Or 'in all of', but the sense is probably not that the 'sum' of all work equates to nothing: Qohelet claims that there are no gains, rather than that gains are balanced by losses. The preposition -ב here may be the *beth pretii* (GKC §119 p): 'what profit is there for the price of all the work?' (so, e.g., HCM). It has also been suggested, though, that the sense must be 'from', as purportedly found sometimes in Ugaritic;²¹ Qohelet is not, however, speaking either of what remains from the work itself, or of what the work has left remaining from something else, which would be the probable connotations if -ב were here equivalent to מן (cf. Lev 2.3; Exod 10.5). If we insist on labels, the most likely use of the preposition here, in fact, is instrumental (GKC §119 o): 'what profit is achieved by means of all the work?'²²

1.3 his] The suffix on עמלו is not reflected explicitly in α' κόπῳ ᾧ ἐκοπίασεν, 'toil in which he toils', or S ܠܡܠ 'ml'; M is supported, however, by the other versions. Goldman views M as an assimilation to the form found in 2.22, 24; 3.13; 4.8; 5.14, 17, 18; 8.15, and proposes not only to delete the suffix, but also to add an article on the basis of 2.20 (although this would arguably be required anyway, once the suffix is deleted), so *BHQ* suggests emendation to הֶעָמָל, '(all) the labour'. The grounds for this emendation seem slight, however. G attests the suffix and does not reflect the proposed article, while, as Kamenetzky, 206-207, observes, S may have regarded the suffix as redundant before the following relative clause. Although it is possible, moreover, that Aquila's source lacked the suffix, hexaplaric readings preserved as marginal glosses do not always convey more than the basic information required to delineate a variant, and the gloss here may simply not have included a suffix even if it was to be found in the original text of α'. Neither S nor α', therefore, provides a strong reason to emend.

---

²¹ So, e.g., Schoors, *The Preacher* I, 193, citing Dahood, 'Phoenician Background', 265, cf. 281. James Barr has raised some important questions about the wider identification of *b* = 'from' within the Ugaritic texts, and doubts that such a sense is to be found in Hebrew; cf. his *Comparative Philology*, 175-77.

²² Jenni, *Die Präposition Beth*, puts this use in his section 442 (p. 345), alongside those in 2.24; 3.13; 5.17; 8.15 (which are to do with taking pleasure 'in one's work'); the section is formally: 'Modalisation-Handlungsabstrakten-Konkrete Aktivitäten, ohne m-Präformative'. Krüger inclines rather to grouping it with the uses in 2.22; 3.9; 4.9; 9.9, which come under the heading of *beth pretii* in section 1856 ('Lohn [für Leistung]'), p. 156. I agree that it is more closely related to these uses, but not that they are clear examples of *beth pretii*.

1.3 business] The negative associations of עמל have been noted by many commentators, and the noun can be used almost as a general term for hardship or trouble (e.g. Num 23.21). Those connotations are hardly absent from Ecclesiastes, in which Schoors (*The Preacher* II, 139) notes 22 occurrences of the noun, and 13 of the verb, but the book generally retains a specific reference to work and the products of work.[23] Expressions similar to the עמל שיעמל of this verse, varied to fit their context, are found also in 2.11 (ובעמל שעמלתי, alongside the comparable מעשי שעשו), 18 (עמלי שאני עמל), 19 (עמלי שעמלתי), 20 (העמל שעמלתי); 5.17 (עמלו שיעמל); 9.9 (ובעמלך אשר אתה עמל); cf. the more extended 2.22 (עמלו...שהוא עמל). This is, then, a formulation very characteristic of the book, although the occurrence in 5.17 is as part of a longer quotation from this verse: בכל עמלו שיעמל תחת השמש. For the translation of עמל adopted here, see the note 'business which I had worked to achieve' at 2.11.

1.3 at which he works] The relative -ש is used frequently in Qohelet—Wright counts 68 instances against 89 of אשר—but some interchange between the two is visible in a comparison of M with the Qumran fragments, and should warn us against investing too much in the proportions, or in the originality of specific cases.[24] Only Song of Songs uses the word with similar frequency, but its appearances are not wholly confined to late texts, and it is usually viewed as an ancient, rarer alternative to אשר. It has naturally played a significant role in the discussions about the date of Ecclesiastes, since the use of -ש, virtually to the exclusion of אשר, is a characteristic of very much later Hebrew. It is still notably unusual, however, even in some late biblical literature such as Chronicles, as well as in the Qumran materials (cf. Schoors, *The Preacher* I, 54-56), so date may be only one factor in Qohelet's usage, alongside aspects of dialect or register.[25] The combination ש-יעמל here was

---

[23] See especially Foresti, '*'āmāl* in Koheleth', who draws a sharp distinction between the senses found in Ecclesiastes and the more common biblical sense 'affliction', and who takes this difference to affirm the late date of the book, since Qohelet's usage is more in line with that of Hebrew and Aramaic texts from the Persian period and later.

[24] 4QQoh[a] has -ש for M אשר twice in 7.19-20, and perhaps also in 6.12; 4QQoh[b], on the other hand, has אשר for M ש- in 1.14.

[25] The differences between -ש and אשר have been variously evaluated. Schwarzschild, 'The Syntax of אשר', sees some distinction in usage posited on his belief that אשר retained a nominal status. Curiously, he gives figures of 'at least sixty-seven' and eighty-eight for -ש and אשר respectively in Ecclesiastes (8): the lower figure for -ש arises from questions about the parsing of בשכבר in 2.16, but it is not clear which instance of אשר he has excluded, or why. More persuasively, Robert Holmstedt in 'The Grammar of ש and אשׁר' and in his *The Relative Clause*, 215-47, has suggested that the distinction is basically diachronic, but has been influenced by other factors. These include the retention of אשר in later texts because it is more classical, and the occasional use of -ש in earlier texts to depict characters who use it as foreign.

reportedly pointed with metheg under the ש alone by ben Naphtali, but under both ש and ׳ by ben Asher (see Lipschütz).

Since the verb עמל does not seem to take a direct object in biblical usage (cf. Jon 4.10), the expression here is probably elliptical for שעמל בו; cf. שלא עמל בו in 2.21, and J-M §158 ha. G μόχθῳ αὐτοῦ ᾧ μοχθεῖ reflects a slightly different understanding: the Greek verb can take a direct object in the accusative, so the dative here probably reflects the intransitive use, 'his work by/in which he is worn out', cf. the explicatory G^S ἐν ᾧ. In this respect, it differs from the use of the same verb with a cognate accusative in, e.g. Euripides, *Helen* 1446, which Lohfink believes has influenced the Hebrew; I doubt that, but it is possible that G is deliberately echoing the classical phrase. The biblical usage of μόχθος is explored at length by Rizzi, 'Tradizione', 249-51, n. 125.

1.3 beneath the sun] The use in Ecclesiastes of both תחת השמש and the more familiar, graphically similar תחת השמים ('beneath the heavens') has led to textual confusion at various points. Here M is supported by G, T, Hie, and V, with only one manuscript of S stepping out of line to read ܫܡܝܐ *šmyʾ* ('heaven'). That this manuscript is the important Codex Ambrosianus hardly outweighs the probability of a simple scribal error here, despite Goldman's inclination to prefer its reading against all the other witnesses.

תחת השמש appears in 1.3, 9, 14; 2.11, 17, 18, 19, 20, 22; 3.16; 4.1, 3, 7, 15; 5.12, 17; 6.1, 12; 8.9, 15 twice, 17; 9.3, 6, 9 twice, 11, 13; 10.5. We might also note the expressions found in 7.11, לראי השמש, and 11.7, לראות את השמש: to look on the sun, i.e. to be beneath it, is to be alive. This is not necessarily good: 7.12 goes on to talk about the need for protection from the sun, and in about half of its occurrences, furthermore, תחת השמש is connected with work or deeds, as here. Like some other favourite expressions in Ecclesiastes, this one is very frequent in the book itself, whilst appearing nowhere else in the Hebrew Bible. The old view that it is based on, or at least influenced by the Greek ὑφ᾽ἡλίῳ or ὑπὸ τὸν ἥλιον has been defended by some recent commentators (e.g. Lohfink, cf. Schoors, *The Preacher* II, 137), even though the expression is found elsewhere in the region, most notably in two sixth-/fifth-century BCE Phoenician inscriptions. That of King Tabnis warns those who would disturb his corpse that they will have no 'seed among the living under the sun (בחים תחת שמש), or resting place with the shades' (*KAI* 13.7-8); that of ʾEshmunʿazar uses precisely the same phrase (*KAI* 14.12). Seow and others cite similar examples from further afield and from rather earlier texts; if not proof that this was a long-established way of speaking about the world of the living, as opposed to the underworld, these texts at least furnish local analogies for the usage in Ecclesiastes.[26] In the absence of still closer analogies, it is hard to say whether the phrase would have had other resonances,

---

[26] We may note, however, the unconvincing attempt of Ginsberg to turn this evidence the other way, by suggesting that since 'under the sun' is 'an

such as the oppressiveness identified by Janzen, in 'Under the Sun', who sees a symbol of mortality in the inevitable setting of the sun, and believes that the sun would have been seen in eschatological terms as a temporary substitute for the rule of God himself.

unmistakable Hellenism', the inscriptions must themselves reflect a Phoenician borrowing from Greek, and can correspondingly be no earlier than the late fourth century. See his review of Harris' grammar, 142, and 'King of Kings', 71.

INTRODUCTION TO 1.4-11

EVIDENCE FROM THE WORLD

(1.4)   One generation goes, another generation comes,
        while the world stays forever constant.
(1.5)   And the sun has risen, and the sun gone down,
        and returned to its place—but then it rises there,
(1.6)   going southward, and turning northward.
        Turning. Turning. The wind goes,
        and on to its surroundings, the wind comes back again.
(1.7)   All streams go to the sea, but the sea is never filled:
        to the place where the streams go, they go again.
(1.8)   When all words are worn out, can a man no longer speak?
        An eye will not be too sated for seeing, nor an ear filled
        with listening.
(1.9)   What will be, will be whatever has been,
        and what will be done, whatever has been done–
        with nothing new beneath the sun.
(1.10) Though when speaking someone might say,
        'Look—this is new',
        it has already been, in the aeons which have existed apart
        from us.
(1.11) There is no memory of the earlier times,
        and likewise there will be no memory of the later,
        which have yet to happen
        —or of those which are going to happen later still.

To explain and justify the claims that he has made in 1.2-3, Qohelet draws on two sources: the common human experience of the world, and his own experience of life and work. Although his account of each has implications for both parts of the challenge, the first relates more directly to his statement that everything is *hebel* and the second to his question about the profit from human labour. In 1.4-11, accordingly, the scope of the evidence that he employs shows that by 'everything' he really does mean everything in the world, although the sense in which it can be called *hebel* is not immediately or explicitly defined. It is striking also, though, that the emphasis in the closing vv. 9-11 seems to be primarily on the future: the evidence Qohelet adduces, and the situation he describes, is not presented simply as an explanation of the world, but as an argument for its constancy, so that by the end of v. 11 it has been made clear already that any 'profit' from human labour can never include real change to the world, innovation within the world, or the prospect of a lasting memory within the world.

The verses begin by drawing a distinction between humans and the world: they come and go while it continues (1.4). What they see in the world, however, is not obviously static or monolithic, and in 1.5-7 Qohelet singles out three examples of natural phenomena that are highly mobile: the sun, the wind, and rivers.[1] The point he seeks to make from these examples is that mobility should not be equated with change, progress or completion. The sun, wind and rivers all do what they are supposed to do, and so might be said to accomplish particular tasks, but their accomplishments do not result in any actual consummation. Each goes on to repeat or to continue what it is doing, because what it is doing has no finality and brings no end. Qohelet's second, shorter set of examples (1.8) is drawn not from nature, but from human communication and perception, which he uses to make a similar point. Speaking, seeing and listening all involve the accomplishment of individual tasks, but these tasks move towards no conclusion, and speaking does not use up words, any more than seeing and hearing progressively fill the eyes and ears. Such actions are like the actions outlined in the previous verses: they are accomplished constantly or repeatedly without contributing in any way towards the fulfilment of some greater task.

Extrapolating from these examples, Qohelet invites us to understand the whole world in such terms. It is not progressing or

---

[1] Behind the choice of examples, many commentators see a reference to the four classical elements of earth, air, fire, and water, perhaps intended to express the idea that all nature is included. Perry, 'Poetics', 10, even suggests that the order of their appearance here has been shaped by a deliberate reference to Gen 1.2. Allowing that the sun might represent fire, however, this seems a little forced: for 'earth' (both here and in Genesis) we would really expect אדמה, while ארץ is not set in parallel with the other phenomena, and may be supposed to incorporate them. Ibn Ezra links the idea solely to 1.4, interpreting it, in terms of Gen 3.19, to suggest that as life breaks down after death into the four constituent elements, humans return to the earth from which they are made.

developing, and nothing is fundamentally altered by everything (or anything) that is happening: events are just events, that may happen again and again without anything greater accruing from them—and it is striking that the many verbs of motion that characterize 1.4-7 are replaced by references to 'being' or 'existing' in the claims of 1.9-11 (cf. Asurmendi, *Du non-sens*, 25-26). We should not hold our breath, therefore, for the day when the wind has blown enough on everything, or the sea has finally been filled. Qohelet states the matter simply in 1.9: because the world never really moves on, nothing can be new, and the future is going to be the same as the past and present.[2]

The closing verses, 1.10-11, may look like a simple elaboration of this general assertion, but they return to the earlier contrast between the different sorts of existence enjoyed by humanity and the world, addressing a consequence that will be of great significance to Qohelet. Since the world is constant and humans are not, they can see only a snapshot of it, which can easily lead them to a misapprehension of its character, through a misinterpretation of what they see. Just as a mayfly might assume that the sun only crosses the sky once, because it never lives to see the process repeated, so humans lack the perspective to understand that everything is like this. Accordingly, when someone proclaims anything to be new, and so asserts implicitly that the world has changed, they can never be right—because nothing can ever truly be new. The limits on human perception are not offset by some collective memory, moreover, and just as the distant past is already forgotten, even the future, and the future beyond the future, will one day be forgotten. Humans each exist only for a brief moment, in a world that stretches vast distances into the past and future beyond them, and this sets significant limits upon their comprehension of that world and, as will become clear, their place within it.[3]

---

[2] Enns (9) says, 'The sun, wind, and streams labor, but in the end they are no better off than when they started. There is no profit or surplus to their struggles.' That is undoubtedly true, but I think the point here is that the phenomena model not the human inability to find a profit, but the context that gives rise to the inability.

[3] It is important to be clear that although Qohelet contrasts the impermanence of humans with the permanence of the world, he considers humans to be a part of the world, and to play a role within its processes. In emphasizing that point against longstanding traditions of interpretation that see an invitation in the book to disengage humans from the world, it is possible, however, to go too far in the

Qohelet will return to such issues in ch. 3, where he identifies the constancy of the world and the ignorance of humans as results of direct divine intention or intervention. Things are supposed to be this way, and there is nothing in these verses to suggest either that Qohelet abhors the nature of this world or that he believes there to be any way to remove the limits on human perception of it—although he will shortly describe some aspects in much more negative terms (1.14-15). The situation that he has outlined does, however, set up a problem that will soon become clearer from his next account: it is only because they fail to perceive, or at least to think through the consequences of a changeless world lasting beyond them, that humans believe they can affect this world. This is a key aspect of his complaint that everything is *hebel*: the world can be perceived but not actually grasped, leading humans to miscalculate their relationship with it.

On attempts to dismiss these verses as secondary, see the commentary on 1.2-3, above. I see no good reason to reject their authenticity, but their character and position does make it easy to think of 1.4-11 as a sort of prologue, sitting outside the main speech. This impression might be strengthened, moreover, by the probability that they are written in a quasi-poetic style,[4] although without the

---

other direction. Müller suggests that Qohelet moves towards actively merging the human and the natural here, in a quasi-mythical way, both through the juxtaposition of natural and human processes, and through a personification of the sun in v. 5, which attributes emotion to it. See Müller, 'Der unheimliche Gast', 443. It is not clear, however, either that Qohelet anywhere actually seeks to assert the significance of humanity for nature (Müller speaks of a 'gegenseitige Integration von Menschenwelt und Naturwelt', 'a mutual integration of the human and natural worlds'), or that it is a deliberate purpose of 1.4-11 directly to associate human with natural phenomena.

[4] Hertzberg (73) takes it to be 'in schlichter, edler Sprache geschrieben, lauft es in rhythmisch freier Form ab, meist in Dreiern und Zweiern, die zwanglos und doch in metrischer Absicht geordnet sind'—'written in a simple, fine style, it proceeds in a rhythmically free form, mostly in tristichs and distichs that are informal, but set out with an eye to metre'. Gordis speaks of 'rhythmic prose', and Verheij suggests that the passage 'is at a rather blurred part of the borderline between poetry and prose'; cf. Verheij, 'Words Speaking for Themselves', 183. Verheij draws attention to the pervasive use of assonance and repetition which is characteristic of vv. 4-7, and similar devices are explored in the more wide-ranging study of 1.3-11 by Tin-sheung, who also identifies different types of parallelism and other patterns, but who works with too absolute a distinction between poetry and prose; cf. Tin-Sheung, 'Qoheleth 1:3-11'.

formal consistency of a discrete poem, which gives them a certain rhetorical force—even if it is hard to discern the tight structuring that is often attributed to them.[5] Of course, similar features have generally been identified in, for example, ch. 3, which is clearly not a prologue, and it might be better to adopt the simpler assumption that Qohelet employs such a style at times for reasons that have little to do necessarily with marking the broader structure of the work. What suggests that these verses form a prelude is not so much the way they are expressed, as the fact that they seem to portray Qohelet's developed view of the world, formed through reflection on the experiences that he will start to describe in 1.12, and so stand outside the memoir that will shape the rest of his monologue.[6]

---

[5] There have been various attempts to analyze the literary structure of the section, and these tend to bring out the close correspondences of theme and vocabulary across the verses, without offering any consensus as to its overall structure. Indeed, a comparison of the similar studies by Auffret and Rousseau throws more light on the subjectivity of their methods than on the organization and parameters of the 'poetry'; cf. Auffret, 'Rien du tout de nouveau'; Rousseau, 'Structure'. Those studies do not apparently see any difficulty in the often highly irregular sizes of the units which they propose or adopt, but if this material really is constructed as a separate poem, we might reasonably expect some greater consistency and distinctiveness, or at least patterning, in such matters as the length and number of stichs. Loretz's rather different analysis, which involves a stichometric component, similarly demonstrates some coherence of length and structure within individual verses or strophes, but no overall regularity or coherence, and his understanding of vv. 4-8 as a separate poem owes as much to exegetical supposition as to analysis of the formal characteristics. See his 'Poetry and Prose', 165-67, and also his 'Anfänge', 226-32. Lohfink offers a simpler analysis, in which he breaks the material down into four units: v. 4 (2 stichs), v. 5 (2 stichs), vv. 6-8 (3+4+4 stichs), and vv. 9-11 (3+4+4 stichs), within which he discerns various connections, and which as a whole he presents as a chiastic scheme (Geschichte–Kosmos–Kosmos–Geschichte, History–Cosmos–Cosmos–History). Many aspects of this scheme, however, seem to be driven by interpretative concerns (Lohfink explicitly integrates his concern with the progression of ideas), and in formal terms are rather arbitrary. See Lohfink, 'Wiederkehr'. Since there is no general agreement even as to whether vv. 9-11 are in verse, let alone as to whether they belong together with vv. 4-8, it can hardly be said that we are dealing with a self-evidently separate and formally coherent poem, which stands out against a context of prose.

[6] It does not seem necessary to adopt the proposal of Glasser, *Le Procès*, 33, that the prologue was only written after the rest of the work was complete. Qohelet's thought is portrayed in the monologue as changing and developing, but that does not mean that the author initially had no idea where it would end up.

Their rather grand style may be a clue, however, to the fact that Qohelet relies less on logic than on rhetoric in these verses. It is a leap, in particular, from accepting Qohelet's observations about his chosen phenomena to accepting his more general claim that they represent the whole nature of the world: from the fact that some processes are endless, it does not follow that everything must be part of an endless process. When we reach v. 9, furthermore, Qohelet himself jumps from statements about the lack of an end to claims about the lack of a beginning. Again, even if it is true that nothing really ends, it does not follow that nothing can begin. In terms of his broader thought, it is possible, perhaps, to understand what Qohelet means by the seemingly outrageous statements about novelty and memory to which this jump brings him, and we might paraphrase the claims rather differently: nothing has come out of nowhere, even if our short-sightedness leads us to suppose that it has. Qohelet himself, however, makes no attempt to explain or to qualify these stark assertions, and 1.4-11 as a whole make no effort to lead us through a series of propositions. If we can speak of an argument here at all, therefore, it is an argument by analogy. Qohelet puts forward a vision of a world in which constancy is masked by movement, and within which apparent beginnings or ends are in fact mere checkpoints on the way. In various respects, the phenomena that he adduces show how processes within that world might be envisaged and understood, and in doing so they speak to the plausibility of the vision, but they do not in themselves actually offer evidence of its reality. Given the breadth of the term, it would be difficult to deny that this material is in some sense 'philosophical'—but any such description must be qualified by a recognition that it does not rest on any serious attempt to develop a logical argument.

That said, it is important to Qohelet's case that his examples should not be open to challenge here: if he does not win the assent of the audience to his observations about specific phenomena, then he will not gain their assent to his broader propositions. This in itself is a potential argument against interpretations of the text which endow those phenomena with unusual characteristics, and that is why it is curious to find in almost all modern translations and commentaries the assumption that in 1.6 Qohelet talks about the wind blowing in circles, which hardly corresponds to normal human experience, or a barely less common interpretation of 1.8 that makes Qohelet see everything as worn out—a characteristic that would presumably be beyond human observation, even if it did not sit uncomfortably with the picture he is trying to draw. Those instances, and others, will be discussed in the notes and comments below, but before rushing to condemn such readings on the basis of an overall interpretation of Qohelet's intentions here, it is important to note that they arise not just from difficulties in the text, but at least in part from attempts to align his analogies with a widespread and very different understanding of 1.4-11, which has had a profound impact on exegesis for many centuries.

According to this understanding, Qohelet is indeed opposed to a linear, progressive understanding of the world, but the changelessness that he sees instead is rooted specifically in a cyclical worldview. Accordingly, 1.9 should be read not as a statement that everything stays the same, but as a claim that everything is repeated, while 1.10 can be taken to assert quite literally that every thing (or person) has enjoyed, in some sense, a former existence. This reading takes its cue in large part from the cyclical character of the sun's journey in the first of Qohelet's examples, although some commentators see it already in the coming and going of 1.4. It runs into exegetical difficulties in 1.6, however, with the need to present the travel of the wind as circular, and into more specifically linguistic difficulties in 1.7, where the Hebrew can hardly yield the required sense of rivers flowing back somehow to their origin; 1.8 is generally discounted as an aside. The problem that these difficulties present for the reading as a whole lies in the fact that every analogy cited by Qohelet has to be cyclical for it to work. A looser concept of non-progression in the world can incorporate cyclical phenomena—it does not matter whether rivers flow in loops or not so long as they fail ever to fill the sea—but a cyclical concept cannot incorporate other, non-cyclical phenomena. At the very least, therefore, it seems difficult to reconcile the way Qohelet expresses himself, especially in 1.7, with any supposition that he is actively promoting a cyclical worldview. It is also hard, moreover, to identify such a perspective anywhere else in the book as a significant component of his worldview, so this reading tends to detach 1.4-11 and to have it make a point about the world that will never be picked up again. As will already be evident, my own view is that this effort to find a pattern results in no great exegetical insights, but it does lead to much forced and unsympathetic reading of the text.

Whether or not there is a cyclical aspect to Qohelet's presentation of the world, this presentation lacks, and possibly excludes any idea that the world is developing or moving toward an end. It will become clear, at least by ch. 3, that Qohelet's views are not anti-teleological—indeed, they turn out to be strongly deterministic—so the continuity that he portrays here should not be understood to result from any absence of divine plan or purpose. Qohelet shows no sign, however, of any belief that God's plans involve an eschaton or other significant future change to the world, and although his claim that the world will persist 'forever' in 1.4 has naturally provoked resistance and re-interpretation by more eschatologically minded readers, he clearly expects the current state and nature of the world to persist at least into the distant future. Although this stands in contrast to the expectations of much other early Jewish literature, there is no clear indication either that Qohelet is deliberately opposing himself to, say, contemporary apocalyptic writers and earlier eschatological ideas (cf. Krüger, 'Dekonstuktion'; Perdue, 'Wisdom and Apocalyptic'),[7] or that the perpetuity of the world is itself at the front of his thinking. If his principal concern is more probably to emphasize the impermanence of humans, and their correspondingly limited perception, then his statements about the permanence of the world may be intended more as a foil to his statements about humans than as declarations of belief in themselves.

In this introductory sketch of the world, none of the natural phenomena are associated with divine activity or creation, and Qohelet evinces no interest in their createdness, as such. When he returns to these issues in ch. 3, he will introduce God as an actor and emphasize the permanence and inalterability of divine works (3.14-15), but also the inability of humans to perceive the entire scope of what God has done (3.11)—apparently with an implication that his actions and achievements are already in place, rather than moving toward some future fulfilment. It is difficult to extrapolate anything precise from this, but what Qohelet appears to sketch is a world that functions more as a finished, self-contained machine, created and

---

[7] I have touched on some specific claims elsewhere, but there is an extensive literature on this topic that cannot be considered in detail here. Much has been reviewed in Schultz's recent 'Was Qohelet?', and I tend to share the scepticism of that article about suggestions that Qohelet deliberately engages with, or rejects, eschatological and apocalyptic claims.

maintained by God (cf. 3.15), than as a work in progress. Accordingly, the determinism that governs human lives arises not from some divine attempt to shape history toward a particular end, but from the role of humans as cogs within that machine. Given the way in which he presents them here, furthermore, Qohelet may well not believe that the world has in any sense been set up for the benefit of humans or with any particular concern for them other than as components. His monologue is anthropocentric inasmuch as it is concerned with human lives, but the whole thrust of his questioning suggests that these lives are not lived in an anthropocentric world. Indeed, it is the very fact that this world is so much bigger and more enduring than humans that makes it a challenge for them to find something for themselves within it.

1.4

One generation goes, another generation comes,
while the world stays forever constant.

Commentary

The Hebrew conjunction which links the two parts of the verse can be used to mean 'and' or 'but'; to adopt either translation, however, would be to impose a contrast or a correlation between the two statements, and it is not clear that either of these is intended. Fox is right, on the one hand, to reject any idea that Qohelet is setting the transience of humanity in opposition to the permanence of the world: it is human individuals, not the species, who have a more temporary character than the world. On the other hand, it is not easy to ignore the basic contrast inherent in the verbs of motion applied to humans and the description of the world as fixed, or stationary. I have taken the verse, then, to be indicating not the difference between humanity and the world as a whole, but the problem which the nature of the world poses for the humans who each encounter it so briefly. Qohelet is concerned here neither with the ephemerality of humans in itself, nor with some cyclical aspect to human existence, but with the problem posed by human mortality in the face of the world's permanence, and with the fact that each human life is too short to observe the true character of the world (physical and human), while each human memory is too short for humanity as a whole to accumulate such an understanding.[1] The brevity of our lives allows us to see no more than a snapshot of things that started long before us, and will reach no end before we die.

Samet ('Qohelet 1,4') has drawn attention to a reading adopted by Rashbam and by Ibn Ezra, which links the second part of the verse to the idea expressed in 12.7, that humans will return to the dust

---

[1] Lohfink, 'Wiederkehr', 127, also argues for an understanding of the poem which links the passing of generations to forgetfulness, but takes the unifying theme here to be the lurking shadow of death and mortality.

from which they were created, and according to which there is not a contrast here between humans and the world through which they pass, but a suggestion that humanity is constantly recycled from the 'earth'. For those keen to find 'cycles' in these verses (who include Samet), that interpretation offers a way potentially to deal with an apparently static earth. It is not one that was picked up by earlier readers, however, probably for the reason that it requires a certain imprecision: humans are not actually made from 'earth' in 12.7—or in 3.20, where the idea is also evoked—but from 'dust', which merely returns to the earth, and the words are distinct in Qohelet's Hebrew. Although the imagery is very attractive, therefore, it is unlikely that we are supposed to make such a connection. If we do, moreover, then the 'earth' is still merely the background against which human transience is portrayed, not explicitly the material from which generations are perpetually formed and re-formed.

Notes

1.4 generation] Although דור is often used in relation to long periods of time, it does not lose its specific reference to human generations (compare, e.g., Joel 2.2 with Joel 1.3), and so this is not simply a reference to the passing of ages (and correspondingly, it does not embody the ambiguity suggested by Crenshaw and Ingram).[2] Equally, it is not a reference to cyclical movements illustrated in the following verses, as Ogden suggests.[3] Piotti, 'La descrizione',

---

[2] Ingram, *Ambiguity*, 59. The word may express long periods of time in terms of the generations which occupy them, but it does not mean 'age' in some more general way, and although a number of commentators who believe the word to have such a sense cite D. N. Freedman and J. Lundbom, 'דּוֹר, *dôr*', 3:169-81 (174), this article makes it very clear that any reference to eras is grounded firmly in the idea of human generations. That there may sometimes be a more extended poetical sense seems possible, and Whybray, 'Wonders of Nature', 154; cf. 159, makes the case for a less literal understanding in Isa 41.4; 51.9. Those debatable cases, however, hardly affirm his view that the noun has 'a cyclical connotation', and we may reasonably ask why a society with no geological perspective or concept of a long pre-human history would have distinguished specific 'eras' or 'ages', except in relation to human life and activity.

[3] See Ogden, 'The Interpretation of דור', and the response by Fox, 'Qohelet 1.4', who points out that 'דור, whatever its etymology, never means "cycle" in Hebrew (or in any other Northwest Semitic language); and it is not cycles that "go and come", but rather things within cycles' (I am not sure how Longman interprets this response as agreement with Ogden's understanding of דור). Ackroyd, 'The

ultimately rejects the idea that Qohelet is talking specifically about cycles and circular movements in 1.4-7, but notes (215-16) the Akkadian *dūru* (*dūru* A in *CAD*), which is used of city-walls and for, as Piotti puts it, 'parti del corpo di forma tondeggiante', 'parts of the body which have a roundish shape'. Roundness or circularity, however, is not a primary connotation of that noun, and the body-parts in question are all clearly comparable to walls. Another noun, *dūru* B, which Piotti also notes, is more plausibly related to the Hebrew, but is used to connote permanence, and that sense is hardly possible here.

1.4 goes…comes] Although either could be read in the consonantal text as *qatal*, the verbs have rightly been taken by the versions as participles which express continuous action (J-M §121 c)—which is the form of most of the verbs in vv. 2-7 (on those in v. 5a, see below). The association with birth and death is found also in 5.15 and 6.4, although it is not a particular implication of the pairing, and is probably absent in 8.10. Fox, 'Qohelet 1.4', makes the point that we would expect the verbs to appear in the reverse order if the emphasis here were on mortality *per se*; this is also an obstacle to understanding the verse in terms of the birth and death of a single generation (see Lohfink, 'Wiederkehr', 132 n. 11).

1.4 world] Fox emphasizes that הארץ does not specifically suggest the physical world, and characterizes it as '"le monde" rather than "la terre"', citing Gen 11.1; 1 Kgs 2.2; and Ps 33.8. However, the word ארץ really incorporates both ideas, not unlike 'the world' in English. Again, it seems unlikely that this constitutes a deliberate ambiguity, as Ingram, *Ambiguity*, 60, maintains: the dual reference is only an issue if one reads into this passage a specific contrast between the physical and human worlds, which, admittedly, many commentators have been inclined to do. Going to the other extreme, HCM see a type of synecdoche here, with the container referring to the contents (just as, they say, we might use 'keg' to talk of the beer inside a keg). This is part of a reading that takes the second part of the verse to accord with, not contrast with, the first, so that the going and coming of generations is a way of expressing the continuity of humankind, and 'world' actually just means 'people'. Especially in view of what follows, that seems too restrictive, even if we allow the possibility that such a device is being used. הארץ is neither just humanity nor just everything except humanity.

1.4 forever] On the usage of לעולם, see Schoors, *The Preacher* II, 221-25. HCM note that its position in the clause gives it the focus, as we might expect given the contrast with more transient 'generations' that is apparently intended here (although they prefer not to read the verse that way). Some understandings of the term owe more to theological presupposition than to lexicographical precision, and we need not engage with questions of

Meaning of Hebrew דור Considered', 9-10, expresses serious reservations about connecting the term to cyclic concepts of time, and notes the broader problems involved in assigning meanings on an etymological basis.

its relationship to philosophical concepts of infinity or eternity, which it is not Qohelet's purpose to assert. Here, as often, the sense is 'in perpetuity' (so McNeile). G's εἰς τὸν αἰῶνα is rather more loaded; cf. σ' γῆ αἰώνιος ἕστηκε,[4] '(the) earth stands forever', and note Jerome's shift from *in saeculo* (Hie) back to *in aeternum* (V), which is the rendering he had adopted in his earlier revision of the Old Latin.[5] Lohfink's supposition that this is a liturgical allusion, drawing on statements about God, is speculative but not entirely implausible; it offers a slim basis, however, for his notion that we are dealing here with an acclamation of the cosmos coloured by Greek pantheistic ideas. See also his 'Wiederkehr', 133.

1.4 constant] Lit. '(is) standing' (participle). A discussion of this word is reported in Midrash Qohelet: מה הוא עומדת מעמדת, 'What does it mean, "it stands"? (answer:) "It causes to stand"', with subsequent rabbinic explanations that the earth preserves its commands and preserves produce. Euringer, taking this to invite an emendation,[6] explores and rightly rejects the possibility that it reflects an original hiph'il, from which the initial מ has been lost. עמד can connote endurance, but it can also mean 'stand still' (e.g. Josh 10.13): both senses are in play here, but perhaps especially the latter.

---

[4] Although αἰώνιος is secure, the full citation has to be treated with some caution: as Field and Marshall point out, Montfaucon cites it as the reading of 'one codex', which is not specified and which has not subsequently been identified. See Montfaucon, *Origenis Hexaplorum quae supersunt*, 56.

[5] Caspari, *Hiob*, 6; Leanza, 'Le tre versione', 90. Jerome uses *in saecula* or similar expressions elsewhere (e.g. Ps 78.69 V) to express an indefinite period of time in the future, but he uses the singular *in saeculo* of activity within the present world or age (e.g. Ps 73.12 V; 4 Esd 3.34 V) or in a future age (Mk 10.30 V; Lk 18.30 V). Accordingly, *in saeculo* has less implication than does *in aeternum* of a world that will continue forever in its present form.

[6] It is unlikely that it was intended that way; cf. Alexander, 'Why No Textual Criticism?'

1.5-6

(1.5) And the sun has risen, and the sun gone down,
and returned to its place—but then it rises there,
(1.6) going southward, and turning northward.
Turning. Turning. The wind goes,
and on to its surroundings, the wind comes back again.

Commentary

Although emendations are often made to bring them into line with each other, there are distinctions between the verb forms in v. 5 which emphasize that we are dealing with a sequence of events: the sun has completed its round and returned, then rises again. As the text stands, it does not explicitly 'return', but reaches its place using a verb that is often translated in terms of 'panting'—a translation that underpins both such renderings as the RSV's 'hastens', and a more general supposition that Qohelet is personifying the sun here. There is no strong reason, however, to believe that the verb can have any such sense, and it probably appears here as the result of a simple (but early) error. More significant problems surround the question of what happens next: does the sun simply rise, or does it rise and then travel to the south and north? To put it another way, when does Qohelet stop talking about the sun, and start talking about the wind?

We cannot just work this out from the form. The observations in the preceding v. 4 consisted of one line (two stichs, if we think in terms of poetry here), while those that will follow in vv. 7 and 8 each consist of two lines, or four stichs. Here, in vv. 5-6, we have two observations, one about the sun, the other about the wind, but seemingly three lines (probably six stichs) to divide between them; in structural terms, therefore, the crucial material in the middle, 'going southward, and turning northward. Turning. Turning', could readily belong to either.[1] Accordingly, the RSV translates: 'The

---

[1] Rousseau, 'Structure', 203, divides vv. 5-6 unconvincingly into four pairs of stichs, some of which are very short indeed, others much longer. It is not

sun rises and the sun goes down, and hastens to the place where it rises. The wind blows to the south, and goes round to the north; round and round goes the wind.' If this material refers to the wind, however, then it is important to note that 'the wind' does not appear in the Hebrew until long after 'going southward' (and that the RSV's first reference to 'wind' translates nothing in the original text). Depending on how one treats the prepositions, there are some six to eight words between the first verb and its supposed subject, and these include four more verbs, only to the last of which is 'the wind' attached. Since readers would expect a new subject to be specified straight after the first verb, it is more natural for them to assume that the sun remains the object right up to the point that the wind takes over explicitly. If the wind is actually supposed to be the subject from the outset, therefore, then the delay in specifying it seems so extreme that this must be considered a deliberate device—and some commentators have indeed supposed that Qohelet is luring the reader into an initial misreading of the text (although they have offered no very convincing explanations as to why he should be doing so).[2]

Despite that difficulty, there is virtual unanimity amongst modern scholars that the subject of 6a is the wind;[3] Murphy and Lys, for instance, both describe this as 'certain', and few trouble even to

straightforward to achieve a neat division into stichs here, which in itself supports the view that we are dealing with something less formal than carefully structured verse.

[2] So, e.g., Wilson, 'Artful Ambiguity', who sees here 'an example of deliberate, purposeful, artful ambiguity' which 'gives the reader cause to reflect' (358)—although he does not make it clear what exactly we are supposed to reflect on. Of course, the text is only really 'misleading', as Wilson suggests, if the sun is not actually the subject of the clause. Whilst happy to agree, moreover, that Ecclesiastes shows no reluctance to engage in a variety of devices, I am not quite sure what the point of this one is supposed to be in this context. Good, 'The Unfilled Sea', 66-67, sees not ambiguity but a delay which is 'affective': 'a continuity of image...masks a discontinuity of subject'. Again, one may accept the possibility of the device, but still be left wondering 'Why here?'

[3] Notable exceptions include Whitley, although he would delete 5b altogether as intrusive, and Graetz, who offers no specific justification, however, for his translation: 'Die Sonne...geht dort (wieder) auf, geht gen Süden und wendet sich gen Norden' ('the sun rises there again, goes toward the south and turns toward the north'). Rather earlier, Clarke also linked v. 6a to v. 5, noting the evidence of the older versions, and remarking that, 'the author refers to the approximations of the sun to the northern and southern tropics, viz., of Cancer and Capricorn'.

discuss the alternative as a possibility.⁴ The reason usually given is simply that, as Good puts it: 'At the right time of year in Palestine the sun is in the south. But when we read *wĕsôbēb ʾel-ṣāpôn* we know that the subject of v. 6 cannot be the sun. In the northern hemisphere, one never looks north for the sun, except in Arctic latitudes' ('The Unfilled Sea', 66). In other words, because the sun does not appear in the north, Qohelet must be talking about the wind even if this requires an unnatural reading of the Hebrew.

It is very important to note, however, that almost all ancient commentators adopt a quite different understanding and take the sun to be the subject of 6a, with a degree of unanimity close to that of the contrary modern consensus. Sara Japhet ('Goes to the South', 291) notes 'the vigorous life and wide distribution' of this interpretation, 'which dominated many generations and schools of exegesis far removed from one another.' To be sure, the interpretation of 6a in terms of the wind may be attested as early as Symmachus, is implied by the Masoretic punctuation, and is later affirmed both by the midrashim on Qohelet and by Ibn Ezra. It was for centuries, however, very much the minority view.⁵ If this seems difficult to understand, given that ancient commentators saw the same movement of the sun across the sky as do modern ones, then we need to understand that they were looking beyond the most visible aspects of that movement.

As it happens, the sun does essentially go round to the north after setting, even if we cannot see it; it also moves northward and southward seasonally, rising and setting due east and due west at the equinoxes, but at points more than 20 degrees north or south of those points at the solstices—a very visible shift, with which ancient observers were familiar. Modern assumptions about what Qohelet might have said are posited on a view that he would or could have had no awareness of such movements—but that seems to be contradicted by the willingness of early readers to accept the sun as subject here even though they were presumably no better

---

⁴ Loretz, 'Poetry and Prose', 165, even suggests we may 'assume' that there was originally an explicit reference to 'the wind', subsequently omitted through scribal error.

⁵ Japhet, 'Goes to the South', 309-10, takes the great turning-point to have been the appearance, during the Reformation, of translations based on Masoretic texts, and shaped by their presentation.

informed than Qohelet about the insights of modern astronomy. Grammatically and stylistically, the text strongly favours taking the sun as the subject, so if we are to take the wind instead, or even to acknowledge an ambiguity, we need a good reason to suppose that the author would not have put into Qohelet's mouth any reference to northward travel of the sun, and that means, in effect, that we have to establish what the author himself might have believed—which is easier said than done.

To those raised with an understanding that we were all flat-earthers before Columbus, it can be a surprise to discover just how close Hellenistic and Roman writers could come to modern descriptions of such matters, even if their wider cosmological understandings differed in important respects from our own.[6] Writing in the first century BCE, for example, Cicero (*De Natura Deorum* 2.19, my translation) was able to say of the sun that:

> Its motion is such that it first fills the countries of the earth with a flood of light, and then leaves them in darkness now on one side and now on the other; for night is caused merely by the shadow of the earth, which intercepts the light of the sun. Its daily and nightly paths have the same regularity. Also the sun, by at one time slightly approaching and at another time slightly receding, causes a moderate variation of temperature. For the passage of about 365¼ diurnal revolutions of the sun completes the circuit of a year; and by bending its course now towards the north and now towards the south the sun causes summers and winters and the two seasons, of which one follows the waning of winter and the other that of summer.

Considerably earlier, Herodotus (*Histories* 4.42) reports, although himself cast doubts on, the claims of Phoenician sailors in the seventh century to have seen the sun in the north as they sailed around Africa (and so were in the southern hemisphere). Although

---

[6] Although heliocentric models of the solar system were not unknown in the ancient world, they were not widespread. Along with Josh 10.12-13, where the sun and moon stand still in the sky, this passage from Ecclesiastes was, in fact, much later to become a scriptural obstacle to the adoption of the Copernican view which underpins modern understandings, and the ways in which the problem was addressed by followers of Copernicus offer insights into the changing relationship between science and scripture in the course of the sixteenth century. See especially Giostra, 'Accomodar i pronunciati'.

explanations of the wider structures differed, most educated people in the Hellenistic and Roman worlds would have thought of the earth as a sphere around which the sun travelled, effectively in an orbit that varied slightly across the seasons—and would correspondingly have had no trouble believing that the sun passed behind the earth to the north. What everybody else thought is more difficult to say. When Vergil (*Georgics* 1.231-256), writing around the same time as Cicero, described a world divided into five zones by the effect of the sun—ice at each extreme, intense heat in the middle, with just two temperate strips left habitable for humans—he was probably reflecting a popular, if slightly less precise understanding; when he talks elsewhere (*Aeneid* 12.113-115) about the chariot of the sun emerging from the depths of the ocean at the start of the day, however, he is probably drawing on mythological motifs for the sake of poetry. It is difficult to gauge the extent to which such motifs remained influential, but they certainly should not be considered normative.

One particular idea, often mentioned by commentators, is that the sun passed through some underground or underwater route, or more specifically the underworld itself. This idea does indeed seem to have persisted at least widely enough for it to be noted by rabbinic sources (*b. Pesaḥim* 94b, in a lengthy discussion of such matters, attributes it to non-Jewish scientists), and was probably derived either from earlier Egyptian or Mesopotamian ideas. We have no reason, however, to suppose that it would have been held widely in the Hellenistic world, let alone by Jews of the Persian period or earlier, despite Whybray's unqualified assertion that this is the idea underpinning 1.5 ('Wonders of Nature', 107-108). The principal ancient alternatives to Hellenistic ideas of the sun circling a spherical earth seem instead to have depended more generally on Mesopotamian ideas that the sun entered and left through gates or other entrances in the sky, with no clear consensus about the direction it took, or where it spent its time between these. The *Astronomical Book of Enoch* (1 En 72–82) describes in great detail the entrances and exits of the sun through a series of gates that correspond to its north/south movement across the year, and 72.8 tellingly declares, moreover, that the sun sets and returns *via* the north in order to rise again in the east. This text, probably composed no later than the third century BCE, shows that at least one other Jewish writer, most likely close in time to the author of Ecclesiastes, was both fully aware of seasonal movement northward, and convinced that the sun moved to the north daily when it was out of sight.

As Japhet (291-93) has argued, furthermore, an understanding of 1.6 in these terms seems to underpin several rabbinic sources that draw on a common earlier source, and, even much later, Rashbam understands the sun's journey not as semi-circular, but as circular: once it has set, and so dropped out of sight, it does not cut directly across from west to east, but passes through those points of the compass which it has not traversed during daylight hours. Correspondingly, in the course of a whole day, it travels southward from the east (where it has risen), sets in the west, and then travels to the north, from where it moves round once again to rise in the east. There are vaguer or dissident opinions in Jewish sources: *b. Baba Batra* 25b has R. Joshua (citing 1.6) argue that the world is like a tent, on which all sides except the north are open, and the sun moves round to the north, behind the tent and so out of sight, but it also records the view of R. Eliezer, that the sun simply reverses direction after setting, and returns 'above the firmament', while *b. Pesaḥim* 94b takes the traditional Jewish understanding to be just that the sun returns 'above the sky'.[7] The Targum, on the other hand, melds a version of the idea that the sun passes through 'windows' with the notion that it passes through 'the deep' to create a complicated, and very probably confused account of its movements.

What all this boils down to for our present purpose, though, is that it seems perfectly reasonable to suppose that the author of Ecclesiastes would quite readily have spoken about movement of the sun through the north, whether he was influenced by Hellenistic perceptions or by more eastern traditions. As 1 Enoch in particular shows, and various rabbinic discussions also affirm, Jewish intellectuals were well aware both of seasonal movements of the sunrise and sunset along the north–south axis, and of the idea that the sun

---

[7] The tractate does, however, also describe a seasonal movement that permits the sun to pass over mountains, settled areas, seas and deserts at different times of year. There is a similar discussion in the Midrash Rabbah on Genesis at 6.8, which describes three different rabbinic opinions: the sun returns above the firmament, below it, or above it in summer and below it in winter (which is why wells are respectively cooler or warmer than the air at those times of year). See Simon-Shoshan, 'The Heavens Proclaim', 82-83.

completed a circuit through all four points of the compass on its daily round. There is really no reason on that basis, therefore, to run against the language of the text, and to suppose that the subject has changed from sun to wind in 1.6 long before the wind is mentioned.

If we allow that Qohelet is probably still talking about the sun in the first part of v. 6, this means, of course, that there is no simple presentation of two cycles here—one based on the east–west movement of the sun, the other on a north–south movement of the wind—and it becomes harder to discern any cyclical pattern in the account. It does, however, give a more specific point to the statements about the sun, which is presented not as travelling endlessly, but as travelling *again* after completing its circuit. It also relieves us of the need to account for a description of the wind that bears no resemblance to the normal behaviour of the wind, either in Palestine or anywhere else.[8] It remains difficult, however, to pin down precisely where Qohelet stops talking about the sun, and it is striking that the early interpreters who saw a continued reference to the sun in v. 6a generally understood Qohelet to be talking about the

---

[8] A useful summary is offered by Orni and Efrat, 'Atmospheric Pressure and Winds'. The prevailing winds in the area are not north/south, as claimed by, e.g., Plumptre: rather, during the summer, the wind typically blows eastward from the Mediterranean during the day, and then, more lightly, westward toward the Mediterranean at night: this is a matter of relative temperature and air pressure over the sea and the land (which retains heat after the sun has set). Correspondingly, when Hertzberg, 'Palästinische Bezüge', 113-14, suggests that the wind may pass through the north or south as it shifts between the west and east, so that the verse refers to those transitions, he shows a misunderstanding of the factors that drive the wind direction: the summer breezes do not involve the wind veering, but display a simple reversal. The winter weather comes closer to the mark: at that time of year, cyclonic conditions can give rise to winds which blow initially from the north- or south-east, and then veer to the west, the north-west, and ultimately the north-east once more, as the cyclone itself moves. However, the wind does not blow directly from the south as part of this process, and it is questionable, furthermore, whether anyone would present such conditions as typical of the wind's behaviour in the region. It is also doubtful, on the other hand, that the description can serve as a useful datum for setting the book's place of composition outside Palestine, as argued by Humbert, *Recherches*, 113. The problem is really that the wind simply does not lend itself anywhere to a description in terms of fixed, changeless cycles. Margoliouth, 'Prologue', 468-69, suggests that the book has imported an opinion from Aristotle (*Meteorologica* 361a), which is simply inappropriate to Palestine. For Aristotle, though, the wind does not turn through these points: they are each the origin of a separate wind.

sun right up to the end of v. 6. They did so by taking the mentions of 'wind' in 6b either as references to the 'spirit' or 'will' of the sun, or in the sense 'direction/side'. These are legitimate understandings of the word *rwḥ*, 'wind' (although 'side' is an Aramaic, rather than a Hebrew usage), and 1 En 72.5, moreover, speaks of the chariot of the sun being driven, in some sense, by the wind. Such readings should not, therefore, be dismissed as fanciful or forced, and his choice of vocabulary suggests that even the Septuagint translator may have understood the text in these terms. It is not clear, however, why Qohelet should have switched from talking about the sun itself to the wind that moves it, if that is what we are supposed to understand, while any reference to 'sides' or somesuch requires significant syntactical *legerdemain*. It seems likely, therefore, that such interpretations emerged not primarily because they offered the most natural reading of the text, but because, if the text were taken to be talking directly about the wind, then the depiction offered seemed unnatural or unrealistic.[9]

This is not such a problem if we dispense with the idea that cycles, rather than movement, are the issue here. Letting go of that understanding also makes it simpler to read the last part of the verse in terms of normal Hebrew usage, so that the wind blows again 'upon its surroundings', rather than giving a special sense to a common word and having the wind move 'on its circuits'. That special sense corresponds well to an understanding that Qohelet is trying to illustrate perpetual, closed circularity, but not so well to the common human experience of the wind, which may move through different points of the compass under certain conditions, but does not characteristically move in fixed circles. As Krüger points out, against Lohfink and Whybray ('Wonders of Nature', 108), Qohelet will himself later note the unpredictability of the winds in 11.5, and it is unlikely that he is trying to portray their movements here as fixed. It remains difficult, however, to say whether the 'turning, turning' in the middle of the verse refers to the sun or to the wind (or should maybe even be split between them). We have to mark the break with punctuation, but, free of such constraints, the author has perhaps deliberately made it possible to read the expression with reference

---

[9] It is important to be clear that the interpretation of the subject as the sun in the first part does not depend upon rejecting any mention of the wind in the second part, as Dell, 'Cycle', 184 n. 15, seems to suggest in response to Japhet.

either to the sun or to the wind, so that 'turning, turning' provides both a transition and a connection between the two accounts. In any case, I take the sense of 6b to be that however much the wind twists and turns, it never finishes blowing on what is around it, so that, like the sun, it expends its effort on an endless task.

Notes

1.5 sun] In those places where the gender can be determined, שמש occurs slightly more often as masculine than as feminine; here it is masculine, while in 12.2 it is feminine, but not too much should be read into the difference: cf. Sir 43.2 (masc.); 50.7 (fem.).

1.5 has risen] Some scholars have proposed that וזרח (pointed as qatal in M) is the result of metathesis within an original participle וזרח (e.g. Lauha, Longman, *BHS*), or have simply vocalized the existing consonants as a conjunction + participle (e.g. *BH³*, Krüger); with similar adjustments to the following ובא, either approach would bring both verbs into line with the surrounding participles, although it is not strictly necessary to do so in order to retain a sense 'rises...sets'—as Salters, 'Textual Criticism', 61, observes, the consecutive perfect in this context 'produces the required frequentative tense'. On my own preference for a past tense, and a distinction between these verbs and the others, see the note 'it rises there', below. The witness of the versions suggests that they all read זרח, but it is unlikely that they all interpreted it as a consecutive perfect, as Seow suggests.

G καὶ ἀνατέλλει retains the conjunction (although it has been omitted, probably as superfluous, in many manuscripts) and reads a present indicative verb, which is what it uses for the surrounding participles. Elsewhere in Ecclesiastes, apparent consecutive perfects (cf. Schoors, *The Preacher* I, 88)[10] are twice rendered with aorist indicatives (and probably not read as consecutive): ἤργησαν, 12.3; ἐκύκλωσαν, 12.5; elsewhere, they are translated contextually as present subjunctive (διαφθείρῃ, 5.5), aorist subjunctive

---

[10] The issue of consecutive perfects in Ecclesiastes has become rather confused. Whitley, 129, and Dahood, 'Qoheleth and Recent Discoveries', 305, both claim that there are none, merely perfects with conjunctive *waw*. This assertion is picked up in J-M §119 za, which cites Isaksson, *Studies*, 43, 93-105, on the subject. Isaksson, however, explicitly rejects the view of Dahood: 'what is commonly called "perfect consecutive" or "converted perfect"—that is, a specific usage of the SC [suffix conjugation] in conjunctive position—is an undeniable syntactical reality in the language of Qohelet' (p. 105). It is not clear that all of these scholars are working with the same definitions, and the question cannot readily be disassociated either from broader questions about this form in biblical Hebrew, or from the interpretation of specific passages.

(ἴδῃ, 3.13; φθάσωσιν, 12.1; ἐπιστρέψωσιν, 12.2; διαστραφῶσιν, 12.3; συντροχάσῃ, 12.6), or future indicative (πίεται...δείξει, 2.24; πίεται, 3.13; σκοτάσουσιν, 12.3; κλείσουσιν, 12.4). It seems highly unlikely, therefore, that G took this to be a consecutive perfect, and καὶ ἀνατέλλει probably indicates that G read וזרח as a conjunction + participle, וְזֹרֵחַ. This seems to be the direction in which Yi (187-88) leans.

Hie, V *oritur*, 'rises', probably also reflects a participle, with the conjunction either absent from the source or omitted (it is noteworthy that Jerome's revision of the Old Latin did preserve the conjunction in *et oritur*, so he was aware of the reading; cf. Caspari, *Hiob*, 6; Leanza, 'Le tre versioni', 90). It is difficult to judge such cases in Syriac, but Kamenetzky, 207, thinks that the lack of a conjunction points to S ܕܢܚ *dnḥ* reflecting a consecutive perfect; the readings for α' and σ' in Syh (cf. Marshall) are distinguished only by dots above and below the word, which, if accurate, indicate that α' read a past tense (ܘܕܢܚ Syriac perfect *wdnḥ*; presumably καὶ ἀνέτειλε), and σ' present tense (ܘܕܢܚ Syriac participle *wdnḥ*), as G. T's וידנח could probably reflect either a participle or a consecutive perfect here. We might also note that some later manuscripts of M point the verb as a participle; cf. Ginsburg, *Writings*.

The vocalization in M may reflect an attempt to deal with the unexpected conjunction, rather than being 'a deliberate link of the activities of humanity with the movement of the natural elements' (Seow). Isaksson, *Studies*, 93-94 thinks that it reflects a perceived 'conceptual parallelism' between vv. 4a and 5a, but given the variety of senses that can be attached to the consecutive perfect, and the looseness with which it can sometimes be used, perhaps we should not strain too hard to identify some specific connection with v. 4. If M is accepted as the original reading with the intended vocalization, the most interesting point is the differentiation of 5a from the descriptions which follow, and the implication, perhaps, that the key part of the illustration lies in 5b (and, I think, 6a).

1.5 gone down] for the use of בוא to describe the setting of the sun, see Gen 28.11, and probably Ps 104.19. The reading of ובא as participle or consecutive perfect will depend on the approach taken to וזרח: see the previous note. Grossman, 'Form and Content', 51, makes the interesting suggestion that the contrasting uses of the verb in this verse (for 'disappearing') and in the last (for 'appearing') is supposed to signify that 'neither "coming" nor "going" makes any real difference; they are all but interchangeable'—although the contrast is only so visible, perhaps, when we have to translate the text, and the point is vulnerable to the same criticism as Krüger's assertions about ambiguity in 1.4-7 more generally (see p. 305 n. 3, below).

1.5 and returned] M שׁוֹאֵף is unexpected here: שׁאף is not a verb of motion, and is nowhere otherwise used with אל, while its normal meanings do not comfortably fit the context. One such meaning has to do with persecution, and more specifically perhaps with trampling (e.g. Ps 56.2-3 ET 56.1-2): in this sense, the verb overlaps with שׁוּף, and BDB, in fact, attributes such uses to a separate homonym, II שאף (although *HALOT* identifies only a single verb).[11] The other uses fall broadly into two categories. In Jer 2.24 the verb is used of a jenny in heat, and in 14.16 of wild asses in a time of drought, who are said to be like jackals when they שאף like this: in each of these verses the verb takes רוח as a direct object, and the animals are apparently, therefore, in some way inhaling or exhaling air. Although jennies do, in fact, open and close their mouths when in heat, it seems likely that the image in both verses is of animals trying to catch a scent: the jenny is seeking a mate, the asses are sniffing around like jackals because their eyes are failing. A comparable use is often identified in Isa 42.14, where God famously promises to act like a woman in labour, and where אשאף stands alongside אפעה and אשם. Both the other verbs are very difficult themselves, however, and the disinclination of the ancient versions to read any reference to breathing or panting in that verse has recently been supported very persuasively by Goldingay and Payne.[12]

The uses of the verb with רוח have to be considered alongside the second use, with other nouns, in Job 5.5, where שאף apparently takes חיל, 'strength' or somesuch, as its object, in Job 7.2 where the object is צל, 'shade' (and ישאף stands in parallel with יקוה), and in Job 36.20 where the object is הלילה, 'the night'. None of these verses is itself straightforward, and Job 5.5 is especially difficult, but it is generally, and probably correctly, understood that in each of them שאף connotes some type of longing or anticipation. Of course, that connotation is hardly absent from the references in Jeremiah, where the animals are in heat or are seeking food and water, but the uses without רוח in Job should probably not be understood in precisely the same terms: שאף רוח is used of seeking a scent, שאף with other nouns of wanting something, or seeking its proximity, and it is likely that the former is a particular idiomatic usage of the latter. In this respect, the remaining use at Ps 119.131 is particularly interesting, because here the speaker claims that he has opened his mouth and will שאף because he desires God's commandments. In the light of other references to 'opening the mouth' (פער פי) as a way of catching food or drink in Isa 5.14 and Job 29.23, the image presented here is probably of seeking to draw in the commandments—the psalmist wants to suck in God's

---

[11] As Pinker, 'Anthropomorphic Conception', notes, Zer-Kavod takes the sense of 'trampling' to understand that the sun is 'treading' here. That is not really the sense of the verb, though, and few commentators have adopted this approach. Gordis notes an unpublished suggestion that a link should be made with the Akkadian *šēpu*, 'foot', to achieve such a sense, but although that word is often found in connection with movement, it is rarely if ever used as a verb.

[12] See Goldingay and Payne, *Isaiah 40–55*, 244-46. With the versions, Goldingay and Payne see a reference to childbirth in the first part of the verse only, and they interpret ואשאף here in terms of crushing; note that 1QIs[a] has ואשופה, suggesting a derivation from שוף.

words, rather as one might catch a breath or scent; cf. the Septuagint εἵλκυσα πνεῦμα, 'I drew breath', where M has merely ואשאפה, and no רוח. Ibn Ezra, citing Jer 2.24, similarly understands the point here to be that the sun sucks up the wind in its desire to return.

There is absolutely nothing to suggest, however, that שאף means 'breathing' more generally, let alone that it refers to 'panting', as is often supposed, and such renderings have probably arisen from a combination of Jeremiah's asses with a desire to draw a link between Eccles 1.5 and the 'racing' sun of Ps 19.6 (ET 19.5).[13] Correspondingly, and despite the fact that this would tie in well with certain interpretations of 1.8, שאף not only has no *necessary* connotation of exhaustion or 'struggling' (as, e.g., Seow asserts), but apparently never has such a connotation at all, and there is absolutely no reason, furthermore, to suppose that the verb might even be used of hurrying. Used of inhalation, it refers to drawing in a long, deep breath, generally to catch or savour a scent.

It is a recognition of this, perhaps, that has influenced the accentuation in M[L] and most of the other principal manuscripts of M, where the setting of the disjunctive accent *zaqeph qaton* on מקומו groups שואף with זורח and implies a reading 'The sun rises, and the sun goes down even to its place; שואף it rises there'. This accentuation makes the verb suggest longing, anticipation, or just possibly 'taking a deep breath' before the new rising, rather than exhaustion following the previous circuit—whether or not that is the meaning of the text, it is at least compatible with other uses of שאף.[14] Of course, this involves treating the conjunction on ואל rather awkwardly as emphatic, and, as Wickes points out, the versions and key rabbinic sources instead reflect a disjunction after שואף, i.e מקומו שואף, which is the reading found in many late manuscripts.[15]

---

[13] The only possible path to that sense would be to take שואף as a curious spelling of, or error for a form from שוף being used in its later sense as an equivalent to נשף, but even that would be forced: used this way, the verb always refers, like נשף, to the wind blowing, not to exhalation.

[14] Lohfink believes that the Masoretes had in mind the impatient snorting of Helios' horses; see 'Wiederkehr', 135. This picks up an idea advanced in more general terms by earlier scholars who were conscious of the *equis...anhelis*, 'the panting horses' of the sun in Vergil, *Georgics* 1.250. Whether or not Qohelet might have conceptualized the sun in these terms, however, it is important to note not only, as I have argued, that שאף does not mean 'pant', but that it is the sun itself which would be the subject of the verb here.

[15] Wickes, *Accentuation*, 141. Wickes suggests that: 'The accents, although respected and generally followed, were not regarded as of final authority'. Carasik, 'Exegetical Implications', suggests that such unexpected accentuation in Ecclesiastes may reflect exegetical concerns, as very possibly in some passages elsewhere. In this case, he draws attention (pp. 147-48) to an interpretation of שואף in Midrash Zutta 1.8 (absent from Midrash Rabbah) which emphasizes the direct divine control of the sun, and he suggests that the accents are intended to show

This implies that the sun reaches its place שואף, and then subsequently rises, which makes better sense of the conjunction, and Schoors is not the only commentator to insist that, with such a division, 'the verb can only have a meaning such as "comes panting"', although it might be better to think in terms of a pregnant construction: the sun 'pants to its place'.

Other usage, however, permits no more than 'comes longing' or, at most, 'comes sniffing', and in the complete absence of any evidence of a sense 'pant' for the verb, the only real way to take שואף with אל מקומו is to treat אל as equivalent to -ל in its use to mark the object of verbs expressing desire (as, e.g., למצותיך יאבתי in Ps 119.131). This is by no means impossible (see, e.g., ואל זרעי ייחלון in Isa 51.5), and would give the sense 'the sun rises and the sun sets, and with longing for its place it rises there'. In a context where אל is going to be used of movement four times in the next two verses, however, the awkwardness of taking it differently here is such that we might easily sympathize with Whitley's rejection of 5b as altogether secondary, a rejection that rests largely on his sense that the application of שאף to the sun is 'unusual and forced', or we might at least seek another reading of the text.

It is difficult to say, however, whether or not the versional evidence encourages us to do so. Certainly, much of it puts the antiquity of M's reading beyond doubt, and Jerome's commentary, for instance, both reports the Hebrew directly as *soeph* and attests that the reading of α' was εἰσπνει, 'breathes in (or on)'. There are two variants in T: שחיף, 'crawl' (like a snake, so just possibly reflecting a supposed derivation from שוף, cf. Gen 3.15),[16] and the more probably original שאיף, which Knobel, *The Targum of Qohelet*, translates as 'glide', but which is most likely just an imitation of the Hebrew; cf. the rendering of ישאף in Job 7.2 by דשאיף. Both of these affirm the reading of M. G εἰς τὸν τόπον αὐτοῦ ἕλκει is harder to assess. For the use of ἕλκει to render שואף, it is not difficult to point again to Jer 14.6, where εἵλκυσαν ἄνεμον = שאפו רוח, and to Ps 119.131, where εἵλκυσα πνεῦμα = ואשאפה. It is important to note, however, that in both places the Greek verb is used with a noun specifying the breath or air that is 'drawn': no such noun is present here, and if G intends 'draw breath' or 'pant', then we have to reckon not so much with literalness (Goldman), as with a very harsh ellipsis of πνεῦμα or some similar word. Such an ellipsis would be odd, and the Greek would more

that the referent of the suffix on מקומו is no longer the sun, but God: the sun is going to *his* place, i.e. where he wants it to go. This seems tenuous, especially in the absence of any explicit reference to God.

[16] This connection seems to have been made in the Midrash Rabbah on Genesis at 6.8, where the idea that the sun שף ברקיע, 'slides through the sky', probably an allusion to our passage, is contrasted with an assertion that in fact it passes through it noisily, like a saw through wood. On the ideas behind that, see Simon-Shoshan, 'The Heavens Proclaim', 83-84.

naturally be understood as 'it keeps going to its place'.[17] It is difficult to say, however, whether the translator is actually dealing with a different Hebrew text, is adopting a different understanding of שאף, or, as seems most likely, is attempting to deal with a perceived problem by slipping between different senses of ἕλκειν.

In his revision of the Old Latin and in the lemma to his commentary, Jerome explicitly follows G by rendering *ducit* (although the Latin can more readily just mean 'go' than can the Greek), but as well as reporting the Hebrew and the reading of α' (see above), Jerome also reports the readings of σ' and (the usually rather conservative) θ' as *recurrit*, 'runs back': Field conjectures that the Greek was ἐπαναστρέφει, which is frequently used to render forms from שוב. This would appear to have influenced Jerome's own later translation *reuertitur*, 'turns back', in V.[18] S ܬܘܒ *t'b* also means 'return', but it is important to note that it lies in the context of a much longer text: S has 'The sun rises and the sun sets, and to the place at which it rose there it returns, from whence again it will rise'. This is obviously much closer to the description of the streams in 1.7, and although there are significant differences between the two in S, it is generally suspected that this text has arisen from a desire to forge an analogy with that verse; Kamenetzky, 207, suggests also that the translator did not understand שואף, and, somewhat implausibly, that he therefore rendered it with the 'similar sounding' ܬܘܒ *t'b*. It is interesting to observe that T has a plus which similarly has the sun rise twice: the sun 'rises on the morrow from the place whence it rose the day before'. Overall, just as it was difficult to assess what G is doing here, so it is also difficult to tell whether σ', θ' and S actually reflect a different Hebrew text with a form from שוב, or whether they are simply offering their own 'corrections' to a text with שואף which they find incomprehensible, and arriving independently at the same solution, either under the influence of 1.7 or as a response to the demands of the context.

---

[17] ἕλκειν, 'drag' or 'draw', can certainly be used of air when the context demands, and in Theophrastus, Περί Σημείων (*de Uentis*), 29, the verb is used of windows creating a draught as air is forced through a narrow space: καὶ αἱ θυρίδες ἕλκουσιν ἀεὶ καὶ πνοὴν παρέχουσι ('windows always draw in and produce a draught'). It can be used of breathing or inhaling also: for instance, Hippocrates tells us (*De aere aquis et locis* 19.22) that the Scythians characteristically 'breathe a moist, thick air' (τόν τε ἠέρα ὑδατεινὸν ἕλκοντες καὶ παχύν). It seems unlikely, however, that readers who saw ἕλκειν used absolutely, as here, in conjunction with a locative expression, would naturally see any reference at all to breathing, and they might more obviously look to the idea of 'dragging on' or 'lasting', which perhaps underpins occasional uses of the verb to refer to the flow of rivers (cf. BDAG).

[18] This is one of the instances listed by Cannon, where 'the dependence of Jerome on Symmachus cannot be doubted'. He suggests that σ' had read שוב, or אך שוב; see his 'Jerome and Symmachus', 191.

What we can say is that, even if they read שואף, almost all the ancient versions seem reluctant to accept it—and none of them connects it with panting. The most popular emendation is that originally proposed by Graetz, which takes שואף to be an error for שב אף, giving a sense 'and it returns to its place then rises there'.[19] Even simpler than this is the suggestion of Burkitt, that the ו of שואף should be deleted, and שאף read as אף + -ש; taking the first הולך from 1.6 with this clause, he then translates, 'and to its place where also it rises does it go. To the South and round to the North...'[20] This is a good sense, but the suggestion would be more compelling were the combination אף + -ש less unlikely, and it should be noted that Burkitt himself understands it in the context of a translation from Aramaic, which might justify such clunkiness. Claiming to base himself more directly on the readings of σ', θ', S, and V, Martin Rose (*Rien de nouveau*, 80-81) has proposed reading simply a form from שוב and taking this with זורח as an expression of the sun's repeated rising: he translates 'Le soleil apparaît; le soleil disparaît dans sa demeure; de là il se met en route pour réapparaître', 'The sun appears; the sun disappears into its abode; from there it sets itself on course to re-appear'. This solution, however, not only fails to explain the emergence of the form שואף, which Rose simply dismisses as secondary, it also involves the removal, apparently without comment, of the conjunction before אל, and Rose does not read שב but ושב: in order to achieve the sense he wants, in other words, Rose has to make a series of adjustments that leaves the text looking significantly different, and for which the versions offer little support.

Where Rose surely is correct, however, is in his criticism of the way in which Graetz removes almost all force from the word אף, which is not, after all, a common term in the book, and which clearly has more force than 'and' or 'then' on the single occasion when it does appear, in 2.9. The same is not true of a similar proposal in Pinker, 'Anthropomorphic Conception', to read אף שת (from שית), with a sense that the sun is stopping or stationing itself before then rising. Such a sense is not attested for that verb, however, and Pinker has to resort to the palaeo-Hebrew script for an explanation of the graphic confusion.

My own translation takes שואף to be an error not for שב אף, but for שב ואף, and I understand ואף to have a strong emphatic sense: the sun rises and sets, and it returns to its starting point—*but then* it rises again. Although the sun has completed a whole circuit, in other words, it is going to pass through that circuit all over again. If this emendation is not actually supported by σ', θ', S, and V, then it is at least in line with their own speculations.

---

[19] This is suggested also, perhaps independently, by Joüon, 'Notes philologiques', 419, and still noted as a possibility by *BHS*; its wide influence on a later generation of commentators is noted by Salters, 'Textual Criticism', 61.

[20] See Burkitt, 'Is Ecclesiastes a Translation?', 26. Montgomery, 'Notes', 242, repeated the suggestion a few years later, again apparently independently.

1.5 to] Jerome's revision of the Old Latin has *in locum suum*, lit. 'into its place' (contrast Hie, V *ad*), which more precisely captures the idea that the sun actually returns to its position, rather than just heading towards it.

1.5 but then] I read וְאָף: see the previous note on 'and returned'.

1.5 it rises there] There are no text-critical or other grounds for the suggestion in *BH³*, *BHS* that this clause is an addition. Ehrlich supposes that in place of זורח הוא שם we should read אָרח הַשֶּׁמֶשׁ, to give the sense '(and hurrying to its place,) the sun devours the route', but this is speculative and improbable. Derenbourg, 'Notes', 173 n. 1, curiously wishes to emend שם to שב. If we retain the text as it stands, however, the participial form זורח stands in contrast to the preceding זרח and ובא (if we do not take those as participles themselves—see above), suggesting that we should not read it as part of the same sequence ('rises…sets…rises [again]'). Many commentators, in fact, regard this as an asyndetic relative clause; cf. RSV '(hastens to the place) where it rises'. That would give a better parallel to the similar v. 7b, where the participle הלכים is found, but the position of שואף in the text as it stands, between מקומו and זורח, tells strongly against such a construal, and any reading along those lines would seem rather to necessitate 'to its place (where) it שואףs (and) rises there', which raises other obvious problems—not least the lack of a conjunction.

If we emend שואף to שב ואף, as proposed above, then שב can be read as either a perfect, in line with זרח and ובא, or as a participle in line with זורח: I take the latter to be more probable, as I think that ואף imposes a disjunction. On this reading, the sun, having risen, set and returned to its place, completing a circuit which is described using verbs in the perfect, then proceeds to rise once more and embark upon another circuit, which is described using participles. The point of the shift may be to indicate that we are moving on from what the sun does in a single day to what it does habitually, but I think that there is also a distinction of tense involved, which I have tried to catch in the translation: the sun *does* these things after it *has done* them already. The distinction is lost in Hie, where Jerome uses *oritur* (var. *orietur*), as at the beginning of the verse, but his revision of the Old Latin (*oriens*; cf. Caspari, *Hiob*, 6; Leanza, 'Le tre versione', 90) and V (the more interpretative *renascens*, 'returning renewed') both have participles. With respect to the pointing here, ben Naphtali reportedly used no *metheg* under the ה of זורח (see Lipschütz).

1.6 going southward] When used of direction, the preposition אל need not imply location at a particular point. It is commonly used of turning, facing or pointing 'toward' something (e.g. Josh 8.18; 1 Sam 17.30; 1 Kgs 8.30), but can also have implications of movement, as when the little horn of Dan 8.9 grows toward the south and east, or the various chariots of Zechariah 6 patrol in different directions (cf. vv. 6, 8); it is often difficult to distinguish travel *towards* from arrival *at* (e.g. in Ezek 47.8). In any case, if the subject here is the wind, then it is blowing towards the south (i.e., it is a north wind); if the subject is the sun, then it is moving southwards on its course.

If we insist on regarding the subject of 6a as ambiguous (see the commentary), then it is not clear that G, S, V can help: they do not explicitly take the subject of 6a to be the sun (as, e.g., Barton, Seow suppose). Jerome reflects this understanding in his commentary, although his Vulgate translation leans more clearly this way than does the lemma in the commentary itself. S simply agrees with M (cf. Kamenetzky, 207). The case of G is complicated by the punctuation of the text in the manuscript tradition, which commonly sets ἀνατέλλων αὐτὸς ἐκεῖ as the start of a new sentence in v. 6 (it is a verbatim rendering of זורח הוא שם at the end of v. 5 in M). This is somewhat variable (G^S notably breaks the text after ἀνατέλλων, so that αὐτὸς is the start of the new sentence), but since the text was certainly read as referring to the sun by early commentators, it could simply reflect an interpretative development within the Greek tradition, which found expression in the subsequent punctuation of the text. Even if it was the intention of the original translator, though, the manuscripts may have been open to different readings, and this problem extends to some other versions. Jerome, who in fact shows no knowledge of that placement in G, reports σ' as *uadit ad meridiem et circumit ad boream perambulans uadit uentus et per quae circumierat reuertitur uentus*, 'it goes to the noonday south and comes round to the north, traversing goes the wind, and the wind returns through (those ways by) which it had come around'; this certainly takes the wind to be the subject in 6b, but that σ' might have considered it to be the subject in 6a too is only implied by the way Jerome has selected the text. The Targum is clearer, and not only identifies the sun in the first part, but relates the rest of the verse to a (now muddled—see Knobel, *The Targum of Qohelet*, 22) account of solstices and equinoxes, in which the winds have become no more than indications of direction.[21]

None of the versions, incidentally, supports Ehrlich's proposal to emend the verbs to הָלוֹךְ and וְסָבוֹב. The term דרום (also in 11.3) is an alternative to the more common word for 'south', נגב; it is used most commonly by Ezekiel (13 times), but appears also in Deut 33.23; Job 37.17. Schoors, *The Preacher* II, 355, like BDB, characterizes it as 'late and poetic'.

1.6 Turning. Turning] M points סובב סבב as two qal participles, the first written *plene*,[22] and separates them with *paseq*. The sign, as it is used here

---

[21] Knobel notes links with the Talmud, where this verse is understood in terms of the sun's seasonal rising and setting to the north or south of due east and west, except at the equinoxes; cf. *y. ʿErubin* 5,1; *b. ʿErubin* 56a. Japhet, 'Goes to the South', discusses the context of these passages in more detail, and notes the appearance of the same material in the corresponding passage of the Tosefta. For the use of רוח to mean 'side' or 'direction', which facilitates the interpretation, see, e.g., the Targum of Ezek 42.16.

[22] It is difficult to know whether the striking juxtaposition of the two spellings is supposed to indicate some distinction in meaning. On the general question of *plene* spellings of the qal participle, see Barr, *Variable Spellings*, 64-81, and

and in 7.24 (its only other occurrence in Ecclesiastes) is clearly an instance of what Wickes calls *paseq homonymicum*, which is employed 'where a word is repeated, in the same or similar form'.²³ It occurs regularly in the expression סביב ׀ סביב, 'round about', which is found at 2 Chr 4.3 and frequently in Ezekiel (e.g. 8.10; 37.2), so that usage may have influenced the decision to make use of it here.

Gordis, indeed, suggests that סביב ׀ סביב should be read in this verse, so that the wind 'goes round about' (so too Ehrlich, while Delitzsch supposes that the expression in Ecclesiastes has the same sense). That reading is not attested, however, by any of the ancient versions, and they probably support M, although only T (מחזר מחזר) offers a precise match. Jerome reports the reading of σ' as *perambulans*, and himself paraphrases with *lustrans universa circuitu*, 'traversing' or 'illuminating all around' (var. *in circuitu* 'in a circuit') in V. The other versions, however, all reflect two words, making it unlikely that we are dealing with an accidental repetition, the preservation of two variant readings in the text, or a secondary addition (so Zimmerli). Interestingly, these versions all render each of the words as a different form of the same verb: so G, θ' κυκλοῖ κυκλῶν, for instance, means 'it goes round, going round', and Hie *gyrans gyrando*; S (cf. also Syh) ܡܬܟܪܟ ܡܬܟܪܟܐ *mtkrkw mtkrk* mark comparable distinctions. The reading of α' is attested as κύκλου κύκλον/κυκλῶν in Greek manuscripts, but Field retroverts κυκλῶν κύκλον, perhaps 'circling a circle', from Syh (against Middeldorpf κυκλοῖ κύκλον), and Marshall supports this as the most probable original reading; in any case, α' likewise differentiates the words.

It seems unlikely that G read סֹבֵב סָבִיב, as Gordis suggests, but that might well be the understanding behind α'.²⁴ Otherwise, G, θ', S have taken the first participle to be acting as a continuous present, like other participles in the section, and the second to be more strictly participial; because S would normally use the participle for the present itself, it has marked the distinction by using an infinitive for the first verb. These versions, then, support the text of M, but read an independent verbal clause: 'It turns, turning; it goes…' (S correspondingly adds a following conjunction). Hie has taken both words to be participial, and marked the orthographic distinction by using a gerundive for the second. Although we cannot exclude the possibility that the text preserves what were originally two variant readings of the same word, we also cannot affirm it: the versions provide no basis for emendation, or for the

---

note esp. 76. If a distinction is intended here, it may be that we are supposed to understand סובב as syntactically parallel with וסובב and הולך, but סבב as a strictly participial attribute of the subject (and this is what some of the versions read).

²³ Wickes, *Accentuation*, 123; pp. 120-29 offer a thorough treatment of paseq in its various uses.

²⁴ See Gentry, 'Relationship', 69-70, who suggests that α' either read this, or translated with sensitivity to context.

deletion of סבב which *BH³*, *BHS* propose as a possibility, and if this is a double reading, then it arose early.

It is harder to say whether it is the sun or the wind that acts as the subject of one or both instances of the verb. The intention here may be to synthesize from the preceding statements a more general observation, that the sun is in constant motion. The subsequent statements about the wind, however, seem rather thin if we are being told only that it goes and comes back. The words are intended, perhaps, to serve for both, and if it does address what follows, then I take the point to be that the wind is always turning—not revolving or rotating like a whirlwind, or even shifting direction continually, but rather passing at different times through different points of the compass. The representation of directions as a surrounding circle, which underpins the classic form of the compass, has its origins in ancient descriptions of the winds which blow from different sides, and this interplay of wind and direction has also informed the interpretation in T, which sees in 1.6 no separate observation about the wind, but a further specification of the points through which the sun will pass. The verb itself can signify a variety of movements and positions, even in Qohelet's own usage, from turning oneself around (2.20) through to surrounding something (9.14) or just going about (12.5), and cannot itself be used to pin down the sense here more precisely.

1.6 wind] Like שמש, the word רוח is found as both masculine and feminine in biblical Hebrew; it is apparently masculine here and in 3.19, feminine in 3.21; 10.4; 12.7 (Schoors, *The Preacher* I, 70, has rightly rejected Ginsberg's attempt to find different senses for each). The semantic range of the term enables the understanding of it as 'spirit', which is a component in some of the readings of 6b as referring still to the sun. So Jerome claims that *siue ipsum solem spiritum nominauit*, 'as though he has called the sun itself a spirit'—because the sun has the qualities of a living creature, or because (he cites the *Aeneid*) *spiritus intus alit*, 'from within a spirit nourishes' (the world and the heavenly bodies). Japhet, 'Goes to the South', 302, suggests that some such idea must also inform G, and it is certainly striking that πνεῦμα is used here, but ἄνεμος in the unambiguous references to wind at 5.15 and 11.4. If we do take G to have understood 'spirit' here, however, we have no way to know quite what the translator took that spirit to be, and it is possible that he is making a connection with 12.7 (see on 'blows again', below) and thinking in terms of 'breath'.

1.6 and on to its surroundings] *BH³*, *BHS* speculate, with no versional support, that the whole clause ועל סביבתיו שב הרוח may be an addition. The sense of G ἐπὶ κύκλους αὐτοῦ ἐπιστρέφει is probably 'returns to its rounds' rather than 'on' them; the active of the verb with ἐπί elsewhere indicates '(re)turning to' or 'toward', not returning on a certain path (e.g. Deut 31.18, 20; Sir 17.29; Zech 1.16; 8.3; Jer 29.3 [M 47.3]; Bar 2.30; Dan 11.9). There are only slender grounds, however, for any emendation of על to אל (as Siegfried): ἐπί only corresponds to אל in 12.6, and even there is probably translating the

עַל for which it is normally used (see the note there on 'the windlass spun free toward the cistern'). At the same time, Jerome's *in circulos suos* (Hie, V) is interpretative, cf. σ' (as reported by Jerome): *et per quae circumierat reuertitur uentus*, 'and the wind returns through (those ways by) which it had come around', which is an attempt to align the movements of the wind with those of the sun.[25] S ܘܠܚܕܪܬܗ *wlḥdrth* (var. ܘܠܚܪܬܗ *wlḥrth*) is the only evidence that leans strongly that way, but it too may be interpretative. Siegfried rests his case on the use of ἐπὶ by θ', which is no more conclusive. As, e.g., Ginsburg has pointed out, שׁוּב may anyway be construed with עַל in the sense 'to'; cf., e.g., Prov 26.11; Mic 5.2; Mal 3.24 (hiph'il).[26]

All the same, some scholars have found the usual meanings of עַל difficult here, and Dahood, 'Phoenician Background', 265, followed by Whitley, supposes that it should be read in the sense 'from'. Schoors, *The Preacher* I, 201, merely accepts that as a possibility, but in his commentary Schoors declares it his preferred option, translating 'and from its rounds the wind returns'. Such a sense, however, can hardly be considered well-established in Hebrew, and even if it were, there is nothing in the context to require it, or to make that a natural reading of the verse. In his earlier work, Schoors also found attractive the proposal of Ellermeier, according to which עַל has here the sense 'wegen, um…willen' ('for the sake of'), so that the expression indicates not *where* the wind returns, but *why*: 'der Wind schlägt um—nur um zu drehen', 'the wind veers round—merely to turn', and some other commentators have translated in terms of cause.[27]

---

[25] Jerome is reported to have used earlier a singular *in circulo suo conuertitur*, cf. Caspari, *Hiob*, 6; Leanza, 'Le tre versione', 90. Since κύκλου is attested as a variant in the lemma of Olympiodorus' commentary, it is just conceivable that this is an Old Latin reading preserving a rare G variant, but more likely that it arose as an error after the first 's' dropped out in *circulos suos*.

[26] It is interesting to observe in 12.7 that the verb is used with both prepositions, of the dust returning to (עַל) the ground and the breath/spirit returning to (אֶל) God. Schwienhorst-Schönberger cites this as evidence that the expressions are equivalent, but if anything that verse probably implies a distinction between them: the components of life return in different directions to their sources.

[27] Ellermeier, *Qohelet I.1*, 199-201. Seow cites Ellermeier to support his translation, 'And on account of its rounds, the wind returns', and explains that 'it returns again and again *because* it has its rounds', although Ellermeier suggests that the preposition 'gibt…weniger den Grund an als den Zweck', 'presents less the basis than the purpose'. Seow's translation is, perhaps, closer to Zimmerli's 'und weil er umschlägt, bläst wieder zürück der Wind' ('and because it turns back the wind blows again'), or Krüger's 'und weil er sich dreht, kehrt er wieder, der Wind' (ET 'and because it turns, it returns, the wind'). Unlike Ellermeier, such renderings take עַל to have its common connotation of cause, rather than as equivalent to -לְ.

While such a sense cannot be excluded *a priori*, I think it misses the meaning of סביבתיו, which is important here, but seldom given much attention. Were the word a fresh coinage from the verb, it would indeed be *hapax*, as Whybray suggests, but there is no reason not to identify it as a very widely attested noun—or, strictly, a plural form with ת(ו)– formed from the noun סביב; it is most commonly used adverbially to mean 'around' or 'about', but can be used as a substantive. In Jer 17.26, for instance, it means 'the environs (of Jerusalem)', and in Ezek 16.57; 28.26; 34.26; Dan 9.16 it similarly refers to 'neighbouring' areas or people; in both usages, it generally takes a suffix pronoun, as here, referring to whatever is being surrounded. So, e.g., Ps 44.14 (ET 44.13): תשימנו חרפה לשכנינו לעג וקלס לסביבותינו: 'You have made us a reproach for our neighbours, into objects of mockery and derision for those around us'. Unless we feel compelled by the context to suppose that in Ecclesiastes alone it has a sense unattested in the many other uses, the noun must refer not to the actions or paths of the wind (its 'turnings' or 'circuits'), but to those things which are around it, and upon which it therefore blows—an idea for which על seems very appropriate.

1.6 comes back again] Lit. 'returns'. This is close to the expression in 12.7, where the רוח returns to God at death, and some scholars have seen significance in the correspondence (e.g. Carasik, 'Qohelet's Twists and Turns', 194-95).

1.7

(1.7) All streams go to the sea, but the sea is never filled: to the place where the streams go, they go again.

Commentary

Many commentators note the exchange in Aristophanes, *Clouds* 1279–1295, where Amynias, having been coaxed by the ingenuous Strepsiades into explaining the nature of interest on a loan, is then tricked into declaring that it would be quite wrong for the sea to grow greater; this gives Strepsiades his chance to declare that if the sea should become no greater, despite the flow of rivers into it, then Amynias can hardly expect his loan to grow greater (from the compounding of interest). The context is very different, but the analogy is similar to Qohelet's next illustration, in which the sea is never filled despite the continual flow of every river into it.[1]

Again, many commentators, ancient and modern, have attempted to see this as the depiction of a circular movement, in which the focus is upon the flow of the rivers rather than the constant level of the sea. On this reading, the rivers flow into the sea, but then return somehow to their sources, from which they will flow again—like the sun returning to the place where it rises. The Vulgate accordingly renders: *ad locum unde exeunt flumina revertuntur ut iterum fluant*, 'to the place whence the rivers come out, they return that they may flow again', and a similar understanding is apparently reflected in all the ancient translations. This is picked up in some much later

---

[1] Curiously, commentators do not normally note the various other points in classical literature where the problem of the sea's constant level, despite the flow of rivers, is discussed as a scientific problem. In addition to Seneca's presentation, outlined below, note, e.g., Pliny the Elder's assertions in his *Naturalis Historia* (2.46) that waters are driven back up through the earth by its weight—*qua ratione manifestum est, quare tot fluminum cotidiano accessu maria non crescant*, 'by which explanation it is made clear why the seas do not increase with the daily inflow of so many rivers'. More in line with modern ideas, Aristotle, in *Meteorologica* 355b, puts the constant level of the sea down to evaporation.

but no less influential versions, and the KJV, for example, has 'unto the place from whence the rivers come, thither they return again'. A number of scholars have rightly observed, however, that this is not the probable sense of the (admittedly difficult) Hebrew, which does not readily yield '(the place) *from* which', or '*whence*', but more naturally means that the rivers continue to flow to the place at which they discharge their waters. To focus on the return of these rivers, moreover, relegates the statement about the sea to little more than a passing comment: if it is the circularity of the system that is the point here, then its effect on the sea is barely relevant.

As with the movement of the sun, it would be helpful here if we had a better understanding of the original author's own presuppositions. Later Jewish interpreters offer several ideas. The Midrash Rabbah on Qohelet, for instance, offers an interesting discussion of the distillation and return of water to the earth through evaporation and condensation, and this is the way in which Ibn Ezra also understood it to return. Such an understanding, broadly in line with modern understandings of the water cycle, has an ancient pedigree: it was espoused by Aristotle (*Meteorologica* 346b-347a) and has earlier roots in pre-Socratic Greek philosophy—but it is also touched on in the passage from the *Clouds* mentioned above, and was probably not an idea confined to intellectual circles. The connection between clouds and rain, noted in 11.3 and 12.2 (cf. Judg 5.4; 2 Sam 22.12; 1 Kgs 18.44-45; Job 26.8; 36.27-28; 37.11; 38.34; Pss 18.12 [ET 18.11]; 77.18 [ET 77.17]; 147.8; Prov 16.15; 25.14; Isa 5.6; Ezek 1.28; Zech 10.1), would presumably have been obvious to all ancient peoples, and rainfall as an origin for river-water perhaps no less so (cf. 1 Kgs 17.7; 2 Kgs 3.17). The origin of clouds, however, is less obvious, and observers who noted, for instance, the continued flow of some rivers even in the absence of rain, or the presence of water in deep wells, could reasonably be forgiven for believing that water circulated in other ways as well.

Accordingly, the Targum here speaks of the rivers flowing into Oceanus (the sea that surrounds the world), and thence to the 'Deep', an image that is evocative both of the subterranean waters of the *abzu/apsû* in Mesopotamia, and of the underground tunnels through which Plato believed water to circulate around the earth (*Phaedo* 112; the idea is roundly rejected in Aristotle, *Meteorologica* 356a). Such ideas, involving the re-circulation of water *as water*, are often assumed to reflect an earlier biblical understanding, and there is nothing new about this assumption: until surprisingly recently, Christian writers looking at the water cycle tended to argue in favour of subterranean circulation, alongside or instead of evaporation, on the basis of their belief that this was a biblical opinion. This belief, however, seems largely to have originated in nothing more than an understanding that Eccles 1.7 itself makes such a claim, which has often been influenced by the Vulgate rendering in particular. An anonymous cosmography, written in Ravenna around 700 CE, is not untypical when it cites the Vulgate of this verse almost verbatim, treating what it says not as dogma, but as a valuable explanation for a phenomenon otherwise invisible to humans.[2] It is much harder, in fact, either to find evidence for any specific belief in the subterranean circulation of water in other early Jewish writings, or to determine specifically what models the biblical writers and their successors might have had in mind.

Seneca's discussion of the matter in book 3 of his *Naturales Quaestiones* (written in about 65 CE) reviews a number of different ideas involving the provision of water to rivers, which he doubts can be entirely put down to rainfall, and he attributes some of these to the much earlier Thales of Miletus, who was active in the late seventh to early sixth centuries BCE. Seneca himself prefers the idea that air, trapped underground, is transmuted into fresh water, and he rejects as a *ueterem et rudem sententiam*—an 'outdated and crude idea' (3.14)—Thales' image of the earth as like a boat floating on an enormous ocean, into which water can leak from outside. This is probably not so very far, however, from the ideas that inform our few biblical sources on the matter: these acknowledge both the sky and an underground deep as sources of water (e.g. Gen 7.11; Prov 3.20), and they probably share with, for example, the Babylonian *Enûma Elish*, the concept of a single mass of water that in some way surrounds the world (cf. Gen 1.6-8) and finds different points of entry. Later, 4 Esd 4.7, which was probably written around the end of the first century CE, poses the deliberately unanswerable

---

[2] Pinder and Parthey, *Ravennatis Anonymi Cosmographia et Guidonis Geographica. Ex libris manu scriptis*, 15-16 (§1.6). With an eye to the seventeenth and eighteenth centuries in particular, Tuan, *The Hydrologic Cycle* traces the extent to which the modern scientific model of the water cycle 'was a handmaiden of natural theology as much as it was a child of natural philosophy', and notes frequently the influence of Ecclesiastes.

question 'How many dwellings are there in the heart of the sea, or how many springs are there in the source of the deep, or how many springs are there above the firmament...?' (4.7).[3] If we can extrapolate any general picture at all from this and the biblical sources, then that picture is of a world watered from above and below, by rains and by a vast aquifer that are both somehow replenished from waters around and outside it.

It might seem that such a model of the world would at least implicitly have involved the return of river waters, if only *via* some much larger pool. Even this, however, is far from certain. Later writers who attempted to defend the subterranean transfer of water often recognized the difficulty posed by the salinity of sea-water, which had somehow to be transformed in the course of re-circulation. This was a strong argument in favour of explanations based on evaporation, although Seneca notes an alternative opinion, that the sea does not grow because it immediately restores to the earth whatever waters have flowed into it, through hidden, endlessly winding channels in which they are filtered and dashed about in a way that somehow restores their freshness.[4] Interestingly, however, alongside its discussion of evaporation, the Midrash offers another interpretation of our text which gives salinity a very different role: the ocean is never filled by the rivers not because their waters pass through it and out, but because its saltiness enables it to absorb them without growing in volume; an anecdote goes on to describe an experimental demonstration of this idea. While it is difficult to assess its antiquity, this belief may have had much wider currency—not least in Palestine where, as Hertzberg notes, the Dead Sea furnishes a graphic example of 'disappearing' water—and it demonstrates one

---

[3] From the Vulgate version: *quantae habitationes sunt in corde maris aut quantae uenae sunt in principio abyssi aut quantae uenae sunt super firmamentum*. The term *uena* ('vein', it is also used of blood-vessels) classically describes a channel for water, but in his translations from Hebrew Jerome often uses it as equivalent to מקור, and that sense 'spring' or 'source' is more in line with the other versions than would be 'stream' or 'water-course'.

[4] *Quidam iudicant terram quicquid aquarum emisit rursus accipere et ob hoc maria non crescere, quia quod influxit, non in suum uertunt sed protinus reddunt. Occulto enim itinere subit terras et palam uenit, secreto reuertitur, colaturque in transitu mare, quod per multiplices terrarum anfractus euerberatum amaritudinem ponit et prauitatem: in tanta soli uarietate saporem exuit et in sinceram aquam transit* (*Naturales Quaestiones* 3.4-5).

obvious (albeit wholly fallacious) way in which waters from above and below could be understood to persist in the world, without ever returning to their external sources.[5]

Although, then, many readers and translators have tried to find an analogy to the cyclical course of the sun in Qohelet's description of the rivers and sea, there is no explicit indication of this in the Hebrew, and we have no good reason to suppose that the original readers would have presumed some cycle to be implicit. Even if they thought, indeed, that rivers were fed from some vast pool into which they also discharged—which is far from certain—then this would be circularity of the very loosest sort (as would some reference to evaporation and condensation, such as Provan sees here), and it would require considerable poetic licence to suggest that, on this model, the rivers were themselves flowing back to their own sources. It is not impossible that Qohelet is laying the ground for his much broader statements, beginning in vv. 9 and 10, that the world is in some sense a closed system, into which nothing new can be introduced. This verse, however, does not place its emphasis on the re-use of water—if it refers to it at all—but on the failure of the rivers to fill the sea, and the consequent continuation of their flow: like the sun and wind, they fulfil their function continuously, without ever reaching a conclusion to their work.

A less common interpretation of these verses finds within them an emphasis not so much on cycles or constancy as on change. Knopf ('Optimism', 196) takes the key characteristic of *hebel* as 'vapour' to be 'restless, unceasing change', and finds in the book a broader engagement with the ideas of Heraclitus, who is famously supposed to have declared that 'everything flows', and that one can never step twice into the same river (see Jarick, 'Book of Changes', 84-85 n. 8). To be sure, 1.7 bears a superficial resemblance to that image, but it is making a very different point, and when Jarick finds

---

[5] Much the same idea is found in Ephrem the Syrian's commentary on Genesis, cited in *Wright*, 'Commentary': 'Rivers flow down into seas lest the heat of the sun dry them up. The saltiness [of the seas] then swallows up [the rivers] lest they increase, rise up and cover the earth. Thus the rivers turn into nothing, as it were, because the saltiness of the sea swallows them up.' The Midrash, incidentally, offers a number of other interpretations, one of which is also reported as a Jewish interpretation in Jerome's commentary; cf. Ginzberg, 'Die Haggada', 23. According to this, the rivers are a metaphor for the dying, who enter Sheol but never fill it (cf. Prov 27.20).

(85-86) the 'notion of change' in 1.9 and 3.15—which could hardly be clearer statements of changelessness—or in 6.10, then he seems deliberately to be ignoring what the book *says* in favour of what he thinks it *implies*. Heard ('The Dao of Qoheleth') similarly sees all the phenomena here as 'pictures of inconstancy, not constancy', emphasizing the constant change within each process. This fits badly, I think, both with Qohelet's opening statement that the earth stands forever (which Heard places in parallel, not contrast, to the coming and going of generations) and with the explicit conclusions that he will draw in 1.9-10. For Qohelet, inconstancy may be an aspect of the way in which humans experience the world, but his point is that the movements we see do not really entail progression or change at all: perhaps it is never the same water twice, but it will always be the same river, doing the same thing.

Notes

1.7 go to the sea] The late variant הלכים שם noted in Lavoie and Mehramooz, 'Le texte hébreu et la traduction judéo-persanne', 498-99, is simply an error, caused by the subsequent appearance of that combination.

1.7 but the sea is never filled] Lit. 'and the sea, it is not filled'; Schoors, *The Preacher* I, 151, discusses the fondness in Ecclesiastes for the construction אין + suffix + participle (1.7; 4.17; 5.11; 6.2; 8.7, 13, 16; 9.2, 5, 16; 11.5, 6). The position of the subject (הים) here, before איננו, is similar to that in 5.11, and in both places the purpose may be to emphasize and to distinguish it, so the sense would be 'but as for the sea...' (cf. HCM). Used of water, מלא may indicate overflowing, cf. Josh 3.15.

1.7 to the place] This echoes the expression in v. 5, but מקום has no suffix here, and, as e.g. Barton, Lauha note, is in the construct before the following relative clause (see GKC §130 d; J-M §129 q; and cf. 11.3).

1.7 where the streams go] Although some recent commentators (e.g. Whybray) continue to assert that the relative -ש might mean 'from which' in this expression, it has long been recognized by most that this pushes the Hebrew beyond its natural sense, and is grammatically improbable. McNeile points to the similar expressions with אשר in Num 13.27 and 1 Kgs 12.2, which strongly favour the sense 'to which'. Matters are complicated by the subsequent שם, which the accents would take with הם שבים. If that word does indeed belong to the last clause ('to the place where the streams go, thither they return...'), then there is merit in Ehrlich's proposal that it should be emended to שמה (with ה lost through haplography with הם). There are, though, many places cited in BDB where שם itself seems to bear the sense 'thither', suggesting that emendation might not be required to yield that sense. Delitzsch and Wright point to Jer 22.27, where both שם and שמה are used for 'thither' with שוב, which makes that point in general, although it is notable that in that particular verse, שמה is used in the clause that is analogous to our *second* clause here.

On balance, it is probably simpler to take שם with the preceding relative clause, lit. 'the place which the streams are going there'; cf., e.g., Gen 13.3, 14; 2 Sam 11.16. In that case, however, שם is a further serious obstacle to any understanding of the verse as a statement that the rivers are returning to their sources, rather than continuing to their destinations. Ginsburg's idea that שם simply equated to משם will hardly do, and it seems improbable that משם could be considered implicit. Correspondingly, to extract the sense 'from which' requires emendation of the text, to restore either משם or משם שם (Crenshaw raises the possibility of restoring מ- before the relative instead, but that would be very ugly).

It is not difficult to see how such an error might have occurred in the midst of so many final *mems* (as Döller, 'Altorientalisches Weltbild', 364, argued long ago), but the versional support for emendation is slight. Fox and others point to V *ad locum unde exeunt flumina reuertuntur*, 'to the place whence they come out the rivers return', and σ' εἰς τὸν τόπον ἀφ' οὗ οἱ ποταμοὶ πορεύονται καὶ ἐκεῖ αὐτοὶ ἀναστρέφουσιν (var. ἀποστρέφουσιν), 'to the place whence the rivers come, there also they return', which seem to offer at first sight a compelling double witness. In fact, however, these versions cannot be considered independent: σ' exerts a strong influence on Jerome's work in many places, and V *unde* probably depends on σ' ἀφ' οὗ (cf. Euringer). So may Hie *de quo*, if it is not La or an interpretation of G οὗ. In any case, both V and σ' tend to translate interpretatively, so are not strong witnesses (note how σ' goes on to add a facilitatory conjunction before ἐκεῖ); they are probably just attempting to render the relative in the light of their presuppositions about the text. It is interesting to note that S, which here deviates from M more than any version except T in pursuit of circularity, offers appropriate differential translations of הלכים/ללכת (ܐܙܠܝܢ ... ܕܐܙܠܝܢ ... ܠܡܐܙܠ *rmyn...d'zlyn...lm'zl*; cf. Kamenetzky, 207-208) and adds a preposition, '*to* there' (ܠܬܡܢ *ltmn*), but still does not attest משם.

In sum, there is considerable consensus that the text cannot mean 'whence the streams flow' without emendation, and there are no good grounds for emendation. There have been some attempts to see a reference to the rivers returning to their sources without reading 'whence' or 'from which'. Allgeier, for instance, suggests that the verb here must refer to the emergence of the rivers from their sources: 'to the place where the rivers emerge, there they return'. However, Ps 104.10, which he cites, tends actually to contradict that understanding, which would anyway require הלכים to have a different sense in each half of our verse. The Hebrew refers most naturally either to the general course of the rivers, or, more probably, to their destination (the sea); there is no apparent reference here to them returning to their sources. Tyler's 1874 translation is clumsy but clear and correct: 'to the place whither the streams flow, thitherward they repeat their flow.

1.7 they go again] If we had just שבים here, the obvious sense would be 'return', and the verb is used of going back to the place from which one set off in, e.g., 1 Kgs 12.24; 13.17. With ללכת, however, the issue is more complicated, since it has long been recognized that שוב can be used to connote repetition in coordination with other verbs (GKC §120 d; J-M §102 g; §177 b), and that, similarly, the construction שוב + -ל + infinitive can mean to do something again (so, e.g., Delitzsch, citing Hos 11.9; Job 7.7). Consequently, שוב ללכת could mean either 'return to go', or 'go again', and the precise understanding of what the streams are doing will depend on how the verse as a whole is understood.

Arguing for a cyclical image here, Min ('How Do the Rivers Flow?', 228) supposes that the verb can only 'be used for completed actions repeated after an interval', although his argument then requires him to stretch this definition far enough to encompass a continuous flow which passes through its own starting-point; Whybray ('Wonders of Nature', 109) limits the range of the verb in almost identical terms, but prefers to discard the sense of repetition altogether, so that the rivers simply 'return'. This insistence that the verb must express *staccato* rather than *legato* repetition is open to question (see, e.g., Neh 9.28; Lam 3.3, albeit with a different construction), but more importantly it misses the point that rivers do not act like other subjects when used with verbs of motion: if we observe, say, that the Thames 'goes' to London, we do not thereby imply that it leaves Oxford dry. Here the rivers each repeatedly reach the sea, inasmuch as each new unit of water within them comes to the end of its journey, but each arrival and completion is followed immediately and seamlessly by another, so that the rivers reach their destination over and over again. Tyler tries to resolve the question rather differently by imposing a rather parochial view on Qohelet: 'The reference is not so much to perennial rivers as to streams intermitting with the summer's heat, such as were generally the streams of Palestine'.

1.8

(1.8) When all words are worn out, can a man no longer speak? An eye will not be too sated for seeing, nor an ear filled with listening.

Commentary

Most commentators see a break at this point, and Whybray expresses the views of many when he says that, 'The first clause of this verse has the function of drawing together and summing up the thought introduced in v. 4 and exemplified in vv. 5-7, while the remainder of the verse stresses the overwhelming effect on the observer of the ceaseless activity of natural phenomena: they leave him speechless...the eye and the ear are also inadequate to take in what they perceive'. This understanding gives rise to such translations as the RSV's 'All things are full of weariness; a man cannot utter it; the eye is not satisfied with seeing, nor the ear filled with hearing'.

Of course, despite the popularity of such readings, it is not entirely clear how the exclamations are supposed to fit together. The most common interpretations of the first sentence make it claim either that the human is stunned into silence by the state of the world, or that it is all beyond the capacity of speech to describe. The clearer second half of the verse, on the other hand, talks not about the inabilities of the eye and ear to see or hear, but about the fact that they can never be sated by doing so: their owner is not overwhelmed, but left unsatisfied. If these are not just two separate points, then Qohelet has to be saying for some reason that our speech is stopped, but our senses unfulfilled. Any such reading imparts to the text a quality of wonder, and although many scholars see something negative here as well—it is not the scale or business of the world, but its weariness that stuns us—the point remains that humans can barely comprehend what is before them.

There are several problems, however, with taking this verse to be an exclamation along these lines. The most obvious is that it certainly does not, as Whybray suggests, draw together or sum up what has gone before, but makes a quite separate point about its effect on humans which interrupts the progression to further statements about continuity in 1.9. In short, it has to be read as parenthetical, or even as an outburst. The second is that, in order to find a purpose for it here, we have to understand all that has been said so far in terms of something astonishing or overwhelming, in order to justify such human wonder. However much the world may actually fill us with such wonder, though, that is never elsewhere a concern of the book, and it is difficult to see why Qohelet should be concerned with it here. The point that he is more obviously trying to make will be expressed in the next verse, 1.9, and the descriptions in 1.5-7 are usually, rightly, thought to lead up to that point: the sun, wind and streams all exemplify what is actually the character of the world as a whole. In that case, it is surely Qohelet's contention that these are everyday phenomena, which all reveal something deeper, rather than that they are in any sense beyond comprehension or description.

The most important objection, however, is that to see an exclamation here is to ignore or reject the considerable continuity in style and content between 1.8 and the preceding 1.7—an issue that goes to the heart of this verse's meaning and position. It is particularly striking that this verse starts in precisely the same way as the last ('all' + plural noun + participle),[1] but in the second part of the verse we can also see an obvious correspondence, noted by a number of scholars, between the ear that will not be filled by listening, and the sea which is never filled by the rivers. Such indications of continuity suggest very strongly that, rather than making tangential comments about the ineffability of the world, Qohelet is actually here making further observations about speech and senses which are similar to those made about the sun, wind, and sea (so, e.g., Enns). In that case, 1.8 stands not as an exclamation and aside, but as a part of the description on which 1.9 is based.

---

[1] Grossberg, 'Form and Content', 50, notes that 'The reiteration of the chain… at the beginning of two consecutive verses connects the two verses and underscores their equivalence'. Atkinson, *Singing*, 193-94, also discusses the resemblance, and sees more than an exclamation of wonder. He understands the link, however, to indicate not a parallel, but a contrast: human speech does not flow like the rivers, but is distorted by loquacity and self-glorification, while sounds 'go in one ear and out the other', so these verses are about the 'tainted' human perception of the world more generally.

It seems likely that this would be a more usual understanding of the verse if it were not that the first sentence in 1.8 seems to fit it badly.² It is not difficult, after all, to see in the descriptions of the eye and ear a functional equivalence with the previous verse: just as rivers keep flowing but the sea is not filled, so the eye keeps seeing and the ear keeps hearing without either of them ever reaching capacity. What precedes those descriptions does present some problems of its own at the outset, and scholars argue both about whether the subject of the first clause is 'words' or 'things' (the Hebrew term can have either meaning), and about whether this subject is being described as 'tired out' or 'tiring' (the former is much more likely: see the note). The second clause, however, seems to say quite uncontroversially that 'a man will be unable to speak'. This, of course, is what gives rise to the idea that Qohelet is talking about ineffability, and to the consequent interpretation of the whole verse in such terms, although even that understanding often imports a certain nuance to the claim: it is not that a man is struck dumb and cannot speak at all, but that he cannot speak adequately (so, e.g., 'no one can successfully speak', according to Krüger, who sees a link with the ἀφασία of Pyrrhonist scepticism and a rejection here of empiricism).³

If we set that idea aside, however, and read the sentence in the light of the material around it, then it is not difficult to see that Qohelet might be talking about speech in the same way that he talks about rivers, eyes, and ears. The constant use of words may wear them out, or perhaps even use them all up, but that doesn't prevent them being used again—speech doesn't stop because all the words run out. If the sentence actually seems to be saying the opposite, that someone's speech can run dry because there are

---

² Treier, in fact, suggests that these lines do fit 'within the cosmic cycles' and address the insatiability of human desire: 'the eye and the ear become vehicles through which our longings likewise become monotonous'. He offers no explanation, however, for the first sentence.

³ The point then would be that 'the words of human language cannot do justice to the complexity of experienced reality', and Krüger sees an attempt to embody this in the ambiguities and multiple senses of the same words in 1.4-7. He does not explain how this is supposed to align with the subsequent references to the insatiability of the eye and ear, and the general assertions about ambiguity are open to the criticism levelled by Piotti, 'Osservazioni sul Metodo', 132-38, that polysemia is not the same as ambiguity.

no words left, then this is not only a direct reversal of the other illustrations, but also patently absurd and untrue. That is a clear signal, I think, that we are actually dealing with a question, not a statement, or at least with a claim supposed to provoke incredulity, and it was probably intended by the writer to be taken as such (questions in Hebrew are quite commonly not marked explicitly). By taking the sentence this way, we achieve a consistent presentation throughout 1.4-8.[4]

Should we choose not to, then Bundvad (*Time*, 55-56) offers another alternative to the problematic reading of an exclamation, according to which the verse marks the temporal limitations of humanity: in the time allotted to us, we shall never be able to say enough, see enough, or hear enough. While such limitations are undoubtedly a concern for Qohelet, however, it is not clear how the weariness of words or things is supposed to fit into this explanation.

Notes

1.8 when] I take the first clause to be circumstantial or conditional (cf., e.g., 6.7): there is no temporal conjunction in the Hebrew. The construction overall achieves the same effect as, e.g., Amos 3.6, where rhetorical questions are framed within explicit conditional clauses (*contra* J-M §161 d, which takes אם exceptionally to be interrogative).

1.8 all words] דברים can, of course, mean 'things' or 'words', and most older commentators see a generalizing reference here to what has preceded: all things are worn out, in the way that the sun, wind and rivers are. Even if we allow that Qohelet might believe that, he has so far said little which might imply it, and the clause here is immediately followed by a reference to speaking, which uses the cognate verb (לדבר), so the context points strongly to 'words' (cf., e.g., Ginsburg; Schoors, *The Preacher* I, 269-70; Fox). Lauha points out also that the plural דברים elsewhere in Ecclesiastes always has that sense (citing 5.1, 2, 6; 6.11; 7.21; 9.16; 10.12, 13, 14; similarly, Seow), although see the note on 'many words' at 6.11.

1.8 worn out] The text of 4QQoh[b] is compatible with the יגעים of M here, and Puech ('Un nouveau fragment', 621) rightly questions the יגע with a

---

[4] This understanding has been accepted by Bennett. Heard, in 'The Dao of Qoheleth', 86, does not offer a detailed justification for his interesting translation 'All words are wearisome. People never stop talking. Eyes are never satisfied with seeing. Ears never have their fill of hearing', which he glosses as 'The last word is never said, the last sight never seen, the last saying never heard', and apparently understands very much in the terms I have outlined above.

following *vacat* which Ernst and Lange ('4QFragment') read on the fragment 4Q4681. See the Introduction, p. 133, above.

יָגֵעַ is an adjective found only here and in Deut 25.18; 2 Sam 17.2, although the similar יָגִיעַ occurs in Job 3.17, and both words are cognate with the well-attested verb יגע, 'toil', 'grow weary' (found in the pi'el at 10.15). When the noun יְגִיעָה appears in 12.12, it clearly has a causative sense, 'wearying', 'wearing out', and various attempts have been made to find such a meaning here: a number of commentators translate as 'wearisome', which implies that sense (e.g. Crenshaw, Murphy, Longman),[5] and Backhaus (*Den Zeit*, 37-39; cf. 39) has put forward an ingenious argument, based on the supposition that יָגֵעַ can only refer to humans, so that this must mean 'Alles (alle Sachverhم alte) ist (sind) ermüdend [für den Menschen]', 'all things are wearisome (for humans)'. This last permits the sense of the adjective to remain stative, but the overall meaning of the clause to be equivalent to a causative use; its semantic basis, however, is highly questionable.

Seow also wants to have it both ways, and claims that the distinction weary/wearisome is an English one, not present in the Hebrew; if so, we might well ask why the causative sense is apparently confined to the pi'el and hiph'il stems of the cognate verb, while the stative sense appears only in the qal—this is not true in מלא or ירא, which he proposes as analogies (and in the latter, the distinction is anyway between transitive and intransitive uses, a rather different matter). The other biblical uses of יגע give no grounds to suppose that it has a causative implication, but rather connote the weariness or weakness of the subject; later usage of the related terms is similar, although it is interesting to note that the Midrash Rabbah interprets this clause consistently in terms of speech which is wearying for people.[6]

Ogden's attempt to read יְגֵעִים as a participle from the verb, rather than as the attested adjective, is not morphologically problematic, but does not achieve his desired end, since the verb itself connotes weariness, and not just work; had the author wished to say merely that 'everything is toiling', he had plenty of less loaded verbs to choose from (the same objection may be raised against, e.g., Whybray, Lohfink).[7] Perles, 'Miscellany', 130, also appears to

---

[5] The treatment of the issue in Hasel, 'יָגֵעַ, *yāgēa'*, is striking, but not untypical. After an excellent review of general usage, which amply demonstrates the term's usual stative sense, a causative meaning is asserted for this verse wholly on interpretative grounds. The use of 'wearisome' in the ET of Krüger, it should be noted, is misleading; like Lauha and others, he renders 'mühen sich ab', 'weary themselves'.

[6] Salters, 'Textual Criticism', 61, notes that Rashi also takes it this way, but that Ibn Ezra is strongly critical of the interpretation as causative.

[7] Whybray seeks affirmation of the sense 'labour' from the usage of the cognate noun יְגִיעַ, which most commonly connotes the products of work, but may also indicate work itself. There is often a pejorative implication of hardship

be reading a participle when he suggests the sense '"All words are toiling," that is to say, no words are adequate to express it fully', but there is no reason to suppose that the verb can mean 'struggle to achieve something', and it does not have that sense in Sir 43.30, which he adduces in support. Ehrlich's proposed emendation to a pi'el participle is entirely speculative, but may offer the best route for those who insist that the sense must be causative (Salters, 'Textual Criticism', 62, notes that it might be possible to invoke haplography of מ in an original הדברים מיגעים).

1.8 can a man no longer] Lit. 'will a man not be able to'; on the form of the verb in the yiqtol, see J-M §75 i. The use of איש brings the account back to the world of humans. Clearly, the context is not gender-specific, and the appearance of איש rather than אדם is a little striking, given Qohelet's generally strong preference for the latter. The intention is presumably to make it clear that he is speaking about the ability of an individual in this situation: אדם could give the sense that every human is silenced. Whatever the distinction between בני אדם and בני איש in Ps 49.3 (ET 49.2), it offers no biblical basis for Perry's claim (reiterated in his *Book of Ecclesiastes*, 45) that איש has the sense 'great person' here, or his subsequent translation 'even a great person cannot'.

Galling's proposed emendation of לא יוכל to לאִ־יְכַלֶּה in both editions of his commentary (cf. *BHS*) gives the sense 'nobody can complete speaking', that is, 'speak adequately'. It has no versional support, and is an attempt to avoid the apparent difficulty of M when the sentence is read as an assertion. Whether or not Puech, 'Un nouveau fragment', 618, has correctly identified and restored the first line of 4Q468l, moreover, there is probably no space for the additional character. Some of the versions themselves struggled with the expression: S replaces it with ܠܐ ܢܣܒܥ *lʾ nsbʿ* to give 'will not be sated (by speaking)', which is a simple borrowing of the next verb; V *non potest eas homo explicare sermone*, 'a human cannot explain them in words', refers the statement to what has gone before, making language inadequate to describe all the difficult things of the world (a strategy close to that of some modern commentators); T links with what follows, so that the impossibility lies in speaking about the future. G corresponds to M word for word, but σ' has the curious ἀδύνατόν ἐστιν ἄνθρωπον ἐκνικῆσαι λέγοντα, 'it is impossible for a human to prevail by speaking'; variants among the witnesses to this are discussed by Marshall, but all attest what Euringer observed to be a double

---

or weariness in the uses of this noun too, however (as in, e.g., Gen 31.42), and it hardly supports even his view that 'the notion of purposeful or effective *activity* is thus a strong possibility here' (which is itself some way from the sense 'labour'), let alone his subsequent adoption of this as the certain sense. See his 'Wonders of Nature', 107, and the detailed refutation in Piotti, 'Osservazioni sul Metodo', 142-45. Lohfink, 'Wiederkehr', 139, seems to see tiredness as an optional connoetation of the verb, which is favoured anachronistically by world-weary modern translators.

translation of יכל by ἀδύνατον and ἐκνικῆσαι. This is similar in sense to V, and may have influenced it. Derenbourg, 'Notes', 173 n. 2, thinks instead that σ' read לגבר.

In any case, there is quite a lot of divergence between the versions, but none points to a different Hebrew text here; indeed, the problems they have with it, and the solutions which they adopt, indicate that they were dealing with a text identical to M. Without emendation, however, there is no easy way around the curious statement that no-one can speak (unless we wish to follow Derenbourg in reading יוכל as a hoph'al of כול, which would not give the sense of 'measuring' that he claims). As Symmachus has clearly observed, יוכל can have the senses 'prevail' or 'succeed', and a reinterpretation of the verb offers one way out, but it would not be natural to understand the text in terms of these alternative meanings when יוכל is followed by ל- + infinitive, since this is the standard and common construction for 'be able to'.

Seow, in a different attempt to avoid the problem, and taking rather the same line as T, describes the phrase here as 'elliptical': the content will become clear as one reads on into the next verse, and realizes that it is novelty and the future about which one cannot speak. That, though, is hardly ellipsis in the normal sense, and if Qohelet intends such a device, it is problematically interrupted by v. 8b.

1.8 speak] Nishimura, 'Un mashal', tries to assign the very specific sense 'make a proverb' here, noting that this is the reference of the verb in 1 Kgs 5.12-13 (ET 4.32-33). Piotti, 'Osservazioni sul Metodo', 141-42, sets out the arguments against this in detail, but it is obvious that such a meaning is not required, even if it is possible. Piotti also notes (146-47) the connection that Vílchez Líndez makes here with Gen 2.19-20 and the uniquely human capacity to speak. Vílchez Líndez himself thinks that there is an implicit criticism here of a wisdom movement that prided itself on its mastery of speech.

1.8 too sated for seeing] There is considerable versional (G, S, T) support for a conjunction before לא השבע (although Hie, V = M), and it seems probable, at least, that this was read in some early Hebrew manuscripts (it appears in a number of later ones: see de Rossi, Ginsburg, *Writings*). The conjunction is most likely an addition influenced by the subsequent ולא, but it is not impossible that it was original.

Schoors, *The Preacher* I, 192, notes that 'Qoh 1,8 is the only instance where שבע is complemented by an expression with ל', but rightly rejects Dahood's notion ('Qoheleth and Northwest Semitic Philology', 349-50, drawing on the use with מן in 6.3) that this must be an instance of מן = ל-, comparable to a presumed 'Ugaritic-Phoenician' usage; cf. Piotti, 'Usi Linguistici', 52-53. The use of the verb more generally in Ecclesiastes is explored by Fox (118-19), who suggests that with מן it means 'derive satisfaction from', and with a direct object means 'get enough of' or 'be sated with'—the sense which he understands here. It is possible, as Fox implies, that לראות is an object infinitive, in which case it would be used analogously with the common construction of verbs such as החל or יסף (cf. J-M §124 c). There are, however, no other instances of such a construction with שבע, and it is more likely that the main verb is absolute here, with the infinitive used in a prospective or consecutive sense, or as a gerund. Ellermeier, *Qohelet I.1*, 207, considers the idea of an object infinitive, but ultimately opts for 'einen Konsekutivsatz..."Nicht wird das Auge satt, so daß es sieht"', 'a consecutive sentence...: "the eye will not be satisfied so that it sees"', rightly rejecting any implication that the eye will derive no satisfaction *from* seeing. In any case, the most likely sense is that the eye will not reach a point of being sated, either with respect to seeing or when it comes to seeing more.

Euringer notes that T does not directly render תשבע, but ולא יכילא עיינא למחזי כל מא דעתיד למיהוי בעלמא, 'and the eye will be unable to see all that will be in the world', probably reflects an understanding of it.

1.8 filled with listening] The construction of תמלא...משמע raises issues similar to those in the last clause, since מלא does not usually use a preposition at all to indicate the substance with which something is filled; cf. 11.3 אם ימלאו העבים גשם, 'if the clouds are filled *with* rain'. In fact, though, מן is employed in a few places (Schoors, *The Preacher* I, 192, notes Isa 2.6; Jer 51.34; Ezek 32.6; Ps 127.5), where there is no discernible difference in the sense, and it seems likely that the motive for using it here was to prevent this clause from being construed in the same way as the last: Qohelet varies his expression so that the eye is too sated to see, but the ear simply filled by what it has heard. It is noteworthy that, although Syh has ܡܢ ܫܡܥܐ *mn šmʿʾ*, 'from hearing', the Origenic manuscripts of G read τοῦ ἀκοῦσαι, 'to hear', instead of ἀπὸ ἀκροάσεως, 'from listening', reflecting a tradition in which there has, in fact, been just such an alignment with the syntax of the previous clause. Kamenetzky, 208, takes the change of preposition in S ܠܡܫܡܥ *lmšmʿ*, 'to hear', to be an adaptation to Syriac usage, but there are other points of contact with the O-group manuscripts, and this may reflect their influence on the transmission of the Syriac text.

1.9-11

(1.9) What will be, will be whatever has been,
and what will be done, whatever has been done—
with nothing new beneath the sun.
(1.10) Though when speaking someone might say,
'Look—this is new',
it has already been, in the aeons which have existed apart from us.
(1.11) There is no memory of the earlier times,
and likewise there will be no memory of the later,
which have yet to happen
—or of those which are going to happen later still.

Commentary

Now Qohelet does sum up, implicitly deducing from his examples what has already been asserted in v. 4, that the world is constant, so that it will not change, although he adds the further assertion that it can contain nothing which has not already happened or been done. It is difficult to render the Hebrew verbs of v. 9 using English tenses, but the basic purpose of the first two clauses is to assert that whatever will happen at any given time is the same as what has been happening already. The sun comes up and goes round, just as it always has and always will, while the wind blows, the rivers flow, words are used, eyes see, ears hear: these actions are not the backdrop to more exciting events, but the epitome of everything that happens; no instance of existence or action is isolated.

The verse finishes with an assertion that is presented as though it were a logical corollary of what has gone before: if every future is the same as what preceded it, then no future can contain anything which did not exist before. Lohfink ('Wiederkehr', 143) is probably right to emphasize that modern attitudes toward novelty and progress should not lead us to presume that an ancient reader would have been dismayed by such a statement; it is, however, a grave over-generalization when he supposes that 'all the cultures shaped by archaic religion' would have viewed innovation with suspicion, and that we should take this statement, therefore, to be triumphant.¹ This is an initial conclusion, which reminds us by its reference to 'under the sun' that Qohelet is still addressing the question of v. 3, but which is really only laying the ground for the following verses.

The Hebrew of v. 10 is a little awkward, but the sense of vv. 10-11 clear enough. Qohelet accepts that it may not be unusual for someone to say that something is new. If such an observation were really valid, then novelty would exist, and each period of time would have to be able to include things which existed at no previous time; correspondingly, there would be beginnings even if there were not ends. His response is simply to reject all this: we might *talk* about novelty, but novelty is not real, and we perceive something to be new only because human memory is too short to comprehend the whole scope of history. On the face of it, though, this objection seems absurd. If I sit at my desk and make a paper dart, that dart is surely new: it did not exist before I folded it into shape. Even if we want to conjure up some very particular view of history, in which my exact counterpart made an identical dart in some long-lost era, then the dart may have been identical—but it is not the *same* dart: my dart is new.²

Qohelet does not explain himself directly, and this has provoked a certain amount of discussion around the possible senses of the Hebrew word for 'new'. The apparent absurdity does not end there, however, since Qohelet goes on immediately to claim that there is no memory of earlier times, despite the fact that, issues around human memory aside, people had already been recording things in writing for at least two thousand years in the Near East before

---

[1] Lohfink goes on to talk about unspecified New Year festivals etc., having already drawn in supposed influences from sources so diverse as Egyptian religion and classical mythology, and his 'archaic religion' seems little more than a selective synthesis of elements culled from several very different religious traditions.

[2] Crenshaw, *The Ironic Wink*, 3, notes the similar protests of Wislawa Szymborska in her Nobel Prize acceptance speech: 'that's what you wrote, Ecclesiastes. But you yourself were born new under the sun. And the poem you created is also new under the sun, since no one wrote it down before you. And all your readers are also new under the sun, since those who lived before you couldn't read your poem.... There's no poet in the world who can say this, least of all a great poet like yourself.' A full English translation is currently available online at https://www.nobelprize.org/prizes/literature/1996/szymborska/lecture/, and the relevant section is excerpted in Segal, 152.

Ecclesiastes was composed. A similar claim is going to be made again in 2.16, a little later. At a certain level, we probably have to acknowledge that Qohelet is making deliberately provocative assertions, which cannot stand up even to the briefest scrutiny without considerable qualification.[3]

Qohelet probably intends both ideas to be understood, however, in terms of the picture he has just painted, of a world filled with endless, unresolved activity, which humans can each glimpse only briefly. If everything in that world is part of such activity, then in some sense it may indeed be true that nothing is new: my dart may only just have taken its current form, but it came from a sheet of paper that existed before, which came from a tree, and so on. If I throw it accidentally into the fire, it will enjoy a new form as ash and smoke. Whether Qohelet means us to accept that nothing is new, in this sense that nothing comes from nothing, or whether (less probably) he actually does believe that the world has already worked its way through every permutation of existence, his point is that nothing stands outside: everything in the world is implicated in some broader process or processes. When humans fail to understand this, it is because of the limitations placed upon them by their own brevity, which Qohelet describes in terms of there being no memory. Bundvad (*Time*, 57) speaks of humans here as 'strikingly unable to forge links between what should be our past, present, and future', and thinks that '1:11 describes human beings as unable to transcend the present in which they live'.

Accordingly, when Qohelet refers to memory, he is probably not thinking of traditions, records or histories, but of the direct human

---

[3] Krüger, 'Dekonstruktion', 111-14, citing Kaiser, 'Sinnkrise', 100, thinks that Qohelet is alluding deliberately to Isa 43.18-19 and 65.17, in order to address ideas about 'a new heaven and a new earth'; cf. also, e.g., his 'Le Livre', 157-61, Mazzinghi, 'Enochism', 158-61; and a more nuanced approach in Barbour, *The Story of Israel*, 51-54. There are resemblances to those passages, but I am not persuaded by the ideas that a writer in the third century would have had to address apocalyptic and eschatological concerns, or that novelty was so prominent a theme in prophecy (so Ravasi and Manfredi 'Qohelet', 301) that we must read specific intentions into any such resemblances. Because the author of Ecclesiastes never explicitly engages with such concerns, it is hard to say whether he knew of them or saw any contradiction between them and Qohelet's claims, so we should be wary of reading some sort of subtext just because we take them to be contradictory; cf. Schultz, 'Qoheleth and Isaiah', 61-64.

recollection that informs our understanding and action—his understanding is closer, perhaps, to the idea of experience. Bianchi (in 'La Storia, la memoria', 66) puts it well: 'This belief leads Qohelet to think that experience is unique and personal, and that it cannot be passed from one generation to another because "the law of time" is different for every person. Each human is therefore an island with respect to the generations that have been and those that are to come.'[4] Nothing is new, because it has already enjoyed an existence during the vast span of time from which each individual human has been excluded—but nobody alive experienced it then.

These themes will be picked up again in 3.14-15, where the nature of the world and the limitations of human knowledge are linked explicitly to divine activity and intention, and where Qohelet indicates more precisely that the world is sealed: nothing can be added or taken away.

Notes

1.9 will be…has been[1, 2]] The two parallel clauses are each probably to be read as tripartite non-verbal clauses ('*x* הוא *y*', meaning '*x* = *y*'; cf. J-M §154 j), with relative clauses acting as the substantive elements ('*that which... = that which...*')—although there is another way to construe the Hebrew: see the note on 'whatever', below. There is considerable variety, but the usual word-order in such tripartite clauses is predicate–pronoun–subject, so the statements are probably to be read as statements about the nature of the future, not about the past/present (cf. Ellermeier, *Qohelet I.1*, 208). This is the reverse of the natural order in English, and so I have transposed the elements in translation: מה שהיה is rendered 'whatever has been', שיהיה 'what will be', מה שנעשה 'whatever has been done', and שיעשה 'what will be done'. There are no reasons to emend the consonantal text, even though S lacks equivalents to the second -ש in each clause (suggesting, perhaps, that it is following G here).

Hebrew does not easily express such finely graded distinctions of tense as does English, which creates issues for the translator in a number of places. There are more serious interpretative problems involved as well, however. Here, it is clear that the imperfect forms (שיהיה, שיעשה) must refer to the future (*contra*, e.g., Ginsburg, Ehrlich, who take them to indicate present tense), but the perfect may refer to the past or present (at least when it is referring to

---

[4] 'Questa convinzione spinge Qohelet a pensare che l'esperienza sia unica e personale e non possa essere trasmessa da una generazione all'altra poiché «la legge dei momenti» è diversa per ogni uomo. Ciascun uomo è dunque un'isola rispetto alle generazioni che furono e a quelle che verranno'.

states, not actions). In principle, therefore, what Qohelet is saying could be understood as a statement either that things in the future will remain the way they always have been, or that things from the past will recur in the future. To put that in other terms, he could be talking about continuity or about cycles. Following what has been said already, I take continuity to be the more likely implication, but it is not clear that cycles can actually be excluded.

Relevant to this are questions that have been raised about שנעשה, in respect both of its sense and its construal.[5] The issues are discussed in detail by Isaksson, *Studies*, 69-76, who contrasts the virtual unanimity among commentators that נעשה should be rendered here by a past tense,[6] with their strong tendency to translate it using a present tense in other places (e.g. 1.14; 2.17). He also notes that the perfect היו in 7.19, for instance, is clearly not referring to the past, so היה here cannot be used to determine the time-reference of נעשה (and we may note that in 10b, where the first היה has explicitly to express the past, this is indicated by כבר). I accept Isaksson's point that a translation of the perfect forms with the present tense here might well be more accurate, and certainly more consistent with translations required elsewhere, but it is important to note also that Ecclesiastes is imposing no actual distinction between past and present, and the declaration can embrace both.

As regards the parsing of נעשה, Fox (in his discussion of 8.11) claims that 'The MT regularly points ʿSH-niphʿal as the perfect *naʿăśāh*, even where the participle (*naʿăśeh*) seems appropriate', and his discussion of this verse suggests that he considers 1.9 to be just such an instance. A similar line is taken by Schoors, *The Preacher* I, 96-97, who approaches the question *via* the versional evidence. With some resort to variant readings in the G tradition, he concludes that all the versions translate the different occurrences of the word fairly consistently: G with the past tense,[7] V with the present, T and S with perfect forms of the verb. This, to be sure, says something about the inclination of the translations to render the consonantal text with consistency, but it is doubtful that it demonstrates anything more. The participle is certainly used

---

[5] It is not relevant to the tense, but we may note in passing that here, in 1.14, and in 2.17 ben Naphtali reportedly pointed שנעשה with *metheg* under the ש, ben Asher with *metheg* under the נ here and in 2.17, and under both the ש and the נ in 1.14 (see Lipschütz).

[6] There are exceptions, e.g., Podechard, Fox (although the issue is complicated in the latter's case by his construal of נעשה). The versions seem all to have read past tense (with future for the imperfects); note especially the very explicit σ' (as retroverted from Syh by Field; the words preserved elsewhere in Greek are underlined): ὃ προάγον ἐστὶν αὐτὸ <u>τὸ ἐσόμενον</u> καὶ ὃ προσεγένετο αὐτὸ ἐστι <u>τὸ μέλλον ἔσεσθαι</u>, 'what has gone before is what will be, and what has happened is what is going to be in the future'.

[7] G in fact uses perfect participles: the perfect because it has parsed the verb as qatal, the participle because that is how it represents the construction with מה ש-; cf. 8.7; 10.14.

in 4.1 נעשים (in contrast to the שנעשו of the similar 1.14), and the construction with אין in 8.11 would seem to require a participle rather than the perfect of M, but it seems unlikely that we can extrapolate from those instances a general conclusion either that M is vocalizing incorrectly in many other places, or, as Samet supposes, vocalizing participles as though this were a lamedh-aleph verb, so that they are indistinguishable from the perfect.[8]

Isaksson, *Studies*, 73, suggests that 'in some uses the *sens linguistique* of the author did not make a sharp distinction' between perfect and participle forms of the niph'al in this verb. To put that in rather different terms, we might observe that the author of Ecclesiastes expected his readers to be following an unvocalized text, in which the forms could not be distinguished except with reference to their context; in those places where the context gives no clue and no other guidance is offered, therefore, it is reasonable for us to assume that he would have seen no problem with either vocalization, and in such cases neither the participle nor the perfect is really 'wrong'.[9] In fact, though, 1.9 does offer some contextual guidance: the parallel היה—which is very unlikely to be a rare participle from that verb—suggests that we are dealing with a perfect. Although a participle would certainly affirm a present tense here, and therefore tend to exclude a cyclical reading, there is no reason to regard the vocalization in M as less plausible, and it is, after all, the same way most of the versions took the verb.

Finally, as regards the difference between the statements, Wright and Barton suggest that Ecclesiastes typically uses היה of natural phenomena and עשה of human actions; this idea is difficult to sustain even in some of the passages cited (e.g. 3.22; 6.12), and it seems unlikely that such a precise distinction was intended.

1.9 whatever[1, 2] מה is probably to be taken here as an indefinite, not an interrogative pronoun (see GKC §137 c; J-M §144 f-g). It is used this way in Ecclesiastes principally in the combination מה ש- (1.9 twice; 3.15, 22; 6.10; 7.24; 8.7; 10.14), which is itself largely confined to the expressions מה שהיה / מה שיהיה, the second use in this verse being the exception (Schoors, *The Preacher* I, 59). Although, however, τι in Greek can likewise function as indefinite or interrogative, the translator of G has apparently understood מה to be interrogative, and has taken the Hebrew in each part to mean 'what (is) that which...?': accordingly, his rendering is most naturally read as questions with answers: 'What is that which...? It is that which...' The Codex Graecus Venetus similarly sees here a pair of questions and answers, and although less

---

[8] Samet, 'Validity', 1069-70. This is not one of the places where she believes a participle to be required, but she claims (n. 14) that 'even if one tends to interpret some of the occurrences of נַעֲשָׂה as perfect forms which refer to the present tense, one still has to admit that this interpretation does not hold true for all cases'.

[9] On the constraints which operate in unvocalized texts in this respect, see especially Barr, 'Reading a Script without Vowels'; also his 'Vocalization'.

likely than the reading as indefinite, this is by no means an impossible way to understand the Hebrew. That construal makes no great difference to the sense, although it shifts the emphasis from identifying the future to identifying the past/present. On Jerome's renderings of the construction, see the note 'whatever exists' at 6.10. Here we may observe that there is a conjunction before the second *quid* in Hie *quid est quod fuit ipsum quod erit et quid est quod factum est ipsum quod fiet*, which corresponds to M, G, S: this is absent from his revision of the Old Latin, which is otherwise identical (see Caspari, *Hiob*, 6; Leanza, 'Le tre versione', 91), and from V. John Cassian's *Collationes* (8.21), however, cites the Latin text here as *quid est quod fuit ipsum quod est et quid est quod factum est ipsum quod fiet*, which exchanges *erit*, 'will be', for *est*, 'is', but does have the conjunction: its loss is more likely a product of the Latin transmission than the reflection of a variant in G (although it is lacking in one Coptic text as well).[10] Jerome's renderings should probably also be read as questions, and so Hie as 'What is there that has been? The very thing that will be! *And* what is there that has been done? The very thing that will be done.'

1.9 with nothing new] Lit. 'and there is not/will not be anything new'; expressions with אין are non-verbal clauses, which derive their tense from context. Although I think this is most naturally read as a further statement about the future, it may be more general. Many late manuscripts omit the conjunction (see de Rossi, Ginsburg, *Writings*), perhaps because it may have seemed redundant.

Krüger suggests that the Hebrew means not 'there is (absolutely) nothing new', but, less radically, 'there is nothing absolutely new', with כל in effect qualifying חדש. His justification of this with reference to the accents imputes to them a more interpretative character than they probably possess here, and that evidence anyway goes only to the understanding of those who placed the accents. The suggestion is attractive, all the same, but none of the other versions has read the text that way, and it would require us to suppose a highly unusual use of כל (perhaps as in the difficult כל הבל of Ps 39.6?). Other uses of אין כל (cf. Num 11.6; 2 Sam 12.3; Prov 13.7) do not furnish precise parallels, but point to the conventional understanding.

Cook ('Aspects', 489) includes this clause in the very short list of places where he believes that the translator of G broke with his habitual consistency, in order to 'nuance his translation', and Aitken too ('Rhetoric and Poetry', 61), has seen deliberate stylistic variation in the translation of חדש here by πρόσφατον ('fresh', 'recent'; cf. La, Hie *recens*), but by καινόν in the next

---

[10] See Michael Petschenig (ed.), *Iohannis Cassiani Conlationes XXIIII* (CSEL 13; Vienna: Sons of Carl Gerold, 1886), p. 236; PL 49, col. 756. Cassian continues *et non est omne recens sub sole*, 'and there is not anything fresh under the sun', which is the same as Hie, and it seems likely that Hie in this verse overall is close to La.

verse (α', σ' read καινόν here). This may be more than variation for the sake of it, as οὐκ ἔστιν πᾶν καινόν might well have conveyed the unwanted implication 'there is nothing remarkable', but it leads G to suggest that everything under the sun is stale.

1.10 Though when speaking someone might say] I take the literal sense to be either 'there is someone talking who might say' or, less likely, 'there might be an utterance which says', and I have translated a little loosely to cover both possibilities: my understanding is not dissimilar to Longman's even looser 'Here is a common expression', although I see a more specific contrast between what might be claimed in casual conversation, and what Qohelet views as the reality. On the more common rendering, 'there is a thing about which someone says', see below.

The general sense here is not in doubt: Qohelet claims that, though it may be said of something that it is new, this something is not really new. The clause sets up a hypothetical situation, and must be understood either with an implicit conditional, temporal or concessive construction ('If/when/though there is...'), or simply by taking the first part of the verse to be a question ('Is there...'; so, e.g., σ', Hie, RSV; cf. Fox). In any case, the initial יש does not here simply state a fact. That much is essentially undisputed, but it is harder to pin down precisely how the author intended his words to be construed.

M vocalizes דָּבָר, 'thing' or 'word', and the following verb as qal, to give the literal sense 'a thing/word that will say', which is undoubtedly the simplest and most natural way to read the consonants. If we retain that literal sense, then דבר must presumably be 'word', since things do not speak, and the looser implication would be something like 'if a statement is made, claiming that something is new'. G ὃς λαλήσει καὶ ἐρεῖ, 'whoever will speak and say',[11] is, on the face of it, very different, and has led to proposals that the translator must have read שידבר ויאמר (McNeile, 138) or שידבר וישאמר (Euringer), with the characters of יש in metathesis, and understood as the initial characters of a separate verb (so, e.g. Seow; Yi, 20-21). Since this text would presumably have arisen through error, there is little weight in Gordis' objection that such expressions are impossible Hebrew, but he may well be correct anyway to suppose that G is actually vocalizing דבר as a participle, דֹּבֵר, rather than reading a yiqtol (for the participle used substantively in the sense 'someone speaking', see, e.g., Esth 10.3; Ps 5.7 [ET 5.6]; 15.2; Prov 16.13; Amos 5.10; and note especially Job's 2.13 אין דבר אליו, lit. 'there was no talker/ no-one talking to him', from which a translator might readily deduce that יש דבר should mean 'there is/was someone talking'). In that case, we might suppose either that G's source-text had merely lost the initial yodh of יש, leaving שדבר (and G itself then discarded the second relative as redundant), or, as Gordis

---

[11] Cassian (see the notes on the previous verse) has *quod loquatur et dicat*, which renders the awkward ὅς of G loosely. S is certainly following G too, although it paraphrases slightly to read '(as for) everyone who will speak and say'.

prefers and I think probable, that it was identical to M. Goldman similarly suggests that G has recognized the function of שׁ, and tried to reflect this in its own construction, so that '(if/when) there is one speaking' becomes '(if/when) someone should say', which in turn forces a rendering of the subsequent relative as a conjunction (to give a construction rather like the English 'if someone is talking and says').

In that case, G construes דבר differently, but actually ends up with a sense that is close to the literal sense of M: both envisage a situation in which someone speaks and makes a claim, and they differ merely in their identifications of דבר as the speaker or the speech. G has probably been pushed toward 'speaker' because speeches do not usually 'speak', but M is not impossible in that sense, and אמר quite commonly specifies the content of a דבר (see, e.g., 1 Kgs 2.30; 22.9; Neh 2.20). S ܗܠ ܕܢܡܠܠ ܘܢܐܡܪ *kl dnmll wn'mr*, '(as for) anyone who will speak, and say', is in the same ballpark, although it is probably not a separate translation of the Hebrew here, but an interpretation of the Greek (with ὅς taken as an indefinite pronoun; so Ginsburg, 501, by implication; Schoors, 'Peshitta', 354; Goldman). V paraphrases, but *nec valet quisquam dicere*, 'nor is anyone able to say', seems to suggest a similar approach. Later, it seems likely that the Midrash construed the clause in much the same way as G: the דבר is someone who makes the claim, but it is countered by חברו, 'his colleague' or 'fellow scholar', who מוכיח עליו, 'proves against him' (with a matching participle).

Two of the other ancient versions, however, read the Hebrew differently, taking דבר not as the speaker or speech, but as the 'thing' about which the claim is being made. So T has אית פתגם דיימר אנשׁ, '(If) there is a word/thing about which a man will say'. Similarly, σ', although it renders the overall construction as a question, has ἆρα ἔστιν τι ὃ ἐρεῖ τις, 'is there something of which someone says?', and this has influenced the reading of Hie also, although not in a simple way.[12] This construal reads שׁיאמר with an indefinite

---

[12] The reading as given is explicitly attested for σ' by Nobilius in Field; Marshall notes the sources as mss 161, 248. Jerome, however, cites σ' as *putasne est qui possit dicere*, 'is there someone able to say?', and Field himself observes that this would seem instead to reflect ἆρα ἔστι τις ὅς ἐρεῖ, 'is there really someone who will say?' (which would be closer to G); this is in turn comparable to V *nec ualet quisquam dicere*, 'nor is anyone able to say', which converts it into a statement. From the fact that σ' frequently influences V, Goldman infers that the reading cited by Jerome is genuinely σ', while the reading of the manuscripts is falsely attributed, and most likely α'. To be sure, attributions are sometimes incorrect in the manuscripts, but it is striking that the lemma of Hie, which itself frequently reflects σ', here corresponds to their reading with its *estne uerbum de quo dicatur*, 'is there a word about which it may be said?' This means that the influence of σ' on Jerome can be used as an argument in favour of either reading, but it is most economical to suppose that there were never two separate readings, and that Jerome has misread σ', or his own notes on σ'.

subject, and takes the relative clause as elliptical for שיאמר עליו or suchlike (cf. McNeile, 56; he notes similar ellipses in 12.1 and Exod 22.8, although in neither of those is there any comparable scope for confusion about the subject). A similar sense might be achieved by a vocalization of שֶׁיֵּאָמֵר as שֶׁיֵּאָמֵר, the niphʻal, as Ehrlich proposes; commentators, however, have been inclined not only to retain the vocalization in M, but to assume that M shares this understanding—which is very far from certain—and the approach found in T and σ' has dominated more modern translations.[13]

It would be wrong to describe this approach as forced, but it seems much more complicated and less natural than taking דבר here as a reference to speech or speaking, and as the active subject of the following verb. Were there something in the context that might drive us to import an indefinite or impersonal subject, and to assume a subsequent ellipsis, the relative complexity might be forgiven. As often in this book, however, the context is of limited help. In a very broad sense, we might say that Qohelet is talking about general phenomena, and so the idea of a 'thing' here would not be inappropriate. On the other hand, we might equally say that the more immediate context tells against this: as in v. 8, putting דבר close to a verb of speech is not the clearest way to indicate that it should be understood in its less common sense of 'thing' or 'matter'. I have opted in the end for the construal that seems simplest, but, although both understandings yield a similar meaning overall, I think it is likely also that a translation in terms of speech brings out a nuance in Qohelet's point. He is not merely trying to pre-empt some potential exception to his claims, but acknowledging that people quite often speak of something or another as 'new': that this is a commonplace of discourse, he asserts, does not make it true. Perhaps, indeed, he is even suggesting that simply to use the word 'new' of anything is always to misrepresent reality.

Like the אין which precedes in v. 9, ש does not specify tense, and we could continue to translate as future (cf. G λαλήσει), but I take the following יאמר to have, in effect, a modal sense.

1.10 Look—this is new] Ecclesiastes uses ראה זה in 7.27, 29 also. In those verses it is followed by a verb, and must be understood either as a freestanding exclamation, lit. 'Look at this: I have found' (which is how I take it there), or as part of an asyndetic relative clause, 'Look at this (which) I have found'. Those uses might tell against detaching the pronoun from the verb

---

[13] Atkinson, *Singing*, 195, notes the strong reluctance of commentators to render דבר as 'word', but his own preference is to adopt that sense while retaining the construal designed to allow 'thing'. Comparing Rev 21.5, he tries to draw from the text a christological reading, 'There is a Word of whom one says, "Behold this one! New he is"', and sees in the passage an invitation to find in creation a witness to divine providence.

here, to read an imperative followed by a tripartite nominal clause 'Look! This (זה), it (הוא) (is) new!' (cf., e.g., Ginsburg, Delitzsch, McNeile, 56, Fox). The conventional translation, 'Look at this (זה)! It (הוא) is new', is also favoured by the accents and was apparently the understanding of the Masoretes, as well as of T and S. On the other hand, זה...הוא is a favourite expression of Ecclesiastes (Barton notes 2.23; 4.8; 6.2; cf. also 5.18, with היא), and the book commonly uses it to form just such nominal clauses, with the predicate between the two pronouns (cf. J-M §154 i). Strictly speaking, G ἰδὲ τοῦτο καινόν ἐστιν and Jerome's Latin renderings (Hie *uide hoc nouum est*; V *ecce hoc recens est*) could be read either way, but they marginally favour 'Look! this is new', and hence the reading as a tripartite clause. The Hebrew is genuinely ambiguous and has been taken both ways, therefore, but in 7.27 and 7.29 there are reasons to suppose anyway that ראה זה זה means little more than 'Look', or 'Look here', serving as a call to pay attention to what follows, rather than as an instruction to examine something specific. If we take that to be a plausible meaning here as well, then both understandings come to much the same thing, and the only reason to insist on 'Look at this' would be a desire to have זה pick up the preceding דבר, taken in the sense 'thing'.

The speaker here need not be pointing to an object or phenomenon: ראה can be used of giving consideration to something in a more general way than 'looking' at it, but the imperative in particular often also has a reduced force, as in, e.g., Gen 27.27, where the free-standing imperative invites consideration of a claim (and sight is certainly not involved), or in 2 Sam 15.27-28, where it simply introduces an instruction and then a statement, with no implication that real observation or thought is needed for either. In such places, it almost seems to serve merely as a discourse marker (comparable to the use of 'look' in English expressions like 'Look, I really ought to go now', or to uses of הנה and הן in Hebrew), and it is striking that such instances usually seem to occur in direct speech. See similarly Gen 31.50; 39.14; Exod 7.1; 10.10; 16.29; 31.2; 33.12; 35.50; Deut 1.8, 21; 2.24, 31; 4.5; 11.26; 30.15; Josh 6.2; 8.1, 4, 8; 23.4; 1 Sam 25.35; 2 Sam 7.2; 14.30; 15.3; 2 Kgs 6.32; Jer 1.10; 40.4; Ezek 4.15; Zech 3.4; 6.8. As well, perhaps, as using ראה זה this way in 7.27, 29, Qohelet possibly uses the simple imperative similarly at 7.14 also—though in that verse, as in some others of these, there may be an actual invitation to take stock and consider. Apart from the fact that it has *uide* for *ecce*, Hie *uide hoc nouum est iam fuit in saeculis quae fuerunt ante nos* is identical to Cassian's text (see the preceding notes), and suggests that Jerome is staying close to the Old Latin here (interestingly, he does in fact use the *uide* found in Cassian when he translates the verse in V).

1.10 already has been] כבר is used frequently in Ecclesiastes (1.10; 2.12, 16; 3.15 twice; 4.2; 6.10; 9.6, 7), but not elsewhere in biblical Hebrew; it occurs in later Hebrew and in Aramaic (cf. T here, and the ܟܒܪ *kbr* of S), but Schoors, *The Preacher* I, 116, observes that attestations in Aramaic are mostly late, so it may not be an 'Aramaism' in Ecclesiastes. Whitley's idea that the temporal use has developed from Hebrew כברה, 'a distance' (cf. Gen 35.16; 48.7; 2 Kgs 5.19), is speculative and unconvincing.

Although the subject could be implicit in the verb, we might expect a pronoun in this clause (since הוא should be read with the previous), and it is interesting to observe ἤδη αὐτὸ attested in Origenic manuscripts, in Syh (ܐܝܬܘܗܝ ܗ݂ܘ ܗ݂ܘ ܗ݂ܘ: *'ytwhy h' ܗ݂ܘ hw* ✓ *hw'*—the pronoun is under lemnisk),[14] and in a correction to G^S. This is probably, however, a facilitation rather than an original reading.

1.10 aeons] לעלמים is written *plene*, לעולמים, in 4QQoh^b line 1, but the reading supports M against the possibility that G ἐν reflects an original -ב in the source-text (as McNeile, 138, suggests, although he also wonders if it might be an accidental repetition of the previous syllable). The first ܡܢ *mn* in S ܡܢ ܥܠܡܝܢ ܕܡܢ ܠܩܘܕܡܝܢ *mn 'lmyn dmn lqwdmyn*, lit. 'from the aeons which (are) from before us', has probably arisen as a result of the second.

Ecclesiastes uses עולם unusually elsewhere (see the notes at 3.11; 12.5), but Jenni's belief (in 'Das Wort 'ōlām', part 2, 23-24) that its freestanding position in this verse must reflect the influence of the Greek αἰών seems to be exaggerating the distinctiveness: for all that the noun generally appears in construct expressions or with an adverbial sense, it is not a great leap to this use from those found at, e.g., Ps 145.13; Jer 28.8.

1.10 have existed] M has a disagreement between the singular verb היה and its apparent subject, עלמים, which has a plural form. *BH^3*, *BHS*, comparing a similar case in 2.7, would emend the verb accordingly to plur. הָיוּ with a few Hebrew manuscripts cited by de Rossi (on which, see Goldman). The readings of those manuscript witnesses are almost certainly just facilitative (cf. Delsman, 'Inkongruenz', 28), but although the singular verb is better attested and seems *difficilior*, it could itself simply be the result of influence from the preceding היה. The versions are of little help, showing only appropriate adaptation to the usages of the various languages. Correspondingly, there are plural verbs in G τοῖς γενομένοις, T דהוו, Hie and V *quae fuerunt*;

---

[14] 'Lemnisk' is the term commonly used for a symbol in Syh that resembles an 'S' turned on its side; its use is not fully understood and has been much discussed: see Field lxiv–lxvii, and the bibliography given by Marshall in his footnote to this passage. It occurs four times in Ecclesiastes (the other uses are in 2.15, 17; 11.9), and Gentry, 'Hexaplaric Materials', 22, notes that 'Since all four instances in Ecclesiastes mark text not in MT, we have no clear evidence here for a function different from that of the obelus'. He goes on to observe, though, that 'All four instances in Ecclesiastes...may involve doublets and one wonders if the lemnisk is signalling a circumstance such as this' (n. 28). Middeldorpf, *Codex Syriaco-Hexaplaris*, 648, understood the Syriac to reflect τοῦτο, rather than αὐτὸ, but that seems improbable in the light of the other witnesses.

S, on the other hand, omits the verb altogether as unnecessary, while Field retroverts σ' as the similarly verbless τῷ αἰῶνι τῷ πρὸ ἡμῶν—although the citation in Jerome's commentary, on which this is largely based, does read a singular verb: *in saeculo quod fuit ante nos* 'in the age which was before us'.

It is possible that the noun, although plural in form, was usually construed as singular (HCM speak of its 'noncount semantics' overriding the plural morphology), but again the available evidence is of little help. Whitley considers Isa 26.4; 45.17; Dan 9.24 suggestive of singular usage, but their evidential value is questionable, and it is certainly not the case, as Seow less cautiously asserts, that these passages show עלמים sometimes to have been 'treated as singular'. Gordis offers two possible explanations which would permit us to read the singular of M while avoiding the problem of disagreement altogether, but neither is convincing. The first, also proposed by some earlier scholars and more recently supported by Schoors, *The Preacher* I, 158, is that היה may have been used impersonally here ('the ages which it/there has been'). Gordis compares ועלטה היה in Gen 15.17; ארבע הידות יהיה in 47.24; and תורה אחת יהיה in Exod 12.49, but none of these, we may observe, entails the use of an impersonal verb after a relative pronoun. The second of Gordis' suggestions is that the verb has been attracted to the number of the relative pronoun, but for this he is able only to adduce parallels from later liturgical usage, and it seems, in any case, to be more a way of explaining an error than of justifying a reading. We might add a third possibility, that אשר היה מלפננו is an independent relative clause which specifies עלמים ('in the aeons—that which has...'). This cannot be considered a natural reading, however, any more than can the attempt in Kamano, *Cosmology*, 47, to take אשר as causal and read 'It has already...because it has'.

I think there is a risk of striving too hard to preserve the singular here when it is not self-evidently the better reading. Not only is it manifestly simpler to consider היה an error for היו, but it is difficult to identify any satisfactory sense which does not involve taking עלמים as the subject of the verb. Only if strong reasons can be presented for that noun having been construed as singular (in this case or generally) should we retain היה.

1.10 apart from us] מלפני is not used in any other passage to express time (but cf. Isa 41.26 מלפנים), and usually appears in the context either of separation from the presence or sight of someone, or of, e.g., fear, humility when confronted by someone. These normal senses are found elsewhere in Ecclesiastes (3.14; 8.12, 13; 10.5), but G notably renders with ἀπὸ ἔμπροσθεν here (reading as לפני + מן), rather than with the ἀπὸ προσώπου which it uses in those places, and most modern commentators have also seen a basic equivalence with לפנינו; see, e.g., Gordis, Schoors, *The Preacher* II, 308. I think, however, that it is difficult both to assign an abnormal temporal sense, and to overlook the word's usual connotation of separation. Correspondingly, I take the clause to foreshadow the next verse: the ages are, as it were, out of our sight and presence, and so we can know nothing of them.¹⁵ I understand the usage, then, to be analogous to that in, e.g., Gen 23.4, 8, where Abraham wants to bury his dead in a place which is 'separated from' him: ואקברה מתי מלפני.

1.11 memory] Elsewhere in biblical Hebrew, when -ל is used to indicate possession of a זכרון, the possessors are not those who will *be* remembered, but those who will remember; so in, e.g., Josh 4.7, the stones will be a memorial *for* (-ל) the Israelites, not *of* them (cf. Exod 12.14; 13.9; 28.12; Num 17.5). That is akin to the idea of a 'subjective genitive': those who possess the memory are remembering. The context here demands, however, that the meaning must be objective in both cases; that is, those who possess the memory are the ones being remembered (so also in 2.16).

Despite the inclination of some commentators (e.g. Schoors, *The Preacher* I, 63; Krüger; HCM) to see זְכָרוֹן here and in 2.16 as an alternative to the normal form of the absolute state (זִכָּרוֹן), it seems unlikely that alternative vocalizations would occur together in this verse, and altogether more probable that זְכָרוֹן points the noun as being in the construct state (so *HALOT*, BDB). See the discussion in the Introduction, p. 163, above. The -ל which directly follows each means that it cannot strictly be in a construct relationship with the subsequent noun, but the use of construct forms before prepositions is a phenomenon attested elsewhere, and is not inherently problematic (cf. GKC §130 a and J-M §129 n); biblical and mishnaic examples are cited by, e.g., Barton, Gordis, and Whitley. It is tempting to speculate in this case that the pointing is a Masoretic attempt to address the subjective/objective ambiguity of זכרון.

With regard to the μνήμη of G, it is not clear what Vinel is attempting to suggest by emphasizing its gender: 'le substantif fém...traduit dans l'*Ecclésiaste* le féminin *zikkārōn*', 'the feminine noun...translates in Ecclesiastes the feminine *zikkārōn*'; we should perhaps note, though, that the Hebrew noun is in fact masculine, here and elsewhere.

1.11 the earlier times...the later] The contrast between ראשנים and אחרנים is here between earlier and later, not first and last (as, e.g., Isa 48.12; cf. 1 Chr 29.29 etc.—such uses have influenced G πρώτοις...ἐσχάτοις). The precise reference, however, is uncertain: many scholars (e.g. Barton, Seow,

---

¹⁵ Cf. Cohen, ''aššūrênû', 141: 'il n'y a plus de place pour aucune évoque dès que l'on a affaire aux formes diversement composées de *lipnê* et telles que *millipnê*... Toutes ces formes dénotent *exclusivement* l'adverbe de lieu "devant". Jamais un adverbe de temps. Il nous paraît donc arbitraire de donner en Qoh. i 10b une valeur temporelle à la forme de *millᵉpānênû*, 'there is no room for any ambiguity...all these forms denote exclusively the adverb of place, "before". Never an adverb of time...' He concludes that if the context for the word in Ecclesiastes demands a temporal sense, then it must be considered an instance of מלפנים 'mal résolu'.

Krüger, Bennett) have argued that these cannot be former things or events, both because it would then be more natural to use feminine forms (cf., e.g., Isa 41.22; 43.18; conversely, Lev 26.45; Ps 79.8; Eccles 4.16), and because things do not remember. Correspondingly the reference must be to people, who in each era fail to remember the people who preceded them. The context of the claim here, though, has been established in the previous verse, which is denying the novelty of words or things, not people (cf. Fox). It is possible that the plurals are a generalization of the דבר in v. 10, but more likely, I think, that the terms here are intended to represent everything and everyone in each timeframe, a notion which is difficult to express in English. We should note both the apparent use of הראשנים with reference to 'previous times' (Ps 89.50 [ET 89.49]; differently, Num 6.12), along with, perhaps, the similar future sense of אחרנים in Isa 41.4, and also the possibility that the verse is evoking the עלמים of v. 10. If those are not considered compelling grounds for taking the reference to be to the times themselves, a translation in those terms at least reflects the comprehensiveness of Qohelet's claim.

1.11 likewise...the later] Lit. 'and also the later which are going to be, there will be no memory of them'.

1.11 which are yet to happen] M is supported by 4QQoh[b] and by most of the versions. However, whilst a number of Greek manuscripts (especially the Origenic ones) read the future γενησομένοις, and Jerome reports G as *qui futuri sunt* both here and later in the verse, G* appears to have been the perfect γενομένοις. McNeile, 138, suggests that this reflects שהיו, and claims support for that reading from one manuscript in de Rossi, and from S ܗܘܐܘ *dhwyn*. Although this is attractive, the manuscript support is weak, and if S does support G, it is not necessarily doing so as an independent witness to the Hebrew. G may be attempting to distinguish the tenses in the two occurrences of שיהיו, to give a more explicit presentation of three different periods.

Yi, 109 (cf. 152), notes the unexpected absence of an article before γενομένοις, and suggests that ἐσχάτοις must be read accordingly as attributive, not substantive, giving 'those born later'. If this was indeed the intention of the translator, it would accord with such a differentiation of tense. It should also be noted, however, that there is considerable scope for errors of transmission in this passage, both because of the preceding γενομένοις in 1.10, and because of the multiple occurrences of the sequence ΤΟΙΣ.

1.11 memory of the later] As noted above, this is lit. 'the later...there will be no memory of them', with להם for 'of them'. For the equivalent in G, Rahlfs reads αὐτοῖς, which would correspond to להם, but αὐτῶν is so much more strongly attested in the manuscript tradition that it has a reasonable claim to be G* (cf. Gentry), even if McNeile, 156, regards it as 'foreign to the style of the translation'. Against the obvious objection that it may have emerged as a variant simply because Greek uses the genitive of things remembered, it can be noted that the other datives in the verse (τοῖς πρώτοις καί γε τοῖς ἐσχάτοις γενομένοις) have undergone no such conversion, although their very presence, of course, must force us to ask why the genitive should have been chosen in just this single case. If it is original, then it seems possible that αὐτῶν was used to clarify the sense in what is a very complicated construction.

1.11 or of] Lit. 'along with'. The preposition עם here is commonly taken to mean 'among', and the clause construed as a statement that the memory will not persist among those coming still later. That sense would be unusual, although not impossible (cf., e.g., Gen 23.4), and it is the sense adopted in Hie, V *apud eos* (cf. σ' παρὰ τοῖς ἐσομένοις). However, in 2.16 we find a very similar statement: אין זכרון לחכם עם הכסיל לעולם. There, the same preposition has its common meaning 'along with', and it recurs later in the verse: both uses establish the parity of the wise man and the fool, while the verse itself makes a clear reference back to this verse. In view of such strong links, it would seem strange to impute different meanings to the preposition in each verse, and we should read it here as it is clearly to be read in 2.16—despite the affirmation of the traditional reading in Schoors, *The Preacher* I, 201, against the similar observations by, e.g., Wildeboer, who translates '*ebensowenig* wird ein Andenken sein *an diejenigen, die darnach leben werden*', 'nor will there be a remembrance of those who will live later'. Correspondingly, this verse does not say that there is no memory of the first period, and will be no memory of the second period amongst those in a third; rather, it says that there is no memory of the first period, and will be no memory of the second period, along with the subsequent period(s?).

1.11 later still] לאחרנה is elaborated in eschatological terms by T, and G εἰς τὴν ἐσχάτην, 'at the last', might lend itself to that interpretation.[16] σ', on the other hand, opts for the much vaguer μετὰ ταῦτα, 'after these things', and is probably right to perceive that the Hebrew does not connote 'the very end', but is associated with position in a sequence (cf. Krüger). So, for instance, on the only other occasion that לאחרנה is used (Num 2.31), it indicates that the Danites should set out last when the tribes all move, and in Deut 17.7 באחרנה is used of taking a turn: the witnesses are first to attack someone condemned, and the people באחרנה ('after that'). The probable reference here, then, is to those who come next in sequence, and the context suggests that the expression may be supposed to embrace all subsequent members of the sequence—those who will exist on into the future.

---

[16] So Holm-Nielsen, 'Interpretation', 171, 'it is not possible to decide whether the translator meant this eschatologically... But the wording could be understood in this way, and definitely it was understood in this way by the translator into Vulgate's Latin: *in novissimo*. This gives the whole context another sense.'

Introduction to 1.12–2.11

Evidence from Experience

(1.12) When I, Qohelet, became king over Israel in Jerusalem, (1.13) then I applied my mind to inquiring and exploring through wisdom, regarding everything which is done beneath the heavens: is it a bad job which God has given humans to work at? (1.14) I looked at all the achievements which are achieved beneath the sun, and behold, it was all an illusion, and wishing for the wind: (1.15) bent, it was beyond fixing, and as a loss, it was beyond counting.

(1.16) I conversed with my heart, saying, 'Behold, I have amplified and increased wisdom to a point beyond anyone who was in Jerusalem before me, and my heart has seen much wisdom and knowledge: (1.17) now let me set my heart to knowing wisdom and knowledge, mindlessness and obtuseness.' I understood of this, too, that it is worrying about the wind, (1.18) for in much wisdom is much exasperation, and whoever gains in knowledge gains in pain. (2.1) I said in my heart, 'Come on then, I shall stuff you with pleasure, and you must examine the benefits!' But behold, it too was an illusion. (2.2) Of fun, I said 'Mindless!', and of pleasure 'What does it do?'

(2.3) With my heart I researched how to sustain my body with wine and my guiding heart with wisdom, and how to keep a hold on obtuseness until I should see what is good for humans to do beneath the heavens, for the limited duration of their lives. (2.4) I accomplished great things: I constructed buildings for myself, planted vineyards for myself; (2.5) I made for myself nurseries and groves, and I planted in them a tree for every kind of fruit; (2.6) I made for myself pools of water, from which to irrigate a forest sprouting timber; (2.7) I acquired servants and maidservants, and home-born slaves. I also had livestock for myself—cattle and herds: I had more for myself than all who were before me in Jerusalem. (2.8) I accumulated for myself also silver and gold, along with kingly possessions and provinces. I put together for myself singers, men and women, and those human luxuries, a fine wine-table and settings. (2.9) And I made myself rich, going beyond anyone who was before me in Jerusalem. My wisdom remained with me, moreover, (2.10) and nothing which my eyes demanded did I keep out of their reach—I did not hold my heart back from any pleasure, for my heart was pleased in all my business, and this was what was mine from all my business.

(2.11) Then I looked round among all my achievements, which my hands had achieved, and at the business which I had worked to achieve—and behold, it was all an illusion, and a wishing for the wind, and there was no profit under the sun.

From 1.12 onward, Qohelet's monologue is more obviously a speech, which begins with a first-person account of his activities and reflections on those activities. This extends to the end of ch. 2, and after that Qohelet's reflections on a wider range of themes frequently draw on his personal claims to knowledge and experience. This shift to the first person, however, does not mark an immediate change of direction after the less personal material that precedes it, and it is clear from the outset that his initial 'memoir' is intended to address the same issues that were set out in 1.2-3 and pursued in 1.4-11. With reference now to his own life, rather than to the basic character of the world, Qohelet again asks what humans can accomplish, and reaches the conclusion in 2.11 that all his own, very considerable achievements were actually *hebel*, and brought him no profit.

It is a commonplace of modern interpretation that, in the course of this account, Qohelet deliberately associates himself with Solomon, so that the purpose is at least in part to demonstrate that even someone so wise, wealthy and powerful is unable to achieve what he wants. If that was indeed specifically the author's intention, however, he has set about it in a very strange way. Qohelet does indeed speak of coming to the throne of Israel in 1.12, but not a single thing that he is then described as doing corresponds to other accounts that we have of Solomon's activities, except when he speaks vaguely of constructing some unspecified buildings in 2.4—which would be a curiously modest way of referring to the Temple and other major building projects attributed to Solomon over a period of more than twenty years in 1 Kings.[1] The commentary below on 2.4-11 will look at the matter in more detail, and also at the way in which such readings tend to presume that Qohelet's purpose involves, above all, a search for physical gratification and material prosperity—a presumption in line with (and probably shaped by) a very old understanding that Ecclesiastes is all about rejecting worldly pleasures. Suffice it to say here that, if there is any connection with Solomon, it is only of the loosest sort, and does not justify attempts to read the account here in terms of events described elsewhere.

If we are to understand what is actually going on, then it seems important to pay attention to the ways in which Qohelet begins and ends his account—even if that is not made any easier by some significant difficulties in 2.1 and 2.3, which partially obscure the sequence. What we seem to have before 2.1, though, is a recollection of Qohelet's attempts to apply his personal wisdom to two different issues: the benefits, if any, to be achieved by humans from their own activities (1.12-15), and the nature of wisdom, knowledge, and their opposites (1.16-18). He finds no benefit in achievement, only loss, and understands the gain from wisdom to be only pain and frustration. In 2.1-2, as I understand it, he then tackles a third issue, immersing himself in pleasure to see what good that can do, and again reaches a negative conclusion: it is neither a loss nor painful, like achievement and wisdom, but it does seem pointless.

I take 2.2 then to mark the end of Qohelet's initial examinations, and the difficult 2.3 to mark the start of something new—references to wine and flesh have led many readers to think that he must still be talking about pleasure, despite having already stated his conclusions, but I think that is a misunderstanding. What Qohelet sets out to do now is to undertake not another examination, but a long-term experiment, in which he will cover all three of the issues that he has examined already: he is going to achieve things himself, making use of his wisdom, and, as 2.10 will make clear separately, he will allow himself any pleasure. Correspondingly, he builds up a series of successful businesses, which then enable him to live a life of wealth and luxury. When the time comes to assess the results of

---

[1] As Condamin, 'Études', 9:41-41, observes, contrasting the much more detailed correspondences in the book of Wisdom, any other king, or even a member of the public, could claim everything that Qohelet claims in 2.4-9.

this experiment in 2.11, however, he finds no more benefit in his own, considerable achievements than he found earlier in any other human achievements (there is a close echo of 1.14). As we shall see later, his review will not only involve an explanation of this failure, when we learn more clearly what Qohelet understands to be truly beneficial, but will also lead him to question the usefulness of his wisdom, so that of the three subjects that he first set out to examine, it is only in relation to pleasure—specifically the pleasure that he found in his work—that Qohelet hints at a change of mind. This may be no more 'useful' than he considered it to be earlier, but it is at least something genuinely his own in 2.10. This will become an important issue as the book progresses, and the themes both of human achievement and of wisdom's shortcomings will also figure throughout, so it would not be an exaggeration to say that 1.12–2.2, and the account more generally, are programmatic, and set out for us Qohelet's agenda.[2]

In any case, though, Qohelet presents himself in these verses not as a wealthy man suddenly taken aback by questions about the meaning of life, but as a man intrigued by those questions, who has cultivated his own wisdom to an extraordinary degree from the outset, and then, when that wisdom fails to do so, has set out to achieve the life and lifestyle that he hopes will answer them. The disappointment of that hope supplies a pretext for the subsequent discussion, and sets it in a loose narrative framework, which will be picked up again in 7.23.

---

[2] Scholars have observed this programmatic aspect on a smaller scale, and Ravasi, for instance, tabulates correspondences between knowledge and understanding in 1.12-18 and 2.12-16, and between enjoyment and action in 2.1-11 and 17-26 (although that particular division, I think, divides the text unnaturally, and misunderstands 2.3-10). I doubt, however, that we should see this as a simple structural matter: having announced his interests, Qohelet will go on to explore each of them, but not subsequently in any particular order, or to the exclusion of other concerns.

1.12-13

(1.12) When I, Qohelet, became king over Israel in Jerusalem, (1.13) then I applied my mind to inquiring and exploring through wisdom, regarding everything which is done beneath the heavens: is it a bad job which God has given humans to work at?

Commentary

1.12] The book has previously announced that its words are those of Qohelet, but Qohelet now introduces himself as a king of Israel. Unless he is using 'Israel' loosely, the claim that he was king of Israel in Jerusalem would seem to identify him as a king of the United Monarchy; the earlier datum in 1.1, that he is a 'son of David', narrows this down to Solomon, or perhaps Rehoboam at a stretch. For some early readers, that identification may have sat a little uncomfortably with the subsequent assertion in 1.16, that Qohelet came to surpass all his predecessors in Jerusalem: unless he is reaching back to pre-Israelite times, there were not many such predecessors. All the same, this introduction has long been understood as an indirect claim to have been Solomon, and it was probably intended as such.

Taking the Solomonic attribution seriously, and understanding this verse to be a declaration that he 'had' been king, the Targum here tells a story of how Solomon became Qohelet. His pride while on the throne led him to break the law and incur divine anger, so that God sent Asmodeus, king of the demons, who drove him from the throne and took his signet ring. Qohelet now wanders the land, weeping and pleading.[1] In his commentary, Jerome also notes the Jewish association of Ecclesiastes with Solomon's penitence after offending God.[2] We may reasonably assume these to be later legends,

---

[1] On the background to the legend, and other references to it, see, e.g., Knobel, *The Targum of Qohelet*, 23 n. 14; Taradach, 'La figure insolite'.

[2] Ginzberg, 'Die Haggada', 23-24, links this to the much vaguer statement in the Midrash, which describes Solomon as having passed through three phases (variously understood), and to be speaking at a point when he is worth nothing.

which have been applied retrospectively to the interpretation of this verse, or which have, perhaps, arisen under its influence. It is possible, though, that they do reflect an important original element in the presentation of the character: some scholars have emphasized the similarities between this self-introduction and those found in a significant number of royal inscriptions from the ancient Near East (see, e.g., Seow, Fox). This link may be important, inasmuch as such inscriptions frequently have an autobiographical and testamentary aspect, which would lend weight to any suspicion that the author is portraying Qohelet as looking back over his experience from a viewpoint at the end of his life. As we saw in the Introduction, it is doubtful, however, that the author has borrowed language that was confined specifically to 'royal' memoirs, as a way to reinforce the Solomonic persona: this is an aspect of a broader question that will be considered below.

1.13] Qohelet's quest is to investigate all worldly activity ('beneath the heavens', a variation on 'under the sun' found also in 2.3 and 3.1) by means of his own wisdom, with the specific purpose of determining whether what humans have been given to do by God is inherently worthless—and therefore, presumably, incapable of generating a profit for them. The term he uses, *'nyn r'*, 'a bad job', will subsequently be associated both with *hebel* (4.8) and with activity that leads to loss (5.13). He presupposes that human activity, or the context in which it happens, has been established in some way by divine power, but he does not assert, at this stage anyhow, that whatever limitations exist are specifically a result of God's will. Equally the 'giving' to humans of work has no specific implications of either compulsion or permissiveness (he will return in 3.10 to the whole matter of God giving tasks to humans). The subject of Qohelet's study at this stage remains the value of human action, not the constraints placed upon it in any other respect. On the reading of a question at the end of the verse, see below.

Notes

1.12 When] See the note on 'became', below.

1.12 I, Qohelet] This could also be taken as a separate non-verbal sentence: 'I (am) Qohelet' (so, e.g., HCM). Ecclesiastes uses the first-person pronoun frequently, and always in the form אני rather than אנכי. The affinities with later literature in this respect are discussed by Schoors, *The Preacher* I, 47-48; see also Seow, 'Linguistic Evidence', 661.

1.12 became] Discussions of the tense here are reviewed by Schoors, *The Preacher* I, 172-73. It is possible to read הייתי as an expression (by a live, dying, or dead Qohelet) of the sense 'I was' or 'I have been (but am not now)', and this is essentially the understanding of T, which elaborates its narrative about Solomon's deposition from the throne by the demon Asmodeus, and of the Midrash. More recently, it has been picked up by Bolin (in *Ecclesiastes*, 49-51), who suggests a link with Greek stories about kings who achieve wisdom only at the end of their reigns, and who understands Qohelet to be looking back on his reign with self-loathing (in a portrayal that is perhaps informed by Greek prejudices about oriental monarchies).

The perfect form of the verb can also indicate a state that began in the past but persists into the present (cf. v. 9, and see especially Isaksson, *Studies*, 50-51, who notes, e.g., Ps 88.5 [ET 88.4]); if that usage were to be understood here, however, it would really require a translation along the lines of 'I am become king'. Some scholars who see a more explicit reference to the past simply see a retrospective aspect to the account (so, e.g., Schoors), which is presented, therefore, as the king looking back over his reign, while Seow cites a number of ancient inscriptions to support his translation 'I have been a king'.

Those inscriptions, however, point to the more probable reading here, in terms of a narrative sequence (so, e.g., Krüger, and cf. G ἐγενόμην). When Mesha, for example, says, …אבי מלך על מאב שלשן שת ואנך מלכתי אחר אבי ואעש, he means 'My father (was) king over Moab for thirty years; *then I reigned after my father, and I built…*' (*KAI* 181.2-3). I take this clause to be the beginning of such a sequence, in which the verb conveys a simple past tense, but also introduces the circumstances of the investigation. Literally the sentence means 'I became king…and I set my heart…', but the implication is that Qohelet is looking back to his actions immediately after becoming king.[3]

1.12 over Israel] The usual expression is simply 'King of Israel': the lack of the preposition in V, and in a number of Greek manuscripts, probably reflects assimilation to that more familiar form (so Euringer). This expression with על is not actually uncommon, however, and it may be no coincidence that 1 Kgs 4.1 describes Solomon as 'king over all Israel' (cf., e.g., 1 Kgs 1.34, 35; 6.1).

1.13 Then] Lit. 'and': see the note 'became', above.

1.13 applied my mind to] Lit. 'gave my heart to'. The expression—on which see especially Seow and Schoors, *The Preacher* I, 85-86—is found also in 1.17; 7.21; 8.9, 16. Used with nouns in 7.21 and 8.9, it always has an association with examining or investigating. In the other instances, as here, it is followed by an infinitive, and the contexts suggest: 'I applied my mind to the task of'. This would fit with the common association between heart and

---

[3] Cf. Longman, *Fictional Akkadian Autobiography*, 121: 'The early sections of the book…refer to a vital young man who actively pursues the answer to his urgent question about the meaning of life'.

the intellect or emotions in biblical literature (which is so strong that North, 'Brain and Nerve', 592-97, suggests we should not, perhaps, identify לב literally as the heart, but as something more like the nervous system!). The heart is also, however, associated with the will, and we should note the similar usage in passages like 1 Chr 22.19; 2 Chr 12.14. These likewise involve seeking, but their primary emphasis is upon determination or intention, not intellectual endeavour, and they suggest the simpler meaning 'I set out to' (so, e.g., Krüger); cf. V *et proposui in animo meo*, 'and I proposed in my mind', which is probably based on σ' καὶ προεθέμην (ἐν τῇ καρδίᾳ μου), 'and I proposed (in my heart)'; see Cannon, 'Jerome and Symmachus', 191. It is unlikely, though, that we can see here an expression of outright commitment, which would justify Treier's '"gave his heart"…to the search'.

The Leiden edition of S assumes that the translator originally eliminated the redundant conjunction on the verb, which would make the common variant ܘܢܒܥܘ *wyhbt* an assimilation to the reading of M and G—but it is possible, of course, that it is the elimination that was secondary.

1.13 inquiring and exploring] Delitzsch usefully distinguishes the words in terms of depth and breadth: דרש is to do with getting to the heart of a matter, תור with exploring its breadth. The latter, found also in 2.3; 7.25, is used, e.g., of the reconnaissance to be made by spies in Num 13.2, 16, 17, and Whitley speaks of 'mental exploration'. This sense is picked up in G κατασκέψασθαι, and probably in Hie *considerandum*, α' ἐξερευνῆσαι (cf. LSJ on ἐξερευνητικός); σ'(?) διαθρῆσαι is more intellectual,[4] cf. V *inuestigare*.

1.13 through wisdom] The -ב is usually considered instrumental, but both דרש (e.g. 1 Sam 28.7) and תור (Judg 1.23) sometimes apparently take the preposition,[5] leading some commentators to view חכמה as the object either of both verbs (e.g. Ginsburg: 'to enquire diligently into wisdom respecting all…') or of the first (cf. Lauha: 'nach Weisheit zu suchen und zu forschen in Hinsicht auf alles…', 'to seek after wisdom and to investigate in respect of everything…'; cf. Müller, 'Theonome Skepsis', 3-6). Schoors, *The Preacher* I, 198, is sympathetic to this approach, not least because על seems awkward before the object after these verbs, but he later changes his mind (Schoors, *The Preacher* II, 10-11), rightly noting the instrumental uses of wisdom in 2.3, 21; 7.21; 9.15 (cf. also Seow). To this objection, we might add the observation that when דרש takes -ב, the preposition is used not of the object into which the

---

[4] διαθρῆσαι is unattributed here, but the same rendering is attributed to σ' by mss 161 and 248 at 7.25. See Field, *Auctarium*, 25, and Marshall.

[5] The instance in Judg 1.23 is not clear cut, in part because the verb is, very unusually, in the hiph'il, and in part because the subject בית יוסף has to be differentiated from the similar object, בית אל. On doubts about the certainty of the reading itself there, see Fischer, 'Beobachtungen', 75, who also argues that -ב is not used with the verb in CD 2.16 to mark the object.

enquiry is being made, but of the source through which an answer is being sought: one inquires *of* (-ב) someone about something. If בחכמה is understood in those terms, then the preposition is effectively instrumental anyway.

With regard to the noun itself, it is interesting to observe that בחכמה is pointed in M with the article (although the pointing is very variable in later manuscripts; cf. Ginsburg, *Writings*, and his *Massorah*, 4:388-89 for a Masoretic note on the subject); prepositions are similarly pointed with the article before חכמה in 2.3, 13; 7.23 (but not in 2.21). חכמה does not generally take an article elsewhere, except when it refers either to the specific skill required for a task ('the wisdom to': cf. 1 Kgs 7.14; 1 Chr 28.21), or, anaphorically, to wisdom which has previously been mentioned (2 Chr 1.12; this may be the reason for the article in 2.13—see below). When לחכמה is pointed with the article in Prov 2.2; 7.4, this is against the normal usage in Proverbs, and may reflect an understanding of the wisdom as that specifically contained within the father's instruction; if the ה in והחכמה at Job 28.12, 20 is not interrogative, then it too is exceptional, and perhaps emphatic. Given the general biblical usage, the various occurrences of חכמה without the article in Ecclesiastes, not all of which are explicable contextually (e.g. 1.17; 2.12; 7.25), and the use of מ- rather than מן ה- at 7.10 and 10.1, this tradition of vocalization is unlikely to reflect the intentions of the author throughout, although it may have been inspired by the occurrences of החכמה in 7.12 (twice), 19 (on which, see below).

That said, Ecclesiastes does apparently use the article with the equally abstract סכלות at 2.13 and 7.25 (but see the notes there), and elsewhere uses the article rather erratically at times (see Schoors, *The Preacher* I, 164-69), although this is usually a matter of unexpected omission. It is interesting to note, moreover, that G's use of the article with חכמה supports that of M quite closely: it is only in 2.3 and 7.10 that they fail to correspond.[6] Rashbam, writing on 2.13, suggests that חכמה pointed as definite is החכמה הרגילה וצריכה לעולם, 'wisdom which is commonplace and always needed', as opposed to the (indefinite) חכמה עמוקה ויתירה, 'profound and extraordinary wisdom'—a distinction which is difficult to sustain.

1.13 regarding] תור almost always takes a direct object, and this is the most common usage with דרש also. In 2 Chr 31.9, however, דרש takes על (described by the Masoretes as the 'western' reading here, cf. Baer; Ginsburg, *Writings*) both with the people of whom an enquiry is being made (cf. 2 Chr 24.6) and with the object of the enquiry (cf. 2 Kgs 22.13); it can take אל (the 'eastern' reading) in both senses also: cf. Job 5.8; Isa 8.19. The preposition is probably not necessary for the syntax, but may be intended to clarify the structure of the sentence after בחכמה, especially if we take the last part of

---

[6] Barr, 'Determination', draws attention to a number of issues relevant here. See esp. 316-19 on the problems surrounding use of the article with abstract nouns, and 325-33 on the pointing of the article with the prepositions ב, כ, and ל.

the verse to be specifying the nature of the inquiry, in which case Qohelet is stating (and having to differentiate) the method of his inquiry, the subject-matter of the inquiry, and the specific question which he is asking. 4QQoh[b] preserves only ל, so could have read על or אל; G uses περὶ for על elsewhere, so perhaps marginally favours that reading, as do S and T. I am aware of no actual attestations of the 'eastern' אל.

1.13 everything which is achieved] On the debate about the vocalization of נעשׂה generally, see on 1.9, above. As Gordis notes, G γινομένων (cf. Hie, V *quae fiunt*, 'which happen') probably reflects an understanding of the word here as a participle. It seems unlikely, as Krüger asserts, that to read a perfect here would oblige us to limit the scope of the expression to the actions of Qohelet's predecessors, but I agree with him (against, e.g., Fox, Murphy, Seow) that the reference in this context is to human actions, and not simply to everything which happens in the world.

G tends to translate כל as plural, so πάντων τῶν γινομένων is a translational adaptation, not the reflection of a variant reading in the Hebrew.

1.13 beneath the heavens] Or 'under the sun'. M is supported by G*, but a number of Hebrew[7] and Greek manuscripts read 'sun' here, as do Hie, V, T, and most manuscripts of S. It is hard to disentangle this, although there is a general consensus that M is probably original, and the variants an assimilation to the more common form (so, e.g., Goldman). It seems highly likely that both readings co-existed in the Hebrew manuscript tradition from an early stage, and the distribution of the variant 'sun' within the Greek tradition suggests hexaplaric influence. Against Lane in the Leiden edition, *BHQ* and Kamenetzky, 197, both support the originality of Ambrosianus' ܫܡܝܐ *šmy'* within S, and if that is right, the majority reading ܫܡܫܐ *šmš'* has most likely arisen from correction toward a variant Greek reading.

1.13 is it] After 'heavens', M has הוא, which is commonly taken to form a nominal clause with ענין רע—'this is wretched work'; the following clause is then attached as an asyndetic relative clause—'(which) God has given'. In what is surely a reference back to this verse, 3.10 speaks specifically of הענין אשר נתן אלהים לבני האדם לענות בו, which (given the context set by 3.9) tells against the idea of many commentators (e.g. Fox, Seow, Schellenberg, 'Qohelet's Use', 147) that הוא refers to Qohelet's enquiry, or to the broader human quest for understanding. The similar construction in 3.14 would likewise point to 'everything which is done' being the antecedent if the sentence is construed this way, and we might note also the reference in 8.16 to את הענין אשר נעשה על הארץ; so, similarly, Fischer, 'Beobachtungen', 76-77.

The same considerations, among others, make it difficult to accept Krüger's understanding, that investigation of the world is a bad business which God has left up to humans, without any concern for it himself. Krüger

---

[7] Miletto finds the reading in four Babylonian manuscripts, as well as listing those noted by Kennicott and de Rossi.

does make the important point, however, that we do not expect the result of Qohelet's investigation to be announced before the account of its execution. If we construe the sentence in the usual way, but accept that it is difficult to understand the pronoun as referring to the investigation, then it is also necessary to understand this verse as an immediate statement of conclusions, upon which Qohelet merely elaborates in the next. That is unsatisfactory, and sits uncomfortably before the הנה of v. 14, which should lead us to wonder whether the sentence should not, in fact, be construed differently.

Lohfink's rendering of 13b as an indirect question is hardly possible in the absence of אם, but makes excellent sense: Qohelet inquires about everything to see whether it is a bad business; cf. also Maussion, *Le Mal, le bien*, 19-20. I understand this part of the verse similarly, but take the question to be direct (and perhaps marked by the prepositioning of הוא); cf. Schwienhorst-Schönberger, *Nicht im Menschen*, 47 (although he takes a different approach in his commentary). The objection of Lavoie, 'Activité', 101-102, and Kamano, *Cosmology*, 55, that Qohelet always marks his questions with an interrogative particle, involves, of course, a circular argument.

In any case, the pronoun has clearly caused difficulties for the versions. Hie, V *hanc occupationem*, 'this occupation', reads it as though it were an attributive demonstrative, S apparently ignores it (perhaps taking it as resumptive within the previous clause),[8] and G, very curiously, reads ὅτι. Kamenetzky, 208, takes this last to be a free rendering of the pronoun, and Euringer claims that all the versions depend on M. Yi, 76-77, similarly regards G as interpretative: the translator has understood הוא to refer to what Qohelet has discovered, and turns what follows into an explanatory comment on this: 'for an unhappy preoccupation God has given to human beings with which to be preoccupied.' Not only, however, would this be rather a free rendering by the standards of G, it also seems forced: the Greek reads more naturally as a declaration *that* Qohelet was going to find it to be an unhappy preoccupation. McNeile, 139, rightly I think, suspects a Hebrew variant, and *BHQ* suggests that G may have found a (probably erroneous) כיא in its source-text.

With regard to the Three, we have no specific information for α', θ'; Marshall points out that ὅτι is not in fact present in the σ' attribution on ms 252, as Field had suggested. Syh attests ܚܠܝܢܐ ܗܘ ܒܝܫܐ ܗܘ ܕܝܗܒ ܐܠܗܐ '*nyn*' hw byš' hw dyhb 'lh' for σ', 'the/that bad occupation that God has given', and Goldman observes of this that ܚܠܝܢܐ ܗܘ '*nyn*' hw 'most likely points toward the possibility of interpreting the pronoun in the text of M as both copula and demonstrative', but ܗܘ hw may reflect no more than the article, and Field retroverts the Syriac as τὴν ἀσχολίαν τὴν πονηρὰν ἣν ἔδωκεν ὁ θεὸς, 'the evil occupation which God gave' (Marshall argues persuasively that κακὴν, 'bad', is more likely than πονηρὰν, 'evil').

---

[8] The treatment of the pronoun in Hie, V, S enables them all to take ענין רע as the direct object of נתן.

1.13 bad] The pointing of עִנְיַן is apparently as construct, which would imply that M^L takes רָע as a noun, and the literal sense to be 'job of badness', although the consonantal text would mean the same were we to read עִנְיָן as absolute and רָע as an adjective (as does, e.g., D'Alario, 'L'assurdità', 180); cf. GKC §128 w. All the other ancient versions use an adjective: it is hard to say whether this is translational, or represents a different vocalization (in which case, this instance could be added to the others listed in the Introduction). Sassoon 1053 supports M^L, but Ginsburg, *Writings*, notes a number of later manuscripts which point עִנְיָן as absolute; the expression occurs again in 4.8 and 5.13, where the pointing of M^L is supported by Sassoon 1053 and by Or 9879,[9] but the other versions again read an adjective and Ginsburg again notes later variants.

The context of 5.13 suggests that the expression refers there to an unhappy set of circumstances through which money is lost, most probably an unsuccessful venture. It seems likely that the sense of 'bad' is the same in all three places: it means broadly 'sub-standard' (cf. esp. Prov 20.14), not 'evil', although perhaps with some implication that it causes unhappiness. The link with הבל in 4.8 (cf. 2.21), and the context of both this verse and that, indeed, may suggest that a עִנְיַן רָע is a job or venture which fails to achieve an aim; if so, Qohelet may be using the language of commerce once again.

1.13 job...to work at] On the face of it, Ecclesiastes uses a verb cognate with the noun, which is difficult to translate (the common 'business...to be busy with' captures the effect, but not really the sense). Neither the verb (ענה, cf. also 3.10, and probably 5.18) nor the noun (עִנְיָן; cf. also 2.23, 26; 3.10; 4.8; 5.2, 13; 8.16) is used by other biblical writers, and although the noun does occur quite frequently in rabbinic literature, usually indicating a 'point' or subject of discussion (cf. Jastrow, *Dictionary*), the verb appears nowhere else. Only its possible relatedness to the Syriac ܥܢܐ *'ny*, which can be used of being occupied with something, tells against the suspicion that it is a new coinage. Gordis suggests, though, that Qohelet is actually making a pun (here and in 3.10) on the more common ענה = 'be afflicted', which should be read as the primary connotation, and T has probably taken the text that way (although it paraphrases too much here to be very reliable).

It is hard to judge the weight of the argument from silence, not least since Ecclesiastes employs a lot of very rare vocabulary, but Gordis' suggestion cannot be excluded as a possibility. G, S, Hie, σ', however, have all taken the verb and noun simply to be cognate, and I have retained that more common rendering. We can only really establish what Qohelet means by the terms from

---

[9] In Sassoon 1053 the vowel is actually smeared at 4.8, and it is possible that this is an attempt to correct (immediately) an initial writing of עִנְיָן with *qameṣ* rather than *pataḥ*: the *qameṣ* in this manuscript is commonly written ָ with a very short bar or dot beneath the horizontal, and the smear covers the area where that would have been.

his use of עניו elsewhere (see Schoors, *The Preacher* II, 427-32), and in this respect 2.26 and 5.13 are important: the first uses it to mean a 'task' (gathering and piling up for others), the second (where it is 'bad', as here) probably uses עניו of a business venture. In other passages, עניו can be vexatious (2.23), a bad עניו can be associated with הבל (4.8), and a mass of עניו stands in parallel with a mass of words (5.3); 8.16 tells us only that עניו is done on earth, and may possibly be associated with sleeplessness (cf. 2.23). The Greek translators use περισπασμός ('preoccupation', 'distraction', 'work done with focus':[10] G, α', θ') and ἀσχολία ('occupation', 'busy-ness': σ'), along with the associated verbs (περισπᾶσθαι, ἀσχολεῖσθαι), while Jerome translates variously according to context, but here uses *occupationem...occuparentur* in both V and Hie, following σ'.[11] As these renderings suggest, there seems to be a strong mental element to עניו—it is something which can preoccupy and upset—but there is a physical aspect also, which means that it can be used of a task or venture. The context here, and the similarity of expression with 2.26, suggest that the primary sense is of a task which humans have been set, and on which they are, perhaps, expected to focus. Schellenberg ('Qohelet's Use') argues that the noun is used in the book particularly in connection with human attempts to acquire knowledge, but even she concedes that such a sense is inappropriate for some of the uses, and her arguments are sometimes unpersuasive—8.16, for instance, does not imply that what Qohelet is investigating (as opposed to his investigation itself) must be something that 'can be carried out at night' (152). Correspondingly, while by no means excluding the possibility that enquiry might be a form of עניו, there seems no good reason to suppose that עניו refers particularly to enquiry.

---

[10] Lampe cites the noun in the sense of the assiduous work done by servants (Eusebius), and notes a second-century BCE papyrus where the associated verb is used for 'occupy', 'detain'—so it need not necessarily have the sense of 'worry' (Tob 10.2 S). See also Gwynn, 'Notes', 119, which cites numerous earlier examples.

[11] Symmachus' rendering ἀνομίας at 5.2 arises from an error (see the note there on 'worrying'), but he otherwise appears to have been consistent. His influence on Jerome here is beyond doubt; cf. Hie^comm: *uerbum* anian *Aquila Septuaginta et Theodotion* περισπασμὸν *similiter transtulerunt quod in* distentionem *Latinus interpres expressit eo quod in uarias sollicitudines mens hominis distenta lanietur. Symmachus uero* ἀσχολίαν *id est* occupationem *transtulit*: 'Aquila, the Septuagint and Theodotion all translate the word *anian* alike as περισπασμὸν, which the Latin translator has expressed as *distentio* (a distending) because the human mind is stretched apart by various cares; Symmachus, however, translated ἀσχολίαν, which is *occupatio* (business, occupation)'. See Cannon, 'Jerome and Symmachus', 191, and also Gentry, 'Propaedeutic', 159-60. Elsewhere (*Ad Iouin* 1.13) as here, Jerome attests *distentionem* as La, and it may be under that influence that he uses forms of *distentio* in his commentary at 4.8 and 5.13 (cf. V at 3.10 *distendantur*).

At the end of the verse, Euringer notes a Coptic plus, 'in pleasure'. He remarks that it is difficult to understand either how this came to be added, or what it could mean here, but we may reasonably suppose it to have originated as a marginal gloss, aligning the verse with Qohelet's later remarks about finding pleasure in work.

1.13 God has given] Krüger notes the construction of נתן with -ל of person + -ל + infinitive in Esth 3.11; 8.11; 2 Chr 20.10. None of these offers strong support either for his view that God is leaving it up to humans to do this job, or for the view of Lohfink, that he is compelling them to do it. As Schoors, *The Preacher* II, 93-98, 157-58, observes, God is very frequently the subject of this verb in Ecclesiastes (cf. also מתת אלהים in 3.13; 5.18); it is used principally to express aspects of the divine dispensation, but the verb does not in itself specify whether he is permitting, assigning or commissioning human actions. The use of the qatal also leaves open a number of theological questions. Although this form can be used to express present states, its reference is primarily to the past (which is how the versions have taken it here), and it is questionable whether we can take it to suggest that God is continually giving in the present, even if we assume on other grounds that Qohelet does not hold predestinarian views (as Isaksson, *Studies*, 83-84, attempts to argue with respect to נתן in 5.17).

G always reads the article with θεός, except in the expressions δόμα θεοῦ (3.13; 5.18) and ὅρκος θεοῦ (8.2). This seems to reflect adherence to an established norm, rather than slavish adherence to its source-text, and on several occasions M lacks a corresponding article (1.13; 3.10; 7.18; 8.13). All the same, Goldman has argued that in such cases M has deliberately omitted the article; for this instance, he suggests that M is 'stressing Qohelet's faith in God and personal relationship with him, in a context where people not acquainted with paradoxical thought could see a kind of philosophical relativism'. It is hard to see, however, that omission of the article would achieve any such thing: as Pinçon, 'Le Dieu', 414-16, has pointed out, the many other biblical uses make it unlikely that האלהים would have connoted 'the deity' in some abstract way. The inconsistency in M is interesting, but it is hard to see any clear distinction between the passages where it is lacking, and similar passages where it is not, so it is questionable whether we should even see the differences as deliberate, let alone read so much into them.

Salters ('The Word for "God"') has drawn attention to a curiosity in the rendering of 'God' by S, which has ܡܪܝܐ *mry'* here and in 2.24, 26; 3.10, 11, 13, 14 twice; 5.17 (ET 18), 18 (ET 19); 8.12; 9.5, 9; 12.7, 13, 14. This word is normally used, like the 'LORD' of the English versions, to render the tetragrammaton, which the Hebrew of Ecclesiastes never uses. Furthermore, S does use the expected ܐܠܗܐ *'lh'* as well as ܡܪܝܐ *mry'* (cf. 3.15, 17, 18; 4.17; 5.1 [ET 2] twice, 3 [ET 4], 5 [ET 6], 6 [ET 7], 18 [ET 19], 19 [ET 20]; 6.2 twice; 7.13, 18, 26, 29; 8.2, 13, 15, 17; 9.1, 7). As Salters points out, it is difficult to identify any contextual or other factor which distinguishes the usage of the words, and he suggests that ܡܪܝܐ *mry'* has been added secondarily, to give the book a more orthodox, Jewish flavour. The Targum consistently renders 'God' in Ecclesiastes with the divine name.

1.13 humans] Lit. 'sons/children of (the) human', as found often in Ecclesiastes (cf. 2.3, 8; 3.10, 18, 19, 21; 8.11; 9.3, 12) and elsewhere. G renders consistently with υἱοὶ τοῦ ἀνθρώπου, but in half the occurrences, there is a strongly attested variant with the plural τῶν ἀνθρώπων, 'of humans'; this is not infrequently attested for the Three as well, and although θ' = G here, σ' seems to have read τοῖς υἱοῖς τῶν ἀνθρώπων (see Gentry, 'Relationship', 73-75). The difference is translational, and does not reflect a Hebrew variant. Among the Hebrew manuscripts themselves, the only variant of note is the use in several of אדם, which is the more common biblical usage in this phrase, rather than האדם. See Miletto, and cf. similar examples in 2.8 and 3.21 noted by Lavoie and Mehramooz, 'Le texte hébreu et la traduction judéo-persanne', 501.

1.14-15

(1.14) I looked at all the achievements which are achieved beneath the sun, and behold, it was all an illusion, and wishing for the wind: (1.15) bent, it was beyond fixing, and as a loss, it was beyond counting.

Commentary

1.14] The investigation is described very briefly, and is followed immediately by a summary conclusion: Qohelet looks at everything, and sees that it is 'wishing for the wind'—labouring for the unattainable. His claim is probably not literally to have seen or considered every single thing that is made or done: the point is rather that he is looking at the world as a whole, or in the round.

1.15] The 'everything' which has just been characterized in terms of its futility is now described as broken beyond mending. Far from achieving any lasting gain, or profit, it represents a serious loss—expenditure without return. Some scholars have noted a resemblance to an image in Egyptian literature, where education is compared to the straightening of a stick by a woodworker,[1] but even if the image might have been familiar, Qohelet is not citing, or even parodying, some common aphorism. His point is not that *anything* bent is beyond straightening, but that *what he has seen* is too bent to be straightened; equally, most deficits can at least be quantified, but this one cannot. The version found in the Qumran text 4QQoh[b] may have elaborated this further: everything is too bent even to be straightened by a strong man. The imagery of crookedness will be picked up in 7.13, when Qohelet associates it directly with the work of God, but the financial imagery, of making a loss, looks more immediately backward, to the initial question about profit posed in 1.3.

---

[1] See Quack, *Die Lehren des Ani*, 125; Lichtheim, *Ancient Egyptian Literature II*, 145.

Notes

1.14 I looked at] Or 'I saw', 'I have looked at/seen'. With 47 occurrences, the verb ראה is found as often as היה in Ecclesiastes, and only עשה, with 43, otherwise comes close to such frequency. Seow notes, moreover, that on 26 of these occasions, it is Qohelet or his heart who is doing the seeing, and Schoors, 'The Verb ראה in the Book of Qoheleth', 230, that on no fewer than 18 the verb is in the first-person singular of the qatal. As part of his broader attempt to show that Qohelet is depicted as adopting a classic 'wisdom' style of developing his ideas, Oh, *Sprachliche*, 69-106, describes these uses as formulaic, discusses their construction in great detail, and notes that they tend to introduce passages where Qohelet will go on to reason. As Schoors himself goes on to argue, however, it is doubtful that any single sense should be attached to these uses: they are neither all about simple observation, nor all about critical evaluation (as Michel, *Untersuchungen*, 25-29, 35-38, would have it), but the frequency of the statements lends a strong, superficially empirical flavour to the work. The context here probably suggests that the idea of examination is uppermost, and that Qohelet is referring to the investigation he has just announced, so there is no good reason to translate more generally 'I have seen'.

1.14 which are achieved] For M שנעשו, 4QQoh^b l. 6 has אשר נעשו; Kennicott notes that reading in two later manuscripts also. It is difficult to judge the originality of either reading, but cf. M at 8.9 לכל מעשה אשר נעשה תחת השמש: it seems likely that the usage would originally have been consistent across both passages, and that slightly favours the 4QQoh^b reading.

Aitken ('Rhetoric and Poetry', 63) notes the striking alliteration which G achieves by translating with a participle: πάντα τὰ ποιήματα τὰ πεποιημένα (cf. 2.17); it is also worth noting that G uses the perfect, interpreting this as all the things which *have* been achieved.

1.14 it was] The non-verbal clause here is governed by והנה, and describes what Qohelet saw when he looked. Accordingly, it inherits its tense from ראיתי, although Qohelet presumably does not intend to suggest that it has subsequently ceased to be הבל.

1.14 wishing for the wind] On the expression רעות רוח, see the Introduction, pp. 22-24, above. As Jerome remarks in his commentary (where he translates *praesumptio spiritus*, 'presumption of spirit', and transliterates the Hebrew word as *routh*), the προαίρεσις πνεύματος, 'purpose/desire of the spirit', used by G renders רעות on the basis of Aramaic (in which רעו/רעותא is used of, e.g., the 'will' of God). He also reports that α' and θ' have νομή, 'wandering, grazing', and σ' βόσκησις, 'feeding (of animals)'—presumably linking the word with רעה—and that his Hebrew teacher understood the word in terms of misery or affliction (cf. T תבירות רוחא, 'breaking/sadness of spirit'; V *adflictio spiritus*, 'affliction of spirit'; S ܬܘܪܦ ܕܪܘܚܐ *twrp' drwḥ'*, 'vexation of spirit'), so it is clear that the expression evoked a number of different interpretations even amongst very early readers; see also Ginzberg, 'Die Haggada', 24.

In the context of later patristic thought, προαίρεσις πνεύματος would have been understood as a reference to free will (cf. Vinel), and it is striking also that G translates in terms of 'spirit' rather than 'wind' (the Three employ ἀνέμου). This leads Bertram, 'Hebräischer und griechischer', 47-48, to suppose that the rendering of G is a deliberate theological interpretation, which imports the notion of misguided and sinful human autonomy. Murphy (xxv) counters that the translation 'might well be an honest effort that is inept rather than tendentious', and, although 'inept' may be unfair when the meaning of the Hebrew is so unclear, it is indeed unlikely that the translator would have associated with προαίρεσις the theological connotations that the term was later to acquire. Holm-Nielsen, 'Interpretation', 170-71, 173, curiously claims that 'while the Hebrew author says that it is useless for man to try to find the meaning of life, the Greek translator comes to the conclusion that it is harmful to the spirit of man when he cannot find it', and he associates G with the rendering in S, suggesting that he somehow connects προαίρεσις with pain or harm, rather than preference.

In any case, it is striking that G makes no distinction between the רעות found in 1.14; 2.11, 17, 26; 4.4, 6; 6.9 and the less common רעיון used in 1.17; 2.22; 4.16. T similarly treats them all the same, while S makes a distinction only at 2.22, where רעיון is not being used formulaically, and Jerome varies his translations somewhat in Hie and V, but not specifically in relation to the variation in the Hebrew. It is harder to judge the readings of the Three, but there is again no sign of a systematic distinction. In his commentary at 1.17, where M has רעיון, Jerome says *de praesumptione spiritus, siue pastione uenti, quia saepius in hoc libro dicitur, supra disseruisse sufficiat*, 'concerning the "presumption of spirit" or "grazing of the wind": as it appears often in this book, let the previous discussion suffice'—referring back to his comments on *routh* at 1.14, with no indication that he sees any distinction. It may well be, of course, that all these various translators viewed רעות and רעיון as completely synonymous, but we should also consider the strong possibility that they found only רעות in their source-texts.

1.15 bent] Or 'broken'. The singular forms in G διεστραμμένον... καὶ ὑστέρημα... open up the possibility of reading 'something distorted... something lacking...' as a free-standing saying, with the implication that nothing can be repaired, and this has been influential in subsequent interpretation and translation of the Hebrew. Crenshaw, for example, translates: 'The crooked cannot be straightened, and the missing cannot be counted'. Jerome has taken a slightly different path, and Hie *peruersus* reflects a reading of מעות as 'the perverted man', whilst V *peruersi difficile corriguntur* generalizes this to refer to 'the perverse', who can only be corrected with difficulty. This may be the result of influence from Jewish exegesis: T also sees here a reference to a rebellious man (who cannot be set right after death if he has not repented), and a similar understanding underpins the various interpretations offered by the Midrash. It is surely more natural, however, to read מעות and חסרון alongside הבל and רעות רוח as further predicates of the preceding הכל—and in G, indeed, the equivalents could certainly refer back to τὰ πάντα. Ehrlich, followed by Gordis, has pointed out that we would expect the words to take an article (both in Hebrew and in Greek, we might add), if this were the sort of proverbial saying (or perhaps parody thereof) which many commentators assume it to be.

The verb עוה (which appears also in 7.13; 12.3) is generally found in the piʻel or puʻal (12.3 hithpaʻel), and it refers to bending, or being bent. So, for instance, in Ps 146.9, God 'makes the way of the wicked twisting'. It is far more commonly used, however, with the sense of perverting or subverting justice (so, e.g., Job 8.3; Lam 3.36), and Amos 8.5 uses it of falsifying measures. There is probably, then, a strong implication in the term that everything is in a state where it seems to function incorrectly, giving, as it were, the wrong results: Piotti's detailed studies ('Percezione I'; *Ricerca*, 80-98) lead him to conclude that it has a connotation of 'disorder'. Gordis (cf. Kamenetzky, 197) suggests that the curious S ܡܒܘܕܐ *mdwdʾ*, 'what/who disturbs', is a corruption of ܡܒܪܐ *mdwr*, 'spoiled', here and in 7.13. It is also possible that it is interpretative, reflecting a tradition like that in T; Holm-Nielsen, 'Interpretation', 173, would understand it to mean that someone worried cannot be raised up, and so to entail a sort of 'spiritualization'.

1.15 it was beyond[1, 2]] G renders each לא יוכל in this verse with the future tense δυνήσεται, but the Hebrew expresses a prospective aspect rather than a simple tense, and in the context 'it was not going to be able to' is better than 'it will not be able to'.

The various opinions about what 'it' might be here are reviewed in Lee, 'A Specific Application', 1-3, and in Pinker, 'The Principle', 392-96. The most obvious grammatical reference would be to the 'everything' that has just been mentioned, and, beyond that, to 'all the achievements' which are the antecedent of הכל; Pinker, 391-92, notes Altschuler's interpretation in these terms at the end of the eighteenth century, which makes the verse say that humans cannot correct what they have done wrong. It seems more likely, though, that Qohelet is responding to the question posed in 1.13: in this context, it does not seem probable that human achievements would themselves be described in these terms, and there is no obvious reason to relate the description to Qohelet's quest in some more general way. In 7.13, a similar expression will be used to characterize what God has achieved, and here it is likely that Qohelet is describing the work that God has given to humans, which offers them no ultimate benefit. Lee reaches a similar conclusion by a rather different route. Pinker, on the other hand, opts to read the verse as a general statement about irreversibility, so that it is not saying that anything in particular is bent, but talking about 'whatever is bent'. That is not technically impossible, or even implausible, but if Qohelet were saying that *nothing* can be mended and *no* loss measured, the claim would be either a deliberate exaggeration or a palpable untruth.

1.15 fixing] In the current form lit. 'it cannot become straight/straightened' or 'be put right', but an early variant seems to have read '(even) a strong man could not fix it' (see below). M points לִתְקֹן unexpectedly as qal. The verb only appears in biblical Hebrew elsewhere at 7.13 and 12.9, where it is pi'el, and in context means 'straighten' or 'put in order' (cf. Sir 47.9), so we would expect the qal to connote being or becoming straight. Many commentators have proposed, however, that a passive form is required here, in view of both the similar 7.13, and the niph'al לְהִמָּנוֹת which stands parallel in this verse. Correspondingly, *BHS* would emend to niph'al לְהִתָּקֵן (so also, e.g., Siegfried, McNeile, Lauha, *HALOT*); it might be possible to retain the present consonants if we assumed syncopation of the ה. Others (e.g. Driver, 'Problems and Solutions', 225; Seow) prefer to vocalize as pu'al לְתֻקַּן, which would avoid changing the consonantal text, and correspond to the pi'el usage elsewhere, while Goldman and Gordis would retain the qal, respectively understanding it as stative or passive (so also Lavoie, 'Activité', 89).

The pointing in M as qal is consistent across manuscripts, and some later texts and editions write the word plene as לתקון, which only tends to affirm it (see Ginsburg, *Writings*). Goldman claims that it this is 'the *lectio difficilior*', and that the Masoretes would not have vocalized as qal unless driven to do so by a tradition of pronunciation, but it is not actually difficult to understand such a vocalization in the light of Aramaic usage, where the corresponding base stem is used of standing firmly or being proper: it seems likely that the reading as qal merely reflects the understanding found in other sources and noted above, that the subject here is a crooked or perverse man. It is also clear that the other versions show no common awareness of any such traditional pronunciation, and among them only S ܠܡܬܩܢ *lmtqn* seems clearly to reflect a qal (cf. Kamenetzky, 208). G ἐπικοσμηθῆναι (cf. Hie *adornari*) is passive, but the active form of the verb chosen, ἐπικοσμῆσαι, would have a sense close to the pi'el as it is used in 12.9, and the translator has probably vocalized as a pu'al.[2] T לית ליה רשו לאיתקנא, 'there is no permission for him to be

---

[2] The Greek ἐπικοσμηθῆναι probably does not have the same potential implications of 'ordering' as κοσμηθῆναι, and it commonly refers to giving honours, or to improving something aesthetically. This is even more certainly true of Jerome's *adornari*. It seems likely that the choice of verb has been influenced by the use in Aramaic (and sometimes in post-biblical Hebrew) of words from the root תקן with reference not just to ordering but to ornamentation: cf. תיקון in the targums to Exod 33.4, and ותקיני יתכון בתקון in the Targum Jonathan to Ezek 16.11. In any case, however, the result is that G and Hie refer most obviously not to the repair or restoration of what is twisted, but to its decoration, so that the statement here becomes

straightened out', has probably also taken the Hebrew as passive, although it is difficult to say whether or not it read a qal or a puʻal. The reading of 4QQohᵇ is uncertain here, but it most likely understood the verb as piʻel, and perhaps had לוא יוכל גבור לתקן, 'a strong man is unable to straighten (it)'; see the Introduction, p. 135 above. This is a much easier reading, but for that very reason is suspicious, despite its relative antiquity. Since גבור, furthermore, would not obviously be an appropriate subject for the second יוכל, we would have to assume either that a second, more appropriate noun has dropped out as well, or that each יוכל is being used differently. If 4QQohᵇ is not to be reconstructed in some other way, which is very possible, it seems likely that it reflects a secondary clarification of the statement. Indeed, if גבור is taken merely as 'a man', which is a common use, then perhaps it too shares the understanding 'perverse, a man cannot be proper/straightened', and the reading would then be intended to make that understanding explicit.

Ultimately, unless we go down that path ourselves then the puʻal has the best claim. Of course, while 'being straight(ened)' corresponds to the sense of מעות here and עותו in 7.13, the use in 12.9 shows that the meaning of the verb is not limited to the idea of being straight, and Rosenthal has sketched the extraordinary breadth of its use in later Hebrew also, where it refers not just to repairing or putting things right, but to getting things sorted out or brought to their best possible state.³ It seems likely that it was evolution in the sense of the word which stimulated understandings in terms of propriety and morality, and obscured what might earlier have seemed a more obvious reading.

1.15 as a loss] Lit. 'a loss'. חסרון itself is *hapax* in biblical Hebrew, but it is probably related to a number of other words: חֹסֶר, which is used in Deut 28.48; 28.57; Amos 4.6 to indicate 'want' or 'absence', especially of food (cf. also חֶסֶר in Prov 28.22; Job 30.3); the more common מַחְסוֹר, which has a similar meaning; and, of course, the verb חָסֵר, which means not only to 'want' or 'lack', but 'to be absent' or 'be deficient' (so 9.8; 10.3; and cf., e.g., Gen 8.3; 1 Kgs 17.14, 16. In Eccles 4.8, the piʻel is used for 'deprive oneself'). The probable connotation in this context, then, is of absence or shortage, and Jastrow, *Dictionary*, offers numerous examples from later Hebrew of חָסְרוֹן/חִסָּרוֹן being used to indicate a deficiency (of e.g. money, rain, organic material). In general, the usage points to the term meaning a shortage of something, rather than specifically an absence. Some scholars suggest very

equivalent to the English saying 'You can't make a silk purse out of a sow's ear': however it is dressed up, nothing good can be made from what is inherently bad. The choice instead of κοσμῆσαι in 7.13 reflects the translator's understanding of that verse in very different terms, despite the similar vocabulary: see the note 'who can straighten what he has bent?' there.

  ³ See Rosenthal, 'Tikkun ha-Olam', which looks more generally at the devel‖opment of a famous Jewish concept which Qohelet would undoubtedly have dismissed as הבל.

plausibly that it was used as a commercial term,[4] and a counterpart to יתרון: Seow (citing Porten and Yardeni, *Textbook*, 1:4.3.8-9) notes a use of the Aramaic חסרן which apparently has this sense. If precisely the opposite of יתרן, it would indicate the loss made on a deal or activity, in contrast to the surplus or profit. On the curious rendering *stultorum* in V, see the next note.

1.15 it is beyond counting] Lit. 'it cannot be counted'. If a חסרן is a loss or deficiency, then parallelism with the previous clause would suggest that it is too great to be recouped. This might be expressed either in terms of its immeasurable size, or in terms of the difficulty which would be involved in making it good. Many commentators have felt that the context demands the latter, and suggested appropriate emendations to a form לְהִמָּלוֹת from מלא, 'fill' (so, e.g., *BHS*). Gordis, indeed, picks up a report noted already by some modern commentators, and suggests that 'the emendation is actually suggested in the Talmud; cf. *b. Ḥagigah* 9b: אמר לו בר הי הי להלל האי להמנות להמלות מיבעי'. This is also cited by Goldman, and would be extraordinary were it true. However, the statement has to be read in context. Ben Hê-Hê is expressing doubt in *b. Ḥagigah* 9b that Eccles 1.15b can be applied to the case of a failure to make feast-offerings before the feast is complete. If that were the case, he is saying, then the verse would not say 'counted' but 'fulfilled'; the verse should instead be applied to the man who does not want to be counted among his colleagues for a duty. He is apparently making a play on words here (להמנות/להמלות), and is certainly not suggesting a different reading—quite the contrary.[5]

It is similarly questionable whether σ' supports such an emendation, as is also often claimed: the reading ὑστέρημα μὴ δυνάμενον ἀναπληρῶσαι ἀριθμόν, lit. 'a deficiency is not able to fill up a number', looks as though it conflates both 'count' and 'fill'. σ' is probably, however, just using two words to render להמנות (cf. Euringer, Fox), taking it to mean that a deficit cannot be reduced ('filled up') to reach the proper number: ἀναπληρῶσαι is regularly used of 'making up numbers'. Of all the versional readings, only S ܠܡܬܡܠܝܘ *lmtmlyw*, 'be filled', seems to support the proposed emendation, but it is hard to be sure that this is not a facilitative adaptation of the graphically similar ܠܡܬܡܢܝܘ *lmtmnyw*, 'be counted', which is well-attested as a variant.

In short, the evidence for emendation is slender, and M makes good sense as it stands. The impossibility of counting the deficit is understood to be the proper sense by both G ὑστέρημα οὐ δυνήσεται τοῦ ἀριθμηθῆναι (cf. Hie *et imminutio non poterit numerari*) and θ', whose reading is retroverted by Field

---

[4] So Plumptre: 'there is an "incompleteness" which we cannot remedy, any more than our skill in arithmetic can make up for a deficit which stares us in the face when we look into an account'.

[5] Fox also objects to the use of this account as evidence for emendation, but I doubt that his characterisation of Ben Hê-Hê's comments is quite accurate either: the point is not that the verb is 'a peculiarity requiring an exceptional interpretation'.

as καὶ τὰ ὑστεροῦντα οὐ δύνανται ἀριθμηθῆναι ψήφῳ (or ψηφισθῆναι), 'and the things that are lacking cannot be counted by number (or numbered)'. It is also supported indirectly by the understanding of T, where a man lacking in Torah will not be 'counted' among the righteous after death. After it has generalized מעות to *peruersi* (see above), V now has *et stultorum infinitus est numerus*, 'and the number of fools is infinite', which probably (so Vaccari, 'Stultorum', 81-82) associates חסרון with the expression חסר לב, 'lacking in understanding', found a number of times in Proverbs, and takes it as a reference to individual deficiency in a way that is not unlike the approach of T. Even though it is paraphrasing heavily, however, this reading also reflects a basic understanding of M in terms of something that cannot be counted.

1.16-18

(1.16) I conversed with my heart, saying, 'Behold, I have amplified and increased wisdom to a point beyond anyone who was in Jerusalem before me, and my heart has seen much wisdom and knowledge: (1.17) now let me set my heart to knowing wisdom and knowledge, mindlessness and obtuseness'. I understood of this, too, that it is worrying about the wind, (1.18) for in much wisdom is much exasperation, and whoever gains in knowledge gains in pain.

Commentary

Qohelet does not spell out the reason for his choice of subjects, and in the comments on 2.1-2 we shall see that the account is probably motivated by an attempt to highlight the way in which certain of his ideas were transformed by his subsequent experiences. If there is any implicit pretext for his switch to an investigation of wisdom here, though, it is probably that, having found nothing for humans in 1.12-15, Qohelet wants to look at the tool that he had used in that investigation, treating it now not as a means, but as an end in itself. His conclusion, that it is a source of pain, marks the beginning of an ambivalence towards wisdom that will continue throughout the book, but it is an outright positive evaluation when compared to the views that he will express in 2.15, after his more active engagement: in that verse, he will question whether there was ever any point in the acquisition of wisdom about which he is now so proud. In respect of these attitudes, it is important to observe that although he sometimes speaks of it as an asset to be possessed, rather than as an inherent quality, Qohelet does not treat wisdom as an abstract entity that extends beyond the wisdom of individuals, except perhaps in the difficult 7.23-25. Accordingly, the critique here is not in itself an attack on the sort of concept promoted by Proverbs 1–9 and picked up by Ben Sira, which presents wisdom as a divine gift that facilitates knowledge of God's will.

1.16] As in the previous investigation, Qohelet 'sets' (lit. 'gives') his heart to undertaking the investigation (see also 8.9, 16; and cf.

9.1), but here he also talks with his heart, and speaks of his heart's accumulated experience in wisdom. Similar internal conversations will follow in 2.1, 15; 3.17, 18, when Qohelet speaks 'in' his heart. Here the two are presented almost as separate entities, as perhaps also in 2.1, 3 and 7.25, and to understand this as meaning simply 'I thought to myself' would be to lose a significant aspect of Qohelet's imagery. As the organ associated with thought, commitment, and decision-making, the heart, for Qohelet, is not a separate personality, but is a part of the self that can influence behaviour (e.g. 5.1; 8.11; 9.3; 10.2) or alter mood (e.g. 5.19; 11.9). He depicts himself, however, as completely in control of his own heart: even when his heart despairs, in 2.20, he has made it do so, and when it takes pleasure, in 2.10, it is with his permission; in 2.3, his heart is both tool and life-line. Although Qohelet is speaking explicitly of his wisdom here, then, he is also demonstrating his self-awareness and control (at least as he perceives them). Correspondingly, his purpose is not simply to brag. His quest to understand wisdom is based on his belief that he is in an exceptionally strong position to do so, and this position is expressed in terms of having achieved greater wisdom than his predecessors. There are some textual variations here that affect the precise nature of the claim. If Qohelet were indeed saying that he has become wiser than all who were before him 'over' Jerusalem (which is the reading of the early Masoretic texts, but of no other ancient witnesses), then this would be open, as often observed, to the pedantic objection that there were few such kings, unless he is including the Jebusites (although, as Bolin, *Ecclesiastes*, 43-44, notes, a similar expression in 1 Chr 29.25 suggests that we should not push that objection too far).

1.17a] Unlike most commentators, I take the first part of this verse to be a continuation of the direct speech, and, correspondingly, Qohelet himself to be depicted declaring his intentions—which he then implicitly carries out, initiating an investigation to which he will refer again in 8.16-17, where he summarizes his conclusions. Qohelet has spoken of his wisdom and knowledge, and in the next verse he will offer characterizations of those same two things. Here, however, he sets out to examine also forms of foolishness, about which no explicit conclusions are reached: this has led many scholars to assume that the words have been added here later, pre-empting the subsequent investigation which begins in 2.12. That is not impossible, but if the text has been changed, the change was very early, and no reading without them is reflected in the ancient versions (some of which had rather different reservations about the words). We should note also that 2.12-16 does not investigate these bad qualities in isolation, but alongside wisdom; the conclusions reached there, indeed, will be rather more about wisdom than anything else. It seems reasonable to suppose that something similar is involved here: Qohelet sets out to look at wisdom and knowledge alongside attributes that denote the absence of wisdom and knowledge. One cannot, after all, properly assess the value of something without understanding what difference it makes. If this is indeed the case, and it certainly seems to be in the next chapter, then it is important to understand that Qohelet does not understand 'mindlessness' and 'obtuseness' to be qualities chosen as alternatives, by individuals who might otherwise stay neutral. Rather, wisdom is an accomplishment which moves one out of the state of being unwise, and consequently its worth depends on the value of such a move. This rather distinctive understanding may be reflected in the book's use of terms which occur nowhere else in biblical literature, but the meaning of which could be deduced from more familiar, related words.

1.17b-18] This is not an investigation which requires either the 'seeing' of the last one, or the experimentation of the next. Qohelet already possesses abundant wisdom and knowledge, so having put his heart to the question, and having already 'seen' much wisdom and knowledge (in much the same way as he previously 'saw' every deed), he 'knows' the nature of wisdom and knowledge. Whereas human activity was $r^cwt\ rwḥ$, 'wishing for the wind', wisdom and knowledge are $r^cywn\ rwḥ$, 'worrying about the wind': the similarity of the phrases links the two. Human effort was unproductive, and a positive loss; wisdom is similarly ineffectual, and a positive source of anger and pain. As we shall see when he returns to it later, Qohelet does not mean that wisdom makes no difference, but that it brings with it the pain of understanding, while enabling no real change to be effected.

Notes

1.16 I] Lit. the clause begins '(I) conversed, I with'. Miletto notes the absence of אני in two Babylonian manuscripts, but there is no good reason to doubt its authenticity. The use of the first-person independent pronoun after a first-person verb seems, in fact, to be a feature of the book's individual style (and is probably not just a mark of date; cf. Seow, Schoors, *The Preacher* I, 160-61; *contra* GKC §135 b). In a detailed discussion, Holmstedt, 'Syntactic Encoding', 4-5, notes that Ecclesiastes uses such pronouns with more than a quarter of the first-person verbs, which is far more often than they are used in other books, and all but twice places the pronoun after the verb, which is a reversal of the normal order. Such pronouns do not add emphasis to the subject, and generally have no impact on the sense, so, at least in syntactical terms, it is reasonable to say that they are mostly pleonastic (as, e.g., Barton). Those commentators who reject that description generally do so because they see a stylistic or structural purpose. J-M §146 b, for instance, views the usage as an 'indication of a meditating philosopher's ego' (§146 a also notes the use of the first-person pronoun in texts where the speaker is boasting). Lauha (writing about 2.1), on the other hand, connects the construction with contexts in which Qohelet sets himself challenges, while Isaksson, *Studies*, 63-171, concludes from a very thorough review of the usage that Ecclesiastes uses it to mark a break in the narrative, when a conclusion is reached or a new theme introduced—although it is hard to see how all the instances (e.g. 2.15b) fit such a description. There may be some nuance that fits the author's characterization of Qohelet, but we should probably not try to understand the peculiarity in terms of a particular rule that the writer applies to his composition—or even necessarily to understand every example in the same way. Isaksson is undoubtedly right to see the writer drawing breath, as it were, in many of the instances. Here, at least though, Qohelet may simply be emphasizing a distinction between himself and his heart, and while it is possible that we should, with HCM, construe the clause as equivalent to 'I and my heart spoke, saying', I think it is more probable that Qohelet depicts himself as speaking *to* his heart: see the next note.

1.16 conversed with my heart] A number of prepositions can be used with לב in expressions of thought, purpose etc. It is surely not that usage which governs the construction here, however, but the quite common use of עם with דבר pi‘el to mean 'talk with', 'converse'. The usual implications of that expression, alongside the use of דבר rather than אמר, and the fact that Ecclesiastes does not use -ב here, as in 2.1, probably suggest that the direct speech which follows is being set in the context of a longer exchange.[1] Qohelet is not just thinking to himself, but portraying an internal conversation—even if it does appear to have been one-sided.

The ἐν καρδίᾳ ('*in* the heart') of G stands in contrast with α' μετὰ τῆς καρδίας, and σ' μετὰ τῆς διανοίας (both 'with'; on the attribution, see

---

[1] The prepositional constructions with דבר are considered by Malessa, 'Vergleich', who concludes (339) that 'Mit אל"ל ist דבר stärker inhaltsbezogen ['more strongly connected to the content'], mit את"עם dagegen stärker handlungsbezogen ['more strongly connected to the action'].'

Marshall); S ܐܡܪ *'m* and Hie *cum* also reflect the עם of M (although Hie is perhaps influenced by α', σ'; cf. Marshall). If G read a variant with -ב, then that may have left a mark also on V *in*, and T's paraphrastic ליבבי בהרהור, although we should not discount in any of these the possibility of assimilation to the form in 2.1.

1.16 saying] As Isaksson, *Studies*, 62, points out, this is the only use in the book of לאמר, which is common elsewhere in biblical literature, and it signals that what follows is direct speech.

1.16 behold, I] The pre-positioning of אני and ואני (or once אנכי) before הנה, usually with a subsequent verb in the perfect, is found sometimes elsewhere (Gen 17.4; Exod 31.6; Num 3.12; 18.6, 8; Jer 1.18; 7.11 [גם אנכי]), always, as it happens, with God as the subject. We only find anything similar with a third-person pronoun in Ezek 37.11, where the following verb is, however, a participle (and the second-person pronouns are not used this way). The construction is more distinctive than the simple addition of the pronoun after a verb, as at the beginning of the verse and in 2.1 etc., but it would be hard to claim that there is really any clear difference in meaning from passages where the pronoun follows הנה. The usage may sometimes be merely euphonic, but the almost complete restriction to the first-person suggests that the construction is idiomatic, and it perhaps conveys some nuance of formality or grandeur.

Dahood's proposed vocalization ('Phoenician Background', 266-67) of אני here as a defective writing of אוֹנִי, 'my wealth', has won the qualified support of Whitley, but it is unnecessary and unsupported by any versional evidence; it would also make the word-order strange. Miletto again notes the omission of the pronoun altogether in two Babylonian manuscripts.

1.16 amplified and increased wisdom to a point] For the first verb, M has a hiph'il form of גדל, and the verb can be read in parallel with the next, so that both take wisdom as their object. Many commentators have also considered the verbs coordinated, to give the meaning 'I (have) greatly multiplied' (so, e.g., McNeile, Barton, Gordis). However, the versions seem largely to have read the first verb as intransitive: contrast G ἐμεγαλύνθην ('I have become great') with the transitive ἐμεγάλυνα ('I made great') used for the hiph'il in 2.4, and cf. Hie *magnificatus sum*, 'I am magnified', V *magnus effectus sum*, 'I am made great', S ܝܪܒܬ *yrbt*, 'I have grown great' (although these may all depend on G). Because of this, there has been wide acceptance of Graetz's suggestion that the Hebrew should be emended to the qal form found in 2.9, with the initial ה regarded as a dittograph.

Goldman has pointed out, however, that G's reading may simply reflect assimilation to 2.9, where we find the similar וגדלתי והוספתי (although in that verse, the verbs stand without a direct object, and the comparison uses מן). In fact, I think, 2.9 may have guided the translator of G in a more significant way: since the hiph'il הוספתי must have an intransitive sense there, and since the hiph'il of גדל may also sometimes be intransitive (cf. 1 Chr 22.5; Dan 8.4-11; Schoors, *The Preacher* I, 30 and *The Preacher* II, 313), he has taken this to be the basic meaning of the expressions in both verses, and translated identically in each: ἐμεγαλύνθην καὶ προσέθηκα ('I have become great and added'). On that understanding, σοφίαν here is not a direct object, but an accusative of respect; cf. σ' καὶ ὑπερέβαλον σοφίᾳ, 'and in wisdom I have gone beyond' (probably the basis for V *et praecessi sapientia*; cf. Cannon, 'Jerome and Symmachus', 192).

The versional evidence in itself, then, gives slender grounds for emendation at best, although analogy with 2.9 might still push us that way. I prefer to retain M, and to understand that in 2.9 Qohelet is speaking more generally. The similarity, however, does tell slightly against treating the verbs here as co-ordinate, and it is possible, indeed, even that we should understand the clause in the way that G has taken it, with the hiph'il used intransitively (or 'inwardly transitive', as HCM prefer to put it).

1.16 beyond anyone] The translator's characteristic rendering of על by ἐπί in ἐπὶ πᾶσιν οἳ ἐγένοντο, makes it possible to understand G as 'I have added wisdom to all who were', but the Hebrew expresses a comparative, as in, e.g., Ps 89.8 (ET 89.7), and the translator probably intended something like 'over and above'. The preposition is also used in an unattributed marginal note in Syh, reflecting ἐπὶ παντὶ τῷ γενομένῳ, 'over everyone having been'; this uses a singular participle with an article in place of G's relative clause with a plural verb. Another unattributed reading, found in Greek, has τοῖς γενομένοις—a plural participle—and the two readings may well be related, as Marshall suggests; he suspects influence from σ'.

1.16 who was in Jerusalem] M כל אשר היה לפני על ירושלם makes the point of the comparison that Qohelet has become wiser than any previous ruler of the city. Almost without exception,[2] however, the versions read 'all who were before me *in* Jerusalem', and very many Hebrew manuscripts similarly read ב- for על.[3] A change in number might be put down to a general tendency (by G in particular), to translate כל as plural (cf. on 1.13, above), although Dahood, 'The Language of Qoheleth', 227, sees different construals of a defective spelling. The change of preposition could reflect assimilation to 2.7 (so, e.g. Salters, 'Textual Criticism', 63; *BHS*) or to a more familiar form (Euringer):

---

[2] There is anonymous marginal note in Syh (with the singular): ܚܠ ܗܠ ܡܢ ܕܗܘ *'l kl mn dhw'* (= ἐπὶ παντὶ τῷ γενομένῳ, 'over everyone who was'); see Marshall, Field.

[3] Perowne, 'Ecclesiastes', 71, notes the use of על in Ps 68.30 (ET 68.29) to indicate that the preposition 'does not necessarily mean "over" in such a collocation as this', which is certainly true, but it is doubtful that it means 'in' even there, or that it would have been understood to have that sense by the versions, so such usages do not, as Perowne supposes, lessen the probability that G and the others read ב- here. For the Hebrew manuscript readings, see, conveniently, Miletto, and the discussion in the Introduction, pp. 180-81, above. 'In' is also read by Codex Graecus Venetus.

although על ירושלם is found used of kings in Ezra 4.20, however, and of a governor in Neh 7.2, it is hardly common, even if Dahood, 'Phoenician Background', 266, is able to cite Phoenician/Punic parallels.

Goldman has raised the possibility that M reflects adaptation toward Solomonic authorship, adopting על in order to specify Qohelet's royal status, and adopting a singular because Solomon had so few (Jewish) predecessors. While that latter problem, of course, might have driven adaptations in the opposite direction, on balance, I think, the data are most easily explained on the assumption that the original reading was כל אשר היה לפני בירושלם, which is so widely attested. The versions have translated normally, and על can be explained either as an error arising from the previous occurrence, or, as Goldman suggests, as an affirmation/clarification of Qohelet's royal status. It is clear, though, that על and ב- co-existed as variants in the Hebrew text tradition from an early time.

1.16 before me] Rudman, 'Qohelet's Use', argues that here and in 2.9, לפני must have the same 'spatial' force that many commentators find in 4.16, so that Qohelet is referring not to those who preceded him, but to those ruled by him. As we shall see, however, it is highly unlikely that the expression has that force even in 4.16.

1.16 seen…wisdom and knowledge] It is not clear whether Qohelet is saying that he has great experience of his own wisdom and knowledge, or reporting that he had already seen many instances of wisdom in action (there is a similar issue in 2.12). If the former, the use of ראה would suit the general emphasis on 'seeing' in Ecclesiastes, but the verb would have to have the sense 'experienced'; for a similar application of ראה to something invisible, cf. Jer 2.31. When Qohelet talks of 'seeing' wisdom in 9.13, however, he is referring to an instance of somebody else's wisdom, and that is probably the case here: Qohelet is not just expressing the same estimation of his own wisdom in different terms.

1.16 much] The use of the hiphʿil infinitive absolute הרבה as an adverb, or in effect often as an adjective, is not uncommon elsewhere, but it is a favourite expression of Ecclesiastes (e.g. 2.7; 5.6, 11, 16, 19). The use in this verse is commonly considered adverbial, but Schoors, *The Preacher* II, 265, notes that the word is often used adjectivally before the noun in later Hebrew, and that gives a better sense here.

1.17 now let me set my heart] Lit. 'and let me set'. This is usually considered one of only three imperfect consecutives in Ecclesiastes (the others being at 4.1, 7, where they constitute a rather special case), and it has been read as such by the versions. Gordis explains that the verse 'is introduced by a Vav consecutive in order to express the idea that after years of experience, Koheleth one day decided to draw the logical conclusion'. The problem with seeing 1.17 as the start of a new phase, however, is that it is clearly supposed to be tied closely to 1.16: the preceding speech is surely the immediate motivation for what Qohelet does, so we would expect any such nuancing of the tense with דבר there, not נתן here. Isaksson actually takes the connection with the speech to be the purpose of the consecutive form here, paraphrasing 'Once in my life I thought, "I have acquired...", and hence I applied my mind' (Isaksson, *Studies*, 62). This is far more likely, but if Ecclesiastes is willing to use the consecutive imperfect that way, then its rarity elsewhere in the book becomes very difficult to understand. At the risk of further reducing an endangered species, I think it is simpler and more satisfactory to see this as a plain cohortative with simple *waw* (cf. 7.23), and to understand the speech as extending until before ידעתי.

The beginning of the verse (καὶ ἔδωκα...γνῶσιν) is lacking in many manuscripts of G, and, more significantly, is under asterisk in Syh (indicating that it was not found in the text of G used by Origen); some manuscripts transpose it with καὶ καρδία...γνῶσιν in the previous verse. It seems probable that these errors have arisen from the similarity of the two clauses, and that the loss arose through homoioteleuton. McNeile (139, 156) thinks that it was either lost in the pre-Origen Greek and restored from the other hexaplaric translations (as the Syh asterisk would suggest), or originally lacking in the Hebrew, where it arose as a doublet.[4] The latter is very unlikely, but omission of the material in early texts of G might help to explain another problem (see below).

Lavoie and Mehramooz, 'Le texte hébreu et la traduction judéo-persanne', 500, note a late variant with את before לבי. This variant is reported in a number of manuscripts by Kennicott also, and in two by Ginsburg, *Writings*. G does not use σύν when translating את לבי, so is no help here. We cannot exclude the possibility that the reading is original: this is Qohelet's usage elsewhere when he uses the same verb with לבי (cf. 1.13; 8.9, 16). On the other hand, the appearance of את here might just be a response to those other uses. The sense, of course, is unaffected.

1.17 knowledge] דַּעַת can be construed either as an infinitive or as a noun: M expresses its preference for reading ודעת as a second infinitive, parallel to לדעת, by setting the disjunctive accent *zaqeph* on the preceding חכמה, yielding a sense 'to knowing wisdom, and to knowing...' Modern commentators, however, have generally followed the versions in reading דעת instead as a noun, parallel to חכמה, which seems more likely in the absence of a second -ל; *BHQ* would accordingly move the accent, and read וְדַעַת (cf. also Salters, 'Textual Criticism', 59). Gordis' subsequent understanding of the sentence is as 'to know that wisdom and knowledge are madness and folly', so that the last two nouns act as predicates for the first two, but this is awkward, and has attracted little support.

---

[4] This latter idea is misrepresented by Barton, who speaks of McNeile's claim that the material is 'a corruption introduced into the text from 𝔊'. McNeile is suggesting that it entered the Greek tradition after arising secondarily in the Hebrew, and so that is why it was lacking in early Greek texts.

As in the next verse, there are some significant differences here between Hie and V, with the latter substituting *prudentiam atque doctrinam* for the earlier *sapientiam et scientiam*—although those nouns are preserved in v. 18, so that V has four different words in total. These distinctions were to play into subsequent interpretations, especially among medieval commentators who did not take them as virtual synonyms; see Dahan, 'L'Ecclésiaste', 217-19. Such strong distinctions are probably not intended in the original: 'wisdom' and 'knowledge' are not identical, but the terms appear often together in biblical literature, and are not clearly or consistently to be distinguished in terms of the topics they might address or the personal qualities they might represent.

1.17 mindlessness and obtuseness] הוללות and סכלות (here שכלות, see below) are paired also in 2.12 and 7.25; neither is found in biblical Hebrew outside Ecclesiastes, and although סכלות does occur in 1QS vii, 14, it is not impossible that they are new coinages.[5] הוללות, however, (vocalized הוֹלֵלוּת in 10.13) is clearly related to the verbal forms מהולל and יהולל which are found in 2.2 and 7.7 respectively, and the verb הלל (cf. *HALOT* iii הלל) is more widely attested. In the qal (cf. Pss 5.6 [ET 5.5]; 73.3; 75.5 [ET 75.4]), participles from the verb stand in parallel with terms for 'the wicked'; the po'el is used of making people look stupid, or deriding them (Job 12.17; Isa 44.25; Ps 102.9 [ET 102.8]); most strikingly, the hithpolel is used of acting recklessly, drunkenly, or as though mad (1 Sam 21.14 [ET 21.13]; Jer 25.16; 46.9; 50.38; 51.7; Nahum 2.5 [ET 2.4]). Although Schoors, *The Preacher* II, 442-43, suggests that Ecclesiastes frequently places הוללות in opposition to concepts like wisdom, its affiliations elsewhere seem to point away from the connotation being 'a state of ignorance or stupidity', and more, perhaps, toward behaviour which is both bad and badly thought-out. Alter, *Wisdom Books*, 348, thinks it suggests 'a wild and unruly indulgence of the senses in which lucidity is lost', which captures some of that sense, although his translation 'revelry' seems both too limiting and too concrete.

The other term, סכלות (cf. Schoors, *The Preacher* II, 193-96), is clearly related to סָכָל (see the note on that term at 2.19), the uses of which in Jer 4.22; 5.21 tie it firmly to contexts of ignorance and unwillingness to learn (note also the cognate verb, discussed in Roth, 'Study'). Another noun, at 10.6, is pointed סֶכֶל and traditionally understood to mean 'folly', but may be a further instance of סָכָל; see the note there. The verb סָכַל, cognate with these terms, does not appear in Ecclesiastes, but is used elsewhere in the qal and hiph'il of making foolish errors, with potentially bad consequences (qal: 1 Sam 13.13; 2 Sam 24.10 = 1 Chr 21.8; 2 Chr 16.9; hiph'il: Gen 31.28; 1 Sam 26.21); the pi'el is used in 2 Sam 15.31 of turning Ahithophel's advice into bad advice, and, alongside הלל in Isa 44.25, similarly of turning the knowledge of wise men into something useless. Again, stupidity is not really the key point: this

---

[5] Proposals for the meaning of the words are helpfully reviewed in Pinker, 'Qohelet 2,12b', 96-98.

verbal usage is all to do with making the wrong decisions or giving the wrong advice, while the noun סָכָל is used of people who seem determined perpetually to do the wrong thing, and not to learn any better. In 1QS VII, 14, the use of סכלות is in the expression אשר ישחק בסכלות להשמיע קולו, and describes laughter or clowning about of some sort, which is loud enough to be heard. This could simply be 'foolish', but the context suggests more that it is inappropriate—someone enjoying a private joke during a serious meeting. T-S Misc. 28.74 translates the noun in 2.13 as χωρικίαν, and the כסיל of the next verse as χωρικός, terms that originally denoted being 'rustic', but by this time had acquired a connotation of being ignorant or unsophisticated; this perhaps captures the implication of 'oafish' in the Qumran use quite well.

In all, then, these concepts of הוללות and סכלות are probably not quite synonymous, and the usage of related terms might suggest that הוללות is acting badly without thought, סכלות the unwillingness or incapacity to do the right thing or act with propriety.[6] Here, their juxtaposition with wisdom and knowledge, has seemed inappropriate to many commentators (e.g. Ginsburg, Lauha, Fox), who have consequently viewed the pair as a secondary anticipation of 2.12 or 7.25. There is no versional support for deletion, however, and there is a danger of forcing the verse to fit preconceptions about its theme. Matters are not straightforward, however, with respect to the versions. Hie and V agree with M, but G reads a positive παραβολὰς καὶ ἐπιστήμην, 'parables and understanding', for הוללות ושכלות, and G is undoubtedly the basis for the similar S ܘܡܬܠܐ ܘܣܘܟܠܬܢܘܬܐ *wmtlʾ wskwltnwtʾ*. In part, this reading must go back to a spelling שכלות, as found here in M. It is a curious coincidence that שָׂכַל, 'understand', means almost the opposite of the סָכָל which we have just been considering, but is spelled similarly; indeed, ש/ס exchanges are common in Hebrew orthography (cf. Lavoie, 'Activité', 91) and the usual spelling of this other word in later Hebrew was סכל. It is surely not by chance, however, that סכלות came to be written שכלות in this one passage, and it is likely that a scribe, understanding the context to be a list of Qohelet's (Solomon's)

---

[6] Although in 7.17 סכל is used alongside רשע (but not as an equivalent to it), there is no obvious basis for Gordis' assertion (at 2.3) that סכלות has any connotation of 'sin, unrighteousness', or that הוללות can similarly mean 'sin'. Indeed, Fox, 'Words for Folly', 10, describes it as 'obtuseness and ignorance, with no necessary connotation of moral turpitude'. Maussion, *Le Mal, le bien*, 63-64, considers סכל in Ecclesiastes to be something beyond simple folly, independent of human will, but something incorrect done by humans, bad and contrary to wisdom, while הוללות 'connote la bêtise humaine dans toute sa splendeur, le manque d'intelligence et de savoir, par opposition à la sagesse et la science', 'human folly in all its splendour, the lack of intelligence and knowledge, in opposition to wisdom and science'. For the Targum's understanding of הוללות in terms of court intrigues, see Midrash Qohelet at 2.14, where rabbinic definitions are offered for both words: הוללות is the intrigues of power (R. Ḥanina b. Papa) or the madness of heresy (R. Simon); סכלות is trouble (b. Papa) or inanity (Simon).

qualities, chose a spelling that might enable the word to be understood in a positive sense (cf., e.g., Goldman; I am not persuaded by the assertions of Seow and Lys, in his commentary and in 'L'Être', 252, that this spelling goes back to the author, so is intentionally ironic and ambiguous). This is undoubtedly the source of ἐπιστήμην in G.[7] What then of παραβολὰς? Despite the reversal of order that is required, παραβολὰς must correspond to הוללות, the translation of which by G is variously attested as forms linked to παραφορά, 'frenzy, 'derangement', or περιφορά, 'revolution', 'circuit', 'passing around'; see the note 'mindless' at 2.2, below. Graetz suggested that this too was an error that arose in the Hebrew tradition, although he took the positive meaning to be original, and argued that הוללות must have displaced an original משלות. Most commentators, however, have looked to the Greek transmission, so that Gordis and Gentry, for example, understand ΠΑΡΑΒΟΛΑΣ to be a graphical error for ΠΑΡΑΦΟΡΑΣ (Gordis, 'Ecclesiastes 1:17'; Meade and Gentry, 'Evaluating Evaluations') or ΠΕΡΙΦΟΡΑΣ (Gentry, earlier in 'Propaedeutic', 160-61), a possibility which Goldman disputes. It is certainly true that G usually translates the term as singular,[8] and that such a slip is not an especially easy one, but it is not only probable that a scribe found himself with a list including ἐπιστήμην, which would make a putative παραφοράν/ς the odd term out, but also possible (see above) that the scribe was aware of manuscripts that lacked the first part of the verse, leaving: καὶ καρδία μου εἶδεν πολλά σοφίαν καὶ γνῶσιν παραφοράν/ς καὶ ἐπιστήμην ἔγνων. In either case, he might well assume that the word was an error by someone else, and hyper-correct on the basis of its resemblance to παραβολὰς, perhaps under the influence of, e.g., 1 Kgs 5.12 (ET 4.32). Note that there is a further such unexpected translation in the next verse. In 2.12, G renders the terms with singular nouns, and *BHQ* suggests that both should be read with the

---

[7] Codex Graecus Venetus has παραφροσύνην καὶ νόησιν, 'derangement and intelligence', which retains the order of G, but replaces the dubious παραβολὰς.

[8] The readings of the Three for הוללות are attested as follows: 1.17 α' πλάνας; θ' παραφοράς or περιφοράς (see Marshall; Meade and Gentry, 'Evaluating EvaluE ations', add new evidence favouring the former); 2.12 α' πλάνας (var. πλανήν); σ' πλανήν; θ' πλάνας; 7.25 α' πλάνας (var. πλανήν); σ' ἔννοιαν θορυβώδη; 9.3 α' πλάναι (var. πλάνη); 10.13 α'? πλάνησις (cf. Marshall); σ' θόρυβος. It is probable that α' regularly rendered as plural, except in 10.13 (cf. M זה- there), and it is likely that θ' did the same, while σ' tends to use a singular, as G. This evidence has to be treated with caution, not least because a number of variants are attested, but the other Greek versions give no strong grounds for supposing either that the Hebrew might have been understood as varying in number (except at 10.13), or that they were aware of a tradition that the plural should be read in 1.17 specifically. The early Masoretic Codex Sassoon 1053 writes הוללת at 1.17, הוללות elsewhere, and we may wonder whether it was a comparable orthographic irregularity in its source-text that led G to translate the term with a different number and perhaps a different word here.

ending ־וּת- throughout. While they should certainly be vocalized consistently, however, the witness of the versions is very mixed in this respect, and it might be unwise to place too much weight on their renderings.

1.17 I understood] We might, perhaps, expect a conjunction here, but the conjunctions in V and S probably reflect only that expectation.

Goldman takes ἔγνων ἐγώ in some important manuscripts of G to be G*, and perhaps to reflect the original Hebrew. Whilst that cannot be excluded, and the reading is strongly attested, it is hard to see why the Hebrew pronoun would have been lost, while this plus can be understood readily as a partial dittograph in the Greek.

1.17 worrying about the wind] On the expression, see the Introduction, pp. 22-24, above, and the note 'wishing for the wind' at 1.14. Ambrosianus in S reads ܗܒܠ ܘܬܘܪܦ hbl' wṭwrp',[9] 'vanity and excitement (of the wind)', while a similar Hebrew variant הבל ורעיון רוח is attested in Kennicott and de Rossi. Jarick, 'Theodore and the Text', 379, notes another similar reading in the Syriac text of the lemma in Theodore of Mopsuestia's commentary, and if this does not reflect the S variant, it might suggest the reading existed in the G tradition also. These would all seem to be adaptations to the expected form with הבל. V *labor et adflictio spiritus* is harder to explain, but probably anticipates *laborem* in the next verse (if it has not been influenced by 2.22).

1.18 in much] For the use of ברב to indicate proportionality, see, e.g., Pss 66.3; 94.19; Prov 10.19; Isa 47.9; Jer 13.22.

1.18 exasperation] The noun כעס (כַּעַשׂ in Job 5.2; 6.2; 17.7; 10.17) and corresponding verb are found also in 2.23; 5.16; 7.3, 9 twice; 11.10. Elsewhere, the verb is most commonly used in the hiphʿil, of provoking God to anger by certain actions (e.g. Deut 4.25; 1 Kgs 14.9; Isa 65.3), but sometimes in the qal, of anger which has been provoked (e.g. Neh 3.33 [ET 4.1]). The story at the beginning of 1 Samuel offers a vivid illustration of both verb and noun, when the childless Hannah is reduced to tears by her rival wife's needling, and speaks to Eli of her כעס (cf. 1 Sam 1.6, 7, 16). There is a useful survey in Tremblay, 'Qohélet 1,18', 9-10, which concludes that 'frustration' would be the best English translation.

G elsewhere translates כעס with forms of θυμός 'anger', so we would expect θυμοῦ here (as α', θ'; σ' has ὀργή, which is the reading also of the much later Codex Graecus Venetus), and the translation γνώσεως is unexpected. It is almost certainly G*, however, and Jerome reflects the La *multitudo scientiae*, 'great amount of knowledge', derived from it in his *Dialogue against the Pelagians* (although his earlier commentary here has *multitudo furoris*, 'great amount of anger').[10] When we find a similar error at 8.6, γνῶσις reflects the confusion of דעת with רעת. Some scholars suppose a similar—although

---

[9] Lane, 'Lilies', 482, observes that this is an assimilation.

[10] *Dial. Adv. Pel.* 2.5.39-40: *In multitudo sapientiae multitudo scientiae* (one ms *doloris*) *et qui addit scientiam addit dolorem*, 'in much wisdom, much

necessarily less straightforward—graphical error here (e.g. Vinel, *BHS*),[11] but others suggest that it anticipates the following דעת (Seow), or that it has been influenced by occurrences in the previous verse (McNeile); Euringer speaks simply of a *lapsus calami*, a 'slip of the pen'. Given the problems in the previous verse, it would not be astonishing if G used a source-text in which the word had been changed for what Goldman here calls 'theological' reasons (it is unlikely to be a deliberate change by the translator, as Bolin, *Ecclesiastes*, 83, suggests). Curiously, one Kennicott manuscript (152, dated to the beginning of the fourteenth century and said to have many variant readings) has בינה, which can hardly be a graphical error, and seems to reflect a similar interpretation.

1.18 gains...gains] Similar expressions are found in Prov 12.17; 18.22, and there is no dispute about the general sense. The form יוֹסִיף, however, is parsed in various ways: setting aside Dahood's improbable suggestion of a yiph'il infinitive construct form in 'Qoheleth and Northwest Semitic Philology', 350-51, the main question is whether in each case the verb is a participle or a hiph'il imperfect (a matter greatly complicated by the blurred boundaries, of sense and form, between the qal and hiph'il of יסף; cf. Schoors, *The Preacher* I, 93-94). Subsidiary questions then follow: if it is a participle, then is it a qal participle (cf. Isa 29.14; 38.5 for the vocalization), or an irregular hiph'il participle? If, on the other hand, it is a hiph'il imperfect, then is it being used elliptically ('[he who] increases'), with an indefinite/impersonal subject ('one who increases'), or as a nominalized/substantivized finite verb ('that one increases [is]')? Lauha defends the parsing as qal participle, but the view that both occurrences are hiph'il imperfects seems to have prevailed amongst recent commentators.

If we accept that view, which has the virtue of simplicity, then there are clearly several ways in which the sentence can be construed. Probably the most elegant solution is to read it as an asyndetic relative (Schoors, *The Preacher* I, 78-79) or conditional (Fox) construction, with an indefinite subject, but J-M §167 a notes the similar Prov 18.22 as an instance of simple juxtaposition (establishing equivalence). All the versions make the indefinite subject explicit, using a relative pronoun or particle (T גבר די, 'a man who'). G has further translated each occurrence of יוסיף in a different way: ὁ προστιθεὶς... προσθήσει ('he who increases...will increase'). This may well be an attempt

---

knowledge (var. grief), and who adds knowledge adds grief'. See Moreschini, *Adversus Pelagianos*, 60-61. Cf. Euringer; Gentry, 'Propaedeutic', 162. See also Vaccari, 'Recupero', 120-21.

[11] Gentry, 'Propaedeutic', 162, discusses the graphical issues, and notes the difficulties, concluding that 'the rendering in OG might be due partly to palaeographic and partly to contextual factors'. Graphical confusion is certainly not 'l'opinion unanime des spécialistes', as Tremblay, 'Qohélet 1,18', 13, asserts (before he confusingly acknowledges that some take a different view).

to render the sense clearly, rather than an indication of how each verb was parsed, and, similarly, we should not read too much into the participles of T and S, or the present indicative form of Hie *apponit*. V also differentiates the forms as indicative and subjunctive, with *qui addit...addat* (cf. the preceding *multa sit indignatio*), but this is an attempt to change the sense ('...*may* add'), not bring it out, and Jerome also changes the object of the verb to *laborem*, 'labour' (cf. Hie *dolorem*, 'anguish', which = G, M). On the reading of V here, see Vaccari, 'Recupero', 120 n. 2.

1.18 pain] מכאוב is probably best known from Isa 53.3, where the איש מכאבות is the 'man of sorrows'. The term denotes severe suffering, physical or mental (e.g. Lam 1.12, 18) but Ecclesiastes uses it both here and in 2.23 to provide a parallel or counterpart for כעס (Schoors, *The Preacher* I, 361), and this perhaps indicates either some weakening of the sense or a certain hyperbole (as when we say that something merely annoying is 'torture').

Lys raises the possibility that, without possessive pronouns attached to the nouns, the suffering here need not necessarily be that of whoever is actually gaining in wisdom and knowledge. Although that is certainly a possibility, however, it does not seem likely to have been the intended meaning, and Lys himself acknowledges the difficulty of reading the first part of the verse in such terms. Attempting to present the verse in the terms of formal logic, Méthot ('Remarques') considers the range of such theoretical possibilities, including the idea that the knowledge and suffering may pertain to everybody.

Jerome's translation with *laborem* in V (see the last note) significantly changes the sense: his earlier and more accurate *apponit dolorem* in Hie seems to have been inherited from the Old Latin (see Vaccari, 'Recupero', 120-21, and the note on 'exasperation', above, for Jerome's rendering in *Dialogue against the Pelagians*). Probably under La influence, *dolorem*, in fact, persisted as a variant—indeed, as the more common reading—in the V tradition, and is discussed by several medieval correctors and commentators who note that it corresponds better to the Hebrew text. Tremblay, 'Qohélet 1,18', 6-7, 17-18, accordingly defends *dolorem*, but the interpretative *laborem* is usually, and probably rightly, considered original; see Dahan, 'L'Ecclésiaste', 212.

2.1-2

(2.1) I said in my heart, 'Come on then, I shall stuff you with pleasure, and you must examine the benefits!' But behold, it too was an illusion. (2.2) Of fun, I said 'Mindless!', and of pleasure 'What does it do?'

Commentary

After Qohelet's failure to find something good for humans in a general way, it was possible to understand his turn in 1.16 toward an examination of wisdom, the tool of his research. It is less obvious why he should now turn to pleasure, except perhaps as a possible counterweight to the pain brought by wisdom. Wisdom and pleasure will remain linked, however, when Qohelet talks of his experiences in 2.9-10 and when he subsequently goes on to speak about divine dispensation in 2.26, where there is no implication that pleasure is supposed somehow to offset wisdom. The two make an odd couple, and if Qohelet is working to some implicit list of things that might be considered valuable ends in themselves for humans, then that list seems very short, and its contents rather disparate.

We should probably recognize, therefore, that the whole account is in some sense a device, sketching a background for Qohelet's subsequent conclusions. Here, an initial reaction to pleasure condemns it as useless, but in 2.10 Qohelet will acknowledge that he actually got something out of his work in the form of pleasure, immediately before condemning the uselessness of his achievements, and in 2.26 he will identify pleasure as something deemed to be given by God. When Qohelet's ideas about pleasure emerge more fully formed in 3.12-13, therefore, we have followed a development in his thinking from outright dismissal of its usefulness through to acceptance of its value as all that humans can get. If his experiences will shift Qohelet's attitude to pleasure in one direction, however, they will also move his ideas about wisdom in the other: in this prior investigation, wisdom is merely painful, but by 2.15 Qohelet will be wondering why he ever bothered with the wisdom of which he is currently so proud. Wisdom and pleasure appear here, therefore, because it is his ideas about each of them that are going to change most visibly as a result of the experiences to come: they are what we are supposed to watch if we are to appreciate the impact of those experiences on him.

2.1] Considerable difficulties surround the vocabulary of Qohelet's address 'in his heart', and most of the ancient versions have seen here a reference to Qohelet somehow testing his heart with pleasure. Since, however, the point of the enquiry is evidently supposed to be the value of pleasure, rather than the nature of Qohelet's heart, most modern commentators have tried to find various ways in which the sentence can be made instead to say that Qohelet will test pleasure, or give his heart experience of pleasure—none of which has been very convincing. Perhaps in recognition of the problem, or under the influence of Jewish interpreters, Jerome moved from a translation 'test you' in his commentary to a different construal of the verb in the Vulgate, so that Qohelet was now going to 'pour out' delights. It is difficult, however, to make pleasure the direct object in that way, when the text clearly says that Qohelet was doing something 'in' or 'with' pleasure. My own translation takes Qohelet to be using a verb that is attested in the sense of filling someone with food (using precisely the construction found here), but that may have been rare enough to have been overlooked by the early translators. I have not ventured so far, but if this construal is correct, then there is a strong possibility that the second verb should also be read differently and Qohelet's words understood as 'I shall stuff you with pleasure, and you shall drink your fill of good': this gives a pleasing symmetry, and does not strictly require emendation of the text. If we do not go down that path, then the construction 'seeing in/with good' has to be understood in terms of investigation, not as a way of saying 'take pleasure'—despite the fact that very many commentators assert that sense. The conclusion, 'it too was an illusion', differs slightly in the Hebrew from what is going to become a refrain in this chapter and in the book, 'this too was an illusion', probably because Qohelet is delivering a verdict specifically on pleasure, rather than on a situation.

2.2] At first glance, the verdict here seems to stand in direct contradiction to Qohelet's famous calls to take pleasure in what one does, and it has often been hailed as a prime instance of Qohelet's self-contradiction. Strictly speaking, in fact, Qohelet is never going to retract the opinions voiced here: when he adopts a more favourable attitude to pleasure, it is not because he sees any more point in it. More importantly, though, his conclusions at this stage, which have more than a little of the 'bah, humbug!' about them, belong in the context of his initial quest, where wisdom and pleasure are considered almost in isolation and as ends in themselves. Looking to the monologue as a whole, I have much sympathy with Lee's position that

> Qohelet is not endorsing a "pleasure principle" that is intent on avoiding pain and maximizing pleasure. Nowhere does he encourage pursuit of pleasure. No, enjoyment, for Qohelet, is much more profound. It has to do with living life to the full—with full recognition of life's travails and woes—and making the most of every God-given opportunity. (*Vitality*, 34)

Unlike many other commentators, though, I do not see any continuation in 2.3 of Qohelet's specific investigation of pleasure, so it stands here almost as an abstraction, and he does not even indicate what the sources of his pleasure are to be. In this passage alone, then, there is a pursuit of pleasure for pleasure's sake, and Qohelet's position is going to change not only as a result of his coming experiences, perhaps, but because the pleasure he will later commend is a pleasure *in* things, not a simple sensualism.

Notes

2.1 I said in my heart] The initial conjunction attested in key manuscripts of S (cf. 2.15) is lacking in many of the other witnesses, and is unlikely to be original.

On the use of אני cf. 1.16, above; the expression, however, is slightly different: there Qohelet spoke עם, 'with', his heart, here he speaks -ב, 'in', it, as at 2.15; 3.17, 18. S follows that reading in those other verses, but has ܠܠܒܝ *llby*, 'to my heart', here. This is unlikely to reflect an early Hebrew variant, and is probably a facilitation: M is supported by the other versions. אמר is also used by itself here, rather than in the combination לאמר...דבר used at 1.16, so Qohelet is not reporting another more general conversation with his heart.[1]

---

[1] On the distinctions in usage of the two verbs, see conveniently Malessa, 'Vergleich', 335.

2.1 Come on then] The expression לכה נא (with paragogic ה-) is used by Balak in his efforts to persuade Balaam (Num 22.6; 23.27; cf. 23.13 Qᵉrê), and in Judg 19.11, where a servant makes a suggestion to his master: it probably expresses polite exhortation (cf. J-M §48 d n. 9), and, like the equivalent English expression, has no necessary implication of movement.²

2.1 I shall stuff you with] The verb אנסכה is most naturally read as a cohortative form of נסך, 'pour', which is how V *affluam* has taken it. Cannon, 'Jerome and Symmachus', 198, suspects Jewish influence on Jerome here: this was later the interpretation of Ibn Ezra, and it is also adopted by Codex Graecus Venetus (against the understanding in G). The subsequent בשמחה, however, cannot be a direct object, and an absolute use of the verb would probably imply the pouring of libations (although Rashi takes it to refer to the mixing of wine, comparing Prov 9.2 מסכה). That does not seem to suit the context, unless the text is emended to link the verb with the wine mentioned in v. 3, and Tur-Sinai, in fact, proposes to move ביין את בשרי ולבי נהג from there.³ This conjecture is given serious consideration by Gordis, who also suggests the possible emendation/re-pointing of the following verbs to accord with this (נהג to ינהג; וראה revocalized as a 'consecutive' infinitive absolute), and translates the result as 'Come, let me anoint my body with wine and let my heart act in joy and see pleasure'. There is no strong basis for such radical changes, however, and it is not clear, furthermore, that נסך can be used of anointing something with a liquid, as opposed to pouring a liquid (despite the obscure Ps 2.6). Rashbam's attempt to read another נסך, cognate with נסיך, 'prince', has found little support: he has to imagine Qohelet indulging in some specifically 'royal' form of enjoyment.

Many more commentators have preferred, therefore, to follow G πειράσω σε, taking אנסכה to be a piʿel imperfect/cohortative from נסה, 'test', with a second person object suffix written plene: 'I shall/let me test you'. This is probably the reading implied by the pointing in M, and is apparently the understanding of Hie and S also,⁴ while the Targum and Midrash may have read or understood אֲנַסֶּה, 'I will try it', which *BHS* proposes as an emendation (and Euringer, more plausibly, takes as an error for the reading of M).⁵

---

² Correspondingly, it does not have to mean 'go', as Pinker insists in 'Experimenting', 20, although we could perhaps equally translate 'go on then'.

³ Tur-Sinai, 'Dunkle Bibelstellen', 279-80; see also his 'דברי קהלת', 402. Ginsberg, *Studies*, 7-8, accepts the suggestion, but implausibly emends אנסכה to א(י)שט(י)בה, rendering 'I will gladden my flesh with wine'.

⁴ S ܐܒܩܝܟ *ʾbqyk* may be following G here; as Kamenetzky, 210, notes, S elsewhere uses the cognate Syriac verb to render נסה; cf. 7.23 ܢܣܝܬ *nsyt* for נסיתי.

⁵ Pinker, 'Experimenting', 22, proposes that there has been an error in two stages: אנסכה is 'a scribal correction of אסנה', but אסנה is itself an error for a simple imperative נסה, which has been influenced both at its beginning and its end by the preceding נא. It is not clear why this vague and complicated second stage

The plene writing of the second-person suffix is rather unusual in Masoretic manuscripts, but by no means unprecedented, and it would have to refer either to Qohelet's heart or to Qohelet.⁶ That he is speaking 'in', and not 'with' or 'to' his heart might favour the latter, but he is, either way, talking to himself. The main objection to this reading is, again, one of sense rather than morphology: if Qohelet is testing something here, the context shows that it is not himself but forms of pleasure, upon which he then comments in the next verse, so the suffix gives an inappropriate sense: 'I will test *you*'. Attempts simply to ignore or delete this suffix (e.g. RSV 'I will make a test of pleasure'), run into the further problem that נסה does not take an object with -ב, so בשמחה cannot be the direct object.⁷ This has provoked some ingenuity: Whybray, for instance, tries to make the suffix an indirect object, citing GKC §117 x, but merely creates thereby two indirect objects.

A slightly stronger case can be made for the idea that נסה may be used not of testing but of giving experience, and Greenberg ('נסה in Exodus 20:20') has argued that to 'test' X with (-ב) Y means to give X experience of Y, citing in particular Exod 20.20; Judg 3.1, and this passage. His conclusion is picked up by, e.g., Fox and Seow, who correspondingly take the sense here to be 'let me make you experience pleasure'. Schellenberg renders 'Versuch es mit Freude', 'give joy a try!', but says that the literal sense here is 'Ich will dich Freude versuchen lassen', 'I want to let you try good': she does not explain, but since there is no causative form of נסה attested, she is presumably adopting a similar understanding. Greenberg's examples, however, point to something less experiential than formative: just as in 1 Sam 17.39 David uses the verb to indicate that he is not 'experienced' in wearing armour, so in Judg 3.1, the enemies are left to make the new, inexperienced generation of Israelites 'experienced' fighters, not just to permit them the sensation of fighting. With this sense of the verb, then, the preposition is simply instrumental, and our clause would have to mean 'I shall use pleasure to make you experienced'. When -ב is used with נסה elsewhere, it similarly indicates the means (cf. Judg 2.22; 3.1, 4; 1 Kgs 10.1 = 2 Chr 9.1) or the location of a test (cf. Pss 78.18; 106.14), and Qohelet actually uses it to indicate the method by which he has

is necessary for his broader interpretation of the passage, but an emendation that retains only נס from the original אנסכה must be regarded as, at best, a last resort.

⁶ There are apparent instances of the spelling at, e.g., Gen 27.7; Exod 7.29; 13.16; Deut 28.27, 28, 35; 2 Sam 2.22; 1 Kgs 18.44; Prov 24.10; Jer 29.25. These alone may suffice to show that, as with so many orthographic variants, it is impossible to identify any particular reason for the use of that form, or to establish its originality. Correspondingly, we should not read too much into the occurrence here, although it is possible that the spelling was intended to overcome a perceived ambiguity.

⁷ The usage does not correspond, incidentally, to the German idiom *es mit etw. versuchen* adopted by a number of commentators, e.g. Bertram, 'Hebräischer und griechischer', 40: 'ich will's bei dir mit der Freude versuchen'.

tried or tested something at 7.23.⁸ If we derive אנסכה from נסה, therefore, the sense would have to be either 'let me make you experienced using pleasure' or 'let me test you using pleasure'.

The former is clearly inappropriate here, but Lavoie, in 'L'expérimentation', 158, 171, concludes that Qohelet is, in fact, testing himself, to find out what humans more generally can gain from pleasure, and so essentially making himself the subject of an experiment. It is true that in 7.23 we probably do need to grant נסה a broader sense than it possesses elsewhere (see the notes there), but there is no reason to suppose that the verb ever had such a meaning: it is used of testing the qualities or loyalty of someone, but not of measuring the effect of something upon them (making them a 'test-subject'), and the implication here would have to be that Qohelet was using pleasure to establish his own value, rather as the Queen of Sheba uses questions in 1 Kgs 10.1 to determine how wise Solomon is. That is clearly not the case, and so the context would seem to exclude both 'make experienced' and 'test'. Accordingly, it is unlikely that we are dealing with a form from נסה.

A final possibility is that the verb to be understood here is אנס. This can be used of compulsion or constraint more generally, but it is used in Esth 1.8 specifically of forcing people to drink, and in Sir 31.21 (*sub* 31.22 in ms B) of filling oneself or being filled (niph'al) with (-ב) too much food.⁹ This offers

---

⁸ Pinker, 'Experimenting', 22-23, tries to avoid the problem by suggesting that ב is not a preposition here, but an abbreviation for בית (cf. the בית שמחה in 7.4), so that in combination with his other emendations, he can read 'I said, I within myself, please go, try the house of mirth, see the good in it, and here, it too is vanity'. This is very ingenious, and not unattractive, but even if we were to allow that the verb might be used of trying something out like that, the reconstruction would be somewhat literal-minded, and open to the same objections as the many other emendations to the book that have been proposed on the basis of supposed abbreviations.

⁹ There may also be, perhaps, an echo of this connotation in Rashi's interpretation of ואנסין in ʿArakin 16a as compelling someone to offer hospitality. The cognate noun is found with the more general sense of 'constraint' in Sir 20.4 when עושה באונס משפט is compared with a eunuch embracing a girl; in ms B, where it appears *sub* 30.20, it is implausibly glossed with בגזל in the margin, possibly under the influence of Qoh 5.7, as well as later legal usage (on which, cf. Jastrow, *Dictionary*). CD 16.13 forbids the votive offering of anything אונס, but the precise implication there is unclear. To my earlier proposal of this reading (in *Ecclesiastes and Scepticism*, 58-59), Lavoie, in 'L'expérimentation', 146, has objected that the verb simply means 'constrain' in Esther and Sirach, but whether or not it has a particular nuance when associated with food, Qohelet can be said to be constraining his heart with pleasure in a way precisely analogous to the way a body is 'constrained' by too much food in Sir 31.21. Lavoie's second objection, that none of the ancient versions has taken it this way, would have more force if any of the versions made more sense here.

an appropriate sense: Qohelet is seeking deliberately to indulge heavily in pleasure—to force-feed it to himself, as it were; it also retains the natural role of the suffix as a direct object and explains the following preposition without resort to desperate measures. I take the original intention, therefore, to have been that אֲסֻכְךָ or אֲסֻכְּכָה should be read as an imperfect qal from that verb with a second-person suffix. It is not necessary to presume an original (ה)אֲסַנְאָ, which would involve an emendation, since in first-person imperfect forms of פ״א verbs, the radical א is usually dropped; see GKC §68 g.

2.1 pleasure] The noun שִׂמְחָה and related forms play a prominent role in Ecclesiastes. Here, the context suggests that the connotation of 'pleasure' or 'enjoyment' is uppermost (cf. Lavoie, 'L'expérimentation', 158-59), rather than rejoicing or happiness.

2.1 and you must examine] Lit. 'and look into!', as G, although Hie, V, T all replace the imperative with a first-person verb, presumably to facilitate the translation (cf. Euringer). S omits the preposition, but since the preposition does appear in the translation of a similar expression at Ps 27.13, as Kamenetzky, 210, notes, this is less likely to be a reflection of Syriac usage than a secondary assimilation to the expressions without -בְּ in 3.13; 5.17; 6.6 (cf. also הראה את נפשו טוב in 2.24), which are all concerned with taking pleasure. There is no good reason to delete the preposition, therefore, but its absence in those other verses does raise three questions: (1) Are we actually dealing here with the same sort of expression, in which ראה means 'see'? (2) If so, does the preposition in itself imply some difference in the sense? (3) Does ראה בטוב as a whole have some special implication? I shall deal with the last of these in the next note.

As regards question (1), it is worth noting Ginsberg's suggestion in his commentary on 6.6, that ראה there might be a variant of רוה, 'drink one's fill'. I doubt that reading is necessary in 6.6, but it is undeniable that some confusion between the two verbs does seem to be visible elsewhere (cf. Job 10.15; Prov 11.25), and it may be that this is a matter of variant spellings or pronunciations rather than of actual errors in the consonantal text. Given the understanding of אֲסֻכְּכָה proposed above, such an understanding would provide a good parallel here, and would explain the use of -בְּ with ראה in this instance. It would not be not far-fetched, in other words, to understand 'I shall stuff you with pleasure, and you shall drink your fill of good'. Alter, *Wisdom Books*, 352, in fact, understands ראה here (and וְהִרְאָה in 2.24) precisely that way, associating it with רוה. I have retained the usual understanding, but consider this reading a strong possibility; what stands against it most strongly is the improbability that the author would originally have used a spelling with א for רוה here, given the scope for confusion, and so we would have to assume that this spelling arose as an error and emend the text without versional support. Of course, however, that presumes that both options for spelling were open to the author.

In considering the use of -בְּ with ראה more generally, in response to question (2), we can obviously set aside instances where the -בְּ is clearly instrumental (usually seeing 'with' one's eyes) or locative (as, e.g., 1 Sam

6.19; Eccles 12.3), and also the particular idiomatic usage of ראה ב- to connote 'gloating' over enemies (Pss 22.18 [ET 22.17]; 59.11 [ET 59.10]; 112.8; 118.7; Ezek 28.17; Obad 12; Mic 7.10). Elsewhere, the expression most often connotes seeing which is especially attentive or emotionally charged. So, a significant number of the uses relate to the observation of good or bad situations, frequently from a standpoint of anticipation;[10] where particular people, objects or events are involved, these are extraordinary, or are visited specially.[11] Besides these instances, though, the expression can also be used of careful examination. So, in Ezek 21.26, a liver is studied for the purpose of hepatoscopy, and the examination in 1 Sam 14.38 is also linked to divination; in Judg 16.5, the Philistines are hoping to see the source of Samson's strength. Correspondingly, Deut 1.33 uses the hiph'il of the verb with ב- of showing a route. Elsewhere in Ecclesiastes itself, careful examination is clearly involved in 11.4, where the clouds are being watched or scrutinized, not merely seen. In 3.22, on the other hand, the reference is to observation of the future.

In short, the evidence suggests quite strongly that ראה ב- means something different from ראה with a direct object, both in this book and elsewhere. Accordingly, we should be wary of assuming that ראה בטוב in this verse means just the same as ראה טוב / ראה טובה in other verses, and of taking enjoyment to be the principal connotation here. Whether or not ראה בטוב has a special meaning (see the next note), ראה ב- implies observation or examination, rather than just experience.[12] We should note, in passing, that Strobel, very implausibly, takes ראה as equivalent to הנה, and the preposition as *beth essentiae*

---

[10] So, the expression is used of things which are dreaded (Gen 21.16; 44.34; Num 11.15; Esth 8.6 twice), or eagerly awaited (Pss 27.13; 50.23; 91.16; 106.5; Isa 66.5; Jer 29.32; Mic 7.9; perhaps also Ps 128.5). Existing, bad situations are observed attentively in Exod 2.11; 1 Sam 1.11; Ps 106.44; Isa 33.15. In the first of those, it is interesting to note how Moses looks upon (with ב-) the burdens of the people—a general situation—then sees (without ב-) the specific instance of an Egyptian beating an Israelite. In Judg 16.27, the expression is used of a crowd looking on while something is happening, and something similar may be true in Ps 64.9 (ET 64.8).

[11] For visiting or following to look at something, cf. Gen 34.1; 2 Kgs 10.16; Job 20.17; Ct 6.11; Isa 66.24. In Hab 1.5, the invitation is to observe extraordinary events, while 2 Chr 7.3 describes the people watching flames descend from heaven.

[12] Fox, noting the similar observations by Podechard and BDB that the expression indicates special scrutiny, objects that 1 Sam 6.19 and Esth 8.6 both use it of merely glimpsing something. In the former verse, though, it is surely not those who have just glimpsed the Ark in Bethshemesh who die (otherwise much of the town would have been killed), but those who go up and examine it, or look inside it. In Esth 8.6, on the other hand, the reference is to anticipation of a dreadful situation. Fox is right to observe that scrutiny, as such, is not always the sense, but the expression means more than glimpsing or catching sight of something.

(cf. J-M §133 c), translating 'Siehe, sie ist das Glück', 'behold, it is good fortune'; if that were the intended sense, we might reasonably expect some more explicit statement of the subject.

2.1 the benefits] Lit. 'a good'. The last question (3) raised in the previous note concerned the sense of ראה בטוב as a whole. When this expression occurs in Ps 27.13, the psalmist expresses his confidence, in the face of adversity, that he will live to see 'the goodness of YHWH', that is, the results of divine favour towards him; Ps 106.5 expresses a similar hope of seeing the טובה of God's chosen ones, when he has delivered them, and Jer 29.32 promises that Shemaiah will have no descendants alive to see the טוב which God will do his people. The only other use of the expression, in Ps 128.5, is in a blessing for the future: 'may you see the טוב of Jerusalem all the days of your life' (// 'May YHWH bless you from Zion'). In its occurrences outside Ecclesiastes, then, ראה בטוב is linked to seeing (especially surviving to see) a state of prosperity arising from divine favour, and it does not seem implausible to suggest that Qohelet is similarly inviting his heart to observe whatever beneficial condition may be achieved by filling it with pleasure. G supports the vocalization as indefinite, and the indeterminate nature of the טוב suggests that the implication might be 'observe *what* benefit (there is)'. At the very least, the implications of ראה ב-, outlined in the previous note, make it clear that Qohelet is telling his heart to examine, not to enjoy the good.

2.1 it too] גם occurs very frequently in Ecclesiastes (cf. Schoors, *The Preacher* I, 128-29; Whitley), and the expression גם זה הבל appears in 2.15, 19, 21, 23, 26; 4.4, 8, 16; 5.9; 6.9; 8.10. Here גם הוא הבל is unexpected, not only because it uses הוא instead of זה, but also because nothing else specific has yet been characterized as הבל, so the גם seems redundant. If we are not to consider it emphatic or adversative, גם probably refers back to the general characterizations of all work and deeds in 1.2, 14. The pronoun suggests that Qohelet is not labelling a situation, as often, but something more specific to which he has just referred, and טוב is the most likely candidate; Fox, similarly, sees the antecedent as 'the experience of pleasure'.

2.2 Of...of] אמר ל- could indicate speaking *to* somebody, and G, Hie, V, S seem to have taken Qohelet's comments to be addressed directly to שחוק and שמחה—as evidenced by their use of second-person verbs in 2b. The preposition is regularly used, however, to denote the topic of speech (e.g. Deut 33.9); cf. GKC §119 u; §143 e.

The words used by the Greek translators (helpfully listed and translated by Jerome) are discussed below, but it is worth noting here their syntax. In 2a, σ' probably read εἰς τὸν γέλωτα εἶπον θόρυβον, 'to/toward laughter I spoke confusion' (cf. ms 161, Syh for the first word), although his readings (and those of θ') for 2b are uncertain. His use of the accusative θόρυβον, however, suggests that, like G τῷ γέλωτι εἶπα περιφορὰν ('To laughter I spoke περιφορά'), he did not understand מהולל to be in direct speech. The reading of α' is attested as both πλάνησιν and πλάνησις ('wandering', 'error');

Marshall argues that the syntax requires an accusative, but it is possible that α' did take the speech to be direct in 2a, as do most modern translations, in which case the nominative might be original.

2.2 fun] שחוק is often used of mockery, but is essentially a neutral term for laughing. The cognate verb can have a more general sense of playing, partying or clowning about, which I take to be the real meaning here: Qohelet is not just talking about the physical act of laughing.

2.2 mindless] For the connotations of הלל, see on 'mindlessness and obtuseness' at 1.17, above. S here has ܡܢ ܗܢܝܢ *mn' hnyn*, in which Janichs, *Animadversiones*, 6, took ܗܢܝܢ *hnyn* to be a participle from ܗܢܐ *hn'*, so that the text might reflect מה הועיל in the source-text, rather than M מהולל. However, the Syriac probably means just 'what are these?' Euringer attributes this translation simply to the influence of the question which follows in 2b, and that may indeed have inclined the translator to vocalize a defectively written מהלל as though it were the mishnaic מה הללו, which Gordis suggests. This seems more likely than Goldman's view, that S actually found מה הללו as a variant in the consonantal text.[13]

T paraphrases here, linking the statement to Solomon's life, and does not reliably suggest that there was a substantive in its *Vorlage* (as Goldman also claims). It is interesting to note, however, that G περιφοράν translates מהולל in the same way that הוללות is rendered in 2.12 and 7.25 (cf. also 1.17), although it uses περιφέρει to translate the verb at 7.7. Nominal forms are found too in α' πλάνησιν, 'error', (cf. V *errorem*) and σ' θόρυβον, 'confusion' (probably here of mind, cf. LSJ), which are attested by Jerome; he also notes that θ' follows G (Hie itself has *amentiam*). It seems less likely that this reflects a different Hebrew text, than that this po'al participle (in some manuscripts pu'al, but Hie[comm] cites as *molal*) was regarded as a substantive—perhaps on the basis of the context, since the form is unattested elsewhere.

The corresponding po'el, used in 7.7 (cf. also Job 12.17; Ps 102.9 [ET 8]; Isa 44.25) seems to be used of making something foolish, or seem foolish, and, by extension, of deriding something; we might expect the po'al, therefore, to indicate that something is 'foolish' or 'mindless', and I have translated accordingly. Despite their preference for a substantive, some such understanding underpins most of the versions (T ליצנותא picks up instead the sense 'derision'). The meaning of περιφορά in G, θ', however, is far from

---

[13] S does not offer support for Seow's proposed reading מה הולל, 'what does it boast?', and actually points up the way in which the second question is more likely to have led scribes to read another question with מה here than to read מהלל. The suggestion is adapted by Pinker, 'Experimenting', 27, who reads the pu'al of הלל, and translates 'Concerning laughter, I said "how praised it was (sarcastically)?" and regarding happiness "what does it produce?"' (although he presumably intends 'how!', not 'how?'). Both Seow's proposal and Pinker's development of it involve emendation, while offering a sense no better than מהלל.

straightforward, and although the textual evidence points to its originality here and elsewhere, it would be less surprising if the translator had used παραφορά, which appears frequently as a variant in G.[14]

2.2 What does it do?] It is worth noting the characteristic use of זה rather than זאת here, as throughout the book (although there is some minor variation between manuscripts in this respect). This is the regular feminine demonstrative pronoun in mishnaic Hebrew; it apparently appears also at 2 Kgs 6.19; Ezek 40.45, as well as in the expression כָּזֹה וְכָזֶה (Judg 18.4; 2 Sam 11.25; 1 Kgs 14.5), but can hardly be considered a common form in biblical Hebrew. For a fuller discussion, see Schoors, *The Preacher* I, 52-54, and note also the issues raised in the Introduction, pp. 160-62, above.

The expressions מַה זֶּה and, more often, מַה זֹּאת are both used in questions, where they form, in effect, a non-verbal clause picked up in the subsequent sentence (cf. J-M §143 g). The literal sense here, then, is 'what (is) it, (the thing that pleasure) is doing?', and the question, although it uses a participle, is similar to those found in, e.g., Gen 3.13; 12.18; 26.10; 29.25; Jonah 1.10. The feminine pronoun is essentially 'neuter' in this usage, and Barton is probably wrong to understand that the participle עשׂה (pointed as feminine in M) agrees 'with זה which represents שׂמחה': the agreement is with שׂמחה itself. The verb, accordingly, is not being used absolutely, as at Dan 8.24, and the object is represented by זה.

Isaksson, *Studies*, 127, comparing the question posed in 8.4, speculates that the participle is used here because an imperfect would have given a different nuance, 'What is it actually doing?' We should not exclude, though, the simpler possibility that the form has been used to match the preceding participle מהולל, and analogy with that previous assertion may suggest that Qohelet intends not to proclaim the pointlessness of pleasure, so much as to express bafflement at it.

G, S, Hie, V have a second-person verb, understanding the question to be addressed directly to pleasure. This rendering has been influenced by an understanding of the preposition -ל to mean 'to' rather than 'about' (see above); it does not, therefore, imply the existence of a variant in the Hebrew.

---

[14] As one would expect, περιφορά, περιφέρω and cognate terms connote 'carrying around', and most of the extended meanings are clearly derived from that basic sense—it is often used of revolving. Lampe notes some instances where the passive of the verb describes the way in which a drunk or a punch-drunk boxer stagger about, and it is just about conceivable that the usage in G is somehow related to that usage. It seems altogether more likely, however, that περιφορά is merely acting as a substitute for παραφορά. The translator's Greek is surely too good for this to have been a simple malapropism, and it is possible that this paronymy represents a usage that had already become established in his context. If it was indeed recognized and accepted by θ' also, then this usage may have been quite widespread.

The reading of σ' was also second-person according to mss 161, 248, but Marshall argues that the presence of the Syh marginal reading ܥܒܕ 'bd' (participle) only makes sense if σ' and θ' had something different from G, and that they probably read third-person ποιεῖ. T 'what benefit is there for the man who does it (pleasure)?' may have vocalized the Hebrew participle as masculine, but is anyway paraphrasing. V *quid frustra deciperis*, 'why do you beguile to no end?', moves beyond paraphrase to the substitution of a wholly interpretative reading.

2.3

(2.3) With my heart I researched how to sustain my body with wine and my guiding heart with wisdom, and how to keep a hold on obtuseness until I should see what is good for humans to do beneath the heavens, for the limited duration of their lives.

Commentary

There are no significant text-critical issues, and the vocabulary presents no serious difficulties, but this verse has caused terrible problems for translators and commentators since ancient times. In part, this has been the result of presuppositions about the content: many have viewed the reference to wine, for instance, as an indication that Qohelet must be continuing his investigation of pleasure, despite having already delivered his verdict. In part, it arises also from the use of figurative language: all the pulling, steering and holding on here may reflect some underlying metaphor based on driving, but the different possible implications of each verb used in this way have sown much confusion—is Qohelet really trying to get hold of folly for himself, for example, as the Hebrew would allow? And what does 'pulling' one's body (or 'flesh') entail?

In the light of Qohelet's discourse so far, the clearer second half of the verse is most plausibly to be taken as a statement that, whatever he is doing, Qohelet is doing it in order to establish whether there is anything good for humans to do in their lives, and so he is again approaching the main question that has so far dominated the monologue. It is also apparent that he is planning to do something 'until' he has achieved his answer, suggesting that the something might take a long time. The view, popular among commentators, that Qohelet intended somehow to find the answer by getting drunk and 'laying hold' of folly is not inherently unattractive, and is often linked to an idea that the following 2.4-10 is primarily about self-indulgence. It is difficult to extract this sense from the Hebrew, however, and it turns the idea that his wisdom is still somehow 'steering' Qohelet into an almost comical contradiction—a claim that he's still in control, when the point is that he should not be.

Commentators have also struggled to explain, of course, why a plan to get drunk—or at least to drink[1]—should require research, and some have felt obliged to render the beginning of the verse in terms quite outside the scope of Qohelet's normal usage.

I take Qohelet's use of wine here, therefore, to be as a stimulant, and not an intoxicant, and his intention to be not that he will embrace folly, but that he will try to keep it at bay. This verse is not about some second attempt to explore pleasure and/or folly, but about Qohelet's careful planning of his next actions. In place of the brief examinations that have so far yielded no answers to his questions, he now looks into hunkering down for a much longer trial of living, in which he will actually build and accumulate for himself, supplying possessions and the wherewithal for a life of luxury. For this, he needs to keep himself going, and to develop ways of ensuring that he remains focused on his objectives—guided by wisdom without slipping into folly. In short, the verse describes his preparations for what is to follow: an experiment that will require time, effort, and some fortifying wine, in place of his previous armchair ruminations and indulgences. It marks a break, therefore, with what has gone before, and serves as a prelude to the activities that will follow.

There is no shortage of references to the intoxicating effects of wine in the Hebrew Bible or in other ancient literature, but wine was also widely regarded as healthy and as energizing: many people would have drunk it as a staple part of their diet, and the Talmud (*b. Baba Batra* 58b) was later to quote as a saying: בראש כל אסוון אנא חמר באתר דלית חמר תמן מתבעו סמנין, '...I, wine, am at the head of all healing; it is where there is no wine that medicines are needed'. The Romans were especially enthusiastic, but probably not altogether untypical. In his *De Agricultura* 57, written around 160 BCE, Cato the Elder lists specific daily wine-rations for slaves working in the fields at different times of year, and recommends an annual allowance (apparently before dilution) of around 180-260 litres of wine

---

[1] Although it may not be so widely held as Longman suggests, it is worth noting Leupold's genteel view that this is 'a reference to a consumption of wine which enables a man to get the highest possible enjoyment by a careful use of it, so that appetite is sharpened, enjoyment, enhanced, and the finest bouquets sampled and enjoyed. Approximating or falling into drunkenness is plainly not under consideration.' On such a reading, Qohelet is somehow turning to wine as the quintessence of gentlemanly pleasure, not as a means to some other end.

per year, with around 820 ml per day—more than a bottle in modern terms—for three months of the year. Lucius Columella, in his first-century CE *Res Rustica* 2.3, even speaks of pouring wine down the throats of oxen after ploughing. It is Pliny the Elder, however, writing in the same century, who identifies the drawback: 'human strength, blood and complexion are nourished by wine', and 'by a little wine the sinews are strengthened', but 'by a greater amount they are damaged—so too the eyes'.[2] Qohelet's research involves, perhaps, finding the proper balance that will enable him to keep his body strong but his 'guiding heart' alert, and it may be his very use of wine, indeed, that brings with it the risk of becoming obtuse. The parallel clauses suggest that Qohelet intends wisdom to be to his heart as wine will be to his body—metaphorically almost a foodstuff or fuel.

Qohelet's purpose here, then, is not to achieve or to experience a particular state, but to learn how to sustain himself for what may be a lengthy quest. Abandoning his previous attempts to evaluate qualities or experiences that came to him pre-packaged, as it were, his intention is now to live a life that will, he hopes, lead him to encounter something worthwhile for humans to do—and, indeed, to live that life until he encounters it. More precisely, he apparently expects to undertake some activity that he will be able to commend to others as worthwhile.

Notes

2.3] The verse is preceded in many manuscripts of S by a plus: 'And I turned to comfort my heart'. This is apparently a double translation, perhaps of v. 20a, where it also appears as a variant, and it may have migrated as a marginal note; cf. Kamenetzky, 210; Lane, 'Lilies', 483. Janichs, *Animadversiones*, 7, sees it as two renderings of תרתי בלבי.

2.3 with my heart I researched] Seow believes that the rendering of תרתי by all the versions in terms of intellectual activity suggests that they struggled

---

[2] *Naturalis Historia* 23.22: *Uino aluntur uires, sanguinis colosque hominum... uino modico nerui iuuantur, copiosiore laeduntur; sic et oculi.* Pliny goes on to cite the view of the physician Asclepiades that *utilitatem uini aequari uix deorum potentia posse*, 'the usefulness of wine can hardly be equalled by the powers of the gods'. Elsewhere, at 7.37, he praises Asclepiades, who was active in the late second and early first centuries BCE, for having discovered how to treat diseases successfully using wine.

to understand the term, but they are merely being consistent with their perfectly proper understanding of the same verb in 1.13, where the exploration is similarly mental (see there under 'inquiring and exploring'). Attempts to make it mean simply 'go about', or to link it (as Fox does) with the expressions using סבב or שוב in, e.g., 2.20; 4.1, result from the exegetical problem that what commentators take Qohelet to be attempting does not require investigation, rather than from any inherent lexical difficulty.

G is difficult here, with most manuscripts attesting καὶ κατεσκεψάμην εἰ ἡ καρδία μου ἑλκύσει, 'and I examined whether my heart would draw'. Rahlfs, however, emends to κατεσκεψάμην ἐν καρδίᾳ μου τοῦ ἑλκύσαι, 'I examined drawing in my heart', in line with Hie and M (and probably following a suggestion by Klostermann, in *De libri Coheleth*, 58); Gentry similarly reads καὶ κατεσκεψάμην ἐν καρδίᾳ μου ἑλκύσαι, like Klostermann, omitting the definite article. As Goldman notes, much rests on the slender and ambiguous evidence of the early ms 998, which attests ΕΛΚΥΣΕ, possibly a writing of ἑλκύσαι, after a lacuna. If the majority text is G*, rather than the result of an early sequence of errors in the Greek tradition, it would presumably have to reflect something like ותרתי אם לבי ימשוך, and McNeile, 139, suggests that this is itself a potential corruption of an original ותרתי אני בלבי משוך. On balance, however, it seems easier to accept here an inner-Greek development, perhaps with a misreading of ἐν (and with the following ὡς οἶνον, see below) leading to subsequent adaptation of the verb, than to posit a wholly unattested Hebrew text which inexplicably develops in two quite different directions.

The conjunction which precedes the verb in the Greek tradition, on the other hand, is just as likely to reflect a variant in the Hebrew source-text as to have arisen from dittography of the following κατ-. It is supported by σ', θ' καὶ διενοήθην (σ' possibly ἐνοήθην, see Marshall) ἐν τῇ καρδίᾳ μου, 'I considered in my heart'.

2.3 sustain] I adopt the same understanding here as, e.g., Crenshaw and Driver, 'Problems and Solutions', 225-26. משך is used principally of pulling or stretching, sometimes literally, of animals drawing a plough or cart (e.g. Deut 21.3, cf. Isa 5.18), for example, or of humans pulling on a rope, fishing-line or bow (e.g. Jer 38.13; Job 40.25 [ET 41.1]; 1 Kgs 22.34), but often also in the figurative senses of luring someone (e.g. Judg 4.7; Ps 10.9), or especially of prolonging some activity or situation (e.g. Exod 19.13; Jer 31.3). This range of meanings is reflected also in α', θ' ἑλκύσαι, and in G's use of the same verb; cf. Hie *traherem*. T also follows the Hebrew closely with לנגדא, but Jerome's Vulgate rendering *abstrahere a uino carnem meam*, 'to withdraw my flesh from wine' is interpretative (cf. Goldman).[3]

---

[3] Compare Lohfink, 'Technik und Tod', 31, 'ich meinen Leib vom Wein wegzog'. The authors of the *Temperance Bible Commentary*—a more scholarly work than one might expect—are naturally intrigued by Jerome's rendering, and

Although Kamenetzky, 238, seeks to link it with an original Hebrew לִבְשׂוֹם or לְבַשֵּׂם,[4] S ܠܡܒܣܡܘ *lmbsmw*, 'delight, refresh' is probably interpretative as well. Goldman explains this rendering in terms of Delitzsch's supposition, that the verb can mean 'refresh' in Mishnaic usage, and that idea has also been picked up in *HALOT*;[5] most recent commentators, however, recognize that this is probably a misreading of *b. Ḥagigah* 14a, where the point seems not to be that the Haggadists refresh the hearts of their hearers like water, but that they attract or draw them out, either as easily as one draws water (so, e.g., Jastrow, *Dictionary*, Corré, 'Epispasm', 416 n. 2), or with all the force that water can exert (so Seow).

The Syriac reading, like Rashi's 'invigorate' (לעדן) or Rashbam's 'indulge' (להתענג), probably results rather from the same source as the many modern attempts to emend the verb or assign to it a new sense—the difficulty of envisaging just what it means to 'draw out' one's flesh with wine, especially if one sees the verse as a reference to inebriation. Joüon, 'Notes philologiques', 419-20, thus declares that emendation is permissible, because no-one has found a plausible sense for the verb, and proposes to read לְשַׂמֵּחַ, 'to rejoice', a view which has attracted little support, despite the attribution of this effect to wine in Ps 104.15. An emendation to לְשָׂמוֹךְ = לִסְמוֹךְ, 'support', is also suggested by *BH*³, *BHS*, but although the use of that verb in Ct 2.5 makes the correction attractive, it remains entirely speculative. Among the various efforts to extend the sense of משך itself, Alan Corré's is surely the most memorable: he thinks Qohelet is referring to the drawing down of flesh over the penis to conceal circumcision, and emends the following word (in line with G, see below) to כיין, which he then takes to be an error for כיון; Qohelet, on that reading, sought to render himself 'uncircumcised like the Greeks' ('Epispasm', 417). Whatever pleasure such an action might or, more likely, might not have induced, the statement hardly seems appropriate to the context. A close runner-up, perhaps, is Köhlmoos' understanding that 'drawing my flesh through wine' is equivalent to the modern 'bathing in champagne'. Less vivid, but also unusual, is Seow's attempt to make the verb mean 'induce', with reference to the bravado of youth. It is not really clear, however, what his 'induce my body with wine' actually means, especially when he later glosses it as 'indulged himself with wine'.[6]

imply very cautiously that he might have read a different Hebrew text; the use of *in uino* in Hie, however, makes this very unlikely. See Lees and Burns, 'The Book of Ecclesiastes', 147.

[4] See Jastrow, *Dictionary*, under בסם: the term, which is post-biblical, commonly refers to perfuming or embalming, but is, strikingly, used of drunkenness in some stems.

[5] See also Driver, 'Problems and Solutions', 225, which invokes the cognate Arabic verb in support of Delitzsch's view.

[6] Some similar extension of meaning seems to be going on in the ET of Lohfink's commentary, where an original 'indem ich meinem Leib mit Wein

I take the context here to be temporal (see the discussion above), and the use of משך to be similar to that found in Job 24.22; Pss 36.11; 85.6; Prov 13.12; Isa 13.22; Jer 31.3; Ezek 12.25, 28: Qohelet is seeking to sustain ('prolong') his body, in the sense of keeping it going until he has achieved his aim. This is not far from the sense that Gesenius assigned to the passage in his *Thesaurus* (p. 826 of the 2nd ed.), where he understood Qohelet to be saying that he would make his body hard, or durable, or 'take care' of it. That interpretation, however, is partly posited on a connection with a supposedly cognate Syriac verb which in fact has more to do with drying out or shrivelling than with hardening.

Schoors, *The Preacher* I, 181, cites with approval the view of Aalders, that the -ל + infin. cs. here is gerundial, that is, Qohelet seeks not 'how to draw' his body, but 'by drawing it'.[7] This understanding, though, seems less natural, and depends heavily on the assumption that Qohelet is seeking here to inebriate himself as a means to his end. Isaksson, 'Background Information', 43-45, also offers a different understanding: drawing on Arabic grammar, and pointing to possible analogies in Gen 2.3; 24.63; 1 Sam 20.36, he argues that both infinitives in this verse are offering supplementary, background information, and translates, 'in that I cheered my body with wine...in that I laid hold on folly'. The analogies are not persuasive, however, and the proposed sense is very strange.

2.3 with wine] On V *a uino*, see the previous note. Despite Rahlfs' emendation εἰς οἶνον, 'to wine', the ὡς οἶνον, 'as wine', which dominates the Greek manuscript tradition is most probably original, and suggests that the translator of G read כיין, rather than ביין. Aitken, 'Rhetoric and Poetry', 61 n. 19, observes that εἰς can be used instrumentally in koine Greek, but such a meaning would be very unnatural after ἑλκύσαι, so the preposition is not likely to have been merely an unusual rendering of -ב. G accordingly understands Qohelet to be drawing his body 'like wine'. Syh reports the reading of θ' as ܐܝܟ ܚܡܪ *'yk ḥmr'*, which is to be retroverted ὡς οἶνον, as G (cf. Field, Marshall), but the other versions support M, and ביין should be retained.

Just as he read בית שמחה in the previous verse, Pinker ('Experimenting', 33) here again reads ב as an abbreviation for בית, and reconstructs a dialogue in which Qohelet asks his heart whether he should 'drag his body' to the 'house of wine'. To the existing complications, this adds the problem that much of what follows has to be divided into separate speeches by 'I' and 'my heart', in which the heart confusingly speaks also as 'I'. He also has to read נהג (see the next note) as an infinitive absolute serving as an imperative.

lockte', 'as I drew/lured my body with wine' (which is different from his earlier translation, see above), is rendered rather misleadingly as 'in order to bathe my body in wine'.

[7] Aalders himself draws an analogy with the common use of לאמר (cf. J-M §124 o).

2.3 guiding heart] נהג is pointed as a participle in M, and the corresponding ܪܢܐ *rnʾ* is probably to be read that way in S also, as Kamenetzky, 198, suggests (cf. also Goldman, who notes that Codex Ambrosianus marks it as such with a diacritical point). An interpretive rendering is offered by σ' ἵνα τὴν καρδίαν μου μεταγάγω εἰς σοφίαν, 'that I might transport my heart to wisdom', followed by V *ut animum meum transferrem ad sapientiam* (cf. Cannon, 'Jerome', 192), and it is difficult to say whether this represents a different parsing of the verb, but G ὡδήγησεν probably reflects a reading of it as qatal, cf. Hie *deduxit*, and T דבר. Most modern commentators have opted to follow M, but Fox has suggested that it should be read as an infinitive absolute, co-ordinated with the two infinitive constructs in the verse. That suits his understanding of the verse, but if this verb truly stands in parallel with the others, we should more naturally expect ולנה(ו)ג את לבי. Following M, I read נהג as a participle, but one used as an attribute qualifying לבי rather than as a predicate.

The verb itself is used commonly of herding people and flocks, and a number of commentators take that to be the primary implication here; Fox talks of the 'submerged' image being that of a shepherd leading an animal on a cord. The verb can, however, refer to driving as well (cf. 2 Sam 6.3; 2 Kgs 9.20), and some other commentators have noted the possible correlation between the preceding משך, used of pulling a cart and נהג used of driving one. Fox also notes that the verb is always transitive in biblical usage, and, indeed, the uses which he notes in Sir 3.26; 40.23 are not intransitive, as he supposes—the first is probably passive, and the second has an implicit object (a friend guides *one* well, but not so well as a sensible wife). It is doubtful, therefore, that the much later, intransitive sense of 'conducting oneself' or 'behaving' should be understood here, as suggested by, e.g., Whitley, and although there is no direct object present, I take the verb to have its usual transitive sense: Qohelet's heart is what guides him, or, perhaps more specifically, is what conducts the current investigation.[8] Indeed, if we are to give weight to the corresponding senses of the verbs, then the heart is driving as he pulls his flesh along.[9]

2.3 with wisdom] In the famous Isa 11.6, the predators will co-exist with the prey, and a little child be נהג בם: the verb elsewhere requires no preposition to mark its object, and, whatever precisely the expression means in Isaiah (perhaps 'a shepherd amongst them'), it does not show that נהג can take a

---

[8] As understood, perhaps, by S. Although Kamenetzky, 210, suggests that the rendering ܪܢܐ *rnʾ* has taken the Hebrew נהג to be derived from הגה, its correspondence to ܕܘܢܝ *rnyt* (for תרתי) at the beginning of the verse surely indicates that S is connecting the function of the heart here to its broader role in the verse.

[9] Perowne, 'Ecclesiastes', 169-70, paints a vivid picture of the flesh as a chariot, drawn by a horse that is wine, representing sensuality more generally, and driven by wisdom as its charioteer.

direct object with ב. When the verb is followed by the preposition in Sir 3.26, indeed, the preposition clearly does not mark the object. Correspondingly, it is unlikely that Qohelet or his understanding is 'leading his knowledge to pasture', as Lohfink suggests ('mein Verstand das Wissen auf die Weide führte'; cf. 'Technik und Tod', 31, 'mein Geist aber weidete das Wissen'); that proposal is discussed and rejected in Schoors, *The Preacher* II, 402-403. The preposition might be indicating the nature of the guidance, and it is commonly understood that the heart is guiding 'wisely', but I think the sentence-structure here demands that בחכמה be read as parallel to ביין in the preceding clause. On the pointing of בחכמה, see the note at 1.13, above.

2.3 how to keep a hold on obtuseness] Its form indicates that ולאחז must stand in parallel with למשוך, both verbs being governed by the initial תרתי: 'I researched how to...and how to...' That might suggest that the following ב should be read instrumentally, like that on ביין, which stands in the corresponding position previously. אחז, however, commonly takes the preposition with its object, and so סכלות here is more naturally what Qohelet seeks to grasp, not the means by which he intends to grasp it. Perhaps unhappy with the idea that Qohelet should be seeking to grasp obtuseness, or under the influence of the preceding 'wisdom' (so Euringer), S renders בסכלות as though it were בשכלות, 'in prudence' (and probably includes it in the description of 'my heart', cf. Salters, 'Textual Criticism', 63); V *devitaremque stultitiam*, 'and that I might avoid folly', simply reverses the meaning.

The reading of G is again problematic, with the manuscript tradition attesting ἐπ' εὐφροσύνῃ (or -ην), for בסכלות.[10] As Goldman notes, this is unlikely to be a reflection of בשכלות, like S's rendering, since εὐφροσύνη, 'joy', would more probably reflect שמחה, as in the preceding two verses. Most commentators, in fact, take it to be an inner-Greek corruption of ἐπ' ἀφροσύνῃ, 'on folly', and some such corruption seems probable; the error has, perhaps, been influenced not so much by the proximity of σοφίᾳ, 'by wisdom' (so, e.g., Gordis), as by the apparent difficulty of the statement.

If G offers no grounds to emend M, however, it does render the Hebrew curiously with κρατῆσαι ἐπ', 'seize *on*': the verb does not take ἐπί in normal Greek usage (or elsewhere in the Septuagint). The translator, moreover, uses ἐπί only in an idiom at 11.6 to represent anything other than על, and perhaps אל, probably never employing it for ב.[11] Some manuscripts actually have ἐν here, and although these may simply reflect assimilation to the Hebrew, there is a strong possibility that this was actually the original reading (cf. 7.18, where G renders תאחז בזה using τὸ ἀντέχεσθαί σε ἐν τούτῳ), since

---

[10] The noun is attested also in the later Codex Graecus Venetus.

[11] See 1.6, 12, 16; 2.17, 20; 3.14, 17; 5.1 three times, 5, 7 twice; 6.1; 8.6, 14, 16; 9.8, 12, 14; 10.4, 7 twice; 11.1, 2, 3, 9; 12.6, 7. In 9.14 and 12.6, G may have read על for M אל. In 11.6, the translator uses the Greek expression ἐπὶ τὸ αὐτὸ, 'together', for כאחד, or perhaps יחדו.

it is unlikely that the translator found על in his source-text. If not, and if the unusual use of ἐπ' is original, then the Greek might more naturally be understood as 'prevail over and against' rather than 'lay hold of', and might represent an attempt to get past the interpretative problem whilst staying close to the Hebrew; in 9.12, where there is no such problem, the translator twice uses θηρεύειν, 'catch', contextually for the same verb.

Some modern commentators also regard the clause as problematic, and *BHS*, following Galling as often, speculatively suggests a possible emendation to the negative ולא אחז; that has been accepted by, e.g. Seow and Fox (in his 1989 commentary, although not in his later work). Driver, 'Abbreviations', 123, tries to read the same by arguing that a לא, abbreviated to 'ל, has been misread. This would be a curious turn of phrase, however, and has no support from the versions. In fact, the verb may not be so very difficult: it is essentially a neutral term for holding or grasping something, which imputes no particular motive and is used for fastening, catching or restraining (as at 9.12), as well as for seizing on something (as at 7.18). It is not used directly in parallel with משך elsewhere, but the difference between them may be illustrated by a comparison of Ct 1.4, where one lover is to pull (משך) the other after him in haste, with Ct 3.4, where one clutches (אחז) the other, and will not release him before bringing him to her mother's house. Here it is reasonable to suppose that we are dealing with a similar distinction, in which the first of the parallel infinitives sets the context for understanding the second: Qohelet seeks, figuratively, to pull his body and heart along, but to catch and contain obtuseness (Lohfink speaks of 'imprisoning' it). On the sense of the term סכלות, see on 1.17, above.

2.3 until] The expression עד אשר appears with לא in 12.1, 2, 6, where it has the sense 'while not yet'. Without the negative particle, it is commonly used to express the continuation of action until a certain event, with the imperfect used if that event is in the future (e.g. Gen 33.14; 1 Sam 22.3; 1 Chr 19.5).

2.3 what] Lit. 'where (there is)' or 'which (is)'. אי זה appears again in 11.6, when it is used of not knowing which seed sown will be successful. That sense is in line with the familiar later use of the expression to mean simply 'who?' or 'which?', and Schoors, *The Preacher* I, 57-58, observes, in the course of a detailed discussion, that such usage can be identified earlier. It is doubtful, therefore, that the expression can be viewed merely as a reinforced form of אי, 'where?', as BDB and *HALOT* suggest, and the versions here notably do not translate with 'where?' (G ποῖον, probably intended to have the sense 'what?', 'which?', rather than 'what sort?'; Hie, V *quid*; S ܐܝܢ *'yn'*; T אי דין מנהון, perhaps influenced by 11.6).

Whatever the origins and later application of the term, though, it is generally used in the biblical literature to inquire about location, often in conjunction with terms for 'way' or 'place', or with reference to a specific building (so, e.g., Job 38.19 אי זה מקמו...אי זה הדרך; see also 1 Sam 9.18; 1 Kgs 13.12; 2 Kgs 3.8; 2 Chr 18.23; Job 28.12, 20; 38.24; Isa 66.1; Jer 6.16), but also absolutely (see 1 Kgs 22.4, which differs in this respect from the parallel 2 Chr 18.23; Isa 50.1). In Esth 7.5, the reference is not necessarily to place, and location is not primary in Qoh 11.6, but if we are to accept the arguments for seeing a basic sense 'what?' or 'which?', as do most recent commentators, then we must also recognize that biblical usage largely limits the expression to certain contexts, perhaps because of associations with אי, and that אי זה is not a simple equivalent of מה, even though that is used in the similar clause at 6.12. In that verse, 'what is good' might be anything (and is not necessarily an activity to be undertaken by humans). Here, however, Qohelet is more likely looking out for something among the experiences that he is about to undergo, and his hope is that he will spot something, rather than that he will attain some heightened knowledge or perception. More loosely, we might understand that he is setting out to see 'where' that good is to be found.

2.3 good] Jerome's interpretation of this as *utile*, 'profitable', in V may owe something to the interesting rendering of σ', τὸ σύμφορον, 'what is in one's best interests'.

2.3 humans] On the plural variants for ἀνθρώπου in G, see on 1.13 'humans', above. The Three all have ἀνθρώπων here.

2.3 to do] Lit. 'which they might do'. The meaning of 'doing good' (עשה טוב) is disputed in 3.12 (see the note there), but the sense of 'doing well' or 'prospering' that many commentators affirm in that verse is hardly appropriate here. In 7.20, the only other verse where the expression occurs, Qohelet doubts the ability of the righteous to 'behave well' all the time without sinning, but does not apparently regard the human ability to do good, in that sense, as fundamentally problematic. If he is sceptical about the existence of a good, or of the ability to recognize what is good *for* or *in* humans, Qohelet allows, nevertheless, that good is something which they can *do*, and such action is explicitly exempted from the general denial of good in 3.12. It is tempting, therefore, to take the relative clause as referring not to the 'good', but to the humans, and so to translate as: 'any good for humans, who work beneath heaven…'—a possibility which is noted by Krüger, and which is left open by the absence of a resumptive pronoun. The tense of the verb, however, tells in favour of the traditional understanding, as does the book's disinclination to use עשה absolutely.

2.3 beneath the heavens] G reads 'under the sun', and is followed by S, Hie, V. Only T supports M (where 'sun' appears only in one or two late manuscripts; see de Rossi; Ginsburg, *Writings*), but *BHQ* is probably correct to see the other versions as the result of assimilation to the more common expression.[12]

---

[12] *BHS* observes that two Hebrew manuscripts have this reading. One of these is noted by de Rossi as a straightforward variant; the other appears in Kennicott with a note that the characters ים- have been deleted, representing correction

2.3 for the limited duration] Lit. '(during) the number of the days'; with some variations, the expression recurs in 5.17 and 6.12, and the idea is found also in Job 14.5: humans have a fixed number of days to live.

toward the standard text. Lavoie and Mehramooz, 'Le texte hébreu et la traduction judéo-persanne', 499, observe that the variant occurs also in the Hebrew text and in the translation of a medieval Judeo-Persian manuscript.

2.4-11

(2.4) I accomplished great things: I constructed buildings for myself, planted vineyards for myself; (2.5) I made for myself nurseries and groves, and I planted in them a tree for every kind of fruit; (2.6) I made for myself pools of water, from which to irrigate a forest sprouting timber; (2.7) I acquired servants and maidservants, and home-born slaves. I also had livestock for myself—cattle and herds: I had more for myself than all who were before me in Jerusalem. (2.8) I accumulated for myself also silver and gold, along with kingly possessions and provinces. I put together for myself singers, men and women, and those human luxuries, a fine wine-table and settings. (2.9) And I made myself rich, going beyond anyone who was before me in Jerusalem. My wisdom remained with me, moreover, (2.10) and nothing which my eyes demanded did I keep out of their reach—I did not hold my heart back from any pleasure, for my heart was pleased in all my business, and this was what was mine from all my business. (2.11) Then I looked round among all my achievements, which my hands had achieved, and at the business which I had worked to achieve—and behold, it was all an illusion, and a wishing for the wind, and there was no profit under the sun.

Commentary

Qohelet's enquiries so far have been conducted entirely in or with his heart (1.13, 16, 17; 2.1)—they have been essentially intellectual in character, even if they have involved some element of experience. What he does now is quite different, even if the ground for it has likewise been laid with his heart (2.3). Verses 4-7 describe the establishment of a business and household, which allow Qohelet both to accumulate vast wealth and to live a life of luxury (2.8-9a). As planned in 2.3, his wisdom remains with him, and he investigates everything, holding his mind back from none of the pleasure that he encounters in his work (2.9b-10): this is an attempt to find something for himself, and, by extension, for any human. Throughout the whole passage, accordingly, Qohelet emphasizes that what he makes or acquires is 'for himself', and the

Hebrew expression *ly*, 'for me', occurs no fewer than eight times in vv. 4-8, and then again in v. 9 when he says that his wisdom literally 'stood for me'. When he steps back to review his accomplishments in 2.11, in the hope of finding what he set out in 2.3 to discover, Qohelet will dismiss everything as 'vapour', and that review will provoke anger and despair in the verses that follow. Before this, however, he observes for the first time in v. 10 something that is going to become central to his ideas: all this work that he undertook was a source of pleasure to him, and this pleasure was genuinely his own (literally, 'his share').

This is not true of everything, or even anything else. Just as the preceding verses had stressed that Qohelet worked *for* himself, v. 11 labours the point that *he* had done the work: '*my* achievements, which *my* hands had achieved, and at the business which *I* had worked to achieve'. Qohelet does not tell us explicitly just why those achievements are not themselves his 'share', but 2.12 is going to introduce the issue of inheritance, and of human achievements passing to others (to become their 'share', 2.21), which ties in to the themes of 1.4-11. Qohelet's accomplishments will outlast him, and will not pass with him when he dies: they will instead persist in the world to become the possession of others, and so are 'his' only for the time being, despite the fact that they result entirely from his own work. Indeed, if we look at the works that underpinned his wealth and lifestyle, then this is clearly true, and is drawn out in the text. Qohelet's business is not ephemeral, and he makes his wealth not from, say, buying low and selling high or from providing services, but from vineyards, orchards, timber and livestock. The sustainability of this business is emphasized in 2.6-7: Qohelet creates an irrigation system for his trees, while the fact that he has 'home-born slaves'—born into slavery as the children of slaves—means that even his workforce is self-sustaining. Since the same is presumably true of his livestock, and since neither his buildings nor his vineyards, orchards and plantations are likely to vanish before his death, then they will be his only for so long as Qohelet himself is alive—which means, in his terms, that they are not truly 'his'.

When he declares it all to be 'vapour' in 2.11, therefore, it seems unlikely that Qohelet is talking about the transitoriness of worldly possessions: it is not those possessions that will pass away swiftly, but Qohelet himself. What he is condemning here is all the effort and aspiration that led to no real, lasting profit. His experience of pleasure in his endeavours does mean, of course, that there is one chink of light in the darkness, and this will eventually become the focus for a more positive strand in Qohelet's thinking (cf. 3.22; 5.17-18; 9.9), even if its benefits are confined to this world (cf. 9.6: the dead have no share in anything). We might legitimately ask, though, what else Qohelet could possibly have hoped to gain from this whole exercise. He has demonstrated from the very outset of the monologue an understanding that the very nature of their place in the world prevents humans from making the sort of profit to which he aspires, and so his conclusions here seem preordained, and a product not so much of his experience as of the way he defines 'profit'.

An answer to that question should naturally, of course, take into account the fact that this is a fictional, literary device. Qohelet is not a logician, genuinely working through a problem, but a character in a book, whose experiences are designed by an author. At one level, the author is simply reiterating key points from the first chapter, linking them now not to generalities about the world, but to the specific experiences of his protagonist. At both a literary and an intellectual level, however, there is more involved here. Without living through his achievements, the Qohelet who was so swift to dismiss pleasure as 'useless' in 2.2 would not have caught on to it now as the sole benefit of his experiences. In what follows, furthermore, Qohelet will be portrayed as genuinely angry, upset and frustrated, to the point of questioning the very value of the wisdom that has guided him so far (2.15), and of hating his own life (2.17). This is not the same individual who made his calculations at the beginning of the memoir, and Qohelet's long experiment, with its focus on experience, has perhaps given him an investment in living, lending an urgency to his questions.

With all that is going on here, it may be surprising to find that most commentaries are dominated by an attempt to find links between Qohelet's account and the life of Solomon, as depicted in the biblical histories or in subsequent traditions. This is hardly provoked by the text itself. Indeed, it would be fair to say that there is not a single detail here that would make a reader think of Solomon had they not been led to think in those terms by 1.1 and 1.12. To be sure, Solomon did build buildings, according to those traditions, but if 2.4 is really referring to the famous complex in Jerusalem and to the Temple, then 'I constructed buildings for myself' is, to say the least, rather underselling the matter.¹ Other points of contact are few and far between, if they exist at all. Solomon, according to the biblical histories, made his money from a trading partnership by sea with Hiram (1 Kgs 9.26-28; 10.11, 14, 22), after almost bankrupting the state with his projects and having to sell cities in the Galilee (1 Kgs 9.10-14). He supplemented this with tax income (1 Kgs 10.15) and gifts (1 Kgs 10.25), not with vineyards, orchards and livestock.² Solomon did not simply buy slaves, as does Qohelet in 2.7, but, according to 1 Kgs 9.21-22, enslaved the non-Israelite population. A very obscure expression in 2.8, that I have translated cautiously as 'a fine wine-table and settings' is often rendered as 'concubines', which might give some link between Qohelet and Solomon—but it turns out that the translation 'concubines' is inspired principally by the expectation of such a link, so can hardly be used to endorse it (see the notes). Even if we refrain from asking why, in the same verse, Solomon should be boasting that he acquired 'kingly possessions' (literally, 'the personal wealth of kings'), which, great or small, would have been his—by definition—from the moment he became a king anyway, it is hard to find a fit here.³ Accordingly, many commentators settle for generalities, and paint a picture of luxury and grandeur simply commensurate with Solomon's

---

¹ It is important to emphasize also that Qohelet's buildings, like his other works, are explicitly built for himself: there is no reference here to the sort of public works that dominate the biblical account of Solomon's projects, or about which royal inscriptions elsewhere commonly boast; cf. Weeks, *Ecclesiastes and Scepticism*, 26-27; Bolin, *Ecclesiastes*, 45.

² Koh, *Royal Autobiography*, 33, understands 1 Kgs 5.3 (ET 4.23) to be referring to Solomon's possession of flocks: it does not. Cattle and sheep are merely listed among the daily provisions for Solomon which are provided by his officers, apparently through provincial taxation. 1 Chr 27.27 does in fact associate vineyards with David (not Solomon, as, Murphy suggests), at least insofar as a royal official in charge of vineyards is named, and the surrounding verses include similar mentions of flocks and herds, but they also refer to cultivated fields, olive and sycamore trees, oil, camels and she-asses, while saying nothing of most of the items in Qohelet's list. We could hardly claim, therefore, even that Qohelet's list is supposed to be some generalized description of the royal estate.

³ A few commentators observe the lack of direct correspondence, but interpret it to suggest that the account here was formulated originally to reflect a more generic royal lifestyle, becoming associated only secondarily with Solomon; see, e.g., Lauha at 2.7. I share these suspicions about the originality of the Solomonic association, but if that is discounted then it becomes even harder, I think, to find any reason to understand the account here in specifically 'royal' terms.

lifestyle, in which orchards become royal gardens, irrigation pools become lakes, livestock are quietly forgotten, and the whole passage becomes an account of hedonistic luxury.[4]

It is awkward, but not impossible to understand Qohelet in the role of Solomon here. Although some modern commentators have attributed more complicated motives or effects to a 'Solomonic fiction',[5] such readings have traditionally tended, however, to elide the different elements of the account into a single point: that Qohelet can speak from the perspective of someone famously wise and powerful, who has had it all and rejected it. If even Solomon's life is circumscribed in this way, such a reading asserts, then how much more so is that of other humans. Seow, for instance, claims accordingly that 'Qohelet itemizes the king's many accomplishments only to show that even Solomon, Israel's most glamorous king, is no better off than ordinary people in some ways... By appealing to the successes of the king, indeed, the wise king *par excellence*, the author shows the limitations of human successes'. (I would reiterate in passing that he does not, in fact, explicitly 'itemize' a single one of Solomon's accomplishments.) Farmer likewise says that 'Someone like Solomon, who could be said to have done almost anything he wanted to do and to have possessed everything his eyes and his heart desired, makes a convincing witness to the ultimate lack of satisfaction such things give to the one who has them'.

That phrase, 'the ultimate lack of satisfaction', reflects another assumption that is often associated with this interpretation, although it does not depend upon it. Noting the use of 'for myself' in the first part of the account, Fox claims that 'This repetition puts great emphasis on the self-centered drive for acquisition, a sort of intense consumerism. Yet the love of possessions cannot be filled by possessing them... Qohelet works obsessively to fill a massive craving, but his real desire is not for material goods.' Long before

---

[4] Even scholars well aware of the way in which preconceptions can influence readings seem to fall into this trap. Salyer, *Vain Rhetoric*, 189, talks of Qohelet's 'Disneyland-like estate', while Koosed, *(Per)mutations*, 60-61, claims that Qohelet's focus is 'on his own physical enjoyment of what he is creating' and that a 'life of wealth, leisure, and sexual pleasure is portrayed here'. Qohelet mentions nothing that is inherently luxurious until 2.8, nor his own pleasure until 2.10.

[5] See, e.g., Vignolo, 'Maschera', which draws out ways in which the reader might be led to identify with the protagonist and his critique, and Lux, 'Ich, Kohelet'.

that, Ginsburg (rightly) denied that Qohelet's actions are 'to gratify an avaricious propensity', but then similarly claimed that 'the complete gratification of every desire' proves 'utterly insufficient to quiet the mind craving after higher enjoyments, and to secure lasting happiness'—and other such statements are to be found in a wide variety of commentaries. They suggest that Qohelet is looking for something that transcends the material, whether he is aware of it or not, and whether that is to be expressed in spiritual, religious terms or in the modern vocabulary of self-fulfilment.

There has been no mention, however, of any such quest, and when 2.3 spoke of 'what is good for humans' to do, it left the matter entirely open. Indeed, it has been a feature of Qohelet's discourse, certainly up to this point at least, that his concept of value is tied wholly to his concept of possession. Qohelet has shown no interest in finding an alternative to material wealth, and said nothing to suggest that he finds wealth unsatisfactory in any way: he is, and will remain, profoundly materialistic. Unless we read a great deal into 'vapour' there, even 2.11 contains no statement that his accomplishments have somehow proved unfulfilling, while the preceding verse, on the contrary, suggests that he found in them everything that he could have wanted—except, it becomes clear, actual ownership. The problem remains not that humans can find no good in possessions, but that they have no way truly to possess them as their own. To put it another way, there is no inadequacy or limitation inherent in the material world that makes material possessions unsatisfactory to humans, but there is a limitation in the relationship of humans to the world that means they can never truly satisfy their desire for material possessions.

Later, of course, and particularly in the second half of ch. 5, Qohelet will observe some of the problems connected with the desire for, and retention of, wealth. It is a message of the monologue as a whole, moreover, that the human attachment to wealth is ultimately misguided. Qohelet never suggests, however, that this is because there is something better or 'higher', and the fault of the desire lies in the fact that it can never be met. That is why, when he first realizes in 2.10 that he has actually gained something for himself from the pleasure that he found in work, he does not recognize it as an answer to his questions, and it does not inhibit his negative declaration in 2.11. The order here does not allow us to understand him as saying, 'I found everything vain, but then realized I could benefit from pleasure', and while Qohelet ultimately has to settle for happiness, that is not what he sets out to find, even unconsciously. Luther, who was well aware that to see a denigration of materialism in Ecclesiastes was to invite the very rejection of the world by Christians to which he was himself so strongly opposed, gives a much better 'Solomonic' reading in terms of human control over possessions:

> Is it not the greatest vanity, that a king who has so much wealth, and all things in such plenty, cannot enjoy anything in particular from so many according to his own plans, while any that he does enjoy, he enjoys just fleetingly? We likewise can control, govern, or comprehend nothing according to our own plans.[6]

Luther pre-empts, perhaps, some other ideas in the book, but, he captures the essential point: Qohelet's experience of creation, ownership and enjoyment of his own wealth leaves him more convinced than ever that it is not, in fact, really his own wealth in any meaningful way—and from that point of view, it is largely irrelevant whether we are supposed to see him as Solomon or not.

Going further than just an association with Solomon, Davis claims that '"Solomon" is here comparing his creation to God's creation of the world'—a claim that is based first on Jewish traditions supposedly associating the Temple with Eden, and then on an analysis of the account that finds seven poetic couplets. The latter idea has been echoed in Leithart ('Postmodern', 447-48), who finds correspondences between, for example, 'Yahweh places man in garden' (Gen 2.15) and 'The king collects men and women'. Setting aside questions about Eden and the Temple, given that there is no clear mention of the Temple here, and that Qohelet's buildings are separate from his 'gardens', we may observe that simply dividing a list into pairs does not turn it into poetry. If there are seven pairs here, or, as Leithart suggests, Qohelet '"makes" things seven times', then we might also recall that God in Genesis 1 only 'makes' things for *six* days. It is possible that the author had a fondness for lists that were multiples of seven in length (see the

---

[6] Nonne est maxima uanitas: regem, qui habet tantum opum, et tam omnibus rebus abundat, non tamen uel una aliqua re, ex tam infinitis, secundum sua consilia frui posse? Et si quibus fruitur, raptim fruitur. Adeo non possumus res nostro consilio regere et gubernare. aut comprehendere.

commentary on 3.1), but if there is really an allusion to creation here, it is well hidden.[7]

2.4] Qohelet's initial claim, to have accomplished great things, is literally 'I made great my work(s)' in the Hebrew, and it possibly picks up his earlier claim to have made great his wisdom (1.16), as will 2.9. If the echo is deliberate, then it reinforces the switch here from the intellectual to the practical.

2.5-6] The 'forest' in v. 6 might be a reference to the trees in v. 5, and commentators often treat them as one, but Qohelet's choice of vocabulary points much more strongly toward there being two separate items here: trees that are grown for fruit, and trees grown for timber—although if the Palestinian setting is to be taken seriously, we should probably think of the latter more in terms of coppices than large plantations.[8] The 'pools' are explicitly for the benefit of the trees, and their purpose is presumably to store rain- or spring-water (which, again, is likely to have been practicable only for a relatively small area of trees). Although they may represent, therefore, a substantial investment of effort for a relatively long-term reward, we should not envisage some large-scale public project—even if the name 'Solomon's Pools' has traditionally been attached to the three large reservoirs southwest of Bethlehem that formed part of an impressive water system built under the Hasmoneans, Herod, and the Romans to supply Jerusalem.[9] Equally, these pools are not boating-lakes.

2.7] Although the noun in the first clause could refer to servants more generally, the verb is used of purchasing slaves elsewhere (e.g. Gen 39.1), and the fact that their children will be born into servitude (see above) makes it clear that Qohelet is talking about slaves here. He himself makes no comment on slavery, beside the acceptance of the institution that is implicit, and his emphasis is more probably

---

[7] Verheij, 'Paradise Retried', makes a simpler observation that the vocabulary in 2.4-6 includes some six words or expressions that are found in Gen 1–2 (cf. also Meek, 'Meaning', 247-48; Treier). Although he likewise sees a reference to the Genesis stories, both texts probably just draw on the same terminology to depict similar activities: the shared vocabulary is confined to the first, more agricultural part of Qohelet's account.

[8] See Lipschitz and Biger, 'The Timber Trade in Ancient Palestine'; Liphschitz, *Timber in Ancient Israel*.

[9] Bishop, 'A Pessimist in Palestine', 34-35, sees a certain continuity between these pools and the works described here.

on the fact that his workforce became self-sustaining—something that goes without saying when he talks of his animals in the second part of the verse. Modern readers, of course, may react differently, although few commentators have engaged with the issue (Bennett is a rare exception), or with Qohelet's juxtaposition of slaves and cattle. Treier does note, however, Gregory of Nyssa's fierce attack on slavery at the beginning of the fourth of his *Homilies on Ecclesiastes*, which is provoked by this verse, and Gregory is particularly incensed by the way Qohelet talks of slaves and animals almost in the same breath. Beyond the fact that both reproduce, Qohelet probably lists them together, and separates his slaves from his singers, because the role of those slaves is to be understood not in the context of the luxurious lifestyle that he sketches in the next verse, but as a key component of his businesses: although it is possibly implied by their position in the list that he only acquired them after some initial success, it was presumably these slaves who built his buildings, picked his fruit, dug his cisterns, harvested his timber, and tended his cattle.

2.8] The Hebrew refers to 'the wealth and provinces of kings', not 'the wealth of kings and provinces', and the context suggests that these are acquired through Qohelet's success in business, not as the result of conquest or the submission to him of actual kings. The point is, therefore, that he has achieved a level of prosperity that would usually be associated with rulers (and since that would only be extraordinary for a commoner, there is some tension between this claim and any identification of Qohelet as Solomon). The term used for 'wealth' is often rendered 'treasure', but it does not imply a particular amount: I have translated 'possessions' because it really indicates those things that belong personally to the kings themselves, as opposed to public money that they might control. There is nothing inherently problematic about the singers that follow: the same expression, 'male singers and female singers' is used in 2 Sam 19.36 (ET 19.35), where the context implies that they provide a common luxury, while a similar expression at Ezra 2.65 and Neh 7.67 refers to singers being brought back by the exiles, along with servants. After that, however, the verse becomes famously difficult. As already noted, many commentators have wanted to find a reference to Solomon's women here, but the expression used to describe the last people or things on Qohelet's list is otherwise unknown to us, and the only clue offered is in the preceding description of them. This is fairly obscure in itself, but probably says no more than that they are 'a human luxury'. My translation is based on those of Aquila and Symmachus, mostly because the latter seems to have something quite specific in mind, rather than just to be guessing like everybody else. Of course, he could be wrong, but the idea that we are dealing with something so specific as a fashionable style of wine service would explain the obscurity of the term—and philologists of the distant future may struggle no less with the concept of a 'cocktail table' at Jay Gatsby's parties, just as few people even now would recognize either the name or the function of an absinthe fountain. It would also allow the list to close, of course, with a reference to the wine with which Qohelet intended to sustain himself from the outset (2.3).

2.9-10] There is another echo here of 1.16: Qohelet's efforts mean that he has achieved the sort of pre-eminence in material terms that he had already achieved in wisdom. Verse 9 perhaps notes that he retained that wisdom alongside his new wealth, but the last clause is more probably to be connected with v. 10, where Qohelet's purpose is, in the first instance, to affirm that nothing has been left out from his examination: he has stayed wise, and has neither refrained from looking into anything that caught his eye, nor held his mind ('heart') back from any pleasure. This is not some purposeless hedonism, and the language remains that of intellectual inquiry: the claim is not that Qohelet denies himself nothing that he wants, nor is he making any explicit effort to seek out potential pleasures. As v. 10 makes clear, he does not need to restrain his mind from pleasure, because it finds pleasure in the very work that he has been doing. This leads him, as we have observed, to an important conclusion. In the next verse, and in much of what follows, Qohelet will affirm that all he has achieved is pointless in itself, at least in so far as it cannot permanently be his: everything that he built 'for myself' will eventually belong to someone else. The only thing that is exclusively, inalienably his own, is the pleasure that he found in his activities—the Hebrew says literally that this was his 'share' or 'portion'.

This is going to become a very significant aspect of his ideas, but Qohelet does not immediately appreciate what it is that he has found: it is only in the next verse that he is going to turn to review his achievements, and only in the subsequent discussion that he will come to appreciate the utter failure both of those achievements and of his own wisdom to answer the question posed in 1.3 or to provide the 'good' that he set out to find in 2.3. When he comes back in 3.22 to this idea of pleasure in work as a 'share', indeed, it is because he has effectively ruled out every other possible gain for humans: the pleasure on which he here remarks almost in passing, is all that will then remain standing. Between this point and that, he will talk in 2.21 of work produced by one person becoming the 'share' of another, and in 3.12-13 will characterize the pleasure that people find in their work as a sort of payment from God. Only in 3.12, however, will Qohelet declare explicitly that *enjoyment* in work, providing a 'share' for oneself as it does, offers the most that humans can expect from life—a theme that is followed up, using the same terminology, in 5.17-18 and 9.9, with a note in 9.6 that no such share is available to the dead.

2.11] Qohelet literally 'turns to face' his accomplishments, and in the next verse will similarly 'turn to face' his wisdom; in 2.20 he will 'turn away' and leave behind what he has done. Although his reflections are intellectual and emotional, therefore, they are presented using the imagery of a physical inspection, and this also implies the end of his experimenting, along with a return to the questions that had originally provoked it. Much as he is enjoying what he does, therefore, Qohelet now detaches himself from it, and finds on inspection that it has provided none of the profit that he was seeking: it is 'vapour' and wishing for the wind.

Notes

2.4 I accomplished great things] Lit. 'I made great my work(s)'. M points מעשי as plural, both here and in 2.11, and G at 2.11 correspondingly renders ποιήμασίν μου; here, however, it renders as singular ποίημά μου, 'my work', whereas T, Hie, V, σ' all have a plural like M (and S marks it as such with seyame). This probably does not reflect a different consonantal text (cf. the form מעשׂך in Deut 15.10: G has read an analogous מעשי with the י taken simply as a pronoun), and both readings are legitimate interpretations of the consonants: the singular and plural can, in any case, be used somewhat interchangeably (compare, e.g., Jer 25.6 with 44.8). The singular is unexpected, however, and unless the translator has simply been swayed by an existing reading tradition, it may suggest that he is making a connection with the other use of הגדלתי at 1.16, as Goldman proposes: Qohelet would then be becoming as great in work as in wisdom. If that connection was intended, however, it is difficult to see why G would have rendered the verb as transitive here, but intransitive in that previous verse (cf. 2.9). If the singular does not just reflect an early error for the plural ποιήματα, its purpose may be to prevent an understanding in terms of individual works or actions, like that of T (אסניתי עובדין טבין, 'I increased good works'), and to relate the statement more generally to Qohelet's achievements. Such a general understanding suits the context well: the initial claim then embraces the whole of the list which is to follow, and I have translated in those terms. The verb appears twice in 1 Kings 1, but is used of Solomon's throne (vv. 37, 47), not his works.

In Ecclesiastes, as in other biblical usage, מעשה can refer both to the act of working and to the works produced, to deeds and to accomplishments, and the emphasis here is surely upon the latter. Qohelet is not claiming to have worked hard so much as to have accomplished a great deal, although the Hebrew, perhaps, implies both. It may be too imprecise to see a more specific statement that he has increased his property and wealth, as Schoors, *The Preacher* II, 165, would have it, and when Qohelet considers what he has done, in 2.11, his מעשים are things created by his hands—things, in other words, which he has made.

2.4 for myself] Gordis characterizes the repeated ל־, here and in the following verses, as an 'ethical dative', which 'subtly conveys the sense of Koheleth's limitless capacity for activity, directed only to the end of his own pleasure'. The notion of a *dativus ethicus* in Hebrew is questionable, however, and the term at least misleading; cf. J-M §133 d(2). Equally, the usage here does not really correspond to the so-called *dativus commodi*, which imparts a reflexive nuance, usually to intransitive verbs (GKC §119 s[2]; J-M §133 d). Although the repetition is striking, and the instances surely to be connected, ל־ occurs in vv. 4-8 not only with verbs of creation or acquisition but also in expressions of possession with היה (cf. v. 7), where the *dativus commodi* can be ruled out. It seems simplest to see here a consistent reiteration of purpose and possession: Qohelet makes or gets these things for himself, to be his.

2.5 nurseries and groves] גנות is commonly translated as 'gardens', but that term may be misleading for modern readers, if it conjures up associations with flowerbeds and lawns. Although Bennett, like many others, declares on no evidence that 'the gardens are not vegetable gardens but parks', the usage elsewhere shows that the גנה is more typically a place where crops of various sorts may be grown, and the term is sometimes linked to vineyards or fruit-trees, as here (see, e.g., Amos 4.9; 9.14; Ct 6.11), or with the consumption of produce (Jer 29.5, 28); much the same is true of the related גן, and, although royal 'gardens' closer to the modern idea certainly did exist in the ancient world, there is no clear reason to suppose even that the 'garden of the king' referred to in, e.g., 2 Kgs 25.4; Neh 3.15, would have been without such a functional aspect, whatever other purposes it may have served.[10] Since גנות

---

[10] By locating it between the city wall of Jerusalem and the waters of Siloam, the Targum apparently draws on Neh 3 in particular to identify the land here

here is sandwiched here between references to vineyards and fruit-trees, with subsequent mentions of timber and livestock, the text itself offers no compelling reason to think in terms of formal or monumental gardens, rather than the much more common agricultural 'gardens': it is only in v. 8 that Qohelet will turn from the constituents of his business to the luxuries earned from it.

The second term, פרדסים, from פרדס, is more uncommon, and is of interest as a probable loanword from Persian: we have already looked at the issues around its origin in the Introduction, pp. 65-68, above. In Neh 2.8 the word refers to a plantation managed for the Persian king, from which timber may be harvested, but in Ct 4.13 the reference is to a pomegranate orchard, and this latter, in particular, accords broadly with the late, very common use of the word in Greek (see 70-71, above), as well as with subsequent Hebrew usage. Even in its original Persian usage, the term probably referred to areas that were more orientated to the functional than the aesthetic, even if they might evoke admiration and provide pleasure, and the 'parks' of, e.g., RSV, is again misleading for a modern reader. Whilst any of the items here might be pleasant, or even cultivated to give pleasure, the context and juxtaposition of terms, not to mention the explicit planting of fruit-trees, all suggest that Qohelet is trying to grow crops, not to provide a horticultural treat for his senses.[11]

with that 'garden of the king'. It is interesting to note also the juxtaposition of הכרם והגנת, 'the vineyard and the nursery (or nurseries)', in line 4 of the much earlier Ammonite inscription on a bronze bottle from Tel Siran, which apparently commends King Amminadab for having similarly undertaken such agricultural projects, and which may go on to speak of irrigation projects as well. In this respect, see especially Smit, 'The Tell Siran Inscription'. The long-term nature of those projects (and perhaps a commemorative function of the inscription) may be picked up in the final lines (7-8), which speak of gladness ביומת רבם ושנת רחקת, 'in many days and distant years'. The Tel Siran text is sometimes taken to be poetic, and a literary creation: Müller, 'Kohelet und Amminadab', noting also a possible reference to Amminadab in Ct 6.12, suggests that the texts are drawing on similar motifs to portray luxurious living, and he picks this up subsequently in 'Travestien', drawing more widely on themes of bucolic escapism in ancient literature. There may be an element of that in Song of Songs, but I think it is a mischaracterization of Qohelet's account here. Interestingly, though, *Les Conseils de Sagesse*, an extraordinarily popular seventeenth-century book, probably by Michel Boutauld, presents Solomon in just such a bucolic context, retiring from the royal court to his country house, where he can contemplate eternity surrounded by forests and rocky streams—an image that has perhaps been influenced by this passage, as well as by the ideals of its own period.

[11] Rütersworden's idea that the concept of a 'paradise' in the Hellenistic period belonged to the sphere of 'Lebensfreude, Genuß und Luxus', 'taking pleasure in life, self-indulgence and luxury', appears to be derived entirely from his reading of 2.5 as an illustration of useless vanity; see his 'Erwagungen', 1156.

2.5 a tree for every kind of fruit] Lit. 'a tree of every fruit', or 'trees of every fruit' (the noun can be used collectively). G has ξύλον πᾶν καρποῦ 'every tree of fruit', and Jerome apparently refers to the La version of this when he attempts to clarify the sense in his commentary: *plantantur arbores, non omnes fructiferae, ut in Latinis codicibus habemus; sed omnes fructus*, 'trees are planted—not all "fruit-bearing", as we find in the Latin codices, but "of all fruits"'; Hie also, though, has *lignum omne fructiferum*. T has supplemented this passage extensively (not least by adding fragrant trees brought from India by demons), but וכל אילני עבדי פירין, 'and every fruit-bearing tree', seems to reflect a similar understanding. So, probably, does the κάρπιμον, 'fruitful' (evocative of Gen 1.11-12, cf. Vinel) attested for α'—whether the full reading was (πᾶν) κάρπιμον, 'everything fruitful', as Field, or (ξύλον) κάρπιμον, 'fruitful tree', as Marshall. These renderings are probably translational, and perhaps influenced by, e.g., Gen 2.9, but the possibility of a variant with עץ כל פרי rather than the עץ כל פרי of M cannot be excluded. S supports M, although it has put both nouns in the plural to represent the collective sense (cf. Kamenetzky, 211).

2.6 pools] The term ברכה is used of reservoirs or cisterns, often explicitly human-made, which channel or contain water for practical purposes (see, e.g., 2 Kgs 20.20; Isa 22.11; Nah 2.9). G renders with κολυμβήθρα, a term more often associated with pools for swimming or diving (cf. Vinel), but this equivalence is found elsewhere (e.g. 2 Kgs 18.17; Neh 3.16; Nah 2.9), and should not be taken necessarily to reflect a different understanding of the pools.

2.6 from which] The suffix pronoun on מהם is masculine, while ברכות is feminine, and so the two do not agree. This happens elsewhere in 2.10; 10.9 (probably); 11.8; and 12.1, and it may reflect a more general tendency, especially in later texts, to discard the feminine plural forms (cf. GKC §135 o and §145 u; J-M §149 b). Dahood, in 'Canaanite-Phoenician', 43-44, notes that the corresponding feminine suffix is, in fact, never used in Ecclesiastes, although his resort to Phoenician for an explanation is hardly necessary (cf. Whitley; Schoors, *The Preacher* I, 162-63). If the presence of this tendency in Ecclesiastes as a whole seems undeniable, however, it is worth pointing out that the suffix pronoun could, in this case, refer to the masculine מים rather than to ברכות.

2.6 a forest sprouting timber] Or 'sprouting with timber': although the versions render it as a direct object of צמח, the qal of the verb is elsewhere intransitive, and so the noun should be read as qualifying the participle—'sprouting (with respect to) timber' (cf. GKC §118 q, and perhaps §117 y or z; J-M §126). צמח can be used of things sprouting on plants (e.g. Gen 41.6; Ezek 17.9), as well as of plants themselves sprouting. Ehrlich would delete עצים, partly on the grounds that the plural is used elsewhere in the absolute almost exclusively with reference to wood or timber, not live trees, but that would seem actually to be its function here. The 'forest', which is undetermined, is not a reference to the fruit-trees of the previous verse, and יער is used not of orchards, but of wild forests where timber can be cut (e.g. Deut 19.5; 2 Kgs

19.23; Isa 10.34); so, in Ct 2.3, the beloved stands out among other young men like an apple tree in a forest—an image which could hardly work if יער meant 'orchard'—and in Isa 29.17, the יער is the opposite of a כרמל. G δρυμός, which itself refers to wild woodland, is commonly used elsewhere to render יער, and since the verb can be used transitively, δρυμὸν βλαστῶντα ξύλα can readily be understood also as 'a wood sprouting timber'.[12] In his commentary, Jerome translates *saltum germinantem lignum*, 'a forest sprouting wood'— *lignum* usually means 'timber', and although Jerome does use it of fruit-trees in V at Gen 1.11 and elsewhere, he goes on here to discuss the irrigation requirements explicitly of non-fruiting trees, so is more certainly drawing a distinction.

2.7 I acquired] Given the constant repetition of לי in these verses, we might expect it here. In fact, it is found in some late manuscripts (see de Rossi, Ginsburg, *Writings*), and 'for me' occurs in both S and the Coptic, raising the possibility that it was found in some early Greek manuscripts. Those readings, however, may reflect no more than the expectation of its presence (so Goldman), and are not a strong basis for emendation.

2.7 home-born slaves] Lit. 'children of the house(hold)'. The singular appears in Gen 15.3, and although the sense there is complicated by the mysterious בן משק ביתי in the preceding verse, most commentators associate the term with the similar, more common יליד בית, the meaning of which is clear from Gen 17.12-13. This is certainly how G οἰκογενεῖς (literally a slave 'born in the household') takes it, cf. Hie *uernaculi*, which means the same as the Greek (although V renders this as a claim simply that Qohelet had a large *familia*, or 'household'). We find a similar expression a number of times in the Aramaic texts from Palmyrene, e.g. PAT 0318 (= *CIS* 3972), line 4 and PAT 0379 (= *CIS* 4033), line 6: ובני ביתה.

2.7 I also had] The first היה לי is commonly taken to belong with the preceding ובני בית, as indicated by the accentuation. This requires us, however, to explain the singular verb either as impersonal/neuter[13] or as an error (the

---

[12] On the form of the verb, see Thackeray, *Grammar*, 226. That ξύλα is lacking from some witnesses (including the important mss B and 998) is probably attributable to a simple error, perhaps homoioteleuton, despite Seow's strange claim that 'LXX[BP] (supported by Copt)…are probably translating somewhat freely'. It is possible, though, that some scribes found the expression awkward: Jarick, 'Theodore and the Text', 379, notes a conjunction in Theodore's lemma, which gives 'a sprouting forest *and* trees'; other scribes might simply have omitted the word as redundant.

[13] GKC §145 u, commonly cited in support of this approach, says of such cases that the verb 'remains undefined in gender (masc.), although the noun precedes for the sake of emphasis'. Of this verse in particular, it says further that it is 'as if the sentence begins afresh *and servants born in my house…there fell to my lot* this possession also'. Delsman, 'Inkongruenz', 28, speaks of היה acting as a 'frozen' form here.

suggestion of, e.g., Barton, that it results from attraction to בית, seems improbable, as does that of Glasser, *Le Procès*, 42, that the servants are considered a collective entity—like 'the staff' in English). As an impersonal construction, this would be awkward, especially since the second היה לי is probably not to be construed that way, and the versions offer support for emendation, with G, S, T and Hie all employing plural verbs (V's interpretative and collective *multamque familiam*, the 'large household' mentioned in the last note, hardly supports M, as Goldman believes); the plural is also found in some late Hebrew manuscripts (see de Rossi). If the reading היה is secondary, then the error would presumably have arisen through assimilation to the second היה לי, the singular number of which is supported by the versions; if it is original, on the other hand, then the plural forms are as readily understood as facilitative. As at 1.16, Dahood, 'The Language of Qoheleth', 227, blames a defective spelling for the confusion.

Schoors, *The Preacher* I, 158, considers the suggestion of Vattioni, 'Due note', 162, that היה לי should instead be taken with the following מקנה, which solves the problem of agreement. He rejects it on the basis that the בני בית would then become objects of קניתי, and that leads to a problem of sense: although קנה does not necessarily imply purchase as such, it generally involves acquisition through a transfer of ownership, and home-born slaves are not acquired that way. This is a pertinent objection, but it seems no harder to accept that the writer is using the verb a little loosely than that he has employed an awkward and unusual impersonal construction for no apparent reason. I have, therefore, taken היה לי to introduce the next clause, while accepting that emendation to היו לי presents a strong alternative solution. None of the options makes any significant difference to the sense.

After 'to me', S adds ܣܘܓܐܐ *swg'*, 'much', whilst retaining ܣܓܝ *sgy* as equivalent to the הרבה of M later in the verse. Goldman, comparing *multam familiam* in V, observes that the adverb seems more necessary here than there, and such a perception may have motivated the addition.

2.7 livestock...cattle and herds] מקנה is used to describe a stock of almost any domestic animals (cf., e.g., Gen 47.17; Exod 9.3), and so includes those embraced by the following two terms, which themselves refer more specifically to cows or oxen (בקר), and to sheep or goats (צאן). The sense is clear—Qohelet has livestock (consisting of) cattle and flocks—but the grammatical relationship between the words less so. G and θ' κτῆσις βουκολίου καὶ ποιμνίου, 'a possession of herd and flock', apparently understands a construct relationship between them (cf. Hie, S, T), while σ' has a conjunction before the second noun, suggesting that Symmachus took the three items to be absolute and in parallel. M points מִקְנֶה, which would usually be the absolute form, but which is taken by many commentators to be an unusual vocalization of the construct (usually מִקְנֵה); there is a similar difficulty with the first מקרה in 3.19. In favour of reading as construct, cf. the expressions מִקְנֵה־צֹאן וּמִקְנֵה בָקָר (Gen 26.14) and

וּמִקְנֵה־צֹאן וּבָקָר (2 Chr 32.29), but מקנה could also be taken as absolute, with the following nouns in apposition (cf. GKC §127 h), and that is, perhaps, the construal behind the pointing in M. The consonantal text, of course, permits both understandings.

Gordis notes the vocalization of the conjunction in וָצֹאן, which he takes to be pausal, in apparent contradiction to the word's conjunctive accent. As GKC §104 g points out, this vocalization in pairs of related nouns can normally be attributed to considerations of stress, and where we find בקר וָצֹאן elsewhere, it is always with a disjunctive accent on צֹאן (Lev 27.32; Num 22.40; 2 Chr 31.6—contrast 1 Chr 12.41). Gordis overstates the case, perhaps, when he claims that the vocalization implies a caesura before הרבה, but a characterization of such instances as 'pre-pausal' (cf. J-M §104 d) raises as many questions as it answers.

2.7 more] The hiph‘il infinitive absolute of רבה is used to mean 'much' or 'many' (cf. at 1.16, above), and it can be employed in comparative expressions with מן to mean 'more' (e.g. Jon 4.11). In 2 Sam 12.2, the rich man has צאן ובקר הרבה מאד, and, although הרבה stands at some remove in our verse from מקנה, it is usually considered to qualify it, yielding a similar sense: Qohelet has more livestock than any who preceded him. If we take מקנה with the first היה לי, as suggested above, then this sense can be retained: 'Qohelet has livestock...he has more (livestock) than...' It is possible, however, that the sense is broader, since הרבה can be used absolutely as a substantive; cf. 2 Chr 25.9, where הרבה מזה means 'much more than this', or Jer 42.2, where מעט מהרבה means 'a few of many'. Schoors, *The Preacher* II, 266, recognizes the substantivization of the word in 5.11, and it cannot be objected that the usage would be alien to Ecclesiastes. So, although this may just be a claim that Qohelet had more livestock, it is also possible that he is claiming more sweepingly to have 'had more than anyone'.

2.7 all who were] In 1.16 the similar expression is singular, 'everyone who was', as in 2.9, and many late manuscripts read that here (see de Rossi; Ginsburg, *Writings*). Despite Goldman's appeal to them in support of M, the ancient witnesses are unhelpful, since the versions use the plural in those other verses also, but the grounds for emendation are slight. De Regt, 'Signs of Redactional Development', 86, notes the inclination of some modern versions to translate 'anyone...before me' (his particular target is the New International Version), and the fact that this obscures the difficulties which the plural expression raises for the tradition of Solomonic authorship.

2.8 and gold] καί γε χρυσίον, in place of καί χρυσίον, 'and gold', is quite strongly attested in the Greek manuscript tradition, and Goldman suspects that it may be G*. We would expect καί γε to indicate גם or וגם, '(and) also', here, instead of the simple conjunction in M, so it is striking to find גם in one Kennicott manuscript, and in two manuscripts noted by Ginsburg, *Writings*. That gives a sense 'both silver and gold', which would suit the position of the preceding גם, and I think there is a very strong possibility that such a reading is original. The other versions and early manuscripts support M^L, however, and it is a little easier to explain how both the Greek and the later Hebrew traditions might have gained a word under the influence of the preceding expression than to see how the word might have been lost.

2.8 kingly possessions and provinces] It is possible that Qohelet is claiming actually to have obtained things belonging to kings, through purchase or conquest, but it seems more likely that he means just 'appropriate to kings' or 'kingly' (so, e.g., Seow, 'fit for kings'). The particular idea that this is a reference to the tribute received by Solomon *from* kings and provinces (so, e.g., Longman; cf. 1 Kgs 5.1 [ET 4.21]) is difficult to sustain—both because the Hebrew is likely to be talking about 'the wealth and provinces of kings', not 'the wealth of kings and provinces', and because the term used for 'wealth' refers to private and not public finances.

The first of these points hinges on the relationship between the three Hebrew words וסגלת מלכים והמדינות. To be sure, G renders καὶ περιουσιασμοὺς βασιλέων καὶ τῶν χωρῶν, 'and abundances of kings and of (the) lands', effectively reading the construct סגלת as 'owned' by both מלכים and המדינות, and most modern translations and commentaries have followed suit. That interpretation is difficult, however, both grammatically and in terms of sense. Although Hebrew is able to string together a series of nouns each connected to a single noun in the construct state (e.g. Num 20.5), the construction is relatively uncommon, and we would not expect one such noun to be determined while another in parallel is not, as here. Indeed, the article would tend to coordinate that noun with the (implicitly determined) noun in the construct state, as in Gen 40.1's משקה מלך מצרים והאפה, 'the butler of the king of Egypt and the baker' (cf. J-M §129 a), so that we would here read 'the סגלה of kings and the(ir) מדינות'. Whilst it is true that Ecclesiastes can sometimes seem erratic in its use of the article within lists (examples are given in Schoors, *The Preacher* I, 166), only 7.25 furnishes a close potential parallel (הסכלות), and that verse is itself difficult to construe.

The problem has led to a number of proposed emendations: Ehrlich, for instance, would emend המדינות to חמדות, 'precious things'; Graetz, noting the expression משמני מדינה in Dan 11.24, suggests that a word has simply been lost, and *BHS* (probably following Podechard) would accordingly supply ושרי, as found in Esth 1.3; Zimmerli proposes המון מדינות, and is followed by Galling 1969 and Lauha. These are all speculative, and only in the case of Ehrlich's proposal is it at all easy to see how such an error might have occurred.

Other commentators have been troubled less by the definite article on המדינות, and more by the lack of correspondence in sense between 'kings' and 'provinces'. Dahood, 'Phoenician Background', 268, proposes that מדינות may have come to have the sense 'governors', and links it to Ugaritic *mdnt*, which he translates as 'prefects'. That view is accepted by, e.g., Whitley and Crenshaw, but this is an improbable rendering of the Ugaritic, and there is no other attestation of the Hebrew with this connotation.[14] In fact, a more serious problem of sense is posed by סגלה, which is almost universally translated as 'treasure' or somesuch. Within the Bible, this term is most commonly found in descriptions of Israel's special relationship with God: unlike others, Israel has been chosen by him to be his own (e.g. Exod 19.5; Deut 7.6; 14.2). Its sole use in the secular sphere is in 1 Chr 29.3, which is commonly cited for the sense 'treasure', since David there declares himself to possess a סגלה 'of gold and silver'. The point in that verse, though, is that he is distinguishing his personal fortune from the valuables which he has provided (and previously listed) for the Temple: he is now offering that fortune as well, and inviting contributions from others.

This nuance of specific private ownership is found in the post-biblical usage also. In *b. Baba Batra* 52a there is a discussion of property which is in the possession of an individual, but does not belong to his estate: in the context of this discussion, the advice is offered that money received for safekeeping on behalf of a minor should be made into a סגולה, that is, some distinct item of property against which a claim can later be lodged (a Torah-scroll or date-palm are both subsequently suggested as possibilities). Similarly, Jastrow, *Dictionary*, lists numerous uses of the verb סגל to indicate money set aside for oneself out of an allowance, or put aside as savings. In both biblical and later Hebrew, then, the term connotes not high value but distinct or private ownership.[15] It is doubtful, therefore, that a province could be said to have a סגלה, but a king could have both private, personal property, and public provinces—the two together constituting the totality of his wealth. This further favours taking מדינות to be coordinated not with מלכים but with סגלה, or else taking it as a separate item, and I have attempted to preserve that

---

[14] The context of the only occurrence (*KTU* 1.3 ii 15f.) is Anat's massacre of participants in a battle between two towns. Wyatt, *Religious Texts*, 74, translates 'townsfolk', and cites Pardee's rendering 'opponents'. At the very least, there are unlikely to have been many governors engaged in the battle.

[15] It is difficult to say how far this is recognized in the various renderings by the ancient versions. G περιουσιασμοὺς seems to refer at first glance to wealth or abundance, but the term is used at Ps 135.4 (Septuagint 134.4) for סגלה, where 'wealth' would obviously be inappropriate, as is περιούσιος elsewhere (even in the NT: cf. Tit 2.14), and the rendering may be conventional. The Peshitta, on the other hand, uses a number of different terms (cf. Kamenetzky, 211), and ܩܢܝܢ *qnynʾ* here seems to render סגלה straightforwardly in terms of individual property, as does α′ οὐσίας (which has probably influenced Hie, V *substantias*). Very interestingly, σ′ uses the unusual word πεκούλια: this is derived from the Latin *peculium*, which is used in a technical sense to mean much the same as סגלה—property which forms part of an estate, but is owned separately by an individual. The later Codex Graecus Venetus uses σφετερισμὸν βασιλέων, probably to be interpreted along the same lines here, as a coinage from σφέτερος, 'one's own'.

ambiguity in my translation. These items are obtained in addition to the silver and gold mentioned previously, despite the arbitrary characterization of the initial conjunction as explicative by, e.g., Galling 1969 and Lys.

2.8 I put together] The use of עשה here is curious. One can 'make' money in Hebrew as in English (e.g. Gen 31.1; Isa 19.10; Ezek 28.4), and one can similarly 'make' a name for oneself (e.g. Jer 32.20; Isa 63.14), but עשה is no more a general verb of acquisition than is 'make'. Instances of its use for other types of gain, in fact, are few and far between, and usually reflect a specific nuance. In Ezek 38.12, for instance, Gog will plunder people who have 'made' cattle and possessions for themselves, and the verb there perhaps emphasizes that those people have earned their property through work, as opposed to looting. Alternatively, it is being used in a way similar to that in Gen 12.5, which speaks more obscurely of the נפש which Abraham and his family have 'made' in Haran: this unusual use of נפש recurs in Gen 14.21, and in both places it is contrasted with רכוש, so probably means that part of the property which consists of slaves and servants (as opposed to that consisting of animals and inanimate objects). It is, then, a *collection* of people which Abraham and Sarah have 'put together', or 'made', rather as in 1 Kgs 1.5 Adonijah 'makes' for himself a רכב, a company of chariots: the individuals are not 'made', but the group is 'made' out of the individuals. I take that to be the sense here: Qohelet has not acquired individual singers, but created a group of them (Longman speaks of him forming a choir, which catches the idea—though perhaps not the style of singing). G ἐποίησά, 'I made', simply renders the Hebrew literally (cf. Hie, V *feci*), but T makes the verb refer to the manufacture of musical instruments, and S uses ܥܒܕ *'bd*, which can have the sense 'appoint'.

2.8 singers, men and women] Lit. '(male) singers and female singers': the Hebrew uses masculine and feminine forms of the same participle. Seow, considering them to be out of place here, raises the possibility that we should understand שרים ושרות as types of jewellery (cf. שירות in Isa 3.19), but this is unnecessary, and it would be difficult to avoid reading the verse as a statement that Qohelet made jewellery.

2.8 those human luxuries] Qohelet also makes for himself תענוגת בני האדם, an expression which describes or is described by the mysterious phrase שדה ושדות which follows, and which presents problems of its own.[16] The verb ענג is usually used, principally in the hithpa'el, of taking pleasure, or indulging one's self in something (fatness: Isa 55.2; peace: Ps 37.11; the milk of Jerusalem's breasts: Isa 66.11; God: Isa 58.14; Ps 37.4; Job 22.26; 27.10). It can be

---

[16] Some significant manuscripts of G omit the conjunction at the beginning of the expression, which would permit it to be read instead as a description of the preceding singers, but there are no compelling grounds to take this as G*, let alone as the original reading of the Hebrew.

used more negatively, so that 'delighting over' someone in Isa 57.4 refers to pulling faces, and having fun at their expense. The puʻal participle is used of the 'daughter of Zion' in Jer 6.2, alongside the problematic נוה (= נאוה?), and the hithpaʻel infin. cs. is employed with the related adjective ענג, to refer in Deut 28.56 to a woman so genteel and delicate that she will not put her foot on the ground. The adjective occurs also in the preceding Deut 28.54 (used of a man who is similarly genteel) and in Isa 47.1; in all three verses it is linked to רך, which connotes tenderness or delicacy. It is difficult, then, to pin down a single nuance for words from this root, which might aid our interpretation of the noun תענוג itself, although there is frequently some connotation of comfort, luxury, or soft living.

The noun appears in the singular at Prov 19.10, as something unsuitable for a fool, but is elsewhere used in a plural form. At Mic 1.16, the inhabitants of Mareshah are addressed as a woman, told to mourn over the בני תענוגיך who are going to go into exile, and in Mic 2.9 (with which a Masoretic note in M^L links this verse, apparently affirming a defective spelling rather than the current plene; cf. Goldman, 40*) God complains about the women each driven from בית תענגיה, so that his glory is taken away from her children. Finally, in Ct 7.7 the lover is described as אהבה בתענוגים, which apparently means something like 'beloved in her comforts', if the reading is original. Much play is made of this last instance by commentators who wish to see an erotic implication in תענוג, but it is far from certain even that it has that nuance in Song of Songs, and such a sense would seem inappropriate to all the other uses. We certainly cannot claim with Dörsing, *Lehre mich doch*, 37, that Qohelet is here asserting sexual intercourse to be the greatest human joy. It seems more likely that the noun refers to a certain level of comfort or luxury, which fools do not deserve, which the victims in Micah associate with their lost children and houses, and which characterizes the background of the lover in Song of Songs. The Greek versions almost certainly recognize that connotation here: note especially σ′ σπατάλας ('dainties'—a term used of soft living, luxury and feasting, and α′ τρυφάς ('delicacies', 'luxuries'); G ἐντρυφήματα is a rarer form (cf. Aitken, 'Rhetoric and Poetry', 72), correspondingly harder to define precisely, but probably similar in sense.

It is difficult to be certain whether any significance should be attached to the fact that most of other instances of the noun in Hebrew use it with a masculine plural ending, where here it has a feminine ending ח-, pointed as plural in M, and taken that way by most of the versions (although S apparently reads as singular, and the interpretation as plural could easily have arisen from context). Most nouns with preformative ת are feminine, in fact (cf. J-M §88 L o, u), so such a variation would not be surprising, and should not be assumed to imply that the comforts are actually feminine, but it may make us wary of identifying the use here too closely with the idiom employed by Micah and Song of Songs. The noun stands in a construct relationship with בני האדם ('humans', lit. 'children of the human'), a term that Ecclesiastes uses elsewhere (1.13; 2.3; 3.10, 18, 19, 21; 8.11; 9.3, 12), quite often to distinguish the human from the divine or animal, so it, conversely, has no particular implication of masculinity (and it is doubtful that אדם itself has that sense anywhere in the book, although some have seen it at 7.28; cf. Schoors, *The Preacher* II, 45).

S reads ܒܒܢܝ ܐܢܫܐ *bbny 'nš'*, '(delight) *in* humans', which probably represents not a variant in its source-text, but an interpretation of the construct relationship as an 'objective genitive'; it then repeats ܥܒܕܬ ܠܝ *'bdt ly*, 'I appointed for myself', so separating this expression from the following שדה ושדות. That repetition is attested in no other versions, and probably reflects an attempt to deal with the problems of the verse rather than a variant in the source-text or error in transmission.

2.8 a fine wine-table and settings] שדה ושדות is a notorious crux, and no translation can be offered with any certainty. The problems may have arisen, at least in part, from textual corruption, but (although the vocalization שִׁדָּה וְשִׁדּוֹת in M may be regarded with some suspicion) there are no strong grounds for emendation of the consonantal text. Jerome's commentary gives the Hebrew as *sadda et saddoth*, and the various renderings in the versions can all be understood in terms of those consonants. Jerome's citation of the Hebrew, indeed, shows that his own use of plural forms for שדה (Hie *ministros*; V *scyphos*) is interpretative, while his description of Symmachus' rendering (*species mensarum*) need not imply that σ' had a plural form also. There are no grounds, therefore, to suppose that a variant שדם existed for שדה, as Goldman suggests: like the widely attested G variant οἰνοχόους (probably the reading of θ'; cf. Marshall) for οἰνοχόον, Jerome's plurals represent alignment to the following word and to the preceding 'singers'.

More drastically, Jastrow and Ginsberg both take the whole expression to be a corrupt doublet of שרים ושרות: this is not impossible, since an initial daleth/resh confusion in either word might have given rise to שדים ושדות, but it is difficult to see what would then have caused the substitution of ה for ם, unless the scribe had some familiar expression in mind. Like attempts to view שדה ושדות as an interpretative gloss,[17] this ultimately shifts the problem, rather than solving it, and such text-critical issues cannot really be considered without reference to the meaning of the term. Before engaging with the lexical problem, however, it is important to note a few points about the context and form of the expression:

---

[17] Galling 1969 (slightly differently in 1940) reads the conjunction on תענוגת as explicative, so that 'human comforts' becomes a description of the singers, with שדה ושדות as a secondary interpretation. Less arbitrarily, Driver, 'Problems and Solutions', 240, thinks that שדה ושדות was originally an attempt by a disapproving scribe to gloss שרים ושרות by an expression referring to furniture (on that sense for שדה, see below).

(1) If שדה ושדות do not constitute an adverbial expression, then they apparently specify the nature of the תענוגת בני האדם, to which they stand in apposition, and must, therefore, be something which could be regarded by humans as a comfort or luxury.

(2) The sentence as a whole is governed by עשיתי לי, which, as we have seen above, does not connote simple acquisition. שדה ושדות תענוגת בני האדם, therefore, must be something which can be made, or a group/set which can be assembled (like the parallel singers).

(3) In the discussion of הבל הבלים at 1.2, above, we have already had cause to examine the idioms which involve collocation of two forms from the same substantive to give a 'superlative' or iterative sense. שדה ושדות does not correspond to any of these, since it does not consist of a construct expression (like הבל הבלים), of a singular and plural form juxtaposed without a conjunction (like דור דורים), or of two singular forms joined by a conjunction (like דור ודור). It does not seem sound method simply to ignore the conjunction (as does, e.g., Schoors, *The Preacher* I, 73), and there are no grounds to suppose that the linking of a singular form to a plural by ו itself constitutes a specific construction of that type. In any case, only the difficult רחם רחמתים in Judg 5.30 potentially offers the sense of plurality, rather than iteration, which many commentators seek here. (This does not, of course, exclude the possibility that שדה ושדות is an idiomatic expression in its own right, but that is a different matter.[18]) It follows that we should not assume שדה ושדות to be equivalent to 'many שדות', or suchlike, but should take seriously the possibility that the noun can have appropriate but distinct senses in the singular and plural.

The ancient versions largely seem to have associated שדה with the Aramaic verb שדי / שדא, which is used of pouring or sprinkling liquid. So G οἰνοχόον καὶ οἰνοχόας, 'a cupbearer and jugs', or maybe 'a male cupbearer and female cupbearers',[19] and perhaps α' κυλίκιον καὶ κυλίκια (var. κύλικας), usually rendered 'goblet and goblets' (but see below). Jerome discusses the translations at length, associating with them the translation by Symmachus (*mensarum species et appositiones*, 'types of tables and settings'),[20] and opting himself in

---

[18] Delitzsch, noting the difficulty, compares the use of the feminine and masculine together to express totality in, e.g., Isa 3.1, משען ומשענה (cf. GKC §122 v), but that is, again, a different expression with a different sense.

[19] See Aitken, 'Rhetoric and Poetry', 60, citing Gwynn, 'Notes', 116; Gentry, 'Relationship', 70. The Origenic manuscripts of G (probably with θ'), read οἰνοχόους καὶ οἰνοχόουσας, bringing out more clearly the male/female distinction which is discussed by Jerome.

[20] Jerome notes that Symmachus may not have been able to find an appropriate corresponding word, and so it is likely that σ' actually had εἶδος τραπεζῶν καὶ θέματα or something similar (for the last word, cf. V at Sir 30.18).

his commentary for *ministros uini et ministras*, 'wine waiters and waitresses', and in V, *scyphos et urceos in ministerio ad uina fundenda*, 'cups and pitchers in a table-service for the pouring of wine'. The same etymology gives rise to a different interpretation in T, which speaks of bath-houses, in which different spouts pour out warm and hot water.²¹ S is usually translated in similar terms, although Goldman has suggested that ܫܩܘܬܐ ܘܫܩܝܬܐ *šqwtʾ wšqytʾ* should be rendered as 'canals and irrigated fields'. This seems unnecessary: the Syriac stem is regularly associated with drinks and drinking (οἰνοχόος is rendered with ܫܩܝܐ *šqyʾ* at Tobit 1.22), and this is probably an attempt to imitate the Greek (in the variant form with οἰνοχόους, cf. Kamenetzky, 211, and possibly with οἰνοχόουσας).

Other etymologies are found in later discussions. In *b. Giṭṭin* 68a, it is reported that שדה ושדות is understood in Babylon to refer to male and female demons (so linking it with שד / שיד), but in Palestine read as 'boxes' (from שידה or שידתא, interpreted as coaches by Rashi and Rashbam—the rabbinic usage is discussed in detail by Delitzsch, who is attracted by the idea that it may mean a palanquin for women). A lengthy story about the demons follows; they appear more briefly in the Midrash, where they have the job of heating the תענוגת (understood to be baths, cf. T).

Most of the more recent commentators see a reference here to wives or concubines, an idea which draws more on context than etymology, rooting itself in part on Solomon's notorious associations with women, in part on the use of בתענוגים in Song of Songs (which is often assumed to be erotic), and in part on the reasonable perceptions that we might expect some reference to persons here, in parallel to the singers, and that the gender of the nouns would make those persons female. The lexicographical arguments in support of this suggestion, however, are as weak as they are varied: some of them might help offer an explanation for שדה ושדות, but none of them would independently compel us toward such an interpretation. So, for instance, Ibn Ezra ties שדה to שדד, 'capture', arguing that it must mean a female captive, and this idea is picked up by such modern commentators as Ginsburg and Lys, sometimes elaborated by a perception that the verb may imply rape (although it is not attested with that sense elsewhere). Others (e.g. Gordis, Provan), connect שדה with שד, 'breast', used uniquely here as a part representing the whole,²² or else simply emend the word to שרה, 'princess' (so, e.g., Euringer, Podechard). Suggested links with Ugaritic and Akkadian terms are problematic, to say the

---

²¹ A similar interpretation appears in the tenth-century Karaite commentary of David ben Abraham al-Fāsī, while Lavoie and Mehramooz note a variation in slightly later Judeo-Persian manuscripts: these are baths for men and baths for women. See Vajda, *Deux commentaires*, 202-203, and Lavoie and Mehramooz, 'Étude de quelques mots obscurs', 186.

²² Schwienhorst-Schönberger actually translates 'Brüste über Brüste', 'breasts upon breasts'!

least, and analogies with words in Arabic or Ptolemaic Egyptian smack of desperation.[23]

I am not myself persuaded by any of these efforts, and the context really does not seem to demand such an understanding. If the reference is indeed to concubines, moreover, then not only is it awkward that they are called 'human' luxuries, rather than specifically male ones, but it is also difficult to understand the form of the expression. Ginsberg's conjecture 'wife and concubines' will hardly do, and most other commentators resort to an equation with idioms like דור דורים to yield 'many concubines' although such an equivalence, as we have already seen, is far from straightforward. Amongst the various other possibilities, two are attractive. A simple repointing to שָׂדֶה yields a noun (employed by Qohelet at 5.8) which can be used in the singular and plural (and corresponds better to Jerome's transliteration), but the sense would be, 'land and properties' (on the use of the feminine plural ending cf. J-M §90 e).[24] This seems awkward contextually, neither fitting well into the list at this point, nor really constituting a luxury. Alternatively, Seow has resurrected the rabbinic association with chests, which would permit us to understand this as, essentially, an adverbial expression: Qohelet gets luxuries 'by the chestload';[25]

---

[23] The late Babylonian term *šūdadu/šudātu*, 'lover', is cited by Wildeboer (as *šadadu*) from a suggestion by Friedrich Delitzsch; the existence of the term, however, is doubtful; cf. Görg, 'Paronomasie', 5 n. 6, and especially the detailed account in Ellermeier, 'Der Harem Qohelet/Salomos', 23-25. The apparent Akkadian or Canaanite gloss *ša-di-tum* in an El Amarna letter (369 l. 8), cited by, e.g., Gordis, is no longer commonly read or understood that way (cf. Ellermeier, 'Der Harem Qohelet/Salomos', 25-27; Moran, 'Amarna Glosses', 151 n. 2, citing *CAD* under *ṣaburtu*; Schoors, *The Preacher* II, 454; *HALOT*). The Ugaritic *št*, 'lady', is better established, but that word is phonetically somewhat distant, and it is difficult to see, as Görg, 'Paronomasie', 6, points out, just what relevance a supposed original derivation of the term from a primitive root *šdt* might have for the understanding of שדה in the very much later language of Qohelet. Görg's own connection with the late Egyptian *šdt*, 'wet-nurse' (sometimes used in an extended sense of nourishment for titles and epithets), relies on a wholly speculative assumption that the term might have developed to describe women of a different sort, who educate the princes of the royal household. Leaving aside unanswerable questions about the likelihood of borrowings from Egyptian at the time when Ecclesiastes was composed, we may note that Görg also seems unaware of the extent to which Late Egyptian has itself imported Semitic loan-words (which are rarely if ever marked by group-writing, as he suggests). This seems likely to be just such a case, and he may be postulating travel in the wrong direction.

[24] As suggested by Luzzatto, 57; cf. Schoors, *The Preacher* II, 453.

[25] Ewald reaches the same idea by a different route, taking שדה to mean a 'pile' or 'heap', so that Qohelet has 'heaps and heaps' of luxuries. There is no clear foundation for that translation of the term, but I do wonder if Codex Graecus Venetus is speculating along the same lines with its σύστημα καὶ συστήματα, which could be understood as 'a collection and collections'.

that, of course, requires that we take the construction of the phrase to imply plurality, but it does bring the list to a suitably climactic conclusion.

Although there is something to commend these, I have opted in the end, like some other modern commentators, to take my translation from amongst those offered in the ancient versions.[26] The feminine form and singular number of שדה make it hard to accept that we are dealing with the male and female cupbearers of G, which feels like an assimilation to the preceding statement about the singers, but something in that sphere would be apt. Here Symmachus' translation stands out, not only because it offers a sense which is appropriate to the context, while not wholly driven either by contextual or etymological conjecture, but also because he apparently has in mind something so specific that he cannot find an appropriate Greek word for it. This makes his rendering very credible, and unlikely to be a simple guess, but it leaves us, of course, with the problem that we cannot know quite what sort of table and settings are meant.[27] From the form of the expression, שדות might constitute the items from which the שדה is constituted (rather as 'plates' make up a component of 'the plate' in old-fashioned English usage), while the possible link with שדי/שדא might lead us to conjecture that the function is more to do with drinking than eating. In this respect, Aquila's rendering is also striking. Although his κυλίκιον has commonly been interpreted as a bowl or vessel, at least since Jerome, a κυλικεῖον is also a 'sideboard' or 'stand for drinking-vessels'. That sense is well-attested and sufficiently early (cf. LSJ), raising the strong possibility that Aquila shares much the same understanding as Symmachus, and is trying to recreate the effect of the Hebrew by using κυλικ(ε)ῖον, 'drinking-stand', in conjunction with κυλίκια, 'little cups' (the diminutive form of κύλιξ).[28] This shared understanding may, of course, be incorrect, but it is early, appropriate, and, I would venture, the most firmly

---

[26] So, e.g., Bons, '*šiddā w=šiddōt*', who opts for 'Kellnerinnen in großer Zahl'—'a great many waitresses', and Schoors, *The Preacher* II, 454-55.

[27] In his commentary, Jerome extrapolates from Symmachus: *Siue igitur urceos, siue scyphos, siue crateres, qui in ministeriis ordinantur. auro gemmisque distinctos Salomonem habuisse credendum est; et quod ex uno* κυλικίῳ, *id est cratere, aliis* κυλικίοις, *minoribus scilicet uasculis, hauriretur; et per ministrorum manus potantium uinum turba susciperet*; 'Solomon must be thought of as having cups, pitchers, or mixing-bowls, which were laid out in table-settings, adorned with gold and jewels. And what is drawn from one κυλίκιον, that is a large mixing bowl, into other κυλίκια, obviously smaller vessels, is received by the crowd of wine-drinkers from the hands of waiters.'

[28] ε and ει are essentially interchangeable in the orthography even of early biblical manuscripts, cf. Thackeray, *Grammar*, §6, 24, and if the words were originally differentiated in this respect, the writings are likely to have been assimilated to each other quite quickly in the transmission of α'. The variant κύλικας found in mss 161 and 248 may be a secondary attempt to differentiate the words (as Marshall notes, Syh ܟܣܐ ܘܟܣܐ *ks' wks'* distinguishes them only by seyame),

grounded that we are likely to get. The context suggests that these are luxury items, and I have included that nuance in my translation, even though there is, of course, no separate term for 'fine' in the Hebrew.

2.9 I made myself rich, going beyond] Lit. 'I became great/rich and I continued more than'. This is similar, of course, to the expression in 1.16 (see above), but differs from it in lacking any explicit object, and in using מכל rather than על כל for the comparison. Those two differences are probably connected, since על is used to indicate excess of quantity in comparisons (and more specifically addition 'to' with the hiph'il of יסף, e.g., Deut 4.2; Isa 38.5): in 1.16 Qohelet increases wisdom to *a quantity beyond* that achieved by others, but here he simply becomes greater *than* others.

That may tell against any attempt either to supply an implicit object here for both verbs (although T inserts טובא, 'goodness', and עותרא, 'wealth', respectively for each), or, as Siegfried suggested, to emend וגדלתי to the הגדלתי of 1.16 (and 2.4) in line with some late manuscripts (see de Rossi). The apparently intransitive sense of וגדלתי והוספתי overall, however, cannot readily be understood simply in terms of two parallel, intransitive verbs, as at 1.16. The qal of גדל does not present a problem in this respect, since it can just mean 'become rich' (e.g. Gen 24.35), or 'powerful', but the hiph'il of יסף does not have this sense, and when used absolutely at Ps 115.14, it means 'make rich', as we should expect, not 'be rich'. It is often used in coordination with another verb to express continuation or repetition (e.g. Gen 25.1, ויסף אברהם ויקח, 'Abraham took again'; cf. GKC §120 d), and a number of scholars have seen such a construction here—hence McNeile translates 'I grew great and continually greater'; cf. Kamano, *Cosmology*, 64, 'And I have increasingly become the greatest'. Fox presumably understands something similar when he speaks of the second verb having 'adverbial force', and translates 'I grew far greater'. The idea of Lys, that the mere juxtaposition of verbs with a similar sense 'constitue une sorte de superlatif', 'constitutes a sort of superlative', is presented without evidence, and merely takes even further the apparent determination of commentators to abuse the grammatical concept of a 'superlative' that we noted at 1.2.

It is interesting to note, however, σ' μεγέθει ὑπερέβαλον, 'I surpassed in greatness' (cf. V *supergressus sum*; Cannon, 'Jerome', 192); that is a paraphrase (as the rendering of the first verb with a noun shows), but it corresponds to Fox's other suggestion, that the verb can mean 'exceed' or 'do more than'. It is difficult to substantiate that suggestion, since the two examples which he cites can be construed rather differently: in 1 Kgs 10.7, Solomon's חכמה וטוב may indeed surpass what had been reported, but literally he has 'increased (them as direct objects) beyond'; in 1 Kgs 16.33, Ahab

but it is not impossible that this form is original. The strange textual variants for Jerome's citation of the Greek (e.g. συλισια) apparently arise from transliteration and re-transliteration: κ → c → σ.

may be worse than his predecessors, but the verb is co-ordinated with the following infinitive, so that he 'goes on' provoking God, or intensifies that provocation—the comparative aspect arises from the clause with מן, and is not inherent in the verb. Although it may be that we should simply see the wealth of the preceding verses as an implicit object here (as Schoors, *The Preacher* II, 314), so that Qohelet 'grew rich and increased (riches)', I am inclined to think that the thought here is, in fact, similar to that second passage: Qohelet grew rich and continued or intensified his doing so, to a point beyond that achieved by his predecessors.

2.9 anyone who was before me] As at 1.16, the versions render as plural; see the discussion there, and also the note on 'before me'.

2.9 moreover] אף has a range of meanings, and is often difficult to translate. We are probably not simply being told, however, that Qohelet kept his wisdom in addition to his wealth (Gordis), and the particle may mark a new thought. HCM remark that the item modified by the word '"adds" information related to the preceding' but translate it as 'even' on interpretative grounds, believing Qohelet to 'recognize that his past acquisitions represent folly'. I doubt that is true, or that אף can have such a sense (except possibly in the expression אף כי at Neh 9.18).

2.9 remained with me] In 1 Kgs 20.38, עמד ל- is used of 'waiting for' someone, but there is no obvious reason to suppose that Qohelet had set his wisdom aside while he was making his fortune. Even on the more usual understanding that עמדה here means 'remained' (cf. V *perseueravit mecum*), the statement seems strange if it is connected to the foregoing account: why should Qohelet's wisdom not have remained? Rashi suggested that the verb here connoted service: his wisdom 'helped' Qohelet, and this idea seems to be implied in the double translation found (with minor variants) in T, where wisdom both remains and assists: חכמתי קמת לי והיא סייעא יתי. The idea has been picked up subsequently by Ginsburg (whose arguments are refuted by Podechard; cf. also Schoors, *The Preacher* II, 12) and, still more recently, by Seow. The latter notes, somewhat disingenuously, that 'the idiom *ʿāmad lĕ*- means "to attend to" or "to serve"', but the examples which he gives illustrate two different expressions: עמד לפני, 'to act as a servant to someone' (1 Sam 16.22; 1 Kgs 1.2; Ezek 44.11), and עמד ל-, 'to perform a function', with the preposition signifying that function (Ezek 44.24; Ezra 2.63; Neh 7.65; the last two are apparently a technical expression for consulting Urim and Thummim). It is not at all clear that service or assistance is a possible connotation here, let alone that it would represent a natural reading of the text.

It may be that Qohelet is referring back to his similar claim in 1.16, so that the point would be merely to affirm that he is now both richer and wiser than others. Despite the punctuation of M, however, it seems to make better sense to take the clause with the next verse, to which it is linked anyway by a conjunction, than to read it in connection with the preceding account or as a free-standing assertion.

2.10 eyes] T רבני סנהדרין, 'rabbis of the Sanhedrin', draws on a tradition found in the Targum and Midrash Rabbah of the Song of Songs, where 'eyes' refer to the Sanhedrin because they are the 'eyes of the congregation' (an expression found in Num 15.24); see Taradach and Ferrer, *Un Targum de Qohélet*, 103; Knobel, *The Targum of Qohelet*, 25. This has then been elaborated in terms of legal questions posed by those rabbis.

2.10 keep out of their reach] Lit. 'remove/keep back from them'. אצל can be used of removal (cf. Num 11.17, 25; Sir 42.21), but in Gen 27.36 it refers to the keeping back of a blessing. Some light is shed on this apparent inconsistency by Ezek 42.6, where the term refers to the way in which parts of a building are 'set back': the basic connotation is probably of separation, and that separation may be achieved either by keeping things back or by moving them away.

The manuscripts of G are torn between ὑφεῖλον (lit. 'take from under', preferred by Rahlfs and Gentry) and ἀφεῖλον (lit. 'take away from'); the former often has some implication of underhandedness, and renders גנב at Job 21.18; 27.20 (cf. Epist Jer 1.10). It is hard to be sure which is G*, but both imply removal (cf. Hie *non tuli ab eis*, 'I did not take from them'), while S, T, V all interpret less precisely in terms of prohibition.

There is probably a lack of agreement between the eyes and the suffix pronoun which refers to them in מהם (so, e.g., Barton; Köhlmoos refers mysteriously to a masculine 'preposition', which is presumably an error): עין is found as both masculine and feminine, but in Ecclesiastes is certainly feminine in 1.8 and 4.8. The confusion over gender might have caused a simple change to the text here in the course of transmission, but there is a broader pattern of such disagreement; see 'from which' at 2.6, above. Rendsburg's suggestion, that הם here is a 'common' dual form, neither specifically masculine nor feminine ('Personal Pronouns', 47) has largely been overlooked, and so has found no takers, as Delsman, 'Inkongruenz', 30, observes. It is not implausible, but seems unnecessary.

2.10 not] *BHQ* notes that S and T have a conjunction before the second לא; its claim that the same is implied by Hie, V *nec* seems less clear cut. A number of later Hebrew manuscripts have a conjunction in the same place (see Kennicott, Ginsburg, *Writings*), but it is likely that it rose independently as a facilitation in each tradition.

2.10 hold my heart back from] Like the English 'hold back...from', מנע מן can be used either of withholding something from someone or of holding someone back from something: contrast Amos 4.7 ('rain from [-מ] you') with Num 24.11 ('you from [-מ] honour').[29] Qohelet is not refusing to deprive pleasure of his heart, so the second is meant here (cf. Barton, Wildeboer).

---

[29] Barton and Schoors, *The Preacher* I, 193, cite Gen 30.2 מנע ממך פרי בטן as similar to Num 24.11, but it actually follows the same pattern as Amos 4.7, with, to use Schoors' terms, accusative of the thing and ablative (מן) of the person.

2.10 pleasure] The variant 'my pleasure' (+ μου) is attested early in the G tradition, but probably arose from the frequency of the pronoun elsewhere in the verse; cf. McNeile, 139, Euringer.

2.10 pleased] M points as the verbal adjective שָׂמֵחַ. It is difficult to determine how the versions took the word; G's use of the passive εὐφράνθη (cf. Hie *laetatum est*) might reflect a similar understanding, but that form often renders the verb itself elsewhere.

2.10 in all my business[1]] M^L has מכל, the usual reading in M, which is supported by σ' ἐκ πάσης φιλοπονίας μου (lit. 'from all my love of work') but G, S, Hie (and probably T) seem to have read בכל, and a few Hebrew manuscripts also have that reading; Miletto notes relatively strong support for it among Babylonian copies. The majority reading with -מ is difficult, since שמח and derived forms normally use -ל or -ב, sometimes על of the source from which pleasure is derived: only Prov 5.18 and 2 Chr 20.27 seem to show clear instances of -מ/מן. Elsewhere, Ecclesiastes talks of pleasure 'in' (-ב) work (cf. 3.22; 5.18). This leads to some scholarly gymnastics: Galling 1969 and Lauha, for instance, take the preposition -מ to have its comparative sense here, and understand Qohelet to be claiming that his pleasure 'outweighs' his effort and expenditure; more tentatively, Krüger suggests 'after' for -מ, citing Jer 31.13 (but there the hiphʻil is being used of creating joy from sorrow). It is simpler to assume, however, either that the majority text of M has assimilated the first to the second occurrence of the phrase, or (less probably) that this is one of those rare instances where the construction uses מן, and has been employed to create a parallel with that second occurrence. In either case, we should translate 'in'. S marks ܥܡܠܝ *ʻmly* as plural, but Kamenetzky, 198, rightly rejects the seyame as secondary. On the translation of עמל, see the note on the next verse.

2.10 what was mine] Lit. 'my portion'. חלק is the portion assigned to someone from the whole, their 'share' of it, so the term is often associated with the assignment and distribution of land, booty or inheritances, but it can also be used of having a 'stake' in something (e.g. 1 Kgs 12.16), or throwing in one's lot with others (Ps 50.18; Isa 57.6). At 11.2 it is used of the fractions into which something is to be divided, and in 9.6 of the stake which the dead no longer have in the world, but Qohelet regularly uses it of something to be found in work (2.21; 3.22) or in living more generally (5.17-18; 9.9). The following -מ is partitive, and does not imply that the חלק has been removed from the work in some way.

2.11 I looked round among] Lit. '(turned to) face in'. פנה means to face, or turn to face, in a particular direction, and it can take a direct object or mark the direction with a preposition, just as in English we can 'turn/face north', or 'turn/face toward the north'. Naturally, that preposition is usually אל, and the use of -ב twice here instead has led most modern commentators to see this as a pregnant construction, implying that Qohelet turned and fixed his attention on his מעשים, which is probably the sense of פנו בי in Job 6.28 (see, e.g., McNeile, 59; Gordis; Schoors, *The Preacher* I, 193). G καὶ ἐπέβλεψα ἐγὼ ἐν perhaps understands that to be an implication of the verb anyway (cf. καὶ ἐπιβλέψω ἐφ' ὑμᾶς for ופניתי אליכם at Lev 26.9), but ἐν is no less odd in the Greek (the preposition is also preserved at both places in S, T, and in the second only in Hie; it is replaced by *ad* in V, and absent from the rendering of ובעמל by σ': καὶ τὸν πόνον, 'and the toil').

Although the construction may well be pregnant, however, the uses of the verb here and in the next verse are surely to be considered as part of an image, which is continued by וסבותי in v. 20: Qohelet turns to face what he has created, turns to look at wisdom, and then finally turns away in despair. Where ופניתי אני לראות certainly implies close scrutiny in v. 12, I think that -ב here is being used locatively: his accomplishments and the products of his labour are not gathered in a single place, towards which Qohelet faces from a distance; rather, he stands or walks among them, turning to face each. On the use of אני, see at 1.16, above.

2.11 all] בכל was reportedly pointed with *metheg* under the כ by ben Naphtali (see Lipschütz).

2.11 my achievements] The suffix pronoun is not reflected in V *uniuersa opera* ('all the works', contrast Hie *omnia opera mea*, 'all my works') or in S ܥܒܕ 'bdʾ. This absence is translational in both cases: it has been regarded as redundant. Kamenetzky, 212, notes that this avoids double determination of the noun in S, and also that seyame has probably been lost in error—the word should be marked as plural (so too Euringer).

While מעשה can have a more general connotation of work or deed, the specification that Qohelet's מעשים have been done 'with his hands' aligns the usage very closely with the many other biblical references to 'works of the hands', which are things that have been made (e.g. Deut 4.28; Lam 4.2; Hag 2.7). Qohelet is not, therefore, looking back on his past activities, but surveying the products of those activities.

2.11 business which I had worked to achieve] Lit. perhaps 'at which I had worked achieving'. The expression echoes 1.3, and will recur with adaptations in 2.18, 19, 20, 22; 5.17; 9.9 (on the form, and on similar expressions, see the notes at 1.3, above). Except in the last case, these other instances consistently refer to 'all' the עמל, and it is that familiar usage which has probably led to the addition of a second ܘܒܟܠ *wbkl*, 'and at all', here in S and παντὶ in some witnesses to G. Since the term עמל is clearly important to Qohelet, we should assume that there is some reasonable consistency in his usage, while making some allowance for the range of meanings covered by the word, and this is the first place where the context permits us to be more specific about what Qohelet has in mind.

We have already noted that the מעשים which stand in parallel here are probably the concrete accomplishments of Qohelet's activity, which suggests that עמל here is itself unlikely to be just Qohelet's work, viewed in retrospect. Whitley, in fact, argues that the term must here connote 'wealth' or 'gain', and translates 'all my wealth, which I strove to acquire', and this is acknowledged as a potential understanding by, e.g., Krüger. It is true that עמל must indeed mean more than just 'toil' at some places in Ecclesiastes, and at 2.18-19 it is apparently something which can be conveyed to another person. Ginsberg, *Studies*, 3 n. 2, argues from Sir 14.14-15, where terms for labour are used for things inherited, that there must be a reference to gain; Dahood, 'Phoenician Background', 3, also notes the Aramaic inscription of Barrakib (*KAI* 216 7-8), but the statement there, that B.'s father's house [ע]מל מן כל, is in the context of statements about loyalty to Assyria, and there is no good reason to suppose that it means 'amassed more than any'. Whitley himself notes the association between wealth and עמל כפים in 1QS 9.22, and the various rabbinic uses of עמל which are listed in Jastrow, *Dictionary*. None of this evidence really adds up to proof, however, that עמל means 'wealth', as such.

In 2.19, the man who will acquire Qohelet's עמל will not simply acquire it, but will have specific rights over it, expressed by the (possibly technical) term שלט (on which see the note at 2.19, below), and the עמל itself is not spoken of as something which might be dispersed, like a pile of gold, but as something which constitutes a specific entity. The rabbinic usage, furthermore, seems to link the term not to wealth *per se*, but to income, or sources of income. In the lengthy discussions about collection of a daughter's share from an estate in *b. Ketubbot* 69a (cf. *b. Baba Batra* 67a), mention is made of the עמל of houses, i.e. the rental income which they produce (this could be collected because it was, in some sense, a part of the land). Rainey's idea (in 'A Second Look at Amal'), that עמל refers to one's 'trade', seems rather forced and limited, and it fits badly the use in Ps 105.44, which is often adduced as evidence for עמל meaning the product of work. That text, however, also seems to demonstrate that more than just wealth is meant: when God gives Israel the lands of the nations and they thereby 'come into possession of the עמל of the peoples', it surely does not mean simply that they get to take whatever piles of money or crops are lying around. Rather, Israel takes over the fields, vineyards, and all the other mechanisms which have been produced by the work of the peoples, and which will now be worked to create their own produce. The verb used there of acquiring the עמל is ירש, regularly used of dispossessing others, as in, e.g., Deut 2.12 and Jer 8.10 (where the dispossessors take over the fields, just as others take over the wives). In short, the key uses of עמל to indicate something other than labour do not point to it being simply the income derived from that labour after its completion: it is, rather, the continuing income, or sources of income, established by that labour. The English 'industry' or 'business' capture some of this. In this context, the term would presumably refer to the flocks, groves, forests etc. which Qohelet had created—the infrastructure of his fortune.

The interpretation of the construction with לעשות will inevitably depend on the understanding adopted for the previous words, but the infinitive is probably acting like a gerund here (cf. GKC §114 o; J-M §124 o), as many commentators have recognized: Qohelet is toiling by setting up his business

(Gen 2.3 is often compared). Alternatively, this is an expression of purpose, so that Qohelet is toiling in order to set it up, but we might then expect a resumptive pronoun.

2.11 and behold…wind] I have translated with a past tense to match the context. In the Hebrew this precisely echoes 1.14, aligning the conclusions about Qohelet's achievements with those about human achievements more generally, just as the following clause seems to answer directly the question in 1.3. On the expression 'wishing for the wind', see the corresponding note at 1.14.

Most scholars have been content to understand the 'all' here as a reference to what Qohelet has just said that he is reviewing. Kamano, 'Character and Cosmology', 421, sees the judgments here and in v. 17, however, as proleptic anticipations of 'a general conclusion that will become apparent later (2,18-23)'. This is hardly natural or necessary, and loses the point, I think, that Qohelet's general assertions are rooted in the specifics of his experience.

Introduction to 2.12-26

Reflections on Experience

(2.12) Then I looked round to observe:
wisdom, and mindlessness, and obtuseness;
what the person will be who comes after me,
what he will bring that he has achieved already.

(2.13) And I saw that there was a gain for the wisdom over the obtuseness like the gain from light over darkness: (2.14) the wise man—his eyes are in his head, while the fool goes along in darkness. But I knew myself that the same things will happen to them both, (2.15) and I said in my heart, 'What happens to the fool will happen to me, even me, so why was I needlessly wise back then?' Then I said in my heart that this also had been an illusion, (2.16) because there is no memory of the wise man forever, along with the fool, since, already in the days that have come, everything has been forgotten, even how the wise man dies along with the fool. (2.17) Then I hated life, for achievement achieved under the sun seemed bad to me, as it is all an illusion, and wishing for the wind.

(2.18) And I hated all my business, at which I had been the one working under the sun, that I shall leave it behind for the person who will be after me—(2.19) and who knows whether he will be wise or obtuse, yet he will have the rights over all my business, for which I have worked and for which I have been wise under the sun. This too is an illusion. (2.20) So I turned away, letting go of my concern with all the business at which I had worked under the sun. (2.21) For there may be a person whose work has been with wisdom and with knowledge and with aptitude, but it is going to be to a person who has not worked on it that he will give it, to be what is his. This too is an illusion, and utterly bad. (2.22) What is there for the person in any of his business, and in the worrying of his heart about that at which he is the one doing the work under the sun? (2.23) For through each of his days, pains and exasperation have been his job; at night, too, his heart has not relaxed. This too, it is an illusion.

(2.24) There is no good in the person who eats and drinks and lets himself take pleasure in his business. This too have I observed, that it is from the hand of God (2.25) who eats and who worries, besides me. (2.26) That he has given wisdom, knowledge, and pleasure to a person he favours, and has given the job of piling and accumulating to the disfavoured, to give to one God favours—this too is an illusion, and wishing for the wind.

Qohelet begins by explaining why, in the light of what he had now learned, he first turned his attention once more to qualities that he had already assessed, more briefly, in 1.17-18. In what follows most immediately (2.13-17), he will describe how death levels everybody, so that, despite his achievements, his wisdom has ultimately given him no advantage over a fool. This is the examination 'of wisdom, and mindlessness, and obtuseness'. His death, however, will have a further consequence: what he has achieved is going to persist beyond him, and pass to somebody who may have done no work for it, so he states at the same time his intention to examine that issue. There are two connected problems here, in other words: it is clear not only that wisdom ultimately yields no personal benefit, but also that the possession of material benefits need not depend on hard work or the possession of wisdom—they will simply pass to somebody else regardless of that person's qualities (2.18-21). It follows that all the anxiety attendant on work is, in effect, a waste of time (2.22-23), while security and enjoyment of life are a matter not of individual worth, but of divine dispensation (2.24-26).

These discussions seem rather specific, but they open up much bigger questions, and this is arguably one of the most important sections of the book. Having earlier set out his plan to answer various questions through living a life geared to attainment, Qohelet has reached in 2.11 the conclusion that all his achievements are a mere vapour, in which there is no profit to be found. Revisiting the topic and vocabulary of that earlier investigation (cf. 1.17-18), Qohelet now finds more than just exasperation in wisdom: it is pointless, because it will ultimately deliver him only to the same destination as a fool, offering him merely the questionable advantage that he, unlike the fool, can see where they are both headed. This is as helpful, perhaps, as facing the firing-squad without a blindfold. Asking why he had himself been so wise, if wisdom is so useless, leads Qohelet back to the issue of humans' failure to learn from what has happened, and to a declaration that all achievement is like this.

The review of what he has physically accomplished is no more re-assuring, because although Qohelet himself, like the fool, is going to pass away, the business that he has created is going to remain behind, and become the property of someone else. This picks up some key points from the prologue—that the world outlasts each human, and that everything in that world persists as part of some longer process—but gives them a new twist. What troubles Qohelet here is not just the issue that his property will cease to be his own, so that he cannot take it with him, but the fact that it will become the possession of another. If anyone can potentially acquire, through inheritance or otherwise, a business and a lifestyle for which they have themselves done no work—and which they might even have been incapable of creating for themselves—then it follows that there can be no simple connection between prosperity and character. This leads him to ask whether there is really any point in all the toil and anxiety that can arise from business, but it also leads him to the conclusion that anybody who instead enjoys what they have and do, does so as the result not of anything inherently good in them, but of a divine providence that has nothing to do simply with rewarding some or punishing others.

It is not entirely clear just what Qohelet has in mind at this point, and any interpretation has to be offered with some caution—not so much, for once, because there are significant difficulties in the text or vocabulary, but because there are various different ways in which we might understand Qohelet's distinctions between those who create wealth and those who enjoy it, between those who please or do not please God, and also, before that, between those who find pain or exasperation in work, and those who find pleasure. It is difficult to know how far our difficulties with these conclusions arise from our own presuppositions or failures to catch Qohelet's nuances, but it would not be wholly unfair to suggest alternatively that they are supposed to be ambiguous, confusing, and maybe confused, perhaps as Qohelet himself is portrayed trying to juggle all these different issues and categories, or that this section is more about raising significant questions than about providing a tidy analysis.

With that in mind, we should pay attention not only to the rhetoric of reason here, which attempts to persuade us that we are being led through a logical sequence of thoughts, but to Qohelet's statements about his own feelings. Up to this point, after all, Qohelet's wisdom has been both a source of pride and the lens through which he has viewed the world, even if he acknowledges that it can bring pain (cf. 1.16-17). Now suddenly, in 2.15, it seems to have been a complete waste of time. Looking at things from his new perspective, in 2.17, he declares his hatred for life, and, in the next verse, his hatred for his business and all that he has achieved—or at least for the fact that he has to pass them on. In v. 20, this leads him to detach himself from his accomplishments, letting go of any further care for them, but there is a strong implication that he had previously felt just the sort of powerful, painful involvement in his affairs that is described in v. 23. The language used is strong, and especially striking after the positive, optimistic tone that dominated the previous account of his achievements. Qohelet is portrayed as rejecting and turning against all that he had been and all that he had done, so the closing declarations about God and providence should perhaps be read neither as calm reflections nor as pleasant pieties, but as a position of fatalism to which Qohelet has been forced, by his resentment and by his intense loss of belief in the value of anything that he had experienced or accomplished.

2.12

(2.12) Then I looked round to observe:
wisdom, and mindlessness, and obtuseness;
what the person will be who comes after me,
what he will bring that he has achieved already.

Commentary

I take 2.12 to be introducing the two discussions that follow: wisdom and folly in vv. 13-16 and the problem posed by inheritance in vv. 17-21. It is not an easy verse to understand, however, and the last part is arguably the most difficult passage in what has proved a difficult chapter already: Ehrlich, indeed, declared most of it *heillos verderbt*, 'hopelessly corrupt'. As it stands, the Hebrew of that part might be translated very literally as: 'for/that what the man who will come after the king whom/what already they have made'—which gives some indication of the difficulties. There are text-critical and linguistic problems involved in some of the words (and these are discussed in the notes, below), but the key problem is a shortage of verbs, and the most common solution has been either to insert or to understand a verb in the first part which can also govern the second: 'What *will he do*, the man who follows the king? What they have already done.' The existing verb in the response is then usually read as a singular form—'What he (the king) has already done'—or else as an impersonal construction, equivalent to the passive—'What has already been done'.

All of that, which wanders some distance from the text as it stands and requires significant, largely speculative emendation or reading-in, yields a declaration that no-one who follows the king can accomplish more than the king himself has done. If such a declaration makes reasonable sense, however, it hardly seems appropriate to its present position, where Qohelet is describing his observation of wisdom etc. (which has led some scholars to move it), and it doesn't make a point that Qohelet seems keen to pursue anywhere else—indeed, even if he considered himself wiser and wealthier than his predecessors, we have no reason to suppose that he believed it impossible for anybody to surpass his own achievements.

It is difficult, in fact, to arrive at any plausible understanding which does not involve either a very forced construal of the text or some degree of emendation. I have argued the case for two possibilities in the notes, one reading the text as it is, the other emending it very slightly (with support from the ancient versions). The latter underpins my translation, but both readings see the last clause as a further part of Qohelet's question: he is interested in the character of his successor not in some general way, but in terms of his prior achievements. Qohelet, accordingly, looks at the problem of his accomplishments from two different but related angles: (1) they will not in the end yield any return on his wisdom, leaving him no better off than a fool, and (2) they will pass to a successor no matter what their previous accomplishments.

Notes

2.12 mindlessness, and obtuseness] On the terms, see at 1.17. In the next verse, Qohelet only compares חכמה and סכלות, and Fox takes הוללות וסכלות to be a hendiadys here, 'inane folly', which would be equivalent to סכלות alone. Qohelet certainly links the two terms elsewhere, but הוללות can appear by itself, and it would seem wrong to blur whatever distinction the book sees between them. As at 1.17, Gordis here wants to see an identification: 'that wisdom was madness and folly' (cf. also Hitzig). This requires, however, either removing the conjunction from והוללות, or taking it to be correlative with the next ('*both* madness *and* folly'), a sense which is not impossible, but which is hardly either demanded or indicated by the text. We might also, as Delitzsch observes, expect such predication to be marked by והנה.

2.12 what the person will be] I have not directly translated כי. The expression כי מה is used a number of times in contexts where the כי has no obvious force, except to emphasize the מה (see, similarly, my discussion of כי מי in the note 'who...who' at 2.25, below). This may be the case when Ecclesiastes uses כי מה elsewhere in 2.22, and possibly in 6.8 (depending on whether we follow M there, and how we understand the verse); cf. also, e.g., 1 Sam 26.18; 28.13, although the wide range of ways in which כי can be used makes it possible to attribute different nuances to the expression in many such cases.[1]

---

[1] For a detailed discussion of the particle, see especially Schoors, 'The Particle כי'. In the face of the relentless labelling of different flavours, however, it is important to bear in mind also the sensible comments of Aejmelaeus, 'Function'. Although the particle undoubtedly has different nuances in different positions and in particular expressions, as here, many of the issues revolve around the various ways in which we must translate it, rather than in separate, inherent meanings. At

Of the versions, however, only V fails to render כי here, and commentators have been inclined to view it as either explanatory or asseverative, depending on how they relate this second part of the verse to the first (cf. Schoors, *The Preacher* I, 103). It might be possible to take כי instead to follow the preceding לראות. When Ecclesiastes uses a similar construction at 4.4, in which ראה takes עמל and כשרון as direct objects, the clause introduced by כי is used to comment upon them ('I observed x and y, [and saw] that they are...'; see also, possibly, 2.24; 8.17). That particular usage does not suit the present context, but since Qohelet is going to talk separately in the following verses about wisdom and obtuseness, on the one hand, and about the qualifications of any putative successor, on the other, I take the purpose of כי here simply to be the announcement of a second object.

Pinker's proposal (in 'Qohelet 2,12b', 103) to emend כי מה to יכמה, from the obscure כמה found only in Ps 63.2 (ET 63.1), gives a very complicated sense: Qohelet is turning to the wisdom etc. that should be desired by the heir to the king by delving into historical precedents. If we allow the emendation and the obscure poetic term, this still presents not only a problem of order (which Pinker acknowledges), but a statement that seems to relate to nothing else in the broader context.

מה האדם is unexpectedly rendered τίς ἄνθρωπος, 'who *a* person', in most manuscripts of G, and where τίς ὁ ἄνθρωπος, 'who *the* person', does appear, the article is probably a correction toward the Hebrew. Since G usually renders the article with great fidelity, this has led Goldman to conclude that the ה was lacking in G's source-text (perhaps lost through haplography), while Rahlfs and Gentry, 'Propaedeutic', 163, both take τίς ὁ ἄνθρωπος to be G*, presumably on the grounds of translation technique, which would make the loss of the article an inner-Greek error. While it is possible that τίς is an interpretative rendering of מה, we should probably, in fact, expect τί here as well, and it is tempting to speculate that an original ΤΙΟ has been corrupted to the more natural ΤΙC at an early stage, as suggested by Klostermann, *De libri Coheleth*, 58. In any case, there is no good reason to doubt M, or to assume that G read a variant מי אדם (as McNeile suggests).

The sense of מה here has, nonetheless, provoked some discussion amongst commentators. The sentence bears a superficial resemblance to the deprecatory questions found in, e.g., 2 Kgs 8.13, 'What is your servant...that...', or Ps 8.5, 'What is humankind...that...', and Gordis has used this link to suggest that מה here might have the sense 'what value is...?'. The typical accompanying clause with כי is lacking, however, and even if מה does have such a sense within those questions, which is debatable, it is doubtful that the meaning can simply be transferred to other contexts. It is doubtful also that מה can be

least in Qohelet's usage, indeed, it seems often to serve principally as a way of affirming rather than defining the connection of a clause to what has preceded it, and it is frequently tempting to render it with punctuation rather than a word.

regarded as equivalent to מי (which Ecclesiastes could anyway have used here if the sense 'who?' was required), and although it can be used of people, as in the deprecatory questions noted above, and, e.g. in 1 Sam 29.3; Ct 5.9, it is not used to query identity.

The use of מה, along with the perception that a verb is required to govern the subsequent relative clause with את אשר, has led *BHS* and a number of commentators to propose that a verb must be inserted or understood here (to give, e.g., מה יעשה האדם), while some others would re-arrange the order of the sentence. Despite the curious assertion of Ogden, however, that 'other textual traditions' argue for such an addition, the versions offer no support for emendation, and ellipsis of a verb here would be very unnatural. Ginsburg, indeed, speaks (admittedly with more justice than elegance) of 'an exceedingly harsh ellipsis, and, even if it could be shewn that it ever takes place, which is very questionable, ought not to be resorted to unless absolutely necessary, which, however, is not the case here'.

Hertzberg's characterization of the omission as 'aposiopesis' (accepted by, e.g., Lauha, Schoors, *The Preacher* I, 156 n. 53, Krüger) does not overcome the problem at all. That device (cf. GKC §167 a) refers to the abrupt breaking off of a sentence—properly, to give a certain effect for rhetorical or stylistic reasons. Biblical examples generally involve ellipsis of the apodosis in a conditional sentence (e.g. 1 Sam 12.14; 1 Chr 4.10), and are rather like the English 'if only it would stop!' or suchlike. Ellipsis of elements earlier in a sentence does occur, of course, especially in exclamations (cf. GKC §147 c, although it is questionable whether there is any real ellipsis at all in some of the examples given there, such as the response אין to the question היש פה איש in Judg 4.20), but that is not strictly aposiopesis, and the missing words can generally be supplied from context. It is difficult to adduce any true parallel for the ellipsis proposed here. Accepting M as it stands, then, we should read a direct or indirect question, 'what (is/will be) the person who...?' (cf. 3.22 לראות במה שיהיה אחריו).

2.12 comes after] When בוא is used with אחרי elsewhere it can connote pursuit (e.g. Exod 14.17; 1 Sam 26.3) or support (2 Sam 20.14; 2 Kgs 11.15), and these two types of 'following' someone are found more generally in uses of אחרי with verbs of motion (cf. 1 Sam 14.37; 2 Sam 20.2; Hos 2.7). G and σ' adopt something like the first in their notion of 'following advice' here (see below), as does S in its curious ܕܢܥܘܠ ܒܬܪ ܡܠܟܐ ܒܕܝܢܐ *dnʿwl btr mlkʾ bdynʾ*, 'who will enter after the king in judgment'. In principle, it would be possible to understand the person in question to be someone who is subordinate to the king (a 'follower'), but Ecclesiastes elsewhere uses אחרי so much with respect to the future that an idea of succession is more likely here, and can be linked to the subsequent discussion. It is interesting to wonder, nonetheless, why the person 'comes' here, when 2.18; 3.22; 6.12; 10.14 all use היה, and the only other use with a verb of motion (12.2) does not concern the future (although the form is אחר there).

Presumably influenced by the use of the verb, T has the man following the king in order to intercede with him—belatedly, since the verdict has already been decided—and this interpretation is found in Rashbam too. Perry also imputes a sense other than succession to the expression, taking it to imply imitation, and translating 'who is the man that can outdo the king?', but that seems to go well beyond the evidence.

2.12 me…that] If the first parts of the verse are difficult, the last is another notorious crux. It is difficult to make any sense of the Hebrew as it stands, and the versions have clearly struggled with it. There is a high probability, indeed, that the text is corrupt, and became so at a relatively early point in its history. I shall start, though, by looking at ways to read it as its stands, which tend to hinge on understandings of את אשר, before turning to what I think is a simpler solution. We may note that a few late Hebrew manuscripts have sought to resolve the problems simply by omitting the את (see de Rossi, Ginsburg, *Writings*), which enables a sense 'after the king who has already done it', but there is no evidence for the antiquity of that reading.

When the object-marker את is affixed to the relative pronoun, it governs the subsequent relative clause as a whole, rather than the object of a verb within that clause. So, we might find 'I heard *what* (את אשר) he had done', but את אשר would not typically be used in '*What he had done* was good', since there the clause is the subject, not the object, or in, e.g. 'What is it *that he has done*?'.[2] This usage immediately rules out certain proposed translations, such as Ginsburg's 'For what is the man that will come after the king, who has been made long ago?' If את אשר marks an object-clause, however, then it must have an antecedent verb, and there is no transitive verb preceding it apart from לראות, while וראיתי, which follows in 2.13, clearly begins a new sentence. Those modern commentators who prefer to insert or understand יעשה in the preceding מה האדם can understand the relative clause as a second object for that verb: 'What can the man do…? That which…' Even if we allow that emendation or ellipsis, however, the resulting sense is not compelling: this is not an obvious moment for Qohelet to be remarking that no successor will be able to do more than a king, and it is not an issue that he picks up later. Other scholars have accordingly sought instead to read המלך as a verb, or to emend it, as, e.g., Lys 'Car que sera l'homme qui succédera au roi, régnant sur ce qu'il a déjà réalisé?', 'for what will be the man who succeeds the king, ruling over that which he has already accomplished'. Such readings are probably impossible, however, because מלך as a verb is not used that way.[3]

---

[2] In the apparent exception at Num 22.6, noted by J-M §158 m, את אשר תברך is, in fact, governed by ידעתי, although it takes מברך as a predicate. The following clause then shows the normal usage: 'I know he whom (את אשר) you bless (that he is) blessed, and whom (אשר) you curse is cursed'.

[3] Lys emends המלך to מֶלֶךְ מֹלֵךְ, adding a participle. Similarly but more simply, Bickell, Ginsburg, *Studies*, 9, Fox and Seow re-point the consonantal text as a

Some other commentators, have therefore attempted to take את not as the object-marker but as a preposition. Gordis reads it with שיבוא, and cites Deut 31.7 (rather implausibly) for the sense 'go with' = 'bring'; that leads him to suppose that the question concerns what the man can bring in addition to what his predecessor had already accomplished. This seems forced, and such a sense would surely have been expressed more readily by a suffix on the preposition, rather than attachment of the preposition to the relative pronoun (see, e.g., Ruth 2.19). Ewald, on the other hand, seeks a particular nuance in את, suggesting that it indicates a comparison with the man's predecessor ('what type of man might it be who would follow the king, *compared with him whom one has made just before?*).[4] Even were that plausible, it would be extremely awkward—although the reading of את as a preposition probably is supported by S, which integrates the clause into its broader interpretation of the verse as a reference to disputation. If we do want to take את as prepositional, then we might be able, at a stretch, to read the clause as parallel to המלך, so that it refers to the person will follow the king 'along with' what the king has achieved.

There are also, of course, places where את seems to act neither as an object-marker nor as a preposition; see, e.g., 1 Kgs 8.31, where את אשר יחטא איש is picked up, as it were, by ואתה תשמע in the next verse. Such uses sometimes share common features, and J-M §125 j notes, for instance, the unexpected appearance of את in several lists, and before nouns which stand in apposition to other nouns with prepositions. If these represent idiomatic or stylistic usages, however, we should not extrapolate from them distinct meanings for the particle. So the fact it stands in place of a conditional expression in 1 Kgs 8.31, does not mean, for instance, that את אשר actually is a conditional conjunction, as Smelik, 'A Re-interpretation of Ecclesiastes 2,12b', supposes—let alone that we can then just read our text as 'if he has already done it'. More generally, though, these peculiar uses of את are unusual, and the sense of the texts where they occur is usually obvious, not baffling.

We may also note that את can sometimes mark an accusative, but not specifically or simply a direct object. Indeed, G σὺν τὰ ὅσα (the σὺν is

---

verbal form, and Rose, *Rien de nouveau*, 183, emends it to וַיִּמְלֹךְ. The problem, as Fox acknowledges, is that מלך does not take a direct object, even in Esth 1.1, which Lys and Rose both cite. Seow takes the construction here to show that the verb is transitive, but that merely begs the question, and he adduces no Hebrew parallels (the unusual Syriac use which he cites, furthermore, itself employs an indirect object with a preposition!). Rose's more plausible characterization of the following clause as an accusative of specification, rather than a direct object, may well be correct, but if that is true, then we do not really need to take המלך as a verb in the first place.

[4] Schoors, *The Preacher* I, 202, attributes this to Elster, remarking that nobody has followed him, but Elster is, in fact, citing Ewald 1837 directly here.

lacking in many manuscripts, see Gentry, 'Propaedeutic', 164) may be trying to render the expression here as an indirect accusative ('with respect to as many things'; as also at 8.9, where it seems to have encountered את אשר in place of M עת אשר). The resulting Greek is far from lucid, but σὺν τὰ ὅσα is apparently an accusative of respect, and the idea that the clause might qualify or specify the preceding one is attractive in this context. Constructions comparable to the Greek accusative of respect are, of course, to be found in Hebrew also (cf. GKC §118; J-M §126), which is what has permitted G to understand the text in this way. Whether they are very common with את (cf. J-M §125 e), is harder to say because it is often difficult to construe possible uses: the only really clear-cut cases, though, of the particle's use with the so-called accusative of specification—which Aalders would read here—are at Gen 17.11, 14; 1 Kgs 15.23 and concern body-parts. In a similar usage, sometimes classed not uncontroversially as 'the accusative of subordination', an object marked with את seems to be 'subordinate to and not co-ordinate with, the object with which it is connected by the Waw Conjunctive', and the most obvious case is 1 Kgs 11.1, where the particle specifies the 'foreign wives' who collectively constitute the direct object of the verb; cf. Wilson, 'The Particle אֶת in Hebrew', 221-22. Of course, though, we do not have a conjunction here.

In the end, the use of את אשר to mark an object clause or accusative is so very common that to take it any other way must be regarded as unnatural, and as something of a last resort. So if we wish to take the text as it stands and do not regard the preceding כי as an obstacle (see the note on 'what', above),[5] then the clause with את אשר should be read either as qualifying the previous clause through an accusative construction, or acting as a second, different sort of object for לראות—את אשר is quite commonly used to mean 'the fact that' or 'how', as a way of introducing verbal clauses in indirect speech or similar contexts (e.g. Josh 5.1; 9.24; 1 Sam 24.11, 19; 2 Sam 11.20; 2 Kgs 8.5; cf. Jer 38.9). On both readings, we are dealing with a reference to observing what the preceding man has done, or how he has acted. Neither reading, however, can be described as easy or elegant, and the difficulties justify supposing that the text is corrupt.

If we are to emend it without resorting entirely to speculation, then we have to step back to המלך, the ancient understandings of which offer the only clue to an alternative reading. This word is, of course, awkward in itself: even if Qohelet is supposed to be posing as a king, there is no very good reason for him to be speaking of himself as king at this point, or referring to himself in the third person. If, on the other hand, he is making some more general statement, then he seems quite unnecessarily to be limiting his questions about succession by making this a matter of royal succession. When Qohelet

---

[5] As does Pinker, 'Qohelet 2,12b', 101, who sees the כי as the principal objection to Zer-Kavod's reading of the verse in these terms, with Qohelet looking at human actions in the present, future, and past.

actually does turn subsequently to the matter of succession, furthermore, he talks simply about 'the person who will be after me' (v. 18). M המלך is supported, nonetheless, by all the versional renderings except G τῆς βουλῆς ('counsel', 'plan') and σ' βουλήν (Gentry, Marshall) or βουλῇ (Field; on the problems surrounding the attributions of material to the Three here, see Marshall and Gentry, 'Propaedeutic', 164-65, but α' and θ' appear to support M).[6] These exceptions seem to reflect an understanding that the noun should be read not as the common Hebrew word for 'king', but as the Aramaic term מְלַךְ, 'counsel' (found in the Bible only at Dan 4.24 ET 4.27, but cf. the verbal וימלך in Neh 5.7).

This reading is puzzling, because that Aramaic word is not generally used in Hebrew, and anybody encountering מלך as a noun in a Hebrew text would have needed a very good reason not to understand מֶלֶךְ, 'king'. Their understanding, however, does not appear to have been forced by the way either translator understood the rest of the sentence: σ' τί δὲ ὁ ἄνθρωπος ἵνα παρακολουθήσῃ βουλήν ('what the man that he might pay attention to advice') apparently, indeed, paraphrases the rest to suit 'counsel', while G ὅτι τίς ὁ ἄνθρωπος ὃς ἐπελεύσεται ὀπίσω τῆς βουλῆς ('for who the man who will come after the advice') is not self-evidently more comprehensible with βουλῆς, 'counsel', than it would have been with βασιλέως, 'king'. There is no evidence that they even share a common understanding, let alone that they have both been constrained by some specific tradition of interpretation. It is far more likely, therefore, that both have felt obliged to read Aramaic here because they found in their source-texts something that was not המלך. In fact, by the time of these translators, the Aramaic word was commonly written מֵילַךְ in Jewish texts, reflecting a slightly different pronunciation and offering a distinction from מלך, 'king'. Were the translators to have encountered המילך, therefore, they would have construed it as a Hebrew article affixed to an Aramaic loanword with the sense 'counsel', and been left, as they evidently were, with no option to read 'the king'. Though they would have read such a text that way, however, the earlier author would not have written it that way, using the later orthography, even if he wished to use the Aramaic term for some reason. These Greek sources very probably reflect a variant המילך, therefore, but that variant is almost certainly an error.

Of course, המילך could just be an error for המלך, but, introducing a character and turning a common word into a wholly unexpected one, it would not have been a particularly easy error to make. It is simpler to suppose, in fact, that the text of M reflects an adjustment of מילך, either through the

---

[6] Kamenetzky, 212 and, more recently, Goldman have rightly dismissed Euringer's suggestion (following Janichs, *Animadversiones*, 7), that S ܡܠܟܐ ܒܕܝܢܐ (*mlk' bdyn'*, 'king in judgement') has attempted to combine the readings of M and G, although the interpretation may have been influenced by the ἐπελεύσεται of G (which can have combative connotations).

imposition of a defective spelling מלך, subsequently understood as 'king', or directly by correction to 'king', understood as Solomon. If המילך arose in another way, however, then the fact that it was comprehensible as a word would have allowed it to persist, even if, or perhaps especially if, the change made the text as a whole much harder to understand. I think, in fact, that it is most readily understood as the result of a simple metathesis of מ and ה in the sequence מהילך, which would mean that the text originally read מה ילך את אשר. There are other problems around כבר עשוהו, which we shall consider below, but an emendation in those terms yields a much easier text, in which Qohelet asks parallel questions with מה: what will the man be, and what (reading the verb as hiph'il) will he bring that he has already accomplished—which is essentially what Qohelet will go on to pick up in 2.18-19 and 21.

Since such an emendation dissolves המלך, we should also need to vocalize the preceding אחרי with a first-person suffix (as, e.g., Galling 1969 prefers anyway), which brings the initial expression האדם שיבוא אחרי much closer to the one which will be used in v. 18: לאדם שיהיה אחרי. My translation presumes this emendation, but, except for the absence of 'king', it offers a sense that is actually very close to what I proposed above for the unamended text.

2.12 he has achieved] A significant number of later manuscripts omit the first ו from עשוהו, making the verb singular (cf. de Rossi), while S ܕܥܒܕܗ *d'bdh* and Hie, V *factorem suum* (both mean 'his maker'), seem likewise to have read a singular form. The reading of G is less clear cut: the singular ἐποίησεν is widely attested, but Gentry, 'Propaedeutic', 165-66, puts a case for G* having been ἐποίησαν, and that is the probable reading too of θ' (retroverted by Field as σὺν τὰ ὅσα ἐποίησαν αὐτήν, lit. '(regarding) such things as they have done it'). T has probably read the plural, as M^L, but renders it as an impersonal construction ('they have done to him' = 'done to him'). It seems likely, in any case, that both עשוהו and עשהו existed in early manuscripts. Hitzig, followed by Euringer, supposed that both were writings of an original infinitive absolute with suffix (עֲשׂוֹהוּ; cf. Exod 18.18), which came to be vocalized separately as forms of the perfect, while *BHS* notes the possibility of emending to עָשָׂה הוּא, the option advocated by Zimmermann. Although Gordis' objections to it are overstated, few commentators have found Hitzig's proposal convincing, and most have opted for a reading as singular or plural qatal, according to their own understandings of the context.

Text-critically, עשוהו can probably claim some edge as the *lectio difficilior* (so, e.g., Seow), despite Goldman's proposal that it may be a theological correction to avoid the suggestion that a human has made a human (it actually raises a different theological problem for the Midrash Rabbah, which has to explain here why there seems to be more than one creator, and the issue was subsequently picked up by Maimonides and in some other sources). It is difficult, however, to identify an appropriate plural antecedent, unless we take Qohelet to be saying that הכמה והוללות וסכלות have shaped or created the man or the king. Whilst that idea is not unattractive, he does not express such a notion anywhere else, and עשה has been used very heavily in the preceding verses to characterize Qohelet's own activities and accomplishments—a consideration that motivates Fox's speculative emendation to עשׂיתיו, which is, again, more attractive than plausible (cf. Rose's proposed יְדֵי עָשׂוּ; *Rien de nouveau*, 184). Those scholars who retain the plural form of M usually take the subject to be a general 'they', as in 7.21 ידברו (so Ibn Ezra, writing on Isa 2.20). If the point is, however, that 'people' established the king (as, e.g., Lohfink would have it), then we might well ask just what people were in a position to accomplish such a thing, and why it is being mentioned here. If it refers to what has been accomplished, then it is important to bear in mind that purely impersonal constructions, truly equivalent to the passive, are rare in biblical Hebrew (cf. J-M §155 c), so this might mean 'what people have done', but is very unlikely to mean 'what has been done (by the king or his successor)' (against, e.g., Schoors, *The Preacher* I, 157). It is altogether simpler to assume that, of the two early variants, עשהו is more likely to be original on grounds of sense, and that we should read 'what he has done': עשוהו probably originated as a graphical error.

2.12 already] Finally, M is also suspect with regard to כבר, which is consistently present in Hebrew manuscripts but is rendered by none of the ancient translations except T. Kamenetzky, 212, suggests that S مـ *kn* (here signifying something like 'let alone with') may correspond to it, but the position and sense are different, making this unlikely, while there is no sign at all that G or Hie found the word in their source-texts (unless it has somehow provoked the *ante* of the latter, as Goldman suggests); it is not attested in Syh, or in the Syh witness to θ', and was probably not known to Origen. There is no evidence, therefore, that it was to be found in any Hebrew text before the second half of the first millennium, and this suggests either that it is a relatively late gloss, or that it was for a long time preserved only in texts that happened to be beyond the reach of the translators—although in either case its subsequent, apparently universal acceptance might seem hard to explain. On my understanding of what Qohelet is saying, its presence or absence makes no great difference, but G, in particular, is unlikely to have omitted it as optional, and there is little strength more generally in Euringer's protest that it is more likely to have been omitted than added. We can no more get to the bottom of this by weighing probabilities, though, than by explaining the data. In the end, I have included 'already' in the translation because, whether כבר is original or not, the English word at least clarifies the sense.

2.13-17

(2.13) And I saw that there was a gain for the wisdom over the obtuseness like the gain from light over darkness: (2.14) the wise man—his eyes are in his head, while the fool goes along in darkness. But I knew myself that the same things will happen to them both, (2.15) and I said in my heart, 'What happens to the fool will happen to me, even me, so why was I needlessly wise back then?' Then I said in my heart that this also had been an illusion, (2.16) because there is no memory of the wise man forever, along with the fool, since, already in the days that have come, everything has been forgotten, even how the wise man dies along with the fool. (2.17) Then I hated life, for achievement achieved under the sun seemed bad to me, as it is all an illusion, and wishing for the wind.

Commentary

2.13-14] Qohelet's comparison of wisdom with light, and its opposite with darkness, probably draws on established imagery (e.g. Job 12.24-25; Ps 119.105; Prov 4.18-19; 6.23). His observation here, however, is not phrased as a proverb, and refers back to the previous verse: there he looked at wisdom and obtuseness; here he sees the nature of the advantage which the former has over the latter.[1] Even if he is borrowing the imagery, moreover, Qohelet is arguably subverting it. Particularly in Proverbs, the virtue of 'light' is that it provides those who possess it with a well-lit path to follow, distinct from the dark and murky path of those who do not. Qohelet's point, however, is that everybody ends up in the same place, so might as well be following the same path: all that such light offers, therefore, is the chance to see where one is going. 'Gain' here is Qohelet's favoured term *ytrwn*, and although the

---

[1] The link with what precedes is affirmed by the unusual use of the definite article with the nouns (see the notes, below), and this tells against any attempt to read this as an aphorism that Qohelet is examining (Michel) or citing (Gordis), with a view to refuting.

verse can be understood more generally in terms of the advantages offered by wisdom (and it is often translated that way), Qohelet is literally talking about the profit made by wisdom.

2.15-16] On Qohelet's speaking 'in his heart', see the note at 3.16. He seems to use the expression when his understanding of a situation contradicts the evidence of his eyes, so here he 'sees' an advantage (2.13), but understands that in fact there is none, and that this is 'vapour'. If it does not offer a way to change direction, or deliver him to a destination different from that of a fool, then Qohelet's wisdom appears useless to him, and after laying so much emphasis on his acquisition and use of wisdom since the beginning of the memoir, he now questions the very point of it. It seems likely that this wasted effort is what he first describes as an illusion ('vapour'), but the explanation that follows is complicated. Evoking the language and ideas of 1.11, Qohelet speaks about the forgetting of the wise as well as the foolish, and about the forgetting of the fact that both of them will die. This forgetfulness is not just something that will happen in the future, but is a present reality—and it is apparently connected with Qohelet's failure to understand much earlier the uselessness of his wisdom. Of course, we might ourselves observe that this understanding rests on his ideas about death, and so he could have reasoned his way at anytime to this conclusion. The book, however, portrays Qohelet as reaching it as a consequence of reviewing his experiences, and Qohelet blames his earlier failure upon a universal human failure to observe the common end of the wise and foolish, and to assimilate the implications.

2.17] These reflections culminate in a rapid intensification of Qohelet's feelings: he declares that he came to hate life: everything done in the world is bad, because it is all vapour, and misplaced effort. There is perhaps, however, a certain train of thought visible here. From the perception of wisdom's inability to change anything, Qohelet moves to a rejection of his own efforts to acquire wisdom as pointless, from there to a perception that he must have been deluded, and have fallen victim to the common human failure to learn from the past, and finally now to a claim that all achievement in the world reflects a similar delusion. Since this is sandwiched between the references to his own wisdom in 2.15-16 and to his own business in 2.18, Qohelet's assertion here is probably not supposed to be read principally as a statement about the achievements of all humans—although he surely does not doubt that it is true of all humans—but as a continuing reflection on his own life and work. What was true of his wisdom is, by extension, true of everything that he has done or might do, and so he hates life, just as in the next verse he will hate the passing of his business to another.

Notes

2.13 and I saw] Michel, *Untersuchungen*, 28-30, suggests that the verbs which Qohelet uses of his own activities in vv. 12-15 are carefully formulated to distinguish knowledge from observation, so that he is not claiming an insight based on observation here, but rather examining a view which has been expressed by others. Fox dismisses this on the grounds that

> *raʾah* with a 'that'-clause always introduces a proposition the speaker believes true. When the direct object is a noun, on the other hand, *raʾah* means 'see,' 'look at,' 'consider,' and the like; and since the object of observation has no propositional content, the verb does not imply validity. It is special pleading to assign this statement to another viewpoint while leaving other affirmations of wisdom's value (such as 7:11f.) to Qohelet.

That response sets up a distinction between substantives and substantivized clauses which would be difficult to maintain (cf. 4.4), and itself attempts, in the first sentence, to assign a linguistic basis to what is, in essence, an exegetical conclusion. It is unlikely that the verb itself inherently conveys either acceptance of what follows, or distancing from it. Michel may well be right, therefore, to reject assumptions that וראיתי is necessarily an expression of empiricism, but his rather speculative analysis gives no secure basis for concluding that Qohelet cannot here be reporting his own observations.

The personal pronoun is omitted in S; Kamenetzky, 236, suggests that it was lacking in the source-text (as in a few known Hebrew manuscripts, cf. de Rossi), but acknowledges elsewhere (212) that the rendering of this verse may, in any case, be rather free.

On the construction with -ש, see the note at 3.18, below.

2.13 for the wisdom] G renders לחכמה with a dative τῇ σοφίᾳ, which has possibly inspired the ܒܚܟܡܬܐ *bḥkmtʾ*, 'in wisdom', of S (if that is not simply interpretative); in any case, neither offers any reason to emend the text. G supports the M pointing of לחכמה with the article. On that more generally, see the note at 1.13, above, but this is an instance where the pointing may well represent the original intention of the author, since הסכלות also has an article (which has probably guided the reading of M and G), and the articles are explicable; see below on that word.

The construction of יתרון with -ל is essentially the same as that used in 1.3; 5.15; 10.11, which each speak of the gain accruing *to* someone, and similar to the construction with יותר in 6.8: מה יותר לחכם מן הכסיל. Where the gain is more probably *from* something at 3.9 and 5.8, a simple construct relationship is used. It is possible that the use of -ל here may be mandated in part by a desire to make יתרון indefinite, as Podechard suggests, but Qohelet is not, strictly speaking, making any direct statement that humans may achieve יתרון *from* wisdom, but talking about the profit made by wisdom (even if that amounts to the same thing in the end). It is difficult to know how much significance we should read into the fact that the parallel כיתרון האור here does not use the preposition, but it is plausible to suggest that, although he is comparing them, Qohelet is also distinguishing between a gain that accrues to wisdom and an advantage that is offered by light. The meaning of יתרון here is probably closer to 'advantage' or 'superiority' than the usual 'profit', but we should perhaps think in terms of the 'surplus' or 'difference' between wisdom and obtuseness, on the one hand, and light and darkness, on the other. G, interestingly, uses περισσεία (cf. on 1.3) consistently for יתרון, but also contextually for יותר at 6.8; 7.11 (and probably 6.11), so apparently sees an overlap between them; see Gentry, 'Role of the Three', 180-82.

2.13 the obtuseness] הסכלות strikingly takes an article also in 7.25, when it appears in a sequence of undetermined nouns, and where the article has no versional support: there the ה really demands either deletion (cf. *BHQ*), or explanation in other terms, and it might be tempting to conjecture that הסכלות is a separate coinage from the hiphʿil (like, e.g., הנחה or הצלה in Esth 2.18; 4.14, cf. GKC §85 c; J-M §88 Lb) were the situation as difficult in this verse. It seems probable, however, that the articles here are to be explained by reference to Qohelet's statement in the previous verse: these are the wisdom and obtuseness which he turned to observe there, rather than just those qualities in the abstract.

2.13 like the gain] The pointing כִּיתְרוֹן with quiescent י is found in M^L and has strong support among early manuscripts over against the variant כְּיִתְרוֹן (cf. Ginsburg, *Writings*; *BHS*). On the form, cf. Schoors, *The Preacher* I, 44-45; GKC §24 e.

2.13 light…darkness] Barr, 'Determination', 332, notes a marked tendency for חשך to be undetermined (especially when the Masoretic vocalization of prefixed prepositions is discounted), and אור is likewise found most commonly without an article. When the two appear together and with articles at, e.g., Gen 1.4-5, 18, the reference is to the light and dark which have specifically been mentioned already; even references back to the light and dark of Genesis, though, do not require articles (e.g. Job 26.10; 38.19). Ecclesiastes, however, does use an article explicitly with אור at 11.7 and 12.2 and with חשך at 11.8, so the use of articles here as well may be a characteristic of the author's style. Presumably aware that they are unusual, T apparently interprets these articles in terms of specific references to 'the light of day' and 'the dark of night'.

2.14 the wise man] The noun is in *casus pendens*, with a nominal clause following; cf. J-M §156 b: GKC §143 a speaks in terms of a 'compound sentence'. The use of *casus pendens* in the book is discussed at length in Backhaus, 'Pendenskonstruktion'. With this instance, compare, e.g., Gen 34.8; Ps 104.17; Nah 1.3. This construction allows Qohelet to draw a clear comparison between the wise man and the fool, with each standing at the head of the clause which describes them. The order is imitated in the versions.

2.14 his eyes are in his head] 'And are the fool's eyes in his feet?', asks the Midrash, sarcastically but not unreasonably pointing out that this seems a statement of the obvious. It goes on to interpret ראש in the sense 'beginning' (noting also the suggestion that it might mean 'end', or 'culmination'), so that this becomes a reference to the wise man's foresight: he can see the end of a matter when he is still at its start. The same interpretation is adopted by T: חכימא מסתכל ברישא מא דעתיד למיהוי בסופא ('the wise man understands in the beginning what is going to happen in the end'). That understanding is not unattractive, but is probably excluded by the suffix pronoun on ראש, which is supported by all the other ancient versions. Although somewhat inelegant in Greek, the expression was widely cited by the Church Fathers (see Vinel), and many witnesses omit the *first* αὐτοῦ, which improves the style; G, however, offers no grounds for emendation, or for deletion of the second suffix pronoun in particular. From the context, it seems likely that the expression is simply a familiar colloquialism or turn of phrase, meaning that the wise man is observant, or looks where he is going. Since people's eyes are supposed to be in their heads, though, it may also imply that this is something normal, rather than extraordinary.

2.14 fool] This is the first use of כסיל in Ecclesiastes, and when it appears subsequently the noun is frequently contrasted with חכם, as often in Proverbs: see 2.15, 16 (twice); 4.13; 6.8; 7.4, 5-6; 9.17; 10.2, 12. There is an overlap with סכל (see especially 10.12-14), but the terms are probably not interchangeable. It is harder to say precisely what each would have connoted. The סכל is presumably characterized by סכלות, on which see the note 'mindlessness and obtuseness' at 1.17. The כסיל here is clearly in some sense the opposite of 'wise' (cf. 4.13; 6.8; 7.4, 5; 9.17; 10.2, 12), but Pinker, 'Reevaluation', has rightly resisted attempts to portray the fool as innately stupid or mentally deficient—although I am not persuaded by his understanding that folly for Qohelet is simply a different, more intuitive approach to solving problems.

2.14 myself] The sentence as a whole is clearly to be contrasted with the previous statement: the wise man and the fool appear to be different, *but* are going to the same end. This is accomplished in the Hebrew simply through the context and the conjunction on the verb. The idea of Ginsburg and others, however, that גם here is also adversative (cf. RSV 'and yet I perceived'), has gained some support among more recent commentators (so, e.g., Gordis, Seow, Schoors, *The Preacher* I, 128-29). If it is intended to contrast Qohelet's knowledge with the previous statement, though, then its position in the sentence is very strange (as was long ago pointed out by Delitzsch and Barton): it should precede the verb, if it is at all comparable to the other, rather infrequent instances usually cited for adversative גם (e.g. Ps 129.2; Ezek 16.28). A similar consideration applies to Podechard's alternative suggestion, that if it does not govern the verb, then it may govern the subsequent proposition. If, on the other hand, it is only the pronoun which is governed, as the position of גם would seem to demand, it is difficult to see why this must be adversative at all. In the light of the next verse, where גם אני serves as an emphatic 'I, myself',[2] it would seem more natural to read it that way here also, and this is apparently how the versions have taken it (so G, albeit mechanically, καί γε ἐγώ; T אוף אנא. S has just the pronoun ܐܢܐ 'n', although Kamenetzky, 212, suggests that it probably rendered גם originally, as it does in the next verse; cf. Hie *ego*). This does not exclude the possibility that Qohelet is contrasting his own opinion with that of others.[3]

2.14 the same] Lit. 'one', but the point is commonality, not singularity; compare, e.g., Exod 26.2; Esth 4.11. The same expression is used in 3.19; 9.2, 3.

2.14 things will happen] As Fox has emphasized, the verb קרה and the associated noun מקרה do not convey any specific notion of fate or predetermination in their common usage (see, e.g., Gen 42.29; Ruth 2.3; 1 Sam 6.9), and the Greek translators have avoided terms connected with τύχη, 'fate' or 'providence': G uses συνάντομαι / συνάντημα ('occurrence'—used negatively of plagues in Exod 9.14 and 1 Kgs 8.37, as Vinel notes, but essentially neutral), while σ' uses the similar ἀπαντάω / ἀπάντημα (but σύμβαμα, 'happening', at 3.19). Even Rudman (*Determinism*, 36) allows that קרה 'is not itself a deterministic term', although he believes that 'In the final analysis, √קרה as it is used in Ecclesiastes cannot refer to a chance occurrence. The fact of death, to which it refers in the great majority of cases, is not a matter of chance: it is the one event that is guaranteed to come to all.' D'Alario, 'Liberté', 462, also wants to retain a sense of 'natural destiny', arising from the subordination of every human generation to a cycle. If it were clear that Qohelet is indeed referring to the single event of death here and in 3.19; 9.2-3, then it might be better to translate in terms of the 'outcome' awaiting all, but מקרה אחד in 3.19 may encompass the list of shared attributes which follows, while the language of 9.3 links the problem of a single מקרה to the problem set out in 8.10-14, that wrong-doers can escape death, at least for a while. The verb is used in 9.11 to describe the action of chance in a wide range of

---

[2] The use is comparable to, e.g., Jer 4.12; Ezek 5.8; Hos 4.6. Note also, though, how גם אתם is used in Neh 5.8 to mark both contrast and emphasis: 'We have bought…while *you* sell'.

[3] So, e.g., Whybray, 'Identification and Use', 448. In his commentary, Whybray explicitly rejects an adversative use of גם in favour of an emphatic one.

contexts, and Krüger is surely right to observe that death may be the example *par excellence* of מקרה in Ecclesiastes, but that death is not the limit of the term's scope in the book.

2.14 both] Lit. 'all'.

2.15 I said in my heart] The same expression was used at 2.1; cf. also 3.17, 18.

2.15 what happens to the fool will happen to] M's pointing of מקרה as construct is accepted by most modern commentators and corresponds to the understanding found in the versions (except perhaps V, which paraphrases). The sense is clear, but the construction of the sentence difficult. We might take יקרני as impersonal (so, e.g., Podechard, Barton, and, apparently, G), to give 'it will befall me as what befalls the fool', or else understand the expression to be elliptical, requiring another מקרה to be supplied (so, e.g., Ginsburg, Seow): '(a fate) like the fate of the fool'. Following a similar line, T, Hie supply words for 'so' or 'such' (כ...כוותיה; *sicut...ita*). This may be unnecessary, as the preposition -כ lends itself to some very economic forms of expression elsewhere, and sometimes has an almost substantival character in its own right (cf. GKC §118 s; J-M §133 g-h). In view of, e.g., 1 Sam 20.3; Isa 10.14; Lam 1.20, it might be possible simply to take this as 'the like of the fate of the fool'.

2.15 me, even me] Or 'me, me too'. גם אני is placed before the verb, in *casus pendens* and in apposition to the suffix on the verb (cf., e.g., Gen 24.27), which gives it a strong emphasis. De Rossi notes a variant כן אני in one codex: this is a facilitation.

2.15 was I...wise] σ' renders καὶ εἰς τί μοι ἡ σοφία μου, 'and for what to me my wisdom?', which parses חכמתי as a noun with first-person suffix. This might simply be translational, but more probably rests on a different pronunciation. In any case, even though Jerome reads a verb, σ' has likely influenced V *quid mihi prodest* ('what good does it do me?'; cf. Cannon, 'Jerome and Symmachus', 192).

2.15 needlessly] Or 'superfluously'. יותר, which is related to יתרון, appears also in Ecclesiastes at 6.8, 11; 7.11, 16; 12.9, 12. Elsewhere in the Bible, it is found only at 1 Sam 15.15, where היותר refers to 'the rest' of the animals, and Esth 6.6 where יותר ממני means either 'apart from (i.e. beyond) me', or 'more than me' (יותר מן is used commonly in mishnaic Hebrew for 'more'). Ecclesiastes seems to use the term quite variably. In 6.8, 11, מה יותר ל- seems to mean 'what more is there for?', in the sense 'what advantage does (someone) have', which is probably the sense also in 7.11. In 12.9, on the other hand, יתר שהיה is probably a reference to something left over, while in 12.12 יתר מ- means 'beyond', 'more than'. The advice in 7.11 links יותר with the verb חכם as here, and places it in parallel with הרבה, but, since the connotation of superfluity or excess over is never absent elsewhere, it probably does not just mean 'very'. Both here and at 7.11, in fact, Qohelet refers to the acquisition of wisdom to an extent which is unnecessary or superfluous, but whereas in 7.11 this idea is very general, with no specific point of comparison, here the context suggests something more precise. Since the wise man shares the fate of the fool, any wise man's acquisition of wisdom serves no evident purpose: it is redundant, superfluous and unnecessary.

2.15 back then] Most modern commentators read אז יותר as a continuation of Qohelet's question, with אז serving as a logical 'then', and יותר as an adverb qualifying חכמתי: lit. '(why have I been wise) then, very much?'. Despite, however, Schoors' declaration that he cannot see a problem here (*The Preacher* I, 29), the word-order is awkward—and even while accepting this construal, HCM acknowledge that the positions of אז and יותר are 'very odd'. Although the sense of אז is usually temporal ('at that time', past or future), subsequence sometimes becomes consequence, so that the clause governed by the word can become, in effect, the apodosis to an actual or virtual conditional sentence (so, e.g., with לולא / לולי in 2 Sam 2.27; Ps 119.92; with אם 1 Chr 22.13; Isa 58.13; with אשר Josh 22.31; Ps 69.5; with no conditional particle Exod 12.44). Whether or not such 'logical' uses are really comparable to the sense usually proposed here, it is important to note that אז usually governs clauses; although it may be preceded by other adverbial expressions (as, e.g., 1 Chr 16.7), it almost always, furthermore, stands at the head of its clause, as we should expect. The exceptions are few, and fall into two groups. Genesis 12.6; 13.7, which place אז between subject and predicate, are noting a different situation which pertained in the past ('Back then, it was the Canaanites in the land'), while the similar 2 Sam 23.14 (= 1 Chr 11.16) is establishing the position of David and the Philistines at a particular time, since this is crucial for understanding the subsequent story. It is the subjects which are out of position in these cases; they are moved forward for emphasis, and אז still precedes the verb which occurs in Gen 13.7. In Josh 14.11 (ככחי אז וככחי עתה) and Hos 2.9 (טוב לי אז מעתה), on the other hand, אז is not being used to govern the clause at all, but to give a specific reference to the past, contrasted with the present (cf. מאז in 2 Sam 15.34, and, indeed, the more general uses of מאז for '(from) of old', e.g., Ps 93.2; Prov 8.22; Isa 48.3, 5). I take the sense here to be similar: Qohelet is not trying to say 'why then was I wise?', but 'why was I wise *then*?'; in the light of what he now knows, he wonders retrospectively what caused him to behave as he did in the past.

Other commentators have opted for emendation. Joüon, 'Notes philologiques', 420, suggests that אז and the preceding אני are doublets, each a corruption of an original אין, so he would emend to אין יותר (cf. *BHS*; Joüon does not propose אז אין יתרון, as Gordis claims); Kamenetzky, 213 n. 1, on similar lines, suggests that אז may have arisen as a corrupt dittograph of אני. Whitley suggests emending אז to אי, 'where?', which is similar to Dahood's suggestion ('Canaanite-Phoenician Influence', 205, and 'The Language of Qoheleth', 227, following Zapletal) that the text arose from a defective writing of אי זה—and that is similar in turn to Driver's suggestion ('Abbreviations', 123) that an abbreviation א 'ז has been misunderstood. Dahood himself, on the other hand, later proposed an alternative explanation, that אז

is, in fact, the demonstrative pronoun with prothetic א (Dahood, 'Phoenician Background', 268). Siegfried, differently again, would insert a verb to read אז תרתי, 'then I researched' (cf. 2.3). These suggestions are unpersuasive, not least because they seem unnecessary.

The text-critical evidence is complicated. Jerome cites G in Latin as *tunc abundanter locutus sum*, 'then I spoke abundantly', but τότε (= *tunc*, 'then') is lacking in important early manuscripts, and is not certainly G*; Goldman suggests that G omitted it, as did Hie, V, S, for the sake of elegance, and McNeile doubts that it was in G's source-text. Deliberate omission by G seems unlikely, given the version's usual translation technique, but if τότε is not G*, it is possible that the word had been lost in the source-text through haplography (note the sequence אזיאני). G does not reflect at all the subsequent conjunction on ודברתי, which might again reflect a variant in its source (so Euringer), although it seems more likely that a καί has dropped out when the inclusion of a gloss (see below) led τότε περισσόν to be read as the beginning of a new sentence (as in Jerome's rendering of G). Jerome's own omission of both אז and יתור in Hie is curious, especially since he is suspicious of G here (*apertius in hoc loco sensum Hebraicum Septuaginta interpretes transtulerunt, licet uerborum ordinem non secuti sint*, 'The Septuagint translators rendered the sense of the Hebrew more plainly here, although they did not follow the Hebrew word-order'). In the body of his commentary, indeed, he appears to reflect both, by paraphrasing 'quid mihi *ergo* prodest, quod secutus sum sapientiam et *plus ceteris* laboraui', 'what good does it do me *therefore*, that I have followed wisdom and worked *more* than others?' (cf. Euringer); he later renders יתור but not אז in V *quod maiorem sapientiae dedi operam*, 'that I have dedicated more work to wisdom'. S may have been influenced by a text of G without τότε, or may be trying to represent the force of אז by placing ܟ *'n* at the beginning of the question. The versions, in short, suggest the possibility that G is based on a faulty Hebrew text, but furnish no real grounds for emendation of M.

2.15 and I said²] The first 'said' in the verse was ואמרתי; here Qohelet uses ודברתי (cf. 1.16), a stylistic variation which is difficult to reproduce in English. It is doubtful that there is any significant difference in sense here. One Hebrew manuscript, noted by de Rossi, has וראיתי, 'and I saw', which is presumably a reminiscence of v. 13. On the absence of the conjunction in G, see above.

2.15 in my heart] G and S include a plus which is variously placed in the Greek manuscripts either after ἐν καρδίᾳ μου, 'in my heart', or at the end of the verse (which is where S has it; it is conventionally labelled the start of 2.16). With slight variations, this reads in G διότι (ὁ) ἄφρων ἐκ περισσεύματος λαλει, 'because a fool speaks from excess'; S ܡܛܠ ܕܣܟܠܐ ܡܢ ܝܬܝܪ ܡܡܠܠ *mṭl dskl' mn ytyr mmll* is a direct equivalent, and probably a translation of G (so Janichs, *Animadversiones*, 7). Euringer ventures the possibility that this is a double translation, but there is general agreement that it is in fact a gloss. Many commentators have pointed to Mt 12.34, ἐκ γὰρ τοῦ περισσεύματος τῆς καρδίας τὸ στόμα λαλεῖ, 'for the mouth speaks out of the excess of the heart', and the related Lk 6.45, ἐκ γὰρ περισσεύματος καρδίας λαλεῖ τὸ στόμα αὐτοῦ, 'for his mouth speaks...', suggesting a Christian origin, but the context and content of those texts shed little light on the purpose of the gloss, and the resemblance extends only to ἐκ...περισσεύματος...λαλεῖ. The thought is much closer to 10.14, as Kamenetzky, 203, notes (and we might add 5.2 also), but the language used there is very different in both M and G. Whatever its origin, this gloss is unlikely to be G*, derived from a Hebrew variant, although it seems to have entered the Greek tradition very early. Equally, it is almost certainly not part of a reading strategy imposed by the G translator himself (as implied by Bolin, *Ecclesiastes*, 67-68), which would be quite out of line with the general character of the translation. The purpose is obscure, but not necessarily polemical (as McNeile): if originally situated at the end of the verse, it may have been intended to attribute the words in 2.16 to a fool, rather than Qohelet; Bolin thinks that it represents Qohelet as immediately repenting of what he has just said. The reading of Syh is even more complicated: it has the addition found in G placed after the statement about vanity (so, at what would be the end of the verse in other versions), but then has (under lemnisk) 'and behold, this too is vanity', generally retroverted as καί ἰδοὺ καί γε τοῦτο ματαιότης.[4] Consequently, it has two almost identical declarations about vanity sandwiching the addition, and perhaps reflecting the different positions of the statement in the Greek tradition. As we would expect, the gloss is not present in the Jewish T-S Misc. 28.74, which tends to affirm its independence from the G tradition.

2.15 had been] The tense is not specified by the Hebrew. Since the declaration is distant from the statements about the wise man and the fool, it probably refers, as e.g. Fox suggests, to Qohelet's acquisition of wisdom. I take it not to be a statement that becoming wise was הבל, however, but that what motivated Qohelet was rooted in הבל; in a sense, then, it is a response to his question.

2.16 no memory of] On the expression -ל זכרון אין and the pointing of the noun, see the note at 1.11. This verse clearly evokes the language and ideas expressed there.

2.16 along with] See the note at 1.11. References by some commentators to the untypical use of עם in a simile (Job 9.26—but see the note 'along with' at 4.15) seem inappropriate here, and it is not clear that any special sense of the preposition need be asserted. Although they are sometimes rendered more smoothly in English as comparisons, indeed, the analogies often cited involve simple conjunction or collocation, not comparison (e.g. 1 Chr 25.8, מבין עם תלמיד, 'the teacher with the pupil', but RSV, 'teacher and pupil alike'; cf. Ps 106.6, and perhaps 88.5, where the verb might rather demand 'among').

---

[4] ܘܗܐ ܐܦ ܗܢܐ ܗܒܠܘܬܐ ܗܝ *wh' 'p hd' sryqwt' hy*. On the use of the lemnisk, see the note 'already has been' at 1.10.

To translate as a comparison can actually be misleading: Qohelet is not taking forgetfulness about the fool for granted, then expressing shock that the wise man is similarly forgotten, but stating simply that neither of them is remembered.

2.16 since, already] The expression בשכבר is only found here, but is clearly a compound כבר-ש-ב. T-S Misc. 28.74 (see the Introduction) seems to have taken the כבר element either as כבד (cf. Exod 8.20; Isa 21.15) or, more likely, as the כביר of, e.g., Isa 28.2, to give a sense 'in the fullness of days'. That element is usually understood, however, as 'already', and most commentators take בש to be the equivalent of באשר, which apparently means 'since' or 'inasmuch as' at 7.2 and 8.4 (cf. Gen 39.9, 23), although it can also be used with other meanings (cf. 3.9, 'in that which'), and commonly, indeed, means 'where' (e.g. Gen 21.17; Judg 5.27; 17.8). S has ܐܟܡܐ ܡܛܠ ܕܗܢܘܢ ܝܘܡܬܐ ܕܡܢ ܟܕܘ ܐܬܝܢ *'yk ywmt' dmn kdw 'tyn* ('likewise for the days that have already come'), which seems to reflect כשכבר (although a variant in one ms., ܕܗܒܘ ܗܘ ܐܝܟ ܝܘܡܬܐ ܐܬܝܢ ܡܢ ܩܕܡ *dkbr h' ywmt' 'tyn*, 'since the days already come before', does not). Against Euringer, Kamenetzky, 236, is probably right to doubt that this could have arisen from the καθότι of G, but Euringer also cites the interesting observation of Ibn Ezra, that בשכבר should be read as though כשכבר—an opinion which S may have shared. Two manuscripts with that reading are, however, noted by de Rossi, and it is not impossible that S actually found this much earlier as a Hebrew variant. בשכבר was reportedly pointed with *metheg* under the ב by ben Naphtali (see Lipschütz).

Hie *eo quod ecce*, 'because look!', is curious. It is unlikely that Jerome read הנה for כבר, and this is probably an aural slip based on the Greek, maybe ἰδέ for ἤδη.

2.16 in the days that have come] Many translations equate הימים הבאים with the English future 'days to come' or 'coming days', and, as we shall see in 11.8, Hebrew can indeed use the idea of 'coming' to express the future. This is not, however, a requirement: an attributive participle derives its tense from the context, and הבאים most often, as it happens, refers to 'those who have/had come' (e.g. Gen 46.8; Ezra 8.35; Jer 36.9; in the difficult Isa 27.6, the subjects are presumably Jacob and Israel, 'when they have come they will'). Since the expression is preceded here by כבר and followed by a verb in the perfect (נשכח—unless we accept Ginsburg's improbable assertion that this should be read as a participle), it would seem hard to deny that the reference here is in some sense to the past. This leads a number of commentators to think in terms of Qohelet putting himself in the future and looking back, so that this becomes a sort of future perfect, but that is unnecessary, and it is manifestly simpler to assume that he is speaking from the present about what has already happened: past things and people are forgotten now, already, so that lessons are not learned from them. In the examples just cited, however, for הבאים used in the past, there seems to be a stative nuance: they refer to people who were somewhere, having previously arrived there. Perhaps, therefore, we should see a similar nuance here, and think of 'the days that have already arrived', or more literally 'days that are come', rather than 'days that came'.

The expression as a whole is temporal, probably the so-called accusative of time (cf. GKC §118 i; J-M §126 i), although it is possible that the prefix ב in בשכבר has temporal force. G, however, apparently takes αἱ ἡμέραι αἱ (> many manuscripts) ἐρχόμεναι with τὰ πάντα, as a subject of ἐπελήσθη: 'the days that were coming—everything was forgotten' (in Greek too the tense of the participle is relative to that of the main verb, which is why the present participle can be used here with the aorist). This is hardly equivalent to an accusative of time, as Vinel suggests, and the awkwardness has provoked emendation to the dative in many manuscripts. S also avoids an expression of time: it takes the days to be past times—everything will be forgotten, just as they are. T, paraphrasing, splits the days into those which will come and those which were in the life of a man.

2.16 even how] An exclamatory איך is used in laments, taunts, and similar contexts at 2 Sam 1.19, 25, 27 (the famous 'How are the mighty fallen!'); Isa 14.4, 12; Jer 9.18 (ET 9.19); 48.39 (twice); 49.25; 50.23 (twice); 51.41; Ezek 26.17; Obad 5, 6; Mic 2.4 (if the איך-clause is not a question); and Zeph 2.15—in Hos 11.8, the context is similar, but the use not exclamatory. The exclamatory use is not wholly confined to such contexts (see Ps 73.19; Prov 5.12), nor is איך the only term used in this way: the related איכה is found in Isa 1.21; Jer 48.17; Lam 1.1; 2.1; 4.1, 2. When used this way, the particles draw attention to an event or situation (almost invariably described using a past tense), and perhaps express regret, albeit often ironically, but they do not function adverbially or adjectivally to modify the sense of the clause that follows them. It is not inconceivable that this last clause of 2.16 should be understood in such terms, and it is often taken that way. On such a reading, Qohelet evokes the language of laments to cry out against the shared fate of the wise and foolish. Stylistically, the interpretation is awkward, however, requiring us virtually to discount the initial conjunction, and perhaps also the tense of the verb.

In terms of sense, it is not clear that the exclamatory uses of איך connote in any way the wrongness of the situations which they describe, so Qohelet might be expressing sadness, but, if that is the usage here, it is unlikely that his words could be read as a protest. For that implication, some other commentators look to the more basic use of איך as an interrogative particle, and interpret this as a rhetorical question; Gordis, for instance, translates, 'Yet how *can* the wise man die just like the fool!' Again, this is possible, but both the exclamatory and rhetorical interpretations turn this last clause into a somewhat disconnected cry of sorrow or complaint. I prefer to understand it as a part of the answer to the question which Qohelet has already posed in the previous verse, and take the use of איך to be similar to the indirect uses found in Ruth 3.18 ('learn *how*'); 2 Kgs 17.28 ('taught them *how*'); Jer 3.19 ('thought *how*'); 36.17 ('tell us *how*'). Everything is forgotten, and so it is forgotten how the wise man dies along with the fool—which is why Qohelet came to invest so much effort in the accumulation of wisdom, ignorant of its ultimate pointlessness. Since this fact is a part of everything, the initial conjunction cannot logically have a simple additive force. I have translated with an emphatic 'even', but the literal implication is probably closer to 'together with' or 'including'.

2.17 I hated] Some manuscripts of G and M (see de Rossi; Ginsburg, *Writings*) follow the verb with a first-person pronoun, as do S and T; אנא ('*n*' = ἐγώ) also appears in Syh, under lemnisk (see the note 'already has been' at 1.10 for the significance). In view of ושנאתי אני in the next verse, we might expect that pronoun here, but it is probably such expectation which has led to its appearance as a variant (so, e.g., *BHQ*), if it is not just a virtual repetition of the preceding -אתי.

2.17 achievement achieved] המעשה שנעשה תחת השמש echoes כל המעשים שנעשו תחת השמש in 1.14, which are likewise pronounced הבל ורעות רוח; a similar expression in 8.17 uses אשר. This may also pick up מעשי שעשו in 2.11. On the general form, see the notes at 1.3, above. The singular is used in 4.3, which itself, perhaps, picks up this verse, and of divine activity in 3.11 (cf. 7.13; 11.5), while the righteous and wicked each have a מעשה in 8.14. Qohelet is clearly not talking about a single event when he uses the singular, but it may not be right to see here 'a collectivity of events', as Fox would have it. The singular is not used as an equivalent to the plural, but rather as a generalisation or abstraction, much as we might speak of 'human achievement', or 'divine action'.

2.17 seemed bad to me] Lit. '(was) bad on me'; cf. G πονηρὸν ἐπ' ἐμέ; Hie *malum super me*. S also renders the Hebrew exactly, as does T (עלי עובדא בישא, 'an evil burden upon me', although it has translated רע once already, to speak of 'evil life'), but a verb is supplied by σ' to give what is undoubtedly the correct sense: κακὸν γάρ μοι ἐφάνη τὸ ἔργον, 'the work appeared bad to me'. We need hardly understand this as Qohelet feeling 'an evil pressure' upon himself (as Ginsburg). The expression רע על is not itself found elsewhere in biblical Hebrew, but טוב על appears in 1 Chr 13.2; Esth 1.19; 3.9. Similar expressions are common in Aramaic (cf. Dan 4.24; 6.15), and found also in later Hebrew. Although the idiom is probably late, therefore, it is worth noting that the expression here might also be understood in terms of the usage found at Jer 8.18. See J-M §133 f. On Qohelet's use of רע in such contexts, see the note at 1.13, above: he is expressing the inadequacy or uselessness of achievement, not declaring it evil.

2.17 wishing for the wind] See the corresponding note at 1.14. T-S Misc. 28.74 reads κακότηταν, 'badness', for רעות, suggesting that it connects it with רעה, and uses the same translation for רעיון in 2.22.

2.18-23

(2.18) And I hated all my business, at which I had been the one working under the sun, that I shall leave it behind for the person who will be after me—(2.19) and who knows whether he will be wise or obtuse, yet he will have the rights over all my business, for which I have worked and for which I have been wise under the sun. This too is an illusion. (2.20) So I turned away, letting go of my concern with all the business at which I had worked under the sun. (2.21) For there may be a person whose work has been with wisdom and with knowledge and with aptitude, but it is going to be to a person who has not worked on it that he will give it, to be what is his. This too is an illusion, and utterly bad. (2.22) What is there for the person in any of his business, and in the worrying of his heart about that at which he is the one doing the work under the sun? (2.23) For through each of his days, pains and exasperation have been his job; at night, too, his heart has not relaxed. This too, it is an illusion.

Commentary

There is no suggestion that Qohelet's successor will necessarily be either capable or useless, and although Brown, for instance, speaks of Qohelet 'leaving the fruits and legacies of his labors for successive generations to waste and abuse', that concern is nowhere voiced here. The matter can be complicated by the Solomonic identification: although Jerome notes simply that Rehoboam was not like his father, and illustrates that we can never know the qualities of those that follow us (with apparent reference to the parable in Luke 12.16-21), Crenshaw claims that Qohelet is possibly, but not necessarily, alluding to Rehoboam, 'whose folly was the subject of ridicule in the official story that circulated in the southern kingdom'. The Targum makes a similar point rather differently, noting that Solomon is going to bequeath his kingdom to Rehoboam, but that it will end up in the hands of Jeroboam, so that we have no control even over who our successors will be. Even without the Solomonic complication, however, Bartholomew draws on v. 21 to claim that '...since this person has not worked for what he receives, he may be thoroughly foolish in how he handles his inheritance'—taking that to be the implication of his not having worked for it, and Qohelet's broader point again to be that we have no control over our successors.

Commonplace though they are, however, such interpretations read into the text something that is not there, and that is alien to Qohelet's perspective: he shows no interest at all in the fate of his estate itself (beyond the fact that it will no longer be his), and no desire to be able to nominate a suitable successor. Since he is going to be dead anyway, none of that is relevant to him (cf. 9.6), and neither the possible ruin of what he has created nor his lack of control over it is the issue at hand. The point is rather that his property will pass to somebody else *regardless* of their qualities (2.19) and of whether they have made any contribution to it (2.21). What outrages Qohelet is that his own hard work will be for the benefit of somebody else, and he does not care whether they are able or not. All this is treated, essentially, as an injustice, which opens a path to the claims of 2.24-26, that what we have results from divine dispensation rather than from our own inherent qualities. If people can possess property without working for it, after all, is there any value in work? If even idiots can do so, moreover, can there really be any direct connection between personal and financial worth? In the course of these verses, however, Qohelet will move from his own reaction to the issue of succession in particular, through to the further problem that, in relation to their work, different people find themselves in different circumstances.

2.18] Qohelet's resentment spills over into what had been flagged by 2.12 as the second topic he was planning to review. He probably does not declare, however, simply that he hates *his business* because it is going to pass to another, so much as that he hates *the fact* that he will leave it to that other. The Hebrew also emphasizes already here that he, Qohelet, was the one who had done all the work to establish it, and so sets up the point that will be drawn out in the next verse, that whoever acquires it will be enjoying the fruits of *his* labour, not their own. His choice of words itself betrays his attitude: Qohelet is not going to 'bequeath' his estate but will be forced to abandon it, and, as elsewhere, he shows no interest in the idea that humans might be motivated by a desire to improve things for the next generation. Tamez misses the point, however, when she associates this directly with expropriation of property: the deprivation that Qohelet foresees is simply the inevitable consequence of his own mortality.

2.19] The use of 'wise or obtuse' indicates the continuing connection between this and the preceding discussion of wisdom. While the wise man and the fool will always come to the same eventual end, matters are a little more differentiated here: not every wise man or every fool will inherit property. There is a similar general point, however, in that their wisdom or folly will make no difference. Someone of no ability can find themselves in the same position as Qohelet, without having put in the years of working wisely. 'Who knows' is used in 3.21 and 6.12 also, with a similar usage in 8.1. It is a conventional, and quite common expression—a rhetorical question that is usually equivalent to 'nobody knows'. When, however, Qohelet declares at the end of the verse that 'this too is an illusion' (vapour) he is probably talking not about this uncertainty, but in some sense about the situation that will arise: his property is going to pass to somebody else even though he had worked for it himself. As in the next verse, the 'vapour' might lie in the injustice of that situation, but I think (given what is said in the next verse) that Qohelet is applying it more directly to his work, the whole point of which is called into question by what will happen.

2.20] Despite Qohelet's apparent anger, the Hebrew here probably does not mean that he gave himself up to despair, although it is often translated that way, or that he succumbed to disillusionment. The implication is rather that he made the decision no longer to care about his business and, in effect, walked away from it emotionally—perhaps having just characterized his efforts as 'vapour'. We might say, indeed, that this verse marks the end of Qohelet's experiment, and that having reviewed all his achievements negatively, he simply moves on. Its position, however, makes it difficult to see this simply in terms of tying up loose ends: it follows a statement about succession in 2.19, but is then apparently explained by another such statement in v. 21. There are, to be sure, slight differences between those other verses in terms of the points that they make, but Qohelet's abandonment of his business seems explicitly to be connected to the statements that surround it. The most obvious reason for his suddenly ceasing to care, therefore, is that the ability of others to acquire the same as him without needing any wisdom of their own makes caring seem pointless. This will be hammered home in the next verse by his claim that all the effort put into a business may prove simply to be for the benefit of someone who makes no effort of their own. Of course, we might again question the strict logic of Qohelet's position, which is apparently that the unearned good fortune of the undeserving somehow renders meaningless everything that the deserving have earned for themselves. Again, though, this is a narrative account of Qohelet's changing perspective, not an exercise in reasoning, so we should not, perhaps, pick at it too finely.

2.21] We have already encountered Qohelet's use of hypothetical individuals and situations in 1.10, and he will go on to use them again, most clearly in 4.8; 5.12-16; 6.2-6; 7.15; 8.14. One reason for the use of this device here is presumably that Qohelet's point would not stand as a general statement: whatever the precise context that we are supposed to envisage for Qohelet himself, most heirs in the ancient world probably would, in fact, have worked alongside their parents (on farms, or in trades and businesses), perhaps for long periods before taking control themselves. Qohelet cannot claim, therefore, that it would be normal for someone's business to pass to somebody that had done no work for it. If we read 2.22-23 as suggested below, however, then Qohelet is using this situation not to make a general point about humanity, but, on the contrary, as a way to move from the issues of succession that might affect anybody through to questions that arise from the difference between human experiences. Those verses will add the information that our hypothetical person has found nothing but pain in their work, and so this individual not only surrenders their achievements to another who has done no work for it, but has also in the meantime derived no pleasure from it. Through these verses, therefore, Qohelet sets up the case of one person whose work has provided them with no discernible benefit, and in v. 24 he will turn to their counterpart, who 'eats and drinks' and finds pleasure in their work. The closing verses of the chapter will have Qohelet dismiss conventional explanations for the different circumstances of each, and lead him to his next theme.

If all that were the only purpose of v. 21, however, then it is hard to see why Qohelet should lay so much stress here on the difference between the person who has worked hard, and their successor who has made no contribution. This point is somewhat different from his previous concerns about the unknown quality of heirs, but his purpose may be in part to reinforce earlier conclusions. The man here has notably worked with wisdom, knowledge and some further quality that I have rendered 'aptitude' (the sense of the Hebrew is uncertain): these, of course, are going to prove of no benefit to the man himself. The succession to his estate, furthermore, illustrates a disconnection between what one has done and what one has, that is analogous to Qohelet's previous point that possessions can be achieved regardless of one's qualities. The most likely reason for the particular details supplied in this verse, however, is that they again foreshadow what is to come—looking ahead this time to v. 26, where Qohelet addresses the idea that someone may be set up by God to work for the benefit of somebody else.

2.22-23] Since 'the person' could readily mean 'a person', these verses are very commonly read as a general question about humanity, comparable to 1.3. So, for instance, the RSV translates 2.22 as 'What has a man from all the toil and strain with which he toils beneath the sun?' If we read them in that way, however, then shortly after talking in 2.10 about the pleasure he found in his own work, and just before talking in 2.24 about another who finds the same, Qohelet would seem to be suggesting in 2.23 that work, on the contrary, is a source of endless pain and exasperation for *all* humans. No less importantly, a reprise of his general question has no obvious place here: the verses that follow offer no direct response, and it would cut them off from the previous discussion. It is better, therefore, and certainly more natural, to see 'the person' as the same person that Qohelet has introduced in the preceding 2.21, and v. 22 accordingly as a rhetorical question about that person: if all their work has been for the benefit of another, what good is for them in any of that work? Picking up a point about worry in v. 22, the following v. 23 then supplies the additional information that the person has found nothing but stress and anxiety in their labours, and so seals off any possibility that they might have gained some benefit from enjoying it. In a transition from the theme of succession through to the points that he is going to make about divine dispensation, Qohelet uses his hypothetical situation as a way to define the human for whom it may be said definitively that work has provided no benefit.

Notes

2.18 business] See the note at 2.11, above.

2.18 at which I had been the one working] Lit. 'which I (was) working'. This second occurrence of עמל has probably been read correctly as a participle by G μοχθῶ; cf. α', θ' κοπιῶ (a reading which has found its way into some early manuscripts of G); Hie *laboro*. Some witnesses to G have an aorist, through assimilation to the more common form in 2.11, 19, 20; similarly V *laboraui*; S ܡܠܬ *'mlt*; T דטרחית. Like a number of other verbs, עמל displays features associated with both stative and non-stative verbs (cf. J-M §41 b), and the M pointing עָמֵל here (cf. 2.22; 3.9; 4.8; 9.9) is probably that of the verbal adjective, which comes to function as a participle for such verbs (cf. J-M §41 c; Isaksson, *Studies*, 135-36; Whitley speaks of the 'stative participial' form). In 2.21-22 and 4.8, as here, a contrast is drawn between the person doing the work and the person who will benefit from it; there is also an emphasis on the person in 9.9 (Isaksson, *Studies*, 136). The fact that this construction can shift the emphasis away from the action and on to the actor, rather than any different nuance of tense or duration, is probably the reason for its use here instead of שעמלתי. I have translated accordingly.

2.18 that I shall leave it behind] None of the versions (except perhaps V, which is paraphrasing here) takes -ש to be a simple relative referring back to עמלתי: cf. G ὅτι ἀφίω; Hie *quia dimitto*; S ܡܛܠ ܕܫܒܩ *mṭl dšbq*; T בגין דאשבקיניה. Although Ecclesiastes does not use -ש elsewhere to express cause (and it does not clearly have that sense in Ct 1.6), אשר may be taken that way in 4.9 and 8.15, and this, along with the absence of a conjunction before the -ש, is probably the basis of the versions' understanding, which most subsequent commentators have followed. The sentence has been examined in considerable detail, however, by Ellermeier, *Qohelet I.1*, 277-83, who concludes that such a sense is unacceptable, and points out that cause is indicated using כי in the previous verse. Like some earlier commentators, he takes the clause which begins with שאניחנו as the object of שנאתי, so that the basic structure is 'I hated (the thought) that I was going to leave it'; את...השמש is then the object of שאניחנו, placed in anticipation.

This has a certain elegance as a solution (and is praised in Schoors, *The Preacher* I, 215-16); Ellermeier translates: 'Verhaßt ward mir der Gedanke, daß ich meinen ganzen mühsamen Gewinn...dem Menschen lassen muß, der nach mir kommt' (p. 281): 'The thought was hateful to me that I must leave all my hard-won profit...to the person who comes after me'. If usage in the previous verse is an argument against reading -ש as causal, however, then it is fair to point out also that את indicates the direct object of שנאתי in that verse, making it a fair presumption that it should do so in this verse also. If it actually marks instead the object of שאניחנו, indeed, left hanging before the verb that governs it, then the reader is misled until halfway through the verse, for no very obvious reason. Although a causal sense cannot really be excluded, I suspect that, insofar as there is any stylistic device employed here, it actually lies in the parataxis which results from the absence of a conjunction. Qohelet begins by expressing his resentment of his work, just as he previously expressed his resentment of life, but adds a second, sharper source of resentment. He does this asyndetically, so that the new clause specifies the first, rather than standing in parallel with it: 'I hated my business, the fact that I'm going to leave it...', not 'I hated my business along with the fact that I'm going to leave it...'.

שאניחנו itself is from נוח, which has two distinct forms of the hiph'il, with separate senses (cf. GKC §72 ee; JM §80 p). The form used here has quite a wide range of meanings to do with placing or leaving. It probably does not, however, mean 'bequeath': Ps 17.14, which is sometimes cited for that sense, is certainly connected with inheritance, but is speaking very generally about an abundance sufficient for one generation to leave some over for the next; another psalm (119.121) demonstrates that the sense of the verb can extend to 'abandon' in a much more negative way, as the righteous man pleads not to be left to his oppressors. Qohelet himself uses the verb of 'abandoning' one's place in 10.4, and, in general, the parallels suggest that Qohelet is not actively 'giving' his עמל to his successor, so much as leaving it behind for him to pick up. On the tense of the verbs which render שאניחנו in G and S, see the next note.

2.18 the person who will be after me] Although the verb is different, this is clearly evocative of 2.12. G, interestingly, rendered שאניחנו with ἀφίω and now uses τῷ γινομένῳ (which is apparently also the reading of θ') for שיהיה; these are both present tense, even though G used a future for שיבוא in 2.12 and for שיהיה in 1.9; 8.7. At 3.22 an aorist subjunctive is used with ἄν or ἐάν for שיהיה, but we meet a similar oddity at 10.14, when the aorist participle τὸ γενόμενον is found. Here and at 10.14, some witnesses substitute future forms, but these are probably secondary assimilations to the Hebrew or to the context (although Syh here notably seems to be translating the present; cf. Marshall). The issue is further complicated by the fact that the present participle γινομένος seems elsewhere to be used in G only to render the niph'al of עשה (1.13; 4.1; 8.11), although in 2.22, γίνεται is used for היה. It is possible that G has read a form other than imperfect for either שאניחנו or שיהיה, and adapted its rendering of the other accordingly, but more likely that its translation here reflects an interpretative understanding, according to which Qohelet is actually at the point of these actions, not looking to the distant future—in other words, he is either at the end of his life or, since he is going to give up on his business in 2.20, simply preparing to pass it on immediately. This might also explain the rendering of וישלט by another present, ἐξουσιάζεται, in the next verse.[1]

---

[1] Yi, 153-54, doubts that γινομένῳ is original, preferring the future γενησόμενῳ that is quite widely attested in the textual tradition. It is not difficult to see how the future might have arisen secondarily, however, and the present is the *lectio difficilior* here. He concedes that 'If the present is original, the Translator

S ܟܠܗܘܢ ... ܐܘ ܕܒܬܪܗ *dšbq 'n'...dhw'* probably follows the tense of G. The personal pronoun is translational, although ἐγώ is found here in a few Greek witnesses. In the closing words, ܒܬܪܝ ܡܢ *mn btry*, the ܡܢ *mn* is probably also an adaptation to Syriac usage; it is lacking in many manuscripts, and Lane, 'Lilies', 482, apparently regards it as secondary. Kamenetzky, 198, however, noting its use at 3.22 and elsewhere, regards it as part of the original translation, probably correctly.

Rashbam reads a variant אחריו in his text—perhaps the result of dittography from the next word; see Japhet and Salters, *Commentary*, 111 n. 23.

2.19 who knows] This conventional expression of uncertainty is used also in Ecclesiastes at 3.21 and 6.12; in 8.1, the object is a nominal expression, not a clause (cf. Ps 90.11; Prov 24.22). Elsewhere, see 2 Sam 12.22; Esth 4.14; Joel 2.14; Jonah 3.9. The implication here, of course, is that 'nobody knows', although Crenshaw (in 'The Expression *mî yôdēaʿ*') has argued that outside Ecclesiastes (and Prov 24.22), the expression is used rather differently, 'leaving the door open', as it were, and expressing hope for change. He also observes similar usages ('variants of the expression') at 8.4, 7, 12; 9.1, 5; 11.5, 6.

BHQ notes the reading ܢܕܥ *ndʿ* in S (over against ܝܕܥ *ydʿ* in the other occurrences of the expression); this is probably a graphic error (ܝܕܥ *ydʿ* is well represented as a variant), and does not attest to an imperfect in the source-text. V *quem ignoro*, '(of) whom I do not know', is a paraphrase; the version renders the expression differently at each use in Ecclesiastes.

2.19 whether he will be wise or obtuse] The construction with the interrogative ה and או is used also in the indirect question at 11.6 (where a third option is introduced by אם). Disjunctive (either/or) questions more commonly use אם(ו)...ה (e.g. Gen 24.21), and when או is used, it is generally before -מ (GKC §150 g suggests that this is for euphonic reasons), but note Judg 18.19. Since the construction with או is more common in mishnaic Hebrew, Schoors, *The Preacher* I, 209, suspects that this might be a late feature.

This is the first place where Ecclesiastes uses סָכָל, which is found also in 7.17; 10.3 (twice); probably 10.6 (see the note there); and 10.14. It is used substantively in the first occurrence in 10.3 and in 10.6 (if that is the reading), but is certainly an adjective in the only occurrences outside Ecclesiastes, at Jer 4.22; 5.21. It does not appear in Proverbs, and סכל is not conventionally

---

may have understood the situation not as future but as contemporary time and viewed the action as on-going'. For the ἐξουσιάζεται of the next verse, however, Yi, 162, prefers a 'futuristic present': 'The future event is described as though it were already present.... By utilizing the present indicative the Translator depicted the future scene as an on-going process with vividness.' Curiously, Yi does not note that the future tense is attested widely in the tradition for this verb as well, or attempt to make a case that it was original. It is likely, of course, that the same considerations motivated the translator in both places.

opposed to חכם, like כסיל. G, nevertheless, generally uses ἄφρων / ἀφροσύνη for סכל and סכלות as for כסיל and כסל (but see the notes at 7.17 and 7.25), treating them effectively as synonyms; so, apparently does σ', with ἀνόητος. The sense is presumably close to that of סכלות, on which see the note at 1.17.

2.19 he will have the rights] שלט, from the Arabic cognate of which the word 'sultan' is derived, is used also in 5.18; 6.2; and 8.9 (only the last is in the qal, as here). Outside Ecclesiastes, it is found in biblical Hebrew only at Neh 5.15; Esth 9.1 (twice); Ps 119.133, but it appears seven times in the Aramaic portion of Daniel (2.38, 39, 48; 3.27; 5.7, 16; 6.25), and elsewhere in Aramaic. The related noun שלטון is found at 8.4, 8 and Sir 4.7, and שליט at 7.19; 8.8; 10.5; it also appears at Gen 42.6, where it is widely considered to be a later gloss (cf. *HALOT*; the opinion is influenced by the assumption of a late date for the word, however, so cannot be used to exclude that usage from discussions of date without some risk of circular argument). Note also שלטה in Ezek 16.30. Despite Dahood's suggestion that the origin might be more ancient ('Canaanite-Phoenician', 205), these terms have almost certainly entered Hebrew from Aramaic, and probably at quite a late date.[2]

A particular use of שליט in Aramaic has attracted special attention amongst recent commentators: in legal documents, שליט ב is used to express general legal rights over someone or something. This is probably related to the use of the cognate verb in Akkadian texts from the neo-Assyrian and neo-Babylonian periods, where it refers more particularly to creditors' rights, and the development of the clause is studied in detail by Gropp, '*šallīṭ* Clause'. One of Gropp's conclusions (34), is that the term comes to be replaced by רשי after the Persian period, when the sense of שליט came to be restricted to the sphere of politics. This is an important datum for Seow, who notes (in 'Linguistic Evidence', 654) the use of שלט in Ecclesiastes to refer to control of assets, links this to the Aramaic legal usage, and infers that Ecclesiastes cannot, therefore, have been written later than the Persian period. Fox, who favours a Hellenistic dating, responds that the legal sense is only discernible here in 2.19, and that the less specific usage elsewhere in the book supports, if anything, a later date. Such arguments embrace a questionable assumption that meanings stop and start rather abruptly; since the more general sense of the word was certainly in use before Hellenistic times, and since Rudman, 'Note', has demonstrated that the technical use of שליט in fact persists long after the Persian period,

---

[2] See esp. Wagner, *Aramaismen*, nos. 306-309; Hurvitz, *Concise Lexicon*, 228-30. Also, e.g., Salters, 'Qoh 6$_2$', 285. As ever, we cannot exclude the possibility that the late attestations belie much earlier usage, and Fredericks, *Qoheleth's Language*, 239, is keen to point out the use of the root in Neo-Assyrian, which might have led to its use in Hebrew during the periods of Assyrian or Babylonian domination. That is very speculative, however, and the evidence suggests, at least, that it was not common in Hebrew until a later period.

Qohelet's apparent use of it, here at least, cannot be used to date Ecclesiastes exclusively to either the Persian or the Hellenistic period.

G renders the verb ἐξουσιάζεται, with a present tense,[3] although the preceding יהיה has been translated with the future ἔσται; this is curious, even if G has read the verb with waw-conversive, and is not really comparable to the case which Gentry cites in 7.7. Against McNeile, 140, it probably does not reflect a variant source-text, and it should probably be considered in the light of the forms used in the last verse: see the note on 'the person who will be after me' there. α' does have the future, reading κυριεύσει (not ἔσται κύριος; cf. Marshall).

2.19 over] Lit. 'in'. G ἐξουσιάζεται is construed with a following ἐν, as at 8.9, although we would expect a simple genitive or ἐπί, and Vinel is probably right to see a calque on the Hebrew. On the tense of the Greek verb, see the note on 'the person who will be after me' at 2.18.

2.19 for which I have...wise] A number of commentators, including Longman, see a hendiadys here, so that this means 'I toiled wisely'. In view of the fact that Qohelet has just separately considered his עמל and his חכמה, it seems better, however, to retain a distinction between the two here.

Many manuscripts of G omit the second ᾧ in ᾧ ἐμόχθησα καὶ ᾧ ἐσοφισάμην ('at which I laboured and at which I was wise'); this is probably a stylistic improvement, but the word may have been absent in α' and θ' also (cf. Gentry, 'Propaedeutic', 150-51). Some manuscripts of S introduce a first-person pronoun, but this is, again, secondary. An equivalent to ושחכמתי is lacking altogether in the Greek T-S Misc. 28.74, probably as the result simply of an error.

2.19 this too] S has ܘܐܦ *w'p*, 'and also', although some manuscripts omit the conjunction, and Hie *sed et hoc*, 'but this too', might also suggest וגם instead of M גם here, but it is impossible to tell whether G καί γε reflects גם or וגם, and T ף דין הבלו או(י)למימר ותבית, 'and I again said "this also is vapour"', has probably read just גם. The readings with a conjunction may reflect assimilation to the form of the expression found at, e.g., 5.15; 7.6.

2.20 I turned away] In vv. 11-12, Qohelet used פניתי, 'turning his face' towards his achievements, then wisdom etc. Here he uses סבותי, as later in 7.25, where he gives up one approach to try another. The verb suggests turning around, rather than toward, so probably suggests that he is turning away from what he was looking at before, an idea that V picks up with *unde cessaui*, 'and I left off'.

G ἐπέστρεψα and S ܘܗܦܟܬ *whpkt* are the verbs used by each to render ושבתי in 4.1, 7; 9.11, and they both use different terms for סבותי at 7.25 (ἐκύκλωσα and ܐܬܟܪܟܬ *'tkrkt*); see Kamenetzky, 213, and Schoors, 'Peshitta', 354,

---

[3] Gentry, 'Relationship', 71-72. The future is found in a number of manuscripts, and is taken as G* by Klostermann, *De libri Coheleth*, 58, but this probably repree sents assimilation to the Hebrew.

and note also Hie *conuersus sum*, 'I turned round', here and 4.7, with *uerti*, 'turned', at 4.1 and 9.11, *circuiui*, 'went around', at 7.25. Although G may have influenced S and Hie, there is a strong possibility that this reflects the existence of an early Hebrew variant ושבתי. Note the defective וסבתי attested (in Hebrew) by T-S Misc. 28.74. Kennicott lists many other instances of this spelling, which would have facilitated a change from ושבתי to וסבותי, or *vice versa*, especially if the ש were read as *śin*, not *šin*.

2.20 letting go of my concern with all the business] יאש is generally used in the niphʻal, where it is used of giving up or abandoning an effort (1 Sam 27.1; Job 6.26; Isa 57.10; Jer 2.25; 18.12). In later Hebrew, the verb is found with direct objects, used of accepting that something is lost (usually possessions, but at *m. ʾAbot* 1.7, the idea of divine justice!). Of the other usage, Whitley declares that it 'hardly represents the force of the term in Koheleth', but that remark demonstrates, more than it validates, the gulf between the attested meanings and the more general sense of despair and disillusionment which most commentators find here: insofar as יאש refers to 'despair' at all, it is in the very restricted sense 'despair of achieving something', and it does not describe emotional turmoil, as such.[4] We have the piʻel here, but despite the interpretation offered in *HALOT*, there are no grounds for taking the verb in this stem to be causative, and Qohelet is probably not causing his heart to do something. As Whitley also notes, the rabbinic usage embraces the related hithpaʻel form, and the noun יאוש, used of accepting loss (see Jastrow, *Dictionary*), seems to be derived from the piʻel itself. I take the object of the verb to be the expression לבי על כל העמל, where לב על is not a reference to the heart with which Qohelet often converses, but is an idiom connoting the interest or attachment which Qohelet feels toward his עמל. There are similar uses at 2 Sam 14.1; Ezra 6.22; Jer 22.17; Mal 3.24 (twice).

If לב is taken alone, the construction here is difficult, and this is reflected in the versional evidence. Since ἀποτάξασθαι usually takes the dative, Rahlfs' reading ἀποτάξασθαι τῇ καρδίᾳ μου ἐπὶ παντὶ τῷ μόχθῳ would seem to indicate that G thought Qohelet was renouncing his heart (it is unlikely to mean 'renounce *in* my heart', as Vinel suggests). Many manuscripts, however, attest what is the more probably original reading τὴν καρδίαν: G seems to have intended an accusative of specification or somesuch ('renounce with my heart'); this was mistaken secondarily for the object, and converted to the more grammatically correct dative. A desire to improve the Greek may also have driven the replacement of the subsequent ἐπὶ by ἐν in many

---

[4] It is an irony that Bolin (in *Ecclesiastes*, 85) understands a shift from 'despair' to 'renounce' in G to be an instance of the translation toning down the original Hebrew: 'despair' is not the natural sense of the Hebrew, and might be considered a prime example of scholarly eisegesis. It is presumably based on an understanding that Qohelet must find something inherently and distressingly futile or wrong in his worldly business.

manuscripts, if that has not just been influenced by the expression ἐν παντὶ μόχθῳ μου in the previous verse—which has almost certainly given rise to the variant addition of μου, also found in many witnesses (cf. Hie *in omni labore meo*); this is likely to have happened independently in the single Hebrew source noted by de Rossi that has על כל עמלי here.

There are some textual difficulties in S as well, where many manuscripts replace ܐܡܠܒܫ *lmpsw*, 'give permission', with ܕܐܫܝܫ *d'šyš*, 'comfort', which Lane, 'Lilies', 489, describes as 'exactly the wrong sense', and considers to have originated in a perceived resemblance between ܫܝܫ *šyš* and the Hebrew יאש. Most of the same manuscripts have a following ܝܬ (*yt* = את); Kamenetzky, 204-206, notes that elsewhere the use of this particle corresponds closely to the rendering of את by σύν in G, and may depend upon it, but that cannot be the case here. Since it is almost certainly secondary, both words of the variant ܕܐܫܝܫ ܝܬ *d'šyš yt* point, therefore, to a revision based on the Hebrew. This rendering appears as a gloss in 2.2 also; see the note there. T corresponds closely to M (although there is an alternative version attested, which enlarges upon the wisdom of Qohelet's heart).

2.20 at which I had worked] As *BHS* notes, many manuscripts add ושחכמתי (cf. de Rossi, Ginsburg, *Writings*), which is reflected also in both versions of T, but not in G, S, Hie, V. It is a secondary reminiscence of the previous verse.

2.21 For] The sequence of sentences beginning with כי here in vv. 21-23 is striking. Michel, *Untersuchungen*, 205-207, is keen to define each, except perhaps the first here, as 'deictic' (others prefer the less confusing term 'asseverative' for this usage), so that Qohelet is making a progressive series of points in each verse, rather than giving a series of reasons. This is in part an interpretative and translational matter, but the default implication of כי in such positions is causative/explicative, and there are no compelling reasons to exclude that meaning here, nor any obvious clues to readers that they should not adopt it.

2.21 there may be a person] יש is used here as it was at 1.10, to posit a hypothetical situation (see also 4.8; 6.11 and perhaps 7.15). Whether this can be characterized as an asydnetic conditional clause (so, e.g., Schoors, *The Preacher* I, 213) seems more questionable: the situation outlined is something which *may* happen, not something which necessarily *will* happen if someone has worked in this way.

2.21 whose work] Ben Naphtali is reported to have pointed שעמלו with *metheg* under the ש (see Lipschütz).

For G here, Rahlfs reads ἄνθρωπος οὗ μόχθος αὐτοῦ, 'a person whose labour', apparently on the basis of Hie *homo cui labor*. This reading is attested in no Greek manuscripts, although it does enjoy support in Coptic, and the proper reading should be with ὅ τι, not οὗ according to Gentry, 'Propaedeutic', 169. Such a way of dealing with -ש is attested in 6.3 also, but the syntax of that verse is very different, and the rendering is in conjunction with a different vocalization of the text. If we read ὅ τι here, then G apparently does not read the relative as referring to the man, but instead understands: 'there is a man: that which is his work…'—a rendering that would be comprehensible if the work were then picked up as the object of 'give' in the second part of the verse, but the Greek is problematic there also (see below). If we try to read the Greek rather as the single word ὅτι, then the clause becomes a simple parallel to the first, as though there were a second כי in the Hebrew: 'For there is a man, for his work…'. It is very difficult, however, to see why the translator should have taken the Hebrew in either way, and he does not struggle with the similar construction ארץ שמלכך in 10.16 and 10.17, which is rendered, as one would expect, using a relative pronoun in the genitive: ἧς ὁ βασιλεύς σου. It is also difficult to identify any potential variant in the Hebrew that might lie behind such Greek, unless כי was indeed repeated by the source-text in place of -ש, and it is easier to explain the origin of any error in terms of the Greek rather than the Hebrew. We may reasonably suspect, therefore, that Rahlfs' reading does in fact represent the original translation, even if that reading has been extinguished from the manuscript tradition following an early confusion between οτ and οτι.

2.21 with] Although this is just a matter of labelling, it is not clear why Seow wants to understand the prepositions here as *beth pretii*; the use is surely instrumental, as most commentators assume. It is interesting to observe, though, that עמל can take an indirect object with -ב, as at Jonah 4.10, and this appears to be the usage in עמל בו, later in the verse. There is a potential ambiguity here, therefore: the person could be working 'at' or 'on' wisdom etc., and Ewald actually takes that to be the intended sense. TS Misc. 28.74 has υπο σοφιας here, even though it uses ἐν with the other nouns, and it is possible that the translator is trying to forestall such a reading.

2.21 aptitude] The noun כשרון is only found in Ecclesiastes, and it is not clear precisely (or, truth be told, even very broadly) what it means. Words from the root כשר are used in later Hebrew principally to indicate suitability or fitness (often ritual legitimacy, hence 'kosher'), although the sense of 'being pleasing', found at Esth 8.5, also persists. TS Misc. 28.74 uses ἐν εὐθυοτητᾱν here, which probably picks up this idea of suitability (cf. Lk 9.62 εὔθετος, 'suitable', and the discussion of that term in MM). Some usage suggests, however, that there could be a connotation of vigour (as sometimes in Syriac ܟܫܪ *kšr*, ܟܘܫܪܐ *kwšr'*, etc.), and in Sir 13.4 השכר is used in contrast with תכרע. This may well be the sense of the verb when it is used by Qohelet at 11.6 (on the use in the obscure 10.10, see the note there), and an understanding in those terms probably explains why G uses ἀνδρεία, lit. 'manliness', for the noun כשרון here and on its other occurrences in 4.4 and 5.10, and for the verb at 10.10. σ' similarly uses γοργότης, 'vigour' or 'vehemence', here and at 4.4 (cf. γοργευσάμενος at 10.10) and ἀνδραγάθημα at 5.10 (see the note there on the sense of that word). Hie *uirtus* (2.21; 4.4) and *fortitudo* (5.10; 10.10) lie in the same sphere.

Although preferred by some commentators, the connotation of 'success' or 'prosperity' (as opposed to 'prospering') is less firmly established: בכושרות in Ps 68.7 seems to be something positive, but its precise sense is uncertain, as is its relationship with כשר, and little else points this way, so translations in these terms are based largely on the usage in Ecclesiastes itself. That usage, however, actually points in the direction of כשרון being something required for achievement, not something achieved as a result of work: here it is set alongside the mental qualities of wisdom and knowledge, applied to work, and in 4.4 it is aligned with an emotion; in 5.10, 'looking on' is the only כשרון for the owner as others enjoy his prosperity. These suggest that כשרון is something in the mind, not the pocket. 'Skill' is often suggested, but it is not clear what sort of skill might be meant here which is not covered by חכמה or דעת, and the sense seems inappropriate for the other occurrences. Given both the attested meanings of כשר, and the renderings by the versions, I think the reference is more probably to attitude, motivation, or aptitude, than to ability or achievement: such a meaning seems appropriate to 4.4, in particular, but also fits comfortably here. In 5.10, a slightly different nuance seems required, but the basic sense seems the same.

2.21 it is going to be to a person] Lit. 'and to a person who has not worked'. I have tried to reproduce the emphasis which the Hebrew achieves by placing the clause in anticipation before יתננו.

For לאדם, G does not render the preposition: see the following notes.

2.21 who has not worked] Although Rahlfs has ἄνθρωπος ὅς, most witnesses to G have ἄνθρωπος ᾧ, and Gentry prefers that reading (cf. 'Propaedeutic', 169-70, where he argues also that ᾧ is probably the reading of θ' too). It is regarded as an error, however, by, e.g., Euringer and McNeile, 157. Gordis, conversely, thinks that ἄνθρωπος should be dative also, although the dative is found in no witnesses.⁵ If G is following its source-text closely as usual, then perhaps it has read a corrupt ואדם שלו לא where M has ולאדם שלא (*via* an earlier שלוא?). If, on the other hand, it has used the nominative ἄνθρωπος deliberately, to stand more directly in parallel with the previous ἄνθρωπος, then the dative has probably to be understood as a result of attraction to the subsequent αὐτῷ; on the face of it, though, the Greek literally means 'and a person to/for whom he did not work in it, he will give to him his portion', with the original person as the subject of both verbs. Hie, S, T support M.

For the first verb, some manuscripts of G have the first-person ἐμόχθησα, an error caused by the occurrence in the previous verse. It is harder to explain the rendering by α' in the present tense (since that is what the pointing of ܠܐ *lʾ* as a participle in the Syh note would usually imply); Gentry, 'Relationship',

---

⁵ Klostermann, *De libri Coheleth*, 58, would read ἀνθρώπῳ ὅς, which is grammatically simpler; there is no manuscript support, however, for ἀνθρώπῳ.

72, wonders whether he vocalized עמל as the verbal adjective/stative participle (on which, see the note at 2.18, above). The context would seem to demand a past tense, as M, G.

2.21 he will give it] Isaksson, *Studies*, 119-20, speaks of the verb having 'a nuance of compulsion' (cf. also Longman), but, apart from that being an attempt to present exegesis as grammar, it misses the point. Qohelet is not claiming that the man himself may even resent passing on what he has achieved: the problem lies in Qohelet's own perception that there is something wrong.

G is again awkward, but it usefully highlights a syntactical problem in the construction. The suffix pronoun on יתננו in M is usually taken to refer to the עמל which is given (so, 'he will give it'), but G renders δώσει αὐτῷ, 'he will give to him', apparently connecting it with the person (cf. also S ܝܗܒ ܠܗ *yhb lh*; it is not clear whether Hie *illi* reflects בה or the suffix pronoun); the variant δώσει αὐτόν, 'he will give it', is secondary, and is attested in Syh as the reading of the Three (perhaps also of Origen: see Marshall). G* αὐτῷ is probably driven by a perception that the verb already has a direct object in חלקו, and, in fact, G and S are not alone in this perception: as Schoors, *The Preacher* I, 91, notes, Ibn Ezra took the suffix to be datival (just as we might say 'give him it' in colloquial English), and Dahood, 'Qoheleth and Northwest Semitic Philology', 352-53, defended such a reading with strong analogies. That the suffix could play this role seems clear: J-M §125 ba cites Judg 1.15 = Josh 15.19; Isa 27.4; Jer 9.1 (although the last two involve the same idiom מי יתנני). Such instances are rare, however, and Seow rightly notes, moreover, that Ecclesiastes commonly uses -ל with נתן for the person to whom something is given (1.13; 2.26 [twice]; 3.10; 5.17, 18; 6.2; 8.15; 9.9; 11.2).

It is more likely that the basic clause here is similar to that in, e.g., Gen 48.4 'I will give this land to (ל) your descendants, (as) a possession'; Deut 2.9, 'to (-ל) the sons of Lot I have given Ar (as) a possession', or Ps 2.8 'I will make (אתנה) nations your inheritance': the verb regularly takes two 'accusatives' when it implies the transformation of something into something else, while retaining -ל for the person on behalf of whom this is done (cf. Exod 7.1, 'I have made you Elohim to Pharaoh'). Accordingly, the suffix pronoun here is the object of the verb, with חלקו a predicate of that object, and לאדם the person 'for' whom it becomes his חלק.

2.21 to be what is his] Lit. '(as) his portion'. On the sense and translation of חלק, see the note 'what was mine' at 2.10, above. In the construction adopted by G (see the previous notes), αὐτοῦ in μερίδα αὐτοῦ most naturally refers to the first person, who gives 'his portion' to the second; Hie *partem suam* should probably be understood in those terms as well, and among modern commentators this reading is preferred by, e.g., HCM. The Hebrew could be read that way if the suffix on יתננו were taken as datival, or חלקו understood to be simply in apposition with that suffix, but in view of the usage noted above, the understanding of T למיהוי חולקיה, 'to be his portion', which makes it explicit that the עמל is intended to become the portion of the second man, is probably correct. I have translated similarly.

2.21 utterly bad] Lit. 'much badness'. This is the only time Qohelet uses רעה רבה in one of his characterizations, although similar expressions appear in 4.8 and 6.2. G πονηρία μεγάλη imputes a 'wickedness' that is probably not intended by the Hebrew, and σ' κάκωσις πολλή[6] seems closer to the mark (on the attribution of the second word, see Marshall): this is something wrong and faulty, not evil. See the notes on 'bad' at 1.13, and on 'a lot for humans to deal with' at 6.1.

2.22 What is there for] I have not translated the initial כי: as noted in v. 12, above, the word frequently has little force before מה and מי. This verse does stand in a sequence of sentences beginning with כי, and is not entirely disconnected from what has preceded it, but a translation as 'for' would imply a much stronger explanatory link with 2.21 than is suggested either by the content or the Hebrew.

De Rossi notes a variant הוא for הוה in a single witness, and Kennicott lists several with a *plene* הווה: perhaps surprisingly, neither has found the more common היה as a variant. As noted in the Introduction, however, that reading does appear in the early Babylonian Masoretic text Berlin Or. Qu. 680 / JTS 510, with a *Qᵉrê* הוה. On the assumption that it is not simply a scribal error, the unusual הוה may be used here for no more reason than to prevent the question being misunderstood as 'what has happened to'; cf. 7.10, and the corresponding future at 11.2 (although G, Hie have, perhaps, understood it in just that way). The verb appears rarely in biblical Hebrew, where it never means 'happen', and the uses outside Ecclesiastes (Gen 27.29; Isa 16.4; Neh 6.6) all refer to the adoption of a status. Although the two verbs become more interchangeable in later Hebrew, the participle of הוה is commonly found with a connotation of existence or endurance, and if the reading of the verb is correct at 11.3, that would seem to be its sense there. The pointing as a participle in M is probably affirmed by the present tenses of G and Hie (contrast σ' περιγέγονεν, '[what] has been left?', see below). Michel, *Untersuchungen*, 33, comparing this question with that posed in 1.3, sees in the replacement of יתרון by this participle an emphasis on what is lasting and enduring, while Lys, 'L'Être', 253, thinks that the nuance is 'what sort of existence is there?' Michel's idea has been supported by Fox, and is attractive, although it is also possible, if this vocalization is what the author intended, that he wished only to mark a break with the events of the previous verse.

G again presents some textual difficulties, since the ὅτι τί γίνεται ('for what happens?') of Rahlfs, which was suggested earlier as an emendation by Klostermann, *De libri Coheleth*, 58, is not attested in the manuscript tradition, where ὅτι γίνεται is always found (τί appears only as an addition to one

---

[6] In addition to Field and Marshall, see also Labate, 'Catena Hauniense', 57.

codex, according to McNeile, 158, and Goldman), although cf. Hie *quid enim fit*. This leads Goldman to suppose that G did not find מה in its source-text, and, indeed, to commend in *BHQ* the reading כי הוה as more probably original than M. He would then read הוה as the noun הַוָּה, translating 'For it is vain desire (emptiness) for a man in all his trouble and project of his heart!' It is certainly simpler, however, to see the reading of G as resulting from an early error (as most commentators have assumed, e.g., McNeile, Euringer), with τί lost in the sequence οτιτιπ, so that Rahlfs correctly offers the G* reading.

The reading of σ' is attested in Greek as ὅτι γὰρ περιγέγονεν, 'for because it remains over', by two sources, and this is the only other support for Goldman's reading. As Marshall points out, though, it is improbable that σ' rendered כי twice, with both ὅτι and γάρ, so this is most likely itself an error for τί γὰρ περιγέγονεν, 'for what remains over', perhaps influenced by the reading of G. M should not, then, be emended.

Kamano, *Cosmology*, 72, speaks of a possible omission here of יתרון or טוב: from his earlier discussion (42), it is not clear whether he means that a word has been omitted accidentally from the text, or whether he believes that either word could be understood. T does, in fact, have מא הנאה, 'what profit/ benefit?', but this is explicatory, and not good evidence for an actual omission in the Hebrew.

2.22 the person] The general use of 'the person' where we would say 'a person' (e.g. 3.11) means that M's vocalization of לאדם as definite (supported by G), does not necessarily make this a reference to the man of the previous verse in particular. Accordingly, the verse is very often understood and translated as though it were a variation on the question in 1.3. On contextual grounds, however, I take it in fact to be picking up the situation that has been described in the previous verse, so that here we are dealing with the same person, to whose specific circumstances Qohelet now applies his more general question. If there is an ambiguity, it may be to some extent deliberate.

A few Greek witnesses precede τῷ ἀνθρώπῳ with ἐν, and since one of these is G^B, it appears in Swete's text. Barton, and apparently McNeile, 140, see it as evidence for a variant source-text with באדם, but it is probably an inner-Greek error, caused either by the frequency of the preposition in the preceding verse (so Euringer), or by its use before the two subsequent datives in this verse.

2.22 in any of] See the note at 1.3.

2.22 worrying] On the sense of רעיון, see the Introduction, pp. 22-24, above. It is used as a counterpart to רעות in the phrase רעיון רוח at 1.17 and 4.16.

2.22 heart] As *BHQ* notes, M^L omits the holem from the waw: read לִבּוֹ, as in, e.g., Sassoon 1053.

2.22 about that at which he is the one doing the work] It seems unlikely that שהוא עמל can be simply equivalent to שעמל in the now familiar variations on עמל שעמל, not least because it is separated from עמלו by רעיון: whatever the precise meaning of that word, it is clearly not something at which one works. In fact, since רעיון can take an object, it is more natural to read the relative clause as that object. שהוא עמל might then simply be equivalent to אשר הוא עמל in 3.9. Given the context, though, I think that there may be some emphasis on the fact that he is the one doing the work, as in 2.18 (see the note there), and have tried to give that inflection to the translation. It is probably an attempt to align this with the more familiar expressions that has led one Hebrew witness, noted by de Rossi, to read שיעמול.

2.23 through each of his days] The sentence could also be construed 'all his days were pains, and exasperation was his job', which is how G and Hie have taken it (cf. V; T and S are themselves probably ambiguous, while α' βάσανος καὶ θυμός, 'torment and anger', could belong to either understanding, or to neither). This reading is also indicated by the disjunctive accent on מכאבים in the pointing of M. Indeed, the use of that plural מכאבים ('pains'), which aligns it with 'days', might be considered a nudge toward that reading by the author, especially since Qohelet used the singular in 1.18. On the other hand, the sentence is followed by one in which the days clearly correspond to the expression בלילה, which means, unambiguously, 'at night'. The latter consideration has led many modern commentators to favour taking כל ימיו itself as an expression of 'time during which' (cf. GKC §118 k; J-M §126 i), as did Ibn Ezra, and as I do here.

2.23 pains and exasperation] The terms echo those used in 1.18, where these things are gained in proportion to increases in wisdom and knowledge. The author may simply like the pairing (although it is avoided in 5.16), but the fact that wisdom and knowledge have just appeared in v. 21 suggests that the allusion to the earlier verse may be deliberate. On the terms themselves, see the note at 1.18. The rendering βάσανος for מכאבים by α' (on the attribution, see Marshall) is vivid: it presumably takes the plural to indicate continuous torment, or perhaps even a session of torture. The plural is found elsewhere, at Exod 3.7; Ps 32.10; Isa 53.3, 4, and the usage does not really support Ginsburg's contention that this is an abstract 'grief' (although the abnormal form מכאבות at Isa 53.3 may have such a sense); the reference is more probably to a constant accumulation of problems (cf. especially Ps 32.10).

The pointing of the conjunction on the other term as וָכַעַס attracted a certain amount of discussion in the older modern commentaries; it is probably linked to the pause induced by the subsequent disjunctive accent *zaqeph* (cf. GKC §29 i; J-M §32 f), which has much the same effect as the *'athnah* at, e.g., Lev 18.5 (cf. GKC §104 g; J-M §105 d). Ginsburg speaks of the conjunction with this pointing being used to join words in pairs (and so takes it for an argument in favour of מכאבים and כעס being taken together as predicates of ענינו), but, as GKC §104 g points out, this is something which arises from the typical position of such pairs in relation to the accents, and is not some special sense conveyed by the vocalization.

2.23 job] On the sense of עִנְיָן, see the note at 1.13. Hie very curiously renders *curarumque*, 'and of cares', leading Goldman to wonder if Jerome has read a plural עִנְיָיו. Euringer, focusing instead on the fact that the suffix pronoun has not been translated, explores the possibility that he has divided the consonants עִנְיָן וְגַם. In the same vein, we might remark that *-que* could imply an initial ו, but it seems evident that the translation is driven by Jerome's conviction that עִנְיָן here refers to the troubles, not to work (cf. *sollicitudinem* in v. 26): he has made the noun plural because he considers it collective, and *curae* would not do, and he has omitted the possessive either as redundant or for the reason suggested by Euringer. In V, he seems to omit the word altogether: Goldman's reference to 'the pl. in his two translations' suggests that Jerome translates with a plural in this version also, but *pleni sunt* is just a translational facilitation agreeing with *cuncti dies*, and the only other plural, *doloribus*, renders מַכְאֹבִים.

2.23 at night, too] It is possible that גַם has an emphatic force, 'even at night' (so, e.g., Schoors, *The Preacher* I, 132), but the normal additive sense will surely do just as well.

2.23 relaxed] Lit. 'lie down': his mind will not, as it were, go to bed. The tense of the verb is the only indication of tense in the verse as a whole. Read as perfect, it probably looks back on the life of the person (so Krüger), but does not necessarily indicate the end of that life or situation. G, Hie, V translate with the present, suggesting that they are reading a participle, as in the previous verse, and Joüon, 'Notes de syntaxe', 226, would prefer to vocalize the text that way. As Schoors, *The Preacher* I, 186 observes, however, the perfect of a stative verb can bear much the same meaning.

2.23 This too, it is an illusion] This is the only place where Qohelet's characteristic declaration includes the pronoun: גַם זֶה הֶבֶל הוּא (cf. Jer 10.3). That is not reflected in S, Hie, V, but is found in T, and is probably what has led G, also untypically, to include ἐστίν. The variation seems to be stylistic and it makes no significant change to the sense, although HCM render 'This too—it is a הֶבֶל', which brings out the difference.

2.24-26

(2.24) There is no good in the person who eats and drinks and lets himself take pleasure in his business. This too have I observed, that it is from the hand of God (2.25) who eats and who worries, besides me. (2.26) That he has given wisdom, knowledge, and pleasure to a person he favours, and has given the job of piling and accumulating to the disfavoured, to give to one God favours—this too is an illusion, and wishing for the wind.

Commentary

There are many difficulties in these verses, and many different interpretations of them. Qohelet's reflections so far, however, have led him to see a fundamental disconnection between the situations in which human individuals find themselves, and the efforts that they have made toward their own self-improvement. This leads him here to a realization (or perhaps better, in the light of his initial assumption at 1.13, an acceptance beyond the purely intellectual) that humans are not, in fact, really in control: what people have, do, or experience is determined by God. That in turn sets the stage for a calmer discussion of determinism in ch. 3, which will take this line of thought much further.

2.24] Ancient copyists and modern commentators alike have tried to read this verse as a statement similar to those in 3.22 and 8.15, where Qohelet declares 'There is nothing better than that a person', or that 'there is nothing good for a person to do except' take pleasure. Indeed, the pressure to make it conform has had an influence on the textual tradition that is significant, and probably very early. Despite the complications, however, it is almost certain that the earliest readings available to us say no such thing, and that if we want to make this verse say the same as those others then emendation is required—a fact acknowledged even by many modern supporters of that reading (although such an emendation would need to be more substantial than commonly allowed). In 3.12 we find a similar reference to good *in*, rather than *for* the person, and, although there has been a corresponding pressure to emend that verse also, we should recognize that Qohelet is in fact making a point in both 2.24 and 3.12 that is different from that in 3.22 and 8.15. Here, indeed, the context makes the point very clear, and it is one that Qohelet has emphasized ever since he began his review of his achievements: the situation of humans does not correspond properly to their qualities or efforts, whether it be in the case of the wise who die just like fools, with respect to those who acquire property regardless of their wisdom or work, or, most recently, in the matter of the person whose work went to another without them ever enjoying it. Having asked rhetorically what good there could possibly be *for* that person, Qohelet now perhaps plays on the wording of his own question to declare that there is nothing good *in* their counterpart, somebody who 'eats and drinks'—that is, takes proper advantage of their life[1]—and finds pleasure in their work. Their ability to do this derives from no virtue of their own, but from the same divine dispensation that condemned the first, undoubtedly worthy individual to a life without such benefits. In 3.12-13, Qohelet will make a similar point, using much the same language, that is likewise set firmly in the context of divine activity, and the theme will be elaborated further in 5.17-18—where Qohelet will use a different construction again, 'good *that*' instead of 'good *for*' or 'good *in*': such variations are a characteristic of the book's style. For Schwienhorst-Schönberger (cf. his *Nicht im Menschen*, titled after this verse, especially 303), this is a crucial statement of the book's central message.

2.25] Verse 25 is as difficult as it is short. Its link to the preceding verse is unclear and the meaning of its second verb uncertain, while it is difficult to determine from the textual witnesses whether Qohelet originally said 'apart from me' or 'apart from him'. These issues are discussed at length in the notes, but any translation must necessarily be offered with caution, and it would be unwise to base too much on any particular interpretation. Qohelet's 'apart from me', in any case, is probably not intended to align him specifically with any group here, or to exempt him from the divine dispensation, but to

---

[1] See also 3.13; 5.17; slightly differently 8.15; 9.7. Although he associates the expression with statements about pleasure and joy, Qohelet may use it more to imply getting on with life, as opposed to worrying about it, and that is indicated by the contrast drawn here in 2.25. The implication is not so much of physical or sensual satisfaction from consumption, as of having one's needs supplied.

signal that he is drawing conclusions from his personal experience that apply to all humanity. The sense, then, is 'I have observed this to be true not just of me,' or 'true of people besides me.'

2.26] This verse presents difficulties of a different sort. On the face of it, Qohelet seems to have moved, suddenly and without warning, to a position like that expressed in Job 27.16-17, aptly cited by Rashbam: the wicked pile up wealth, but the righteous enjoy it (cf. also Prov 13.22). Even setting aside Qohelet's own case, that would seem to mean that the man who worked so diligently a few verses ago, but never got to enjoy his wealth, is no longer a cause for outrage, or even a victim of divine caprice. Rather, he is being punished by God, just as those who do enjoy their wealth are being rewarded—despite the fact that there is supposedly 'no good in' them. Matters are complicated further by Qohelet's linking of wisdom and knowledge with pleasure here, despite his recent characterizations of wisdom as painful and ultimately useless. It is possible to make the distinction less sharp (although the text arguably more confusing) by seeing a different sort of wisdom here, as does Fox, or by judicious removal of words, but it is not surprising that many commentators have dismissed the whole scheme as a pious gloss, added later to the text.

The passage seems all the stranger when read in the light of what has preceded more generally, because if there are supposed to be two classes of person described, then Qohelet himself would seem to belong to both of them: he possesses wisdom and knowledge, and he has taken pleasure in his work, but he also clearly perceives himself as having produced something that others in the next generation will enjoy. Indeed, it seems to follow from his observations so far that anyone who accomplishes anything must fall into the class of those who gather for somebody else, whether they themselves have wisdom and pleasure or not: there is nothing in what Qohelet has said to suggest that he would regard the two categories here as mutually exclusive. Far from providing a logical conclusion to his account and reflections, therefore, this verse seems almost precisely to contradict them. Since it also provides a transition, however, to the theme of divine providence that will dominate the next chapter, it seems unlikely that it is simply a secondary addition, designed to impose some view alien to Qohelet's own.

If we are supposed to read this verse strictly in terms of reward and punishment of some sort, then there is a further contradiction with v. 24, and with his preceding statements about deserving and undeserving heirs: Qohelet has apparently moved rapidly from saying that a person's situation may be unrelated to their character, to a declaration that it depends on whether they please God or not. This contradiction is a little easier to address: the person who is literally 'good before' God may be no more than a person who God deems appropriate for a particular role—the language is careful, and does not explicitly describe the person as righteous or pious. It is harder to remove all implications of culpability, however, from the description of that person's counterpart, which uses a term more commonly associated with committing sins. Qohelet, moreover, is going to use similar expressions in 7.26, where I understand his point to be that, ironically, whoever is 'good before' God will escape becoming trapped by wisdom, and it is the one who 'sins' that will be ensnared. It is unlikely, therefore, that he is using the language simply of being 'right' or 'wrong' for a job in either verse, and there is some implication of divine favour or disfavour, although not, perhaps, anything so strong as a statement about divine judgment.

It would not be impossible to discount the problems here by suggesting that we are making too much of them, and extrapolating too precise an account from what are merely illustrations of Qohelet's main point, that human life is governed by divine, not human choices. There is a degree of precision in the language, though, that seems to invite such extrapolation, and I think that in this case we need to pay particular attention to the closing statement, that what has been described is, in fact, an illusion. Qohelet is in effect, I think, rejecting a particular assumption twice. First, in vv. 24-25, he does so in general terms: human benefits do not come from the inherent worth, in any respect, of those who enjoy them, but from choices made by God. That might be taken merely to suggest, however, that God is rewarding humans for their worth, giving good things to those who have pleased him, bad to those who have not—an idea that stands in complete contradiction to the thrust of Qohelet's discourse so far, although he will touch on the issue again in 6.2. Accordingly, that more conventional idea is dismissed as 'vapour', and it is this dismissal that more precisely takes us to the issues that will concern him in ch. 3.[2]

---

[2] After a helpful survey of the issues and opinions, Pinker, 'Ecclesiastes 2.26', concludes rightly that '2:26 is a quote that Ecclesiastes rejects, or that it was added

Notes

2.24 There is no good in the person who] In 8.15, when Qohelet suggests that there is nothing good except eating, drinking, and taking pleasure, the expression used is אין טוב לאדם...כי אם לאכול, while 3.22 declares that אין טוב מאשר ישמח האדם. The ability to do these things is characterized as a gift of God in 3.13 and 5.17-18, and it is clear that the combination of actions forms something of a *leitmotif* in the book. It is also clear, however, that Qohelet is not trying to make the same point each time, so we must be wary (as Backhaus, *Es gibt*, 106-107, emphasizes) of attempting to harmonize the various statements. It is probably a reminiscence of 8.15 (and perhaps of 6.12) which has led some Hebrew manuscripts (de Rossi lists only three) to read לאדם in place of the more difficult באדם here, and this may also have happened in the source-text of G (as McNeile, 140, and Goldman suppose), although it is very possible that ἐν (τῷ) ἀνθρώπῳ is G*, and that the preposition independently dropped out in much of the Greek tradition for similar reasons (alternatively, as McNeile also points out, its position in the sequence ΘΟΝΕΝΑΝΘ might have led to a simple error, if the article is not original). S ܠܓܒܪ *lgbrʾ* may render the G variant (τῷ) ἀνθρώπῳ, so is not itself a reliable witness to an early Hebrew variant לאדם. Although it is peculiar, באדם corresponds to בם in the similar expression אין טוב בם at 3.12, which enjoys firmer support from the versions, and there are no strong reasons to emend here.

Most commentators, however, do seek to emend the next word from שיאכל, 'that he eat', to משיאכל, 'than that he eat', on more substantial versional evidence. It is indeed possible that the initial מ might have dropped out through haplography after the preceding מ of באדם (although this would not have been so straightforward when final-form ם was in use), but of the similar texts commonly cited in support of emendation, only 3.22 uses the comparative -מ, while 3.12 and 8.15 both use כי אם.[3] The choice of construction in 3.22, furthermore, is linked to the connection of האדם directly with the verb, rather than to the אין טוב clause as at 3.12 and 8.15 ('that a man eats' rather than 'for a man to eat'). Since אדם belongs with the אין טוב clause here, we should, correspondingly, expect a comparison here to use כי אם, not -מ—and that is a very much more challenging emendation. G uses εἰ μή to render both constructions in 3.12, 22; 8.15, and a significant number of manuscripts

by a pious glossator.' I think that 'quote' is too precise here, if it evokes the idea that Qohelet is dismissing a particular saying or statement, as opposed to himself putting into words an opinion with which he disagreed, but this is one place where we might accept that the monologue contains views that are not Qohelet's own.

[3] The description of Qohelet's 'better than' sayings in Ogden, 'Qoheleth's Use', 340, conflates the prepositions that may follow אין טוב to mark the recipient or possessor of the good, with the prepositional מן that marks what it is better *than*—to confusing effect.

read εἰ μή ὃ φάγεται or πλὴν ὃ φάγεται in this verse (the latter appears as an unattributed variant in the margin of Syh, and may be hexaplaric in origin; see Marshall). The best witnesses, however, read only ὃ φάγεται, the reading reflected in Syh itself, and this is probably G*. The readings of Hie *nisi quod comedat* and S ܐܠܐ ܕܢܐܟܘܠ *ʾlʾ dnʾkwl* (both 'except that/what he eats') might simply reflect the variant in G, but T, strikingly, also reads 'except': אילהין דייכול. This may well suggest that a Hebrew text existed with such a reading.

Contextual issues aside, however, if we are to take that text as original then Ecclesiastes either had אין טוב באדם משיאכל, which makes an easy emendation but has no parallel, or אין טוב באדם כי אם לאכ(ו)ל, which has close parallels but is an unlikely source for the present text. Although even Euringer would emend to באדם משיאכל here, and Fox regards the emendation as beyond doubt, it seems easier to view the longer texts as a consequence of harmonization to some of Qohelet's most famous statements than to change M, which makes good sense in this context as it stands (so, similarly, Krüger; see also his 'Qoh 2,24-26', 131-36). If we do not actually emend, we can hardly assume some ellipsis of 'except', as Seow suggests, and retaining the current text makes it difficult to see Qohelet's claim here as a response to the question asked in 2.3, as Kamano, 'Character and Cosmology', 421, proposes.

'Good' here might be a virtue, but in biblical usage טוב is not usually a quality attributed to humans, and when attributed to God seems to connote his beneficence more than his own inherent 'goodness' (e.g. Neh 9.35)—although there may be some elision of the ideas (e.g. Ps 145.7). Backhaus, *Es gibt*, 108, understands a 'beth constitutionis', and takes the point to be rather that humans have no power over what is good for them (in English we might say, 'they do not have it in them to'). That is possible in principle, although the interpretation is driven in part by a desire to understand טוב as 'good fortune'. In the light of what follows here, however, I take Qohelet to be saying that there is nothing in or about these humans that might make them 'good' or 'deserving' before God, and this is the basis of his denial in 2.26, that the possession of pleasure is a mark of divine favour.

2.24 eats and drinks and lets] The sequence of verbs שיאכל ושתה והראה (cf. 3.13; 5.17; and, with a different final verb, 8.15) appears to consist of an imperfect with two consecutive perfects, although the actions are clearly supposed to be contemporaneous rather than sequential (cf. Isaksson, *Studies*, 94), and G, S, T correspondingly translate them all as future (Syh attests the infinitive for the first verb in σ', cf. V, and the present in θ', cf. Hie).

G and S also attest a relative before each verb, however, and the reading of the last verb in α' is similarly attested in Syh as ܘܡܗ ܡܒ ܕܢܚܘܝܗ *whw mʾ dnḥwʾ* (= καὶ ὃ δείξει), 'and what he shows'. Although the second and third relative pronouns have been omitted in many manuscripts, they are clearly G*, leading McNeile to suspect an early reading with relatives in Hebrew (he suggests ושישתה ושיהראה on pp. 60-61, but ושתה ושיראה on p. 153). G's translation (which apparently takes each relative pronoun as the object of its verb, rather than as a reference back to the person) would certainly be easier to understand if its source-text had ושישתה ושיהראה, since G renders the similar Hebrew at 3.13 with just ὃς φάγεται καὶ πίεται καὶ ἴδῃ ἀγαθὸν, 'who eats and drinks and sees good', rather than the ὃ φάγεται καὶ ὃ πίεται καὶ ὃ δείξει, 'what he eats and what he drinks and what he shows', used here; S similarly lacks all but the first relative in 3.13. Such a text might have arisen through a confusion of the ש on ושתה with the relative ש, and subsequent adjustment, but it is also possible that the relatives are original, and that M has been assimilated to 3.13.

2.24 himself take pleasure in his business] Lit. 'and causes his self to see good in'. The expression וראה בטוב was used in 2.1, but with a rather different sense (see the note there). The usage here is apparently similar to that in 4.8, where מחסר את נפשי מטובה is a reference to self-deprivation (cf. איננו חסר לנפשו in 6.2), and in 6.3's ונפשו לא תשבע מן הטובה. Although it can just mean 'self', there is, perhaps, a nuance to נפש here which is difficult to capture in English: the term can refer to the gullet and physical appetite (see the note at 6.3), so the juxtaposition with eating and drinking may imply a more specific image of feeding oneself well.[4] Alter, *Wisdom Books*, 352, would read והראה here as a form from רוה, 'drink one's fill'; cf. the note 'and you must examine' at 2.1.

As Kamenetzky, 214, observes, S ܠܢܦܫܗ *lnpšh*, lit. 'to the soul', replaces the double 'accusative' of the Hebrew with a more usual Syriac idiom, although it might also have been influenced by the dative τῇ ψυχῇ of G; it does not suggest a variant לנפש.

For בעמלו G has ἐν μόχθῳ αὐτοῦ, 'in his labour': σ' ἀπὸ κόπου αὐτοῦ, 'from his toil', is translational, and has probably influenced V *de laboribus* ('from his labours'; cf. Cannon, 'Jerome and Symmachus', 192).

2.24 This too have I observed, that] Ecclesiastes commonly uses גם זה in the characterizations of phenomena as הבל (see 2.15, 19, 21, 23, 26; 4.4, 8, 16; 5.9; 6.9; 7.6; 8.10, 14), or at least in similar expressions (1.17; 5.15), which tends to tell against assigning גם some special sense as adversative here (so Delitzsch). When it is used with ראיתי in 9.13, זה points forward to what follows, and it is likely here that the pronoun similarly anticipates the clause which follows, כי מיד האלהים היא; cf. Gordis, Schoors, *The Preacher* I, 160. Certainly, the pointing of זֹה as feminine in most manuscripts of M links it

---

[4] Some caution is needed, however. The comment in BDB, that Ecclesiastes uses נפש only in the sense of hunger, thirst or appetite, is probably based principally on a particular interpretation of 6.1-9 in these terms, but whether it is the primary connotation even there, let alone here and in 4.8 or 7.28, is questionable. נפש is not so much a word with different meanings as a complicated concept with different facets, and this makes it difficult to define, let alone to translate into other languages. With due sensitivity to the familiar problem of 'illegitimate totality transfer', therefore, it is important to avoid the assumption that only one 'meaning' of the term is ever in play, even if the necessities of translation force us to privilege only one aspect at a time.

to the subsequent היא (which may explain the pointing), although masculine forms of both are attested in the manuscript tradition (de Rossi notes a number of witnesses with זֶ, and a very large number with הוא—although, interestingly, not all of the former are included among the latter). On the feminine הׄי as a rare alternative to זאת, see the note on 'What does it do?' at 2.2, and note also the discussion in the Introduction, p. 161 n. 177, above. Ginsburg, *Massorah* III, 71, lists זי as a $Q^e r\hat{e}$ here, and it is found with that spelling in the text of a few manuscripts (see de Rossi, Ginsburg, *Writings*): the same will be true in 5.15, 18; 7.23; 9.13.

Correspondingly, כי probably indicates 'saw *that*' after the verb. On the construction, see the note on 'that it is' at 4.4.

S seems to have omitted translation of אני (cf. Kamenetzky, 214, 236), which is supported, however, by the other versions.

2.24 hand of God] The expression is used of divine power over humans (e.g. 1 Sam 4.8; 2 Chr 30.12; cf. the more common יד יהוה), most commonly in negative contexts of punishment. It appears again in 9.1-2, where the common מקרה of all is linked to all people being in the hand of God. Other usage suggests, therefore, no connotation of divine care here: the phenomenon which concerns Qohelet is simply being attributed to the exercise of divine power in the world.

2.25 who…who] כי here is usually taken to be explanatory, and the sentence understood as a rhetorical question: matters are in the hands of God because nobody can eat etc. without him. This reading requires us to read חוץ ממנו, which is less probable than חוץ ממני, and to understand חוץ in a poorly attested sense (see below on both points), so we might reasonably wonder whether it is not in fact כי מי which requires closer examination. In fact, it is striking that the כי in כי מי has no obvious force at all when the expression appears in 6.12 and 7.13, unless it is to emphasize the מי, and similar instances can be found elsewhere (e.g. Jer 15.5; Zech 4.10); see the note at 2.12 on כי מה. It is far from certain, then, that this verse has to be read as an explanation of the last, and there is a range of ways in which כי might be understood here. I take the particle, in fact, to be nominalizing the sentence, so that it stands in apposition to, and reveals the content of, the preceding זה…היא: 'I have seen this too, that it is in the hand of God *that*…'. The construction, then, is essentially similar to that in, e.g., Job 13.16, גם הוא לי לישועה כי לא לפניו חנף יבוא, 'this will be a salvation for me, *that* a godless man will not come before him'; other examples are noted in BDB (under כי, §1a) and Schoors, 'The Particle כי', 261. On that understanding, מי is then used indirectly, as in, e.g., Gen 43.22; 1 Kgs 1.20; although it commonly involves a verb of knowing or suchlike, that use need not do so where a question or option is implicit (cf. Josh 24.15).

2.25 worries] The word יחוש here is a notorious crux, and the meaning very uncertain. That the reading is original seems likely, although the difficulties of interpretation are reflected in a certain amount of confusion amongst the witnesses. Two readings are asserted for G: φείσεται, 'will refrain' (i.e., who will eat and who will not), and πίεται, 'will drink'. The former is the probable reading of α' and σ' (see Marshall and Gentry, 'Propaedeutic', 172); it is not actually attested in any manuscript of G, but is taken as G* by Rahlfs on the basis of Hie *parcet* and Syh ܢܚܘܣ *nḥws*. Both of these sources have probably been influenced, however, by α' or, in the case of Hie, more probably σ',[5] and Gentry, 'Propaedeutic', 170-73, presents an incontrovertible case for rejecting φείσεται as G*.[6] The translation probably originates, as many commentators have suggested, in a reading of יחוש as equivalent to יחוס.

The origin of πίεται is less clear, although this dominates the G tradition, and is also attributed to θ'; S ܢܫܬܐ *nšt'* is probably derived from G (so Janichs, *Animadversiones*, 8). Gentry, 'Propaedeutic', 171, following Waard, 'The Translator', 522, picks up Hertzberg's idea (1932 and 1963) that this is a *Verlegenheitslesart*, a reading born of desperation: the Greek translator struggled with the verb, and substituted a rendering based on the context, which was then retained by θ'; so, similarly, Salters, 'Textual Criticism', 65. That itself feels like an explanation born of desperation, however, and we cannot exclude the possibility that G found ישתה in its source-text. Some commentators have gone so far as to see this as the original reading (so Graetz, Podechard, Kamenetzky, 238), even if it is clearly the *lectio facilior*: Kamenetzky supposes that חוש arose as a dittography of the following חוץ, and presumably believes that it then displaced ישתה. If ישתה was found as an early Hebrew variant, however, it more probably arose as a careless reminiscence of the previous verse. McNeile's suggestion (158) that φείσεται and πίεται might both go back to an original πείσεται, 'will suffer' (not 'persuade'), is untenable, but it is conceivable, if G did not find ישתה, that πίεται is a very early corruption of that word, likewise caused by assimilation to the previous verse. We have no direct evidence, however, that the reading πείσεται ever existed.

In short, יחוש has caused the versions problems, but they offer no grounds for emendation of M. Nevertheless, with no versional support, Ginsberg emends to the Aramaic יחשה (cf. Dan 3.16; Ezra 6.9; 7.20), assuming that the

---

[5] Gentry, 'Propaedeutic', 173, suggests α' τίς φάγεται καὶ τίς φείσεται, 'who will eat and who refrain', as Jerome's source for his translation *quis enim comedet et quis parcet*, 'for who will eat and who refrain' (in the body of the commentary we also find *quis enim uel comedere uel cum opus est parcere potest*, 'for who can either consume, or, as needs must, abstain'). There is no strong reason, however, to prefer α' as a source over σ' τίς ἀναλώσει καὶ τίς φείσεται, 'who will consume and who refrain', especially as *comedere* shares the ability of ἀναλίσκειν to connote both consumption and wasteful spending—a double meaning that is drawn out in Jerome's comments.

[6] Podechard argued a similar case quite independently, which has been overlooked in much of the subsequent literature.

following חוץ has caused both haplography of the final ת and the introduction of a spurious ו; he then translates 'who uses?' (cf. his *Studies*, 11, for the English). This is gratuitous, as Schoors, *The Preacher* II, 384, remarks, and Ginsberg presents no substantial evidence for his assertion that the Aramaic can have the meaning 'use' as well as its normal sense 'need' (he draws an analogy with German *brauchen* and *gebrauchen*).

For the most part, modern scholars have otherwise retained M, and have translated in terms of either indulgence in / abstention from food, or enjoyment / unhappiness, which all suit the context, and which offer synonymous or antithetical counterparts to the preceding 'eat'. The earlier Jewish commentators associated the verb with חוש, 'hurry', but that is awkward, and only adopted by Ginsburg amongst the modern writers (he compares Hab 1.8); other suggestions have been made from time to time without winning wider support, and Seow's suggestion 'gather' = 'glean', based on a presumed Arabic cognate looks likely to fall into that category.[7] Of the more common interpretations, that involving indulgence in food or drink is least persuasive, resting as it does almost solely on other presumed Arabic cognates.[8] Gordis also appeals to Arabic for the sense 'abstain', although that can be achieved, as Ehrlich notes, by reading יחוש = יחוס, as did α', σ'.

The general sense 'enjoyment' has been accepted by significantly more scholars, although it too depends largely on presumed cognates in other languages: the mishnaic חשש and הוש, as Gordis observes, are not generally used of positive emotions, while the Ugaritic *ḫšt* (*KTU* 1.16 i 4), adduced by Dahood, 'Qoheleth and Recent Discoveries', 307-308, is itself obscure: see, e.g., Wyatt, *Religious Texts*, 219 n. 196. This really leaves only the Akkadian *ḫašāšu*, 'swell with joy', 'rejoice', suggested as a cognate by Levy.

The strongest evidence is on the side of taking יחוש to mean 'worry', 'be unhappy', a sense which is firmly attested in mishnaic Hebrew, which can probably be understood for חושי in the difficult Job 20.2, and which is also found for the apparent Akkadian cognate *ḫâšu*, as Ellermeier has been at some pains to point out (see especially *Qohelet I.2*, which is an expanded version of his article 'Das Verbum'). This is probably the understanding of T, which takes the verb in the sense 'be anxious'. It may be going too far to say, with Schoors, *The Preacher* II, 386, that Ellermeier has 'settled the

---

[7] See especially Waard, 'The Translator', for a survey of proposals; also Schoors, *The Preacher* II, 384-86. To these should be added the suggestion in Pinker, 'Qohelet 5:17-19', 76 n. 37, that 'the MT as well as Aquila and Symmachus reflect an original with the *Pual* imperfect masc. of שוח, "to bend (as in toiling, Ps 44:26, Lam 3:20)", which by metathesis became יחוש. In this case, יחוש, like the English "he broke his back," would stand for "hard work".'

[8] So Ewald, who considers G, S to have translated accurately as 'drink'; differently, Reider, 'Etymological Studies', 129-30, who proposes 'be full of food'.

476   ECCLESIASTES

debate', but his view has been accepted by some recent commentators (e.g.
Fox, although he wrongly associates the reading of α', σ', and Syh), and is
much better supported than the alternatives. I doubt that we can exclude the
alternative possibility of reading as יחוס here, but it is the only real rival. In
the light of the difficulties, it seems hard to accept Byargeon's suggestion (in
'Ambiguity', 369-70; cf. also Noegel, 'Word Play', 17) that the word would
freely have been read either to mean enjoyment or worry, producing a deliberate and provocative ambiguity. It is not certain that the audience would have
recognized either meaning, let alone both.

2.25 besides me] As De Waard, 'The Translator', has emphasized, the way
in which we understand this verse as a whole should depend very much on
the way we understand this expression. In practice, however, we again have
to face both text-critical and lexical obstacles which mean that the sense of
the expression is more often itself understood on the basis of the presumed
context. There are two basic problems. The first is that the majority text of
M here reads חוץ ממני, with a first-person suffix, and is supported by T בר מיני
and V *ut ego*, but it seems apparent that G πάρεξ αὐτοῦ, S ܠܒܪ ܡܢܗ *lbr mnh*,
and Hie *sine illo* all reflect חוץ ממנו, with a third-person suffix (which is also
found in a handful of Hebrew manuscripts, cf. de Rossi). Such י/ו confusions
are common, and in many hands the two would be indistinguishable except
by reference to context.

The versional readings with the third-person suffix cannot simply be
dismissed as the result of any desire to interpret the verse in specific theological terms; indeed, it is not certain that they all take it to be about God. To be
sure, judging by the remarks in his commentary, Jerome clearly does associate
the pronoun with the preceding אלהים (he goes on to speak of eating *absque
deo*, 'without God', in a eucharistic context), but it is less clear that S and G
do so. In the case of S, this is because ܠܒܪ ܡܢ *lbr mn* has such a wide range
of meanings that it could refer either to God ('without him') or to the man
described in the previous verse ('except him'), and the translation leaves the
issue open. G πάρεξ, on the other hand, does not generally mean 'without' or
'apart from' in the way that, say, χωρίς does, but 'except' or 'besides' (so, e.g.,
the Septuagint Ruth 4.4; 3 Kgdms 3.18; Hos 13.4; and cf. the Syh rendering
of the Greek with ܣܛܪ ܡܢ *str mn*), which would seem to limit the reference
to the man. The translation is probably driven, however, not by a particular
understanding of the context, but by a desire to imitate the Hebrew as closely
as possible: like חוץ, πάρεξ has the basic sense 'outside', while its common
sense 'except' corresponds to the usual sense of חוץ מן in mishnaic Hebrew (see
below). If the third-person readings are not driven by any obvious interpretative motive, it is equally difficult to see any such reason for the first-person
ones, although they do, as I shall indicate, give a less ambiguous sense. In
short, our first problem is that the versional evidence supplies no grounds for
choosing between the variants ממני and ממנו: whichever one is secondary, it
probably arose early in the transmission of the Hebrew text, and perhaps as a

result of nothing more than the lack of any clear cue in the context for copyists to read the final character as י or ו.

Our second, closely related problem is one of sense. The translation by G does tend to affirm, at least, that the translator considered חוץ מן unlikely to mean 'without', let alone to bear the sense 'without the action/approval of' which underpins common interpretations of this verse in terms of general divine providence. Indeed, the sense 'without' is uncommon for חוץ מן in mishnaic Hebrew, and was most likely restricted to particular usage.[9] For that meaning, we should probably have to look to Aramaic rather than Hebrew, and see here an imitation of the broader בר מן, which is the formal equivalent of חוץ מן, and is used in their renderings here by S and T. That would permit 'without', but 'except' or 'besides' would still be the more common and natural sense. This could conceivably be stretched to mean, as Delitzsch puts it, '*praeter eum (Deum), i.e.* unless he will it and make it possible'. Such a sense would correspond to some of the ways in which the earlier Hebrew term בלעדי is used (e.g. Gen 41.44; 2 Kgs 18.25), but it is also, however, some distance beyond the attested meanings of חוץ מן itself, and the common interpretation of this passage in such terms is correspondingly speculative.

Although not in themselves conclusive, such considerations of sense can, perhaps, help us with the text-critical problem. If we can reasonably suppose that a contemporary reader would have taken 'except' or 'besides' as the most obvious sense of חוץ מן, then that might in itself tell against reading ממנו here, since the superficial sense would then have been 'Who eats…except God?'. This was hardly the writer's intention, and the fact that the man of the preceding verse might furnish a potential (although surely no less probable) alternative referent for the pronoun only adds ambiguity to the mix. If ממנו was

---

[9] The expression is not used elsewhere in biblical Hebrew. In later Hebrew it almost always means 'except', or 'excluding', commonly qualifying כל ('all/none except'), and the use may be illustrated with some typical examples from *b. Berakoth*: ואין כל בריה יכולה...חוץ מבלעם, 'and there is no creature has been able, *except* Balaam' (7a); כל המצות האמורות בתורה חוץ מן התפילין, 'all the commandments set down in the Torah *except* the Tefillin' (11a); הכל בידי שמים חוץ מיראת שמים, 'everything is in the hands of heaven *except* the fear of heaven' (33b). For the meaning 'without', Jastrow, *Dictionary*, and Levy, *Wörterbuch*, each cite only the Midrash Rabbah on Genesis, where, in parashah 49, a series of parables addresses the question of why God should consult Abraham before destroying the cities of the valley. A number of times in this sequence the expression עשה דבר חוץ מדעת is used, e.g. איני עושה דבר חוץ מדעתו and בקש המלך לעשות דבר חוץ מדעתן. Each time it refers to an action performed 'without' informing or consulting another party (in one instance, somebody is locked away so that they will not find out about it), but this seems to be a fixed expression of questionable relevance to the sense of חוץ מן more generally, and it may involve a dependence on the more basic, literal sense of חוץ: this is action 'outside' the scope of someone's awareness.

original, in other words, the expression may have been difficult and confusing from the outset. If the writer intended ממני, on the other hand, then the sense is much clearer.[10]

Some commentators (recently including Willmes, *Menschliches Schicksal*, 108-109) have attempted to retain both the first-person reading of M and a statement of divine providence here, by making this an unmarked quotation of God's words: this is motivated by an insistence that חוץ must mean 'without', and seems very contrived. If we are willing to dispense altogether with any reference to divine action, however, then it is straightforward to understand חוץ ממני as 'except me, Qohelet'. This is the interpretation adopted by, e.g., Rashi and Rashbam, who see here a continuation of Qohelet's concern about his possessions being enjoyed by others 'outside of' him, and take the verse to justify not the statement about God, but the preceding statement about eating and drinking. This is read as a commendation: I should eat and drink what is mine, because who else deserves to? The Midrash, on the other hand, has Qohelet boasting: who has eaten, drunk, or done as much as me? (which is essentially the interpretation adopted more recently by Lohfink).

In short, then, ממני, with the sense 'except me' or 'other than me', provides a clear and unambiguous sense, which the medieval Jewish commentators have found unproblematic, although they have related it to the context in different ways. The difficulties which are caused by ממנו, on the other hand, suggest that it arose as a simple error. This error opened the possibility of reading here a statement of divine providence, upon which many subsequent readers have been quick to pounce, but that reading, influential though it has been, is not certainly even a natural reading of the text.

The theory of Dahood should be mentioned here, finally. In 'Qoheleth and Recent Discoveries', 306, he suggested tentatively that ממני might actually be a Phoenician spelling of the third-person suffix pronoun, which would make it simply an equivalent of ממנו. He took this up more forcefully in 'Qoheleth and Northwest Semitic Philology', 353, citing an unpublished study by Moriarty along with a list of other possible biblical instances, and the opinion is accepted by Whitley. The lack of correlation with actual Phoenician usage, however, has been demonstrated by Zevit, 'Arguments' (cf. also Schoors, *The Preacher* I, 50-51), and the opinion can hardly be sustained.

2.26 That] How we understand כי naturally relates to the relationship that we see between the first part of this verse and the surrounding context. Ellermeier, *Qohelet I.2*, 10 n. 1 remarks that this verse is hardly the justification for the preceding verse, but takes vv. 25 and 26 (excluding the final clause) together as the justification for 24b; correspondingly, he takes כי here as emphatic, although on that reading it might simply be an explicative 'for' (cf.

---

[10] Such considerations make it difficult, I think, to support M simply on the basis that there might have been theological reasons for a change from first to third person, but not *vice versa*, as, e.g., Fischer, 'Zur Übersetzung', 223.

Schoors, *The Preacher* I, 103), or stand in parallel with the ‫כ‬ of v. 25. I take its function rather to be the substantivization of the sentence that follows, so that it can be picked up by the subsequent ‫זה‬: 'That X happens: this is an illusion'. Of course, this is not the most natural reading, which is why, I think, the verse has caused such problems for subsequent interpreters: the author has relied too much, perhaps, on the willingness of his audience to recognize the many ways in which it contradicts what Qohelet has said so far, and to understand that this is a position he could not countenance. That they have been reluctant to do so is in part, perhaps, because if it is viewed as Qohelet's opinion, then its links to other texts make him seem, for once, attuned to a broader canonical view.

2.26 has given] M points as perfect, and this is the translation adopted by all the ancient versions (on the reading of S, cf. Kamenetzky, 198). Joüon, 'Notes de syntaxe', 225, would vocalize instead as a participle, to give a more general sense, and Isaksson, *Studies*, 78-79, is keen to emphasize that Qohelet is not talking simply about an event in the past, in part because that would seem to introduce a notion of predestination. It is true that, if we follow M then the qatal does not exclude any sense that God continues to make such dispensations. It is also true, though, that the Hebrew could quite legitimately be read as a statement of pre-destination, and although I doubt that this was Qohelet's intention, we cannot remove the possibility just by classifying it as a different sort of perfect. While it seems best to avoid translating 'gave', therefore, Isaksson's preferred 'gives' is no less of an interpretative imposition on the text. The Hebrew really leaves the matter open.

2.26 wisdom, knowledge] Lit. 'wisdom and knowledge'. Galling would omit these words as having no corresponding contrast in the other part of the antithesis (see also his 'Kohelet-Studien', 288 n. 3), and is followed by Ellermeier, 'Das Verbum', 217 n. 112. This would certainly ease some of the exegetical problems, but seems arbitrary.

2.26 a person he favours] Lit. 'a human who (is) good before his face', or 'before him'. This is not a common expression found elsewhere, although the similar 'good in the eyes of God' expresses divine approval in Lev 10.19; Mal 2.17 (cf. Seow), while the psalmist declares to God in Ps 143.2 that no-one alive can be righteous before his face. σ' τῷ ἀρέσκοντι αὐτῷ, 'to one who pleases him', is interpretative but captures the probable implication. I have translated the clause out of order; in the Hebrew, this stands at the beginning to give it emphasis and enhance the contrast.

2.26 job] On ‫עניו‬, see the note at 1.13, above. Bertram, 'Hebräischer und griechischer', 45-46, takes the use of περισπασμός (see at 1.13) by G here to result in a significant, if possibly accidental, change of sense.

2.26 accumulating] This is the verb which Qohelet used of his own activities in 2.8, and there seems no reason to impose any different sense here. As the link suggests, he is probably referring to the acquisition of wealth and property.

2.26 the disfavoured] Lit. perhaps 'the one who is wrong'. Again, I have translated out of order: this stands before the second 'given' in the Hebrew, drawing a strong contrast with the preceding 'person he favours'. Although it can have a general reference to 'sin', the verb חטא, from which the participle used here is derived, has a more fundamental sense of doing something wrong (like missing a target, Judg 20.16, or overlooking a problem Job 5.24), or of wronging somebody (e.g. Gen 42.22; 1 Sam 19.4). It is rarely devoid altogether of moral content, however, and it seems unlikely that we could understand 'bungler' or 'loser' here, as Seow suggests, or 'fool', as Levy renders it. To be sure, it does relate more to the actions than to the nature of the individual, so that it is possible to do wrong unconsciously (e.g. Gen 20.6; Lev 4.2), or for a good person to do wrong (e.g. Neh 6.13), and so to be a 'sinner' is not necessarily to be 'wicked' in some more general way. Indeed, a few times the implication seems to be merely of being 'wrong' or blameworthy in somebody else's opinion.[11] There is an implication here, however, that someone characterized this way will actively have displeased (so Bickell, 74: 'mißfällig') or offended God, and while the previous 'one who seems right' might conceivably mean 'one he deems suitable', it is unlikely that this expression could correspondingly mean 'one he deems unsuitable' (through no fault of their own), as Galling, 'Kohelet-Studien', 289, would like. Fox's suggestion, that the 'wrong' lies in the very act of working too hard, seems to read more into the text than is really there: it is hard to presume that the original readers would have recognized hard work and the accumulation of wealth as foolish per se, and Qohelet says nothing here about excessive toil or ambition. More importantly, though, it is hard to see how this would be a wrong before God, which is clearly what we are supposed to understand here. Not dissimilarly, Ramond, 'Y a-t-il de l'ironie?', 635-36, raises the possibility, largely on the basis of 7.26, that the 'sinner' is actually the wise man who seeks sense in existence. Leaving aside the question whether an audience would have understood the text in such a way before encountering 7.26, this again seems to fit poorly with what Qohelet has said so far: it is clearly not always the wise who gather.

The vocalization of חוֹטֶא with *segol* in M[L] results from treating it as a lamedh-he verb (cf. 8.12; 9.2, 18, but not 7.26); it is pointed with *ṣere* in the early BM Or 9879, and in a number of later manuscripts noted by Ginsburg, *Writings*. See the discussion in the Introduction, pp. 161-62, above.

---

[11] In Gen 43.9; 44.32 the verb is used with -ל, as when more specifically 'wronging' someone, and it is difficult to determine whether this nuance might be involved elsewhere in contexts without explicit statements of duration. Note also, though, the expression נשׂא חטא, 'bear guilt', and the interesting claim of Bathsheba, in 1 Kgs 1.21, that she and Solomon will be regarded as 'sinners' after his death, if David does not proclaim Solomon his heir.

2.26 to give] S, V add a conjunction, making לתת part of the sequence with the preceding verbs: 'piling and accumulating and giving'. Kamenetzky, 236, thinks S found the conjunction in its Hebrew source-text, and notes (214) that the variant is found in some Hebrew manuscripts (cf. de Rossi). It probably arose as a simple error, influenced by the preceding verbs. G τοῦ δοῦναι, 'to give', σ' ἵνα δοθῇ, 'that he might give', both agree with M, as do Hie and T (although they use passive constructions). In view of the preceding context, it seems likely that Qohelet has in mind the acquisition of property through inheritance, rather than the actual employment or enslavement of one class by the other.

2.26 to one who seems right] After V translated the expression literally at the beginning of the verse, *ei qui placuit* probably now follows the paraphrase by σ' ἐκείνῳ ᾧ ἀρέσει ('to him who pleases'; cf. Cannon, 'Jerome and Symmachus', 192).

2.26 this too] G here has ὅτι καί γε, lit. 'for also indeed': this is never elsewhere used to render גם זה alone, but appears for כי גם (4.14, 16; 8.12) and שגם (1.17; 2.15; 8.14, 16; 9.12). Such a reading appears in no other versions, although some manuscripts of S do have a conjunction here which is absent in the Hebrew, and V has *sed et hoc*, 'but also this'. It seems unlikely that this is an interpretative addition by the translator, which would be out of character, and it is not obvious how it might have arisen as an error. The additions in S and V might conceivably have the same origin, but it is probable that all reflect secondary attempts to connect the last clause to what precedes, and that this is an addition which either crept into the G tradition very early, or was found in G's source-text. Strikingly, the reading כי גם זה is found in the Complutensian Polyglot, and such a text could very easily have been the basis of G. That reading, however, enjoys only very limited support among the manuscripts collated by Kennicott and de Rossi, and although a similar כי זה has been noted in a Persian manuscript by Lavoie and Mehramooz, 'Le texte hébreu et la traduction judéo-persanne', 501, both may simply reflect the same pressure to make a connection.

2.26 wishing for the wind] See the corresponding note at 1.14.

Introduction to 3.1-15

The Work of God and Humans

(3.1) Everything has an occasion, and every matter beneath heaven a time:
(3.2) A time for birth and a time for dying;
a time for planting and a time for pulling out what is planted;
(3.3) A time for killing and a time for curing;
a time for wrecking and a time for building;
(3.4) A time for weeping and a time for laughing;
a time of mourning and a time of dancing;
(3.5) A time for throwing stones down and a time of gathering stones up;
a time for embracing and a time for avoiding an embrace;
(3.6) A time for seeking out and a time for letting slip;
a time for keeping and a time for throwing out;
(3.7) A time for ripping and a time for stitching;
a time for being silent and a time for talking;
(3.8) A time for loving and a time for hating;
a time of war and a time of peace.

(3.9) What is the lasting gain from the worker in that at which he toils?

(3.10) I have seen the work God has given to humans to work at: (3.11) he has made everything fine in its time; he has also put 'forever' into their heart, for lack of that which no human can discover: the achievement which God has achieved from start right through to finish.

(3.12) I know that there is no good in them except taking pleasure and doing good in one's life, (3.13) and also that every person who eats and drinks and finds good in all his business—this is a payment from God.

(3.14) I know that everything God achieves is what will exist forever: there is no adding to it, and there is no subtracting from it—and God has achieved their fear before him. (3.15) This already is whatever is, and what is to be already is, and it is God who will seek whatever is to be pursued.

If Qohelet's description of the world in the first chapter might be considered a prelude to his memoir, then ch. 3 presents its aftermath. Throughout this chapter, the material retains a continuity that will often be lacking after the start of the next, as Qohelet wraps up his account of the situation in which humans find themselves, and lays the ground for more miscellaneous remarks about its consequences. The set-piece presentation in vv. 1-8, however, marks a distinct break with the tone of his conclusions in ch. 2, and a return to something more like that of 1.4-11. Qohelet continues to remind us that these are his conclusions and observations, dropping in the fact that he has 'seen' the work of humans (3.10), and that he 'knows' certain things about humans and about God (3.12, 14), but he is no longer reflecting directly on his own experiences or emotions, and his points are stated once again as universal truths.

By the end of the last chapter, the author had portrayed Qohelet as being forced by his experiences into a realization that what individual humans have and do must be a result not of their own qualities or actions, but of divine dispensation. Chapter 3 now begins with a strong statement that all actions, accordingly, must in some sense be 'right'. If it is the case that what we do is in fulfilment of some divine plan or mandate, then no action is in itself inherently good or bad, but each must be the proper thing to have been done at the time when it was done: as Jerome puts it (at 3.11), *uicissim iuxta dispositionem dei bonum est unumquodque cum opus est*, 'each thing in turn, according to God's arrangement, is good when the need (for it) arises'. When Qohelet in 3.9 returns to his question from 1.3, therefore, he now asks not what profit humans can have from their work, but what profit that work can yield at all when all of it is done on God's behalf, as part of a much broader divine activity within an essentially changeless world. Humans have an awareness that this bigger picture exists, but no knowledge of it (just as, in 1.4-11, the brevity of their lives prevented them from properly understanding the world). Rather than profit, he goes on to speak again of the one thing that he had found positively to be his own in 2.10: the pleasure that can arise from living and working. If humans are employed by God, on tasks that ultimately yield no gain, and the real reasons for which are beyond their understanding, then this, at least, is their wage.

3.14-15 allude more specifically again to 1.4-11, in a way that re-states the impossibility of human influence: God's achievements are unalterable, and the world unchangeable. These achievements include, Qohelet notes, human fear of God—and the context may suggest that this should be connected with God's withholding from them of knowledge about his own actions: we fear God because we do not comprehend what he is doing. Along with an attempt to impose some notion of divine justice in the face of the determinism that he espouses, Qohelet will pick this point up again in the closing 3.16-22, where the inability of humans to understand their own position will lead him not just to observe that humans must find pleasure in what they do, but to commend such pleasure in the face of an unknowable future.

3.1-8

(3.1) Everything has an occasion, and every matter beneath heaven a time:
(3.2) A time for birth and a time for dying;
a time for planting and a time for pulling out what is planted;
(3.3) A time for killing and a time for curing;
a time for wrecking and a time for building;
(3.4) A time for weeping and a time for laughing;
a time of mourning and a time of dancing;
(3.5) A time for throwing stones down and a time of gathering stones up;
a time for embracing and a time for avoiding an embrace;
(3.6) A time for seeking out and a time for letting slip;
a time for keeping and a time for throwing out;
(3.7) A time for ripping and a time for stitching;
a time for being silent and a time for talking;
(3.8) A time for loving and a time for hating;
a time of war and a time of peace.

Commentary

This is without doubt the most famous section of the book—and going beyond the obvious reference to the Pete Seeger song, 'Turn! Turn! Turn! (To Everything There Is a Season)', which draws its lyrics directly from the text, Ravasi offers a particularly varied and interesting list of modern allusions to it; see also Christianson, *Ecclesiastes through the Centuries*, 164-73. Interpreters, however, have long been divided over its meaning, and have fallen, broadly speaking, into two camps. For some, the message is that there are right times and wrong times at which to do things, and Qohelet's words are sometimes understood to be affirming an ancient 'science of times', which sought to understand the proper times for action and inaction. For others, this is a statement almost of the opposite: what Qohelet suggests is that no action can ever be 'wrong' because every action contributes to the fulfilment of God's plan or wishes. The difference between the two understandings might be stated in terms of the relationship between divine and human activities: is Qohelet urging humans to align what they do with some underlying process, so that what they do may succeed, or is he telling them to accept that whatever they do will be a part of that process, whether they like it or not?

The 'science of times' option is attractive only in as much as it avoids imposing a sort of moral neutrality on human activities. This is found elsewhere in the book, however, most obviously in the suggestion of 9.7, that what one has done must somehow have been approved already by God. As we shall see shortly, Qohelet struggles to reconcile his determinism with an insistence that God judges humans—and that tension between human freedom and destiny remains a significant theological problem. If this passage is advocating proper choices, however, then it is odd that it should start with statements about birth and death: humans generally have very limited choices when it comes to the timing of those particular events. Most of the other actions are more compatible with the notion of choice, but, even so, there is something unsettling about the idea of making calculated decisions to laugh or weep, love or hate. Ultimately the most important consideration is that in the following verses Qohelet will emphasize the subordination of human action to God's will, and 3.10 links the fact that everything has been made 'fine in its time' quite explicitly to divine achievement, and to God's employment of humans for his own ends.[1]

---

[1] Against the 'science of times' interpretation more generally, see Lavoie, 'Il y a un temps', 33-35, although I do not share his view that the passage is intended to convey frustration. Some scholars have tried to find a middle path. Gammie, Stoicism', 175, is being highly selective, however, when he claims that the list actually asserts the freedom of humans to do certain things ('when to plant, when to weed', etc.) even within a framework of determinism. Bundvad, *Time*, 95-106, seems to be arguing that 3.1-8 reflect a 'science of times' understanding, but are then rejected in 3.9-11, which limit the human capacity to engage with such a scheme; that is an interesting way to deal with apparent incompatibilities between the two passages, but Bundvad does not address the problems associated with that understanding, and this approach seems unnecessarily complicated. Segal is similarly reluctant to align Qohelet with either 'description' or 'prescription', as he characterizes the two approaches, and he thinks that these verses 'glide' between the two, 'floating' on 'a sense of order beyond control'. His reservations are provoked by the admitted difficulty of seeing a thoroughgoing determinism across the book as a whole (which would render much of the subsequent advice irrelevant), but I doubt that the tensions in Qohelet's thought more generally should be

Whether they constitute a 'poem' as such,[2] or a less formal set piece, these verses should be understood as the iteration through different examples of a single basic point: no actions are 'bad' simply because they are the opposites of actions we consider 'good', since the 'goodness' or 'badness' of actions lies not in their own nature, but in their correspondence to the divine will at the point when they happen. Since nothing can happen except in correspondence to that will, everything is, in effect, 'good'. The point is emphasized by the mixture of actions that is presented, and by the variation of order: we are not simply given a list of things that we might consider positive, each followed by some more negative counterpart, and in some cases it is perfectly clear that, even on a human reckoning, the 'goodness' or 'badness' of some actions will depend entirely on their context.[3] From the fact that it might be good, say, to 'throw out' when we are spring-cleaning, or to 'pluck up' when we are gardening, we are supposed to understand that all actions can be of similar value when considered in the context of God's intentions, even if they seem more negative, somehow, than keeping or planting. Just as every dog has its day, so every action has its proper moment.[4]

---

read into each passage; as Segal himself observed earlier (3), 'one should not jump to the conclusion that the book offers a philosophy or a theology'.

[2] The colometric analysis in Loretz, 'Anfänge', 233-34, shows a general degree of consistency in the length of lines, but exceptionally long clauses, especially in v. 5.

[3] I am, correspondingly, unconvinced by the attempt in Loader, 'Qohelet 3,2-8', to distinguish 'desirable' and 'undesirable' actions, and then to identify patterns in the order of presentation. Even the 'favorable' and 'unfavorable' that he adopts in his later commentary are a stretch. Naturally, the use of complementary or antithetical actions in each pair means that one may consist simply of not doing the other, or of doing something that is more destructive than constructive, but the very variations that Loader identifies seem likely to have been intended to counter simple divisions into 'good' and 'bad'. Loader's suggestions are picked up in Wright, 'For Everything There Is a Season', which advances a similar analysis, and cf. Jarick, 'The Dao of Qoheleth', 86-98. Sicker describes the actions in each pair as being like the two sides of a coin, which is, I think, a better way of looking at them.

[4] From that analogy, it may be clear that I do not think we can extrapolate from these verses the sort of strong determinism that might schedule, say, 'plucking up' to happen at a fixed time on a certain date—but, equally, they do not exclude such an idea. Qohelet's point here does not encompass such questions. In a thoughtful study, which avoids fruitless attempts to find some greater precision in

Masoretic manuscripts present vv. 2-8 in stylized formats, although not all in the same way. Codex Leningrad, followed by *BHQ*, places the word for 'a time' or 'and a time' at the end of each column, with each clause spread across two lines:

	a time
for birth	
	and a time
for dying	
	a time
for planting	
	and a time
for pulling out what is planted	

In Ms Or. 9879, on the other hand, there are two clauses on each line, with space between them (which seems to have been a more common pattern), so that the clauses are justified to the right and left sides of the column:

a time for birth	and a time for dying
a time for planting	and a time for pulling out what is planted

There are similar formats to be found at, most notably, Esth 9.7-9, which is a list of names each prefaced by the accusative marker, and Josh 12.9-24, a list of kings with each name followed by the word for 'one'.[5] The presentations appear to be a response to

the Hebrew terminology, Fox, 'Qohelet's Catalogue', distinguishes 'actual time' from 'right time', and deduces from 7.17 that Qohelet must be talking about the latter, since a death must be able to happen when it is not 'the right time' for it. Such an understanding may indeed be required in 7.17, but here I think we are dealing with neither 'actual time' nor 'right time', but with something more like the sort of time involved when we say that someone has their 'moment in the sun' or their 'fifteen minutes of fame'. As Clines, 'Predestination', 532, puts it: 'The variegated experiences of life do not occur by human design but when their "time" arrives'. Qohelet is not interested in the nature of the timing, but in the fact of the certain occurrence. Gorssen, 'La cohérence', 290-92, argues, not dissimilarly, that the point here is the sheer number of possible outcomes or occurrences, not the timing of each, although he goes on to suggest that Qohelet is interested in the disquieting effect on humans of so many possibilities, which, I think, reads more into the text than is there.

[5] See also the special spacings used variably in different manuscripts for the list of David's warriors in 1 Chr 11.26-47. These are discussed by Penkower, in 'Codex', 105-106, who also notes (103) the special layouts used by two early manuscripts to deal with repeated words in Jer 51.20-23.

multiple repetitions close together of a single, short word, and their original purpose was probably to prevent the errors of reading or transcription that can happen easily in such contexts, although there is, perhaps, a decorative aspect as well. The Talmud (*y. Megillah* 3.7; *b. Megillah* 16b) describes them in terms of bricks and half-bricks arranged like a wall, and explains more fancifully that in Joshua and Esther the purpose is to prevent the listed individuals ever rising again, perhaps because such a wall, unlike one built of solid text, would be so unstable. Here, 3.1 is not included in the special presentation, probably because the word for 'time' is varied rather than repeated in the second part.

The lists in Esther and Joshua are certainly not poetry, and (as Hobbins, 'Poetry', 167, emphasizes) we should not use the formatting itself to identify 3.2-8 as verse. I doubt even that, in any sense other than graphic, 'it shows that the Masoretes distinguished this material from the surrounding text', as Linafelt and Dobbs-Allsopp suggest in 'Poetic Line Structure', 249 n. 1 (pedantically, it seems likely that this was, in any case, a scribal convention rather than a Masoretic innovation; cf. Bar-Ilan, 'Writing', 31).

3.1] Whether or not we are dealing with verse as such, however, there is no doubt that the passage is highly stylized—and, as Linafelt and Dobbs-Allsopp observe, 3.1 lies outside the carefully balanced structure, even though it clearly serves to introduce it. Their response is to overrule the Masoretic accentuation which drives the conventional construal of the verse, and they propose to read either 'To everything, a season, / and a time for every matter / under the heavens', or, better, 'For everything, a time and a season, / for every matter under the heavens' (similarly, HCM). Both are attractive and legitimate readings of the text, and I have retained the normal understanding in my own translation only because it seems slightly more natural—and I am not entirely persuaded that 3.1 is supposed to be poetic.

Corley, 'Qoheleth and Sirach', 151, notes that 3.1 has seven words, while in the list that follows there are 28 occurrences of the word for 'time'. He may be right to suggest that the design deliberately evokes another aspect of time by using the numbers of days in a week and a (four-week) month, but it is difficult to exclude coincidence in such cases. Lohfink ('Gegenwart', 4) interprets the 28 differently, as the number of perfection (7) combined with the four cardinal points, and Crenshaw (*The Ironic Wink*, 72) more simply takes the 14 antitheses as twice that perfect number—both of which seem less plausible. Schwienhorst-Schönberger notes that the numerical value of the word for time (עת) is 70 + 400 = 470, and relates this to the roles of 4 and 7—a relationship that is clearer, perhaps, to modern readers using Arabic numerals, and that could surely not, as Köhlmoos suggests, have served a mnemonic purpose.

In 3.17 and 8.6, Qohelet will recall the statement here, that 'there is a time for every matter' to make a point that everything will be judged—that there is, in other words, 'a time of judgment' for everything. That sense is highly unlikely here, however, not least because it is hard to imagine what judgment could be delivered on actions like birth and death, and it seems that Qohelet is using his later evocations of this verse to suggest a continuity between ideas that actually stand in tension with each other (see the comments at 3.17). Equally, though, we should not suppose that the claim in this verse might be summarized simply as 'everything will happen': the Hebrew has the more specific sense that 'everything has its own time', when it should happen, which will be nuanced in 3.11 by Qohelet's further claim that God has made everything 'fine' in its time.

3.2-8] Whybray ('Time to Be Born', 475) is surely right to reject the idea that each pair of activities in this list is intended to 'express completeness or totality' (as Crenshaw puts it), by representing everything that might lie between them, and that the 'twenty-eight items cover the spectrum of human activity' (Crenshaw, again). He is also right to note the lack of formal and thematic consistency across the list as a whole. There is little weight, however, in his suggestion that it must therefore have evolved from a collection of originally independent sayings: although, to be sure, any one of these sayings might have been created to make the sort of point that Qohelet is making, it is hard to imagine that they constituted some sort of popular genre—and quite unnecessary to do so. There probably is an intention to represent a wide range of actions and events—to exemplify the fact that *every* action and event is implicated—and this in itself drives the thematic and, in turn, the formal variety. Any insistence on consistency in both respects, however, is just a demand that the list correspond to our own ideas of what it should look like.

3.2] The Hebrew uses verbs here, but it is difficult to capture the sense using verbs in English: a translation 'being born' would give a more precise parallel to 'dying' (and many commentators understand that sense here), but the Hebrew verb could be understood either way, and I have tried to preserve that neutrality. Of course, one is not usually given a conscious choice about the time to 'be born', and few actively choose a specific time to die (cf. 8.8; 9.12), so this verse, and its prominence at the beginning of the list, present a significant obstacle to the idea that Qohelet is talking about identifying the right times for action. Blenkinsopp ('Ecclesiastes 3.1-15') tries to turn this argument on its head: since every act here must be under human control, he suggests, Qohelet must be referring here to suicide, and quoting a Stoic source.

3.5] The Midrash apparently understands the first antithesis in sexual terms: stones are to be thrown when one's wife is ritually clean, gathered when she is not. Levy, in an appendix to his commentary (144-52), and in 'Das Steinewerfen', seeks to demonstrate that this is a more widely used figure, and that it should be understood as the original sense here. His evidence, though, is far from compelling, and the view has rightly been rejected by most subsequent commentators (Gordis, and, more recently, Schwienhorst-Schönberger being among the notable exceptions); it continues, all the same, to find some other supporters (e.g. Dorp, 'Enkele aantekeningen'; Jarick, 'The Dao of Qoheleth', 89). The Targum, in fact, interprets the *second* antithesis in terms of embracing a wife (as, very plausibly, does the Testament of Naphtali; cf. Lange, 'In Diskussion', 123-24), and we may be dealing with an error in the textual transmission of the Midrash, through which an exegesis of the second part has been transferred to the first.[6] Whether that is the case or not, it seems unlikely that an erotic tone was originally intended, or that we can use this verse as a key to unlock other sexual metaphors in 3.2-8, as does Brenner ('M Text Authority'), who finds love poetry here (cf. Koosed, *[Per]mutations*, 69-71, which is critical of Brenner, but finds desire represented here in

---

[6] Treier suggests that the interpretation of stones in sexual terms is to be found among early Christian commentators also. He cites only Augustine *On Marriage and Concupiscence* 14, however, where 'embracing' in this verse is understood sexually, but no reference is made at all to stones.

a different way). Galling ('Das Rätsel der Zeit', 10) discusses the interesting possibility that the reference is to pebbles used as pieces in a board-game or as tokens, while Provan thinks that Qohelet is talking about precious stones, and so about the accumulation, distribution, and, subsequently, the embrace of wealth. There is no such specification here, however, and there are, of course, many other circumstances in which stones of many different sorts might be gathered or discarded.

3.7] The Hebrew verb for 'ripping' is used most often of tearing clothes as a sign of mourning, and Levy sees a reference here to that practice, followed by the repair of the clothing after the period of mourning is finished. Though he does not note it, this is, in fact, precisely the interpretation of the Targum. Gordis finds Levy's view attractive, although he accepts that there is some distance between this verse and the preceding references to mourning. It is difficult to see, however, why we should limit the scope of the verse to that context alone, and most subsequent scholars have been wary of doing so. There is, equally, no very good reason to adopt Provan's association of the imagery with the 'opening' and 'sealing' of the mouth that he finds implicit in the second pair of verbs.

Notes

3.1 Everything has] Lit. 'for everything an occasion'. The right time 'for' doing something can be expressed using an infinitive cs. with ל- (e.g. Hos 10.12), but ל- can also be used with a following substantive to express possession, classically when what is possessed is indeterminate (like *a* time), and what possesses is not. Since the list that will follow suggests that 'everything' here is to be understood in terms of 'every action', there is an initial ambiguity in the syntax: Qohelet might be saying that there is a time 'to do' every action, or that every action 'has' a time. From 3.4 onwards, the preposition is omitted a number of times in the list, and although it is difficult to say whether this, strictly speaking, resolves the ambiguity, the final items in 3.8 are nouns, and the expressions are more certainly expressions of possession. The author may have played on the similarity of the constructions, or perhaps not even have been especially conscious of a difference between them, so we should probably not use 3.8b as a template to parse everything else in the list. Equally, though, the applications of ל- זמן and ל- עת to כל in this verse, where they can again only be, strictly, expressions of possession, do not favour an understanding that Qohelet is using 'time to' clauses throughout. Barton speaks accordingly of -ל representing the 'genitive relation', and cf. V *omnia tempus habent*, 'all things have a time'. If, however, we can more or less resolve the syntactical ambiguity in favour of reading expressions of possession, this does not in itself tell us whether Qohelet is talking about times when things should be done, or about times when things happen: עת in a possessive construction like this can indicate both (contrast, e.g., Gen 29.7 with Gen 38.27)—although the latter is more common.

The possessive constructions in this verse may also indicate how the syntax of each clause in this verse is to be construed. Although translators commonly opt for a statement of existence (e.g. RSV 'For everything there is a season'), and Qohelet himself uses יש for a similar claim at 8.6, it is difficult to find any close analogy elsewhere for 'there is' simply being understood. On the other hand, in the twin clauses of Hag 2.8, for example, there are some obvious parallels to non-verbal statements of possession with -ל. With the predicate placed first, these naturally put the emphasis on the possessor (cf. J-M §154 ff), so that לי הכסף means 'the silver is *mine*', and if we read our clauses here in such terms, then we would expect them likewise to be emphasizing that 'a time (belongs) to *everything*'. That seems quite appropriate: Qohelet's purpose, after all, is probably not to show that there are many times, but to declare that nothing is without a time.

T כל גבר distinguishes the first כל as a reference to 'every man', while the second is כל עיסקא, 'every matter'; the Midrash notably illustrates the first with a list of times at which particular people had to perform certain actions, so may share that interpretation. Although G renders the first as plural, to give τοῖς πᾶσιν...τῷ παντὶ πράγματι ('for all...for every deed'; so also Hie, probably following La),[7] there is no reason to suppose that it too intends such a distinction.

3.1 an occasion] Almost all manuscripts of G read an article here before χρόνος, to give 'the time' (although not before the subsequent καιρὸς), and it is easier to explain the loss of that article through assimilation in those that do not than to see how it might have arisen secondarily. It has a fair claim to be G*, then, although it is rejected by Rahlfs and Gentry, and McNeile argues that it reflects a reading in the source-text of G. The other versions offer little assistance here, although σ' παντὸς ὥρα, 'a proper time for everything', does support M.

The term זמן itself is generally regarded as a loanword from Aramaic (which may itself have borrowed it originally from Akkadian; cf. Schoors, *The Preacher* I, 60-61; *The Preacher* II, 382), and it appears commonly in later Hebrew. The noun and cognate verb, however, are found elsewhere in

---

[7] Hie in 3.1-3 is identical to the text of Jerome's earlier revision of La, see Caspari, *Hiob*, 6; Leanza, 'Le tre versione', 91.

biblical Hebrew only at Ezra 10.14; Neh 2.6; 10.35; 13.31; Esth 9.27, 31. זמן refers to times which have been set for events or appointments, but the other usage suggests no reason to emphasize strongly either the predetermination or the appropriateness of those times; when Nehemiah sets a זמן in Neh 2.6, it is simply the proposed date of his return to court.

3.1 matter] The usual meaning of חפץ in biblical Hebrew is 'pleasure' or 'what one wants', and Ecclesiastes uses it that way in 5.3; 8.3; 12.1, 10. Here, however, and in 3.17; 5.7; 8.6, the book clearly intends a different sense, and G distinguishes the uses by translating with πρᾶγμα, a 'deed' or 'matter', instead of θέλημα, 'will' or 'what one wills', which it uses in 5.3; 12.1, 10, or its cognate terms (cf. also S, which uses ܨܒܘ *ṣbw*—5.7 ܨܒܘܬܐ *ṣbwtʾ*—instead of the related ܨܒܝܢ *ṣbynʾ*: that gives a distinction of sense similar to that in G). This meaning is not certainly to be found anywhere else in biblical Hebrew, although it is sometimes understood in Prov 31.13; Isa 58.3, 13.

Its attestation in later Hebrew is also less clear cut than is sometimes assumed. The Greek version renders חפצך, 'your work' (τὸ ἔργον σου), in Sir 10.26, but the normal sense would do just as well. The same is true in the Aramaic Sefire inscription III, 8, cited by Whitley, Seow, and Schoors, *The Preacher* II, 212, where, for לכל חפצי, Fitzmyer (*Aramaic Inscriptions*, 96) has 'my business' but Donner and Röllig (*KAI* 224.8) 'was mir gefällt', 'whatever I like', which certainly suits the tone and context. Elsewhere in Hebrew, Schoors, *The Preacher* II, 213, cites Sir 11.23 (Ms A *sub* 11.21) and 43.7, in addition to 10.26. In 11.23, though, the expression refers to need or desire, and in 43.7 the sense is unclear, but has something to do with the phases of the moon. Seow cites uses in the Damascus Document (CD 14.12) and Treatise of the Two Spirits (1QS 3.17) as references to 'specific assignments or tasks of individuals', but in the former, the context makes it clear that כל חפציהם is a reference to the 'needs' or 'wants' of the many, for which money is to be set aside; in the latter, יכלכלם בכול חפציהם might refer to the conduct of affairs (cf. Ps 112.5), but more probably, again, refers to providing for 'needs'. In rabbinic usage, חפץ can mean a 'thing', but generally connotes an actual object. Jastrow, *Dictionary*, cites *b. Moʿed Qaṭan* 9b, חפצי שמים, for the sense 'heavenly affairs (religious deeds)', but this is a discussion of Prov 3.15; 8.11, and personal desires are being contrasted with religious requirements using the vocabulary of the biblical texts. In short, Qohelet's dual usage of the term is clearly recognized by the translators of Ecclesiastes, but is apparently idiosyncratic, and cannot be shown, on current evidence, to reflect some broader usage. His use of חפץ to connote a 'deed' or 'matter' may have been influenced by the two senses of the Aramaic צבו, rather than being a parallel semantic development in Hebrew (as Wagner, *Aramaismen*, 58, suggests). σ' πάσης χρείας may be an attempt to capture both meanings, as χρεία can refer to both need and activity.

3.1 heaven] Lit. 'beneath the heavens'. The expression has been used already, in 1.13 and 2.3. S, along with some Hebrew and many Greek manuscripts, reads 'sun' here, but this is an assimilation to the more common idiom.

3.1 a time] עת is a more general word for time than is זְמָן, but there is no apparent intention to distinguish their senses here. S, indeed, renders both Hebrew words with ܙܒܢ‎ *zbnʾ* (as does Syh their Greek equivalents), and Hie similarly uses *tempus* for each. Despite much discussion of the sense (cf. Schoors, *The Preacher* II, 111-19), the precise meaning in Ecclesiastes is something which must be determined through interpretation of the passages in which it is used, rather than through broader lexical considerations: the word is used in biblical Hebrew to connote many different sorts of 'time', from experiences and destiny through to the time of day. V paraphrases here: *et suis spatiis transeunt universa sub caelo*, which is difficult to translate, but means something like 'and all things pass under heaven at the times when they are to be done'.

3.2 for birth] Lit. 'for birthing'. Jerome's use of gerunds in his translations catches well the sense of the infinitive constructs throughout the list, but his indecision between 'giving birth' or 'becoming a parent' (Hie *pariendi*) and 'being born' (V *nascendi*) also sums up a problem which has been much discussed by modern commentators. If the reference is to being born, then the verb must be understood as passive, or at least intransitive, against the normal use of the qal stem. If, on the other hand, it is to giving birth, then it is a less satisfactory parallel to the subsequent 'dying'. Fox points out that the infinitive is neutral with respect to voice, citing J-M §124 s, and would read the verb as intransitive on the basis of context. Grammatically, the point is a fair one, but since the writer had the option of the well-attested niphʿal stem if he wished specifically to indicate 'being born' (and, arguably, of the hiphʿil for a transitive sense), it seems better to retain the neutrality than to force the sense: this is probably a reference to the act of birth, not to the actions of either the parent or the child in particular. That is difficult to render in English using a verb: Seow opts for 'birthing', but I have chosen to use a noun instead.

Dyk and Talstra, 'Paradigmatic', 160, argues that the syntax of the pairs here and in the following verses should be understood in terms of verbless clauses expressing existence ('[there is] a time to be born') and rejects the idea that the infinitive could be a 'predicate complement' (yielding 'to be born has a time'). The insistence that other examples of the infinitive being used in this way would be needed to demonstrate such a sense, however, should be considered in the light of the facts that (1) they present no comparable example of a verbless clause expressing existence without any modifier or particle of existence, and (2) there is absolutely no reason in principle why the infinitive should not be used that way. The peculiar nature of what is being said here does make it difficult, of course, to adduce clear parallels, but if we wanted to identify a 'predicate complement' construction, then Job 39.1 probably offers grounds to do so ('do you know what time belongs to giving birth by mountain-goats?').[8] I think it is altogether simpler, however, to suppose that we are not actually dealing with 'statements' in these verses at all, but with a plain list of items, separated into pairs: if there were an over-arching construction, it would be inherited from 3.1 (on which, see above), and that verse does not involve the complication of infinitives. Accordingly, I doubt that we should translate each item either with 'a time exists for x', as do HCM, or with 'x has a time', which would probably be closer to the intended sense.

3.2 for planting] The infinitive construct of נטע with -ל is usually לִנְטֹעַ in biblical Hebrew and לִטַּע in the later language, so לָטַעַת here is exceptional. As often noted, Bauer-Leander §52 h sees the forms with נ in the infinitives of pe-nun verbs as a new formation, based on the strong verb (while allowing the possibility that the variation is dialectal), but the aphaeresis of נ in these verbs is sufficiently erratic that we should probably not read too much into the use of a particular form here. The final ת occurs as compensation after the aphaeresis, and the vocalization with *patah* results from the medial guttural; cf. J-M §72 c-d.

3.2 for pulling out] This is the only biblical occurrence of עקר in the qal stem; it is more commonly found in the pi'el, used of hamstringing animals (e.g. Gen 49.6; 2 Sam 8.4). The niph'al is found at Zeph 2.4, where it stands in parallel with a form from גרשׁ, 'expel', and is a play on the name Ekron. The context does little to reveal the sense, but the Greek rendering there is ἐκριζωθήσεται, 'will be uprooted', or 'rooted out'; in our text, G has ἐκτῖλαι, which refers to plucking out or off, and both renderings correspond to the sense of the cognate Aramaic verb.

Dahood, 'Phoenician Background', 270, notes, however, the use of עקרת in one of the Karatepe inscriptions (*KAI* 26.1.1), for which Donner and Röllig, following Bossert, suggest 'Speicher' ('storehouse'). This leads him to suggest that the Phoenician term has arisen because the verb can mean 'harvest', and he then transfers that sense to Ecclesiastes—an argument which is accepted by Whitley, but which is self-evidently tenuous: the meaning of the noun is uncertain, its derivation unknown, and its relationship with the Hebrew word unclear. The pulling-up of plants may well be in the context of harvesting them, and we need not insist that this describes an act of wanton destruction (cf. Willmes, *Menschliches Schicksal*, 112-13), but the antithesis here is between putting them into the ground and taking them out of it.

---

[8] The constructions used with עת and similar nouns are studied in considerable detail by Kotjatko-Reeb, 'Infinitive und Verbalnomina', where the infinitives are characterized as epexegetical, but the parallel constructions with nouns described in terms of a construct relationship. Kotjatko-Reeb (71) looks to 1 Chr 20.1 for a similar juxtaposition of both constructions.

3.3 killing...curing] The slight imprecision of the antithesis has led S to render לרפוא with ܠܡܚܐ *lmḥyw*, 'saving', and some commentators to emend להרג to להרוף or to להרוס. That last is quite tempting, since it would give an opposition between destroying and repairing, as in 1 Kgs 18.30 (cf. Gordis), but it would thereby also, arguably, render the second part of the verse redundant. M is generally supported by the versions, and should be retained, but an early Latin reading *tempus infirmari et tempus sanari*, 'a time to be ill and a time for healing', is noteworthy as an attempt to improve the antithesis in a different way.[9]

3.3 wrecking] לפרוץ might have been chosen in part for assonance with the preceding לרפוא, but it can also be used specifically of demolishing structures (cf. Isa 5.5), and this connotation is drawn out in T לפכרא בניינא.

3.4 of mourning...of dancing] The infinitives lack -ל, as will כנוס in the next verse. Although G makes no attempt to differentiate between the forms with and without the preposition in its translation, this hardly proves that its source-text was different (as McNeile suspects), and there are no text-critical grounds for emendation. A number of commentators have supposed that the preceding prepositions are doing 'double duty' here, and functioning with these verbs as well as those to which they are attached (so, e.g., Schoors, *The Preacher* I, 203-204; Dahood, 'Phoenician Background', 270). This seems to be stretching the principle set out in GKC §119 hh, but does not, in any case, address the more fundamental question of why the preposition should only be omitted in these three cases. In the absence of any grammatical explanation, it seems likely that the motive here is euphonic (enhancing the assonance between the terms which is noted by Ginsburg).

Levy argues that רקוד might refer to singing, but dancing is not a bad antithesis to mourning (and Seow notes the opposition between the two in Ps 30.12 [ET 30.13], albeit with a different verb).

---

[9] This reading appears in the context of Jerome's revision of the Old Latin in Codex Sangallensis 11, but as part of a double translation with the normal 'kill' and 'heal': *tempus occidendi et tempus sanandi, tempus infirmari et tempus sanari*; cf. Caspari, *Hiob*, 6. It does not appear in the otherwise identical reproduction of 3.1-8 in John Cassian's *Collationes* (XXI, 12, 3): see Petschenig, *Conlationes*, 586, and PL 49, col. 1186. Leanza ('Le tre versione', 90-91) suggests plausibly enough that it represents the unrevised La. Vaccari, 'Recupero', 115, on the other hand, takes the rendering to be a marginal gloss of less specific origin, which has slipped into the text. There is a similar double rendering in 3.7: see below. If this is indeed La, then it seems to have used infinitives, following G, where Jerome opts for gerunds, but Vaccari shows in connection with a different point (119-20) that the second part of 3.5 is quite widely attested with gerunds in early Latin sources. Unless we allow that the treatment of the verbs may have been quite inconsistent in the La rendering of the list, then we should be wary of characterizing this translation simply as 'the Old Latin'.

S and Syh here exploit the dual meanings of the Syriac cognate ܪܩܕ *rqd* (hafel = 'lament', pael = 'dance') to achieve a play on words (cf. Kamenetzky, 214). Jerome represents the 'happy' verbs (*ridendi...saltandi*, 'laughing... dancing') consistently here, but Hie, V adopt *flendi* to represent weeping and *plangendi* for mourning, where Jerome's revision of La used *plorandi* and *lugendi*—probably the verbs employed originally (cf. Caspari, *Hiob*, 6; Leanza, 'Le tre versione', 91).

3.5 for throwing stones down] As Jerome notes in his commentary, G βαλεῖν suggests the deliberate hurling of stones, and he prefers 'scatter' (*spargendi*) in Hie, V, making this a less violent act, whilst retaining a greater precision than the *mittendi* ('sending off', 'letting go') used in his revision of La (Caspari, *Hiob*, 6; Leanza, 'Le tre versione', 91). This is probably more in line with the sense of the Hebrew: שלך is used of casting things down or away, rather than of throwing weapons (cf. the unattributed marginal reading ῥῖψαι in mss 161, 248). As Schoors and others point out, 'stones' is probably repeated to avoid using the same verb absolutely here and in the next verse, but some commentators have seen it as a gloss. Glasser, *Le Procès*, 58-59, offers a complicated explanation for the gloss in terms of the early Jewish interpretation of these verses as a reference to the history of Israel: the stones are then a reference to the scattered stones of Lam 4.1.

3.5 for avoiding an embrace] Lit. 'for keeping one's distance from an embrace / from embracing' or 'being far from an embrace / from embracing'. G, Hie and S seem to read חבק as a substantive (cf. also V, which makes it plural), perhaps the חֲבֻק of Prov 6.10 = 24.33 (to which there may be a reference in 4.5), while M points it as a pi'el infinitive. Since the need for an infinitive corresponding to the preceding לחבוק has already been met by לרחק, vocalization as a noun seems very plausible, but חבק could also be read either as M reads it, or as a defectively written qal infinitive: the consonantal text leaves all these possibilities open, and none makes a significant difference to the sense.

The construction with רחק and מן is not problematic, and although it usually indicates simply being far from something (e.g. Deut 12.21; Ps 119.50), it can also imply deliberate distancing (e.g. Exod 23.7; Prov 22.5; Sir 7.2 [ms C; ms A has hiph'il]). While in principle it should be able to take an infinitive (which would hardly be 'unhebräisch', as Ehrlich claims), in practice it does not do so elsewhere, which might again support reading a noun here. That, at least, would be simpler than Ehrlich's own preference, which is to vocalize as a pi'el participle מְחַבֵּק, 'someone who would embrace (you)', and take לרחק as a pi'el infinitive לְרַחֵק, so that the reference is then to keeping a potential embracer away from oneself.

3.6 seeking out...letting slip] The order is reversed in S (see Janichs, *Animadversiones*, 8), which Goldman considers an attempt to create a more logical sequence (cf. Kamenetzky, 214), but Euringer finds arbitrary. This reversal is also found in Origenic manuscripts of G, however, so may not be an independent development in the Syriac, even if S does not adopt the subsequent reversal of the next verbs, also found in most such manuscripts.

Although it is often used in contexts of destruction, the second verb, אבד, basically refers in the qal to disappearance or cessation of existence, with the pi'el having a causative sense—G finds a good equivalent with ἀπολέσαι here and the middle ἀπολεῖται in 5.13. The qal is used of 'lost' sheep in Jer 50.6; Ps 119.176 and of lost donkeys in 1 Sam 9.3, 20, while Ezek 34.4, 15-16 uses it when speaking metaphorically of seeking (בקש, as here) lost sheep. Although Gordis, followed by some other commentators, has suggested that the corresponding sense of the pi'el must be 'giving up for lost', we do have direct evidence for the usage which makes that unlikely: in Jer 23.1, the pi'el is used of causing or allowing sheep to stray, while Prov 29.3 uses it figuratively of squandering resources.[10] These references suggest that the connotation is waste or neglect, not conscious surrender, so that the antithesis here is between seeking something out and letting something slip away.

Jerome is inconsistent: in his revision of La, he used, or retained, *expellendi* (cf. Caspari, *Hiob*, 7; Leanza, 'Le tre versione', 92), while Hie has *proiciendi* and V *abiciendi*. These reflect a loose progression from 'casting away' to 'letting go'.

3.6 keeping...throwing out] S is again different here, reading ܘܒܢ ܠܡܩܛܪ ܘܙܒܢ ܠܡܫܪܐ *zbn' lmqṭr wzbn' lmšr'*, 'a time for binding and a time for loosing'. This is reminiscent of Matt 16.19; 18.18, but the Peshitta there has ܠܡܫܕܐ *lmšd'* for ܠܡܩܛܪ *lmqṭr*, so the resemblance may be coincidental. As Euringer notes, we might expect ܠܡܢܛܪ *lmnṭr*, 'keep', and ܠܡܫܕܐ *lmšd'*, 'throw', emendations which are proposed also by Kamenetzky, 201. The second would be straightforward, assuming a simple √ר (*d/r*) confusion, although it is harder to see how *n* might have become *q* in the first. In any case, it is interesting to see here, as in G ἐκβαλεῖν and Hie *proiciendi* (cf. V *abiciendi*), an apparent differentiation in the translations of להשליך between this verse and the last, avoiding the repetition of M; T paraphrases, but also uses different verbs in each case. The context here suggests that the sense is throwing out or away, as in, e.g., 2 Kgs 7.15; Jer 7.29.

---

[10] Levine, 'Semantics of Loss', 154, interprets Jer 23.1-4 in terms of the shepherds actively driving the sheep away, and would accordingly translate 3.6 as 'A time to seek out and a time to drive away'. It is true, of course, that the hiph'il of פוץ, with which אבד is linked in Jer 23.1, can refer to the deliberate scattering of people or things, but if we are supposed to see the image in terms of shepherds actively dispersing their flocks, this sits uncomfortably both with ולא פקדתם אתם, 'you have not attended to them', in 23.2, and with the declaration in 23.3 that it is God himself who has driven the sheep to other countries. Jeremiah's point is that the people were dispersed into exile because their leaders failed to do their job properly, not that the leaders actively chased them away into exile.

Both T and the Midrash illustrate with nautical examples, the former noting that it might be necessary to throw merchandise overboard in a storm, the latter telling the story of a merchant who throws his money into the sea in order to avoid being killed for it by the crew. Where the first part of the verse speaks of casual loss, this part speaks of deliberate disposal.

3.7 ripping...stitching] Hie, V have *scindendi...consuendi*, 'tearing... stitching together', but Jerome's revision of La uses the more general *disrumpendi...sartiendi/ sarciendi*, 'breaking...repairing' (Caspari, *Hiob*, 7; Leanza, 'Le tre versione', 92).[11]

3.7 being silent...talking] Levy, again followed by Gordis, cites the Midrash Rabbah here as עת לחשות בשעת האבלות ועת לדבר לאחר האבלות, 'a time to be silent in the period of mourning and a time for speaking after mourning', which would support his own interpretation of the theme in this verse as mourning. This reading, however, is absent from the standard text, and Levy has perhaps derived it from the gloss on the midrash in Epstein's *Torah Temima*. T interprets in terms of refraining from or engaging in argument.

3.8 loving...hating] Aitken, 'Rhetoric and Poetry', 68, notes that G elsewhere renders אהב with ἀγαπᾶν (5.9 twice; 9.9), which α' uses here. As he suggests, the use of φιλῆσαι instead may result from a stylistic concern to achieve a better phonetic match with μισῆσαι, and it lends some weight to his observation that ῥῆξαι...ῥάψαι may have been chosen for a similar reason in the previous verse. It is also possible that in this context the translator wants to emphasize physical expression rather than just emotional state: φιλῆσαι could mean 'kiss'. Hie *amandi...odiendi*, 'loving...hating', retains the terms used in Jerome's revision of La (Caspari, *Hiob*, 7; Leanza, 'Le tre versione', 92), and imitate G. V *dilectionis...odii*, 'love...hatred', on the other hand, uses substantives, bringing this first part of the verse into line with the second.

3.8 war...peace] The list ends with a switch to nouns in place of the preceding infinitives. These are not preceded by -ל, and עת stands in a construct relationship with each, indicating possession. The change to nouns is largely reflected in the versions, but T inserts verbs, so that the reference is to 'starting' war or 'making' peace.

---

[11] Although it is presumably covered by his general comment about double renderings in Sangallensis 11 (p. 90 n. 9), Leanza, 'Le tre versione', does not explicitly note that the codex here has both *disrumpendi...sartiendi/ sarciendi* and *elidere...saluandi* ('to break...of saving'); cf. Vaccari, 'Recupero', 115. The second is absent in Cassian's text (see the note at 3.3, above): on Leanza's reckoning, this is the original, unrevised La, although one might expect *saluare* rather than *saluandi*, to match *elidere*, and the form may have been influenced by the verbs in Jerome's revised version.

3.9-15

(3.9) What is the gain from the worker in that at which he toils?

(3.10) I have seen the work God has given to humans to work at: (3.11) he has made everything fine in its time; he has also put 'forever' into their heart, for lack of that which no human can discover: the achievement which God has achieved from start right through to finish.

(3.12) I know that there is no good in them except taking pleasure and doing good in one's life, (3.13) and also that every person who eats and drinks and finds good in all his business—this is a payment from God.

(3.14) I know that everything God achieves is what will exist forever: there is no adding to it, and there is no subtracting from it—and God has achieved their fear before him. (3.15) This already is whatever is, and what is to be already is, and it is God who will seek whatever is to be pursued.

Commentary

With a variation of the question that he first posed in 1.3, Qohelet now asks, in effect, what can be gained from any effort, and probably suggests that no such gain is possible. As in the first chapter, though, he does not address the question directly in what follows, but offers a context within which it is to be understood. This initially recalls an idea that he earlier presumed in 1.13, that humans are employed by God—which has more recently, of course, been the substance also of the idea that he rejected in 2.26, and so after the set piece of vv. 1-8, he is returning to a central issue. He links this new discussion to those verses by adding that God has made everything 'fine in its time', but then adds a further, new observation: God has in some sense put 'forever' into the mind or ambitions of humans, but has not given them a corresponding insight into the whole scope of his own achievements, which they cannot discover for themselves. If he is in part drawing threads together, then, Qohelet is also introducing an assumption or conclusion that denies any possibility of human independence: what we do is for God, and although we are motivated to act by ideas about the impact of our actions, we cannot begin to understand their real place in the greater scheme of things.

As with 2.24, commentators have tried to find in 3.12 a claim that there is 'nothing better *for* humans' than that they should take pleasure, but there is little textual support for an emendation to bring this into line with 3.22. If in 2.24 the issue was one of possessing worth, however, Qohelet seems to be working with a broader notion here, and talking neither about potential benefits to humans, nor strictly about their qualities, but simply about the limitations imposed on them by their position: finding pleasure and doing something good (or doing well) is all that they can achieve, and they have the ability to do that only as a sort of wage from God. Qohelet is building up towards a commendation that humans accept that limitation, but here he is still at the point of observation.

Returning to the ideas of 1.9-10, he contrasts the position of God: it is *his* actions that will persist, without any change by others, and it is *God* who will 'seek what is pursued'. This expression (perhaps an idiom more familiar to the original readers than to us) seems to use the imagery of hunting, and it is difficult to know for sure just what it is that God is said to track down. If he is not just seeking to round up anything that threatens to escape from the continuity of his world, however, then perhaps the implication is that, if there is any particular goal towards which things are moving, then it is God who directs them. What distinguishes the claims here from those in 1.9-10, after all, is principally the fact that constancy in the world is portrayed not just as inherent, but as the consequence of divine action: as mere instruments of that action, humans are doing nothing for themselves, and understand nothing of what they do.

At the end of 3.14, Qohelet remarks almost parenthetically that God has achieved human fear 'before him', and 3.11 has already claimed that God put 'forever' into the human heart without a matching capacity to comprehend his actions, or perhaps by withholding such a capacity. Qohelet does recognize that God might act deliberately to inhibit or confuse humans, and 7.14 probably asserts just such action, as may 8.17. The statements here leave that possibility open, but probably do not make explicit or unambiguous claims that God has actually set out to disadvantage humans.

Indeed, the slightly contorted expression of 3.11 may even reflect an effort to avoid such a claim: God has given humans a certain awareness, and although that awareness is limited, the limitation is not itself made the point of his action. In 3.14, the Hebrew is not awkward or difficult so much as ambiguous: God has made 'what they fear' or God has made 'the fact that they fear'. Although often translated in terms of purpose, however, it probably cannot mean God has acted 'so that they might fear'. In context, Qohelet's point is probably that, as one of his 'achievements', the human fear of God will be as changeless and perpetual as all the others.

Crenshaw ('Eternal Gospel', 44) compares other ancient texts 'describing a god's jealousy lest human creatures achieve a status or power that threatens the deity'. Throughout this discussion, however, Qohelet's intention is apparently not to portray God as oppressive or manipulative, so much as to set human efforts within the context of a world that humans cannot properly understand, and in which they depend on God even for the ability to live their lives well. Lavoie ('Puissance', 286-87) similarly sees the gifts of work and 'forever' as poisoned chalices, but there is no explicit indication that God seeks to harm or even simply to suppress humans, and any resentment that we might feel flows simply from a sense that our role should be different. Given the way that Qohelet himself comes to feel about wisdom, in fact, it is not clear that the human incapacity that he describes here is even necessarily to be taken as a bad thing. As Paulson remarks, echoing Luther and looking at the book more generally, 'We are shown...that we are not to look to our own efforts for anything that lasts. We are freed from the tyranny of making more of ourselves than we should, more than we can. God has given us good things in life to enjoy, and once we are freed from the necessity of finding ultimate meaning in these things, we are freed to find the joy that God has intended for us' ('The Use of Qoheleth', 308-309). Provan ('Fresh Perspectives', 404) similarly thinks that Qohelet 'is trying to persuade his hearers of the futility of this ongoing human quest and thus to save them from a life that is itself characterized by futility'.

3.9] It is not impossible to read 'What is the gain *for* the worker?', which is the common understanding of the question here, but the wording is not the same as in 1.3, and usage elsewhere in the book favours 'from'. Neither the list that precedes, moreover, nor the subsequent points made in 3.10-11, seem directly relevant to the broader problem of human profit. The question is, however, followed immediately by a statement that God gives humans work to do, and in 3.14-15 by emphatic claims that God's achievements are unalterable, and that it is God who will do whatever needs to be done. In this context, and after he has made the point that the value of all human works lies in their conformity to divine intentions, it seems likely, in fact, that Qohelet is echoing his earlier question, but addressing a very different issue: the objective value of human work, in a world where only divine work can make any difference. Humans are given their tasks by God, motivated by him, and paid by him, and those tasks are 'fine' inasmuch as they have been appointed by him, but if they generate any sort of gain, that is only in terms of advancing the divine agenda. If we are supposed to read the question as rhetorical, furthermore, demanding the answer 'none', then Qohelet may even be suggesting that there is no 'gain' from work even in those terms: his earlier depiction of a world that is in constant movement, but that never changes, is also echoed in these verses, and there is little reason to suppose that he believes God to be seeking any sort of profit or improvement—either from his own work, or from that which he gives humans to do.

3.10-11] There are strong echoes of 3.11 in 8.17, where Qohelet talks of human efforts to discover all that has been achieved under the sun, using the Hebrew verb *'ml* to describe those efforts. This has encouraged a number of commentators to adopt an attractive, though almost wholly speculative, emendation to the text here, and to read *'ml* in place of *'lm*. That would mean that God puts 'work' into human hearts, and Fox explains 'The arduous task that God has placed in man's heart is defined by the rest of the verse. It is the attempt to understand "what God has brought to pass"'—he himself links this to the work set by God in the last verse. The emendation involved is very slight—the swapping of two characters—and it would achieve an interesting continuity between vv. 10 and 11, as well as strengthening the link with 8.17. Verse 11, however, begins with a reference to God making things fine in their time, and ends by talking about God's achievements 'from start right through to finish': it is not difficult to see that Qohelet might be talking here about God's shaping of human attitudes to time, even if the nature of that shaping has provoked much discussion. The emendation offers an attractive alternative, but is hardly, therefore, necessary.

The connection between 3.10 and 3.11 lies in God's making everything 'fine' (not just 'appropriate', as some would have it): the work set by God for humans consists of all their actions, each made so fine when it happens by the very fact that God set it. What 3.11 then goes on to suggest is that God has not only 'given' work to humans (3.10), but has also, literally, 'given' them something else 'in their heart'—which probably means that he has inspired them with it, or inspired them to want it. If we do not emend the word, as already discussed, the most straightforward understanding of this something is as 'perpetuity', or perhaps 'the long term': God has given humans things to do, but he has also given them a reason to do things, so that they are not mere marionettes, and act on what they take to be their own behalf.[1] It is the motivation offered by the prospect of accomplishment, advancement or even changing the world that leads them to act, although, in doing so, they are unwittingly working for God. Humans work, therefore, because of their own sense of the future, but they possess no insight into the broader sweep of divine accomplishments to which their own work will contribute.[2] The Hebrew is difficult, but probably implies that God has inculcated this sense of the future (or the desire to work, if we choose to make the emendation) not just 'without' a knowledge of his own achievements, but by means of that ignorance. If humans knew the reality of their world, and of their situation within it, then they would have no such aspirations.[3] Alternatively, it is

---

[1] I am not persuaded that 'forever' would have had negative connotations, read against a background of eschatological speculation (as Janzen suggests, in 'Under the Sun', 479-80), or even that the expression can 'make sense only if considerably amplified' (as Fox puts it). As Azize, 'The Genre of Qohelet', 133, says, it 'makes sense. It is dense, even poetic, perhaps even enigmatic, but that is no argument against the natural reading: it only signifies that the natural reading is dense, poetic, or enigmatic.'

[2] Again, this obviously does not align with the revelatory claims of apocalyptic literature, but it is not clear that it actively and consciously contradicts them, as supposed by D'Alario, 'Qohelet e l'Apocalittica'; Lavoie, 'Puissance', 287. Integral to the claim of apocalyptic that it 'reveals' divine secrets, is the assumption that they are secret, and otherwise unknowable.

[3] Machinist, 'Reflections', 172-73, similarly understands what is set in hearts to be 'the ability to consider and reflect on the concept of eternity', although he attributes that sense just to the word 'forever', rather than to the expression as a whole. He goes on differently, however, to understand the point to be that humans

just possible (if we derive the key Hebrew word from a root that is attested, but parse it as a form that is not) that we are to understand what God gives in a quite different way, and that the affirmation is much simpler: God has put into their hearts a darkness or obscurity, because they lack a knowledge that they cannot attain for themselves (see the notes).

3.12-13] The meaning of 'good' is a problem here. In 2.24, I suggested that the sense was connected to the subsequent idea of being 'good before God', and that the term was therefore suggestive of 'worth', but the statement as a whole here seems almost to contradict that verse, despite both standing in similar contexts. In 2.24, Qohelet saw no good in the person who took pleasure, but here he sees no good in the person *except* in doing just that, and in 'doing good'—a notion that adds a further complication, which will be compounded in the next verse by a reference to 'seeing good'. Backhaus (*Es gibt*, 110-11) tries to see two different perspectives at work, linked to the impossibility of gaining a profit, but the possibility of living a happy life. That requires us, however, to read in much that is unstated. More probably, I think, Qohelet is qualifying his previous statement. In 2.24, he was concerned with the idea that humans do not deserve what they receive, and to counter a simplistic idea that their individual circumstances correspond to God's perception of each. After his expressions of determinism in ch. 3, Qohelet now wants to make the point that God is actually involved, but not in such a simple way. Broadening the sense of 'goodness' from 'worthiness' to incorporate notions of enjoyment and virtue, he allows that humans do have the limited capacities to find things good and to act with good intentions, so that there *is* 'goodness' in them. Their capacity for pleasure in particular, though, is itself something they receive from God, and the term used of his giving it is a very neutral one: humans get that capacity as a gift or as a

are given a knowledge of what is beyond their limitations, and hence of those limitations. Hankins, 'Internal Infinite', suggests that God has placed infinity within finite humans, engendering a conflict within them, and giving them the sense that God's deeds are concealed from them—'causing frustration and inciting desire' (50). Certainly Qohelet has that sense, but it is not clear to me that he portrays it as something common to all humans.

wage for their work, not necessarily as a reward for worthiness. This point will be echoed in the rather different 3.22, then reiterated and expanded at the end of ch. 5, before Qohelet turns, at the beginning of ch. 6, to the problem that some people may possess the outward trappings of wealth without the ability to enjoy it; the issue will then be addressed once more in 8.15. It might be fair to say, therefore, that what we have here is the second stage in a continuing attempt to qualify and elaborate the claim of 2.24. Since 'good' in 5.17 will take on another sense again, shifts of meaning, or perhaps some playing on the terms, seem to be an aspect of that attempt, and although they are often discussed together, we should certainly not view these various passages simply as different presentations of the same, static claim: they are, at the very least, variations on a theme.

3.14] As sometimes elsewhere, Qohelet avoids the religious cliché 'fear God' in favour of an expression closer to 'be afraid of God', and so this should not be read simply as a claim that God has made everybody pious. Seow is keen to emphasize that the expression 'does not connote absolute terror. Rather, the concept of the fear of God here…stresses the distance between divinity and humanity'—and the particular wording of the expression in Hebrew might indeed lend itself to some implication of 'distance'. It is less clear, though, that terror is actually absent from its connotations, and Longman ('Fear of God', 21) speaks of Qohelet 'urging those listening to him to be afraid of God and to minimize one's exposure to him'. Murphy adds another note when he speaks of 'the proper attitude which God wants to evoke in creatures by means of his mysterious action.… According to Qoheleth, one is caught between the nearness of a God who fixes times and the mystery of a God whose work is unintelligible; in this situation fear of that God is the proper response.' Ellis ('Reconsidering', 61-66) has linked this to Rudolph Otto's concept of *mysterium tremendum*—the experience of deity as a wholly mysterious other, which provokes terror and humility in humans—and that does not seem inappropriate here. Crenshaw ('Eternal Gospel', 44) goes further to suggest that 'it signifies cold terror', while Piotti ('Percezione III', 13) speaks of it as 'rispettoso, ma freddo e guardingo', 'respectful, but cold and guarded'. Contextualizing it a little differently, and drawing out the practical consequences, Sneed ('[Dis]closure', 120) observes,

'Essentially, one responds to God as one would an arbitrary despot (5.1-7 = 8.2-6). Caution, moderation, and avoiding irritating the deity are the chief virtues.'

3.15] The Hebrew is no easier than the English translation would suggest here; partly in an attempt to echo 1.9, perhaps, it is concise almost to the point of obscurity. Qohelet's initial point, however, seems to be that the divine accomplishments described in the last verse already constitute the present reality: there is nothing in existence that is not a product of what God has done. He goes on after that to make a further assertion, also in line with his claims in the previous verse and elsewhere, that the future will be the same: whatever is going to exist is already in existence. The third statement is more difficult, but most probably emphasizes that whatever course needs to be pursued to ensure this continuity, it is God who will pursue it. This matches, in other words, Qohelet's previous claim that God's achievements are unalterable, but adds a more dynamic dimension: God has not just made the world the way it is (and will be) then left it to run, but continues working to ensure its future without help or interference from others. Qohelet implies, through this emphasis on exclusive divine action, that whatever humans choose themselves to pursue, they will have no effect on the course of the world, so they are subordinate to God not only on account of their fear of him, which constitutes one of God's achievements, and so will last, but also because they are powerless to shape the future for themselves.

Notes

3.9 from the worker] The use without -ל suggests that this should be the יתרון derived from the worker, rather than that which accrues to them; contrast 1.3; 2.22; 5.15; 6.11; 10.11; also see the notes at 2.13 and 5.8. G reflects the distinction by using the genitive instead of the dative. V *quid habet amplius homo de labore suo*, 'what has man more from his work', reflects not just free translation (as Goldman), but assimilation to 1.3 and other such passages. This has happened more drastically in S, where the principal witnesses have ܠܒܪ ܐܢܫ ܒܥܒܕܐ ܕܗܘ ܥܡܠ *lbr ʾnšʾ bʿbdʾ dhw ʿml*, 'for a human in the work at which he works', and finish the verse with ܬܚܝܬ ܫܡܫܐ *thyt šmšʾ*, 'under the sun'; as Kamenetzky, 198, notes, however, the additions are probably secondary.

Ginsburg, *Massorah* III, 71, lists העושה written *plene* as a *Qʿrê* associated with the eastern tradition, and this spelling is very commonly found in manuscripts and editions, although in the list presented by M^L, the *plene* is given as the western reading.[4] In any case, both spellings clearly co-existed as variants from an early time.

3.9 in that at which he toils] Or possibly, 'in that he toils'. On the form of עמל, see at 2.18 above.

3.10 the work] On the Hebrew term, see the note above at 1.13. A significant number of G manuscripts have σὺν πάντα τὸν or similar. This addition of 'all' is found in none of the other versions, and has probably been influenced by the next verse, or by 1.14 and similar expressions (cf. 4.1, 4, 15; 7.15; 8.9, 17). The early attestation in G raises the possibility that the variant occurred in the translator's source-text (cf. McNeile), but neither Rahlfs nor Gentry treats it as G* (and Klostermann, *De libri Coheleth*, 58, rejects it).

3.10 God has given to humans] As at 1.13, Goldman believes that M has omitted an article before אלהים: see the notes on that verse above, with regard to this and the expression as a whole. As also in 1.13, there is a common variant in the G tradition: τῶν ἀνθρώπων, 'of the humans', for τοῦ ἀνθρώπου, 'of the human'. Here the singular is also attested for σ', the plural for α'θ'.

3.10 to work] T uses לאיסתנפא in 1.13, but לסנפותהון, 'to wear them out' here, and Krüger suggests that it has vocalized the Hebrew as a causative form. It is difficult to know quite why T renders this verse so differently from 1.13, but the translation of the verb is part of a broader shift, in which the idea of punishments is introduced, so the changes may be interpretative. Jerome rather differently moves from *occupentur* ('be employed') in Hie to *distendantur* in V ('that they may be distracted by it'—contrast 1.13 *occuparentur*); Cannon, 'Jerome and Symmachus', 198, suspects Jewish exegetical influence.

3.11 he has made everything] When עשה takes a 'double accusative' with two nouns, it generally means 'make x into y' (cf. Gen 27.9; Num 11.8; 17.3; Judg 17.4; Ps 104.4; Hos 8.4), or refers in some other way to the making of something out of something else (e.g. Exod 28.31; 39.30). J-M §125 w suggests that such constructions must be viewed as the causative equivalent of clauses with היה, and, extrapolating this to the rarer use with adjectives, we might expect a similar sense 'he made x become y' (so, e.g., 1 Sam 17.25). Accordingly, when God in Ezek 31.9 states that he 'made (the cedar) beautiful', the point is not that he created it beautiful, but that he made it develop into something beautiful, as the subsequent qualification 'in the abundance of its branches' shows. Likewise, the point here is not that everything has a fineness that is intrinsic and inherent in its creation, but that God

---

[4] See Ginsburg, *Introduction*, 236; Ginsburg mistakenly associates the reading with 3.13.

makes it, or has made it, 'become' fine or proper in its time. Equally, though, עשה in this construction does not refer simply to action, and when Kamano, *Cosmology*, 99, translates 'He does everything appropriate in its time', he wrongly limits the scope.

The verb is pointed as qatal in M, and read that way by the versions. This does not exclude reference to the present, and Isaksson, *Studies*, 79-81, argues that it must refer to the continuous activity of God, not simply to a past creation (so, similarly, Fischer, *Skepsis*, 230-33), leading him to translate 'Everything he makes'. As Schoors, *The Preacher* I, 175, points out, however, there seems to be an inconsistency in his subsequent translation of נתן as past tense, and Schoors himself would translate both as present (cf. Schoors, *The Preacher* II, 95), referring to a continuous creation. Joüon, 'Notes de syntaxe', 225, would simply vocalize as a participle to give a similar sense. It is the translation into other languages that forces us to impose a precision that is absent from the Hebrew, and although I have translated using an English perfect tense, I take Qohelet to be talking primarily about the constant fitting of event to circumstance, something that presumably stretches across both past and present: it would not be inappropriate to translate 'he has always made', if that did not potentially confuse discussion of what follows.

Especially given the lack of closer specification in the Hebrew, it seems unlikely that the writer had some special concern to articulate the timing of God's actions, and it is questionable, indeed, whether there is really any reference to creation here at all, at least in any technical sense. The verb עשה is used often in the book, and God is its subject some seven times elsewhere (later in this verse, 3.11; 3.14 twice; 7.14, 29; 8.17; 11.5). Most of these references are to his achievements in general, and two of the rest to his accomplishment of human fear and ignorance of his activities. Setting aside the difficult 7.29, which is often considered to refer to creation, only the reference in 7.14, to the making of bad times to match good ones, involves anything specifically creative, but that is hardly talking about 'the creation'. In short, when we see עשה associated with God, the usage in the book gives us no reason to make an automatic link with some theological notion of creation, except insofar as any activity or achievement can be called 'creative'.

Although it is consistent as to tense, the text of G is complicated here, with many important manuscripts reading σύμπαντα or τὰ σύμπαντα in place of σὺν τὰ πάντα (which is adopted by Rahlfs and defensible on grounds of translation technique [cf. 7.15; 10.19; although also 11.5], but only poorly attested). The variant itself makes little difference to the sense, but most manuscripts then follow the expression with a relative ἅ, giving the sense 'all the things *that* he made'; the relative is found also in S, which may have taken it from the Greek. Goldman believes that it may be G*, derived from a reading את כל אשר עשה in the source-text, and he is inclined to prefer this to M's את הכל עשה. It seems easier, however, to envisage an early corruption of G through dittography of the alpha and/or assimilation to a familiar phrase (e.g. 1 Kgs 15.31, and many times), than to explain such a change in the Hebrew.

3.11 fine] Even in quite late biblical usage, יפה refers to beauty (e.g. Esth 2.7), and when God, as we have already noted, makes the cedar יפה in Ezek 31.9, it is its physical perfection which provokes envy. In later usage, though, it can also connote goodness or value more generally, and it seems to be used this way in 5.17, where it stands in parallel with טוב (which is also substituted for יפה at Sir 39.16, 33, as, e.g., Crenshaw, Seow note, if that is actually the recollection of this verse that some scholars take it to be). There is no reason to suppose, however, that it ever took on the specific sense 'appropriate' or 'fitting', as is quite commonly asserted by commentators. If, on the other hand, there is a deliberate allusion to the proclamation of creation as 'good' in Gen 1.31, as Lauha and others suggest, it is unclear why טוב itself has not been used. Scippa, 'Il tutto fece bello', sees a more general reference to creation and cosmic ordering, and the statement here is clearly not simply aesthetic—equally, though, it is not explicitly moral or functional. Taylor, 'On Some Verses', 296-99, takes the sense to be simply 'pleasant' or 'agreeable'. Qohelet is saying no more than that all things have an appreciable, even admirable value in their time, and he probably implies no specific claim beyond that.

3.11 in its time] Analogous uses of בעתו involve, e.g., the falling of rain in the rainy seasons (Deut 11.14; 28.12; Jer 5.24; Ezek 34.26), the threshing of grain at harvest (Job 5.26), and the production of fruit in season (Ps 1.3). Ecclesiastes uses the negated בלא עת at 7.17 with reference to dying 'before one's time' (cf. Job 22.16; Sir 30.24 of premature old age), and the expression probably implies, then, the time when something is supposed to happen. Proverbs 15.23 famously speaks of דבר בעתו, 'a word in season', to speak of a response or intervention made at the appropriate time.

Although Crenshaw notes that it is impossible to determine whether the suffix pronoun here refers to God ('his time', so e.g. Müller, 'Wie sprach', 514: 'die Zeit Gottes', 'the time of God') or the 'all'. The usage of the expression, however, points strongly to the latter, and an elliptical 'his time (when he has determined that each thing should happen)' seems forced. Symmachus makes the reference of the pronoun quite explicit: καλὸν ἕκαστον ἐν καιρῷ ἰδίῳ, 'each fine in its own time'.

3.11 also] An adversative translation of גם is preferred by some commentators (see Schoors, *The Preacher* I, 131), but the context hardly requires such an unusual sense for the word. Taylor, 'On Some Verses', 300-301, renders 'Yea—he hath thus given...'. Whether or not that is the implication of the accents, as he claims, such a rendering of גם as emphatic only really suits an interpretation where עלם refers to the world (see below).

3.11 put...into their heart] Some commentators, including Lohfink, Lauha, and Ellermeier, *Qohelet I.1*, 320-21, have taken this to be a reference to הכל rather than to the humans mentioned in the previous verse. This is not grammatically impossible, and might yield the sense that God has imbued all things with a certain quality, but it is improbable. First there is the number. Although a single late Hebrew manuscript noted by Kennicott has a singular suffix (בלבו), and a number of Greek ones have αὐτοῦ for αὐτῶν, 'his' for 'their', there are no compelling grounds for emendation to the singular. A plural suffix could still refer to כל, of course, which Ecclesiastes elsewhere treats variously as singular or plural (compare, e.g., 2.7 with 2.9), but we might expect consistency in the space of a few words, and in בעתו a singular suffix is used. Ellermeier explains that כל is being treated collectively in one case, but distributively in the other, with each individual component having its time, but it remains hard to see why the author should not simply have made the suffix singular in each case, and thereby prevented a potential misreading, especially when the situation is already complicated by the use of לב in the singular (as at 8.11).

The sense is no less important: biblical Hebrew does not use 'in the heart of' to mean 'within', or even, commonly, to mean 'in the midst of' (except, perhaps, in the expression בלב ים / בלב ימים in, e.g., Exod 15.8; Ezek 27.4; Ps 46.3 [ET 46.2]; cf. the similar לב השמים of Deut 4.11). There would be no obvious precedent for it to mean that actions possess a certain quality, or for the usage that Ellermeier requires in his otherwise ingenious reading, whereby God 'has put time without limit in the heart of everything' (*Qohelet I.1*, 307-22). *BHS* is uncomfortable with בלבם altogether, and demands that it be deleted as a dittographic corruption, to be replaced by בו or בם; Galling similarly deletes it, and in 1940 preferred לו (a solution favoured also by Jenni, 'Das Wort 'ōlām', 26), in 'Das Rätsel der Zeit', 4, בו or לו, and in 1969 בו or בלבו. There are no solid grounds, however, for emending M, which is accepted by most commentators. If we assume that the text should stand, and that בלבם does mean that God put something into human hearts, the expression is not unusual, but does require some explanation.

In other biblical usage, to put (נתן) something into someone else's heart is to inspire them with an ability (Exod 35.34; 36.2; 1 Kgs 10.24 // 2 Chr 9.23), an emotion (Ps 4.8 [ET 4.7]; Jer 32.40; cf. Lev 26.36), or a desire to do something (Ezra 7.27). It is, roughly speaking, the causative counterpart of having something in one's heart (e.g. Exod 4.14; Lev 19.17; 1 Sam 2.35; 14.7; Ps 28.3; Prov 14.33; Isa 10.7). We might also take into consideration such similar uses as 1 Sam 21.31 and Job 22.22, where placing (שים) something in one's own heart involves 'considering' it, although Ecclesiastes seems to prefer נתן אל לב for that sense (7.2; 9.1). The precise nuance assigned here will depend on the understanding of the object, העלם, but I take the sense to be that God has made humans desire perpetuity, or become focused upon it—rather as in 8.11 human hearts are 'filled' with the desire to do wrong, and in 9.3 with הוללות also.

If there are no grounds to emend the text, the rendering in V is, nevertheless, striking. In Hie, Jerome opted for *saeculum dedit in corda eorum*, 'he gave the/an age into their hearts', but the V tradition is torn between *mundum tradidit disputationi eorum* and *mundum tradidit dispositioni eorum*, 'he handed the world over for their debate' or 'into their management'. On the translation 'world', see the next note; already in his commentary, Jerome had glossed the text as *dedit quoque deus mundum ad inhabitandum hominibus*, 'God also gave the world to humans to inhabit', and associated his understanding of the passage as a whole with the views of his Hebrew teacher. If the original reading of V was with *disputationi*, then it seems possible that he had subsequently encountered a Hebrew text with ברבם instead of בלבם (cf. Dubarle, 'Ἀράξασθε παιδείας', 512), but the probability is that *disputationi* actually arose secondarily from *dispositioni* (cf. Elliot, 'Temporality', 84-86), and that V merely extends the idea expressed in the commentary: humans are given the world not just to live in but to run.[5]

3.11 forever] ע(ו)לם usually means a long period of time, and it can be employed in a wide range of expressions which refer to things existing from the distant past, or into the distant future.[6] The unusual use of the term by itself, outside such expressions, has already been found in 1.10, where the plural עלמים referred to past ages, and there is no reason, in principle, why the noun should not stand here as the object of נתן.[7] In practice, though, it is unclear what it actually means in such a context. Although functionally equivalent to 'for ever' in many uses, it is not certain that עולם can bear the sense 'eternity' (like the similar αἰών, which G uses here), let alone that it could mean 'the concept of eternity', which is often understood. The problem has long provoked attempts to seek new meanings or nuances.

Rashi notes the defective spelling and adduces a connection with the verb עלם, 'conceal' (used at 12.14), a connection found in the Midrash as well, where one interpretation is in terms of the secret divine name; ideas of concealment also appear in the highly interpretative rendering of this verse in T.[8] In view of the variability in biblical orthography that we explored in the Introduction, it might be unwise to make too much of the spelling itself, but it is very possible that the writing here reflects a similar scribal interpretation. In any case, though, the qal participle of עלם is found at Ps 90.8, used of secrets, and the Ugaritic cognate *ǵlm* is associated with darkness (cf. Dahood,

---

[5] Whitley, in fact, suggests that Jerome has read ברבם, but his *disputationi eorum* here does not resemble his translation of that expression at Job 31.13.

[6] See Jenni, 'Das Wort 'ōlām', the most comprehensive study of the term. Also, Barr, *Biblical Words for Time*, 117-18.

[7] This use in 1.10 seems in itself to raise a significant objection to Gerleman's idea that עולם in 3.11 refers to a barrier set by God, and that the בית עולם of 12.5 is a 'locked house', whatever the merits or otherwise of the broader hypothesis in Gerleman, 'Die sperrende Grenze', 341-42.

[8] The word is, in fact, attested with a *plene* spelling העולם in many manuscripts; cf. Kennicott, Baer, 81. Ginsburg, *Massorah* III, 71, lists it as an 'eastern' reading.

'Canaanite-Phoenician', 206), so a sense of concealment is not impossible (and Youngblood, 'Dark House', goes so far as to suggest that this is the implication of עולם in 12.5, 14, as well), although it is difficult to identify any other biblical use of a substantive from this root (as Piotti, 'Osservazioni su alcuni I', 171, observes, the use that Dahood identifies in Job 22.15 does not have to be understood that way).[9] It is difficult, moreover, then simply to make this imply 'ignorance', as Barton and many other scholars would like, enabling a simple statement that God keeps humans in the dark: Holland, 'Heart of Darkness', 93, speaks of '"darkness" in the sense of ignorance', but this is hardly a normal sense of 'darkness', which can cause us to be ignorant by preventing us from seeing, but which is not in itself a manifestation of that ignorance. Gault, 'Reexamination', 57, shows better the sort of understanding that is required by glossing the text as 'has obscured humanity's knowledge, placing darkness in their hearts, so that they cannot discover His divine program', and much earlier Hodgson spoke of 'the darkness which he spreadeth over men's hearts'. Such interpretations, however, have to deal with the problem that what follows, although admittedly difficult, seems to distinguish human ignorance from עלם, not to identify the two or to make עלם the source of ignorance (let alone, as Hankins, 'Internal Infinite', 49, would have it, to play on potential senses of עלם in order to identify 'the finite appearance of concealment' as 'the essence of the infinite'). Were we to adopt this sense for the word, the point would have to be that God has put a darkness or concealment in human hearts *by* withholding knowledge of his own actions.

Both Rashi and the Midrash also associate the noun with the later use of עולם to signify 'world' (cf. the reading of V, discussed above), and that sense has likewise proved popular with more modern commentators. Such a use of the word, however, would be unusually early (unless we find that meaning in the ms A version of Sir 3.18, and accept its originality; cf. Levy). It should be noted, moreover, that this usage is largely in the context of expressions like 'the world to come', 'the present world' and suchlike: it more readily connotes an 'age', 'era', or state of being for the world than the actual, physical world. Most of the other suggested readings of עלם are more speculative and far less plausible.[10]

---

[9] There are some grounds for supposing that עולם might refer to the underworld, and that idea is often associated with the expression בית עולמו at 12.5; cf. Niehr, 'Semantik'. If so, an association with 'darkness' rather than 'eternity' cannot be excluded, but that would make it less likely that such a substantive could refer to confusion. The alternative idea, that God here might be causing humans to think about death, is not unattractive, but fits poorly with what follows.

[10] They include a suggestion made earlier by, e.g., Spohn, but picked up most famously by Hitzig (initially in 'Ueber die Stelle Prediger 3,11'), that the word should be read עֵלֶם and associated wih an Arabic word meaning 'knowledge'—on

Other scholars have resorted to emendation of the text. M עלם is essentially supported by the versions, although G is complicated by the fact that key manuscripts have σύμπαντα or σὺν πάντα for σὺν, which some scholars have taken to be a G* rendering of a Hebrew variant את כל עלם (see, e.g., Barton, McNeile, but contrast Klostermann, *De libri Coheleth*, 58); this is not impossible, although there is some indirect evidence for Rahlfs' σὺν τὸν αἰῶνα, and Syh gives that reading in a Greek marginal note (see Field). The most commonly proposed emendation, however, concerns עלם itself, which Macdonald, Kamenetzky, and later Günther all independently proposed should be emended to עמל, a view more recently accepted by Fox.[11] The latter sees an echo of this verse in 8.17, with the עמל put into human hearts here corresponding to יעמל האדם לבקש... there; allowing that there is a reminiscence, though, the wording is not so close that it really makes the case. While it is interesting to note that the reading of Codex Ambrosianus for S in our verse is ܥܡܠܐ '*ml*' = עמל, which might support the case text-critically, this is usually taken to be an independent error, and most manuscripts of S read ܥܠܡܐ '*lm*' = עלם.

With so many approaches for which a more or less plausible case can be made, context becomes an important consideration, and if עלם is not an error for עמל then both the preceding בעתו and the subsequent מראש ועד סוף suggest very strongly that the word should be read in a temporal sense: the writer would otherwise have been positively misleading his readers. Emendation to עמל is tempting, both in the light of 8.17, and because it would make a straightforward counterpart to the ענין of 3.10, but the versional support is very slight, and עלם clearly the *lectio difficilior*. For a true parallel to 8.17, moreover, one might expect the עמל to be identified with the subsequent human quest, but it is difficult to read the sentence here that way, and the two seem rather to be distinguished. Ultimately, as Isaksson, *Studies*, 180, points out, 'the context of the word *ʿōlām* is decisive for its meaning. And in this context time is present everywhere.... An interpretation that retains a temporal meaning in *ʿōlām* must therefore be given priority.' Mazzinghi, 'Il mistero del tempo', seeks accordingly to understand a play on words here, so that עלם has connotations of both time and secrecy, and the reference is to an epistemological limitation. Even if it were entirely clear what 'the mystery of time' would connote here, however, such an approach seems merely to add a further complication, and 'forever' or something similar seems most appropriate to the context. 'Darkness' or 'concealment' would fit well with the subsequent qualification (see below), but the existence of a noun עלם with that sense has not been sufficiently demonstrated.

---

which see Grimm, 'Ueber Koheleth 3, 11ᵇ', 275. Van der Palm, in the same period, guessed from context that עלם must be a 'seal', set by God on human hearts.

[11] See MacDonald, 'Old Testament Notes', 212-13; Kamenetzky, 238; Günther, 'Der Zusammenhang in Koh 3 11-15'.

3.11 for lack of that which] Crenshaw notes the resemblance between מבלי and the preceding בלבם, understanding there to be a play between the words. Graetz, on the other hand, views מבלי as a virtual dittograph of בלבם, and therefore secondary. It is true that G ὅπως μὴ εὕρῃ, 'so that he might not find', could be understood as a translation simply of אשר לא ימצא (cf. 7.21), as might α' ὡς οὐχ εὑρήσει, 'that he will not find', while Kamenetzky, 214, notes that the Peshitta usually renders מבלי with ܡܢ ܒܠܝ *mn bly*, which is absent here—although S ܐܝܟ ܕܠܐ *'yk dl'*, 'so that...not', could just reflect the influence of G (cf. Hie, V *ut non*). It is noteworthy, however, that in 7.14 G renders what would be a very similar שלא ימצא האדם with ἵνα μὴ εὕρῃ ὁ ἄνθρωπος, so we should not exclude the idea that it read מבלי here, and the Hebrew word is elsewhere rendered very variably. Since their readings could, therefore, reflect attempts to translate the phrase as it stands in M, it would be wrong to say that the versions demand a reading without מבלי, although they allow the possibility that a variant Hebrew text existed without the word. If there was such a text, however, it seems at least as likely that it arose through omission in the confusing sequence בלבממבלי as that מבלי itself arose through dittography, and there are no compelling text-critical grounds for emendation. A more remote possibility should also be mentioned, that the versions did in fact read מבלי, but not the subsequent לא, which could have arisen in M as a consequence of similar passages (see the next note). It is generally acknowledged, however, that M should be retained.

Despite this, many commentators have tended to translate the verse as though מבלי were absent, and those who do not ignore it often assign it a new sense from context. This is strange, because the term is not rare, and its meaning is well-attested: like the more common בלי, אין expresses non-existence, and correspondingly מבלי is used like מאין to mean 'without' (the two are used interchangeably in an expression found at Isa 5.9; 6.11; Jer 2.15); it often also has a similar causal implication, 'for want of', or 'because...not' (e.g. Deut 9.28; Job 31.19; Hos 4.6). In fact, מבלי is used together with אין in a set expression, המבלי אין...ב, 'is it because there is/are no...in...?', which is found at Exod 14.11; 2 Kgs 1.3, 6, 16.

That set expression is probably not a simple instance of double negation (as e.g. J-M §160 p suggests), although the matter is complicated both by the fact that interrogative use turns expressions of non-existence into affirmations of existence (so by itself, אין would mean 'Is/are there not...?', as in, e.g. Judg 14.3; 1 Kgs 22.7), and by the ironic imputation of motive in all the instances. In fact, מבלי is probably to be taken with the following verb in each case, so that in 2 Kgs 1.3, for example, Elijah is to say, 'Is it not because (you think) there is no God in Israel that you are going...?', or more literally, 'Is it without "There is no God in Israel", your going...?' In any case, though, the expression is used in very restricted contexts, and hardly provides a basis for the common assertion that מבלי in our current verse is being used as a double negative with the subsequent לא, allowing us to translate 'so that the human might not', or somesuch.

Elsewhere מבלי does not take אשר, but there are no grounds for assuming, furthermore, that the presence of the relative here might change the sense, and when, e.g., Schoors, *The Preacher* I, 147, asserts that the word must have a final or consecutive implication found nowhere else, this is no more than an effort to facilitate the reading of a difficult verse. Equally, there is no obvious basis for Isaksson's assertion (*Studies*, 181) that, when followed by אשר, מבלי 'becomes a conjunction meaning "except that", or "yet so that"' which 'signals an *exception* or a *restriction*'.[12] Cazelles, 'Conjonctions', 22, offers another study that begins with the presumed sense ('because' for Cazelles), and works backward: it lists half a dozen superficially similar but unrelated Aramaic expressions to support that sense.

It is possible that אשר itself is causative here, and merely reinforces מבלי. Since, however, we would usually expect a noun or equivalent (e.g. an infinitive or substantivized participle) after מבלי, the most natural approach is either to take אשר as 'that which (the human will not discover)', or to construe the relative clause itself as substantivized: 'that the human will not discover' (cf. 3.22; 7.18, 29; 8.11, 12, 14). I take the former to be more likely, and would read literally either 'God set...without that which no human can discover', or, more probably, given the common causative sense of מבלי, 'God set...for lack of that which no human can discover'.[13] This is similar to the understanding in, e.g., Taylor, 'On Some Verses', 301-302. Gorssen, 'La cohérence', 293-94, also accepts the reference to lacking, but thinks that this requires a reading of עלם in terms of 'ignorance': the fact that humans do not know is the very 'lack' at stake here, and the statement simply specifies the nature of the ignorance. It is hard to see why the following clause would require negation on that reading, but it might be possible alternatively to understand 'an ignorance (which is) without that which no human can discover', and so to read the sort of specification found in, e.g., Jer 9.10 (ET 9.11).

3.11 no human can discover] Lit. 'the human will not find'. The same expression is found at 7.14, where it refers to the inability of humans, resulting from divine action, to see what will follow them. In 8.17, the human is unable to see what has been achieved under the sun (again, apparently as a result of divine action): לא יוכל האדם למצוא; furthermore, they will seek, but not

---

[12] This in turn becomes the (insecure) basis for his interesting suggestion that the clause restricts what precedes, so that humans are given עלם in their hearts, that is 'the eternal work' (183), but are prevented from discovering God's work. Cf., much earlier, Grimm, 'Ueber Koheleth 3, 11ᵇ', 279.

[13] Frydrych, *Living*, 75 n. 63, comes to the correct conclusion, I think, that מבלי is causative, but then renders 'because of which a person is not' (as Kamano, *Cosmology*, 100, points out with respect to similar renderings by Crenshaw and Whitley, that is an expression of result, not cause). Frydrych's confusing description of the לא as 'pleonastic', citing Exod 14.11 etc., suggests that he also understands a double negation.

find: יעמל האדם לבקש ולא ימצא. Although יכל is not used here, the parallels suggest that human inability is implicit. The use of מצא 'epistemologically' has received a certain amount of attention, and in passing, Mazzinghi, 'The Verbs', 111, glosses 'what man is incapable of finding' as what he 'is incapable of understanding'—a way of construing the sense that is found amongst some other commentators—and in his conclusion Mazzinghi suggests that it is sometimes equivalent in effect to ידע. I see no evidence for that, or any reason to suppose that Qohelet ever uses מצא to mean more than 'find' or 'discover', albeit sometimes intellectually rather than physically. Here the point is not that humans would not know or comprehend any divine action should they encounter it, but that God's overarching activities are beyond the scope of human senses or investigations.

3.11 the achievement which God has achieved] Similar expressions are found at 1.14; 2.11, 17; 4.3; 8.9, usually with reference to human deeds 'under the sun'. For reference to divine action, see 8.17, and cf. 7.13; 11.5.

3.11 from start right through to finish] ראש is literally 'head' or 'top', but is commonly used for 'start'; סוף is much rarer, and appears outside Ecclesiastes only at 2 Chr 20.16, referring to the end of a valley, and at Joel 2.20, where ספו is contrasted with פניו, and refers to the northerner's 'back'.[14] Ecclesiastes uses it also at 7.2 and 12.13 to refer to an end or conclusion, which corresponds to later use, but the pairing with ראש here may imply literally 'from front to back'. The construction used, מ-...ועד is common, and implies extent: everything from point A to point B; see, e.g., Exod 28.42; Lev 13.12; Num 4.3; Ruth 2.7; Ps 131.3. Given the preposition, it is difficult to see how this qualifies as a merism (cf. Schoors, *The Preacher* I, 218), but the sense is clear: Qohelet denies the possibility that humans can discover the whole extent of what God has achieved. Fox claims that this means humans cannot 'find it at all', but the expression more naturally suggests, in fact, that they cannot 'find it all'. T understands a reference to death: a human will not know from the outset what will happen at the end.

3.12 good in them] The expression טוב ב- has already been used in 2.24; see the note there. In this verse, the preposition is supported by all the versions except Hie and V, which do not render בם at all; there are, therefore, no grounds for emendation to ל- טוב, as at 2.3; 8.15. The reference of the suffix pronoun 'them', however, is less clear cut, especially in the light of the singular pronoun on the subsequent בחייו. The parallel with 2.24 has suggested to most commentators, ancient and modern, that 'they' must be humans (T נשא בבני בהום makes the identification explicit, as do two late Hebrew manuscripts listed by Kennicott, which have באדם); the plural seems strange, however, sandwiched as it is between singular האדם in both vv. 11

---

[14] Hurvitz, *Concise Lexicon*, 188-90, argues that the term is late despite its appearance in Joel.

and 13. Emendation to באדם has often been suggested, therefore, not least in *BHS*, with Driver even suggesting ('Once Again Abbreviations', 80) that בם was an early abbreviation of that expression. There is no versional support for such an emendation, however, and the supposed error is not readily explained; Gordis' proposal to delete בם altogether as dittography from the surrounding ב and כ is no more persuasive, although it can at least seek support from Jerome's omission and from the theoretical possibility of מ/כ confusion in the old script (מ/כ)—although it is far from certain that the book was ever copied in that script.

If we retain M, then it is possible to see the reference of the suffix elsewhere, and Goldman has argued that it picks up את הכל in 3.11, with the divine action considered a collective concept; this is in line with Rashbam's interpretation in terms of 'all these times and events', and if בם is not considered equivalent to לם, then it makes good sense. In the end, though, we have plural suffixes on בלבם in the previous verse and on בם here, along with a plural subject for שיראו in v. 14, all without explicit specification. Humans are probably the subject of the first and of the last, reflecting the continuing relationship between these verses and 3.10: it seems hard to believe that the author would have so confused matters by making the referent different here.

There is no versional or textual support for an understanding 'nothing better...than' here, although that is assumed by many commentators even in the absence of a comparative מן (contrast 3.22). The construction here is similar to that of 2.24, and closer to 8.15 than 3.22, but despite their formal similarities, Qohelet uses his statements with אין טוב to make a series of rather different claims.

3.12 except] Schoors, *The Preacher* I, 136 rightly rejects the suggestion of Aalders, that כי אם should be split, and the כי taken as adversative, to give the sense 'maar, als', 'but if'. At the very least, one might expect a main verb to follow in that case. Vinel, 'Accumulation', 394, notes that this is the only place where G does not render כי with ὅτι (contrast, e.g., 8.15 and cf. Yi, 340), despite its tendency to use that translation even when ὅτι is pleonastic or misleading.

3.12 doing good] The juxtaposition with לשמוח has led many commentators to suppose that the sense of לעשות טוב here is not 'doing good', but 'doing well'—experiencing prosperity or enjoyment (and some have even sought speculatively to emend it to לראות טוב, the expression used in the next verse). Correspondingly, it has often been linked to the Greek εὖ πράττειν, and even seen (e.g. by Tyler) as a borrowing from the Greek. Elsewhere, however, Ecclesiastes apparently contrasts יעשה טוב with יחטא (7.20), and in 2.3 the quest for a טוב לבני האדם אשר יעשו is surely not for prosperity or pleasure. Attempts (by e.g. McNeile, Gordis) to argue from the use of the opposite עשה רעה in 2 Sam 12.18 are similarly vitiated by Ecclesiastes's own use of that expression at 4.17; 8.11-12, where it clearly means 'doing wrong' (cf. Krüger)—and in the 2 Samuel passage it may have a sense more like 'do something stupid' than 'be in a bad way', or 'be miserable'. Although an ethical sense (cf. Rosenmüller's *recte facere, non peccare, a malo recedere*, 'act properly, not sin, refrain from evil', in *Salomonis regis*, 2:91) is probably not demanded here by the Hebrew, it is certainly not excluded. Lee, *Vitality*, 41, appears to find a double meaning, so that 'enjoyment of life is...a matter of ethical duty. Enjoyment *is* doing good.' Even if we allow that there may be an ambiguity here, however, such ambiguity does not imply equivalence.

3.12 one's life] S ܒܚܝܝܗܘܢ *bḥyyhwn* makes the suffix pronoun plural, most likely in order to conform with the preceding ܒܚܝܘܢ *bḥwn*. The suffix in the Hebrew is probably to be regarded as 'impersonal' (so, e.g., Gordis); cf. הולדו in the difficult 7.1. Alternatively, the singular is distributive, and indicates that these are things done not by humans *en masse*, but each individually, in their own life.

3.13 and also that] In terms of both its construction with an anacoluthon and its content, this verse is similar to 5.18. The latter starts with גם, but here there is a conjunction, and וגם has been rendered many ways, according to different understandings of the sense (cf. Schoors, *The Preacher* I, 131): even among the ancient versions, V opts for *enim* ('for'; contrast Hie *et quidem*, 'and indeed' = G καί γε). I think the verse is most naturally read as an additional thing which Qohelet 'knows', and so follows ידעתי כי in the previous verse, with גם taking its normal, additive sense.

3.13 every person] The definite article in כל האדם is reflected in only a few manuscripts of G, where the use of an article is erratic across all occurrences of this expression; cf. Ziegler, 'Gebrauch', 102. Goldman rejects it as G* both here and in the similar 5.18, while of 7.2 he claims that 'G no longer reflects the article before אדם' (which is true only to the extent that it is lacking in some of the earliest manuscripts and many cursives). Gentry, 'Relationship', 73, would retain the article on the basis of translation technique, but that presumes, of course, that the translator found it in his source-text, which Goldman denies (cf. his note on 5.18). McNeile, 144, indeed, asserts that the article has been added to אדם throughout M, as a result of secondary recension, and he notes also 6.7; 8.17 twice; 10.14; however, the article at 6.7 has now been confirmed by 4QQohª (II, 5), and that claim is hard to sustain.

Overall, the evidence is hard to assess, and it may be telling that there is so little consistency amongst the manuscripts of G, with no single group favouring the article where M has כל האדם, and no single translation found for any one manuscript in every passage. The simplest explanation for this is that G*, probably following its source-text, had the article in some cases but not others, and that this led to subsequent confusion in the early course of transmission. 3.13 and 5.18 are the instances where it is hardest to make a case for originality of the article in G on the basis of the manuscript evidence (with only G^B and a couple of minuscules attesting it in the former, and the article in the latter looking very like the result of hexaplaric influence). That accords well, in fact, with the common observation that an article would not usually be expected after כל when the sense is 'any person' or 'every person', rather than 'all the people'; cf. GKC §127 b, and e.g. Num 16.29; Josh 11.14; Zech 8.10 (although Schoors, *The Preacher* I, 168, notes a number of exceptions, and we may concede that the matter is not always clear cut). HCM have seen the peculiarity as a reason to suppose that כל האדם is an elliptical expression meaning 'the whole (portion) of man': see the note at 5.18.

I am inclined to suspect that the article appears here and in 5.18 as a result of influence from 7.2 and 12.13, rather than as an attempt to impose some special nuance (Lys, for instance, thinks that the connotation is 'quiconque', 'whoever', as opposed to 'quelqu'un', 'someone', or humanity in general). The source-text of G probably maintained the distinction, but when taken up into G, it led to confusion within that tradition as well, exacerbated in 5.18, at least, by revision toward the changed Hebrew text.

3.13 who] The construction of the sentence is difficult, and some commentators have taken the function of ‑ש not to be as a simple relative, but as a way of substantivizing the subsequent clause, so it is 'the fact that one may...' which is the מתת אלהים; see, recently, Seow, and the alternative translation suggested by Krüger. This would seem to leave כל האדם stranded, however, and, on that reading, the pre-positioning of this expression would introduce the confusing possibility of reading ‑ש as 'who', whilst serving no obvious purpose. HCM follow a similar line, but address the problem of כל האדם by taking it to mean 'the everything of the human', which is the probable sense in 12.13 (and which they find in 5.18 also). Accordingly, they read it as the subject of a non-verbal construction, with the ‑ש clause as a substantivized predicate: 'the whole (portion) of man is that he eats...'. This is clever, and by no means impossible, but it is important to observe that the construction in 12.13 is signalled by זה. With no comparable indication here, it is so natural to take כל האדם as 'every human' and the ‑ש as relative that the reader would be positively misled almost till the end of the verse if something else were intended. I take the construction in 5.18 to be similar, with גם כל האדם followed by a more complicated relative clause, or sequence of clauses, but clarified there by the addition of זה. The source of the awkwardness here, and perhaps the reason why there is no matching זה, is that the sentence is governed by ידעתי כי in the previous verse; see the note above, and compare the construction with ראיתי כי in 2.24.

3.13 eats and drinks and finds good] The sequence of verbs is similar to that in 2.24 שיאכל ושתה והראה, with waw-consecutive forms used despite the apparent simultaneity of the actions (see the note there). The only obvious difference lies in the use of the qal instead of the hiphʻil for the final verb, so it is strange that G seems to render ὃς φάγεται καὶ πίεται καὶ ἴδῃ, 'who eats and drinks and might see', here, where it used ὃ φάγεται καὶ ὃ πίεται καὶ ὃ δείξει, 'what he eats and what he drinks and what he shows', in 2.24, with the sparsely attested variants seeming to indicate no more than assimilation by some manuscripts to the relatives used in that verse. As noted above, this may suggest that the source-text of G differed from M in 2.24, but it also suggests that G understood the sense to be different here, with the use of the aorist subjunctive ἴδῃ in place of a future especially striking: we should perhaps understand an interpretative 'whoever eats and drinks—it is a gift of God that also he should see good in all his toil'. There may be a similar distinction between the verbs made in Jerome's comment that *neque se putet plus de suo labore lucrari posse, quam cibum et potem et si quid de opibus suis in bonis operibus expenderit, hoc solum Dei donum est*, '...than food and drink and whatever he might spend on good works...'.

Here we have ב- טוב ראה, rather than the ראה בטוב of 2.1 (see the notes there on 'and you must see' and 'what good it does'). This expression (with טובה instead of טוב) will be used again in 5.17, and it literally means 'see good in'; ראה טובה is found in 6.6 without any qualification of the place where it is to be found. The whole sequence of verbs, in fact, appears again in 5.17, constructed with infinitives: לאכול ולשתות ולראות טובה בכל עמלו. Finding good in one's work is replaced by simply 'taking pleasure' in the sequence at 8.15: לאכול ולשתות ולשמוח.

3.13 in all his business] There is no 'all' in V *de labore suo*, and a number of late manuscripts similarly have בעמלו rather than בכל עמלו (see de Rossi; Ginsburg, *Writings*). It is possible that this error had crept into the Hebrew tradition as early as Jerome, and is perpetuated in the late sources, but it may, of course, have arisen independently in different traditions (and the word is also missing in one manuscript of Hie).

3.13 this is] היא (הוא in some late manuscripts; see Kennicott, Ginsburg, *Writings*) is not matched by a pronoun in G* (manuscripts with τοῦτο δόμα are assimilating to the Hebrew or to 5.18), which instead uses ἐστιν, as earlier at 2.24 and later at 5.18. Hie imitates this, although S, V, T do all have an equivalent pronoun. S, in fact, has two pronouns ܗܕܐ ܡܘܗܒܬܐ ܗܝ ܕܡܪܝܐ, *hdʾ mwhbtʾ hy dmryʾ*, 'this is a gift; it is of the Lord'. *BHQ* judges the first 'explicatory', and links it with the *hoc*, 'this' of V (which is surely derived, however, from the Hebrew, as an equivalent to היא), and Kamenetzky, 198, sees assimilation to 5.18, but the position of the pronouns in this double rendering suggests that it might be an attempt to combine separate readings based on the היא of M and on the Greek variant with τοῦτο.

3.13 a payment from God] Or 'a gift of God', but the conventional translation 'gift' for מתת here and in 5.18 may be misleading, as the Hebrew probably bears no implication that what is offered has not been earned. In Sir 42.7, where the context is trade or financial accounting, a מתת is an expenditure or disbursement, as opposed to a receipt (לקח), and the מתת promised in 1 Kgs 13.7 is a financial payment or reward. This fits also the uses in Ezek 46.5, 11, where מתת ידו is apparently equivalent to the more familiar uses of נשא with יד (cf. 46.7), to indicate the limit of one's means, while in Prov 25.14, a

מתת שקר is most likely a false promise of payment. It is less clear in Sir 41.19, 22 what מתת is to be given on request or not followed up with an insult, and the noun appears in Phoenician for an offering made to a deity,[15] but the scope of the term is clearly broader than 'gift', and it is probably not synonymous with מתן or the more common מתנה (which is used instead at 7.7). Here the מתת is offered in the context of the work assigned by God (3.10), and it might be characterized as what God offers in return for that work, or as the way in which he sweetens the deal, rather than as a simple gift.

3.14 which God achieves] With the exception of T, all the versions have a past tense here. *BHQ* sees this as interpretative, but if so, they have resisted the temptation to make a similar change at 11.5, and it seems more likely that this reflects a variant עשה for M יעשה.[16] Since the divine action is past tense throughout the preceding verses, and in the light of the subsequent עשה in this verse, we might perhaps expect the qatal[17]—which would be a legitimate argument in favour of M as *difficilior*, although it seems no less likely that M has been influenced by the tense of the following יהיה. In any case, the statement is probably intended to be general, rather than a reference solely to past or future actions, so it is not necessary to choose between them. Views on the scope of the description are helpfully surveyed in Pinker, 'Qohelet 3:14-15', 255-58.

3.14 is what will exist forever] Lit. 'this will be forever'. Fox is right to criticize the view of Jenni, 'Das Wort 'ōlām', 22, that עולם here, uniquely, implies unalterability, although his own translation, 'whatever God makes happen is always what will be', seems a little forced itself, and it is doubtful that עולם can have that sense of 'always' ('always' in English can mean both 'for ever' and 'constantly', an ambiguity that is absent from the Hebrew). His point seems valid, however, that the interest of the verse is not in perpetuity

---

[15] See *KAI* 29.2, and the notes there. Dahood attempts ('Canaanite-Phoenician', 46) to use this as evidence of a fondness for Phoenician noun-formations in Ecclesiastes, but its wider currency in Hebrew hardly permits such an inference; cf. Schoors, *The Preacher* I, 68.

[16] It is true, though, that Cassian (*Collationes* VIII, 24, 2) appears to have emphasized the past character of the divine action for polemical purposes by adding *ab initio* to his La text: he is concerned to offset claims that God might have made improvements subsequent to the creation; see Petschenig, *Conlationes*, 244; PL 49, col. 766. Cassian's text in this verse, *cognoui quoniam omnia quae fecit deus ab initio ipsa erunt in aeternum super illa non est quod addatur et ab illis non est quod auferatur*, is otherwise close to Hie, although the latter preserves the infinitives of G in the second part.

[17] As rightly observed by Zimmermann, 'Aramaic Provenance', 40, who does not note, however, the versional evidence: this offers a simpler solution than his supposition that an original Aramaic participle has been misinterpreted.

as such, but in the resistance of divine achievements to change, and I have translated accordingly. Symmachus probably makes the same point by using διαμενεῖ, 'persists', for ἔσται (Cannon, 'Jerome and Symmachus', 192, thinks this influenced V *perseverent*).

3.14 there is no] The use of אין with -ל and the infinitive construct to imply prohibition or impossibility is well-attested in late Hebrew (see, e.g., Esth 8.8). Schoors, *The Preacher* I, 183 offers a lengthy list of examples, but it is clear from these that the construction does not always have the same meaning: in 1 Chr 23.26, for instance, the sense of ללוים אין לשאת is apparently that 'there is no carrying for the Levites to do' (cf. 2 Chr 35.15), while in 2 Chr 5.11 the priests sanctify themselves אין לשמור, 'without paying regard to', their divisions, and in 14.10; 20.6; 22.9 the אין always expresses the absence of someone to do something (cf., e.g., 1QH 7.28-29; 12.30-31). Qimron suggests that at Qumran this is effectively just a means to negate the infinitive, and most of the biblical instances can be understood in that general way.[18] We should be wary, therefore, of imposing here the specific sense that 'no adding is possible', since the construction could equally imply 'there is nobody who can add' or maybe even 'no adding is needed': the author has picked a very broad expression, and it seems best to retain that breadth in translation.

3.14 adding...subtracting] The verbs יסף (in the hiph'il) and גרע occur together also in Deut 4.2 and 13.1 (ET 12.32), and it seems likely that we are dealing with a formulaic expression (so, e.g., Crenshaw), to which there is perhaps also a reference in Prov 30.6. Some scholars have seen the origins of this expression in ancient injunctions against the alteration of texts.[19]

3.14 achieved their fear] Lit. 'that they fear'. When -ש appears directly after a transitive verb, it seems most natural either to read it as a simple relative serving as the object ('God has made that which they fear'—a possibility considered by Krüger; cf. Dan 11.24), or to take the clause which it governs as the (substantivized) object ('God has made [the fact] that they fear'). This verse, however, is most commonly translated 'God has acted *so that* they may fear', or somesuch. The observation that the ancient versions seemingly understand -ש here to introduce a purpose clause has been considered to offset the problem that it is not elsewhere used that way, and it is by no means impossible, of course, to take עשה as being used absolutely (the verb can be used this way of divine action, cf. 1 Sam 14.6; Ps 119.126).

To support this understanding, appeal is often made, furthermore, to the apparent use of אשר in purpose clauses (cf. GKC §165 b; J-M §168 f), but

---

[18] Qimron, *Hebrew of the Dead Sea Scrolls*, 79. The construction is discussed at length in Hurvitz, *Concise Lexicon*, 36-39, which distinguishes it from the usage in 1 Sam 9.7, and argues for its late date.

[19] See especially Herrmann, 'Zu Koheleth 3, 14', but note also the reservations expressed in Vonach, 'Die sogenannte Kanon- oder Ptahotepformel'.

that usage is not straightforward. In Ezek 36.27, for example, the את in ועשיתי את אשר בחקי תלכו shows that אשר is functioning not as a conjunction, but to substantivize the clause which follows, 'and I will achieve (the situation) that you walk in my statutes', not literally 'and I will act *so that* you…'. In Deut 6.3, where Israel is urged to take care לעשות אשר ייטב לך ואשר תרבון מאד, we may understand a similar construction rather than ellipsis of the object or an absolute use of the verb followed by two final clauses: they are to take care 'to achieve (the situation) that it goes well with you and that you multiply greatly'. Of the other instances commonly cited, none necessarily involves taking אשר as a conjunction introducing a purpose clause, and in most it is probably to be taken simply as a relative pronoun.[20] With the use of אשר so problematic in this respect, it seems hard to presume that ש- can be taken in such a way.

The evidence of the versions is also less clear cut than it seems at first sight. G uses ἵνα also in 5.14, where מאומה...שילך is rendered οὐδέν…ἵνα πορευθῇ, 'nothing…that might depart'; it is difficult to believe that this is intended to be an expression of purpose, and G is probably just displaying the considerable breadth of meaning which ἵνα had come to possess in Hellenistic Greek, often simply creating substantivized clauses. With our present verse, we might compare John 11.37 or Col 4.16 in the NT, where ποιεῖν is used with ἵνα and the subjunctive to mean 'achieve (the situation) that…'—much the same sense that we saw for עשה with אשר in Deut 6.3; Ezek 36.27. When G translates ש- with ἵνα here, then, it was not necessarily intending to express purpose, but adopting a Greek construction broadly equivalent to the Hebrew; S does the same in Syriac, and although Hie *fecit ut timeant*, 'he has acted that they might fear', *does* express purpose, it probably rests on an understanding of G rather than a specific reading of the Hebrew. None of these versions, therefore, reflects a clear or independent understanding of the Hebrew as a purpose clause, and, other than Jerome, only T has obviously read the text in this way—it adds punishment as the object of the divine action,

In short, the grounds for reading a specific expression of purpose here are rather slight, and other uses of עשה with a relative suggest that we should understand this to be a statement that God has made or achieved a situation in which 'they fear'. Although intention may be implicit in this, it seems

---

[20] Gen 24.3; 2 Kgs 22.16; and Neh 8.14f. do not clearly include purpose-clauses at all, but expressions of the content of oaths and laws, and in Josh 3.7 אשר is most likely a relative pronoun referring to Israel. Although there are implications of purpose, it is probably a pronoun in Gen 11.7 also (lit. 'confuse their language, who will not (then) understand'), and in Deut 32.46 ('the words which I am…which you may…'); Deut 4.10 may also be understood in those terms, and in Deut 4.40 the second אשר, followed by an impersonal verb, probably stands as a pronoun in parallel with the first ('his commandments which I command…[by] which it will go well…'; a true purpose clause with למען then follows).

doubtful that it can be stretched to embrace Fox's idea that God intends to provoke fear without imposing it. V *timeatur* understands the 'they' to be impersonal, but even if that is the intended reading, it is difficult to see who would be doing the fearing if not humans, and I take the reference to be once more back to the humans of 3.10.

Noegel, 'Word Play', 18, thinks there is a pun here: the verb could be read as from ראה, so that humans would 'see' God, or perhaps 'learn from him' (comparing Judg 7.17). That is possible in principle, but it is hard to see what the point would be.

3.14 before him] מלפני was used in 1.10 to express the separation of distant aeons (see the note there). As well as 10.5, where it has its basic sense of going 'out from the presence' of someone, Ecclesiastes also uses it with ירא twice in 8.12-13. The verb usually takes a simple accusative or מן, and although מפני is not uncommon, מלפני is found elsewhere only at 1 Sam 18.12. Although in that passage the context might suggest 'afraid to be in the presence of', it is difficult to know whether some special sense is implied in any or all cases, and we should note that the expression occurs with other verbs of fearing in 1 Chr 16.30; Esth 7.6; Ps 114.7, and in connection with other emotions in 1 Sam 8.18; 1 Kgs 21.29; 1 Chr 16.33; 2 Chr 33.12, 23; 34.27; 36.12.

It is correspondingly hard to say whether we can treat the expression here as though it were identical simply to 'fear God', the simpler and more common expression found in commands at 5.7 and (in the epilogue) at 12.13. In 8.12-13, those who 'fear God' are also those who 'fear before him', and someone who has 'no fear before God' is their opposite. The concepts would seem to be aligned, therefore, but if the statement in 8.12 is not wholly tautologous, then there must be some distinction between them. Perhaps the best we can say is that Qohelet does make some use of the very well-known expression 'fear God', but likes also to use one that is not a familiar cliché, in which the idea of actual fear has not been swallowed up in a more general notion of piety. We might ourselves distinguish between being 'God-fearing' and being 'afraid of God', even if the same person could be both.

3.15 This already is whatever is] There is an obvious echo of 1.9, but the construction is different. In the usage of Ecclesiastes, כבר precedes what it qualifies (cf. especially 6.10), so the first element is probably just 'whatever is/ has been' (see the note at 1.9 on the tense), not 'whatever already is/has been'. Although G renders הוא with ἐστιν, 'is', like היא in v. 13, it is not, of course a verb, and its relationship to that first element is unclear. If we read 'what is/ has been: it already (was/is)', taking הוא to be resumptive of מה שהיה, we are left with a statement of the blindingly obvious.

T, V, Hie (perhaps also G) try to distinguish two different periods to make sense of this: what was in the past and what continues more recently or in the present, but הוא can hardly carry any connotation of tense, and 1.9 has probably influenced their understandings. Jerome's readings (cf. the note on 'whatever exists' at 6.10) are complicated by the fact that neither in Hie nor in V does he have any direct equivalent to כבר here, although it is possible that Hie *ipsum quod est* is supposed to represent הוא כבר: הוא alone was represented by *ipsum* in 1.9. Joüon, 'Notes philologiques', 420, would emend הוא to היה, or שהיה to שיהיה, and Zimmermann predictably sees a translation error here: 'the Hebrew translator failed to distinguish properly *huʾ* and *hawaʾ*, the letters being identical. The verse should read: *ma dehuʾ kebar hawaʾ*: "whatever is now, already was".'

It seems to be better, however, to take this as a bipartite non-verbal sentence, with הוא referring back instead to the divine action of the previous verse: what God has achieved is already whatever exists. If it seems awkward for כבר to qualify a non-verbal equivalence, then the normal order (and the accents) might be ignored to take it with היה, which is apparently the way in which S has read the Hebrew. That changes the sense only slightly: it 'is whatever exists already'.

Having rejected an interrogative sense in 1.9, where G reads a question, Barton now adopts one here, where it does not: 'What is that which is? Already it has been.'

3.15 and what is to be] The infinitive construct with -ל commonly has a prospective aspect, looking to the future from the perspective of the subject, hence its use for expressions of purpose, obligation etc. (cf. the various uses discussed in GKC §114 g-l). The use here is similar to that in, e.g., Gen 15.12 ויהי השמש לבוא, 'the sun was about to set', or 2 Kgs 4.13 מה לעשות לך, 'what (is) to be done for you?'. To be quite precise, it is not equivalent to, or a periphrasis, for the imperfect here (so Seow), but there is obviously an overlap between the two.

Joüon, 'Notes philologiques', 420, considers the repetition of היה to be weak, and suggests the possibility that it should be emended to יהיה with a present frequentative sense, 'that which will happen, happens already'. That is not only arbitrary, but unnecessary.

S ܘܟܠ ܡ *wkl mʾ* (cf. Syh ܘܟܠܗܘܢ *wklhwn*) is probably an interpretation of G καὶ ὅσα, although another unexpected 'all' occurs in v. 22 also (see the note there).

3.15 will seek] S has two verbs: ܢܒܥ ܠܪܕܝܦ *nbʿ lrdypʾ*, 'is about to/ seeks to seek out'; Kamenetzky, 215, and Euringer see the second (which is from the same verb as the object) as an explanatory gloss. Lucifer, *De Sancto Athanasio*, I, xxxv, cites the text in Latin as *et deus requiret*, 'and God will seek out', or 'seek out again'; cf. the later Hie *et deus quaeret*, 'and God will seek for'.

3.15 whatever is to be pursued] Or 'what is pursued', perhaps 'what may be pursued'. See below.

את is not reflected in G (= α') or S, and we might expect a definite article, but there are no real grounds for emendation, even though the versions reflect considerable variety.²¹ G τὸν διωκόμενον, 'the one who is pursued', and Hie *eum qui persecutionem patitur*, 'he who suffers persecution', understand the subject of נִרְדָּף to be human, in line with early interpretations of the text as a reference to divine care for the persecuted (cf. Sir 5.3; also T and the Midrash);²² this may also be the understanding of σ', (ὁ δὲ θεὸς ἐπιζητήσει) ὑπὲρ τῶν ἐκδιωκομένων, 'but God will seek on behalf of those persecuted', where it becomes plural. Modern commentators do not generally see a reference to a human (although Zimmermann thinks that Qohelet is referring to himself: 'God hounds him without cessation'). The modern view, and that of earlier commentators such as Ibn Ezra, is better encapsulated in V (*deus instaurat) quod abiit*, 'God restores what has passed', with God maintaining the continuity of events.²³

The verb can be used of scattering by the wind (Job 30.15 niphʿal, as here; cf. Isa 17.13 puʿal), and it can have a general sense of seeking (e.g. Deut 16.20; Hos 6.3), but it generally connotes pursuit, usually hostile pursuit, and can be used in association or parallel with בקש (cf. Josh 2.22; Judg 4.22; 1 Sam 23.25; 25.29; 26.20; Ps 34.15 [ET 34.14]; Isa 51.1; Hos 2.9). Other proposals for the sense of נִרְדָּף are unpersuasive,²⁴ and the collocation of the

---

²¹ Salters, 'Ecclesiastes 3.15b', 419, points out that the readings of G and α' reflect 'what is desiderated', and cannot be used to justify restoration of the missing article; he notes a similar case in 7.7 (את לב). He also observes that the את is lacking in Sir 5.3 כי יי מבקש נרדפים, which he takes to depend on our passage, and speculates that Ben Sira 'read a text which was similar to MT, and was forced to emend it himself in quotation'. Kamenetzky, 238, would move the last four words of the verse to the end of v. 17, and read הָרֹדֵף.

²² So similarly Salters, 'Ecclesiastes 3.15b', 420-21, who notes that Rashi and Rashbam stand in the same tradition of Jewish interpretation. That interpretation is rare today, but see Garrett, 'Use and Abuse', 160-62, which links the statement here to 3.16-17. That link was also made by Lucifer (see above).

²³ In his commentary, Jerome cites G as τὸ διωκόμενον, an attested variant, and explains that it is 'that which has passed away, which has been expelled, has ceased to exist' (confirming, incidentally, that he read the neuter, against the masculine attested for the Greek in some texts of the commentary). He distinguishes, however, the strict sense of the original, which forms the basis for his translation in terms of persecution. Bianchi, 'La Storia, la memoria', 62-63, takes Jerome's characterization of G as a stage in the development of his own thinking, which leads ultimately to the rendering in V.

²⁴ Montgomery, 'Notes', 242, suggests that נִרְדָּף should be connected instead with an Arabic term which refers to someone who rides behind another, and so refers to consequence. This seems tenuous, to say the least; the idea was later developed in Driver, 'Problems and Solutions', 226, with a more subtle interpretation ('each succeeding moment of the future as it becomes present and of the present as it becomes past'), but little more plausibility. Driver additionally argues that the preceding את originated as an abbreviation of אותו. Wright and Delitzsch

verbs points strongly to both having some such connotation of pursuit here. Ogden proposes that we should, in fact, understand '(God requests) that it be pursued', or even that we should parse the verb as first-person plural imperfect qal, to give 'that we pursue (it)'. Even if, at a stretch however, we allow his assumptions that את might be equivalent to את אשר,[25] and the clause parallel to the -ש clause at the end of v. 14, either reading would surely require a pronoun to mark 'it', and the form of the verb (however pointed) would be very odd if the first were intended. Even 'God requires that we pursue' would involve a wholly unexpected switch from the third person, and make no obvious sense in context; Qohelet, moreover, does not elsewhere use the first person plural to associate himself with other humans, or, indeed, at all.

If we accept the normal construal of the word as a niphʻal participle, that leaves open a number of different ways to understand the expression, both because what is 'pursued' remains unspecified in the text, and because passive participles can express a range of meanings. J-M §413 i notes, for instance, such gerundial implications as '(an animal that) may be eaten', or '(God who is) to be feared' attached to niphʻal participles, and GKC §116 e adds further examples, with an even broader range. In principle, then, Qohelet might be describing not just something that *is* pursued, but something that 'might be', is 'fit to be', or 'ought to be' pursued. In that case, of course, it is possible to understand the pursuit itself in a correspondingly broad range of ways—and it will be clear from my translation that I consider just such a gerundial nuance to be required here. It remains a stretch, however, to find the simple reference to God maintaining or restoring the past, which most commentators prefer on contextual grounds, because it is difficult to see how things or events that have ceased, or might cease, are, or should be, in any sense 'pursued'.

I take the very lack of specification here, in fact, to suggest that Qohelet's concern is not with *what* God pursues, but with the fact of the pursuit. This is not a new approach in itself. Levy, for instance, paraphrases the statement as '„Gott erstrebt das schon einmal von ihm Erstrebte wieder", er führt nichts Neues herbei', '"God strives for what he has striven for already", he brings about nothing new', and Michel understands the point to be that only God

---

appeal to Arabic, and to much later Hebrew, for the different sense 'analogue' or 'synonym', with the implication that God seeks to restore continuity with the past, but Delitzsch admits that ancient attestation of that meaning is lacking. Eaton notes rabbinic uses of the passive participle to mean 'swift', but this sense is nowhere attested for the niphʻal. Pinker, 'Qohelet 3:14-15', 270-71, suggests that there is an error here for שאת פני, and translates 'God desires (looks for) respect': he does not explain how this became the graphically very different, and much harder את נרדף.

[25] In the second edition of his commentary, Ogden speaks mysteriously of a '*še* in v. 15b [which] is a truncated form of *ʾet-*ʾ*ăšer*'; from the first edition, it is clear that he is referring to the את.

is equipped to pursue those intellectual quests that humans undertake. Both those understandings, to be sure, import new specifications of their own: the text lacks any explicit reference to God doing what he has 'always done' or has 'done before', while it is tenuous to extrapolate from Qohelet's uses of בקש elsewhere that the verb must refer to intellectual enquiry. I think, however, that Levy is right to see the seeking and pursuit as virtual synonyms, with a broad reference, and Michel to understand that the emphasis here is on divine, as opposed to human, action; that emphasis is affirmed by the position of האלהים before the verb. Qohelet's point is that, whatever end or purpose needs to be pursued, perhaps to ensure that the future will remain the same as the present, it is God who will pursue it.

Introduction to 3.16-22

Hidden Distinctions

(3.16) And again, I saw beneath the sun the place of justice—guilt was present there—and the place of innocence—guilt was present there. (3.17) I said in my heart, 'The innocent and the guilty: God will make a judgment—as there is a time for every matter—and about everything that is done there'.

(3.18) I said in my heart concerning humans, 'God is going to separate them, while they see themselves as animals'. (3.19) For what happens to humans, and what happens to animals, just one thing happens to them: as the death of this one, so the death of that, and there is one breath for all. Then what a human has more than an animal—it's gone, since all is illusion. (3.20) Each goes to one place: each came into being from dust, and each returns to dust. (3.21) And who knows the breath of humans—does it rise upward?—and the breath of animals—does it sink downward to the ground?

(3.22) Then I saw that there is nothing better than that a person rejoice in his achievements, since that is what is his: who can bring him to see what will be after him?

The very grand declarations of 3.1-15, in which human activity is wholly subordinated to the divine, seem to be leading up to 3.22, in which Qohelet finally declares that humans can do no better than to enjoy what they achieve. It is a little surprising, therefore, when Qohelet suddenly turns to a different topic in 3.16-17, and starts talking about divine judgment. The language in the second half of 3.17, however, makes an explicit reference back to 3.1, so we are clearly invited to see a connection. When 3.22 does make its declaration about enjoyment, furthermore, it connects it not directly with the key points made in 3.1-15, but rather with the issue of human ignorance about the future; this itself picks up 3.11, but it also informs the difficult 3.18-21. There is supposed to be some basic continuity here, and these links seem to assert that Qohelet is tacking towards his destination, not simply changing course.

His purpose, in fact, seems to be to introduce further issues that arise both from the relationship between God and humans, and from the limitations set on human knowledge. In 3.16-17 the concern is apparent injustice in the world, and Qohelet (speaking once more 'in his heart') expresses a confidence that God will, in fact, judge between the innocent and guilty. Qohelet does not draw an explicit conclusion from those verses, perhaps because he wishes to associate them with what follows. However, his second observation, made in the difficult 3.18-21, represents a shift to a somewhat different topic: the inability of humans to see for themselves that they are actually any different from animals—although Qohelet again reassures himself that they are. What unites 3.16-17 and 3.18-21 is not their subject-matter, therefore, but the fact that they each identify a particular sort of situation, in which (Qohelet believes) the very real distinctions that will inform divine actions or decisions are hidden from humans.

This, of course, underpins the point in 3.22, that humans are ignorant of the future—whether it be the coming divine judgment, or the difference between their death and that of animals. Qohelet himself, of course, is not averse to claiming an insight that is unavailable to others, but even he cannot act as a guide for his fellow humans in this respect, because the problematic situations that he identifies are problematic whether his own views on them are right or wrong. The issue lies not in the very fact that guilt seems to be pervasive, or that human death is indistinguishable from the death of animals, but in the problem that any information that might shed a different light on each situation is unavailable, so that humans can do no more than hold unverifiable beliefs about them. Qohelet will later take this in a slightly different direction, and in 8.10-14, for example, the contradiction between what people can see and what he himself believes to be going on leads him to suppose that, ignorant of their own ignorance, people respond wrongly to such situations because they misunderstand them. Here, though, that point is pursued no further than the suggestion that people wrongly see themselves as animals.

We can see, then, that there is in fact a certain continuity between all this and the preceding 3.1-15: where the earlier part of the chapter drew out the subordination of human work to God's activities, these last verses now pick up a particular point about human ignorance, even of their own nature. Qohelet wants to make it clear that the limitations on human activity include both a lack of control and a lack of understanding. Although it was restated in 3.9, therefore, Qohelet's standing question about profit has given way to a more comprehensive dismantlement of human aspirations, and when we finally reach 3.22, Qohelet no longer even troubles himself to dismiss profit as a possibility, or to contrast the 'share' available with the profit he seeks. Here instead he associates his commendation of pleasure with a different point, which is itself a rather neglected *leitmotif* in the monologue: that humans cannot know what will happen after them. This is not a way of saying that they cannot know what is going to happen to *them*, or simply that life is unpredictable, but states something closer to Qohelet's earlier ignorance about his successor: humans cannot see how things will be in the world after they have left it.

It is not immediately clear what this restriction in itself has to do with enjoyment of work being the best thing available to humans, and the point made by the question does not furnish a direct explanation for the whole statement that precedes it. It is likewise difficult to establish the connection between the different elements which we will encounter later in 6.12, where Qohelet follows a question about the good for humans with a similar rhetorical question, again rejecting the possibility that anybody might tell them what will come, but there interposing an additional observation about the finitude of human life. The very fact that we find the same association in both places, however, suggests that it is meaningful to Qohelet, while its association with brevity of life as well as with human good in 6.12 raises the possibility that this meaning lies not in its value as an explanation, but in its role as a further, parallel limitation. In other words, there is nothing better for humans than enjoyment *and* no way for them to know what will come. As often elsewhere, however, our understanding of the connection rests on the significance and weight that we place on the Hebrew particle *ky* that links the two parts here. If we insist that this is an explanation, then we have to imagine that Qohelet restricts the justification for his claim here to the point that humans can make no plans for the future beyond them, so should find contentment within the more limited span of what they are doing—even if that sits uncomfortably with his earlier observations that individuals can find no benefit for themselves anyway in such a future.

3.16-17

(3.16) And again, I saw beneath the sun the place of justice—guilt was present there—and the place of innocence—guilt was present there. (3.17) I said in my heart, 'The innocent and the guilty: God will make a judgment—as there is a time for every matter—and about everything that is done there'.

Commentary

3.16] A number of commentators understand the sense here to be 'in place of judgment was guilt, and in place of innocence was guilt'. This is an attractive reading, and an influential one (not least because Jerome adopted it for his Vulgate translation), but it is hard to make the Hebrew yield such a sense, especially if we intend it to have the particular implication that Qohelet saw guilt *instead of* justice and innocence.

Although each can be used more broadly, all of these terms have a forensic or judicial implication, and the use of them together like this suggests that Qohelet might have such a context in mind. If he is thinking in terms of a trial or law-court, then the 'place of judgment' could be the spot where the judges are, as often suggested (and this was, in fact, Jerome's understanding in his earlier commentary). Then the claim would be that the guilty stand where the judges should. It is harder, though, to make sense of the second 'place' in those terms: trials might typically have a specific place for those who are being tried, but there is no spot for the innocent, as such. If the person in the dock, as it were, is in fact guilty, then the dock is not the 'place of innocence', and we end up having to adopt some rather contrived understanding of it as a spot where the guilty are 'being pronounced' innocent, or *vice versa* (which would make 'place of innocence' an extremely economic usage, to say the least).

From the next verse, it seems likely that Qohelet is trying to suggest a confusion in the world between the innocent and the guilty, which will be resolved by divine judgment, rather than simply to make a point that guilt is endemic or the judicial system corrupt. Accordingly, his observation is probably a general one, that in *every* place where there is justice or righteousness, guilt is also present. Indeed, the Hebrew could be vocalized as 'the guilty man', which is how the Greek translator read it, and this would give a more vivid image of the guilty mingling among the just and righteous.

3.17] Qohelet spoke 'in his heart' at 2.1, 15, and will do so again (for the last time) in the next verse. In 2.1, he seems, in effect, actually to have been speaking 'to' his heart, but elsewhere the expression appears simply to mean 'I thought to myself'. It is probably not a specific nuance of the idiom, but 2.15; 3.17, 18 all use it to introduce an idea that contradicts the evidence of Qohelet's eyes (2.13; 3.16): he sees something, but expresses his belief or understanding that, in fact, there is something else going on.

Divine justice is a tricky area for Qohelet: the determinism that he has just expressed so strongly raises significant questions about the basis on which God might judge humans (if whatever they do is being done in pursuit of his own designs), and Qohelet's various statements affirming such judgment often seem more like attempts to engage with an established belief than a central part of his thinking (I have explored this in 'Divine Judgment')—many scholars, indeed, have doubted that they are an original part of the monologue (so, recently, Berne, 'Der Ferne Gott'). There is potentially a certain *chutzpah* involved, therefore, in his apparent evocation here of 3.1, particularly if the determinism that might undermine divine judgment is being presented as the basis for affirming it.

At one level, the claim might be taken simply to be a syllogism that reverses the logic of 3.1; as Farmer puts it: 'he concludes that if God truly has "appointed a time for every matter" (v. 17), then it logically follows that God also has appointed a time for judging between the bad and the good'. It is important to note, however, the connection of 'time' with 'judgment' also in 8.6, which uses very similar language: both here and in that verse, Qohelet effectively changes the meaning of 'a time for every matter', so that it no longer means 'an occasion for everything' but 'a time of reckoning for everything'. Accordingly, the words of 3.1 are being evoked, but not their sense, and by playing on different connotations of 'time', Qohelet gives an appearance of continuity while making a point that is very different—and perhaps contradictory.

Commentators generally take 'everything that is done there' to be set in parallel with 'every matter', so RSV, for instance, speaks of 'a time for every matter, and for every work', but it is difficult to reach this without emendation, even if we go against all the versions by vocalizing the last word as 'appointed' instead of 'there' ('he has appointed a time for…and for…'; see the notes). If we retain 'there', as we most likely should, then the reference may be to the world 'beneath the sun', with Qohelet claiming that God will judge all actions done in that world, or perhaps more precisely to the 'places' that he has just mentioned.

Notes

3.16 and again] Although it is not normally used this way in biblical Hebrew, ועוד here seems to be introducing a new point (the use in 2 Chr 17.6, perhaps, is most comparable). Rather than a simple 'moreover', though, it may be picking up the preceding ראיתי in 3.10, so that Qohelet 'saw again'. The more common usage would lead us to read 'while I was yet seeing' or similar, and does not point to the sense 'constantly' or 'continually' preferred by a few commentators.

3.16 place of] The objects of ראיתי have been variously understood. If they are simply מקום המשפט and the corresponding ומקום הצדק, then the two clauses שמה הרשע describe each מקום attributively or predicatively (cf. Delitzsch): 'I saw the place…(where) הרשע was', or 'I saw the place…(that) הרשע was there'. A number of commentators (including Seow) have preferred, however, to take מקום in each case not as the object, but as an adverbial expression introducing a clause, with the clause itself serving as the object of ראיתי. The clause would then have a structure similar to that commonly read in the last part of 11.3. On such an understanding, Qohelet is saying something like: 'I saw (that in) the place of…was הרשע'. In support of such a reading, it is often noted that the accents of M place a disjunction before מקום, and suggested that this tells against the Masoretes having taken the noun as the object of ראיתי. If that is true, however, the rule is hardly absolute, and some other commentators have pointed out that there is disjunction before the object in no less a verse than Gen 1.1. We may also observe that only V among the other ancient versions takes מקום to be adverbial. The issue may seem to be trivial, since there is no strong distinction of sense, but if we do take מקום to be an adverbial 'accusative of place' then it is important to note that 'in the place of' does not mean 'instead of', a sense which is only possible for the term at Hos 2.1, and not certain there.

3.16 justice] The terms משפט, רשע, and צדק all have general connotations of justice, wickedness, and righteousness respectively, but they also have legal, forensic meanings, which are often taken to be in play here. So in Deut 25.1, for example, המשפט is the court in which disputes are judged; those found guilty are רשע, while the vindicated are צדיק; see also, e.g., 2 Chr 6.23. On that reading, the מקום המשפט is either the court or the place within the court where the judges sit. For reasons outlined in the commentary above, I think it is difficult to see something so precise as a court setting here, but the context of divine judgment does make a forensic translation of רשע and צדק appropriate, even if Qohelet has something more general in mind than criminal liability. I have retained 'justice' for משפט, however, because 'place of judgment' implies something too specific in English. There is a detailed discussion of the book's uses of משפט and צדק in Laurent, 'Les Paroles'.

3.16 guilt...guilt] On the translation 'guilt', see the previous note. On both occasions here, M reads רשע as רֶשַׁע, guilt or wickedness, rather than as רָשָׁע, a guilty or wicked person, and this reading is supported by Hie, V, and probably S. All of these, however, use a different noun on each occasion (*impietas* then *iniquitas* in the Latin versions, ܪܘܫܥܐ *rwšʿ* and ܥܘܠܐ *ʿwlʾ* in S). On stylistic grounds, Graetz suspected that the second term was originally פשע (which would be 'crime' or a 'criminal' in this context), a suggestion which is by no means far-fetched, and which has since been made by others (see especially Hertzberg, in 1932 and 1963). Some such variation might explain the distinctions made by these versions, and עול (cf. S) would be another candidate, although it is graphically more distant. The grounds for emendation are slim, however, and this can remain no more than a suspicion. It is no less likely that Jerome and S are imposing a variation for their own reasons of style. T probably understands רָשָׁע both times.

Matters are more significantly complicated by G, which reads the first occurrence as רָשָׁע (ἀσεβής), but then has, in almost every manuscript, εὐσεβής, 'the pious man', for the second. Vinel (35) wonders if this was a deliberate choice by the translator, attempting to make sense of the passage, but that would be uncharacteristic, and it is usually assumed that the reading has arisen either as a careless error in the transmission of G (so, e.g., Euringer, Goldman), or as a deliberate alteration ('in the cause of orthodoxy', McNeile, 158). The change must have been early to have so permeated the manuscript tradition, and it remains largely uncorrected: Syh ܫܦܝܪ ܕܚܠܬ *špyr dḥltʾ* and the Origenic manuscripts both reflect εὐσεβής (Gentry, 'Propaedeutic', 167, suggests that the five manuscripts which read ἀσεβής do so as a result of influence from Jerome or Aquila), as does the La *illic impius...illic pius*, cited in Lucifer, *De Sancto Athanasio* 1.35. If we take G* to have been ἀσεβής, as seems likely, then G (like T) understood רָשָׁע in both places where M has רֶשַׁע.

Goldman thinks that the original intention was רָשָׁע in the first occurrence, רֶשַׁע in the second, but it is difficult to see how such a distinction could have been signalled in the consonantal text. משפט, and probably צדק (see below), point to 'guilt' rather than 'guilty' here, but whichever is read, the same should be understood in both places.

3.16 was present there] The Hebrew has no verb, and it is not clear whether שמה implies 'thither' (cf. 9.10) or 'there': both senses are possible, although the former is more common (cf. Schoors, *The Preacher* I, 101-102). The usage is probably similar to Ezek 32.29-30, and the implication that הרשע

is 'present at' these places, but Qohelet could conceivably be saying that he saw injustice 'heading towards' them. Michel, *Untersuchungen*, 250-51, takes this much further, to argue that Qohelet is speaking of a divine tribunal, 'to which' injustice must go, and Schwienhorst-Schönberger also advances this as a possibility. Of course, any such reading has to account for the fact that Qohelet is claiming to have seen something 'beneath the sun', but that could only anyway be the unambiguous sense if שמה always meant 'thither'.

3.16 innocence] α′ τῆς δικαιοσύνης supports M הצדק, as do Hie and V *iustitiae* (although possibly influenced by α′). On the other hand, G τοῦ δικαίου ('of the righteous man'; plural in some manuscripts) and T suggest הצדיק, a reading found in two late Hebrew manuscripts (see de Rossi; they have perhaps been influenced by T), and preferred by *BHQ*. Dahood, 'The Language of Qoheleth', 228, put the difference down to an originally defective spelling. Gentry, 'Propaedeutic', 167, suggests, however, that the translator of G used an adjective not to reflect his source so much as to match his approach to הרשע, and the parallel משפט would certainly lead us to expect הצדק. M should probably be retained, therefore, although it may be that the 'place of innocence' is anyway to be understood as the position occupied by the innocent man (whatever we might understand that to be: see above).

Although משפט is often famously paired with צדקה (e.g. Isa 5.7; Amos 5.7, 24), it is not clear that we are dealing with a 'distributed word-pair' here, as Fox would have it, with מקום המשפט and מקום הצדק together characterizing the law court as the place of righteous judgment.

3.17 I said in my heart] The same expression is used in 2.1, 15, and will be used again in the next verse. As in 2.1, there is some versional attestation of an initial conjunction (S, P, V, some key manuscripts of G); it is possible that this goes back to a Hebrew original (cf. Kamenetzky, 236, on S; Barton). Some manuscripts of G instead insert ἐκεῖ, which is probably an error for καὶ, influenced by the preceding clause (McNeile, 141), or by the start of the next verse (see below).

3.17 the innocent and the guilty] All the versions read the adjectives here. Some manuscripts of S mark both as plural with *seyame*, but this is a secondary generalization. Galling would delete the whole text ...הצדיק את האלהים as an interpretative addition, which is entirely arbitrary; he marks it as redactional in his 1969 edition.

3.17 God will make a judgement] M ישפט האלהים. S transposes the words, so that the subject precedes the verb: the change may be stylistic, but that reading is found in Coptic as well, and might reflect a variant in G. The word-order is unusual in the Hebrew, and I have attempted to reflect that in the translation.

3.17 there is a time] Lit. just 'because a time'. In 8.5-6 משפט is used in conjunction with עת (cf. the discussion in Schoors, *The Preacher* II, 233-34), and the quotation of 3.1 here, also in the context of divine judgment, may impart a more precise nuance to the word.

3.17 and about] If the two phrases לכל חפץ and ועל כל המעשה are taken to be set in parallel, it is difficult to understand why we have על in the second, where we might expect simply another -ל, and although S does indeed assimilate to the preceding לכל, M ועל כל is supported by G, Hie, T. Even if the two tend to converge in later Hebrew (cf. Schoors, *The Preacher* I, 100-101), we should still not expect על to express possession like -ל in this context, or to find such a variation in a single sentence.[1] It is possible that the text is corrupt, and that we should either delete the ע or else insert a ת to read ועת לכל; Driver, 'Abbreviations', 122, indeed, suggests that an abbreviation ועׄ, intended to be read ועת, has been misread. Any emendation, however, would be speculative. Furthermore, of the various proposals to understand or emend שם (see below), those which might explain the על are not really tenable on other grounds.

We have שפט here, rather than הביא במשפט, but it is noteworthy that 11.9 and 12.14 each construe the latter with both a direct object (of the act or person to be judged) and על, apparently used to mark the basis of judgment (in fact, על כל is used in both cases). This suggests the possibility that ועל כל המעשה שם is not supposed to stand in parallel with לכל חפץ, but rather that כי עת לכל חפץ is a parenthetical explanation, with ועל resuming the statement about divine judgment. I have adopted that understanding in my translation, and if it lacks a certain elegance, it at least avoids speculative emendation.

3.17 that is done] Lit. 'all the achievement' or 'all the behaviour'. Fox suggests that we should perhaps read the niphʻal הנעשה for M המעשה, and this might be supported by Hie *factum*. All the other versions, however, agree with M (including σ' πάσης χρείας, 'every activity'; on the attribution, see Field, Marshall: the manuscripts assign this to α'—who does, admittedly, use χρείας at 12.10).

3.17 there] Commentators have long found שם awkward here: it adds a specification that seems both unnecessary and imprecise. Some important manuscripts of G place ἐκεῖ at the start of the next sentence (as in Rahlfs' edition), perhaps reflecting a similar sense on the part of the scribes, although

---

[1] Podechard puts the problem well: 'il est une singularité que personne n'explique d'une manière satisfaisante, c'est que des deux noms régis par עֵת, le premier soit précédé de לְ et le second de עַל. Del[itzsch] dit bien, et avec raison, qu'en hébreu tardif עַל en est venu à remplacer אֶל et לְ à peu près dans tous les sens. Mais cette équivalence ne prouve pas qu'on ait accoutumé d'employer dans la même proposition לְ et עַל, immédiatement à la suite l'un de l'autre et dans le même sens, après un seul nom, ou verbe, non répété.' That is, 'It is a curiosity for which nobody can furnish a satisfactory explanation, that of the two nouns governed by עת, the first should be preceded by -ל, the second by על. Delitzsch has said well, and correctly, that in late Hebrew על came to replace אל and -ל in almost every sense. But this equivalence does not show that one might be in the habit of using -ל and על in the same statement, one straight after the other and with the same meaning, following a single, unrepeated noun or verb.'

this is complicated by the fact that some other manuscripts have read καὶ as well or instead (and the Origenic manuscripts read a plus, ὁ θεός). In the light of M and the other versions, it seems unlikely that G* had καὶ but not ἐκεῖ, as McNeile suggests, and the reverse was probably true. There are no text-critical grounds for emendation, therefore, and although Hertzberg raises the possibility that we should correct to זְמָן (cf. 3.1), this is motivated by considerations of sense. The same is true of Podechard's proposed מִשְׁפָּט (cf. 8.6), which Fox finds attractive, although he concedes that 'the emendation is perhaps too extensive'. (Podechard himself wonders, without enthusiasm, whether שָׁם might have arisen from corruption of an abbreviation.) McNeile, 63, suggests the possibility that שָׁם should simply be deleted, as a corrupt doublet of the preceding -שֶׁ or following אֲמָ-.

The lack of a verb after כִּי is awkward, and has led many commentators to read שָׂם, 'he has appointed',[2] which would require only a different vocalization, rather than emendation of the text. Although this corresponds to the understanding of none of the versions, it is attractive, and the objection that it should appear earlier in the sentence seems weakened by the similar pre-positioning of the objects in the previous clause.[3] The lack of a verb, however, aligns the clause with 3.1, and so there is no need to introduce one; indeed, to do so would make the allusion less obvious.

It has also been suggested that we should read a substantive here, construing the clause as 'a time for every matter, and for every achievement a שָׁם', which would be reminiscent of the chiastic sentence structure commonly read in 3.1. *BH³* and *BHS* suggest substantivized participles, שֹׂמֵר, and מֵשִׂים respectively (for the latter, cf. Job 4.20 מֵשִׂים, but the form and sense 'observatio' are dubious). Dahood, in 'Qoheleth and Northwest Semitic Philology', 354-55, proposed a passive participle שֻׂם, '(something) appointed' = 'an appointment', then later, in 'Phoenician Background', 271, suggested a noun שֻׂם, '(proper) place'. Vílchez Líndez and Gorssen, 'La cohérence', 305 n. 79, accept the latter, but both suggestions are speculative. Whitley undercuts the Amarna evidence used to support Dahood's '(proper) place', and himself goes in a different direction, suggesting that שָׁם may have an interjectional, and hence an additional force, so that it could mean 'also'.[4] If so, we might expect

---

[2] Goldman, curiously, seems to believe that most scholars read the participle, rather than this qal perfect, and cites Houbigant as the source of that idea; Hertzberg, though apparently Goldman's own source, cites Houbigant specifically as 'hat er gesetzt'.

[3] Galling 1969 curiously reads this verb in the next verse instead, not at the beginning but after לִבְרָם, so that God is the subject. In his 1940 edition, he more simply replaced שָׁם here with תַּחַת הַשָּׁמַיִם. It would be hard to say which solution is less plausible.

[4] See also his article 'Has the Particle שָׁם an Asseverative Force?', 396. Whitley is followed by Longman.

it to be more common, and would certainly expect to find it in a different position here. Seow, citing Dahood's earlier proposal, is also inclined to see a derivative from the verb שׂים/ שׂום with the sense 'determination' or 'destiny', equivalent to Akkadian *šīmtu*, but he presents no evidence for the existence of such a word, which, again, we might expect to find elsewhere if it were established enough for the original readers of Ecclesiastes to have recognized it. His alternative suggestion, that we read שֵׁם, 'name', is more attractive in the light of 6.10, but awkward with עַל.

Despite all these suggestions, many commentators prefer to retain שָׁם, with M and the other versions. Knobel, *The Targum of Qohelet*, and a few others have assigned a temporal sense 'then', which it is doubtful that the particle can possess. V *tunc*, which might be adduced in support, is interpretative; cf. Hie[comm] *ibi; id est in iudicio quando dominus coeperit iudicare*, '…there, that is, in the judgment when the Lord will begin to judge': Jerome understands the point to be that God's judgment is reserved for a future point at which everybody will be judged simultaneously.

3.18-21

(3.18) I said in my heart concerning humans, 'God is going to separate them, while they see themselves as animals'. (3.19) For what happens to humans, and what happens to animals, just one thing happens to them: as the death of this one, so the death of that, and there is one breath for all. Then what a human has more than an animal—it's gone, since all is illusion. (3.20) Each goes to one place: each came into being from dust, and each returns to dust. (3.21) And who knows the breath of humans—does it rise upward?—and the breath of animals—does it sink downward to the ground?

Commentary

The Hebrew of 3.18 is extremely difficult, and clarity, especially in the second half of the verse, seems to have been sacrificed by the author in an effort to give the language a polished assonance, structure and rhythm (Enns sees 'one of the more beautiful examples of alliteration' in the book). Although 3.19-21 are more straightforward, commentators have been left, therefore, struggling to understand the claim for which these verses are presented as a justification, and many different ideas have been put forward. These generally, though, have Qohelet suggest in some way that God is testing humans or otherwise demonstrating to them that they are no different from animals. On this understanding, 3.18 is an extrapolation from the preceding verses: the earthly confusion of innocence and guilt exists to show people that they are no more significant than beasts. 3.19-21 are then taken to affirm this, by pointing out that humans and animals die in the same way.

It is very difficult to reach such a meaning, however, without emending the text or understanding words and grammatical elements in ways that are either unattested or extremely unusual. Perhaps more to the point, though, a reading in those terms seems to neglect the rhetorical question posed in 3.21, where Qohelet suggests that nobody can actually know whether the breath ('spirit') of humans and animals travels in different directions after death—the point there being that humans would indeed be different if their breath returned to God, unlike that of animals. This is not simply a way of saying that it does not, and the most coherent understanding of 3.19-21 is that these verses are talking about appearance: humans die like animals and in doing so visibly lose any advantage over animals that they might have possessed in life. It is indeed true, therefore, that human and animal lives come ultimately to the same thing (cf. Ps 49.13 [ET 49.12]), but the factor that might actually make them very different, the human possession of a spirit from God, is invisible. Nobody can simply judge the matter solely from appearances, therefore, even if appearances seem to suggest no distinction. This is not an argument in favour of the idea that humans are just animals, but an illustration of the problem that visible evidence does not permit humans to distinguish themselves from animals.

Accordingly, I think that Qohelet does in fact believe there to be a difference, and this will much later be confirmed by his unequivocal suggestion in 12.7, that human breath does return to God. Just as he was willing in the preceding verses to assert the reality of divine judgment despite the evidence of his own eyes, so now Qohelet suggests that humans are different from animals, despite all visible indications to the contrary. The issue for him lies in the fact that his fellow humans may not share his belief, given the little that they can see: God genuinely is going to treat them separately from animals at death (or possibly has already marked them out), but they do not know it, and cannot discern that fact from what they observe in the deaths of others. Without emendation (but making allowance for its stylization), the claim in 3.18 can be read literally, in accordance with this understanding, as '(I thought that) going-to-separate them (is) God, and going-to-see that-they-animals (are), they for them', or less literally as 'God is going to separate them, but when they look for themselves, they are going to look on themselves as animals'. As in 3.16-17, therefore, Qohelet asserts that there is an underlying reality that contradicts what may be observed, and that cannot be deduced from it. Here he connects the additional, related idea, that humans may correspondingly be misled by what is visible to them.

It is possible to read many implications into the idea of humans seeing themselves as animals, from the negative possibility that they might therefore act in a way that is 'bestial', through to the more positive hope that such a perception might lead them to treat other animals better (and Dell, *Interpreting Ecclesiastes*, 68-75, looks at these verses in the context of animal theology). Whatever we may find there, however, Qohelet shows no interest at all in the consequences, and certainly does not use this as a way to attack human behaviour. It is not wholly clear, indeed, that he believes humans in general actually to think of themselves as animals, and his concerns are expressed narrowly in terms of the situation leading them to do so. Indeed, the lack of any discussion might in itself provoke a suspicion that this issue has been chosen for its heuristic value, rather than because it represents a real, general problem. Qohelet's religious ideas do not extend into the realm of 'souls' or supernatural spirits, but the idea of a divine breath, with which humans are infused and animals are not, provides him with a useful case-study for the way in which the aspects of the world that are visible to humans can actually belie reality.

If some authorial artifice seems likely, then, in the choice of issue here, it is worth pondering also, for a moment, the dynamics behind Qohelet's rhetoric. His human/animal example, like that of divine judgment in 3.16-17, is persuasive only insofar as the audience accepts Qohelet's interpretation of what is really going on: if none of them actually believes that God will judge, or that humans have a divine breath, then he fails to enlist his audience and make his case. Ironically, therefore, the effectiveness of his claim in 3.18-21, that humans might be led to see themselves as animals, relies on the assumption that his audience do not—and we may calculate, as the author surely did, that most contemporary Jewish readers would have backed Qohelet's ideas about both judgment and a divine breath. Where Qohelet appears to be setting himself apart from the mass of humanity, then, he is also exempting his readers. Or perhaps, to turn that round, he is making statements about human perceptions, here and often elsewhere, that his audience would not have recognized as their own, and that would have drawn them to his side in opposition to 'other people'.

3.19] Qohelet observed a similar lack of distinction between himself and the fool in 2.14-15, and will extend this to cover many different groups of humans in 9.2-3: he presents the fact of everybody's death as a particular problem, and uses it to question the reality or significance of distinctions between people. So long as the distinctions in question are distinctions of outcome, to be sure, the problem is a real one, and Qohelet can legitimately question, say, the point of all his wisdom if he is going to die like the fool. When the issue is distinctions of character or nature, however, the logic is more dubious: if you are both going to be eaten by a bird anyway, there may not be any *point* in being a snail rather than a seed, but that does not make a snail the *same* as a seed. That would be a syllogistic fallacy (technically, a fallacy of the 'undistributed middle'). Although the issue was apparently presented as one of identical nature in 3.18, therefore, Qohelet shifts quietly to different ground here: humans lose at death whatever might differentiate them from animals—or, as he puts it, whatever it is that they have over and above what animals have. The problem becomes more specifically, then, that a dead human seems to be the same as a dead animal, which represents a significant narrowing of the perception described in 3.18, to the point that it is almost unexceptionable. If Qohelet is not just deliberately blurring the issues, then we are perhaps supposed to surmise that the concern is not so much with identity of nature after all, as with what will happen to humans at death. One aspect of a difference at that point might be the different direction of their departing breath, as described in the next verse, which stands in contrast to the air shared here by humans and animals in life. Of greater concern, however, even if it is unmentioned here, would be the possibility of an afterlife for humans that might not be available to animals.

3.20-21] Qohelet speaks in 12.7 of dust returning to the ground at death, and breath returning to God—he uses the term *rwḥ* which can be translated, according to context, as 'breath', 'wind' or 'spirit', but which should not generally be thought of as a 'soul'.[1] As already

---

[1] See especially the long discussion in Bidder, *Koheleths Stellung*, which denies absolutely (32) that *rwḥ* can mean 'soul'. In fact, though, in 4Q206 fr. 2 col. II, 3-4, we do find an Aramaic reference to seeing the '*rwḥ* of a dead man'. From other versions of Enoch, this is clearly the spirit that went out from Abel when Cain slew him, which protests eternally, and the *rwḥ* here is the counterpart to the blood that cries out from the ground in Gen 4.10—which likewise has a 'voice'. If the Greek is an accurate representation of its source, the Aramaic probably went on to use *rwḥ* more generally in the lines that followed (now lost in Aramaic), so it seems likely that in this text, probably written around the same time as Ecclesiastes, *rwḥ* was used interchangeably with *npš* to talk about the dead. We cannot exclude such a sense in our text on purely lexical grounds, therefore, but the

noted, this makes his own views on the matter clear, but it also, of course, echoes those of Gen 2.7, where God makes the first human from dust and breathes into him the 'breath of life'—although Qohelet does not use quite the same vocabulary as the writer in Genesis, and is probably not alluding directly to that text (as claimed by, e.g., Anderson, 'Curse of Work', 101). Job 27.3 equates being alive with having 'the spirit of God in my nostrils' (cf. 33.4), just as Job 34.14-15 declares that if God should choose to take back his spirit, then all flesh would die, and humans return to dust, while we also find references to God's life-giving spirit in Isa 42.5 and 57.16 (and cf. the complicated account in Ezek 37.6-14). It is not difficult to suppose, therefore, that some idea of a particular breath given by God and required for life was quite widespread.

The specific belief implied here, that this breath was possessed by humans alone, or at least that humans possess a breath that is different from the breath of animals, may not have been shared by all the biblical writers. In Job 32.8, on the one hand, Elihu identifies the spirit from God as the source of human understanding, which would seem to accord with Qohelet's suggestion if we assume that animals are not supposed to share such understanding, and something similar may be implicit in Prov 20.27, which suggests, conversely, that the breath of a human is a sort of light, by means of which God sees inside them. In Gen 7.21-22, on the other, animals that died in the flood explicitly did possess the 'breath of life' like humans, while Ps 104.25-30 seems to understand that even sea creatures are animated by a breath from God.[2] The references are too few for us to posit any specific historical development in these ideas, and it is difficult to connect them directly to those of other

---

'spirits' in Enoch notably do not rise to God, and are detained in the underworld to await judgement. If Qohelet is deliberately addressing some current belief in an afterlife, then it is not the belief espoused in 1 Enoch, and it is quite unnecessary to suppose that he is doing so at all—let alone to deduce some broader confrontation with apocalyptic literature, as does Fischer, 'Frühe Apokalyptik'; cf. Michel, 'Weisheit und Apokalyptik'; d'Alario, 'Chi sa se lo spirito'. Lux, 'Tod', 56-57 n. 56, argues (rightly, I think) that the context here demands 'breath of life'.

[2] If we take them seriously, the references to animals in Jonah 3.7, 8; 4.11 might imply some similar equality with humans, although I am not persuaded by Hunter's attempt ('Beastly') to link those passages with this (via 10.2), and impute the same view to Qohelet.

cultures.³ We should be wary, however, of assuming that there is any clear reference here to an afterlife or to immortality of the soul. What is envisaged seems more simply to be an animating force that is lent to each creature so long as they survive, and then surrendered when they die.

Notes

3.18 I said] On the initial ἐκεῖ in some presentations of G, see the preceding note on 3.17.

3.18 concerning] There are only a few biblical uses of דברה outside Ecclesiastes. In Job 5.8, Eliphaz declares that he would 'set his דברתי' to God, a statement placed in parallel with seeking or consulting God (דרש אל), and probably concerned with addressing speech to him; in Deut 33.3, מדברתיך is again probably to do with speech. The noun occurs with על only elsewhere in Ps 110.4, where God swears that 'you are a priest for ever על דברתי Melchizedek'; this is usually taken to mean 'of the same type as', or suchlike, but its different form and the obscurity of the reference should warn us against using it to understand על דברת more generally.⁴ In Aramaic, we find the expression על דברת די in Dan 2.30 and 4.14 used of purpose, meaning 'so that', but perhaps with the nuance 'because of the need to'. In Hebrew, the similar על דבר sometimes means simply 'on account of' or 'for the sake of' (e.g. Gen 12.17; 20.11, 18; Ps 45.5 [ET 45.4]; 79.9), and when it is followed by אשר and a verb in Deut 23.5 and 2 Sam 13.22 it correspondingly means 'because'. Often, though, it indicates the subject-matter or content of speech (e.g. Exod 8.8; 2 Sam 18.5), and has to be translated as 'concerning', or 'with

---

³ By way of comparison, in Greek thought both the θυμός (*thumos*), which is closest, perhaps, to the idea of an animating breath found here, and the ψυχή (*psyche*), which is the 'soul', are generally considered to exist in animals as well as humans. Correspondingly, anthropocentrism is rooted not in the exclusive human possession of such things, but in broader ideas of human rationality or resemblance to the gods. See especially Renehan, 'The Greek Anthropocentric View of Man'. The Greek translator uses πνεῦμα (*pneuma*) here, and that term had come to have profound significance in Stoicism. Again, though, its pervasive character in that tradition reflects an understanding very different from that of these biblical texts, as do its more general uses to represent breath and inspiration elsewhere.

⁴ That does not deter Bartholomew from using it to understand Qohelet's use of על דברת in 8.2 in the sense 'as in the manner of'. This is neither the sense of the interpretation in Heb 5.6, 10; 6.20, nor the probable meaning of the original Hebrew (in which there is either a first person suffix or an abnormal form of the construct to be explained), but seemingly takes the traditional English translation 'after the order of' to mean the same as 'in the order of', and to broaden it out from there.

respect to' (which are the meanings of על דבר attested in Aramaic). It has a similar but more general sense in places like Num 17.14; 25.18 (three times) where it describes a set of circumstances and means 'in the matter of', which is perhaps the basic sense from which the others have been derived.

If we turn to the uses of על דברת by Qohelet, then it is immediately clear that he employs על דברת ש- at 7.14 in the way that על דברת די is used in Aramaic, to mean 'so that', not in the way that על דבר אשר is used in Hebrew to mean 'because'. Here and in 8.2, the sense without a following verb is harder to establish, not least because both verses are very difficult, but the word-order in this verse suggests that the clause should be taken with אמרתי, as is now widely acknowledged, so it seems likely that the sense is 'concerning', or 'with respect to' (so, e.g., Cazelles, 'Conjonctions', 22): Qohelet is not embarking immediately on what he said, but specifying the subject-matter of his thoughts. I take the sense to be similar in 8.2, and if the form על דברת emerged in Aramaic, it is very possible that Qohelet only used it in the senses attested for על דברת and על דבר in Aramaic, which would exclude the uses for 'on account of' found in Hebrew.[5]

In any case, however, the term may not have been well-known to later generations, and it has given the versions some trouble. G, Hie, S translate literally, in terms of speech, and G uses περὶ λαλιᾶς again in 7.14, but, contextually, περὶ λόγου in 8.2. Jerome, in fact, takes the idea of speech very seriously in his commentary, taking the point here to be that humans are differentiated from animals by their ability to speak. On the actual reading of Hie, note that the lemma has *de loquela*, but that in the following commentary Jerome unusually sets out to analyse the individual components of what is said, and offers slightly different renderings: for this he has *de eloquio*.

3.18 going to separate them] M לבור in 9.1 leads BDB, *HALOT*, *DCH* and some others to propose a verb בור, with the sense 'examine' derived from the context in that verse; לברם here is then linked to that verb by *HALOT* and Zorell.[6] The reading in 9.1, however, is extremely doubtful (see the note there), and the existence of the verb improbable.

Pinker ('Qohelet 3,18: A Test?') has attempted to dispense with a verb altogether, re-dividing the text to read לבר מהאלהים, 'apart from God', so that Qohelet is seen to reach the conclusion that if humans are considered without the notion of God, they are merely animals, and he offers a further refinement of that reading by suggesting that לבר should be emended to לבד, 'alone'. Although the proposed לבר would have to be taken as a borrowing from Aramaic, this is an attractive and clever solution. It does not really work,

---

[5] It is not impossible that the origin of the form was actually in Phoenician, as Dahood supposes, but its appearance in Daniel makes it likely that it was at least mediated *via* Aramaic. See Dahood, 'Canaanite-Phoenician', 47-48.

[6] See also Driver, 'Supposed Arabisms', 108. Zorell also links the verb with Arabic *bâra*.

however, with the syntax of the verse as a whole, since ולראות then has to be in sequence with אמרתי, and to mean either 'in order to conclude' (which ignores the conjunction and gives an odd sense) or 'and I concluded' (for which the form is inappropriate).

Most commentators parse לברם as an infinitive construct from the geminate ברר, with a prefixed -ל and a third-person plural suffix pronoun.[7] This is how G has read the word, with ὅτι διακρινεῖ reflecting an understanding of the construction as equivalent to the future (there is no manuscript evidence to support McNeile's speculation [158] that this is a corruption of a G* τοῦ διακρίναι), while an unattributed hexaplaric reading τοῦ ἐλέγξαι αὐτοὺς ὁ θεός, 'God to choose them' (probably α'; cf. Marshall), certainly parses the same way, but probably takes the infinitive to follow אמרתי ('I said that God was/would be choosing them'). T likewise reads the same verb and form, with the infinitive expressing purpose. Jerome's readings are complicated: the lemma of Hie has simply *quia separat illos deus*, '(I said)...that God separates them', but in the body of his commentary (see the previous note) Jerome renders *ut eligeret eos deus*, 'that God might choose them', taking human speech as the way in which God separates humans out; V *ut probaret eos deus*, 'that God might test them', employs the same construction with a different verb. From all this, we should probably deduce that Jerome, like T, understood the Hebrew in terms of an infinitive expressing purpose, but paraphrased somewhat in his lemma.

The odd one out amongst the versions, therefore, is S ܕܒܪܐ *dbr'*, which seems to parse לברם as a finite verb form from ברא, 'create' (cf. Kamenetzky, 215), and this foreshadows two opinions that are less common amongst modern commentators: that we should read the verb as from ברא,[8] and that we should understand it to be qal perfect, perhaps with an emphatic or asseverative -ל (e.g. Gordis, who translates 'Surely God has tested them'; Whitley, Seow). For the sake of completeness, we should note also Ehrlich's suggestion, that לברם should be emended to לא ברם, '(God) has not chosen/ distinguished them', which is commended by Gordis and Fox, but accepted by neither; also the proposal by Ginsberg, echoed in *DCH* (under ברר I), that we should read מהאלהים, with Qohelet as the subject of the verb.

With regard to these various suggestions, it should be observed first that the subsequent ולראות is certainly an infinitive. Whether or not this is coordinate with לברם, its presence tells strongly against the -ל of לברם being emphatic

---

[7] On the form and pointing, see J-M §82 l, and the discussion in Bianchi, 'Teologia della prova', 168-69.

[8] See especially Irwin, 'Ecclesiastes 3,18'. In a later exchange, published by the same journal, Frank Zimmermann noted that the suggestion had already been made not just by S but by Ibn Ganah, and Irwin responded with a further citation of Eitan; see Zimmermann, 'On Eccles. 3:18'; Irwin, 'A Rejoinder'. The opinion has been defended most recently by Goldman, who commends it in *BHQ*.

or asseverative: the author would be inviting confusion, quite unnecessarily; correspondingly, it is difficult to take לברם as a finite form. Where Qohelet has previously used אמרתי אני בלבי (2.1, 15; 3.17), he has followed this with direct speech, but it may be true, nevertheless, that לברם should be considered an object of אמרתי, and perhaps an expression of indirect speech (a possibility considered by Goldman, and almost certainly the way in which G construed it). There are several places in the book where Qohelet could be understood to use such a construction, in each case with a future or prospective nuance (see the note 'they have no idea when' at 4.17), although it is not the usual way of expressing such things in Hebrew.[9] Alternatively, the construction is that of, e.g., Isa 38.20; Jer 51.49, where the infinitive construct with ־ל serves to represent the future in place of a finite verb form (perhaps with ellipsis of היה; the construction is reminiscent of the Latin *coniugatio periphrastica*): we have seen something similar already, with אשר להיות in v. 15.[10] In the context, tense may not, of course, be the only nuance, and although the future fits the comment on future divine judgment in the previous verse, the infinitives in this verse may imply that the actions are consequent upon the situations which Qohelet describes. In any case, however, if we do not take the verb as finite, the construction seems to connote an action that is prospective, if not actually in the future: God is/was going to do something.

This makes it very difficult to read לברם as the infinitive of ברא, since the divine creation of humans is clearly not a future activity. On balance, the issue here is not, then, whether we are dealing with the infinitive construct of ברר, but what precisely that verb might mean in this context. The sense 'test', adopted by some commentators, is found as early as V *probaret*, and is understood in T. It is not really an attested meaning for the word, however, which is fundamentally concerned with ideas of purification and selection (the link between the ideas is demonstrated in, e.g., Ezek 20.38, where the rebellious are selected and driven out). It is the latter which is picked up in the translations of G, Hie and α' (see above on the last), and the biblical usage points to

---

[9] Bühlmann, 'Thinking in Greek', 103, who argues for the more general influence of Greek diction on Qohelet's expression, sees an example here in the use of a construction with accusative (האלהים) and infinitive (לברם) after a verb of speech, and it cannot be denied that, if this is indeed the construction, it looks more Greek than Semitic. It would not be wholly out of line with some other Hebrew uses of the infinitive, however (cf. especially 2 Chr 6.20), and it is interesting to wonder whether such phenomena as the many future infinitives used this way in the Hebraizing Greek translation of Judith might not conceal other instances.

[10] Schoors, *The Preacher* I, 112, and Schwienhorst-Schönberger adduce Num 24.23 as a comparable example of the infinitive construct with an object-suffix and subsequent subject. While this illustrates the word-order, however, it is less clear that משמו is serving in place of a finite verb there: 'Who will survive from God doing this?' seems gerundial.

selection or separation. Backhaus, *Den Zeit*, 136, suggests that the meaning therefore should be 'Gott hat sie ausgesondert'—God has separated humans from other animals, a distinction which Qohelet himself then denies; although he does not note it, this is quite close to the understanding of Ibn Ezra, who speaks of humans as chosen by God. That the distinction lies between human and animals is also assumed by Jerome, as we noted above.

Schoors, *The Preacher* II, 353-54, is attracted to Backhaus' solution, and notes the many other commentators who have imputed this meaning to the verb, but understood the separation to be between humans and God. Schoors himself, however, prefers to draw on the later use of ברר in rabbinic literature to mean 'clarify' or 'bring to light', so that he views לברם here as parallel to, not in contrast with ולראות, and proposes 'God brings to light and shows'. This is itself an old solution, found in Rashi, the Midrash, and many of the earlier modern commentators. However, both understandings, of course, require לברם to be understood as a reference to some past or continuous action, and this is a sense for which the infinitive construct with -ל would seem an extremely strange choice. Since ברר later means 'clarify' not 'inform', furthermore, the suffix is awkward, and Schoors is forced to the suggestion that it is proleptic, for the subsequent subject of לראות (if humans are the subject of that verb); this is a suggestion which seems more ingenious than plausible.

The general line taken by Backhaus can, however, be understood slightly differently in future terms: God is, in fact, going to treat humans differently ('separate them out'), but what he shows them, or what they see, is that they are just like animals. This distinction, between the reality of human difference and the perception that all creatures share one fate, suits the implicit declaration of human ignorance in v. 21, and is analogous to Qohelet's later concern, in 8.10-14, that human behaviour is affected by the apparent deferral of judgment. The contrast within the sentence is signalled by the statement of separation here, followed by the subsequent statement of identity.

3.18 while they see] Lit. 'while they are going to see'; on the tense, see below. M points ולראות as qal, and T reads it that way, understanding a reference to God seeing. The other versions also take God as the subject, but translate as causative 'show', presumably vocalizing as לַרְאוֹת, a hiph'il (with syncope of the ה). Either is possible (despite the claim of Salters, 'Observations on the Septuagint', 170, that the context demands the hiph'il), although the consonantal text favours reading the more obvious qal (unless there was an actual variant להראות). The matter is complicated not only by the interpretative problems elsewhere in the verse, but also by much scholarly speculation about the syntactical function of this verb.

The infinitive construct with -ל can be used almost like a finite verb in continuation of a previous verb (GKC §114 p; J-M §124 p), but not so straightforwardly as can the infinitive absolute, and most of the instances cited are really not of 'finite' usage, which must be considered at best a rather rare phenomenon, but of common non-finite uses, perhaps in syntactically awkward positions.¹¹ Correspondingly, we cannot just treat ולראות in our verse as though it were virtually equivalent to וראיתי, a course proposed by Levy and a number of subsequent commentators, who take Qohelet to be the subject of the verb, and see here a continuation from אמרתי.¹² Whitley, for instance, translates 'I considered in my heart concerning the sons of men...and saw that they are beasts', while Goldman similarly believes that 'Qohelet, thinking about the human condition...is led to see that..."they are beasts"'.

Gordis accepts the analysis, but considers the distance between those verbs too great; he correspondingly sees ולראות as a finite continuation from לברם, so (reading a hiph'il) translates 'and He has shown'. He is compelled to this view, it seems, by the fact that he has already construed לברם as a qal perfect with emphatic -ל, and has now to explain away a second infinitive, which is not amenable to that treatment. It does seem obvious, indeed, that all these readings are driven by exegetical concerns. When an infinitive construct is followed by another, two words later, and the second has waw-conjunctive, we should expect to read them as coordinate, and the presence of each makes it difficult to read the other as some different form. If the writer wished to make a distinction between them, he could have done so very easily, and was under no clear obligation to employ either a rare usage of -ל or an even rarer periphrasis for a main verb. To have used one would have been clumsy and misleading, but to have used both, as Gordis supposes, would have been bizarre.

---

¹¹ Jer 44.17-19 furnishes an interesting example, where the infinitive construct להסך suddenly appears in place of the infinitive absolute within a list of actions that is repeated three times, a change that is presumably linked to the different syntactic context within which the list appears in v. 19.

¹² In the cases adduced by the grammars (which are not numerous), the infinitive usually seems either to specify rather than to continue the previous clause (e.g. 2 Chr 7.17; Job 34.8; Ps 104.21; Amos 8.4), or else to contain a specific prospective nuance, often an idea of purpose (e.g. 2 Chr 30.9; Hos 12.3). To take an example of the latter, J-M §124 p cites as finite ולכפר in 1 Chr 6.34 (ET 6.49), but there the priests do not make sacrifices *and* make atonement, but make sacrifices *for* the מלאכה of the Holy of Holies, *and for* atonement for Israel: these are two purposes, set in parallel. For instances at Qumran, see Qimron, *Hebrew of the Dead Sea Scrolls*, 71-72. Many of his examples, again, have a modal or prospective aspect. It is possible to quibble over some of the instances, and Levy was appropriately cautious in claiming that the usage was occasional. The extent of the phenomenon, however, is sometimes exaggerated by commentators: for his claim that it is 'a usage particularly common in later Biblical Hebrew' Gordis cites GKC §114p, which speaks merely of 'a number of instances - especially in the later books'; he then muddies the waters by including references to the infinitive absolute used this way, which is a very different matter. Schoors, *The Preacher* I, 180, cites Gordis' opinion as a fact, almost *verbatim*.

I think, accordingly, we must treat both verbs in parallel.[13] In that case, we might expect the subject to be God, who would be going to 'see' or 'show'. Goldman supposes that the reading of the verb as causative in most of the versions is driven by a theological desire to avoid any implication that God might need to see anything about humans which he did not already know (although T, interpreting in terms of judgment, has no problem reading a qal, with God as subject). In fact, however, I think that the subject was more probably marked by the subsequent המה (on which, see below), so that it is the humans themselves who will do the seeing.[14] Literally, then, we should read 'Going-to-separate them (is) God, and going-to-see that-they-animals (are) they for them'. Qohelet is not only trying to contrast the authors of the actions, but also the actions themselves, and the postponement of the subject arises from this emphasis on the verbs. In fact, the two clauses correspond in order (verb-object-subject), and their different lengths arise from the expression of the object as a suffix pronoun in one, but a clause in the other; the subject would have been a great deal clearer had המה preceded that object-clause. The versions which read לראות as causative have rightly perceived, perhaps on the basis of what follows, that the issue here is human perception, but have misunderstood the syntax; this misreading has been influenced by, or else has given rise to problems over, the reading and placement of המה להם.

If we treat the verbs together, then it would seem to follow that the future tense implied by the sense and form of the first should be shared by the second. If I have understood the overall meaning correctly, however, then there is, strictly speaking, something of a mismatch: God is going to separate humans, but their perception of themselves will precede that separation, and is in essence a present reality. Matters are already complicated, of course, by the degree of stylization in the verse more generally, but I think the intention of the alignment here is more probably to connote not tense, as such, but simultaneity, for the sake of contrast. In other words, the humans are not, strictly, going to start seeing themselves as animals only at some point in the future, but that will be their existing view when God separates them. I have tried to convey that in the translation by using 'while'.

---

[13] So Bianchi, 'La Storia, la memoria', 165 (cf. 169), is properly consistent in reading both לברם and לראות as 'indicative' infinitives ('Dio li mette alla prova e gli fa vedere che...', 'God puts them to the test and shows that...'), but it is hard to see why they should have been used to express a present continuous nuance.

[14] Bühlmann, 'Thinking in Greek', 102-104, suggests that the writer has been thinking in terms of Greek infinitive clauses, so that the construction is equivalent to αὐτοὺς κρίνειν τὸν θεὸν ὥστε ἰδεῖν αὐτοὺς κτήνη εἶναι, which he renders 'that God governs them in such a way that they themselves think that they are cattle'. The suggestion may be a little too ingenious, but I think it does catch something of the way in which the verbs are being used here.

3.18 as animals] Lit. 'that they (are) animals.' To clarify that this is a comparison, rather than an identification, S adds ܐܝܟ *'yk* and T an initial -כ, while V *similes esse bestiis*, 'to be similar to beasts', paraphrases along the same lines.

Montgomery, 'Notes', 242, suggests that שהם means 'whether', comparing Syriac ܕܐܢ *d'n*, but this relies on the highly improbable assumption that הם is a conflation of Aramaic הן and Hebrew אם. For the use of ש- in a syndetic object clause after ראה, cf. 2.13; Ecclesiastes also uses it after ידע in 1.17; 2.14; 9.5, and it is effectively equivalent to using אשר in such contexts (cf. GKC §157 c; J-M §157 c).

The term for 'animals', בהמה, is commonly used in the singular, which makes 'cattle' attractive as a translation. Although it can be used in that sense, however (cf. G κτήνη), it refers to animals more generally, or at least to mammals (cf., e.g., Gen 1.24; 1 Kgs 5.13).

3.18 they...themselves] M המה להם ends a sequence שהם בהמה המה להם which may be regarded either as ingeniously assonant or suspiciously repetitive: although its stylistic features have not gone unobserved, there have been many proposals to delete words within it, or to re-divide the text. Partly on the basis that G does not appear to reflect it (so, e.g., Crenshaw), many commentators have deleted המה in particular as a dittograph. G reads, however, ὅτι αὐτοὶ κτήνη εἰσὶν καί γε αὐτοῖς, which indicates that its source-text had וגם or גם either in place of המה or in addition to it. If גם(ו) is original (as *BHQ* supposes), then המה may be an error for it, or may have dropped out after it; if גם(ו) is secondary, then it is presumably an addition or an error for המה. G offers possible grounds for emendation, therefore, but in neither case does it justify the simple deletion of המה.[15]

Because it is attested in all the versions, attempts to emend or delete להם are less common, but Barton follows Siegfried in rejecting it as an explanatory gloss, Ginsberg views it as the product of 'vertical dittography' from להם in the next verse, and Fox considers its letters a 'partial dittography' of המה (which he would retain). These are all speculative, and present excuses rather than reasons for deleting the word. Much the same is true of Driver's drastic

---

[15] In fact, I doubt that we should follow G. Goldman remarks of the presumed original גם(ו) that 'it is hard to imagine why it would have been introduced into the text if it is not the original reading'. It becomes easier to imagine, however, when we bear in mind that the manuscript traditions of G and S associate להם with the next verse; if such an understanding existed in the Hebrew tradition before G, then the appearance of a facilitatory גם in G's source-text would hardly be astonishing. As regards המה, Schoors, *The Preacher* I, 113-14, argues that G εἰσὶν renders it as a 'copula' (compare its treatment of הוא in, e.g., v. 15), and it is certainly possible that the translator was simply concerned to catch the sense here, rather than to match each pronoun. Euringer, in fact, takes G καί γε to be an interpretative translation of 3.19 כי—which seems improbable; see below.

re-division ('Problems and Solutions', 227), which quietly adds a ב and reads the text as מִשֶּׁהֵם־בָּהֶם הֵמָּה לָהֶם, '(to see) what they are in themselves, whether they are (true) to themselves'; Driver also considers the possibility that בהמה 'is a mere dittograph'.

If we retain the text as it stands, the sense of המה is straightforward: it is either the subject of the preceding infinitive (as I take it to be), or resumptive of the הם in the preceding object-clause. There has been more discussion of להם, which fits a little awkwardly into those construals of the verse that take God to be the subject of לראות, not least because Hebrew does not typically use -ל with those people 'to' whom something is shown, and so the preposition is often viewed as somehow connecting המה to להם.[16] I take them to be essentially separate, with להם following the subject המה, as in the similar sequence at 1 Kgs 14.23 ויבנו גם המה להם, where המה marks the subject, and להם indicates that they built 'for themselves'. That '-ל of advantage' might broadly be understood here, as might the indirect reflexive construction, where -ל is prefixed to a pronoun agreeing with the subject of the verb,[17] or even conceivably a use of -ל to indicate the object (J-M §125 k). Alternatively, we might consider the common use of the preposition to mean 'with regard to' (Delitzsch), or the suggestion of Ibn Ezra, that they are animals 'to themselves', that is, in their own estimation.[18] Both would suit my construal:

---

[16] It does seem likely that σ' καὶ τοῦ δεῖξαι αὐτοῖς, 'and to show to them', took להם as the indirect object of the verb, but it is possible that this is a paraphrase: the rest of the verse is not attested. G αὐτοῖς is probably to be read with the next verse.

[17] That construction is often characterized misleadingly as an 'ethic dative' (*dativus ethicus*). Muraoka calls it 'centripetal', placing a special, isolating focus upon the subject; cf. J-M §133 d, and especially Muraoka, '*dativus ethicus*'. It should be emphasized that this usage requires both a verb and a correspondence between the pronoun and the subject of that verb (cf. GKC §119 s), so it is puzzling to find that so many commentators speak of an ethic dative here while taking God or Qohelet to be the subject of לראות (e.g. Levy, Crenshaw, Krüger, Schwienhorst-Schönberger; Schoors, *The Preacher* I, 114). Even if that were possible, it would not yield the sense 'even they', or similar. Whitley's argument for an 'emphatic lamedh' here (cf. also Eaton)—with just such a meaning—cites as analogous only 1 Sam 26.11-12, which most would take to be an instance of the ethic dative. In any case, however, the boundary between the -ל of advantage (*dativus commodi*) and this construction is somewhat fluid, especially in the case of transitive verbs (cf. BDB 515b; Muraoka, '*dativus ethicus*', 498, would exclude those, suggesting that they might be an intermediate stage between the -ל of advantage and his 'centripetal' -ל).

[18] I think there may well be such a use in 9.4. Some of the other senses proposed, however, are improbable. Gordis, for instance, sees an equivalence to -ב here (cf. Lys), so that the expression means 'in themselves' or 'essentially'. This

the preposition has a wide range of meanings or uses, but if להם is to be construed with לראות, then one way or another the expression is equivalent to saying that the humans 'see themselves', 'see for themselves', or 'see themselves in their own reckoning'. Its effect is to qualify the statement, so that humans are not said to be recognizing (the fact) that they are animals, but merely to be perceiving themselves as such.[19]

Frank Zimmermann's suggestion that להם means 'cattle' (based on an Ethiopic usage) should be mentioned, although more for the entertaining exchange with W. A. Irwin which it precipitated than for any inherent plausibility; see Zimmermann, 'Notes', 303-304, and on the exchange, see above, n. 8.

3.19 for[1]] M כי is supported by Hie, T, and probably S (if its ܡܛܠ *mṭ'* is corrected to ܡܛܠ ܕ- *mṭl d-*, the reading of Syh, cf. Kamenetzky, 201; McNeile, 141). G presents a more difficult picture: a significant number of manuscripts have no equivalent to כי, and those that do are divided between reading οὐ and ὡς; Rahlfs read ὅτι (as did Klostermann, *De libri Coheleth*, 58) on the basis of Syh, but the other direct evidence for that reading is slight. It is difficult to relate the readings οὐ and ὡς to each other, although Euringer suggests that the former was to be read as a question, 'Is not...', and ὡς substituted to soften the implication. Considered in its own right, however, ὡς may be understood as a rendering of כ in place of כי, which leads Goldman to suppose that it is G*, and based on a faulty source-text with כמקרה, an assimilation to the subsequent כמות. (Siegfried actually takes this to be the original Hebrew, although he does not cite G.) McNeile, 142, also accepts that possibility, while suggesting that it may alternatively have arisen as a dittograph of the preceding οις; McNeile himself, though, leans to the view that the Hebrew originally lacked כי altogether, and that G* reflected this. If either of these solutions is correct, however, then οὐ is difficult to explain except as a dogmatic correction; that is not impossible, but the word's credentials are good (including mss B, 998), and such corrections are hardly widespread in the early text of G, despite plenty of opportunities for them. It seems better to understand ογ as a corruption of G* οτι, perhaps facilitated by the troubling nature of the statement, ὡς as a subsequent correction toward a Hebrew text with כמקרה, and the reading with neither, perhaps, as the consequence of a perceived incoherence arising from either change.

3.19 what happens to[1,2]] The term מקרה (on the meaning of which, see the note at 2.14, above) was used in a similar way previously in 2.15, where it was

usage would be without parallel and, as Fox suggests, 'has no particular meaning'. Delitzsch discusses Luther's attractive understanding that there is an implication of reciprocity here, that this is how they see each other, but that sense is unlikely.

[19] This seems to be the implication of Strobel's translation, 'äußerlich gesehen' ('viewed superficially'), although he does not offer a justification.

pointed as construct מִקְרֵה; here M^L apparently points all three uses as absolute מִקְרֶה. Seow considers that a mere inconsistency in the vocalization, and would read this as an alternative pointing of the construct (a possibility accepted by Goldman also); many other commentators would revocalize the first two occurrences to the form found at 2.15 (cf. *BHS*, *BHQ*). This accords with the understanding of the versions. Wright proposes, on the other hand, that the absolute should be retained, and translates: 'For a chance are the children of men, and a chance is the beast, and the same [lit. one] chance happeneth to them'. This takes account of the troublesome conjunction before the third מקרה (see below), and although it is not probable in the light of 2.14-15 and 9.2-3, such a reading may reflect the rationale behind the pointing of M^L; Siegfried, followed by Goldman, sees this as a dogmatic change, making both humans and animals subject to, instead of sharing, the same fate (so similarly, e.g., Maussion, *Le Mal*, 156, citing Podechard). Before we make too much of the issue, however, we might note that M does not speak with a single voice here: the early manuscript BM Or. 9879 points the first מקרה with *segol*, then the second two with *ṣere*: if we were to insist that the former is absolute and the latter construct, then this would have to imply the nonsensical 'fate (is) the human, and the fate of the animals and the fate of the one'; for later variants, see Ginsburg, *Writings*. It seems most likely that the forms are effectively interchangeable in the M tradition, although the confusion has undoubtedly been exacerbated by the presence in that tradition of the conjunction with the third מקרה.

3.19 just one thing happens to them] Lit. 'and one happening (is) to them' (cf. 2.14-15; 9.2-3). The initial conjunction, lacking in many later manuscripts (see de Rossi), is not reflected in the versions, except possibly in V *idcirco unus interitus est hominis et iumentorum et aequa utriusque condicio*, 'for that reason, the annihilation of the human and of cattle is one, and the situation of each equal' (so *BHQ*, Seow, Schoors, *The Preacher* I, 125, but Jerome is paraphrasing, and it is difficult to determine equivalence). It has been explained syntactically in various ways (surveyed in Schoors, *The Preacher* I, 125): as explicative (GKC §154 a), emphatic (so Gordis), comparative (e.g. Krüger; cf. GKC §161 a; J-M §174 h), or as a *waw apodoseos* (so Schoors himself, Seow; cf. GKC §143 d; J-M §176). As often, the distinctions between these different usages can be rather blurred, but if we retain the ו then the last category is the most probable here, with the conjunction resumptive after a long *casus pendens* (as Schoors; cf. J-M §176 c, h). *BHQ*, on the other hand, would delete the ו altogether as a secondary, dogmatic addition (see Goldman), and it is certainly not difficult to see it simply as an error caused by the preceding ומקרה. It is not important for the sense whether we delete or retain it, but the omission in G, especially, does make it very suspect.

Certainly secondary is the addition of 'all' in S ܠܟܠܗܘܢ *lklhwn*, which may perhaps not be a free translation (Kamenetzky, 215; Euringer), but the result of influence from G, where πᾶσιν is attested as a variant.

3.19 death...death] The use of the noun implies, perhaps, not that they both die, but that the deaths of each are the same, so RSV 'as one dies, so dies the other' may be misleading.

S adds an ܐܦ *'p*: 'so the death *also* of that'; again, a corresponding variant οὕτως καὶ is attested for G, but they may be independent clarifications.

3.19 breath] σ' καὶ ἀναπνοὴ ὁμοία πᾶσιν, 'and breath(ing) (is) the same for all', avoids the suggestion that humans and animals share a spirit (M רוח; G πνεῦμα), and V *similiter spirant omnia*, 'all breathe alike' (perhaps influenced by σ', cf. Cannon, 'Jerome and Symmachus', 192), likewise makes this strictly the physical act of breathing.

Mishael ben Uzziel records here that the traditions of ben Asher and ben Naphtali were in agreement over the pointing of כן מות זה, over against another Masorete, Moshe Moḥa, who preferred כן־מות זה, with a *maqqeph*.

3.19 then what a human has more than an animal ceases] Lit. 'and the abundance of a human more than the animal: there is not'. To connect (the abnormally vocalized) אין, which stands independently at the end, we have either to understand '(as regards) the abundance of a human more than the animal, there is none' (so, e.g. Seow; cf. T), or else '(what is / is there) the abundance of a human more than the animal? there is none'. G takes the latter approach, reading a question and answer (cf. Judg 4.20): καὶ τί ἐπερίσσευσεν ὁ ἄνθρωπος παρὰ τὸ κτῆνος; οὐδέν, 'And in what respect does the human have an advantage over the animal? None.' The readings of σ', καὶ τί πλέον ἄνθρωπος κτήνους, 'and in what is a human more than an animal?', and θ', καὶ τί περίσσεια τῷ ἀνθρώπῳ, 'and what is the advantage to the human?', are similar, and although θ' has aligned the sense with passages like 6.8, there seem no firm grounds to suppose that these versions possessed a source-text with a variant ומה יותר (so, e.g., McNeile, 154; *BHQ*—Barton, Vinel suppose ומי).[20] That notion cannot be excluded, but the readings are explicable as interpretations of the text as it stands in M, and G offers a quite legitimate way of reading that text.

I take the point, in fact, to be a little different: humans undeniably have a מותר over animals in life, but when they all die, it ceases to exist. מותר is not used elsewhere in Ecclesiastes, and is not, perhaps, precisely equivalent to יתרון. In Prov 14.23; 21.5, the only other two places where it is found, it is used as an antonym for the more common מחסור, 'lack', 'need', or 'shortage', and here it probably denotes not wealth or profit—hardly to be expected of animals—but those aspects of human life which are lacking in the existence

---

[20] Yi, 18-19, suggests implausibly that the translator had the consonants of M, but construed מותר as an interrogative מה followed by a hiphʿil.

of animals. The idea of cessation is not, of course, implicit in אין, but is to be derived from the context of the statement.

3.19 since all] Although הכל refers to the humans and animals in the next verse, Schoors, *The Preacher* II, 4, doubts (*contra*, e.g., Crenshaw, Lohfink) that in this verse it can mean 'both (humans and animals)'; he is right to do so, inasmuch as Qohelet does not typically characterize beings as הבל. The scope here, however, may not be 'everything' as often elsewhere, but the מותר of the previous clause, which ceases to exist at death just because it is הבל.

Despite Ogden's argument that characterizations as הבל almost always act as concluding clauses (accepted in Schoors, *The Preacher* I, 103), we really do not expect a concluding clause sandwiched between this verse and the next, which continues it, so there is no need to read the כי as asseverative rather than causative.

3.20 goes] Although הולך is reflected in the other versions (for α', θ' cf. Marshall), G πορεύεται is lacking in some early manuscripts, and McNeile, 142, believes that the verb was missing in the original Hebrew, with הולך restored under the influence of 6.6. That is possible, and the Hebrew would be meaningful without the verb; it is also possible that G's source-text had lost the word, as a consequence of the sequence הכלהלכ. On balance, however, it seems more likely that the error was within the G tradition.

3.20 dust] V *de terra...in terram* may have been influenced by σ'. This has τῆς γῆς for G τοῦ χοός, giving a clearer implication of 'earth as distinct from porous clay or sand' (cf. Gwynn, 'Notes', 121); contrast Hie *de humo... ad humum*.

3.20 returns] As McNeile, 142, notes, G ἐπιστρέφει is replaced in many manuscripts by a future ἐπιστρέψει; he speculates that the Hebrew originally read ישב. As McNeile himself concedes, however, graphic Φ/Ψ errors are not hard to explain, and the context might have led copyists to expect a future form.

3.21 and who knows] The interrogative is preceded by a conjunction in G, S, Hie, with only T and V supporting the usual reading of M, without one. Goldman again sees a deliberate theological revision in the M tradition, but the conjunction is present in many later manuscripts of M, and if it is original, then its omission in other manuscripts may have been a simple error. The presence or absence makes no real difference to the sense. On the expression as a whole, see the note at 2.19, above.

3.21 spirit[1, 2]] Although we might expect them on grounds of translation technique, there is significant manuscript evidence against reading articles with each occurrence of πνεῦμα in G, and Rahlfs accordingly omits them, although Gentry would read articles in both places; Klostermann, *De libri Coheleth*, 59, would omit the article only before the second instance of πνεῦμα. If the articles were indeed lost, it may have been because they seemed awkwardly to suggest a single πνεῦμα for all humans.

3.21 does it rise upward...does it sink downward] M points the participles הָעֹלָה and הַיֹּרֶדֶת, as though the initial -ה on each were the definite article, but the other versions have read each -ה as interrogative (although on T, see below). Few modern commentators have tried to defend the reading with articles, which seems to affirm that the breath of humans and animals does indeed travel in different directions (as in the KJV). Among those who do, Eaton associates the thought with 8.11, and Aalders attempts to link it to the issue raised in v. 18, that God will separate them, but that humans do not really know their fate. Hence he translates 'Wie bespeurt, dat de adem van de menschenkinderen omhoogstijgt naar boven, en dat de adem van de beesten nederdaalt naar beneden in de aarde?', 'Who detects that the breath of humans...and that the breath of animals...?' See similarly Laurent, 'L'homme', 33. This would, however, be an extremely strange way of making that point in Hebrew, and most commentators have followed the other versions, reading *he interrogative*.

If there has been any significant disagreement, it is about the reason for the pointing in M, with some scholars disputing the long-established view that it is dogmatically motivated, and suggesting that these may be legitimate, if unexpected, pointings of the interrogative. So, e.g., Gordis points out (against GKC §100 m) that 'before Aleph and Yod, there was a tendency to vocalize the interrogative *He* with full vowels and dageš'; he cites examples from Gen 19.9; Lev 10.19; Num 16.22 and Job 23.6. This possibility (long ago rejected by Ibn Ezra) has been accepted by Seow, but most commentators would understand the proper pointing to be הַעֹלָה and הֲיֹרֶדֶת, and it does seem odd that two exceptional pointings of the interrogative would occur together.

The consonantal text could, in fact, be read as an indirect question in similar terms: 'who knows the breath of humans, whether this is the one rising upward, and the breath of animals, whether this is the one sinking'—which arguably offers a more interesting sense. T, which puts אִין, 'whether', before the 'breath of humans', could likewise be understood in this way, which is possibly the understanding that lies behind the pointing in M—but if it were the reading that the author intended, we would probably expect a corresponding אם at that point in the Hebrew, and so the reading with interrogatives is to be preferred.

For the use of the personal pronoun after the participle compare 7.26; 8.12, but here the cause is the use of anticipated subjects (see Schoors, *The Preacher* I, 213-14, who sees anticipation as a characteristic of the book's style). S does not reflect the pronoun on the second occasion.

3.22

(3.22) Then I saw that there is nothing better than that a person rejoice in his achievements, since that is what is his: who is going to take him to visit what will be after him?

Commentary

The point made here about human ignorance will be summarized by 6.12, in particular, when in response to the question 'Who knows what is good for the human in life?', Qohelet declares: 'The days of his life are vapour, and he spends them as a shadow: who is there who can tell the human what will be after him under the sun?' This is expressed (later in 8.7 and 10.14, as well as here and in 6.12) using a rhetorical question, 'Who will...?', but it is probably not Qohelet's intention in such passages specifically to attack any sort of prophecy or claim to prediction—even though 7.14 connects such ignorance to a deliberate divine purpose that would seem to exclude such possibilities. Here, that issue is not at stake, since the claim being made by Qohelet is that no human can actually be taken to examine that future for themselves—as though by some Ghost of Christmas Yet to Come—and it seems unlikely that anyone could have taken exception to such a claim.

In all these passages, 'after him' refers to the period after the death of the human, and in 6.12 it is made explicit that 'after him' means 'after him in the world'—the terminology is similar to that used of succession in 2.12, 18. The point is not, therefore, that humans are ignorant about what will happen to them later in life or in some afterlife, and Qohelet's intention here, as noted earlier, is apparently to stress the importance of enjoying one's own life, rather than attempting to influence the unknowable future world that will follow it.

Notes

3.22 better] S adds ܒܗܘܢ *bhwn*, 'in them', probably from v. 12 (cf. Kamenetzky, 215), although Gordis suggests that the reading may have arisen in Hebrew, from dittography of the במ in טובמאשר.

3.22 since that is what is his] הוא must refer to the substantivized clause אשר ישמח האדם, rather than the plural מעשיו. That suits the idea expressed at 2.10 (cf. 5.17-18; 9.9).

On חלק, lit. 'his portion', see the note on 'what was mine' at 2.10, above.

3.22 who] I have translated the כי only with a colon. As already noted at 2.12 and 2.25, the כי in כי מי and כי מה often has little if any force, especially in Qohelet's usage, so although this rhetorical question may be offered as an explanation for the preceding claim, it would be unwise to emphasize that role here.

3.22 can take him] Lit. 'will take him', or 'bring him'. The hiph'il of בוא is used in Isa 37.26; 46.11 of bringing a promised situation to pass, and although it is just conceivable that Qohelet is conjuring with an image of bringing someone back from the dead, it is more likely that the verb is being used of guiding someone into a position where they can see what will follow. In similar questions at 6.12 and 10.14, Qohelet uses יגיד, 'inform'.

3.22 to visit what] Or 'to look into what'. On the construction of ראה with ב, see the note at 2.1, above, which refers to the uses of the expression to mean 'visit' in places like Gen 34.1. I take that to be the likely implication here, although there is undoubtedly also a nuance of 'examining' the future.

On the pointing of מֶה, see GKC §102 k, but also J-M §37 d-f.

S reads ܒܟܠ ܠܡܚܙܐ *lmḥzʾ bkl*, 'to look at everything', which is reminiscent of its plus at v. 15; Kamenetzky, 201, suggests plausibly, however, that ܒܟܠ *bkl* is an error for ܒܡܐ *bmʾ* (cf. the Serto ܒܟܠ / ܒܡܐ).

3.22 after him] Although it is found in a more obscure context at 9.3, אחריו is used similarly in 6.12 and 7.14 to express the inaccessibility of the future to humans; cf. 10.14, which uses מאחריו. We should expect a consistent sense, so it is odd, therefore, that here at 3.22 Seow says it must mean 'when they die', and explicitly denies that it can refer to 'a future point in a person's life', that later in 6.12 he interprets it as a substantive, with the sense 'their end' or 'their destiny', and that in 7.14 he then refers back to his note at 6.12, and glosses 'they can know nothing of the future in one's lifetime', comparing 3.22—where he has denied the possibility of such a meaning!

That sort of confusion reflects a marked hesitance on the part of many scholars to read the expression in the most obvious way as 'after him', which goes back at least to Symmachus' τίς γὰρ αὐτὸν ἄξει θεάσασθαι τὰ ἐσόμενα μετὰ ταῦτα, 'For who will take him to see what will be after these things' (Jerome cites this in Latin in his commentary, describing it as a looser translation). This is motivated by a sense that Qohelet should be talking about the inability of humans to see what will happen to them (in life, or perhaps beyond), which leads Levy, Gordis and others to propose that the suffix is 'petrified', and that the term correspondingly means 'afterwards'. Schoors' examination (*The Preacher* I, 118-19) does affirm that difficulties of agreement could well lead us to find that sense for אחריו in Jer 51.46 and several times in Neh 3.16-31, although the formulaic character of the latter should surely warn us against placing too much weight on that text.

Schoors himself is inclined to give full weight to the suffixes when אחריו is used by Qohelet, however, and the sense 'afterwards' is unlikely in the vast majority of cases where the expression is used elsewhere. It is important, furthermore, to note such uses as that in Job 21.21, where אחריו refers specifically to the situation after one's death, or the many references to 'descendants after one' (e.g. Gen 17.7-10; Exod 28.43; 2 Sam 7.12), all of which suggest that the text here is most naturally taken to imply that humans cannot know what will happen in the world (cf. 6.12) after they have died.

Introduction to 4.1-16

Work and Other People

(4.1) Then again I observed all the extortion that goes on beneath the sun. And behold, the tears of those who suffer extortion—and there is no-one to comfort them; and from the hand of those who extort from them, strength—and there is no-one to comfort them. (4.2) And I commended the dead, who have already died, over the living, who are living still; (4.3) and—better than either—anyone who has not yet come into existence, who has not seen the wretched achievement which has been achieved beneath the sun.

(4.4) Then I observed all the business and all aptitude in activity, that it is a passion which separates one person from another. This too is an illusion, and wishing for the wind. (4.5) It is a fool who cups his hands to eat his meat: (4.6) better a palmful of respite than two hands filled with business and with wishing for the wind.

(4.7) Then again I observed an illusion beneath the sun: (4.8) there may be a single person, no second, nor has he any son or brother; yet there may be no bounds to all his business, nor will his eye be sated with wealth—and who have I been working for, or giving up happiness? This too is an illusion, and it is a bad job.

(4.9) Two are better than one, when they get well paid in their work: (4.10) for if they fall, one will lift their fellow, while if it were someone alone who fell, then there would be no second to lift them. (4.11) Also, if two lie together, then it will be warm for them, but how can just the one be warm? (4.12) And if one man might be outmatched, two will stand before him—and a three-plied thread is not readily snapped.

(4.13) A poor and wise child is better than an old and foolish king, who still does not know how to take care: (4.14) because one may leave the poor-house to become king; because the other, even in his kingship, was born impoverished.

(4.15) I have seen all the living, those who go about their business beneath the sun, along with the next child who is going to stand in the place of each. (4.16) There is no end to all the people, to everyone who has been before them, and those coming later will take no pleasure in them, because this too is an illusion, and worrying about the wind.

After the relatively long units that made up chs. 1–3, it becomes much more difficult in the following chapters to see a clear structure in Qohelet's monologue, and there is a danger of imposing classifications on the material that are so broad in themselves as to be meaningless, or else so narrow that they force the text into a straitjacket. It does seem, however, that although the pessimism of 4.1-3 sets a negative tone for the rest of the book, what Qohelet picks up most immediately from these verses is not their implication that human life is hardly worth living, but rather their reference to the isolation of those who have been exploited by others—which is the aspect of their situation emphasized in the first verse. Accordingly, 4.4-6 first identifies the problem that work separates humans from each other, and commends time out from it, while the rest of the discussion deals in different ways with the significance of working for, or with, others. In 4.7-8 the issue is the pointlessness of working on behalf of nobody else, while 4.9-12 asserts the benefits of cooperation.

The meaning of 4.13-16 has been much debated, but I take the theme to be succession, and the purpose to be a qualification of what has just been said.[1] Qohelet begins with a saying or parable that commends the potential of the young by contrasting a child in utter destitution who may yet be king, with an actual king who has never managed to raise himself from his own poverty of mind. Pretending, however, to observe their children alongside all who

---

[1] Although Wright, 'The Youth', reads 4.13-16 very differently, I am in agreement, therefore, with the conclusion that those verses are intended 'to qualify the examples in vv 9-12' (150).

are now alive, he characteristically sets the succession of each generation in the context of an endless process, and remarks that no generation will feel the same affection toward its predecessors as each generation feels toward its descendants. In short, then, we should not let work separate us from others, may find more purpose in our work if it is on behalf of others, and will benefit from working alongside others. On the other hand, we stand in an endless line of succession, and should not be deluded into thinking that any future generations for whom we work will ultimately care about us at all.

Stephanus ('Qohelet') places 4.1-16 at the heart of the book's concerns, and Lavoie is probably right to think that her analysis has been influenced more by liberation theology than by the text itself ('Analyse de Qohélet 4,9-12', 192-93). Here and sometimes elsewhere though, perhaps most especially in 5.7, Qohelet seems to invite such readings, which have been popular in Latin-American scholarship:[2] he undoubtedly sees human greed and its oppressive effects as a significant cause of misery in the world. It is less clear that such ideas would have been especially distinctive or radical, but Qohelet's take on them is interesting. In these verses, that misery is real, but portrayed as potentially meaningless and unnecessary. Amongst those jostling for resources, it is not only the losers who may be isolated, and even the successful ultimately accomplish nothing for themselves. Although he does not draw out that implication directly here, Qohelet's denial that humans can gain any real profit, or have any lasting influence, also implies that there is no point to all the harm that their efforts do. Accordingly, his

---

[2] There is no space here to explore more generally the very interesting story of the book's reception in political movements, past and present—whether it be in the various contemporary sermons that drew on 10.17 to welcome the 1660 restoration of the monarchy (see the commentary on that verse), or in Schneck's reflections on the 'absurd' Cenepa War, in 'Guerra Amazónica', Tamez's on hopelessness in 'Ecclesiastes 3:1-8', following the end of the revolutionary government in Nicaragua, or Ugwueye's critique of Nigerian society in 'God-Justice'. Through a contrast between Tamez's liberation-theological commentary and an Indonesian commentary by E. G. Singgih, Drewes, 'Prediker', offers some perceptive insights into the way exegetes choose to contextualize their readings in this respect, while Dell, *Interpreting Ecclesiastes*, 76-83, offers some cautionary notes about the receptivity of the text to liberation-theological readings.

observations do not lead him to cry out for reform or for social justice, but, if anything, for self-awareness and a proper sense of perspective.[3]

---

[3] I doubt it is fair to say, as does Longman, that Qohelet simply 'resigns himself to the situation', but there is something unsatisfactory also about Bartholomew's response, that Qohelet is on a 'personal quest for meaning', and is himself horrified by what he sees. The point here, I think, is that Qohelet sees extortion as the consequence of more fundamental attitudes and perceptions, not simply to be repaired by better policing or political change. Cf. Miller, 'Power', 146: 'Qohelet points to individualism (lack of a community orientation) and materialism (the drive to accumulate) as key factors in the persistence of oppression. In their place, he promotes a lifestyle that counteracts rather than perpetuates systems of oppression.'

4.1-3

(4.1) Then again I observed all the extortion that goes on beneath the sun. And behold, the tears of those who suffer extortion—and there is no-one to comfort them; and from the hand of those who extort from them, strength—and there is no-one to comfort them. (4.2) And I commended the dead, who have already died, over the living, who are living still; (4.3) and—better than either—anyone who has not yet come into existence, who has not seen the wretched achievement which has been achieved beneath the sun.

Commentary

4.1] The reference is to the illegitimate extortion of money or property from people, by other people or potentially by the authorities, something with which Qohelet will concern himself again in 5.7 and, perhaps in a more abstract way, in the difficult 7.7. Although this may involve oppression of a more general sort, he is not talking about oppression itself here, even though his words have often been read in such terms, but specifically about such extortion. The text is very probably corrupt in the last part of the verse, and that makes it difficult to be certain about the point as a whole, but two things do seem to be in Qohelet's sights: the willingness of humans to gain for themselves at the cost of others (a point he will pick up later, when he talks about extortion again in 5.7) and, more particularly, the isolation of those who are exploited in this way, and find themselves without even a comforter (much less, the text perhaps went on to say originally, a rescuer).

I am not sure why Fontaine ('Ecclesiastes', 154) sees here and in 5.7-8 'callous dismissals of the plight of the oppressed', or how Manfredi ('Qohelet', 303) identifies a sarcasm that he contrasts with the prophetic willingness to take a stand against injustice—Tamez, in contrast, sees 'a radical critique of the oppressive society', although that description is itself, perhaps, no easier to justify. The worst that can be said on the basis of the text itself, perhaps, is that Qohelet makes no explicit call for change (which, as Segal, 149-50, notes, hardly provides a basis for such accusations), and that there may be some artifice involved in the verse: the language used here of abandonment is very similar to that used about Jerusalem in the first chapter of Lamentations, and may draw on a familiar motif to give the verse the flavour of a lament. In part, Qohelet uses this as a way to introduce the wretchedness of human living, which he will emphasize in the next two verses, but it also provides a dramatic way for him to set the stage for a more general point that human relationships are dysfunctional.

4.2-3] The syntactical connection between these two verses is loose, but their sense clear: Qohelet believes it to be better to be dead, or not yet born, than to have experienced what is going on. In 6.1-6 he will make a similar claim, that a miscarried child is better off than a man who finds no pleasure, while 7.1 declares (although on rather different grounds) that the day of death is better than the day of one's birth. The difficult 9.3-6 may redress the balance a little in favour of life, and Qohelet's outlook arguably becomes more optimistic in this respect when he develops more thoroughly his ideas about enjoyment of life (although, as Crenshaw, 'Shadow', points out, his ideas reflect throughout an ambivalence towards death). For the moment, though, he sounds like Job lamenting the day of his birth in Job 3, and his reaction seems extreme: something makes the world such a bad place that nobody should be born into it. That something is described using the same vocabulary of action and achievement that he has used often already to characterize human and divine activity (e.g. 1.14; 2.11; 3.11), and the point is not about an evil inherent somehow in the world itself, but about wrongful deeds, epitomized in the preceding account of extortion and isolation. In their treatment and neglect of each other, humans make it so terrible to live that the dead seem lucky. This vocabulary will be picked up again in 4.4, when Qohelet seeks to understand human achievement, and comes to believe that the human commitment to work itself drives people apart.

Notes

4.1 Then again I observed] The same construction is used in 4.7, which also uses a wayyiqtol form, and the similar שבתי וראה at 9.11. Qohelet does 'turn' in connection with his observations (2.20; 7.25: Fox talks here of his 'metaphorical geography', and cf. van Hecke, 'The Verbs', 215-17), but שוב

is used in these verses almost as an auxiliary verb, to express repetition. J-M §177 b notes of such usage that 'שׁוּב expresses a movement opposite to the one mentioned previously', and the force is well illustrated in, e.g., Judg 19.7 when the Levite gets up to go, but ends up staying the night again, or in Hos 11.9, when God promises that he will not again destroy Ephraim. Correspondingly Seow is probably right to suggest that this construction marks a discontinuity in Ecclesiastes with what has gone before, and it implies more specifically, in fact, that Qohelet is moving back to the stage of making observations in the world, rather than of drawing conclusions from his observations (which is how וראיתי was used in the last verse); cf. V *uerti me ad alia et uidi*, 'I turned myself toward other things, and saw'. The use of consecutive forms here and in 4.7 is linked to this idiom: Ecclesiastes may not use them at all elsewhere (see the note on 'and let me set' at 1.17). Van Hecke 'The Verbs', 219, believes that, here and in 4.7, Qohelet is talking not merely about observation, but about examination, or 'looking at' (noting that 'under the sun' appears also in 1.14, where that sense is generally accepted). I would not exclude that meaning, but if it is what Qohelet intends, then his attention is drawn rapidly from the extortion to its victims.

4.1 extortion that goes on] Lit. 'extortions that are done'. The scope of the verb עשׁק is quite broad. Jeremiah 50.33 can use it to describe the position of the two kingdoms in captivity, perhaps drawing on an image of hostages held for ransom (cf. Ps 119.134), and Deut 28.33 of the people being עשׁוק ורצוץ, 'exploited and oppressed', by the conquerors who will consume all that they have worked for and produced, while Amos 4.1 famously denounces the 'cows of Bashan...who extort from the poor, who oppress the needy' (...העשׁקות הרצצות), the sort of behaviour that is perhaps described more precisely in Mic 2.2, where property is seized: it can be a catch-all term for economic exploitation or manipulation linked to subjugation, although it is not something that rulers are depicted as doing to their own populations (except possibly in the difficult Prov 28.16). It also refers, however, to more specific sorts of financial crime: Lev 5.21 links 'extortion' to fraud and robbery (cf. Lev 6.4; Deut 28.29; 1 Sam 12.3, 4; Ps 62.11 [ET 62.10]; Jer 21.12; 22.3, 17; Ezek 18.18; 22.29), Ezek 22.12 seems to identify it with the charging of interest, Hos 12.8 identifies it as the crime of a merchant who uses false measures, and in Lev 19.13 and Deut 24.14 it is associated with withholding or delaying payment (cf. Mal 3.5); Isa 33.15 lists rejecting profit from מעשׁקות alongside integrity and the refusal of bribes. What seems to be at stake in almost every case is illegitimate (although possibly legal) deprivation of money or property: someone takes it or keeps it back unjustly from someone weaker, who owns it or has earned it. Although it is often linked to oppression in a more general sense, therefore, עשׁק does not in itself refer to political repression so much as to a type of injustice (cf. 5.7) that is perpetrated by people against each other for the sake of profit (cf. Prov 22.16, עשׁק דל להרבות לו), and that can even, in principle, be perpetrated by the poor (Prov 28.3).

It is interesting that G renders in terms of συκοφαντία (the basis of Hie, V *calumnias*), which had originally to do with false accusations by informers, but which came to have a similar implication of swindling, defrauding, blackmailing or shaking people down (cf. Lk 3.14). As the translator has perceived, Qohelet is not talking about slavery and subjugation here: העשקים are crimes or abuses of the political and judicial system, not specifically manifestations of that system.

In view of נעשים, we probably need to take this first use of העשקים as a reference to the offences themselves (despite σ′ τοὺς συκοφαντουμένους, which refers to those who suffer such crimes), and some commentators (e.g. Barton, Gordis) speak of it as an abstraction. Pinker (in 'The Oppressed'), to be sure, rounds up an impressive list of scholars who take העשקים to be the victims here, and makes a case for that meaning in the other occurrences of the word in Job 35.9 and Amos 3.9 (although he does not note that in the former the Septuagint has συκοφαντούμενοι, and in the latter the Vulgate has *calumniam patientes*, 'those suffering oppression', both of which would have supported that case). Were it not for נעשים, indeed, coherence with the meaning of העשקים in the second part of the verse would be a compelling argument, but it is unlikely that victims could be 'made' in the same way that one 'makes' people slaves (so Ginsburg, presumably referring to the curious usage in Gen 12.5). Qohelet himself does use עשה of people in 2.8, apparently in the sense of assembling together a group of them (see the note for that verse on 'I put together'), but it is doubtful that such a sense could be extended to this verse.

Recognizing this difficulty, Pinker himself makes a speculative emendation to עֲשֻׁשִׁים, and renders 'all the oppressed, that are punished under the sun'. It is interesting to observe, as Pinker does not, that the Greek text renders יין עשוקים in Amos 2.8 with οἶνον ἐκ συκοφαντιῶν, interpreting it as wine gained through extortion, and forms from עשׁק are used metaphorically in Prov 19.19; 22.3 and 27.12, although they refer to 'paying the price for something', rather than more generally to suffering. The emendation is not unattractive, then, but it is only forced upon us if we assume, as does Pinker, that נעשׂים is as inappropriate for העשקים in the sense 'extortions' as in the sense 'victims', an assumption that requires us to suppose, on little or no evidence, that it must refer to a condition that is imposed rather than to actions that are undertaken.

Ginsburg, *Massorah* III, 71, lists העשקים (with the defective spelling) as a *Qᵉrê* associated with the eastern tradition in both the places where it appears in this verse; the western reading, correspondingly, is העשוקים, which appears in many manuscripts. The witnesses to the reading are confused and contradictory, however: see the Introduction, p. 190, above.

4.1 tears] Although it refers to a concept that we might consider inherently plural, the singular דמעה is used, as in, e.g., 2 Kgs 20.5: cf. G δάκρυον (the variant δάκρυων is surely secondary). The plural δάκρυα of σ′ may have influenced Hie *lacrimae*, V *lacrimas*, but is anyway more natural, and S is correspondingly pointed with seyame; T has no reference to tears.

4.1 and there is no-one to comfort them[1]] Lit. 'and there is not for them one who comforts'. The language is very close to that used of Jerusalem in the first chapter of Lamentations (cf. Mazzinghi, 'Violence', 547), where she has tears on her cheeks, and none to comfort her from among her lovers (Lam 1.2, ...אין לה מנחם..דמעתה; cf. 1.9, אין לה מנחם; 1.16, מנחם ממני; 1.17, אין מנחם לה; 1.21, אין מנחם לי); the 'comforting' of one who is weeping occurs also in Isa 22.4, and the absence of comforters in Ps 69.21 (ET 69.20; cf. also Isa 54.11). It is not at all clear, however, that such references would necessarily evoke any idea that Qohelet is alluding here to the absence of God, or point to theodicy as the issue at stake (so Bianchi, 'Essi non hanno'; cf. Lavoie, 'De l'inconvénient d'être né', 301-302; Mazzinghi, 'Violence', 547-48), and God is not certainly the comforter who is missed even in Lamentations 1.

4.1 and from the hand of those who extort from them, strength] There is no verb here, and either we have to read ומיד עשקיהם כח as governed still by ואראה or הנה, or else we have to take it as a non-verbal clause with כח as the subject. Commentators have generally preferred the latter, and understood Qohelet to be saying that the extortioners have possessed or exerted an oppressive power over their victims. This runs into two serious problems, however. Firstly, מיד is used of receiving something 'from the hand' of someone (as in 2.23; cf. e.g. Sam 12.3), or, more often, of rescue 'from the power of' someone (e.g. Judg 6.9; 1 Sam 10.18; 17.37; 2 Chr 32.15; 32.22; Job 5.15; 6.23); it never means 'in the hands of' or 'at the hands of', for which we would expect ביד (e.g. 1 Chr 29.12; 2 Chr 20.6). Secondly, כח is never used of force or violence: it refers to a personal vigour or power that can be spent or used up, but not to something that can be projected or to acts of violence.

It may be a recognition of these constraints that drives the expansive rendering of T, 'and there is none to liberate them from the hand of their oppressors with vigour of hand and with strength': with ומיד עשקיהם we might certainly expect a reference to rescue, perhaps like Job 6.23b, ומיד עריצים תפדוני, or Jer 21.12 and 22.3, והצילו גזול מיד עושק. G and S render the Hebrew word for word (although S lacks the initial conjunction), but Hie has *et in manibus calumniantium eos fortitudo*, 'and strength in the hands of those oppressing them': Goldman asserts with great confidence that *in manibus*, '*in* the hands', must reflect a Hebrew reading with -ב, but there is no reason to suppose that it is anything other than a facilitation, while in V *nec posse resistere eorum violentiae cunctorum auxilio destitutos*, 'and the inability to resist their violence, deprived of the help of any', Jerome paraphrases quite differently.

In an attempt to make sense of the text as it stands, Dahood, 'Phoenician Background', 271-72, argues that ומיד עשקיהם כח must be taken as a construct chain, meaning 'from the grip of their powerful oppressors', and then takes what follows to be a reference to the absence of a liberator (see next note). As Schoors, *The Preacher* I, 170, points out, however, it is difficult to find analogies for the interruption of a construct relationship by suffix pronouns in that way: in the examples that Dahood cites, the pronouns are being used proleptically for the subsequent noun, not with a separate antecedent, and so what he suggests would be, at the very least, extremely awkward. The Hebrew as it stands makes sense only if we understand a verb that would necessitate the מ- of מיד ('comes forth', or somesuch), which is quite a lot to read in, and even then the force of כח is such that it would more probably mean that the extortioners lost or even transferred strength to their victims than that they wielded power over them: it is also an obstacle to the relatively simple emendation ביד.

Pinker's suggestion ('The Oppressed', 402), that we emend כח to מכה is based on no evidence, and gives a strange sense: when it is used of physical violence, מכה does not mean 'a blow', as Pinker would like, but refers to wounds or, sometimes more specifically to lacerations inflicted in the context of corporal punishment (cf. Deut 25.3; Prov 20.30) It seems likely that the text here is corrupt, or at least that something is missing, but we have no firm basis for emendation.

4.1 and there is no-one to comfort them²] The problems observed in the previous note, or the reluctance of many commentators to believe that Qohelet would simply repeat himself here, have long led many to suppose that this second occurrence of ואין להם מנחם must be read, or at least somehow understood, differently from the first. There is some indication of this already in the versions: I have noted the very distinctive renderings of T and V, but S also uses a separate noun (ܡܥܕܪܢ *mʿdrn*', 'helper', var. ܡܦܨܝܢ *mpṣyn*', 'deliverer', instead of the previous ܡܒܝܐܢ *mbyʾn*', 'comforter'), and even Hie replaces *et non est qui eos consoletur*, 'and there is none who consoles them', with *et non est eis consolator*, 'and there is no consoler for them'. It is difficult to be certain that σ' read something different in both places, but for the second occurrence a rendering παρηγορῶν παραμυθούμενος, 'consoling comforter', is attested, and this double rendering seems likely to reflect an attempt to impose a distinction. Only G certainly matches M by making both occurrences identical, and although the variety amongst the other versions makes it unlikely that they are drawing upon some different Hebrew text, we can see that they were uncomfortable with a simple repetition.

Among more modern readers, Haupt was keen to see a distinction without any need even to vocalize the text differently, claiming that 'The Heb. has in both cases: and there was no *menaḥḥém* for them; but *menaḥḥém* means in the first case *comforter*, in the second case *avenger*' (111); cf. more recently Noegel, 'Word Play', 21. A very similar suggestion was made by G. R. Driver half a century later ('Problems and Solutions', 227-28), who would point as a hithpaʿel מְנַחֵם (citing GKC §54 c for the form with assimilated ת), to render 'and none avenging himself on them'. As it happens, the related forms מתנחם in Gen 27.42 and והנחמתי in Ezek 5.13 do both have associations with revenge, but this is a matter of context, and there is no reason to suppose that they have a specific implication of vengeance. Even if it were evident that מנחם could bear that sense, however, this would require a stronger steer from the context than seems to be on offer. Correspondingly, *BH*³ and *BHS* both suggest a possible emendation to מְנַקֵּם, 'one who takes revenge' (so also, e.g., Scott), but this is really no less speculative than Graetz's alternative claim that, on the basis of V and S, 'Man müsste also lesen אין להם מושיע'—'one must therefore read "they had no helper"'.

Dahood's proposal, part of his broader solution to the problems of the verse (see the last note), is actually more plausible, and involves reading מנחם as מְנַחֵם, a hiph'il participle from נחה, with a third-person plural suffix, which would mean 'someone to lead them (from the hand etc.)'; this too, however, requires both emendation (the deletion of the conjunction on ואין, which Dahood ignores), and some good reason to suppose that the original readers would have realized that they needed to vocalize the word differently on this second occasion.

My own suspicion is that this repeated clause, and the awkward כה which precedes it, have indeed displaced a clause that referred to the absence of some rescuer or redeemer, but I see no way to recover the original text that is not entirely speculative.

4.2 commended] ושבח is pointed as a pi'el infinitive in M, but a number of commentators have been reluctant to accept this reading (cf. Schoors, *The Preacher* I, 178 for some of the key alternatives, and the useful summary by Whitley). In the nineteenth century, even Euringer, a strong defender of M's integrity, suggested emending the text to restore a participle, מְשַׁבֵּחַ, and Elster similarly proposed to read it as a participle from which the initial מ had been omitted. Although it is now widely accepted that Ecclesiastes shows itself in 8.9 and 9.11 capable more generally of using the infinitive absolute as a finite verb, the construction of the infinitive with the personal pronoun is not found elsewhere in the book, and is sufficiently rare in biblical Hebrew to raise a question mark here (Whitley notes only Esth 9.1; GKC §113 gg accepts several more cases).

On the basis that, 'There is a well-known rule of Semitic syntax that, when the verb precedes the subject, it may stand in the simplest form, i.e. the masculine singular third person, instead of agreeing with it', G. R. Driver suggested in 'Reflections', 130, that ושבח could instead be read as a simple perfect, and later in 'Once Again Abbreviations', 94, that it might be an abbreviation for ושבחתי, which is the form found in 8.15, where Qohelet seems to be saying something very similar. We may note, indeed, that G has καὶ ἐπῄνεσα ἐγὼ both here and in 8.15, so has either read the perfect, or perceived there to be no difference in meaning. In any case, although the reading of M may be considered suspicious, not least because it is hard to see why Ecclesiastes would not have used the same form here as in 8.15, there are no sufficient grounds for emendation, and the way we parse the verb makes no clear difference to the sense.

Although Qohelet obviously does not use שבח here simply to mean 'give praise to' (as, e.g., Pss 117.1; 147.12), there is nothing in the use of the verb elsewhere (including 8.15) to suggest that it could mean 'consider fortunate': it is usually a way of saying that someone or something is good, not that they are in a good position (σ' ἐμακάρισα), and of declaring the fact to others, rather than of thinking it to oneself. Kugel, 'Qohelet and Money', 44-45, makes the interesting suggestion that the sense in play here is a commercial one, 'raise up in value', which is found in later Hebrew, and that we should translate 'esteem'. The subsequent relative clauses (lacking in V) obviously furnish the grounds for his preference, and we might translate each as 'because they...' (cf. Fox, 'since they'), but Qohelet is not praising the actions directly, or saying that he commends the dead 'for having died' (which is not likely to have been, in any case, a voluntary action on their part).

4.2 the dead] A number of witnesses to G have 'all (σύμπαντας) the dead', which Barton, following McNeile, 142, takes to reflect an early Hebrew את כל המתים, but which Klostermann, *De libri Coheleth*, 59, rejects as G*. In Jerome's commentary on Ephesians, book 3, discussing Eph 6.1, he has *laudaui ego omnes mortuos*, 'I praised all the dead', and it is possible that this was a reading found in the La tradition, but there is no *omnes* here in Hie or in the other versions, and the reading is indeed unlikely to be G*. See the next verse for a similar case.

4.2 who are living] If אשר is serving simply as a relative, then the personal pronoun after אשר is redundant, and Dahood, 'Canaanite-Phoenician Influence', 196-97, notes similar usage both in 7.26 and in several Phoenician texts. Against the suggestion that it must be a Phoenicianism, Hebrew passages such as Deut 1.39 and Ezek 43.19 can be adduced to show that the construction is not unknown in Hebrew (cf. Whitley, 41), but it is the case that in most other instances the pronoun serves more obviously to specify the antecedent when this might be ambiguous or unclear. It is possible, therefore, that we are supposed to give אשר conjunctive rather than simply relative force here, as the basis of Qohelet's preference (cf. σ' ὅτι αὐτοὶ for G ὅσοι αὐτοὶ): 'I commended the dead...over the living, *because* they are living still', or '*in that* they are living still'. Much the same sense can be achieved, though, simply by taking this as a matter of emphasis.

4.2 still] The meaning of עדנה is not in doubt, but the word is found only here, with what is commonly taken to be a shorter form of it, עדן, in the next verse (where with לא it apparently means 'not yet' or 'not now'). In later Hebrew, the equivalent is אדיין, sometimes written as עדיין, עדין, or with various other spellings: Gordis, in his commentary and in 'Was Koheleth a Phoenician?', 111, takes the forms here to be defective writings of this. In Judg 16.13, however, we find עד הנה with the sense 'up to now', and the same expression appears in Ps 71.17; 1 Chr 9.18; 12.9 meaning 'still now', with negative counterparts in Gen 15.16 ('not yet') and 44.28 ('still not since'). Since the medieval Jewish commentators, the forms in Ecclesiastes have been explained by most scholars as contractions of this expression, or variously as contractions of עד הנה and עד הן. That view is not incompatible with linking them also to the later forms, but it is difficult to ignore altogether either the existence of *'dn* in Ugaritic and עדן in Aramaic (e.g. Dan 2.8, 7.25), both meaning 'time', or the fact that we have two separate forms here, even if those have been dismissed as 'merely phonetic-orthographic variants' (Schoors, *The Preacher* I, 117).

Dahood, 'Canaanite-Phoenician', 48, accordingly suggested that they derive instead from the Ugaritic as a simple adverb (עדן), and as an adverb with a terminative *-h* (עדנה). Whitley notes that the different forms in Ugaritic have previously been assigned to different roots (itself a matter for speculation), and it certainly seems unlikely that the words have such an early origin, but it is attractive all the same to suppose at least that עדנה is not simply a variant of עדן, but a form with paragogic ה, used to indicate 'time up to' (cf. מימים ימימה in 1 Sam 1.3)—or, perhaps, if the origin of the expression is actually in עד הנה, that עדן is a back-formation, with the ה removed because it is perceived to be paragogic.

4.3 and—better than either—anyone] Despite the את in M טוב...את אשר, which would most naturally mark the one who has not yet been born as the object of a verb, G reads ἀγαθὸς...ὅστις, 'good...(is) whoever', in the nominative. On the face of it, then, while M seems to set the one who has not yet born in parallel with את המתים in the previous verse, as a further object of שבח, G makes them the subject of a new, non-verbal clause. Hie and S seem to follow suit, but T supports M, while V *feliciorem utroque iudicaui qui necdum natus est*, 'and I judged happier than both he who has not yet been born', tries to retain elements of both M and G by introducing a second verb.

It is possible that G simply did not read את here, but commentators have long observed the awkwardness of the construction in M. If את אשר עדן לא היה is being commended above the שניהם just as את המתים were commended above החיים, we should expect a simple comparison using מן, as before: טוב is intrusive, and seems to mark instead the beginning of a non-verbal טוב... מן expression. If, however, אשר עדן לא היה is the subject of a clause meaning 'better than both of them', as the מן on משניהם would suggest, then why is it marked with את? In order to establish strict grammatical coherence, we have, in effect, to choose between (1) continuing the construction from the previous verse by ignoring or explaining טוב; and (2) beginning a new, 'better...than' construction by ignoring or explaining את. Commentators have generally opted for the latter, which is probably what G chose to do, and many have observed that את ש- can be used in later Hebrew to mark the subject rather than the object of a clause. Always assuming that this option were available to the writer, however (and it is difficult to adduce any clear parallels),[1] no good

---

[1] Many of the cases where את precedes a subject in biblical Hebrew fall into groups which seem to reflect particular idioms or usages (there is a likely instance at 7.26; see the notes there), although the small numbers involved make it difficult

explanation has been offered for the use of a 'nominative אֵת' here, where it is redundant and only serves to confuse the sense.²

I think there is a risk of imputing a greater stylistic purism to the book than is generally on display elsewhere, and that it is simpler to acknowledge a certain looseness of construction: we have את אשר either as a result of attraction to the preceding את המתים, or, more probably, because the טוב מן expression is supposed to stand by itself, parenthetically, and not as part of a non-verbal clause: 'I commended...and, (as better than both), him who has not...'.

4.3 not yet] See the note on 'still' in the previous verse.

4.3 has not seen] In contrast to G, α' and θ' ὃς οὐκ εἶδεν, 'who has not seen', σ' seems to have rendered interpretatively ὃς οὐκ οἶδε, 'who has not known'—although it is possible that this is merely an error in the early transmission of the σ' text; see Marshall, and Labate, 'Catena Hauniense', 57-58.

4.3 the wretched achievement] Many manuscripts of G add 'all', and this reading is reflected in Jerome's commentary on Ephesians (book 3, discussing Eph 6.1: *et non uidit omne opus malum quod factum est*, 'and he has not seen all the evil work that has been done'), although it is absent from Hie here. McNeile's suggestion (154) that this reflects an original את כל is accepted by, e.g., Barton, but it is unlikely that G* had σύμπαν or σύμπαντα, let alone that this reflects the original reading of the Hebrew (and it is rejected as G* by Klostermann, *De libri Coheleth*, 59); it is, rather, a secondary clarification that Qohelet is not referring to a single deed, comparable to the use of the plural in σ' τὰ κακὰ ἔργα τὰ γινόμενα ('all the evil deeds that happen', reflected in V *mala quae...fiunt*; Cannon, 'Jerome and Symmachus', 192).

---

to establish what rules governed such uses. Many other instances are generally attributed to attraction, where there is an actual accusative nearby, or to dependence on what GKC §117 l describes as 'a verbal idea, virtually contained in what has gone before, and consequently present to the speaker's mind as governing the accusative'; that would not be inappropriate here. The discussion in J-M §125 j identifies examples 'before an ordinary subject' in only Judg 20.44, 46; Ezek 17.21; 35.10. GKC §117 m has a slightly longer list, but there is much uncertainty in this area. The only potential analogy to the את אשר used here occurs in Jer 38.16 K*ethîbh*, where, however, אשר has a direct antecedent, and the *Qᵉrê* would eliminate את. Schoors, *The Preacher* I, 192, thinks that in the absence of biblical analogies, 'the parallelism with the mishnaic instances is all the more striking'; others might reasonably feel that it makes a genuine link with those instances look all the less likely.

² Wernberg-Møller, 'The Old Accusative Case Ending', 162-63, sees the use of את in terms of 'an adverbial accusative of specification', which is only strictly the subject of the sentence 'to our way of thinking': he translates literally as, 'but better than both as regards the one who has not yet been', and offers a confusing explanation of the syntax in terms of personalizing an impersonal construction.

Aitken, 'Rhetoric and Poetry', 63, notes the striking alliteration of G τὸ ποίημα τὸ πονηρὸν τὸ πεποιημένον.

4.3 been achieved] M נעשׂה: the versions strongly affirm that a past tense is intended.

4.4-6

(4.4) Then I observed all the business and all aptitude in activity, that it is a passion which separates one person from another. This too is an illusion, and wishing for the wind. (4.5) It is a fool who cups his hands to eat his meat: (4.6) better a palmful of respite than two hands filled with business and with wishing for the wind.

Commentary

4.4] The RSV understands Qohelet to be saying that work is motivated by 'a man's envy of his neighbour', and the Vulgate that human works may inspire such envy: interpretations like this are commonplace, and correspond to an understanding of human motivation that is no less widespread. There are no good grounds, however, to believe that this is what the key Hebrew word (rendered here as 'passion') actually means, either in this verse or when Qohelet uses it later in 9.6. Even though the related verb can be used in contexts of envy or resentment, the reference is more to the powerful sense of attachment or possessiveness that may be provoked by such envy, but that may be felt without any specific provocation—which is why it often refers to the way in which God feels attached to Israel, or humans to God.

It is also difficult to take the Hebrew here as referring to an emotion that is directed *against* another human (the RSV's understanding) or felt *by* them (the Vulgate's): Qohelet is more probably speaking of one that draws the person who feels it *away from* others. His observation, accordingly, is that work and ambition come to constitute an all-consuming passion (we might speak of an 'obsession') that isolates people from those around them—but one which is in itself a form of delusion, and a quest to catch what cannot be caught (a way Qohelet has already characterized human activities, including his own, in 1.14; 2.11, 17, 26—he will use 'wishing for the wind' for the last time with a rather different reference in 6.9). This may pick up the point of 4.1, in which humans extort from others or are isolated from them, but it will also more certainly lead into

4.7-8, where Qohelet describes the futility of working on behalf of nobody else, and the following 4.9-12, where he advocates cooperation with others. More immediately, 4.5-6 will address the aspect of obsessiveness through a commendation of respite from work.

4.5-6] The resumption of 'wishing for the wind' at the end of 4.6 indicates that these verses belong with 4.4, but they have usually been treated separately, and commentators have struggled to explain their coherence both with each other and with the surrounding context—Gordis ('Quotations in Wisdom Literature', 137-38) uses the verses as key evidence for his broader contention that Qohelet quotes and then contradicts the ideas of others. This disconnection, however, is perceived largely because interpretation of the verses has been profoundly influenced by an association with passages from Proverbs, whereby v. 5 is commonly linked to Prov 6.10 = 24.33 (in which the sluggard who rests too much folds his hands, like the fool here), and v. 6 with Prov. 15.16, 17; 17.1 (which all contrast a little with a lot). Read in the light of Proverbs, Qohelet's statements here appear to introduce a sudden observation on the fool's laziness, which then sits uncomfortably with a commendation of a little rest over a lot of work (and this has itself been viewed by some commentators as so self-evident that it is a point hardly worth making).[1] Since the latter can at least be seen as a counter to the claim in 4.4, the reference to the fool appears especially intrusive, and Barton is not the only scholar to view it as a later gloss.

The link between the verses, I think, lies in the imagery, but extends beyond it. After the fool who wraps his hands together, v. 6 contrasts a small palmful favourably with hands that are filled, and if we are not to view this as merely incidental, it seems best to discard the idea that the fool in v. 5 is being depicted as lazy (which is not a charge that Qohelet levels against fools elsewhere), and to understand all these references to hands together in a different context. I take Qohelet actually, therefore, to be talking about moderation at table, and his images to be of people reaching out for food. Still thinking in terms of the work described in v. 4, he conjures the image of a fool who cups his hands to scoop up his

---

[1] Although it comes at the text from a different direction, Piotti, 'Lavoro e pigrizia', likewise sees no contradictions here, and argues that comparisons with Proverbs have to take account of very different socio-economic contexts for each work.

stew, rather than dip his bread in it, then remarks that we should do better to grasp a little rest in one palm than likewise to scoop up business and pointless aspiration in our cupped hands. It is not clear whether the ambiguity is deliberate, but the reference to the fool eating 'his meat' could also be understood as eating 'his own flesh'—and if that sense was intended (which I consider unlikely), then the analogy would suggest that throwing oneself into work is similarly self-destructive.

Qohelet is talking about rest from work (as when he uses the same term in 5.11 and 11.6), not some broader sense of calmness, and he seems also to be talking in particular about work that is accompanied by 'wishing for the wind', so this should probably not be taken as a general claim that peace and quiet is more valuable than hard work. Conversely, though, it is difficult to make the Hebrew imply something so specific as 'satisfaction is better than work that grants no satisfaction'. The idea is something closer to 'it is better to retreat from work than to persist in it when it has become a pointless pursuit'.

Notes

4.4 the business] On עמל in Ecclesiastes, see the note at 2.11. Since G is usually faithful in such matters, Goldman may well be right to suppose that its use of a definite article here (τὸν μόχθον) means that its base text had העמל: if the article were merely translational, we should expect to find an article used with the subsequent ἀνδρείαν as well (cf. θ' τὴν σὺν πᾶσαν). העמל is more correct and would present a better parallel to the following כשרון המעשה, so G may well represent the earlier reading, and I have adopted it here. Both S ܥܡܠ *'ml*' (as currently pointed with seyame, which Kamenetzky, 202, would delete) and V *labores hominum et industrias*, 'the labours and industries of humans', render the nouns as plural, but probably just to indicate the general character of what is being observed.

4.4 aptitude] See the note at 2.21.

4.4 in activity] Lit. 'in what is done'.

4.4 that it is] The predicative construction used here after ראיתי is basically similar to those used in, e.g., Gen 1.4, 'God saw the light, that (it was) good', and Job 22.12, 'See the uppermost of the stars, that they are high': the verb takes a direct object, which is then the implicit or explicit subject of a clause introduced by כי; a similar construction was used in 2.24. GKC §117 h describes such usage in terms of the verb taking a second object, while for JM §157 d this is anticipation of the subject of an object clause. It is probably not simply equivalent, however, to a plain object clause with כי, and the construction exploits the different senses of the verb with and without כי. Correspondingly, it gives a parallel implication 'God *looked* at the light and *saw that* it was good', '*Look* at the uppermost stars, and *see how* high they are'; similarly with ידע, 'You *know* the people, and *are aware that* they are prone to evil' (Exod 32.22). Accordingly, Qohelet is probably saying here that he looked and saw, rather than just that he saw.

היא is not rendered explicitly in S and there is strong manuscript support in G for ὅτι τὸ ζῆλος rather than ὅτι αὐτὸ ζῆλος, but the latter is almost certainly G*, and it is doubtful that there was a variant text כי קנאת איש, as McNeile, 142, suggests. That we have 'it' not 'they' suggests either that עמל and כשרון are being treated collectively, or that it is the latter being described: the gender of היא is unexpected, but it is possible that Ecclesiastes takes כשרון to be feminine.

4.4 a passion] The cognate verb קנא can be used in the piʿel straightforwardly of envy or resentment (e.g. Gen 26.14; 37.11), but it is also used more generally of feeling (or, in the hiphʿil, provoking) the emotion to which the noun קנאה refers. This emotion is a strong feeling of attachment that can encompass, but is by no means confined to sexual or other jealousy and possessiveness (e.g. Num 5.14)—it is because of his feelings of this sort towards Israel, for instance, that Saul tries to slay the Gibeonites in 2 Sam 21.2, while Ct 8.6 declares that 'love is as fierce as Death, קנאה unyielding as Sheol'. Unsurprisingly, it is often used with reference to the feelings of God toward Israel or of humans toward God (Num 25.11 offers a vivid example of both), and Qohelet himself uses it in 9.6 to express a key emotion that humans will cease to experience when they die.

Unlike the verb, the noun is not used of envy *per se* in biblical Hebrew, nor, so far as I can tell, by the rabbis (Jastrow, *Dictionary*, lists that sense, but from the context of the saying that he cites from *b. Baba Batra* 21a, 22a, it is clearly not a reference to envy, emulation or competition amongst scholars, as he suggests, but to the incentive given to a teacher against failure by the *resentment* of a colleague whom he has displaced, or against whom he has set up in competition). Although such a meaning is commonly assumed here, it is difficult to make a case, therefore, that Qohelet must be characterizing work as the product of envy or competitiveness: that is not the primary sense of קנאה, and may not be a sense that it possesses at all.

4.4 which separates one person from another] Lit. 'a person from their fellow'—there is no verb in the Hebrew here. איש...רעהו is a common idiom for 'one...another', with את or a variety of prepositions before רעהו, appropriate to the context (e.g. Gen 11.3; 43.33; Exod 18.7; 21.14, 18; Judg 7.22; Prov 25.18), and this should discourage us both from thinking literally of a man and his neighbour here, and from taking מרעהו to be from מרע, a word used of close companions (e.g. 2 Sam 3.8). When we find איש...מרעהו elsewhere, in Gen 31.49 and Jer 9.3, the use of -מ is explained in each case by the verb involved, but we are confronted with the problem here that we have no verb, and that קנא, the verb cognate with קנאה, never elsewhere takes -מ. This is a further obstacle, incidentally, to the understanding of קנאה as 'envy', because on those occasions when קנא does have that sense, the object of envy is expressed either as a direct object (Gen 26.14; Ezek 31.9) or, more commonly, with -ב (e.g. Gen 37.11; Ps 73.3; Prov 24.1). When it has a broader sense, the person toward whom the emotion is directed can be indicated by -ל.

This problem is widely recognized, and a number of solutions offered: Barton speculates implausibly, for instance, that the preposition must indicate a reciprocity of emotion, and Delitzsch sees it as expressing a comparison that is implicit in the idea of envy—although he does not explain why, in that case, it is not used elsewhere. Schoors, *The Preacher* I, 171-72, has more recently expressed his support for the idea of Podechard, according to which איש is the object of envy directed at him from (מן) his neighbour; that is to say, presumably, that the construct קנאת איש must be understood to express an objective and not a subjective genitive (like Ps 69.10 [ET 69.9]; Isa 26.11, but in contrast to 2 Kgs 19.31; Isa 9.6; 11.13; 37.32). This may be what Hie *aemulatio uiri a sodali eius* takes to be the meaning of G ζῆλος ἀνδρὸς ἀπὸ τοῦ ἑταίρου αὐτου, which itself simply renders the Hebrew word for word, but it seems a convoluted way of expressing the idea. Given the range of meanings that קנאה possesses, moreover, it is not clear that the clause would more naturally express a negative emotion felt against the man than a positive emotion felt toward him, if מן indicated no more than the source of the emotion. I take this rather to be a pregnant construction, of a sort that is quite common with מן (cf. GKC §119 x-z, ff): Qohelet is talking about work as a consuming passion (which draws) one person away from another.

4.4 illusion...wishing for the wind] See the Introduction, pp. 22-24, and the corresponding note at 1.14.

4.5 It is a fool who] Lit. just 'the fool', but I take the position of the subject before the verb to suggest this emphasis here.

4.5 cups his hands to eat] Lit. 'clasps his hands and eats'. There is no specific expression of purpose in the Hebrew, which is similar to that in, e.g., Gen 27.19, 'sit up and eat', but such coordination of actions is better expressed by 'to' in English.

The expression חבק את ידיו, literally 'clasping of the hands', occurs also in Prov 6.10; 24.33, where it is something done by the lazy person as a prelude to lying down or sleeping. That other occurrence is frequently read into interpretations of this verse, although there is nothing elsewhere in Ecclesiastes to suggest that fools are lazy, and no reason to suppose that the action itself is something done only by the lazy. חבק means 'embrace' (cf. 3.5), and חבק את ידיו perhaps entails, therefore, interlacing, or wrapping the fingers of one hand around the other (making a pillow for the head in Proverbs?)—although Jerome's commentary understands a wrapping of the arms across the chest (Negenman talks similarly of the fool sitting with his arms crossed); cf. σ' περιπλέκεται ταῖς χερσὶν αὐτοῦ, 'wraps himself in/with his hands'. The versions otherwise translate literally. In view of what follows, I take the action here to be a cupping of the hands, to form a bowl.

M points this and the subsequent ואכל as participles and σ' supports the present tense that this implies, but G* rendered using aorists (the present tense in many manuscripts of G is a hexaplaric correction): these may be gnomic (so Goldman), but it is also possible that G has vocalized the verbs as perfect. T אזיל ומנפף...ובסיתווא יכול creates its own narrative of a fool who is lazy in the summer and will not eat in the winter, but it is not impossible that the germ of this lies in a reading of ואכל as consecutive. Hie *complexus est...et comedit* also shows a switch of tense, from past to present, which is explained in the commentary when Jerome makes an explicit connection to the lazy man of Proverbs.

4.5 his meat] The expression probably means just 'eats his meat' (most likely in the form of stew), but interpretations of the verse in terms of laziness have driven commentators to understand it in terms of self-cannibalism ('eats his own meat'): a criticism of laziness, after all, would seem to require some negative consequence (although Lohfink speculates that there is a deliberate reversal of expectation here—even the lazy have enough to eat; cf. Ginsburg, who sees an image of relaxed contentment, in contrast to competitiveness). Isaiah 49.26; Mic 3.3; Ps 27.2; and Prov 30.14 are commonly invoked in support of this idea, and these undoubtedly show that the terms can be used in the imagery of cannibalism—although they unsurprisingly furnish no other example of somebody eating their own body. That the same terms can also be used in the normal eating of meat, however, is apparent from passages like Exod 21.28; Isa 22.13; and Ezek 39.18. Attempts to pin down the usage more precisely become semantically or methodologically problematic: the fact that the other uses of בשר in Ecclesiastes (2.2; 5.5; 11.10; 12.12) are references to the body (Seow), would only be significant if Qohelet talked as often elsewhere about meat and used a different word, whilst Fox's observation that suffixes on בשר always refer to the source, not the owner, would require validation through a much broader study of suffixes, not of בשר.

G καὶ ἔφαγεν τὰς σάρκας αὐτοῦ is unenlightening: the plural is translational, because although the old distinctions in meaning between the singular and plural of σάρξ, 'flesh', had been eroded by this time (*pace* Goldman), the plural could still be used for the body. More importantly, σάρξ could also be used as a synonym for κρέας (cf. MM under σάρξ), so its use effectively replicates M's theoretical ambiguity.

Wazana, whose 'Evil Eye', 694-96, reads 4.4-8 in terms of the 'evil eye' associated with envy, observes that cannibalism and the loss of flesh can be associated with demonic activity: by isolating himself, the fool provokes an envy in others that activates the evil eye and leads to the wasting of his flesh. The merits or otherwise of that suggestion do not depend wholly upon the supernatural elements that Wazana sees behind the text, but it does not fully explain why a vivid image of self-cannibalism should be used for a situation in which the fool harms himself only indirectly, and suffers at the behest of others. I am not myself convinced, in fact, that we need to see an image of cannibalism here at all: it is a product, essentially, of the interpretation based on Prov 6.10, and although there is technically an ambiguity in the language, I doubt the context was intended to elicit such a bizarre idea. The possibility cannot, however, be excluded altogether.

4.6] Note that V adds *dicens* so that this verse becomes a quotation of the fool who was the subject of the last (as Ibn Ezra). As Lavoie, 'Repos', 335, observes, a number of other medieval and modern commentators have adopted the same strategy to create some continuity; Lavoie himself prefers to see two proverbs in vv. 5 and 6, with the second approved by Qohelet.

4.6 palmful...two hands filled] מלא כף is the amount that can be held in the open palm of the hand, which, as 1 Kgs 17.12 indicates, is regarded as a small amount; the dual form חפנים represents the slightly larger amount that can be held by cupping both hands together around something (Prov 30.4 offers the interesting image of catching the wind this way, set in parallel with wrapping up the waters of the earth in a garment). In biblical Hebrew, the noun חפן only ever appears in the dual, but the singular in later texts probably indicates a 'fistful', which is hardly to be distinguished from a 'handful': this is why, perhaps G πλήρωμα δρακὸς...πλήρωμα δύο δρακῶν, 'fullness of a hand...fullness of two hands', uses the same noun δράξ to render both Hebrew words here.

Along with the fact that it does not instead use the related term δραχμή, a well-known measure that was originally a 'handful' of something, this suggests that G sees no reference to specific and distinct weights or measures. Seow is right to note that these amounts are both small, but his observations that both כף and חפן are used as official measures in Egyptian Aramaic need to be qualified, therefore, both by the lack of any evidence that the versions recognized them as such, and by the fact that, like the English 'hand', כף seems to have been a measure of length not volume (cf. TAD B3.12 R.8).

In G, the distinction is solely numerical—a handful and two handfuls[2]— and T takes a similar route with חופני...מתרין חופנין. It is not clear, however, that חפנים would naturally have conjured up a picture of 'two hands', and it is interesting to note σ′ πληρώματα ἀμφοτέρων χειρῶν, 'fullness of both hands', and Hie *plenus pugillus...plenitudo manuum*, 'a full fist...fullness of hands', which each render in terms of 'both hands together'. We certainly should not see an explicit numerical progression here. On the other hand, the use of חפנים

---

[2] Cf. the La of Cassian, *Collationes* xxiv, 13, 5: *melius...pugillus unus cum requie quam duo pugilli cum labore et praesumptione spiritus*, 'better...one fist with rest than two with labour and presumption of spirit', which is otherwise close to Hie. See Petschenig, *Conlationes*, 689; PL 49, cols. 1302-1303.

makes it difficult to believe that the primary contrast here is between an open hand, symbolic of giving, and a clenched fist, representing stinginess or strife, as Wazana suggests ('Evil Eye', 696).

4.6 of...with] As 1 Kgs 17.12 shows (cf. Exod 9.8; Lev 16.12), מלא כף with a following noun means 'a handful of something', or, literally, 'fullness of hand as to something': Hebrew can use simple collocation to express measures, and talk about 'two talents silver' (2 Kgs 5.23) where English would use 'two talents *of* silver': see GKC §131 d. Accordingly, the expressions here do not consist of construct chains 'fullness of hand of something', and חפנים does not have to be in the construct state; it follows that the final ם– is not problematic, and does not have to be read as an archaic enclitic mem, as Dahood, 'Qoheleth and Northwest Semitic Philology', 355-56, and Whitley have proposed.

Some commentators, however, have resisted rendering as 'handful(s) of something' for other reasons. Seow, for instance, notes that 'one does not measure rest by handfuls', and Gordis complains that it is too self-evident to be worth saying that a handful of rest is better than two handfuls of work. On my own understanding of the verse, that is not the issue, and Qohelet's point is rather that one should never commit completely to work. It may have been some such considerations, though, that led σ' to translate μετὰ ἀναπαύσεως...καὶ κακώσεως πνεύματος, 'with rest...and distress of spirit', which is partly imitated in Hie *cum requie* and perhaps more fully in V *cum requie...cum labore et adflictione animi*, 'with rest...with labour and affliction of mind'. T uses prepositional expressions to achieve the same sense, and in all of these versions Qohelet is taken to be stating that it is better to have a little, along with good things, than a lot, along with bad—a point rather close to those made in Prov 15.16, 17; 17.1.[3]

Although attractive, it is difficult to extract such a sense from the Hebrew without emendation, however, and the differences between the renderings by σ' and T offer a poor basis simply to insert conjunctions before נחת and עמל, as does Ehrlich (and, more tentatively, *BHS*). A more popular suggestion (by, e.g., Gordis, Murphy, Seow) has been to take these nouns as 'adverbial accusatives' (cf. GKC §118 q). Adverbial accusatives are a problematic concept, however, in a sentence which has no verb (as Krüger points out), and such a construal would require us to assume that a verb is first understood and then modified (cf. Gordis' 'one handful achieved through ease is better than two handfuls won through exertion'). It is doubtful that the Hebrew could bear this weight even were it not clear from the other uses of מלא כף and similar expressions that readers would more naturally have understood

---

[3] It is important to be aware, however, that the reading attributed to σ' includes no equivalent for עמל, and may be incomplete: if Hie *laboris* also followed σ', then the sense of σ' may originally have been 'better is a handful with peace than both hands full of work and affliction of spirit'.

'handful(s) of'. Accordingly, σ' (along with Hie, V) and T should be regarded as interpretative translations.

4.6 respite] G, σ' render נחת with ἀναπαύσεως, cf. Hie, V *requie*, and although it is often asserted that the reference here is to satisfaction, calmness or tranquillity, the Hebrew does have this primary connotation of rest or relief from service (cf. Isa 30.15 of disengaging from conflict; Prov 29.9 of an end to or retreat from an argument; Sir. 11.19 of retirement from work). It is doubtful that it can convey the sense 'satisfaction' by itself (Goldman here, citing Gordis at 6.5), even though the later expression נחת רוח is used of pleasure or gratification (cf. T נפש הניות), but it might plausibly connote 'ease' or a lack of effort. Jastrow, *Dictionary*, lists a number of later expressions in which this is the underlying sense, and this is surely the point of the issue disputed in *b. 'Erubin* 13b, whether נוח לו לאדם שלא נברא יותר משנברא.

That passage has נוח not נחת, but is widely cited as an analogy to 6.5, and read in terms of whether humans would have been happier or more satisfied never to have been created, justifying some similar translation in terms of 'happiness' here. The question actually being addressed in the Talmud, however, is whether it would have been *easier* for them (given the obligations arising from existence). That is certainly a possible implication of Qohelet's own usage of נחת in 6.5, where he attributes it more to the miscarried child, who has never been conscious, than to the man who lived a life without satisfaction, and his point is surely related to the fact that the man has ended up where the child is, but expended more effort getting there. When Qohelet uses נחת for a third time, in 9.17 a contrast between words בנחת and the subsequent 'shouting' seems intended: they may be words spoken 'restfully', 'without effort', or (as I think) 'in respite' from that shouting, and we need not presume that they imply a state of calmness, as such. In short, נחת seems generally to connote a disengagement from effort, which may imply rest or ease, but it does not refer to a state of mind, or actively to pleasure and satisfaction.

In 6.5, the *plene* writing נוחת of 4QQoh[a] (II, 2) does not correspond to the consistent vocalization of the word as נַחַת in M, and that writing is also found in the expression נוחת עולם, used in Sir 30.17. *HALOT* takes it to be a feminine form נוֹחָה from נוֹחַ, but Mizrahi, in 'Qohelet 6:5b', 166, notes similar forms at Qumran, such as תוחת for תַּחַת, and he suspects a simpler assimilation of a qatl to a qutl pattern (cf. Qimron, *Hebrew of the Dead Sea Scrolls*, 65; Reymond, *Qumran Hebrew*, 171-74). On Mizrahi's own preference for reading a participle in 6.5, see the note 'it's easier for it than for him' there.

4.6 business] On Qohelet's uses of עמל, see the note at 2.11. He does not regard it as an inherently bad thing, or use the term pejoratively, so the statement that a handful of נחת is better is not a statement of the obvious.

4.6 wishing for the wind] See the corresponding note at 1.14.

4.7-12

(4.7) Then again I observed an illusion beneath the sun: (4.8) there may be a single person, no second, nor has he any son or brother; yet there may be no bounds to all his business, nor will his eye be sated with wealth—and who have I been working for, or giving up happiness? This too is an illusion, and it is a bad job.

(4.9) Two are better than one, when they get well paid in their work: (4.10) for if they fall, one will lift their fellow, while if it were someone alone who fell, then there would be no second to lift them. (4.11) Also, if two lie together, then it will be warm for them, but how can just the one be warm? (4.12) And if one man might be outmatched, two will stand before him—and a three-plied thread is not readily snapped.

Commentary

A change of direction is signalled by the fact that 4.7 begins in the same way as 4.1: having spoken about the isolating effect of work in the previous verses, Qohelet now commends company, first by affirming in 4.7-8 the pointlessness of work from which nobody else will benefit, and then by asserting the practical value of cooperation with others.

The expression of these ideas is curious. The first begins by evoking what appears to be another of Qohelet's hypothetical situations (cf. 1.10; 2.21), this time involving an individual whose work occupies his whole life and who will never be satisfied with what he has. This is the sort of obsessiveness induced by work that Qohelet spoke about in 4.4, and so is not perhaps to be regarded as unusual: what marks the individual out for discussion here is that they have no partner or potential heir, and the problem that Qohelet highlights is not that they have no assistance, therefore, but that their work, and the surrender of happiness that it involves, is of benefit to nobody—this person will find no satisfaction, and no-one else that they care about gets to enjoy the proceeds. Instead of simply commenting on this, however, Qohelet switches suddenly to first-person speech, either putting words into the mouth of this individual, or revealing that he is actually talking about himself (in the absence of any expression like 'he said', the latter seems more a more natural reading, but commentators have taken it both ways).

The expression of 4.9-12 is noteworthy in a rather different way. Verse 9 qualifies its statement that two are better than one with a clause that has been read since ancient times in two different ways: two are better either *because* they get paid well, or *if* they get paid well. The latter is a slightly easier reading of the Hebrew, and the former would seem intrusive when Qohelet will go on to offer a very different justification, using more explicit language, in 4.10: the stated benefit of being picked up has nothing to do with making more money. It seems, likely, therefore, that Qohelet is entering a rather idiosyncratic note of caution: two are better than one when there is enough income to support them both. This pragmatism might be jarring were it not for the matching absence of sentimentality in the examples used to illustrate his point: there are surely few people who would leap to these as the most important reasons for humans to work together.

4.8] It is difficult to express the effect of the original Hebrew, in which negatives are piled together to emphasize how many things the individual does *not* have. In 4.15, 'second' is used in the context of the 'next' generation, and it is possible that there is some such implication of succession here—but more probable that Qohelet is referring generally to the lack of a partner: this person works with nobody. The reference is not apparently to a spouse, and I have translated 'son' and 'brother' to retain the masculine implications of the text here: Qohelet is not really talking about the absence of family or about this individual's support for a family, but—in a culture where women were conventionally restricted to particular roles—about the absence of anyone else with a direct stake in the business.

Qohelet's last hypothesis, in 2.21, envisaged a person forced to leave his estate to somebody who had done no work on it. The topic here is different, and Qohelet is no longer pursuing the questions raised by the very fact of succession, but this scenario is certainly reminiscent of the last. If the sudden switch to the first person marks the revelation that Qohelet is talking about his own situation, then we might well wonder whether the author is perhaps nudging us to read some of the other hypothetical individuals in the monologue as cyphers for Qohelet himself. It would at least seem to portray Qohelet either as unable to sustain here a device that he uses to distance himself, or as coming to a sudden realization that his description fits his own situation. If the voice is rather that of the individual that Qohelet is describing, the absence of anything to introduce such direct speech by someone else is puzzling: so far as we know, writers had no way to mark speech using punctuation alone, and the words spoken by another in 1.10 were described explicitly as such. Some scholars have used this verse as an opening to suggest that Qohelet actually cites the words of others many times elsewhere—a suggestion that is considered in the Introduction, pp. 45-53—but if this is direct speech by another speaker, it seems more likely that something has been lost from the text.

In any case, though, the portrait painted is of a man whose efforts are on behalf of nobody else, but who sets no limit to what he does, or to his acquisitiveness (in an expression reminiscent of 1.8, his eye never sees enough wealth to be sated). When he understands his situation, he realizes that his work has been of benefit neither to himself nor to others: whatever motivated him to spend his life this way involved a false or thoughtless expectation, and resulted in a bad deal for him. Correspondingly, Qohelet implies that the man might have seen more point to his labours if there had been others who depended upon him—although, engaged as he is here in a discussion of work and the motives behind it, this should probably not be taken as an acknowledgment that, in the broader scheme of things, such altruism would actually have constituted a benefit for the man himself.

4.10-11] Schwienhorst-Schönberger makes the interesting suggestion that 4.10-12 are about old age and death, and while I am not persuaded of that reading as a whole, Qohelet's examples in these verses are certainly curious. In the Introduction, I touched on the fact that he shows no interest in loneliness or companionship for its own sake, but in attempting to illustrate the benefits of a companion he also here points to requirements that seem far from universal: most people do not need help picking themselves up, or more warmth than a fire and a blanket can provide (unless we follow the Targum, and see a potential sexual reference here). Schwienhorst-Schönberger offers numerous analogies to suggest that Qohelet is referring to the needs of the old in particular, and that is not implausible, especially since old age will be a factor in 4.13. It is less clear, however, that 4.9 and 4.12 should be understood in such terms. Wernik ('Will the Real Homosexual?', 61) uses these verses very differently to suggest that, especially in 4.11, Qohelet is talking about friendship between men from a gay perspective: Lyons ('Outing', 197) refutes this (alongside all Wernik's other arguments for Qohelet's homosexuality), but the idea has been picked up in a rather different way by Hügel ('Eine queere Lesart').[1]

4.12] The scenario that Qohelet sketches here has generally been understood in one of two ways: (1) there is a single person who confronts two others and they prevail against him; or (2) there is someone who would prevail over a single person, but not over two. The second of these is more common, but both understand the last clause to be supplementary: if two are stronger than one, then how much stronger still are three. As it is normally read, however, the Hebrew verb in the first clause has a personal suffix, and to achieve these readings this suffix has either to be understood as introducing some otherwise unannounced person for the single one to beat, or else treated as redundant so that the single person, and not that suffix, can be the object of the verb. The Hebrew would be clumsy in either case, and matters are complicated by the fact that the expression in the second clause is much more naturally taken to mean 'stand with someone' than 'stand against'.

Like some other commentators, I take the first verb to have been vocalized wrongly in the Masoretic text, but I also think that the image here is not just of two standing firm where one would be overwhelmed, but of two stepping forward to help the one—so that the threefold cord is actually a reference to this scenario, and not just an afterthought. This has not been a popular understanding among modern readers, but a similar understanding lies behind the interpretation of this verse in an early medieval midrash, which speaks of Solomon passing judgments based on decisions made by the prophets Nathan and Gad ('because the two are better than the one'):

---

[1] Qohelet's 'latent homosexuality' had earlier been deduced by Zimmermann (11, cf. 27, 46, 142), from Qohelet's interest at 3.7 in the essentially 'feminine occupation' of sewing. To a more modern eye, his index entry 'homosexual tendency apparent from sewing' verges on self-parody.

וכת״ אם יתקפו האחד : האחד זה שלמה המלך, השנים : אלו נתן וגד, והחוט
המשולש : אלו שלשתן

And it is written, 'if the one attacks...': 'the one' is Solomon, 'the two' are Nathan and Gad, and 'the threefold cord' is the three of them.[2]

Notes

4.7 Then again I observed] The verse begins in exactly the same way as 4.1. See the note there.

σ' is attested as καὶ πάλιν ἀναστρέψας κατέμαθον, 'and turning again I perceived', and Cannon, 'Jerome and Symmachus', 193, suggests that this has influenced V *considerans repperi et aliam*, 'considering, I found also another' (contrast *uerti me ad alia et uidi*, 'I turned myself to other things and saw', at 4.1, without the participle).

4.8 there may be a single person, no second] Lit. 'there is/was one and there is/was not a second', as G, S, Hie. The Targum is expansive, 'there is/ was a man alone and there is/was not a second apart from him', and V *unus est et secundum non habet*, 'one is, and he has not a second', is perhaps derived from σ' οὗ (possibly ᾧ) μὴ ἔσται δεύτερος, 'there is not a second for him'. There are no verbs, and so the Hebrew expresses no indication of tense until we reach תשבע.

We have already noted, at 1.10 and 2.21, Qohelet's tendency to use שי as a way of positing hypothetical situations, and virtually creating conditional sentences. Here he begins in that same way, and I have opted to translate accordingly: it is only with the revelation that he is talking about himself that it becomes clear to the reader that Qohelet really does have a particular person in mind, and that the שי is not hypothetical.

4.8 no...nor...no...] It is impossible to reproduce idiomatically in English the effect of the Hebrew, which uses אין three times. Literally, *'there is not a second, also a son and a brother is not to him and a limit is not to all his work'*: a limit to work is presented as one in a series of things that are lacking. The use of גם three times, each without a conjunction, also serves to structure the verse: on the last occasion, it merely introduces the formulaic statement about הבל (and may have gained a conjunction in some texts; cf. Ginsburg, *Massorah*, 4:246), but the first two uses coordinate the lack of son and brother with the lack of satisfaction for the eye.

---

[2] The text is from Perles, 'Thron und Circus des Königs Salomo', 133. The midrash was probably composed sometime before or during the tenth century: see now the useful introduction and translation in Mehlman and Limmer, *Medieval Midrash*, 135-48, 161-68. Other understandings of the cord are outlined in Bardski, 'The Snowball and the Cord'.

4.8 son or brother] The reading καί γε υἱὸς καὶ γε ἀδελφὸς, lit. 'and indeed a son and indeed a brother', is attested for almost every manuscript of G, and Goldman (like McNeile) accordingly supposes that the translator read גַם בֵּן (וּ)גַם אָח, noting also T אוּף ברא אוּף אחא לית ליה, lit. 'either son or brother there is not...', which could reflect the same text. T has to be used with caution, however, and it is important to note that Hie, which is usually strongly influenced by G, shows no more knowledge of a second γε or גַם than does S. Rahlfs and Gentry in fact take G* to have been καί γε υἱὸς καὶ ἀδελφὸς, and that second γε, by implication, to have been an early error (there is a potentially similar instance at 2.8), rather than the reflection of a second גַם in G's source-text. It is difficult to judge the issue, but it makes no significant difference to the sense.

Barton draws attention to the unusual pointing of וְאָ֣ין before the conjunctive accent *munaḥ* (we might expect the waw-conjunctive to be pointed with šewa, cf. GKC §104 g), and contrasts the pointing of the word וְאָ֣ין in Prov 17.17, where it has *mer*ᵉ*kha*.

4.8 nor[1]] The גַם may have some emphatic force, 'he does not even have' (so, e.g. Schoors, *The Preacher* I, 132-33; Seow), but it also helps to coordinate elements of the verse (see the note on 'no...no...no...', above).

4.8 no bounds to all his business] On all the occasions when קֵץ, 'limit, end', occurs in Ecclesiastes (here, 4.16 and 12.12), G renders it with περασμός, a term that is found in Greek only in these passages or in subsequent patristic references to these passages; Aitken, 'Rhetoric and Poetry', 72, suggests that the translator may have invented it. Whether or not that was the case, the word is presumably to be derived from περαίνω / περάσθαι, and although it is distinct from the more common πειρασμός, 'testing', it may have been modelled upon it (and many of the manuscripts actually have πειρασμός here). It is possible to get an idea of the sense (and also, perhaps, of the register), from the use of cognate words in, e.g., the discussion of infinity in Aristotle, *Phys.* III.4, 203b: τὸ πεπερασμένον ἀεὶ πρός τι περαίνειν, ὥστε ἀνάγκη μηδὲν εἶναι πέρας, εἰ ἀεὶ περαίνειν ἀνάγκη ἕτερον πρὸς ἕτερον, 'the finite always reaches a limit in something, so there must be no limit if everything must always reach its limit in something else'. When α' uses τέλος instead, the meaning is completely changed, from 'there is no limitation to all his business' to 'there is no purpose in all his business'. There is also a significant difference between Hie *non est finis omni labori eius*, 'there is no limit to all his work', which is quite a good reflection of G, and V *laborare non cessat*, 'he does not cease to work', which shifts the emphasis again toward an implication of unceasing labour.

On the meaning of עָמָל, see the note at 2.11. Given both Qohelet's general usage of this term and the subsequent parallel here, the sense is probably not that the man is toiling endlessly or working too much (as V), but that there is no limit to his acquisition (as G, Hie); cf. the similar expressions at 4.16 and 12.12, which both refer to things that stretch out into the future without reaching any natural end.

4.8 eye] The *Qᵉrê* עינו is apparently singular, as is the verb תשבע with which this must agree,[3] and only V supports the *Kᵉthîbh* dual עיניו: a number of commentators prefer that dual, however, as the *lectio difficilior* (which it is not really, in text-critical terms) and with a view to Prov 27.20. This would make it necessary to suppose that the eyes are being treated as a collective concept for purposes of agreement (Seow). In the light of the versions and especially of Qohelet's own usage in 1.8, the singular is to be preferred. The expression means that he never tires of looking at wealth.

4.8 I] T ולא יימר בליבביה, 'and he does not say in his heart', and V, *nec recogitat dicens*, 'and he does not reflect (on it), saying', try to furnish a context for the sudden switch to the first person, and, although they are similar, these are probably independent explanatory additions or both derived from Jewish exegetical traditions, rather than reflections of a Hebrew text.

4.8 giving up happiness] Lit. 'depriving myself (or my appetite) of what is good'. M ומחסר את נפשי מטובה is close to 6.3 ונפשו לא תשבע מן הטובה, but the precise sense of each is uncertain, since both נפש and טובה have a range of meanings, and G uses the stereotyped ψυχή and ἀγαθωσύνη respectively, which offer little guidance. There is also an apparent echo of this verse in the preceding 6.2, which speaks of a man ואיננו חסר לנפשו מכל אשר יתאוה. Krüger, 'Das Gute', 55-56, argues that the issue at stake in 4.8 and 6.3 is not the denial to oneself of material prosperity, but of finding enjoyment in that prosperity, and Hie, V speak rather interestingly here about 'cheating one's soul' (*fraudo animam meam*) of goodness. I think that in this context, however, the question is still governed by למי: it is not that the man believes himself to be surrendering prosperity, any more than he thinks that he should not be working, but that he wonders why he is not, since there is nobody for whom he can make sacrifices, or to whom he can transfer what he accumulates. Without pushing the distinction between טוב and טובה too far, I think that טובה in Qohelet's usage has a particular connotation of personal contentment or respite from difficulty: see especially 5.17; 6.6; 7.14 and the note on 'but his self is not satisfied by his good fortune' at 6.3.

4.8 bad job] See the note on 'bad' at 1.13.

4.9 Two are better than one] Lit. 'better are the two than the one'. The articles on השנים and האחד have occasioned some discussion: they may indicate that Qohelet is talking about just the sorts of people in singles and pairs that were the subject of the previous verse (so, e.g., Delitzsch, and this may be what Barton means when he says that 'the writer individualizes two persons and one person'), or simply that he is talking about groups—'singles' and 'couples' as it were (cf. Seow). The articles are not used consistently across vv. 9-12, however, and it might be wise to avoid reading anything too general

---

[3] The presence of the verb makes it unlikely that this is simply a matter of spelling conventions, comparable to the use of ידיו / ידו discussed in Barr, 'A New Look at Kethibh-Qere', 29.

into them: in this verse, I suspect, they have a particular grammatical function specifying the antecedents of a relative clause (see below).

Along with the positioning of 'the two' before 'the one', one thing that the articles do seem to achieve is an effective disconnection from the traditional form of numerical sayings. When Ogden says that comparison 'with other numerical sayings from the ancient near east reveals that the lesser digit always precedes the larger unless some specific reason is declared',[4] the proper conclusion to be drawn is not that Qohelet has inverted the order, as Ogden avers, but that this is not a numerical saying, and the use of definite articles helps to prevent us from reading numerals (or 'digits') here.

4.9 when] It is common to read M אשר here in the sense 'because', making the second part of the verse the reason for the first, and there is no doubt either that אשר can sometimes be used in that way (cf. GKC §158 b; J-M §170 e)—although I doubt it is found in Ecclesiastes so often as sometimes asserted (see Schoors, *The Preacher* I, 140-44, for a good summary of suggested cases, and Holmstedt's examinations in 'The Grammar of ש and אשר' and *The Relative Clause*)—or that it was taken that way by at least some of the ancient versions: S is just a calque of M and T substitutes a conjunction, but V has *habent enim emolumentum societatis suae*, '*for* they have the benefit of their company', and this is probably in imitation of σ' ἔχουσι γὰρ κέρδος ἀγαθόν, '*for* they have a good profit'.

G, however, has read a simple relative οἷς ἔστιν αὐτοῖς μισθὸς ἀγαθὸς, 'to whom there is good pay', cf. Hie *quibus est merces bona*, with the same sense, and several modern commentators have ventured alternative ideas. Michel, *Untersuchungen*, 241, sees the אשר here, and often elsewhere, as explicatory or clarificatory, while both Schwienhorst-Schönberger and Lohfink translate it contextually here as introducing a condition: 'two are better than one if there is good pay to both'. This last, I think, catches the point, although the clause is not so much a condition as a qualification: increasing numbers are not a good thing when resources are static, so two are only better than one when there is enough to go round. G shows how the verse should be construed with a relative, which is probably, strictly speaking, the way it should be read:[5] 'two is better than one for those to whom there is good pay', or better, 'the two for whom there is good pay are better than the one' (which offers an explanation for the definite articles also).

---

[4] Ogden, 'The "Better"-Proverb', 499; see also his 'Mathematics of Wisdom', where he claims (451) that 'From a wisdom perspective, mathematics is an imprecise science: "one" may be more than "two" (v. 6) though not necessarily so (v. 9)'.

[5] Despite his reservations about the conjunctive use of אשר, Holmstedt in *The Relative Clause*, 378, accepted a general causal sense here, while insisting that it is implied by the context and position of what remains strictly a relative clause; more recently HCM (Holmstedt is the 'H') simply deny that it is causal.

4.9 they get well paid in their work] On the literal sense, see above. שכר is a reward or wage, which is generally paid 'for' (-ל) work (e.g. Num 18.31; Jer 31.16; 2 Chr 15.7); -ב here implies 'in the course of their work' (cf. 5.14). As Schoors, 'The Word *ṭwb*', 685, points out against Gordis, a שכר טוב is clearly not just the same as a שכר, and the reference is to *good* payment, not just payment.

4.10 if they fall] M יפלו is plural and supported by α'σ'θ' πέσωσιν, but Hie, V and T ('if one falls ill') all have the singular (see below); both G and S are mixed, with the singular in some manuscripts, but each probably read the plural originally. Many commentators have been inclined in the past to approach the problem with an assumption that only one of the companions is supposed to have fallen, and emendations have sometimes been proposed in line with this assumption: S. R. Driver in *BH¹*, for instance, suggests reading יפל האחד השני for יפלו האחד, which is approved by Barton but entirely speculative, whilst Galling 1969 would read a plene singular יפול for יפלו—Horst, in *BH³*, adopts as a suggestion Galling's earlier 1940 proposal instead to insert השנים. Rather differently, a short note by Dahood in 1968 ('Scriptio Defectiva') suggested that in a text which had originally been written defectively, only יפל would have been found, and that this should have been construed as equivalent to יפול, not יפלו (cf. also his 'Hebrew–Ugaritic Lexicography VI', 367). Such a suggestion rests, of course, on some very dubious presuppositions, but it amounts to no more than an attempt to justify what is really a conjectural emendation.

Most recent commentators, however, along with some earlier ones, have taken the perceived difficulty of the plural יפלו to be an indication of its probable originality: it is the *lectio difficilior* (so Goldman), as well as being better attested. Because most also want to retain the assumption that only one companion falls, however, several ways have been suggested to construe the plural form with a singular sense: GKC §124 o, for example, presents this as an example of the plural used to represent an indefinite singular (so too McNeile), and others speak of it as partitive or distributive (e.g. Gordis, Seow: 'if either of them should fall'; Lavoie, 'Analyse de Qohélet 4,9-12', 187, accepts both possibilities). In the absence of any explicit indication to the contrary, however, it is both simpler and more natural to understand that Qohelet is speaking of two companions who fall.

4.10 one will lift] The sense could be 'each will', but Qohelet is more probably trying to suggest that either one of them would lift the other, rather than that they both assist each other. The paraphrase in Jerome's commentary (*alterius ruina alterius auxilio subleuetur*, 'the fall of one is alleviated with the help of the other') shows that Hie *si ceciderit unus eriget participem suum*, 'if one has fallen, he may raise his companion', is not an error for *si ceciderint...*, 'if they have fallen...', as presumed in Goodrich and Miller, *Jerome: Commentary*, 244 n. 25. It is perhaps the position of האחד before יקים (and possibly a knowledge of the G variant πέσῃ / -ει for πέσωσιν) that has

led Jerome to construe it with the previous verb as well as with יקום; cf. T
אין יפול חד...חדא יקים, 'if one falls...one will raise', which appears to render
האחד twice. In V *si unus ceciderit ab altero fulcietur*, 'if one has fallen, he is
supported by the other', the second verb is treated as though it were passive.
Podechard inserts השני from v. 15 before יקים, believing it to have been
displaced.

4.10 fellow] Although it is used more often of actual friendship in later
texts (e.g. Sir 37.6), חבר does not generally imply close companionship
in biblical usage, but a looser association or position as a counterpart to
someone, so we must be wary of importing the sort of notion presumed by
Delitzsch, that the rescue will depend upon him being a 'true friend' ('wahrer
Freund'), citing חבר טוב from *m. ʾAbot* 2.9 (where it is the adjective, of course,
that conveys the implication 'true'). G uses μέτοχον: this is probably not
quite so technical as Vinel suggests, but μέτοχος is used widely in Hellenistic
Greek of business partnerships and associations, and G likely understands
the text in the business terms of the previous verse. Hie *participem* and σ'
ἑταῖρον likewise have no particular implication of personal intimacy, and
although α' opts for φίλον, the versions seem generally not to have seen this
as being about the necessity of friendship, as such.

4.10 while if it were someone alone who fell, then] Lit. 'and in the case
that (it is) the one who falls'; or alternatively 'and woe to him, the one who
falls / when he falls'. The alternatives arise because there are two possible
readings of אילו: (1) as an abnormal writing together of two words אי and
לו, yielding the sense 'woe to him' (אי is a late equivalent to אוי; cf. Schoors,
The Preacher I, 149), or (2) as a single word, well-attested as a conditional
conjunction in Aramaic, which has the sense 'in the case that' (it is found
written defectively as אלו in M at 6.6). Most readers, including most of the
ancient versions, have opted for the former; the latter is the understanding of
T and (although M exceptionally gives the word two accents) apparently of at
least some Masoretes (see the notes at 6.6), as well as, most probably, of the
pre-Masoretic scribes who transmitted the letters as a single word—contrast
the writing of אי לך as two words in 10.16. Whether we adopt one or the
other does not, of course, make a great deal of difference to the sense, but the
suggestions of, e.g., *BHS* and *DCH*, that we might read the conjunction here
can be commended on grounds of simplicity: this reading does not require us
either to account for an inconsistency in the writing, or to explain a redundant
suffix ו- as anticipatory of the next word האחד ('woe to him, the one').

If we were to opt instead for the other reading, then the -ש of שיפול could
be understood in several ways, as a simple relative, with a conditional
implication of its own (Lauha), or as temporal (e.g. Seow). All the same, G
ὅταν πέσῃ, 'whenever he falls', is unexpected, and in its other occurrences
at 9.12 and 10.3, ὅταν translates -כש. Whether or not the translator actually
found that reading here (and we have no other evidence for it), he apparently

takes Qohelet to be talking about potentially habitual problems, 'woe to him, the one, whenever he falls without there being a second person (καὶ μὴ ᾖ δεύτερος)'.

If S 'woe to him, to one, for if he falls' is not attempting a double translation of אילו, then it is probably paraphrasing G. Hie *cum ceciderit* and V *cum ruerit* probably likewise imitate G, as does *si ceciderit* in Jerome's revision of La (Caspari, *Hiob*, 7; Leanza, 'Le tre versione', 92). These three versions, however, are rather different from each other: the revision has *uae illi qui solus est si ceciderit* ('woe to him who is alone if he has fallen'), Hie *et uae uni cum ceciderit* ('and woe to the one when he has fallen'), and V *uae soli quia cum ruerit* ('woe to [the one who is] alone, because when he falls'). The absence of the initial conjunction in V and in Jerome's revision may correspond to a variant in G (this absence is probably attested also in the Coptic of Papyrus Michigan 3520, if the line has been correctly reconstructed), and the revision is otherwise generally closest to G here.

4.11 then] M, G have a conjunction here (cf. T). Its absence in S, V is translational, as those versions have adapted the syntax, but it is striking that Hie has *etiam*, 'also', and Jerome's revision of La *et etiam*, 'and also'; see Caspari, *Hiob*, 7; Leanza, 'Le tre versione', 92. These may reflect a variant G text, in which καί γε had been repeated from the beginning of the verse.

4.11 warm¹] M has to be read with an impersonal form of the verb חָמַם in the qal, an understanding of וחם reflected also in two manuscripts of G (possibly influenced by the second part of the verse). However, G* and Hie (the latter probably on the basis of La, cf. Jerome's revision) have read this as the noun חם, 'warmth', and understand 'warmth (will be) for them'; cf. T ושחין להון, where the specification of the two as a man and woman raises the possibility that שחין has a secondary connotation of sexual 'heat', as sometimes elsewhere. Both understandings of the consonantal text are possible, and there is no significant difference in sense between them. S and V paraphrase with (personal) verbal forms.

4.11 how can just the one be warm?] M is literally 'while for one how will it be warm', using an impersonal construction again; this is matched by T ולחד איכדין ישחן, and note also α', θ' καὶ τῷ ἑνί = ולאחד. S and V replace with personal forms once more, but now G also has a personal καὶ ὁ εἶς πῶς θερμανθῇ, 'and the one, how should he be warmed?'. *BHQ* suggests very plausibly that M is assimilating to the first part of the verse, and that an original והאחד is reflected in G and in Hie *et unus quomodo calefiet*, 'how will one be warmed?', but it is difficult, and ultimately unimportant for the sense, to establish whether והאחד or ולאחד is actually the earlier reading.

4.12 And if one man might be outmatched] I take the literal sense to be 'and if they might overpower the one', an impersonal construction of a common sort that means 'and if the one might be overpowered'. The verb תקף connotes aggression or attack in neither Hebrew nor Aramaic, but conveys instead the sense of being or becoming strong. This may sometimes mean 'be too strong for an opponent to beat', so that the translation 'prevail' is appropriate, and the verb may take a direct object in this sense, as at Job 14.20; 15.24 where there is a sense 'overwhelm'. When it is used of 'overpowering' somebody in later Hebrew, it is in contexts where the fact of overwhelming compulsion is significant (e.g. *b. Yebamot* 54a), although it can be used metaphorically, as in *m. ʾAbot* 3.8 where תקפה עליו משנתו is used of somebody's study proving too much for them.

Qohelet is not depicting, then, a sudden attack upon someone, so much as an unequal confrontation, but there is considerable disagreement about who is confronting whom. As noted above in the comments, the problems revolve around יתקפו, which is pointed in M as יִתְקְפוֹ: a third-person singular verb with a third-person singular suffix. If the suffix is the object of the verb, as would seem most natural, then האחד would be the subject, and it is the 'one' who would be overwhelming 'him'. This is clearly the understanding of S ܘܐܢ ܢܚܣܢ ܚܕ *wʾn nʿšn ḥd*, 'and if one is strong', and Hie *si inualuerit super eum unus*, 'and if one prevails over him'. Both render ואם יתקפו האחד with האחד as the subject of the verb, so that the image is of one strong man who can be beaten by two (and this is probably also the understanding that underlies T's lengthy paraphrase). Both have probably also recognized the suffix on יתקפו as the object of the verb (cf. Hie *super eum*), even if S seems to have ignored it, or perhaps just chosen not to render it (Kamenetzky, 216, suggests that its choice of an intransitive verb is the reason).

These readings have probably been influenced by G καὶ ἐὰν ἐπικραταιωθῇ ὁ εἷς, but the meaning of the Greek is complicated by the fact that passive forms of κραταιόω often have an active sense in biblical literature (e.g. in the similar 2 Sam 10.11, ἐὰν κραταιωθῇ Συρία ὑπὲρ ἐμέ...καὶ ἐὰν υἱοὶ Αμμων κραταιωθῶσιν ὑπὲρ σε, 'if Syria is too strong for me...and if the Ammonites are too strong for you'), so if ἐπικραταιωθῇ were read as though it were equivalent to κραταιωθῇ, then G could be understood to mean 'if the one should prevail'—which is how Hie and S probably took it—rather than as 'if the one should be prevailed over'. On that understanding, G has not rendered any equivalent to the suffix, which leads *BHQ* to suppose that it read יתקף rather than יתקפו (and to offer this as a better reading than that of M), but if we insist on reading the suffix while understanding האחד as the subject, then the object of the verb has to be an indefinite 'someone' who will be overwhelmed by 'the one'.

In general, though, translators and commentators have tried to make האחד the object of the verb instead of its subject, so as to give a better parallel to the preceding statements and the better sense that, in a situation where one man might be beaten, two will prevail (the definite article, incidentally, need not imply that האחד is the single man of the previous verse or one of the two who are to be mentioned; see, e.g., Gen 42.27; 2 Kgs 6.3, 5). This is certainly to be preferred in terms of sense, but because the suffix on יתקפו already provides an object for the verb, it is awkward syntactically: most scholars have opted to see that suffix, therefore, as a redundant proleptic or anticipatory suffix attached to an impersonal verb ('if one prevails over him, [i.e.] the one...'). This is grammatically feasible, but it is difficult to see why such a suffix would have been used here, where it does nothing to clarify and much to obscure the sense. This is especially true when the potentially ambiguous role of האחד could easily have been resolved by the use of את to mark it as the object, and when את is used in other passages, such as Exod 35.5, which are commonly adduced as parallels to this proposed construction. If we follow the vocalization in M, then we have to choose either to make האחד the subject, or to treat the suffix as redundant and misleading.

I prefer another option that has sometimes been suggested (e.g. by Lauha), which resolves the problem by vocalizing not as M יִתְקְפוֹ but as יִתְקְפוּ, and thereby reading the consonants not as a singular verb with a suffix, but as a plural verb without a suffix. That verb can then be treated as impersonal (J-M §155 b, c). This is a simpler and more elegant way to understand the text, and the only significant objection to it is that the suffix on the subsequent נגדו would then have to refer not to the indeterminate subject of the verb, but to the 'one' (cf. Seow); this ceases to be an objection if that is indeed the reference intended, as I shall suggest below. Rose, *Rien de Nouveau*, 332-33, proposes to read a niph'al plural, and then to restore a niph'al singular (supposedly lost through haplography), yielding ואם יתקפו יתקף האחד, 'and if they are attacked, he who is alone will be overcome'. This gives a nice connection to the preceding verse, but has nothing else to commend it.

Returning to G and its reading, we noted above that if ἐπικραταιωθῇ is regarded as equivalent to κραταιωθῇ then its sense might well be active, so that 'the one' would be prevailing. As it happens, ἐπικραταιόω (with that spelling) is found nowhere else in Greek, but the more common form ἐπικρατέω can be used quite normally in the passive (as famously in the first section of Polybius' *Histories*, where almost the whole world is ἐπικρατηθέντα by Rome), so we do not have to assume at all that G intended an active sense here. It is very likely, in fact, that the translator meant to say 'if the one is defeated', which would both nicely render a reading of the Hebrew with the plural יִתְקְפוּ and explain the absence of any equivalent to the suffix of M's vocalization: *contra BHQ*, therefore, G did not certainly read יתקפו here, and the translator most likely just vocalized the יתקפו differently, understanding it in the same terms proposed here.

It is more difficult to judge V *si quispiam praevaluerit contra unum*, 'if someone should prevail against one', which is probably influenced by σ' ὑπερισχύσῃ τις ἑνός (this has a similar sense), but Goldman is surely wrong to suggest that *unum*, 'one', renders the suffix in יתקפו and *quispiam*, 'someone', renders האחד, which would be perverse: since they would be no more likely to try to read the suffix as an indefinite subject of the verb, it seems probable that V and σ' also understand an impersonal construction here, and are trying to provide an equivalent to it while at the same time supplying a referent for the suffix on the subsequent נגדו. Joüon, 'Notes philologiques', 420, feels that this suffix on נגדו requires something more precise than האחד, and inserts an attacker by reading תקפו יתקפו (cf. 6.10 for the noun), a suggestion that is picked up by *BHS*, but that seems quite unnecessary.

4.12 stand before him] עמד can sometimes be used of withstanding an assault (e.g. Josh 21.44; Esth 9.2), but in such cases it usually takes לפני or בפני: one stands 'in the face' of an enemy, as Barton noted long ago. נגד is never used in such expressions, and עמד נגד seems to mean 'stand in front of' or 'stand in the presence of' (see Josh 8.33; 1 Kgs 8.22 = 2 Chr 6.12), not 'stand against': it connotes locational opposition or proximity, not antagonism. In some texts, indeed, נגד stands in parallel with עם, to express the idea of being 'with' people (cf. 1 Chr 8.32; 9.38; in a negative sense, Job 10.17), which is perhaps, broadly, the implication of the related כנגד in Gen 2.18, 20. It is interesting to note, conversely, that in Obad 11 עמדך מנגד means 'to stand aloof', 'be disengaged' (cf. Ps 38.12 [ET 38.11], and תתיצב מנגד in 2 Sam 18.13), with the מן making that expression more or less the opposite of standing 'with' someone.[6]

It is much easier, then, to suppose that עמד נגד implies standing up *for* someone, or standing *with* them, than to suppose that Qohelet is talking about standing up *to* someone, and, if only for that reason, we should re-consider the almost universal assumption that Qohelet is talking here of two individuals standing against an aggressor mentioned in the protasis. That assumption is difficult anyway, because if we retain M יִתְקְפוֹ and see the suffix as anticipatory, then the suffix on נגדו would more naturally point, like that suffix, to האחד than to the unnamed and indeterminate subject of the verb, whilst if we vocalize as יִתְקְפוּ (as proposed above, and as I take G to have done), then the referent could only be האחד because the verb would be plural. I take the point not to be that two men can stand up to someone who is very strong, but rather that, if humans work in co-operation with each other, then when one man finds himself confronted by more than he can handle, two others will stand with him, creating an equivalent to the three-plied cord of which Qohelet goes on to speak.

4.12 three-plied] Lit. 'a thread of three' or somesuch: משלש is elsewhere used of animals that are three years old (Gen 15.9; 1 Sam 1.24 emended) and

---

[6] Although נגד clearly retains the implication of being 'in front of', 'before' or 'in line with' in many passages, we may observe that in Ps 16.8, God manages to be both לנגד the psalmist and 'at his right hand', which suggests that this implication can be very weak in some contexts. For מנגד expressing disassociation more literally, see also, e.g., Gen 21.16, where Hagar sits down מנגד her child, so that she does not have to look at him, or 1 Sam 26.20. It often expresses being at a distance sufficient to permit looking on or being seen, but too great to permit involvement, e.g. Deut 32.52; 2 Kgs 2.7, 15; 4.25.

a building with three stories (Ezek 42.6); Aitken, 'Rhetoric and Poetry', 72, suggests that G ἔντριτον, which tries to match this, may be a neologism, and the double translation τετριπλωμένον ἢ τριπλοῦν, 'tripled or triple', of σ' also reflects a certain struggle to render the term (Field suggests that the last two words are a gloss, but Marshall that the double translation may be original). T מגדלא תלת תלת נימין appears to be something plaited from three-plied cords, which strengthens the image, because although a חוט is probably not of any particular thickness, Judg 16.12 implies that it can be broken easily (Samson snaps his ropes 'like a thread [הוט]'), and the image there depends, indeed, on the idea that a single-plied חוט would be very easy to snap.

4.12 readily] In 8.11 Qohelet uses מהרה adverbially, and his use of במהרה instead here probably implies a slightly different nuance: it is not a matter of the speed with which the potential snapper works, so much as of the time that he will take to finish. We should not simply, therefore, regard this as a late equivalent to מהרה (so Barton). σ' οὐκ εὐχερῶς, 'readily' (cf. Hie *non facile*, 'not easily'; V *difficile*; Cannon, 'Jerome and Symmachus', 193), may be trying to make a similar distinction over against G οὐ ταχέως, 'not swiftly'.[7]

---

[7] Although he was purportedly a student of Jerome, Presbyter Philip speaks of the *spartum triplex, quod no(n) cito rumpitur*, 'the threefold rope which is not swiftly broken'—a translation that is much closer to the Greek; see Philippus Presbyter, *In historiam Iob* 181B. There is no adverb cited at all in many early references to the passage (including some by Jerome), suggesting that La texts in circulation read simply 'a threefold cord is not broken', probably as the result of an error either in the source-text or in the transmission of the Latin tradition. Vaccari, 'Recupero', 119, suggests, accordingly, that Philip's reading represents a correction toward the Greek, which he associates with Jerome's revision of La.

4.13-16

(4.13) A poor and wise child is better than an old and foolish king, who still does not know how to take care: (4.14) because one may leave the poor-house to become king; because the other, even in his kingship, was born impoverished.

(4.15) I have seen all the living, those who go about their business beneath the sun, along with the next child who is going to stand in the place of each. (4.16) There is no end to all the people, to everyone who has been before them, and those coming later will take no pleasure in them, because this too is an illusion, and worrying about the wind.

Commentary

These verses have generally been read in one of two ways: (1) separately, with 4.13-14 offering a saying which will perhaps be elaborated or qualified in the observations of 4.15-16, and (2) as a sort of story, in which events described by 4.13-14 form part of a sequence that runs through to 4.16; many of the commentators who take this second approach then identify a reference to specific historical events. My own interpretation is of the first sort, and I understand Qohelet to be picking up once again the issue of succession, in a way that qualifies his enthusiasm for collaboration. In 4.13-14 he uses an illustrative saying to make the point that even someone young and poor may be better than someone old and powerful, when the child is wise and the old man foolish: the one has almost unlimited potential to rise, the other will never be anything but (metaphorically) poor, despite his status.

This saying, which may well have been borrowed, is really about the value of wisdom, but that is not why Qohelet uses it here. Its references to the future potential of each new generation which will replace the last (just as the child may replace the king), instead open the way to Qohelet's own observations in 4.15-16. Here he pretends to see everyone alive who works in the world, along with the child who will succeed them, and the image expands to include the endless generations that have preceded them. Echoing a point that he made much earlier, in 1.11, he claims that future generations will care about none of all these countless people: it is important that we work for others, and it may be important that the potential of each new generation be realized—but this is an endless process in which we are swiftly forgotten. The warning, of course, is that we will all be replaced and displaced; the implication, perhaps, is that we should not view the succession to our own place as in any sense a benefit to us, and that the human rearing of each generation is based on an illusion.

There are various good reasons not to see a narrative here, and not the least of these is that its standard 'Better...than' form surely invites us from the outset to read 4.13 as aphoristic. The considerable complexity of the various narrative readings might also be a strong argument against them, but the text is, to be sure, difficult on any reading. Lavoie ('Ironie en Qohélet 4,13-16', 30-32) enumerates some thirteen different ways in which its message has been understood, and goes on to conclude that the number of distinct issues within it can only be explained as a deliberate strategy by the author, who has consciously provoked his readers to adopt different understandings. I doubt that, but it does seem very likely that exegetes have tried to over-determine these verses, and to find a greater coherence than they were originally intended to possess.

4.13-14] Like Seow and the majority of earlier commentators, I take the two parts of v. 14 each to refer separately to one of the characters introduced by v. 13, and accordingly translate 'the one... the other...' where the Hebrew simply has 'he...he...'. The point is, then, that the wise child, who is poor (in socio-economic terms), may rise from the lowest place in society to become king, while the old king has always been poor (in terms of his ability), despite his royal birth—and that is why he has remained incautious. The saying embodies contrasts between wisdom and folly, youth and old age, and low and high social status, but its principal point seems to be that wisdom offers potential for improvement where folly does not. It is presented as a familiar sort of 'Better...than' saying, a type used already a few verses back in 4.6 and 4.9. The narrative readings popular among modern commentators generally take v. 14 not to refer to each of the characters in turn, but instead to provide a further account either of the child, who is perhaps going to rise despite having been born poor into what will become his kingdom, or of the king, who perhaps managed some similar ascent before becoming foolish. Such understandings are not, of course, impossible (although the latter, in particular, is difficult), but they make v. 14 less effective as an explanation for v. 13's claim that the child is superior—which tends anyway to get rather lost in narrative readings of the passage.

4.15] The Hebrew speaks literally of 'the second child', which probably corresponds to a broader use of 'second' in Hebrew to mean 'next' or 'following', and it says that this child will stand 'in his own place' or, more probably, in the place of his predecessor among the living: the image is of all living people, each accompanied by the young person who will replace them. Those readings that link this verse directly to the last usually take this 'second' instead to be either the child of 4.13 or some new child who is ultimately going to replace that child (although 'second' has also been understood as 'second-in-command'), and the future tense of the verb is then explained in terms of a past prospect: Qohelet saw the child in the past when he had not yet taken over, but was going to do so. None of that is wholly impossible as a reading of the Hebrew, but the awkwardness and unnecessary complexity do suggest that, if a story is being told across vv. 13-16, then it is being told inexplicably badly.

4.16] The text says literally that future generations will find no pleasure in 'it' or 'him', and narrative readings of the passage have tended to take this as a reference back to the 'second child' of the previous verse. It more probably refers, however, to the much closer 'everyone who has been before them': Qohelet is saying that each generation raises the next in an endless succession, but that no generation takes pleasure in its forebears—even implying, perhaps, that they fail to reciprocate the emotional investment made by those forebears (cf. Prov 23.24, where the same expression is used). This is 'vapour', and a frustrating waste of time, at least because it represents an effort that is wholly one-sided, but maybe also, more basically, because Qohelet sees no point in this endless production of new generations—and children are strikingly not listed alongside marriage among the potential sources of pleasure that he will go on to commend in 9.7-10. The link between 'everyone who has been before them' and 'those coming later' is very obvious in Hebrew, which uses contrasting terms for 'before' and 'behind', and narrative readings which take the first expression to mean 'those whom (the king) was ruling' have both to ignore this correspondence and (usually) to demonstrate that 'to be before someone' might mean 'to rule over someone'—which is very uncertain.

Notes

4.13 poor] Ecclesiastes also uses מסכן in 9.15-16, where it refers to a wise man who might stand against a mighty king; it is not found elsewhere in biblical Hebrew (although Gordis would read it in Isa 40.20), but is used widely in Aramaic and in later Hebrew to refer to the poor, which is its sense also in Sir 4.3 and 30.14. In Deut 8.9, the related מסכנת apparently means poverty or scarcity. Dahood, 'Canaanite-Phoenician', 206, observes that it is found as a proper name in Phoenician, which would be odd if it actually existed as a word 'pauper' in that language too, but there would seem to be little reason to question its meaning in this verse.

Seow has claimed, however, that 'the word does not necessarily imply poverty...the issue in our passage is not economics but social status' (183), and Schoors, *The Preacher* II, 444, notes that a similar claim was made earlier by Power (77). This may originally have been true of the Akkadian *muškēnu* from which מסכן is derived, but to insist that it must have preserved this connotation is merely an instance of the etymological fallacy, while the fact that it was probably borrowed by Aramaic independently but with the same sense of 'poor', tends to suggest that its force had changed even in Akkadian.[1] That Ecclesiastes twice contrasts a מסכן with a king does make a reading in terms of social status attractive, but there is no linguistic basis for such a reading.

Pinker, in 'Qohelet 4,13-16', 178-79, has taken a very different path, suggesting that 'poor man' makes no sense in 9.15, and preferring to associate מסכן both here and in that verse with the verb סכן, which is commonly understood to refer to an exposure to danger when it is used in the niph'al at 10.9. We are dealing here, therefore, with a child in danger, to be contrasted with the foolish king who carelessly endangers himself. This is not impossible, but it is speculative and seems unnecessary; certainly none of the ancient versions adopted such an understanding.

4.13 child] Barton and many other commentators note that 1 Kgs 12.8 uses ילד of Rehoboam's contemporaries, even though he, and presumably they, were over forty at the time, according to 1 Kgs 14.21, and were at the very least adults. The translation 'child', correspondingly, has often been

---

[1] The word passed from Aramaic into Arabic, and from there into various other modern languages. In many of these it has retained a reference to poverty or, as in the case of the French *mesquin* or Spanish *mezquino*, to impoverishment of a different sort.

resisted. The use in 1 Kings 12 is unusual, however, and has to be understood in context: these are הילדים אשר גדלו אתו, and the expression obviously connotes something like 'childhood friends'—they are literally 'children who had grown up with him' and in the process ceased to be children. To be sure, a ילד does not have to be an infant, and when Daniel is brought to court with his friends at a point when they are all ילדים endowed with knowledge and competence already, but expected to undergo three more years of education (Dan 1.1-5), it is reasonable to suppose that the boys were in their early teens, or perhaps a little younger; when the seventeen year-old Joseph is described in Gen 37.2, on the other hand, it is using the broader term נער (although his older brothers talk of him as הילד, 'the kid', in 37.30; 42.22). Most of the time, however, ילדים are young children, and it would be odd to use the term of an adult, even quite a young adult, without explanation. Moreover, the very fact of the intended contrast with the king here points to tender years: the king is royal and the ילד poor, the king is foolish and the ילד wise, so it would seem reasonable to suppose that if the king is also old, the ילד must be correspondingly young. G apparently takes the point by translating with παῖς, 'child', as Vinel notes; νεανίσκος, 'youth', will be used in v. 15. Jerome does not attribute the reading *puer pauper*, 'poor boy', to σ' (as Field suggests), but only *pauper*, 'poor' (although it is probable, of course, that *puer* has dropped out or is to be understood).

4.13 still does not know how to take care] The precise implications of לא ידע להזהר עוד are uncertain. In the niphʿal, the verb זהר means to be warned or to be wary (cf. 12.12), and G προσέχειν understands this in terms of paying attention or staying alert. The Three seem to have used forms more strongly suggestive of caution (α' φυλάξασθαι; θ' φυλάσσειν or φυλάξαι? σ' *praecauere uicissitudinem*—Marshall suggests προφυλάξασθαι—all have to do with being 'on one's guard'). Hie and V, on the other hand, both have *providere in posterum*, making foresight the issue.[2]

Although it frequently means 'no longer', לא עוד can mean 'not again' (cf. Gen 6:21; Deut 34:10) or 'still not' (e.g. 1 Kgs 22.44), so whatever it is that the king is failing to do, he may have given up or have ceased to be able to do it, but he may, alternatively, never have been able to do it at all, despite having reached old age. Commentators often conjure up an idea that the king was once able but is now in decline (a reading that depends in part on the next, very difficult verse), but since there is nothing in the text itself to suggest that he was ever anything but a fool, I have taken the contrast to be between one who is wise, despite being young and poor, and one who remains foolish, despite being old and powerful. I also take this to be the reason for the use of

---

[2] The *praeuidere* cited by Cannon, 'Jerome and Symmachus', 193, would make Jerome closer to σ', but is found only as a variant in V, while the *prouidere* of Hie, attested without variants, seems to establish a deliberate distinction from σ'.

לא ידע ל- here: it is not that the king has merely ceased to be careful, but that he has no idea *how* to be careful. A similar expression will be used of fools again shortly, in 4.17, although with a slightly different sense.

T imposes its own story about Abraham and Nimrod, but in that story Nimrod is notably depicted as an old fool who still fails to learn his lesson, even after Abraham has been saved by a miracle. The use of the aorist ἔγνω in G might indicate that that translator also saw a story here, but it is more probably gnomic; α' uses the future γνώσεται, and Hie, V the present, *nescit*.

4.14 because one...because the other] 'One' and 'the other' are not specified explicitly in the Hebrew, which simply has a third-person singular verb in each clause. The two clauses are introduced with כי and כי גם respectively, and the first apparently refers to a humble origin, the second to being born into kingship or a kingdom. They are very commonly taken together as a description either of the youth or, less commonly, of the old king in the previous verse. So, for instance, RSV has 'even though he had gone from prison to the throne or in his own kingdom had been born poor', referring to the king, and Goldman renders 'for he went out of the (womb?) for even in his kingship he was born deprived', while Gordis talks about 'the wise lad of v.13 who is able to supplant the old king in spite of his lowly origin—"from the prison-house he came forth to rule, though he was born poor in his (i.e. the old man's) kingdom"'. Such readings involve, at the very least, the presumption of a back-story, which identifies the youth or the king as having accomplished particular things or having been subject to particular circumstances, so that they are, in effect, qualifications of the previous verse: it is not generally true that a wise youth is better than a foolish king, but true only if that youth has accomplished certain things, or if the king is foolish despite certain things.

This sort of reading, in other words, is difficult to disassociate from attempts to see a historical reference in these verses, rather than to see them as statements of what Qohelet takes to be a general fact. Understandings of כי, and especially of כי גם, are correspondingly geared to understandings of that story—RSV, for instance, has to take both in a concessive sense, and Gordis' rendering effectively discounts the first כי altogether, or treats it as equivalent to אשר. Following this line of interpretation, Torrey, in 'Problem', even feels driven to insert 10.16-17, taking those verses to have been displaced, because the current text offers no account of the youth's rise, or illustration of his wisdom. It is a great deal less convoluted to take the clauses as parallel, with each referring to the youth and to the king respectively, as for instance in Seow's rendering 'for (one) went forth from the prison to reign, while (another), though born into his kingship, is impoverished', or Levy, 'Denn jener "kann" aus dem Gefängnis heraus zur Herrschaft gelangen, während dieser trotz seines Königtums ein arm Geborener ist', 'For that one *may* get out of prison to obtain power, while this one, for all his kingship, is born to penury'. This is the way that T reads the verse, relating the first part to Abraham and the second to Nimrod, and apparently also the understanding behind σ', ὁ μὲν γὰρ ἐκ φυλακῆς ἐξῆλθεν βασιλεῦσαι ὁ δε καίπερ βασιλεὺς γεννηθεὶς ἠπορήθη, 'For the one went out from custody to be king, but the other, though born king, became poor'; cf. V *quis egrediatur...et alius...inopia consumatur*, 'he who goes out...and the other...is consumed by poverty' (Jerome's commentary here includes a Latin version of Symmachus' translation). As Ginsburg suggests, this was for many years the mainstream interpretation of the passage. G and Hie leave both understandings open.

4.14 may leave] M points יֵצֵא qatal, cf. σ' ἐξῆλθεν, 'went out', S, T. However, G ἐξελεύσεται, in the future tense, has apparently vocalized as the yiqtol יֵצֵא, which is how I translate here. The unvocalized text itself, of course, would have been open to both readings, and the reading as yiqtol would have been guided originally, I believe, by the expectation that readers were taking this as an aphorism, not a narrative. Hie, V use the present tense, reflecting just such an understanding, and probably follow the same reading as G.

4.14 poor-house] Lit. 'house of binding', or 'prison'.[3] As Goldman observes, all the ancient versions except T have taken הסורים to be equivalent to הָאֲסוּרִים (cf. Judg 16.21, 25; Jer 37.15), and *BHS* notes that there is some late manuscript support for that reading (although the numbers are not overwhelming: de Rossi speaks with unusual vagueness of 'nonnulli', 'some', manuscripts having that reading, but lists only one; Kennicott lists seven, with two other possibilities, along with some individual variants like האסרים and האס חסורים).[4] The pointing of the article in M presupposes elision of the א (cf. GKC §35 d; Reymond, *Qumran Hebrew*, 85-86),[5] as already noted by Rashi and Rashbam. If this is the proper reading, the meaning is not in doubt, and the expression is found in Aramaic (בית אסירין) as well as Hebrew: as Seow points out, however, citing much evidence, the prison in the ancient world is more typically a place for debtors (and their families, which is why a child might be there) than for criminals, and we are presumably to understand this as an account of very humble origins.

Not all commentators have accepted this reading, however, and T derives from בית הסורים an observation that Abraham came from a family of idolaters, probably linking it with סור and seeing a reference to apostasy. Zimmermann also likes the idea that the background is bad rather than deprived, and draws

---

[3] The distinction is important for Garuti, 'Une Route qui mène', who sees here an echo of the *rex Nemorensis*: to have left the בית הסורים is to have become a fugitive, which qualifies the youth to take up the office by killing the existing holder, until he is killed in his turn by another fugitive.

[4] See also, though, the attestation in Loevy, *Libri Kohelet*, 23.

[5] For the loss of א even at the beginning of a syllable in Qumran texts, Reymond cites, e.g., הרץ for הארץ in 1QpHab XIII, 1 and 4Q79, and, with a reduced vowel following as here, הנשים for האנשים in 1Qsa I, 27; הבנים for האבנים in 1QHª XXIII, 28. He also notes other instances in M: מכלת for מאכלת (1 Kgs 5.25); הרמים for הארמים (2 Chr 22.5); השפות for האספות (Neh 3.13; cf. 3.14).

links with the rebellious connotations of סרי סוררים in Jer 6.28 and of סור in Dan 9.5, 11, and with the uses of forms from Syriac ܐܣܪ *'sr* in connection with conspiracy, to render 'From among conspirators he emerges to be king'. Ewald in 1832 suggested a link here with סורה in Isa 49.21, to give a sense 'house of outcasts', and Hitzig, making a similar connection, offered two translations along the same lines: 'place of fugitives' (in his 1847 commentary, referring to Judg 4.18) and 'place of the estranged' (in his much later 'Zur Exegese', 567, referring to Jer 2.21; 17.13). Ewald's interpretation was picked up by Haupt, who added the observation that 'The Hebrew term *sûrîm* suggests the name of the Syrians, and the idea of apostasy or heathenism', and this link with Syria was pushed further by Schlögl (in 'Qohelet 4, 13-16') who, on the basis of the historical facts that he sees behind the verse, declared (165) that 'In V. 14 richtig zu lesen: *k^emibbêth-hassūrîm*', and rendered 'aus Syriens Königshaus', 'from the royal house of Syria'. Going in a completely different direction, Umbreit translated בית הסורים as 'Dornenbüschen, seiner Wohnung'—'thorn-bushes, his home'—presumably making a connection with הסירים in 7.6.

Others have tried to find a reference to being born, as a parallel to the statement in the second part of the verse. So Dahood, 'Qoheleth and Northwest Semitic Philology', 356-57, takes בית to be a preposition, 'between' (which is very unlikely, cf. Schoors, *The Preacher* I, 121-22), and then implausibly derives סורים from a hypothetical root סרר, taking the whole expression to indicate emergence 'from between the entrails', i.e. birth. Whitley considers Dahood's understanding of בית to be unnecessary, and takes the expression as a whole to indicate the womb, but otherwise interprets along similar lines. Both scholars refer to Rashbam's understanding that this is a reference to birth from the womb, but neither of them observes that Rashbam identifies the בית הסורים *with*, and not *as* the womb. There is a similar double interpretation in Rashi, where הסורים is linked to the 'filth of the womb' by means of the fact that the Targum renders ויבאש, 'putrefied', in Exod 16.20 (cf. 7.21) using וסרי, but this is a symbolic translation, and the literal meaning is still taken to be 'prison'. Rashi is cited by Pinker, 'Qohelet 4,13-16', 180-81, who, appearing to exclude the possibility of orthographic variation, claims that for בית הסורים to be connected with the forms found in Judges 16 and Jeremiah 37, multiple emendations would be required, and who doubts that Qohelet would have used this term anyway to mean 'prison', when there were more familiar ones to hand (he does not discuss possible differences in sense). This leads him to his own emendation of הסורים to סַהֲוֹרָיִם, which he associates with the crescent moon and with the use of סהר in Ct 7.3, and takes to mean 'two crescents'; the 'house of two crescents' would then be the pudenda. It need hardly be said that this is highly speculative, and there is little force in the arguments that he advances for rejecting the sense 'prison' (which does not, strictly, require any emendation at all).

4.14 to become king] The infinitive construct לִמְלֹךְ in M is supported by G, σ' βασιλεῦσαι, S, and probably T. Hie *egreditur in regem*, 'comes out into kingship', and V *egrediatur ad regnum*, 'may come out to a kingdom', are paraphrases, and do not suggest that Jerome read a noun here (cf., e.g. V at 1 Kgs 2.15). Since M makes perfectly good sense as it stands, and has clearly been taken as the natural reading by the versions, alternative readings have generally been driven not by necessity so much as by a desire to make the text fit suppositions about what is going on in the verse as a whole. So, reading the clause as a reference to the king being born, Dahood, 'Qoheleth and Northwest Semitic Philology', 357, followed by Whitley, reads לְמֶלֶךְ, the noun 'king' with an emphatic -ל to give 'even the king went forth' (Whitley 'a king'). Ogden, adopting a very old understanding of the text as a reference to the story of Joseph in 'Historical Allusion', 312-13, connects it to the Aramaic root מלך with the sense 'counsel', and Rudman (followed by Miller), while noting the improbability of that connection, tries in 'Contextual Reading', 64-66, to accomplish much the same by reading לַמֶּלֶךְ, 'to the king', so that both have the youth emerge to act as a royal counsellor. Galling, in 'Kohelet-Studien', 296 n. 1 (and in the 1940 edition of his commentary), simply emends arbitrarily to למלכות, 'to the kingship'.

4.14 even] Or possibly 'also because...'. The combination כי גם does not seem to have any single specific sense beyond those one might expect for גם + כי, and (*contra* Gordis, commenting on 8.12) is not equivalent in Qohelet's usage to גם כי, which often has concessive force. The two words are clearly separable in 4.16, where Qohelet's familiar refrain with גם זה הבל is introduced by כי, and it is questionable whether they ever strictly form a 'composite conjunction', as Schoors describes the combination (*The Preacher* I, 135—he reviews the usage in Ecclesiastes on 134-36; cf. also Fox on 8.12). A concessive force, therefore, is not excluded here but it is not required, and I take the כי to stand in parallel with the preceding כי (see the note, above), while גם is either emphatic or additive, marking the fact that this is a second explanation. σ' καίπερ, 'although', is, in fact, concessive, but in ὁ δε καίπερ βασιλεὺς γεννηθεὶς ἠπορήθη (see above) it qualifies βασιλεὺς γεννηθεὶς, not the clause as a whole: 'he was impoverished despite having been born king', not 'despite having been born poor in his kingdom'.

4.14 in] The suggestion of *BHS*, that we should perhaps emend -ב to -ל, has no versional support, and, given the usual biblical usage of -ל with נולד (e.g. Gen 4.18), would most naturally impute paternity (this, rather than location, is the probable meaning even in 1 Chr 26.6). במלכות has a range of possible meanings, which include the temporal (e.g. Ezra 7.1; 8.1, 'in the reign of': cf. 2 Chr 29.19, and in Aramaic Dan 6.29 [ET 6.28]) and physical (e.g. Ezra 7.13; Dan 11.9), but may extend to supporting David 'in his rule' (1 Chr 11.10), or to the failure of former leaders to serve God 'in their rule' (Neh 9.35).

4.14 his kingship] מלכות can be used, especially in late texts, of the territory ruled by a king, or of those people and things that constitute the kingdom (cf. Esth 1.14, 20 for both those senses; and see Hurvitz, *Concise Lexicon*, 165-70, which understands such a meaning here). Its primary reference, however, is to the kingship itself (e.g. 1 Kgs 2.12), or to royal status (e.g. Esth 1.19; Dan 11.21): this is unlikely to be, therefore, a reference simply to the youth having been born in the old king's realm (as Gordis suggests). The third-person suffix most naturally refers, in any case, to the subject of the clause, and so its antecedent is understood variously by scholars according to their theories about the verse as a whole.

4.14 was born] After using a future tense in the first part of the verse, G ἐγεννήθη now matches the past tense of M, with the other versions. It does not really matter that the king is unlikely to have been a king at birth, the point is that he is born into kingship or royalty (and passages like Esth 1.11; 1.19; 2.17 show that the notion of 'royalty' may extend to other members of the royal family). For scholars who see a depiction of the king's senescence here, however, it is a problem that the king's 'poverty' is from birth, and a number of older commentators took the verb to have here the sense 'become', rather than 'be born', enabling an understanding that the king's situation has declined. T איתעבד...מסכינא, '(when Abraham was king, Nimrud) became poor', suggests such an understanding, and Rashi cites Job 11.12 in support of that interpretation, understanding it to mean that the offspring of the wild ass will 'turn into' a man. It is also defended by some nineteenth-century commentators: Ginsburg, following Herzfeld, compared the two senses 'be born' and 'become' of the Greek verb γίνομαι and Graetz, 182-83, suggested that the verb could have that meaning in later Hebrew, probably under the influence of Greek usage. That suggestion is questionable: in *m. Nedarim* 9.2, פותחין בנולד does indeed mean that release from a vow may be possible (according to R. Eliezer) in the light of unforeseen circumstances; the passage is not talking about 'developments', however, but about a situation coming into existence that was not there before (hence the language of birth). In *m. Temurah* 3.5, על פי שנולדה להם מום similarly refers to a blemish coming into being (cf. Gordis).[6] It was not unreasonable for Tyler, who is misleadingly lumped together with Ginsburg and Graetz in Barton's discussion of the passage, to use both these passages to justify his translation in terms of poverty 'arising'; they do not, however, support the idea that the niphʿal of ילד ever meant 'become', or 'change from one state to another'.

---

[6] Gordis' account of the scholarship around this question has to be treated with caution, though, and is uncharacteristically confusing: he attributes an argument to Ginsburg and a translation to Levy which are difficult to locate in the work of each.

Galling, 'Kohelet-Studien', 296 n. 1 (and in the 1940 edition of his commentary), reads the verb as a participle, to support an idea that Qohelet is saying here that even someone born poor can rise to the kingship.

4.14 impoverished] רש is usually taken to be a participle from רוש, serving as an adjective or substantive: most of its occurrences are in Proverbs, and it often stands in contrast to עשיר (e.g. Prov 14.20). Qohelet may have used it here, instead of simply repeating מסכן from the previous verse, because it has an implication of positive need or of impoverishment (cf. Prov 10.4; 19.7; 22.7; 28.7; and the use of the verb at Ps 34.11 [ET 34.10]), and this is picked up in σ' ἠπορήθη, 'was impoverished', which renders רש as a verb and is imitated in V *inopia consumatur* (cf. Cannon, 'Jerome and Symmachus', 193). Probably in order to strengthen the link with that previous verse, however, rather than because they have read a variant, G uses πένης, as before, while S repeats ܡܣܟܝܢ *mskyn* and T has מסכינא.

The variation in M is used as the basis for Schunck's proposal (in 'Drei Seleukiden', 195-96) that we should in fact read ראש, 'head (of a family)', here: he doubts that Qohelet would have used different terms in this verse and the last, and notes that רש is, in fact, spelled ראש on a number of occasions (e.g. 2 Sam 12.1, 4). The only reason to adopt that reading, however, is to make the text fit better Schunck's own theories about historical allusion in these verses. A less drastic alteration has been proposed by Seow, who wants to parse רש as the qatal of the verb, rather than the participle, and read 'while (another), though born into his kingship, is impoverished'. Although Seow himself does not note the fact, this is identical to the reading of σ', and close to that of V. It involves ignoring the Masoretic accents, to be sure, but facilitates Seow's interpretation, in which the king has declined into folly, rather than been born that way, so that we have parallel reversals of fortune in each half of the verse. The principal objections to be raised against it are that finite forms of the verb are very rare (Ps 34.11 [ET 34.10] is the only example in the qal usually recognized), so readers would have been more likely to take this as a noun or adjective (as did most of the versions), and that there is no reason to suppose that the verb could mean '*become* impoverished': without that nuance of change, reading רש as a verb makes no significant difference to the sense.

Probably the most distinctive modern reading of the passage, however, involves no emendation or unusual parsing: Fox (whose position in his 1999 commentary was previewed in 'What Happens?') takes רש as a noun, but sees no reference to the king's past, or to the poverty of the youth who has already been mentioned: this is a new, third individual, born poor in the reign of that youth, after the youth had succeeded the old king; in the next verse we will be introduced to yet another youth, so Qohelet is establishing a sequence. This requires taking כי as equivalent to a simple conjunction -ו (Fox translates 'while'), and although Qohelet often uses that particle in mysterious ways, its appearance here would be positively misleading if it were his original intention to add a new character. It also has to be taken as implicit both that the previous youth had replaced the old king, rather than ascended a different throne of his own, and that the new poor man is either going to become king himself, or at least possesses the wisdom to do so.

4.15 I have seen] Herzfeld argued long ago that Qohelet is not simply declaring himself to have seen both the living and the second child, but stating that he saw the living to be associated with that child—'I saw that the living were with the second', in other words, rather than 'I saw the living along with the second'. Such a reading underpins many subsequent interpretations, including Gordis' vivid claim that 'The verse describes how all men flock to the youth's banner', and although it is often simply presumed, Fox has more recently made much the same case for it as did Herzfeld. The issue is far from clear cut, however, and boils down to whether Qohelet is 'seeing' or 'seeing that': the verb does not require a predicate, but if it has one, then it should be עם הילד השני. Of course, in some of the places where Qohelet claims to have seen something, it is no less difficult than here to determine whether he is 'seeing' or 'seeing that', but we may note that in 1.14, where the predicate similarly stands at some distance from ראיתי, Qohelet introduces it with הנה, and that he uses a clause with כי in 2.24; 3.22; 4.4; 8.17. More importantly, it seems far more typical of Qohelet's style to state simply that he has seen a thing or things (cf. 2.13; 3.10, 16; 4.1; 5.12; 6.1; 7.15; 8.10; 9.13), and then to extrapolate his point separately. The verse certainly *implies* that the living and the child were together, but I doubt it is the purpose of the verse to *state* that. On the temporal reference here, see the note on 'is going to stand', below.

4.15 all the living, those who go about their business] Lit. 'all the living, the moving'. את כל החיים and המהלכים stand in apposition, and the expression may be understood as an asyndetic relative clause: the article on המהלכים (reinforced by the accents in M) prevents us from reading this as a statement simply that Qohelet saw the living going about with the child. G σὺν πάντας τοὺς ζῶντας τοὺς περιπατοῦντας reproduces the Hebrew verbatim, but thereby creates a relative clause in Greek, 'all the living who walk around', and relative pronouns are introduced explicitly by S, T, Hie, and V; Jerome reports the reading of σ' as *omnes uiuentes qui gradiuntur*, 'all the living who walk about', from which it is difficult to tell whether the original Greek would have had an explicit relative pronoun. The pi'el of הלך can have a specific reference to walking or travelling (e.g. Ps 85.14 [ET 85.13]; Prov 6.28), but it frequently refers to more general movement (e.g. Ps 104.26) or to the to-ing and fro-ing of everyday life (e.g. Job 24.10; 30.28), and Qohelet is not trying to conjure up an image of everybody on their feet or in motion.

4.15 beneath the sun] Galling, 'Kohelet-Studien', 296 n. 1, would move תחת השמש and use it to replace תחתיו at the end of the verse: the successor takes the place of 'the sun', because solar references are part of the Ptolemaic royal titulary. This would be marginally less implausible if 'under the sun' were not such a regular expression elsewhere in the book.

4.15 along with] Fox points to a number of passages in which 'Being "with" (ʿim) someone indicates alliance and support', in order to suggest that the verse refers to the loyalty of the population. He does not note that T, in fact, seems to adopt that understanding, albeit buried within an interpretation of the verse as an account of Jeroboam's rebellion. Although it has also been suggested by Ginsburg, Barton and many others, this is not, however, a natural reading of the expression. It is true that people want God to be 'with them', although in passages like Gen 26.3 and 1 Kgs 8.57, עם may be used because that idea embraces physical proximity as much as it does support. The only passages that Fox cites, however, in which it is a matter of humans being on the side of other humans (2 Kgs 6.16; 9.32), use את, not עם, and in Ps 94.16, indeed, עם marks the enemies against whom the psalmist seeks support. The scope of the word itself aside, of course, such readings have to deal with the issue that Qohelet would very explicitly not then be talking about the loyalty of a particular population to a ruler, but of the whole of humanity.

Other very specific understandings have been proposed. Ewald, for instance, understood עם as comparative, so that Qohelet looks at all the living 'in comparison with' the child, and this reading was expounded a little later by Heiligstedt also. It runs into the difficulty that the interpretation both scholars offer requires not that the living be compared with the child, but that the child be compared with the living. Weisman, much more recently, has suggested in 'Political Satire' that the preposition should actually be understood to mean 'like', in order to achieve a different sort of comparison: 'for even in his own kingdom he became poor…like the second youth who was to stand in his place' (552). In many of the cases cited for that sense of עם (e.g. 2.16; cf. Gen 18.23) it really retains its usual meaning 'along with', and there are very few places where it is actually used to draw an analogy: even in what might seem to be the clearest example, Job 9.26a, the image is probably of a river 'with' boats on it, marking the speed at which it flows (when an actual simile follows in 26b, -כ is used). The principal obstacle to Weisman's suggestion, however, is that it involves an otherwise unwarranted transposition of vv. 15a and 15b, for which there is no versional support or text-critical justification.

4.15 the next child] Lit. 'the second child'. M הילד השני uses the same noun ילד as was used in v. 13, so it is striking that G uses νεανίσκος here, after using παῖς there. Hie, V similarly have *adolescens* instead of *puer* (and that variation probably existed originally in the account that Jerome gives of σ' at 4.13), while S has ܥܠܝܡܐ ʿlymʾ in place of ܛܠܝܐ ṭlyʾ. As previously, when M varied the terms referring to poverty in vv. 13 and 14 but the other versions did not (see the note above on 4.14, 'impoverished'), this may represent an attempt to clarify the text in terms of a particular interpretation. More significant problems surround השני, literally 'the second', which many commentators have found difficult, because it seems to add a further character to the existing child and king of the preceding verses.

If the 'second youth' here actually means 'the second just mentioned, the youth rather than the king' then the expression is the wrong way round, as Hitzig acknowledged long ago: we would expect השני הילד. Gordis tries to find a way round this by turning the apposition into essentially a relative construction, citing Hos 2.9 to justify a rendering as 'the lad, who was second'—an argument that would be stronger were he not to have first to argue for a similar sense in Hosea, and were the usage of שני not so common and well established. Fox's understanding of the text is not constrained by the need to find an allusion to one of the previous characters, but is awkward because this is, on his reckoning, the third and not the second youth: 'Youth[3] is "second" to the previously mentioned one (youth[2]) but third in the sequence'. If that were really the case, then the use of השני here would have to be deemed almost deliberately confusing.

A number of scholars have responded to the difficulty simply by emending the text: Ehrlich, for example, would remove השני as meaningless or nonsensical, and BH^3 suggests that it should possibly be deleted or emended to העני (Galling 1940 and 1969, contrarily, deletes הילד); Irwin, in 'Ecclesiastes 4:13-16', 256 n. 3, is similarly inclined to regard it as spurious, and draws attention to George Dahl's suggestion about a potentially comparable marginal note having been drawn into the text of Joshua ('The "Three Heights" of Joshua 17.11'). Podechard does not delete it, but moves it to v. 10 before קים, believing it to have been omitted then restored in the wrong position, and Whitley would move the whole of 15b, claiming that originally it probably 'stood in close proximity to השנים יעמדו נגדו (v. 12) or else is a disconnected passage from a proverbial source relating to the same theme'. Rather differently, Gordis cites (without reference) the opinion of H. Hirschberg, that השני should be emended to השבי, 'the captive lad'.

Finally, a number of commentators have sought to find a different sense for השני. Levy, most improbably, and ignoring both the meaning of ילד and the rules regarding definite articles in construct relationships, translates as 'the son of the second' ('der Sohn des zweiten'): the reference, in other words, is to Ptolemy III Euergetes, who was the son of Ptolemy 'the Second' Philadelphus. Ginsburg, no more plausibly, reaches back to vv. 8-10 and translates 'sociable', which makes no sense here. In pursuit of his Aramaic theory, Zimmermann ('Aramaic Provenance', 34) argued that the word reflects a failure to understand the secondary sense of Aramaic תנינא, a term that can mean not just 'second' but 'second-in-command'— although he goes on to translate 'crown prince', which seems a stretch away from that sense. Reaching a similar conclusion by a different route, Nachtigal in 1798 talked of הילד 'deputizing' (*Stellvertretend*) for the king, and Ewald similarly, in the 1867 edition of his commentary, argued for an equivalence with המשנה in Gen 41.43, indicating a 'deputy' (*Stellvertreter*) of the king. More recent champions of the idea include Hertzberg, who translates 'dem Zweiten (im Staate)'. Even allowing that השני might have that sense in biblical Hebrew, however, which is quite unproven, it is difficult to make sense of these suggestions in context, whether or not one associates this verse with the immediately preceding verses: there is no reason to suppose that Qohelet has any concern with someone occupying the second slot, and they merely introduce an additional complication.

It is undoubtedly true, however, that the sense of שני often extends beyond the simply numerical: it is used very commonly in expressions of time to mark a succeeding period (e.g. 'the next day', Exod 2.13; 'the following year', Gen 47.18), not one that is strictly 'second' on some scale. Throughout Nehemiah 3, moreover, מדה שנית is 'a further section' of repairs to the wall (cf. vv. 11, 19, 20, 21, 24, 27): each cannot strictly be a 'second repair.' In 2 Sam 16.19, והשנית is used to introduce an additional argument, and in Mal 2.13 זאת שנית is an additional crime. The idea of 'second' has not altogether disappeared in such usage—which means that Fox's adoption of the sense 'next' here does not entirely let him off the hook—but the primary connotation is of one thing following another.[7] It seems best, therefore, to understand this as a reference to the child as one who has succeeded or will succeed another, as does Seow ('the next youngster'; cf. Ellermeier, *Qohelet I.1*, 222), and this has the virtue of simplicity, as well as providing a good fit to context.

4.15 is going to stand] I translate as a future, with G, Hie, T. When Qohelet says ראיתי at the head of the verse, I take him to be making a general statement that he has observed something which is essentially timeless: the current generation accompanied by the next, both standing in an endless succession of generations, as v. 16 will suggest. Among the commentators who do not seek a specific link to the previous verses, Seow, for example, speaks of the verb being frequentative or habitual, and it is possible that it should be understood in this way, rather than simply as a future (cf. perhaps V *consurgit*, although *consurget* [as Hie] is strongly attested as a variant).

If the verse is read instead as a more specific continuation of vv. 13-14, however, and הילד השני taken to be a child in a particular line of succession, then it becomes more important to specify the temporal reference here, and for those many commentators who identify the child here with the child mentioned in v. 13, and see a reference to him taking over from the old king, the form of יעמד poses a particular constraint, because the yiqtol does not naturally refer to the past (despite σ' *surrexit*). It is common for the verse to be read, therefore, as a statement that Qohelet saw the youth 'who was to stand in his place' at a point before he actually took over. This is potentially less of a problem for those who see the succession of a third character, but McNeile, 11, asserts similarly that Qohelet is putting himself back in the past to a point

---

[7] The word does not mean 'other' or 'the other' in a more general way, however, and this is the most obvious weakness in the suggestion by Bühlmann, 'Thinking in Greek', 105-106, that Qohelet is trying to get across a reference that he would have been able to convey in Greek by ὁ νέος ὁ ἕτερος.

where another youth was 'about to oust' the poor and wise one. Such uses of the yiqtol can sometimes be found (cf. GKC §107 k; J-M §113 b; 2 Kgs 3.27 ויקח את בנו הבכור אשר ימלך תחתיו, 'and he took his eldest son who was to reign in his place', provides an interesting analogy). When, however, Schoors, *The Preacher* I, 177, says that 'the imperfect יעמד expresses posteriority, referring to a situation which was future in the past', it is important to be clear that this is a function of the yiqtol within a subordinate clause: it does not have a general prospective aspect outside such clauses, and so the same analogies cannot be found for 4.16 ישמחו, which both McNeile and Schoors would like to read in the same way, as parallel to each other. Schoors does acknowledge that ישמחו could alternatively be understood as a durative past, which is perhaps the only reasonable way of understanding why Qohelet should have adopted such a complicated device: he puts himself in the past in order to claim that he had seen the subsequent reaction for himself. That still does not explain, however, why he should so unnecessarily in this current verse have set himself back prior to the transition from king or first youth to the next youth.

As for the meaning, the verb עמד can sometimes be used of serving in a position (e.g. Neh 12.4), but, *contra* Seow, is not used specifically of taking office: of the examples that he cites, Ezra 2.63 refers to priests being in post, and 10.14 to officials 'standing in for' the people as a whole, while the other examples offered in Schoors, *The Preacher* II, 318, do similarly little to establish a late equivalence between עמד and קום. Even though תחתיו is frequently used in combination with מלך of somebody succeeding to the kingship, there is no reason to suppose that the expression we have here itself carries any connotation more specific than occupying a place or position.

4.15 in the place of each] Or 'in his own place'. In Judg 7.21, ויעמדו איש תחתיו refers to each man holding his own position during a battle, and to die תחתיו is to die where one stands (2 Sam 2.23; Job 40.12; Isa 25.10; Jer 38.9). Although it is very commonly used of substitution or replacement, therefore, תחת by no means always has this sense, and it would not be difficult to justify a translation 'who will hold his ground' (cf. 4.12), if that made any sense in this context. Ogden, indeed, takes it simply to be a reference to the child standing beneath the sun ('under it'), along with all the living, a view that is made implausible by the form of יעמד (which we should expect to find as a participle if it is supposed to match and contrast with המהלכים), but is not linguistically untenable. At the very least, it is important to emphasize that although the implications of אשר יעמד תחתיו are often taken for granted, they should not be considered so clear cut that they drive interpretation of the verse or section as a whole.

The difficulties are not confined to the sense of תחת itself, moreover. For commentators who see a reference to one youth succeeding another, or succeeding the old king, the pronoun on תחתיו has to refer back to the last mention of the individual who will be replaced, in v. 13 or 14—which makes it rather vague, of course, and positively ambiguous if v. 14 is talking about them both. It is the lack of clarity here, indeed, that has made it difficult to argue the case decisively for any one such interpretation over another. Given the distance and the difficulties, I prefer a closer antecedent, and take the singular pronoun here to be distributive (GKC §145 l, m; cf. van der Palm, 145)—Qohelet is talking about the child who will succeed to take the place of each person currently alive. I think it is also possible, though, especially in the light of the examples above, that the antecedent is to be found in הילד itself, and that Qohelet sees with each of the living the child who will go on to find their own place in the world. The overall significance is similar either way.

4.16 people] Qohelet uses עם only here, although it also appears in the epilogue at 12.9. The term is very frequently used to designate particular peoples or groups of people, and though it can mean 'people' in a more general sense (e.g. Gen 50.20), the reference is more specific than the 'living' of the previous verse. Van der Palm suggested in 1784 that the noun should be emended to עמל and then serve as the antecedent to the pronoun in ישמחו בו, which would give a very different reference to work: this is not unattractive, but entirely conjectural. Graetz adopted this suggestion, but with a redivision of the consonants rather than an emendation, so as to read כל עמל rather than עם לכל, and Allgeier, perhaps independently, was later to suggest the same division.

4.16 to everyone who has been before them] As observed by, e.g., Gordis and Whitley, it seems difficult to resist seeing a connection between לפניהם and the subsequent האחרונים, which convey contrasting implications of 'before' and 'behind, after'. This is especially true when היה לפני commonly denotes something that has happened previously (cf. 1.16; Deut 4.32; 1 Kgs 3.12; 14.9; 16.33; 2 Kgs 17.2; 18.5; 23.25; 1 Chr 17.13; Jer 28.8; 34.5). Since ancient times, however, many translators and commentators have been inclined to take the two expressions separately, as references respectively to all those who serve the second child of the previous verse, and to those generations who will follow. Without emendation, this has to involve understanding כל אשר היה לפניהם to mean 'everyone whom he was before', with the new ruler or ruler-to-be, and not כל אשר, as subject of היה—which is a little clumsy without the subject explicitly stated, but not impossible. G τοῖς πᾶσιν ὅσοι ἐγένοντο, however, has taken כל אשר as the subject, and all the ancient versions except T have a plural verb here; S enforces the point with لكلهون *lklhwn*, 'to all of them'. Goldman (at 1.10) takes this to be translational, and although there is no good reason to exclude the possibility either that they have read היו, or that the plural was original, it is possible that the plural has been inspired by the awkwardness of reading a singular form governed by אין קץ. It is interesting to observe in this context that V translates לפניהם with the singular *ante eum* (contrast Hie *ante illos*), and that this reading also appears as a secondary development in manuscripts of G, which have αὐτοῦ for αὐτῶν; this may be why S likewise has ܩܕܡܘܗܝ *qdmwhy*, although Kamenetzky, 216, puts that down to the influence of the subsequent ܒܗ *bh*.

There is, then, a clear interpretative pressure in the tradition to make an association with the ruler, but this is manifested in the treatment of the pronoun, rather than the verb. Zimmermann achieves the reference to rule by proposing ('Aramaic Provenance', 34-35) that an original Aramaic text דְּהוּא was read as דַּהֲוָא, so that the text should clearly have indicated that *he* (was) before them. More radically, Dahood, 'Qoheleth and Northwest Semitic Philology', 357, reads 'to all that were before me' *via* a Phoenician text in which הלפניהם has been parsed to give that sense. Both of these are highly conjectural, and Zimmermann's idea works only if his (highly problematic) overall theory of a translation from Aramaic is correct, whilst Dahood's suggestion, whatever its merits in Phoenician, is surely impossible when transferred to Hebrew.

In any case, if we accept M היה לפניהם as original, it is then necessary to address the problem that 'everyone whom he was before' would seem more naturally to indicate that the ruler was serving them, than that they were serving him (see, e.g., Num 16.16, and especially 1 Sam 29.8). It is not clear what David is doing in 1 Sam 18.16, often cited in support of this reading, when he 'comes and goes' לפני Israel and Judah, but it has to do with his achievement of popularity before he became king, and cannot imply that he stood before them as ruler (which must be used to qualify the sense of the similar expression in 2 Chr 1.10). Of course, God is acting like a ruler of the people when he is 'before them' in Ps 68.8 (ET 68.7), leading them through the wilderness, and we expect rulers to be in front of their subjects in certain circumstances, but servants can just as easily be in front of their masters, as in 2 Sam 19.18 (ET 19.17): this is just a matter of context, not of implicit connotation. So far as we can tell in Hebrew idiom, however, simply to be לפני someone indicates that you are serving them, not ruling them (as van der Palm, 81, pointed out, long ago). On top of the awkwardness of expression and the text-critical questions that surround it, therefore, the understanding of this verse as a reference to the king's rule over his followers has to contend with the difficulty that 'everyone whom he was before' cannot easily be shown to mean 'everyone whom he ruled', and could at the very least certainly be understood to mean 'everyone whom he served'. There is no way to make כל אשר היה לפניהם straightforwardly or clearly mean 'all whom he ruled', and it is far less problematic to read a temporal statement here: 'all who were previous to them', although the Hebrew also permits a more physical representation of this, in terms of a line stretching before and behind. In an attempt to hang on to a connection with the preceding whilst adopting such a reading, Gordis makes 'them' refer to the characters of v. 13, but the more likely antecedent is the much closer כל עם.

4.16 and] M גם here is difficult to translate, but perhaps a little stronger than a simple conjunction like the *et* of V—contrast Hie *et quidem*, reflecting the formulaic G καί γε. Whether, however, one sees it as additive, emphatic, concessive (Seow), or adversative (cf. Schoors, *The Preacher* I, 131), depends on one's construction and interpretation of the verse as a whole. Especially in the absence of an actual conjunction, I take it to be aligning the statement about the endlessness of those who came before with that about those who will follow,[8] whilst also making clear that there is going to be a new point raised in the second, so 'and, further' might do.

4.16 those coming later] Qohelet has already used אחרנים in a similar context at 1.11, of the later things or people of which there will be no subsequent memory, and אחרון is commonly used as an adjective with a temporal sense, e.g., Ps 78.4; Isa 30.8.

4.16 will take no pleasure in them, because] Lit. 'not...in him' or 'not... in it'. For the tense of the verb, see the note at 4.15 on 'is going to stand'. Most commentators see a reference in the pronoun to הילד השני of the previous verse: on the 'ruler' reading of these verses, Qohelet is saying that future generations will find no joy in the ruler who currently attracts so much support. It is not clear why 'joy' in a ruler should be an issue, since even the strongest readings of these verses in such terms have only so far had people align themselves with the ruler, or be on his side, and the expression itself does not mean 'remember fondly'. The association with הילד השני would be possible, of course, even without the rest of that interpretation, making this more purely a statement that people will take no pleasure in a previous generation, but it is still difficult for two reasons. The first is simply distance: a number of potential antecedents have been introduced in this verse (כל אשר היה כל העם, קץ), and it seems difficult to reach back to the child of the previous verse when his presence has not explicitly been marked in this one. The second is that this is the only occasion on which Qohelet precedes his familiar statement גם זה הבל with כי (contrast 2.19, 21, 23, 26; 4.4, 8; 5.9; 6.9; 8.10), and, even if we try to write off that כי as emphatic (so, e.g., Seow), it seems difficult to ignore the fact that גם זה הבל is thereby presented as though it were an explanation for the previous clause.

Whitley, interestingly, takes קץ as the antecedent (he has deleted 15b), although his interpretation suggests that he actually takes the reference to be to the whole idea embodied by אין קץ: 'there is no end...to such numbers, but as this is a feature common to all ages, future generations will see nothing in it at which to rejoice'. I take the pronoun most probably to refer to the closest potential antecedent, כל אשר היה לפניהם (or possibly to כל העם if the original reading was היו), and the point to be that those who come later will find no joy in any who preceded them. Qohelet has used שמח with -ב in 3.22 of taking pleasure in what one has accomplished, and will use it similarly in 5.18 of business (cf. Deut 12.7; 26.11); in 11.8-9, he also speaks of taking pleasure in

---

[8] Cf. Garuti, 'Une Route qui mène', 113: 'le גם non précédé d'une conjonction fait penser à une situation semblable pour les deux groupes', 'the גם without a preceding conjunction leads one to think of a comparable situation for both groups'.

all one's years and in one's youth, but the expression with -בּ may be temporal there (cf. Ps 90.14) and the finding of pleasure more general. It is not an expression confined to the pleasure that can be found in states or actions, however, and it is used by other writers frequently of taking pleasure in God (e.g. Ps 149.2; Joel 2.23), and sometimes of pleasure in people (e.g. Judg 9.19, with ironic exaggeration—'I wish you joy in each other!'; Ct 1.4). The most apposite example is surely Prov 23.24, which speaks of the joy that will be taken by a father in his son, if that son is righteous or wise: for the writer of that saying, at least, this is an emotion to be provoked by one's children.

4.16 worrying] Despite the scope for confusion, and the treatment of the phrase in the other ancient versions (see the note on 'wishing for the wind at 1.14), the Hebrew manuscripts generally maintain the distinction between רעיון and the more common רעות, so it is noteworthy that a number read the latter here; see Miletto.

Introduction to 4.17–5.6 (ET 5.1-7)

Speaking to God

(4.17, ET 5.1) Watch your step, when you go to the house of God, and draw near to listen. A sacrifice is what fools pay, for they have no idea when they'll do what is wrong. (5.1, ET 5.2) Don't run off at the mouth, and don't let your heart be in a hurry to say something in front of God, for God is in heaven and you are on earth. So then, let your words be few. (5.2, ET 5.3) For a dream comes with a lot of worrying, and a fool's voice with a lot of words.

(5.3, ET 5.4) When you vow a vow to God, don't be slow to fulfil it, as nobody has any use for fools—you should fulfil what you vow. (5.4, ET 5.5) It is better that you should not vow, than that you should vow and not fulfil. (5.5, ET 5.6) Don't let your mouth get your body into trouble, and don't say before you have kept your word that it was not meant: why should God be angry with your voice, but ruin what you have achieved with your hands? (5.6, ET 5.7) For when there is a mass of empty dreams and words aplenty, then fear God!

The chapter and verse numbers used conventionally for modern Hebrew and English bibles are out of step here, with the Hebrew taking what is the first verse of ch. 5 in English bibles as the last verse of ch. 4; the English verse numbers for ch. 5 are consequently always one more than the Hebrew verse numbers. See the Introduction, p. 185, above.

After his discussion of relationships between humans, Qohelet turns more briefly to the question of how we should behave before God—not in terms of general ethical or moral behaviour, but in the specific contexts of temple sacrifices and vows, and with a particular concern about speech in these contexts. This embraces issues that might confront anybody in the ancient world, and although there is a probable reference to Deuteronomy in his advice about vows, the questions considered here are not specifically Jewish concerns. The fact that sacrifices and vows recur in 9.2, however, albeit using slightly different terms, does suggest that they might have been of particular interest to the author or his original readers. That verse, which reiterates Qohelet's point that everybody comes to the same end, includes a long list of contrasting pairs—the righteous and the wicked, the good and the bad, and so on—but among the otherwise very general categories, he singles out those who sacrifice and those who do not alongside those who take oaths and those who fear them.

Whatever the common fate of such individuals, however, Qohelet here makes it clear that he regards such activities as potentially dangerous: when one enters the temple, it is best to say as little as possible. If one might be tempted to blurt something out before God, then one should bear in mind that he is not actually there and present, but far away in heaven: blabbering away is what fools do, and it is also fools whose inability to judge their own behaviour compels them to compensate for it with sacrifices. In Deut 23.22-24 (ET 23.21-23), with which this passage is often linked, it is made clear that vows are entirely optional, and his general advice about speech before God suggests that Qohelet would not recommend making them even if one is going to fulfil them (cf. 5.4). If someone has done so, however, then it becomes imperative for them to fulfil the vow as soon as possible, in order to avoid God's anger. In all, therefore, interacting with God in such ways is a hazardous and unnecessary business.

Such advice raises some interesting questions about Qohelet's religious ideas: the God who might react angrily to a broken vow, after all, seems very different from the God elsewhere in the book who governs human actions in accordance with his own plans (which leads Michel, *Untersuchungen*, 257, to dismiss 5.5 as an orthodox gloss). As in his discussions of divine judgment, Qohelet betrays here some of the tensions and contradictions that exist in his own thought (and perhaps much more widely in much ancient and modern religious thought), where notions of determinism would seem to limit both the scope for human influence on God, and the usefulness of advice. For Qohelet himself, however, the main issue is the power of words to cause trouble in this context, and to undo anything that one has accomplished. In the frenetic atmosphere of a temple packed with dreamers and talkers, it is important to be calm and quiet. If one is persuaded, all the same, of the need to make a vow, then it has to be fulfilled immediately. It is in the midst of so much talking and dreaming that there is the greatest potential for danger, and so when Qohelet concludes by warning that it is in just such an atmosphere that one should 'fear God', the familiar language of piety is charged with a reminder that God genuinely is to be feared.

Some commentators have seen a poetic construction within or across this section, although their specifications of its structure rarely coincide with each other: in 'Die Struktuur', 260-62, Spangenberg (who helpfully tabulates various of the opinions that have been put forward) is probably right to see it more in terms of a prose that is sometimes rhythmic, and that is a way in which much of the material in the book could be characterized. Loretz, 'Eiliges Gebet', sees a mixture of poetry and prose. Although we can say quite definitely, therefore, that there is a shift of address in general terms here—Qohelet is suddenly offering direct advice—it is not clear that he is adopting the more consistently poetic style that would associate this advice with instructions or other familiar types of didactic composition. It is correspondingly unhelpful to see what he is saying in terms of discrete units in a series, such as are often found in those works, or to think of the injunctions here as the beginning of separate sayings: they belong together as part of a tightly knit unit.

4.17–5.2

(4.17, ET 5.1) Watch your step, when you go to the house of God, and draw near to listen. A sacrifice is what fools pay, for they have no idea when they'll do what is wrong. (5.1, ET 5.2) Don't run off at the mouth, and don't let your heart be in a hurry to say something in front of God, for God is in heaven and you are on earth. So then, let your words be few. (5.2, ET 5.3) For a dream comes with a lot of worrying, and a fool's voice with a lot of words.

Commentary

4.17, ET 5.1] The Masoretic pointing creates a significant difficulty in the middle of the verse, where it indicates literally 'than giving the fools sacrifice'. This may originally have been an attempt to make it mean 'a sacrifice (is more) than the giving of fools', but many subsequent commentators have tried to draw the previous clause into the comparison, as in the RSV's 'to draw near to listen is better than to offer the sacrifice of fools'. This is very difficult, not least because it introduces the need to supply 'better' (which is absent from the Hebrew), and attempts to get around that need have only added further complications. We might note also that the form and word-order makes 'the sacrifice of fools' impossible, and that the verb 'giving' is not generally used of making sacrifices in Hebrew. Without going into all the problems (I have discussed them in more detail in the notes), it is clearly not easy to construe the text this way.

I have opted to vocalize differently, reading a noun used elsewhere by Qohelet in place of the verb, and understanding the central part of the verse to mean 'sacrifice (is) the gift/payment of fools'. The remainder of the verse is less difficult to read, but causes no fewer problems, because the Hebrew, literally 'they do not know to do wrong', would classically mean 'they do not know *how* to do wrong', and this seems bizarre in context. Fox confesses 'Since the MT is clear and grammatically feasible, I translate the sentence literally without understanding its point'. Matters are easier if one does not have to explain, like Fox and many others, how the ignorance of fools in this respect makes drawing near better than their sacrifice. I take the point to be that fools offer sacrifices pre-emptively or when things go wrong because they simply have no idea whether what they are doing is good or bad, making sacrifice a sort of tax on idiocy, and something that others should be able to avoid.[1] This understanding is possible even if we read 'know how', but I think that Qohelet also uses the construction concerned in a particular way, here and elsewhere, to indicate knowledge about the future more specifically. The message of the verse overall, then, is that one should take care entering the temple, and should approach what is going on with a view to listening, not participation. 'Watch your step' has the same value here that it can have in English: 'be careful'—because this is an environment in which one can easily get oneself into trouble. What one should listen to is unspecified, although it is unlikely that Qohelet is talking about being receptive to God (as, e.g., Tamez suggests). I take his point to be that it is by listening to what is going on that one will understand the pointlessness, or even danger, of joining in.

5.1, ET 5.2] Informal as it sounds, 'run off at the mouth' is quite close to the original, but it is difficult to capture in English the implication of speaking under pressure without due thought—although we might talk even more colloquially about 'blurting something out'. This is not an admonition to speak succinctly, or even to speak at all, but a warning against giving in to such pressure. The statement that God is in heaven has given rise to much discussion, but Qohelet's primary purpose here is not to establish the different status of God so much as to offer an assurance that he is not actually present, so one should not panic at the prospect of appearing before him. Of course, this implies a belief that God is not in any way actually *in* the temple, and that in turn opens up some important

---

[1] It is interesting to compare a saying found on an Akkadian-Hurrian bilingual text from Ugarit, which is difficult in places, but speaks of the man 'ignorant of sin', who rushes to pray to his god, and perhaps makes a similar point that not knowing whether or not one has offended a deity can be a strong incentive to piety; see RS 15.10, lines 10-13, presented conveniently in Cohen, *Wisdom*, 207-11. Strikingly, this is the second of only two sayings on the tablet, and the first is an admonition against breaking an oath, which Loretz, 'Eiliges Gebet', has compared to 5.3-5.

questions about divine presence, concerning which the biblical writers may have held varying opinions. Qohelet is clearly not trying intentionally to make the point, however, that God's distance from humans means that he is unconcerned with human affairs (as Gordis suggests, comparing Job 22.11-14 and, curiously, Ps 14.1— the following verse, 14.2, explicitly contradicts such a notion). This is one of many places in the monologue where we should be cautious not to read more than is meant into what Qohelet says. On the other hand, Gammie, 'Dualism', 363, is right to point out that this verse reflects more clearly than any other a spatial dualism—a separation between the realms of heaven and earth—that is attested elsewhere in Qohelet's frequent references to affairs 'under the sun' or 'under heaven'.

5.2, ET 5.3] In the Vulgate, Jerome translates this verse as *multas curas sequuntur somnia et in multis sermonibus invenitur stultitia*, 'Dreams follow many cares, and in many words will be found folly', and he takes Qohelet to be suggesting that dreams are the consequence of human anxiety or pre-occupation, while folly is, correspondingly, something to which the use of many words gives rise. This understanding has been picked up by the majority of subsequent commentators, and is a possible reading of the Hebrew. It is an awkward one, however, and Jerome smoothes over the problems by paraphrasing the text: the Hebrew speaks not of 'folly' but of 'the voice of the fool'. In order to retain his understanding without such paraphrase, therefore, we have to suppose that the many words give rise to something that 'sounds like' folly. Even if we do so, however, it is difficult to see how the first part of the verse might fit into the context on such a reading, and it really has to be taken as a statement about something completely different, designed to support the second by analogy. So Whybray, for instance, paraphrases it as '*Just as* dreams go with overwork, *so* does the voice of a fool with too much speaking'—but even he then acknowledges that 'the analogy is not particularly apposite or, to the modern reader, particularly effective'.

It is simpler to follow the reading of Fox and some other commentators, which reverses the cause and effect, but which is no less plausible as a reading of the Hebrew. Fox himself comments that the first part '…probably means that the dreams are accompanied by busyness (*'inyan*), rather than that busyness provokes dreams. Construing the phrase in the latter way would mean that in the parallel line, "much talk" was the source of "the fool's voice," whereas the causality is the other way around.' Even so, he introduces the verse as a 'parenthetical remark of proverbial character', the main point of which is to be found only in the second part, and with most commentators, he sees no particular place here for its reference to dreams, except insofar as they are appropriately meaningless.

If all the emphasis is to be placed on the second part of the verse, however, as motivating the preceding advice to 'let your words be few', it is hard to explain why 'dreams' crop up again in 5.6, which is the summary and culmination of Qohelet's discussion. It may be important, therefore, to bear in mind that dreams would have had a religious significance of their own for the original readership (as Brown observes). To be sure, Ben Sira (34.5-8) condemns dreams as a folly, and a source of deception for humans, and the rejection of meaningless fantasy is not unique to the modern world—Lavoie, 'Critique cultuelle', 160-61, adduces a number of similar warnings from other ancient literature. Ben Sira also, however, lists dreams alongside divinations and omens in the same passage, and his advice to ignore them is qualified by an exception: some may actually have been sent from God (34.6). This reflects a long-standing and widespread belief that God could communicate with humans through dreams (for biblical instances, see, e.g., Job 33.14-18; Joel 3.1—and, in a more complicated way, Deut 13.2-4 [ET 13.1-3]), so it is unlikely that readers would have overlooked such an idea when dreams are mentioned twice by Qohelet in this context. The point, I think, is that 5.2 should be taken not just as a general statement, but more specifically as a reference to the tumult of the temple, which Qohelet has advised us to hear but not to join: it is fools who are doing all the talking, and the bustle is of those who think they have heard God. It is in just such an atmosphere that unwise commitments to God may be made, and, as 5.6 will remind us, that we should be most afraid of him.

Notes

4.17 (ET 5.1) watch your step] Lit. 'guard your foot' (or 'feet'). Hertzberg would read the verb as an infinitive, in parallel with קרוב, to draw this part of the verse into a comparison with מתת (on which, see below). It is usually read as an imperative, and if it is not actually the first in the book, as Spangenberg,

'Die Struktuur', 260, seems to suggest (ראה is usually parsed as an imperative in 1.10 and 2.1), it is at least the first to introduce an admonition.

The Qᵉrê singular רַגְלְךָ, 'your foot', is supported by many manuscripts and all the ancient versions against the Kᵉthîbh dual. Schoors, *The Preacher* I, 34, observes that the singular is used in similar expressions (e.g. Isa 56.2; Prov 3.26), but we also find the dual in 1 Sam 2.9. Dahood, 'The Language of Qoheleth', 227, puts the differences down, of course, to an originally defective spelling. Ehrlich notes the rabbinic use of the noun for pilgrimage festivals and prefers to understand the verse in those terms, thinking that the advice is otherwise too obvious ('as if one didn't have to do that even when one goes to the theatre!'), and Jastrow, *Dictionary*, similarly translates, 'Observe thy pilgrimages to the house of God'; cf. earlier but similarly, Derenbourg, 'Notes', 177 n. 1. This, of course, involves pointing רגליך as plural, rather than dual, and fits the context uncomfortably. Tita, in 'Ist die thematische Einheit?', sees כאשר...לשמע as parenthetical, so that the point here is to keep one's feet from giving a sacrifice of fools (= a foolish sacrifice); however, as Hieke notes with some understatement in 'Wie hast du's?', 322 n. 18, linking feet to sacrifice is 'semantically problematic', and it is unlikely that the text was supposed to be read this way.

Given the context, most commentators have seen here an idiom equivalent to, as Fox puts it, 'tread carefully', an interpretation that is broadly supported by 1 Sam 2.9 and Prov 3.26, where, when God 'keeps the feet' of those he is protecting, it is to prevent them from going into the darkness, or falling prey to the snares that are associated with the ruin of the wicked. In that case, it does not matter whether we read singular or dual. This is not incompatible with Gordis' suggestion that the advice is 'Do not run thoughtlessly and over-frequently to the Temple', with which he compares Prov 25.17, but it is difficult to get that meaning directly from שמר.

Pinker, 'Intrusion', finds a wholly different sort of meaning, noting the uses of רגל as a verb to mean 'spy out', and seeing the advice as a warning to be on the look out for spies or informants: 'perhaps it alludes also to one who "watches your feet," i.e., follows you (רַגְּלְךָ)'. We would surely need either a relative pronoun or a piʿel participle, מרגל, for that, however. The Midrash Rabbah takes the expression literally, as an injunction against trailing dust into the temple (cf. Plumptre's association of reverence with the removal of shoes).

4.17 (ET 5.1) when you go] Ehrlich would delete the כ of כאשר as a dittograph, and although he does not note this, there is support for such an emendation in the existence of a Masoretic *Sᵉbîr* / *Sᵉbîrîn* annotation, which suggests that 'some were of the opinion' that אשר should be read (see Ginsburg, *Massorah* III, 326-27, and the apparatus to his *Writings, ad loc.*). The opinions expressed in such notes were sometimes characterized in other sources as *Qᵉrê*, and Ginsburg himself, in his *Introduction*, 187-96, takes them as virtually equivalent to a *Qᵉrê*, but James Barr represents the more common opinion when he says (in 'A New Look at Kethibh-Qere', 23) that they operate 'like our *sic* in English: it means, this text looks strange, there are those who *think* it should be otherwise, reason itself suggests it should be otherwise, but don't alter it, it should really be this way as it stands.' In this instance, there is no manuscript support for the annotation, but if we were to adopt the suggestion, the point would be 'watch the step that you take'. G ἐν ᾧ ἐὰν πορεύῃ reflects a third possible reading, באשר, which would imply 'the foot with which you walk', and this is probably supported by θ'.[2]

Goldman reviews the differences and correspondences between M and G whenever באשר and כאשר occur, showing that they agree in reading באשר only once (at 3.9) and כאשר four times (5.3, 14; 8.7; 9.2b), but that twice G has apparently read כאשר where M has באשר (7.2; 8.4), and three or four times it has read באשר where M has כאשר, as here (4.17; 8.16; 11.5; probably 9.2a). He concludes that 'There is some hesitation in the transmission of באשר and כאשר in Qoh.', which may be an understatement, although it is also noteworthy that of the four places in which G seems to have read באשר where M has כאשר, this is the only one where de Rossi's lists suggest that there was any significant degree of support for באשר in the later Hebrew manuscript tradition. In fact, Barton, 17, notes support for באשר in various rabbinic citations of the verse, and although the reading is not found in modern editions of all the texts that he lists (but see, e.g., *y. Berakot* 67b), it seems likely that this was an early and persistent variant. Just here and in 5.3, T uses בעידן ד-, 'in the time when' where M has כאשר: this is probably a simple paraphrase rather than a reflection of באשר, but it does not exclude that reading.

4.17 (ET 5.1) house of God] Or 'temple'. As a term for the temple in Jerusalem, the precise formulation בית האלהים is largely confined to Chronicles, Ezra and Nehemiah, appearing otherwise only at Judg 18.31 and Dan 1.2. In that last verse, though, we also find בית אלהיו used to refer to the temple of Nebuchadnezzar's god in Babylon, and the same expression appears in 2 Chr 32.21 for the temple of Sennacherib's god. It seems likely, therefore, that Qohelet might be understood in principle to be referring to any temple.

4.17 (ET 5.1) draw near to listen] As G's verbatim rendering καὶ ἐγγὺς τοῦ ἀκούειν shows, it is not difficult formally to read קרוב as an adjective. In Isa 13.33, however, the very similar expression וקרוב לבוא means 'close to coming' (cf. the uses with the hiph'il of the verb קרב at Gen 12.11; Isa 26.17), and it seems clear that Qohelet does not intend such a sense here. If we construe the word as an adjective, furthermore, it is also difficult not to take וקרוב לשמע as a continuation of the כאשר clause, so that Qohelet would be advising caution 'when you go to the temple and (are) near in order to listen': it becomes clear in the next verse, however, that it is speaking, and not listening, that he regards as dangerous. None of this absolutely prohibits

---

[2] See Gentry, 'Propaedeutic', 151-52, who argues that the citation in Syh is intended to show that θ' did not support a rival reading with τῷ πορεύεσθαι.

construal of קרוב as an adjective, but it seems better to read it instead as an infinitive of the verb קרב: this verb can naturally be used of drawing near in order to do something (expressed by ל- with the infinitive construct, e.g., Lev 21.17; 1 Sam 17.48), and the use of the infinitive would make it clear that Qohelet does not intend a simple continuation of the subordinate clause. If קרוב is indeed an infinitive absolute, then it can be taken either as an injunction ('you should draw near'; cf. GKC §113 bb; J-M §123 v) or, as I think more likely given the conjunction, a simple continuation of the instruction that begins with שמר (cf. GKC §113 z; J-M §123 x): both uses of the infinitive absolute are quite common. In either case, I take Qohelet to be suggesting that one should 'take care…and draw near to listen.'

That the clause is often translated very differently has more to do with what follows than with any difficulty inherent in וקרוב לשמע. In the subsequent מתת הכסילים זבח, the first word is pointed in M with a prefixed מן, and in order to deal with that preposition, interpreters have commonly read וקרוב לשמע as the first part of a comparison, so that they can translate what follows as '*than* the sacrificing of fools'.[3] The obvious comparison, 'listening is closer than…', makes no sense, and 1 Sam 15.22, with its declaration that שמע מזבח טוב, has also clearly been on the mind of some commentators, so either the sentence is read outright as a 'better than' expression, in which קרוב is read as an infinitive with טוב supplied ('approaching and listening [is better] than…'), or else a different, more evaluative sense is supplied for קרוב, allowing it to be a substitute for טוב (e.g. Fox, 'to obey is more acceptable'; Seow, 'it is more acceptable to give heed'; cf. V *enim melior est oboedientia*, 'for obedience is better').

Both approaches, however, face some significant obstacles. Not the least of these, although it is often overlooked, is the conjunction on וקרוב, which is supported by G, S, Hie and the hexaplaric reading καὶ ἔγγιζε ὥστε ἀκούειν, 'and approach to listen' (which Marshall believes to be σ', although it is attributed to α' in the manuscripts). This conjunction has either to be ignored (as, e.g., Seow) or else translated in an abnormal way (e.g. Gordis, Fox, who translate 'for'; cf. V *enim*), because its presence most naturally connects קרוב to what has preceded, and is, to say the very least, a disincentive to reading what follows as a comparative clause (although Schmidt, 'Koheleth 4:17', simply takes this to be a new saying, loosely linked to the preceding one). After that, the reading with ellipsis of טוב has to contend with the fact that, although we might just allow the claim of GKC §133 e, that the pregnant use of מן here would drive the reader to insert טוב, it would more naturally lead them to insert

---

[3] As I shall suggest below, it seems likely that M did intend a comparison, but one restricted only to the last part of the verse: 'a sacrifice (is) more than the giving of fools'. Even if one retains the vocalization of M, therefore, it is not strictly necessary to implicate וקרוב לשמע in the comparison.

it where S has done so, immediately before מתת (as *BHS* suggests). S in fact reads 'and approach to listen: (it is) better than (ܛܒ ܡܢ, *ṭb mn*, perhaps under the influence of G ὑπέρ?)', which takes קרוב in the sense that I propose, and deals with the next clause as a separate problem.

Alternatively, those scholars who prefer to suggest that 'closer' means 'better', or that קרוב has some different sense here, have to provide more convincing evidence of such a possibility than has been furnished so far. Closeness to God is naturally something to which many biblical writers aspire, but the fact that something is good does not make it a synonym of 'good', and the many references to divine proximity are irrelevant here. Herzfeld's idea that obedience (לשמע) provides a 'shorter route' (קרוב) to God than sacrifice represents a not uncommon but highly implausible solution. Fox points, rather differently, to 1 Kgs 8.59, where 'words of prayer are said to be "near to the Lord," meaning acceptable to him', and is followed by, e.g., Seow. It is plain, however, that what Solomon wants in that passage is not for his words to prove 'acceptable' (that is not in question), but for them to remain close to God 'day and night, so that he may maintain the cause of his servant…as each day requires'; they are to remain (metaphorically) under God's nose, in other words, so that he will never forget them, and קרוב has its normal sense here, without even any secondary connotation.

Gordis cites with approval the view of M. Seidel, that a root קרב should be distinguished in passages such as Ps 75.2 with the sense 'praise, glorify', and this passage understood as 'it is more excellent to listen', which seems like speculation built upon speculation. The difficulties involved in reading this clause as the first part of a comparative sentence suggest that we might do better, in fact, not to read the sentence as comparative, and it is manifestly simpler to reject the vocalization of מתת in M, which inspires such readings (see below).

4.17 (ET 5.1) a sacrifice] G alone has '*your* sacrifice', θυσία σου. Since it also reads ὅτι, this is not merely a misreading of the subsequent כי, but, if it is not entirely interpretative (which would be out of character), it may reflect a dittograph or deliberate double reading of the כ (see the next note). In an attempt to make sense of the text, V reads interpretatively *stultorum uictimae*, 'the victims of fools'. S has 'the gifts of sacrifices of fools', which is an impossible reading of the Hebrew, but could be derived loosely from G δόμα τῶν ἀφρόνων θυσία (cf. Kamenetzky, 217).

4.17 (ET 5.1) what fools pay] As noted already, M points מִתֵּת: the infinitive construct תת of נתן, with the preposition מן; this vocalization is supported by an unattributed Syrohexaplaric reading (maybe σ′, since the others are accounted for, but Marshall, 362, takes it to be a G variant, and non-hexaplaric) τὸ δοῦναι ἀφροσύναις θυσίαν, 'the giving of sacrifice to follies (ܠܡܬܠ *lštywtʾ*)'. The readings (G ὑπέρ) δόμα τῶν ἀφρόνων θυσία of α′, θ′, and G (cf. Hie *donum*), however, render using a noun, a reading which S follows. It is sometimes proposed that G reflects מתנת, but the translator probably just found מתת, the same consonants as M, and rendered the infinitive תת as a noun.⁴ If the readings attested for α' and θ' imply that they had no ὑπέρ, then they may have read it as a noun מַתָּת (on the meaning of which, see the note on 'a payment from God' at 3.13). A noun is actually easier here syntactically, and מַתָּת was probably the intended reading. M and G have both tried to create a comparison, which is connected with the previous use of σου in G: '(Let) *your* sacrifice (be) beyond the gift of fools'. M is less satisfactory in this respect, because מן does not have quite the clarity or force of ὑπέρ, and results in 'a sacrifice (is) more than the giving of fools' (note that sacrifices are not 'given' in Hebrew, which lends weight to the idea that M confines its comparison to this part of the verse: זבח would be an improbable object of תת).

4.17 (ET 5.1) they have no idea when] Or, 'they have no skill at all (in doing wrong)'. Qohelet uses the construction אין + suffix + participle (GKC §152 l-m) also in 5.11; 8.7, 16; 9.2, 5, 16; 11.5, 6; and אין + participle (without the suffix pronoun) in 9.1. Here and on five other occasions (8.7; 9.1, 5; 11.5, 6) the participle is from ידע, and the construction is used to express absolute ignorance of something (cf. similarly 1 Sam 26.12; 2 Kgs 17.26). It is very doubtful that Qohelet would be using it here merely to express the sense that they act 'without understanding' (so, e.g., Thilo). This ignorance is expressed using an infinitive, and elsewhere in biblical Hebrew, ידע + -ל + infinitive construct always has a particular connotation of being trained, or of possessing a technical skill (Exod 36.1; 1 Kgs 5.20 [ET 5.6]; 2 Chr 2.6-7 ET 2.7-8, 13 ET 14; Isa 50.4). On the basis of general usage, then, we should understand this to mean that the fools have no expertise in doing wrong. Qohelet himself, however, seems to use the expression more loosely in 4.13 to mean 'know how to', and although the contexts of 6.8 and 10.15 are difficult, it almost certainly does not have a specific nuance of expertise in either of those verses, while in 6.8 I doubt even that it means 'know how to' (see the note there). Lohfink, 'Warum ist der Tor', insists that the verse must be understood in such terms of 'not knowing', and that its claim, initially outrageous, is clarified when we reach 5.5, and it becomes clear that these fools are offering the traditional sacrifices for inadvertent, 'unknown' sins. The link between the two verses is far from clear, however, despite the elaborate poetic structure that he identifies as grouping them, and, as Lohfink himself seems to acknowledge (120), the audience would need something of an 'ear' for such structures to get the point.

Other scholars have sought meanings that avoid 'not know how to', and Seow seeks to establish here a sense of acknowledgement ('they do not recognize that they are doing evil'), which is certainly a potential connotation of ידע

---

⁴ Yi, 274, argues that it is the translator's normal practice to render 'a bound infinitive prefixed by מן' using a noun, so the text here need not reflect ממתת rather than מתת. He cites 1.8 (משמע = ἀπὸ ἀκροάσεως) and 3.5 (מחבק = ἀπὸ περιλήμψεως). See also his notes on pp. 13-14.

(e.g. Deut 33.9; Jer 3.13). It is possible that the same sense could be attached to ידע + ל־, although the example that Seow offers from Ps 69.5 (ET 69.6), where he takes ידעת לאולתי to mean 'you recognize my folly', is unpersuasive, and, as Delitzsch noted of older proposals along the same lines, we should really expect עשותם, 'their doing' (cf. דע שאתי in Jer 15.15), for that sense. It is true, however, that the infinitive construct is quite commonly used in object clauses (cf. J-M §124 c), and this is what Aalders probably means when he talks about it being used here with a more gerundial force. That could yield the meaning that the fools have no idea about wrongdoing, or, more specifically, no idea when they are doing wrong. My own suspicion, however, is that אינם יודעים לעשות רע employs the infinitive with ל־ in a more specific way, comparable to the normal use after verbs like יסף, יכל, אבה, and מאז. In such places, it has a prospective aspect, expressing such ideas as 'continuing *to do*', 'being willing *to do*', or 'refusing *to do*', in which the action expressed in the object clause is consequent upon and/or subsequent to the main verb. There is an interesting example of this in 2 Chr 6.20, where God 'has promised *to set*', and the construction is being used, in effect, to express indirect speech. Both verses are difficult, but I think that Qohelet already used ל־ + infinitive construct similarly to express indirect speech in 3.18, and that usage would supply an analogy for an understanding of the construction here as 'know that they are going to'. There may be a more precise parallel, moreover, in 6.8, if יודע להלך means 'knowing that he is going to go', rather than 'knowing how to go', which also seems likely. A not dissimilar sense can be achieved by taking the infinitive as an expression of attendant circumstances ('they are not aware when doing'), as advocated by Eaton, who cites GKC §114 e (although §114 o might be more apposite).

In any case, whether we see a reference to expertise or to something more general, the verse is not claiming that fools never do wrong: on the face of it, the point is either that they have no understanding of the concept or practice of doing wrong, or that they do not understand their own wrongdoing (which may be one of the things that marks them as fools). Some of the ancient versions interpret the verse along these lines: T, for instance, claims that the fools do not know whether they are doing good or evil, and Hie *nesciunt quod faciunt malum*, V *nesciunt quid faciant mali* have them ignorant of the bad they do (Jerome explains in his commentary that they are more particularly unaware that it is wrong to try to satisfy God through sacrifice). G ὅτι οὐκ εἰσιν εἰδότες τοῦ ποιεῖν κακόν corresponds closely to M, but the difficulties with the statement felt by many readers are reflected in the secondary variant καλόν for κακόν in G^S and many other manuscripts: this reverses the sense, making the fools ignorant of how to do good. S ܡܛܠ ܕܠܐ ܝܕܥܝܢ ܠܡܥܒܕ ܕܛܒ *mṭl dlʾ ydʿyn lmʿbd dṭb* is the same; Kamenetzky, 217, argues that this is an independent development because καλόν would have been rendered with ܕܫܦܝܪ *dšpyr*, not ܛܒ *ṭb*, but ܛܒ *ṭb* is, in fact, used for καλόν at 5.17, and this reading probably is, therefore, based on the Greek variant.

Some subsequent commentators have tried to avoid the difficulties in other ways: for instance, Herzfeld's solution, adopted by Ginsburg and others, identifies the subject of the clause ('they') with those who have undertaken to obey (לשמע), so Ginsburg translates, 'they who obey know not to do evil'. It is a considerable stretch, however, to claim that לשמע even has an implicit concrete subject, let alone that this subject could naturally be picked up in such a way. Glasser, *Le Procès*, 83, implausibly takes כי אינם יודעים as a parenthetical description of the fools (who are such because they are ignorant) and who do evil. Many other scholars, though, have opted to make emendations, the most popular of which (going back to Siegfried) has been to suggest that an initial -מ, bearing the sense 'except', has been lost through haplography, and that we should read מלעשות, 'they do not know but to do evil'. The note justifying this in *BH¹* ('idioma Mischnicum, huius libri sermoni haud absonum', 'Mishnaic idiom, hardly unexpected of the language of this book') also draws attention to its weakness: it is not a biblical usage (if it is a Hebrew usage in any period at all, actually), and it is very doubtful that we could legitimately draw that sense from מלעשות, even if we made the change; the suggestion has nevertheless persisted into *BHS*, and G. R. Driver ('Once Again Abbreviations', 79) has added the twist that the error could have arisen through misreading of an abbreviation with one מ rather than two.

Pinker, 'Intrusion', has more recently combined the arguments to propose that the text originally read כי אינם יודעים מה לעשות, with the ה lost through abbreviation and the מ through haplography. This is implausible in itself, but only creates a useful sense anyway if we remove רע from consideration, so that לעשות needs a new object (see the next note). *BH¹* also offered a suggestion initially proposed by Renan (595) and later accepted by, e.g., Wright, which was to read כי אם before לעשות: Renan suggested that it had been omitted by homoioteleuton. This is wholly speculative, and barely easier to justify than Ibn Ezra's insertion of רק in the same place, to give a similar meaning. Ginsberg offers a list of possibilities, including the simple substitution of other words for רע, and a replacement of it by עד (for עוד), which he suggests very tentatively, could be considered on grounds of sense (although Fox complains that it 'does not motivate the advice of v. 17a') and is less difficult graphically than some other proposals. Like all the other emendations, however, it falls squarely inside the territory of scholars trying to change a text simply because they do not like what it says. The versional evidence does not support emendation, and it is inherently unlikely that a text would have changed in the direction of a statement that has proved so unpalatable to so many readers.

4.17 (ET 5.1) do what is wrong] An association with the rare word רֵעַ, found in Ps 139.2, 17, was favoured by some early commentators, and underpins, e.g., the translation *quia nesciunt facere uoluntatem eius*, 'because they do not know how to do his will', in the Pagninus Bible of 1528. That can be excluded both because it is unlikely that one could 'do' a thought or purpose in this way, and because עשה רע is such a well-known expression that no ancient reader would have recognized the less common term in this context. The precise meaning of the expression here, however, has been much discussed, and many commentators have sought a sense that avoids proclaiming fools to be ignorant of wrongdoing. Jastrow's 'for they do not know enough to do any harm' is unlikely. עשה רע can indeed mean 'to do harm (to somebody)' (e.g. Gen 31.29; Ps 15.3; Jer 39.12), but in biblical usage it appears far more frequently in the expression עשה הרע בעיני, 'to do what is wrong in the eyes of' or 'displease' somebody (usually God, but cf. 1 Sam 29.7). Qohelet uses it in a more absolute way of 'doing what is wrong' (8.11, 12), a usage that is largely confined to late texts (cf. 2 Kgs 17.11; 21.9 = 2 Chr 33.9; 2 Chr 12.14; Neh 9.28; Ps 34.17 [ET 34.16]; Prov 2.14; Isa 56.2). More generally, however, רע in the book commonly refers to things that are unfortunate, bad or wrong, but that need not be consciously evil or wicked (see the note on 'bad' at 1.13). Humans in general may do them (8.11), and if 8.12 associates them with the sinner in particular, it also suggests that Qohelet thinks in terms of individual actions, so the expression here is not equivalent to 'be wicked'. Attractive though the reading is, it is also doubtful, however, that the expression could simply mean 'create havoc', as Ogden would like (and he notably swings to the opposite extreme in 8.11-12, speaking of 'pursuing the same evil course', and of a 'descent further into serious evil'). Rashi's proposal, 'harm oneself', is presumably based on 2 Sam 12.18, where David's servants worry about his reaction to hearing that his child is dead: ועשה רעה. Hitzig's proposal, further elaborated by Stuart, draws on the same source for the understanding 'they know not how to be sad', and treats the expression here as the opposite of לעשות טוב in 3.12. On the latter point, see my note on 'doing good' in that verse; for 2 Sam 12.18 we should bear in mind first that the fear of David 'doing something bad' need hardly be taken as an *expression* of something so specific as harming himself or being upset, whatever specific ideas it might *imply*. More importantly, perhaps, רעה is used there, not רע, and although the terms are similar, they cannot be considered interchangeable.

Actual emendations are rare (although see Ginsberg's suggestion, discussed in the last note). Schmidt, 'Koheleth 4:17', 80, however, does suggest repointing to רֵעַ, which he takes to mean 'other', translating 'Denn sie wissen nicht Anderes zu tun', 'For they know not to do anything else'. Apart from the fact that this does not really convey an appropriate meaning here, רֵעַ does not mean 'something else', and we cannot derive that sense from its use in such relational expressions as 'one another' or in contexts like Prov 18.17, where it refers strictly to people and to situations in which one has to be present for there to be another ('his fellow'). Pinker, 'Intrusion', suggests, more drastically, 'that רע resulted from a ד/ר confusion and the word דע, "know," belongs to the next verse', where he translates 'Know, do not be hasty…'. This goes hand-in-hand with his proposed restoration of מה before לעשות (see the last note), while it supposes a series of errors for which there is no evidence, and which we do not need to postulate. Qohelet does use דע in 11.9, as Pinker suggests, but not as an isolated imperative, and it is followed in that verse, as we should expect, by a כי clause.

5.1 (ET 5.2) run off at the mouth] Lit. 'Do not rush on your mouth'. בהל is used principally in the niphʻal, of a panic induced by fear (e.g. Exod 15.15; Jer 51.32), and the piʻel is correspondingly used of causing others to panic (e.g. 2 Chr 32.18). Ecclesiastes uses the expression אל תבהל, which is not found elsewhere in biblical Hebrew, three times (5.1; 7.9; 8.3). Here and in 7.9, M points it as a piʻel, and although it is pointed as a niphʻal in 8.3, many commentators would vocalize it as a piʻel there also. On no occasion, however, is the causative meaning 'Do not terrify' appropriate, and G always renders it with forms from σπεύδω or σπουδάζω, which express eagerness or haste; cf. σ' here: μὴ προπετὴς γίνου τῷ στόματί σου (with minor variants attested), 'Do not be reckless with your mouth' (which is probably the basis of V *ne temere quid loquaris*: see Cannon, 'Jerome and Symmachus', 193). This corresponds to the meaning of the piʻel in Esth 2.9 and 2 Chr 35.21, where it is used of doing something quickly—an idea connected with the puʻal in Esth 8.14 (and perhaps Prov 20.21), and with the hiphʻil in Esth 6.14 and 2 Chr 26.20, if we are to trust the pointing in every case—and there is no doubt that this is a legitimate sense of the verb in late texts. Schoors, *The Preacher* II, 250, notes similar connotations of the root in the Aramaic of Daniel and Ezra, but there it is restricted to adverbial expressions, and the use of main verbs with this sense is common neither in early Aramaic nor in later Hebrew (both at Qumran and in rabbinic texts, בהל seems to retain its earlier meaning of panic or agitation), so whether or not it should be considered an Aramaism, it seems to mark a temporary semantic shift in the Hebrew of a particular period, and a usage with which the Masoretes and their tradition may have had very limited familiarity.

Whether or not we treat the pointing as reliable, however, on all three occasions when he uses אל תבהל, Qohelet seems to do so with the meaning 'do not be too quick', rather than just 'do not be quick', and, at least here and in 8.3, he appears to be talking about a potentially unwise reaction to pressure (7.9 cautions against an unwise reaction to other circumstances), so speed is not the only issue, and the verb seems to retain something of its earlier and more common meaning in the niphʻal.

על פיך is probably not strictly instrumental, 'with your mouth': contrast ברוחך in 7.9, which may have influenced S to render ܒܦܘܡܟ *bpwmk*, 'in/with your mouth', as Kamenetzky, 217, suggests. Generally speaking, to be על פי someone in biblical usage is to be at or under their command (e.g. Exod 17.1; Job 39.27), but that is inappropriate here, and Seow notes mishnaic uses of the term in connection with reading 'out loud'.

5.1 (ET 5.2) to say something in front of] Lit. 'bring out a word in front of'. The hiphʻil of יצא is used quite commonly of speech, e.g., in Neh 6.19, where we also find לפני used of the person to whom the speech is delivered, and Qohelet will use the expression again in 5.5. It is not clear that we need to regard speaking לפני someone as an Aramaism, as Fox suggests (Schoors, *The Preacher* I, 123, is dubious), and in view of what follows, Qohelet is probably using it to give a specific nuance: no human can literally speak 'in front of' God when he is not present, and nobody should feel intimidated by supposing him to be present.

5.1 (ET 5.2) heaven...earth] Many manuscripts of G have τῷ οὐρανῷ ἄνω, 'heaven *above*', and/or τῆς γῆς κάτω, 'earth *below*'. Whilst it is possible that the former, at least, arose from dittography of ΑΝΩ, as McNeile, 159, claims, it is most likely that both variants arose as a reminiscence of the numerous texts like Exod 20.4; Deut 4.39; Josh 2.11 which phrase the contrast in that way. That there is a difference would seem to tell against the claim of Schoors, 'Misuse', 51, that 'Qoheleth here deliberately adapts Deut. iv 39'.

5.1 (ET 5.2) few] The plural מעטים is found only here and in the very similar Ps 109.8; it stands in contrast with the normal, singular usage in 9.14, אנשים מעט בה. In that usage, מעט is a substantive, but here it is apparently treated as an adjective (so Schoors, *The Preacher* II, 474-75), and should possibly be pointed as a passive participle of the verb, cf. mishnaic מָעוּט. Hurvitz, *Concise Lexicon*, 171-72, treats the emergence of the plural as a specifically late development.

5.2 (ET 5.3) a dream] M החלום is lit. 'the dream', in the sense 'all dreams'. G παραγίνεται ἐνύπνιον lacks an article, and although it is possible that the translator has read the ה as part of the verb, taking חלום to be feminine (so McNeile, 154), σ' ἀποβήσεται ὄνειρος also lacks the article. Since there is no article for the parallel קול כסיל it seems likely either that the article is secondary here in M, or that the parallel expressions had been aligned in the source-text of G.

The suggestion of *BHS* (following Joüon, 'Notes philologiques', 421), that we might read הֹלְלוֹת, is not unattractive, but entirely speculative, as is Joüon's accompanying proposal to delete בא as 'mauvaise dittographie' of כי. Rose, *Rien de nouveau*, 347-48 (cf. 'Querdenken', 89-90), proposes to read חלים or חללים, connecting it with the use of חלה in the expression הלה פנים (e.g. Exod 32.11), which Seybold, 'Reverenz', takes to have a ritual significance. All else aside, there is no reason to suppose that the verb alone can have that force, although Rose tries to identify other passages where it might be appropriate.

5.2 (ET 5.3) with a lot of...with a lot of] It is not difficult to find passages such as Lev 16.3 and Ps 66.13, where ב- is used to indicate something that accompanies or is brought by the subject of בוא, as Fox notes, and that would suggest that 'many words' are a product of the fool's voice, just as ענין is an accompaniment to dreams. σ' διὰ πλῆθος, however, makes dreams the result instead of the cause, and this is picked up most explicitly in V *multas curas sequuntur somnia et in multis sermonibus invenitur stultitia*, 'dreams follow many cares and folly is found in many words'. T takes a similar line, and it is probably no less likely, in principle, that Qohelet is claiming that we dream because of our preoccupations, than that our preoccupations arise from our dreams. Texts like Hab 2.4 and Ps 19.12 (ET 19.11), in which ‑ב is instrumental, can be adduced to support that sense (so, e.g., Barton). The Hebrew is ambiguous, therefore, and it would not be impossible to suppose that Qohelet plays on that ambiguity to say something slightly different in each clause. On balance, though, it is more natural to read them both in the same way, and since the logic of the verse and of the context seems to demand that Qohelet is advising reticence because it is through a lot of babbling that the voice betrays its owner's folly, so, correspondingly, dreams must be the source of much ענין, not the result of it.

5.2 (ET 5.3) worrying] On the sense of ענין, see the note at 1.13. Joüon, 'Notes philologiques', 421, would arbitrarily replace it with רעיון.

V and T translate the singular as plural, perhaps because it is easier that way to retain the parallel expressions. Most manuscripts of G have πειρασμοῦ, 'trial' or 'temptation', and none have περισπασμοῦ, but this was almost certainly the original reading (see Bertram, 'Hebräischer und griechischer', 42-43). σ' ἀνομίας, on the other hand, probably represents a confusion of M ענין with עוון (as Goldman suggests).

5.2 (ET 5.3) a fool's voice] Perles, 'Miscellany', 130, feels that 'The second half of the verse is no logical sequel to the first. In the place of קול we rather expect a word which would indicate the consequences of much talking for the fool.' He makes two suggestions: to emend to קלון, 'disgrace', or to read קול as from קלל, noting the use of מִקֵּל at Jer 3.9. The first of these requires a significant change to the text, and the second does not give a good sense, at least if we are to infer the meaning from the isolated occurrence in Jeremiah ('lightness', 'ease with which someone does something'). Perles does have a point, though, about the logic of the verse, and this lends weight to an understanding of the fool's voice as the source, not the product of the many words.

5.3-6

(5.3, ET 5.4) When you vow a vow to God, don't be slow to fulfil it, as nobody has any use for fools—you should fulfil what you vow. (5.4, ET 5.5) It is better that you should not vow, than that you should vow and not fulfil. (5.5, ET 5.6) Don't let your mouth get your body into trouble, and don't say before you have kept your word that it was not meant: why should God be angry with your voice, but ruin what you have achieved with your hands? (5.6, ET 5.7) For when there is a mass of empty dreams and words aplenty, then fear God!

Commentary

The sort of vow envisaged here would have been familiar to many people in the ancient world, but it has often been recognized that there is a close similarity in wording between 'When you vow a vow to God, don't be slow to fulfil it' here and 'If you vow a vow to YHWH your God you shall not be slow to fulfil it' in Deut 23.22 (ET 23.21). It is not inconceivable that this is a coincidence, but the author probably has Deuteronomy in mind, especially bearing in mind that the subsequent verses Deut 23.23-24 (ET 23.22-23) go on to emphasize both the voluntary nature of vowing (cf. v. 4 [ET 5] here) and its character as an action of the mouth (cf. v. 5 [ET 6] here).

The vow itself would have consisted of a commitment to give something to God, usually but not necessarily in the form of a sacrifice, in return for divine favour or assistance. So, for example, Jacob vows in Gen 28.20-22 that if God helps him return safely to his father's house, then he will take him as his god, make the pillar that he has set up a house for God, and return to God a tenth of everything God gives him (cf. Gen 31.13). Similarly, Jephthah in Judg 11.30-31 promises—with tragic consequences—to offer as a burnt-offering the first person to greet him on his return if God gives him a victory, and Hannah in 1 Sam 1.11 asks God for a son, with the commitment that this son will be handed over to God for a lifetime of service. The regulations in Leviticus 27 embrace the possibilities that people might commit humans (for service), animals, houses, or land—allowing the possibility of cash alternatives in most cases. It was also possible to take Nazirite vows (Num 6), which involved observance of a particular lifestyle for a period, and in Ps 61.9 (ET 61.8) the psalmist apparently understands his daily praises of God in terms of fulfilling a vow. Of course, frequent references to votive offerings suggest that sacrifice was the most common form of payment, but the concept of the vow could clearly embrace a wide range of commitments on the part of a human, and probably no less wide a range of requests to God.

Obviously, vows could be made in a temple, but there is no reason to suppose that the priesthood or staff of the temple had a specific role in recording the vow or in its enforcement, beyond receiving pledges and sometimes valuing them when the person who had made the vow wished to offer a substitute. Numbers 30 is interesting in this respect: it deals with vows made by women that can be annulled by their fathers or husbands if they have heard and opposed the vow on the day in which it was made. Whether or not we take literally the references to such vows being made while the woman was in the 'house' of her father or husband (they may just mean that she belonged to their household), the annulment is expressed simply in terms of God releasing her from the vow, and no formal process appears to have been envisaged. It is difficult to see how, indeed, any such process could have dealt with cases where it might be a matter of judgment as to whether God had yet fulfilled a request made of him in return for a pledge. Every indication is that a vow was treated as a matter between the human and God, with the sole sanction being that if God believed the human to be in default, he could punish or 'curse' them (cf. Mal 1.14; in the Akkadian-Hurrian text from Ugarit, RS 15.10, on which see p. 628 n. 1, above, the sanction is that the oath-breaker's wife will never bear him a son). To the extent that there was any formal aspect to this arrangement, it seems solely to have lain in the requirement that a vow be spoken aloud to God.

The basic notion here, then, is that vows offer a simple way to incur divine anger, and that the longer a pledge remains unfulfilled, the more likely it is that God will deem whoever took it to be in default. It is interesting to observe, therefore, that Qohelet's advice is first motivated *not* by a warning about divine punishment, but by an observation about fools. Although often understood in such terms, moreover, this observation is not actually phrased in terms of the reaction that a delay might provoke in God himself (whose principal concern here is anyway with the breach of promise, not the intelligence of whoever made it). Rather, this delay in fulfilment is portrayed as an indication of foolishness, and, as Qohelet essentially puts it, nobody likes an idiot. His principal concern at the outset, therefore, seems to be the need to distinguish one's behaviour from that of the fool, just as in the preceding verses it was important to do so by restraining one's speech in the temple, and (by implication) avoiding the need for sacrifices. Of course, the idiocy of delay has other, potentially ruinous consequences, but these are once more expressed in terms of speech: it is their *mouth* that causes trouble for the rest of the defaulter, and their *voice* with which God is angry. In short, Qohelet seems to have focused on vows here not just because of any interest that he might have in them as a topic, but because their spoken character permits them to exemplify his more general point about the dangers of speaking to God. It is this point, of course, that is picked up in the concluding verse.

 5.3, ET 5.4] On the expression 'nobody has any use for', see the note: it is an impersonal expression, and appears to be an idiom used of things held in general contempt. The context, however, has led many translators and commentators to see in it a reference specifically to God's reaction. Jerome's paraphrase to this effect in the Vulgate (*displicet enim ei infidelis et stulta promissio*, 'for a faithless and foolish promise displeases him') has been, as often, highly influential on subsequent Christian understandings of the text, and a similar construal is also to be found in the Targum. Fox, recognizing that this is not what the Hebrew says, tries to salvage that interpretation by claiming cautiously that 'The impersonal locution…may indicate a hesitancy…to speak of God's emotions directly', but no such hesitancy is visible when Qohelet speaks of God's anger two verses later, and it is better to accept that Qohelet is talking not specifically about God's reaction to fools, but about the reaction to them of everybody. Of course, that may include God, but I take the implication here to be that, like the offering of sacrifices and the use of too many words, the failure to fulfil a vow swiftly is the mark of a fool: Qohelet will only turn directly to the matter of God's response in 5.5.

5.5, ET 5.6] The Septuagint and the Syriac here have 'God' where the other ancient versions have 'the messenger', and both probably existed as variants in the Hebrew tradition. There are no good grounds for the common claim that 'messenger' must have replaced 'God' because some scribe was uncomfortable with the idea of humans talking to God—the Hebrew Bible would look very different if such discomfort were commonplace. My own translation, in fact, rests on an understanding that neither reading is actually original, but that Perles and Dahood (see the note) are right to believe that 'messenger' appeared first, as the result of a difficult expression being misunderstood (which would probably make 'God' a response to confusion about the role of this messenger). If this is correct, Qohelet's original advice was against claiming that the vow was a mistake 'before your fulfilment (of it)'—that one should not, in other words, make a vow then say 'that was just a mistake' and carry on as though nothing had happened.

Despite its wide attestation, 'messenger' causes many problems. From an early time, some commentators have seen a reference to an angel, others to a human. For the former, this is either an angelic intermediary between humans and God, or an angel who interrogates humans on the day of judgment (the view of the Targum), while for the latter, the messenger must be some priest or employee of the temple, responsible for enforcing pledges. As we have already seen, however, there is no reason to suppose that temples would, or could, have enforced vows in such a way, and the evidence for temple 'messengers' of this sort is, to put it generously, extremely tenuous. Since it is also very clear that Qohelet has no belief in a post-mortem judgment, it is difficult to accept that this confrontation might be set, as it were, outside the pearly gates or at the end of time (by which point, the ruination of one's property might hardly be a concern anyway). The idea of an angelic intermediary is more credible, and we might note, for example, the way in which the book of Tobit speaks of seven angels who stand before God and present prayers to him (Tob 12.15, cf. 3.16-17; 12.2), and Job 33.23 of an angel who might speak on a human's behalf: whether or not such beliefs were widely held in whatever context the author wrote, they are at least attested, and attested early enough for him to have attributed them to Qohelet. It is still very far from clear, however, that anybody would have believed that defaulters could expect an angelic visitation, or for that matter, an appearance by God himself, and it remains most likely that the text here has been misread.

In any case, it is difficult to render in English the declaration that one is not supposed to make in these circumstances: where I have translated 'not meant', the Hebrew actually uses a term that has a well-established technical application to crimes or sins that were committed unwittingly, and for which compensation can generally be made (the same term will appear, again in a non-technical context, in 10.5). Qohelet imagines that the defaulter is saying, in effect, 'I didn't mean to do it', and that the vow or the default was a silly, forgivable error—or perhaps something that they can hope to get out of at some lesser price. God's response to the default is depicted as anger toward the defaulter's 'voice', that is, toward what they have said—and I take there to be a deliberate contrast here between the damage done *by* the voice and the damage done *to* whatever one's hands have achieved, just as the verse began with a distinction between the mouth and the rest of the body. Qohelet does not specify whether it is the initial vow or the attempted excuse that constitute the provocative speech, but it is probably the former, or perhaps the combination of the two.

5.6, ET 5.7] On the significance of dreams in this context, see the comments on 5.2, above. Qohelet lists three items—'dreams and vapours and words'—but I take the first two to be a hendiadys, 'vaporous dreams', and so there is quite a close match to that earlier verse. It is also possible that Qohelet is playing on the literal and metaphorical senses of 'vapour', as he does in 6.11, to talk about 'dreams, hot air and words'. Many commentators have tried to see a non-verbal sentence here, like Barton's 'in a multitude of dreams and words are many vanities' or Fox's 'much talk is like a lot of dreams and absurdities', but such readings require an unnecessary emendation of the text.

The construction that links the final command to the list is well attested elsewhere, and is used to indicate action that should be taken in particular circumstances: this means not only that the list can stand without emendation, but also that we should avoid isolating and contrasting the appeal to fear God. Qohelet is not saying that we should ignore all the meaningless dreams and words, but that it is precisely in the midst of such things that we should fear God. Human fear of God has already been mentioned in 3.14 and Qohelet will use the familiar expression 'fear God' later in 7.18 and 8.12-13 to express re-assurance that things will work out for the God-fearing. The imperative, used here, will also appear in the epilogue at 12.13, the last verse of the book, in connection with keeping God's commandments. In all these later passages, it can be understood as a fairly conventional way to express piety, but the context here, immediately after a reference to divine anger and punishment, suggests very strongly that Qohelet is laying real emphasis on the aspect of 'fear'. The point is not that we should just be resolutely pious in the face of what is meaningless, but that in a situation where there are so many words and such risks attached to speaking without thought, a healthy fear of what God might do should help us to keep our mouths shut.

Notes

5.3 (ET 5.4) when] M has כאשר for the כי of Deut 23.22 (ET 23.21). Although it is widely supported in the manuscripts, καθὼς ἄν or καθὼς ἐὰν is not the way in which G usually renders כאשר (cf. 5.14; 8.4, 7; 9.2), and possibly represents some assimilation to the Greek Deuteronomy (where ἐὰν alone is used for כי): G* is most probably καθώς.

5.3 (ET 5.4) God] לאלהים where Deut 23.22 (ET 23.21) has ליהוה אלהיך.

5.3 (ET 5.4) nobody has any use for] Lit. 'there is not delight in' or 'there is no matter in'. This is commonly understood to mean that God has no pleasure in fools or their vows (so T, V), although Barton notes and rightly rejects Plumptre's attempt to make it mean 'there is no fixed purpose in fools'. The expression אין חפץ ב- seems to be an idiom, however, which, at least in the biblical sources, is used especially of unwanted earthenware: it appears in Jer 22.28 and 48.38 used of pots that can be smashed or thrown away because nobody has any use for them, and Hos 8.8 has the nations hold Israel in the sort of general contempt in which such pots are held. There is a related usage, with a specification of the particular person for whom there is no חפץ, in 1 Sam 18.25, where we find אין חפץ למלך במהר, and in Mal 1.10, where God declares אין לי חפץ בכם; Qohelet will use the expression himself this way in 12.1, of the years אין לי בהם חפץ. The expression without such specification of the person is sufficiently well established, however, that we do not need to supply one, and the issue at this stage is probably not the reaction of God but the exposure of oneself to everybody as a useless fool. G renders word-for-word οὐκ ἔστιν θέλημα ἐν, 'there is no will/pleasure in' (cf. 12.1; Mal 1.10; Hie *non est uoluntas in*), but σ' οὐ γάρ ἐστιν χρεία ἀφρόνων, 'as there is no need for fools' captures that sense better. There is little to commend the suggestion of Staples, 'Meaning of *ḥēpeṣ*', 111-12, that the sense here is 'fools have no business (that requires a vow)'.

5.3 (ET 5.4) fools] Joüon, 'Notes philologiques', 421, would arbitrarily replace חפץ כסילים with חפצו עצלים, 'he hates those who are negligent/ late'.

5.3 (ET 5.4) you should fulfil what you vow] Lit. 'fulfil what you have vowed': the first verb is an imperative. In את אשר תדר שלם, M points את as the object-marker אֶת. In all the manuscripts of G, however, we find σὺ οὖν, 'you therefore' (Schoors, *The Preacher* I, 26, is incorrect to say that the reading is restricted to 'some minor manuscripts'), and S here has ܐܢܬ *'nt*, 'you', twice, with a variant ܐܢܬ ܕܝܢ (*'nt dyn* = σὺ οὖν) attested for the first. As McNeile, 159, pointed out long ago, 'The particle οὖν is foreign to the translation'—it occurs nowhere else, which raises a reasonable suspicion that we should treat σὺ οὖν as a corruption of σύν (so Klostermann, *De libri Coheleth*, 59), and this would bring G into line with M. Rahlfs has accordingly made that emendation in his text. However, although the reading of α' is only preserved in Syriac, it seems to have been σὺ ὅσα εὔξῃ, which also has σὺ where we should expect σύν, and although T does have an accusative marker ית in those manuscripts that do not lack the clause altogether, it likewise has a pronoun אנה, 'you'. These variations may indicate that the same consonantal text את has been vocalized by different readers as the object-marker אֶת and as אַתְּ, an orthographic variant of the pronoun אתה, and Goldman suggests, rather tentatively, that G σὺ οὖν might have originated in what he calls a 'conflate reading', the graphically similar σὺ σύν, which embodied both possibilities.

Goldman also believes that the original intention of the writer was for the את to be read as the pronoun. Such writings of the pronoun without ה are uncommon, however, and Schoors, *The Preacher* I, 26, discusses only eight apparent examples in biblical Hebrew, alongside Dahood's theory that this is a Phoenician spelling ('Canaanite-Phoenician', 39-40; 'The Language of Qoheleth', 227). Those eight, to be sure, do include an instance in 7.22, so the author or subsequent copyists of Ecclesiastes were clearly capable of this spelling, but the context there guides the vocalization: to use the shorter spelling of the pronoun here, directly before the object of the verb, would be positively to invite misunderstanding. If the text did have just a single את, it seems more likely that it was the object-marker. The book's stylistic quirk of placing the object of an imperative before the verb itself (cf. Schoors, *The Preacher* I, 160) encourages it to use את for clarification (see 5.6; 12.13; and perhaps 8.2), but as a consequence of this word-order the את is placed first in the clause: that makes it possible for readers mistakenly to take the word as a pronoun in an emphatic position, although it is still not easy to understand why any might have considered that reading more natural.

It may be that Aquila and others simply found a text with אתה instead of את, but that difficulty, along with the book's normal usage and the fact that both G and T can plausibly be taken to embody understandings of את as the object-marker *and* as the pronoun, forces us to take seriously an alternative possibility: that the translators actually found a Hebrew text with אתה את, rather than just את. This could itself represent a conflation of two different variants or understandings, or it could be the result of duplication in a consonantal text like that of M—but it might conceivably be original, and the other versions derived from texts in which one word or the other had been lost. In that case, the purpose of the pronoun would presumably have been to emphasize that 'you' must not act like the fools. Given the uncertainties that surround the text, however, it may be just as well that none of the various possible readings makes any great difference to the sense.

5.4 (ET 5.5) better] σ' has βέλτιον, 'better', for the more literal G ἀγαθὸν, 'good.'

5.4 (ET 5.5) better] M[L] מִשְׁתְּדוֹר lacks the *dageš* which we should expect in the שׁ after a prefixed -מ (GKC §102 b; J-M §103 d): *BHQ* characterizes this as an error, and contrasts other early manuscripts. It seems worth noting, though, that Sassoon 1053 also appears to lack a *dageš*, so this may be an inherited oddity, rather than a simple slip on the part of both *naqdanim*. If so, the cause is unclear, but the omission may have been influenced by vocalizations of -שׁ with *šewa*, or simply a reluctance to have three characters with *dageš* in a row.

5.5 (ET 5.6) don't let] This is a standard classical construction of נתן when it means 'permit', with the person or thing who is permitted serving as direct object of the verb (without -ל, as in, e.g., Esth 8.11; 2 Chr 20.10) and the permitted action indicated by an infinitive with -ל; so, e.g., Gen 20.6; Josh 10.19.

5.5 (ET 5.6) get…into trouble] Lit. 'cause to sin' or 'cause to be condemned'. The context demands a causative form of חטא, and לַחֲטִיא is pointed as equivalent to לְהַחֲטִיא: the hiphʿil infinitive with -ל. Such syncopation of the initial ה is not uncommon in some other forms of the hiphʿil, although this is one of only a few clear biblical instances in the infinitive (see GKC §53 q; J-M §54 b)—the phenomenon is still rare at Qumran, but more common in mishnaic Hebrew (cf. Schoors, *The Preacher* I, 44). The hiphʿil has two related meanings, of causing someone to sin and of exposing them to condemnation or punishment (e.g. Deut 24.4; Isa 29.21). Since the failure to fulfil a vow is not actively a sin committed by the body, many commentators think the latter is more in play here (and there is anyway no need to see a borrowing from Aramaic לחיבא to get that sense, as does Zimmermann, 'Aramaic Provenance', 32-33). There may be a reference to Deut 23.22 (ET 23.21), which says that failure to fulfil 'will be a sin in you'.

5.5 (ET 5.6) your body] Salters, in 'Koh. 5:5', 96-97, argues forcefully that בשרך should be rendered 'you' or 'yourself', which is a position adopted by many commentators from Rashbam onwards. I do not think, though, that Qohelet is saying only that a part of the body can destroy the whole, but also that words have physical consequences—a point drawn out later in the verse—and the distinction that he makes in the Hebrew should be preserved.

Jerome, interestingly, criticizes 'his Hebrew' (who has expounded the text to him) for treating it too loosely, and taking it to mean *non des os tuum, ut non pecces*, 'Do not give your mouth, so that you may not sin', but his objection arises from his own understanding of the passage as a reference to people who blame their sins upon the inherent and irresistible sinfulness of their flesh, and if we are to retain the reference to the body then it is important not to see this in terms of sensuality, or to impose such anachronistic Christian ideas about 'flesh' upon the text (as does, e.g., Zöckler).

5.5 (ET 5.6) say before] לפני is commonly used for the recipient of a speech: see, e.g., Exod 6.30; Deut 26.5, 13; 1 Sam 20.1; Neh 3.34 (ET 4.2); 6.19; Esth 1.16; Ezek 28.9. Correspondingly, it can be understood here as 'say to the messenger' or 'say to God' if we follow the ancient versions. These examples do not really justify the assertion of Ginsburg, that speaking לפני is reserved for speaking to God or some supernatural being, even if, as he asserts, there may be some such distinction made between speaking 'to' and speaking 'before' in Deuteronomy 26. Correspondingly, we could not use the expression to judge the much-debated nature of the addressee in this verse, even if we understood the meaning to be 'say *to*'. For reasons outlined in the next note, however, I take the actual function of לפני to be temporal.

In an article that has gone through several incarnations ("The Angel" in Qohelet 5:5'; 'La formula sapienzale'; 'The Wisdom Formula'), Alexander Rofé argues that we are dealing here with an example of a particular type of saying, which will be exemplified again in 7.10, and which takes the form, 'Do not say "...", for...'. Accordingly, he understands לפני to be the first word of what is said, rather than a preposition indicating the addressee, and he repoints it with a first-person suffix to give the meaning 'Do not say, "before me there is an angel", for this is an error'; with its reference to dreaming, 5.6 then serves as the motive for this injunction. The proposed vocalization is not intrinsically problematic (although it has no versional support), but it would seem odd to describe a simple hallucination as a שגגה, while to impose such a tyranny of form upon Qohelet is not only to presume an unrealistic coherence across the corpus of sayings collections, but also to discount the considerable amount of material in the book that has clearly not been shaped by any such conventions. The main objection to Rofé's suggestion, however, is that it introduces an interruption within the verse, creating an unnecessary break between the parts that precede and follow ואל תאמר...שגגה היא, when those parts obviously belong together.

5.5 (ET 5.6) you have kept your word] Lit. 'your enacting' or 'your fulfilling'; this understanding rests on a minor emendation. M here has המלאך, 'the messenger' or 'the angel', which is supported by α', σ' and θ', who all seem to have had τοῦ ἀγγέλου, and by Hie, V, T, who understand the reference to be to an angel. G, on the other hand, has τοῦ θεοῦ, 'God', which is supported (or more likely imitated) by S. If either of these is original, no very convincing reason has been put forward to explain why it should have been displaced by the other. If, as is frequently suggested, a copyist was uncomfortable with the idea of someone speaking directly to God and so introduced an intermediary, it is difficult to see why they would not have changed the reference in 5.1 as well. There is nothing to suggest in the history of the reception of the passage, on the other hand, that G (or its source-text) would have assumed 'messenger' to be a cypher for 'God', let alone that they would have felt obliged or even free to change it accordingly as some form of clarification.

Efforts to equate the two readings do not really solve the problem: McNeile, 68, may be right to draw attention to passages like Exod 22.8-9, where to bring an issue to 'God' for resolution is actually to bring it to human authorities for judgment, but it seems unlikely either that somebody would have tried to clarify the sense by using 'messenger' if they understood an original 'God' in these terms, or that they would have employed such an obscure and confusing usage to replace 'messenger'. We are left to speculate either that both readings are somehow derived from an original 'messenger of God', for which there is no evidence other than the fact of their coexistence, or, more probably, that the change from one reading to the other was motivated by some particular idea about what happens when one fails to fulfil a vow, and to whom one answers: the reading of G seems to assume that it is simply to God that one must explain oneself, while that of M understands there to be some system of recording and enforcement operated by human or supernatural intermediaries.

Commentators who follow M have long debated the nature of the messenger. Jerome reports the view of 'his Hebrew' that every vow is reported instantly to God by the angel who accompanies each human, and himself translates as 'angel' in both Hie and V. The Targum similarly speaks of an angel, although it relocates the speech to a coming day of judgment, and this view persists amongst some more modern commentators: Ginsburg's note includes a lengthy essay on angelology. Salters, 'Koh. 5:5', 98-100, observes, however, that the angelic interpretation is absent from the Midrash, and that other early Jewish commentators see references here to a human being. He and many other commentators take Mal 2.7 to be an indication that priests, who are responsible in Leviticus 27 for the commutation of vows, could be called 'messenger', and Delitzsch goes so far as to see it as a priestly title (see similarly Piotti, 'Osservazioni su alcuni I', 174-76). Seow likewise points to a votive inscription on a fifth-century incense altar, which describes someone as [ך]המלא, but it must be emphasized that the evidence for this as a title is extremely thin. Other scholars, such as Gordis and Zimmermann, see a more general reference to some sort of emissary or debt-collector from the Temple, but we simply do not know what arrangements might have been in place for the enforcement or annulment of vows: Leviticus 27 is dealing only with the very specific circumstances of people who wish to convert into financial donations to the Temple whatever it is that they have dedicated to God in vows. The strongest probability is that there were none, and, although they might work for the benefit of a temple, we have no good reason to suppose that vows were ever seen as something other than, in essence, a contract made by an individual with God, with the expectation that the terms would be enforced by God. Accordingly, I am inclined to think that G offers what is most likely the later reading, which simply replaces a mystifying reference to some messenger or angel with a statement more in line with usual beliefs. If the strange reading of M is earlier, however, I doubt all the same that it is original: there is nothing except this passage to suggest that anyone sent messengers or angels to check on progress.

A very different approach to המלאך, which underpins the translation I have adopted, is taken by Perles, 'Miscellany', 130, who regards 'the messenger' as 'wholly unintelligible', and who proposes to read מלאך instead as the piʿel infinitive of מלא, with a second person singular suffix, so that the sense would be 'before your fulfilling (it)'. Of course, this requires that the initial ה be considered a secondary addition, supplied when the verb had already been misunderstood as a noun. Dahood, 'Phoenician Background', 282, arrived independently at a similar conclusion, but construed the word instead as a niphʿal infinitive: this has the advantage of explaining the ה without further elaboration, but the more substantial disadvantage that מלא is only used with the sense 'fulfil' in the piʿel (see, most strikingly, Jer 44.25), and, if we are to go down this route, then Perles' suggestion is the better. Such an approach is actually very attractive, turning the verse into an admonition against giving up on the vow, or declaring it void before it has been fulfilled.

It is not clear whether the relative rarity of the proposed construction counts for or against Perles. לפני with an infinitive meaning 'before' occurs only in Gen 13.10; 36.31 (cf. 1 Chr 1.43); 1 Sam 9.15; 2 Sam 3.13, 35; 2 Chr 33.19; Ezek 33.22; Joel 3.4; Mal 3.23, while only in 2 Sam 3.13 and 2 Chr 33.19 does the infinitive take a suffix. If the writer of Ecclesiastes did choose to express himself this way, though, then it is easy to see how readers might have misunderstood what they were seeing (perhaps especially when מלא seems not to have been used with this sense in later Hebrew), and consequently have assigned more familiar meanings to both לפני and מלאך (with the latter later receiving a clarificatory article). A potentially more substantial objection lies in the fact that vv. 3-4 have consistently used the piʿel of שלם for fulfilment of the vow, not מלא. It is very probable, however, that there is some difference of nuance between them, and in this context of problematic speech, it is worth noting that the piʿel of מלא is often found in contexts which emphasize the physical fulfilment or enactment of spoken utterances; cf. 1 Kgs 8.15, 24; 2 Chr 6.4, 15; Jer 44.25, which all talk of doing with one's hands what one has promised with one's mouth. On balance, although it is difficult to choose between the various options here with any assurance, the solution offered by Perles presents a significant improvement in the sense at the cost of a very minor emendation. See also on 'God', below.

5.5 (ET 5.6) not meant] Although Qohelet uses it in an unusual context at 10.5, the word שגגה is elsewhere used either in a fixed expression (מכה נפש בשגגה) to denote individuals who have killed somebody without intending to do so, and who may flee to the cities of refuge for protection until they can be judged (Num 35.11-15; Josh 20.3-9), or, more commonly, of sins that were committed unwittingly, and for which sacrifices can be made in recompense (e.g. Num 15.25; Lev 5.15). This is a term with a strong technical background, and, strictly speaking, to declare either that the failure to fulfil a vow or the original making of that vow was שגגה would be not just to make an excuse, that the fault was unwitting, but to assert that it is a problem that can be resolved. Jerome discusses α' ἀκούσιον, 'an involuntary offence', which captures this technical sense more precisely than G ἄγνοιά, which can mean simply 'ignorance', although in Hellenistic usage it often refers likewise to actions committed inadvertently. Vinel, 'Le Texte Grec', 298, sees in the translation a reference to the Greek version of 1 Kgs 14.24, and puts this in a broader context of supposed echoes: I am not persuaded that these add up to the reflection on the monarchy that she identifies.

5.5 (ET 5.6) why] G renders למה, which generally means 'why' in biblical usage, as ἵνα μὴ, making it equivalent to פן, 'lest'. The same understanding is adopted in Hie, V (although S and T retain the sense 'why'), and these versions can be read as tying the divine anger specifically to the preceding declaration that שגגה היא. On that reading, perhaps, it is not simply the default itself which angers God, but the attempt to excuse it. Dahood, 'Canaanite-Phoenician', 195, links such a meaning to the usage of the Phoenician לם, and Whitley sees analogies in Aramaic, but G translates similarly in 7.16-17 (contrast 2.15), and in all these cases it is difficult to be sure whether the translator actually took למה to mean 'lest', or simply saw Qohelet's rhetorical questions as equivalent to negative final clauses and rendered accordingly. This is a common way to translate למה in the Septuagint (cf. BDB), and it need not imply that the Hebrew expression had actually changed or extended its sense, although in passages like Dan 1.10 and Ct 1.7 it does seem clear that it could mean 'lest' when used with a relative. In any case, there is no particular reason for us to follow G's approach, which excludes, amongst other things, the possibility of reading these words as a continuation of the indirect speech.

5.5 (ET 5.6) God] The suggestion in *BHS* that this might be an addition presumably rests on a perception that it becomes repetitive and redundant if the preceding המלאך is replaced by האלהים (see the note on 'the messenger', above), as *BHS* itself recommends, but that might be considered a stronger argument against that emendation than for the deletion of this second occurrence.

5.5 (ET 5.6) angry with] The object of קצף is regularly expressed with על, so Qohelet is not talking directly about an anger toward the speaker provoked by their voice, but about an anger directed *at* that voice. There is a contrast drawn here between the voice that attracts the anger, and the hands that have achieved what will be lost.

5.5 (ET 5.6) ruin] The pi‘el of חבל is often translated 'destroy', and it can connote an almost total desolation or destruction (cf. Isa 13.5-12), but it can also be used of the sort of damage that foxes do in a vineyard (Ct 2.15), or that can be done to the poor by lies (Isa 32.7). Kugel, 'Qohelet and Money', 33-35, rightly observes that 'the word "destroy" seems here a bit on the violent side', although his own proposal, to read it as from חָבַל, 'hold or seize something taken in pledge', entails a significant shift of meaning. Seow rejects that proposal, but would vocalize the verb as qal here, claiming that 'In postbiblical Hebrew, ḥbl in Qal may mean "to destroy" or "to take away"' (see Jastrow, *Dictionary*, p. 419)'. This claim is not really borne out by Jastrow's entry, which shows only that the qal has taken on the sense 'injure', and that the verb has become confused with or coalesced with its homonym, so that it can be used of seizing pledges. It is not clear that the use for seizing property of the cognate Akkadian *ḥabālu* in the G stem, to which Seow also appeals, is of any particular pertinence here, but it should be noted anyway that the Akkadian is not used of legal distraint, but specifically of wronging somebody, sometimes by, or in connection with, seizing property unlawfully from them. We might take Kugel's point that there could be a reference to pledging here if there were any reason to suppose that vows were seen in those terms, but the point of a vow would seem to be that something is promised to God with the attendant risk of incurring anger if it is not delivered, rather than that God holds or seizes something as surety.

5.5 (ET 5.6) what you have achieved with your hands] Qohelet speaks in 2.11 of 'all my achievements, which my hands had achieved' and the expression appears elsewhere in biblical Hebrew: see the note to that verse on 'my achievements,' which also discusses the sense of מעשה. It is unclear whether the threat is simply to existing achievements, or to future ones as well.

Qohelet speaks variously of 'achievement' or 'achievements', and G normally follows the number of the Hebrew. Here, however, we find plural τὰ ποιήματα (cf. Hie, V, T) for the singular מעשה of M (cf. S), and the same happens in 7.13, with the first occurrence of the noun in 8.17, and in 11.5. In 2.4, on the other hand, G has the singular for M plural (see the note there on 'I accomplished great things'). As Schoors, *The Preacher* I, 23-24, observes, the singular is often translated with a plural elsewhere in the Hebrew Bible, but it is difficult to maintain simply, as he does, that 'this phenomenon is connected with translation techniques and idiomatic features of the receptor languages'. In 8.11, where G construes the word differently, and translates ἀπὸ τῶν ποιούντων, surely it must actually have read מעשי for M מעשה. Here too, it is likely that we are dealing with a Hebrew textual variant (which Dahood, 'The Language of Qoheleth', 227, attributes to an originally defective spelling). In the other places where G has the plural for M singular, there is little support from within the textual tradition of M itself, but in this case de Rossi does note a number of Hebrew manuscripts with the plural, and it is listed as a 'reading of the eastern Jews' (see the Introduction, p. 189, above). It is similarly important to note that T supports the plural of G here against M, but not in those other passages. At the very least, it does seem likely that G was dependant on a well-established Hebrew variant in this verse, and Euringer actually considers the plural to be earlier, suggesting that the singular arose under the influence of other passages, such as Deut 16.15. In any case, we can remove this verse from consideration of the general problem, which makes the variation overall seem much less random, and in 7.13, 8.17, and 11.5, G simply seems deliberately to have changed the singular to plural through a preference for 'works of God' over 'work of God'.

5.6 (ET 5.7) For] Strobel deletes כי as a 'Doppelschreibung' ('a double writing', presumably of the preceding כ), and reads the first part of the verse as a continuation of what has preceded, to give the attractive sense that the work of the hands is destroyed 'in einem Überfluß von Träumereien...', 'in a plethora of dreams'. There is no versional support for the emendation, however, and it would make the sentence unusually long. Lauha treats the כי as emphatic, and translates it as 'Fürwahr', 'indeed', although it is not clear why he feels the need to do so.

5.6 (ET 5.7) when there is a mass of] Without emending the text, it is difficult to read ברב here in the same way as at 1.18, where it indicated proportionality ('in much wisdom is much exasperation'), and some commentators have struggled to find the sense that they want in it. Fox, for instance, simply emends ברב to כרב, so that he can render 'for like much dreams and absurdities are many words', while Schoors, *The Preacher* I, 103-104 follows Gordis in taking the preposition as concessive: 'In spite of all dreams, follies, and idle chatter'. Fox's emendation is accepted by Spangenberg, 'A Century', 87, but has no versional support. The reading of -ב as concessive relies on a use of the preposition which is extremely rare, if it exists at all (BDB cites only Isa 1.15 and Ps 46.3, which can both be construed differently). Gordis cites Ps 94.19 in support, but there ברב שרעפי בקרבי תנחומיך ישעשעו נפשי does not mean 'In spite of the multitude of doubts within me, Thy consolations delight my soul', as he would like, but simply 'When the cares within me are many...'. I take the sense here to be similar: cf. also the similar Prov 10.19, 'When there is a mass of words, transgression never stops'.

5.6 (ET 5.7) empty dreams and words aplenty] Lit. perhaps 'dreams and vapours and words aplenty'. The conjunctions oblige us to take הלמות והבלים ודברים הרבה as a list, despite the redundancy of the last word, and they are read this way by G (ὅτι ἐν πλήθει ἐνυπνίων καὶ ματαιοτήτων καὶ λόγων πολλῶν, 'for in a plentifulness of dreams and *of* vanities and *of* many words': Rahlfs' ὅτι ἐν πλήθει ἐνυπνίων καὶ ματαιότητες καὶ λόγοι πολλοί, 'for in a plentifulness of dreams, and vanities and many words', is based on Hie), as well as by S, T, and Hie. Jerome's rendering in V, however, is *ubi multa sunt somnia plurimae vanitates et sermones innumeri*, 'where dreams are many, vanities (are) plentiful and words innumerable'. This is probably an imitation of σ', which may be retroverted as διὰ γὰρ πλήθους ὀνείρων ματαιότητες καὶ λόγοι πολλοὶ ψεύδων, 'for on account of / in the midst of plentiful dreams, vanities and words of falsehoods are many'. These translations have no conjunction before their equivalents to הבלים, but they also more explicitly echo v. 2, and it would be unwise to presume that they rest on a Hebrew variant, let alone that the conjunction is secondary—however much we might want to delete at least one of the conjunctions here to create a non-verbal clause.

Fox does just that, removing the conjunction before דברים, whilst Lauha not only removes the conjunction but also re-arranges the words to give a proverb: 'bei der Fülle "der Worte" sind Träume und Eitelkeit in Menge', 'with a wealth of "words", dreams and vanity are aplenty'. Barton takes a similar path, swapping הבלים and דברים to create a proverb of his own, 'in a multitude of dreams and words are many vanities', which requires him instead, however, to ignore the conjunction on הבלים. Spangenberg, 'A Century', 87 (cf. 'Die Struktuur', 263-64), deletes that conjunction and reads הבלים twice, claiming that there is an ellipsis, with the many dreams and the many words each described as הבלים. There are other, even more drastic proposals to deal with the text, amongst which we might note the proposal of Hitzig and Knobel to supply ב before דברים, to give 'and also in many words'. This is reluctantly adopted by Wright and elaborated by *BH³*, which would insert עניין after ברב (cf. v. 2) and read ודברים as בדברים, 'for dreams and vanities are in a mass of business and in many words'. Galling's '"Nichtigkeit" ist bei vielen träumen und völlige Nichtigkeit "bei" vielen Worten', 'Vanity is in many dreams and complete vanity in many words', in both editions of his commentary, comes from a similar insertion—this time of הבל at the start of the verse, combined with reading בדברים. Ehrlich would replace ודברים with נדרים, to give 'denn öftere Träumereien und Faseleien führen zu vielen Gelübden', 'more frequent dreams and drivel lead to many vows'.

There have also, however, been attempts to deal with the difficulties without emendation. GKC §143 d, for instance, claims that 'an incomplete noun-clause is appended by wāw apodosis', effectively discounting the first ו as a conjunction, while Whitley treats the conjunction on דברים as an instance of an asseverative or emphatic ו, so that he can translate 'in a multitude of dreams and vanities there are indeed many words'. Zimmermann, quite differently, sees הרבה as the result of misvocalizing an original Aramaic שנין, and translating it as 'many' rather than 'they err'. He renders 'Because in the multitude of dreams, vanities and talk, persons err', which seems only to state the obvious. It is a coincidence, but interesting to note, however, that after 'much speech' most manuscripts of S do add ܕܛܘܥܝܝ, *dṭwʿyy*, 'of error', which Lane, 'Lilies', 482, attributes to the influence of 2 Thess 2.22, but which is also intriguingly similar to the λόγοι πολλοὶ ψεύδων of σ'. Zimmermann might be said to share with at least some ancient readers an inclination to see an emphasis here on the falsehood rather than the sheer quantity of the speech.

Seow offers, I think, the most attractive and ingenious solution: he takes הלמות והבלים as a hendiadys meaning 'vacuous dreams'. Qohelet's use here of the plural הבלים, which has attracted little comment, may support this approach. Despite the widespread use of the singular in Ecclesiastes, the plural otherwise occurs only in the mottoes of 1.2 and 12.8, where it is used and contextualized in the expression הבל הבלים. Outside the book it appears in Deut 32.21; 1 Kgs 16.13, 26; Jer 8.19; 10.8; 14.22, where it refers pejoratively to idols or foreign gods, and in Ps 31.7 and Jonah 2.9, where those who care about הבלי שוא are contrasted with those loyal to Yahweh and the connotation may be similar. Its use here, then, is unexpected, and although by using it Qohelet may, on the one hand, simply be distinguishing his statement here from his more common statements about הבל, the plural binds it tightly to הלמות, on the other, in a way that might well indicate hendiadys.

For the sense, it is worth noting the use in Jer 23.16 of מהבלים, the hiph'il participle of the cognate verb, which refers to the passing on of useless, uninspired visions, and which indicates the sort of thing that Qohelet may have in mind here. Seow's rendering of the sentence as a whole, however, is 'For vacuous dreams are in abundance, and there are words aplenty', which would be more persuasive if we had והרבה דברים or some other indication that הרבה was predicative: if a second non-verbal clause was intended here, it is not signalled at all, and the context pushes strongly toward an understanding of ודברים as an addition to what precedes, rather than as the beginning of a new clause. Although I am persuaded that we should take הלמות והבלים as a single entity, therefore, I think that we are still dealing with a list, albeit a list of two and not three things.

5.6 (ET 5.7) then fear God] The witnesses to G are divided between a reading σύν = M אֶת (supported by Klostermann, *De libri Coheleth*, 59) and σύ, which might represent a reading of את as a Hebrew second-person pronoun אַתְּ (see the note on 'you should fulfil what you vow' at 5.3, above) or possibly a different division of the text as אתה אלהים (which Seow takes to be the proper division). Among the other versions, S and V support the pronoun, while Hie *sed deum time* and σ' ἀλλὰ τὸν θεόν have probably read the object-marker. This is reminiscent of a similar issue in v. 3, but the strong representation of σύν suggests that what has happened here is an early error within the Greek tradition, where an original σύν has been misread as σύ (perhaps because of a supralinear nu, rather than, as Euringer suggests, as a correction). Goldman takes G*, on the contrary, to have been σύ, but it is harder to understand the alien σύν as secondary. There is very little difference in the sense either way.

The bigger question is how this clause should be connected to the rest of the verse, and how, accordingly, we should understand the initial כי. There are no good grounds to delete that word, although it is apparently not rendered at all by S, and Schoors, *The Preacher* I, 104, raises the possibility that it has been repeated deliberately or accidentally from the beginning of the verse (he describes this misleadingly as 'dittography', however, and attributes the opinion incorrectly to Strobel—who sees the first כי as a dittograph, not this one). It has been read as adversative by σ', Hie, V and possibly T; it is explained as such by Rashi, and translated that way by Rashbam, with many modern translations and commentators, such as Lauha and Seow, following suit. Others, such as Gordis, prefer to see it as emphatic, but as Schoors (loc. cit.) sensibly remarks (cf. also Fox), 'in such an interpretation, emphatic and adversative כי are closely related, the adversative force being a specific case of its asseverative function'. The key point is that these readings take Qohelet to be commending fear of God in the face of the circumstances outlined previously, not connecting it to them causally. In fact, the use of כי with a following imperative is interesting and relatively unusual: where we do find it, though, the כי very often serves to provide continuity with what has preceded (e.g. Deut 4.32; Job 8.8; 2 Kgs 5.7; Jer 2.10; 7.12; 9.19), with no adversative or emphatic implication. To the extent that it can usefully be translated at all in such passages, it is usually by 'so' or 'then': typically the sense seems to be 'Such-and-such is the situation, so you should do such-and-such'. I take the point here, therefore, to be that it is precisely in the circumstances of many dreams etc., not despite them, that fear of God becomes most important.

www.ingramcontent.com/pod-product-compliance
Lightning Source LLC
Chambersburg PA
CBHW072017240426
43667CB00043B/1460